This book belongs to:
Jonathan Lawlor (TPS/Investments)
150 Chadacre Road
Stoneleigh
Surrey
KT17 2HG

BUILDING APPLICATIONS WITH MICROSOFT OUTLOOK VERSION 2002

Randy Byrne

PUBLISHED BY
Microsoft Press
A Division of Microsoft Corporation
One Microsoft Way
Redmond, Washington 98052-6399

Copyright © 2001 by Microsoft Corporation

All rights reserved. No part of the contents of this book may be reproduced or transmitted in any form or by any means without the written permission of the publisher.

Library of Congress Cataloging-in-Publication Data
Byrne, Randy.
    Building Applications with Microsoft Outlook Version 2002 / Randy Byrne.
       p. cm.
    Includes index.
    ISBN 0-7356-1273-0
     1. Microsoft Outlook.   2. Time management--Computer programs.   3. Personal information management--Computer programs.   I. Microsoft Press.   II. Title.

HD69.T54 B97   2001
005.369--dc21   2001030707

Printed and bound in the United States of America.

1 2 3 4 5 6 7 8 9   QWT   6 5 4 3 2 1

Distributed in Canada by Penguin Books Canada Limited.

A CIP catalogue record for this book is available from the British Library.

Microsoft Press books are available through booksellers and distributors worldwide. For further information about international editions, contact your local Microsoft Corporation office or contact Microsoft Press International directly at fax (425) 936-7329. Visit our Web site at mspress.microsoft.com. Send comments to *mspinput@microsoft.com*.

ActiveX, FrontPage, IntelliSense, JScript, Microsoft, Microsoft Press, MS-DOS, MSDN, Outlook, PivotTable, PowerPoint, SharePoint, Visio, Visual Basic, Visual C++, Visual InterDev, Visual Studio, Windows, Windows Media, and Windows NT are either registered trademarks or trademarks of Microsoft Corporation in the United States and/or other countries. Other product and company names mentioned herein may be the trademarks of their respective owners.

The example companies, organizations, products, domain names, e-mail addresses, logos, people, places, and events depicted herein are fictitious. No association with any real company, organization, product, domain name, e-mail address, logo, person, place, or event is intended or should be inferred.

Acquisitions Editor: David Clark
Project Editor: Devon Musgrave
Technical Editor: Marzena Makuta

Body Part No. X08-06066

*To my wife, Susan Cohen Byrne—
your laughter, wisdom, and compassion have made the task easier.*

*To my daughters, Lily and Zoe, who make me a very proud dad
and always provide a new perspective.*

Contents at a Glance

Part I Introducing Microsoft Outlook 2002
1	Applications You Can Create with Outlook	3
2	Outlook Design Tools	17

Part II Quick Guide to Building Applications
3	Customize Built-In Modules	41
4	Design a Custom Application	71

Part III Building Blocks of Applications
5	Forms	109
6	Controls, Fields, and Properties	153
7	Actions	211
8	Folders	247

Part IV Beyond the Basics
9	Raise Events and Move to the Head of the Class	311
10	The Outlook Development Environment	383
11	Using Visual Basic, VBA, or VBScript with Outlook	415
12	The Northwind Contact Management Application	531
13	Distributing and Securing Applications	591

Part V Advanced Topics
14	Creating COM Add-Ins with Visual Basic	653
15	Integrating Outlook with Web Applications	711
16	Using Outlook with SharePoint Portal Server	785

Table of Contents

Foreword	xli
Acknowledgments	xliii
Introduction	xlv

Part I Introducing Microsoft Outlook 2002

1 Applications You Can Create with Outlook — 3

Types of Applications You Can Create	5
Forms You Can Create	7
Message Forms	8
Post Forms	9
Built-In Module Forms	10
Folder Applications	11
Folders Based on Built-In Modules	11
Discussion Folders	13
Tracking Folders	14
Reference Applications	14
For More Form and Folder Ideas	16

2 Outlook Design Tools — 17

Help and Web Sites	18
To open the Help And Web Sites folder	18
To open a Web page directly in Outlook	19
To add a page opened in a Web View to your Outlook Bar	19
Outlook Form Design Mode	20
To view an Outlook form in Design mode	20
Properties Dialog Box	21
To view the Properties dialog box	21
Advanced Properties Dialog Box	21
To view the Advanced Properties dialog box	22
The Visual Basic Expression Service	23
To open the Business Card Request form in Design mode	23
To open the Visual Basic Expression Service	23

Table of Contents

Script Editor and VBScript	24
To view the Script Editor	24
Folder View Design Tools	25
To add or remove a column using the Field Chooser	25
Folder Properties Dialog Box	27
To view the folder Properties dialog box	28
Outlook Visual Basic for Applications Design Tools	28
Visual Basic Editor	29
To open the Visual Basic for Applications Editor window	29
To open the Visual Basic for Applications Object Browser	30
To add a UserForm to your Outlook VBA project	31
Add-Ins and Other Design Tools	32
Other Tools and Add-Ins	35
Debugging Tools	35
Development Tools	36
Other Tools	37

Part II Quick Guide to Building Applications

3 Customize Built-In Modules — 41

Overview of the Folder You Create	42
Create New Folders	45
Create the Design Environment Personal Folder (.pst) File	46
To create the Design Environment personal folder	46
Create the Beta Contacts Folder	46
To create the Beta Contacts folder	46
Create Custom Views	47
Create the Potential Beta Participants View	47
To create the Potential Beta Participants view	47
To remove fields	48
To add new fields	48
To drag the Company column heading	49
To drag the fields to the Column Heading row	50
To adjust the column widths	50
Create the Beta Participants View	50
To create the Beta Participants view	51

Table of Contents

To remove fields from the view	51
To add new fields	52
To drag the fields to the Column Heading row	52
To adjust the column widths	53
To create a filter	53
Create Items for the Beta Contacts Folder	54
To switch to the Potential Beta Participants view	54
To create a Beta Contacts item	54
To create a second Beta Contacts item	55
To create third and fourth Beta Contacts items	55
Enter Dates in the Beta Participants View	57
To switch to the Beta Participants view	57
To enter the Beta Agreement Sent date in the fields	57
Customize the Contacts Form	57
Open the Contacts Form	58
To open the Contacts form in Design mode	58
To switch from Design mode to Run mode	58
Rename the New Page	58
To rename and show the page	59
Add Controls to the Form	59
To show the Control Toolbox	59
To add the ComboBox control	59
To set properties for the ComboBox control	60
To add a label	61
To add a TextBox control	61
To set properties for the TextBox control	62
To add a label	63
To add a CheckBox control	63
To create the Current Customer field	63
Set Form Properties	64
To set form properties	64
Test the Form at Design Time	65
To switch from Design mode to Run mode	65
Publish the Form	65
To publish the form to the Beta Contacts folder Form Library	66

Table of Contents

Specify the Default Form for the Folder	67
To make the Beta Contact form the default form	67
Test the Application	67
To select the Potential Beta Participants view	67
To test the Beta Contact form	68
Delete the Items You Created	68
To delete the items in the Beta Contacts folder	68
Copy the Folder to Public Folders	68
To copy the Beta Contacts folder	69
Set Permissions	69
To set permissions for the Beta Contacts folder	69
Release the Application	70
To set administration properties	70
4 Design a Custom Application	**71**
Overview of the Product Ideas Application	72
Create the Product Ideas Folder	75
To create the Product Ideas folder	75
Create the Product Idea Form	75
Open the Post Form	76
To open the Post form in Design mode	76
Edit the Compose Page	76
To remove the Categories control	77
To adjust the Message control	77
To center the Message control horizontally	78
To add the Product Category control	78
To set the properties for the Product Category control	79
To add a Label control	80
To align the Subject and Product Category controls	81
To add a Label control	81
To move controls	82
To add a form graphic using a label control	82
To add a form graphic using a Frame control	83
To add a form graphic using an Image control	83
To save the form graphic for reuse on other pages	84
To set the Tab Order for the Compose page	84

Table of Contents

Edit the Read Page	85
To switch to the Read page	85
To delete controls to make room for new controls	85
To adjust the From and Posted controls	86
To copy the controls from the Compose page	86
To set the tab order	87
Set Product Idea Form Properties	87
To set Product Idea form properties	87
Test the Form at Design Time	88
To switch between Design mode and Run mode when testing	88
Make a Backup Copy of the Product Idea Form	88
To save the Product Idea form	88
To open your backup copy of a form	89
Publish the Product Idea Form	89
To publish the form to the Product Ideas folder	89
Create the Product Idea Response Form	90
Edit the Compose Page	91
To switch to the Compose page	91
To make the Product Category control read-only	91
To clear the Initial Value property	91
To change the label	92
Edit the Read Page	92
To switch to the Read page	92
To make the Product Category control read-only	92
To change the Product Idea label	92
Set the Form Properties	92
To set the form properties	92
Make a Backup Copy of the Product Idea Response Form	93
To make a backup copy of the Product Idea Response form	93
To open your backup copy of a form	93
Publish the Product Idea Response Form	93
To publish the Product Idea Response form	94
Set the Actions	94
Set the Actions for the Product Idea Form	94
To open the Product Idea form in Design mode	94

Table of Contents

To make the Reply To Folder action unavailable	95
To create a new action	96
Make a Backup Copy of the Product Idea Form	97
To make a backup copy of the Product Idea form	97
Republish the Product Idea Form	97
To republish the form	97
Set the Actions for the Product Idea Response Form	98
To open the Product Idea Response form in Design mode	98
To make the Reply To Folder action unavailable	99
To create a new action	99
Make a Backup Copy of the Product Idea Response Form	99
To make a backup copy of the Product Idea Response form	99
Publish the Product Idea Response Form	100
To publish the Product Idea Response form	100
Create the Product Category View	100
To create the Product Category view	101
Remove Fields	101
To remove fields	101
Group Items	102
To group items by Product Category, then by Conversation	102
Sort Items	102
To sort items by the Conversation Index field	103
Arrange the Column Heading Order	103
To arrange the column heading order	103
Specify the Default Form for the Folder	103
To specify that the Product Idea form is the default form	103
Set the Hidden Property for the Product Idea Response Form	104
To set the Hidden property for the Product Idea Response form	104
Test the Application	104
To test the Product Ideas application	104
Copy the Folder to Public Folders	105
To copy the Product Ideas folder	105
About Folder Permissions	106
Release the Application	106
To set Administration properties	106

Table of Contents

Part III Building Blocks of Applications

5 Forms   **109**

- Become Familiar with Designing Forms and Form Components   109
  - Outlook Form Design Mode   109
  - Types of Forms   111
  - Parts of a Form   112
- Fields   115
  - Properties   116
  - Actions   116
  - Form Scripts   117
- Learn How Forms Work   119
  - What Is an Item?   119
  - What Happens When the Form Definition Is Saved with the Item?   120
  - How Is a Form Opened?   122
  - How Do Shared Fields Work?   122
- Create a Folder   123
  - *To create a personal folder*   124
- Open the Form and Switch to Design Mode   125
  - *To create a Message form*   125
  - *To create a Post form*   125
  - *To create a Calendar, Contact, Distribution List, Task, or Journal form*   126
  - *To create a form based on a custom Outlook template*   126
- Edit Form Pages   127
  - The Compose Page   127
  - The Read Page   128
  - About Separate Read Layout   128
  - *To view either the Read or the Compose page*   129
  - *To specify the Separate Read Layout option for a page*   130
  - Hide or Show a Page   131
  - *To hide or show a page at run time*   131
  - Rename a Page   131
  - *To rename a page*   132
- Add Controls   132
  - *To show the Control Toolbox*   132
  - *To add additional controls to the Control Toolbox*   133

xiii

Table of Contents

To add a control to a form	133
To set Display properties for a control	133
To set Advanced Properties for a control	133
Create and Bind Fields	134
Create a New Field and Bind It to a Control	134
To create a new user-defined field	135
Bind a Control to an Existing Field	135
To bind a control to an existing field	135
Select Fields from Other Forms	135
To add a field set from a form to the field list	136
When to Use the Field Chooser	136
To add a field from the Field Chooser	137
Delete a Field	138
To delete a field	138
Polish the Layout	138
Select and Edit Controls	138
Align Controls	138
To align controls	138
Space Controls	139
To space controls	139
Set Tab Order	139
To set the tab order for the Compose page	139
View the Form in Run Mode	140
To switch between Design mode and Run mode	140
Create Help (Optional)	141
To create ControlTipText	141
Edit the Read Page	141
To copy controls to the Read page	141
Set Properties for Controls on the Read Page	142
To make a control read only	142
Set the Tab Order for the Read Page	142
About Viewing the Read Page in Run Mode	142
To switch between Design mode and Run mode	142
Set Action Properties	143
To create actions	143
To set actions	143

Table of Contents

Set Form Properties	143
To set form properties	143
Publish the Form	146
Make a Backup Copy of the Form	147
To make a backup copy of a form	147
To open your backup copy of a form	147
Publish the Form	147
To specify the form name	148
To change the message class	148
To publish a form	149
Test and Release the Form	150
To test a Message form in the Personal or Organizational Forms Library	150
To test a Post form in a forms library in a folder	151
Release the Form	151
Where To Go from Here	151

6   Controls, Fields, and Properties   153

Set Control Display Properties	154
To view the display properties for a control on the Vacation Request form	154
Change Foreground and Background Colors	155
To set foreground and background colors for a control	155
Layer Controls	156
To send a control to a back layer	156
To bring a control to a front layer	157
Set Advanced Control Properties	157
To open the Advanced Properties window	157
Bind a Control to an Existing Field	157
To bind a control to an existing field	158
Create User-Defined Fields	160
To create a user-defined field	160
Location of User-Defined Fields	161
Specify Field Type	162
Changing Field Type	163
To change the type of a user-defined field	163

Table of Contents

Specify Field Formats	163
Create Combination Fields	164
To create a Combination field	164
Create Formula Fields	167
To create a Formula field when you create the field	167
To specify that the field automatically calculates the result	168
Set Initial Field Values	170
Validate and Restrict Data	172
Specify That a Value Is Required for a Field	172
To specify that a value is required for a text field	172
Create Validation Formulas	173
To create a validation formula	174
Set Field-Specific Properties	176
To Field	177
To set the initial value of the To field	177
To add a folder address to an Address Book in your profile	178
To Preaddress the To field to a folder	179
Subject Field	179
To specify the initial value of the Subject field	180
Message Field	181
To insert a file attachment or shortcut in the Message control	183
To insert an item in the Message control	183
To insert a folder shortcut in the Message control	184
To insert a URL shortcut in the Message control	184
To insert a hyperlink in the Message control	184
To insert an object in the Message control	186
About the Control Toolbox	187
Set Control-Specific Properties	188
To install Microsoft Outlook Visual Basic Reference	188
To use controls	189
Label Controls	189
To set the initial value of a Label control	190
TextBox Controls	190
To specify the Multi-Line option for a TextBox control	191
To specify the initial value for a TextBox control	191

Table of Contents

Frame Controls	192
To add a Frame control	192
To add or remove controls from a Frame control	192
To change the caption of the Frame control	192
OptionButton Controls	192
To specify a caption for an OptionButton control	193
To bind an OptionButton control to a field	193
To set the Value property of an OptionButton control	194
To set the initial value of an OptionButton control	194
CheckBox Controls	194
To bind a CheckBox control to a field	195
To set the initial value of a CheckBox control	195
ComboBox Controls	195
To bind the ComboBox control to a field	196
To select a list type	196
To add values to the combo box list	196
To set the initial value of a ComboBox control	197
ListBox Controls	198
To bind the ListBox control to a field	198
To add values to the ListBox control	199
To set the initial value of a ListBox control	200
CommandButton Controls	200
To add a CommandButton control	201
To create a procedure for a CommandButton control	202
To test a CommandButton control Click procedure	202
MultiPage Controls	202
To add a MultiPage control	202
To add controls to the MultiPage control	202
To insert, rename, delete, or move a page	203
Image Controls	204
To add a picture to an Image control	204
To delete the picture in the Image control	204
To size an image in the Image control	204
SpinButton Control	205
To add the TextBox control and bind it to a field	205

Table of Contents

	To add the SpinButton control and bind it to a field	206
	Controls That Require VBScript	206
	Using Custom ActiveX Controls	207
	To add a Date Selection control to your custom Outlook form	207
	Select Multiple Controls and the Dominant Control	209
	Where To Go from Here	209
7	**Actions**	**211**
	Voting Buttons for Message Forms	211
	Overview of the Art Approval Form	212
	Create the Art Approval Folder	212
	To create the Art Approval folder	213
	Create the Art Approval Form	214
	To open the standard Message form	215
	To preaddress the form	215
	To set the initial value of the Subject field	215
	To specify voting buttons	216
	To specify the reply address	216
	To specify where the Tracking item is stored	216
	To publish the form	217
	Test the Art Approval Form	219
	To send the Art Approval form	219
	To vote on the item	219
	To open the response item in your Inbox	220
	To open the Tracking item	220
	Reply Actions for Message Forms	221
	To open the Vacation Request folder	221
	Overview of the Vacation Request Application	221
	To view a Vacation Request form	221
	Actions for the Vacation Request Form	222
	To view the Actions page for the Vacation Request form	223
	To view the Approve Vacation action	224
	To specify a form name	226
	How Field Values Are Copied to the Reply Form	228
	Vacation Request Reply Forms	230
	Publish Reply Forms	231

xviii

To make a backup copy of a form	231
To open your backup copy of a form	231
To publish a form	232
Test the Forms	232
To publish the Vacation Request forms	232
To test the Vacation Request forms	233
Set the Hidden Properties for Response Forms	233
Reply To Folder Actions for Post Forms	235
To open the Training Management folder	235
Overview of the Training Management Application	235
Actions for the Course Catalog Entry Form	237
To view the Actions page of the Course Catalog Entry form	237
To make the Reply To Folder action unavailable	239
To view the Create Offering action options	240
To specify a form name	241
How Field Values Are Copied to the Response Form	242
Create Response Forms	244
Publish the Forms to the Forms Library of the Folder	244
To make a backup copy of a form	244
To open your backup copy of a form	244
To publish a form in the forms library of a folder	245
Test the Forms	245
To test the forms in the Training Management application	245
Set the Hidden Property for Response Forms	246
To set the Hidden property for the Training Management Response forms	246
Where To Go from Here	246

8 Folders   247

To open the Classified Ads folder	248
An Important Reminder About Planning	248
Create or Select a Folder	249
Choose Where to Design the New Folder	250
Create a Folder from Scratch	251
To create a folder	251
Directly Modify a Folder	252
To directly modify a Mailbox or public folder	252

Table of Contents

Copy a Folder Design	253
To copy a folder design	253
Publish Forms in the Folder	254
To publish a form in an Outlook folder	254
Manage Forms	255
To view the Forms page	256
To specify the types of items allowed in a public folder	256
To open the Forms Manager	257
To change the library in the left or right drop-down list box of the Forms Manager	257
To copy a form to a folder	258
To delete a form	258
To update forms published in different forms libraries	258
To view the properties of a form	258
To set the Hidden property for a form	259
Design Folder Views	259
Create a New View	260
To create a new view	260
To show only the custom views created for the folder	261
Create Columns	262
To add a column to a view	262
To remove a column from a view	262
To change the format properties of a column	264
To create a combination column	265
To change a combination column label or formula	266
To create a combination column showing only the value of the first non-empty field	267
To create a formula column	267
To change a formula column label or formula	268
Group Items	269
To group items by using Customize Current View	269
To create groups by using the Group By box	270
Sort Items	271
To sort items	271

Table of Contents

To group items by Conversation	273
To sort items by Conversation Index	274
Filter Items	274
To filter simple message properties	276
To filter by message class	277
To filter by a field value	278
Format Views	279
To format a view	279
In-Cell Editing Views	280
To enable in-cell editing and a new items row	280
Automatic Formatting	281
To create automatic formatting for individual messages in a view	281
View Performance	283
Use Folder Home Pages	283
Folder Home Page Scenarios	284
Folder Home Page Considerations	286
To set a folder home page	286
Offline Use	287
To configure a folder home page for offline use	288
To establish offline Web page settings	289
Set General Properties	290
To set general properties	291
To automatically generate Microsoft Exchange views	291
Test Forms and Views	291
Copy the Folder to Public Folders	292
To copy the folder to a new location	292
Specify Internet Newsgroup	292
To set a Public Folder as a Newsgroup folder	292
Set Administration Properties	293
To restrict access to the folder	293
Initial View On Folder	294
Drag/Drop Posting Is A	294
Add Folder Address to Personal Address Book	294

Table of Contents

This Folder Is Available To	295
Folder Assistant	295
Moderated Folder	296
Set Permissions	296
To open the Permissions page	297
About Distribution Lists	297
To add a user, distribution list, or folder name to the Name list box	297
Assign Roles	298
To assign roles to users	298
To assign a custom role	299
Set Permissions for Subfolders	299
To use Exchange 5.0 or 5.5	300
To use Exchange 2000	300
Design Rules	300
You can use rules to	301
To create rules	301
Specifying Conditions of a Rule	301
Rules Syntax	302
Specifying Simple Conditions	302
To specify simple conditions	302
Specifying Advanced Conditions	302
To specify advanced conditions	303
Specifying That a Rule Applies to Items That Do Not Match the Conditions	303
To specify that a rule applies only to items that do not match the conditions	303
Specifying Conditions with User-Defined Fields	303
To specify custom fields as conditions	303
Specifying Actions for a Rule	304
To specify an action to run when a condition is met	305
Make the Folder Available for Offline Use	305
To create an offline folder file (.ost)	306
To specify folders for offline use	306
Test and Release the Folder	307
To make the folder available to all users with access permission	307
Where To Go from Here	308

Part IV Beyond the Basics

9 Raise Events and Move to the Head of the Class — 311

- The VBA Editor — 312
  - Launching the VBA Editor — 312
  - *To open the Visual Basic for Applications Editor window* — 313
  - ThisOutlookSession Class Module — 314
  - Navigating in the VBA Editor — 314
  - The Outlook Application Object — 315
  - *To view or set references for Project1* — 316
  - Saving Your Outlook VBA Project — 316
  - Securing Your Outlook VBA Project — 317
  - *To protect an Outlook VBA project* — 317
- Writing an Outlook Macro — 318
  - *To create a new Outlook Macro* — 319
  - *To add an Outlook Macro to the Standard toolbar for the Explorer* — 320
  - *To change your Macro Security settings* — 321
  - *To run an Outlook Macro using the Macros dialog box* — 321
- Writing Code to Respond to Events — 321
  - Use the WithEvents Keyword to Declare Object Variables — 321
  - When You Must Use WithEvents to Declare the Outlook Application Object — 322
  - Using WithEvents for Child Objects — 322
  - Where to Instantiate Child Objects Declared Using WithEvents — 325
  - Observing Events in the Example VBAProject.otm — 326
  - *To turn on event tracing in the VBAProject.otm example* — 326
- Application Events — 326
  - ItemSend — 327
  - NewMail — 327
  - OptionsPagesAdd — 328
  - Quit — 329
  - Reminder — 330
  - Startup — 330
  - New Application Events in Outlook 2002 — 331
- Reminders Collection Events — 332
  - BeforeReminderShow — 333

Table of Contents

ReminderAdd	333
ReminderChange	334
ReminderFire	334
ReminderRemove	334
Snooze	335
NameSpace Events	335
OptionsPagesAdd	336
Explorers Collection Events	337
NewExplorer	337
Explorer Events	338
Activate	338
BeforeFolderSwitch	339
BeforeViewSwitch	339
Close	340
Deactivate	340
FolderSwitch	341
SelectionChange	342
ViewSwitch	342
New Explorer Events in Outlook 2002	343
SyncObject Events	344
OnError	346
Progress	346
SyncEnd	347
SyncStart	347
OutlookBarPane Events	347
BeforeGroupSwitch	348
BeforeNavigate	348
OutlookBarGroup Events	348
GroupAdd	348
BeforeGroupAdd	349
BeforeGroupRemove	349
OutlookBarShortcut Events	350
ShortcutAdd	350
BeforeShortcutAdd	350
BeforeShortcutRemove	351

Inspectors Collection Events	351
Exceptions to the NewInspector Event	351
NewInspector	355
Inspector Events	356
Activate	356
Close	357
Deactivate	357
New Inspector Events in Outlook 2002	357
Folders Collection Events	358
FolderAdd	358
FolderChange	359
FolderRemove	360
Views Collection Events	361
ViewAdd	362
ViewRemove	362
Items Collection Events	362
ItemAdd	363
ItemChange	364
ItemRemove	365
Item Events	366
Adding Events to VBScript Behind Forms	368
To add or modify an event	369
The Firing Sequence of Events	370
Preventing Events from Firing	372
The AttachmentAdd Event	374
The AttachmentRead Event	374
The BeforeAttachmentSave Event	375
The BeforeCheckNames Event	375
The BeforeDelete Event	375
The Click Event	376
To create a Click event procedure	376
The Close Event	376
The CustomAction Event	376
The CustomPropertyChange Event	377
The Forward Event	377

Table of Contents

The Open Event	377
The PropertyChange Event	378
The Read Event	379
Before you run this example, perform the following steps:	379
The Reply Event	380
The ReplyAll Event	380
The Send Event	381
The Write Event	381
Firing Order of Events	381
Where To Go from Here	382
10 The Outlook Development Environment	**383**
The Outlook E-Mail Security Update	383
Trusted COM Add-Ins	384
Outlook and VBA	384
VBScript Versions	385
Determining the VBScript Version in Code	386
The Outlook Script Editor	387
To view the Outlook Script Editor	387
An Introduction to Using the Script Editor	388
To create and test a PropertyChange event	388
Jumping to a Line of Code	389
To jump to a line of code	389
Troubleshooting Code Using the Microsoft Script Editor	389
To install the Microsoft Script Editor	390
To launch the Microsoft Script Editor	390
Controlling How a Script Executes	392
Entering a Breakpoint	392
To set or remove a breakpoint	393
Entering Commands at Run Time	393
To enter script commands	393
Viewing the Call Stack	394
To view the call stack	394
Viewing the Locals Window	394
To view the Locals window	394
Viewing the Watch Window	395

Table of Contents

To view the Watch window	395
To display the properties and property objects of the Item object	395
How to Open an Item Containing VBScript	396
Information Resources for Programming Outlook 2002	396
Web Resources	396
Sample Code	396
To open the VBScript Samples folder	397
Microsoft Outlook Visual Basic Reference Help	397
To use Microsoft Outlook Visual Basic Reference Help	397
A Caution About the Outlook Programming Environment	398
The Implied Item Object	399
To test this example	399
Object Libraries	400
Helper Object Libraries	401
Using an Object Browser	402
To use the Outlook 2002 Object Browser to view the Forms Object Model	402
Moving Around in the Outlook Object Browser	402
To move around in the VBScript Object Browser	402
To display the Outlook VBA Object Browser	403
Object Models	403
To view the Microsoft Outlook Object Model	405
To view the Microsoft Forms 2 Object Model	405
Using the Object Hierarchy	405
To test the code samples in the VBScript Samples folder	406
Getting and Setting Properties	407
Using Variables	408
Using the Variant Data Type	409
VBScript Naming Conventions	410
Declaring Constants	411
To add Outlook CONST declarations to your VBScript code	412
Assigning Objects to Variables	412
Referencing Collections and Single Objects	413
Where To Go from Here	414

xxvii

Table of Contents

11	**Using Visual Basic, VBA, or VBScript with Outlook**	**415**
	To open the VBScript Samples folder	416
	The Application Object	416
	Application Object Methods	417
	To display the Query Builder page on the Filter dialog box	423
	To build a filter using the Query Builder page on the Filter dialog box	423
	The NameSpace Object	426
	NameSpace Object Methods	426
	Properties of the NameSpace Object	427
	The Outlook Window (Explorer Objects)	430
	Explorer Methods	431
	Explorer Properties	431
	The Panes Collection Object	432
	Determining Whether a Pane is Visible	433
	The OutlookBarPane Object	434
	The OutlookBarStorage Object	434
	The OutlookBarGroups Collection Object	434
	The OutlookBarGroup Object	435
	The OutlookBarShortcuts Collection Object	436
	The OutlookBarShortcut Object	436
	The CommandBars Collection Object	437
	To use the code in the VBA Samples folder	439
	To run the PrintAllCBarInfo *procedure*	439
	To run the CBShowButtonFaceIDs *procedure*	441
	The CommandBar Object	445
	The CommandBarControls Collection Object	448
	The CommandBarControl Object	449
	To write an event procedure for a command bar control	457
	The CommandBarButton Object	457
	The CommandBarComboBox Object	458
	The CommandBarPopup Object	459
	The AddressLists Collection Object	459
	AddressLists Collection Methods	459
	The AddressList Object	460
	The AddressEntries Collection Object	460
	AddressEntries Collection Methods	460

The AddressEntry Object	462
AddressEntry Object Methods	462
AddressEntry Properties	465
Using CDO to Obtain Recipients	466
Installing Collaboration Data Objects	467
To install Collaboration Data Objects	467
The Folders Collection Object	468
Folders Collection Methods	468
The MAPIFolder Object	469
MAPIFolder Object Methods	470
MAPIFolder Object Properties	470
The Views Collection Object	475
The Items Collection Object	476
Items Collection Object Methods	477
Items Collection Object Properties	481
The PostItem Object	481
PostItem Object Methods	481
The MailItem Object	483
MailItem Object Methods	483
MailItem and PostItem Objects Properties	486
The DocumentItem Object	490
To add built-in document properties to a Folder View	495
To create an Expense Statement Document	495
To add custom document properties to a Folder View	496
The AppointmentItem Object	496
Working with Recurring Appointments	497
The MeetingItem Object	501
Working with Meeting Requests	501
The TaskItem Object	505
TaskItem Object Methods	506
The TaskRequestItem Object	507
Working with Task Requests	507
The ContactItem and DistListItem Objects	509
ContactItem Object Methods	510
The JournalItem Object	512
JournalItem Object Methods	513

Table of Contents

The Item Window (Inspector Objects)	514
Inspector Object Methods	514
Inspector Object Properties	515
The Pages Collection Object	516
The Page Object	516
The Controls Collection Object	517
Methods of the Controls Collection Object	517
Controls Collection Object Properties	518
The Control Object	518
Properties of Control Objects	520
The UserProperties Collection Object	525
UserProperties Collection Object Methods	526
The ItemProperties Collection Object	526
The Recipients Collection Object	527
Recipients Collection Object Methods	527
Automation	529
Where To Go from Here	530

12   The Northwind Contact Management Application   531

Overview	532
Outlook 2002 and Automatic Activity Journaling	535
A User Navigates to the Root Folder	536
A User Searches for a Company	537
Viewing Shared Activities	538
Custom Views on the Shared Activities Page	539
Viewing Sales Data in the Customer Form	540
Recording Shared Activities by Using Links	540
Shared Documents	542
Shared Appointments and Tasks	543
A User Sends Shared E-Mail	544
Setting Up the Application	544
Copying the Application Folders to Public Folders	546
To copy the Northwind Contact Management Application folder	546
Restricting Access to the Application Folders	547
To restrict access to the application folder and its subfolders by using Outlook	547

Table of Contents

Adding the Shared Mail Folder to the Global Address List	548
To add the Shared Mail folder to the Global Address List	548
Setting the Folder Home Page for the Root Folder	548
To establish a folder home page for the application folder	548
Creating Items in Public Folders from the Shared Database	548
To re-create the items in the Companies and Shared Contacts folders	549
Exposing the Shared Contacts Folder as an Outlook Address Book	550
To expose the Shared Contacts folder as an Outlook Address Book	551
Setting the Initial View on the Customers and Shared Contacts Folders	551
To set the initial view on a folder	551
Setting the Default Item for a Folder	552
To set the default form for the Shared Calendar folder	552
Installing the Outlook Shared Activities Add-In	553
To install the Outlook Shared Activities Add-in	553
Setting the Database Connection String	553
To establish a database connection string	555
Loading the Company and Company Contact Forms	555
The Company Form	559
Script-Level Constants and Variables	560
Declaring Form Controls with Script-Level Object Variables	560
Initializing Form Controls	561
Using the Outlook View Control to Display Company Contacts	564
Retrieving the Possible Values for Custom Fields	568
Updating Company Contacts When Values Change in a Company	569
Creating a Create Shared Items Toolbar	570
Tracking Shared Activities	571
Selecting Views in the PivotTable List	572
Determining Whether a User Is On Line	574
Other Application Forms	575
The Company Contact Form	575
The Administration Form	577
Shared Item Forms	577
The Outlook Shared Activities Add-In	578
Displaying an Explorer Toolbar	578
Extending Your Application with Public Methods	583

Table of Contents

Application Folder Views 586
    The Companies Folder 586
    The Company Contacts Folder 587
    The Shared Journal Folder 587
Releasing the Northwind Contact Management Application 587
    Setting Permissions 587
    To set permissions for the Companies folder and its subfolders 587
    Setting Administration Properties 588
    To set administration properties 588
    Setting Forms Properties 588
    To set forms allowed in the folder for the Companies folder and subfolders 589
Customizing the Application 589
Where To Go from Here 589

13   Distributing and Securing Applications   **591**

Distribute Forms 592
    Make Forms Available in the Organizational Forms Library 592
    To submit a form to an Administrator 593
    To clear the Send Form Definition With Item check box 594
    To publish the form in the Organizational Forms Library 595
    Make Forms Available in the Personal Forms Library 595
    To clear the Send Form Definition With Item check box 595
    To save a form as an .oft file 596
    To insert a form (.oft) file as an attachment in a message 596
    To publish the attached form in a Personal Forms Library 597
    To publish a form in your Personal Forms Library 597
    Make Forms Available in a Folder Forms Library 598
    To publish a form in a folder forms library 598
    Changing the Standard IPM.Note Message 598
    To change the default Read message 600
    Use the Send Form Definition With
        Item Check Box to Send a Form to Another User 601
    Distribute Forms in a Personal Folder (.pst) File 601
    Make Forms Available for Offline Use 601
Manage Forms 602
    The Forms Manager 602

Table of Contents

To open the Forms Manager	603
To copy a form	603
To set form properties	603
To delete a form	603
To update forms published in different forms libraries	603
Modify Forms	604
To change the message class of existing forms in a folder	605
To set the Hidden property of a form	606
The Forms Cache	608
To specify the amount of disk space allocated for forms	608
Clearing the Forms Cache	609
To clear the forms cache in Outlook 2002	609
Form Activation	610
Distribute and Manage Folders	611
Make a Folder Available to All Users in Your Organization	611
To create a folder in Public Folders	611
To copy a folder to Public Folders	612
To set permissions for the folder	612
Make a Folder Available for Personal Use	612
To create a folder in your Mailbox or in a personal folder (.pst) file	613
To copy a folder to your Mailbox or personal folder (.pst) file	613
Distribute a Folder in a Personal Folder (.pst) File	613
To create a personal folder (.pst) file	614
To copy a folder to a personal folder (.pst) file	614
To make an existing personal folder file available on your Microsoft Exchange System	615
Making Changes to a Folder	615
Folder Replication Issues	615
Age and Archive Folders	616
To turn on AutoArchiving for Outlook	616
To turn AutoArchiving on for a specific folder	617
Outlook 2002 Security	617
Attachment Security	618
Object Model Security	622
CDO Security	628
Administrative Options	629

xxxiii

Table of Contents

Installing Admpack.exe	630
To install admpack.exe	630
Creating the Outlook Security Settings Public Folder	631
To create the Outlook Security Settings public folder	631
The Outlook Security Form	632
To install the Outlook Security form	633
Deploying Outlook Security Settings to Client Computers	635
To create a new registry key for distribution to client computers	636
Enabling Offline Use	637
User Registry Settings	637
To create a Level1Remove key	637
Administrator vs. User Settings	638
Preventing End User Customization	638
Creating Custom Security Settings	639
Outlook Security Settings Page	639
Programmatic Settings Page	642
Trusted Code Page	644
To specify a trusted COM Add-in	646
Building Trusted COM Add-Ins	647
Outlook Redemption: A Third-Party Alternative	648
The Redemption Object Library	648
Where To Go from Here	650

Part V Advanced Topics

14 Creating COM Add-Ins with Visual Basic   653

Tools Needed to Create COM Add-Ins	654
The COMAddIns Collection Object	655
COMAddIn Object	656
Displaying the List of COM Add-Ins	657
To display the Outlook COM Add-Ins dialog box	658
To add a toolbar button for the COM Add-Ins dialog box	658
To Load or Unload a COM Add-In	658
To Add a COM Add-In	658
To Remove a COM Add-In	659

xxxiv

Table of Contents

Creating an Outlook COM Add-In Project in Visual Basic	659
To install the Outlook COM Add-in project in your Visual Basic 6.0 Projects folder	660
To open a new Outlook COM Add-in project in Visual Basic 6	660
To add your identity to the Outlook COM Add-in project	661
The Outlook COM Add-In Project Template	662
Moving ThisOutlookSession Code to a COM Add-In	663
What Is a COM Add-In?	664
Building a COM Add-In	666
COM Add-In Settings	666
IDTExtensibility2 Event Procedures	670
Adding Property Pages	678
Installing the Sample Page Project	679
To install and open the Sample Page project	679
Loading the Page and Persisting Settings in the Registry	681
Marking the Page as Dirty	682
Applying Changes	683
Compile and Distribute the ActiveX Control	684
Displaying the Property Page	685
Modifying Command Bars	685
Basic Techniques	686
Step-By-Step Summary for COM Add-In Command Bars	686
To create an Explorer command bar button in an Outlook COM Add-in	686
Command Bar Caveats	687
Adding Dialog Boxes	688
Visual Basic Forms	689
To add a Visual Basic form to a COM Add-in	690
Forms 2.0 Forms	690
To add a Forms 2.0 form to a COM Add-in	690
Displaying a Dialog Box with a Public Method	691
The Debugging Process	692
To debug a COM Add-in in Visual Basic 6	693
Compiling Your COM Add-In	693
To compile a COM Add-in in Visual Basic 6	693
Sample COM Add-Ins	694
Outlook View Wizard	694

xxxv

Table of Contents

Outlook Shared Activities	697
Search	698
Test Trust	698
Add-In Registration	699
Providing Security	699
Securing Your Intellectual Property	700
Outlook Macro Security	700
To install the Create Digital Certificate utility	703
To digitally sign a VBA project	703
Object Model Guard and Attachment Security	705
Trusted COM Add-Ins	706
Deploying Your COM Add-In	707
The Package and Deployment Wizard	708
Visual Studio Installer	710
Where To Go from Here	710

15 Integrating Outlook with Web Applications   **711**

What Folder Home Pages Are	712
What Folder Home Pages Are Not	713
Outlook Web Access	713
Outlook and the Web	713
Folder Home Pages Compared to Outlook Web Access	713
Placeholder Folders and Active Folder Home Pages	714
Folder Home Page Security	714
Using Zone Security and Allowing Script Access to the Outlook Object Model	715
Using Zone Security Only	715
The Outlook Today Page	716
To set a custom Outlook Today page	717
Tools to Create Folder Home Pages	717
The Outlook View Control	718
Adding the View Control to a Form	719
To open the Outlook View Control UserForm	719
To add the Outlook View Control to your Control Toolbox	720
To add the Outlook View Control to your form	720
Outlook View Control Properties	721

Outlook View Control Methods	722
Outlook View Control Events	726
Obtaining Views for the Active Folder	727
Using the View Control in an HTML Page	728
Accessing the Outlook Application Object	728
Using FrontPage 2002 with the Outlook View Control	729
To insert the Outlook View Control into a Web page using FrontPage 2002	729
To set properties for the Outlook View Control	731
HTML Markup for the Outlook View Control	732
Outlook View Control Security	733
To use OutlookViewControl.htm as a folder home page	734
Writing Code in a Folder Home Page	735
Maintaining State in a Folder Home Page	738
Using Event Handlers with the View Control	739
Digital Dashboards	740
Glossary of Digital Dashboard Terms	741
Choosing the Digital Dashboard Platform	741
Downloading the Digital Dashboard Resource Kit 3.0	742
Installing the SQL Server Dashboard	742
To install the SQL Server sample Dashboard for the DDRK	743
Installing Office XP Developer Support for SQL Server Digital Dashboard 3.0	743
To install Office XP Developer Support for SQL Server Digital Dashboard 3.0	744
To create a new Dashboard Project with Office XP Developer	744
To import Web Parts into an Office XP Developer Dashboard Project	745
Importing a Web Part	746
To install the sample Web Parts to the file system	746
Creating My Dashboard	747
To create My Dashboard	747
Creating a Nested Dashboard	748
To create the Northwind Dashboard	748
Adding Web Parts from the Web Part Catalog	749
To add Web Parts to My Dashboard	749
To add Web Parts to Northwind Dashboard	751
Features of My Dashboard	752

Table of Contents

Designing Web Parts with Office XP Developer		753
Opening and Designing a Web Part		754
To create a Web Part in Office XP Developer		755
My Inbox HTML		755
The _WPQ_ Token		757
Scripting a Web Part		758
Web Part Localization		761
DHTML Events for a Web Part		761
Writing Outlook Code in a Web Part		762
Maintaining State in a Web Part		764
Providing a Web Part Namespace		764
Exporting Web Parts		765
To export a Web Part		765
The Northwind Digital Dashboard		765
Northwind Dashboard Setup		766
Web Part Flexibility		767
Browser Interface for a Public Folder Application		767
Quick Search		768
Track Shared Activities		769
Communicating Between Web Parts		770
The DDSC Notification Service		770
The Companies Web Part		773
The Shared Activities Web Part		775
The Sales Data Web Part		778
Putting It All Together		781
Setting the Folder Home Page for the Companies Folder		781
To set a folder home page for the Companies folder		781
Navigating to the Companies Folder		782
Where To Go from Here		784
16 Using Outlook with SharePoint Portal Server		**785**
SharePoint Portal Server Evaluation Edition		787
SharePoint Portal Server Platform		787
The Workspace		788
To create the Northwind workspace		788
SharePoint Portal Server Roles		789
To create roles for the Northwind workspace		790

Table of Contents

Document Management	792
Using Web Folders	793
To create a Web folder on Windows 98 or Windows NT	794
To create a Web folder on Windows Me or Windows 2000	794
Check In and Check Out	795
Document Profiling	796
To add a new document profile named Northwind Document	797
To set the Northwind Document Profile as the default document profile	798
Approval Routing	799
To enable approval routing for an enhanced folder	801
Using Categories	802
To add categories to a document profile	803
Content Indexing and Searches	803
Establishing the Default Content Access Account	804
To set the Default Content Access account	804
Indexing Exchange Public Folders	805
To set up a content source on an Exchange server public folder hierarchy	805
Scheduling Updates	807
To schedule content source indexing	807
Searching the Northwind Workspace	807
Using Advanced Search	809
To search using Advanced Search	810
The Power of Subscription	811
Outlook Integration with SharePoint Portal Server	812
Modifying Default Web Parts	812
To allow Web Parts to be removed from a SharePoint Dashboard site	813
Adding a URL to the CRM Administration Form	814
To add the SharePoint URL to the CRM Administration form	815
Publishing a Document with the Company Form	815
Improving Productivity with the Office XP Places Bar	817
To add a SharePoint Document folder to the Office XP Places Bar	818
The Outlook Shared Activities Add-In	819
Calling Methods from the Company Form	819
The *PublishSharePointDocument* Method	820
Web Storage System Properties	823
Handling Keywords	825

Table of Contents

Referencing the PKMCDO and CDO 3.0 Object Libraries	826
Displaying the List of Documents	827
The *ShowDocumentListHTML* Method	828
Working with Web Storage System Date/Time Values	831
The PKMCDO Object Model	832
The KnowledgeServer Object	834
The KnowledgeWorkspace Object	834
The KnowledgeCategoryFolder Object	835
The KnowledgeFolder Object	835
The KnowledgeDocument Object	836
The KnowledgeContentClass Object	836
The KnowledgeVersion Object	836
An Outlook COM Add-In for SharePoint Portal Server	837
Installing the SharePoint Portal Server Add-In	837
To install the SharePoint Portal Server COM Add-in	837
Using the SharePoint Portal Server Add-In	838
To add attachments to a Document folder	839
SharePoint Portal Server COM Add-In Code	840
SharePoint Development Opportunities	845
Where To Go from Here	845
Index	**847**

Foreword

If there was ever any doubt that Microsoft Outlook is the world's most widely used programmable e-mail application, that uncertainty evaporated in May, 2000, when millions of people found messages of affection in their Inbox folders, sometimes from complete strangers. What came to be known as the I Love You or LoveLetter virus—and the many similar viruses that subsequently targeted Outlook—demonstrated just how easy it is to write programs that automate Outlook.

Maybe too easy, concluded Microsoft. As a result, a security patch was issued for Outlook 98 and Outlook 2000, and Microsoft built those security features into Outlook 2002. Dealing with the changes to Outlook automation imposed by these new security features is the single biggest challenge facing Outlook 2002 developers. In this book, you'll find details on how to handle the prompts that the "object model guard" presents to users, how to use the tools for Exchange Server and HP OpenMail environments that allow administrators to trust specific COM Add-ins and selectively turn off the object model guard prompts, and what alternatives are available in situations in which the administrative tools cannot be used.

Despite the tighter security prompted by a world now wary of mail-borne viruses, Outlook remains the most customizable e-mail program available. Independent software developers have built hundreds of applications that either enhance Outlook with new capabilities—such as automatically compressing attachments in mail messages—or use Outlook as the foundation for complex programs that combine Outlook data with information from other sources. Corporate developers have extended Outlook in thousands of additional projects involving custom forms, Exchange Server scripts and event sinks, and COM Add-ins.

Besides being a more secure environment, Outlook 2002 offers some long-awaited object model improvements, including programmable views and searches and new folder properties that facilitate building applications both in Public Folders and for offline use. Outlook's ability to take an Exchange Server–based application off line is one of its critical strengths and has spawned many customer relationship management programs that help a "road warrior" manage data during his or her travels and automatically synchronize it with the server.

Above all, you'll find this book a very concrete guide to application development with Outlook. Randy Byrne is one of those people who isn't content to

Foreword

know only what the program does but wants to explore much further to discover how it might meet practical business and other goals that Outlook developers bring to their projects.

Sue Mosher
Slipstick Systems, Arlington, VA
http://www.slipstick.com

Acknowledgments

This book was almost an entirely different book, but that is another story that does not bear telling here. I want first to thank Chris Kimmell of Microsoft for extending the invitation to write the Outlook 2002 version of this book. Other current and former members of the Outlook team in Redmond deserve thanks for their contributions, including Michael Price, Paul Steckler, Dan Battagin, Ronna Pinkerton, Bill Jacob, Chad McCaffery, Abdias Ruiz, Aaron Hartwell, Florian Voss, Don Mace, David Raissipour, and Brian Trenbeath. On the Exchange team, I've learned from the contributions of Jamie Cool, Jeff Wierer, Mindy Martin, Thomas Rizzo, KC Lemson, Jim Reitz, and the incomparable Charles Eliot. Finally, I want to acknowledge the assistance of Kay Williams and Paul Garner, lead program managers of the Outlook team, and Steven Sinofsky, Senior Vice President of Office. They provided access to material that made this a better book.

Apart from the Outlook team, I want to acknowledge the Microsoft Most Valued Professionals (MVPs) on the Outlook newsgroups who volunteer their time and effort to answer postings from Outlook users. Their ultimate goal is to make Outlook a better product. Thanks to all the members of the Outlook lunatic asylum, including Sue Mosher, Ken Slovak, Jay B. Harlow, Vince Averello, Hollis D. Paul, Jessie Louise McClennan, Ben M. Schorr, Milly Staples, Diane Poremsky, Bill Rodgers, Patricia Cardoza, Russ Valentine, Steve Moede, and the wizard of Extended MAPI, Dmitry Streblechenko. You all have helped me to comprehend pieces of Outlook that escaped my notice or understanding. In the MVP community, I send an immense thank you, once again, to Sue Mosher of Slipstick Systems, whose energy and commitment to Outlook and Exchange is unsurpassed. From the early preview of Office XP through the final beta, Sue has provided a sounding board for ideas and has always provided a clear perspective on developments in the world of Outlook and Exchange. For those of you who live by Outlook (both literally and figuratively), you know that there aren't enough superlatives to describe Sue's contributions.

There are peers who also enriched my knowledge of Outlook, Exchange, and SharePoint Portal Server. I'd like to thank Richard Wakeman, Robert Ginsburg, and Andy Sakalian of IT Factory (formerly ECMS). Additional thanks go to Phil Seeman of TeamScope Software, Jan Cirpka of Compaq Global Services, and Siegfried Weber of CDO Live. Finally, special thanks to David Kane, Vice President of Development at Micro Eye, for providing patient answers to my questions concerning the integration of Outlook with Web technologies.

Acknowledgments

Because a book of this type is by its very nature a group effort, I want to thank the Microsoft Press team behind this book. Thanks to David Clark, my acquisitions editor, for pushing this title through the approval process. Devon Musgrave, my project editor, deserves kudos for keeping me on track and on schedule. You actually made this book like a comfortable ride to an alluring destination instead of a slow uncontrolled descent into the underworld. Marzena Makuta was the technical editor and provided a sharp eye for code and technical errors. Michelle Goodman did the manuscript editing and Holly Viola the copyediting. Dan Latimer served as the principal compositor. Michael Victor pitched in as the buildmaster for the companion CD. Again, I thank all the team for their professionalism and enthusiasm. You did a great job, guys!

For encouragement and support during the writing of this book, I want to thank the following friends and family: Marie Byrne; Barry Byrne, MD; Lou and Harriet Cohen; Davide Atenoux; Chuck Schultz; Susan Brown; Steve Ekstrom; Steve Cohen; Laura Hogan; Karen Kane; Jerry Kaplan; Fern Friedman; and Susan Chainey.

Introduction

Who Should Use This Book

This book is designed primarily for Microsoft Outlook application developers using Microsoft Exchange Server. Many of the examples assume that you'll be deploying workgroup applications in an Exchange Server environment using both public and private folders. It's also assumed that you'll be using Outlook 2002 to run the applications in this book. Although many of the techniques discussed in this book can be used in prior versions of Outlook, you won't be able to take full advantage of the code examples and sample applications unless you've installed Outlook 2002.

Part I, "Introducing Microsoft Outlook 2002," provides you with a broad perspective on what you can accomplish using Outlook as a development platform. You'll learn about some tools and add-ins included on the companion CD that will make your life easier as an Outlook developer. In Part II, "Quick Guide to Building Applications," both programmers and nonprogrammers can pick up this book and find the information they need to develop groupware applications. Part III, "Building Blocks of Applications," gives you a solid foundation on which to build more complex Outlook applications. You'll understand that Outlook applications are developed using the core objects of messages and folders, and you'll learn how to customize Outlook forms to create an Outlook application.

In Part IV, "Beyond the Basics," you'll learn how to use events in the Outlook object model to write event-aware code. After an introduction to the Outlook development environment, you will be able to write Microsoft Visual Basic or Microsoft Visual Basic Scripting Edition (VBScript) code to create more sophisticated applications than you can using Outlook's built-in modules. You'll learn about the critical Outlook E-Mail Security Update that is built into Outlook 2002 and how you can work with this component of Outlook to protect your personal and private data from e-mail worms and viruses. I'll also extend what you've learned in a complete customer relationship management (CRM) sample application that operates both on line and off line. Part V, "Advanced Topics," is for developers who are at an intermediate or advanced level in Visual Basic. Step-by-step instructions are included that show you how to create COM Add-ins that replace Exchange Client Extensions and provide Outlook functionality that you only dreamed of in the past. You'll learn about the new Outlook 2002 View

Control, folder home pages, and integrating Outlook with Digital Dashboards and Web Parts. Finally, you'll see how to add document management and powerful search capabilities to your Outlook applications with SharePoint Portal Server 2001.

More Detail on How This Book Is Organized

This book consists of the following five parts and sample applications.

Part I Introducing Microsoft Outlook 2002

Chapter 1, "Applications You Can Create with Outlook," discusses the processes and problems best suited for Outlook solutions and shows you the kind of Request, Discussion, Tracking, and Reference applications you can build to streamline communications in your organization. Chapter 2, "Outlook Design Tools," showcases the tools available for creating Outlook forms and for building COM Add-Ins and folder home pages by using Microsoft Office XP Developer, Visual Basic, and Microsoft Visual InterDev. Chapter 2 also introduces you to evaluation versions of important third-party tools and Microsoft SDKs that are included on the companion CD.

Part II Quick Guide to Building Applications

Chapter 3, "Customize Built-In Modules," shows you how to create instant groupware applications by modifying the built-in Contacts application, customizing it for tracking customer correspondence related to a beta program, and then copying it to Public Folders on Exchange Server. Chapter 4, "Design a Custom Application," shows you how to build a Discussion application called Product Ideas that makes it possible for users to submit, read, and respond to new product ideas.

Part III Building Blocks of Applications

Chapter 5, "Forms," introduces the form design process and covers fundamental form design tasks such as adding controls and fields, creating new actions, setting form properties, and publishing forms. Chapter 6, "Controls, Fields, and Properties," covers the fundamental skills and information you need to effectively use controls, fields, and properties on a form. It also explains the unique features of each commonly used control and then offers some strategies for implementing these controls and fields in an application. Chapter 7, "Actions," discusses the easiest way to create responses for Message forms, explains how to create custom Reply actions for Message forms, and then shows how to create custom Reply To Folder actions for Post forms. Chapter 8, "Folders," takes an in-depth look at the folder design process, discusses how to make a folder available for offline use, and explains how to create custom views and folder home pages. It also covers setting folder permissions and building rules.

Part IV Beyond the Basics

Chapter 9, "Raise Events and Move to the Head of the Class," explains how you can use all the new events in the Outlook Object Model to write event-aware code in Outlook Visual Basic for Applications or an Outlook COM Add-in. Chapter 10, "The Outlook Development Environment," introduces the Outlook Script Editor for VBScript code behind Outlook forms. This chapter also discusses debugging with the Microsoft Script Editor and shows you the object models used in Outlook development. Chapter 11, "Using Visual Basic, VBA, or VBScript with Outlook," introduces VBScript and provides a wide variety of code examples for the most commonly performed tasks using VBScript or Visual Basic in Outlook. Chapter 12, "The Northwind Contact Management Application," demonstrates how you can apply what you've learned so far in a reusable Customer Relationship Management (CRM) application designed for online and offline use. Chapter 13, "Distributing and Securing Applications," shows you how to distribute forms in folders and provides some techniques for maintaining and securing applications. This chapter also discusses the critical areas of Outlook Object Model and attachment security and illustrates how the Outlook E-Mail Security Update has been integrated into Outlook 2002. Finally, you'll learn how your current and future applications can coexist with the Outlook E-Mail Security Update.

Part V Advanced Topics

The Advanced Topics chapters are primarily for developers who want to use Visual Basic to extend Outlook in a corporate environment where Exchange Server is installed. Chapter 14, "Creating COM Add-Ins with Visual Basic," provides you with practical templates for Visual Basic COM Add-in component creation and discusses the security issues associated with COM Add-ins. You'll also learn how to use Visual Basic to create an ActiveX control that serves as a property page in the Outlook Tools Options dialog box. Chapter 15, "Integrating Outlook with Web Applications," shows you how to use the Outlook View Control in Web pages. You'll also learn how to create Digital Dashboard Web Parts for the Northwind Contact Management Application. In Chapter 16, "Using Outlook with SharePoint Portal Server," you'll discover how you can use the PKMCDO Object Model for document check in, check out, and versioning. You will be able to integrate the Northwind Contact Management application with SharePoint Portal Server document management and search.

Introduction

Sample Applications

The sample application for this book is in the Building Microsoft Outlook 2002 Applications personal folders (.pst) file on the CD that accompanies this book. You can modify the sample Northwind Contact Management application for use in your organization. The Northwind Contact Management application is a CRM application created in Exchange public folders and is suitable for both online and offline use. This application is extended in the Advanced Topics chapters of the book. You can integrate the Northwind Contact Management application with the Digital Dashboard Resource Kit 3.0 or SharePoint Portal Server 2001 as shown in Figure I-1.

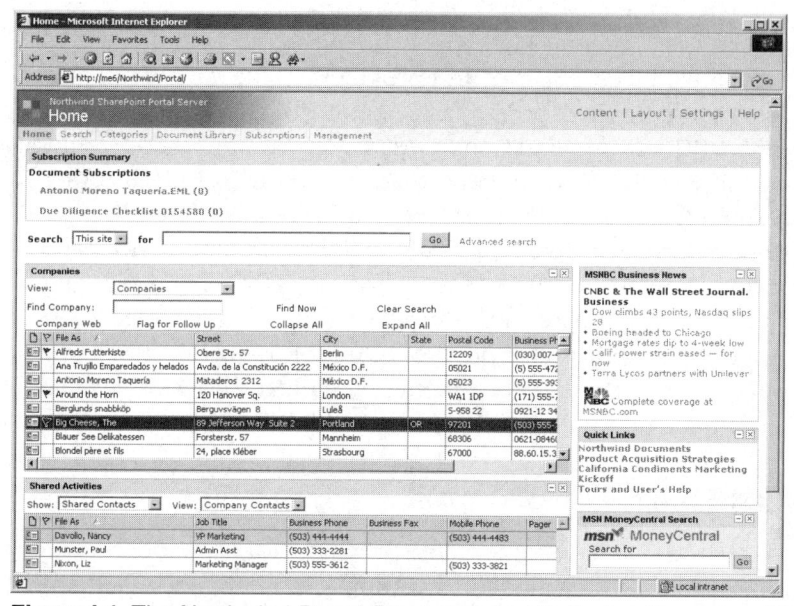

Figure I-1 The Northwind Portal Site integrates Outlook with custom Web Parts and SharePoint Portal Server Document Management.

System Requirements

To run the code on the companion CD, you will need a computer that meets the following minimum requirements:

- Pentium 133 or higher Pentium-compatible CPU

- 32 megabytes (MB) of RAM or more, depending on the operating system, plus 8 MB of RAM per each open Office application

Introduction

- 650 MB hard disk or larger, depending on the operating system
- CD-ROM drive
- Super VGA (SVGA) monitor
- Mouse or other pointing device (recommended)

The following software must be installed on your system:

- Windows NT 4.0, Windows 2000 Professional, or Windows 2000 Server or later
- Microsoft Internet Explorer 5.01 or later (to view the electronic version of this book)
- Microsoft Outlook 2002
- Collaboration Data Objects 1.21

To modify the sample applications, you will need the following software:

- Microsoft Visual Basic 6.0 with Service Pack 3 or later
- Microsoft Visual InterDev 6.0 with Service Pack 3 or later
- Microsoft Office XP Developer

To install the sample applications on Exchange Server:

- Microsoft Exchange 5.5 Server or Microsoft Exchange 2000 Server

To extend the sample applications:

- Microsoft Digital Dashboard Resource Kit 3.0 or later
- Microsoft SharePoint Portal Server 2001

Using the Companion CD

The companion CD contains all the code necessary to run the sample applications discussed in this book, including evaluation versions of several third-party tools, sample COM Add-ins, Web Parts for use in Digital Dashboards or SharePoint Portal Server 2001, the Exchange SDK, and the SharePoint Portal Server SDK. It also includes a sample personal folders (.pst) file, which contains all of the applications and sample code covered in this book.

You might want to make a copy of the applications and dissect the ones you're most interested in to see how they're developed. You can also customize these applications and put them to work in your organization.

Introduction

Run the Setup Program for *Building Applications with Microsoft Outlook Version 2002*

> **Caution** The Setup program requires that you have already installed Microsoft Outlook 2002 on your computer. Microsoft Outlook 2002 is not included on the companion CD. You must install Microsoft Outlook 2002 before you proceed.

To install the book's program files

1. Insert the CD accompanying this book into your CD-ROM drive.
2. If a menu screen does not launch automatically, double-click StartCD.exe in the root folder of the CD-ROM..
3. Click Install Samples to start the Building Applications with Microsoft Outlook 2002 installation to your hard disk. A Welcome dialog box will appear.
4. In the Welcome dialog box, click Next.
5. In the Select Directory dialog box, select the folder where you will install the Building Microsoft Outlook 2002 Applications personal folders (.pst) file. Click the Browse button if you want to select an alternative folder.
6. Click Next to begin the installation process.
7. If Setup detects that you already have a VBAProject.otm file on your system, you will see an Alert message box that informs you that the VBAProject.otm accompanying this book has been renamed and the location of the renamed file. See "Installing VBAProject.otm" later in this Introduction if you see this alert message box during installation. Click OK to dismiss the VBAProject.otm Warning alert box if it appears during installation.
8. Click Finish to complete the installation.

Introduction

Using the Building Microsoft Outlook 2002 Applications Personal Folder (.pst) File

The Setup program installs a Building Microsoft Outlook 2002 Applications file in the destination folder you specified during installation and adds this file as a personal folders file to your current profile. The Building Microsoft Outlook 2002 Applications file is actually a personal folders (.pst) file that contains sample forms and files, links to technical articles and white papers, links to Microsoft Product Support Services Knowledge Base articles that pertain to Outlook development, and all the files necessary to run the sample applications and code examples.

Although it's not required that you add the Building Microsoft Outlook 2002 Applications file to your system, it serves as a valuable reference tool, and the sample applications can be used as a starting point for building applications that can be customized for your environment.

Installing VBAProject.otm

Outlook 2002 supports Visual Basic for Applications as an integral component of the Outlook application environment. All the code for Outlook Visual Basic for Applications is stored in a single file, VBAProject.otm. This file is stored in the locations in the following table depending upon operating system and whether user profiles are operational on your system. If your operating system is installed on a drive other than drive c:\, adjust the location accordingly.

Operating System	Location for VBAProject.otm
Microsoft Windows 98 and Windows Me	*<drive>:*\Windows\Application Data\Microsoft\Outlook
Microsoft Windows NT 4.0	*<drive>:*\Winnt\Profiles*<user>*\Application Data\Microsoft\Outlook
Windows 2000	*<drive>:*\Documents and Settings\Profiles*<user>*\Application Data\Microsoft\Outlook

If you already have a VBAProject.otm on your system, the installation program will display an alert message informing you that it has detected an existing VBAProject.otm. In this instance, the VBAProject.otm that accompanies this book will be renamed to VBABAO2K2.otm and copied to the location of your existing VBAProject.otm. For you to use the sample code in the VBAProject.otm that accompanies this book, you will have to rename your existing VBAProject.otm

li

Introduction

to a name such as MyVBAProject.otm and then rename VBBAO2K2.otm to VBAProject.otm. If you don't have an existing VBAProject.otm, the VBAProject.otm that accompanies this book will be installed automatically and you can ignore the following steps.

> **To install the VBAProject.otm that accompanying this book if you already have VBAProject.otm installed on your Windows 2000 system**

1. If Outlook is running, quit Outlook by using the Exit command on the File menu. You must exit Outlook completely or you will receive a sharing violation when you attempt to rename VBAProject.otm.
2. Click the Start button on the Windows Task bar, click Search, and click For Files Or Folders.
3. Type *vba*.otm* in the Search For Files Or Folders Named drop-down combo box.
4. Select Local Drives in the Look-In drop-down combo box.
5. Click Search Options. Make sure that the Search Subfolders box is checked.
6. Click Search Now.
7. When VBAProject.otm and VBABAO2K2.otm are found on your system, right-click VBAProject.otm and select Rename on the shortcut menu. Type *MyVBAProject.otm* as the new name, and press Enter.
8. Right-click VBABAO2K2.otm, and select Rename on the shortcut menu. Type *VBAProject.otm* as the new name. Press Enter.
9. Restart Outlook. The VBAProject.otm that accompanies this book is now the operational VBA Project for Outlook.

The steps for other operating systems are similar. Simply locate the vba*.otm file on your system, rename it, and replace with the supplied file.

Outlook Macro Security

If Outlook Macro Security is set to High, the macros in VBAProject.otm will be disabled. In Outlook 2002, the default Outlook Macro Security setting is High. For the code in the VBAProject.otm file accompanying this book to run correctly, you must change the Outlook Macro Security setting to Low or Medium. Changing the setting to Low or Medium impacts only your ability to run the code in VBAProject.otm; it does not modify the built-in object model and attachment security mechanisms built into Outlook 2002.

Introduction

To change Outlook Security settings to Low or Medium

1. Select Macro from the Tools menu.
2. Select Security from the Macro submenu.
3. Select the Low or Medium security option on the Security Level page.
4. Click OK to accept your selection.

> **Important** Because Outlook Visual Basic for Applications code is loaded on demand, you must press Alt+F11 to open the Visual Basic Editor the first time you launch Outlook after you install the VBAProject.otm that accompanies this book. Once you press Alt+F11, you'll see the Macro Warning dialog box. Select the Enable Macros button to run the code in VBAProject.otm.

Installing Collaboration Data Objects

Some of the code examples on the companion CD require the installation of Collaboration Data Objects (CDO) 1.21. CDO is not installed with the default Office XP setup. It is recommended that you install CDO before you run the code examples that are provided with this book.

To install Collaboration Data Objects

1. Insert the Office XP CD into your CD-ROM drive.
2. Click Start, click Settings, and then click Control Panel.
3. Double-click Add/Remove Programs.
4. On the Install/Uninstall page, click Microsoft Office XP—the exact title will vary depending on the version of Office XP installed on your computer—and then click Add/Remove on Windows 2000 computers. On Windows 98, Windows Me, and Windows NT 4.0 computers, click Change.
5. In the Microsoft Office XP Maintenance Mode dialog box, click Add Or Remove Features.
6. Double-click the Microsoft Outlook For Windows item to expand the item in the Microsoft Office XP: Update Features dialog box.

Introduction

7. Click the Collaboration Data Objects item under Microsoft Outlook For Windows.
8. Select Run From My Computer in the installation options drop-down.
9. Click Update to complete the installation of Collaboration Data Objects.

Technical Support for the Companion CD

Every effort has been made to ensure the accuracy of this book and the contents of the companion CD. Microsoft Press provides corrections for books through the World Wide Web at the following address:

http://mspress.microsoft.com/support/search.htm/

If you have comments, questions, or ideas regarding this book or the companion CD, please mail or e-mail them to Microsoft Press at the following addresses:

Postal Mail

Microsoft Press
Attn: Building Applications with Microsoft Outlook Version 2002 Editor
One Microsoft Way
Redmond, WA 98052-6399

E-mail

mspinput@microsoft.com

Please note that product support is not offered through the above mail addresses. For support information on Outlook, see the documentation for the appropriate product support phone number.

Part I

Introducing Microsoft Outlook 2002

1 **Applications You Can Create with Outlook** 3

2 **Outlook Design Tools** 17

Chapter 1, "Applications You Can Create with Outlook," discusses the processes and problems best suited for Outlook solutions and shows you the kind of Request, Discussion, Tracking, and Reference applications you can build to streamline communications in your organization. Chapter 2, "Outlook Design Tools," showcases the tools available for creating Outlook forms, building COM Add-ins, and developing folder home pages.

1

Applications You Can Create with Outlook

Microsoft Outlook 2002 offers incremental improvements to Outlook 2000 for collaborative application developers. You can programmatically create and modify Views, create a Search object and iterate over its Results collection, and manipulate Reminders in ways that were impossible in previous versions of Outlook. On the other hand, Outlook 2002 creates security roadblocks that were not present in the initial version of Outlook 2000. These security features will perplex many developers who believe that the Outlook development world has been held captive by the destructive behavior of hackers who use Outlook's object model as a launching pad. Regardless of whether Outlook developers applaud, Microsoft had to respond to the threat of massive disruption of corporate e-mail systems by Outlook-related viruses. Developed in response to e-mail-borne viruses such as Melissa and ILoveYou, the Outlook E-Mail Security Update is built into Outlook 2002 and cannot be removed. On the positive side, Outlook 2002 provides a mechanism to create COM Add-ins that can be trusted by an Exchange administrator and that bypass the security restrictions built into the Outlook object model.

Outlook 2002 supports Microsoft Visual Basic for Applications 6.3. No longer do Outlook developers have to dream of a professional editor and debugger. The full Visual Basic object browser is only a keystroke or mouse click away. Performance improves with strongly typed variables and early binding. ActiveX property pages created in Visual Basic can replace Exchange custom extensions written in C++. Folder home pages and the Outlook View Control offer a means of scripting Active Server Pages to provide Web-based views into Exchange and Outlook public and private folders. COM Add-ins allow you to create commercial or corporate versions of Outlook. The list goes on. On the following page are just a few of the things you can accomplish with Outlook 2002.

- **Share information** You can build applications that allow users to share all types of information, including schedules, tasks, contacts, distribution lists, documents, product ideas, and customer feedback.

- **Structure information** You can build forms and folders to structure information so it's both easy to read and easy to find. For example, you can create a Preferred Vendors public folder so managers can quickly find qualified vendors that have been referred by other managers in the organization, or you can use the Product Ideas application supplied with this book to enable users to submit, organize, and view new product ideas in a public folder.

- **Distribute information** You can create forms that enable users to send announcements, sales reports, documents, and request-for-services items. For example, you can create a Bulk Mailer form so you can automatically notify all users in a particular distribution list when a product update is available.

- **Collect information** You can create forms and folders for collecting information. For example, you can create a User Response Form and public folder for collecting information about a product under development. Or you can use the Classified Ads application supplied with this book to allow users to submit and respond to classified ads.

- **Collaborate on information** One of the benefits of Outlook is that it allows each user to collaborate on the same item. For example, with the Product Ideas application, users from different locations can all participate in an online discussion about a particular product feature. With the Contact Management application, users can collaborate on the pursuit of new customers in a set of linked public folders.

- **Streamline processes** You can create applications that are modeled on paper-based processes in your organization. For example, you can create forms and folders that allow users to electronically submit vacation requests, travel plans, copier requests, purchase orders, time cards, status reports, classified ads, and training class registration. Using the Exchange Workflow Designer for Exchange 2000, you can integrate Outlook forms with folder-based workflow logic and create powerful workflow applications.

- **Work off line** One of the advantages of Outlook over a pure Web mail interface is the ability of mobile users to work off line and consolidate their work later. Remote users can update custom forms and then synchronize their changes when they return to the office.

Types of Applications You Can Create

The two main building blocks of Outlook applications are forms and folders. From an object model perspective, all Outlook applications consist of message and folder containers. Advanced applications elaborate this core model by either presenting data in departmental or corporate databases or by maintaining links to Web documents stored with SharePoint Team Services in Microsoft Office XP.

The design tools described in this book allow you to create a wide variety of Outlook and Exchange applications, ranging from rudimentary applications that leverage the basic Outlook forms to more complex collaboration and tracking applications that are multitiered:

- **Applications that consist entirely of forms**   These are forms that are not associated with a specific folder, such as the While You Were Out form.

- **Applications that consist of a custom folder and standard forms**   When you create a folder, you often will create custom views for that folder while still using the standard Outlook forms. For example, you might create a Contacts folder in a public folder and create custom views for the folder, but not change the standard forms supplied with the folder.

- **Applications created with the Team Folder Wizard**   The Team Folder Wizard lets you create the following types of applications with the ease of a wizard: discussion, frequently asked questions, document library, issue tracking, team calendar, team contacts, team project, and team tasks. Folder home pages for these applications can be customized to go beyond what the wizard provides.

- **Applications that consist of a custom folder and custom forms**   In many cases, you customize both the folder and the form to build an application. For example, the Training Management, Classified Ads, and Contact Management applications all consist of customized forms and folders.

- **Applications that use folder home pages**   Outlook 2002 allows developers to combine the power and flexibility of Web pages with Outlook views and offline support for mobile users. Folder home pages provide users with a graphical way to organize their Outlook information with Web links to related content on either the Internet or a corporate intranet. Active Server Pages and the Outlook View Control let you combine Outlook views with Active Server Page scripting. You can create HTML-based Web views of Exchange folders with links to user instructions, frequently asked questions, or component

Part I Introducing Microsoft Outlook 2002

downloads. Folder home pages can also provide data or pivot table analysis to the user with the new Office XP PivotTable List control. Figure 1-1 shows a Digital Dashboard folder home page in the Companies folder of the Northwind Contact Management Application.

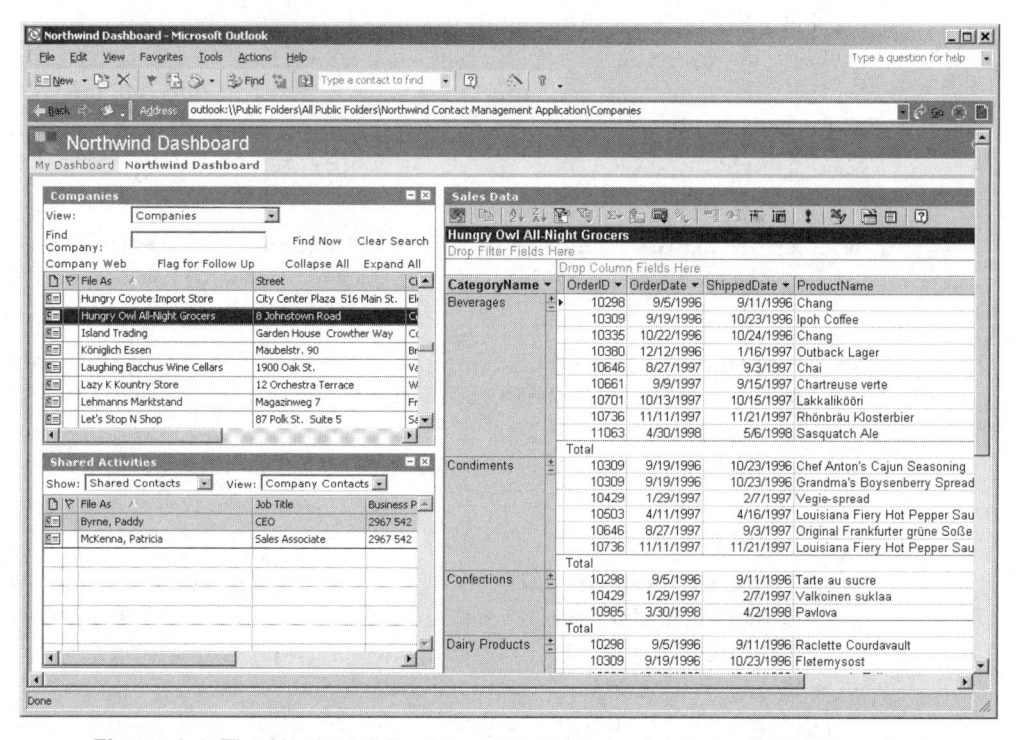

Figure 1-1 The Northwind Dashboard folder home page uses Web Parts to display company information.

- **Applications that use Exchange public folders and Outlook forms through a browser**   Outlook Web Access provides a means for Internet users to access public folders that contain discussions or customer service applications, for example. It lets users send e-mail, manage appointments and contacts, and access Exchange public folders and several standard Outlook forms by using a browser.

- **Applications that modify the Outlook user interface through COM Add-ins**   These applications could best be described as custom Outlook applications that change the normal appearance and functionality of Outlook. COM Add-ins allow you to modify the command bars, the toolbars, and the Outlook Bar to suit specific application requirements. Other programs can be launched from a COM Add-in, such as retrieving data from corporate databases or providing other custom functions.

- **Applications that use Exchange agents to extend a custom folder or custom forms** Certain advanced applications require the use of either Exchange Server scripting or routing on private and public folders. For example, scripting agents (known as Event Sinks in Exchange 2000) are essential when you want to synchronize the contents of an Exchange public folder with a corporate database. Users can create workflow processes for documents and forms (voting, routing) that improve business processes by automating the transfer of information with Exchange Routing Objects available with Exchange Server 5.5 Service Pack 1 or later. If you run Exchange 2000 in your organization, Office XP Developer provides a drag-and-drop workflow designer that lets you create simple workflow applications without coding. You can build advanced workflow applications by writing workflow scripts or by creating server-based components that use the Collaboration Data Objects (CDO) Workflow object library.

- **Applications that provide custom functionality built on Exchange and Outlook** Knowledge Management, Sales Force Automation, and Document Management applications provide customizations of Exchange and Outlook for their target customers.

Forms You Can Create

With the Outlook form in Design mode, you can create a wide spectrum of forms to perform a variety of tasks. When you create forms with Outlook, you never need to start from scratch. Instead, you base the forms you create on a standard form of a specific type supplied with Outlook. Standard form types include Message, Post, Office Document, and built-in modules, such as Appointment, Contact, Distribution List, Journal, and Task. Because most of the functionality is already available in these forms, you can often create custom forms by adding additional fields and controls to the standard forms, or by removing any controls you do not need. You can also create custom forms that bear little resemblance to the base form, such as a Post or Contact form.

In this section, we look at the different types of forms you can create or customize in Outlook. For more information, see "Outlook Form Design Mode" in Chapters 2 and 5 ("Outlook Design Tools" and "Forms").

Message Forms

Message forms are forms that are based on the Outlook Mail Message form. As such, Message forms allow users to send information to other users or to a public folder. Message forms are often used to streamline a request or approval process. Here are some examples of Message forms:

Vacation Request

The Vacation Request application, covered in Part III, "Building Blocks of Applications," contains a Vacation Request form, as shown in Figure 1-2. The Vacation Request form allows a user to send a vacation request to a manager. The Vacation Request application also contains a Vacation Approved form and a Vacation Denied form so a manager can respond to a request.

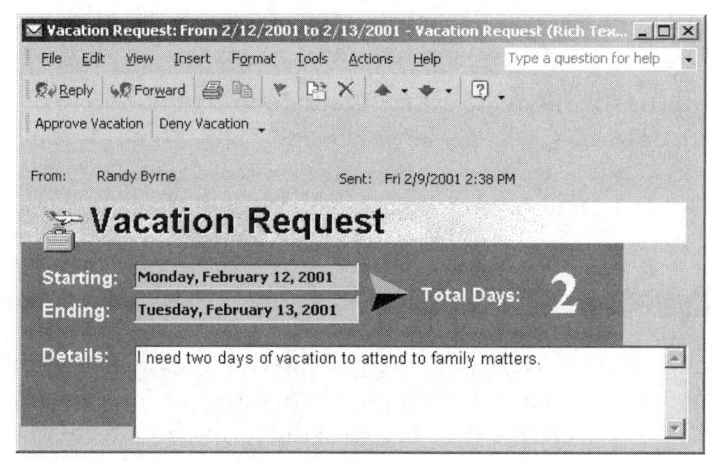

Figure 1-2 The Vacation Request form.

Status Report

You can also create a form that enables users to send weekly or monthly status reports to their managers. Submitted status reports can be stored in a personal folder or public folder and used for reference at review time.

Mileage Report

Forms can be created to make it possible for a user to submit monthly mileage reports to a manager for approval. When approved, the information in the Mileage Report item can be written to a database. This report can be extended to a management-type application with the Exchange 2000 Workflow Designer.

Post Forms

Post forms are used to post items, as well as responses to items, to a folder. Post forms are used in applications that enable users to conduct online discussions, such as the Product Ideas folder discussed in Chapter 4, "Design a Custom Application." As such, Post forms serve as the foundation for creating threaded conversations in views. Post forms are also used for applications that require users to respond to a particular item, such as the Training Management application, in which the Evaluation form is used to post a response to a Course Offering item.

The following sections describe a few ideas for creating Post forms using Outlook in Design mode.

Product Ideas

The Product Ideas application consists of a Product Idea form and a Product Idea Response form, both of which are posted to a public folder as shown in Figure 1-3. Innovative, new ideas are readily shared and recorded in a public folder for all to access.

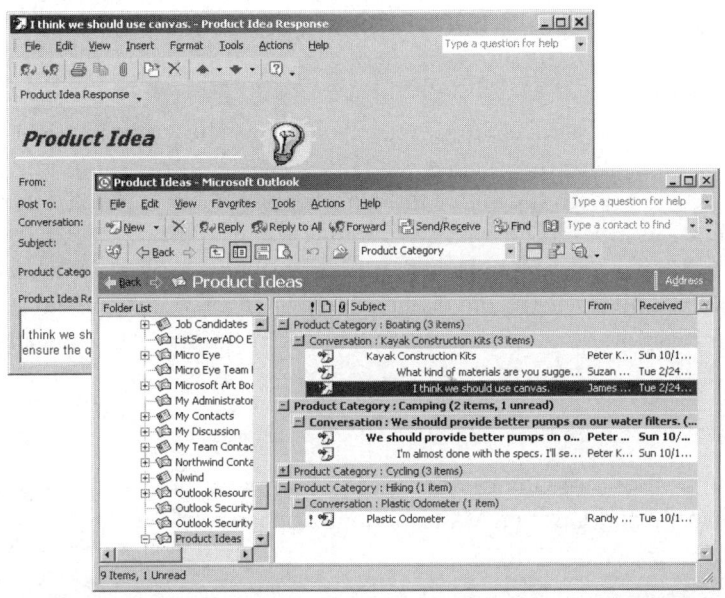

Figure 1-3 The Product Ideas folder with the Product Idea Response form in the background.

> **More Info**   For more information, see Chapter 4.

Job Posting

You can also create a Job Posting form that structures information and makes it possible for Human Resources to post a job opening in the Job Postings folder.

Job Candidate

You can also create a Job Candidates application, which consists of a Job Candidate form and a Response form. A manager or human resources administrator can submit a Job Candidate item to the Job Candidates public folder.

Each user, after interviewing the candidate, uses the Response form to submit hiring recommendations to the Job Candidates folder, where the manager can review the summary of opinions.

Built-In Module Forms

You can customize forms based on the forms in the built-in modules—Appointment, Task, Contacts, and Journal—to take advantage of the specific functionality of the module. The following sections offer a few ideas for the types of forms you can create based on the forms in the Outlook built-in modules.

Company Form

You can create forms such as the Company form, as shown in Figure 1-4, to make it possible to track shared activities, such as a sales call, in relation to a customer or vendor. As demonstrated here, the standard Contact General page has been modified to show related Company Contacts in an Outlook View Control. New pages named Notes and Shared Activities have been added to the form. Other pages on the standard form have been hidden. A custom toolbar lets the user create items in subfolders for shared mail, tasks, appointments, journal items, and documents.

> **More Info** For more information on the Company form, see Chapter 12, "The Northwind Contact Management Application."

Applications You Can Create with Outlook   Chapter 1

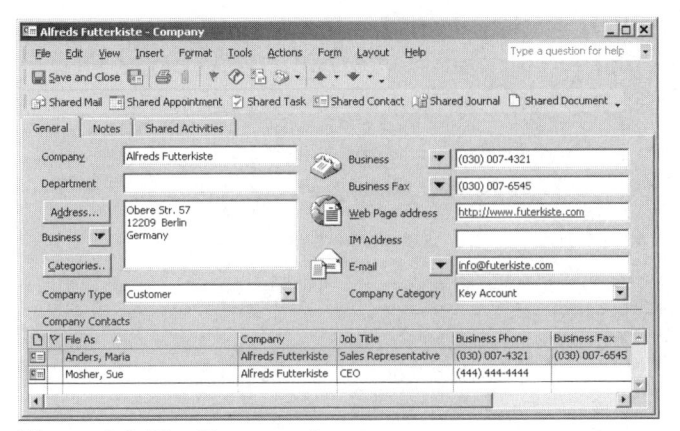

Figure 1-4 The Company form.

Folder Applications

Folders in Outlook are generally used for the following purposes:

- To facilitate online discussions about a particular topic, as demonstrated with the Product Ideas folder.

- To store, organize, and share information, as demonstrated with the Classified Ads and Training Management folders.

- To record and track information that is constantly updated, as demonstrated with the Northwind Contact Management application.

Folders Based on Built-In Modules

With built-in modules such as Appointments, Tasks, and Contacts, instant workgroup solutions can be created simply by creating a folder in public folders. The folder can then be modified for the specific purpose of your workgroup or organization. The following sections offer a few ideas for the types of applications you can build based on built-in module folders.

Beta Contacts Folder

With the Beta Contacts folder, managers can post contacts for a beta testing program. The Beta Contacts folder, as shown in Figure 1-5, is based on the built-in Contacts module.

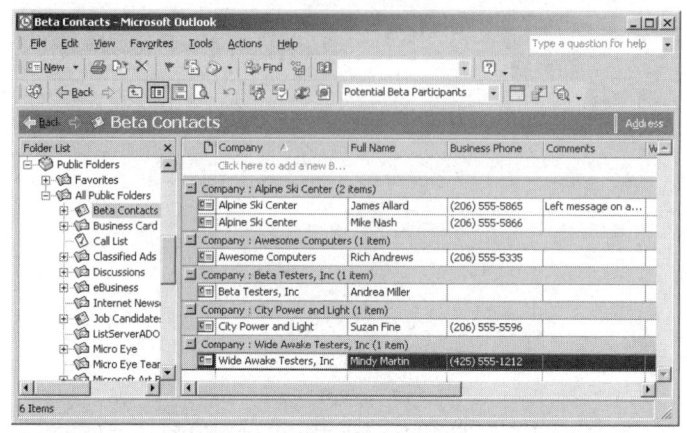

Figure 1-5 The Beta Contacts folder based on the built-in Contacts module.

Shared Calendar Application

You can create a custom Calendar folder in Public Folders, so events relating to a particular group can be easily recorded and shared. For example, you might want to create a shared Calendar that contains events related to the product development cycle so that product announcements, press releases, trade shows, and shipping dates are accessible to the entire workgroup.

> **Note** Exchange 2000 provides a more robust and scalable platform than Exchange 5.5 for Web access to built-in module applications in public folders. Unlike Exchange 5.5 Outlook Web Access (OWA), Exchange 2000 supports public folder contact items in its Web interface. Figure 1-6 shows company contacts stored in the CRM folder.

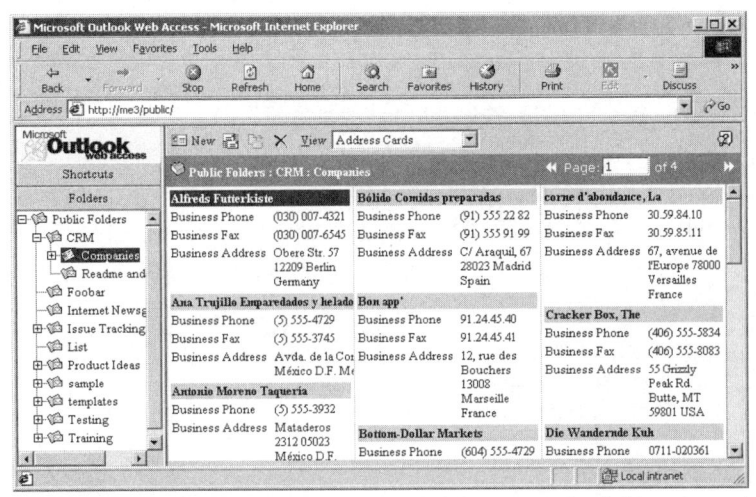

Figure 1-6 Exchange 2000 supports Web access for folders based on the built-in Contacts module.

Discussion Folders

Most often, Discussion folders serve as a central location for users to submit, share, and respond to ideas and information. Discussion folders feature views with threaded conversations, so users can view the history of responses to a particular item.

Product Ideas Folder

The Product Ideas folder makes it possible for users to post and respond to new product ideas. In addition, users can post responses to product idea responses. Responses to a particular item are indented and placed underneath the original item, creating the threaded conversation view.

Training Management Folder

The Training Management folder makes it possible for training personnel to post Course Catalog items in the folder, as shown in Figure 1-7. After a Course Catalog item is posted, training personnel can post a Course Offering item as a response to the Course Catalog item. Users completing a course can post an Evaluation item as a response to the Course Offering item.

Part I   Introducing Microsoft Outlook 2002

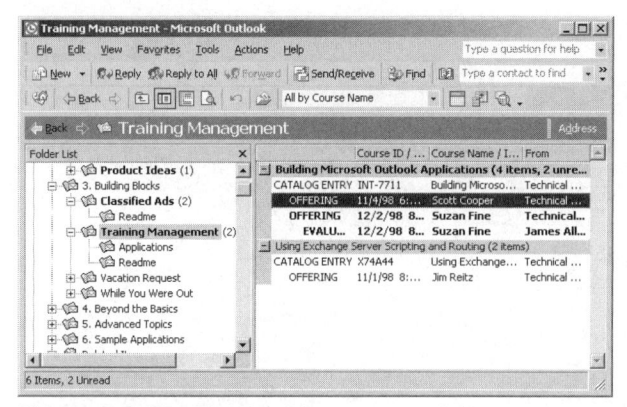

Figure 1-7 The Training Management folder.

Tracking Folders

Tracking folders allow users to record and review information that is constantly updated.

Companies Folder and Related Activities Subfolders

The Companies folder contains Company items that allow the sales force to keep track of activity involving key company contacts. A Company item can be assigned a company type, such as vendor or customer. Separate subfolders record customer-related activities and use Outlook links to tie public folder Appointment, Task, Contact, E-Mail, Document, and Journal items to Company items. See Figure 1-8.

Reference Applications

You can store just about any kind of information in a folder, including product specifications, feature proposals, sales reports, software prototypes, employee status reports, Web site addresses, and training materials. With the addition of folder home pages introduced in Outlook 2000, a folder gains a Web interface, as shown in Figure 1-9. Web views of a folder can be customized with Microsoft Visual InterDev 6 or any other Web development tool.

Specification Library

As development team members work on a project, individuals can store product specifications in a public folder so other members of the team, as well as sales and marketing personnel, can have access to the documents.

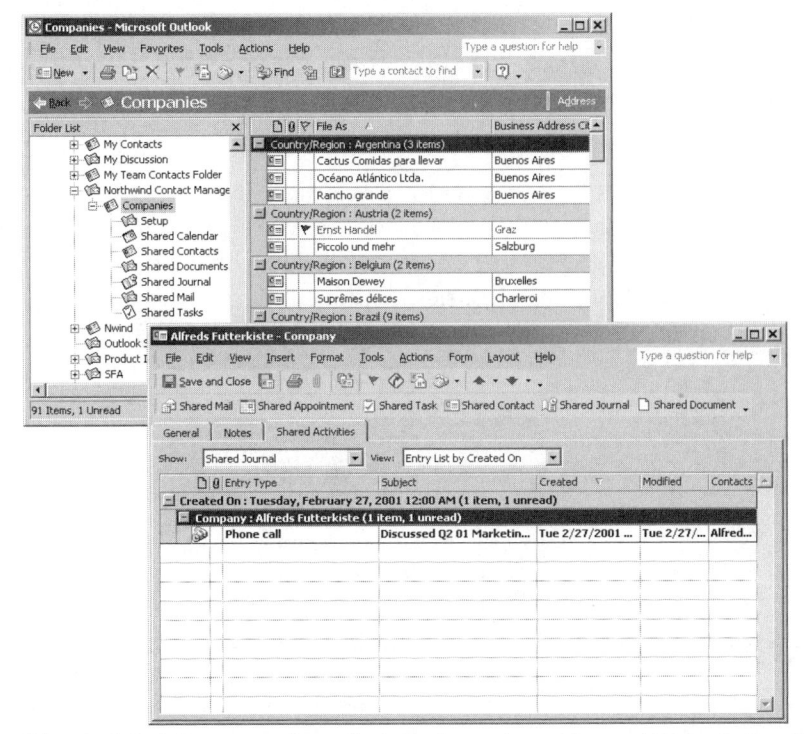

Figure 1-8 A Company form that displays shared journal items in the Outlook View Control.

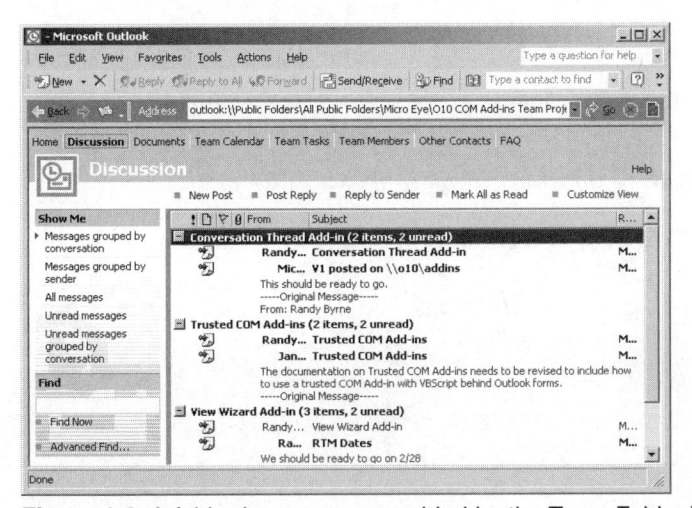

Figure 1-9 A folder home page provided by the Team Folder Wizard.

Status Reports

Managers, as well as employees, may want to store weekly status reports in a public folder for reference at review time.

VBScript Samples

The VBScript Samples folder provides a good medium for collecting communal sample scripts. As shown in Figure 1-10, the VBScript Samples folder contains sample procedures for a variety of commonly performed tasks that can be accomplished using Microsoft Visual Basic Scripting Edition (VBScript).

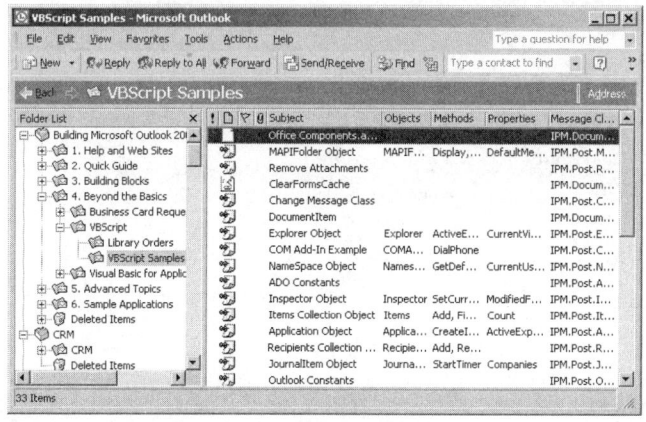

Figure 1-10 The VBScript Samples folder.

For More Form and Folder Ideas

For additional information about the types of applications you can create, visit the following Web sites:

http://www.slipstick.com/addins/mssampleapps.htm

http://www.microsoft.com/technet/download/sample.asp

http://msdn.microsoft.com/office/

http://msdn.microsoft.com/exchange/

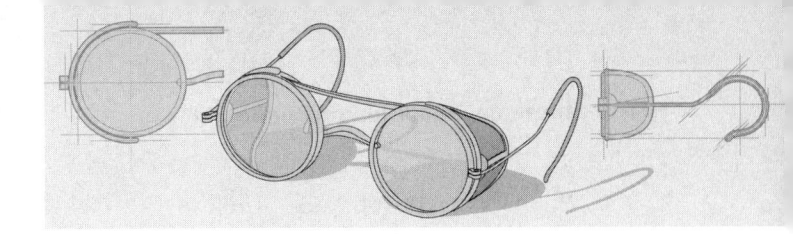

2

Outlook Design Tools

Microsoft Outlook offers easy-to-use design tools for creating custom forms and folders. For example, in Design mode, Outlook provides an AutoLayout feature that automatically positions controls as you add them to a form. In addition, a Script Editor window is provided in Design mode, so you can use Microsoft Visual Basic Scripting Edition (VBScript) in your forms to control folders, forms, fields, and controls. And when working with Outlook folders, you can create custom views directly in the folder by dragging fields to or from the column heading row. In many cases, you don't even need to open a dialog box to create a view.

Microsoft Outlook and Exchange have matured as a development platform, and as a result, Microsoft and third-party vendors offer a variety of new tools to help you create powerful collaborative applications. You can download some of these tools from Microsoft's Web sites. Third-party tools, however, require the purchase of a license. This book's companion CD contains evaluation versions of several of these tools. You'll find them in the Tools And Add-Ins folder that's installed by the setup program on the CD.

If you intend to write advanced, collaborative applications, you'll need some serious development tools. Because this book focuses on Visual Basic programming, I recommend that you add either Microsoft Visual Studio 98, which includes Visual Basic 6, or Microsoft Office XP Developer to your development toolbox. At the time of this writing, Visual Studio.NET and Visual Basic for Applications.NET were still in beta, so it wasn't clear how the.NET platform would influence Exchange and Outlook development.

If you've ever used Office Developer, you'll be impressed with Office XP Developer. Office XP Developer includes the familiar Code Librarian, which contains reusable code nuggets for your projects. New features in Office XP Developer include an improved Exchange 2000 Workflow Designer and the ability to create a Digital Dashboard project for Exchange 2000 Server.

Part I   Introducing Microsoft Outlook 2002

In this chapter, you'll get a quick introduction to the tools that you use to design Outlook applications. Along the way, you'll see some of the features that you can use to make designing applications quicker and easier.

Help and Web Sites

In the Building Microsoft Outlook 2002 Applications folder supplied on the CD that comes with this book, you'll find a Help And Web Sites folder. In this folder, you'll find Readme files with information on how you can install Microsoft Outlook Visual Basic Reference Help, in case you didn't install this file while installing Outlook.

> **Important**   If you have not added the Building Microsoft Outlook 2002 Applications folder, see the Introduction of this book for instructions.

To open the Help And Web Sites folder

- Click Folder List on the View menu. Select the Building Microsoft Outlook 2002 Applications folder, and then open Folder 1. Help And Web Sites folder.

    Here is a quick summary of the contents of the Help And Web Sites folder:

- **Help folder**   This folder contains links to white papers and other documents that relate to building applications with Outlook, Exchange, and SharePoint Portal Server.

- **Microsoft Web Sites folder**   This folder contains links to Microsoft Web sites that pertain to Exchange and Outlook development. The folder also has post items for many of the chapters in this book that contain URLs to Microsoft Knowledge Base articles from Microsoft Product Support Services. These articles contain critical bug reports, workarounds, and code fragments.

- **Third Party Web Sites folder**   This folder contains links to third-party Web sites that offer information relating to Outlook and Exchange development. Microsoft is not responsible for the content or the availability of these sites. However, these sites contain additional information that will be useful to you when you develop applications with Microsoft Outlook.

> **Caution** Past versions of Outlook allowed you to place URL shortcuts in a folder. When you clicked the URL shortcut, a new browser window would open. In Outlook 2002, the Outlook E-Mail Security Update blocks these URL shortcuts. For additional details, see Chapter 13, "Distributing and Securing Applications."

> **Note** Use Microsoft Outlook 2002 Web Views to browse Web pages directly within Outlook without launching your Web browser. You can view Web pages directly in the Outlook window. Click on sites listed on your Favorites menu, or create shortcuts to Web pages that you visit frequently and add them to your Outlook Bar.

To open a Web page directly in Outlook

1. Click the View menu, select the Toolbars command, and then click Web on the Toolbars submenu.
2. Type the URL for the Web page in the Address box of the Web toolbar.
3. Press the Enter key.

To add a page opened in a Web View to your Outlook Bar

1. Use the steps outlined above to display a Web page in Outlook.
2. Right-click in the gray area of the Outlook Bar. Do not right-click on an Outlook Bar shortcut.
3. Select the Outlook Bar Shortcut To Web Page command. Outlook will place an Outlook Bar shortcut for the active Web page in the My Shortcuts group on your Outlook Bar.
4. If you want to rename the shortcut, right-click the Shortcut icon and click the Rename Shortcut command.

Part I   Introducing Microsoft Outlook 2002

Outlook Form Design Mode

The ability to customize and create forms is built directly into Outlook, so opening a form in Design mode is as easy as opening a new form, choosing Forms on the Tools menu, and then clicking Design This Form. When the form is in Design mode, the Form Design toolbar and the Field Chooser appear. As shown in Figure 2-1, you can add fields and controls to the form by dragging the fields from the Field Chooser to the form. When you add a field to a form using the Field Chooser, Outlook automatically creates a control and a label for the field and binds the control to the field. With the Outlook AutoLayout feature, the controls are automatically aligned with existing controls on the form. To enter Run mode, you click Run This Form on the Form menu. In this way, you can easily switch back and forth between Design and Run mode to check the layout of a form at run time.

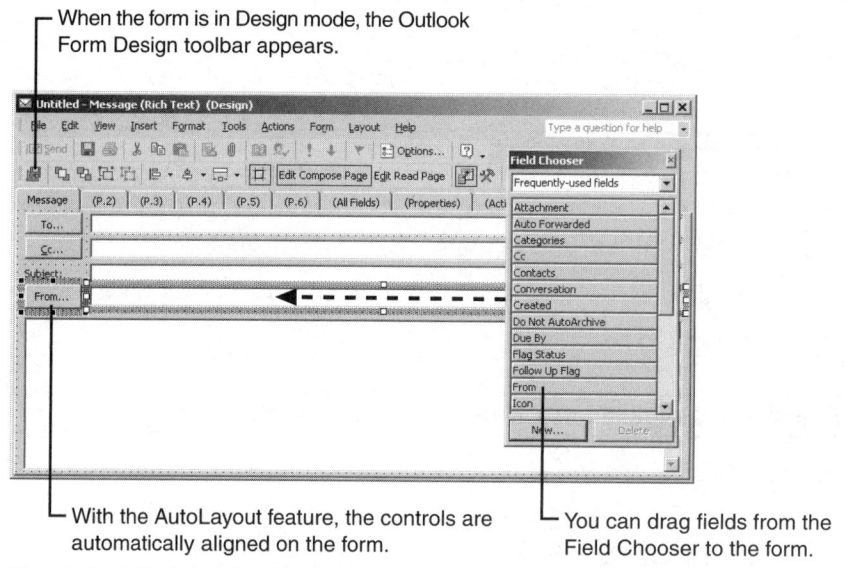

Figure 2-1 Outlook Design mode tools.

To view an Outlook form in Design mode

1. On the Outlook Actions menu, click New Mail Message, or click the New Mail Message icon on the Standard toolbar. You may also select a different form, such as Appointment, which most closely resembles your end application.

2. On the form's Tools menu, choose Forms and then click Design This Form.

> **Note** Message and Discussion/Post forms are fully customizable. You can customize Task, Distribution List, Appointment, and Journal forms by adding additional pages to the forms, but the existing built-in pages cannot be modified. This constraint also applies to the Contact form, but you can modify the first page of a Contact form. See Chapter 5, "Forms," for more information.

Here are just a few advantages of developing forms using Outlook design capabilities:

- **Outlook forms are fully 32-bit forms** So they're fast, and perhaps equally important, they're small, averaging about 1 KB. Attachments and shortcuts add to the average size of the form.

- **Outlook forms are interpreted** So they're easy for designers to keep track of and update. With Outlook forms, designers don't need to worry about searching through folders or directories to find uncompiled source files to make changes to a form.

- **In Design mode, an Outlook form provides a grid and a variety of alignment tools** Including AutoLayout, to make sure your forms have a professional appearance.

Properties Dialog Box

To set properties for controls and fields that you add to forms, you use the Properties dialog box, shown in Figure 2-2, which is accessible while Outlook is in Design mode.

To view the Properties dialog box

- With the form in Design mode, right-click an existing control on the form. For this example, you can right-click the Subject control and then click Properties on the shortcut menu.

Advanced Properties Dialog Box

With the Advanced Properties dialog box, you can set properties for controls. As shown in Figure 2-3, the Advanced Properties dialog box is used to set the ControlTipText property for a control.

Part I Introducing Microsoft Outlook 2002

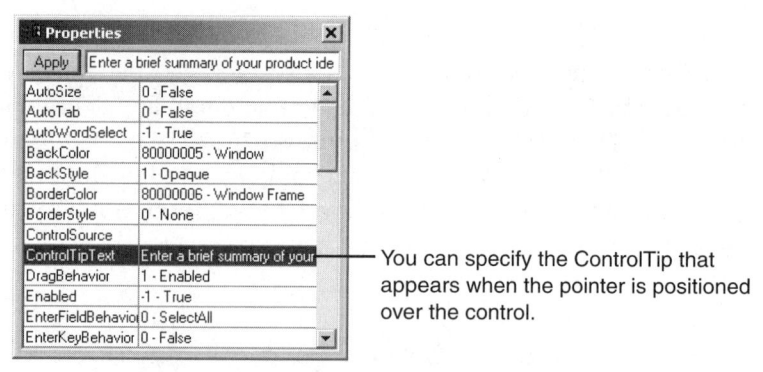

You can specify the ControlTip that appears when the pointer is positioned over the control.

Figure 2-2 The Properties dialog box available in Design mode.

Use this page to set properties for controls.

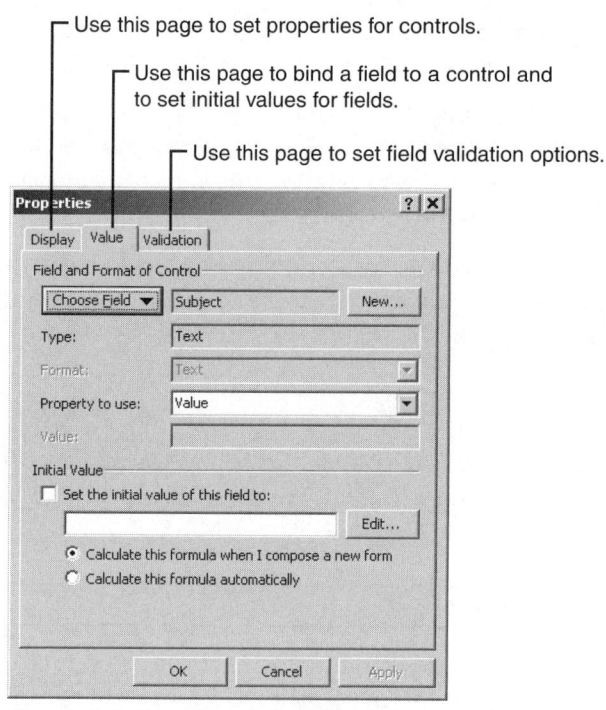

Use this page to bind a field to a control and to set initial values for fields.

Use this page to set field validation options.

Figure 2-3 The Value tab of the Advanced Properties dialog box available in Design mode.

To view the Advanced Properties dialog box

- With the form in Design mode, right-click an existing control (the Subject control in this example) and then click Advanced Properties on the shortcut menu.

> **More Info** For more information about using the Properties dialog box or the Advanced Properties dialog box, see Chapter 6, "Controls, Fields, and Properties."

The Visual Basic Expression Service

Using the Visual Basic Expression Service provided in Outlook, you can create validation criteria for fields, you can create formulas to calculate field values, and you can create formulas that combine text strings in a field.

To explore this capability using the Business Card Request form, open the form in Design mode.

To open the Business Card Request form in Design mode

1. In the Folder List, select the Business Card Request folder under 4. Beyond The Basics.
2. On the Actions menu, select New Business Card Request.
3. To get into Design mode, select Forms on the Tools menu and then click Design This Form.

To open the Visual Basic Expression Service

1. With the form in Design mode, right-click an existing control (in this example, the CardAddress control) and then click Properties on the shortcut menu.
2. Click the Value tab, and then click Edit.

As shown in Figure 2-4, the Visual Basic Expression Service is used to create a formula for a field in the Business Card Request form.

With the Visual Basic Expression Service, you can

- **Validate fields** You can create validation formulas to ensure that a specific value or a value range is entered in a field, or to ensure that a field value is not exceeded.
- **Create formulas for calculating values in fields** For example, you can create a formula for a Total field that multiplies hours by hourly rate.
- **Create Combination fields** You can create formulas that combine field values and text fragments together, or you can create combination fields that show the value of the first non-empty field in the item.

Part I   Introducing Microsoft Outlook 2002

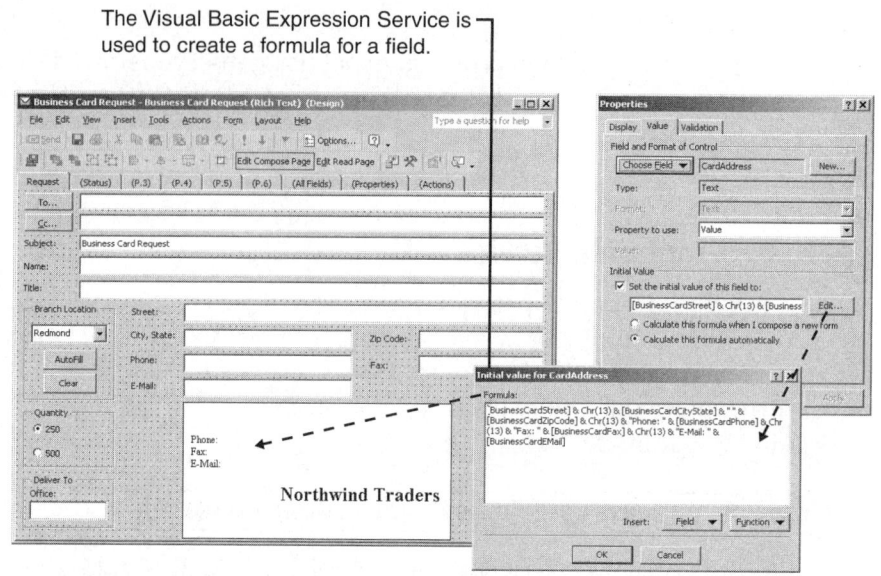

Figure 2-4 With the Visual Basic Expression Service, you can create formulas for fields.

> **More Info**   For more information about the Visual Basic Expression Service, see Chapter 6.

Script Editor and VBScript

With the Script Editor, available in Design mode, you can program Outlook forms using VBScript. VBScript is a subset of the Visual Basic language and is designed to be a small, lightweight interpreted language. Using VBScript, the Outlook 2002 Object Model, and the Forms 2.0 Object Library, you can accomplish a wide variety of programming tasks. For example, you can set the current form page when the form opens in Compose mode.

To view the Script Editor

■   With the form in Design mode, click View Code on the Form menu.

The Script Editor has templates for all the item events. To add an event template to your script in the Script Editor, click Event Handler on the Script menu, click an event name in the list, and then click Add. The appropriate Sub…End Sub or Function…End Function statement is inserted. As shown in Figure 2-5, the *Item_Open* function is added to the Script Editor window for the Business Card Request form, and code is added to the event to hide the Status page of the form when the form is in Compose mode. This code also resolves the hard-coded Business Card Requests recipient address and displays a critical error message box if the address cannot be resolved.

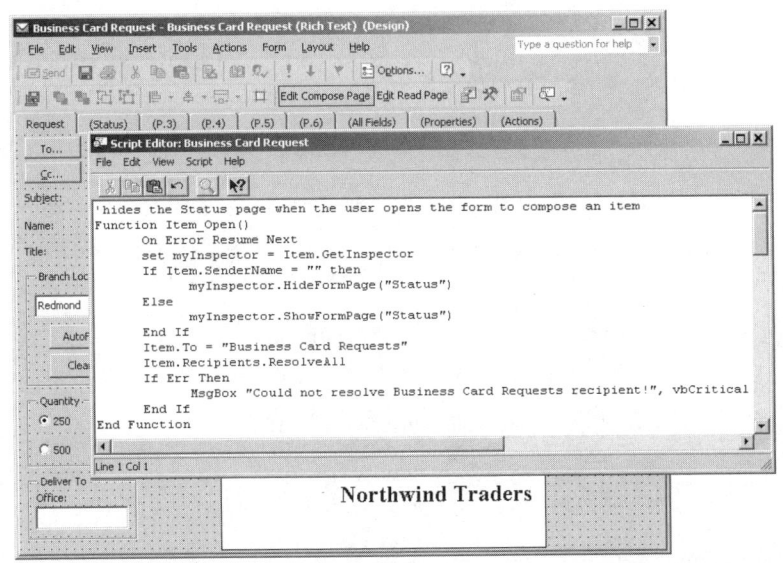

Figure 2-5 The Script Editor window shows the *Item_Open* function.

> **More Info** For more information about using VBScript, see Chapter 11, "Using Visual Basic, VBA, or VBScript with Outlook."

Folder View Design Tools

With Outlook, you can create custom views by adding, removing, and rearranging fields in the Column Heading row of the folder. For example, you can create a column by dragging a field from the Field Chooser to the Column Heading row.

To add or remove a column using the Field Chooser

1. Select a folder on the Folder List. Click Toolbars on the View menu, and then click Advanced.
2. Select Field Chooser from the Advanced toolbar.

Part I   Introducing Microsoft Outlook 2002

3. Drag the field you want to add as the new column to the Column Heading row, as shown in Figure 2-6. Use the double-arrow marker to position the new column heading in the Column Heading row.

4. To remove the column heading, drag the column heading you added away from the Column Heading row until an X appears, and then release the mouse button.

As shown in Figure 2-6, the Business Phone 2 column is created by dragging the Business Phone 2 field from the Field Chooser to the Column Heading row.

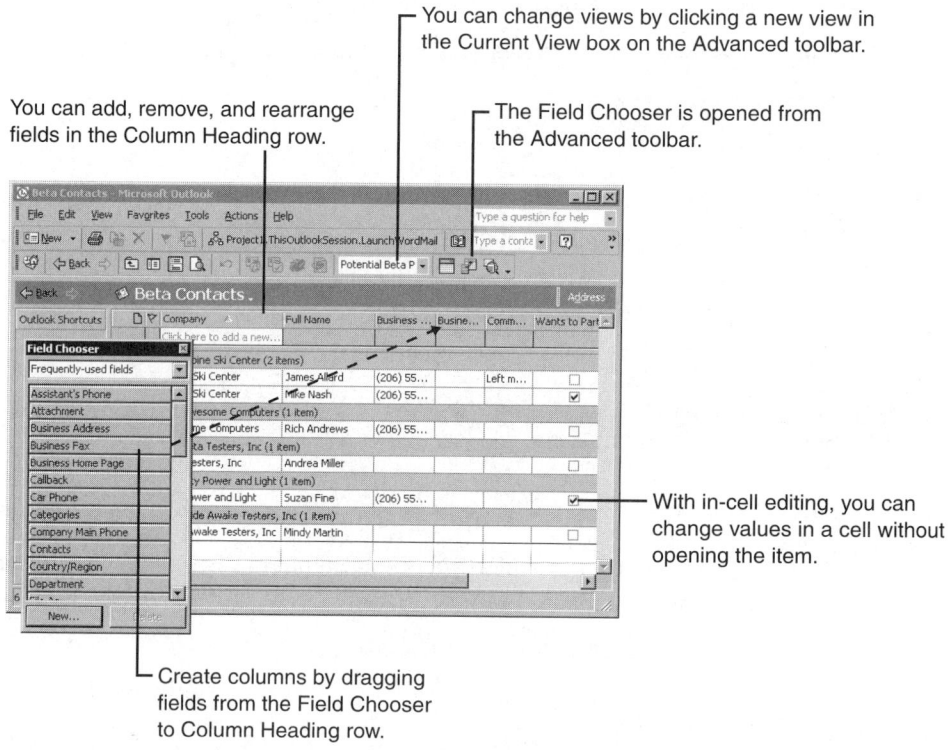

Figure 2-6 The Beta Contacts folder and the Field Chooser.

Drag and drop grouping You can group items in a folder by a particular field simply by dragging the field you want to group by above the Column Heading row. On the Advanced toolbar, click the Group By icon. Click and drag a field from the Field Chooser to the area above the Column Heading row. You cannot group or sort by combination or formula fields.

Format columns The ability to format columns gives you great flexibility in designing views. For example, in many cases, you want the column label to be different than the name of the field the column is based on. To format a column, right-click the column heading and then click Format Columns on the shortcut menu. You can then choose the options you want.

In-cell editing When the in-cell editing option is turned on for a folder, users can edit and enter information in cells within the folder without opening a form. For example, in the Beta Contacts folder, as shown earlier in Figure 2-6, users can click in a Wants To Participate cell on the far right to add or remove a check box icon in the cell. To activate in-cell editing, select Current View on the View menu and then click Customize Current View. Click Other Settings, and then choose the Allow In-Cell Editing check box in the Rows box.

Best fit feature This feature automatically arranges the column size to fit the text in the column heading label. To choose the Best Fit option for a column, right-click the column heading and then click Best Fit on the shortcut menu.

Show only custom views Quite often, users are confused by the large number of views available in a folder. To alleviate this problem, Outlook makes it possible to show only the custom views created for the folder. To select this option, select Current View on the View menu and then click Define Views. Then select the Only Show Views Created For This Folder check box.

Folder Properties Dialog Box

With the folder Properties dialog box, as shown in Figure 2-7, you define folder attributes and behavior. For example, you can define who can access the folder and the functions they can perform, and you can create rules that automatically process items as they arrive in a folder.

> **Note** To view all available Properties dialog box pages for a folder, the folder must be located in your Mailbox or in a public folder where you have owner permissions. Also note that the Outlook Address Book page is available only for contact-type folders.

> **More Info** For more information about designing folders or designing folder views, see Chapter 8, "Folders," and Chapter 15, "Integrating Outlook with Web Applications."

Part I Introducing Microsoft Outlook 2002

- This page sets general folder properties.
- This page opens the Folder Assistant to automatically process items as they arrive.
- This page opens the Forms Manager to set this folder's form properties, such as the Hidden property.
- This page adds the folder as an Outlook Address Book.
- This page specifies who can access the public or Mailbox folders and what they can do in the folders.

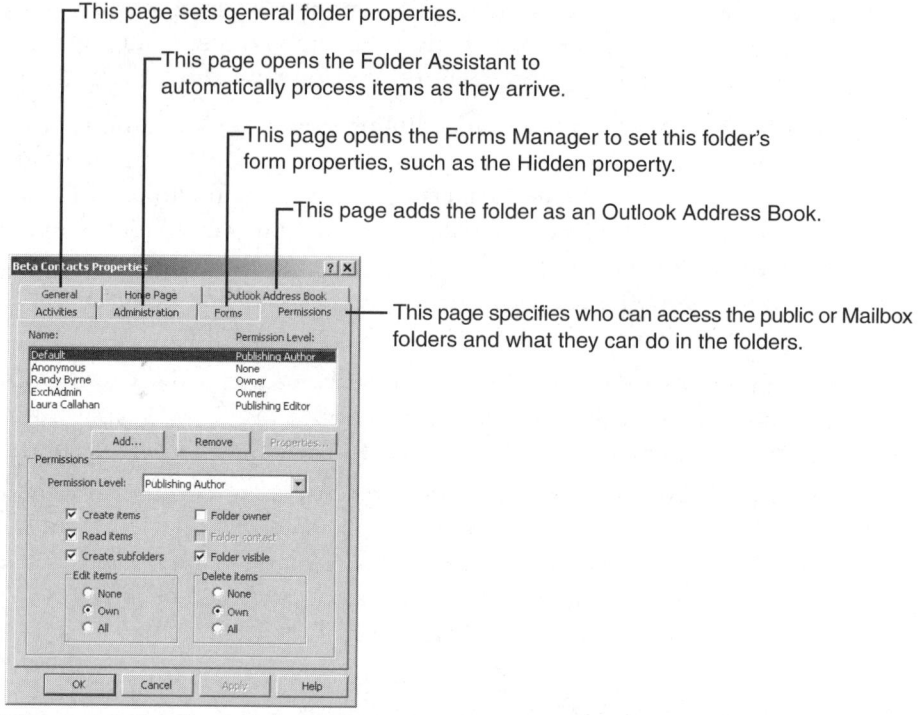

Figure 2-7 The folder Properties dialog box.

> **To view the folder Properties dialog box**

- Right-click the folder, and then click Properties on the shortcut menu.

Outlook Visual Basic for Applications Design Tools

First introduced in Outlook 2000, Visual Basic for Applications (VBA) provides a convenient environment for writing and debugging code. The version of VBA that ships in Office XP is 6.3. Once you have programmed and tested a prototype of your application in VBA, you can take the next step by moving your code to a COM Add-in. Unfortunately, only one VBA project can run in any given Outlook session. This limitation means that VBA code is typically used for prototyping solutions rather than deploying solutions in a corporate environment.

VBA brings many features to the design environment of Outlook, including the ability to display UserForms, create custom command bars for the Outlook Inspector and Explorer windows, and write code in standard and class modules. You need to understand that Outlook VBA does not replace the design tools used in Outlook forms development. You cannot use VBA to program Outlook forms directly. However, VBA provides you with the ability to design new features in the Outlook application environment and to customize the Outlook experience for yourself and your users. Corporate users will prototype COM Add-ins—ActiveX components that replace obsolescent Exchange Client Extensions—using Outlook VBA code and design tools.

Visual Basic Editor

The Visual Basic Editor gives you an integrated design environment for writing and debugging your code. You can now enjoy the same feature-rich editor that users of other Office applications such as Word and Excel have used for quite some time. We'll tour some of the important VBA features in this chapter. In later chapters, you will learn how to use the new objects, properties, and events in the Outlook 2002 object model.

> **To open the Visual Basic for Applications Editor window**

1. On the Explorer or the Inspector Tools menu, click Macro.
2. Click the Visual Basic Editor command. You can also press Alt+F11 to open the VBA Editor window, shown in Figure 2-8.

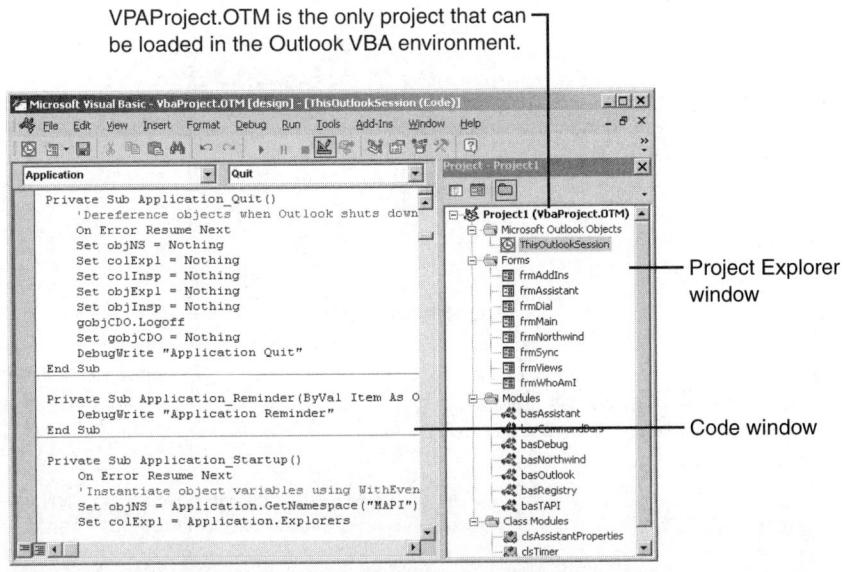

Figure 2-8 The Outlook Visual Basic Editor window.

Auto List Members and Context-Sensitive Help

When you write code in a code window, you can use the Auto List feature to display the properties and methods of objects as you type your code in the code window. Auto List Members enhances your productivity and cuts down on the

Part I   Introducing Microsoft Outlook 2002

tedium of debugging typing errors. When you place the cursor under a Visual Basic keyword or an object type, property, or method and press the F1 key, you'll see context-sensitive help. Figure 2-9 illustrates the pop-up Auto List window that appears after you type the dot operator.

Unlike the VBScript code environment, where all variables are Variants by default, Outlook VBA encourages you to declare strongly typed variables. Early binding of these variables speeds up the execution of your code. You can use the Tools References command to set references to other object libraries such as ActiveX Data Objects so that you can use those libraries in your code. The Visual Basic Object Browser helps you add additional object libraries to your project and lets you quickly find class members and their properties, methods, and events.

To open the Visual Basic for Applications Object Browser

1. On the Visual Basic View menu, click Object Browser.
2. Select the object library that you want to browse in the Object/Library drop-down list.

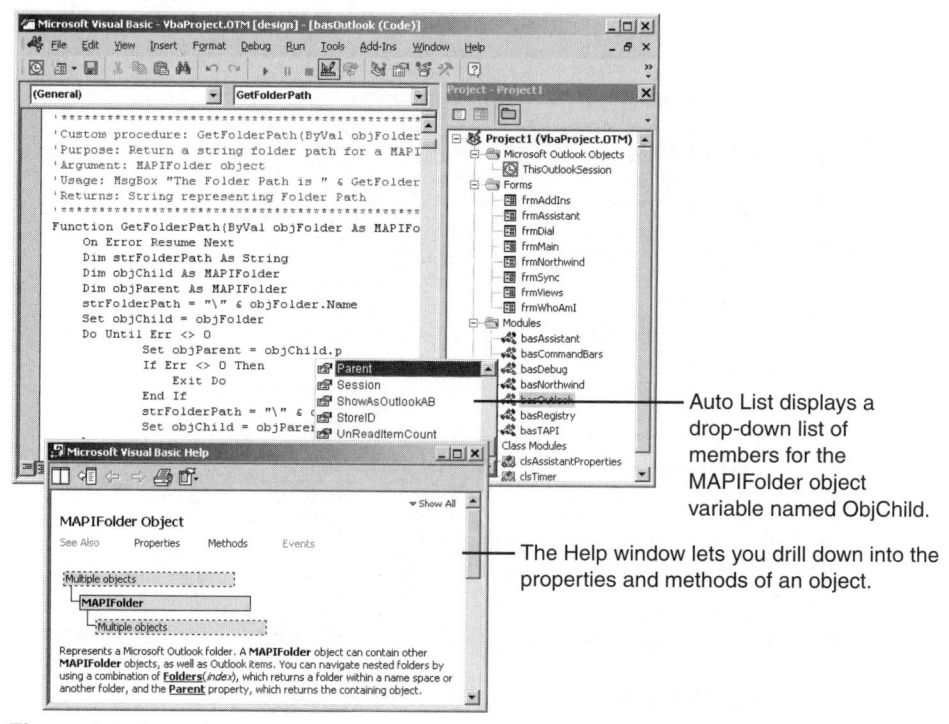

Figure 2-9 Auto List Members saves on typing and reduces errors.

UserForms

Visual Basic UserForms provide dialog boxes in the Outlook application environment. The intrinsic controls that you place on UserForms are the same as the Forms 2.0 controls used with Outlook custom forms. In Outlook VBA, all the properties, methods, and events of the control are exposed when the controls are placed on a UserForm. No longer are you limited to just the Click event of Forms 2.0 controls on an Outlook form. You can also place extrinsic ActiveX controls on your UserForm. Figure 2-10 depicts a UserForm that uses the Outlook View control, an ActiveX control that's an integral component of Outlook 2002. The versatile View control lets you display views on forms or HTML pages.

To add a UserForm to your Outlook VBA project

1. On the Visual Basic Insert menu, click UserForm.
2. On the Visual Basic View menu, click Toolbox.
3. Drag and drop controls from the Control Toolbox onto the UserForm.
4. Select the control on the UserForm, and press F4 to display the Properties window.
5. Set UserForm and control properties in the Properties window.

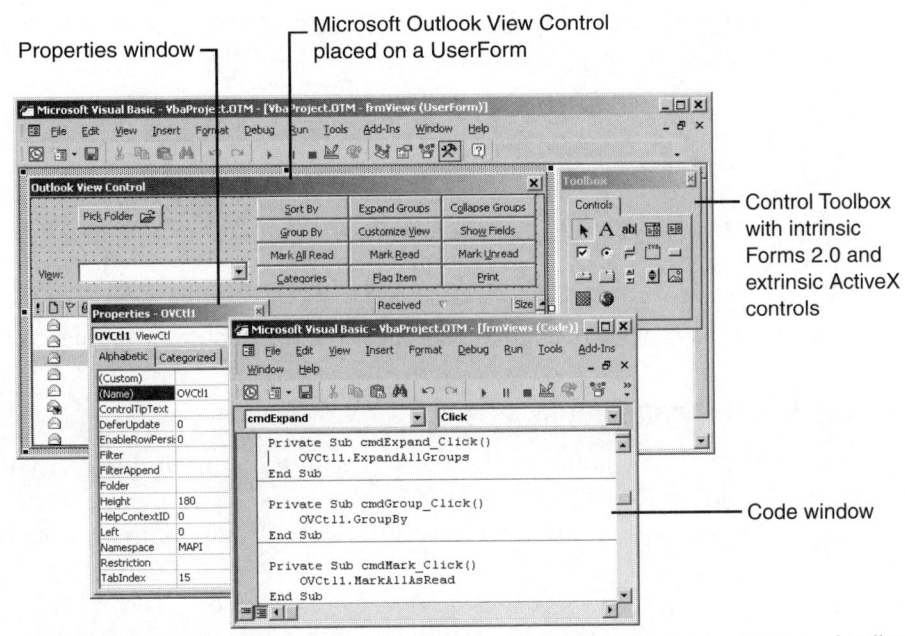

Figure 2-10 VBA UserForms and ActiveX controls let you create complex Application dialog boxes.

Part I   Introducing Microsoft Outlook 2002

Command Bars

Although you might not think of command bars as design tools, they are essential to the design of a custom user interface for Outlook. Command bars are now completely programmable in both the Explorer and Inspector windows. You can program an Outlook command bar to display built-in or custom dialogs, launch other applications, or open custom forms. Figure 2-11 shows two custom command bars in the Outlook Explorer window. The New Call dialog box that you see in Figure 2-11 appears when a user clicks the Dial Phone command bar button on the Create Shared Items toolbar. We'll examine both of these command bars in detail in subsequent chapters.

Like command bars, the Outlook Bar is also completely programmable in Outlook 2002. While not a design tool per se, you should think of the Outlook Bar as a design element when you create a custom application. Outlook Bar shortcuts can go to a URL, open a file on a local or networked drive, or launch an application. Figure 2-11 shows a custom Outlook Bar group that works in conjunction with the displayed Companies folder.

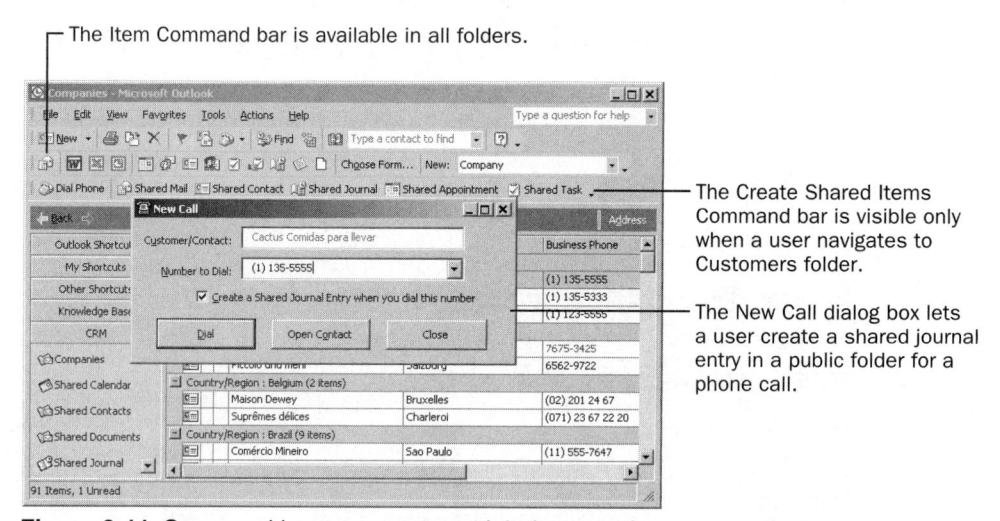

Figure 2-11   Command bars are an essential element of custom application design.

Add-Ins and Other Design Tools

We've just covered some of the basic design tools in Outlook Visual Basic for Applications. Since Visual Basic for Applications supports an add-in extensibility model, add-ins are available for the VBA environment that provide you with additional tools to complete your application design quickly and effectively. VBA add-in design tools are available from Microsoft or from third-party vendors.

Microsoft Office XP Developer

Microsoft offers its add-in design tools in a special version of Microsoft Office XP known as Microsoft Office XP Developer. Figure 2-12 shows the Code Librarian window and a procedure named *LinkExchangeFolder* that creates an Access table linked to the Outlook Contacts folder.

The following add-ins are available when you install Office XP Developer:

- Code Commentor and Error Handler
- Multi-code Import/Export
- Packaging Wizard
- VBA Source Code Control
- VBA String Editor

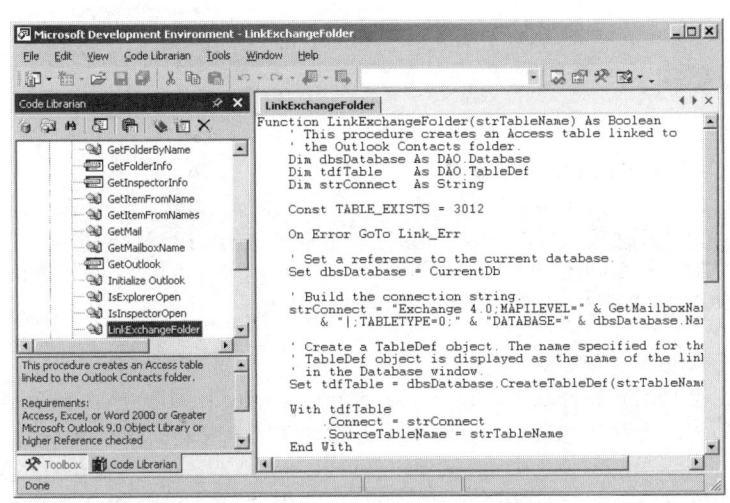

Figure 2-12 The Code Librarian in Office XP Developer contains procedures for use in Outlook, Exchange, and other Office applications.

Office XP Developer also includes several extrinsic ActiveX controls that you can add to your Outlook forms and distribute with your solution. Noteworthy is the DTPicker control that duplicates the functionality of the drop-down calendar control on Outlook appointment and task items.

When it comes to collaboration, other noteworthy Office XP Developer additions include the Exchange Workflow Designer and the Digital Dashboard project. The Exchange Workflow Designer (shown in Figure 2-13) provides a graphical design surface that lets you create simple workflows in a drag-and-drop environment. More complex workflows will require you to write code with the Workflow Designer Code Editor. Be aware that you can design workflows with Office XP Developer only on Exchange 2000 Server. Unlike the cumbersome Routing Objects on Exchange 5.5, workflows in Exchange 2000 are based on synchronous events and offer much greater control over process objects and state transitions.

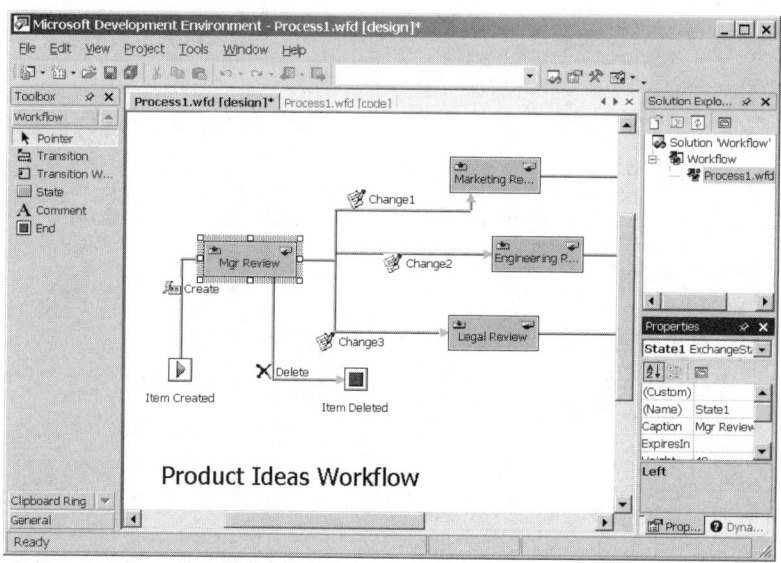

Figure 2-13 The Exchange Workflow Designer adds powerful workflow functionality to Outlook applications running on Exchange 2000 Server.

Microsoft Visual Studio

Discussion of Outlook design tools now must include Microsoft Visual Studio in addition to the Office Developer product. Outlook's development stage has expanded to such an extent that you should now consider Microsoft Visual Studio 6 or later as part of your Outlook development toolbox. The table on the facing page illustrates how you gain additional design resources when you obtain Visual Studio.

Function	Visual Studio Component
Author custom ActiveX controls for use on Outlook forms	Visual Basic 6
Create COM Add-ins that replace Exchange Client Extensions	Visual Basic 6
Create Exchange 2000 event sinks and COM+ components	Visual Basic 6
Create ASP pages and write VBScript to enhance and extend Team Folder Home Pages	Visual InterDev 6
Create store applications for Exchange Server 2000 and SharePoint Portal Server	Visual InterDev 6

Other Tools and Add-Ins

Outlook and Exchange developers now have some great tools and add-ins to assist them—an indicator of the growing maturity of the Outlook/Exchange application platform. These add-ins can be broken into two general categories: debugging tools and design tools. You'll find the debugging and design tools discussed in this section in the Tools And Add-Ins folder installed by the setup program on the companion CD. Most of these are third-party tools, so Microsoft makes no warranties about their use.

Debugging Tools

Debugging tools are for the developer who wants to delve deeper into the workings of Exchange and Outlook. Use these tools when you are looking for an undocumented property or hidden message that can add new functionality to your application. The Web Storage System Explorer can be used only for development of store applications on Exchange Server 2000. As a word of caution, you should be careful when you modify properties with either of these tools. It is strongly suggested that you test your changes thoroughly in an isolated environment before you implement any changes in a production environment.

Outlook Spy

In the past, Outlook developers who wanted to peer into the black box of the Messaging Application Program Interface (MAPI) had to use a tool provided with Exchange Server. This tool has the cryptic name MDBVU32, and it would be an understatement to say that MDBVU32 never won an award for user-interface design and usability. Outlook Spy provides all the low-level information available in MDBVU32 and then some. Using Outlook Spy (shown in Figure 2-14), you can examine hidden messages in folders or explore the hidden properties of messages. If you want to learn more about the inner workings of MAPI, Outlook Spy is an indispensable tool.

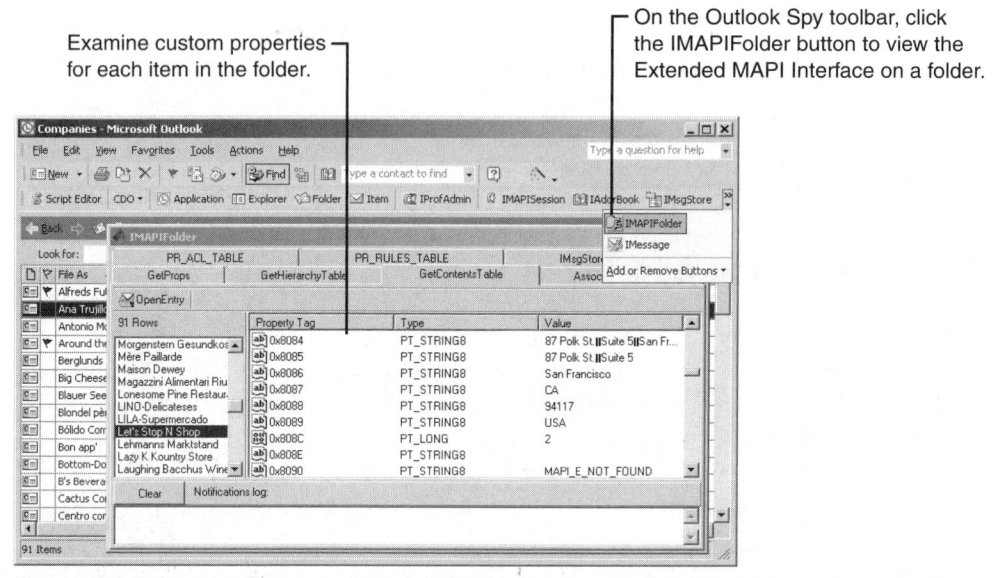

Figure 2-14 Outlook Spy uses Extended MAPI to provide low-level information about profiles, information stores, folders, and messages.

Web Storage System Explorer

The Web Storage System Explorer is a powerful debugging and development tool for the Exchange store. In addition to the Application Deployment Wizard, it is a component of Web Storage System tools. The Web Storage System tools, the Exchange SDK, and the SharePoint Portal Server SDK are included on the companion CD. If you are developing for Exchange 2000 Server or SharePoint Portal Server 2001, you'll find that the Web Storage System Explorer saves you from writing many lines of ActiveX Data Objects (ADO) code. Use the Web Storage System Explorer to create or modify schemas, form registrations, event registrations, content classes, or property definitions.

Development Tools

Once you've used a debugging tool to explore the low-level data structures of Exchange and Outlook, you might also need a development tool so that you don't have to reinvent the wheel. The Outlook Extensions Library provides you with some important ActiveX controls and functionality if you are developing traditional Outlook forms applications. A sibling of Outlook Spy, Redemption offers you a wrapper for Extended MAPI and provides an alternative for developers whose applications need to coexist with the Outlook E-Mail Security Update. IT Factory Development Center is a complete development environment for store applications running on Exchange 2000.

TeamScope Outlook Extensions Library

The Outlook Extensions Library simplifies and extends the development of applications that use traditional Outlook forms technology. Several ActiveX controls are available in Outlook Extensions Library, including a grid and calendar control. You can also add item locking to your applications, encrypt field-level data, access the Microsoft Windows API from VBScript behind forms, and print forms without writing code.

Redemption

Redemption uses Extended MAPI to overcome some of the development limitations imposed by the Outlook E-Mail Security Update. You can also use Redemption as an alternative to Collaboration Data Objects. For additional details about Redemption and the Outlook 2002 Object Model Guard, see Chapter 13.

IT Factory Development Center

IT Factory Development Center is a high-level development tool for Exchange 2000 Server and SharePoint Portal Server applications. An add-in for Visual InterDev 6.0, IT Factory Development Center provides several templates for Exchange 2000 application development. It offers an object-oriented interface for creating content classes and custom properties, and it also features a drag-and-drop query designer that simplifies the creation of complex ADO queries against the store.

Other Tools

Micro Eye ZipOut 2000

ZipOut 2000 is a COM Add-in for Outlook 2000 or Outlook 2002 that automatically compresses attachments to outgoing messages and items stored in your mailbox or personal folders. You can compress attachments on all items in a folder and subfolders, remove HTML stationery, or simply delete attachments from a selection of messages. You can schedule automatic attachment compression in your mailbox based on a single or recurring Outlook task, and display the compression results in an Office Web component. ZipOut fully supports the Microsoft Outlook E-Mail Security Update. Unlike the Security Update, ZipOut will also warn you if .zip files contain potentially harmful files.

Part II

Quick Guide to Building Applications

3   Customize Built-In Modules   41

4   Design a Custom Application   71

Chapter 3, "Customize Built-In Modules," shows you how to create instant groupware applications by modifying the built-in Contacts application, customizing it for tracking customer correspondence related to a beta program, and then copying it to public folders on Microsoft Exchange Server. Chapter 4, "Design a Custom Application," shows you how to build a Discussion application called Product Ideas that makes it possible for users to submit, read, and respond to new product ideas.

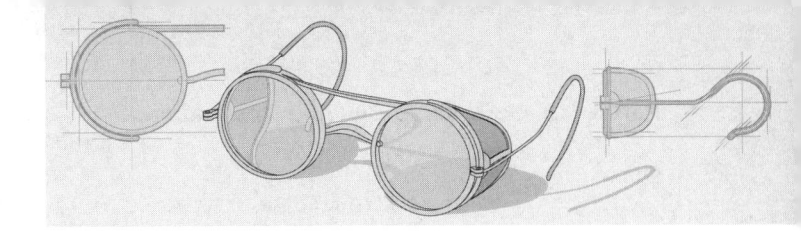

3

Customize Built-In Modules

As a desktop information manager, Outlook provides built-in personal management tools such as Calendar, Tasks, Contacts, and Journal that can significantly increase user productivity. While these modules work great for individual use, their value is dramatically increased when they're located in an Exchange public folder because they allow users to share calendars, schedules, task lists, and customer information among workgroups or across the organization. In fact, with the built-in modules in Outlook, creating groupware is as simple as creating a module in public folders.

> **Note** The examples in this book, and in the companion CD-ROM, require Microsoft Exchange to create and access public folders.

This chapter is designed to show you how to easily customize built-in Outlook modules to suit the needs of your workgroup or organization. You will learn how to transform the Contacts module into a groupware application that allows users to record, share, and track the history of customer correspondence. When you're finished with this chapter, you should have a better understanding of both the limits and possibilities of customizing built-in modules. Perhaps equally important, you should have a whole new set of ideas about the kinds of applications you can create using these modules as a starting point. Here are a few ideas:

- **Calendar** Can be created in public folders and used to post, share, and update schedules for activities such as training classes, sporting events, and company functions. For a product launch, you might want to post milestone events such as trade shows, press tours, and the product ship date to the Calendar folder.

- **Tasks**   Can be created in public folders and used to post and track the tasks completed by each member of a project team. For example, the Tasks folder can be used to delegate responsibilities to a staff of temporary workers or to track workgroup members' hours, billing information, and mileage.

- **Contacts**   Can be created in public folders and used to post contact names, phone numbers, addresses, and company information that can then be shared by a workgroup. With Contacts, users can post and track correspondence with sales contacts, potential customers, vendors, contractors, and coworkers.

- **Distribution lists**   Can be created in either the Contacts folder of a user's mailbox or in a public folder that contains Contact items. A distribution list can contain multiple recipients and is used to send messages to all members of the list. First introduced in Outlook 2000, Distribution List items are meant to replace distribution lists maintained in the Personal Address Book.

- **Journal**   Can be created in public folders and used to log and track information such as the amount of time an individual or workgroup spends on a particular task, on a project, or with a specific customer.

> **Note**   For the Notes module, you can add custom views to the folder but you cannot modify the built-in form.

Overview of the Folder You Create

The Contacts module is designed primarily for individuals to keep track of their personal contacts. As such, it offers a built-in Contact form and a variety of views, including an Address Cards view, a Phone List view, and a By Company view. In this chapter, you transform the Contacts module into the Beta Contacts application shown in Figure 3-1.

In this chapter, you also transform the Contacts module into a groupware application that is used to track correspondence with participants in a beta software program. (For those of you not involved in the software industry, most software companies send early copies of their software to their preferred customers for early testing and feedback. This process, known as beta testing, usually involves close communication between the people running the beta program and the beta participants.)

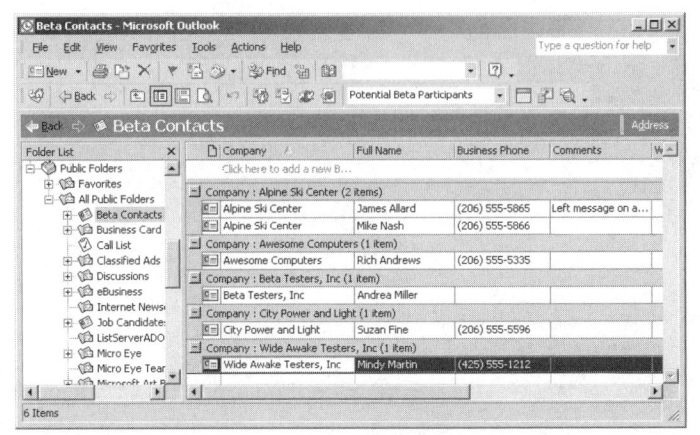

Figure 3-1 The Beta Contacts folder you can create.

To build the Beta Contacts application based on the Contacts module, you first create a new Contacts folder in public folders. Then you rename the folder and add custom views. Next you modify the built-in Contacts form. Finally you set permissions on the folder so that only those individuals involved in the beta program can have access to it.

The Beta Contacts folder This folder is based on the built-in Contacts module. The Beta Contacts folder is created in public folders so that the information in the folder can be shared among members of a workgroup. In this chapter, you first create the Design Environment folder so you have a place for creating and testing applications, as shown in Figure 3-2.

The Potential Beta Participants view As part of the customization process, you create a Potential Beta Participants view. This view groups contacts by company and enables users of the Beta Contacts application to select a check box in a column to specify that the contact wants to participate in the beta program. The Potential Beta Participants view is shown in Figure 3-3.

The Beta Participants view You also add to the Beta Contacts folder a view that uses a filter to show only the contacts that have agreed to participate in the beta program. In addition, you add fields to the Beta Participants view that enable users of the Beta Contacts folder to update and track the status of correspondence either sent to or returned by customers, as shown in Figure 3-4.

Part II Quick Guide to Building Applications

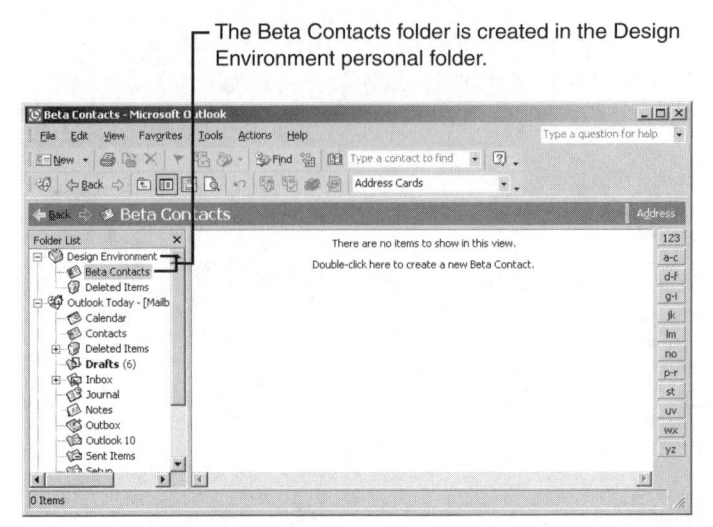

Figure 3-2 The Beta Contacts folder is created in the Design Environment personal folder (.pst) file.

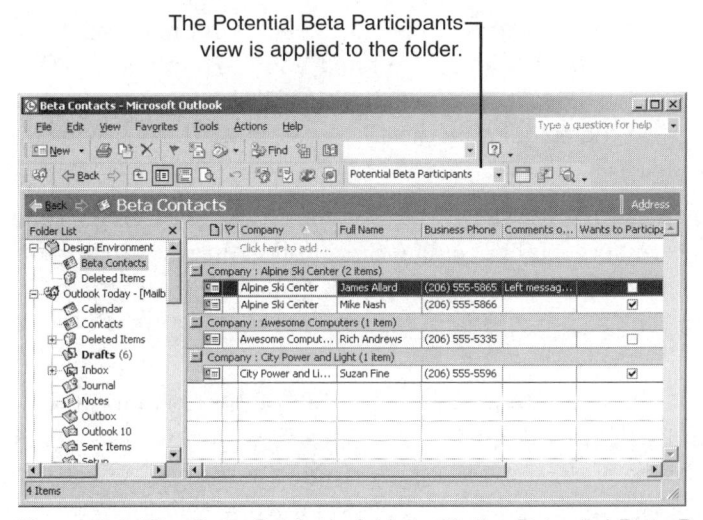

Figure 3-3 The Beta Contacts folder with the Potential Beta Participants view selected.

The Beta Contact form Finally you customize the form that comes with the Contacts module by adding a page to the form. You then add controls to the page and bind the controls to custom fields that you add to the Beta Contacts folder. Figure 3-5 shows the additional page you design for the Beta Contact form.

Customize Built-In Modules Chapter 3

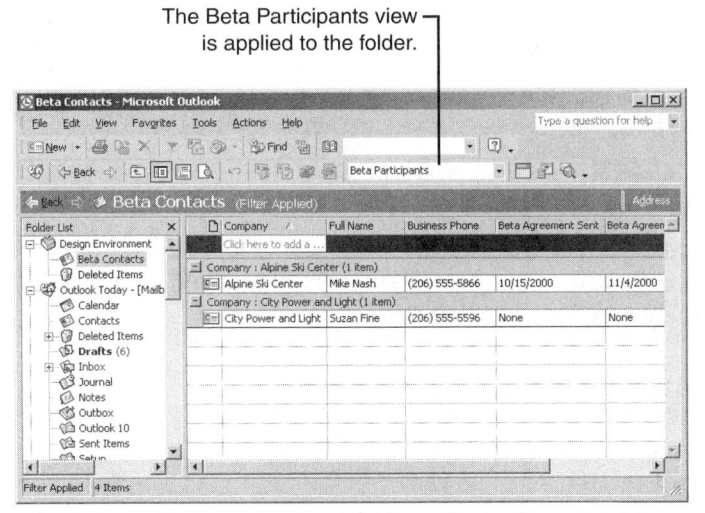

Figure 3-4 The Beta Contacts folder with the Beta Participants view selected.

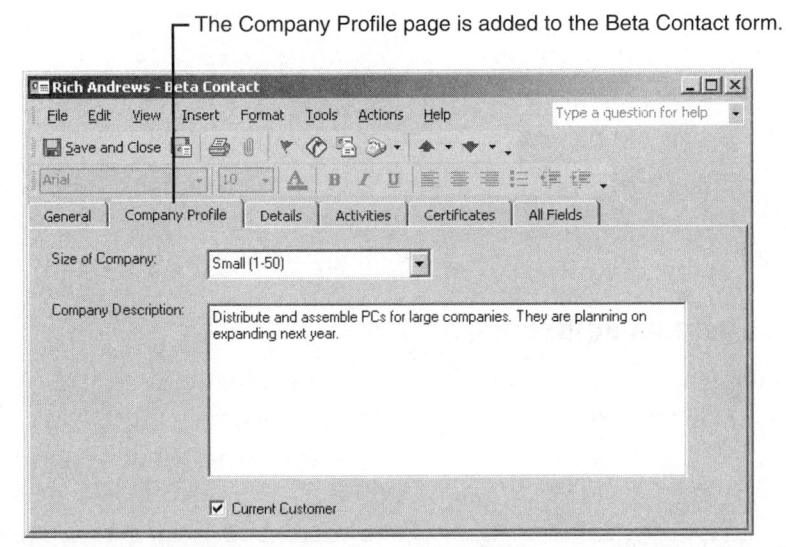

Figure 3-5 The Beta Contact form with the Company Profile page selected.

Create New Folders

To start, you create a new personal folder (.pst) file called Design Environment. This is the folder you use throughout this book for creating and testing folders. We recommend you start building your Outlook applications by creating forms and views in a personal folder (.pst) file. After you've tested the forms and views, you can then copy the folder to a public folder, if necessary.

Create the Design Environment Personal Folder (.pst) File

The Design Environment personal folder (.pst) file you create is a private folder, which means that only you can view its contents. This secure environment is ideal for building applications. A personal folder file can reside on either your local drive or a network drive. In either case, it is always best to back up your Design Environment personal folder file on a regular basis.

To create the Design Environment personal folder

1. Select Outlook Data File from the New menu, and then click OK in the New Outlook Data File dialog box.

2. In the Create Or Open Outlook Data File dialog box, select a location for the .pst file from the Save In folder drop-down list box or accept the default location. This is the folder in which the .pst file will be stored on the file system.

3. In the File Name text box, type *Design Environment* and then click OK. This is the name of the .pst file on the file system.

4. The Create Microsoft Personal Folders dialog box opens. In the Name text box, type *Design Environment* and then click OK. This is the name of the personal folder, as it appears on the Folder List in Outlook.

Create the Beta Contacts Folder

Now you create the Beta Contacts folder as a subfolder of the Design Environment folder. When you create the Beta Contacts folder, you specify that the folder contains Contact items, so the folder automatically inherits the properties and functionality of the built-in Contacts module.

To create the Beta Contacts folder

1. In the Folder List, right-click the Design Environment folder.

2. Click New Folder.

3. In the Name text box, type *Beta Contacts*.

4. In the Folder Contains drop-down list box, select Contact Items.
    When you click Contact Items, the folder automatically takes on the characteristics of the Contacts module.

5. Click OK.
6. If a prompt appears, select your choice in the Add Shortcut To Outlook Bar dialog box.
7. Right-click the Beta Contacts folder, and then click Properties.
8. In the Description text box, type the following:

    This folder contains beta program contacts. It also contains beta program status that shows whether the company is a beta customer, and whether they have returned their beta material.
9. Click OK to close the Properties window.

Create Custom Views

With Outlook, you can create custom views to organize and show information in the folder so users can easily find the information they want. For the Beta Contacts folder, you create two views:

- **The Potential Beta Participants view** Lets users keep track of those people who agree over the telephone to participate in the beta program.

- **The Beta Participants view** Lets users view only those contacts who have agreed to participate in the beta program.

Create the Potential Beta Participants View

Let's assume that you and a few others in your workgroup are responsible for contacting a list of companies to see if they want to participate in the beta program. To keep track of who agrees to participate, you can create the Potential Beta Participants view. To create this view, you add user-defined fields to the Beta Contacts folder. Once you create these fields, you build a view with columns based on these fields.

To create the Potential Beta Participants view

1. In the Folder List, click the Beta Contacts folder in the Design Environment folder.
2. On the View menu, select Current View and then click Define Views.
3. In the Define Views For "Beta Contacts" dialog box, click By Company, and then click Copy.
    In this case, you save time by creating the new view based on the existing By Company view.

Part II   Quick Guide to Building Applications

4. In the Name Of New View text box, type *Potential Beta Participants*.
5. Click This Folder, Visible To Everyone, and then click OK.
6. In the View Summary box, click OK.
7. In the Define Views For "Beta Contacts" list box, click Apply View.

Remove Fields

Many of the fields in the By Company view aren't necessary for the Potential Beta Participants view, so you can remove them by dragging them from the Column Heading row.

To remove fields

- Drag the following column headings away from the Column Heading row until an X appears through the column heading, and then release the mouse button.
    - ❑ Attachment (shown as a paper clip in the column heading)
    - ❑ Job Title
    - ❑ File As
    - ❑ Department
    - ❑ Business Fax
    - ❑ Home Phone
    - ❑ Mobile Phone
    - ❑ Categories

Add New Fields

Next you add the Wants To Participate, Does Not Want To Participate, and Primary Contact fields to the view.

To add new fields

1. Right-click anywhere in the Column Heading row, click Field Chooser, and then click New.
2. In the Name text box, type *Wants to Participate*.
3. In the Type drop-down list box, click Yes/No and then click OK.
4. Click New.

Customize Built-In Modules   Chapter 3

5. In the Name text box, type *Does Not Want to Participate*.
6. In the Type drop-down list box, click Yes/No and then click OK.
7. Repeat steps 4, 5, and 6 to add the Primary Contact field, but in step 5, type *Primary Contact* in the Name text box. Make sure you choose a Yes/No type field.
8. Repeat steps 4 through 6 to add the Comments Or Issues field, but in step 5, type *Comments or Issues* in the Name box. Make sure you choose a Text type field.

Change the Order of the Company and Full Name Columns

With Outlook, you can change the order of column headings by dragging them to new locations.

To drag the Company column heading

- Drag the Company column heading, as shown in Figure 3-6, until a red double-arrow marker appears over the border where you want to place the column.

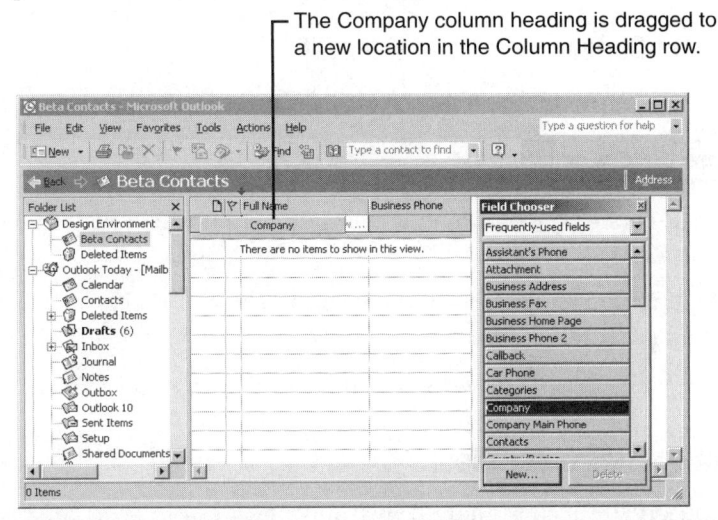

Figure 3-6 The Company column is placed in front of the Full Name column.

Add the Column Headings to the Column Heading Row

To add column headings, you drag the fields you created earlier from the Field Chooser to the Column Heading row.

To drag the fields to the Column Heading row

1. From the Field Set drop-down list box on the Field Chooser, select User-Defined Fields In Folder.

2. Drag the Comments Or Issues field from the Field Chooser to the Column Heading row, and position it to the right of the Business Phone column heading. The red double-arrow marker shows you where the new column heading will be inserted in the Column Heading row.

3. Drag the Wants To Participate field from the Field Chooser to the Column Heading row, and position it to the right of the Comments Or Issues column heading.

4. Drag the Does Not Want To Participate field from the Field Chooser to the Column Heading row, and position it to the right of the Wants To Participate column heading.

5. Drag the Primary Contact field from the Field Chooser to the Column Heading row, and position it to the right of the Does Not Want To Participate column heading.

Adjust the Column Widths to Best Fit

To resize columns, you right-click the column heading and then click Best Fit.

To adjust the column widths

1. Right-click the Comments Or Issues column heading, and then click Best Fit.

2. Repeat for the Wants To Participate, Does Not Want To Participate, and Primary Contact column headings.

3. The view should now look similar to the view shown in Figure 3-7.

Create the Beta Participants View

Next you create a view that shows only the people who are primary contacts and who have agreed to participate in the beta program. This view enables folder users to track what has been sent by beta coordinators and returned by beta participants. For example, once a contact agrees to participate in the beta program, you send him a beta agreement to read and sign. Then, once the beta agreement has been returned, you send him a beta package, complete with the product and necessary feedback forms.

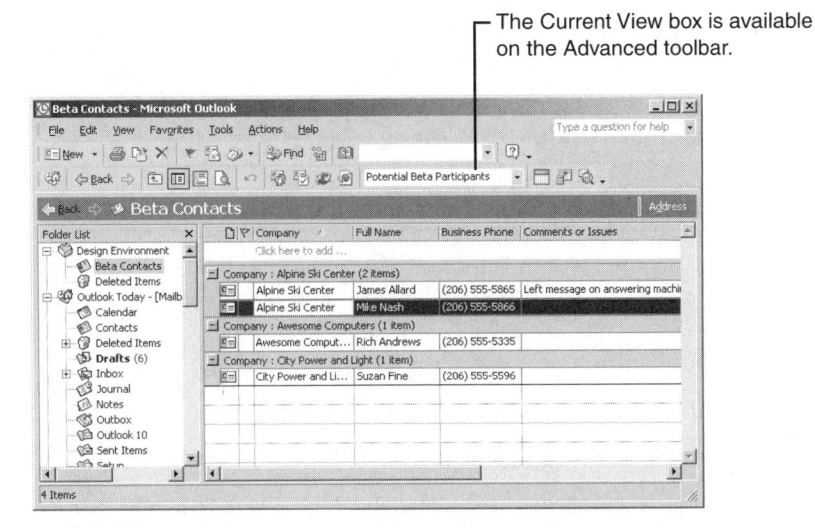

Figure 3-7 The column widths are adjusted for Best Fit in the Potential Beta Participants view.

To create the Beta Participants view

1. In the Folder List, click the Beta Contacts folder.
2. On the View menu, choose Current View and then click Define Views.
3. In the Define Views For Folder "Beta Contacts" list box, click Potential Beta Participants and then click Copy.
4. In the Name Of New View text box, type *Beta Participants*.
5. Click This Folder, Visible To Everyone, click OK twice, and then click Apply View.

To remove fields from the view

- Drag the following column headings away from the Column Heading row until an X appears through the column heading, and then release the mouse button:
    - Comments Or Issues
    - Wants To Participate
    - Does Not Want To Participate
    - Primary Contact

Add New Fields

Next you add the Beta Agreement Sent, Beta Agreement Returned, and Beta Package Sent fields to the view. The user can enter information directly in these fields without opening the form.

To add new fields

1. On the Outlook Advanced toolbar, click the Field Chooser icon.
2. Click New on the Field Chooser.
3. In the Name text box, type *Beta Agreement Sent*.
4. In the Type drop-down list box, click Date/Time.
5. In the Format field, click a date format and then click OK.

    Repeat steps 2 through 5 for both the Beta Agreement Returned and Beta Package Sent fields.

Add the Column Headings to the Column Heading Row

Now you add the new fields to the Column Heading row.

To drag the fields to the Column Heading row

1. Drag the Beta Agreement Sent field from the Field Chooser to the Column Heading row, and position it to the right of the Business Phone column heading. The double-arrow marker shows you where the new column heading will be inserted in the Column Heading row.
2. Drag the Beta Agreement Returned field from the Field Chooser to the Column Heading row, and position it to the right of the Beta Agreement Sent field.
3. Drag the Beta Package Sent field from the Field Chooser to the Column Heading row, and position it to the right of the Beta Agreement Sent field.

Adjust the Column Widths to Best Fit

Next you adjust the column widths for the Beta Agreement Sent, Beta Agreement Returned, and Beta Package Sent column headings.

Customize Built-In Modules   Chapter 3

To adjust the column widths

1. Right-click the Beta Agreement Sent column heading, and then click Best Fit.

2. Repeat for the Beta Agreement Returned and Beta Package Sent column headings.

Your Beta Participants view should now look similar to the view shown in Figure 3-8.

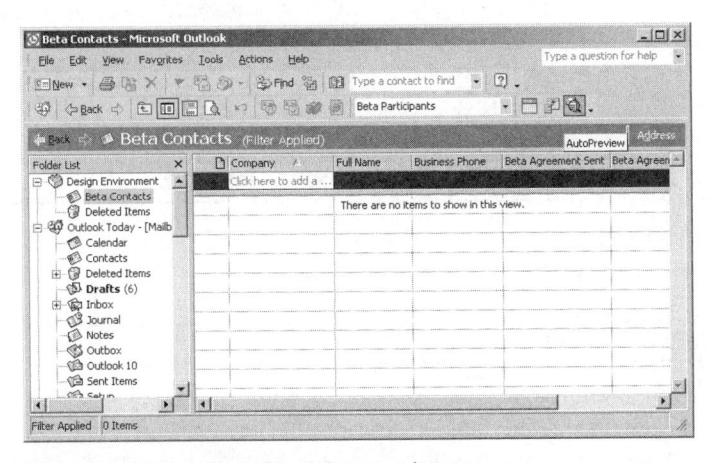

Figure 3-8 The Beta Participants view.

Create a Filter for the Beta Participants View

With a filter, you can create a set of criteria that determines the items that are shown in a view. For the Beta Participants view, you create a filter that displays only items that have a check in the Wants To Participate and Primary Contact fields.

To create a filter

1. On the View menu, select Current View, click Customize Current View, and then click Filter.

2. In the Filter dialog box, click the Advanced tab.

3. Click Field, point to User-Defined Fields In Folder, and then select Wants to Participate.

4. In the Value text box, select Yes from the drop-down list box and then click Add To List.

5. Click Field, point to User-Defined Fields In Folder, and then click Primary Contact.

53

6. In the Value text box, select Yes from the drop-down list box and then click Add To List.

7. Click OK twice.

Create Items for the Beta Contacts Folder

Now let's assume you're ready to call potential beta participants and you want to keep track of those customers who agree to participate and those who do not. You might also want to type the results of your calls, such as "Left message on answering machine," in the Comments field.

Before you create items, you switch to the Potential Beta Participants view. This is the view in which you enter new contacts.

To switch to the Potential Beta Participants view

- On the Outlook Advanced toolbar, select Potential Beta Participants in the Current View drop-down list box.

To create a Beta Contacts item

- In the folder view, click the Click Here To Add A… cell in the Company column, as shown in Figure 3-9, and then fill in the cells. After you finish typing in an item, click outside the cell. The item is then added to the folder. The values for the cells are shown in the table following the figure.

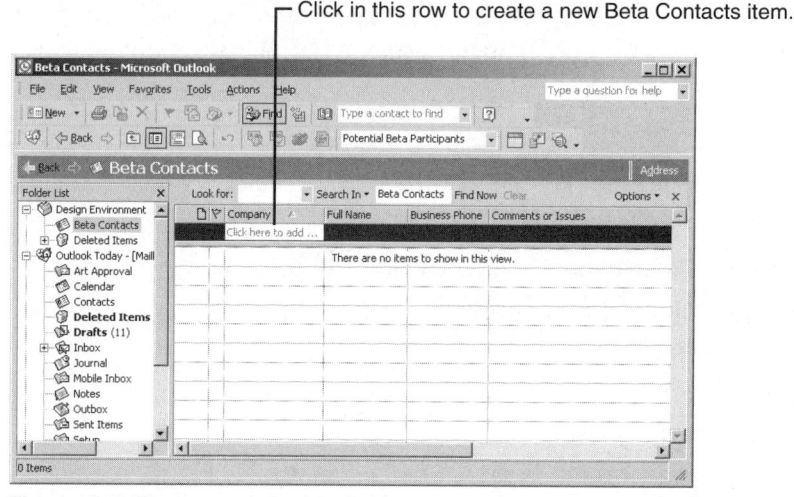

Figure 3-9 The top row in the view lets you create a new item for the view.

Customize Built-In Modules Chapter 3

Cell Column	Value
Company	*Alpine Ski Center*
Full Name	*James Allard*
Business Phone	*(206) 555-5865*
Comments	*Left message on answering machine 7-10*
Wants To Participate	
Does Not Want To Participate	
Primary Contact	

Now let's assume you talked to Mike Nash and he agreed to participate in the program and to be the primary contact for the beta program for Alpine Ski Center.

To create a second Beta Contacts item

- In the folder view, click the Click Here To Add A... cell in the Company column, and then fill in the cells with the values shown in the following table.

Cell Column	Value
Company	*Alpine Ski Center*
Full Name	*Mike Nash*
Business Phone	*(206) 555-5866*
Comments	
Wants To Participate	X
Does Not Want To Participate	
Primary Contact	X

To keep things interesting, let's create some more items.

To create third and fourth Beta Contacts items

- In the folder view, click the Click Here To Add A... cell in the Company column, and then fill in the cells with the values shown in the table on the following page.

55

Part II Quick Guide to Building Applications

Cell Column	Value
Company	*Awesome Computers*
Full Name	*Rich Andrews*
Business Phone	*(206) 555-5335*
Comments	
Wants To Participate	
Does Not Want To Participate	*X*
Primary Contact	

Here's one more to create.

Cell Column	Value
Company	*City Power and Light*
Full Name	*Suzan Fine*
Business Phone	*(206) 555-5596*
Comments	
Wants To Participate	*X*
Does Not Want To Participate	
Primary Contact	*X*

Your view should now look like the view shown in Figure 3-10.

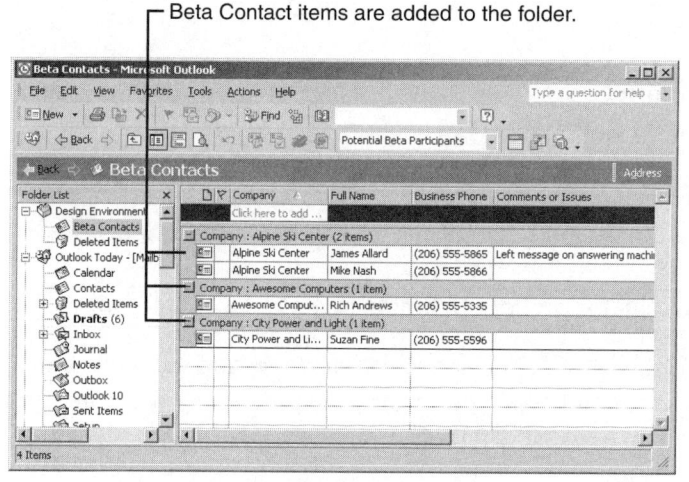

Figure 3-10 The Potential Beta Participants view with the Beta Contact items.

Enter Dates in the Beta Participants View

Now let's assume you want to send beta agreement contracts to those people who agree to participate in the program. To do this, you use the Beta Participants view to enter the date that the beta agreement contracts are sent.

To switch to the Beta Participants view

- On the Outlook Advanced toolbar, click Beta Participants in the Current View drop-down list box.

To enter the Beta Agreement Sent date in the fields

- Click the Beta Agreement Sent field for Mike Nash, and then type the date, as shown in Figure 3-11.

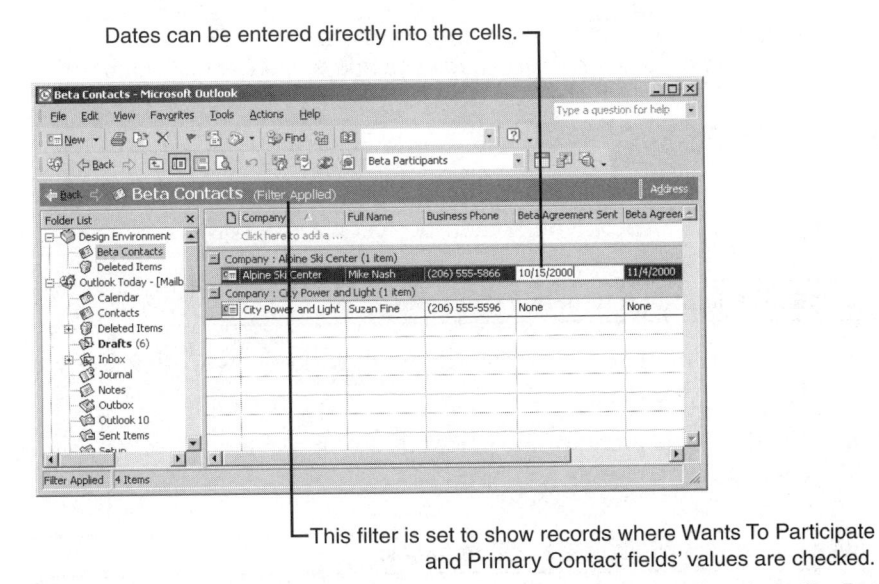

Dates can be entered directly into the cells.

This filter is set to show records where Wants To Participate and Primary Contact fields' values are checked.

Figure 3-11 The Beta Participants view with dates entered directly in the Beta Agreement Sent fields.

Customize the Contacts Form

Up to this point, we've focused on modifying the Beta Contacts application by adding custom views. Now we'll further customize the Beta Contacts application by modifying the built-in Contacts form.

In this example, you add a Company Profile page to the Contacts form, shown in Figure 3-12.

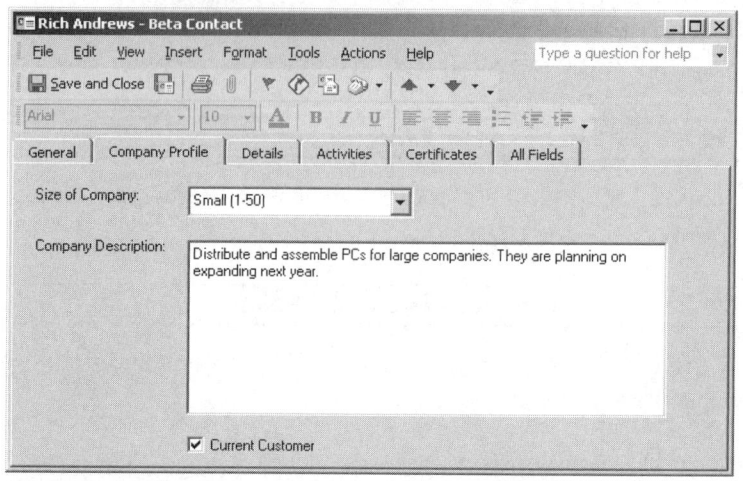

Figure 3-12 The Company Profile page you add to the Contacts form.

Open the Contacts Form

To customize a built-in form, first open it as you would to create a new contact. After the form is open, you switch between Design mode and Run mode.

To open the Contacts form in Design mode

1. While in the Beta Contacts folder, click the New Contact icon on the Outlook Standard toolbar.
2. On the Tools menu of the Untitled - Contact window, select Forms and then click Design This Form.

To switch from Design mode to Run mode

1. On the Form menu, click Run This Form.
2. Close the Run mode window to return to Design mode.

Rename the New Page

The Contacts form provides several additional pages to which you can add controls. Notice that the additional pages are in parentheses; this indicates that the pages are hidden at run time. When you add controls to a page, the parentheses are automatically removed, so the page is visible at run time. For this example, you rename (P.2) to Company Profile.

To rename and show the page

1. In Design mode on the Contacts form, click the (P.2) tab.
2. On the Form menu, click Rename Page.
3. In the Page Name text box, type *Company Profile* and then click OK.
4. On the Form menu, click Display This Page.

Add Controls to the Form

Now you use the Control Toolbox to add controls to the Company Profile page. After you add a control, you create a new field and then bind the control to the field. In Outlook, a control is the physical component on the form in which the user enters, views, or clicks values. The field is the storage area in which the values from the controls are saved or loaded.

To show the Control Toolbox

- On the Form Design toolbar, click Control Toolbox.

Add a ComboBox Control

The ComboBox control you add to the Company Profile page allows users to select and view the size of a company, such as Small (1–50), Medium (51–500), or Large (501–1000+).

To add the ComboBox control

- From the Control Toolbox, drag a ComboBox control to the form. Then drag the sizing handle on the right border of the control until the field is approximately the size of the field shown in Figure 3-13.

Set properties for the ComboBox control   When you set properties for the ComboBox control, you create a Size Of Company field. When you create a new field for a control from the Properties dialog box, the field is automatically bound to the control. When a control is bound to a field, the values in the control are saved to the field when an item is composed. When an item is opened in a folder, the values from the fields are loaded into the controls.

Part II Quick Guide to Building Applications

The Control Toolbox from which you drag controls

The ComboBox control is dragged to the form.

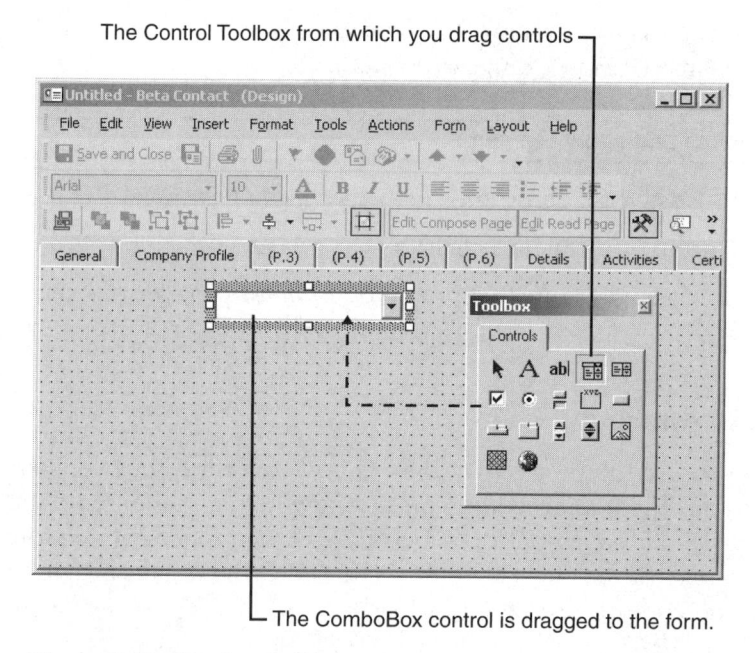

Figure 3-13 The ComboBox control is added to the Company Profile page.

To set properties for the ComboBox control

1. Right-click the ComboBox control, click Properties, and then click the Value tab, shown in Figure 3-14.

2. Click New.

3. In the Name text box, type *Size of Company* and then click OK.

4. In the List Type drop-down list box, select Droplist.
    With a Droplist ComboBox control, the user must select a value from the list. A Dropdown ComboBox control, on the other hand, allows the user to type in the value or choose from the list. If you intend to group fields (for example, by company size) based on values in a combo box, it's usually best to specify that the combo box is a Droplist so that you can control the values by which you group items in the folder.

5. In the Possible Values text box, type the following:
    Small (1-50);Medium (51-500);Large (501-1000+)

6. Select the Set The Initial Value Of This Field To check box, and in the text box below it type *"Small (1–50)"* and then click OK.

Customize Built-In Modules   Chapter 3

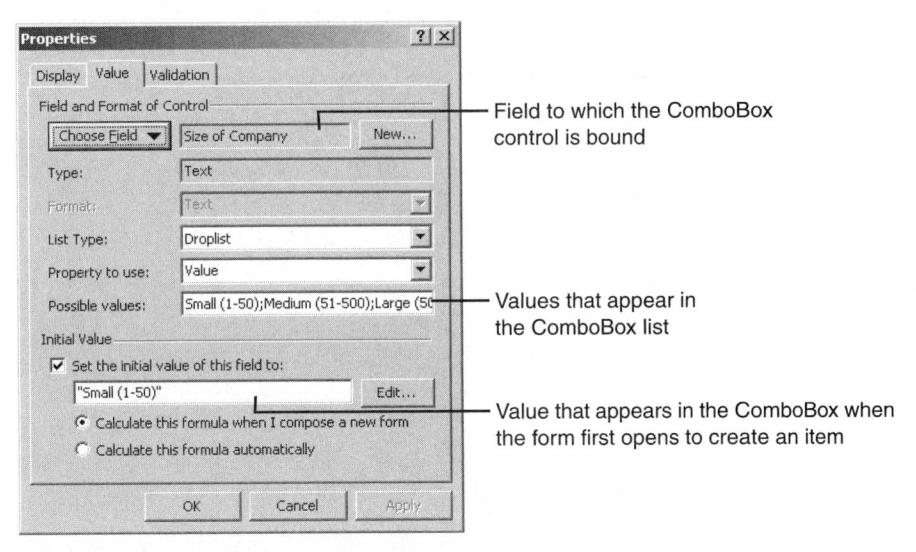

Figure 3-14 Properties for the ComboBox control.

Annotations on figure:
- Field to which the ComboBox control is bound
- Values that appear in the ComboBox list
- Value that appears in the ComboBox when the form first opens to create an item

Add a label for the ComboBox control   Now you add a label for the ComboBox control to identify the control and to help the user understand the purpose of the control.

> **To add a label**

1. From the Control Toolbox, drag a Label control to the form.
2. In the label, select the word Label1 and then type *Size of Company:*, as shown in Figure 3-15.

Add a TextBox Control

Now you add a TextBox control to the Company Profile page. This control allows users to enter and view a company description on the Company Profile page.

> **To add a TextBox control**

- From the Control Toolbox, drag a TextBox control to the form. Then drag the sizing handle on the right border of the control until the field is approximately the size of the field shown in Figure 3-16.

Set properties for the TextBox control   Now you create a Company Description field that is automatically bound to the TextBox control. In addition, you select the Multi-Line check box for the control so the user can enter multiple lines of text in it. You also select the Resize With Form check box so the control size is adjusted to the size of the form.

61

Part II Quick Guide to Building Applications

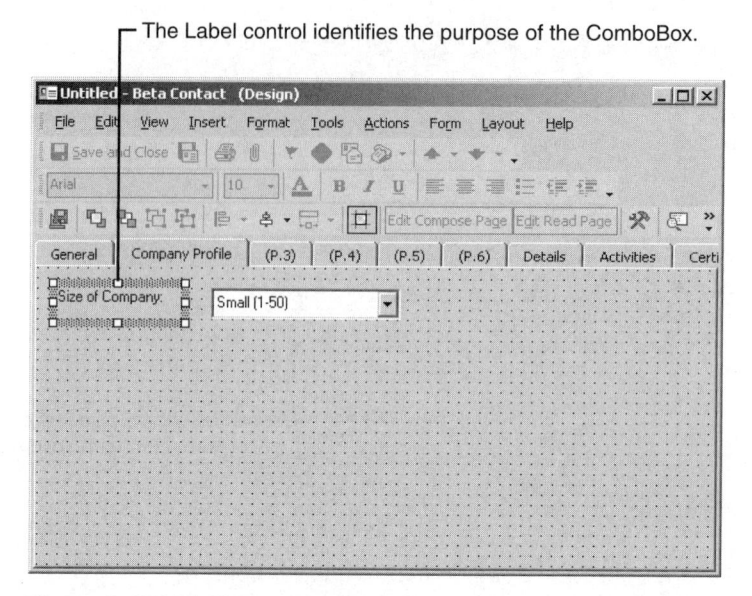

— The Label control identifies the purpose of the ComboBox.

Figure 3-15 A label is added for the ComboBox control to identify its purpose.

— A TextBox control is added to the form.

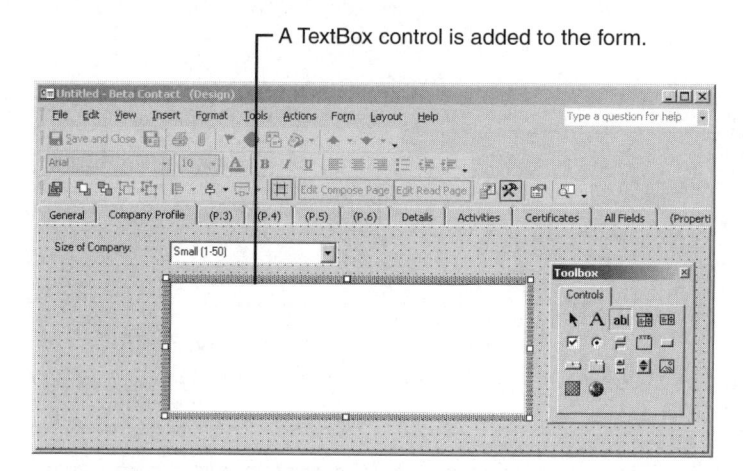

Figure 3-16 A TextBox control is added to the Company Profile page.

To set properties for the TextBox control

1. Right-click the TextBox control, click Properties, and then click the Value tab.
2. Click New.
3. In the Name text box, type *Company Description* and then click OK.

Customize Built-In Modules Chapter 3

4. Click the Display tab.
5. Select the Resize With Form check box.
6. Select the Multi-Line check box.
7. Click OK.

Add a label for the TextBox control   Now you add a label for the TextBox control so users know the purpose of the control.

To add a label

1. From the Control Toolbox, drag a Label control to the form, and position it to the left of the TextBox control.
2. In the label, first select the word Label2 and then type *Company Description:*.
3. To resize the label, drag the sizing handle on the right border of the label until all text in the label is visible.

Add a CheckBox Control

Finally you add a CheckBox control to the form. This control allows users to specify that a company is a current customer.

To add a CheckBox control

1. From the Control Toolbox, drag a CheckBox control to the form.
2. Click the CheckBox control, and then type *Current Customer*, as shown in Figure 3-17.

Set properties for the CheckBox control   Next you create a Current Customer field to which the CheckBox control is bound.

To create the Current Customer field

1. Right-click the CheckBox control, and then click Properties.
2. Click New.
3. In the Name text box, type *Current Customer*.
4. In the Type drop-down list box, click Yes/No.
5. In the Format drop-down list box, click Icon and then click OK twice.

Part II   Quick Guide to Building Applications

A CheckBox control is added to the form.

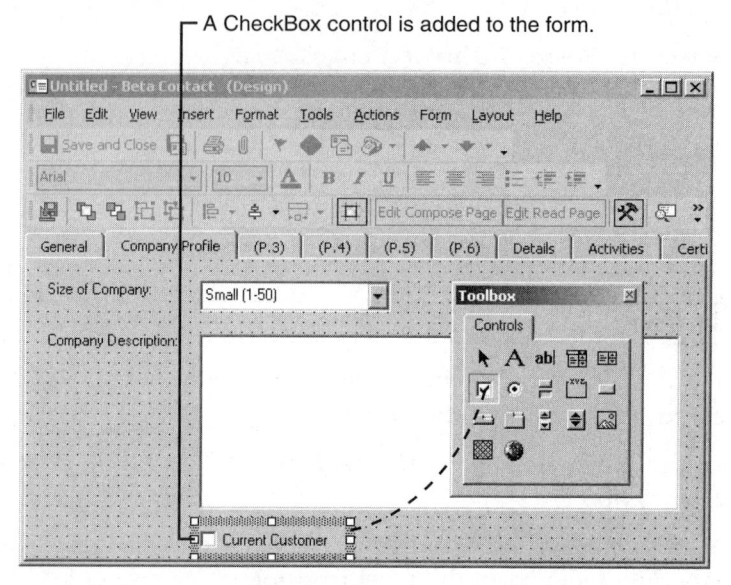

Figure 3-17 A CheckBox control is added to the Company Profile page.

Set Form Properties

The Properties page of the form shown in Figure 3-18 lets you name the form and specify a contact in case someone has suggestions for improvements or problems with the form.

To set form properties

1. Click the Properties tab.
2. In the Version text box, type *1.0*.
3. In the Form Number text box, type *1-1*.
4. In the Contact text box, type your name, and in the Description text box, type the following:

    Use this form to post, view, and update Beta Contact items in the Beta Contacts folder.

Customize Built-In Modules   Chapter 3

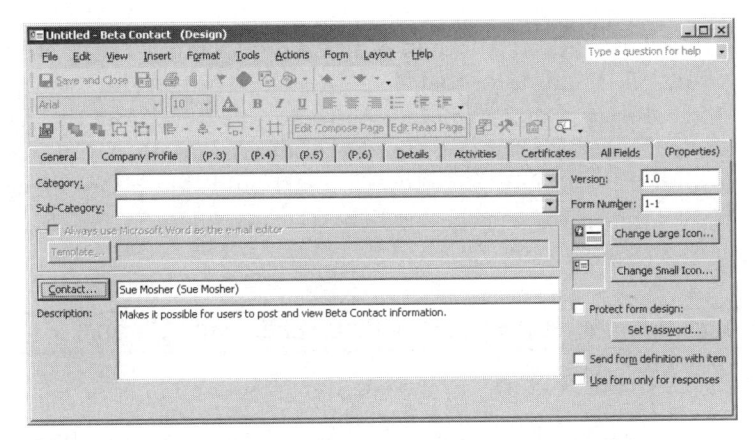

Figure 3-18 The Properties page of the Beta Contact form.

> **More Info**   For more information about setting form properties, see Chapter 5, "Forms."

Test the Form at Design Time

Before you save a form or publish a form to a folder, it's a good idea to run the form to see how the form layout appears at run time. With Outlook, you can easily switch between Design mode and Run mode for the form.

To switch from Design mode to Run mode

1. With the Compose page in Design mode, click Run This Form on the Form menu. View the Compose page of the form.
2. To test the Read page, send the form to your Inbox. Double-click the item in your Inbox to view the Read page of the form.
3. To return to Design mode, close the Run mode window.

Publish the Form

After you run the form and you're satisfied with its layout, you can publish the form in the Beta Contacts folder. When you publish the form, it is saved and registered in the Beta Contacts folder Form Library. Also, a menu item appears for the form on the Actions menu of the folder.

65

Part II Quick Guide to Building Applications

Forms with the same name, but different contents, may produce unpredictable results. For example, the Beta Contacts form in the Beta Contacts folder (Building Outlook 2002 Applications) and the Beta Contacts form in the Beta Contacts folder (Design Environment) should be identical. If they are not, unique names should be assigned, or the forms should be updated using Forms Manager. For further information, see "The Forms Manager" in Chapter 13, "Distributing and Securing Applications."

To publish the form to the Beta Contacts folder Form Library

1. On the Tools menu, choose Forms and then click Publish Form As.
2. In the Display text box and the Form Name text box, type *Beta Contact,* as shown in Figure 3-19.

The display name is visible in the forms library of the current folder where it was published, and in the form title bar.

The form name is reflected in the full Message Class designation.

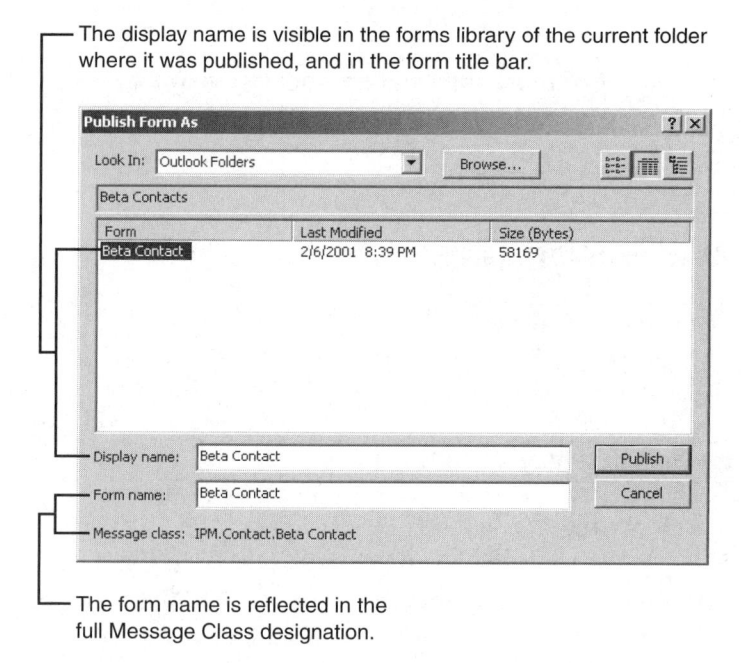

Figure 3-19 The Publish Form As dialog box is automatically filled in for you.

If for some reason the Beta Contacts folder is not selected (in the Look In box), click in the Look In drop-down list box and select the Beta Contacts folder.

3. Click Publish.

4. Close the form. When the message box appears, click No for Do You Want To Save Changes? in most cases. Click Yes if you want to save a backup copy to the Beta Contacts folder.

5. Click the Actions menu to verify that the form is published and available for use.

Specify the Default Form for the Folder

Now that you've created a custom form, you may want to run it to see if it works as expected. However, at this point, there are two possible forms that you can open. One form is the built-in Contacts form that's provided with Outlook. The other is the Beta Contact form you created. If you click the New Contact button on the Standard toolbar, the built-in Contacts form appears. You must click New Beta Contact on the Outlook Actions menu to open the Beta Contact form you created.

To avoid this step, make the Beta Contact form the default form for the folder. Then, when the user clicks the New Contact button, the Beta Contact form will appear.

To make the Beta Contact form the default form

1. In the Folder List, right-click the Beta Contacts folder and then click Properties.

2. Click the General tab.

3. In the When Posting To This Folder, Use list box, click Beta Contact, and then click OK.

Test the Application

Let's test the Beta Contacts application to make sure the Beta Contact form opens when you click the New Contact button. But first, let's switch to the Potential Beta Participants view.

To select the Potential Beta Participants view

- In the Current View drop-down list box on the Advanced toolbar, click Potential Beta Participants.

To test the Beta Contact form

1. While in the Beta Contacts folder, click the New Contact button on the Standard toolbar.
   You should see the Beta Contact form with the Company Profile tab.
2. Fill in the form, click Save, and then click Close.
3. The new item is posted in the Beta Contacts folder.

> **More Info** For more information about how forms and views work together, see Chapter 8, "Folders."

Delete the Items You Created

Before you make the form available to other users, delete the items you created earlier in this chapter. You do this because the items you created earlier in the chapter without the Beta Contacts form will show in the Contacts form when opened.

To delete the items in the Beta Contacts folder

1. Hold down the Shift key, and then click the items in the Beta Contacts folder.
2. Press the Delete key.
3. Click OK in the message box.

Copy the Folder to Public Folders

Now that you've created forms and views for the Beta Contacts folder, and you've tested the folder to make sure it works as planned, you copy the folder from the Design Environment personal folder (.pst) file to public folders so the folder can be shared by a workgroup or across the entire organization. Before you copy the folder, you might want to check with your administrator to determine the best location for the folder. In addition, you might need to get administrative permission to copy the folder to its destination in Public Folders.

To copy the Beta Contacts folder

1. In the Folder List, click the Beta Contacts folder.
2. On the File menu, point to Folder and then click Copy Beta Contacts.
3. In the Copy The Selected Folder To The Folder box, click the location you want the folder copied to, such as All Public Folders, and then click OK.

> **More Info** For more information about distributing folders, see Chapter 13.

Set Permissions

With Permissions, you define who can open the folder and what functions they can perform in the folder. When you create a folder in Outlook, you are automatically given an Owner role for the folder. This means you have full permissions to create, edit, and delete items in the folder, and you have full permissions to change any folder properties.

When you create a public folder under All Public Folders, the Default role is set to Author. If the public folder is a subfolder of an existing public folder, the Default role is inherited from the Default role in the parent folder. The Author default role assignment means that all users in the Microsoft Exchange Server system are automatically given permissions to create and open items in the folder and to delete and edit their own items. The Author role does not have the ability to create subfolders.

The Anonymous role should be set to None in the Beta Contacts folder. The anonymous role assignment means that users who open public folders through Outlook Web Access—under the anonymous Internet Information Services Internet guest account—have no access to the Beta Contacts public folder.

For the Beta Contacts folder, you limit access to the folder to only a few users by first setting the Default role to None. You then give a few of your coworkers a Publishing Author role so they can create, edit, and delete items in the folder.

To set permissions for the Beta Contacts folder

1. In the Folder List, right-click the Beta Contacts folder and then click Properties.
2. Click the Permissions tab. This tab is only available if the folder is an Outlook Mailbox folder or a public folder.

3. In the Name list box, click Default, and then, in the Roles drop-down list box, click None.

   This prevents all users on the Microsoft Exchange Server from opening the folder.

4. Click Add, select several of your coworkers' names from the list, click Add, and then click OK.

5. In the Name list box, hold the Ctrl key down and click each name you want to select. In the Role drop-down list box, click Publishing Author.

6. The Permissions page should now look similar to the illustration shown in Figure 3-20.

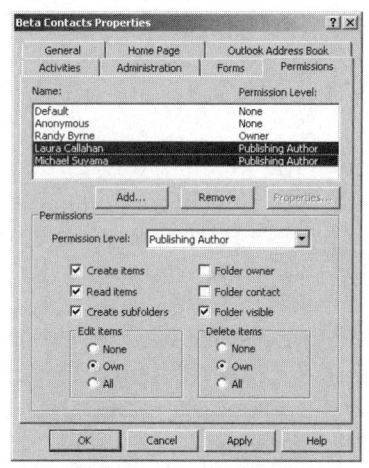

Figure 3-20 The Permissions page for the Beta Contacts folder in Public Folders.

Release the Application

Before you release the application, set the Initial View On Folder property to Potential Beta Participants. This will be the view users first see when they open the Beta Contacts folder.

To set administration properties

1. In the Folder List, right-click the Beta Contacts folder and then click Properties.

2. Click the Administration tab.

3. In the Initial View On Folder drop-down list box, click Potential Beta Participants and then click OK.

   Now that the folder is ready for use, send a message to your coworkers to notify them that the application is available.

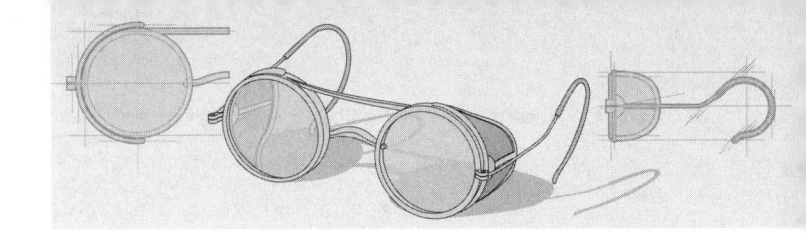

4

Design a Custom Application

The Microsoft Outlook Post form can be used in conjunction with a public folder to build custom discussion applications that let users submit, share, and collaborate on ideas and information. Discussion applications provide a great way to facilitate communication in your organization because they enable users across the enterprise to conduct online conversations. Perhaps equally important, the history of correspondence is saved and organized in a public folder, so important ideas or critical conversations are always available for viewing at a later date. Discussion applications are especially useful for virtual corporations or flexible workgroups where members collaborate on a project but work different hours or in different locations.

In this chapter, you will build a Product Ideas application that lets users submit, read, and respond to new product ideas in a public folder. This application provides a good example of how a discussion application can be used in your organization both to collect, store, and organize ideas, and to foster enterprise-wide dialogue about subjects that are vital to your company's interests.

By the end of this chapter, you should have the basic skills and concepts you need to build one of the most common types of groupware applications—the discussion application. As a result, you will be able to build a wide variety of new applications to foster communication in your company. In addition, you should also have a working discussion application that you can use as a basis for building other information-sharing applications.

Here are just a few suggestions for the types of discussion applications you can build:

- **Product feedback** Allows users to post comments about existing products and features in a public folder. Other users, such as product developers, marketing, or sales personnel, can then respond to existing comment items, thus creating an online discussion. Product planners can review the folder on a periodic basis to get an overall idea of what users like and dislike about a particular product.

- **Technical users group**   Serves as a forum for posting issues and problems, as well as solutions to problems. For example, users who are having difficulty with particular tasks can post problems to the Technical Users Group public folder. In turn, another user can post a solution to the problem item, perhaps suggesting an alternative discovered by working on a similar task.

- **Vendor services application**   Allows members of your organization to post, respond to, and read reviews of professional services provided by your company's vendors. For example, a supervisor looking for temporary word-processing help can search the folder for a highly recommended vendor who has previously been employed by the company.

- **Restaurants and accommodations application**   Allows users to post, read, and respond to restaurant and hotel/motel reviews in a public folder. With this application, your company can quickly develop an online travel guide to help business travelers plan where to eat and stay when they're working away from the office.

Overview of the Product Ideas Application

The Product Ideas application consists of a Product Ideas folder and two forms: the Product Idea form and the Product Idea Response form. Following is an example of how the Product Ideas application might be used by a sports equipment manufacturer to help generate new ideas for products.

Let's assume Peter Krebs in Seattle opens the Product Ideas public folder and then uses the Product Idea form to post an idea for a wooden kayak construction kit. Suzan Fine in Boston reads the idea and then uses the Product Idea Response form to post a response asking what kind of wood is best to use. A few minutes later, James Allard reads the items posted by Peter Krebs and Suzan Fine and uses the Product Idea Response form to post a response to Suzan Fine's item. As shown in Figure 4-1, the resulting conversation is stored and organized in the folder.

The Product Category view   As part of the application design process, you add a custom view to the Product Ideas folder that groups items first by Product Category field and then by the Conversation field, as shown in Figure 4-2.

Design a Custom Application   Chapter 4

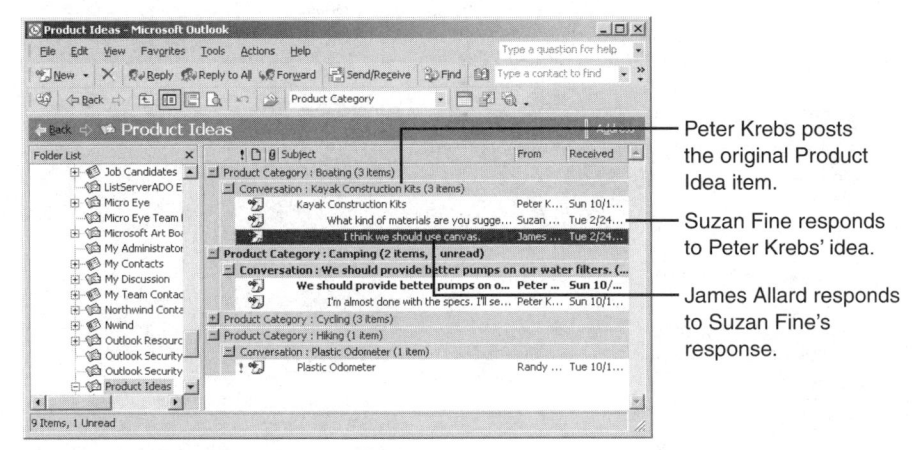

Figure 4-1 The Product Ideas folder.

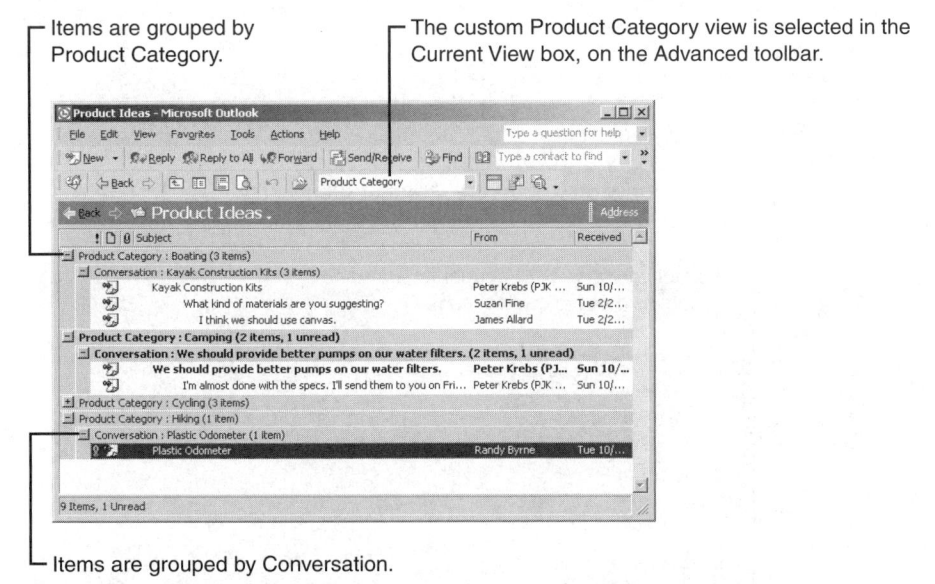

Figure 4-2 The Product Category view in the Product Ideas folder.

The Product Idea form The Product Idea form is a modified Post To Folder form. The New Product Idea form has both a Compose page and a Read page. With the Compose page, as shown in Figure 4-3, the user posts a new item in the Product Ideas folder. With the Read page, the user opens and views a posted item.

The Product Idea Response form The Product Idea Response form, as shown in Figure 4-4, serves two purposes. It lets users post a response to a product idea. It also lets users post a response to the response. We'll take a look at how this is done later in this chapter.

Part II Quick Guide to Building Applications

Users click the Post button to submit an idea to the Product Ideas folder.

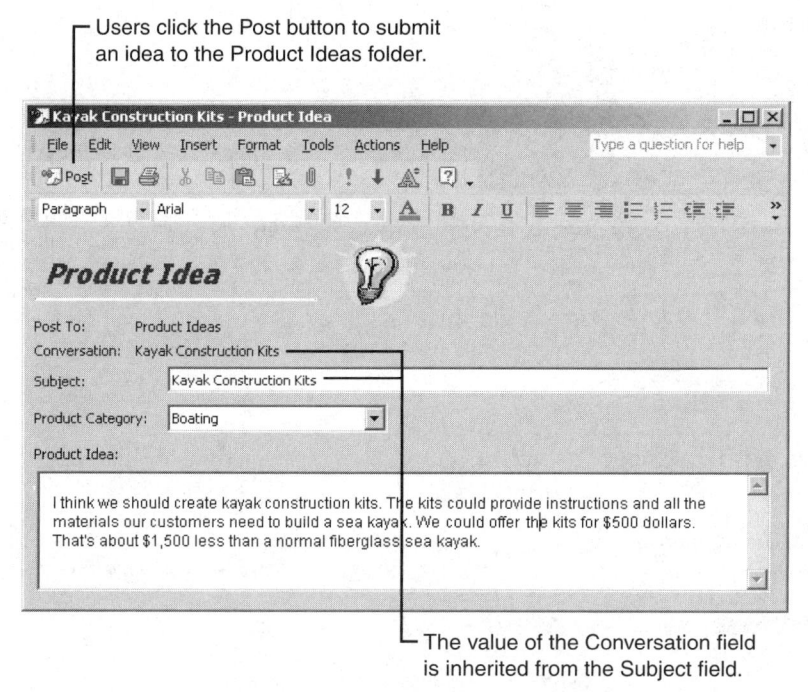

The value of the Conversation field is inherited from the Subject field.

Figure 4-3 The Compose page of the Product Idea form.

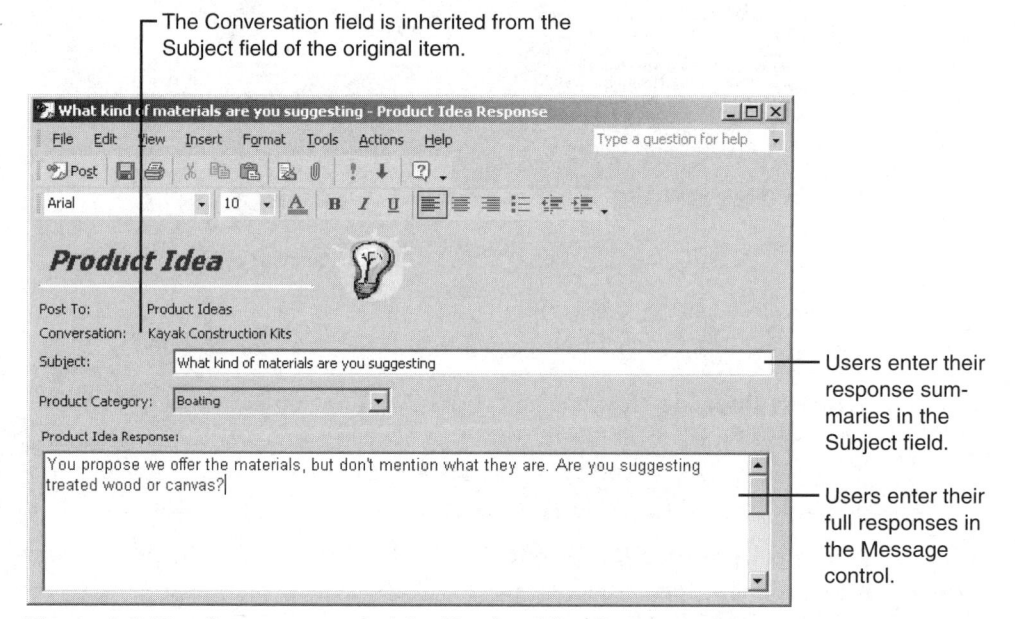

The Conversation field is inherited from the Subject field of the original item.

Users enter their response summaries in the Subject field.

Users enter their full responses in the Message control.

Figure 4-4 The Compose page of the Product Idea Response form.

Create the Product Ideas Folder

To get started, you create the Product Ideas folder in the Design Environment personal folder, shown in Figure 4-5. If you haven't yet created the Design Environment folder, refer to "Create the Design Environment Personal Folder (.pst) File" in Chapter 3, "Customize Built-In Modules."

To create the Product Ideas folder

1. In the Folder List, right-click the Design Environment folder, and then click New Folder on the shortcut menu.
2. In the Name text box of the Create New Folder dialog box, type *Product Ideas*.
3. In the Folder Contains drop-down list, click Mail And Post Items.
4. If a prompt appears, click your desired response in the Add A Shortcut To Outlook Bar? message box.

Figure 4-5 Use the Create New Folder dialog box to create the Product Ideas folder.

Create the Product Idea Form

The Product Idea form that you create will enable users to post new ideas to the Product Ideas folder. The Product Idea form is based on the standard Outlook Post form. The Outlook Post form supplies most of the required functionality—all you need to do to build the Product Idea form is add and remove some controls and then set a few properties for the controls and the form. To design the Product Idea form, you'll modify the Compose page of the Post form, as shown in Figure 4-6.

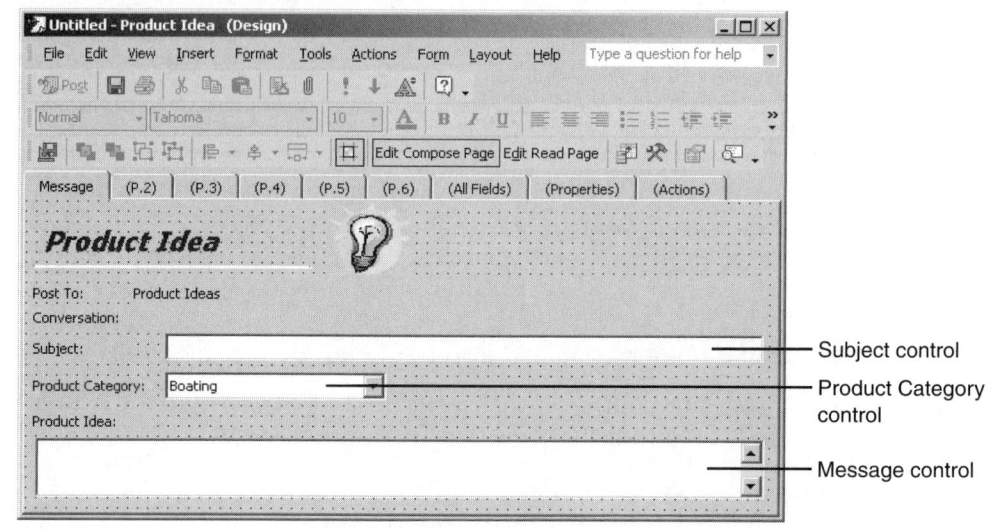

Figure 4-6 The finished version shows the Compose page of the form in Design mode.

Open the Post Form

To build the Product Idea form, you open the Post form in the Product Ideas folder and then switch to Design mode to modify the form.

> **To open the Post form in Design mode**

1. In the Folder List, click the Product Ideas folder.
2. On the File menu, select New and click Post In This Folder.
3. On the Tools menu of the Post form, select Forms and then click Design This Form.

Edit the Compose Page

Most forms consist of two pages—a Compose page for submitting items and a Read page for opening and viewing items. In most cases, the Compose page is slightly different from the Read page. For example, the Compose page has a Post To control that shows where the item is posted, while the Read page has a From control that shows who posted the item.

Design a Custom Application Chapter 4

To edit the Compose page, remove the Categories control, resize the Message control, and then add a Product Category control plus a label, a frame, and an image control to give visual impact to the form. The associated labels for the controls will also be removed.

Remove the Categories Control

For the form you're creating, the Categories control serves no purpose, so you can remove it from the Compose page.

To remove the Categories control

1. Click the Categories edit box, and then press Delete.
2. Click the Categories command button, and then press Delete.

Adjust the Message Control

Now move the Message control and resize it to make room for the Product Category control that you add to the form.

To adjust the Message control

1. Drag the Message control bottom border until it resizes to fill to nearly the bottom of the Compose page.
2. Drag the Message control top border until it is approximately the size and at the location of the control shown in Figure 4-7.

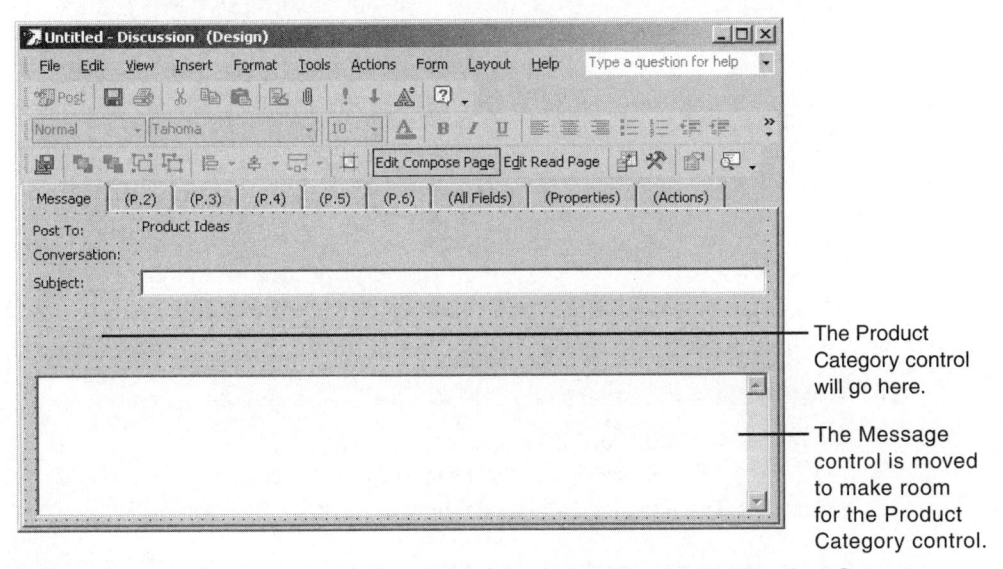

Figure 4-7 The Message control is adjusted to make room for the Product Category control.

Part II Quick Guide to Building Applications

> **To center the Message control horizontally**

- On the Layout menu, point to Center In Form and then click Horizontally.

Add the Product Category Control

The Product Category control is a ComboBox control that lets users select a product category, such as Boating or Fishing, or enter a new product category. Later in this chapter, you will build a view that groups items in the Product Ideas folder by product category. When product ideas are grouped in the folder by product category, it becomes much easier for the user to find ideas about a particular product.

> **To add the Product Category control**

1. On the Form Design toolbar, click the Control Toolbox button.
2. From the Control Toolbox, drag a ComboBox control to the form. Then place the pointer over a sizing handle on the right border of the control and drag the border until the field is approximately the size and at the position of the control shown in Figure 4-8.

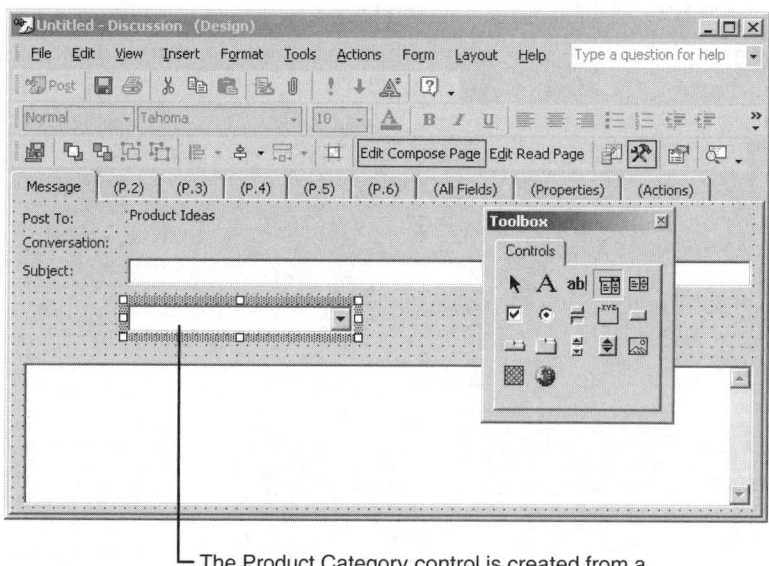

The Product Category control is created from a ComboBox control that you drag to the form.

Figure 4-8 The Product Category control is added to the Compose page.

Set the properties for the Product Category control   When you set properties for the Product Category control using the Properties dialog box, as shown in

Figure 4-9, you name the control and then you create a Product Category field for the control. When you create the field from the Properties dialog box, you automatically bind the field to the control. When a field is bound to the control, the value in the control at run time is saved to the field when the item is posted. The value is loaded into the control from the field when a posted item in a folder is opened.

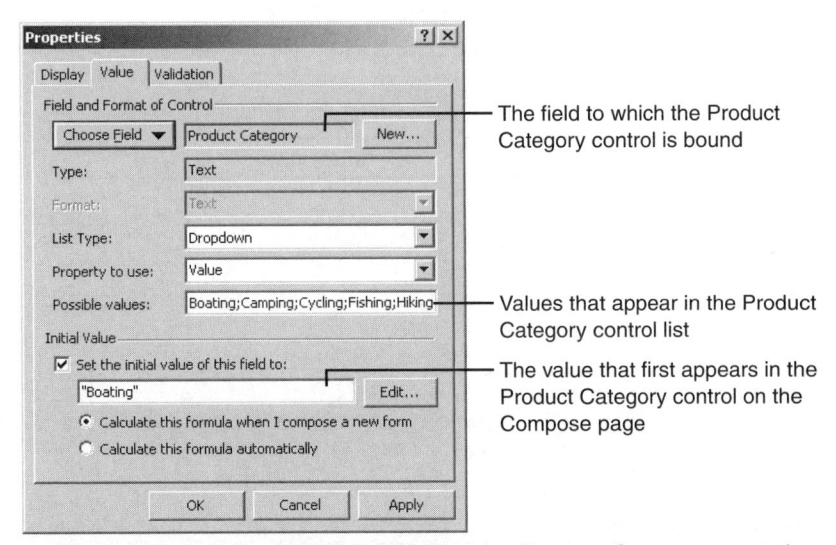

Figure 4-9 The Properties dialog box for the Product Category control.

To set the properties for the Product Category control

1. Right-click the ComboBox control you added to the form, and then click Properties on the shortcut menu.
2. Click the Display tab.
3. In the Name text box, type *Product Category*.
4. Click the Value tab.
5. Click New.
6. In the Name text box, type *Product Category* and then click OK.
    The Product Category control is now bound to the Product Category field.
7. In the Possible Values text box, type: *Boating;Camping;Cycling; Fishing;Hiking;Running*.

Part II   Quick Guide to Building Applications

8. Select the Set The Initial Value Of This Field To check box, and then type *"Boating"* in the text box.

    The initial value is the value that appears first in the control when the form first opens at run time.

9. Click OK.

Add a Label for the Product Category Control

Now add a label for the Product Category control so that users know the purpose of the control.

To add a Label control

1. From the Control Toolbox, drag a Label control to the Compose page, as shown in Figure 4-10.

2. Click the Label control, and then change its text to Product Category.

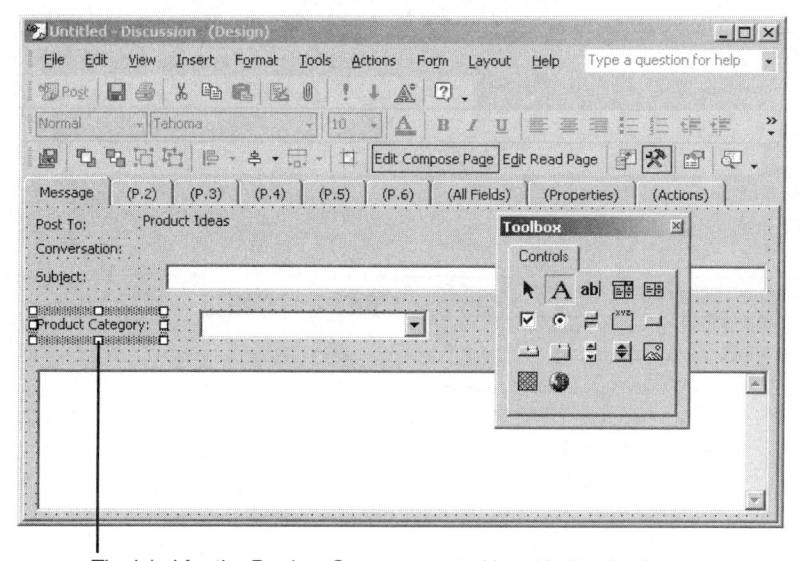

The label for the Product Category control is added to the form.

Figure 4-10 The Product Category label is added to the form.

Align the Subject and Product Category Controls

One way to make sure your forms have a professional look is to align the controls on the form. Outlook offers a variety of layout options, but in most cases you can align items simply by dragging the borders of controls until they are aligned the way you want. For example, on the Compose page, you can align the Subject and Product Category controls by dragging the left edge of the Subject control until it is aligned with the left edge of the Product Category control.

Because the Snap To Grid option is on by default, the Subject control is automatically adjusted for you.

To align the Subject and Product Category controls

- Click the Subject control, and then drag the left border of the Subject control to the right until it is aligned with the left border of the Product Category control, as shown in Figure 4-11.

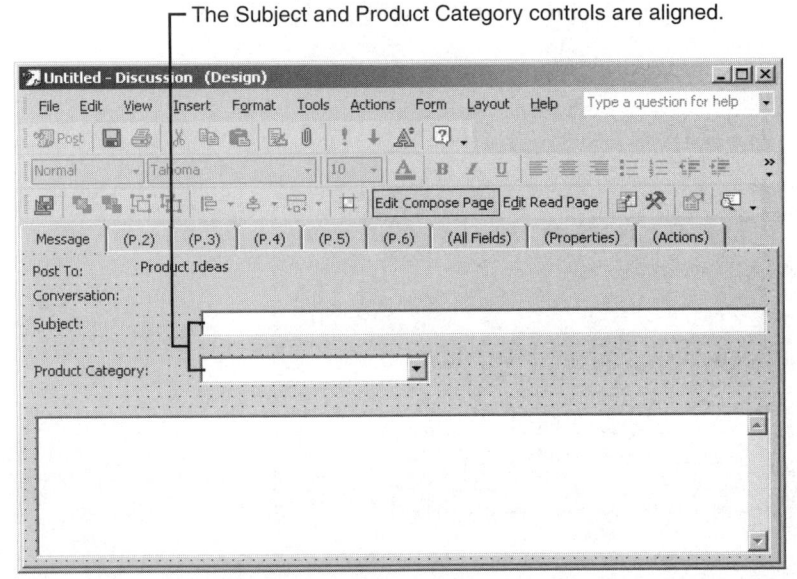

Figure 4-11 The Subject control is aligned with the Product Category control.

Add a Label for the Message Control

Now add a label for the Message control to indicate to users the type of information they're supposed to type into the control. To make room for the label, you may need to make the Message control slightly smaller.

To add a Label control

1. Drag a Label control from the Control Toolbox to the Compose page.
2. Click the Label control, and then type *Product Idea:*.

Move Controls and Add Form Graphics

Next move controls down to make room for the form graphic that consists of a Label, a Frame, and an Image control. You will need to resize the form vertically to add more room at the bottom of the Message tab.

Part II   Quick Guide to Building Applications

To move controls

1. Click the Selector tool in the Control Toolbox.

2. Click in the upper-left corner of the Compose page, and drag the selector box to the lower-right corner of the page. All controls on the page should be selected. Start again and reselect all the controls if they are not selected.

3. Drag the selected controls to the bottom of the form. When you have finished dragging the controls, they will be positioned as shown in Figure 4-12.

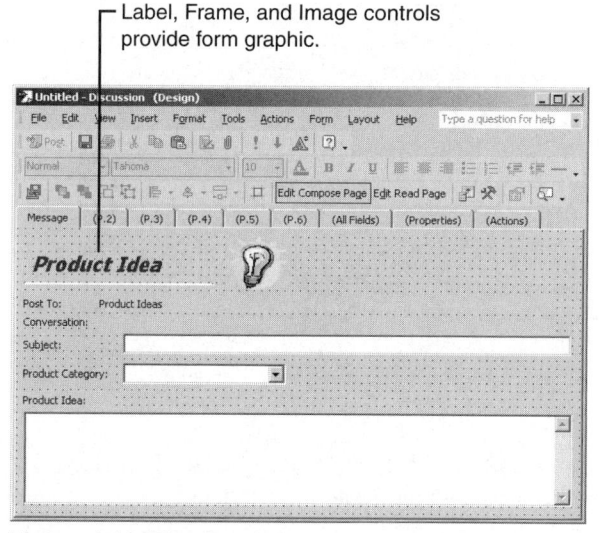

Figure 4-12 The Compose page shows the form graphic consisting of a Label, a Frame, and an Image control.

To add a form graphic using a label control

1. Drag a Label control from the Control Toolbox to the Compose page.

2. Click the Label control, and then type *Product Idea*.

3. Right-click the Label control, and select Properties on the shortcut menu.

4. Click the Display tab, and then click the Font button on the Properties dialog box.

5. Set the font to 16 pt Tahoma, Bold Italic, color Maroon, and click OK twice.

82

6. Drag the Product Idea label to the approximate position shown in Figure 4-12, resizing as necessary.

To add a form graphic using a Frame control

1. Drag a Frame control from the Control Toolbox to the Compose page.
2. Right-click the Frame control, and then select Advanced Properties on the shortcut menu.
3. Double-click the BackColor property, and select White Color Box from Basic Colors. Click OK.
4. Double-click the Caption property, press the Delete key, and then click Apply.
5. Double-click the Height property, type *3* in the edit box, and then click Apply.
6. Double-click the Width property, type *180* in the edit box, and then click Apply.
7. Close the Advanced Properties window. The Frame control is now masquerading as a white line. Select and drag the line to the approximate position shown in Figure 4-12 under the Product Idea label.

To add a form graphic using an Image control

1. Navigate to the Product Ideas Readme folder. This folder is a subfolder of the Product Ideas folder under the 2. Quick Guide folder in the Building Microsoft Outlook 2000 Applications.pst file.
2. Open the Readme post item in the Readme folder.
3. Right-click the attachment icon for idea.gif, and select the Save As command. Navigate to the Desktop folder, and click the Save button to save the file on your desktop.
4. Drag an Image control from the Control Toolbox to the Compose page.
5. Right-click the Image control, and then select Advanced Properties on the shortcut menu.
6. Double-click the Picture property, and then use the Load Picture dialog box to select a picture for the Image control. Click the Desktop folder in the Folder drop-down list box, select idea.gif from the File Name list box, and click OK to confirm your selection. You can delete idea.gif using Windows Explorer or move it to a storage folder for graphics files.

7. Double-click the BorderStyle property to change it to None. Click the Apply button.

8. Double-click the PictureSizeMode property, and the property should change to Stretch. Click the Apply button.

9. Close the Advanced Properties window. Select and drag the image to the position shown in Figure 4-12, just to the right of the Product Idea label. You might need to resize the Image control by selecting and then resizing the control.

To save the form graphic for reuse on other pages

1. Click the Selector tool in the Control Toolbox.

2. Click in the upper-left corner of the Compose Page, and drag the selector box to the right of the Image control until all the form graphic controls are selected.

3. Drag the selection from the Compose page to the Control Toolbox.

Set the Tab Order for the Compose Page

The tab order defines the sequence in which the controls become active on the form when the user presses the Tab key. When you add controls to the form, the control name is added to the bottom of a list of controls in the Tab Order box. For the Compose page, you must move the Product Category control up the list so that it follows directly after the Subject control.

To set the Tab Order for the Compose page

1. On the Layout menu, click Tab Order.

2. In the Tab Order dialog box, click Product Category and then click Move Up until Product Category is above Message.

3. Click OK.

> **Note** Label controls, such as *ConversationLabel* and *SubjectLabel*, are listed in the Tab Order box but are not included in the tab order.

Edit the Read Page

To edit the Read page, you copy the controls you added to the Compose page. Before you do this, however, you must switch to the Read page, adjust the grid settings, and delete existing controls to make room for new controls.

To switch to the Read page

- On the Form Design toolbar, click Edit Read Page, as shown in Figure 4-13.

To delete controls to make room for new controls

1. Click the Selector tool on the Control Toolbox. Click on the Read page just above and to the left of the Posted To label and drag the selection box to the lower right corner of the form so that all controls on the Read page are selected except for the From label, the From control, the Posted label, and the Posted control. If these controls are selected accidentally, you can deselect them by holding down the Ctrl key and then clicking the control that you want to deselect.

2. Press Delete.

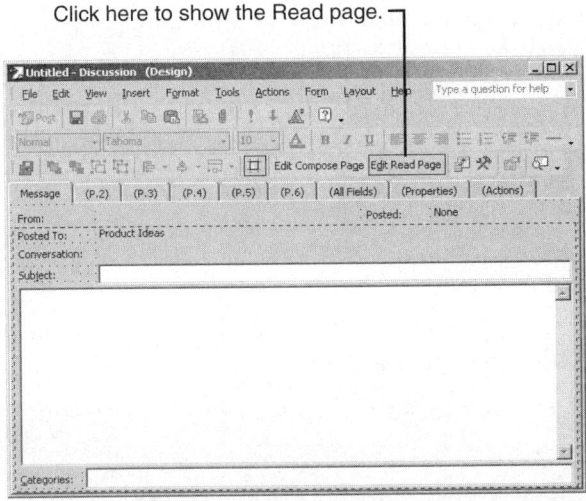

Figure 4-13 Use the Selector tool to remove controls from the Read page of the Product Idea form.

Part II   Quick Guide to Building Applications

To adjust the From and Posted controls

1. Use the Selector tool to select the remaining From and Posted controls on the Read page.
2. Drag the selected controls until the position of the controls is approximately the same as the controls shown in Figure 4-14.

Copy Controls from the Compose Page

Now switch to the Compose page and copy the controls required to complete the Read page. Then switch back to the Read page and paste the controls.

To copy the controls from the Compose page

1. On the Form Design toolbar, click Edit Compose Page.
2. Click the Selector tool in the Control Toolbox. Click just to the top and left of the Post To label, and drag the selection box to the lower right of the page so that all controls on the page—including and below the Post To control—are selected.
3. On the Standard toolbar, click Copy.
4. On the Form Design toolbar, click Edit Read Page.
5. When the Read page appears, click Paste and then position the pasted controls on the page as shown in Figure 4-14.
6. On the Form Design toolbar, click Edit Compose Page again.
7. Use the Selector tool to select the form graphic controls (Product Idea label, Frame control line, and Image control).
8. On the Standard toolbar, click Copy.
9. On the Form Design toolbar, click Edit Read Page.
10. When the Read page appears, click Paste and then position the pasted controls on the page as shown in Figure 4-14.
11. Change the caption of the Product Ideas label to Product Ideas Response.
12. Right-click the Product Category ComboBox, and check the Read Only check box in the Properties dialog box.

Controls are copied to the Read page.

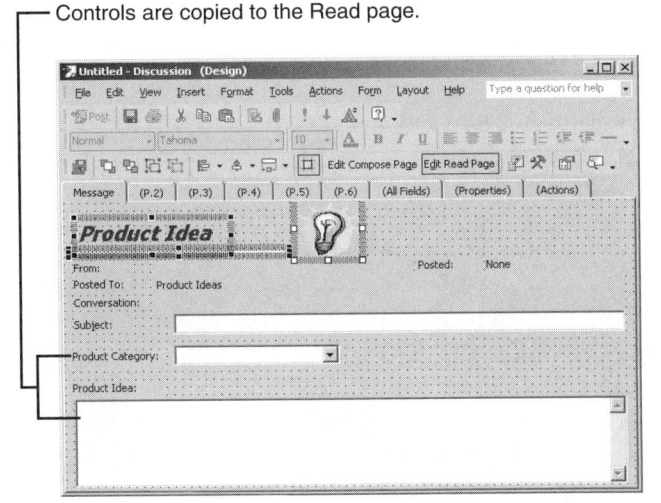

Figure 4-14 The Read page of the Product Idea form.

Set the Tab Order for the Read Page

In designing forms, it is important to remember that when you change a design element on the Compose page, you often need to make the same change on the Read page.

> **To set the tab order**

1. On the Layout menu, click Tab Order.
2. In the Tab Order dialog box, click Product Category and then click Move Up until Product Category is below Subject. Click OK.

Set Product Idea Form Properties

The Outlook Properties tab lets you define the overall attributes for the form, including the Caption property, which appears in the title bar of the form window, and the Contact property, which specifies the individual to contact for upgrades or form maintenance. There are a variety of other properties you can set for the form, but for now, set only the properties listed in a moment.

> **To set Product Idea form properties**

- Click the Properties tab, and then fill in the values shown in the table on the following page.

Part II Quick Guide to Building Applications

Property	Value
Contact	*Your name*
Description	*Use this form to post and view product ideas in the Product Ideas folder.*
Version	*1.0*
Form Number	*1*

> **More Info** For more information about how to set form properties, see Chapter 5, "Forms."

Test the Form at Design Time

Before you save a form or publish it to a folder, it's a good idea to run the form to see how the form layout appears at run time. It's also a good idea to test both the Read page and the Compose page of the form.

To switch between Design mode and Run mode when testing

1. With the Compose page in Design mode, click Run This Form on the Form menu.

2. To test the Read page, send the form to yourself and view the received item in your Inbox.

3. To return to Design mode, close the Run mode window of the Compose page.

Make a Backup Copy of the Product Idea Form

Although it's not absolutely necessary, it is a good idea to make a backup copy of the form before you publish it to a form library.

To save the Product Idea form

1. With the form open, click Save As on the File menu.

2. In the Save In drop-down list box, select the default Outlook template folder. The location of the default Outlook template folder depends upon your operating system. You can also use the My Documents folder if that is more convenient.

Design a Custom Application   Chapter 4

3. In the File Name text box, type *Product Idea* as the name for the form.
4. In the Save As Type drop-down list box, select Outlook Template.
5. Click Save.

To open your backup copy of a form

1. Select New on the File menu, and then click Choose Form.
2. Click User Templates In File System in the Look In drop-down list box, click the form you'd like to open, and then click Open.
3. In the Select Folder window, choose the appropriate folder and click OK.

   The following table lists the location of the default Outlook template folder.

Operating System	Default Outlook Template Folder
Windows 98 or Windows ME	*drive*:\Windows\Application Data\Microsoft\Templates
Windows NT 4	*drive*:\Winnt\Profiles\<*user*>\Application Data\Microsoft\Templates
Windows 2000	*drive*:\Documents and Settings\<*user*>\Application Data\Microsoft\Templates

Publish the Product Idea Form

When you publish the Product Idea form to the Product Ideas folder, you register the form definition in the folder. As a result, a menu command appears on the Actions menu of Outlook when the user opens the Product Ideas folder. This is the menu command that enables users to open the Product Idea form and create a new Product Idea item.

To publish the form to the Product Ideas folder

1. Choose Forms on the Tools menu, and then click Publish Form As.
2. In the Form Name text box and the Display Name text box, type *Product Idea*.
3. If the text in the Look In drop-down list box is not Product Ideas, click the drop-down list box, select the Product Ideas folder, and then click OK.
4. Click Publish.

5. In the Send Form Definition With Item message box, choose Yes if this form will be sent to someone without access to your forms library system. That way, recipients will have a self-contained form that can be viewed independently. Select No if the recipient has the form published in Personal Forms Library or Organizational Forms Library, or has access to the forms library of the folder. This keeps form size down and speeds form opening. For more information, see Chapter 13, "Distributing and Securing Applications."

> **Tip** Click the Outlook Actions menu. You'll notice that the New Product Idea command is added to the menu. Outlook automatically constructs the menu command by combining the word New with the Display Name property Product Idea.

Create the Product Idea Response Form

The Product Idea Response form, as shown in Figure 4-15, is very similar to the Product Idea form. Therefore, to create the Product Idea Response form, all you need to do is modify a few properties of the original Product Idea form, change the form name, and then publish the form in the Product Ideas folder.

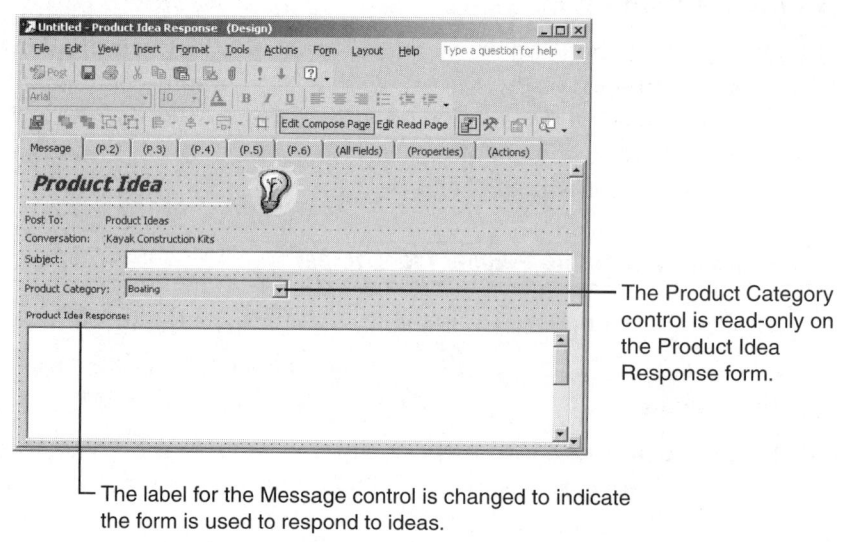

Figure 4-15 The Compose page of the Product Idea Response form.

Design a Custom Application Chapter 4

Edit the Compose Page

To edit the Compose page, you change several properties for the control and you change the label associated with the Message control. First, however, you must switch from the Read page to the Compose page.

To switch to the Compose page

- On the Form Design toolbar, click Edit Compose Page.

Make the Product Category Control Read-Only

On the Product Idea Response form, you make the Product Category control a read-only control so that the product category selected by the person who posted the new idea cannot be changed by individuals responding to the idea.

To make the Product Category control read-only

1. On the Compose page, right-click the Product Category control and then click Properties.
2. Click the Display tab, and then select the Read Only check box.
3. Click OK to close.

Clear the Initial Value Property for the Product Category Field

Now specify that the Initial Value property for the Product Category field is cleared. This ensures that the value from the Product Category field in the Product Idea item is copied to the Product Category field in the Product Idea Response item.

To clear the Initial Value property

1. Right-click the Product Category control, and then click Properties.
2. Click the Value tab, clear the Set The Initial Value Of This Field To check box, and then click OK.

Change the Product Idea Label

Now change the label above the Message control from Product Idea: to Product Idea Response: to clarify the purpose of the Message control on the Product Idea Response form.

Part II   Quick Guide to Building Applications

| To change the label |

1. Click the Product Idea label (located above the Message control), and then click it again.
2. Change the text in the label to *Product Idea Response:*.
3. Resize the label.

Edit the Read Page

Now switch to the Read page, set the Product Category control to read-only, and then change the Product Idea label to Product Idea Response.

| To switch to the Read page |

- On the Form Design toolbar, click Edit Read Page.

| To make the Product Category control read-only |

1. Right-click the Product Category control, and then click Properties.
2. Click the Display tab, select the Read Only check box, and then click OK.

| To change the Product Idea label |

1. Click the Product Idea label (above the Message control), and then click it again.
2. Change the label to Product Idea Response.
3. Resize the label.

Set the Form Properties

Now set the form properties for the Product Idea Response form.

| To set the form properties |

- Click the Properties tab, and then fill in the values shown in the table on the following page.

Property	Value
Contact	*Your name*
Description	*Use this form to post or view a response to a product idea or to post or view a response to a product idea response.*
Version	*1.0*
Form Number	*2*
Use Form Only For Responses	*True (checked)*

Make a Backup Copy of the Product Idea Response Form

Now save the Product Idea Response form in the folder where you saved the Product Idea form.

To make a backup copy of the Product Idea Response form

1. With the form open, click Save As on the File menu.
2. In the Save In drop-down list box, select the default Outlook template folder.
3. In the File Name text box, type *Product Idea Response* as the name for the form.
4. In the Save As Type drop-down list box, select Outlook Template.
5. Click Save.

To open your backup copy of a form

1. Select New on the File menu, and then click Choose Form.
2. Click User Templates In File System in the Look In drop-down list box, and then click on the form you'd like to open.

Publish the Product Idea Response Form

Before you publish the Product Idea Response form, change the Form Name option in the Publish Form As dialog box to Product Idea Response. Then publish the Product Idea Response form to the Product Ideas Form Library.

Part II Quick Guide to Building Applications

> **To publish the Product Idea Response form**

1. On the Tools menu, select Forms and then click Publish Forms As.

2. In the Display Name text box and Form Name text box, change the name to Product Idea Response. The Message Class property automatically updates when you change the Form name. The Display Name field reflects both the form name on the Actions menu of the folder and the caption on the title bar of the published form.

3. Click Publish.

4. Close the Product Idea Response form. In the Save Changes? message box, select No in most cases. Select Yes if you want a backup item in the current folder.

Set the Actions

Actions determine how a form handles responses. For example, the action you create for the Product Idea form will allow users to respond to a Product Idea item with the Product Idea Response form. In addition, the action you create for the Product Idea Response form will enable users to respond to a Product Idea Response item with the Product Idea Response form. In essence, the form will call itself for a response.

Set the Actions for the Product Idea Form

First open the Product Idea form in the Product Ideas folder. Then switch to Design mode for the form and set its actions.

> **To open the Product Idea form in Design mode**

1. Locate the Product Ideas folder in the Folder List, and click once to open it.

2. On the Outlook Actions menu, hold down the Shift key and click New Product Idea.

3. On the Tools menu of the Product Idea form, select Forms and then click Design This Form.

Design a Custom Application Chapter 4

> **Tip** Holding down the Shift key when you open a form for design purposes is a good practice because it prevents any code in the form from executing when the form is opened. Note that the Product Ideas folder must be open for the New Product Idea command to appear on the Actions menu.

Make the Reply To Folder Action Unavailable

When you create a new action for a Post form, you usually make the standard Post To Folder action unavailable. You do this for two reasons. First, you don't want standard Post items in the Product Ideas folder because they won't group correctly in custom views. Second, you want to avoid the confusion of presenting the user with two commands—New Post In This Folder and New Product Idea—that allows them to post an item in the folder.

To make the Reply To Folder action unavailable

1. On the Product Idea form, click the Actions tab.
2. Double-click the Reply To Folder action.
3. Clear the Enabled check box, and then click OK.

    The Actions page should now look like the Actions page shown in Figure 4-16.

The Reply To Folder action is not enabled for the Product Idea form.

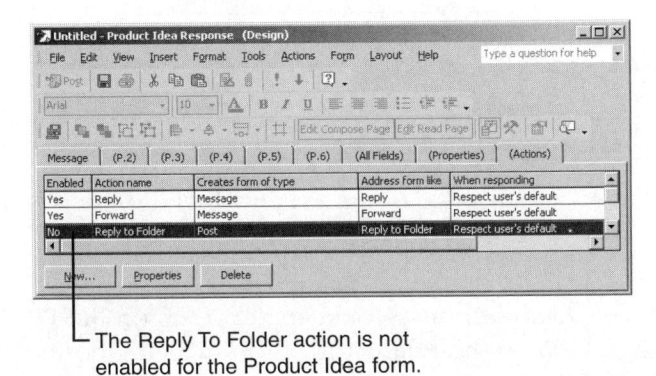

Figure 4-16 The Reply To Folder action is made unavailable for the Product Idea form.

95

Create a New Action

Now create a new action that specifies that a Product Idea Response button appears on the Product Idea form when the user opens a posted Product Idea. When the user clicks the Product Idea Response button, shown in Figure 4-17, the Product Idea Response form appears, which can then be used to post a response in the folder.

The new action causes the Product Idea Response button to be placed on the Read page of the form.

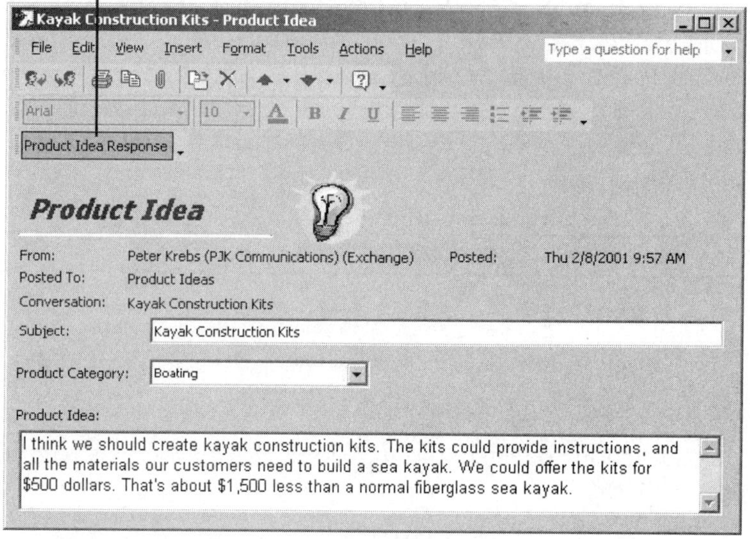

Figure 4-17 The Product Idea Response button is added to the Product Idea form when a Product Idea item is opened in the folder.

To create a new action

1. Click New on the Actions page of the Product Idea Response form.

2. In the Action Name text box, as shown in Figure 4-18, type *Product Idea Response*.

    The Product Idea Response command appears on the Product Idea Response button on the Product Idea form when a posted item is opened. The Product Idea Response command also appears on the Actions menu of the folder when a Product Idea item is selected in the Product Ideas folder.

3. In the Form Name drop-down list box, click Product Idea Response.

4. In the Address Form Like A drop-down list box, click Reply To Folder, and then click OK.

Design a Custom Application   Chapter 4

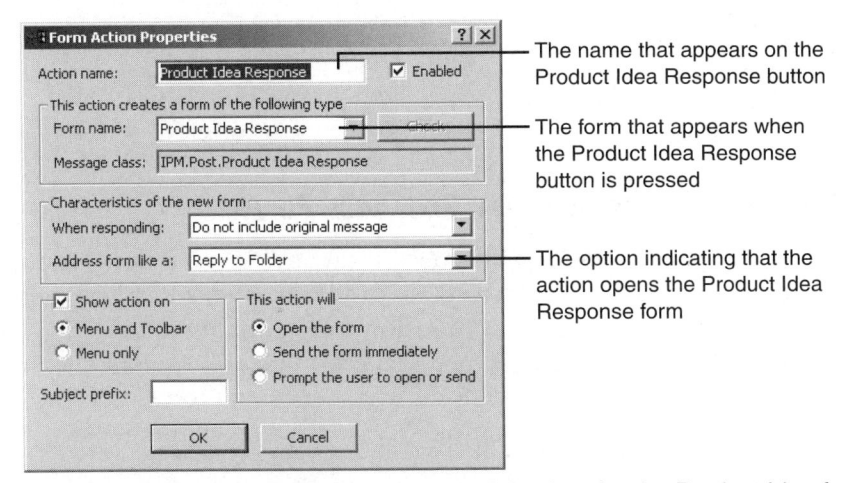

Figure 4-18 The Form Action Properties dialog box for the Product Idea form specifies that the Product Idea Response form opens when a user clicks the Product Idea Response button.

Make a Backup Copy of the Product Idea Form

Before you republish the form, it's a good idea to make a backup copy of the modified form.

To make a backup copy of the Product Idea form

1. With the form open, click Save As on the File menu.
2. In the Save In drop-down list box, select the default Outlook template folder.
3. In the File Name text box, double-click on Product Idea.
4. In the Save As Type drop-down list box, select Outlook Template.
5. Click Save.
6. Select Yes to replace the existing file.

Republish the Product Idea Form

To republish the form

1. On the Tools menu, select Forms and then click Publish Form As.
2. In the window with the list of published forms, double-click Product Idea.

Part II   Quick Guide to Building Applications

3. If you are prompted to replace the existing form, click Yes.

4. Close the Product Idea form. Click No to save changes. Click Yes if you want a backup draft saved to the current folder.

Set the Actions for the Product Idea Response Form

Now open the Product Idea Response form and create a new Product Idea Response action so that users can respond to a Product Idea Response item. In effect, users can create a response to a response by opening another instance of the Product Idea Response form. When you create the new action, the Product Idea Response button is added to the form when a posted Product Idea Response item is opened in the Product Ideas folder, as shown in Figure 4-19.

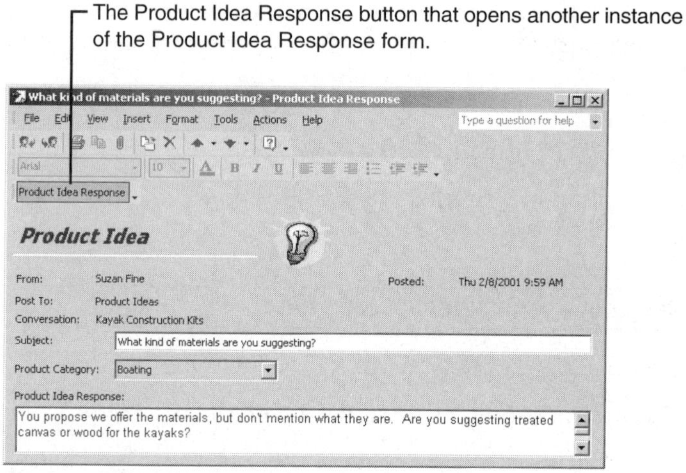

Figure 4-19 The Product Idea Response button appears on the form when the user opens a Product Idea Response item in the folder.

Open the Product Idea Response Form

To create a new action for the Product Idea Response form, you first open the form in Run mode, and then switch to Design mode so that you can add the new actions to the form. Note that the Product Ideas folder must be open for the New Product Idea Response command to appear on the Actions menu.

To open the Product Idea Response form in Design mode

1. On the Outlook Actions menu, hold down the Shift key and click New Product Idea Response.

2. On the Tools menu of the Product Idea form, select Forms and then click Design This Form.

Make the Reply To Folder Action Unavailable

Just as you made the Reply To Folder action unavailable for the Product Idea form, you make it unavailable for the Product Idea Response form.

To make the Reply To Folder action unavailable

1. On the Product Idea Response form, click the Actions tab.
2. Double-click the Reply To Folder action.
3. Clear the Enabled check box, and then click OK.

Create a New Action

Now create a new action that causes the Product Idea Response button to appear on the Product Idea Response form when the user opens a posted Product Idea Response item.

To create a new action

1. On the Product Idea Response form, click the Actions tab.
2. Click New.
3. In the Action Name text box, type *Product Idea Response*.
4. In the Form Name drop-down list box, click Product Idea Response.
5. In the Address Form Like A drop-down list box, click Reply To Folder and then click OK.

Make a Backup Copy of the Product Idea Response Form

It's always a good idea to have a backup copy of the form.

To make a backup copy of the Product Idea Response form

1. With the form open, click Save As on the File menu.
2. In the Save In drop-down list box, select the default Outlook template folder.
3. In the File Name drop-down list box, double-click on Product Idea Response.
4. In the Save As Type drop-down list box, select Outlook Template.
5. Click Save.
6. Select Yes to replace the existing file.

Part II Quick Guide to Building Applications

Publish the Product Idea Response Form

To publish the Product Idea Response form

1. On the Tools menu, select Forms and then click Publish Forms As.
2. Double-click Product Idea Response in the forms window.
3. Close the Product Idea Response form. Close the form, and select No in the Save Changes message box.

Create the Product Category View

Custom views organize information in folders so that the information is meaningful and can be analyzed more quickly. For example, take a look at the Messages view in Figure 4-20. In this view, items are listed chronologically according to the order in which they were posted in the folder. With this flat presentation of information, you would never know that discussions are taking place within the folder.

Now take a look at the same information in Figure 4-21. With the custom Product Category view applied to the folder, items are grouped first by the Product Category field and then by the Conversation field. In addition, each item in a conversation group is sorted by the Conversation Index field, so you can see the history of responses to each item.

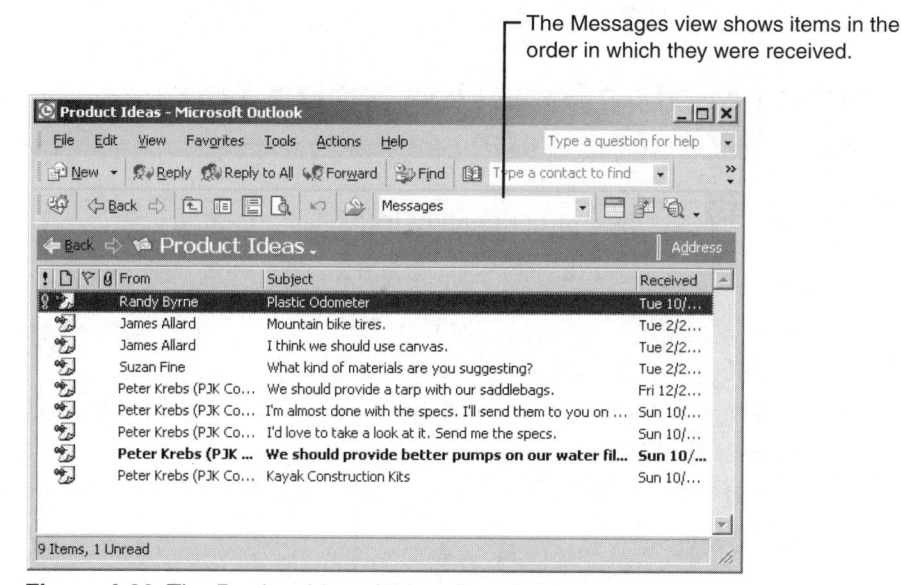

Figure 4-20 The Product Ideas folder with the Messages view selected.

100

Design a Custom Application   Chapter 4

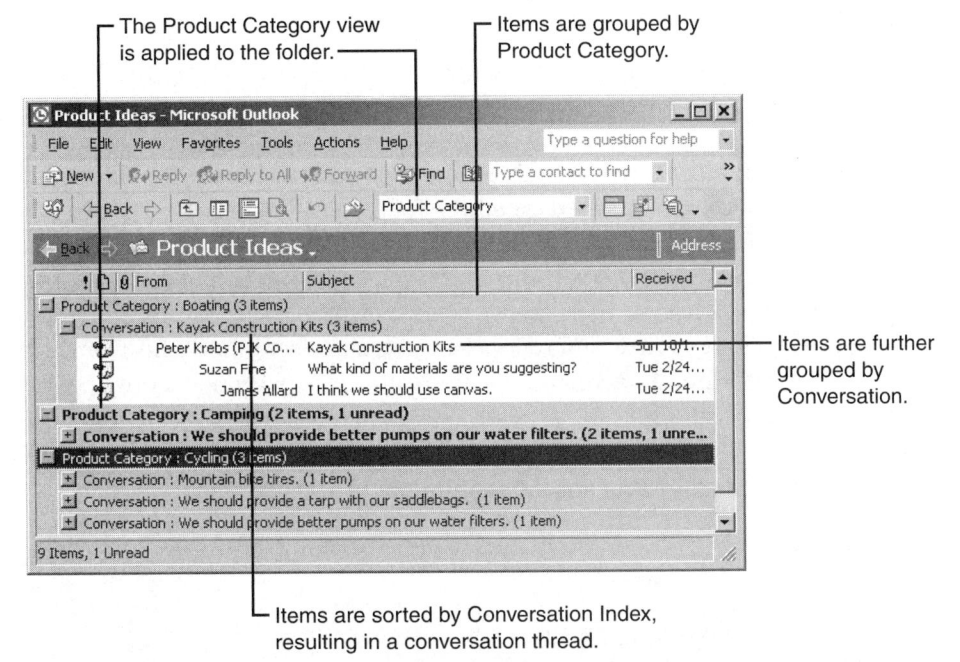

Figure 4-21 The Product Ideas folder with the Product Category view selected.

To create the Product Category view

1. Click the Product Ideas folder in the Folder List.
2. On the View menu, select Current View and then click Define Views.
3. Click New.
4. In the Name Of New View text box, type *Product Category*, click OK twice, and then click Apply View.

Remove Fields

Now remove the fields that aren't necessary for the Product Category view.

To remove fields

- Drag the Flag Status column heading (the column heading with the flag symbol) away from the Column Heading row until an X appears through the column heading, and then release the mouse button.

101

Group Items

For the Product Category view, you group items first by the Product Category field, and then by the Conversation Topic field.

When you group items in a view by product category, all items in the Product Ideas folder that have the value *Camping* selected in the Product Category drop-down list box are grouped together. Similarly, all items that have the value *Fishing* selected in the Product Category drop-down list box are grouped together.

When a user first submits a Product Idea item, the subject of the item becomes the Conversation Topic property. Any response items to the item, whether it is a direct response or a response to a response, inherit this Conversation Topic property value. As a result, all items about a particular conversation topic are grouped together.

To group items by Product Category, then by Conversation

1. On the View menu, select Current View and then click Customize Current View.
2. Click Group By in the View Summary box.
3. In the Select Available Fields From drop-down list box near the bottom of the dialog box, click User-Defined Fields In Folder.
4. In the Group Items By drop-down list box, click Product Category.
5. In the Select Available Fields From drop-down list box, click Frequently-Used fields.
6. In the Then By drop-down list box, click Conversation.
7. Click OK twice.

Sort Items

The Conversation Index field is the field that makes threaded conversations come to life. When you group items by conversation topic and then sort them by conversation index, you can see the relationships between items in a discussion application because a response to an item immediately follows the item. Plus, the response is indented from the associated item so that it's easy for a user who hasn't been part of the online conversation to quickly become familiar with an issue by simply following the thread of conversation up to the last posted item.

To sort items by the Conversation Index field

1. On the View menu, select Current View and then click Customize Current View.
2. Click Sort in the View Summary box.
3. In the Select Available Fields From drop-down list box, click Frequently-Used Fields.
4. In the Sort Items By drop-down list box, click Conversation Index and then click OK twice.

Arrange the Column Heading Order

For discussion applications, the Subject column heading usually precedes the From column heading. In Outlook, you can make adjustments to the view directly in the folder, so changing the column heading order is a simple matter of drag-and-drop editing.

To arrange the column heading order

- Drag the Subject column heading to the left until the double arrow appears, and then drop the column heading.

Specify the Default Form for the Folder

Now make the Product Idea form the default form for the Product Ideas folder so that when a user clicks the New button on the Outlook Standard toolbar, the Product Idea form appears.

To specify that the Product Idea form is the default form

1. In the Folder List, right-click the Product Ideas folder.
2. Click Properties.
3. Click the General tab.
4. In the When Posting To This Folder, Use drop-down list box, click Product Idea and then click OK.

Part II   Quick Guide to Building Applications

Set the Hidden Property for the Product Idea Response Form

Before you test the Product Ideas application to make sure it's working as expected, you set the Hidden property for the Product Idea Response form. This ensures that users can only open the Product Idea Response form by first selecting or opening a posted item. Therefore, the Product Idea Response form can be used only for posting responses, not for creating new items to start a conversation topic.

When you set the Hidden property of the Product Idea Response form, you remove the Product Idea Response command from the Outlook Actions menu. With the Hidden property set, the Product Idea Response form can only be opened by clicking one of the action commands you specified for the Product Idea and Product Idea Response forms.

To set the Hidden property for the Product Idea Response form

1. In the Folder List, right-click the Product Ideas folder.
2. Click Properties.
3. Click the Forms tab, and then click Manage.
4. In the Forms list box on the right, click Product Idea Response and then click Properties.
5. Select the Hidden check box, and then click OK.
6. Click Close twice.

Test the Application

Before you copy the Product Ideas application to public folders and make it available to other users, it's a good idea to test the application to make sure everything is working as expected.

To test the Product Ideas application

1. With the Product Ideas folder open, click New Product Idea on the Outlook Actions menu.
2. Fill in the form, and then click Post.
3. The new item is posted in the Product Ideas folder.
4. Double-click the Product Idea item you posted.

5. When the Product Idea form appears, click the Product Idea Response button on the form.

6. Fill in the Product Idea Response form, and then click Post.

7. Close the Product Idea form.

8. In the Product Ideas folder, double-click the Product Idea Response item you just posted.

9. When the Product Idea Response form appears, click the Product Idea Response button.

10. Fill in the Product Idea Response form, and then click Post.

11. Close the Product Idea Response form.

12. Repeat steps 1 through 7 several times. Each time you perform step 2, click a different value in the Product Category box and enter different text in the Subject text box.

Copy the Folder to Public Folders

Now you've created forms and a custom view for the Product Ideas folder. You've also tested the folder to make sure it works as planned. Now copy the folder from the Design Environment personal folder to public folders so that the folder can be shared by a workgroup or across the entire organization. Before you copy the folder, you might want to discuss with your administrator the best location for the folder. In addition, you might need to get the appropriate permissions to copy the folder to its destination in public folders.

To copy the Product Ideas folder

1. In the Folder List, click the Product Ideas folder.

2. Delete any test items or draft forms from the folder before copying. Select the items, and press the Delete key.

3. On the File menu, point to Folder and then click Copy Product Ideas.

4. In the Copy The Selected Folder To The Folder list box, click the location you want the folder copied to, such as All Public Folders.

5. Click OK.

Part II Quick Guide to Building Applications

About Folder Permissions

When you create the Product Ideas folder, you are automatically given owner permissions for the folder. In addition, all users are given Publishing Author permissions so that they can post and open items in the folder and modify and delete items they create. At this time, you can leave the folder permissions alone.

> **More Info** For more information about how to set permissions, see Chapter 8, "Folders."

Release the Application

Before you make the application available to coworkers, you set the Initial View On Folder property to Product Category. This is the view users first see when they open the folder.

To set Administration properties

1. In the Folder List, right-click the Product Ideas folder and then click Properties.
2. Click the Administration tab.
3. In the Initial View On Folder drop-down list box, select Product Category. Click OK.

Now that the folder is ready for use, you can send a message to your coworkers to notify them that the application is available.

> **More Info** For more information about releasing applications, see Chapter 13, "Distributing and Securing Applications."

Part III

Building Blocks of Applications

5 Forms   109

6 Controls, Fields, and Properties   153

7 Actions   211

8 Folders   247

Chapter 5, "Forms," introduces the form design process and covers fundamental form design tasks such as adding controls and fields, creating new actions, setting form properties, and publishing forms. Chapter 6, "Controls, Fields, and Properties," covers the fundamental skills and information you need to effectively use controls, fields, and properties on a form. It also explains the unique features of each commonly used control and then offers some strategies for implementing these controls and fields in an application. Chapter 7, "Actions," discusses the easiest way to create responses for Message forms, explains how to create custom Reply actions for Message forms, and then shows how to create custom Reply To Folder actions for Post forms. Chapter 8, "Folders," takes an in-depth look at the folder design process, discusses how to manage forms, and explains how to create custom views and folder home pages. It also covers setting folder permissions and building rules.

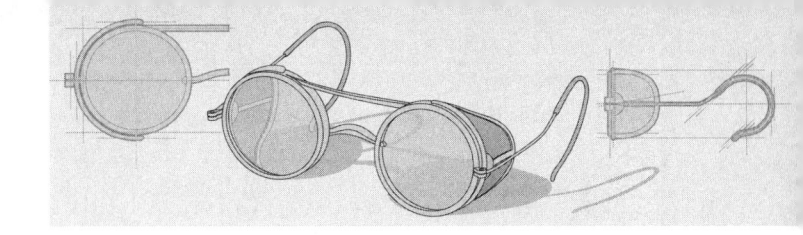

5

Forms

With Outlook forms in Design mode, you can build custom forms to streamline request processes, collect and distribute information, and save and show information that is structured so that it's both easy to find and easy to read. For example, you can create travel request forms to automate the approval of business travel plans. You can create product response forms to collect valuable information from your customers. Or you can create job candidate forms to post information about a potential employee so that other members of your organization can view the candidate's background before interviewing the candidate. After the interview, interviewers can post their impressions of the candidate in a public folder, so a manager can quickly get an overall impression of the candidate.

This chapter discusses form design concepts, introduces the form design process, and then covers fundamental form design tasks such as adding controls and fields, creating new actions, setting form properties, and publishing forms. When you have completed this chapter, you should have the basic knowledge and skills you need to create and publish forms in your organization.

Become Familiar with Designing Forms and Form Components

This section covers the components of forms in Design mode and discusses the parts of an Outlook form.

Outlook Form Design Mode

The following elements are available while Outlook forms are in Design mode:

- **Form Design window** To show the various pages of the form and the form properties and actions.
- **Toolbox** To add new controls (such as buttons) to the form.

Part III Building Blocks of Applications

- **Field Chooser** To select fields for the form.
- **Properties dialog box** To modify a control or field.
- **Script Editor** To program or automate the forms.

The last four elements are shown in Figure 5-1. For more information on how to open a form in Design mode, see "Outlook Form Design Mode" in Chapter 2, "Outlook Design Tools."

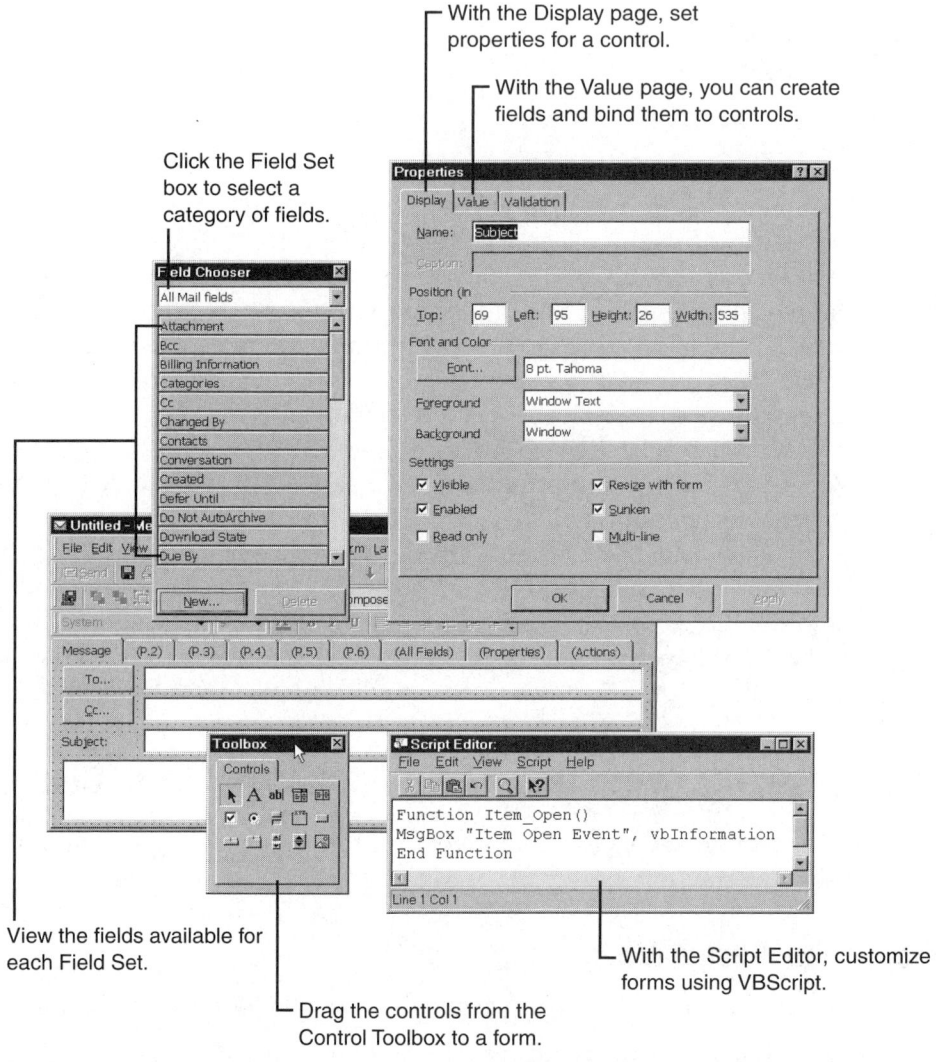

Figure 5-1 These elements are available while Outlook forms are in Design mode.

Types of Forms

Outlook provides four basic types of forms to use as starting points for all forms that you build. To design forms effectively, you need to know the basic characteristics of these four types: Message, Post, Office Document, and built-in forms.

Message and Post forms can be fully customized. Although Office Document forms can't be directly modified, you can add VBScript to the form to customize it. Task, Appointment, and Journal forms can be customized by adding pages to the forms, but the existing pages cannot be modified. This also applies to the Contact form, but you can modify the first page of a Contact form.

For a detailed description of form components, see "Parts of a Form" later in this chapter.

Message Form

Use the Message form shown in Figure 5-2 as a starting point for building forms that allow users to send information to other users, to a distribution list, or to a folder. The Message form can be fully customized. When Message forms are sent, they travel through the messaging transport system and are then routed to the specified address. Examples of Message forms are the Vacation Request form, the While You Were Out form, and the Business Card Request form.

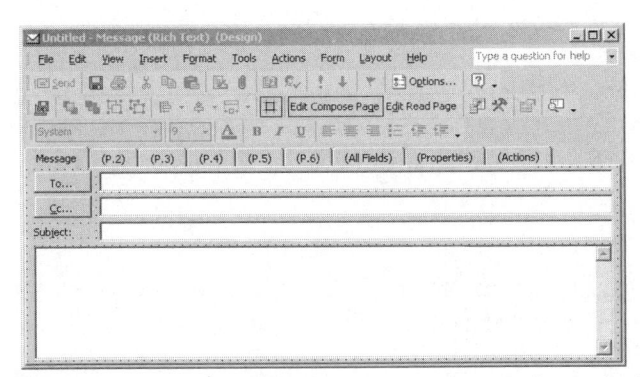

Figure 5-2 The Mail Message form is the starting point for Message forms.

Post Form

Use the Post form shown in Figure 5-3 as a starting point for building forms that allow users to post, open, and respond to information in a personal or public folder. The Post form can be fully customized. Post forms submit items directly to the active folder. For this reason, Post forms are tightly integrated with folders. Examples of Post forms are the Product Idea and Product Idea Response forms found in the Product Ideas application, which is discussed in Chapter 4, "Design a Custom Application."

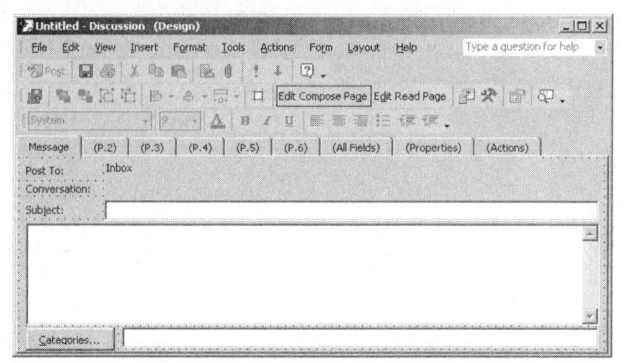

Figure 5-3 The Post form is the starting point for forms that are integrated with a personal or public folder.

Built-In Forms

You can modify built-in forms in Calendar, Contacts, Distribution List, Journal, and Task modules by showing additional pages on the form. You can then add controls and fields to the form to suit the needs of your application. (See Figure 5-4.) The default page cannot be modified, with the exception of the Contact form's default page.

The characteristics of each built-in form vary, depending on the application. For example, with the Task Request form, users send a Task Request to other users. With the Task form, however, users save the task in the current folder.

Parts of a Form

Before you get started designing forms, you need to know about the different components of a form and what each component is used for. This section dissects a form and discusses the purpose of each of its components.

The Compose and Read Pages

An Outlook form can consist of a single page, but in most cases, it consists of two pages: a Compose page and a Read page, as shown in Figure 5-5. Although the Compose and Read pages are often similar in appearance, they serve very different purposes. The Compose page enables users to create items and to send or post items. The Read page lets users open and read submitted items in a folder, and to respond to items.

Forms Chapter 5

You can show additional pages and add controls to them.

The first page of built-in forms cannot be modified, with the exception of the first Contact page.

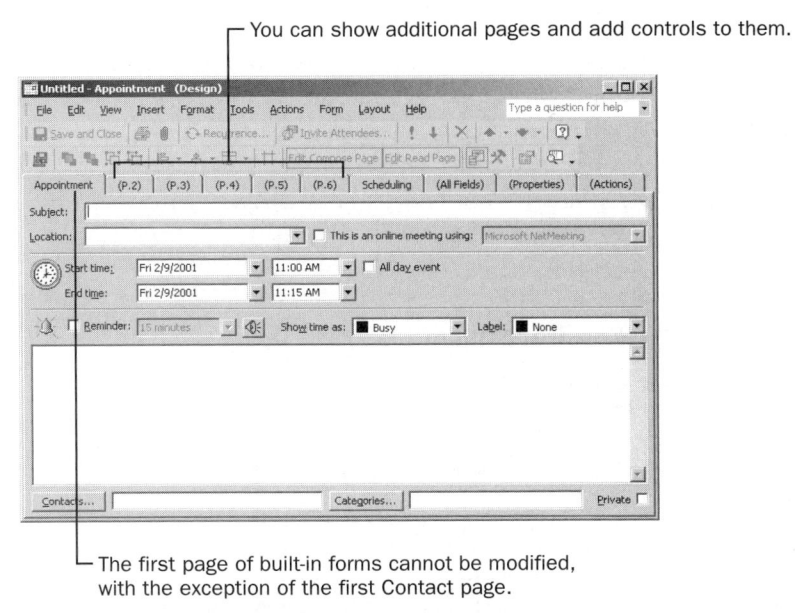

Figure 5-4 The built-in Appointment form can be customized to meet your personal needs or those of your workgroup or organization.

With the Compose page, users can create an item and send or post it.

Users enter information on the Compose page.

With the Read page, users view and respond to information.

Users view submitted information on the Read page.

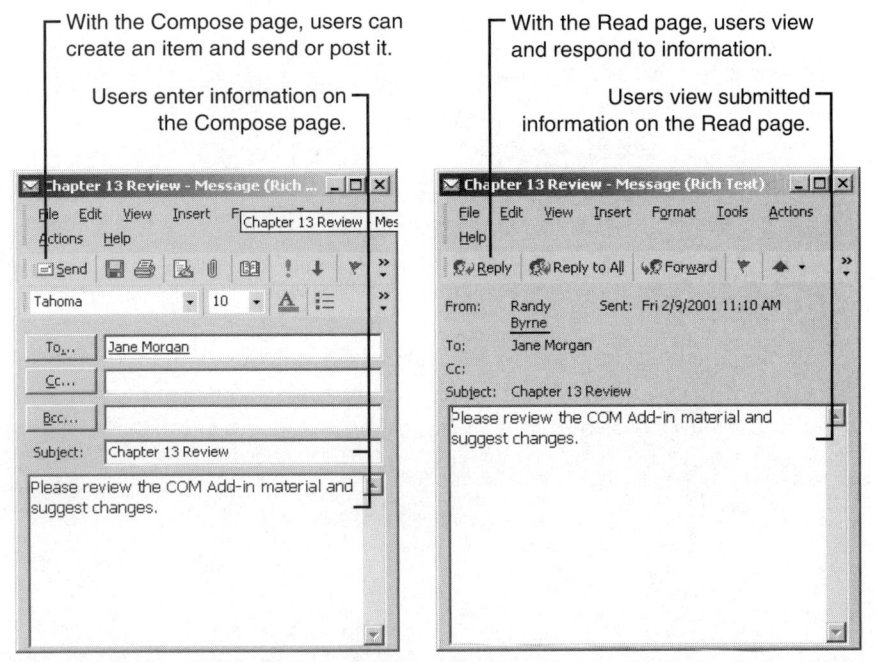

Figure 5-5 The Outlook form consists of a Compose page and a Read page.

Pages

Forms also have a series of pages that you view by clicking their respective tabs. In addition to the default Message or General page, forms have five custom pages that you can add controls to. Forms also have pages such as the Properties and Actions pages that enable you to set properties for the form to define how it functions, as shown in Figure 5-6. The All Fields page allows you to view all fields and field values for the form. You can even update some of these properties, which is useful for testing.

Standard Message (or General) page

You can hide or show additional pages and add controls to them.

Use this page to view all fields and field values for the form.

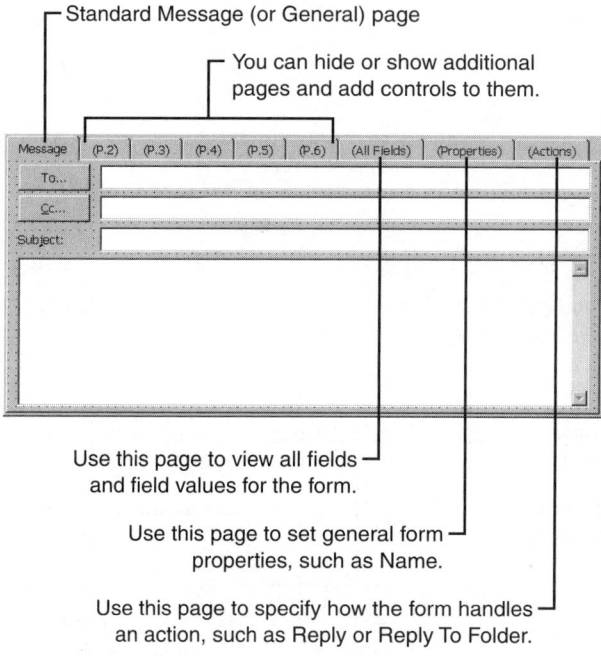

Use this page to set general form properties, such as Name.

Use this page to specify how the form handles an action, such as Reply or Reply To Folder.

Figure 5-6 Pages of the Message form.

Controls

Controls are the components of a form that allows users to enter and view information. Controls are the means through which users interact with the form. You add controls to the form by dragging them from the Control Toolbox. (See Figure 5-7.)

Forms   Chapter 5

- The Label control is used to show text that users cannot change.
- The TextBox control enables users to enter and view text.
- Users can add controls to the form by dragging them from the Control Toolbox.
- The Frame control groups similar information, such as OptionButton controls.
- The ComboBox control lets users enter values or select from a list.

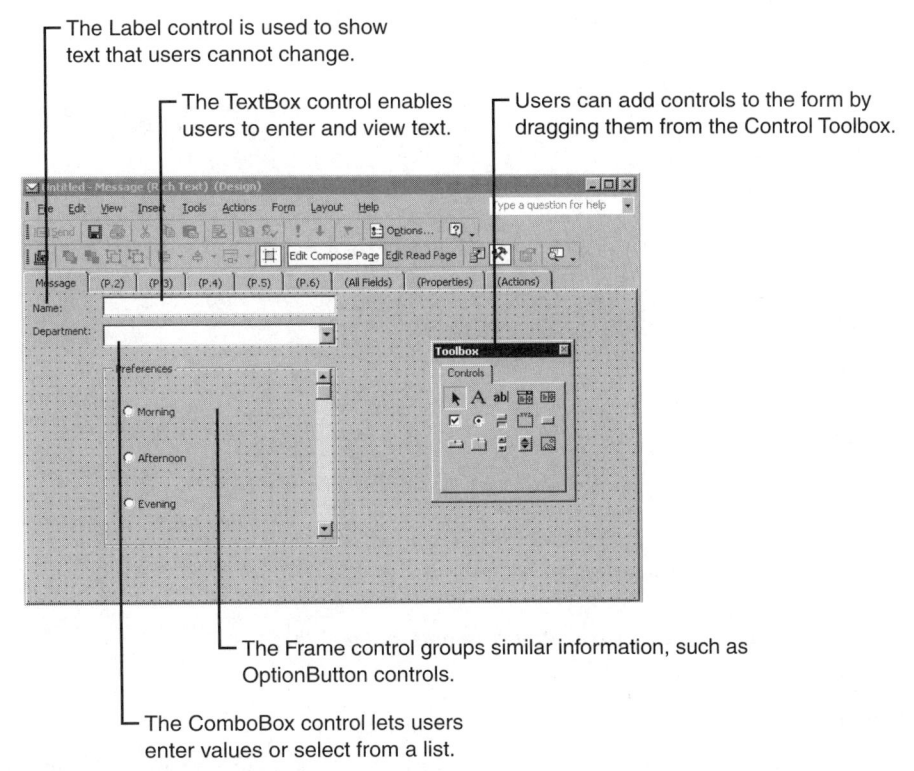

Figure 5-7 Controls and the Control Toolbox.

Fields

A form field defines how information in a control or in a folder is saved and displayed in messaging applications. In addition, the field is a physical storage location in the item where the specified data is saved. To specify that the information in a control is to be saved, you bind the control to a field. For example, as shown in Figure 5-8, the TextBox control is bound to the Name field so that the information in the control is saved to the field when an item is sent, saved, or posted. When the item is opened, the information is loaded from the field into the control.

Part III   Building Blocks of Applications

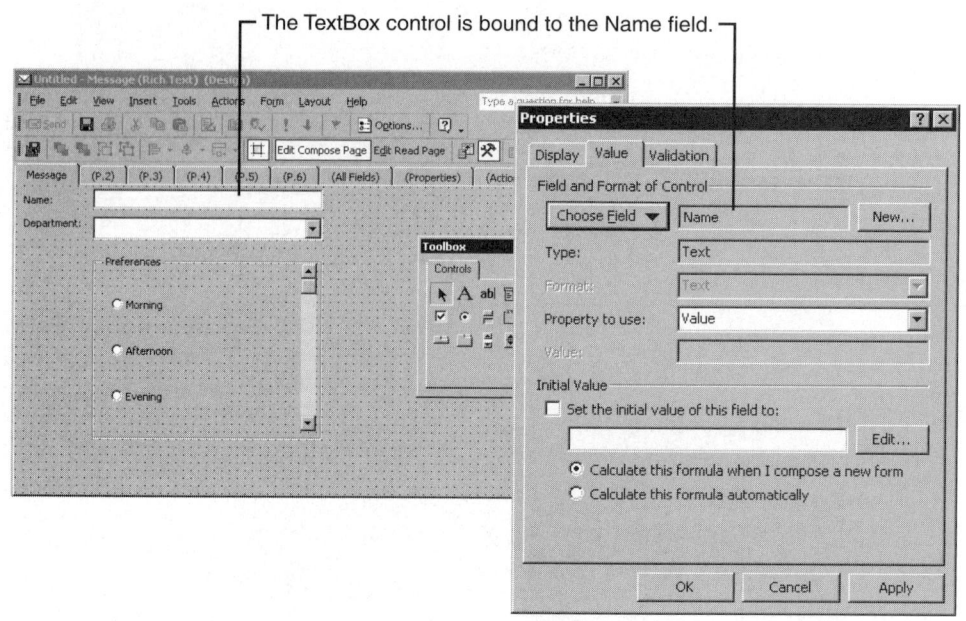

Figure 5-8   The TextBox control is bound to the Name field.

Properties

Properties define the characteristics of form components. With Outlook, you can define properties for forms, controls, and fields. Figure 5-9 shows display properties that are set for the Name control.

Control properties are accessed by right-clicking on the control or field and then selecting Properties. Form properties are modified in the Properties dialog box while in Design mode.

Actions

Actions define how a form handles responses. You can modify existing actions or create new actions. For example, you can modify an action to specify that a custom form is opened when the user clicks the Reply button on a form. You can also create a new action that adds a custom response button to the form. As shown in Figure 5-10, new actions have been created for the Vacation Request form that allow users to respond to a Vacation Request item by clicking an Approve Vacation or Deny Vacation button on the form.

Forms   Chapter 5

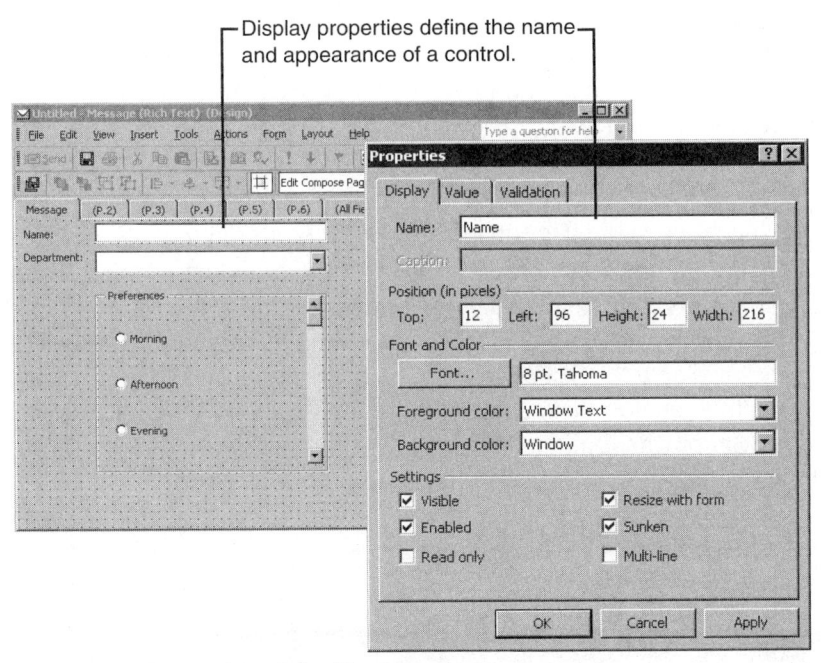

Figure 5-9 Properties of the Name control.

Figure 5-10 The Actions page for the Vacation Request form.

Form Scripts

With the Script Editor, you can use Microsoft Visual Basic Scripting Edition (VBScript) to add functionality to a form. You can add code for a command button

117

Part III Building Blocks of Applications

that creates and sends a response item, call the properties and methods of an ActiveX component, launch other applications from a form using Automation, or create procedures that automatically fill in or clear values on the form, as shown in Figure 5-11.

> **Important** Outlook 2002 includes a COM Add-in that allows you to use Visual Basic for Applications (VBA) to program the running instance of Outlook. VBA is especially useful when you want to respond to events that occur within the Outlook application environment. However, VBA is not available for Outlook forms. You still must use VBScript to program Outlook custom forms. See Chapter 11, "Using Visual Basic, VBA, or VBScript with Outlook."

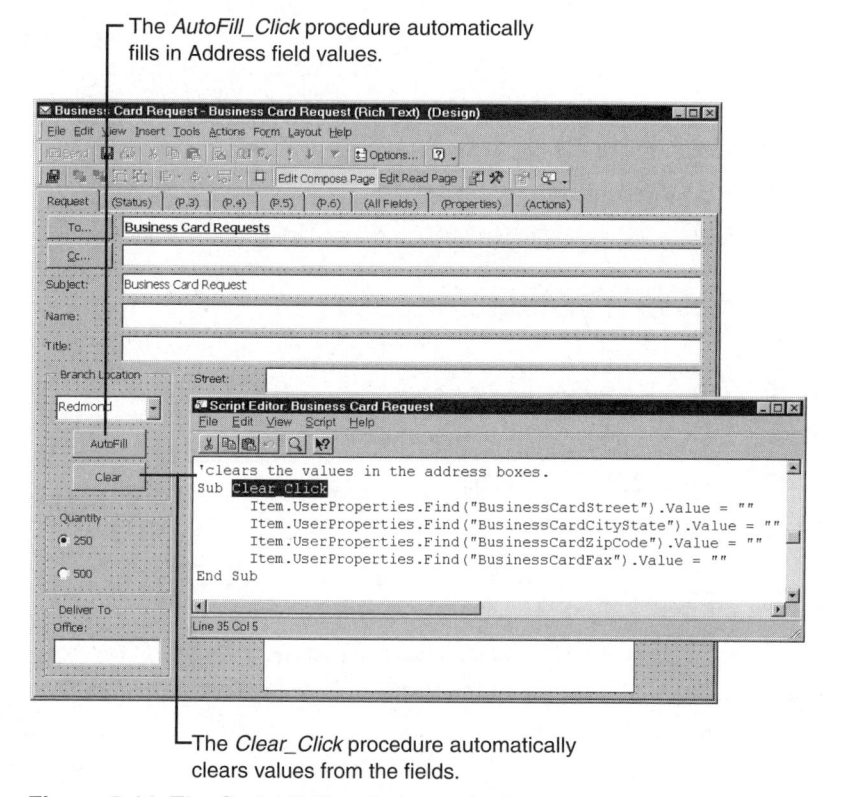

The *AutoFill_Click* procedure automatically fills in Address field values.

The *Clear_Click* procedure automatically clears values from the fields.

Figure 5-11 The Script Editor shows code that automates a Business Card Request form.

Learn How Forms Work

This section briefly covers some fundamental form concepts, such as the meaning of the term *item,* how saving the form definition with an item affects the form, and how shared fields work.

What Is an Item?

Throughout the book, the term *item* is used often. In the past, an item was simply called a message. So why change the terminology? Because the term *message* can no longer encompass the vast array of information that can be included in an item. In Outlook, an item is a container for information. In addition to text and number values entered by users, this container can hold just about anything, including Uniform Resource Locators (URLs), voice mail, office documents, video clips, PowerPoint presentations, and so on. An item also contains properties that define the item—such as message class—and that associate the item with a specific form.

> **Note** You may be wondering where items are stored. If you are running Outlook as a client for Microsoft Exchange Server, public folder items are stored in a public information store on an Exchange server. Typically, mailbox items are stored in a private information store on an Exchange server. If you have configured Outlook for offline use, both public folder and mailbox folder items will be stored in an offline store or in an .ost file when you work offline. If you do not use Exchange Server in your organization, mailbox items are stored on a local or network drive in a container known as a personal information store, or .pst file. The limitation of using a .pst file is that it does not support simultaneous access by more than one user. Mailbox items are stored either in a .pst file or in a private information store on an Exchange Server. The important point to remember is that .pst files, .ost files, and public and private stores on Exchange Server are containers for a collection of items with diverse message classes. In all cases, you cannot access a message item in a public or private folder by simply opening a file on your local drive C, as you would with a Word document.

What Happens When the Form Definition Is Saved with the Item?

> **Note** Due to the new security protections in Outlook 2002, forms that have the Send Form Definition With Item option selected function differently in Outlook 2002 than in previous versions of Outlook. Forms that have this option selected are known as one-off forms. These forms have not been explicitly trusted to a forms library by either an Outlook user (Personal Forms library) or an Exchange administrator (Organizational Forms library). Since one-off forms have not been explicitly trusted, a hacker can use them to damage the recipient's system or to spread a virus to other users. In Outlook 2002, the code behind one-off forms is disabled by default. For additional information regarding one-off forms and Outlook security, see Chapter 13, "Distributing and Securing Applications." The following discussion of the Send Form Definition With Item option applies only to forms that will be opened in Outlook 97, Outlook 98, Outlook 2000, or Outlook 2000 SR-1 without the Outlook E-Mail Security Update. If you are using Outlook 2000 SP-2 or Outlook 2002, you will not be able to trust the code in a one-off form.

In Design mode, Outlook provides an option on the form Properties page called Send Form Definition With Item. The Send Form Definition With Item option serves two purposes:

- **It enables users to send Message forms to other users** When the Send Form Definition With Item option is selected for a Message form, the form definition is included in the item. This allows users who receive the item to view the item in the custom form, even though they do not have the custom form published in a forms library on their system. Thus, this option provides a useful way to send items created with custom forms to locations outside your immediate system. For example, you may want to send a customer response item over the Internet to a customer site. If the Send Form Definition With Item option is selected, customers see the item in the custom form when they open it, even though they do not have the form published on their system. Saving the form definition with the item also has the side effect of not giving your item a unique message class.

- **It provides a security measure** If a user opens a Message form that has the Send Form Definition With Item option selected, and the form is not available on the server or on the user's Outlook system, and the form has VBScript included with it, the user sees the Macro Warning dialog box, as shown in Figure 5-12. Remember that the Macro Warning dialog box will not appear for Outlook 2000 SP-2 or Outlook 2002. All Outlook VBScript macro code is disabled by default in those two versions of Outlook. In earlier versions of Outlook, the Send Form Definition With Item option provides a security measure to prevent a user from opening a potentially harmful form. (See the discussion above and in Chapter 13.) When you finish designing a Message form, you can:

- Clear the Send Form Definition With Item option and publish the form in the Personal Forms Library or in a forms library in a folder.

- Submit the form to an Exchange administrator, who checks it for harmful macros. If none exist, the administrator clears the Send Form Definition With Item check box and then publishes the form to the Organizational Forms Library.

Figure 5-12 Users see the Macro Warning dialog box when they try to open an item that contains the form definition and VBScript.

> **Important** By default, the Send Form Definition With Item option is turned off to keep form size small and reduce network traffic and form loading time. A form designer can enable the Send Form Definition With Item option when the form is published.

> **More Info** For more information about the Send Form Definition With Item option, see "Set Form Properties" later in this chapter.

How Is a Form Opened?

By default, the Send Form Definition With Item check box is cleared. The question then arises: If the form definition doesn't travel with the item, how is the form opened? The answer is that the form is launched from a Personal or Organizational Forms Library, or from the forms library of a folder, when the user attempts to create or view an item associated with the form. The form is associated with the item by its message class. Each form has a message class that identifies it internally to the Outlook messaging system. For example, the standard Post form has the message class IPM.Post, while the standard Contact form has the message class IPM.Contact. When an item is created, the message class of the form used to create the item is saved as one of the attributes of the item. When the user double-clicks an existing item to open it, the form definition for the message class of the item is retrieved from a personal folder, or Organizational Forms Library, and is then used to display the form associated with the item within Outlook.

Publishing a form registers its definition. If the form definition doesn't exist in the user's forms libraries, Outlook will substitute the next class in common. For example, if IPM.Note.Myform.ThisForm does not exist, Outlook will try to open IPM.Note.Myform. If that form definition does not exist, IPM.Note will load and the user will see a standard message form.

As shown in Figure 5-13, when a user opens the form to create a Volunteer Registration item, the form is launched from the Organizational Forms Library. The item, and not the form, is then sent to a recipient. When the recipient opens the item in his or her Inbox, the Volunteer Registration form is launched and the information from the item is shown in the form.

For More Information About	See
Sending the form definition with an item	"Set Form Properties" later in this chapter
Submitting a form to an administrator	Chapter 13
How forms are cached	Chapter 13

How Do Shared Fields Work?

If you're new to designing forms, it helps to understand how the form saves information in the item and how it loads information from the item to the form. One of the central concepts behind the storing and loading of information is shared fields. A shared field is a field that is bound to controls on both the Compose and Read pages of a form. As shown in Figure 5-14, the Name control is bound to the Name field on the Volunteer Registration form.

Shared fields can also be used between forms. For example, when a user creates a response to an item, the information in fields that are common to both forms is copied from the first-opened form to the response form.

> **More Info** For more information about creating shared fields, see Chapter 6, "Controls, Fields, and Properties."

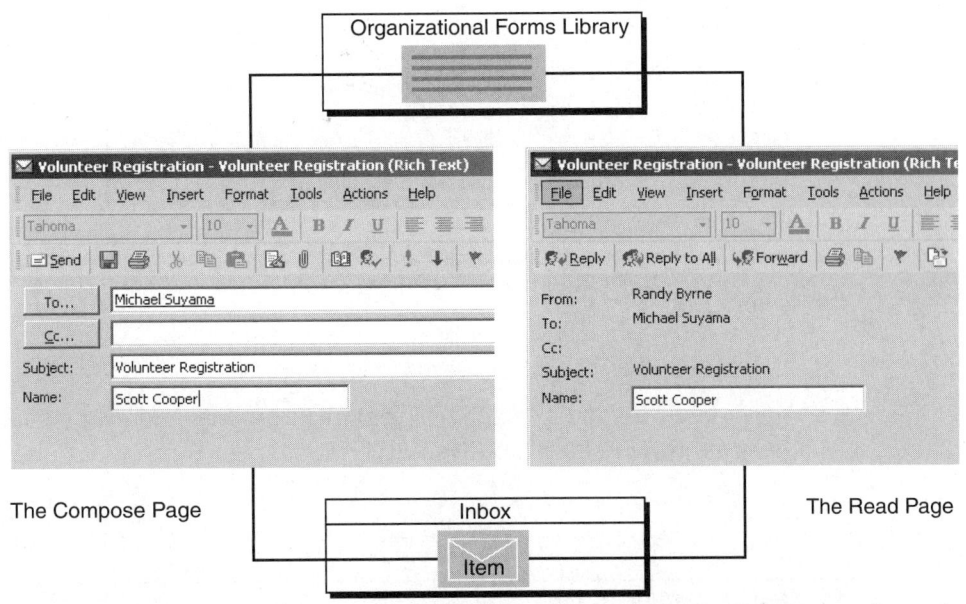

Figure 5-13 The Compose page creates and sends the item. The Read page shows the item. The form is loaded from the Organizational Forms Library.

Create a Folder

Generally, it is a good idea to create a form in a personal folder. This method offers a couple of advantages. First, it lets you store forms in a central and private location while you're designing them. Second, it makes it easy to test the form. To test the form, open the form by clicking the menu command that Outlook adds to the Actions menu of the folder when you publish the form in the folder's forms library.

Part III Building Blocks of Applications

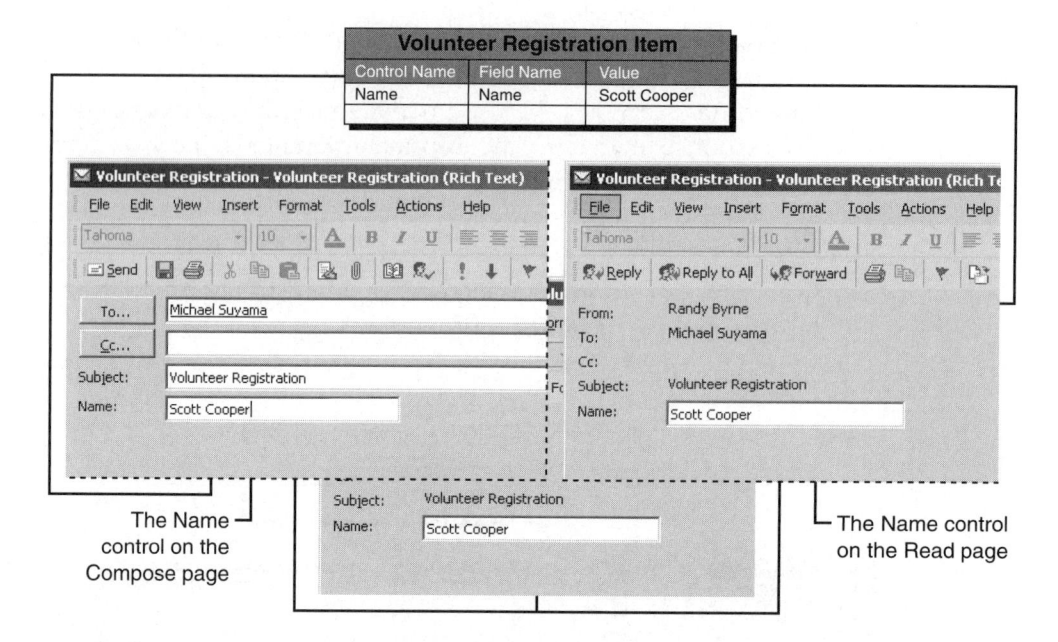

Figure 5-14 When the item is created and sent, the information is saved from the control to the field. When the item is opened, the information is loaded from the field into the control.

> **More Info** If you have not yet created a personal folder (.pst) file, see "Create New Folders" in Chapter 3, "Customize Built-In Modules."

To create a personal folder

1. In the Folder List, right-click a personal folder under which you want to create a folder, and then click New Folder.

2. In the Name text box, enter a name for the folder.

3. In the Item Type list box, do one of the following:

    ❑ Click Mail And Post Items to create a folder that will contain items created with Message, Post, or Office Document forms.

    ❑ Click Calendar, Contact, Journal, Note, or Task to create a folder for items of that type. Then click OK.

> **More Info** For more information about creating folders, see Chapter 8, "Folders."

Open the Form and Switch to Design Mode

When you design an Outlook form, you always start with an existing form. Outlook lets you choose from a variety of standard and custom forms. In addition to forms supplied in Outlook, you can design forms based on custom templates created by others in your organization.

- To open a form and switch to Design mode, first select the folder in which you want to create the form. Then select the type of form you want to open, such as those in the following sections.

- To close a form, click the Close button. When you save Message, Post, or Office Document forms, they become items in the Drafts folder of your mailbox. Other forms are saved to the current folder.

To create a Message form

1. On the Outlook Actions menu, click New Mail Message. To create a Message form, you must be in the Inbox folder or a folder that contains Mail items.
2. On the Tools menu of the form, select Forms and then click Design This Form.

To create a Post form

1. On the Outlook File menu, select New, and then click Post In This Folder. To create a Post form, you must be in the Inbox folder or a folder that contains Mail items.
2. On the Tools menu of the form, select Forms, and then click Design This Form.

Part III Building Blocks of Applications

To create a Calendar, Contact, Distribution List, Task, or Journal form

1. Select the folder in which you want to create the form. Typically you will create a custom item in a folder that is designed to hold items of the same message class. For example, you would create a Contacts folder to hold custom contact items. However, folders that contain mail or post items are generic containers—they can contain items of any message class.

2. On the File menu, point to New, and then click the appropriate form type. You can also click the New button on the Standard toolbar. The New button defaults to the item type that is the default item type for the current folder.

3. On the Tools menu of the form, select Forms, and then click Design This Form.

> **Important** If you want to design a custom Distribution List, you must first switch to a Contacts folder. Distribution List items can reside only in Contact folders.

> **Caution** You cannot design a custom Notes form. Be sure not to confuse the sticky notes form, using the message class IPM.StickyNote, with the standard mail message form, using the message class IPM.Note.

To create a form based on a custom Outlook template

1. On the File menu, select New, and then click Choose Form.
2. In the Look In drop-down list box, select User Templates In File System.
3. Double-click the template you want.
4. If the template is a Post template, select the folder with which the form will be associated.
5. On the form Tools menu, select Forms, and then click Design This Form.

For More Information About	See
Creating a Message form	Chapter 8
Creating a Post form	Chapter 4
Modifying a built-in form	Chapter 3

Edit Form Pages

Forms usually consist of two pages: a Compose page and a Read page. There are other pages contained within the Compose or Read page, such as (P.2)–(P.6), that you can customize or use to set properties on the form. These pages are covered later in this chapter. Each of these individual pages of the form has its own Compose and Read pages, depending on whether Separate Read Layout has been selected for that page.

The Compose page appears when the user opens the form to create an item. The Read page appears when the user double-clicks an existing item and opens it. When you create forms, you usually edit both the Compose and Read pages. In fact, when you first start designing forms, it's a common mistake to make adjustments to the Compose page but fail to make the same adjustments to the Read page. When working with forms, you can switch back and forth between the Read and Compose pages by clicking the Edit Compose Page or Edit Read Page button on the Form Design toolbar, as shown in Figure 5-15. Although the Compose and Read pages look very similar, they each have unique characteristics that you need to be aware of.

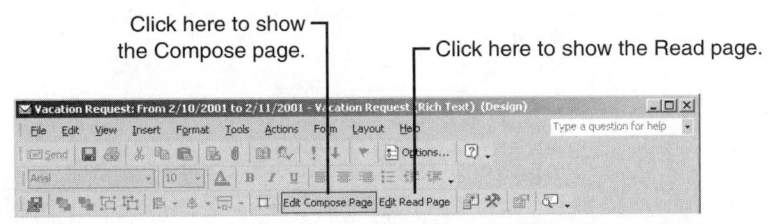

Figure 5-15 The Edit Compose Page and Edit Read Page buttons.

The Compose Page

The Compose page of a form contains controls in which the user enters information. For example, in Figure 5-16, the user can enter information in the Starting and Ending text boxes of the Vacation Request form. When the item is sent or posted, the information in these controls is saved in the item. In addition, the Compose page of Message forms provides controls such as the To button and To text box that allow users to specify an address for an item.

Part III   Building Blocks of Applications

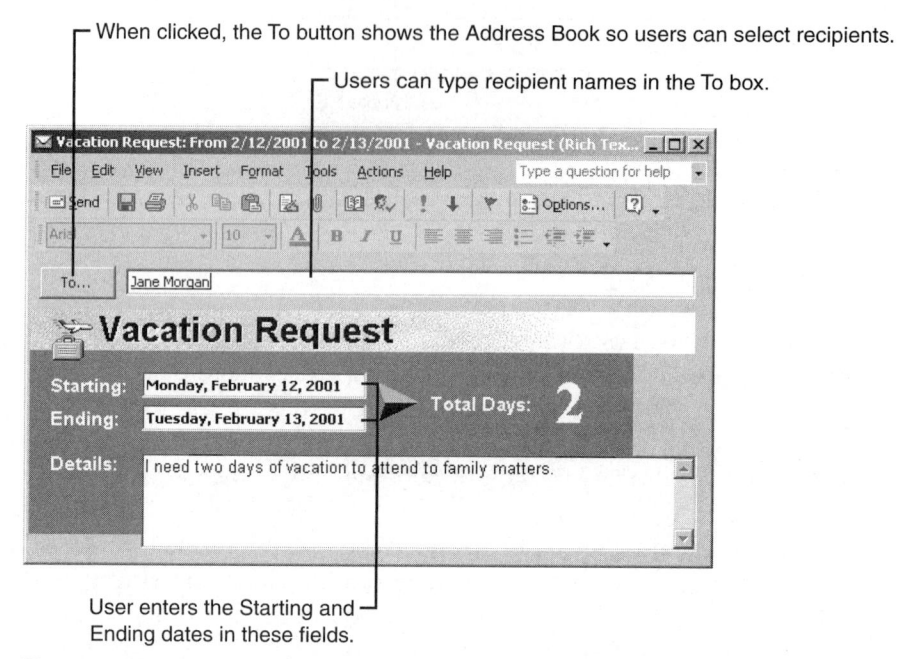

Figure 5-16 The user enters information in the controls on the Compose page.

The Read Page

The Read page of a form lets the user open and read an item. Quite often, many controls on the Read page are read-only, especially when the form involves financial or sensitive information. As shown in Figure 5-17, the Starting and Ending text boxes on the Read page of the Vacation Request form are read-only, so the reader cannot change them.

About Separate Read Layout

While a form is in Design mode, Outlook provides a Separate Read Layout option that lets you specify if an individual form page has a Read page layout that is different from the Compose page layout. By default, the Separate Read Layout option, located on the Form menu, is selected for the Message page of Message and Post forms. However, for a custom page, this option is not automatically selected.

Forms   Chapter 5

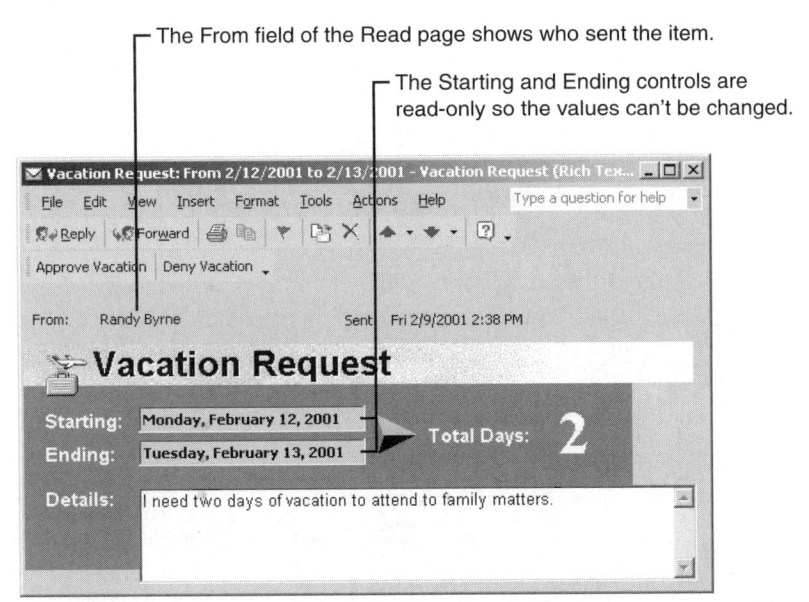

- The From field of the Read page shows who sent the item.
- The Starting and Ending controls are read-only so the values can't be changed.

Figure 5-17 The Read page of the Vacation Request form. Many of the controls on the Read page are read-only, so they cannot be changed by the reader.

Most often when designing forms, you edit the Compose page first, and then you edit the Read page. When you open a Message or Post form, the Message page is visible. For many of the forms you create, the Message page may be the only page you edit. However, you can also edit pages P.2 through P.6, as shown in Figure 5-18.

To view either the Read or the Compose page

1. Open the form and put it in Design mode.
2. On the Form Design toolbar, click the Edit Compose Page or Edit Read Page button.

> **Important**   If you decide to add controls to a custom form page, you must select the Separate Read Layout option (Form menu) if you want the Compose layout of this page to be different from the Read layout of the form page, as shown in Figure 5-18.

129

Part III Building Blocks of Applications

When a control is added to a page, the
page is automatically visible in Run mode.

Pages in parentheses are visible in
Design mode but not in Run mode.

When you add controls to an additional page, click
Separate Read Layout if you want the Read page
layout to differ from the Compose page layout.

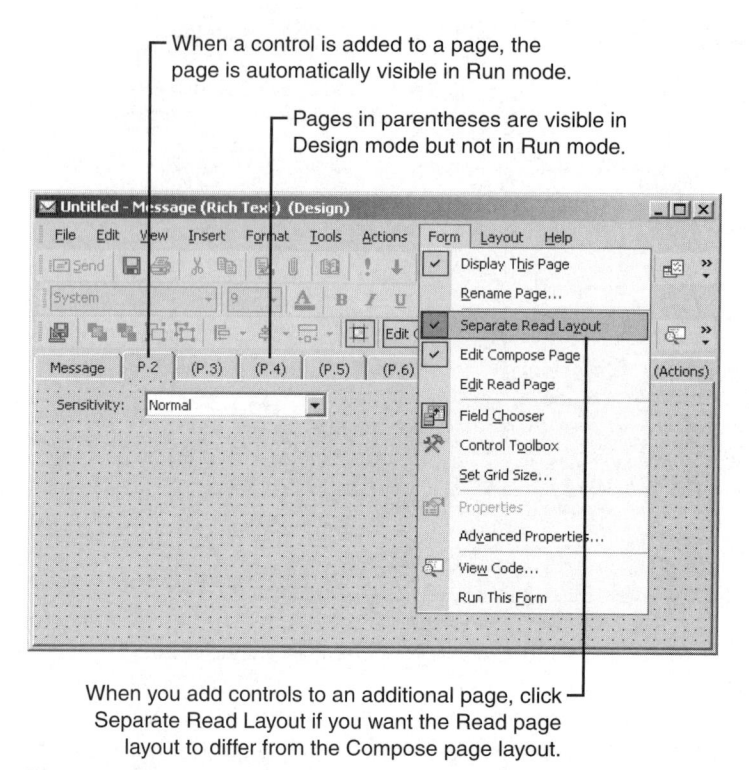

Figure 5-18 For the Message form, the Separate Read Layout option is selected for the custom page.

> **Note** If the Separate Read Layout option is not selected for a page, you cannot switch between the Compose and Read pages when the individual page is active.

To specify the Separate Read Layout option for a page

1. Click the page for which you want to specify the Separate Read Layout option.
2. On the Form menu, click Separate Read Layout.
3. Repeat for each individual page of the form.

Hide or Show a Page

Outlook uses parentheses to designate the pages that are hidden at run time. For example, in the preceding Figure 5-18, notice that the tab label text for pages 3 through 6 is in parentheses to indicate that these pages will be hidden at run time.

The ability to hide and show pages gives you great flexibility in designing forms. For example, quite often there isn't enough room on the Message page for all the controls you need to add. In this case, you can add controls to a custom form page. When you add controls to a page, the parentheses are removed from the text on the page's tab, indicating that the page will be visible at run time.

For some forms, you may want to hide the Message page. This can be especially useful for preaddressing forms. For example, you can specify an address in the To field of a form at design time and then hide the page. This prevents the user from changing the address and also lets users submit items without ever seeing the destination address on the form. In addition, you may also want to hide a second page of the form. Keep in mind, however, that at least one page must be visible on the form.

To hide or show a page at run time

1. In Design mode, click the desired page.
2. On the Form menu, click Display This Page.

> **Note** If you drag a field or a control to a hidden page, Display This Page will turn on automatically. To hide the page, deselect Display This Page on the Form menu.

For More Information About	See
Preaddressing forms	"To Field" in Chapter 6
Hiding and showing pages	"Hiding and Showing a Form Page" in Chapter 11

Rename a Page

When you make a page visible, you should rename it to convey the purpose of the page.

Part III   Building Blocks of Applications

To rename a page

1. In Design mode, click the page.
2. On the Form menu, click Rename Page.
3. Type the new name for the page.

Add Controls

Controls are the means through which users enter and view information on the form. When creating forms with Outlook, you usually add controls to the Compose page of the form first. Then, if you want the information in the controls to be saved to the item, you create a field for the control and bind the field to the control.

To add controls to the form, you use the Control Toolbox.

To show the Control Toolbox

- In Design mode, on the Form Design toolbar, click the Control Toolbox icon.

With Outlook, you can add third-party .ocx controls and Microsoft ActiveX controls to the toolbox to provide added flexibility on your forms. Figure 5-19 illustrates the addition of several Microsoft ActiveX controls to the Outlook Control Toolbox.

> **Note** Be aware that almost all of the events for third-party ActiveX controls do not fire within the Outlook forms container. However, the properties and methods of those controls are accessible using Outlook VBScript. See Chapter 6.

> **Caution** If you add ActiveX controls to your custom form, you must ensure that those controls are correctly installed and registered on your user's system. If the controls are not registered properly, an error message will appear when the user opens the form containing the embedded custom control.

Forms Chapter 5

Controls selected in the Additional Controls dialog box will be added to your Outlook toolbox.

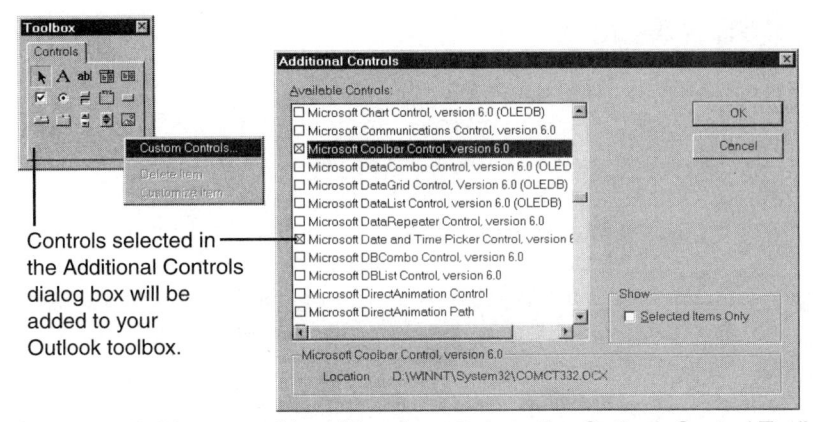

Figure 5-19 You can add additional controls to the Outlook Control Toolbox by using the Custom Controls command and selecting controls in the Additional Controls dialog box.

To add additional controls to the Control Toolbox

1. Right-click the bottom of the Controls page in the Control Toolbox, and then click Custom Controls on the shortcut menu.

2. Under Available Controls, click the controls you want to enable, and then click OK.

To add a control to a form

- Drag the control from the Control Toolbox to the form.

To set Display properties for a control

1. Right-click the control, and then click Properties.

2. On the Display page, set the properties you want.

To set Advanced Properties for a control

1. Right-click the control, and then click Advanced Properties.

2. In the Properties window, set the properties you want and then close the window.

Part III   Building Blocks of Applications

Create and Bind Fields

Fields are the means through which information in a control gets saved and shown in an item. Therefore, you need to create fields only for those controls containing information that you want to save in the item. For example, you generally don't need to create an associated field for a Label control, as shown in Figure 5-20, because there's no reason to save the values in such controls to the item. However, for controls in which users enter information, such as the TextBox and ComboBox controls, you usually create a new field or bind an existing field to the control so that the value in the control is saved to the item.

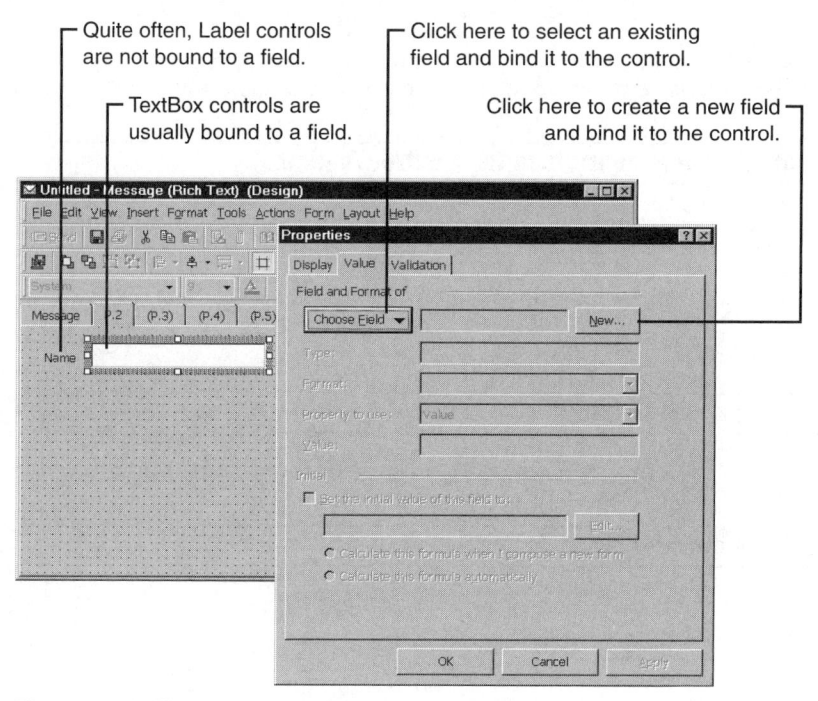

Figure 5-20 Fields in which the user enters or selects information are generally bound to fields.

Create a New Field and Bind It to a Control

When you create a new field by using the Properties dialog box, the field you create is automatically bound to the currently selected control. In addition, the field you create is automatically added to the User-Defined fields in the Folder field set.

To create a new user-defined field

1. Right-click the control, and then click Properties.
2. Click the Value page.
3. Click New.
4. In the Name text box, type the field name.
5. If necessary, change the Type and Format of the field, and then click OK twice.

> **More Info** For more information about specifying the type and format for a field, refer to Chapter 6.

Bind a Control to an Existing Field

In addition to the user-defined fields that you create, Outlook supplies several different sets of fields that you can use. These field sets include Frequently-Used fields, Address fields, Date/Time fields, and All Mail fields. These are built-in fields that, in most cases, perform advanced functions not easily attained with user-defined fields. To select an existing field to bind to a control, you use the Properties dialog box, as shown previously in Figure 5-20.

To bind a control to an existing field

1. Right-click the control, and then click Properties.
2. Click the Value tab.
3. Click Choose Field, point to the set of fields you want, and then click the field.
4. If necessary, change the format and set the initial value of the field, and then click OK.

Select Fields from Other Forms

Outlook conveniently categorizes fields by the forms with which they're associated. This is often useful if you want to create a form that has many of the same fields as another form. Rather than looking through the User-Defined fields in the Folder field set, you can view a shortened list of fields for a form.

Part III Building Blocks of Applications

To add a field set from a form to the field list

1. Right-click the control, and then click Properties.
2. Click the Value tab.
3. Click Choose Field, and then click Forms.
4. In the upper left library drop-down list box, click the forms library that contains the forms you want, as shown in Figure 5-21.
5. In the left forms list box, double-click the form to add it to the Selected Forms box.
6. Click Close, and then click OK.

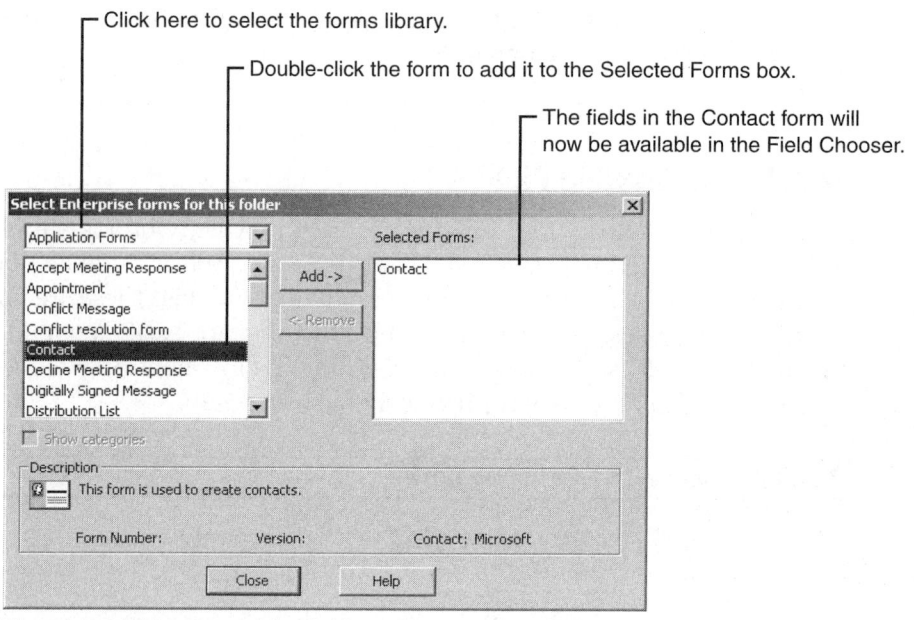

Figure 5-21 You can add a field set from another form to the field list.

When to Use the Field Chooser

The Field Chooser allows you to view, add, and delete fields. You add a field by dragging it from the Field Chooser to the form. When you drag a field from the Field Chooser, Outlook adds a control and a control label to the form and automatically binds the control to the associated field. It then automatically positions the controls on the form if the AutoLayout option is selected on the Layout menu. The control added to the form depends on the field you add. For example, if you add a Yes/No type field to a form from the Field Chooser, a CheckBox control is added to the form. If you add a Text type field, a TextBox control is added to the form.

In addition to providing a shortcut for adding TextBox and CheckBox controls to a form, the Field Chooser serves several other purposes:

- If you accidentally delete a standard control such as Message, To, or From on a form, you can add it back to the form by dragging it onto the form from the Field Chooser.
- The Field Chooser allows you to delete fields.
- The Field Chooser allows you to view fields available in the active folder and in other forms, as shown in Figure 5-22.

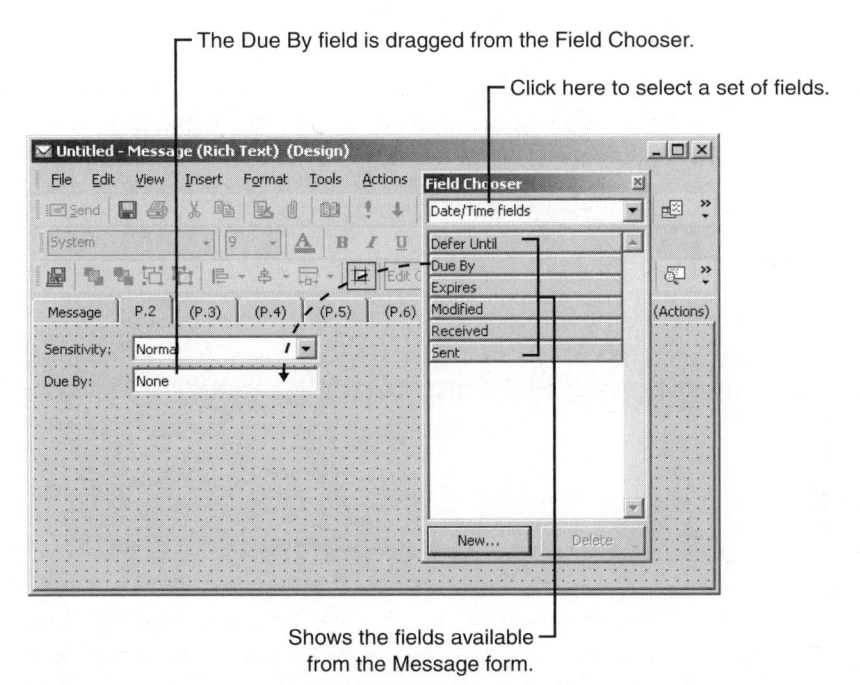

Figure 5-22 You can drag fields directly from the Field Chooser to the form.

To add a field from the Field Chooser

1. On the Field Chooser, click the set of fields you want.
2. Drag the field from the Field Chooser to the form.

Delete a Field

To delete a field, you use the Field Chooser.

To delete a field

1. On the Field Chooser, click the set of fields you want from the drop-down list box.
2. Click the field you want to delete, and then click Delete.
3. In the message box, click Yes.

Polish the Layout

After you add controls to the form, you can use Outlook's layout options to add professional polish to your forms. Outlook provides a great set of layout options that will save you countless hours of finish work. This section covers how to select, edit, align, and space controls. You are encouraged to experiment with the remainder of the layout options.

Select and Edit Controls

To select a control on a form, click the control. To edit the control, click it again. For example, to select a Label control, click it once. To type text into the label, click it again and then type the text. To exit Edit mode, click outside the Label control.

Align Controls

With Outlook alignment options, you can align the borders of a control. When you align controls, the alignment is always based on the last control selected. The sizing handles of the last control selected are white, as opposed to black sizing handles on the other controls, to indicate the control on which the alignment is based.

To align controls

1. Hold down the Ctrl key, and then click each of the controls you want to align.
2. On the Layout menu, point to Align, and then click one of the alignment menu commands from the Align submenu.

Space Controls

After you align the controls, you can space them so they are evenly separated.

To space controls

1. Hold down the Ctrl key, and then click each of the controls you want to space.

2. On the Layout menu, point to Horizontal Spacing or Vertical Spacing, and then click one of the spacing options from the menu.

Set Tab Order

The tab order defines the sequence in which the controls become active on the form when a user presses the Tab key. When you add controls to the form, the control name is added to the bottom of a list of controls in the Tab Order dialog box, as shown in Figure 5-23.

Label controls, such as *ConversationLabel* and *SubjectLabel,* are listed in the Tab Order dialog box but are not included in the tab order at run time. Also, when the Message control is active, pressing the Tab key will cause the insert bar to advance to the next tab stop in the control. If possible, it's usually best to place the Message control as the last control in the tab order.

> **Tip** You can select more than one control at a time in the Tab Order dialog box. To move multiple controls, hold down the Ctrl key, click the controls you want in the Tab Order list box, and then click the Move Up or Move Down button.

To set the tab order for the Compose page

1. In Design mode, on the Layout menu, click Tab Order.

2. In the Tab Order list box, click Move Up or Move Down to put the controls in the proper tab sequence and then click OK.

Part III Building Blocks of Applications

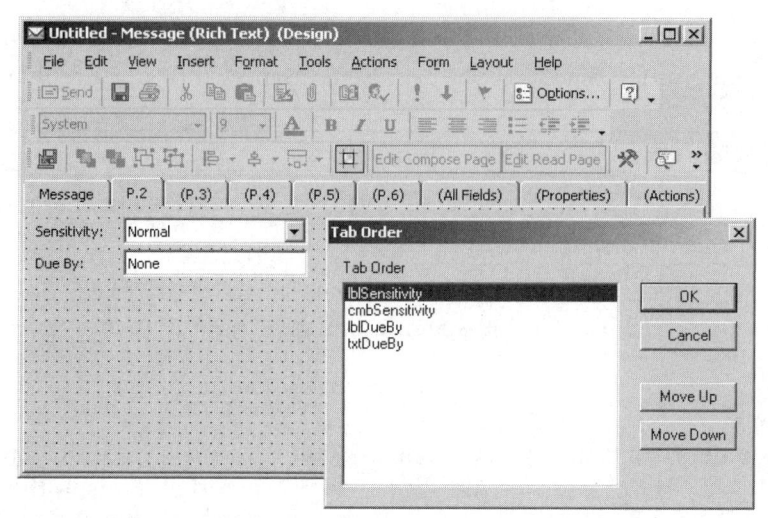

Figure 5-23 Use the Tab Order dialog box to change the tab order of controls on a page.

> **Note** If you intend to use the Tab Order dialog box to rearrange the tab order, it is good form design practice to use a standard naming convention to name the controls on your form. Otherwise, you will be confused as to the identity of the controls referenced by *TextBox1, TextBox2*, and so forth. Consider adopting a standard control-naming convention that is used throughout your organization. Figure 5-23, shown previously, uses a typical Visual Basic naming convention.

View the Form in Run Mode

When you've finished with the layout of a page, it's a good idea to switch from Design mode to Run mode to see how the form will look at run time.

To switch between Design mode and Run mode

1. On the Form menu, click Run This Form.
2. Click the Close button to return a form to Design mode.

Create Help (Optional)

Not all forms require TipText help. In fact, most forms should be simple enough that TipText help is not required. In some cases, however, you may want to specify ControlTipText for a control. With ControlTipText, the TipText appears when the user positions the pointer over the control.

To create ControlTipText

1. In Design mode, right-click the control you want to specify ControlTipText for, and then click Advanced Properties on the shortcut menu.
2. Double-click the ControlTipText cell, and then type the text you want in the text box next to the Apply button.
3. Click the Apply button to insert the text into the cell.
4. Close the Advanced Properties dialog box.

Edit the Read Page

Quite often, the Compose and Read pages of a form are very similar. As a result, you can design most of the Read page by copying controls from the Compose page. As a rule, you must edit the pages of the Read page if the page has a separate read layout.

> **Important** Each individual page of the form has its own Read or Compose page if Separate Read Layout was selected for that page.

To copy controls to the Read page

1. On the Form Design toolbar, click Edit Read Page.
2. Click the individual page you want to edit.
3. Adjust or remove any unnecessary controls on the page to make room for the controls you want to copy from the Compose page.

4. On the Form Design toolbar, click Edit Compose Page.
5. Click the individual page that contains the controls you want to copy.
6. Hold down the Ctrl key and click the fields that you want to copy, or use the selector tool to select a group of fields.
7. Click the Copy button.
8. Click Edit Read Page.
9. Click the Paste button.
10. Repeat steps 2 through 9 for each Read page you want to edit.

Set Properties for Controls on the Read Page

Quite often, you make many of the controls on the Read page read only. This prevents readers from changing the contents of an item after it has been sent or posted.

To make a control read only

1. Right-click a control, and then click Properties.
2. On the Display page, check the Read Only box.

Set the Tab Order for the Read Page

With Outlook forms, you must set the tab order for the Compose and Read pages separately. In addition, you must the set the tab order for each individual page separately. For instructions on setting the tab order for a page, see "Polish the Layout" earlier in this chapter.

About Viewing the Read Page in Run Mode

To view the Read page in Run mode, you must first send or post an item with the form. For some built-in forms, you must save an item. Consequently, you should test the Read page after you publish the form. Publishing and testing the Read page of the form is discussed later in this chapter.

To switch between Design mode and Run mode

1. On the Form menu, click Run This Form.
2. Close the form in Run mode to return to the form in Design mode.

Set Action Properties

With form action properties, you specify how a form handles responses. Form actions are one of the most important aspects of Outlook because they enable users to respond to existing items in an Outlook folder.

> **Important** Throughout this book, the term *response* is used to encompass Reply, Forward, Reply To All, Reply To Folder, and all user-defined response actions.

With Outlook actions, you can specify

- Whether a Reply, Reply To All, Forward, Post To Folder, or custom menu command appears on the Outlook Actions menu and the form Actions menu
- Whether an Action button appears on the form toolbar
- The form to activate to enable the user to send or post a response
- Whether the action opens the response form or sends the response immediately, or whether the user is prompted to open the response form

To create actions

- See "Create a New Action" in Chapter 4.

To set actions

- See Chapter 7, "Actions," which provides a detailed discussion of how to set actions for Message and Post forms and provides several detailed examples to help you understand how actions can be applied in applications.

Set Form Properties

With the form's Properties page, you give the form a name and a description and you specify whom to contact with questions about the form.

To set form properties

- With the form open in Design mode, click the Properties page, as shown in Figure 5-24.

Category Allows you to create or specify a category for forms to help organize the forms in the New Form dialog box.

Sub-Category Allows you to create or specify a subcategory for the form.

Always Use Microsoft Word As The E-Mail Editor Allows you to specify that Microsoft Word runs in the Message control of the form, so users have spell checking, thesaurus, and full formatting options that are available with Microsoft Word. The Word editing features are available only to recipients who use Word as their e-mail editor.

Template Allows you to specify the Microsoft Word template that is used to format the text in the Message control of the form.

> **Note** The Always Use Microsoft Word As The E-Mail Editor option and the Template edit box are disabled on the Properties page of your custom form if your default mail format is either Plain Text or HTML and you are using Outlook 2000. If you're using Outlook 2002, you can enable Always Use Microsoft Word As The E-Mail Editor for all default mail formats (Plain Text, Rich Text, and HTML). In versions of Outlook earlier than Outlook 2002, you can specify a Word template for use in the message body of your custom form only if you have selected Microsoft Outlook Rich Text as the default mail format for outgoing messages. To change the default mail format, select the Options command from the Tools menu and click the Mail Format page in the Tools Options dialog box.

Contact Click the Contact button to select the names of those people who are responsible for maintaining and upgrading the form. When the form is published, contact information shows in the form's Properties page and the form's Properties dialog box selected from the Form Manager.

Description Type a description for the form. The form description shows in the form's About dialog box on the Help menu and also in the Properties dialog box for the form.

Change Large Icon Click to change the icons for the form. Large icons appear in the form Properties dialog box.

Change Small Icon Click to change the icons that appear in the Outlook folder to represent an item of the type created with the form.

Forms Chapter 5

— Shows who is responsible for maintaining the form

[Screenshot of Vacation Request form Properties page]

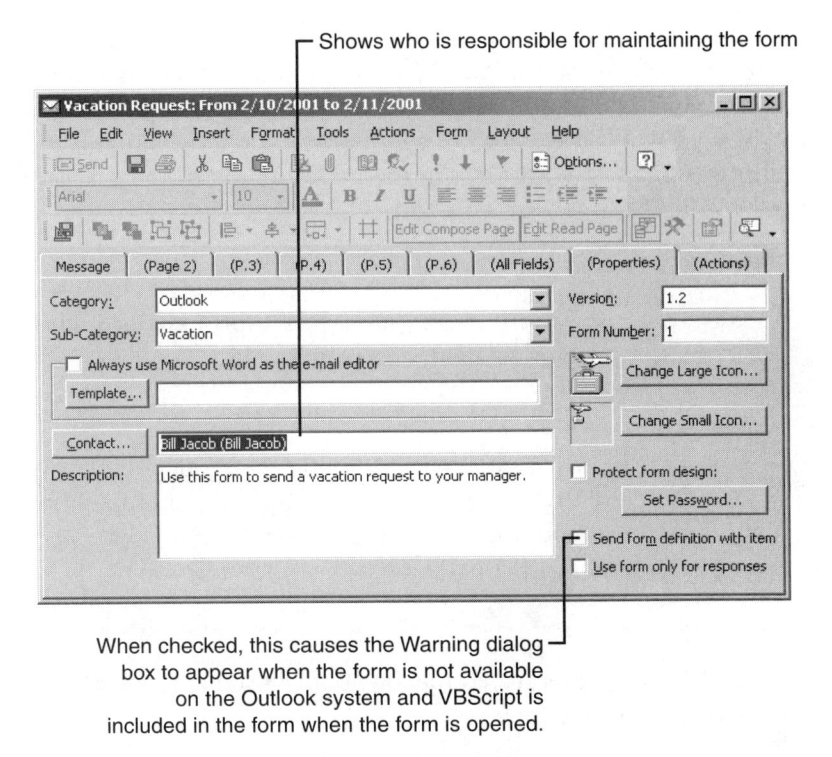

When checked, this causes the Warning dialog box to appear when the form is not available on the Outlook system and VBScript is included in the form when the form is opened.

Figure 5-24 The form's Properties page.

> **Note** Outlook 2000 and later versions provide both large and small icons for all the built-in Outlook forms in a language-specific folder under the Forms folder. For example, if you are using the U.S. English version of Outlook 2002, the language-specific identifier is 1033. Look for the icons in C:\Program Files\Microsoft Office\Office 10\Forms\1033.

Protect Form Design Select this check box to have password protection enabled for your form. This prevents other users from changing the form after you've published it.

Send Form Definition With Item Specifies that the form definition is included with the item. To speed opening the form, this check box is cleared by default. However, it may be selected when the form is published.

Part III   Building Blocks of Applications

This option provides limited security for forms that are opened in Outlook 2000, Outlook 98, or Outlook 97. If you attempt to open a one-off form (a form that sends its definition with the item), you will not see the Macro Warning dialog box and all VBScript code will be disabled by default. Remember that if an Outlook 2002 user wants to run the code behind a one-off form, he or she will have to publish the form to a forms library.

> **More Info**   For more information about form security and managing forms in your organization, see Chapter 13.

Use Form Only For Responses   Certain forms, such as the Approve Vacation and Deny Vacation forms, are used solely for responding to existing items. As a result, these forms are opened only if a related item is first selected or opened. They also don't appear in the dialog boxes allowing you to compose a new form.

> **More Info**   For more information about this option and creating response forms, see Chapter 7.

Publish the Form

When you finish designing a form, you publish it to a forms library. Optionally, you can make a backup copy of the form, although it is not required.

- When you publish a form, you register the form in a forms library and expose the form to the Outlook user interface. For example, after the form is published, the form menu commands and form name are visible in the Outlook user interface.

- When you make a backup copy of the form, you save the form definition as an Outlook Form Template or .oft file.

Outlook forms are interpreted, not compiled. Therefore, there's no source code to worry about. Since only the form definition is saved, rather than the form and all of its associated controls, the message size for forms where the form definition is not saved with the item averages 1 KB per item. If your custom form contains one or more file attachments, the message size will increase accordingly.

Make a Backup Copy of the Form

Before you publish the form, you may want to make a backup copy of the form on your hard disk or on your organization's server. When you make a copy of the form, you save it as an .oft file in much the same manner as you would save a Microsoft Word template.

To make a backup copy of a form

1. With the form open, click Save As on the File menu.
2. In the Save In drop-down list box, select the default Outlook template folder.
3. In the File Name text box, type a name for the form.
4. In the Save As Type drop-down list box, select Outlook Template (.oft).
5. Click Save.

To open your backup copy of a form

1. Select New on the File menu, and then click Choose Form.
2. Click User Templates In File System in the Look In drop-down list box, and then click on the form you'd like to open.

Publish the Form

When you publish a form, you accomplish three things:

- You make the form available to be run in Outlook.
- You register the form in the designated form library.
- You expose the form's properties, such as form name, description, and menu commands in Outlook.

About the Form Name and Message Class

When you click the Publish Form button on the Form Design toolbar and type a name in the Display name text box, Outlook adds the name to the Form Name text box and sets the message class for the form by appending the form name to IPM.*xxx*. For example, if the form is a Message form and you type *Business Card Request* in the Form Name text box, Outlook constructs the message class for the form by appending the form name to IPM.Note. Thus, the message class would become IPM.Note.Business Card Request. The message class is the internal identifier of the form and is used to locate and activate a form when an item associated with the form is created or opened.

To specify the form name

1. On the Form Design toolbar, click Publish Form.
2. Type a name in the Display Name text box.

To change the message class

- In the Form Name text box, change the name of the form. The Message class is automatically updated.

Publish to a Forms Library

When you publish a form, you publish it to a forms library. After the form is published in a library, you can then open the form to compose, submit, and read items in a folder. Where you publish the form determines how the form will be available to other users. The following table provides a description of the forms libraries where you can publish forms.

> **Important** When publishing and naming forms, the form names should be unique, or unpredictable results may occur. Also, if the form is published in more than one forms library and you make changes to the form, the form must be updated in all the forms libraries in which it is published unless the form definition is sent with the item. To update forms libraries, use the Forms Manager. For more information, see "Manage Forms" in Chapter 13.

Location	Advantage	Description
Organizational Forms Library	A public container of forms that is located on an Exchange Server. It is not connected with a specific application folder.	Allows forms to be used by anyone who has access to the Exchange Server.
Personal Forms Library	A private container of forms. It is not connected with a specific application folder.	Allows forms to be available for personal use. Also handy for designing and testing forms.

Location	Advantage	Description
Public Folder Forms Library	A public container of forms. Each public application folder has its own forms library. The container exists in the folder in a Public Information Store on an Exchange Server.	Allows forms to be used by anyone with access to the Exchange Server and whoever has permission to use the application folder.
Personal Folders Forms Library (in a .pst file)	A private container of forms. Each application folder has its own attached forms library located on a local or network hard disk drive. Can be opened only by one user at a time.	Allows forms to be organized in a personal folder. Also allows designers to distribute a large number of forms and folders by using a .pst personal folder or file.
Offline Folder Forms Library (in an .ost file)	A private container of forms that is associated with the security context of a mailbox account, located on a local hard disk drive. Each folder has its own attached forms library. Synchronized manually or programmatically with an Exchange Server.	Allows forms to be organized in an offline store folder. Users in remote locations can use forms as if they were connected directly to the server. Folders can then be synchronized between the local hard disk and the server.

> **More Info** For more information on updating or synchronizing forms published in multiple locations, see "Make the Folder Available for Offline Use" in Chapter 8. For more information on publishing and distributing forms, see "Manage Forms" in Chapter 13.

To publish a form

1. In Design mode, select Forms on the Tools menu, and then click Publish Form As.
2. In the Display Name text box and Form Name text box, type the name for the form.

3. To change the location (library) where the form is stored, click Look In, and then do one of the following:

   ❑ To publish a form in the Organizational Forms Library, click Organizational Forms Library in the Look In drop-down list box, and then click OK.

   ❑ To publish a form in the Personal Forms Library, click Personal Forms Library in the Look In drop-down list box, and then click OK.

   ❑ To publish a form in a public or personal folder, choose Outlook Folders, click the Browse button, select the folder in the Look In drop-down list box, and then click OK.

4. Click Publish.

5. In the message box, choose No for most cases where users have access to the same libraries as you. Choose Yes if this form will be sent to someone outside your system who needs the definition to view the form.

> **More Info** For more information about how to make forms available to users, see Chapter 13.

Test and Release the Form

After you publish the form, you need to test it to make sure it works as expected.

To test a Message form in the Personal or Organizational Forms Library

1. On the Folder List, click Inbox.

2. On the Outlook Tools menu, select Forms and then click Choose Form.

3. Select the forms library from the Look In drop-down list box, and then double-click the form in the list.

4. Fill out the form options, and then send the form to yourself.

5. When the item arrives in your Inbox, double-click it to make sure the Read page of the form works as expected.

Forms   Chapter 5

> **To test a Post form in a forms library in a folder**

1. In the Folder List, click the folder that contains the form you want to test.
2. On the Outlook Actions menu, click the form's associated menu command to open the form.
3. Fill out the form options, and then click Post.
4. After the item is posted in the folder, double-click it to open it and make sure the Read page of the form works as expected.

Release the Form

> **More Info** For more information about releasing forms, see Chapter 13.

Where To Go from Here

Microsoft Knowledge Base Articles Microsoft Knowledge Base articles are available on the Web at *http://support.microsoft.com/support*. Also see "Forms (Chapter 5) KB Articles" in the Microsoft Web Sites folder under the Help and Web Sites folder on the companion CD.

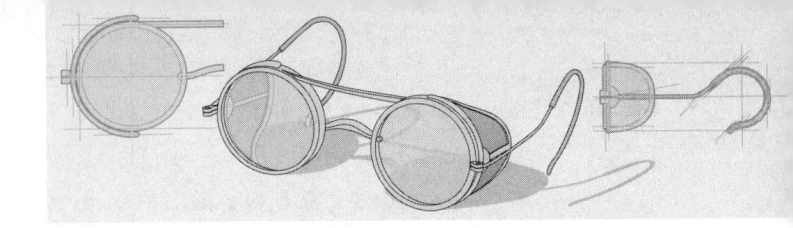

6

Controls, Fields, and Properties

In this chapter, you'll get the fundamental skills and information you need to use controls, fields, and properties effectively on a form. In addition, you'll take a look at the unique features of each commonly used control and then learn some strategies for implementing these controls and fields in an application.

Specifically, we'll cover how to

- **Set display properties for controls** Including foreground and background colors.

- **Set advanced properties** Such as the BackStyle, BorderStyle, ControlTipText, and WordWrap properties for a control.

- **Create combination fields** That show the results of combined text strings.

- **Create formula fields** That automatically perform calculations and show the results in the field. For example, for a Grand Total field, you can create a formula to show the result of adding the value of the Total field to the value of the SubTotal field.

- **Set initial values** In a field to determine the value that appears in the field when the form first appears at run time.

- **Validate and restrict information in a field** And learn how to create validation formulas that Microsoft Outlook checks before it closes the form. For example, you can create a validation formula that shows a message box if a value in a field exceeds a certain number.

Part III   Building Blocks of Applications

- **Use the To, Subject, and Message fields**   And see how to preaddress a form by setting the initial value of a To field. You will also look at how the Subject field works, and how to insert files, items, and hyperlinks to Web pages in the Message field.
- **Set control-specific properties**   And learn how to create check boxes, bind option buttons to a field, and create list boxes so users can select multiple values.

Set Control Display Properties

Each control, regardless of whether it is bound to a field, has a unique set of display properties that you can change. With display properties, you can change the name of the control, specify its exact position on the form, set its foreground or background color, and specify settings such as read-only or multi-line, as shown in Figure 6-1.

Since the Vacation Request form is the example used in this chapter, select the Vacation Request folder from the Folder List. To do this, click the Actions menu, and choose the Vacation Request form from those listed at the bottom of the menu.

To view the display properties for a control on the Vacation Request form

1. In Design mode, right-click the control, and then click Properties on the shortcut menu.
2. Click the Display tab.

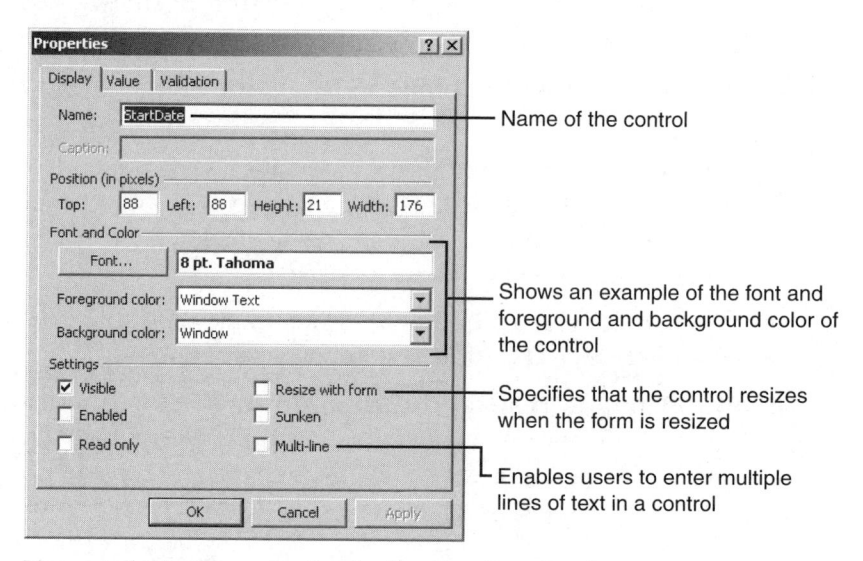

Figure 6-1 Display properties for the StartDate TextBox control.

> **Tip** When you add a control to a form, the control is given a default name such as TextBox1, Label1, and so on. If you'll be referencing the control in Microsoft Visual Basic Scripting Edition (VBScript) procedures for the form, it's a good idea to give the control a unique name, as shown previously in Figure 6-1.

Change Foreground and Background Colors

The background or foreground color for a control corresponds to the color specified for the component on the Appearance tab of the Display icon in Windows Control Panel. As shown earlier in Figure 6-1, the foreground color of the StartDate control is set to Window Text, so the color of the foreground text in the StartDate control matches the color of Window text in the Display Properties dialog box. Similarly, the background color of the StartDate control matches the color defined for Window. If you have Window defined as green on your system, the background of the control is green.

To set foreground and background colors for a control

1. Right-click the control, and then click Properties.
2. Click the Display tab.
3. In the Foreground Color or Background Color drop-down list box, click the component to which you want to map the control.

The Vacation Request form shown in Figure 6-2 provides a good example of how color effects can be achieved on a form. The background color for the Label8 control is set to Button Shadow so that it will have a dark gray color for almost all users. Also, many of the controls on the form have a white background. In this case, the background color is set to Window, which maps to white in the Windows Control Panel. Notice that most of the controls actually sit on top of the Label8 control. Controls are layered in Design mode, using Bring To Front and Send To Back options from the icons in the Form Design toolbar. For this form, the Label8 control is sent to the back layer of the page.

> **Tip** Generally, you can make a dark gray background for a control by setting the background color to Button Shadow. You can make a white background by setting the background color to Window.

Part III   Building Blocks of Applications

Layer Controls

The Label8 control on the Vacation Request form provides a good example of how you can layer controls on a form. As shown in Figure 6-2, several controls, such as StartDate and EndDate, are located on top of the Label8 control. This is done by using the Send To Back and Bring To Front buttons on the Form Design toolbar. With these buttons, you can layer controls by bringing them to the front layer or sending them to the back layer.

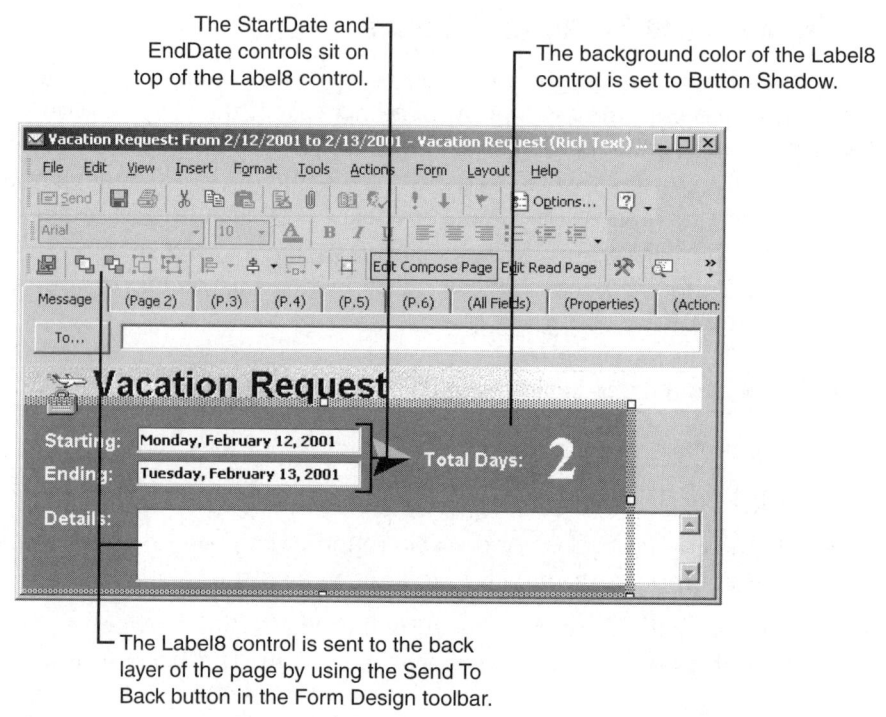

Figure 6-2 The Vacation Request form.

To send a control to a back layer

- Click the control, and then click the Send To Back button on the Form Design toolbar, or select Order from the Layout menu.

To bring a control to a front layer

- Click the control, and then click the Bring To Front button on the Form Design toolbar, or select Order from the Layout menu.

> **More Info** For more information about setting control display properties, see "Set Control-Specific Properties" later in this chapter.

Set Advanced Control Properties

The Advanced Properties window provides even more ways to customize a control. For example, with the Advanced Properties window, you can

- Define a transparent background for a control.
- Specify the ControlTipText property—the text that appears when the user moves the pointer over the control.
- Specify whether the control has the WordWrap property turned on.
- Specify the BorderStyle property for the control.

To open the Advanced Properties window

- Right-click the control, and then click Advanced Properties on the shortcut menu.

In the example shown in Figure 6-3, the Label2 control sits on top of the textured Image1 control. However, the text appears to be part of the image because the Label2 BackStyle property is set to Transparent. The BackStyle property for a control can be set only in the Advanced Properties dialog box.

Bind a Control to an Existing Field

In many cases, you can bind a control to an existing field rather than creating a new field. For example, you can bind a control to a field supplied by Outlook, or you can bind a control to an existing user-defined field. You can view a list

Part III   Building Blocks of Applications

The textured Image1 control sits on the back layer.

The Label2 control has a transparent background and sits on top of the Image1 control.

The Label2 BackStyle property is set to Transparent in the Advanced Properties dialog box.

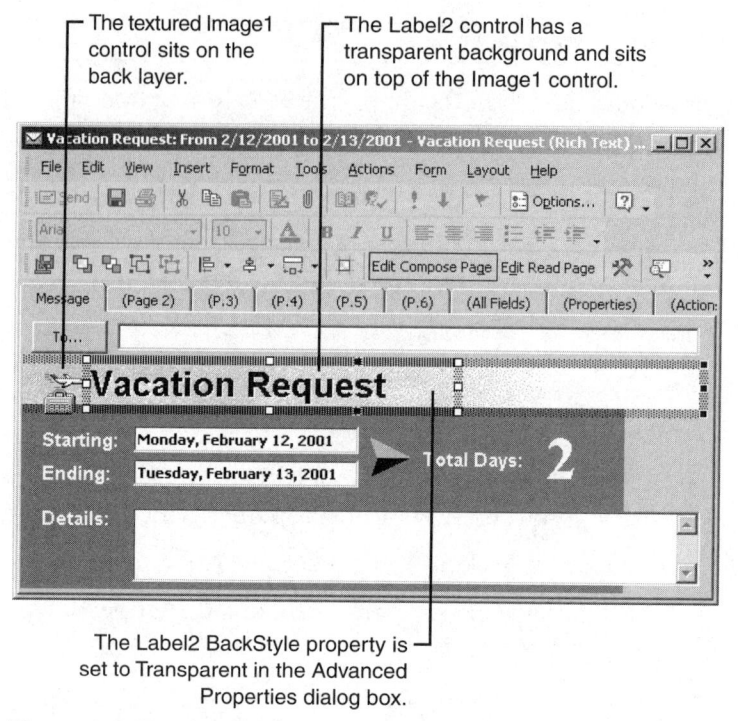

Figure 6-3 The BackStyle property of the Label2 control is set to Transparent, so the control appears to be part of the Image1 control behind it.

of available fields in the field list in the Properties dialog box, as shown in Figure 6-4.

To bind a control to an existing field

1. Right-click the control you want to define a field for, and then click Properties on the shortcut menu.
2. Click the Value tab.
3. Click Choose Field, point to the set of fields you want, and then click the field.

The sets of fields available in the field list in the Properties dialog box differ for each type of form. For example, if you create a Message form, the field list does not show the field categories for built-in forms, such as All Contact fields, All Appointment fields, and All Task fields. In addition, when you create a Message form, all user-defined fields are created in the Inbox, regardless of the active folder.

Controls, Fields, and Properties Chapter 6

- Click this button to view available field sets.
- The field list shows the fields you can select.
- When creating a message form, all user-defined fields are created in the Inbox, regardless of the active folder.
- Click Forms to add a new set of fields to a list.

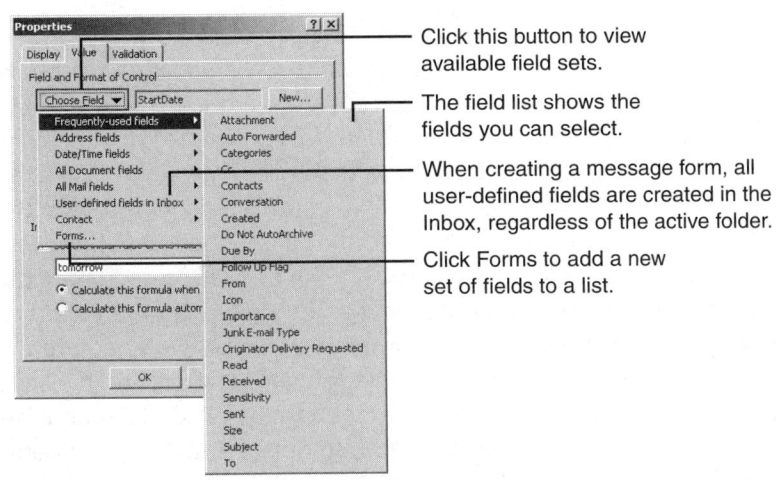

Figure 6-4 The field set and field list in the Properties dialog box.

The following table shows the field sets that are available for each type of form, and where the user-defined fields are created for the form. It also shows whether the Field Chooser is available for the form type.

Form Type	Available Field Categories	User-Defined Fields Are Created In	Field Chooser Available
Message	Field sets from built-in forms, such as Appointment, are not available	Inbox	Yes
Post	All Post fields	Active folder	Yes
Office Document	Not applicable	Active folder	Yes
Built-in	All	Active folder	Yes

> **More Info** For more information about creating built-in or custom document properties in an Office document, see the online Help for the specific application.

159

Part III   Building Blocks of Applications

> **Important**   For Office Document forms or Office documents posted directly to an application folder, you must create fields in the document itself using the built-in or custom document properties of the application (Microsoft Word, Microsoft Excel, or Microsoft PowerPoint). For example, you would use the Word Forms toolbar in a Word document to add linked fields to a bookmark in the document. You can then use the Properties command on the File menu to add built-in or custom document properties and link them to the bookmarks in the Word document. In a similar manner, you can link defined names in an Excel workbook to custom document properties that you define for the Excel document. Any built-in or custom document properties you create in the document are exposed as user-defined fields in the folder containing the document. However, you must explicitly create those built-in or custom document properties; they are not created automatically.

Create User-Defined Fields

You can create fields with Outlook in two ways. You can use the Field Chooser, which offers the advantage of automatically creating and positioning controls for you when you drag fields onto the form. You can also use the Properties dialog box, which enables you to edit field properties. In this section, we explain how to use the Properties dialog box to create new user-defined fields. Before you can create a field using the Properties dialog box, however, you must first select a control on the form to which you want to bind the field.

> **Note**   When creating a Message form, all user-defined fields are created in the Inbox, regardless of which folder is active.

To create a user-defined field

1. Right-click the control you want to define a field for, and then click Properties on the shortcut menu.
2. Click the Value tab.

Controls, Fields, and Properties Chapter 6

3. Click New.
4. In the Name text box, type a name for the field.
5. In the Type drop-down list box, click a field type.
6. In the Format drop-down list box, select a format, as shown in Figure 6-5.

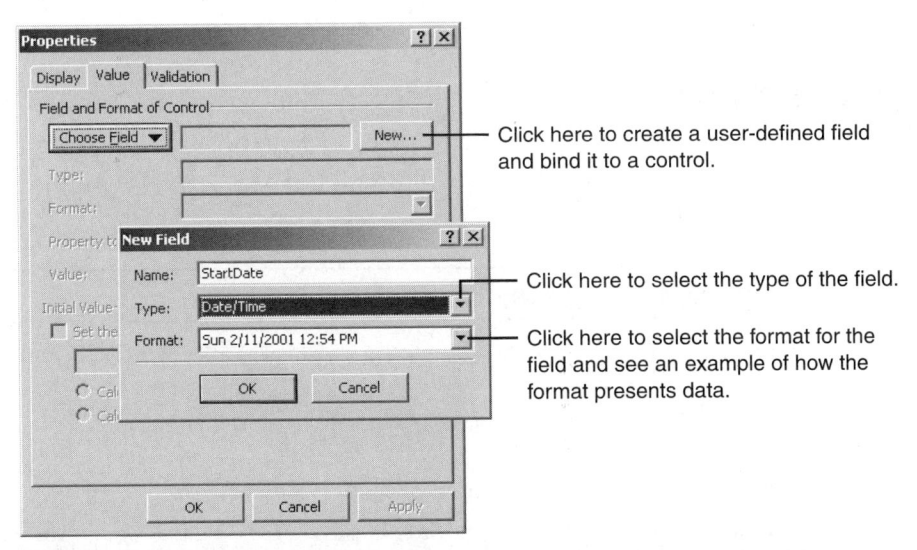

Figure 6-5 You can create user-defined fields from the Properties dialog box.

> **Note** After you create a field, you cannot change its type. Rather, you must create a new field with a different name and with the desired properties. You can then delete the old field. To delete a field, use the Field Chooser.

Location of User-Defined Fields

A user-defined field can be created in several different locations, depending on how you create the field. The following table specifies where user-defined fields are created.

161

Part III Building Blocks of Applications

Action	Field Added To
Use the New button on the Field Chooser in a view	Folder
Use the New button on the Field Chooser in form Design mode	Folder
Drag a field from the Field Chooser to a form	Item
Use the New button in the Properties dialog box of a control when binding the control to a field	Item and Folder

Specify Field Type

When you create a new field, you use the Type property to specify the type of data stored in a field in the item. The following table describes the uses for the various field types.

Field Types	Description
Combination	Fields that show the result of combined text strings. Combination fields are read only.
Currency	Numeric data as currency or mathematical calculations that involve money.
Date/Time	Date and time data.
Duration	Use to show time expired. This control has no inherent intelligence built in.
Formula	Fields that show the result of a formula. For example, a Totals field might contain a formula that multiplies the value of the Hours field by the Hourly Rate field. Formula fields are read only.
Integer	Nondecimal numeric data.
Keywords	Fields that are bound to a ListBox control from which the user can select multiple values.
Number	Numeric data used in mathematical calculations, with the exception of currency.
Percent	Numeric data as a percentage.
Text	Text or numbers that don't require calculations, such as phone numbers.
Yes/No	Fields that are bound to a CheckBox control.

Changing Field Type

After you create a field, its Type drop-down list box is disabled, so you cannot easily change its type. When you create a user-defined field with the Properties dialog box, it is created in the folder where you are creating the form and with a user-defined field in your custom form. If you haven't specifically defined a folder for the form by publishing the form in the folder's forms library, you will create the folder-level user-defined field in your Inbox. Even if you delete the control containing the user-defined field from your form page, a copy remains at the folder level. Any attempt to delete the control and then redefine the user-defined field with the same name and a different field type will result in an error message informing you that a user-defined field with this name already exists in the folder. You can circumvent this problem by following these steps.

To change the type of a user-defined field

1. Select the control bound to the user-defined field that you want to change, and press Delete to delete the control.
2. In the Field Chooser window, select User-Defined Fields In Folder from the drop-down list box at the top of the Field Chooser.
3. Select the user-defined field that you want to redefine.
4. Click the Delete button.
5. You will see a prompt stating, "The field <Name> will be removed from the list of available fields but will remain in all items in which it was used. Do you want to continue deleting the field from the available fields?" Select Yes to delete the user-defined field on the assumption that you have not published your form and are still in the initial design phase. If you are deleting a user-defined field in a form that has been published to a folder and that contains data in the form, select No. You will have to write VBA code to perform the type conversion.

You can now re-create the user-defined field that you removed in step 2 and use a different field type for the field.

Specify Field Formats

Field formats determine how information is saved and shown in a control. Each field type has a different set of formats that you can choose from. Each format in the Field Format drop-down list box, as shown earlier in Figure 6-5, includes an example of how the format displays information in the control.

Part III Building Blocks of Applications

Create Combination Fields

With Combination fields, you can create a formula for a field that combines string values from other fields and then shows the results in the control bound to the field. This section describes the general procedure for creating Combination fields and provides several examples of the types of Combination fields you can create.

To create a Combination field

1. Right-click the control that you want to bind to a Combination field, and then click Properties on the shortcut menu.
2. Click the Value tab.
3. Click New.
4. In the Name text box, type a name for the field.
5. In the Type drop-down list box, click Combination.
6. Click Edit.
7. Do one of the following:
    - Click Joining Fields And Any Text Fragments To Each Other to show combined string values in the field.
    - Click Showing Only The First Non-Empty Field, Ignoring Subsequent Ones if you want only the first value entered in the specified fields to show in the Combination field.
8. Type text in the Formula text box, or click Field to specify the fields you want inserted in the expression. Click OK.
9. To make the formula update automatically, select the Calculate This Formula Automatically button on the Value page.

> **Note** The Showing Only The First Non-Empty Field, Ignoring Subsequent Ones option is generally used in the context of folder fields. For example, when you have a folder that contains different types of items, one type of item may have the user name in the Author field, while another type of item may have the user name in the From field. To combine these two field values into one field in the folder, you can use the Showing Only The First Non-Empty Field, Ignoring Subsequent Ones option.

Combine Field Strings

With the Visual Basic Expression Service provided with Outlook, you can easily build expressions for Combination fields without worrying about concatenating values. As shown in Figure 6-6, the FullName control shows the combined values from the FirstName and LastName fields.

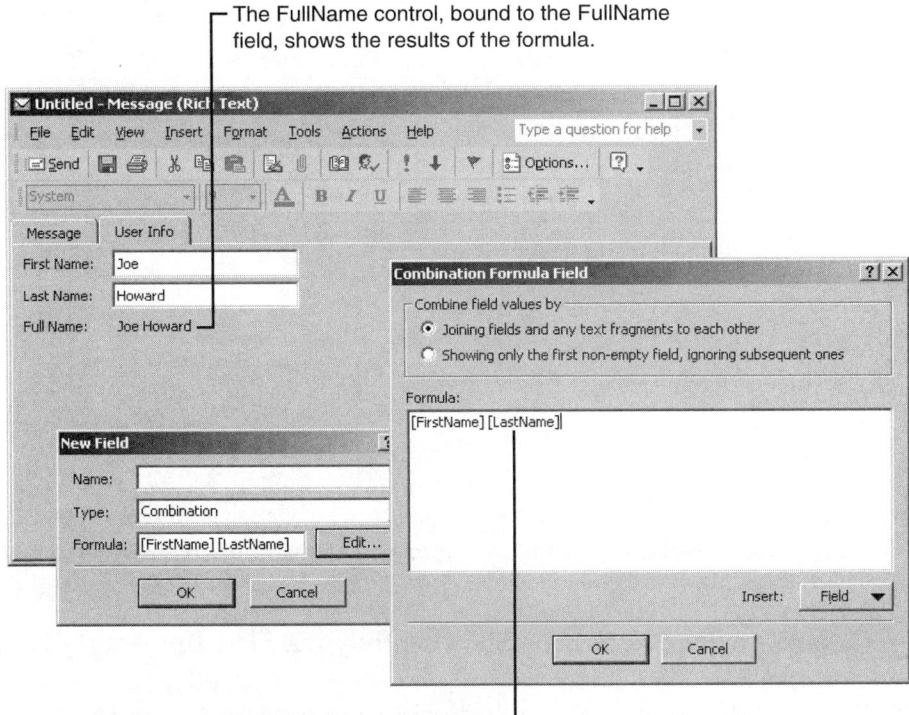

The FullName control, bound to the FullName field, shows the results of the formula.

The formula for the FullName field combines the values of the FirstName and LastName fields.

Figure 6-6 The formula for the FullName field combines the values from the FirstName and LastName fields and shows the results in the FullName control. Notice that the field is read only.

Combine Field Value Strings with Text Fragments

Quite often, you combine text fragments that you type into the Formula text box with string values from other fields. In the following example, the Combination field named UserName is located on the Read page of a form. At run time, when the user opens a submitted item, the value of the From field is combined with the User Name: fragment to create the result shown in Figure 6-7.

Part III Building Blocks of Applications

The UserName control is bound to the UserName field in the form. Notice the field is read-only.

Shows the User Name: text fragment in the UserName field.

Shows the value of the From field in the UserName field.

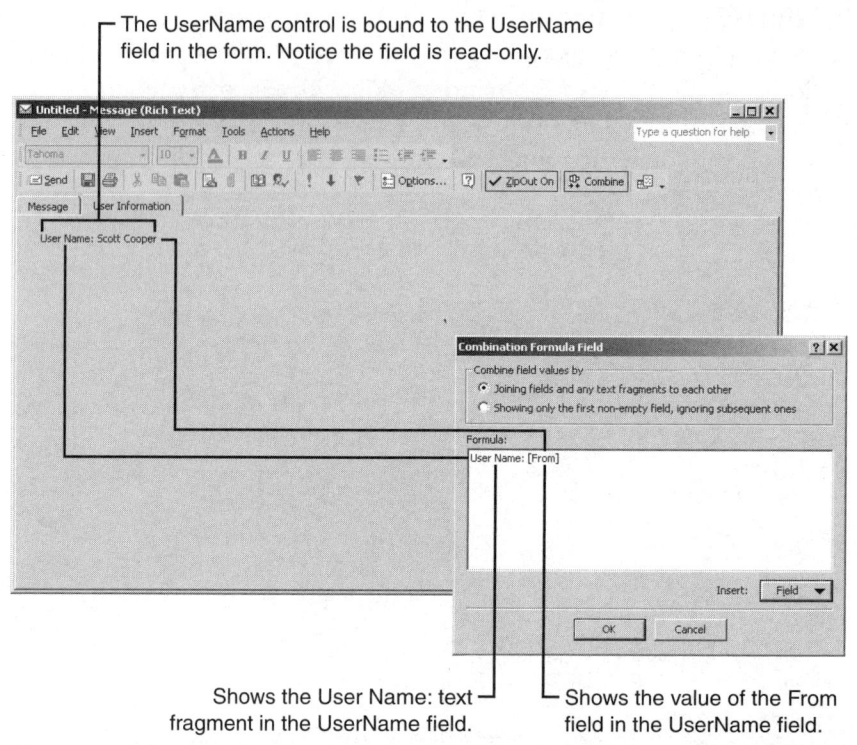

Figure 6-7 The User Name: [From] formula automatically combines the text fragment with the value in the From field.

Combine Field Values by Showing Only the First Non-Empty Field

In general, this option makes more sense when applied to a folder than when applied to a form. In fact, it is described in detail in Chapter 8, "Folders." However, it can have some use when applied to a form. For example, let's assume a folder contains items created with a form having a variety of phone number fields, such as home phone, car phone, business phone, and fax number. Also assume that you want to create a new form that consolidates the numbers so that only the primary phone number shows on the form. To do this, you can create a Combination field named Primary Phone that combines the phone numbers but only displays the value in the first non-empty phone field in the item.

> **Important** Combination fields appear with the default format of the data type used. To display a data type with a custom format, you must create a formula field and use the Format function. Furthermore, you cannot sort, group, or filter the contents of a combination field.

> **More Info** For more information about using Combination fields in folders, see Chapter 8.

Create Formula Fields

With Formula fields, you can create formulas that automatically calculate values and show the result in a control. Here are a few examples:

- **For a Time Card form,** you can create a formula for a field that totals the hours for the day and then totals the hours for the week, showing the results in the Totals field.

- **For the sample While You Were Out form,** the Subject field contains a formula that combines the values from several fields into a message that shows in the Subject field.

- **For the Vacation Request form,** the TotalDays field contains a formula that automatically calculates the number of vacation days by finding the difference between the Starting date and the Ending date.

- **For an Invoice form,** you can create a Totals field that contains a formula that shows the results of the number of hours multiplied by the hourly rate.

Although you can create a Formula field using the Type property, it's just as easy to create a formula for a Text, Number, or Currency field. As a result, there is no compelling reason to create a Formula field. Instead, it's preferable to create the type of field you want and then create the formula for the field. As you'll see in the examples in this section, the fields include formulas but are not defined as Formula fields.

To create a Formula field when you create the field

1. In Design mode, right-click the control you want to bind to the Formula field, and then click Properties on the shortcut menu.
2. Click the Value tab.
3. Click New.
4. In the Name text box, type a name for the field.

Part III   Building Blocks of Applications

5. In the Type drop-down list box, click the type of field you want. You do not have to select Formula. You can select any type of field—Currency, Number, Date/Time—and then click OK.

6. On the Value page, click Edit.

7. In the Formula text box, type in the formula or use the Field or Function button to insert the field or function you want. Some samples follow.

Specify That the Field Automatically Calculates the Results

After you create the formula for the field, you must set the Calculate This Formula Automatically option so the field is updated when field values referenced in the formula are changed. For example, for the Invoice form shown in Figure 6-8, the TOTAL field automatically updates when the values in the Hours or Hourly Rate controls change.

To specify that the field automatically calculates the result

1. Right-click the control that you want to create a formula for, and then click Properties on the shortcut menu.

2. On the Value page, select the Set The Initial Value Of This Field To check box.

3. Click Calculate This Formula Automatically.

4. To make the control read only, click the Display tab, and then select the Read Only check box.

Calculate Totals

In Figure 6-8, the TOTAL field is a formula field that shows the result of the expression

[Hours] * [Hourly Rate]

This expression multiplies the number of hours in the Hours field by the value in the Hourly Rate field and shows the result in the TOTAL field.

Build Text Strings

The While You Were Out form shown in Figure 6-9 gives an example of a Formula field showing the results of combined values in the Subject field—which is not visible on the form at run time. When the While You Were Out item is created, the values from the You Received and Please Contact fields are combined with the You Received text fragment to create the value in the Subject field. This is the value that appears in the user's Inbox when they receive the message.

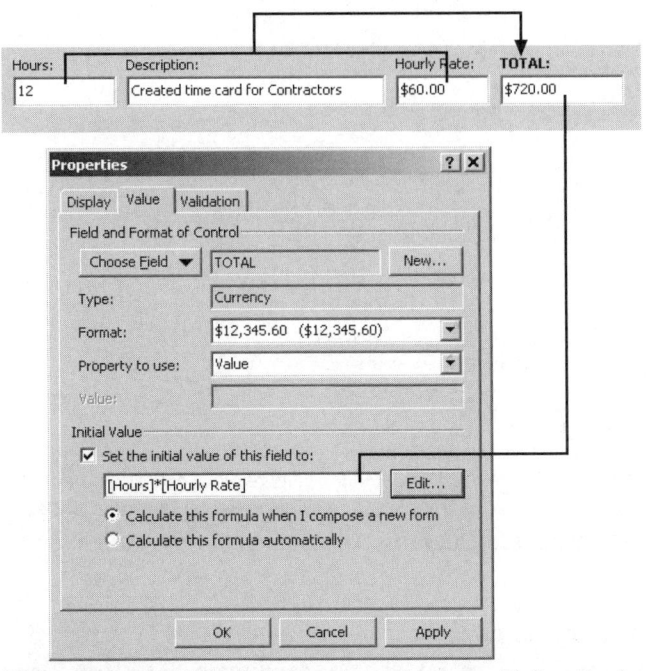

Figure 6-8 The TOTAL field automatically multiplies the hours by the hourly rate and shows the results.

When the item arrives in the user's Inbox, the Subject field shows the following result:

You received a Phone Call; contact Siegfried Weber.

In the formula, as shown in Figure 6-9, the *IIf* function evaluates the expression and returns one of two parts, based on whether the expression evaluates as *True* or *False*. For example, if the Message Type field value is not *Other*, the Subject field shows the value of the Message Type field (a phone call). In the next line, if the Please Contact field is not empty, the value of the Please Contact field is added to the Subject field.

For more information, take a look at the Microsoft Outlook Visual Basic Reference Help.

Part III Building Blocks of Applications

The value of the Message Type field.

The value of the Please Contact field.

The formula is found in the Subject control on Page 2 of the While You Were Out form. Its result is calculated from elements on the Compose page and viewed on the Read page.

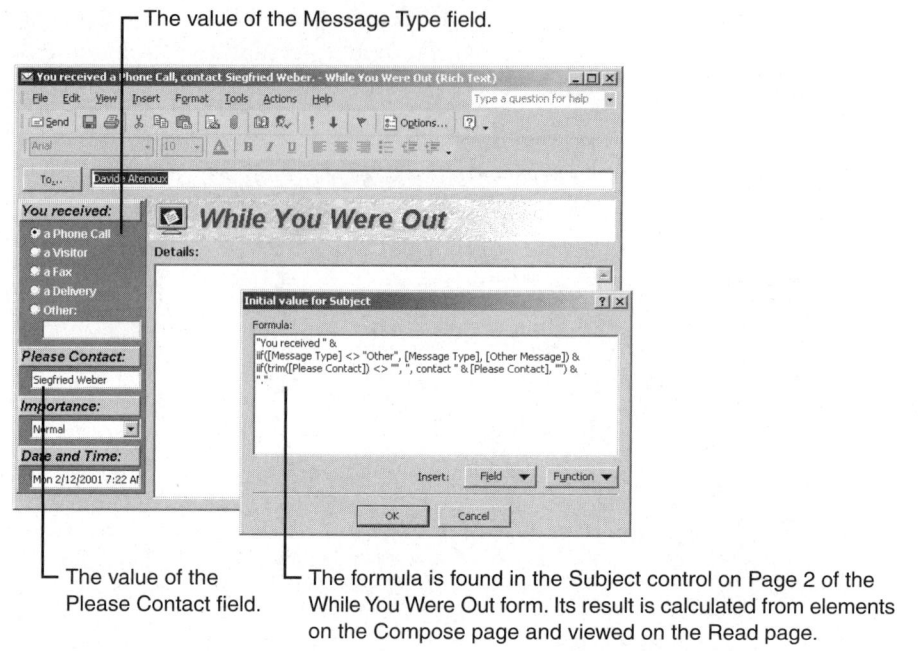

Figure 6-9 The While You Were Out form. The Subject field is hidden on the form at run time.

Calculate Date Differences

On the Vacation Request form, as shown in Figure 6-10, the TotalDays field contains a formula that automatically calculates the difference between the Starting and Ending date fields and shows the result.

> **Tip** The StartDate and EndDate fields in the Vacation Request form offer Microsoft IntelliSense. For example, if you enter Next Tuesday into the EndDate field, Outlook translates Next Tuesday into the correct date.

Set Initial Field Values

When you create an initial value for a field, you specify the values that are available in the field when the user opens the form to create a new item. With Outlook, the way the initial value is set varies somewhat depending on the control to which the field is bound. As a result, we'll cover the general concept of initial values in this section and then cover how to set initial values for each control separately.

Controls, Fields, and Properties   Chapter 6

— The StartDate control shows the value in the StartDate field.
— The EndDate control shows the value in the EndDate field.

— The TotalDays control shows the results of the formula that calculates the data difference.

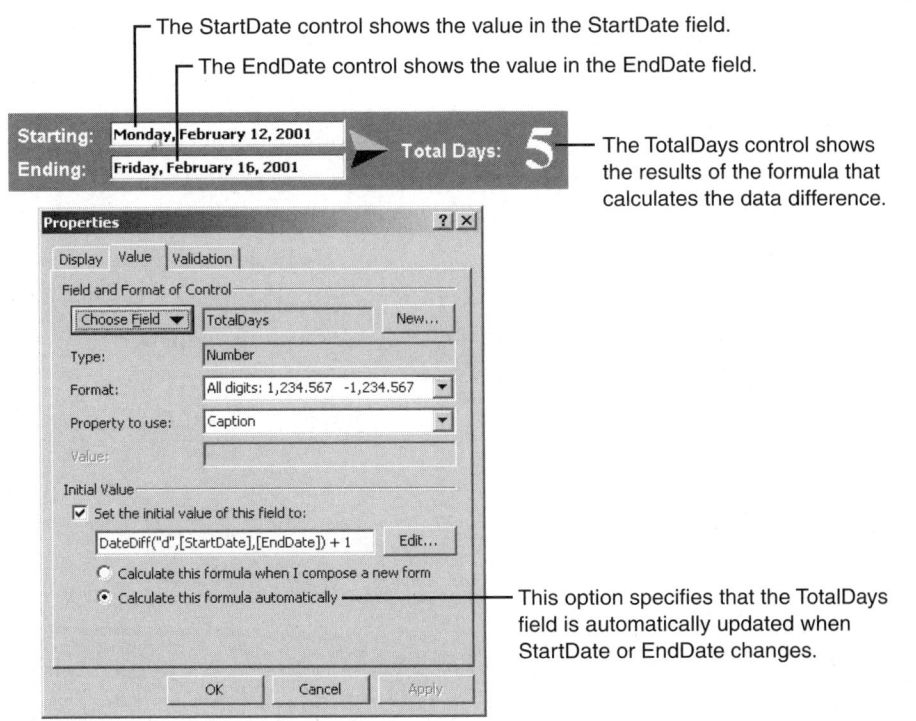

— This option specifies that the TotalDays field is automatically updated when StartDate or EndDate changes.

Figure 6-10 The TotalDays field calculates the difference between the StartDate and EndDate fields and adds 1.

Here are a few examples of why you set initial values for fields.

- To set the default values in Label, TextBox, ComboBox, ListBox, CheckBox, and OptionButton controls.

- To set the initial value of the Subject field of a form to summarize the content of the form. For example, for an Art Approval form, you can set the initial value of the Subject field to Art Approval.

- To set the initial value of the To field on a Message form to preaddress the form. For example, for an Employee Feedback form, you can preaddress the To field to an Employee Feedback public folder so that all responses are automatically routed to that folder.

The following table lists the sections in this chapter that explain how to set initial values for the control to which the field is bound. Therefore, each control contains a separate section on how to set the initial value.

To Set the Initial Value For A	See Later in This Chapter
To field	To Field
Subject field	Subject Field
Message field	Message Field
Field bound to a Label control	Label Controls
Field bound to a TextBox control	TextBox Controls
Field bound to an OptionButton control	OptionButton Controls
Field bound to a CheckBox control	CheckBox Controls
Field bound to a ComboBox control	ComboBox Controls
Field bound to a ListBox control	ListBox Controls

Validate and Restrict Data

Outlook provides a couple of ways to validate and control how information is entered into a form.

- At the simplest level, you can specify that a value is required for a field. As a result, if the user tries to submit or save the item and no value is in the field, a message box appears, saying that a value is required in the field.

- You can create a validation formula for a field. If the field validation fails, a message box appears, showing the types of values allowed in the field.

Specify That a Value Is Required for a Field

Many forms contain Text fields in which the user is required to enter information. For example, on the Business Card Request form, as shown in Figure 6-11, the Name field requires a value. If a value is not entered in the Name field when the user attempts to send the form, Outlook shows a message box that tells the user that a field on the form requires a value.

> **To specify that a value is required for a text field**
>
> 1. Right-click the control that is bound to the field, and then click Properties on the shortcut menu.
> 2. Click the Validation tab.
> 3. Select the A Value Is Required For This Field check box.

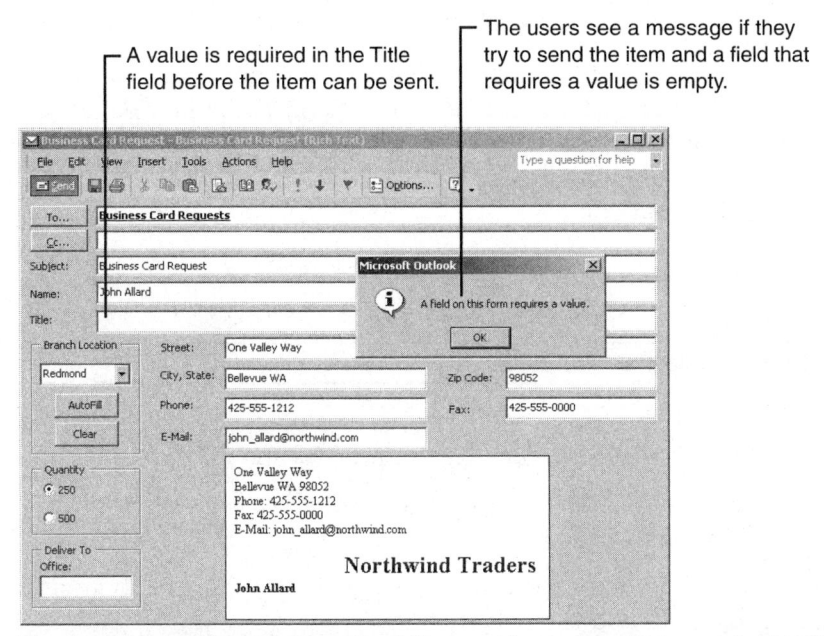

Figure 6-11 On the Business Card Request form, a value is required in the Title field. If no value is entered, users see a message when they attempt to send the item.

> **Important** Many of the Outlook field types automatically supply a value in the field by default. For example, the Date field has the value None by default. For field types such as Date, Currency, and Number that automatically supply a value, you must create a formula or use a script to validate that the field contains the specified information.

Create Validation Formulas

Outlook performs field validation when users attempt to save, send, or post an item. In addition, Outlook performs field validation when users attempt to close a form. With validation formulas, you can limit the type of information that can be saved to the item. For example, you can define

>=10 And <=100

as the validation formula for a Number field that accepts only values from 10 to 100. When users attempt to submit or save the item, they see a message only if the number entered in the field does not fall within the range of 10 to 100.

> **Tip** If you want to validate the field immediately after users enter information in the field, you can do so by writing VBScript code for your form and using the PropertyChange event or CustomPropertyChange event. For more information, see Chapter 11, "Using Visual Basic, VBA, or VBScript with Outlook."

To create a validation formula

1. Right-click the control you want to create a validation expression for, and then click Properties on the shortcut menu.
2. Click the Validation tab, and then, under Validation Formula, click the Edit button.
3. Type the validation formula or use the Field or Function button to build the formula, and then click OK.
4. In the Display This Message If The Validation Fails text box, type the message you want to appear in the message box the user will see if the validation fails.

Formulas That Validate Amounts

For many forms, you can create field validation formulas to check whether a value in the field is more or less than a specified value. For example, in Figure 6-12, the validation formula for the Amount field in the Charity Donation form specifies that the value in the field must be at least $1. If the user enters a value less than $1 in the Amount field, a message appears.

> **More Info** Note that the *CCur* function (Currency Conversion) is used in the validation formula. For more information on the *CCur* function, see Microsoft Visual Basic Help.

Validation Formulas That Compare One Field Value with Another

In some cases, you might want to create a validation formula that compares one field value against another field value. For example, for the Vacation Request form shown in Figure 6-13, the value of the StartDate field is compared with the value of the EndDate field to make sure the EndDate value falls after the StartDate value.

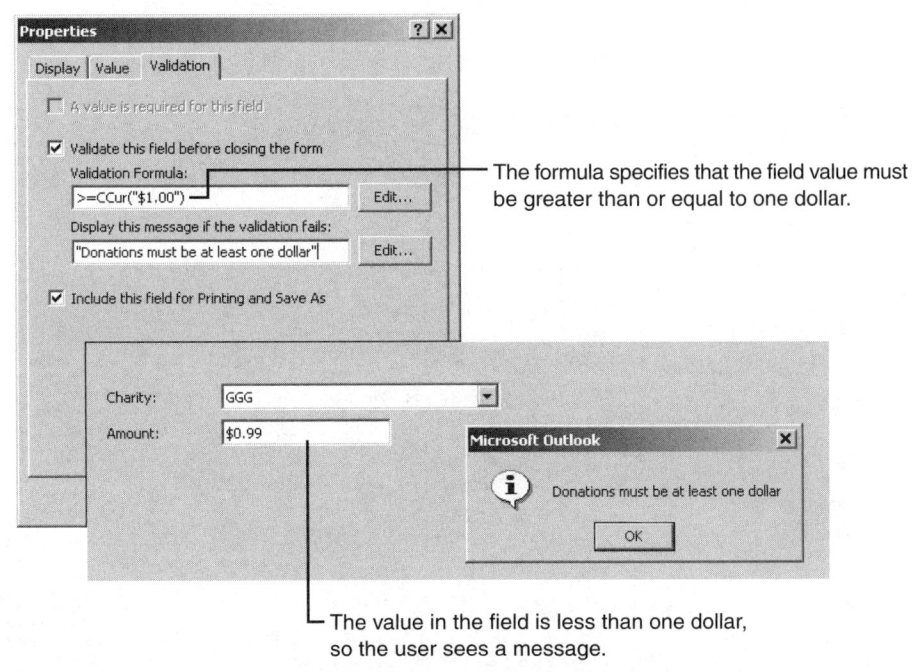

Figure 6-12 The Amount field contains a value that is less than one dollar. When the user attempts to send the form, a message box appears, indicating what is acceptable in the field.

> **Caution** Validation formulas can sometimes cause unexpected results in your forms. If you delete a bound control that uses a validation formula but then fail to delete the underlying user-defined field in the folder, you may experience validation messages that don't appear to have a source. Normally, the focus changes to the control that has triggered the validation error. However, if the control is not on the form page that has the focus, the user will not be able to determine which field value is causing the error. Writing VBScript code to control validation is more difficult than using validation formulas, but it can lead to a more consistent experience for your users, and it can accommodate more complex validation scenarios.

Part III Building Blocks of Applications

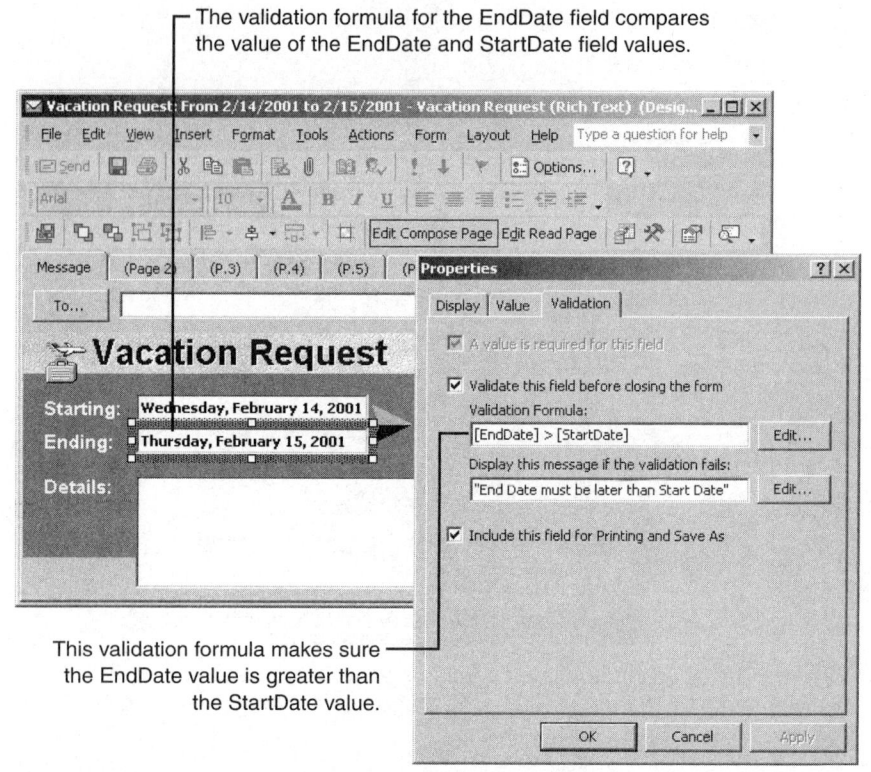

Figure 6-13 The validation formula for the EndDate field specifies that the validation passes if the value is greater than the StartDate field.

Set Field-Specific Properties

The Message page of standard Message and Post forms contains three Outlook-supplied fields that provide fundamental functionality on the form. These fields are

- **To field** Used to address the form.
- **Subject field** Used to summarize the message. The text in the Subject field appears in the Title bar of the Form window. The value in the Subject field also sets the value of the Conversation field in the item.
- **Message field** Used to enter text or insert files, items, or objects or insert shortcuts to them.

This section describes how the To, Subject, and Message fields work and then describes strategies for effectively using these fields in a form.

To Field

With Outlook, you can preaddress forms by setting the initial value of the To field. Preaddressing a form is much like providing a self-addressed envelope. Because the address is already provided on the form, the user just fills in the form and clicks the Send button.

Preaddress a Form to a Distribution List or Person

In some cases, you want to preaddress a Message form to a distribution list or to a user. For example, you want to preaddress a form such as a Weekly Schedule form to a distribution list. In addition, you may want to preaddress a Reply form so that the item created with the form is sent to your Inbox.

> **To set the initial value of the To field**

1. On the Outlook Actions menu, click New Mail Message.
2. On the form, click the To button.
3. Double-click the desired names or distribution list name to select recipients, and then click OK. If the Exchange distribution list you want to specify does not exist, you must ask your Exchange administrator to create it. If you create a Personal Distribution List or use an existing Personal Distribution List, the form will work correctly only on your computer. Also, if you use a Personal Distribution List item in your Contacts folder, the form will work correctly only on your computer.
4. On the Tools menu, select Forms, and then click Design This Form to switch to Design mode.
5. Make additional modifications to your form, and then save and exit.

Preaddress a Form to a Folder

In some cases, you might want to preaddress a form to a folder. For example, the Business Card Request form, as shown in Figure 6-14, can be opened from the Organizational Forms Library. However, the form is preaddressed to the Business Card Request folder, so the user can submit the item automatically by simply clicking the Send button.

Part III Building Blocks of Applications

```
┌─ The user simply clicks        ┌─ The To field is preaddressed to the
   the Send button to send          Business Card Requests folder.
   the item to the folder.
```

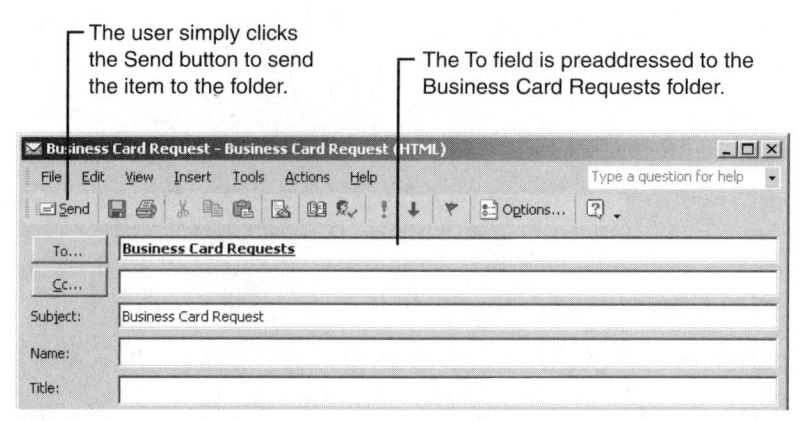

[Screenshot of Business Card Request form window with To field filled with "Business Card Requests" and Subject field "Business Card Request", plus Name and Title fields.]

Figure 6-14 The Business Card Request form is preaddressed to the Business Card Request folder.

Before you can preaddress a form to a folder, the folder address must exist in the Global Address Book or in an Address Book in your profile. If the folder address does not exist in the Global Address Book, you can ask your Exchange administrator to make the folder address available in the Global Address Book, or you can publish the folder address to an Address Book in your profile.

> **Important** To publish a folder address in an Address Book in your profile, the folder must be located in Public Folders.

To add a folder address to an Address Book in your profile

1. In the Folder List, right-click the folder, and then click Properties on the shortcut menu.

2. Click the Administration tab. (You will see the Summary tab if you do not have owner permissions to modify this folder.)

3. Click Personal Address Book to add this item to a Personal Address Book in your profile. Unlike previous versions of Outlook, which would add a public folder address only to your Personal Address Book when you clicked the Personal Address Book button, Outlook 2000 and later will add the folder address to the Address Book selected in the Keep Personal Addresses In drop-down list box on the Addressing page of the Services dialog box for your Exchange profile.

Controls, Fields, and Properties   Chapter 6

> **Note**   In Outlook 2002, the Services dialog box is no longer available under the Services command on the Tools menu. Instead, you can access the Properties dialog box of your profile with the E-Mail Accounts command on the Tools menu. To set the addressing options for your profile, use the Options command on the Tools menu of the Address Book dialog box. To display the Address Book dialog box, select the Address Book command on the Tools menu.

To Preaddress the To field to a folder

1. On the Outlook Actions menu, click New Mail Message.
2. On the Message form, click the To button.
3. In the Show Names From The drop-down list box, click the name of the Address Book that you've selected to keep personal addresses in the Addressing dialog box.
4. Double-click the folder name in the list, and then click OK. The folder name should appear in the To field.
5. On the Tools menu, select Forms, and then click Design This Form to switch to Design mode.
6. Modify the form as desired, and then save and exit.

> **More Info**   For more information, see "Add Folder Address to Personal Address Book" in Chapter 8.

Subject Field

The Subject field provides several important functions on a form:

- It summarizes the information in the item.
- It sets the value of the Conversation field. The Conversation field is the field used to create threaded conversations in views.
- The value in the Subject field appears in the title bar of the window.

Part III Building Blocks of Applications

Set the Initial Value of the Subject Field

In some cases, you may want to set the initial value of the Subject field. For example, for single-purpose forms such as the Business Card Request form, you can set the initial value of the Subject field to Business Card Request.

To specify the initial value of the Subject field

1. Right-click the Subject control, and then click Properties on the shortcut menu.
2. Click the Value tab.
3. In the Value text box, type a value or click Edit to build an initial value formula for the Subject field, as shown in Figure 6-15.

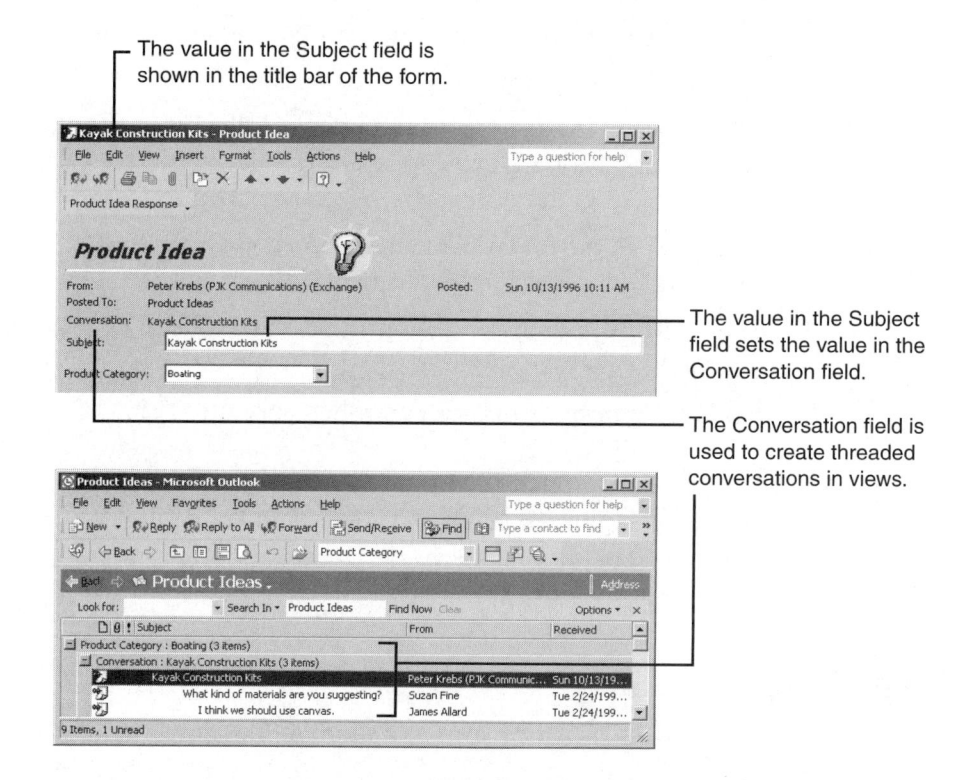

Figure 6-15 Shows how the Subject field functions in the New Product Idea form.

Message Field

With the Message field shown in Figure 6-16, you can insert the following types of items. Each of these scenarios is covered in more detail in later sections.

- **File attachments and shortcuts**   For example, for a Copier Request form, the user can insert attached files into the Message field. If the files are too large to send through the Exchange Server system, the user can insert shortcuts to the attached files instead. In addition, you—the designer—can insert files, file shortcuts, and hyperlinks. For example, you may want to insert attachments for ReadMe files that explain how to use the form or application. Or you may want to insert a hyperlink to a file or folder address.

- **Item attachments and shortcuts**   This allows users to insert messages from other users into the Message field.

- **Shortcut to a World Wide Web page**   Recipients must have a Web browser installed on their computer to use the shortcut.

- **Linked or embedded objects**   These objects can be Word documents, Excel workbooks, PowerPoint presentations, or any other valid ActiveX object supporting object linking and embedding.

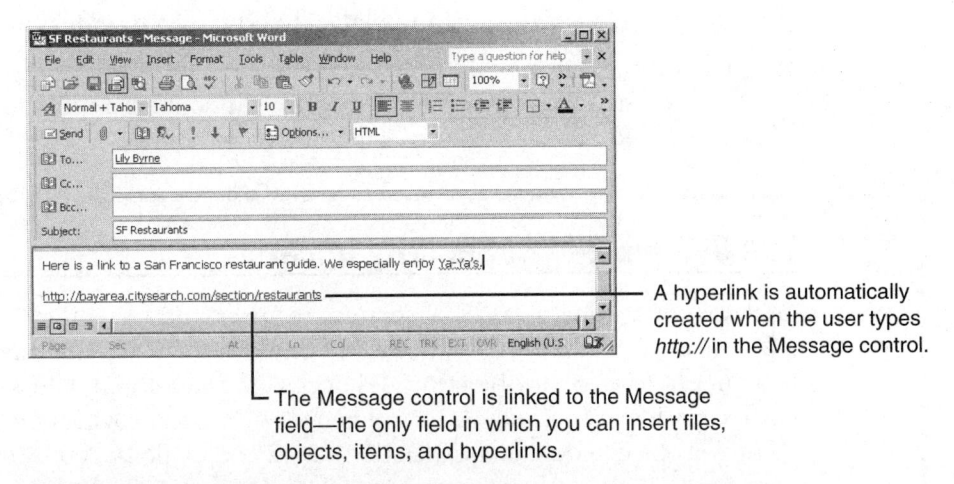

Figure 6-16 At design time or run time, you can insert files, items, hyperlinks, and objects in the Message field.

A hyperlink is automatically created when the user types http:// in the Message control.

The Message control is linked to the Message field—the only field in which you can insert files, objects, items, and hyperlinks.

> **Caution** Due to the attachment security feature of Outlook 2002, you should not insert many of the file types listed in this section into a message body. The same warning applies if you have upgraded Outlook 2000 or Outlook 98 with the Outlook E-Mail Security Update. Outlook 2002 attachment security prevents access to the following items inserted into a message body:
>
> - .lnk (Exchange shortcut)
> - .url (Internet shortcut)
> - Embedded OLE objects
> - Level 1 attachments
>
> For additional details, see Chapter 13, "Distributing and Securing Applications."

Restrictions and Rules for Message Control Usage

When working with the Message field and Message control, there are a few guidelines you should be aware of:

- The Message control is automatically bound to the Message field.

- Each form can contain only one Message control per page. For example, the Compose page of a form can contain a Message control and the Read page can contain a Message control.

The Outlook E-Mail Security Update

Outlook 2002 contains a set of security features known as the Outlook E-Mail Security Update. Introduced to combat e-mail viruses that use an attachment to exploit object model access to the Global Address List or Contacts folder, the Outlook E-Mail Security Update provides both attachment and object model guards. Outlook 2002 and Outlook 2000 SP-2 or later contain the Outlook E-Mail Security Update; Outlook 2000 SR-1 requires that you install the Outlook E-Mail Security Update. For additional details on this security update, including how to set administrative options in a Microsoft Exchange Server environment, see Chapter 13.

- You cannot have a Message control on the Message page and a duplicate control on page 2 or following the Compose or Read page.
- If the form does not have the Separate Read Layout option selected on the Form menu for the page that contains the Message control, the form can contain only one Message control.
- The Message control is the only control on a form in which you or the user can insert files, items, or objects.
- The form must be in Run mode to enter information into the Message control.

> **Note** The default e-mail format in Outlook 2002 is Rich Text, and Word is the default e-mail editor. Most of the instructions that follow pertain only to using Outlook as the default e-mail editor. You can change the default e-mail editor and format on the Mail Format page of the Outlook Tools Options dialog box.

To insert a file attachment or shortcut in the Message control

1. In Run mode, click in the Message control where you want to insert the file attachment or shortcut.
2. On the Insert menu, click File.
3. Locate and click the file you want to insert.
4. Under Insert, click an option. If you are using a version of Outlook with the Outlook E-Mail Security Update installed, you cannot insert a folder shortcut.
5. Click OK.

To insert an item in the Message control

1. In Run mode, click in the Message control where you want to insert the item.
2. On the Insert menu, click Item.

3. In the Look In drop-down list box, click the folder that contains the item you want to insert, and then click the item.

4. Under Insert As, click an option. If you are using a version of Outlook with the Outlook E-Mail Security Update installed, you cannot insert a folder shortcut.

5. Click OK.

To insert a folder shortcut in the Message control

- In Run mode, using the right mouse button, drag the folder from the Folder List to the Message control. If you are using a version of Outlook with the Outlook E-Mail Security Update installed, you cannot insert a folder shortcut.

To insert a URL shortcut in the Message control

1. First create a Uniform Resource Locator (URL) shortcut on the Windows desktop using your Web browser.

2. In Run mode, drag the URL shortcut from the desktop to the Message control. If you are using a version of Outlook with the Outlook E-Mail Security Update installed, you can drag the URL into the message body. However, you can't be certain that the message recipient will able to see the URL shortcut. This is because URL shortcuts are treated as Level 1 attachments by the Outlook E-Mail Security Update. (For additional details, see Chapter 13.) For this reason, inserting a hyperlink in the Message control is preferable.

To insert a hyperlink in the Message control

- In Run mode, type the hyperlink in the Message control. When you type *http://* or one of the supported protocols, the text is automatically underlined and the color is changed to blue by default. For example, to create a hyperlink to the Building Microsoft Outlook 2002 Applications root folder using the Outlook protocol, you specify the following hyperlink in the Message control:

    Outlook://Building Microsoft Outlook 2002 Applications/

Controls, Fields, and Properties   Chapter 6

> **Important**   If the hyperlink includes spaces, you must enclose the entire address in angle brackets <>. If you are using WordMail, you should end the hyperlink with a carriage return after the closing angle bracket (>). Notice in the examples below that file names use the forward slash (/) instead of the traditional backslash (\). If you want the hyperlink to open an item in the folder rather than in an Outlook Explorer displaying the hyperlinked folder, place a tilde character (~) in front of the subject for the item that you want to open. Duplicate subjects in the folder can yield unpredictable results. For information about URL addressing in Exchange 2000, see the Exchange 2000 sidebar on page 187. Valid hyperlink examples are as follows.
>
> *<file://c:/program files/microsoft office/office/msowcvba.hlp/>*
> *<outlook://public folders/all public folders/Product Ideas/*
>   *~Kayak Construction Kits>*
> *<outlook:inbox/>*
> *<http://msdn.microsoft.com/exchange>*
> *<file:////ServerName/ShareName/exchsrvr/bin/cdo.hlp/>*

> **Note**   If you want the hyperlink to point to default folders in the current user's mailbox, don't add the double forward slash (//) after outlook: protocol. Valid examples are *outlook:Contacts* and *outlook:Tasks*.

Here are the supported protocols:

Protocol	Description
file://	A protocol used to open files on an intranet. If you are using a version of Outlook with the Outlook E-Mail Security Update installed, you will see the Opening Mail Attachment dialog box when you click the file URL. You have the option of saving the attachment or opening it directly.
ftp://	File Transfer Protocol (FTP), the most common method used to transfer files over the Internet.

(continued)

Part III Building Blocks of Applications

Protocol	Description
gopher://	Gopher protocol, by which hyperlinks and text are stored separately.
http://	Hypertext Transfer Protocol (HTTP).
https://	Hypertext Transfer Protocol Secure; a protocol designed to provide secure communications using HTTP over the Internet.
mailto://	A protocol used to send mail to an e-mail address. When the recipient clicks this hyperlink, a new message opens with the mailto e-mail address filled in.
news://	A protocol used to open an Internet newsgroup for recipients who are connected to an NNTP server.
nntp://	Network News Transfer Protocol, a protocol used to distribute, inquire about, retrieve, and post Usenet articles over the Internet.
outlook://	A protocol used to open an Outlook folder or an item or file in Outlook. This protocol is supported only in Outlook.
prospero://	A protocol used to organize Internet resources in your personal set of hyperlinks that go to information on remote file servers; for your personal virtual file system.
telnet://	The Internet standard protocol for logging on from remote locations.
wais://	Wide Area Information Servers protocol, a distributed information system used to retrieve documents based on keywords you supply.

To insert an object in the Message control

1. In Run mode, click in the Message control where you want to insert the object.

2. On the Insert menu, click Object. If you are using a version of Outlook with the Outlook E-Mail Security Update installed, the Object command will be unavailable and you will not be able to insert an embedded object. If your message recipient is using a version of Outlook with the e-mail security update installed, he or she will not be able to access the embedded object.

3. In the Insert Object dialog box, click the Create From File button.

4. In the Create From File text box, type the name of the file that you want to link or embed in the Message control, or click Browse to select from a list.

    ❑ To create a linked object, select the Link To File check box.

    ❑ To show the object as an icon, select the Display As Icon check box.

    You can see the Link To File check box when Create From File is selected.

About the Control Toolbox

The Control Toolbox identifies the controls you can add to a Frame or page of a form. You can customize the Control Toolbox in many ways, including the following:

- Add pages to the Control Toolbox. Right-click on the Control Toolbox page tab, and select the New Page command.

- Move controls from one page in the Control Toolbox to another. Right-click on the Control Toolbox page tab, and select the Move command.

- Rename Control Toolbox pages. Right-click on the Control Toolbox page tab, and select the Rename command.

- Change the properties of a control in the Control Toolbox. Right-click on the icon for the control, and select the Customize *<ControlName>* command. You can change the ToolTip text for the control and the image that represents the control.

- Add other controls—including ActiveX controls—to the Control Toolbox. Right-click in the body of the Control Toolbox, and select the Custom Controls command.

Exchange 2000 URLs

One of the core features of Exchange 2000 is that you can use URLs to access all items in public and private folders. You do not need to use the cumbersome and error-prone tilde (~subject) convention shown earlier to open an item with a URL. The *cmd* parameter in the URL tells Exchange 2000 to perform an action (such as new or open) or to open the item using a specified form.

Here are some valid examples of Exchange 2000 URLs:

http://corpmsg-01/exchange/RByrne/Contacts/FriedmanFern.eml? Cmd=open

http:// corpmsg-01/public/Product%20Ideas/Kayak%20Construction%20Kits.EML

http://me3/apps/rpa/?cmd=new

http://me3/apps/rpa/{8FF20CF7-7D10-4F76-909B-3CFDA66D96A0}.EML?cmd=open

http://corpmsg-05/public/exec/financials/2001Q3Budget.xls

http://smf-msg-03/workflow/governor/budget/fy2002title238.eml? cmd=docprep.asp

- Copy modified controls from a form to the Control Toolbox. Use the selection tool to select a group of controls, and drag them to the Control Toolbox to create a controls template. Drag the controls template from the Control Toolbox to a form in design mode to re-create the controls.

- Import or export all the controls on a page in the Control Toolbox. Right-click on the Control Toolbox tab, and select the Import Page or Export Page command. Toolbox pages are saved with the .pag extension.

> **Note** When you add a control to a form by using the Control Toolbox, the control is not initially bound to a field.

Set Control-Specific Properties

Each of the controls in the Outlook Control Toolbox serves a unique purpose. As a result, the properties for each control are set in a slightly different way. This section covers setting the properties for the most commonly used controls.

> **More Info** For more information about all Outlook intrinsic controls, see the Microsoft Outlook Visual Basic Reference Help. The Microsoft Outlook Visual Basic Reference Help (vbaol10.chm) is available on the Microsoft Office XP installation CD. If the Outlook Visual Basic Reference Help is not available, follow these steps to install it.

To install Microsoft Outlook Visual Basic Reference

1. Click the Start button, select Settings, and then select Control Panel.
2. Double-click the Add/Remove Programs icon.
3. Select Microsoft Office XP in the list of installed programs, and click the Change button if you're running Windows 2000 or the Add/Remove button if you're running Windows 98, Windows ME, or Windows NT 4.
4. Click Add Or Remove Features, and click Next.

Controls, Fields, and Properties   Chapter 6

5. Open the Microsoft Outlook for Windows item under the Microsoft Office root item.
6. Click the Visual Basic Scripting Support item.
7. Select Run From My Computer.
8. Click Update.

> **To use controls**

1. Open the form in Design mode by selecting Forms on the Tools menu and then clicking Design This Form.
2. Click the Control Toolbox button on the Advanced toolbar.
3. Drag the desired control to the form page.
4. Modify the control using the following guidelines.

Label Controls

Label controls can be used to show text on the page. Thus, they are useful for company logos, address information, or a heading on a form page, as shown in Figure 6-17.

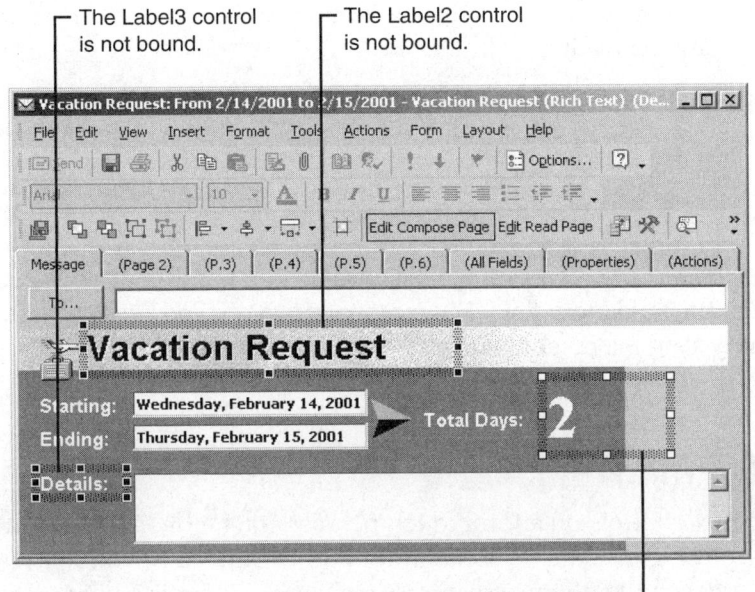

Figure 6-17 Label controls on the Vacation Request form.

When to Bind a Label Control

Generally, you bind Label controls to fields when you want to save the value to the item. For example, in the Vacation Request form, as shown in Figure 6-17, the Total Days label is bound to the TotalDays field. In this way, the value in the field is saved to the item when the item is saved or sent. However, also notice that Label2 and Label5 are not bound. As a result, the value in the Vacation Request field is not saved to the item. Rather, it exists in the form definition and is re-created each time an instance of the form is activated.

Set the Initial Value of a Label Control

In some cases, you may want to set the initial value of a Label control. For example, in the Vacation Request form, the TotalDays Label control on the Compose page contains a formula that automatically shows the result in the field.

To set the initial value of a Label control

1. In Design mode, right-click the control, and then click Properties on the shortcut menu.
2. Click the Value tab, and then type the initial value in the Initial Value text box, or click Edit to create an initial value formula.
    - ❑ To automatically calculate a formula, click Calculate This Formula Automatically.
    - ❑ To show the initial value in the Label control when the form is opened to create an item, click Calculate This Formula When I Compose A New Form.

> **Note** Before you can set the initial value of a Label control, the control must be bound to a field. For more information, see "Bind a Control to an Existing Field," earlier in this chapter.

TextBox Controls

Use TextBox controls on a form to let the user enter, edit, and view information, as shown in Figure 6-18. For example, you can place a TextBox control on a Compose page to let the user enter information and on the Read page to let the user view information.

Controls, Fields, and Properties   Chapter 6

> **Note** In some cases, you may want to insert attachments, shortcuts, or hyperlinks. To do this, you must use the Message control. For more information about the Message control, see "Message Field" earlier in this chapter.

The TextBox control has a variety of display properties that give you great flexibility in determining how the TextBox control looks and functions. For example, you can specify the Multi-Line property so the user can enter more than one line of text in the control. Before you can specify the initial value for a control, it must be bound to a field.

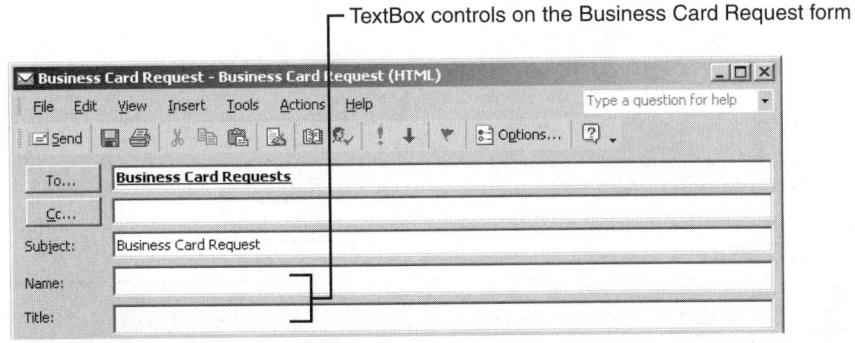

Figure 6-18 TextBox controls on the Business Card Request form.

To specify the Multi-Line option for a TextBox control

1. In Design mode, right-click the control, and then click Properties on the shortcut menu.
2. Click the Display tab, and then select the Multi-Line check box.

Initial values for text boxes can be specified on the Value page of the Properties dialog box for that control.

To specify the initial value for a TextBox control

- On the Value page, type a value in the Initial Value text box or click Edit to build an initial value formula for the field.

Frame Controls

Use the Frame control to contain controls that are logically related, as shown in Figure 6-19. Frame controls are often used to contain OptionButton controls, but they can also contain other controls such as CheckBox, ComboBox, Label, and TextBox controls.

> **Tip** You can use the Frame control to create a line on the form. Set the height or width to 2, depending on whether it is a horizontal or vertical line.

Use the Frame control to group related controls on the form.

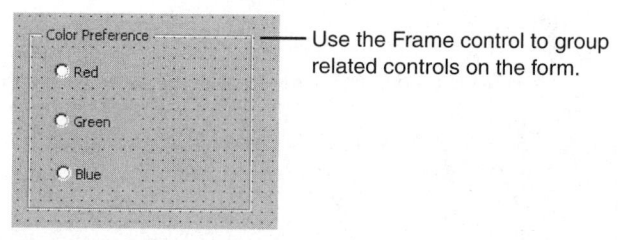

Figure 6-19 The Frame control.

To add a Frame control

- Drag the control from the Control Toolbox to the form.
  Controls within the Frame can be easily removed by dragging and deleting.

To add or remove controls from a Frame control

- To add a control, drag the control into the frame. To remove a control, drag it outside the border of the frame, right-click the control, and then choose Delete on the shortcut menu.

To change the caption of the Frame control

1. Right-click the border of the Frame control, and then click Properties on the shortcut menu.
2. In the Caption text box on the Display page, type a new caption for the Frame control.

OptionButton Controls

Use OptionButton controls on a form when you want to give the user a limited number of choices. For example, on the Business Card Request form, Option-

Button controls are used to enable users to select the quantity of cards they want, as shown in Figure 6-20.

OptionButton controls offer a choice of mutually exclusive options.

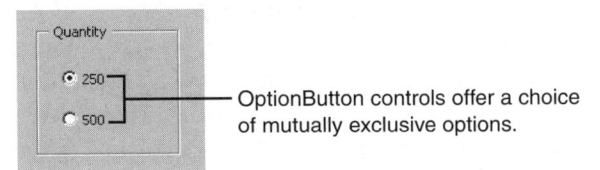

Figure 6-20 OptionButton controls on the Business Card Request form.

To specify a caption for an OptionButton control

1. In Design mode, drag the OptionButton control from the Control Toolbox to the form.

2. Click the OptionButton control. When the insertion pointer appears, type a caption for the control.

Set Value Properties for an OptionButton Control

To group OptionButton controls together, you bind the controls to the same field. For example, the OptionButton controls in Figure 6-20 are bound to the Quantity field. When you bind one OptionButton control to a field, all other option buttons in the group are automatically bound to the same field. Option buttons on pages that are not included in a container, such as a Frame or MultiPage control, are grouped together automatically. Option buttons in a Container control are grouped with the option buttons in that container.

To bind an OptionButton control to a field

1. Right-click the control, and then click Properties on the shortcut menu.

2. Click the Value tab.

3. Do one of the following:

    - Click New to create a new field. You can create a Currency, Text, or Number field. Choose the type of field to match the data in the control. In this example, the Quantity field is a Number field.

    - Click Choose Field, point to User-Defined Fields In Folder, and then click the field to which you want to bind the OptionButton control. In this example, the OptionButton control is bound to the Quantity field. The folder name changes depending on which form is being designed.

Part III Building Blocks of Applications

When you bind one option button in the group to a field, all option buttons in the group are bound to the same field automatically.

Set the Value property of each option button separately After you bind the option buttons in a group to an existing field, you must set the Value property of each option button separately. The Value property is the value that is written to the field when the option button is selected at run time. This value appears in folder views to represent the option button if it is selected in an item.

To set the Value property of an OptionButton control

1. Right-click the OptionButton control that you want to set the Value property for, and then click Properties on the shortcut menu.
2. Click the Value tab.
3. In the Initial Value text box, type a value for the option button.
4. Click OK.

To set the initial value of an OptionButton control

1. Right-click the OptionButton control that you want as the default button when the form first appears at run time. Then click Advanced Properties on the shortcut menu.
2. Click the Value cell, and then type *True*.
3. Click Apply, and then close the Advanced Properties window.

CheckBox Controls

Use CheckBox controls to give the user an On/Off or Yes/No choice, as shown in Figure 6-21. Because check boxes work independently of each other, the user can select any number of check boxes at one time.

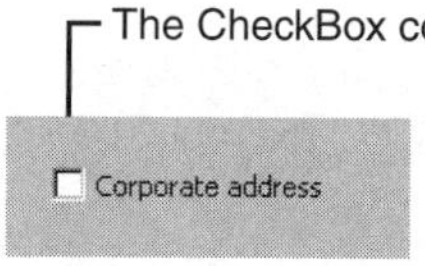

The CheckBox control provides an On/Off or Yes/No choice.

☐ Corporate address

Figure 6-21 A CheckBox control.

Controls, Fields, and Properties   **Chapter 6**

To bind a CheckBox control to a field

1. Right-click the CheckBox control, and then click Properties on the shortcut menu.
2. On the Value page, do one of the following:
   - ❑ Click New to create a new field. You can create a Yes/No, On/Off, True/False, or Icon field. When you select a Yes/No field, the selected value appears in the cell in the folder. If you select Icon, the CheckBox icon appears in the folder as selected or cleared.
   - ❑ Click Choose Field, point to User-Defined Fields In Folder, and then choose the field to which you want to bind the CheckBox control. In this example, the CheckBox control in Figure 6-21 is bound to the Corporate field.

> **Note** The CheckBox control must be bound to a Yes/No field type for the check box to operate properly.

To set the initial value of a CheckBox control

1. Right-click the CheckBox control, and then click Advanced Properties on the shortcut menu.
2. Click the Value cell, and then type *True*.
3. Click Apply, and then close the Advanced Properties window.

ComboBox Controls

Use ComboBox controls so users can either choose a value from the list portion of the control or enter text in the edit box portion of the control, as shown in Figure 6-22. When working with the ComboBox control, you create the control, bind it to a field, and then specify the values for the items in the combo box list.

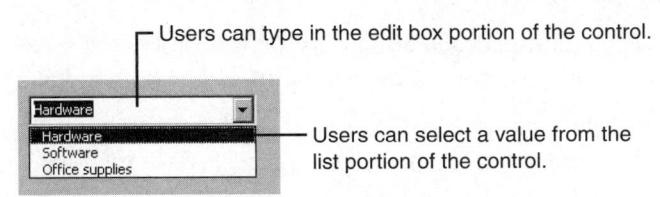

Figure 6-22 A Dropdown ComboBox control.

195

To bind the ComboBox control to a field

1. Right-click the ComboBox control, and then click Properties on the shortcut menu.

2. On the Value page, do one of the following:

   ❑ To create a new field, click New.

   ❑ To bind the ComboBox control to an existing field, click Choose Field, point to User-Defined Fields In Folder, and then click the field to which you want to bind the ComboBox control.

To select a list type

- In the List Type drop-down list box on the Value page, click either Dropdown or Droplist.

   Outlook provides two types of combo boxes that you can use. You can set the combo style at design time on the Value page of the field's Properties dialog box, or you can set the style at run time by programmatically setting the Style property. The ComboBox also supports the same ListStyle property as the ListBox control. See the ListStyle table under "ListBox Controls" later in this chapter.

Style	Description
DropDownCombo	Users can either select a value from the list or type a new value in the combo box.
DropDownList	Users must select a value from the list. Users cannot type a new value in the combo box.

To add values to the combo box list

- In the Possible Values text box on the Value page, type the values you want to appear in the list. Separate each value with a semicolon (;), as shown in Figure 6-23.

- You can also programmatically add items to the ComboBox. See Chapter 11 for examples. Use one of the following programmatic methods:

   ❑ The *AddItem* method allows you to loop through a collection and add the items one at a time. This method works well for a small number of items.

Controls, Fields, and Properties   Chapter 6

❏   The List and Column properties let you set or retrieve an array of values. List and Column properties are especially useful when you want to create multicolumn lists or combo boxes. If you assign a variant array to the List property of the control, you will enhance the performance of programmatically populating controls.

To set the initial value of a ComboBox control

■   In the Initial Value text box on the Value page, type the value that you want to appear in the edit box portion of the control when the form first appears, as shown in Figure 6-23.

You can set the MatchEntry property to determine how a ListBox or ComboBox responds to user input at the keyboard. Use the Advanced Properties dialog box at design time to set the MatchEntry property for a selected control or programmatically set the property at run time.

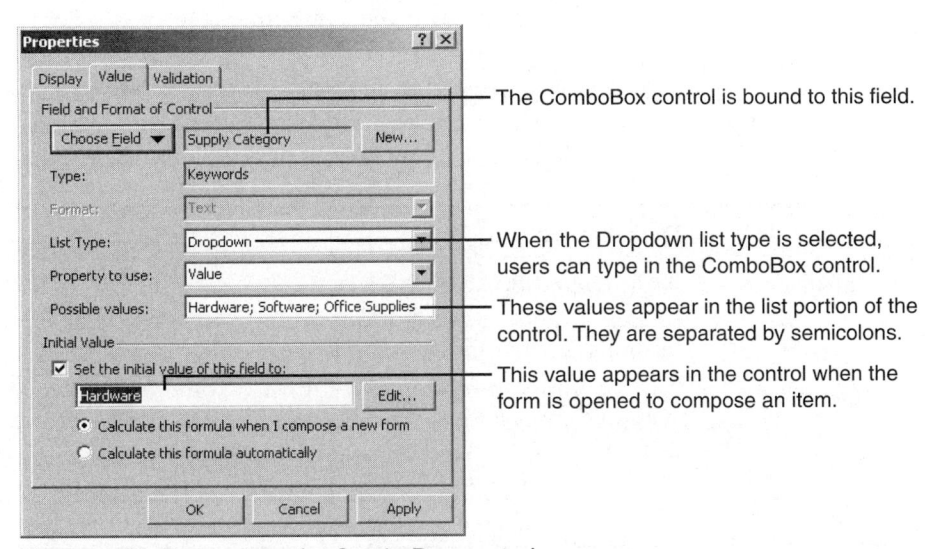

Figure 6-23 Properties of a ComboBox control.

Set the Match Entry Property To	To
None	Provide no matching.
FirstLetter	Compare the most recently typed letter to the first letter of each entry in the list. (The first match in the list is selected.)
Complete	Compare the user's entry and an exact match in an entry from the list.

> **Note** The matching feature resets after two seconds (six seconds in the Far East version). For example, if you have a list of the 50 United States and you type *CO* quickly, you will find Colorado. If it takes you longer than two seconds to type *CO*, however, you will find Ohio first because the auto-complete search resets between letters.

ListBox Controls

Use ListBox controls to show a list of values from which the user can select one or many values. To create a list box that enables users to select more than one value, you must bind the ListBox control to a Keywords field. List boxes that are bound to Keywords fields have check boxes that allow users to select multiple values, as shown in Figure 6-24. When the user selects multiple values in the ListBox control, the values appear in the view in an Outlook folder as comma-separated values.

Outlook provides two presentation styles for the ListBox control. You can set the style at design time by using the Advanced Properties dialog box for the control or at run time by programmatically setting the ListStyle property.

ListStyle	Description
Plain	Each item in the list box is in a separate row. Depending on the setting of the MultiSelect property, the user can select either one row or multiple rows in the control.
Option	An OptionButton or CheckBox appears at the beginning of each row. With this style, the user selects an item by clicking the option button or check box. Check boxes appear only when the MultiSelect property is set to either Multi or Extended.

To bind the ListBox control to a field

1. In Design mode, right-click the control, and then click Properties on the shortcut menu.

2. On the Value page, do one of the following:

    ❑ To bind the ListBox control to an existing field, click Choose Field, point to User-Defined Fields In Folder, and then click the field to which you want to bind the ListBox control. Items selected from this list will appear in the field to which this list is bound.

❑ To create a Keywords field, click New, and then click Keywords in the Type drop-down list box. With Keywords you can place several values in a single field, depending on what the user selects. These values can be used to group items within a folder, similar to the Categories field of Task items.

❑ To create a ListBox control without a Keywords field, click Text, Number, Currency, or Date/Time in the Type drop-down list box and then, in the Format dialog box, click to select a format. This information is transient and not stored in a field, but it can be accessed and manipulated by VBScript code. For more information, see Chapter 11.

When a ListBox control is bound to a Keywords field, multiple values can be selected in the control.

Multiple values in a Keywords field appear as comma-separated values in an Outlook view of the folder the user-defined field was created in. If this is in a Message form, the user-defined fields are created in the author's Inbox.

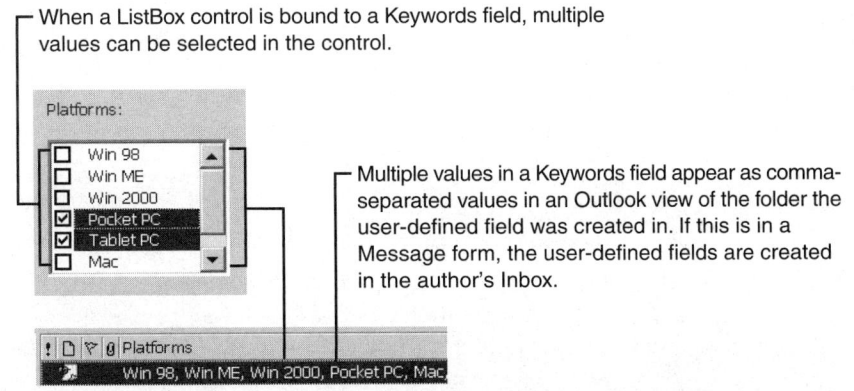

Figure 6-24 Values selected in a list box bound to a Keywords field are shown as comma-separated values in an Outlook view.

> **Note** Do not bind the ListBox control to a Yes/No, Combination, or Formula field.

To add values to the ListBox control

■ In the Possible Values text box on the Value page, type the values you want to appear in the list. Separate each value with a semicolon, as shown in Figure 6-25. You can also use the *AddItem* method or the List and Column properties to add items programmatically to the control.

Part III Building Blocks of Applications

To set the initial value of a ListBox control

- In the Initial Value text box on the Value page, do one of the following:

    ❑ To set the initial value to a single value, type the value that you want to appear as checked in the ListBox control when the user opens the form to compose an item, as shown in Figure 6-25.

    ❑ To set the initial value to multiple values, type the values that you want to appear as checked in the ListBox control when the user opens the form to compose an item. Separate each value in the Initial Value text box with a semicolon.

> **Note** The ListBox control can also display multiple columns, at which point it behaves more like a grid than a list box.

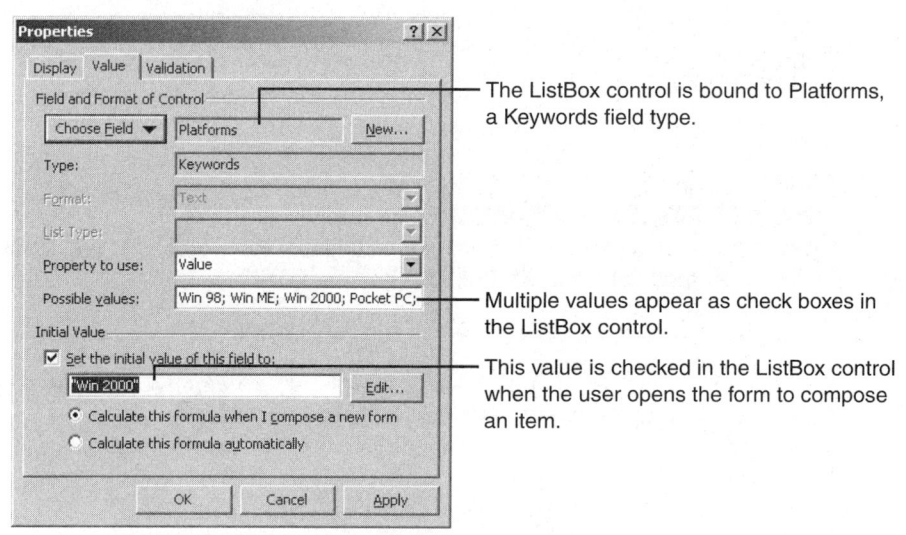

Figure 6-25 The values that you want to appear in the list are typed in the Possible Values text box.

CommandButton Controls

The CommandButton control, when clicked, triggers the Click event. Thus, you can write VBScript Click event procedures in the Script Editor for each CommandButton control, as shown in Figure 6-26.

200

Controls, Fields, and Properties Chapter 6

> **Important** Outlook supports only the Click event for most of its intrinsic controls. Some third-party extrinsic ActiveX controls might not support even the Click event, but most extrinsic ActiveX controls do support this event.

Users click the CommandButton control to trigger VBScript procedures.

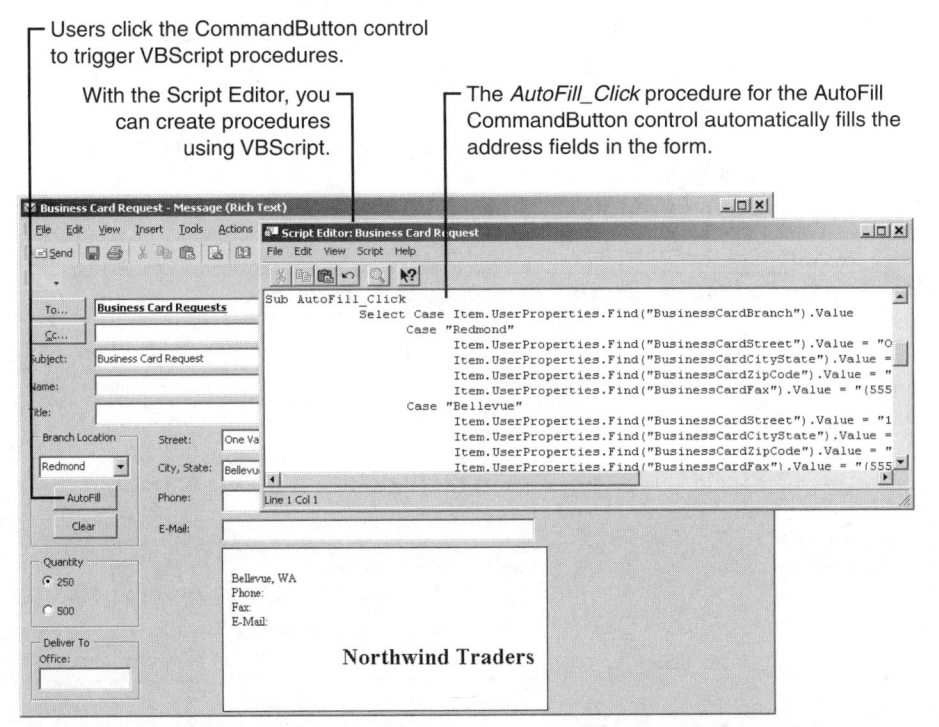

With the Script Editor, you can create procedures using VBScript.

The *AutoFill_Click* procedure for the AutoFill CommandButton control automatically fills the address fields in the form.

Figure 6-26 CommandButton controls on the Business Card Request form.

To add a CommandButton control

1. In Design mode, drag the control from the Control Toolbox to the form.

2. To set the caption for a CommandButton control, click the control. When the edit pointer appears, type the name in the control.

3. To specify a name for the CommandButton control, right-click the control, and then click Properties on the shortcut menu.

4. In the Name text box on the Display page, type a name, and then click OK.

Part III Building Blocks of Applications

To create a procedure for a CommandButton control

1. Click the View Code button on the Form Design toolbar.

2. In the Script Editor window, type *Sub* followed by a space, followed by *CommandButton1_Click*, where *CommandButton1* is the name of the control.

3. Add the necessary code to the procedure.
   End the procedure with an End Sub statement, as shown in the following example:

   ```
   Sub CommandButton1_Click
     MsgBox "This is a procedure for a CommandButton control"
   End Sub
   ```

4. Close window.

To test a CommandButton control Click procedure

1. On the Form menu, click Run This Form to switch the form into Run mode.

2. Click the command button.

3. To switch back to Design mode, close the Run window.

> **More Info** For more information about creating procedures for forms using Visual Basic Scripting Edition, see Chapter 11.

MultiPage Controls

Use MultiPage controls to provide multiple pages of information on a form, as shown in Figure 6-27.

To add a MultiPage control

- Drag the MultiPage control from the Control Toolbox to the form.

To add controls to the MultiPage control

- Switch to the page you want to add controls to, and then drag the controls you want from the Control Toolbox to the MultiPage control.

Controls, Fields, and Properties Chapter 6

Figure 6-27 The MultiPage control on the Compose page of the Get Info From Address Book form.

To insert, rename, delete, or move a page

- Right-click a tab on the MultiPage control, and then click Insert, Delete, Rename, or Move on the shortcut menu, as shown in Figure 6-28.

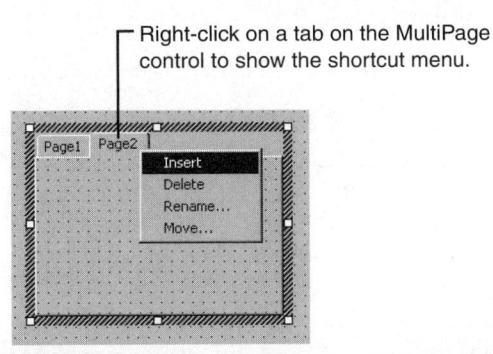

Figure 6-28 The shortcut menu of the MultiPage control.

How the TabStrip Control Differs from the MultiPage Control

With a MultiPage control, each page on the control usually contains a different set of controls. With the TabStrip control, however, each page contains the same controls. For example, you might use a TabStrip control to display the addresses of various companies. You set the title of each tab to the name of the company, and then you write code that, when you click a tab, updates the controls to show the address of that company.

203

Part III   Building Blocks of Applications

Image Controls

Use Image controls to contain graphic images, as shown in Figure 6-29.

To add a picture to an Image control

1. Right-click the Image control, and then click Advanced Properties on the shortcut menu.
2. Double-click the Picture cell, and then select the image.

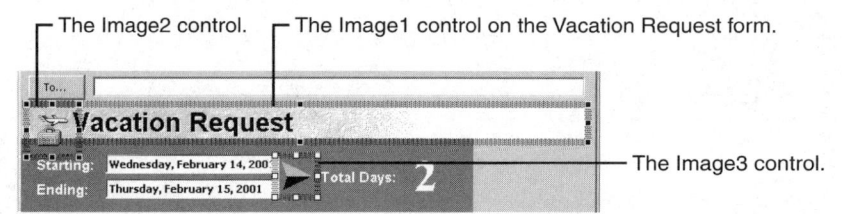

Figure 6-29 Image controls on the Vacation Request form.

To delete the picture in the Image control

- You must delete the Image control, so click to select the Image control, and then press the Delete key.

To size an image in the Image control

1. Right-click the Image control, and then click Advanced Properties.
2. Do one of the following.

To	Do This
Automatically size the control to the picture	In the AutoSize cell, click True.
Maintain the size of the picture, regardless of the size of the Image control	In the PictureSizeMode cell, click Clip.
Stretch the picture to fill the Image control	In the PictureSizeMode cell, click Stretch.
Enlarge the picture but still maintain the PictureAlignment property setting	In the PictureSizeMode cell, click Zoom.

> **Tip** The Click event fires for Image controls. You can create large command buttons containing graphics by using the Image control as shown in Figure 6-30. Drop an image on your form using the Control Toolbox, add a picture, and then stretch the picture using the PictureSizeMode property above. The image will have the appearance of a command button if you set the SpecialEffect property to Raised in the Advanced Properties dialog box. Write code for the image's Click event, and the job is complete.

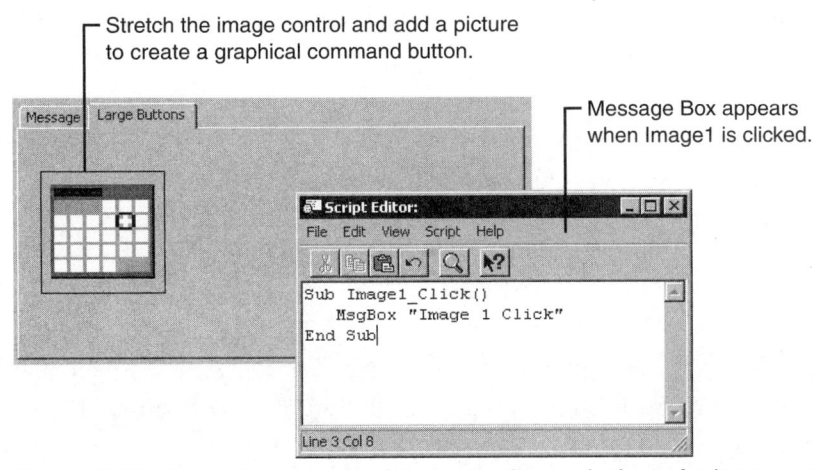

Figure 6-30 Use an Image control to create the equivalent of a large command button.

SpinButton Control

Use the SpinButton control to enable the user to increase or decrease numbers in a control. Although you can write script for the SpinButton control, it is not required to create a SpinButton control. To create a spin button for a control, you can bind the spin button to the same field that a TextBox control is bound to. Here is an example of how you can create a SpinButton control.

To add the TextBox control and bind it to a field

1. From the Control Toolbox, drag a TextBox control to the form.
2. Right-click the TextBox control, and then click Properties on the shortcut menu.

Part III   Building Blocks of Applications

3. Click the Value tab, and then click New.
4. In the Name text box, type a name for the field.
5. In the Type drop-down list box, click Number.
6. Click OK. If you want, select Calculate This Field Automatically, and then click OK again.

To add the SpinButton control and bind it to a field

1. From the Control Toolbox, drag a SpinButton control to the form and position it to the right of the TextBox control you just added.
2. Right-click the SpinButton control, and then click Properties on the shortcut menu.
3. Click the Value tab.
4. Click Choose Field, point to User-Defined Fields In Folder, and then click the field you just added.
5. Click OK.
6. Hold down the Ctrl key, and then right-click the SpinButton and TextBox controls.
7. On the shortcut menu, point to Make Same Size, and then click Height.
8. To test the SpinButton control, click Run This Form on the Form menu to enter Run mode, and then click the SpinButton control to increase or decrease the number in the TextBox control.

Controls That Require VBScript

In addition to the CommandButton control, the Control Toolbox provides several other controls that require VBScript to operate. These are the ToggleButton, TabStrip, and ScrollBar controls.

> **More Info**   For more information about these controls, see the Microsoft Outlook Visual Basic Reference Help.

Using Custom ActiveX Controls

If the Microsoft Forms controls that are available in the Outlook Control Toolbox do not satisfy your requirements, you can add either Microsoft or third-party ActiveX controls to your Outlook form. You can also use Visual Basic 6.0 or later to create your own custom ActiveX controls for use in Outlook forms. However, this strategy presents several problems that must be addressed in your solution.

- The ActiveX control must be installed and registered properly on every machine where you intend to run the custom form.

- You must possess a valid license to set the properties of the control in Design mode.

- None of the events supported by the ActiveX control—except the Click event—will fire in a custom Outlook form. For example, you cannot write VBScript code in your Outlook form to respond directly to the DblClick event if the user double-clicks a row in a data-bound grid.

- Not every ActiveX control can be bound to an Outlook user-defined field. You should test the ActiveX control's ability to bind its default property to an Outlook user-defined field.

One of the most frequent questions seen in the Outlook newsgroups is how to duplicate the date and time selection controls on the first page of the Appointment, Task, and Journal item forms. If you have purchased Microsoft Office Developer, you can use the ActiveX controls that ship with Office Developer. You can also obtain the same controls if you have a license for Microsoft Visual Basic 6.0 or later. The control that specifically replaces the Outlook date and time selection controls is the Microsoft DTPicker control, shown in Figure 6-31. The following procedure list assumes that you have installed either Office Developer or Visual Basic on your system.

To add a Date Selection control to your custom Outlook form

1. In form design mode, right-click the Controls Toolbox and select the Custom Controls command.
2. Check the Microsoft Date And Time Picker Control, Version 6.0, in the drop-down list box of available controls in the Additional Controls dialog box.
3. Click OK.

Part III   Building Blocks of Applications

4. Drag the DTPicker control from the Control Toolbox to your form.
5. Resize the control on your form if necessary.
6. Set the properties of the control using the Properties dialog box to bind the control to a user-defined or default field.
7. Set the Format property of the control using the Advanced Properties dialog box to specify how the control displays the date or time field to which it is bound.
8. Setting the UpDown property of the control to *True* provides spin buttons for date or time modification. If the UpDown property is *False*, the control will use a drop-down calendar that mimics the Outlook calendar control.

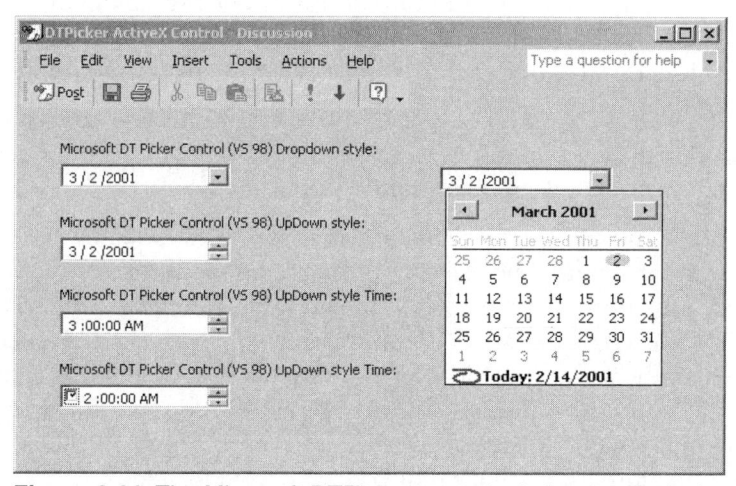

Figure 6-31   The Microsoft DTPicker control mimics the Outlook calendar control.

> **Note**   In addition to the Microsoft DTPicker control, several third-party date and time picker controls are available to Outlook developers. For additional information, visit *http://www.slipstick.com/dev/datepick.htm*. These controls must be installed on each client machine on which your application will run.

Select Multiple Controls and the Dominant Control

You can select multiple controls in three ways. In addition, when you select more than one control, one of the controls becomes a reference for the other controls and is called the dominant control. The sizing frame of the dominant control has black handles. Any other selected controls have white handles.

Selection Method	What Is Selected	Dominant Control
Shift+Click	All controls in an invisible rectangle around the selected controls	First control you select
Ctrl+Click	Individual controls, one at a time	Last control you select
Select Objects pointer in Control Toolbox	All controls that fall within or touch a rectangle you draw	Control nearest the mouse pointer when you begin drawing the rectangle

> **Tip** Use the following special tips when selecting controls on a form page:
> - The Ctrl+Click method may occasionally select additional controls that are near or adjacent to the selected controls. For more accuracy, use the Select Objects pointer method.
> - If you Ctrl+Click twice on a selected control, that control becomes the dominant control.
> - If you select a group of controls and then drag the selection to the Control Toolbox, the selected controls will be available as an item to drag from the Control Toolbox to another page on this form or on a different form. When you drag the icon for these controls to a page, the alignment and size of the controls are maintained.

Where To Go from Here

Microsoft Knowledge Base Articles Microsoft Knowledge Base articles are available on the Web at *http://support.microsoft.com/support*. Also see "Controls, Fields, and Properties (Chapter 6) KB Articles" in the Microsoft Web Sites folder under the Help And Web Sites folder on the companion CD.

7

Actions

Action properties make it possible for you to define custom responses for forms, instead of using the standard Reply and Reply To Folder actions. For example, with the Vacation Request form, a supervisor can reply to a vacation request item by choosing an Approve Vacation or Deny Vacation action, rather than by using the standard Reply action.

This chapter describes the different ways of creating responses for forms. Specifically, topics include the following:

- **Voting buttons for Message forms**   The easiest way to create responses for Message forms is to use voting buttons. An example shows how voting buttons are created for an Art Approval form.

- **Reply actions for Message forms**   As an example, you'll look at how Reply actions are implemented for the Vacation Request form.

- **Reply To Folder actions for Post forms**   As an example, you'll look at how custom responses are designed for the Course Catalog Entry in the Training Management folder.

Voting Buttons for Message Forms

Voting buttons, which are available only with Message forms, provide an easy way for users to collect quick feedback from other users. When you specify voting button options for a form, two important things happen:

- Voting buttons are added to the Read page, as shown in Figure 7-1.

- The location of the Tracking item is specified. The Tracking item contains the voting results and shows them on the Tracking page, which is shown in Figure 7-2.

Part III Building Blocks of Applications

Voting buttons are added to the Read page of the Art Approval form. Reviewers click Approve or Reject to send their response to the artist.

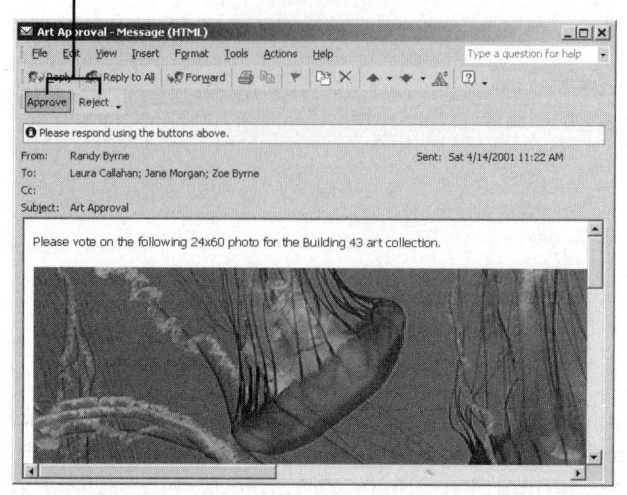

Figure 7-1 The Read page of the Art Approval form. This page is used by members of the Art Approval Committee to approve or reject the art submitted by the artist.

In the following section, you'll create an Art Approval form that has voting buttons and a Tracking item. When you're done, you'll understand how voting buttons work and how they can be used to collect feedback from other users.

Overview of the Art Approval Form

The Art Approval form illustrates the easiest way to create responses for Message forms. It uses voting buttons, which send responses to a folder for review. The Art Approval form, shown in Figure 7-3, is used by an artist to send an attached file of electronic art to users on the Art Approval Committee distribution list for review. The recipients review the attached file and then vote to approve or reject. To see the voting results, the artist opens the Art Approval Tracking item in the Art Approval folder.

Create the Art Approval Folder

Before you create the Art Approval form, create an Art Approval folder in your Mailbox folder. This is where you'll store the Tracking item that tallies responses.

Actions   Chapter 7

The Tracking item is stored in the Art Approval folder in the user's Mailbox folder.

The Tracking item tallies the responses. The user double-clicks the Tracking item to open it.

The Tracking page of the Tracking item.

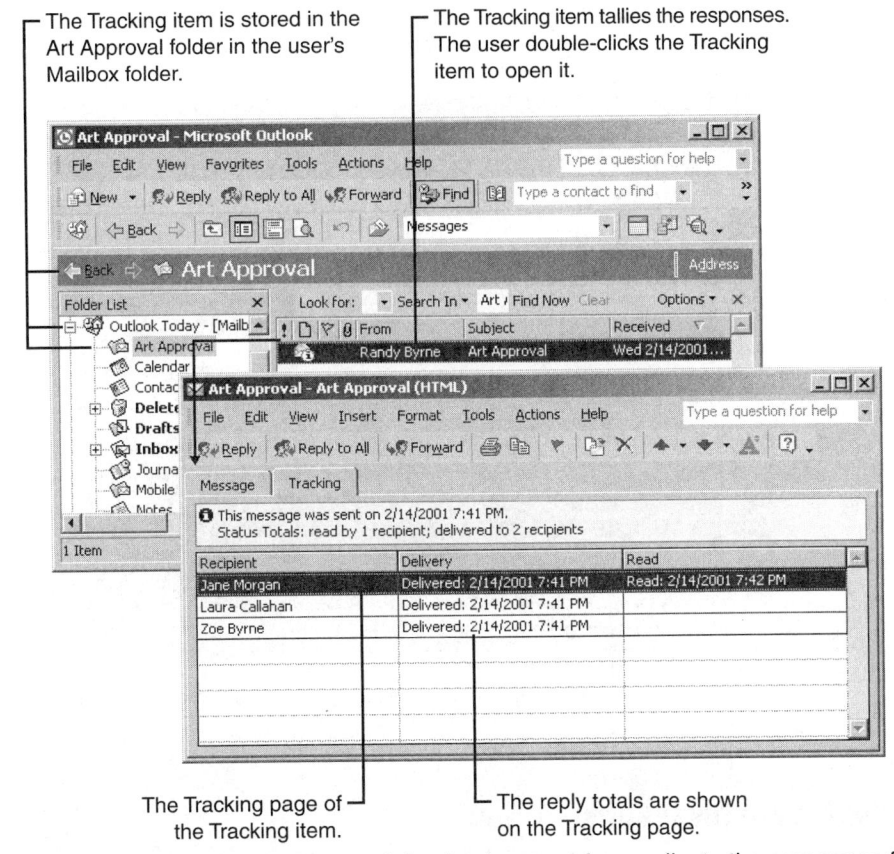

The reply totals are shown on the Tracking page.

Figure 7-2 The Tracking page of the Art Approval form collects the responses from the Art Approval Committee members.

To create the Art Approval folder

1. In the Folder List, right-click the Mailbox folder and then click New Folder.
2. In the Name text box, type *Art Approval* and then click OK.
3. If a dialog box appears asking if you want to Add A Shortcut To Outlook Bar, click No.

213

Part III Building Blocks of Applications

The To field is preaddressed to the Art Approval Committee distribution list.

The initial value of the Subject field is set to Art Approval.

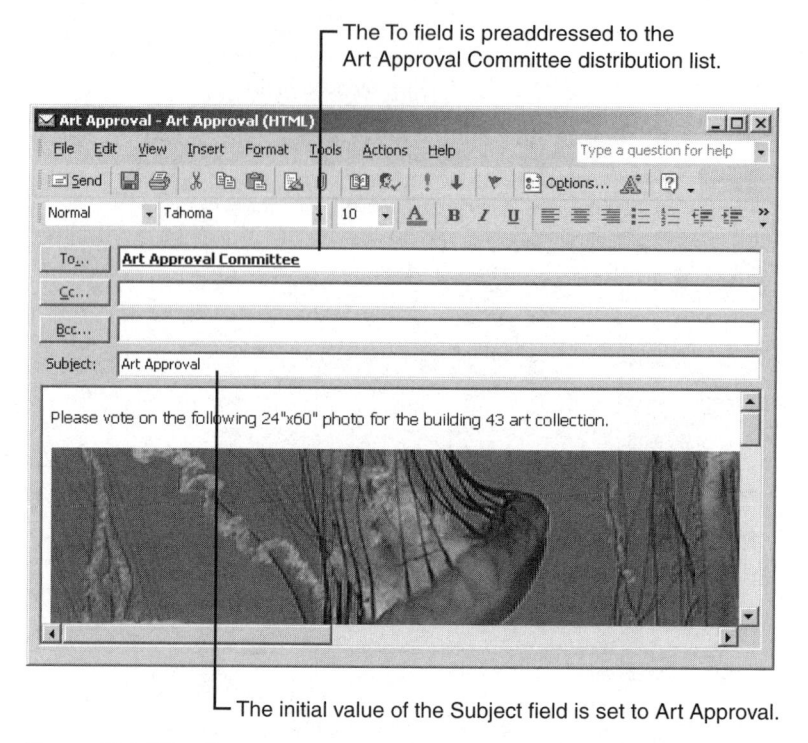

Figure 7-3 The Compose page of the Art Approval form.

Create the Art Approval Form

To create the Art Approval form, first open the standard Message form. Set the initial value of the To and Subject fields. Next specify voting button options for the form. Finally publish the form in your Personal Forms Library.

Open the Form in Run Mode

This form should be built entirely in Run mode.

> **Note** The following instructions assume that you are using Outlook as your default e-mail editor. In Outlook 2002, Word is the default e-mail editor. To change your default e-mail editor, select Options on the Tools menu, click the Mail Format tab, and uncheck Use Microsoft Word To Edit E-Mail Messages.

To open the standard Message form

1. In the Folder List or from the Outlook Shortcut bar, click Inbox.
2. Select New Mail Message from the Outlook Actions menu.

Preaddress the To Field

Quite often, you'll want to preaddress a form to the people you send the form to on a regular basis. To preaddress a form, you set the initial value of the To field. In this chapter's example, the initial value of the To field is set to the Art Approval Committee distribution list. For the form that you create, however, you will preaddress the form to your own address. You must set the initial value of the To field at run time because you cannot open the Address Book from the To field at design time.

> **More Info** To create a distribution list, see Microsoft Outlook Help.

To preaddress the form

1. On the opened form, click the To button.
2. Double-click the address you want to set as the initial value in the To field. (For this example, you can select your own address.)
3. Click OK.

Set the Initial Value of the Subject Field

For forms that serve a specific purpose, such as the Art Approval form, it makes sense to set the initial value of the Subject field. This saves the user the time of filling in the field and ensures that recipients see a consistent subject field each time they receive an Art Approval item in their Inboxes.

To set the initial value of the Subject field

- Type *Art Approval* in the Subject text box.

Set Options for the Art Approval Form

Options are set by clicking the Options icon on the form's Standard toolbar, which opens the Message Options window. Here you specify voting button, menu options, and desired tracking and tallying information. Remember, the Options icon is available only in Message forms.

Set voting button options Voting buttons appear on the Read page of the form and allow the user to respond to the Art Approval item by clicking the Approve or Reject button. The Read page of the form appears when the user double-clicks an Art Approval item in the Inbox.

To specify voting buttons

1. Select the Use Voting Buttons check box.//
2. In the Use Voting Buttons text box, type the text you want to appear on the voting buttons or select the values from the list. If you type values, you must separate each value with a semicolon.

Specify recipients of the replies When you select the Have Replies Sent To check box, your address is automatically added to the text box. You can add additional addresses to the text box, or you can replace your address with another.

To specify the reply address

1. Select the Have Replies Sent To check box.
2. To specify additional names, click Select Names and then double-click the names you want.
3. When the appropriate addresses appear in the Message Recipients box, click OK.

> **Note** When the approval committee votes, their replies will go to the Inbox or Inboxes specified here. The tally of votes (tracking) will be stored in the folder specified in the Save Sent Message To text box.

Specify where the tracking item is stored With forms that have voting buttons, Outlook provides an automatic tally of the voting button responses in a saved item in a folder. This folder must be located in your Mailbox folder. The default folder is the Sent Items folder, but you can change it.

To specify where the Tracking item is stored

1. On the Message Options window, choose Save Sent Message To and then click Browse.

Actions   Chapter 7

2. In the Folders list box, click the Art Approval folder and then click OK.

3. Click Close to save your options.

As shown in Figure 7-4, the Save Sent Message To option is set to the Art Approval folder. So when an Art Approval item is sent, an Art Approval item is also saved in the Art Approval folder in your Mailbox folder. After you receive and open voting responses in your Inbox, the responses are written to the Tracking item in the Art Approval folder. If this seems a little confusing right now, don't worry. You'll go through the process step by step.

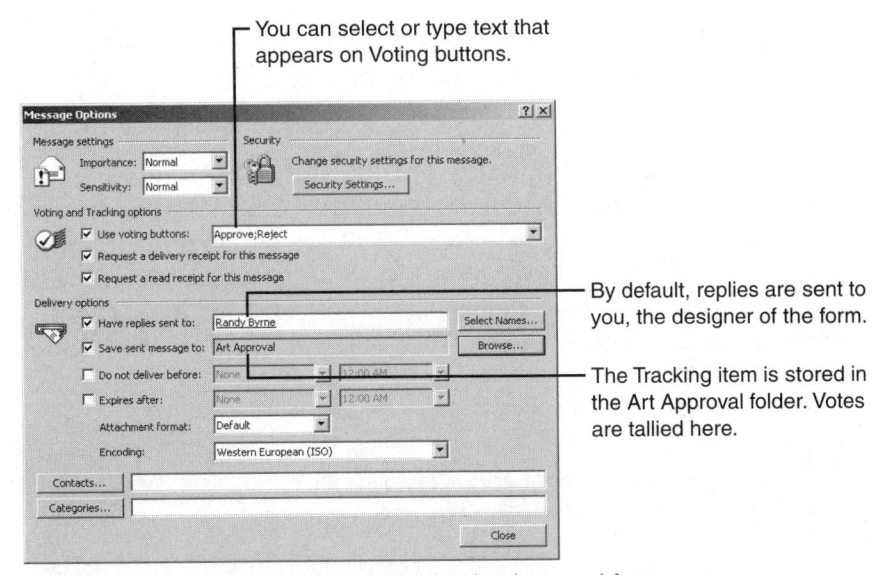

Figure 7-4 Voting button options for the Art Approval form.

Publish the Form to the Personal Forms Library

After the form is created and modified, you publish the form to your Personal Forms Library so that you can open and test the form.

To publish the form

1. Select Forms on the Tools menu, and then click Publish Form As.

2. If Personal Forms Library does not appear in the Look In drop-down list box, click the drop-down list box and select Personal Forms Library from the box.

3. In the Display Name text box and the Form Name text box, type *Art Approval* or whatever you want to name the form, and then click Publish.

217

4. If the Save Form Definition With Item message box appears, choose No for the Do You Want This Checkbox Selected prompt.

5. Close the form. At the Do You Want To Save Changes prompt, choose No for most cases, or choose Yes if you want a backup copy saved in the Drafts folder.

The form is saved in its final form by publishing it. The Save prompt, on the other hand, creates a copy in the Drafts folder.

> **More Info** For more information about where to publish forms, see Chapter 13, "Distributing and Securing Applications."

How Actions Are Automatically Set for Voting Buttons

When you specify voting buttons and publish a form, Outlook automatically adds custom actions to the Actions page. There are two important points to remember about these actions. First, when you specify voting buttons, the Creates Form Of Type property is set to the standard Message form (IPM.Note). Second, the Address Form Like property is set to Response, as shown in Figure 7-5.

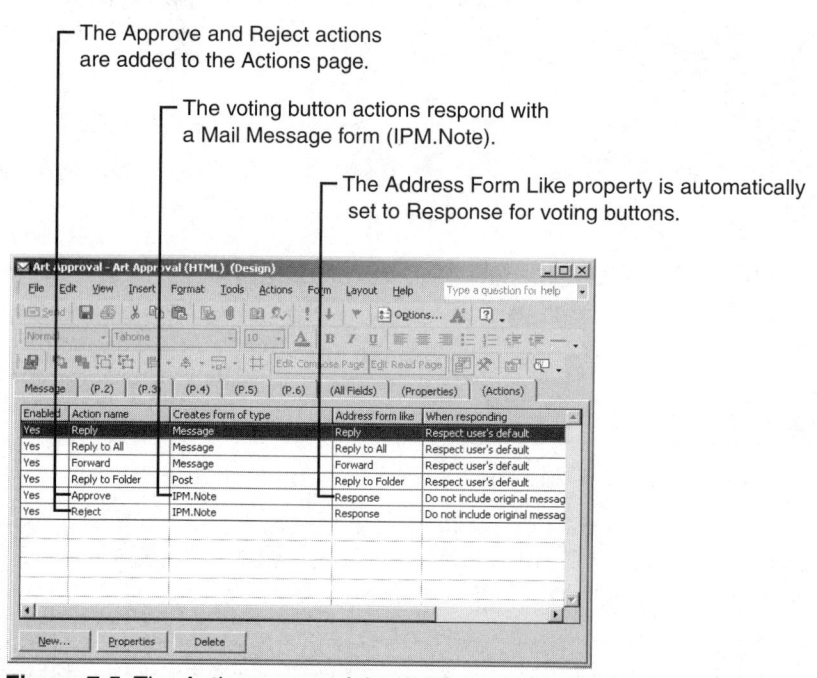

Figure 7-5 The Actions page of the Art Approval form. Approve and Reject actions are automatically added when you specify the voting buttons on the Options page.

Test the Art Approval Form

Now you open the Art Approval form and then send an Art Approval item to your Inbox.

Send an Art Approval Item

Open the Art Approval form from your Personal Forms Library. When you open the form, you will see the Compose page of the form. Using the Compose page, you send an Art Approval item to your Inbox.

To send the Art Approval form

1. On the Outlook File menu, select New and then click Choose Form.
2. In the Look In drop-down list box, click Personal Forms Library and then double-click Art Approval.
3. On the Insert menu, click File and then double-click a file to insert in the message box on the Art Approval form.
4. Click the Send button.

Use the Voting Buttons To Respond

Now you open the Art Approval item in your Inbox. Then you click one of the voting buttons.

To vote on the item

1. Double-click the Art Approval item in the Inbox to which the form was addressed in the To box.
2. Click Approve.
3. Click Send The Response Now, and then click OK.
4. Close the Art Approval form.

Review Replies

Open the Art Approval Reply in your Inbox. Then you open the Tracking item in the Art Approval folder.

> **Important** The voting button responses are tallied in the Tracking item only after the response items are opened in your Inbox. If the items are not opened, the results are not tallied in the Tracking item. If no response items are opened, the Tracking page is not available on the Tracking form.

Part III   Building Blocks of Applications

To open the response item in your Inbox

- In your Inbox, double-click the Art Approval item.

To open the Tracking item

1. In the Folder List, open the Art Approval folder.
2. Double-click the Tracking item, as shown in Figure 7-2 earlier in this chapter.
3. The Tracking item is identified by an information icon, as shown in Figure 7-6.
4. Click the Tracking tab.

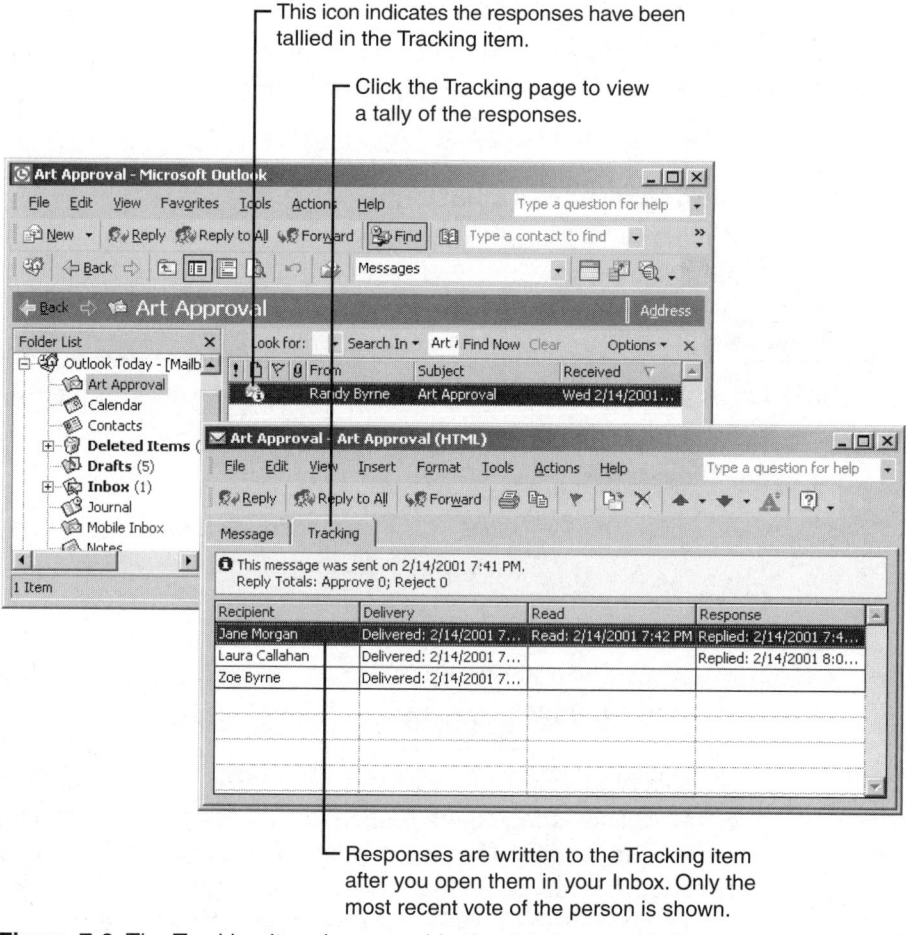

Figure 7-6 The Tracking item is opened in the Art Approval folder.

220

Reply Actions for Message Forms

When creating applications with Message forms, you often create Reply actions that open custom forms instead of the standard Message form. For example, the Vacation Request form has two custom actions: the Approve Vacation action activates the Vacation Approved form, and the Deny Vacation action activates the Vacation Denied form.

In this section, we create custom Reply actions for Message forms. Throughout this section, we use the Vacation Request application for examples of how to implement Reply actions with Message forms.

To open the Vacation Request folder

- In the Folder List, expand the Building Microsoft Outlook 2002 Applications folder and then expand the Building Blocks folder. Then click the Vacation Request folder.

> **Note** If you haven't installed the Building Microsoft Outlook 2002 Applications folder, see the Introduction of this book for instructions.

Overview of the Vacation Request Application

The Vacation Request application consists of four forms: Vacation Request, Vacation Approved, Vacation Denied, and Vacation Report. All forms are intentionally left unhidden in this folder so you can view them.

To view a Vacation Request form

1. On the Actions menu, view the forms at the bottom of the menu.
2. Click New Vacation Request.

Vacation Request form The form opens in Compose page. The user can compose a Vacation Request item and send it to his supervisor. When the receiving supervisor opens the form from her Inbox, she sees the Vacation Request Read page. It contains the Approve Vacation and Deny Vacation buttons, as shown in Figure 7-7.

Part III Building Blocks of Applications

- This action button opens the Vacation Approved form.
- This action button opens the Vacation Denied form.

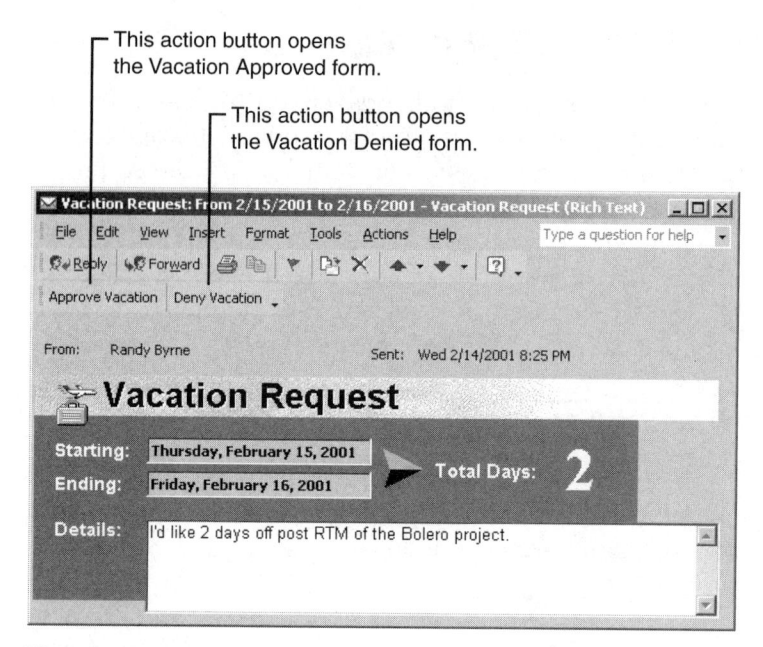

Figure 7-7 The Read page of the Vacation Request form.

Vacation Approved form The supervisor sees the Compose page of the Vacation Approved form when she clicks the Approve Vacation button on the Vacation Request form. She then clicks Send to route the approved vacation request to the user.

Vacation Denied form The supervisor sees the Compose page of this form when she clicks the Deny Vacation button on the Vacation Request form. She can then click Send to route the denied vacation request to the user.

Vacation Report form This form lets the user send the supervisor a report of the vacation days taken. The supervisor can then track the days available for each employee.

Here the discussion focuses primarily on the Vacation Request form and its associated actions. Along the way, you will also see a custom Reply action.

Actions for the Vacation Request Form

To get familiar with actions, take a look at the Actions page for the Vacation Request form, as shown in Figure 7-8.

Actions   Chapter 7

> **To view the Actions page for the Vacation Request form**

- In the Design mode of the Vacation Request form, click the Actions page.

— This action places an Approve Vacation button on the Read page. When the button is clicked, it opens the Vacation Approved form.

— This action places a Deny Vacation button on the Read page. When the button is clicked, it opens the Vacation Denied form.

— Click here to show the Actions page.

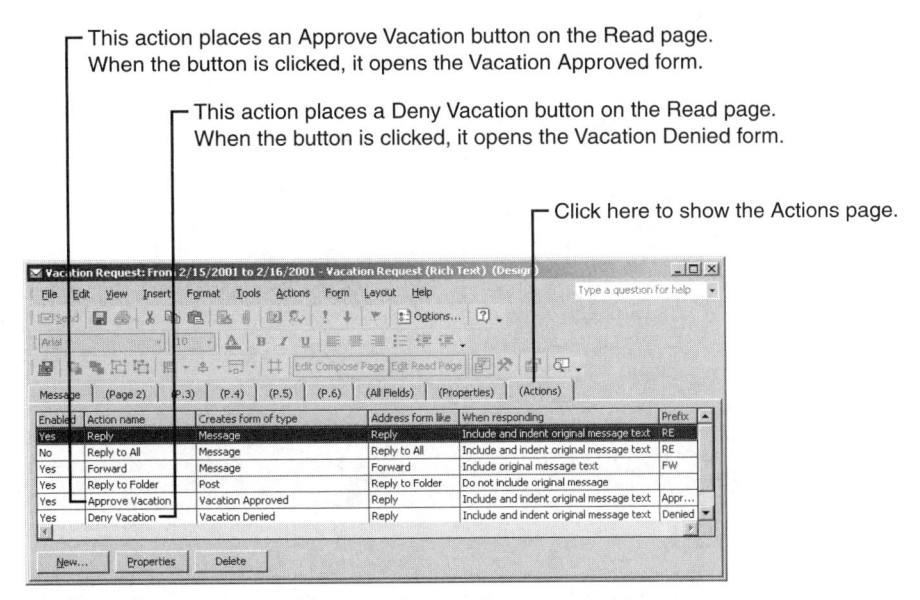

Figure 7-8 The Actions page for the Vacation Request form.

New Reply Actions

When you create new Reply actions, you specify that custom command buttons and menu commands are added to the form. The menu commands and buttons, when clicked, activate a custom form that lets the user reply to an item. For example, the Vacation Request form has a custom Approve Vacation action. When a supervisor opens a Vacation Request form, she can click the Approve Vacation button to open the Vacation Approved form, as shown in Figure 7-9.

The supervisor can then click the Send button to send the Vacation Approved item to the person who requested it. When the Vacation Approved form is opened, the original message is copied from the Vacation Request form to the message box of the Vacation Approved form. Likewise, the From field is copied to the To field, and the values in the StartDate, EndDate, and TotalDays fields are copied from the Vacation Request form to the Vacation Approved form.

223

Part III Building Blocks of Applications

On the Read page of the Vacation Request form, the Approve Vacation button opens the Vacation Approved form.

The supervisor clicks the Send button to send the response to the requester.

The original message is copied to the message box of the Vacation Approved form.

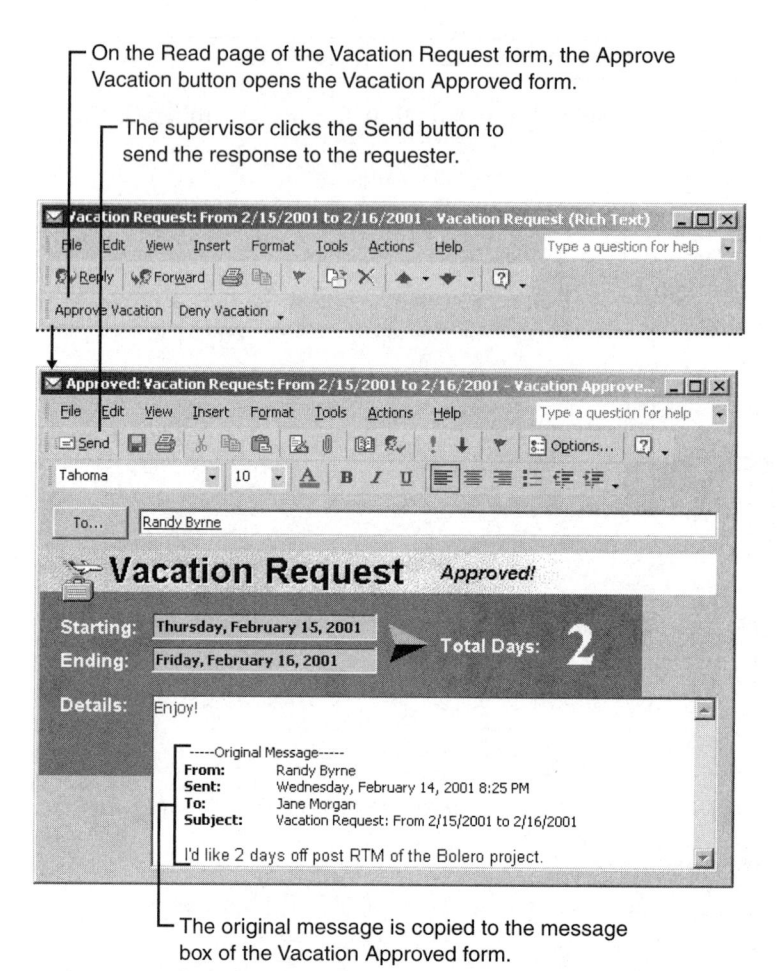

Figure 7-9 The Read page (partial) of the Vacation Request form and the Compose page of the Vacation Approved form.

The Approve Vacation action   Now let's take a look at the properties associated with the Approve Vacation action.

To view the Approve Vacation action

1. Open the Vacation Request form by selecting the Vacation Request folder from the Folder List. Then click New Vacation Request on the Actions menu.

2. In Design mode, click on the Actions page and then double-click the Approve Vacation action.

Actions   Chapter 7

The Form Action Properties dialog box, as shown in Figure 7-10, allows you to create new actions and to modify existing actions. With this dialog box, you specify the text that appears on the action button and menu, the form that appears when the button is clicked, and whether the original message is copied to the Reply item.

- This option determines if action buttons and menu commands are visible on the Read page.
- Text that appears on the action button on the Read page of the form
- Form that is activated when the action button is clicked
- This option specifies if and how the original item is copied to the Reply item message box.
- This option determines how the To, Cc, and Subject fields are set up in the Reply item.
- These options specify if the Reply form is opened or if the item is sent immediately.

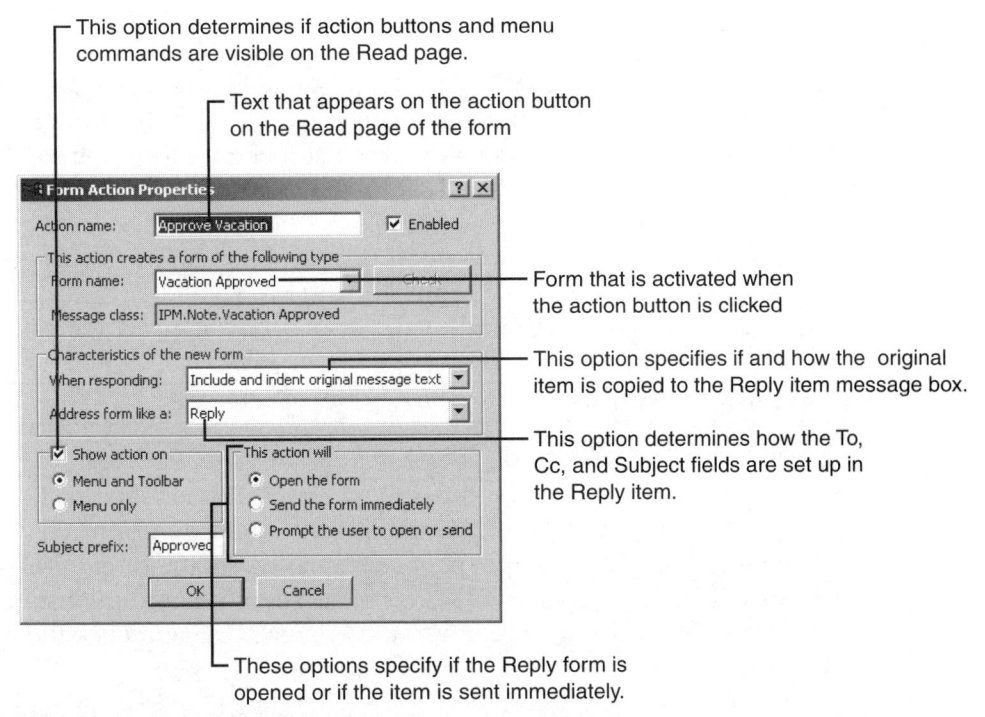

Figure 7-10 The Form Action Properties dialog box.

> **More Info** To create a new Action Item, see "Create a New Action" in Chapter 4, "Design a Custom Application."

Action Name The Action Name text box, as shown above in Figure 7-10, defines the name of both the menu command and command button that open the associated custom Reply form. The custom action button appears on the Read page of the form.

225

The custom menu command appears in two places:

- On the Outlook Actions menu when an item created with the associated form is selected in a folder. For example, with the Vacation Request form, the Approve Vacation command appears on the Actions menu when a Vacation Request item is selected in the Inbox.

- On the Form Actions menu of the Read page.

Form Name and Message Class The Form Name box contains the name of the form that is opened when the menu command or command button is selected. The Message Class box contains the internal identifier for the form. When you select a form in the Form Name box, the message class automatically appears in the Message Class box.

The Form Name combo box contains the names of the forms published in the active folder. In addition, it contains a Forms value that you can use to select from forms in the Organizational, Personal, or Standard Forms Libraries.

To specify a form name

Do one of the following:

- In the Form Name combo box, type a form name and then click Check to search for the form. If Outlook cannot find the form, you see a message box. If this happens, you should create the form before you specify the form name. After you create the form and publish it in a forms library, you can return to the original form and click the name of the form in the Form Name combo box.

- In the Form Name combo box, click a Form Name from the drop-down list.

- In the Form Name combo box, click Forms on the drop-down list. In the Choose Form box, double-click the form you want.

Characteristics Of The New Form Under Characteristics Of The New Form, you can specify whether the original message is copied to the message box of the Reply form. In addition, you can specify how the values in the From, Cc, and Subject fields are copied from the original form to the Reply form.

When Responding For Reply actions, you can specify if the contents of the original item are copied to the message box of the Reply item. You can also specify how the contents of the message box are copied. The default setting for this property is Respect User's Default. In Outlook, the user can set the When Replying To A Message option on the Email Options page of the Options dialog box (Tools

Actions   Chapter 7

menu). By default, this property is set for the user to Include And Indent Original Message Text. Therefore, if you have Respect User's Default selected in the When Responding drop-down list box, you can assume that for most users the message box on the Reply form includes and indents the original message. If you want to override the user's When Replying To A Message preference, click another option in the When Responding drop-down list box to define explicitly how you want the contents of the message box to appear on the Reply form.

Here are a few general guidelines for setting the When Responding option for Message forms.

- If the original message is brief, click Include And Indent Original Message Text. As shown earlier in Figure 7-10, this is the option that is selected for the Approve Vacation action in the Vacation Request form.

- If you want to include a shortcut to the message in the response item, click Attach Link To Original Message.

Address Form Like A   For Message forms, you almost always choose Reply for this option. When you choose Reply, the To field of the Reply form contains the contents of the From field of the original item, and the Cc field is empty. The Subject field, unless otherwise specified, contains RE:, followed by the contents of the Subject field of the original item.

The following table describes how the Address Form Like A options set up the Reply form.

Option	Description
Reply	This sets up the Reply form so the To field contains the contents of the From field of the original item. The Cc field is empty. The Subject field contains whatever is specified in the Subject Prefix box of the Form Action Properties dialog box, such as RE:. It is followed by the contents of the Subject field of the original item.
Reply To All	This sets up the Reply form so the To field contains the contents of the From and Cc fields of the original item. The Subject field contains RE:, or whatever you specify, followed by the contents of the Subject field of the original item.
Forward	This sets up the form so the To and Cc fields are empty and the Subject field contains FW:, or whatever you specify, followed by the contents of the Subject field of the original item.

(continued)

Option	Description
Reply To Folder	This sets up the Reply form so the Post To field contains the active folder address, the Conversation field contains the subject of the original item, and the Subject field is empty. In most cases, the Conversation field is not visible on a form. The Conversation field contains the value of the Subject of the original item.
Response	This is used exclusively for voting button actions.

Show Action On Most of the time, you can leave the default Menu and Toolbar options for a form. However, there may be times when you want to control the placement of the custom action buttons on the form. For example, you may want to add a command button to the bottom of the form and then write a macro for the command button to activate the Reply form when the button is clicked. If this is the case, you can click the Menu Only option, or uncheck the Show Action On box so that it will not show in either the menu or the toolbar.

This Action Will For the Vacation Request form, the Approve action, when initiated, opens the Vacation Approved form. For most actions, you should specify Open The Form under This Action Will. However, there might be cases when you choose the Send The Form Immediately option. For example, you might send a form to a user requesting an updated phone number and address. Rather than opening a Reply form, the user can fill in the fields on the original form and then click the custom action button. The Reply form is then activated but isn't visible to the user. Values from the originating form are then copied to the Reply form. If you specify the Send The Form Immediately option, you must still create the Reply form. Also, you must ensure that the fields you want filled in on the invisible Reply form are included on the original form.

Subject Prefix This shows the prefix that appears in the Subject text box of the Reply form. The prefix is RE: by default. For example, for the Approve Vacation action, the Approve prefix appears in the Subject text box of the Vacation Approved form. When the person who requested the vacation receives the Approved Vacation item in his Inbox, the text in the Subject column in the folder tells him his vacation is approved.

How Field Values Are Copied to the Reply Form

Outlook does not provide a way to explicitly define the field values that are copied from custom fields on the original form to custom fields on the Reply form. Rather, you accomplish this by using the same fields for both forms, as shown in Figure 7-11. When the field is shared between the original and Reply forms, the values are automatically copied from the original form to the Reply form at run time.

For example, the following fields are located on both the Vacation Request form and the Vacation Approved form: Subject, TotalDays, StartDate, and EndDate. When an Approve Vacation action is initiated, the values in these fields are copied from the Vacation Request form to the Vacation Approved form.

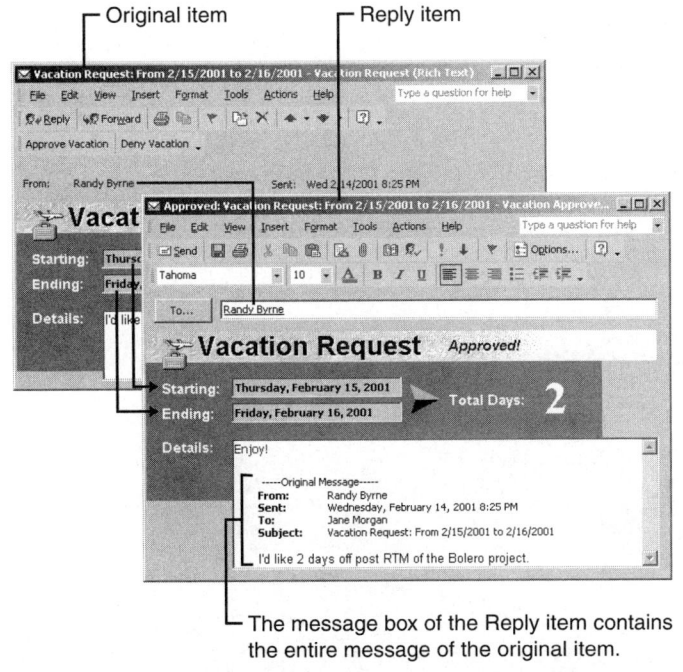

Figure 7-11 Values between fields common to both the original and Reply forms are copied to the Reply form.

> **Important** To ensure that field values are copied between the original form and the Reply form, use the same fields for both forms. For example, for the Vacation Request application, the TotalDays, StartDate, and EndDate fields are used for the Vacation Request form.

Part III   Building Blocks of Applications

> **Note**   In Figure 7-11, the Subject field is not visible. Instead, it is located on page 2, a hidden page. The Subject text, however, is copied from the original item to the Reply item and does appear in the Subject box on the Read page of the Reply item.

Vacation Request Reply Forms

In most cases, the custom Reply form is very similar to the original form. Quite often, you can use the original form as a template for the Reply form. For example, the Vacation Approved form is a Reply form based on the Vacation Request form. Only a few modifications have been made:

- The custom Reply actions are removed.
- The form description is changed, as shown in Figure 7-12.

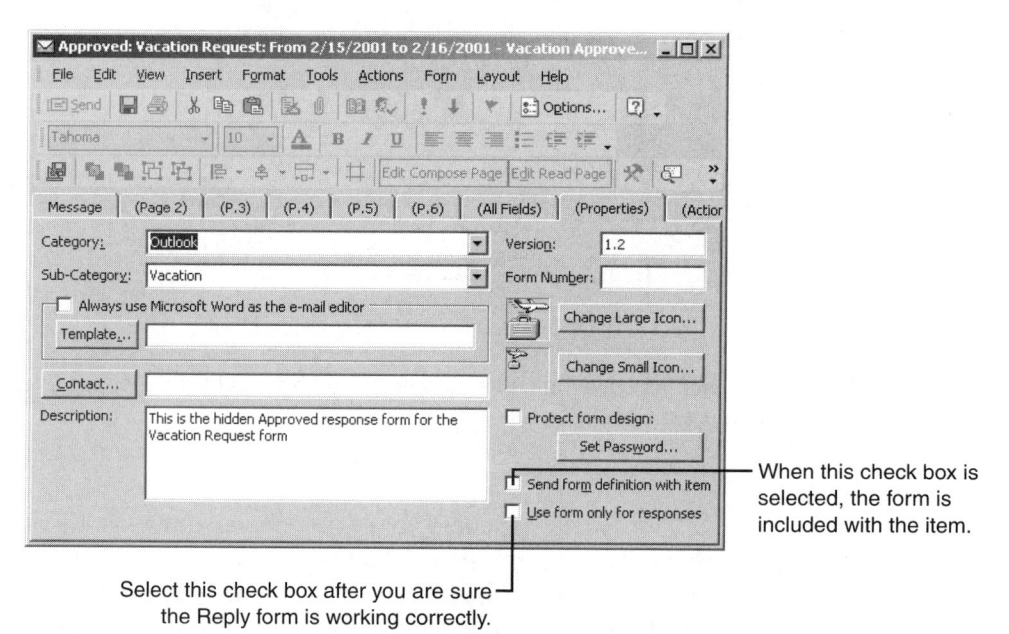

Figure 7-12   The form description is changed for the Reply form.

Actions   Chapter 7

> **More Info**   For more information on creating and modifying forms, see "Open the Form and Switch to Design Mode" in Chapter 5, "Forms."

Publish Reply Forms

For Reply forms to work correctly, they must be available on the user's system. Before you publish the forms, however, it's a good idea to make a backup copy.

To make a backup copy of a form

1. With the form open, click Save As on the File menu.
2. In the Save In drop-down list box, select the default Outlook template folder, such as C:\Documents and Settings*UserName*\Application Data\Microsoft\Templates.
3. In the File Name text box, type a name for the form.
4. In the Save As Type drop-down list box, select Outlook Template (.oft).
5. Click Save.

To open your backup copy of a form

1. Select New on the File menu, and then click Choose Form.
2. Click User Templates In File System in the Look In drop-down list box, and then click the form you'd like to open.

After you make a backup copy of the form, you can publish it to one of the following forms libraries:

- **Organizational Forms Library**   Publish the form in this library if you want the form to be available to all users in your organization.

- **Personal Forms Library**   Publish the form in this library if you intend to use the form for personal use. The Personal Forms Library is also a good place to publish forms when you want to test them.

- **The forms library of a folder**   Publish the form in the forms library of a folder if the form is integrated with the folder.

Part III Building Blocks of Applications

> **More Info** For more information about where to publish forms, see Chapter 13.

To publish a form

1. On the Tools menu, select Forms and then click Publish Form As.
2. Click the Look In drop-down list box, and select the forms library you want to publish in.
3. In the Display Name text box and the Form Name text box, type a name for the form and then click Publish.

Test the Forms

After you publish the forms to a forms library, you should run the forms to make sure they work as expected. For example, here's how you publish and test the Vacation Request forms.

To publish the Vacation Request forms

1. In the Vacation Request folder, click New Vacation Request on the Actions menu.
2. On the Tools menu, select Forms and then click Design This Form to switch to Design mode.
3. On the Tools menu, select Forms and then click Publish Form As.
4. Click the Look In drop-down list box, and then click Personal Forms Library.
5. Type a name for the form in the Display Name text box. The Form Name will be identical by default, but it can be changed if you want.
6. Click Publish.
7. Close the form.
8. On the Actions menu, click New Vacation Approved, and then repeat steps 2 through 7.
9. On the Actions menu, click New Vacation Denied, and then repeat steps 2 through 7.

> **To test the Vacation Request forms**

1. Select New on the File menu, and then click Choose Form.
2. In the Look In drop-down list box, select Personal Forms Library and click Vacation Request.
3. Address the form to yourself, and then click the Send button.
4. When the Vacation Request item arrives in your Inbox, double-click it to open it.
5. Click the Approve Vacation button.
6. Click Send.
7. When the Approved Vacation item arrives in your Inbox, double-click it to open it.

> **Note** Remember to keep forms updated and synchronized with each other by performing the following forms maintenance:
>
> ❑ Keep fields uniform on both Compose and Read pages.
>
> ❑ If form names are changed, update the links between the action and the form. See the section "The Create Offering Action" later in this chapter.

Set the Hidden Properties for Response Forms

After you publish and test the forms, you select the Hidden option for response forms so that the response forms can be opened only as a response to an item. For example, if the Hidden check box is selected for the Vacation Approved form and the form is published in the Personal Forms Library, the Vacation Approved form name does not appear in the forms list in the New Form dialog box. Users can only open the form when an associated Vacation Request item is selected in the Inbox or when the Vacation Request item is opened in Read mode.

To set the Hidden property for the Vacation Approved form and the Vacation Denied form, take the following steps.

1. On the Outlook Tools menu, click Options and then click the Other tab.
2. Click the Advanced Options button.
3. Click the Custom Forms button.

Part III Building Blocks of Applications

4. Click the Manage Forms button.
5. Note that the right-hand Form Library text box is set to Personal Forms.
6. In the right-hand Library list box, click Vacation Approved and then click Properties.
7. Select the Hidden check box, and then click OK.
8. Repeat steps 6 and 7 for the Vacation Denied form.
9. Click Close and then click OK.

> **Note** After forms are hidden, they are no longer visible in the following places:
> - The Choose Form dialog box selected from New on the File menu
> - The Actions menu for that folder

Custom Reply Forms for Users Not on Your Microsoft Exchange Server System

You may occasionally want to create forms that are used between your company and another company over the Internet. For example, let's assume you have a Legal Approval form and a Legal Approval Response form and you want to use the forms between your company and an attorney's office. Also assume that the attorney has Outlook but is not on your Microsoft Exchange Server system. For this scenario to work correctly, the attorney must have both the Legal Approval form and the Legal Approval Response form installed on his or her system—either in the Organizational Forms or Personal Forms Library.

> **Note** If the Reply form specified by an action is not available on the user's system, Outlook opens the standard Message form in its place.

> **More Info** For more information about where to publish forms, see Chapter 13. For information on sending forms to other people, see "Learn How Forms Work" in Chapter 5.

Actions   Chapter 7

Reply To Folder Actions for Post Forms

When creating applications with Post forms, you can create custom actions so users can reply to items in a folder using custom forms, rather than the standard Post form. In this section, we use the Training Management application for examples of how to implement Reply To Folder actions for Post forms.

> **To open the Training Management folder**

- In the Folder List, expand the Building Microsoft Outlook 2002 Applications folder and then expand the Building Blocks folder. Then click the Training Management folder.

Overview of the Training Management Application

The Training Management application allows training personnel to create an entire course catalog in the Training Management folder. To create the catalog, administrators first post Course Catalog Entry items in the folder. Course Catalog Entry items contain a general description of the course. After Course Catalog Entry items have been posted, training administrators can post Course Offering items as responses to the Course Catalog Entry items, as shown in Figure 7-13. After students complete a course, they can post an Evaluation item as a response to the Course Offering item.

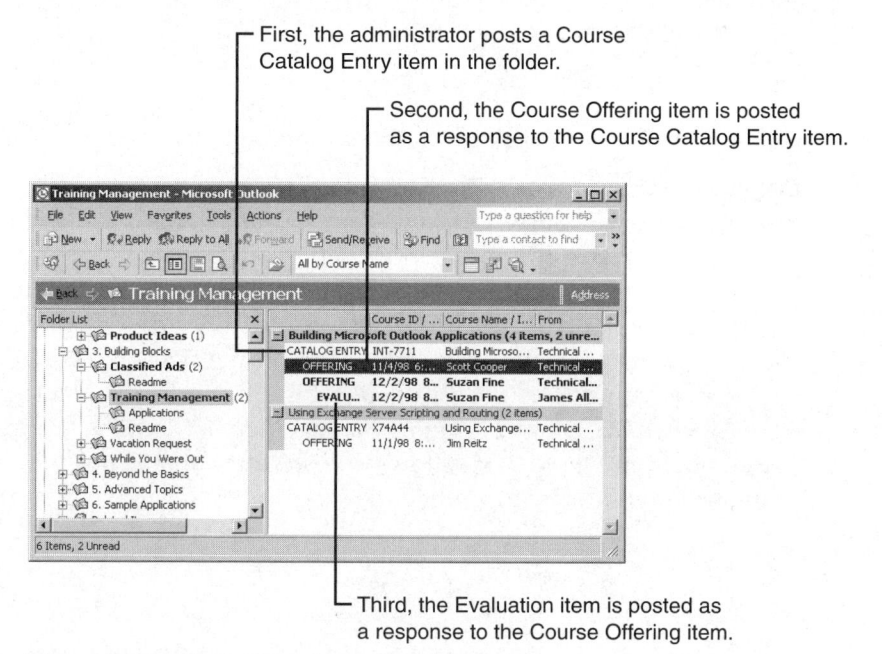

First, the administrator posts a Course Catalog Entry item in the folder.

Second, the Course Offering item is posted as a response to the Course Catalog Entry item.

Third, the Evaluation item is posted as a response to the Course Offering item.

Figure 7-13 The Training Management folder.

235

Part III Building Blocks of Applications

The Training Management application contains the following forms:

- **Course Catalog Entry form**   This form allows the administrator to post an item that contains general information about a course, such as the Course ID, Cost, Name, Target Audience, and Course Description. The Read page of the form, shown in Figure 7-14, allows an administrator to view the course offering information and to open a Course Offering Response item.

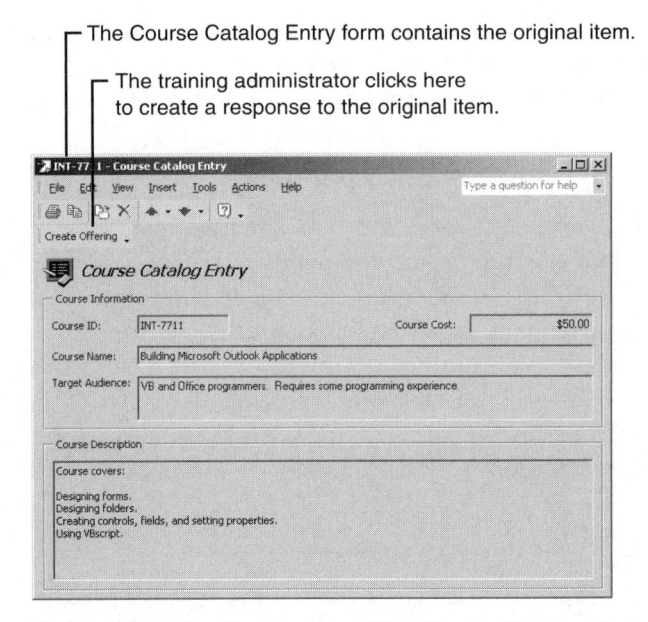

Figure 7-14 The Read page of the Course Catalog Entry form.

- **Course Offering form**   The Course Offering form allows an administrator to post a Course Offering item in the Training Management folder. The Course Offering item, which contains specifics about the course such as class time and instructor, is posted as a response to the Course Catalog Entry item. The Read page of the Course Offering form shows two custom buttons: a Signup button that lets students register for a class and a Course Evaluation button that lets students post a course evaluation in the Training Management folder. The Compose page, shown in Figure 7-15, shows a Post button that sends the form to the specified folder for public viewing.

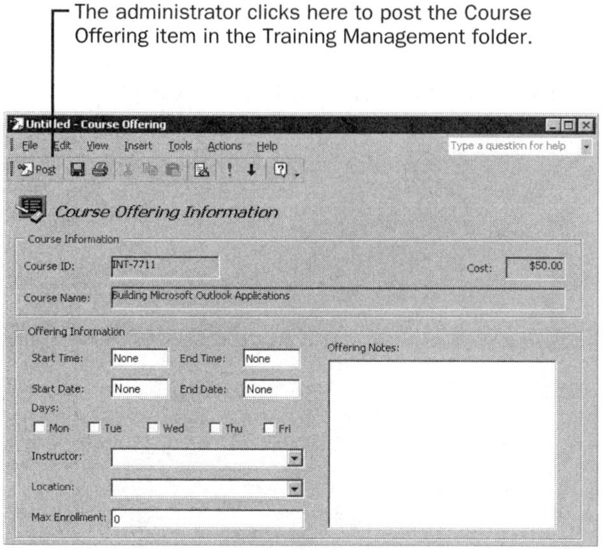

The administrator clicks here to post the Course
Offering item in the Training Management folder.

Figure 7-15 The Compose page of the Course Offering form.

- **Signup form**   This form enables a student to send a Signup item to the Course Registration folder. This part of the application is not covered in this section.

- **Evaluation form**   This form allows students to post an Evaluation item as a response to a Course Offering item. This part of the application is not covered in this section.

In the rest of this section, we'll look at the custom actions of the Course Catalog Entry form. First we examine how the actions work in the folder. Then we look at how the fields are copied from the Course Catalog Entry form to the Course Offering form. Finally we look at how response items are organized in a custom view in the Training Management folder.

Actions for the Course Catalog Entry Form

Now let's take a look at the Actions page for the Course Catalog Entry form, as shown in Figure 7-16.

To view the Actions page of the Course Catalog Entry form

1. On the Actions menu of the Training Management folder, click New Course Catalog Entry.

Part III Building Blocks of Applications

2. On the form's Tools menu, select Forms and then click Design This Form.

3. Click the Actions tab, as shown in Figure 7-16.

The Reply To Folder action is not enabled for the Course Catalog Entry form.

The Create Offering action is a custom action that causes a Create Offering command button to be placed on the Read page of the Course Catalog Entry form.

The Actions page

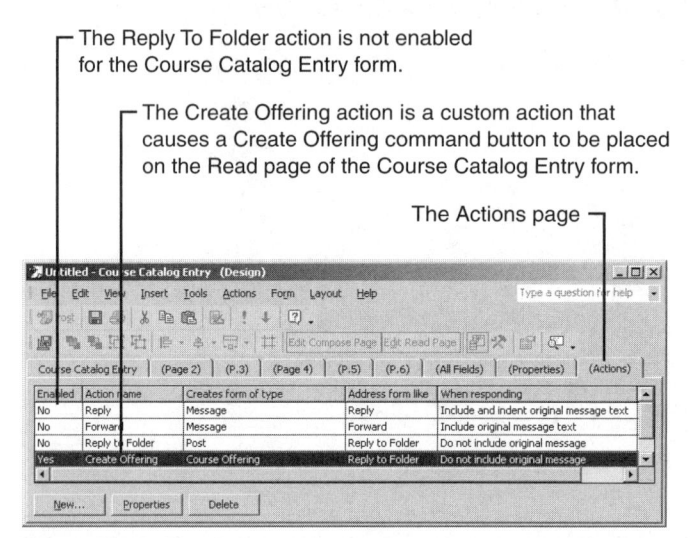

Figure 7-16 The Actions page for the Course Catalog Entry form.

Make the Reply To Folder Action Unavailable

Take note of the following simple rule.

> **Rule** If you create a custom Reply To Folder action for a form, set the Enabled option to No for the standard Reply To Folder so the action is not available.

As shown in Figure 7-16, the Reply To Folder command is not available for the Course Catalog Entry form. This is done to prevent the user from posting standard Post form items in the Training Management folder. You can also do this for the Reply and Forward actions.

> **Tip** If you create a custom Reply To Folder action for a form, set the Enabled option to No for the standard Reply To Folder so the action is not available.

Actions **Chapter 7**

To make the Reply To Folder action unavailable

1. On the Actions page, double-click the Reply To Folder action.
2. Clear the Enabled check box.

New Post To Folder Actions

With New Post To Folder actions, you can specify that custom command buttons and menu commands are added to the form. The menu commands or buttons, when clicked, open a custom form that enables the user to post a response item to the folder. For example, the Course Catalog Entry form has a custom Create Offering action. When an administrator opens a Course Catalog Entry item in his Inbox, he can click the Create Offering button, as shown in Figure 7-17.

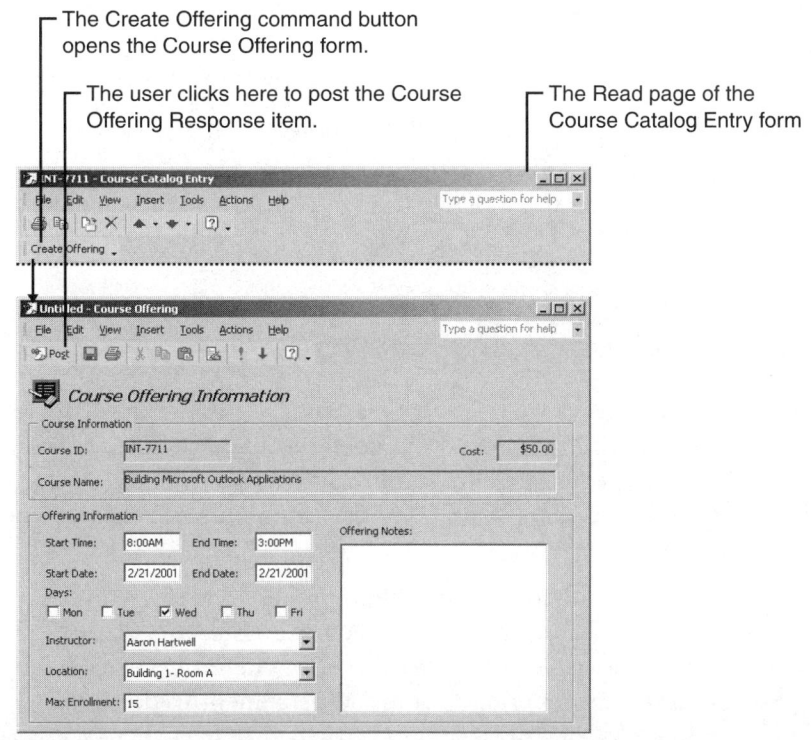

Figure 7-17 The Create Offering button is added to the Read page of the Course Catalog Entry form. When clicked, it opens the Compose page of the Course Offering form.

The Create Offering Action

Now let's take a look at the options that make up the Create Offering action, as shown in Figure 7-18.

239

Part III Building Blocks of Applications

> **To view the Create Offering action options**

1. In the Design mode of the Course Catalog Entry form, click the Actions page.
2. Double-click the Create Offering action to open the Form Action Properties dialog box.

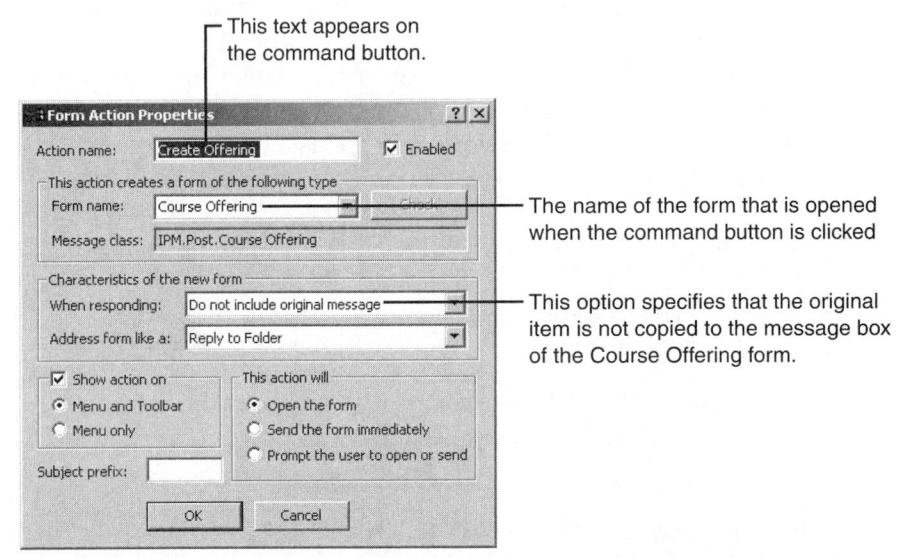

Figure 7-18 The properties for the Create Offering action

Action Name On Post forms, the Action Name option defines the name of the menu command and action button that open the associated Reply To Folder form.

The custom Create Offering command button appears on the Read page of the Course Catalog Entry form. The custom menu command appears in the following places:

- On the Outlook Actions menu when an item created with the associated form is selected in a folder. For example, the Create Offering command appears on the Actions menu when a Course Catalog Entry item is selected in the Training Management folder.

- On the Context menu when you right-click on an item created with the associated form.

- On the Actions menu of the Read page of the Course Catalog Entry form.

Form Name and Message Class The Form Name option holds the name of the form that opens when the command button or menu command is clicked. The

Message Class, the internal identifier for the form, is automatically supplied for you in the Message Class text box. The Form Name combo box contains the names of the forms published in the current folder, so you see the Training Management forms in the Form Name combo box.

To specify a form name

Do one of the following:

- In the Form Name combo box, type a form name and then click Check to search for the form. If Outlook cannot find the form, you will see a message box that explains that Outlook can't find the form. If this happens, you should create the Response form before you specify the Form Name option. After you create the Response form and publish it in a forms library, you can then return to the original form and click the name of the Response form in the Form Name combo box.

- In the Form Name combo box, click a form name to specify the form that is activated when the user clicks an action menu command or command button.

- In the Form Name combo box, click Forms to open the Choose Form dialog box. In the first box, click the library, and then click the form you want in the box below it.

Characteristics Of The New Form Under Characteristics Of The New Form, you specify how values from the original item are copied to the Response item.

When Responding When creating actions, remember that the original message can be copied only to the message box of the Response item. If the Response form does not have a message box, as is the case with the Course Offering form, then the message cannot be copied.

> **Tip** If the Response form does not have a message box, then specify Do Not Include Original Message in the When Responding box.

Generally, with Post forms, you should be very careful about including the original message, especially if the message is very large.

Address Form Like A For Post forms, you always choose Reply To Folder for the Address Form Like A option. Reply To Folder sets up the response form so the Post To field of the Response form contains the active folder address, the

Conversation field contains the subject of the original item, and the Subject field is empty.

Show Action On   Most of the time, you can specify the default Menu And Toolbar option. However, there may be times when you want to place action buttons in a custom location on the form. To do this, you can add a command button to the form and then create a procedure for the command button to open the Response form when the command button is clicked. If this is the case, you can click the Menu Only option or uncheck Show Action On.

> More Info   For more information about creating procedures for forms, see Chapter 11, "Using Visual Basic, VBA, or VBScript with Outlook."

This Action Will   For the Course Catalog Entry form, when the Create Offering action is initiated, it opens the Course Offering form. For most Reply To Folder actions, under This Action Will you should specify Open The Form.

Subject Prefix   When the Reply To Folder option is selected in the Address Form Like A box, the Subject field of the Response item is cleared. So, in most cases, you leave the Subject Prefix box blank when Reply To Folder is selected.

How Field Values Are Copied to the Response Form

Earlier in this chapter, we learned that values from shared fields—those fields that are common between the original item and the Response item—are copied from the original item to the Response item.

When the Reply To Folder option is selected in the Address Form Like A box for an action, the same principles apply. Values from shared fields are copied from the original item to the Response item. However, there is one important exception.

> Important   When the Reply To Folder option is selected in the Address Form Like A box, the value from the Subject field is not copied from the original item to the Response item. Instead, the value of the Subject field of the original item is copied to the Conversation field of the Response item and the Subject field in the Response item is blank.

Actions   Chapter 7

In Figure 7-19, there is no Subject field visible on either form. Instead the Subject field is hidden (on page 2) and bound to the CourseID field, so when a form is opened, the value of the CourseID field appears in the title bar of the form. This is done because the value in the item's Subject field always appears in the title bar of the form. Also, there is no message box on either form, so the original message is not copied to the Response message.

- When the Create Offering action is started, as shown in Figure 7-19, the values in the following fields are copied from the Course Catalog Entry form to the Course Offering form: CourseID, CourseCost, and CourseName.

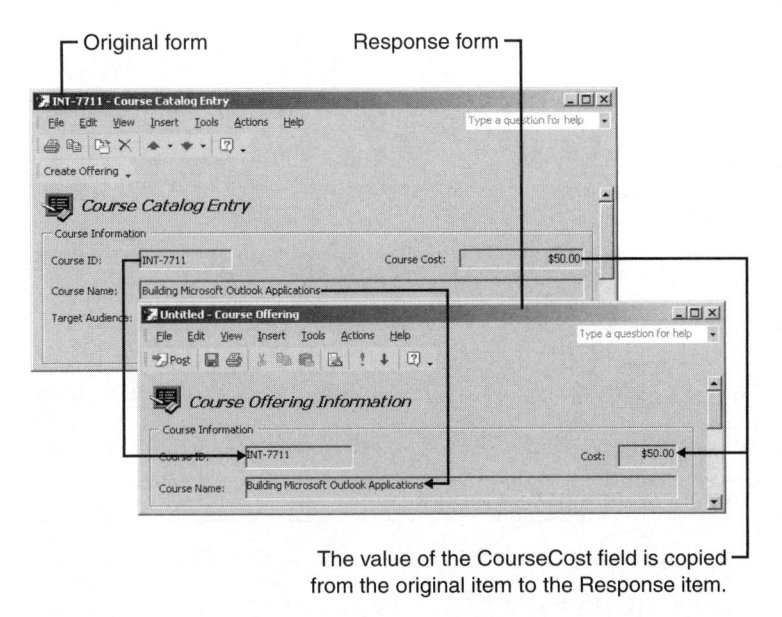

Figure 7-19 Values between fields common to both the original and Response form are copied to the Response form.

Tip   To make sure field values are copied between the original form and the Response form, use the same fields for both forms. For example, for the Training Management application, the CourseID, CourseCost, and CourseName fields are used for both the Course Catalog Entry form and the Course Offering Information form.

Part III   Building Blocks of Applications

Create Response Forms

Generally, it is recommended that you create all Response forms for an application before you create form actions. For example, for the Training Management application, you create the Course Catalog Entry form and then you create the Course Offering form. After you've created the Course Offering form, you then return to the Course Catalog Entry form and create a Create Offering action that specifies the Course Offering form as the Form Name option.

In some cases, the Response form is very similar to the original form, so you can use the original form as a template. At other times, it's quicker to start from scratch. In the case of the Course Offering Response form, either approach can be used.

> **More Info**   For more information on creating and modifying forms, see Chapter 5.

Publish the Forms to the Forms Library of the Folder

When you create actions for a form, you must make sure that the forms that are opened as a result of the action are published in the forms library of the folder. Before you publish the forms, however, it's a good idea to make backup copies of them.

To make a backup copy of a form

1. With the form open, click Save As on the File menu.
2. In the Save In drop-down list box, select the default Outlook template folder, such as C:\Documents and Settings\<UserName>\Application Data\Microsoft\Templates.
3. In the File Name text box, type a name for the form.
4. In the Save As Type drop-down list box, select Outlook Template (.oft).
5. Click Save.

To open your backup copy of a form

1. Select New on the File menu, and then click Choose Form.
2. Click User Templates In File System in the Look In drop-down list box, and then click the form you'd like to open.

To publish a form in the forms library of a folder

1. On the Tools menu, select Forms and then click Publish Form As.
2. If the text in the Look In box does not reflect the active folder, click Browse, select the forms library you want, and then click OK.
3. Type the name of the form in the Display Name text box and the Form Name text box.
4. Click Publish.

Test the Forms

After you create actions and custom forms to respond to the actions, you should run the forms to make sure they work as expected. For example, here is a quick way to test the forms and their actions in the Training Management application.

To test the forms in the Training Management application

1. In the Folder List, click the Training Management folder.
2. On the Actions menu, click New Course Catalog Entry.
3. Fill in the Course Catalog Entry form, and then click Post.
4. In the Training Management folder, double-click the Course Catalog Entry item you just posted.
5. Click the Create Offering button.
6. Fill in the Course Offering form, and then click Post.
7. The Course Offering item is posted as a response to the Course Catalog Entry item. As such, it is indented in the folder.
8. Alternatively, you can double-click the Course Offering item and then click Create Evaluation or Signup on the form. Click Post to put it in the folder.
9. The Signup form is a Message form that routes course registration information to a course administrator or public folder. If you like, you can send the message to your Inbox as a test. The Course Evaluation form is a custom Response form that posts a Response Evaluation item in the Training Management folder.

Set the Hidden Property for Response Forms

After you publish and test forms, you set the Hidden property for the Response forms. For example, the following procedure sets the Hidden property for the Response forms in the Training Management folder.

> **To set the Hidden property for the Training Management Response forms**

1. In the Folder List, right-click the Training Management folder and then click Properties on the shortcut menu.
2. Click the Forms page, and then click Manage.
3. In the right-hand drop-down list box, click Course Offering and then click Properties.
4. Select the Hidden check box, and then click OK.
5. In the right-hand drop-down list box, click Course Evaluation and then click Properties.
6. Select the Hidden check box, and then click OK.
7. In the right-hand drop-down list box, click Signup and then click Properties.
8. Select the Hidden check box, and then click OK.
9. Click Close, and then click OK.

> **Note** After forms are hidden, they are no longer visible in the following places:
>
> ❑ From the Choose Form dialog box selected from New on the File menu
>
> ❑ From the Actions menu for that folder

Where To Go from Here

Microsoft Knowledge Base Articles Microsoft Knowledge Base articles are available on the Web at *http://support.microsoft.com/support*. Also see Actions (Chapter 7) KB Articles in the Microsoft Web Sites folder under the Help And Web Sites folder on the companion CD.

8

Folders

With Outlook, you can create a wide variety of folders to help users share, organize, and track information in your organization. Here are just a few examples:

- **Discussion folders that provide a public forum for users to submit, share, and respond to ideas and information** For example, you can create a discussion folder for posting job openings, job candidate information, and interview responses for a candidate. Or you can create a Technical Users Group folder, such as the HTML folder at Microsoft, where writers and designers can post, read, and share information and solutions to problems.

- **Placeholder folders that provide a logical hierarchy for your application folders** Public folder applications sometimes include placeholder folders that provide a logical means of organizing the application folders that actually hold the documents manipulated by a user. Assign permissions to a placeholder folder, which prevents users from adding, editing, or deleting items in the folder. For example, you might have a top-level placeholder folder named Sales with regional placeholder folders for East, West, South, and Midwest. Under the regional folders you would add application folders named Current Customers and Prospective Customers that contain items holding the data for your application.

- **Reference folders that provide a place to store and organize information** For example, you can create a Product Specification Library that stores Microsoft Word documents. You can use the built-in or custom document properties of those Word documents to create views in the folder. In addition, you can create a Reference Library that stores Web addresses or a Project Library that stores a variety of materials such as Visio documents, PowerPoint presentations, Visual Basic prototypes, or Microsoft Excel workbooks.

- **Tracking folders that allow users to record and review information that is constantly updated**   For example, you can create a Help Desk application so that users and help desk technicians can schedule appointments and track the status of help desk requests.

This chapter takes an in-depth look at creating public folders, discusses how to manage forms, and looks at creating custom views. It also covers how to set folder permissions, create rules for a folder, and establish folder home pages. Introduced in Outlook 2000, folder home pages allow you to specify a URL displaying a Web page in place of a normal Outlook view of folder items. Using Visual InterDev and the Outlook View Control, you can also create custom HTML-based views of a folder's contents.

For the majority of examples in this chapter, the sample Classified Ads folder is used, as shown in Figure 8-1.

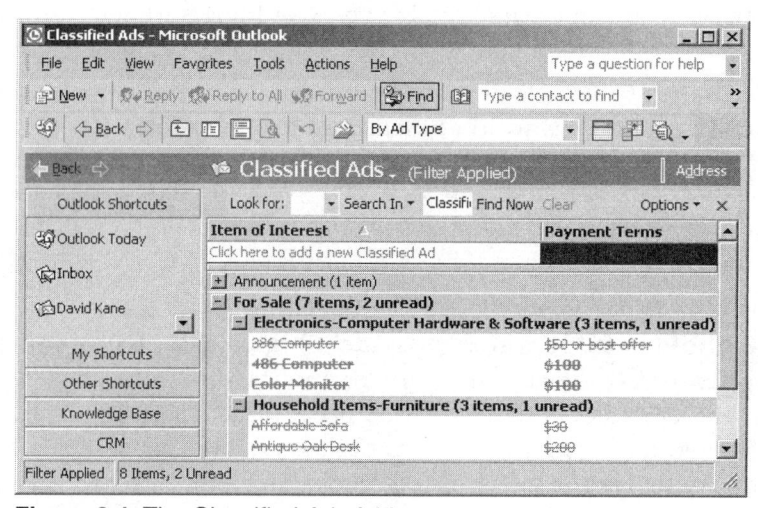

Figure 8-1 The Classified Ads folder.

To open the Classified Ads folder

- In the Folder List, expand the Building Microsoft Outlook 2002 Applications folder, expand the Building Blocks folder, and then click the Classified Ads folder.

An Important Reminder About Planning

To create folders that meet the needs of your users, it is essential to plan them first. If you dive headfirst into creating a folder hierarchy and its contents, you might have to redesign both your folder structure and the custom forms contained in those folders if business rules change or design requirements are overlooked. Careful planning avoids expensive, time-consuming redesigns. Your motto when you approach folder design should be to plan, plan, and plan again. Although planning processes differ with each organization and application, there are general steps you should follow when planning a public folder:

- Determine who will plan, design, and implement the folder.

- When you identify folder users and their needs, evaluate their requirements in terms of public folder roles and permissions. For example, what is the default permission on the application folder? Can your users modify the folder items created by other users? Create a list of user groups that will have access to your folder and determine whether they have permission to create, edit, or delete folder items. You also need to consider which forms will be available in your folders and which users can modify those forms.

- Be aware that folder users do not have to correspond to individual mailbox accounts. Exchange Distribution Lists provide a convenient way for you to manage the users who have been assigned to a public folder permissions role such as editor or author.

- Create a design plan that identifies the problems to be solved and how the folder will solve them. The design plan should include preliminary graphics of form windows or views to be created.

Create or Select a Folder

With Outlook, you can design a folder by using one of three methods.

Method	Use When
Create a new folder from scratch.	You cannot find an existing folder in your organization that closely matches the folder you want to create. In this case, it's quicker to start from scratch.
Modify an existing folder that is in public use.	You want to make minor changes to a folder, such as adding permissions or a view.
Copy the design of an existing folder to a new folder, and then modify the new folder.	You want to create a new folder based on the design of an existing folder, or you want to make changes to an existing folder and those changes will disrupt users' work.

Part III Building Blocks of Applications

Choose Where To Design the New Folder

If the method of folder design you choose requires that you create a new folder, you can create the folder in Public Folders, your Outlook Mailbox, or Personal Folders. The location determines whether the folder is public or private and determines the design properties you can set for the folder.

Designing new folders in a personal folder is recommended for most public folder application designs. After you have tested and refined your application, you can copy the private folders to Public Folders on an Exchange Server. At this point you should set permissions and go through another round of testing before you publish your application.

In a personal folder (.pst), you can create forms and design views, and then test them to make sure they work as expected. After you create forms and design views, you or the administrator can copy the folder to Public Folders, where you can complete the design of the folder by setting permissions and administration properties. At this point you will also publish your custom forms, if any, to an application folder or to the organizational forms registry.

You should be aware that many organizations require that you deploy your public folder application on a test Exchange Server before you move your application to a production server in your Exchange site. If you use Exchange Server 5.5 scripting agents or Exchange Server 2000 event sinks with your application, it is essential to run your application in a test environment before you move the application to a production server.

The following table shows the attributes that you can set in each folder location.

Option	In a Personal Folder	In a Mailbox Folder	In a Public Folder
Activities tab and Outlook Address Book tab on Contact Folders only	X	X	X
Create Exchange Server 5.5 scripting and routing agents or Exchange Server 2000 event sinks and workflow applications		X	X
Copy or install forms	X	X	X
Define rules		Set rules with the Rules Wizard	Set rules with the Folder Assistant

Option	In a Personal Folder	In a Mailbox Folder	In a Public Folder
Design views	X	X	X
Designate the types of items allowed in the folder	X		X
Set administration properties	Can only set the initial view on folder	Can only set the initial view on folder	All
Set folder home page	X	X	X
Set permissions		X	X

> **Note** Personal folders appearing on the Folder List are attached to personal folder (.pst) files saved on your hard disk drive. For more information on creating a personal folder (.pst) file, see "Create New Folders" in Chapter 3, "Customize Built-In Modules."

Create a Folder from Scratch

One way to design a folder is to create a new folder. After you create the folder, you can follow the design process outlined in this chapter, beginning with "Publish Forms in the Folder" (on page 254).

To create a folder

1. In the Folder List, right-click a personal folder in which you want to create a folder, and then click New Folder on the shortcut menu.

2. In the Name text box of the Create New Folder dialog box shown in Figure 8-2, enter a name for the folder.

3. In the Folder Contains A drop-down list box, do one of the following:

    ❑ Click Mail Items to create a folder that will contain items created with Message, Post, or Office Document forms.

    ❑ Click Appointment Items, Contact Items, Journal Items, Note Items, or Task Items to create a folder that will contain items of the associated type. For example, if you click Appointment Items, Outlook creates a Calendar folder.

4. Click OK to close. If a dialog box appears asking if you want to Add A Shortcut To Outlook Bar?, click No if you do not want to add a shortcut to the current group in your Outlook Bar. Otherwise, click Yes to add a shortcut to this folder in the currently selected group.

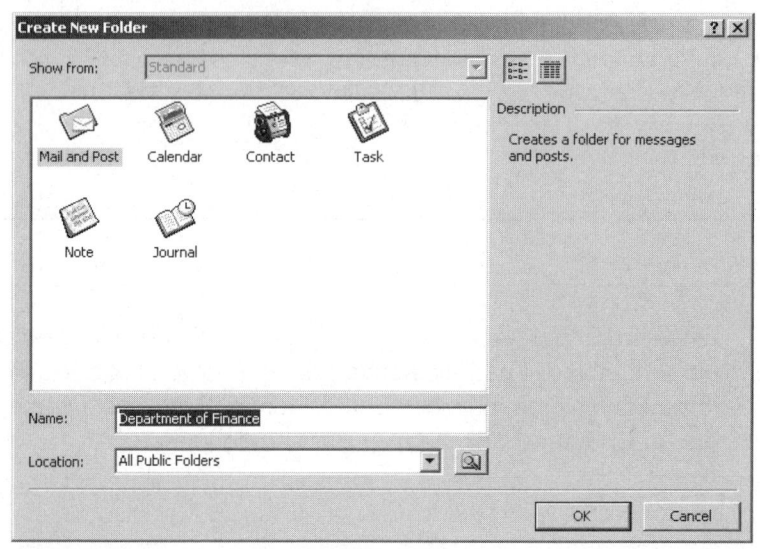

Figure 8-2 The Create New Folder dialog box lets you select the default item type for a new folder.

Directly Modify a Folder

If a folder is in public use, it's best to directly modify the folder only if the changes are minor and will not disrupt another user's work. Minor changes include adding permissions, adding a view, or changing a folder contact.

To make more significant changes—such as modifying forms or rules—copy the design of the folder to another folder, modify the design (as described in "Copy a Folder Design" later in this chapter), and then copy the modified design back to the original folder.

To directly modify a Mailbox or public folder

1. In the Folder List, right-click the folder, and then click Properties on the shortcut menu. You can also right-click the shortcut for the folder if it exists on your Outlook Bar.
2. In the Properties dialog box, make the changes, and then click OK.

> **Note** To modify a folder, you must have owner permissions for the folder. To check your permissions for a folder, right-click the folder, and then click Properties on the shortcut menu. You can view your permissions on the Permissions page of a Mailbox or public folder. If you are viewing subfolders of your Exchange mailbox, you are the folder owner by default. If you cannot see the Permissions page of a public folder, you do not have permissions as a folder owner. If you need to acquire owner permissions, contact your Exchange administrator.

Copy a Folder Design

To create or modify a folder, you can copy the design of an existing folder to a new folder. You can then customize the design of the new folder. Copying a folder design involves copying design components, such as forms and views, from one folder to another. When a folder design is copied, the folder permissions and rules are always maintained, regardless of whether the folder design is copied to or from a folder in a personal or public folder.

When Outlook copies the design to a folder, it merges the design components of the source folder with design components of the destination folder. If two properties conflict—for example, the permissions for a user in the source folder are different from the permissions in the destination folder—the properties in the source folder take precedence. All of the design components in the destination folder are overwritten.

To copy a folder design

1. In the Folder List, select the folder to which you want to copy the design. Remember that you are copying the folder design to the selected target folder from a source folder that you will specify in step 3.
2. On the File menu, point to Folder, and then click Copy Folder Design.
3. In the Copy Design From This Folder drop-down list box, select the folder you want to copy the design from.

Part III Building Blocks of Applications

4. Under Design Copy Of, select one or more of the following.

To Copy	Select
Permissions from the source folder	Permissions
The rules associated with the source folder	Rules
The description of the source folder	Description
Forms and views that are stored in the source folder	Forms & Views

5. Click OK.

Publish Forms in the Folder

Not all folders require custom forms. For those folders that do, however, you must first design the forms, and then publish them in an Outlook folder, such as a Mailbox folder, a public folder, or a personal folder. When you publish a form in a folder, you accomplish two things:

- You make the form available in the folder so that it can be opened by users to compose and view items in the folder.

- You expose the form properties, such as form name, description, and menu commands, in Outlook.

To publish a form in an Outlook folder

1. With the form open, select Forms on the Tools menu, and then click Publish Form As. If you have already published your form to either the Personal or Organizational Forms Library, select the Tools menu, and then click the Select Form command to open the form in order to publish the form to your application folder.

> **Tip** If the form you wish to publish contains code in Microsoft Visual Basic Scripting Edition (VBScript), select the Tools menu, click the Choose Form command, select the form in the Choose Form dialog box, and hold down the Shift key in order to disable macros when the form opens. If you run macros and then publish the form, you might unintentionally create default values for some of the user-defined fields in the form.

254

2. In the Display Name text box, type the name of the form that will appear in the form caption, forms list, and menu command. In the Form Name text box, type the name reflected in Message Class, if different.

   To change the location (library) where the form is published, click the Look In drop-down list box, and then select the folder where you want to publish the form.

3. Click Publish.

> **More Info** For more information about creating and publishing forms, see Chapter 5, "Forms."

Manage Forms

With the Forms page of the folder's Properties dialog box, as shown in Figure 8-3, you can see the forms that are published in the forms library of the folder. In addition, you can specify the types of items that can be created in the folder. You can also use the Forms page to access the Forms Manager. With the Forms Manager, you can copy and delete forms, and view form properties.

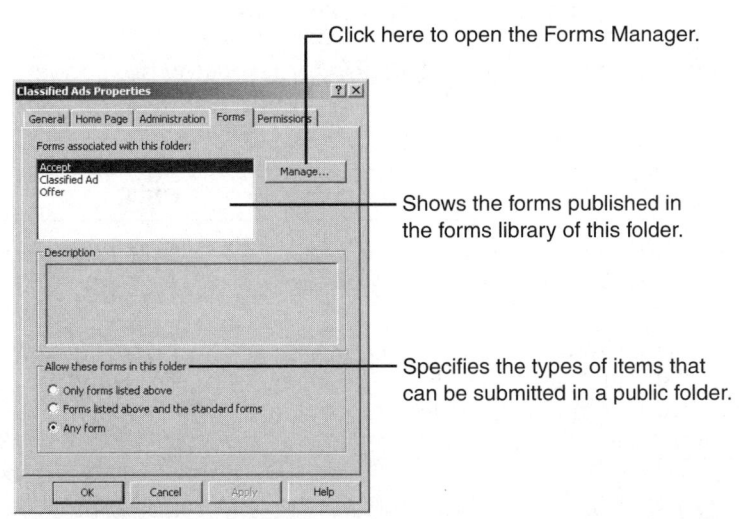

Figure 8-3 The Forms page shows the forms that are published in the current folder.

Part III Building Blocks of Applications

> **To view the Forms page**

1. In the Folder List, right-click the folder, and then click Properties on the shortcut menu.

2. Click the Forms page.

> **Tip** You can also access the Forms Manager by clicking Options on the Outlook Tools menu. You then have access to all forms, not just those in the current folder. Click the Other tab, click the Advanced Options button, and then click the Custom Forms button. Finally, click the Manage Forms button to get to the Forms Manager.

Specify the Types of Items Allowed in the Folder

In many folders, you might want to control the types of items that can be submitted. For example, in the Classified Ads folder, you want to prevent the user from submitting standard Post items to the folder because they are out of context and do not appear correctly in the custom views created for the folder.

> **To specify the types of items allowed in a public folder**

- On the Forms page of the folder's Properties dialog box, under Allow These Forms In This Folder, click one of the following.

To Specify That	Click
Only items created with the forms specified in the Forms Associated With This Folder drop-down list box can be submitted in the folder.	Only Forms Listed Above
Only items created with the forms specified in the Forms Associated With This Folder drop-down list box and standard Post and Message forms can be submitted in the folder.	Forms Listed Above And The Standard Forms
Any type of item can be created in the folder.	Any Form

Copy and Delete Forms or Set the Hidden Property for a Form

You can use the Forms Manager, as shown in Figure 8-4, to copy and delete forms and to view form properties.

Folders Chapter 8

Figure shows the Forms Manager dialog box with the following annotations:
- Click here to select the source forms library for a Copy operation.
- Shows forms in the selected forms library
- Shows the active folder
- Click here to select the destination forms library for a Copy operation. When grey, it manages only the current folder.
- Click to view properties of the selected form, such as the Hidden property.

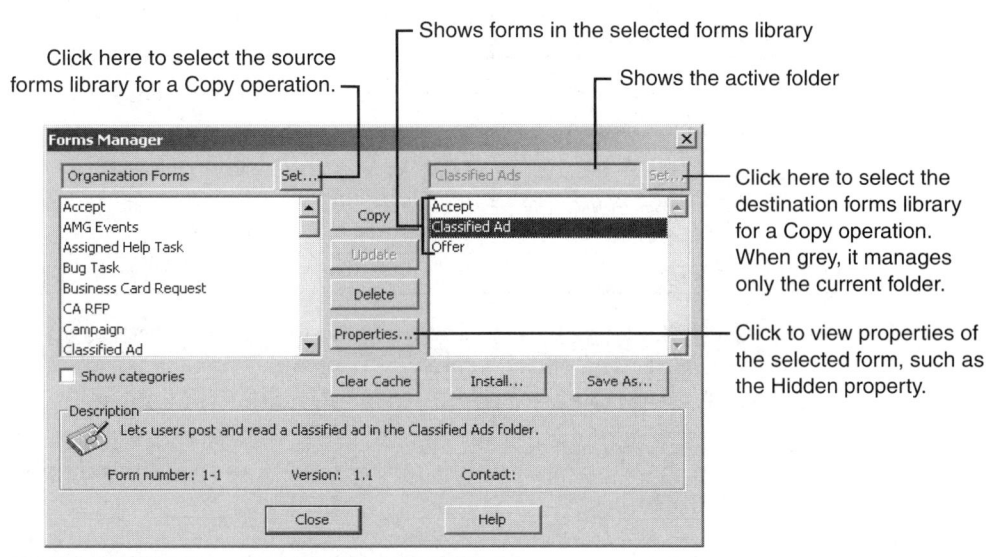

Figure 8-4 The Forms Manager dialog box.

To open the Forms Manager

- On the Forms page of the folder's Properties box, click Manage.

If the form you want to use already exists in your organization and is published in a forms library, you can copy it to the forms library of the folder you're designing. By default, the left drop-down list box in the Forms Manager dialog box shows the contents of the Organizational Forms Library and the right list box shows the contents of the active folder's forms library. The left list box shows the source forms library from which you can copy forms. The right list box shows the destination forms library to which you copy the forms. You can easily change the libraries shown in these boxes.

To change the library in the left or right drop-down list box of the Forms Manager

1. Choose Set for the list box that contains the library you want to change.
2. Do one of the following:
   - ❑ In the Forms Library drop-down list box, click the library you want.
   - ❑ In the Folder Forms Library drop-down list box, select the folder you want.

Part III Building Blocks of Applications

To copy a form to a folder

- In the left drop-down list box, click the form you want to copy, and then click Copy.
    You can copy a form from one forms library to another. You can delete any form from either forms library.

To delete a form

- In the left or right drop-down list box, click the form you want to delete, and then click Delete.
    To synchronize a form with an updated version, select the one you wish to update. For the update process to work properly, the form must be visible in both forms libraries (in both the left and right drop-down list boxes).

To update forms published in different forms libraries

- In the right drop-down list box, click the form, and then click Update. Although you won't see an action, the forms will now be updated.

View Form Properties or Set the Hidden Property for a Form

With the Properties dialog box, you can view a form's properties, and you can set the Hidden property for a form. When you select the Hidden property for a form, you specify that the form's associated menu command is not visible in the Outlook user interface, so users can only create response items with the form or view items with the form. In addition, forms published in the Personal Forms Library or the Organizational Forms Library with the Hidden property selected will not be visible to the user in the Choose Form dialog box. The Choose Form dialog box is available by selecting New on the File menu.

To view the properties of a form

- In the right list box of the Forms Manager dialog box, click the form whose properties you want to view, and then click Properties.

> **Important** The Install and Save As buttons are not valid for Outlook forms. They are intended for use with forms created for Microsoft Exchange Client.

To set the Hidden property for a form

1. In the right drop-down list box of the Forms Manager dialog box, click the form that you want to set the Hidden property for, and then click Properties.
2. Select the Hidden check box, and then click OK.

Design Folder Views

To help users organize and manage the information stored in folders, you can create folder views. With views, users can organize and view the same information in different ways within the folder. With Outlook, you can create table, timeline, card, day/week/month, and icon view types. Outlook 2002 also provides the ability to create and modify views programmatically. For information on adding, changing, and deleting views programmatically, see "The Views Collection Object" in Chapter 11, "Using Visual Basic, VBA, or VBScript with Outlook." The following list describes the features you can use with views.

- **Columns** As shown in Figure 8-5, columns show values for a particular field in an item under the column heading.

- **Groups** With groups, you can create categories of items that share a common field value. Items in the By Category view are grouped by the type of ad, as Figure 8-5 shows. Groups can be expanded or collapsed.

- **Sort** You can sort the items in a group based on the criteria you specify. For example, you can sort items by the date received, field values, or alphabetically.

- **Filter** With Outlook filters, you create criteria to specify the items to be shown in the folder. For example, in Figure 8-5, the filter applied to the folder specifies that only items created with the Classified Ad form are shown in the folder.

- **Format** With the Format dialog box, you can specify fonts, grid lines, and in-cell editing for a folder. With in-cell editing, users can change information in a cell in the folder.

Part III Building Blocks of Applications

The filter shows only items created with the Classified Ad form.

The By Category view in the Current View box is applied to the folder.

Items are grouped by type of ad, and then by category.

Items within each group can be sorted from least expensive to most expensive.

The column heading determines the values that appear in the column below.

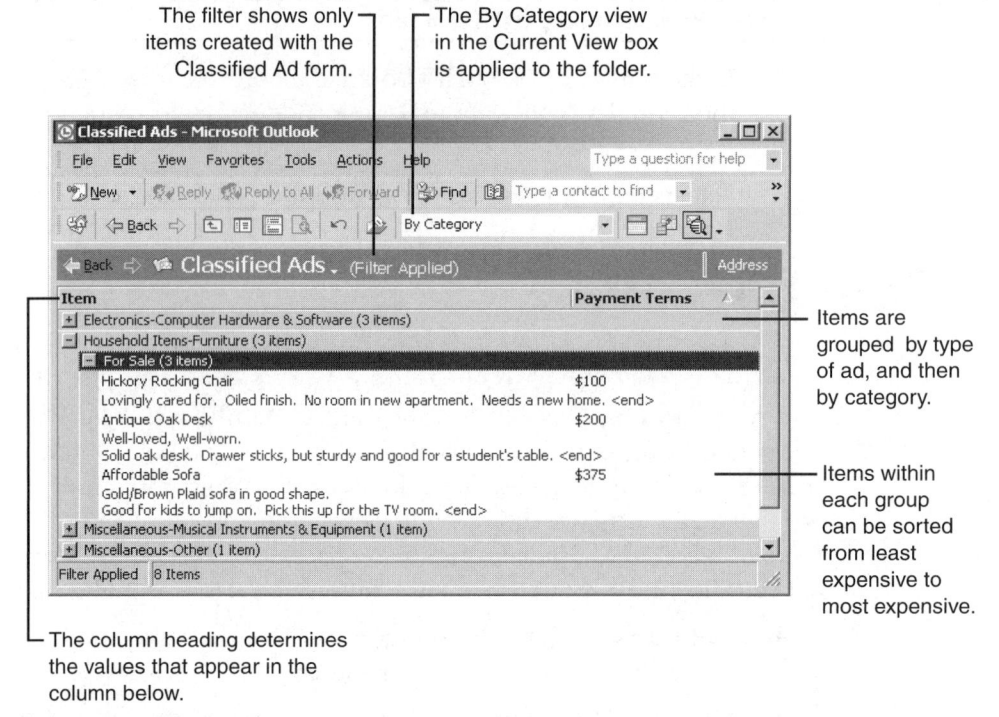

Figure 8-5 The view chosen by the user determines how items are organized in the folder.

Create a New View

Each view you create is given a name that appears in the Current View drop-down list box on the Advanced toolbar, as shown earlier in Figure 8-5. When the view name is clicked in the Current View drop-down list box, the view is applied to the folder and the items in the folder are arranged according to the criteria specified in the view.

To create a new view

1. On the View menu, select Current View, and then click Define Views.
2. Click New.
3. In the Name Of New View text box, type a name.
4. In the Type Of View text box, click the type of view you want.
5. Under Can Be Used On, verify that This Folder, Visible To Everyone is selected.

6. Click OK twice.
7. Click Apply View.

Show Only the Views Created for the Folder

For each folder you create, Outlook provides several standard views in the Current View drop-down list box. In many cases, these views are not relevant to your folder, so you can remove them from the Current View drop-down list box. If you want to remove the standard views from the Current View drop-down list box and show only the custom views you create, you can select the Only Show Views Created For This Folder check box, as shown in Figure 8-6.

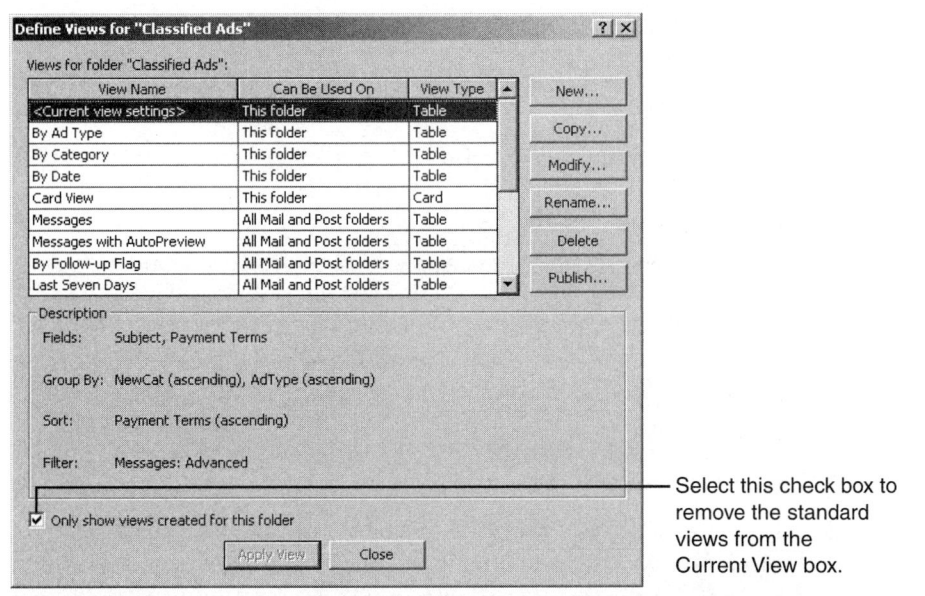

Figure 8-6 The Only Show Views Created For This Folder check box specifies that the standard views are not shown in the Current View drop-down list box on the Standard toolbar.

To show only the custom views created for the folder

1. On the View menu, select Current View, and then click Define Views.
2. Select the Only Show Views Created For This Folder check box.
3. Click Close.

Part III Building Blocks of Applications

Create Columns

With Outlook, you can create columns by dragging fields from the Field Chooser to the Column Heading row. When you add a column to a view, the column shows the value of the field for each of the items in the view, as shown in Figure 8-7.

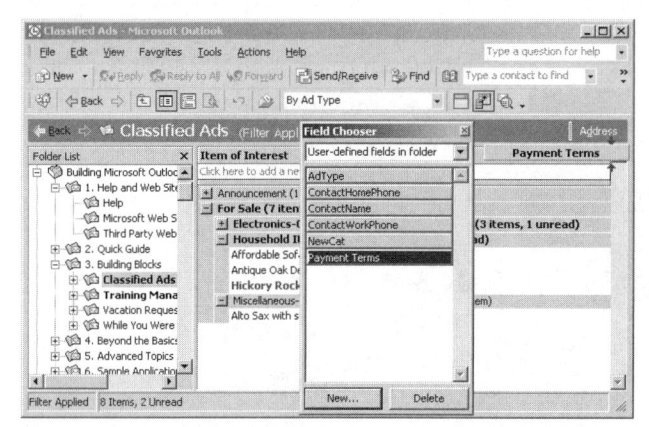

Figure 8-7 Columns for the By Ad Type view in the Classified Ads folder.

To add a column to a view

1. On the Advanced toolbar, click the Field Chooser icon.
2. In the Field Set drop-down list box in the Field Chooser, click the field set from which you want to choose fields.
3. Drag the field you want as the new column heading to the Column Heading row, as shown in Figure 8-8. Use the red double-arrow marker to position the new column heading in the Column Heading row.

To remove a column from a view

- Drag the column heading away from the Column Heading row until an X appears through the column heading, and then release the mouse button.

Format Columns

By default, a column heading has the same label as the field on which it is based. For example, the Payment Terms column heading is identical to the Payment Terms field. In some cases, you might want to change the column heading label so that it's different from the field name. The Item Of Interest column heading in the By Ad Type view shows an example of a changed column heading label.

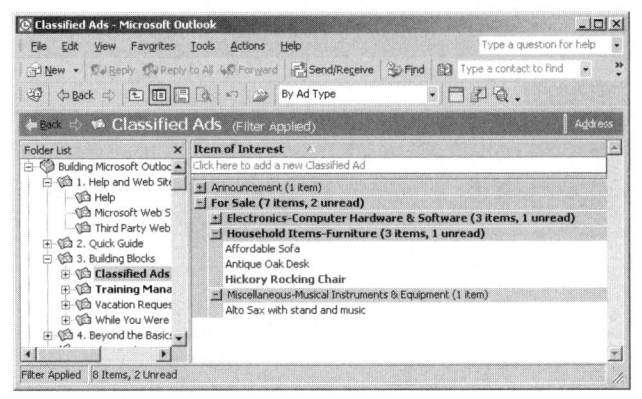

Figure 8-8 The Payment Terms field is added to the Column Heading row.

On the Classified Ads form, the Subject field on the form is labeled Item Of Interest, as shown in Figure 8-9. In this example, the Subject field is used for the form because it provides the unique ability to display its value in the caption on the form window. Just as the label for a field can be changed on the form, the label can also be changed in the column heading of the view. For example, for the By Ad Type view, as shown earlier in Figures 8-7 and 8-8, the column heading for the Subject field is Item Of Interest. To change the column heading label, you change the label for the field in the Format Columns dialog box.

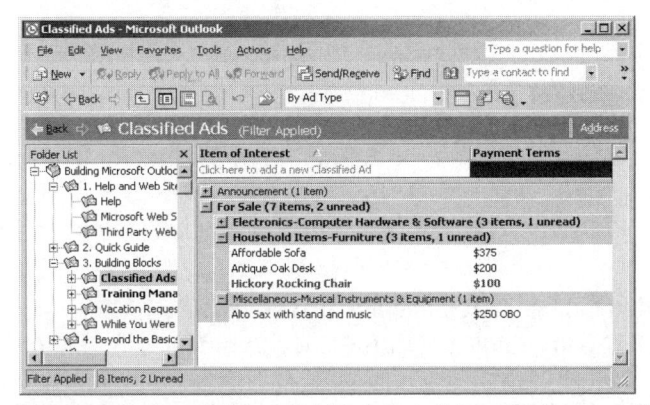

Figure 8-9 The Subject field is labeled Item Of Interest. The value of the field appears in the window caption.

Part III Building Blocks of Applications

> **To change the format properties of a column**

1. Right-click the column heading you want to format, and then click Format Columns on the shortcut menu.

2. In the Available Fields list box, click the field you want to format, and then make the changes you want.

3. Click OK.

Create Combination Columns

In some cases, you might want to add Combination fields to a view. To help demonstrate the point, this section shows you an example of a Volunteer Registration application. Note that this application is merely an example and is not included in the Building Microsoft Outlook 2002 Applications folder.

With the fields on the Volunteer Registration form, as shown in Figure 8-10, a user can enter his or her first name, last name, address, city, and postal code in separate fields.

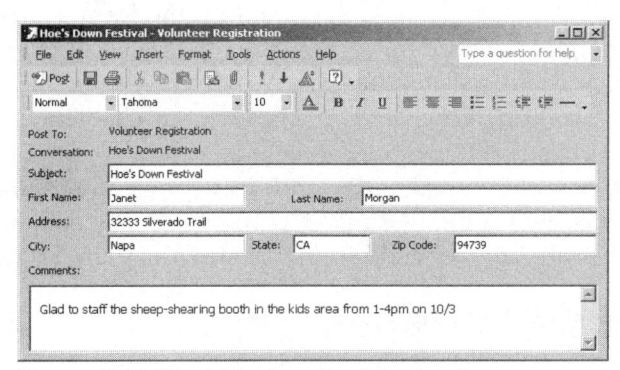

Figure 8-10 The Volunteer Registration form.

Now, assume you want to create a column in the Volunteer Registration view that combines the Fname and Lname field values and shows them in a single Name column, as shown in Figure 8-11. To do this, you create a combination column.

Create a combination column that combines text fragments   There are two kinds of Combination fields you can create: those that combine text fragments and those that show the value of the first non-empty field. This section shows you how to create a combination column that combines text fragments. The next section shows you how to create a combination column that shows only the value of the first non-empty field.

Folders Chapter 8

The Name column combines values from the FName and LName fields.

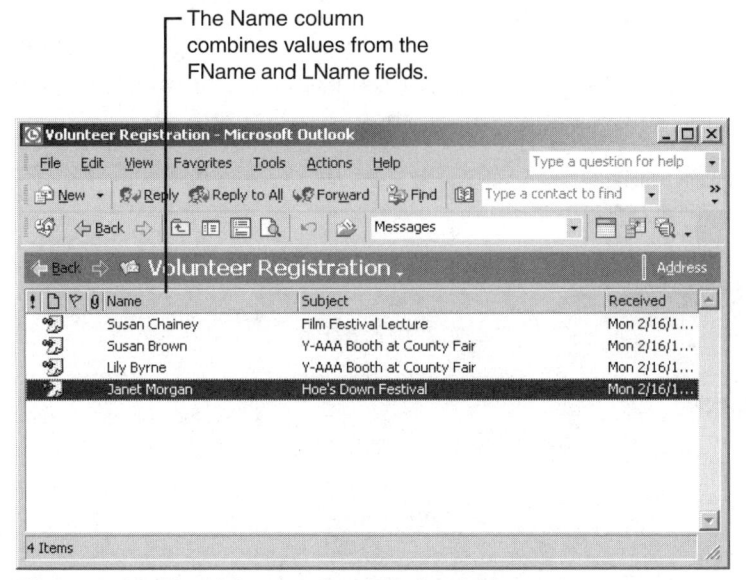

Figure 8-11 The Volunteer Registration folder.

To create a combination column

1. On the Advanced toolbar, click the Field Chooser icon.
2. Click New.
3. In the Name text box, type the column name.
4. In the Type drop-down list box, click Combination.
5. Click Edit.
6. Click Field to add the fields you want to combine, and then click OK twice.
7. From the Field Chooser, drag the field you want as the new column heading to the Column Heading row. Use the red double-arrow marker to position the new column heading in the Column Heading row.

> **Note** Message forms save user-defined fields in the Inbox. Other forms save user-defined fields in the current folder.

265

Part III   Building Blocks of Applications

In some cases, you might want to change the label of the combination column so that it's different from the field name. In addition, you might choose to change the formula specified for the combination column. To do this, you use the Format Columns dialog box, as shown in Figure 8-12.

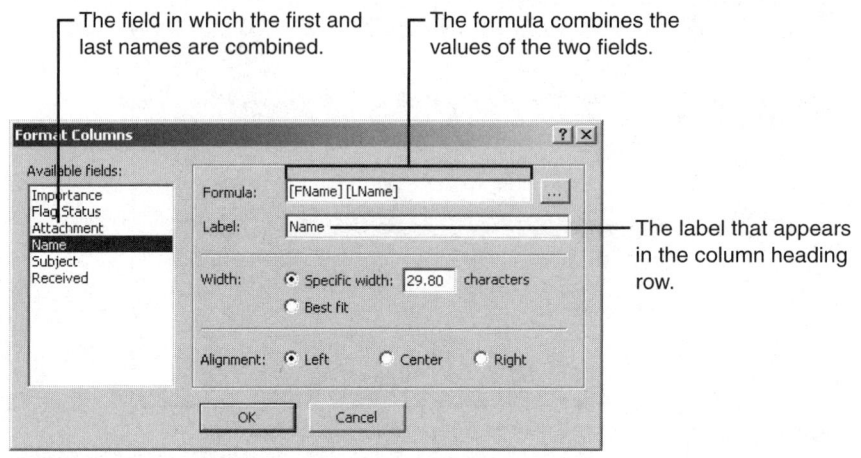

Figure 8-12   The format properties for the Name column in the Volunteer Registration folder.

To change a combination column label or formula

1. Select the folder, right-click the column heading, and then click Format Columns on the shortcut menu.

2. In the Available Fields list box, select the combination field whose properties you want to set, and do one or both of the following:

    ❑   To change the formula, click the button next to the Formula text box.

    ❑   To change the column label, change the text in the Label text box.

3. Click OK.

Create a combination column that shows only the value of the first non-empty field

In some cases, you might want to create a column that shows only the value of the first non-empty field in the item. For example, say you want to create a combination column if you have multiple item types in the folder and the items have fields with similar values but different field names. Assume you have documents and standard post items in a folder and you want to create an Author column. Rather than creating a From column for post items and an Author column for document items, you can create an Author/From field, and then click the Showing Only The First Non-Empty Field, Ignoring Subsequent Ones option.

To create a combination column showing only the value of the first non-empty field

1. On the Advanced toolbar, click the Field Chooser icon.
2. Click New.
3. In the Name text box, type a name.
4. In the Type drop-down list box, click Combination.
5. Click Edit.
6. Click Showing Only The First Non-Empty Field, Ignoring Subsequent Ones.
7. Click Field to add the fields you want to combine, and then click OK twice.
8. From the Field Chooser, drag the field you want as the new column heading to the Column Heading row. Use the double-arrow marker to position the new column heading in the Column Heading row.

Create Formula Columns

For some views, you might want to show different field values in the folder. For example, in the sample Training Management folder, as shown in Figure 8-13, the Course ID/Time and Course Name/Instructor columns are formula columns. In the Course ID/Time column, the value of the CourseID field is shown in the column if the item is a Catalog Entry item. If the item is a Course Offering item, the value of the StartTime field is shown in the column.

To create a formula column

1. On the Advanced toolbar, click the Field Chooser icon.
2. Click New.
3. In the Name text box, type a name.
4. In the Type drop-down list box, click Formula.
5. Click Edit.
6. In the Formula box, specify the formula you want for the column, and then click OK twice.

Part III   Building Blocks of Applications

7. From the Field Chooser, drag the field you want as the new column heading to the Column Heading row. Use the red double-arrow marker to position the new column heading in the Column Heading row.

   You can change the label of the formula column so that it reflects the field values shown in the column. In addition, you might want to change the formula specified for the column.

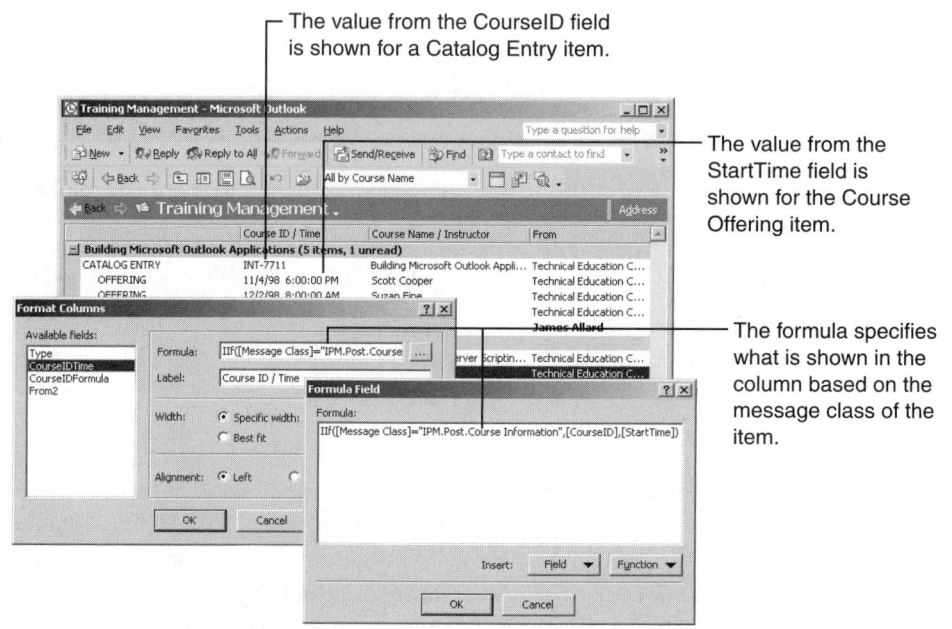

Figure 8-13 The formula for the Course ID/Time column shows a different field value for each message class.

To change a formula column label or formula
---

1. Right-click the column heading, and then click Format Columns on the shortcut menu.

2. In the Available Fields list box, select the field whose properties you want to set, and do one or both of the following:

   ❑ To change the formula, click the button next to the Formula text box.

   ❑ To change the column label, change the text in the Label text box.

3. Click OK.

Group Items

Groups provide a convenient way to organize items that have the same field values in a folder. For example, in the By Ad Type view in the Classified Ads folder, items are grouped by ad type and then by category. As shown in Figure 8-14, items that have a *For Sale* value in the AdType field are grouped together. In addition, items that have an *Electronics-Computer Hardware & Software* value in the Category field are grouped together.

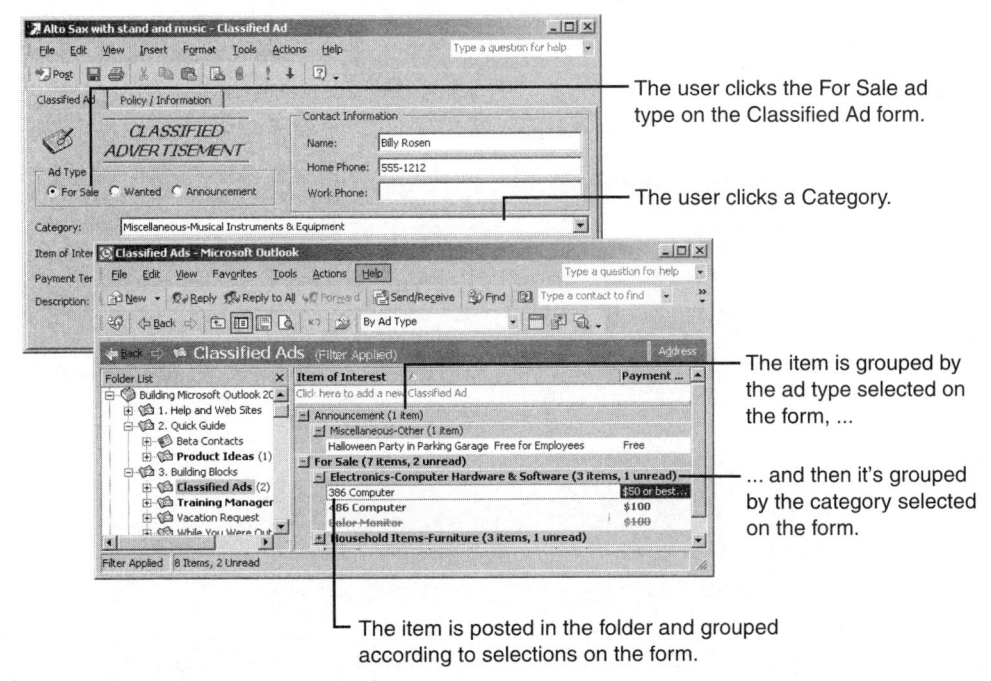

Figure 8-14 The Classified Ad form.

If your application makes use of custom forms, you should consider enforcement of validation rules to ensure that views are complete and logical for the user. A validation rule on a user-defined field requires that a given field have a value, or one value from a range of possible values.

To group items by using Customize Current View

1. On the View menu, select Current View, click Customize Current View, and then click Group By.

2. In the Select Available Fields From drop-down list box, click the field set containing the field you want to group by.

3. Under Group Items By, click the field you want to use to group items.

4. Alternatively, you can click the Show Field In View check box. This option shows the field in the view above the column heading.

5. Click Ascending or Descending. When Ascending is selected, the groups are arranged alphabetically, starting with "A" at the top.

6. To group items into further subsets, click a field in the next available Then By drop-down list box, as shown in Figure 8-15.

7. Click OK twice.

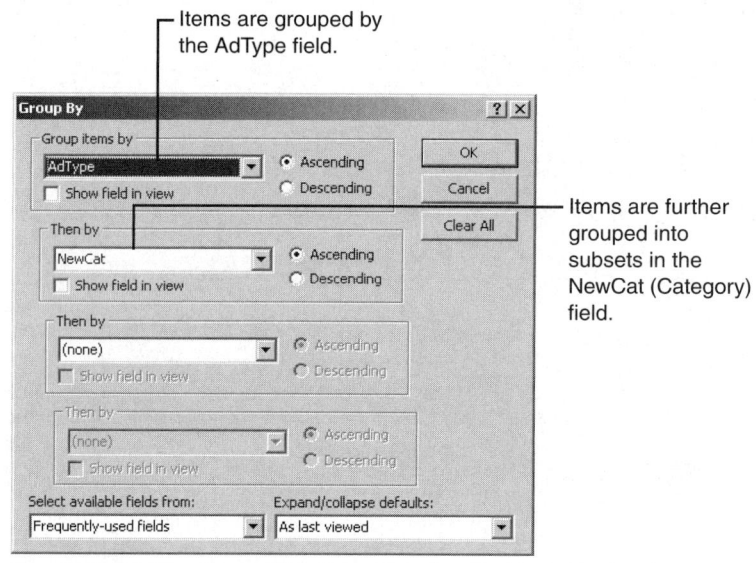

Figure 8-15 The Group By dialog box for the By Ad Type view.

Show or Hide the Group By Box

An easy way to create groups for a view is to show the Group By dialog box, and then drag column headings to the Group By box. You can then hide the Group By box.

To create groups by using the Group By box

1. On the Advanced toolbar, click the Group By icon. The Group By box appears above the column heading area.

2. Drag the fields you want to group by from the Field Chooser, or from the Column Heading row, to the Group By box above the Column Heading row.

3. After you create the groups you want, click the Group By Box icon on the Advanced toolbar to hide the Group By box.

Sort Items

Sorting items provides a convenient way to organize information within a group. For example, you can sort items in a group by the date the items were received, or you can sort items alphabetically. When you specify a field to sort by, you can specify ascending or descending order. Ascending order sorts items in alphabetical order, with the oldest date (or the lowest value) at the top of the list. Descending order sorts items in alphabetical order, with the most recent date (or highest value) at the top of the list. Figure 8-16 shows the items in the By Ad Type view sorted by Subject. Remember that the label for the Subject field is changed in the column heading from Subject to Item Of Interest, as discussed earlier in "Format Columns."

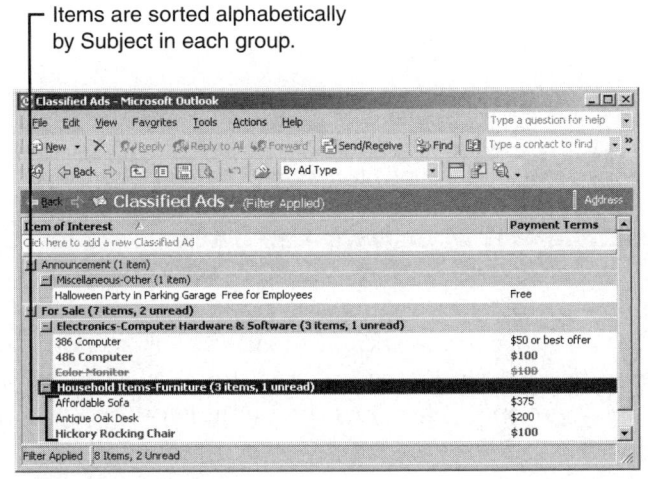

Figure 8-16 Items in each group are sorted alphabetically by Subject in the Item Of Interest column.

To sort items

1. On the View menu, click Current View, and then click Customize Current View.
2. Click Sort.
3. In the Select Available Fields From drop-down list box, click the category of fields containing the field you want to use for sorting.

4. Under Sort Items By, click the field you want to use to sort items by.
5. Click either Ascending or Descending to choose the sort order.
6. To sort items into further subsets, click a field in the next available Then By drop-down list box, as shown in Figure 8-17.
7. Click OK twice.

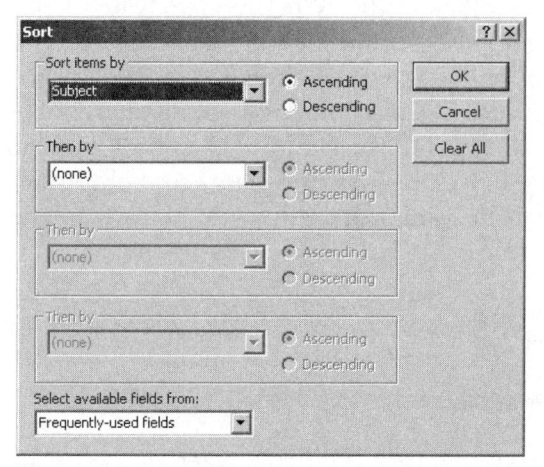

Figure 8-17 Items are sorted alphabetically by the value in the Subject field.

Group by Conversation, Sort by Conversation Index

Conversation and Conversation Index are unique properties that you can use to create views for discussion folders so that people can view the history of responses to an item, also known as a conversation thread. For this section, the Product Ideas folder covered in Chapter 4, "Design a Custom Application," is used to provide an example of grouping by Conversation and sorting by Conversation Index.

Grouping by Conversation Conversation is a unique property that is inherited from the Subject field. For example, if you submit a standard Post item to a folder, the Conversation field of the item is set to the value of the Subject field. Thereafter, any responses made to the item automatically inherit the value of the Conversation field. As shown in Figure 8-18, the items in the Product Ideas folder are grouped by Product Category, and then by Conversation.

Folders   Chapter 8

- Items are grouped by Product Category, and then by Conversation.
- Items within each group are sorted by Conversation Index.

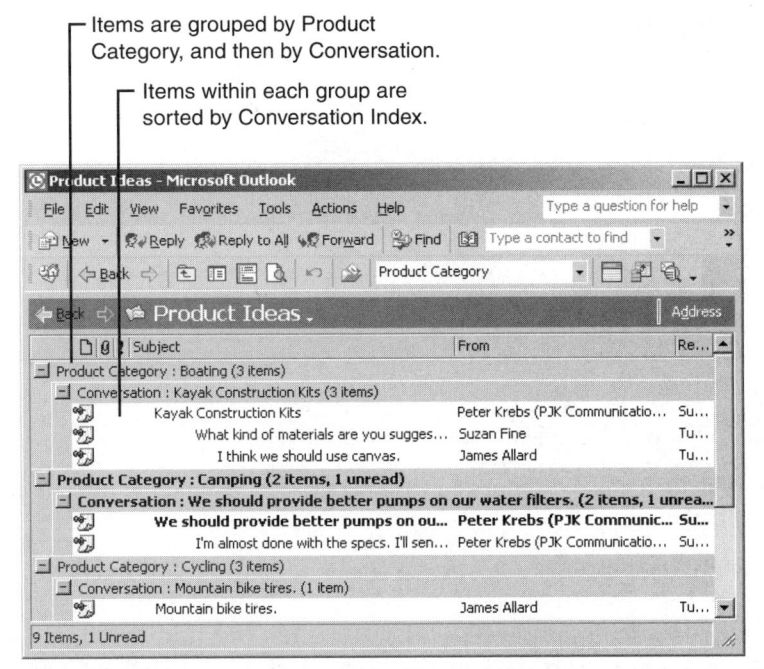

Figure 8-18 Items are grouped by Product Category, and then by Conversation. They are sorted by Conversation Index.

To group items by Conversation

1. On the View menu, select Current View, and then click Customize Current View.

2. Click Group By.

3. In the Select Available Fields From drop-down list box, click Frequently-Used Fields.

4. Under Group Items By, click the field that you want to use to group items by.

5. In the Then By drop-down list box, click Conversation, as shown in Figure 8-19.

6. Click OK twice.

273

Part III Building Blocks of Applications

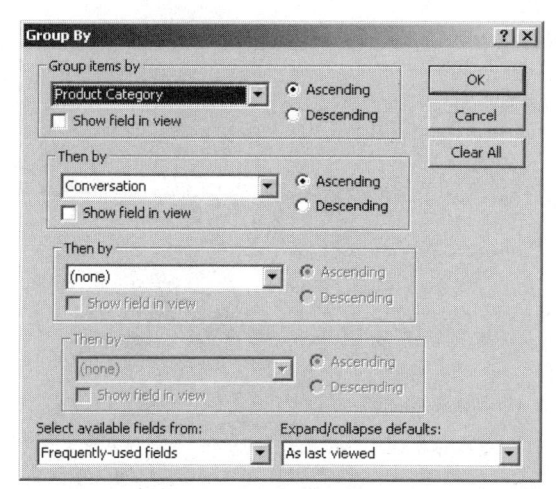

Figure 8-19 Items are grouped by Product Category, and then by Conversation.

Sorting by Conversation Index The Conversation Index property is a way of keeping track of responses. When you sort by Conversation Index, the responses to each item are indented from, and follow directly after, the original item. In this way, users can track the history of responses to an item.

To sort items by Conversation Index

1. On the View menu, select Current View, and then click Customize Current View.
2. Click Sort.
3. Under Sort Items By, click Conversation Index, as shown in Figure 8-20.
4. Click OK twice.

Filter Items

Filters provide a way to find information quickly and easily in a folder. When a filter is applied in a view, only the items that meet the filter conditions show in the folder. For example, as shown in Figure 8-21, the filter created for the By Ad Type view shows only items created with the Classified Ad form (IPM.Post.CreateAd) in the folder.

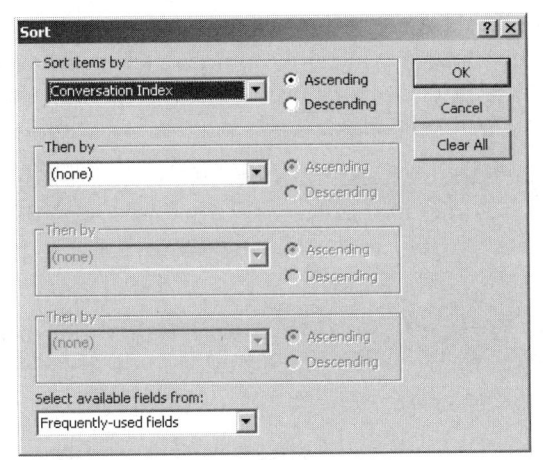

Figure 8-20 When items are sorted by Conversation Index, response items are indented and follow the original item.

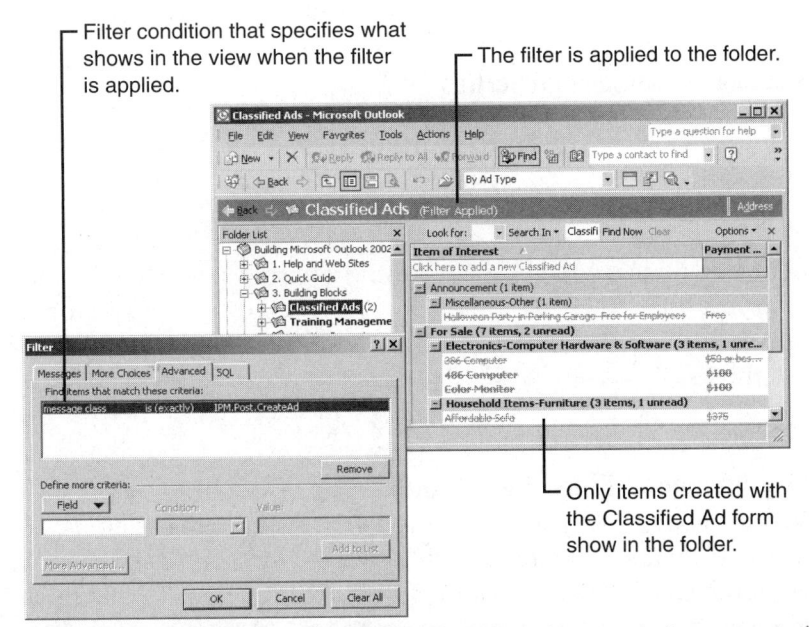

Figure 8-21 The filter for the By Ad Type view shows only items created with the Classified Ad form (IPM.Post.CreateAd) in the folder.

Filters consist of a condition or set of conditions that determine what items are shown in a folder. For example, a condition could be From:Jim Hance. Conditions can have multiple arguments. For example, From:Jim Hance;Don Funk. Here are a few simple guidelines to follow when creating conditions:

- **Multiple conditions are logical AND values**   For example, the condition From:Jim Hance;Subject:GG&G is *True* if the From field of the incoming item contains *Jim Hance* and the Subject field contains *GG&G*.

- **Multiple arguments within a condition are logical OR values**   For example, the condition From:Jim Hance;Karl Buhl;Don Funk;Max Benson is *True* if the From field contains any of the names included in the expression.

Specify Simple Filter Conditions

You can filter messages that meet specific criteria. For example, you can filter all incoming messages from a particular user or about a particular subject.

To filter simple message properties

1. On the View menu, select Current View, and then click Customize Current View.
2. Click Filter.
3. On the Messages page, specify the properties you want for the filter. For example, to create a filter that shows only messages from a particular person, click From, and then double-click the person's name in the list.
4. Click OK twice.

Specify Advanced Filter Conditions

On the Advanced page, you can create a variety of filter conditions. For example, you can specify that only items with a specific message class show in the view. In addition, you can specify that only items with a specific value in a field show in the view.

Filter by message class   When you filter by message class, you specify that only items created with a particular form are visible in the folder. For example, in the

By Ad Type view in the Classified Ads folder, only items created with the Classified Ad form show in the view.

To filter by message class

1. On the View menu, select Current View, and then click Customize Current View.
2. Click Filter.
3. Click the Advanced tab.
4. Click Field, point to All Mail fields, and then click Message Class.
5. In the Condition drop-down list box, click Is (Exactly).
6. In the Value text box, type the message class, as shown in Figure 8-22.
7. Click Add To List.
8. Click OK twice.

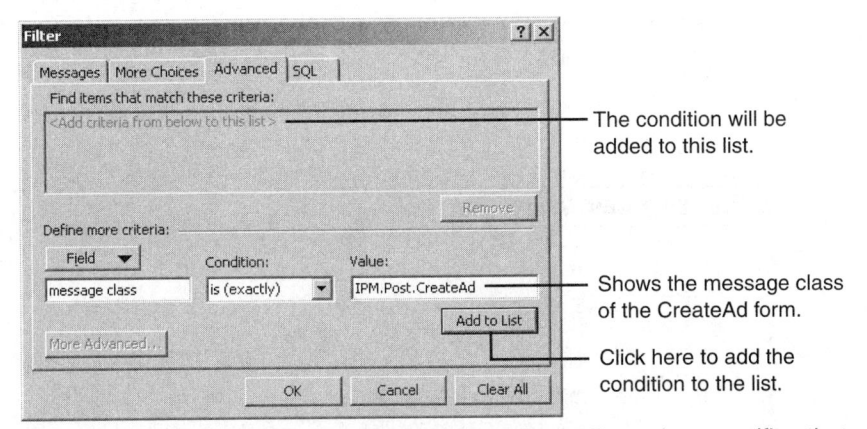

Figure 8-22 The condition for the filter in the By Ad Type view specifies that only items with the message class IPM.Post.CreateAd show in the folder.

Filter by field values   You can create a filter that shows only items that have a specific value in a field. For example, as shown in Figure 8-23, the conditions for the filter specify that only items created with the Classified Ad form and that have the value *For Sale* in the AdType field and the value *Transportation-Cars* in the NewCat field show in the view.

Part III   Building Blocks of Applications

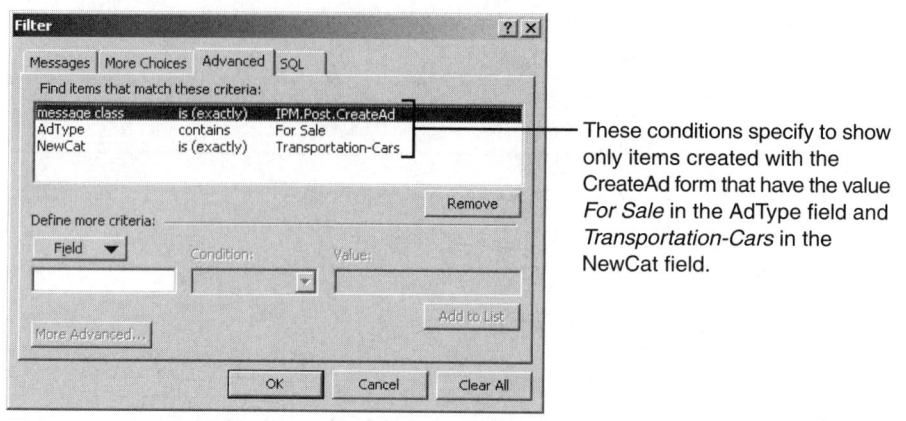

Figure 8-23   Advanced filter conditions for the By Ad Type view.

> **Note**   In Outlook 2002, the Advanced Filter dialog box displays the SQL page visible in Figure 8-23. Do not edit the filter directly on the SQL page unless you are familiar with the construction of SQL queries for Exchange 2000.

To filter by a field value

1. On the View menu, select Current View, and then click Customize Current View.
2. Click Filter.
3. Click the Advanced page.
4. Click Field, point to the field set you want, and then click the field you want.
5. Do one of the following:
   - To filter a single field value, click Is (Exactly) in the Condition drop-down list box, and then type the value you want in the Value text box.
   - To filter multiple values in a field, click Contains in the Condition drop-down list box, and then type the values you want, separated by a comma, in the Value text box.

Folders   Chapter 8

6. Click Add To List.
7. Click OK twice.

Format Views

By using the Other Settings dialog box, accessible from the View Summary dialog box, you can change the fonts in the view, specify grid lines for the view, specify whether group headings are to be shaded, and turn on in-cell editing so that users can enter and edit information in the cells in the folder, as shown in Figure 8-24.

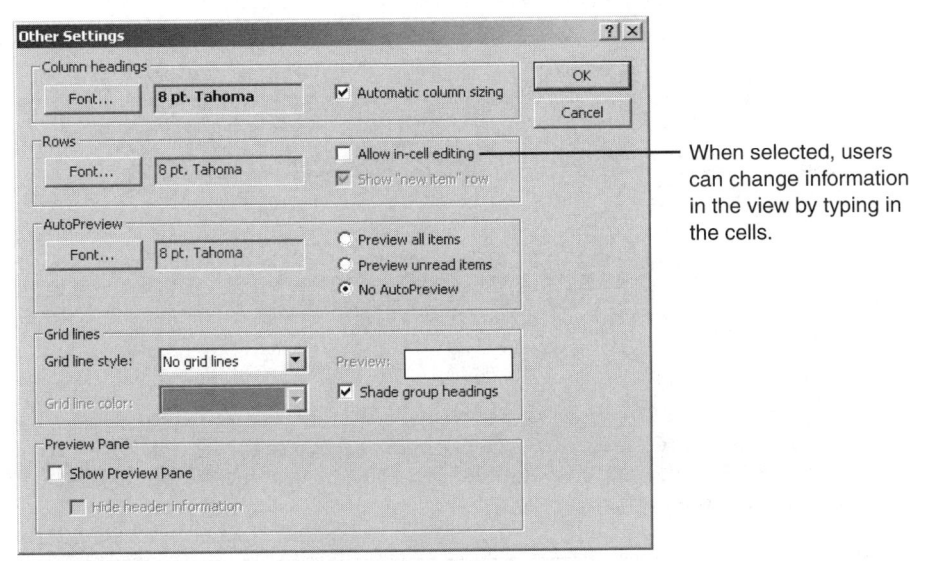

When selected, users can change information in the view by typing in the cells.

Figure 8-24 Format options for the By Ad Type view.

To format a view

1. In the Current View drop-down list box on the Advanced toolbar, switch to the view you want to change.
2. On the View menu, select Current View, and then click Customize Current View. You can also right-click a field heading in the current view and select Customize Current View from the shortcut menu.
3. Click Other Settings.
4. Select the options you want, and then click OK twice.

279

Part III Building Blocks of Applications

In-Cell Editing Views

If you check Allow In-Cell Editing in the Other Settings dialog box, users can edit item information directly from the view. The Beta Contacts sample application discussed in Chapter 3 has both in-cell editing and Show "New Item" Row enabled in the Potential Beta Participants view shown in Figure 8-25. Users do not have to open the form to change field values. You can also expose a new item row so that users can enter new information from the view rather than using the Actions menu to open a new form instance.

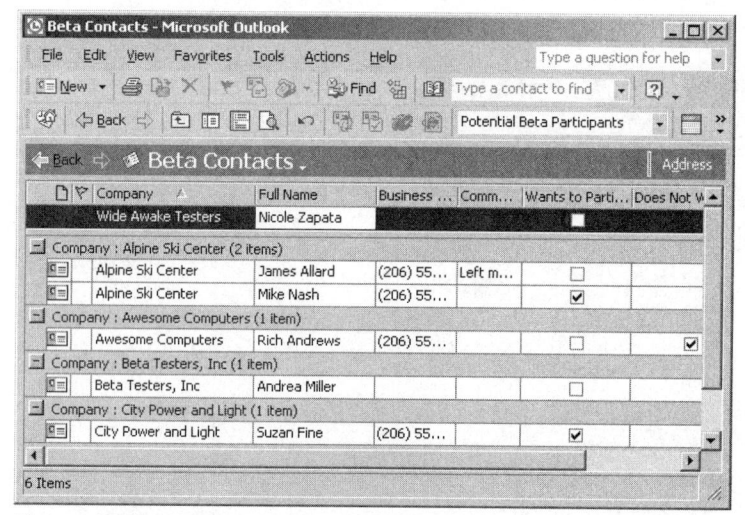

Figure 8-25 In-cell and new item editing allow item creation and modification directly in the view without opening an item.

To enable in-cell editing and a new items row

1. In the Current View drop-down list box on the Advanced toolbar, switch to the view you want to change.
2. On the View menu, select Current View, and then click Customize Current View.
3. Click Other Settings.
4. Check the Allow In-Cell Editing box.
5. Check the Show "New Item" Row box.
6. Click OK twice.

> **Note** Use in-cell editing and the new items row with caution in a public folder. If you are using a custom form (IPM.Contact.Beta Contact) rather than a built-in form (IPM.Contact or IPM.Post), you could experience problems with one-off form creation and the firing of CustomPropertyChange events in VBScript code when you enable in-cell editing. For a detailed explanation of these issues, search for the following articles on *http://support.microsoft.com/support/*:
> - Working with User-Defined Fields in Solutions (*http://support.microsoft.com/support/kb/articles/q201/4/38.asp*)
> - Working with Form Definitions and One-Off Forms (*http://support.microsoft.com/support/kb/articles/q207/8/96.asp*)

Automatic Formatting

You can format the font of the individual items in the row on the basis of built-in rules such as whether the item has been read. You can create your own rules for automatic formatting of an item that depend on a custom set of conditions. Figure 8-26 illustrates a custom condition to highlight items according to special rules in the Classified Ads folder. Custom automatic formatting rules use the Filter dialog box explained earlier to set conditions for the rule. Follow the guidelines shown in this chapter's "Filter Items" section to create rules in a folder to produce automatic formatting.

To create automatic formatting for individual messages in a view

1. In the Current View drop-down list box on the Advanced toolbar, switch to the view you want to change.
2. On the View menu, select Current View, and then click Customize Current View.
3. Click Automatic Formatting.
4. Click Add.
5. Type a name for the automatic formatting rule in the Name edit box.
6. Click Font and select the font name, size, weight, and special effects in the Font dialog box. Click OK to confirm your font selection.

Part III Building Blocks of Applications

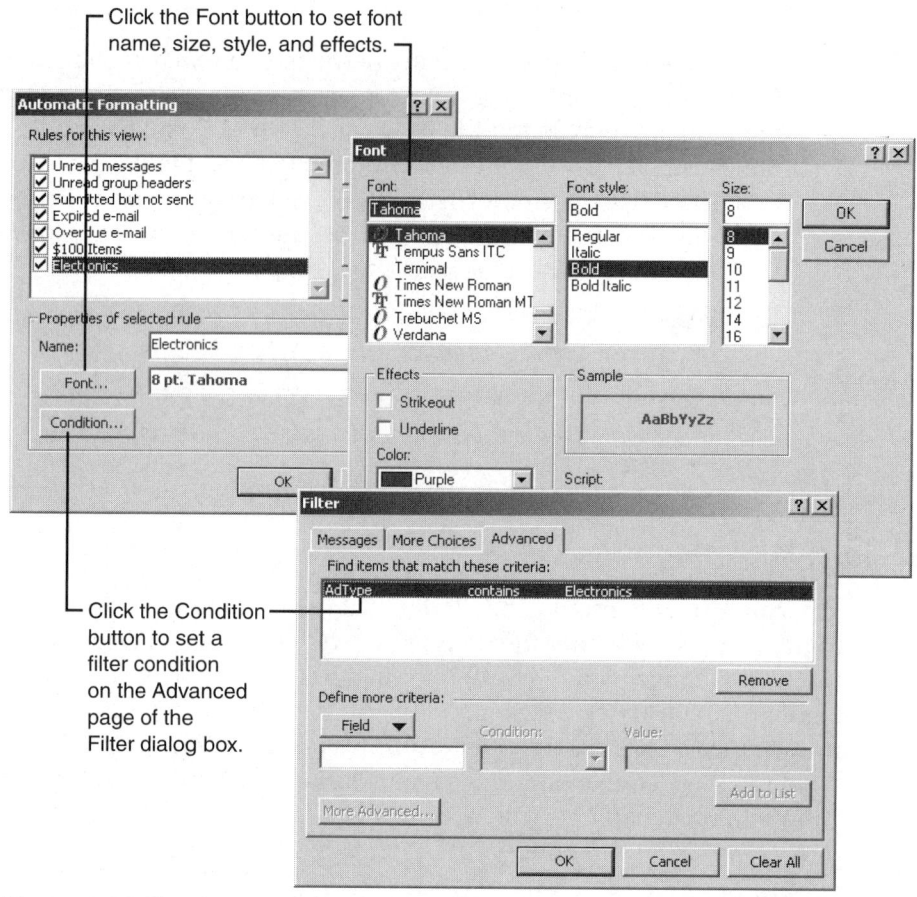

Figure 8-26 The Automatic Formatting dialog box lets you establish font colors and sizes for a folder view.

7. Click Conditions to establish a filter for your automatic formatting rule. Use the guidelines for filters discussed earlier. Click OK to confirm your filter.

8. Click Move Up or Move Down to change the order of precedence by which your rule will be applied to an item for automatic formatting. Note that you cannot move your automatic formatting rule above the default formatting rules for the folder. Each folder type has a given set of automatic formatting rules.

9. Click OK twice.

View Performance

When you design a public folder application, you should consider the time that will be required to build views and present the view to the user in Outlook. Not all views render instantly, especially when there are thousands of items in the application folder. View performance depends on several factors, including the number of items in the folder and the time interval between the current time and the time when the user last inspected the folder using the current view.

Here are some general rules to follow when you design views for an application folder:

- Don't create so many views for the folder that the users have difficulty selecting the correct view for the information they are seeking to display.

- Name your views clearly so that their purpose is easily understood by the user.

- If possible, create the folder views you will need when the number of items in the folder is small. This reduces the time needed to create the original view index.

- Views for online users are cached on the Exchange Server where the public folder is stored. If the view is not used within an eight-day default cache interval, the view must be refreshed and view indexes rebuilt when an Outlook client requests a folder view. Your Exchange Server administrator can change the cache interval to a longer interval, if necessary.

- See Q159197 at *http://support.microsoft.com/support/kb/articles/q159/ 1/97.asp* for details on modifying the registry to control folder index aging.

- Views for offline users will be slower than views for online users. Use filtered synchronization to reduce the number of items in an offline public folder. The Outlook client supports only one index at a time, so it might take a long time to change views off line if the number of folder items is large.

Use Folder Home Pages

Folder home pages are a powerful means to extend views for application folders. Folder home pages let you set a default view on a folder based on a home page URL that points to a page on your Web server containing custom script to render the view in the Outlook Web view pane. See Chapter 15, "Integrating Outlook with Web Applications," for a complete discussion on programming custom folder home pages.

Think of a folder home page as a customizable Outlook Today page for a given folder or a hierarchy of subfolders. You can establish folder home pages for folders in a personal information store, a private mailbox, or Exchange public folders. Folder home page views are available only if you are using Outlook 2000 or later. Users of Outlook 97 and Outlook 98 will see the normal default view on the folder.

Folder Home Page Scenarios

Figure 8-27 shows a folder home page that serves as the default view for the Discussion folder in a Team Project application created by the Team Folder Wizard. Notice that the folder home page provides functionality not available in conventional Outlook views. Customize View and Mark All As Read hotspots let you embed commands directly into your view. By pointing and clicking, a user changes views without resorting to the Advanced toolbar. Find and Advanced Find functionality is simplified in the Discussion Folder Home Page.

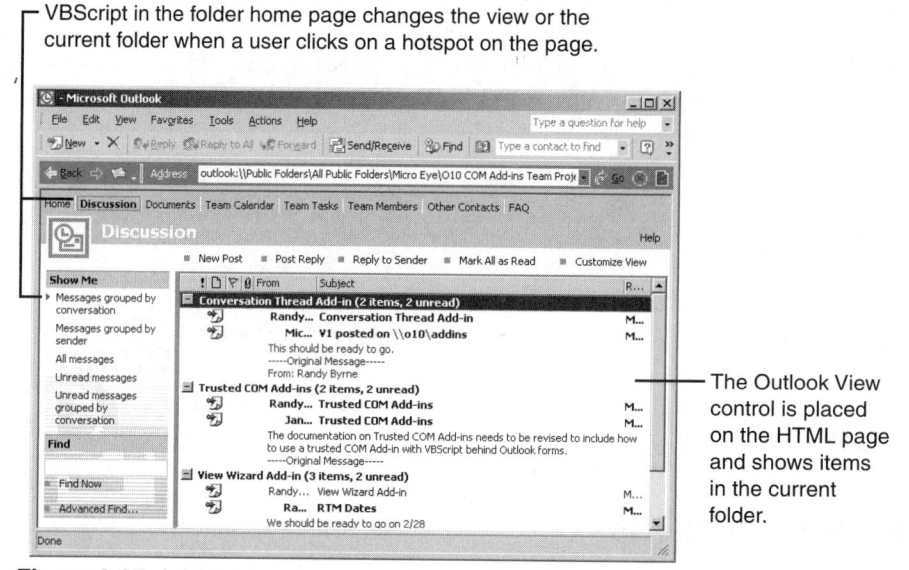

Figure 8-27 A folder home page serves as the default view for the Discussion folder.

Folder home pages can also provide special functionality in a parent folder that contains many subfolders. Figure 8-28 illustrates a folder home page in the Exchange/Outlook Development public folder. This folder is actually a placeholder folder containing many subfolders relating to Microsoft Outlook. The default permission on this folder is none; users are not allowed to post items in this folder.

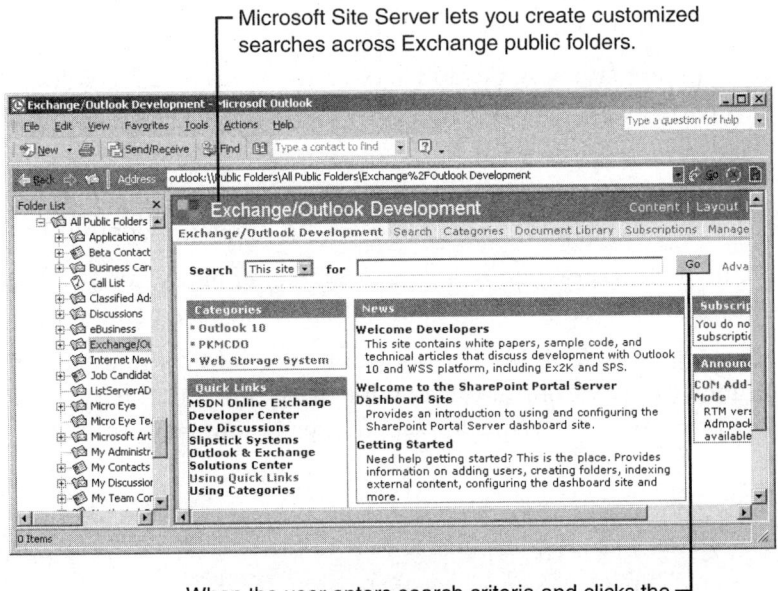

Microsoft Site Server lets you create customized searches across Exchange public folders.

When the user enters search criteria and clicks the Go button, Site Server returns an HTML page that shows all items that satisfy the criteria. You can display the Search page as a folder home page to allow users to search a folder and its subfolders.

Figure 8-28 A SharePoint Portal Server folder home page provides search capabilities, document management, news, quick links, and announcements for its target audience.

A user navigating to the Exchange/Outlook Development folder will encounter a folder home page allowing her to search all the items in the subfolders of the parent folder by using the built-in search capability of SharePoint Portal Server. For additional information on using SharePoint Portal Server with Outlook and Exchange, see Chapter 16, "Using Outlook with SharePoint Portal Server."

Folder Home Page Considerations

Here are important factors to consider when you establish a folder home page:

- A folder owner or application designer might elect to display a folder home page, but an individual user can override this setting and turn off the folder home page.

- Using a COM Add-in can help you ensure that a folder home page will always appear when a user navigates to a folder.

- You can programmatically add a folder to the Application Folders Send/Receive group as well as start folder synchronization. For additional details, see Chapter 11.

- Folder home page settings are established on a per-mailbox basis, independent of the Exchange profile on a given machine.

- Folder home pages can be made available off line as long as Microsoft Internet Explorer 5 or later is installed on the system.

- If you elect to download folder home pages for offline use, you can establish a synchronization schedule, determine the depth of links to synchronize on the page, and set the maximum amount of disk space to use for the offline page.

- Unlike the per-mailbox setting for the display of folder home pages, the offline Web page setting is per machine.

To set a folder home page

1. In the Folder List, right-click the folder you want to set properties for, and then click Properties on the shortcut menu.
2. Click the Home Page tab.
3. Check the Show Home Page By Default For This Folder box.
4. Enter the URL for the folder home page in the Address edit box as shown in Figure 8-29. You must enter a valid URL that points to either a page on your intranet or a page on an external site. External site pages are not recommended because the page might be unavailable. If you enter an invalid URL, your browser will report that it could not open the URL.
5. Click OK.

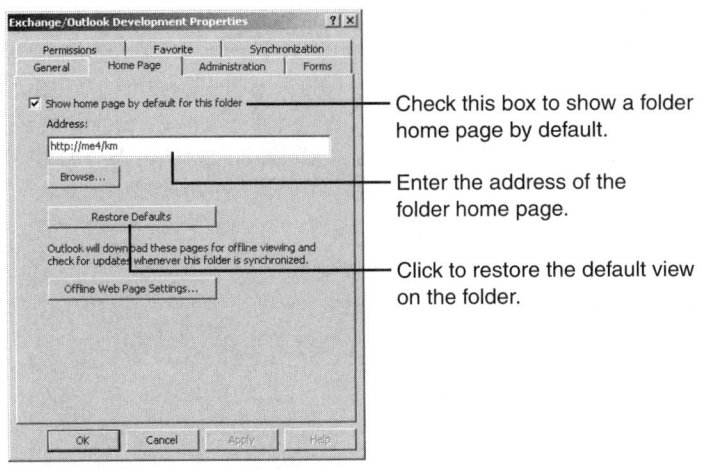

Figure 8-29 Set a folder home page by using the Home Page tab of the Folder properties dialog box.

> **Note** If you want to reset a folder home page view to the default Outlook view, right-click the folder in the folder list and clear the Show Home Page By Default For This Folder check box on the Home Page tab of the Folder properties dialog box. You can also click the Restore Defaults button, which clears the check box and the Address edit box. Unlike Outlook 2000, Outlook 2002 does not have a Show Folder Home Page command on the View menu that lets users hide or show a folder home page. Folder home page settings are established on a per-mailbox basis. If you want to prevent a user from turning off a folder home page, you can create a COM Add-in that always will display a folder home page when a user navigates to the target folder.

Offline Use

Folder home pages can also be configured for offline use. If you use a folder home page to provide help for your application, you can ensure that a user has help whether working on line or off line. If you use a folder home page that retrieves dynamic data from a database, remember that the page might not have the most current information when a user is off line. Outlook 2002 uses Send/Receive groups instead of the Quick Synchronization groups found in Outlook 2000. If you want to establish an offline folder home page for Outlook 2000, consult the online documentation.

Part III   Building Blocks of Applications

To configure a folder home page for offline use

1. To configure a folder home page for offline use in a Public Folder, you must first add the Public Folder to Favorites by right-clicking the folder in the folder list and then selecting the Add To Favorites command. Complete the Add To Favorites dialog box as shown in Figure 8-30, and then click OK.

2. On the Tools menu, point to Send/Receive Settings and then click Define Send/Receive Groups.

3. In the Group Name list box shown in Figure 8-38 on page 307, click a Send/Receive group containing an Exchange Server account and then click Edit. The default Send/Receive group is All Accounts.

4. Under Accounts, click the Exchange Server account.

5. In the folder tree, select the folders that you want to be available off line, as shown in Figure 8-31. Public folders that are available for offline use will appear under the Favorites folder under Public Folders.

6. Select the Make Folder Home Pages Available Offline check box.

7. Click OK, and then click Close.

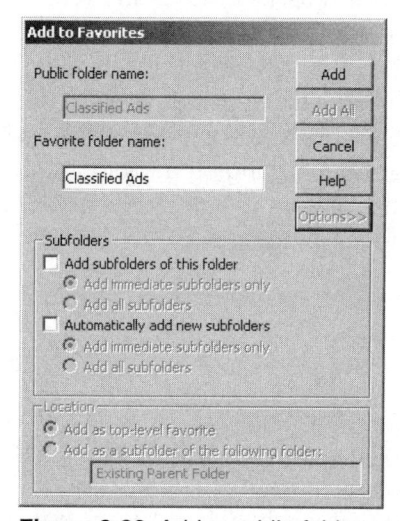

Figure 8-30 Add a public folder to Favorites with the Add To Favorites dialog box.

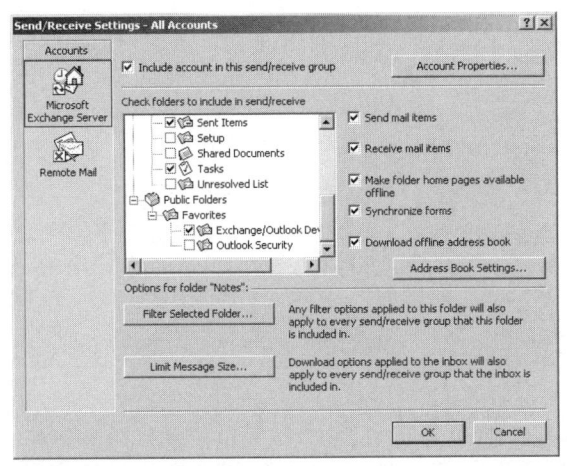

Figure 8-31 Make folder home pages available off line with the Send/Receive Settings dialog box.

To establish offline Web page settings

1. You must install Internet Explorer 5 or later to set a Web page for offline use.

2. In the folder list, right-click the folder you want to set properties for, and then click Properties on the shortcut menu.

3. Click the Home Page tab.

4. Click the Offline Web Page Settings button, as shown in Figure 8-29 (on page 287).

5. Select the Make This Page Available Offline box on the Web Document page of the Offline Web Page Settings dialog box illustrated in Figure 8-32.

6. Use the Schedule page to set a synchronization schedule.

7. Use the Download page to establish settings for depth of links, limits on hard disk usage, and notification of page changes. You can click the Advanced button on the Download page to determine whether to download the Images, Sound And Video, and ActiveX controls as well as Java applets.

8. Click OK twice.

Part III Building Blocks of Applications

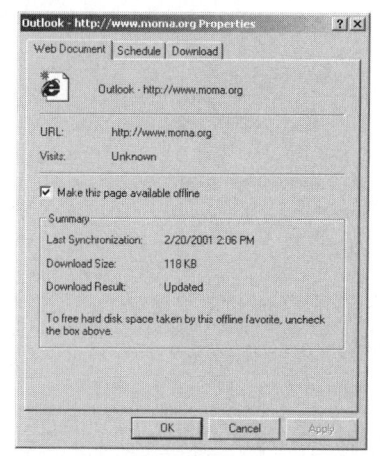

Figure 8-32 The Offline Web Page Settings dialog box provides granular control over offline folder home pages.

Set General Properties

On the General page of the Properties dialog box, as shown in Figure 8-33, you can specify the default form that appears when a user creates a new item in a folder. For example, for the Classified Ads folder, the Classified Ad form appears when the user clicks the New Post In This Folder command on the Actions menu.

- Specifies the form that appears when the user clicks the New Post In This Folder command.
- Generates views for users running Microsoft Exchange Client.

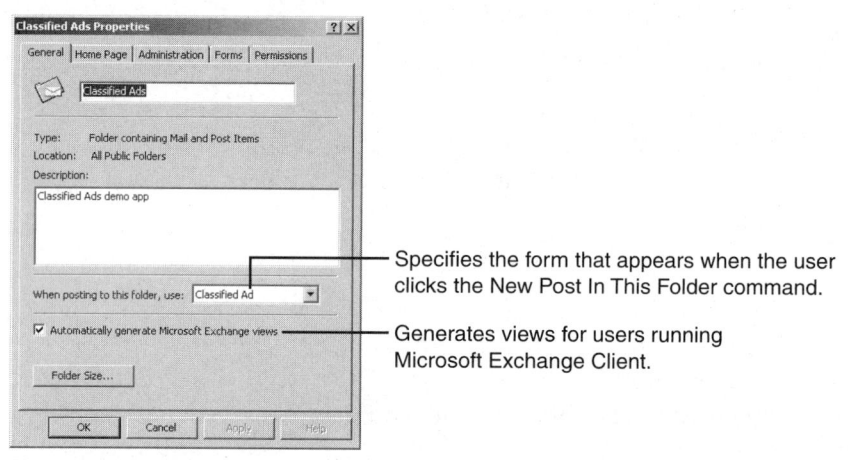

Figure 8-33 The options in the When Posting To This Folder, Use drop-down list box specify which form appears when the New Post In This Folder command is clicked.

To set general properties

1. In the Folder List, right-click the folder you want to set properties for, and then click Properties on the shortcut menu.
2. Click the General page.

To specify the form that appears when the user clicks the New Post In This Folder command

- In the When Posting To This Folder, Use drop-down list box, click the form that you want to appear when the user clicks Post In This Folder after selecting New on the File menu.
    If you do not want a custom form to appear, click Post in the When Posting To This Folder, Use drop-down list box.

To automatically generate Microsoft Exchange views

- If your organization uses both Microsoft Exchange Client and Outlook, select the Automatically Generate Microsoft Exchange Views check box. This option generates Microsoft Exchange views for the folder so that the views can be seen by users of the Microsoft Exchange Client, the predecessor to Outlook.

> **Note** This property is only available for Outlook table views.

Test Forms and Views

After you publish forms and define views for the folder, you need to test them to make sure they work as expected.

To test the forms, open the folder in which the forms are published, and then click the menu commands that are associated with the form on the Actions menu. In the form, enter the information you want, and then click the Post button. After posting the item in the folder, double-click it to open it and make sure it shows information correctly in the form. You should test each form in the folder.

To test views, open the folder you want to test, and then click each of the views in the Current View drop-down list box on the Advanced toolbar. If the folder has multiple forms, you should post several types of items in the folder before testing the views.

Part III Building Blocks of Applications

When you finish testing the forms and views, you can delete the test items you posted in the folder.

Copy the Folder to Public Folders

After adding forms, defining views, and testing their functionality, you are ready to copy your folder to Public Folders. You can then complete the folder design by designating types of items allowed in the folder, setting permissions, setting administration properties, and specifying rules. This step is necessary only if you started the folder design process with a personal folder or a mailbox folder, and not with a public folder.

Depending on the policies of your organization, you might not have permission to add a folder to Public Folders. You might be required to hand off the folder to your administrator, who then copies the folder and completes the design task according to your specifications. Perhaps you'll be given permission to copy your folder to a specific public folder and then complete the task yourself. See your administrator for specific instructions.

To copy the folder to a new location

1. In the Folder List, right-click the folder, and then click Copy Folder Name on the shortcut menu.
2. Select the public folder you want to copy the folder to, and then click OK.

Specify Internet Newsgroup

The Internet News page identifies the folder as an Internet newsgroup folder. Users of Internet newsreader software within a Microsoft Exchange environment can view and post items posted in the newsgroup folder.

To set a Public Folder as a Newsgroup folder

1. In the Folder List, right-click the folder you want to identify as a newsgroup folder, and then click Properties on the shortcut menu.
2. Click the Internet News page.
3. Select the Publish This Folder To Users Of Newsreader Software check box.

> **Note** In order to access the Internet News page in the Folder Properties dialog box, you must have privileges to administer NNTP, and the Internet News Service must be established on your Microsoft Exchange Server. For additional information, see the documentation that accompanies Microsoft Exchange Server.

Set Administration Properties

After you copy a folder to a public folder, it's a good idea to restrict access to the folder while you set folder permissions and test the folder. To restrict access to the folder, you can use the This Folder Is Available To option on the Administration page, as shown in Figure 8-34.

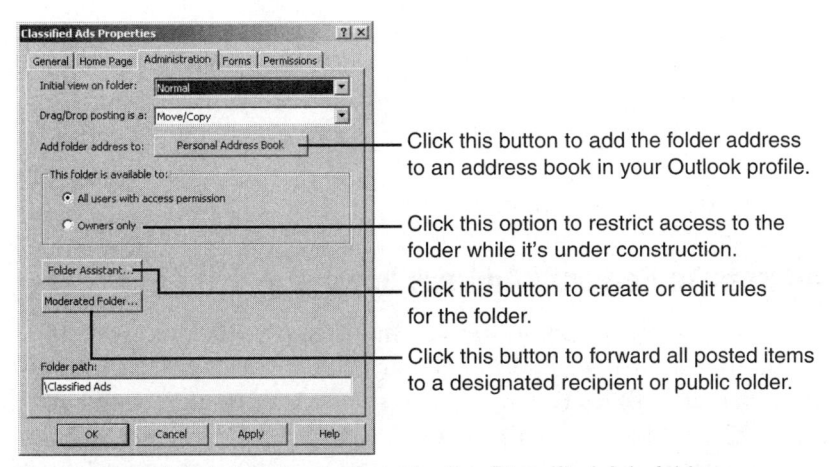

Figure 8-34 Administration options for the Classified Ads folder.

To restrict access to the folder

1. In the Folder list, right-click the folder, and then click Properties on the shortcut menu.
2. Click the Administration tab.
3. Click Owners Only.

Initial View On Folder

You use this option to specify the folder view that you want to display when the user first opens the folder. By default, this view is the Messages or Normal view, depending on the type of items the folder contains.

Drag/Drop Posting Is A

You use this option to specify how Outlook formats items that are dragged to a folder. You can specify that the drag/drop operation formats the posted item in one of the following ways:

- **Move/Copy** This option specifies that when an item is dragged to a folder, Outlook does not reformat the item. For example, if Eric Lang drags an item sent by Clair Hector from his Inbox to the Employee Feedback folder, the item appearing in the Employee Feedback folder is shown as sent by Clair Hector.

- **Forward** This option specifies that when an item is dragged to a folder, Outlook reformats the item to show that it has been forwarded by the user who dragged it to the folder. For example, if Eric Lang drags an Inbox item from Clair Hector to the Employee Feedback folder, the item in the Employee Feedback folder appears as though it has been forwarded by Eric Lang.

Add Folder Address To Personal Address Book

You use this option to preaddress forms. When you click the Personal Address Book button, the folder address is automatically added to an Address Book in your Exchange profile. Unlike previous versions of Outlook, which would only add a public folder address to your Personal Address Book when you clicked the Personal Address Book button, Outlook 2000 or later will add the folder address to the Address Book selected in the Keep Personal Addresses In drop-down list box on the Addressing page of the Services dialog box for your Exchange profile. You can then use the folder address in your Address Book to preaddress a Message form to a folder or to create a rule that automatically forwards items to the folder.

> **Tip** Another way to make the folder address available for preaddressing a form is to ask your Exchange administrator to add the folder address to the Global Address Book. Normally, public folder addresses are hidden from the Global Address Book. However, your Exchange administrator can unhide the public folder address by using the Exchange Administrator program. You can then select the folder name from the Global Address Book to preaddress a form.

> **More Info** For more information about preaddressing a Message form to a folder address, see "To Field" in Chapter 6, "Controls, Fields, and Properties."

This Folder Is Available To

You use this option to make a folder unavailable while it's under construction. You can click Owners Only when you are modifying or creating a folder design. This gives only those people with the Owner role permission to access the folder. After the folder is tested and ready for general use, you can click All Users With Access Permission and make the folder available for public use.

> **Tip** The Owners Only option prevents access to the specified folder, but does not prevent access to subfolders. This way, users can post items in a subfolder while the parent folder is disabled.

Folder Assistant

You can click the Folder Assistant button to create rules that automatically process incoming folder items. Rules are described in more detail in "Design Rules" later in this chapter.

Part III Building Blocks of Applications

Moderated Folder

You can use a moderated folder to cause all posted items to be forwarded to a designated recipient or public folder for review. Permissions must be granted to move these items back into the folder for general viewing once they have been reviewed and approved.

Set Permissions

You assign permissions to users to define the functions they can perform in the folder. You determine who can view and use the folder by adding the user names, distribution list names, or public folder names to the Name list box on the Permissions page. After the names are added to the Name list box, you can assign roles to define the permissions for each user or distribution list, as shown in Figure 8-35.

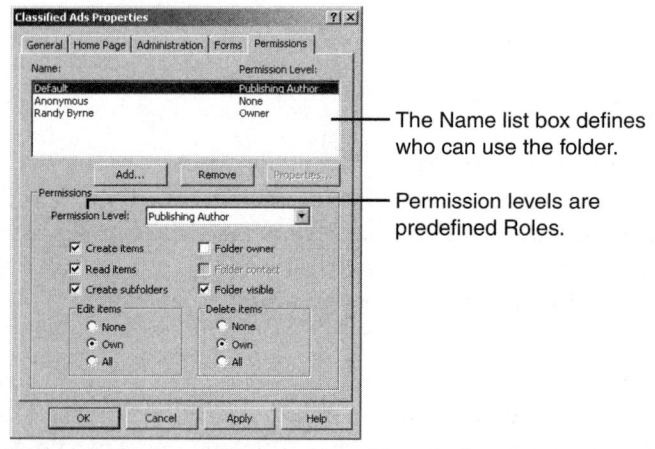

Figure 8-35 Permissions for the Classified Ads folder. Modify the Name List.

> **Note** Permissions can be set for folders in your Mailbox or public folders. Permissions cannot be set for personal folders.

To open the Permissions page

1. In the Folder List, right-click the folder you want to set permissions for, and then click Properties on the shortcut menu.

2. Click the Permissions tab.

The names in the Name list box determine who can view and use the folder. If you create the folder, you are automatically given owner permissions for the folder. With owner permissions, you can add users to, and remove users from, the Name list box. You can also change permissions for selected users.

One name in the Name list box is *Default*. The permissions defined for *Default* are granted to all users who have access to the folder. If you want to give a particular user permissions other than *Default*, add the user's name to the Name list box, and then set permissions for that user.

When you test the folder, it's a good idea to set the *Default* permissions to None in the Roles drop-down list box. Then, grant access to a limited number of users. When you are sure that everything is working correctly in the folder, you can change the *Default* permissions and add names to the Name list box.

You can remove any name from the Name list box except *Default* and, if you are the sole owner of the folder, your name. If you remove *Default* or your name, they will reappear the next time you view the Permissions page.

About Distribution Lists

Distribution lists provide a convenient way to assign permissions to a group of users. For example, rather than enter 50 names in the Name list box, you can enter the distribution list name to assign permissions to all users on the list.

To add a user, distribution list, or folder name to the Name list box

1. On the Permissions page, click Add.

2. Click the user, distribution list, or folder you want to add, and then click Add.

3. Click OK.

> **Note** Public folder permissions are designed to be optimistic. Optimistic here implies the least restrictive set of permissions. The permissions that apply to the user include the set of permissions the user inherits from each of the groups the user belongs to, in addition to the explicit permissions granted directly to the user's individual account. A user's permission level is always the least restrictive of that user's explicit permissions and the permissions of any and all groups to which that user belongs.
>
> For example, users A and B exist on a site. The Exchange administrator creates two distribution lists (DLs): Manager and Sales Team. Both user A and user B are added to the Sales Team DL; only user A is added to the Manager DL. Then, on folder X, the Manager DL is given the Owner role, and the Sales Team DL is given the Author role. User A will ultimately have owner permissions on folder X, even though user A is a member of the Sales Team DL, which has only the Author role. User B is limited to the Author role on folder X.

Assign Roles

When you set permissions for a user, you define the functions he or she can perform within the folder. You can set permissions by using predefined roles or by using custom roles:

- **Predefined roles** Predefined groups of permissions that are available from the Roles drop-down list box.

- **Custom roles** Permissions you set for the user that do not match any of the predefined roles.

To assign roles to users

1. In the Name list box on the Permissions page, click the user name you want to set permissions for.
2. In the Roles drop-down list box, click a role for the user.
3. The following table lists the roles and the predefined permissions that are assigned to each role.

Role	Description
Owner	Create, read, modify, and delete all items and files and create subfolders. As the folder owner, you can change permissions others have for the folder.
Publishing Editor	Create, read, modify, and delete all items and files and create subfolders.
Editor	Create, read, modify, and delete all items and files.
Nonediting Author	Create and read items. This person or group cannot edit, but can delete items and files you create.
Publishing Author	Create and read items and files, create subfolders, and modify and delete items and files you create.
Author	Create and read items and files, and modify and delete items and files you create.
Reviewer	Read items and files only.
Contributor	Create items and files only. The user cannot open the folder.
None	The user cannot open the folder.
Custom	Perform activities defined by the folder owner, from options selected on the Permissions page.

To assign a custom role

1. In the Name list box, click the user name whose permissions you want to set.

2. In the Roles drop-down list box, click the role that most closely resembles the permissions you want to grant to the user.

3. Under Permissions, select the options you want. If the permissions do not match a role, you will see Custom in the Roles drop-down list box. If the permissions match a role, the role will show in the Roles drop-down list box.

Set Permissions for Subfolders

If you want to automate setting permissions for subfolders, use the Exchange Administrator program (Exchange 5.0 or 5.5) or the Exchange System Manager (Exchange 2000) to propagate client permissions for the subfolders of a public folder. Contact your Exchange administrator if you are not allowed to run Exchange administrative tools.

Part III Building Blocks of Applications

To use Exchange 5.0 or 5.5

1. On the Start menu, point to Programs, point to Microsoft Exchange, and then point to Microsoft Exchange Administrator.

2. Navigate to the parent folder under Public Folders (Organization\Folders\Public Folders) in the console tree.

3. Select Properties on the File menu.

4. Check the Propagate These Properties To All Subfolders check box on the General tab.

5. Click the Client Permissions button, and then select the permissions for the parent folder. Click OK twice.

6. Make sure that Client Permissions is checked in the Subfolder Properties dialog box, and then click OK.

To use Exchange 2000

1. On the Start menu, point to Programs, point to Microsoft Exchange, and then point to System Manager.

2. Navigate to the parent folder under Public Folders (Organization\Administrative Groups\First Administrative Group\Folders) in the console tree.

3. Right-click the parent folder, and select Properties.

4. Click the Permissions tab, and then click the Client Permissions button.

5. Select the permissions for the parent folder. Click OK twice.

6. Right-click the parent folder, and then select Propagate Settings from the All Tasks submenu.

7. Check Folder Rights in the Propagate Folder Settings dialog box, and then click OK.

Design Rules

Rules automatically process items as they arrive in a folder. A rule consists of two parts: a set of conditions that are applied to an incoming item, and the actions that are taken if the conditions are met, as shown in Figure 8-36.

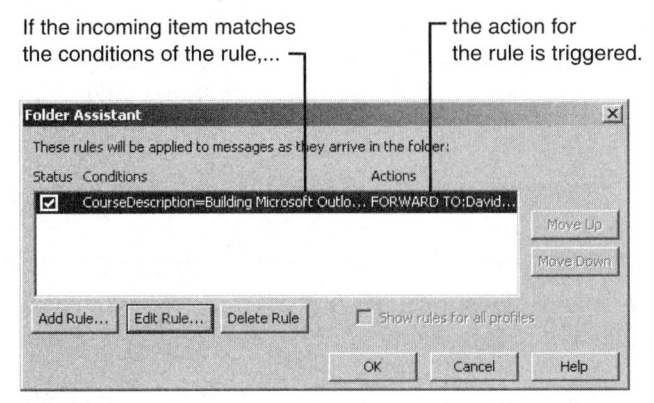

If the incoming item matches the conditions of the rule,... — the action for the rule is triggered.

Figure 8-36 Rules for the Training Management folder.

You can use rules to

- Specify that certain types of items are automatically returned to the sender
- Automatically delete items based on the specified conditions
- Automatically reply to specific kinds of items with a reply template
- Automatically forward specific types of items to another folder or user

To create rules

1. In the Folder List, right-click the folder, and then click Properties on the shortcut menu.
2. Click the Administration tab, and then click Folder Assistant.

> **Note** Folder Assistant is only available for public folders.

Specifying Conditions of a Rule

The conditions of a rule identify the items that are to be processed by the rule. These conditions can range from very simple to relatively advanced. An example of a simple condition is From:James Allard. This condition states that if an item is submitted to the folder and the item is from James Allard, then a specified action is taken. A more advanced set of conditions is Only Messages That Do Not Match This Criteria; From:James Allard;Joe Howard;Scott Cooper. These conditions state that if the items submitted to the folder are not from James Allard, Joe Howard, or Scott Cooper, then a specified action is taken.

Rules Syntax

Before you create rules, there are a few fundamental concepts you need to know:

- A rule consists of conditions and a corresponding action. A rule can have one condition or multiple conditions. For example, From:James Allard is a single condition and From:James Allard;Subject:GG&G are two conditions. Each condition is delimited by a semicolon. A condition can consist of an argument or multiple arguments. For example, From:James Allard is a condition with a single argument and From:James Allard;Joe Howard is a condition with multiple arguments.

- Multiple conditions within a rule are logical AND values. For example, the condition From:James Allard;Subject:GG&G is *True* if the From field of the incoming items contains *James Allard* and the Subject field contains *GG&G*.

- Multiple arguments within a condition are logical OR values. For example, the condition From:James Allard;Joe Howard;Max Benson is *True* if the From field of the incoming item contains any one of the names included in the expression.

Specifying Simple Conditions

You can specify simple conditions based on the contents of the From, Sent, To, Subject, and Message fields of an incoming item.

To specify simple conditions

1. From the Folder Assistant dialog box on the Administration page, click Add Rule, or select the rule you want and then click Edit Rule.
2. Under When A Message Arrives That Meets The Following Conditions, type the criteria in the associated boxes.

Specifying Advanced Conditions

With the Advanced dialog box, you can specify a wide range of conditions, including conditions based on values in user-defined fields in the folder.

To specify advanced conditions

1. In the Folder Assistant dialog box on the Administration page, click Add Rule, or select the rule you want and then click Edit Rule.
2. Click Advanced.
3. Type the criteria in the appropriate boxes.

Specifying That a Rule Applies to Items That Do Not Match the Conditions

You can create rules that take actions if conditions are met and rules that take actions if the conditions are not met.

To specify that a rule applies only to items that do not match the conditions

- In the Advanced dialog box, click the Only Items That Do Not Match These Conditions check box.

Specifying Conditions with User-Defined Fields

In some cases, you'll want to create conditions based on user-defined fields in the folder. For example, for the Training Management folder, you might want to create a rule that forwards a Course Offering item to a distribution list when a Course Offering item that pertains to a specific subject is posted in the folder.

To specify custom fields as conditions

1. In the Advanced dialog box, under Show Properties Of, do one of the following.

To Show	Click
Custom fields of the currently selected forms	Forms, and then select the forms you want
Standard document fields	Document
Custom fields of the currently selected folder	Folder: *folder name*

2. Under Properties, select the check box of the property that you want to use to create a condition.

Part III Building Blocks of Applications

3. In the drop-down list or text boxes to the right of the check boxes, do one or more of the following:

   - If the field to the right of the selected check box is a text box, you can type one or more values in the text box. For example, if you want to create a rule that forwards Training Management items that have the value *Building Microsoft Outlook Applications* in the CourseDescription field, then type *Building Microsoft Outlook Applications* in the text box to its right, as shown in Figure 8-37. If you specify multiple values in the text boxes, separate the values with a semicolon.

   - If a drop-down list box and a text box are to the right of the check box, click the value in the list box first. Then type or click the criteria in the box to its right.

4. Click OK.

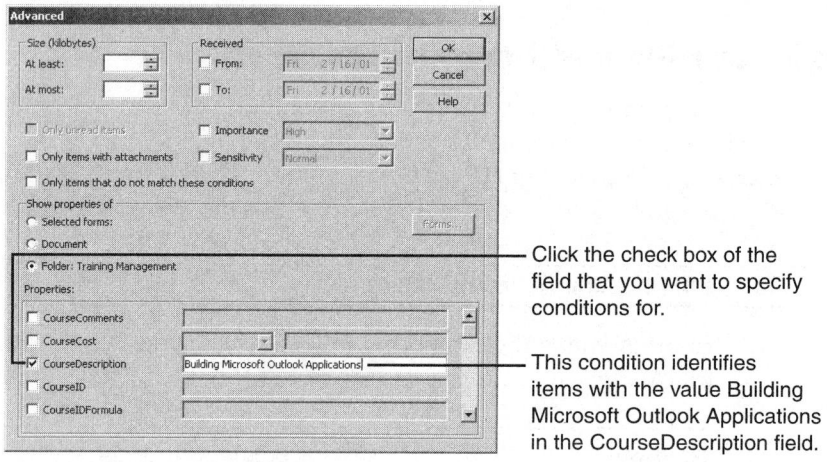

Figure 8-37 With Advanced properties, you can build conditions based on specific field values in a field.

Specifying Actions for a Rule

Actions occur when the conditions of a rule are met. You specify an action for a rule in the Edit Rule dialog box of the Folder Assistant.

To specify an action to run when a condition is met

To Perform This Action	Click
Return the item to the sender if the conditions of the rule are met	Return To Sender.
Delete the item if the conditions of the rule are met	Delete.
Specify the Reply message that is sent if the conditions of the rule are not met	Click Reply With, click Template, and then fill out the message box of the form with the Reply message you want to send.
Forward an item if the conditions of the rule are not met	Click Forward, click To, and then select the user name, distribution list, or folder.

> **More Info** For more information about specifying actions, see Chapter 7, "Actions."

Make the Folder Available for Offline Use

A strong point of Outlook application development is the program's ability to make folders available on line and off line. If your application requires both online and offline use, you will need to make the folder and any custom forms contained in it available for offline use. For an example of an application that operates on line and off line, see Chapter 12, "The Northwind Contact Management Application." By using some of the new properties and methods in the Outlook 2002 object model, you can make a folder available for offline use programmatically. For information about programming the Application Folders Send/Receive group, see Chapter 11.

Before you can make a folder available for offline use, you must create an offline folder file (.ost). An offline folder file acts as a local copy of folders in your mailbox or in the public folders in your Favorites folder. Access to an offline folder file requires authentication. You cannot create an offline folder file if you are not connected to an Exchange server.

To create an offline folder file (.ost)

1. On the Tools menu, click E-Mail Accounts, select the View Or Change Existing E-Mail Accounts option, and then click Next.
2. In the Outlook Processes E-Mail For These Accounts In The Following Order list, click Microsoft Exchange Server, and then click Change.
3. Click More Settings.
4. Click the Advanced tab, and then click Offline Folder File Settings.
5. In the File box, type the path to the file you want to use as the offline folder file. The default filename is outlook.ost. If this file already exists, you will be prompted for a new name.
6. Click OK to dismiss the Microsoft Exchange Server dialog box.
7. Click Next, and then click Finish.

> **Note** Custom forms in folders are not automatically available when off line. If you want custom forms to be available off line, select the Synchronize Forms box, as shown in Figure 8-31 (on page 289).

To specify folders for offline use

1. On the Tools menu, point to Send/Receive Settings, and then click Define Send/Receive Groups.
2. In the Group Name list box shown in Figure 8-38, click a Send/Receive group containing an Exchange Server account, and then click Edit. The default Send/Receive Group is All Accounts.
3. Under Accounts, select your Exchange Server account.
4. In the list, select the folders that you want to use off line in addition to your default folders, as shown in Figure 8-38.
5. If you want to apply a filter to a specific folder, click the folder, click Filter Selected Folder, and then select the options that you want. Filters are an important means of restricting the number of items in an offline folder.

6. If you want to limit the size of messages to download when you synchronize folders, click Limit Message Size, and then click the options that you want.

7. Click OK.

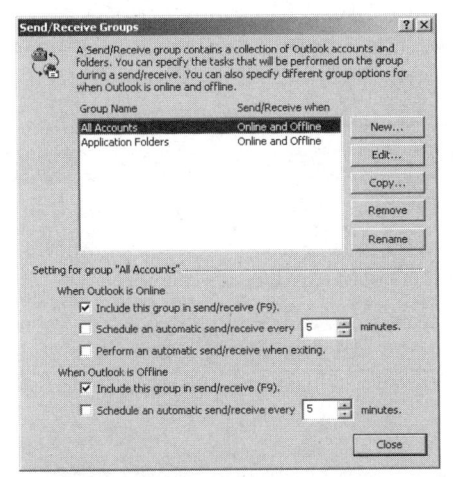

Figure 8-38 Send/Receive groups allow you to define which folders are available off line.

Test and Release the Folder

After you create or modify a folder, you should test it with a few users. When testing the folder, you and the users involved in the test should compose, submit, and open items in the folder and check views, permissions, and rules to make sure they work as planned.

When you're sure the folder is working properly, you can open the Administration page in the folder's Properties dialog box and make the folder available to the general public.

> **To make the folder available to all users with access permission**

1. In the Folder List, right-click the folder, and then click Properties on the shortcut menu.
2. Click the Administration page.
3. Click All Users With Access Permission.
4. Click OK.

307

If you plan to replicate the folder application between servers, have your Exchange Administrator define replication settings using the Exchange Administrator program and then test the folder on a small scale before replicating it on Exchange servers in your organization.

When the folder is ready for public use, send out an announcement to the users who will be using the folder to let them know the folder is available. You can include a link to the folder in your announcement message so that users can easily find the folder.

For More Information About	See
Setting permissions	"Set Permissions" earlier in this chapter
Distributing and maintaining folders	Chapter 13, "Distributing and Securing Applications"
Replicating folders	The Microsoft Exchange Server documentation

Where To Go from Here

Microsoft Knowledge Base Articles Microsoft Knowledge Base articles are available on the Web at *http://support.microsoft.com/support*. Also see "Folders (Chapter 8) KB Articles" in the Microsoft Web Sites folder under the Help and Web Sites folder on the companion CD.

Part IV

Beyond the Basics

9　**Raise Events and Move to the Head of the Class**　311
10　**The Outlook Development Environment**　383
11　**Using Visual Basic, VBA, or VBScript with Outlook**　415
12　**The Northwind Contact Management Application**　531
13　**Distributing and Securing Applications**　591

Chapter 9, "Raise Events and Move to the Head of the Class," explains how to use the events in the Outlook Object Model to write event-aware Outlook VBA or COM Add-in code. Chapter 10, "The Outlook Development Environment," introduces the Outlook Script Editor for Microsoft Visual Basic Scripting Edition (VBScript) code behind Outlook forms. This chapter also discusses debugging with the Microsoft Script Editor and shows you the object models used in Outlook development. Chapter 11, "Using Visual Basic, VBA, or VBScript with Outlook," provides a wide variety of code examples for the most commonly performed tasks using Microsoft Visual Basic or VBScript in Outlook. Chapter 12, "The Northwind Contact Management Application," demonstrates how you can use what you've learned so far in a reusable customer relationship management (CRM) application designed for online and offline use. Chapter 13, "Distributing and Securing Applications," shows you how to distribute forms in folders and provides some techniques for maintaining and securing applications. This chapter also discusses the critical areas of the Outlook Object Model and attachment security and takes a close look at how the Outlook E-Mail Security Update has been integrated into Outlook 2002. Outlook 2002 COM Add-ins can be trusted for privileged access to the Outlook Object Model. Finally, you'll learn how your current and future applications can coexist with the Outlook E-Mail Security Update.

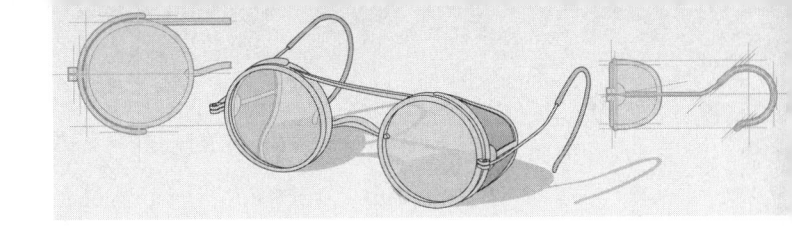

9

Raise Events and Move to the Head of the Class

Previous versions of Microsoft Outlook supported a limited number of form and control level events. To write code to respond to these events in Outlook 97 and Outlook 98, you had to write Microsoft Visual Basic Scripting Edition (VBScript) code behind custom forms. Outlook 2000 introduced events at the application level that you define and program within Outlook's own Microsoft Visual Basic for Applications (VBA) environment. These events let you respond to some great new Application object events, as well as events for child objects in the Outlook Object Model.

At this point, we might do well to ask what exactly an event is from a programmatic point of view. An event results from an action that is typically performed by a user, such as sending a message, switching a folder or view in an Explorer window, or changing either default or user-defined fields in an item—but the action that triggers an event can also be performed by program code, or by the system itself.

Within the context of Outlook, events occur at several different levels. The only events supported in Outlook 97 and Outlook 98 were primarily form-level events such as Item_Open, Item_Write, Item_Close, and a limited control-level event known as the Click event. Form developers could write VBScript event procedure code to respond to the firing of an event. You can continue to write form-level code in VBScript in Outlook 2000 and Outlook 2002. Unlike previous versions of Outlook, however, you can also declare public variables using the WithEvents keyword in Outlook VBA and write code to respond to form-level events within the context of the running Outlook application.

Part IV Beyond The Basics

The primary focus of this chapter is using Visual Basic in Outlook to respond to events. For readers who are not familiar with Microsoft Visual Basic for Applications, we'll cover some of the basic functionality of the Visual Basic for Applications Editor (shown in Figure 9-1) before we move on to the new events in the Outlook Object Model.

The VBA Editor

Outlook 2002 supports all the functionality of Visual Basic for Applications 6.3 in Office XP. Unlike other Office XP applications, where VBA is an integral component of the application, Outlook 2002 provides VBA services through an Office XP COM Add-in. If your company does not want to deploy Outlook VBA to every desktop, you can control the availability of Outlook VBA by using the Custom Installation Wizard or the System Policy Editor in the *Microsoft Office XP Resource Kit*.

VBA allows you to create code ranging in functionality from simple macros to complex application add-ins. Application add-ins can utilize any of the objects, properties, methods, and events in the Outlook Object Model. Moreover, you can use the VBA environment to add references to other object models, and to use Outlook as an automation controller, in addition to its traditional role as an automation server.

> **New to Outlook 2002** You can use VBA code to add custom scripts to the Rules Wizard. However, these script rules are client based, so Outlook must be running for the VBA code to execute.

Launching the VBA Editor

One of the greatest features of VBA is the proximity of the design process to the application you are designing. VBA is only a few keystrokes or mouse clicks away. You have complete and immediate access to all the objects in the Outlook Object Model. Previously, you had to create advanced Outlook and MAPI functionality using C++ code. Now you can operate in an interactive environment that lets you rapidly develop new applications. Follow the steps in the next procedural section to open the Visual Basic for Applications Editor window, shown in Figure 9-1.

Raise Events and Move to the Head of the Class Chapter 9

Figure 9-1 shows the Visual Basic for Applications Editor window in Outlook 2002, with callouts indicating "The VBA Project Explorer," "Outlook 2002 is a full-fledged member of Office with full Visual Basic for Applications support," and "The Visual Basic for Applications Editor window."

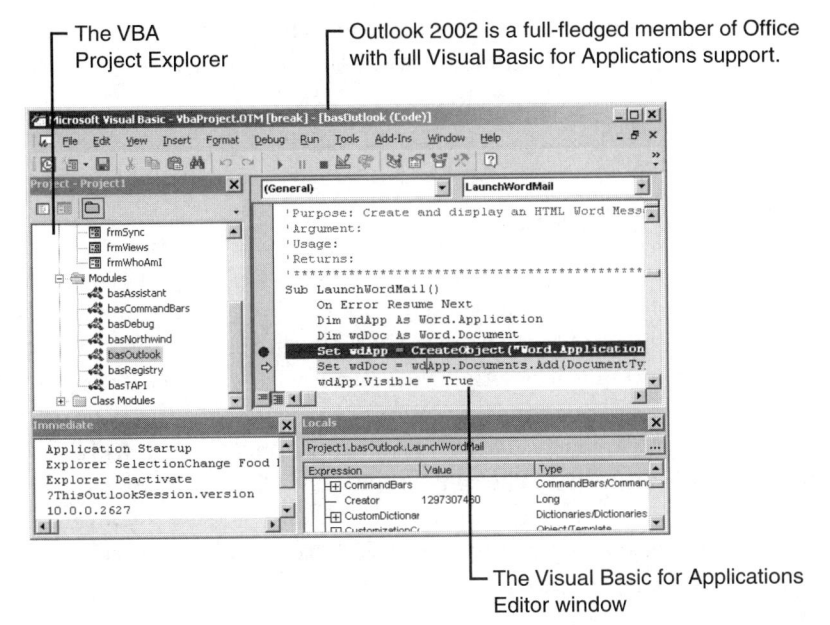

Figure 9-1 The Visual Basic for Applications Editor window in Outlook 2002.

To open the Visual Basic for Applications Editor window

1. On the Explorer or the Inspector Tools menu, click Macro.
2. Click the Visual Basic Editor command, or press Alt+F11 in an Inspector or Explorer window.

You can also customize the Standard and Advanced Outlook toolbars with a toolbar button that launches the Visual Basic Editor. To add a VBA command bar button to the Advanced toolbar for Outlook Explorer, follow these steps:

1. On the Explorer Tools menu, click the Customize command.
2. Click on Advanced Toolbar in the Toolbars list box, and make sure that the Advanced Toolbar is selected.
3. Click the Commands tab in the Customize dialog box.
4. Select Tools in the Categories list box.

Part IV   Beyond The Basics

5. Select Visual Basic Editor in the Commands list, and then drag the Visual Basic Editor item from the Customize dialog box to any position on the Advanced Toolbar.

6. Click Close to close the Customize dialog box.

ThisOutlookSession Class Module

When the Outlook Visual Basic Editor opens for the first time, you will see only one object, under Project1, named ThisOutlookSession, as shown in Figure 9-2. While not explicitly identified as such, ThisOutlookSession is a class module rather than a standard module. Although you cannot view its class properties, the Instancing property of ThisOutlookSession is private and the class cannot be instantiated by using *CreateObject* in another application or with VBScript code running in Outlook forms. The class represented by ThisOutlookSession is the Application object in the Outlook Object Model. The Application object is the parent of all other classes in the Outlook Object Model. All other class objects are derived from the Outlook Application object.

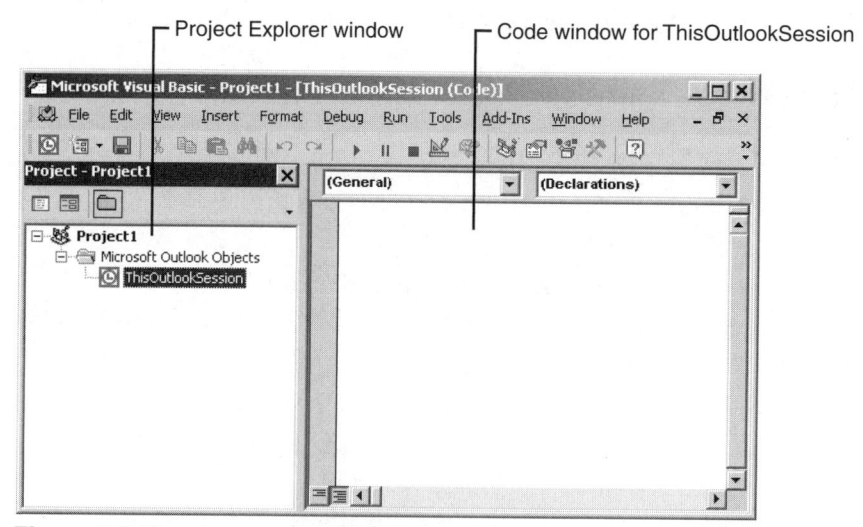

Figure 9-2 The class module ThisOutlookSession is initially empty when you launch the Outlook Visual Basic for Applications Editor for the first time.

Navigating in the VBA Editor

A very brief tour of the VBA Editor is helpful for developers who are new to VBA. The Project Explorer window contains a tree view of the class modules, standard modules, and UserForms in your project. The Code window shows the functions and Sub procedures for the currently selected object in the Project Explorer. The

Properties window lists the design-time properties for a selected form, control, class, project, or module. The Object Browser window displays all the objects in the current project, along with their properties, methods, and events. The Immediate, Locals, Watch, and Call Stack windows are invaluable when it's time to debug your code.

Individual windows in the VBA Editor can be docked or undocked. A window is docked when it is attached or anchored to one edge of the screen, application window, or another dockable window. When you move a dockable window, it snaps to a docking position at the top, bottom, left, or right of the Editor window. Every developer will have personal preferences about configuring the window elements of their project. The following table is a quick guide to keystrokes that will help you navigate the different windows in VBA.

Press	To
Ctrl+G	Display the Immediate window. You can execute statements or examine variable values in the Immediate window.
Ctrl+L	Activate the Call Stack window.
Ctrl+R	Activate the Project Explorer window.
F2	Activate the Object Browser.
F4	Activate the Properties window for the currently selected form, control, class, or module object.
F7	Activate the code window for the currently selected object in the Project Explorer.
Alt+F11	Return to the Outlook Application window.

The Outlook Application Object

The Outlook Application object is the top-level object in the Outlook Object Model. All other objects in the object model are derived from the Application object. Also, the Application object is the only object that can be created by using the *CreateObject* statement in another application. For additional information regarding the Outlook Object Model, see Chapter 10, "The Outlook Development Environment."

From the perspective of VBA in Outlook, the Application object is directly available in the VBA Editor code window for the ThisOutlookSession object. Remember that the ThisOutlookSession object is equivalent to the Outlook Application object. When you write VBA code for Outlook, you do not have to explicitly set a reference to the Outlook object library. Figure 9-3 illustrates how both the Office and Outlook object libraries are automatically referenced in the References dialog box for your VBA project.

Part IV   Beyond The Basics

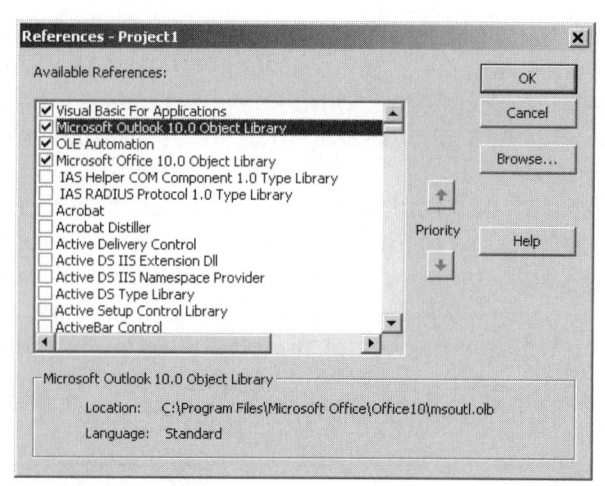

Figure 9-3 VBA automatically sets references for both the Office and Outlook object libraries.

To view or set references for Project1

1. If the Outlook application window is active, press Alt+F11 to open the VBA Editor window.
2. On the Tools menu of the VBA Editor, select the References command.
3. Select additional object libraries to reference in your VBA project by checking the box next to the name of the object library you wish to reference in the Available References list box.
4. Click OK when you have finished selecting references.

Saving Your Outlook VBA Project

If you have written code for ThisOutlookSession or added code modules to Project1, you will be prompted to save the project when you quit Outlook. If you answer Yes to the alert box that prompts you to save the project, you will save the project in a file named VBAProject.otm. You cannot change the name of the file in which an Outlook VBA project is saved. Unlike project files in Visual Basic, VBAProject.otm is a binary file, and you should not attempt to edit it with a text editor. You also cannot change the folder location in which VBAProject.otm is stored. VBAProject.otm is stored in the following locations depending upon the operating system you are using:

Operating System	Location for VBAProject.otm
Microsoft Windows 98 and ME	*drive*:\Windows\Application Data\Microsoft\Outlook
Microsoft Windows NT 4	*drive*:\Winnt\Profiles\<*user*>\Application Data\Microsoft\Outlook
Microsoft Windows 2000	*drive*:\Documents and Settings\<*user*>\Application Data\Microsoft\Outlook

Securing Your Outlook VBA Project

You can secure an Outlook VBA project to protect it from unauthorized changes by others. However, you should keep in mind that an Outlook VBA project lacks the same level of security that you can achieve with an Outlook COM Add-in. The compilation of a Visual Basic COM Add-in project into an ActiveX DLL protects your source code. Only one VBA project can be associated with an Outlook application. Like their predecessor Exchange Add-ins that use .ecf files, multiple COM Add-ins can run in a single Outlook session. Remember that Outlook VBA is more a personal development tool rather than a vehicle for deploying commercial or corporate Outlook Add-ins. If you want to protect your VBA code, you can prevent users from viewing the code unless they have a password to open the project for editing. Don't lose this password, or you will be prevented from viewing and editing the code for the project.

To protect an Outlook VBA project

1. If the Outlook application window is active, press Alt+F11 to open the VBA Editor window.
2. On the Tools menu of the VBA Editor, select the Project1 Properties command.
3. Check the Lock Project For Viewing check box, as shown in Figure 9-4.
4. Supply a password to allow viewing of project properties, and then confirm the password.
5. Click OK to accept the Project1 Properties. The project is not actually locked for viewing until you quit and restart Outlook.

Part IV Beyond The Basics

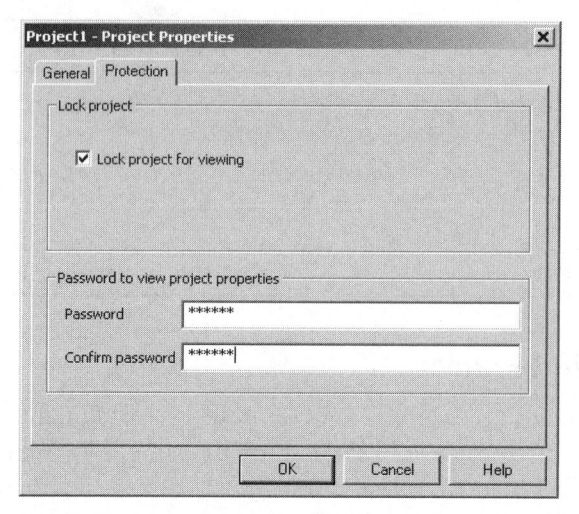

Figure 9-4 The Protection tab of the Project Properties dialog box lets you lock your Outlook VBA project.

> Note Outlook VBA projects can be digitally signed with a security certificate. On the Tools menu, select Macro and then choose the Security command to set the security level for your Outlook session. If you are developing VBA code for Outlook, it is recommended that you temporarily set the security level to Low so that you don't have to bypass the Macro Warning dialog box when Outlook launches. By default, the Macro Security setting is High for Outlook 2002. If you require additional information on developing solutions with security certificates, see Chapter 13, "Distributing and Securing Applications," and Chapter 14, "Creating COM Add-Ins with Visual Basic."

Writing an Outlook Macro

Outlook 2002 supports macro code that automates repetitive tasks. Unlike some other members of the Office XP family, Outlook does not feature a macro recorder that will write VBA code in response to user commands and actions. From the standpoint of Outlook VBA, an Outlook macro is a public Sub procedure without arguments in a standard module. If you add arguments to your module-level Sub procedure, it will no longer be available as a macro. An Outlook macro cannot utilize a Function procedure or private Sub procedure. Also, you cannot place macro code in a class module such as ThisOutlookSession or a form module. Remember that ThisOutlookSession represents a class module rather than a standard module. If you want to write a Sub procedure that you can use as a macro, you must first insert a standard module into your Outlook project and then insert a Sub procedure into that module. Follow these steps to create a macro that launches Microsoft Word 2002 and creates a Word mail message:

To create a new Outlook Macro

1. In Outlook, point to Macro on the Tools menu and then click Visual Basic Editor.

2. On the Tools menu, click References. Use the References dialog box to set a reference to the Microsoft Word 10.0 Object Library. Click OK.

3. Select Project1 in the Project Explorer. If you want to insert a new module, click Module on the Insert menu of the VBA Editor window. Otherwise, double-click the name of the module where you want to insert the macro in the Project Explorer window.

4. On the Insert menu, click Procedure.

5. In the Name box, type *LaunchWordMail* for the macro name, as shown in Figure 9-5. The name cannot contain spaces.

6. Click OK.

7. The LaunchWordMail Sub procedure appears in the Code window.

8. Type the following code in the body of the Sub procedure:

```
Sub LaunchWordMail()
    On Error Resume Next
    Dim wdApp As Word.Application
    Dim wdDoc As Word.Document
    Set wdApp = CreateObject("Word.Application")
    Set wdDoc = _
        wdApp.Documents.Add(DocumentType:=wdNewEmailMessage)
    wdApp.Visible = True
    wdApp.ActiveWindow.EnvelopeVisible = True
End Sub
```

Part IV Beyond The Basics

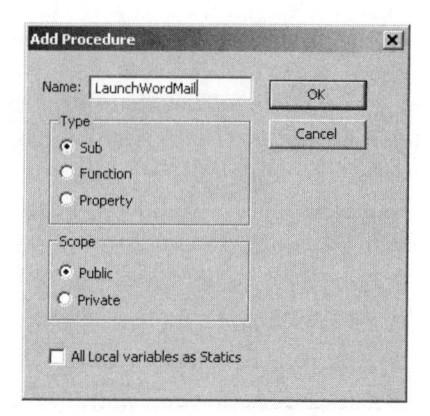

Figure 9-5 Use the Add Procedure dialog box to create a Sub procedure for an Outlook macro.

Once you have created your macro procedure and debugged it, you'll want to customize either an Explorer or Inspector toolbar so that you can run the macro with a mouse click. Be aware that you must lower your Macro Security settings to Low or Medium in order to run any VBA macro code. In order to test the LaunchWordMail macro, you can simply insert the cursor into the LaunchWordMail Sub procedure in the Code window and select Run Sub/UserForm on the Run menu on the Visual Basic Editor toolbar. To continue with the LaunchWordMail macro example, use the following steps to create a toolbar button to run the macro:

To add an Outlook Macro to the Standard toolbar for the Explorer

1. In the Outlook Explorer, select the Customize command on the Tools menu.

2. Select Macros in the Categories drop-down list box on the Commands page.

3. Drag the LaunchWordMail macro to the position on the Standard toolbar where you want the toolbar command button to appear.

4. Right-click the Project1.LaunchWordMail toolbar button, and set its properties. For example, you might want to rename the button to WordMail.

If you have created a number of Outlook macros, adding macros to the toolbar can be impractical and can pose a security risk. You can also use the Macros dialog box to run an Outlook macro, provided that your Macro Security settings are either Low or Medium.

> **To change your Macro Security settings**

1. Point to Macro on the Tools menu, and select Security on the Macro pop-up submenu.

2. In the Security dialog box, change the Security Level to Low or Medium. Changing the Macro Security setting does not alter the built-in attachment and object model guard security for Outlook 2002. These security protections remain in place no matter how you set Macro security.

> **To run an Outlook Macro using the Macros dialog box**

1. Press Alt+F8 in an Outlook Explorer or Inspector window.

2. Double-click the macro name in the Macros dialog box.

Writing Code to Respond to Events

Outlook macros are very useful for simple repetitive tasks. However, macros are only a snack compared with the banquet of events available in the Outlook 2002 Object Model. For Visual Basic developers, the key to writing code that responds to events is learning how to use the WithEvents keyword in Visual Basic.

Use the WithEvents Keyword to Declare Object Variables

The WithEvents keyword is used to dimension an object variable in a class module. If you attempt to use WithEvents in conjunction with an object declaration in a standard module, your code will raise an error and will not compile. By declaring an object using WithEvents, you notify Visual Basic that you want to respond to events for the instance that is assigned to that object variable. You can use the WithEvents keyword only with objects that support events, and only in a class module such as ThisOutlookSession.

> **Note** If you want to use C++ to write code supporting the new events in Outlook 2002, you should see the Microsoft Product Support Services sample COM Add-in at *http://support.microsoft.com/support/kb/articles/Q230/6/89.ASP*. It comes with an Office COM Add-in template for Visual C++ that you can use to develop Outlook COM Add-ins in C++, should you so desire. This template contains complete instructions for implementing the IDTExtensibility2 interface in Microsoft C++ Version 6.

Part IV   Beyond The Basics

Because the class module ThisOutlookSession represents the Outlook Application object, you do not have to explicitly declare an Outlook Application object using the WithEvents keyword when you write Outlook VBA code. If you examine the code window for ThisOutlookSession, you'll notice that all the events for the Outlook Application object are available in the Procedures drop-down list box. Figure 9-6 shows the Application object in the code window for ThisOutlookSession.

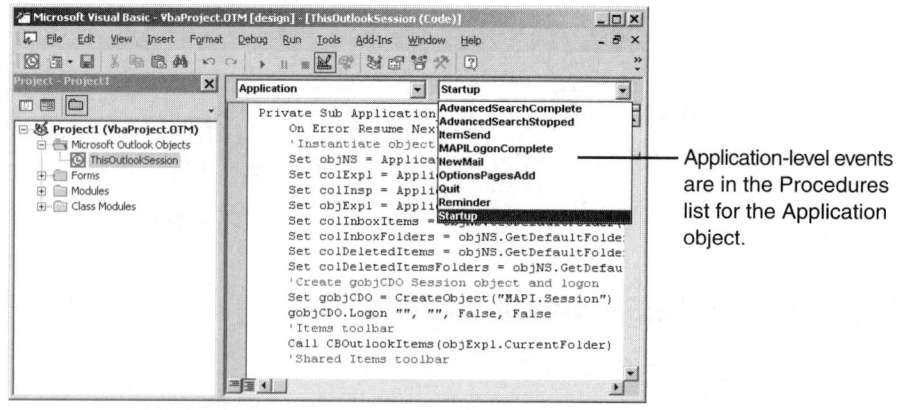

Figure 9-6 Select an Application event from the Procedures drop-down list box to create an application-level event procedure.

When You Must Use WithEvents to Declare the Outlook Application Object

If you are writing a COM Add-in that traps Outlook events, you must explicitly declare an Outlook Application object using the WithEvents keyword. COM Add-ins are beyond the scope of this chapter; they are discussed in depth in Chapter 14. The technique you should use to create child objects of the Application object, however, applies equally to COM Add-ins and Outlook VBA code. Many of the child objects of the Application object can also raise events. You might be wondering how you write event procedures for those child objects. The trick is to declare these objects using the WithEvents keyword and to instantiate those objects in the correct event procedures. Object-related events beget additional event-aware objects and their event procedures.

Using WithEvents for Child Objects

As discussed previously, all objects in the Outlook Object Model are child objects of the parent Application object. Not every Outlook object supports events. Consult the Object Browser in Outlook VBA or the Microsoft Outlook Visual Basic Reference Help to determine which Outlook objects raise events. The following table lists application-level events in Outlook 2002 and the objects that raise those

Raise Events and Move to the Head of the Class   Chapter 9

events. The events and objects that are new to Outlook 2002 appear in bold. Note that certain events are cancelable, meaning that you can write code to roll back the event depending on the conditions you evaluate during event processing.

Object	Event	Cancelable
Application	**AdvancedSearchComplete**	No
	AdvancedSearchStopped	No
	ItemSend	Yes
	MapiLogonComplete	No
	NewMail	No
	OptionsPagesAdd	No
	Quit	No
	Reminder	No
	Startup	No
NameSpace	OptionsPagesAdd	No
Explorers	NewExplorer	No
Explorer	Activate	No
	BeforeFolderSwitch	Yes
	BeforeItemCopy	Yes
	BeforeItemCut	Yes
	BeforeMaximize	Yes
	BeforeMinimize	Yes
	BeforeMove	Yes
	BeforeSize	Yes
	BeforeViewSwitch	Yes
	Close	No
	Deactivate	No
	FolderSwitch	No
	SelectionChange	No
	ViewSwitch	No
SyncObject	OnError	No
	Progress	No
	SyncEnd	No
	SyncStart	No
OutlookBarPane	BeforeGroupSwitch	Yes
	BeforeNavigate	Yes

(continued)

Part IV Beyond The Basics

Object	Event	Cancelable
OutlookBarGroup	GroupAdd	No
	BeforeGroupAdd	Yes
	BeforeGroupRemove	Yes
OutlookBarShortcut	ShortcutAdd	No
	BeforeShortcutAdd	Yes
	BeforeShortcutRemove	Yes
Folders	FolderAdd	No
	FolderChange	No
	FolderRemove	No
Inspectors	NewInspector	No
Inspector	Activate	No
	BeforeMaximize	Yes
	BeforeMinimize	Yes
	BeforeMove	Yes
	BeforeSize	Yes
	Close	No
	Deactivate	No
Items	ItemAdd	No
	ItemChange	No
	ItemRemove	No
Reminders	**BeforeReminderShow**	Yes
	ReminderAdd	No
	ReminderChange	No
	ReminderFire	No
	ReminderRemove	No
	Snooze	No
Views	**ViewAdd**	No
	ViewRemove	No

To raise events for these child objects, you should follow these coding practices:

- Dimension the object as a public object variable, and use the WithEvents keyword in a class module. If you're writing Outlook VBA code, declare the child object variables using WithEvents in ThisOutlookSession.

- Instantiate the child object variable in an appropriate event procedure, or use a Sub procedure in module-level code to instantiate object variables that raise events. For example, you should instantiate the NameSpace object and the Explorers and Inspectors collection objects in the Application Startup event so that the events supported by these objects will be available throughout the life of the application. The following code illustrates this technique:

```
'Place these declarations in ThisOutlookSession
Public WithEvents objNS As Outlook.NameSpace
Public WithEvents colReminders As Outlook.Reminders
Public WithEvents colViews as Outlook.Views
Public WithEvents colFolders As Outlook.Folders
Public WithEvents objExpl As Outlook.Explorer
Public WithEvents colExpl As Outlook.Explorers
Public WithEvents objInsp As Outlook.Inspector
Public WithEvents colInsp As Outlook.Inspectors
Public WithEvents colInboxItems As Outlook.Items
Public WithEvents colDeletedItems As Outlook.Items

Private Sub Application_Startup()
    Set objNS = Application.GetNamespace("MAPI")
    Set colFolders = objNS.Folders
    Set colReminders = Application.Reminders
    Set colExpl = Application.Explorers
    Set colInsp = Application.Inspectors
    Set objExpl = Application.ActiveExplorer
    Set colViews = objExpl.CurrentFolder.Views
    Set colInboxItems = objNS.GetDefaultFolder(olFolderInbox).Items
    Set colDeletedItems = _
        objNS.GetDefaultFolder(olFolderDeletedItems).Items
End Sub
```

Where to Instantiate Child Objects Declared Using WithEvents

It's important to determine the correct event procedure when you create additional child objects. For example, if you want to raise events for an Explorer object, you can either set a reference to an Explorer object in the Application Startup event or you can use the NewExplorer event of the Explorers collection object. The NewExplorer event passes an Explorer object to the NewExplorer event procedure. Using the code example above, a reference is set to *objExpl* in the Application Startup event. This Explorer object refers to the ActiveExplorer object of the Application object when Outlook launches. Either users or code can cause multiple Explorer objects to display for a given Outlook Application object. If you want to trap events such as FolderSwitch or BeforeShortcutAdd for another instance of an Explorer, you must either create a new Explorer object that you can instantiate in the NewExplorer event or reuse the existing *objExpl* object and set *objExpl* to the Explorer object that you receive in the NewExplorer event. Many of the examples in the following section will discuss strategies and options for raising events on child objects of the application's parent object.

Observing Events in the Example VBAProject.otm

Because it writes a statement to the VBA Immediate window when an event procedure fires, the VBAProject.otm project accompanying this book lets you observe events for most of the available events in the Outlook Object Model. Following the firing sequence of events in the Immediate window is an excellent way to learn about the new events in the Outlook Object Model. To observe event tracing in the VBA Immediate window, you must follow these steps:

To turn on event tracing in the VBAProject.otm example

1. Select Macro from the Tools menu.
2. Select Security from the Macro submenu.
3. On the Security Level page of the Security dialog box, click the Low option. If you click Medium, you will have to click Enable Macros in the Security Warning dialog box every time Outlook starts.
4. Click OK.
5. Press Alt+F11 to open the VBA Editor.
6. Select Project1 Properties from the Tools menu.
7. In the Conditional Compilation Arguments edit box on the General page of the Project 1 – Project Properties dialog box, enter *conDebug = 1*.
8. Click OK.
9. Press Alt+F11 to return to Outlook.
10. Select Exit And Log Off from the File menu.
11. Restart Outlook. Event tracing will be turned on, and you can observe the firing sequence of events in the VBA Immediate window.

Application Events

Application-level events are most useful when you write code for an Outlook COM Add-in. You cannot respond to application-level events in VBScript code behind an Outlook form.

ItemSend

The ItemSend event occurs when an item is sent either because a user clicked the Send button on the item or because code causes an item to be sent. Typically the Application_ItemSend event occurs after the form-level Item_Send event and before the form-level Item_Write and Item_Close events. You should apply user-interface elements such as alert and dialog boxes with care in the ItemSend event. If you use the Cancel argument to cancel sending the item and the item has already been sent from an open Inspector, the Inspector will remain in its previously displayed state. The item's Inspector will not close as it normally would when the Send button is clicked. The following example unobtrusively strips all attachments from outgoing mail messages:

```
Private Sub Application_ItemSend(ByVal Item As Object, Cancel As Boolean)
    Dim oAttach As Outlook.Attachment
    If Item.Attachments.Count And Item.MessageClass = "IPM.Note" Then
        Do Until Item.Attachments.Count = 0
            Set oAttach = Item.Attachments.Item(1)
            oAttach.Delete
        Loop
    End If
End Sub
```

> **Note** The example above assumes that you are writing code directly to the explicit Application object in VBA. If you are writing a COM Add-in or using an event handler to instantiate an Outlook Application object that has been declared using WithEvents, the name of the Application object will differ but the code will remain the same.

NewMail

The NewMail event occurs when an item arrives in the Inbox of the current logged-on user. The NewMail event will not occur if an item arrives in the mailbox of a user for whom the logged-on user has delegate permissions. NewMail is a generic event that notifies you that mail has arrived in the Inbox. Unlike the ItemSend event, it does not pass an Item object representing the item or items that have arrived in the Inbox. If you want to raise an event for the arrival of a specific item in a folder, you should declare an Items collection object using WithEvents. Assign the Items collection object to the Items property of the folder that you want to monitor, and then write an event procedure for the ItemAdd event of the Items collection object. If the Explorer window is minimized, the following NewMail example causes the Explorer window to display with a normal window state.

Part IV Beyond The Basics

```
Private Sub Application_NewMail()
    Dim olExplorer As Outlook.Explorer
    Dim olFolder As Outlook.MAPIFolder
    Set olFolder = _
      Application.GetNamespace("MAPI").GetDefaultFolder(olFolderInbox)
    Set olExplorer = Application.ActiveExplorer
    If olExplorer.WindowState = olMinimized Then
        If olExplorer.CurrentFolder <> olFolder Then
            olExplorer.CurrentFolder = olFolder
        End If
        olExplorer.WindowState = olNormalWindow
        olExplorer.Display
        olExplorer.Activate
    End If
End Sub
```

OptionsPagesAdd

OptionsPagesAdd is the one event in the Outlook Object Model that appears at first examination to be misnamed. This event occurs after a user selects the Options command on the Tools menu of the Outlook Explorer and before the Tools Options dialog box actually displays. Consequently, you may prefer to think of the OptionsPagesAdd event as the BeforeOptionsPagesAdd event. From the perspective of the Application object, the OptionsPagesAdd event refers to the property pages of the Tools Options dialog box. You can use this event to add custom property pages to the Tools Options dialog box. Previous versions of Outlook required complex C++ coding to add property pages to this dialog box. See Chapter 14 for a complete example of how to create an ActiveX control and use this control as a property page that stores and retrieves settings from the Windows registry.

Figure 9-7 illustrates a property page with the caption *Sample Page* that has been added to the Tools Options dialog box. Be aware that creating an Outlook property page requires a complete understanding of how to create ActiveX controls and how to read and save registry values. Typically, you will want to use the Windows registry to preserve user settings on controls in your property page.

The Programmatic ID of the ActiveX control that contains the controls on the property page is PPE.SamplePage. The Programmatic ID is also known as a ProgID and results from the combination of ProjectName.ClassName in the ActiveX control project that implements the property page. The syntax for using the *Add* method of the PropertyPages collection object is as follows:

```
Private Sub Application_OptionsPagesAdd(ByVal Pages As PropertyPages)
    Pages.Add "ProgID", Caption
End Sub
```

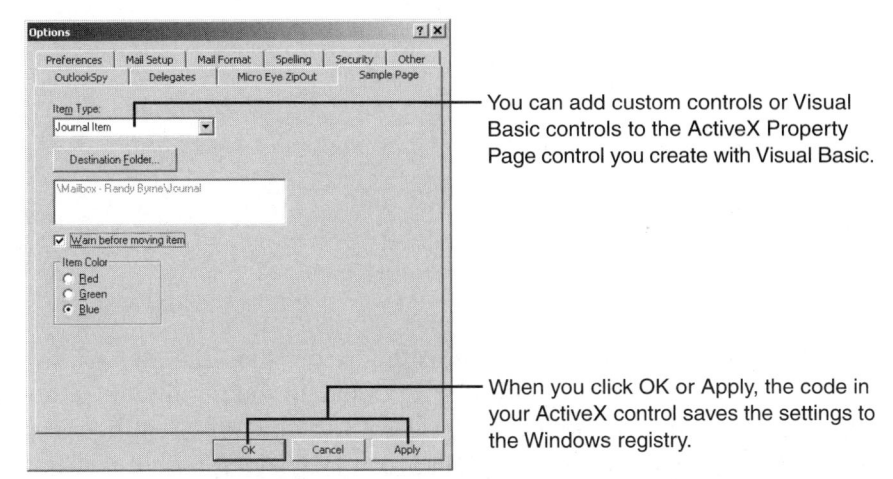

Figure 9-7 The Sample Page property page is added to the Tools Options dialog box.

Although alternative syntaxes are proposed for the PropertyPages *Add* method in the Microsoft Outlook Visual Basic Reference, the use of the Programmatic ID and the Caption will provide the most trouble-free coding practice. Be aware that if you use the ProgID argument with the *Add* method, the Caption argument is mandatory rather than optional. If you omit the Caption argument, Outlook will raise an internal error.

Here is a one-line example of using the OptionsPagesAdd event to add a property page with a caption of *Sample Page* to the property pages in the Outlook Tools Options dialog box. The ActiveX control that implements the property page has been compiled so that its ProgID is PPE.SamplePage. The actual code that makes this property page behave as expected is part of the SamplePage ActiveX control.

```
Private Sub Application_OptionsPagesAdd(ByVal Pages As PropertyPages)
    Pages.Add "PPE.SamplePage", "Sample Page"
End Sub
```

Quit

The Application Quit event takes place when you exit Outlook. This event provides a location for you to clean up any objects that you have created in the Startup event. It is good programming practice to set any global object variables you have created to Nothing in the Quit event. The following code example illustrates this technique.

```
Private Sub Application_Quit()
    On Error Resume Next
    Set objNS = Nothing
    Set colExpl = Nothing
    Set colInsp = Nothing
    Set objExpl = Nothing
    Set objInsp = Nothing
End Sub
```

Reminder

The Reminder event occurs immediately before the reminder for an item is displayed. Outlook passes a generic Item object to the Reminder event procedure. If you want to determine the type of item for which the reminder is going to be displayed, examine the Item's Class property to determine the specific Outlook item type.

```
Private Sub Application_Reminder(ByVal Item As Object)
    Select Case Item.Class
        Case olMail
        MsgBox "You are about to receive a message reminder.", _
            vbInformation
        Case olAppointment
        MsgBox "You are about to receive an appointment reminder.", _
            vbInformation
        Case olTask
        MsgBox "You are about to receive a task reminder.", vbInformation
    End Select
End Sub
```

> **New to Outlook 2002** The Reminders collection object offers more granular control over Reminder events than the Reminder event on the Application object. If you instantiate a Reminders collection object, you can trigger ReminderAdd, ReminderChange, ReminderFire, ReminderRemove, and Snooze events.

Startup

The Startup event fires when Outlook starts and after any Exchange or COM Add-ins have been loaded. Consequently, you can use the COMAddIns collection object to determine which COM Add-ins have been loaded on startup for the Outlook Application object. The Startup event is also the place where you'll want to create instances of other global object variables that you've declared using the

WithEvents keyword. Object variables that are leading candidates for instantiation in the Startup event are the Inspectors collection object, the Explorers collection object, and the Items collection object for any folders where you want to write event procedure code when an item is added, changed, or removed in a specified folder.

The following example adds a command button to the Standard toolbar of the Outlook Explorer. Outlook 97 and Outlook 98 required C++ coding to achieve the same result. This toolbar button opens the While You Were Out template located in the file system.

```
Private Sub Application_Startup()
    Dim objCB As Office.CommandBar
    Dim objCBB As Office.CommandBarButton
    Set objCB = Application.ActiveExplorer.CommandBars("Standard")
    Set objCBB = objCB.Controls.Add(msoControlButton)
    With objCBB
        .TooltipText = "Open While You Were Out Form"
        .Style = msoButtonIcon
        .FaceId = 1757
        .OnAction = "cmdWhile_Click"
    End With
End Sub

'This OnAction procedure must reside in module-level code
'rather than in ThisOutlookSession
Sub cmdWhile_Click()
    Dim objMsg As Outlook.MailItem
    Dim objInsp As Outlook.Inspector
    Set objMsg = Application.CreateItemFromTemplate _
        ("C:\ My Documents\while you were out.oft")
    Set objInsp = objMsg.GetInspector
    objMsg.Display
    'You must display the message before you set WindowState
    objInsp.WindowState = olNormalWindow
End Sub
```

New Application Events in Outlook 2002

The following events are new to Outlook 2002. The AdvancedSearchComplete and AdvancedSearchStopped events are critical to the functioning of programmatic search using the AdvancedSearch method of the Application object.

AdvancedSearchComplete

The AdvancedSearchComplete event occurs when the *AdvancedSearch* method has completed. Use this event to determine when a programmatic search has finished or to start a new procedure upon the completion of the search. The following example displays the Subject for each Results item in the Immediate window when the search is complete:

```
Private Sub objOutlook_AdvancedSearchComplete _
    (ByVal SearchObject As Search)
    Dim colResults As Results
    Set colResults = SearchObject.Results
    For Each objItem In colResults
        Debug.Print objItem.Subject
    Next
End Sub
```

AdvancedSearchStopped

The AdvancedSearchStopped event occurs when the *Stop* method is called on a Search object. If you call the *Stop* method on a Search object, the Results collection object might not contain complete results for the search.

> **Note** Both the AdvancedSearchComplete event and the AdvancedSearchStopped event will fire only if the *AdvancedSearch* method is called programmatically. These events do not occur for a search that executes when a user invokes the Advanced Find dialog box in the Outlook user interface.

MapiLogonComplete

The MapiLogonComplete event occurs after the Application Startup event. When MapiLogonComplete occurs, it means that a valid MAPI session object has been created and that you have full access to all the objects, events, and properties in the Outlook Object Model.

Reminders Collection Events

The Reminders collection object is new to Outlook 2002 and is a child object of the Outlook Application object. The Reminders collection object represents all the Reminder items stored in the hidden Reminders folder of the mailbox of the user who is logged on. Reminder items include appointment reminders, task reminders, and follow-up flags for Mail and Contact items. Several new events for the Reminders collection object give you granular control over Reminder items.

Because the Reminders collection object is a child of the Application object, you should instantiate it in the startup procedure for your COM Add-in or VBA code.

The Reminders collection object is the programmatic sibling of the new Reminders dialog box in Outlook 2002. The Reminders dialog box, shown in Figure 9-8, eliminates the clutter caused by individual reminders in previous versions of Outlook and places all pending reminders into a single dialog box.

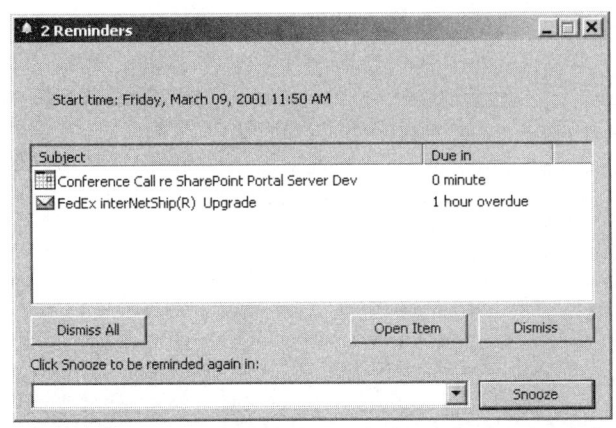

Figure 9-8 The Reminders dialog box allows convenient access to all pending reminders.

BeforeReminderShow

This event occurs just before the Reminders dialog box is displayed. The following example sets the *Cancel* argument to True and displays a Custom Reminders dialog box named *frmReminders*:

```
Private Sub colReminders_BeforeReminderShow(Cancel As Boolean)
    Cancel = True
    'Show Custom Reminders dialog box
    frmReminders.Show
End Sub
```

ReminderAdd

This event occurs when a Reminder item is added to the Reminders collection. The following example changes the default reminder sound, depending on the Item class of the ReminderObject passed to the *ReminderAdd* event procedure. All appointment items play the Utopia sound, and all task items play the Splash sound. You cannot set the ReminderSoundFile property for Mail and Contact item follow-up flags.

```
Private Sub colReminders_ReminderAdd(ByVal ReminderObject As Reminder)
    Dim objAppt As AppointmentItem
    Dim objTask As TaskItem
    Set objItem = ReminderObject.Item
    Select Case objItem.Class
        Case olAppointment
            Set objAppt = objItem
            objAppt.ReminderOverrideDefault = True
            objAppt.ReminderSoundFile = "c:\sounds\utopia.wav"
            objAppt.ReminderPlaySound = True
            objAppt.Save
        Case olTask
            Set objTask = objItem
            objTask.ReminderOverrideDefault = True
            objTask.ReminderSoundFile = "c:\sounds\splash.wav"
            objTask.ReminderPlaySound = True
            objTask.Save
    End Select
End Sub
```

ReminderChange

This event occurs after a Reminder item is changed in the Reminders collection. The item containing the reminder must be saved before the ReminderChange event will fire.

ReminderFire

This event occurs just before a Reminder item fires. The following example sends a notification to a pager device when the reminder fires:

```
Private Sub colReminders_ReminderFire(ByVal ReminderObject As Reminder)
    Dim strBody As String
    Dim objNotify As MailItem
    strBody = ReminderObject.Caption
    Set objNotify = objOutlook.CreateItem(olMailItem)
    objNotify.Body = strBody
    'Must use trusted COM Add-in to prevent OM guard prompts
    objNotify.To = "5551212@mobile.att.net"
    objNotify.Send
End Sub
```

ReminderRemove

This event occurs when a Reminder item is removed from the Reminders collection. Because the ReminderRemove event does not pass a ReminderObject, you cannot determine which reminder has been removed from the Reminders collection. A reminder is removed from the Reminders collection when any of the following events occur:

- A reminder is dismissed programmatically or by a user action.
- A reminder is turned off programmatically or by a user action in the item containing the reminder.
- The item containing a reminder is deleted.
- A reminder is removed from the Reminders collection with the *Remove* method.

Snooze

This event occurs when a user snoozes a Reminder item, either through the Outlook user interface or programmatically. The following example changes the text in the FlagRequest property if a user snoozes a flagged message that's marked High Importance:

```
Private Sub colReminders_Snooze(ByVal ReminderObject As Reminder)
    If ReminderObject.Item.Class = olMail Then
        Dim objMI As MailItem
        Set objMI = ReminderObject.Item
        If objMI.Importance = olImportanceHigh Then
            objMI.FlagRequest = "Urgent - Do not snooze!"
            objMI.Save
        End If
    End If
End Sub
```

NameSpace Events

Events that follow Application events are not available in the VBA Editor window unless you explicitly declare object variables and use the WithEvents keyword. If you look at "Using WithEvents for Child Objects" earlier in this chapter, you'll see that the NameSpace object is declared as a public variable in ThisOutlookSession using the WithEvents keyword. However, mere declaration of the variable is not sufficient. You must instantiate the NameSpace object variable in the Startup event of the Application object or use an event handler procedure to create an instance of the NameSpace object. If you don't instantiate the child object in another procedure, the event code that you write for the child object will not actually fire when the event occurs.

OptionsPagesAdd

Oddly enough, the NameSpace object supports only one event, the OptionsPagesAdd event. This event is the first cousin of the OptionsPagesAdd event for the Application object. OptionsPagesAdd for the NameSpace object occurs before a Folder Properties dialog box is displayed for a folder. The folder for which the Folder Properties dialog box is displayed is then passed as a MAPIFolder object to the event procedure for OptionsPagesAdd. You can use the OptionsPagesAdd event of the NameSpace object to add property pages to the Folder Properties dialog box for a given folder. If the folder passed to the OptionsPagesAdd event is the default Contacts folder, the following example displays the property page shown in Figure 9-9:

```
Private Sub objNS_OptionsPagesAdd(ByVal Pages As PropertyPages, _
    ByVal Folder As MAPIFolder)
    Dim strCaption As String
    'Only display for default Contacts folder
    If Folder = objNS.GetDefaultFolder(olFolderContacts) Then
        strCaption = Folder.Name & " Sample Page"
        Pages.Add "PPE.SamplePage", strCaption
    End If
End Sub
```

Notice that with the Folder object passed to the procedure, you can change the caption of the property page to reflect the folder name, as shown in Figure 9-9.

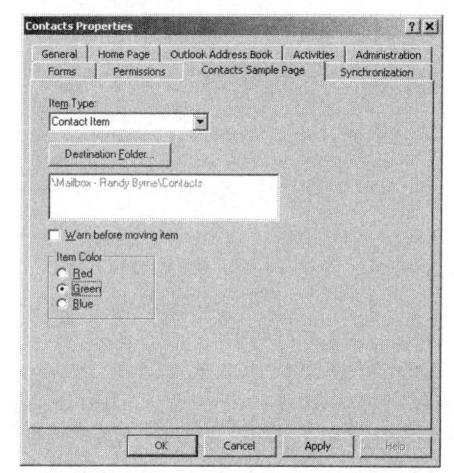

Figure 9-9 The Sample Page property page is added to the Contacts folder properties dialog box.

> **Note** For a complete listing of the procedures required to create an ActiveX control that serves as a container for an Outlook property page, see Chapter 14. You can also examine the source code for the Sample Page ActiveX control in the Sample Page Property Page Example folder under the Creating COM Add-Ins With Visual Basic folder in the Building Applications With Microsoft Outlook 2002 personal folders (.pst) file accompanying this book.

Explorers Collection Events

There is only one event for the Explorer collection object: the NewExplorer event.

NewExplorer

The NewExplorer event fires after a new Explorer window has been created and before it is displayed. A new Explorer window can be created through a user action or through your code. If you have dimensioned an Explorer object variable using WithEvents, the NewExplorer event is the correct location to set a reference to that Explorer object. Outlook passes an Explorer object to the NewExplorer event procedure. The *cmdNewExplorer* procedure shown next runs as an Outlook macro in a VBA code module. Once the code runs, the NewExplorer event causes the Explorer window for the Contacts folder to be displayed in the upper left corner of the display.

```
Sub cmdNewExplorer()
    Dim colExplorers As Outlook.Explorers
    Set colExplorers = Application.Explorers
    Set objFolder = Application.GetNameSpace("MAPI").GetDefaultFolder _
        (olFolderContacts)
    Set objExplorer = colExplorers.Add _
        (objFolder, olFolderDisplayNavigation)
    objExplorer.Display
End Sub

Private Sub colExpl_NewExplorer(ByVal Explorer As Explorer)
    Set objExpl = Explorer
    With objExpl
        .Left = 0
        .Top = 0
    End With
End Sub
```

Explorer Events

Explorer events provide you with a great deal of control over the Outlook user interface. You can now control the size and window state of Explorer windows, respond to selection changes through the new SelectionChange event and the Selection object, and determine when the user has changed her view or the current folder. Outlook 2002 adds a group of events that provide a granular level of control over the Outlook application window. These events are BeforeMaximize, BeforeMinimize, BeforeMove, and BeforeSize. The *IsPaneVisible* and *ShowPane* methods allow you to show or hide the Folder List, Outlook Bar, and Preview pane. The BeforeFolderSwitch and BeforeViewSwitch events are cancelable, so you can prevent the user from moving to a folder or activating a view. If you combine the Explorer events with the new events and programmatic control for the Outlook Bar and Office command bars, you have complete programmatic control over the Outlook user interface. You can customize the Outlook Explorer to suit the requirements of your organization.

Activate

The Activate event occurs when an Explorer window becomes the active window. Be careful not to overload this event procedure with code because the Activate and Deactivate events fire many times during an Outlook session. Each time a user opens an Inspector for an item, the following event sequence occurs:

1. Explorer Deactivate
2. Inspector Activate
3. Inspector Deactivate
4. Explorer Activate

The following code example shows you how to use the Activate event to make a command bar named Contacts visible or invisible, depending on the current folder in the Explorer:

```
Private Sub objExpl_Activate()
    On Error Resume Next
    If objExpl.CurrentFolder.Name = "Contacts" Then
        objExpl.CommandBars("Contacts").Visible = True
    Else
        objExpl.CommandBars("Contacts").Visible = False
    End If
End Sub
```

BeforeFolderSwitch

The BeforeFolderSwitch event occurs when the Explorer navigates to a new folder, either as a result of user action or through program code. This event is cancelable, so you can prevent users from navigating to prohibited folders. Of course, you can prevent users from opening prohibited folders through Exchange folder permissions, but with this event, you can also customize the Warning dialog box. The following code tests whether the current user is a member of a distribution list. If not, the user is prevented from switching to a public folder named Salary Guidelines.

```
Private Sub objExpl_BeforeFolderSwitch(ByVal NewFolder As Object, _
  Cancel As Boolean)
    If NewFolder Is Nothing Then Exit Sub
    Set objAE = Application.GetNamespace("MAPI").CurrentUser
    If IsDLMember("HR Admins",objAE) = False Then
        If NewFolder.Name = "Salary Guidelines" Then
            MsgBox "You do not have permission to access this folder." _
            & vbCr & "If you believe you should have access to this folder," _
            & vbCr & "please contact your departmental HR supervisor.", _
                vbCritical
            Cancel = True
        End If
    End If
End Sub
```

> **Note** If *NewFolder* is a folder in the file system, then *NewFolder* is Nothing. Your code should provide for this possibility.

BeforeViewSwitch

The BeforeViewSwitch event is similar to the BeforeFolderSwitch event, except that it occurs before a view is switched to a new view, either through a user action or programmatically. If a user changes from the Contacts folder to the Tasks folder but does not explicitly change the view with the View selector, the BeforeViewSwitch event will not fire, even though the default views on the two folders have different names. This event is cancelable. The event procedure on the following page prevents the user from switching to the view named Message Timeline if there are more than 500 items in the current folder.

```
Private Sub objExpl_BeforeViewSwitch(ByVal NewView As Variant, _
    Cancel As Boolean)
    If NewView = "Message Timeline" Then
        If objExpl.CurrentFolder.Items.Count > 500 Then
            Cancel = True
        End If
    End If
End Sub
```

Close

The Close event occurs when an Explorer object closes as a result of a user action or program code. Don't confuse this event with the *Close* method, which causes the Explorer window to close. The following example sets several Outlook Bar objects to Nothing when the Explorer window Close event fires:

```
Private Sub objExpl_Close()
    Set objPane = Nothing
    Set objContents = Nothing
    Set colOutlookBarGroups = Nothing
End Sub
```

Deactivate

The Deactivate event fires when an Explorer or Inspector window ceases to be the active window, either as a result of user action or through program code. You should treat this event with caution! If you display user interface elements such as a message box in the Deactivate event procedure, Outlook might exhibit unpredictable behavior. The following procedure simply writes a string to the VBA Immediate window when the Deactivate event occurs:

```
Private Sub objExpl_Deactivate()
    Debug.Print "Explorer Deactivate"
End Sub
```

> **Note** You should not display a message box, dialog box, or any other user interface element during the Deactivate event of an Explorer or Inspector object. Showing a user interface element in the Deactivate event may disrupt the activation sequence and make Outlook behave unpredictably.

FolderSwitch

The FolderSwitch event occurs when the current folder changes in the Explorer, either through a user action or a programmatic change. In the following event procedures, a toolbar button is added to the Standard toolbar in the Application Startup event. If Explorer's current folder is Nwind, the FolderSwitch event makes the New Nwind CommandBarButton visible. Otherwise, the button is hidden on the Standard toolbar. This toolbar button is declared as a CommandBarButton using the WithEvents keyword in the Declarations section of ThisOutlookSession.

```
'Place these in declarations section of ThisOutlookSession
Public WithEvents objExpl As Outlook.Explorer
Public WithEvents objCBB As Office.CommandBarButton

'Instantiate objExpl and objCBB in Application Startup event procedure

Private Sub Application_Startup()
    Dim objCB As Office.CommandBar
    Set objExpl = Application.ActiveExplorer
    Set objCB = objExpl.CommandBars("Standard")
    Set objCBB = objCB.Controls.Add(Type:=msoControlButton)
    With objCBB
        .TooltipText = "New Nwind Contact"
        .Style = msoButtonIconAndCaption
        .FaceId = 1099
        .Caption = "New Nwind"
        .Visible = False
    End With
End Sub

'This event procedure hides and unhides the button
Private Sub objExpl_FolderSwitch()
    If objExpl.CurrentFolder = "Nwind" Then
        objCBB.Visible = True
    Else
        objCBB.Visible = False
    End If
End Sub

'Event handler for the button adds a new custom item to the folder
Private Sub objCBB_Click(ByVal Ctrl As Office.CommandBarButton, _
    CancelDefault As Boolean)
    Dim olNwindItem As Outlook.ContactItem
    Set olNwindItem = objExpl.CurrentFolder.Items.Add("IPM.Contact.Nwind")
    olNwindItem.Display
End Sub
```

SelectionChange

The SelectionChange event answers many requests from Outlook developers for a means to determine which items are currently selected in the Explorer. The SelectionChange event occurs when the selection changes in the current view in the active Explorer window. Be aware that this event does not fire if you iterate over a collection of items in the current folder programmatically. The event is not triggered if the current folder in the Explorer changes due to a user action or code. However, if the user then changes the selection with a mouse click or an arrow key after he changes folders, the SelectionChange event occurs. When the SelectionChange event fires, use the Selection Property object of the Explorer object to return the items that are selected. The following example tests the Selection object to determine whether Contact items are selected and then displays the number of selected contacts in a message box:

```
Private Sub objExpl_SelectionChange()
    Dim intContacts As Integer
    For i = 1 To objExpl.Selection.Count
        If objExpl.Selection.Item(i).Class = olContact Then
            intContacts = intContacts + 1
        End If
    Next
    If intContacts Then
        MsgBox "You have selected " & intContacts & " contacts.", _
            vbInformation
    End If
End Sub
```

ViewSwitch

The ViewSwitch event occurs when the view in the Explorer window is switched, either through user action or programmatically. Like the FolderSwitch event, this event helps you to control the Outlook user interface by notifying you when either a view or a folder has changed. The following example uses the *ShowPane* method to hide or display the folder list depending on the current view:

```
Private Sub objExpl_ViewSwitch()
    If objExpl.CurrentView = "Message Timeline" Then
        objExpl.ShowPane olFolderList, False
    Else
        objExpl.ShowPane olFolderList, True
    End If
End Sub
```

New Explorer Events in Outlook 2002

To bring the events available for COM Add-ins to parity with the events used by Exchange Client Extensions, Outlook 2002 introduces a series of Explorer window events. A similar set of window events is available for the Inspector object. The Explorer window events determine when an Explorer window has been minimized, maximized, moved, or sized. Additional events for Explorer enable you to perform copy, cut, and paste operations.

BeforeItemCopy

This event occurs before an item is copied from a folder to the clipboard. When an item is selected in Explorer, BeforeItemCopy corresponds to the Edit Copy command. This event is cancelable.

BeforeItemCut

This event occurs before an item is cut from a folder and moved to the clipboard. When an item is selected in Explorer, BeforeItemCut corresponds to the Edit Cut command. This event is cancelable.

BeforeItemPaste

The BeforeItemPaste event occurs before an item is pasted from the clipboard. This event also occurs when a user attempts to drag an item from one folder and drop it into another. This event is cancelable. The following example prevents a drop (or a paste) operation from being performed on a specific folder:

```
Private Sub objExpl_BeforeItemPaste(ClipboardContent As Variant, _
    ByVal Target As MAPIFolder, Cancel As Boolean)
    Dim strPath As String

    strPath = "\\Public Folders\All Public Folders" _
        & "\Northwind Contact Management Application\Companies"
    If objExpl.CurrentFolder.FolderPath = strPath Then
        If TypeOf ClipboardContent Is Selection Then
            MsgBox "You cannot drag items from this folder.", _
                vbCritical
            Cancel = True
        End If
    End If
End Sub
```

BeforeMaximize

This event occurs before the Explorer window is maximized. This event is cancelable.

BeforeMinimize

This event occurs before the Explorer window is minimized and is cancelable.

BeforeMove

This event occurs before the Explorer window is moved and is cancelable.

BeforeSize

This event occurs before the Explorer window is resized. BeforeSize does not fire when a window is restored. This event is cancelable.

SyncObject Events

A child object of the NameSpace object, SyncObject represents a Send/Receive group that controls offline synchronization in Outlook 2002. In Outlook 2000, a Send/Receive group is known as a Quick Synchronization group. You cannot establish a SyncObject programmatically by using an *Add* method of the SyncObjects collection object. Both the SyncObjects collection object and the SyncObject object are read-only objects, meaning that you cannot change the properties of a SyncObject or create a new SyncObject programmatically. You can, however, create a SyncObject (known in Outlook 2002 as a Send/Receive group) through the Outlook user interface. For additional information about creating and modifying Send/Receive groups, see "Make the Folder Available for Offline Use" in Chapter 8, "Folders."

> **New to Outlook 2002** Although you cannot create a SyncObject programmatically, there is one SyncObject you can modify programmatically in Outlook 2002: the Application Folders SyncObject. By using the InAppFolderSyncObject property of a MAPIFolder object, you can programmatically synchronize folders for the Application Folders SyncObject. If the Application Folders Send/Receive group does not exist when you set InAppFolderSyncObject to True, the Application Folders SyncObject is created automatically. The user does not have to create this group through the Outlook user interface. Keep in mind that other properties of the Application Folders Send/Receive group must be modified through the user interface. You cannot programmatically control other Send/Receive settings such as Synchronize Forms, Download Offline Address Book, or Make Folder Home Pages Available Offline.

Raise Events and Move to the Head of the Class   Chapter 9

If you need to enumerate the defined SyncObjects for the current logged-on user, use the SyncObjects collection object of the NameSpace object. Figure 9-10 illustrates a UserForm populated with Send/Receive groups. The following code block demonstrates how to populate a list box with SyncObjects and start synchronization when the user clicks the Start Sync command button. Notice that a default group of All Folders is defined, in addition to custom Send/Receive groups.

```
'Place this declaration in the general section of frmSync code window
Dim colSyncObjects As Outlook.SyncObjects

Private Sub cmdCancel_Click()
    Unload Me
End Sub

Private Sub cmdStart_Click()
    Set ThisOutlookSession.objSyncObject = _
        colSyncObjects.Items(lstSync.ListIndex + 1)
    colSyncObjects.Item(lstSync.ListIndex + 1).Start
    Unload Me
End Sub

Private Sub lstSync_DblClick(ByVal Cancel As MSForms.ReturnBoolean)
    Call cmdStart_Click
End Sub

Private Sub UserForm_Initialize()
    Set colSyncObjects = ThisOutlookSession.objNS.SyncObjects
    For i = 1 To colSyncObjects.Count
        lstSync.AddItem colSyncObjects.Item(i)
    Next
End Sub
```

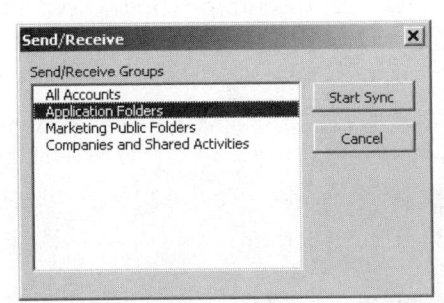

Figure 9-10 Show a UserForm to select and start the synchronization of a Send/Receive group.

OnError

The OnError event fires when an error occurs during synchronization of a Quick Synchronization group represented by a SyncObject. The following code example displays a message to the Help Desk when the OnError event for a SyncObject fires. Notice that *objSyncObject* is instantiated in the Quick Synchronization group's UserForm example shown earlier. When the user selects a synchronization profile in the UserForm and clicks the Start Sync command button, a reference is set to *objSyncObject* declared in ThisOutlookSession.

```
Private Sub objSyncObject_OnError(ByVal Code As Long, _
ByVal Description As String)
    Dim objMsg As Outlook.MailItem
    strText = Now() & " Sync Error " & CStr(Code) & Space(1) & Description
    Set objMsg = Application.CreateItem(olMailItem)
    With objMsg
        .Recipients.Add ("Help Desk")
        .Recipients.ResolveAll
        .Body = strText
        .Display
    End With
End Sub
```

Progress

Use the Progress event to inform a user about the completion percentage of a synchronization job for a Send/Receive group. Notice that the Progress event provides several values that let you provide information to the user. The *Value* variable specifies the current value of the synchronization process based on the number of items synchronized; *Max* represents the total number of items to be synchronized; and *State* identifies the current state of the synchronization process where state has one of two values representing whether synchronization has started or stopped. The following example updates the label named *lblCaption* on *frmProgress* during the synchronization process:

```
Private Sub objSyncObject_Progress(ByVal State As Outlook.OlSyncState, _
    ByVal Description As String, ByVal Value As Long, ByVal Max As Long)
    Dim strCaption As String
    If State = olSyncStarted Then
        strCaption = "Synchronization started: "
    Else
        strCaption = "Synchronization stopped: "
    End If
    strCaption = strCaption & Str(Value / _
        Max * 100) & "% " & Description
    frmProgress.lblCaption = strCaption
End Sub
```

SyncEnd

The SyncEnd event takes place when the synchronization of a Send/Receive group is completed. The code example unloads a UserForm that showed the synchronization progress to the user.

```
Private Sub objSyncObject_SyncEnd()
    Unload frmProgress
End Sub
```

SyncStart

The SyncStart event takes place when the synchronization of a Quick Synchronization group begins. The code example displays a UserForm that uses the Progress event to inform the user about synchronization progress.

```
Private Sub objSyncObject_SyncStart()
    frmProgress.Show
End Sub
```

OutlookBarPane Events

You can use cancelable Outlook Bar events to prevent navigation from Outlook Bar groups or shortcuts. (For a detailed discussion of the properties and methods of the OutlookBarPane, OutlookBarStorage, OutlookBarGroup, and OutlookBarShortcut objects, see Chapter 11, "Using Visual Basic, VBA, or VBScript with Outlook.") If you dimension the correct object variables using the WithEvents keyword, your code can raise events when Outlook Bar groups and shortcuts are added to or removed from the Outlook Bar.

If you raise events on Outlook Bar panes, groups, and shortcuts, you'll need to instantiate object variables during event procedures for other objects in the Outlook Object Model. The table below suggests event procedures where you should set a reference to the object variable.

Object	Set Object Reference in This Event Procedure
objPane	*objExplorer_Activate*
colOutlookBarGroups	*objExplorer_Activate*
colOutlookBarShortcuts	*objPane_BeforeGroupSwitch*

BeforeGroupSwitch

The BeforeGroupSwitch event occurs before Outlook switches to a different Outlook Bar group, either because of user action or a programmatic change. Because this event is cancelable, you can prevent users from changing to a prohibited group on the Outlook Bar. The following example instantiates a collection object for OutlookBarShortcuts and then prevents the user from switching to the Real Estate Division group on the Outlook Bar:

```
Private Sub objPane_BeforeGroupSwitch(ByVal ToGroup As OutlookBarGroup, _
    Cancel As Boolean)
    Set colOutlookBarShortcuts = ToGroup.Shortcuts
    If ToGroup = "Real Estate Division" Then
        MsgBox "You cannot switch to " & ToGroup.Name _
            & " on the Outlook Bar!", vbInformation
        Cancel = True
    End If
End Sub
```

BeforeNavigate

The BeforeNavigate event occurs before Outlook navigates to a folder or launches an Outlook Bar shortcut, either because of user action or program code. Because this event is cancelable, you can prevent users from navigating to folders or launching shortcut URLs or executables.

```
Private Sub objPane_BeforeNavigate(ByVal Shortcut As OutlookBarShortcut, _
    Cancel As Boolean)
    If Shortcut.Name = "Financial Services" Then
        Cancel = True
    End If
End Sub
```

OutlookBarGroup Events

The events in this section fire when an OutlookBarGroup object is added or removed, either programmatically or through a user action.

GroupAdd

The GroupAdd event occurs after a group has been added to an Outlook Bar, either because of a user action or through program code. The following example adds shortcuts for all the members of a distribution list named Shared Calendars to a new group named Workgroup Calendars. All the members of the Shared

Calendars distribution list must grant at least Reviewer permission on their calendar folders for this example to work correctly.

```
Private Sub colOutlookBarGroups_GroupAdd(ByVal NewGroup As OutlookBarGroup)
    DebugWrite "OutlookBarGroups GroupAdd " & NewGroup.Name
    Dim myFolder As Outlook.MAPIFolder
    Dim myRecip As Outlook.Recipient
    Dim myDL As Outlook.DistListItem
    On Error Resume Next
    Set myFolder = objNS.GetDefaultFolder(olFolderContacts)
    Set myDL = myFolder.Items("Shared Calendars")
    For i = 1 To myDL.MemberCount
        Set myRecip = objNS.CreateRecipient(myDL.GetMember(i).Name)
        myRecip.Resolve
        If myRecip.Resolved Then
            Set myFolder = _
            objNS.GetSharedDefaultFolder(myRecip, olFolderCalendar)
        End If
        NewGroup.Shortcuts.Add myFolder, "Calendar - " & myRecip.Name
    Next
    NewGroup.Name = "Shared Calendars"
End Sub
```

BeforeGroupAdd

The BeforeGroupAdd event occurs before a group is added to an Outlook Bar, either because of user action or through program code. This example prevents a user from adding groups to the Outlook Bar.

```
Private Sub colOutlookBarGroups_BeforeGroupAdd(Cancel As Boolean)
    Cancel = True
End Sub
```

BeforeGroupRemove

The BeforeGroupRemove event occurs before a group is removed from an Outlook Bar, either because of user action or through program code. The code in this example cancels an attempt by a user or program code to delete the Outlook Shortcuts group.

```
Private Sub colOutlookBarGroups_BeforeGroupRemove _
  (ByVal Group As OutlookBarGroup, Cancel As Boolean)
    If Group.Name = "Outlook Shortcuts" Then
        Cancel = True
    End If
End Sub
```

OutlookBarShortcut Events

The OutlookBarShortcut events occur when an OutlookBarShortcut object is added or removed, either programmatically or through a user action.

ShortcutAdd

The ShortcutAdd event fires after a shortcut has been added to an Outlook Bar group, either because of user action or through program code. The following event procedure adds the name of the logged-on user to the shortcut name if the user adds a shortcut to his or her Calendar folder:

```
Private Sub colOutlookBarShortcuts_ShortcutAdd _
  (ByVal NewShortcut As OutlookBarShortcut)
    On Error Resume Next
    Dim objFolder As Outlook.MAPIFolder
    Set objFolder = NewShortcut.Target
    'Bail out if not a folder shortcut
    If Err Then Exit Sub
    'Test EntryID's to determine if folder shortcut
    'is for user's calendar folder
    If objNS.GetDefaultFolder(olFolderCalendar).EntryID = _
      objFolder.EntryID Then
        NewShortcut.Name = "Calendar - " & objNS.CurrentUser
    End If
End Sub
```

BeforeShortcutAdd

The BeforeShortcutAdd event takes place before a shortcut is added to an Outlook Bar group, either because of user action or through program code. This example prevents users from adding a shortcut to the Web Links group. Objects representing the current group on the Outlook Bar and the collection of shortcuts for the current group are instantiated in the BeforeGroupSwitch event of the Pane object.

```
Public objCurrentGroup As Outlook.OutlookBarGroup

Private Sub objPane_BeforeGroupSwitch(ByVal ToGroup As OutlookBarGroup, _
    Cancel As Boolean)
    Set colOutlookBarShortcuts = ToGroup.Shortcuts
    Set objCurrentGroup = ToGroup
End Sub
```

```
Private Sub colOutlookBarShortcuts_BeforeShortcutAdd(Cancel As Boolean)
    If objCurrentGroup.Name = "Web Links" Then
        Cancel = True
    End If
End Sub
```

BeforeShortcutRemove

The BeforeShortcutRemove event takes place before a shortcut is removed from an Outlook Bar group, either because of user action or through program code. The code in this example cancels an attempt by users or program code to delete a shortcut from the Financial Services group.

```
Private Sub colOutlookBarShortcuts_BeforeShortcutRemove(Cancel As Boolean)
    If objCurrentGroup.Name = "Financial Services" Then
        Cancel = True
    End If
End Sub
```

Inspectors Collection Events

The Inspectors collection object provides the gateway to item-level events in Outlook 2000 and Outlook 2002. Although this collection object has only one event that occurs when a new Inspector is displayed through either a user action or program code, the NewInspector event lets you instantiate item-level objects declared using the WithEvents keyword. In Outlook 97 and Outlook 98, the only supported events were form-level events for customized Item objects, also known as custom forms. Any form-level item for which you write VBScript code is, by definition, a custom Outlook form. VBScript code in those forms could respond to events such as Item Open, Close, Read, Send, Write, Reply, Reply All, Forward, PropertyChange, CustomPropertyChange, and CustomAction. The important departure Outlook 2000 and Outlook 2002 make from previous versions is that they now enable you to write VBA code in ThisOutlookSession or develop a COM Add-in to respond to item-level events. If you raise events using the item-level objects in the Outlook Object Model, you are no longer constrained by VBScript when you write code for item-level events in Outlook custom forms.

Exceptions to the NewInspector Event

Unfortunately, there are some exceptions to this freedom that should be clearly explained at this point. If an item in a folder does not utilize an Inspector object, then you will not be able to write item-level event code in Visual Basic for this object. Certain e-mail editors do not support an Inspector object or the NewInspector event. For example, if you use Word as your e-mail editor and the format of the message you are composing is plain text, the NewInspector event does not fire in Outlook 2000 because an Inspector object is not added to the Inspectors collection when you create the mail message. The default editor selected on the Mail Format page of the Tools Options dialog box determines whether the default MailItem with the message class IPM.Note supports the Inspector object. The following table indicates which types of MailItems support an Inspector object, depending on your default mail editor and Outlook version.

Message Format	When Your E-Mail Editor Is Outlook 2000	When Your E-Mail Editor Is Word 2000 (Office Mail)	When Your E-Mail Editor Is Outlook 2002	When You E-Mail Editor Is Word 2002
HTML	Supports Inspector	Does not support Inspector	Supports Inspector	Supports Inspector
Rich Text Format (RTF)	Supports Inspector	Supports Inspector	Supports Inspector	Supports Inspector
Plain Text	Supports Inspector	Does not support Inspector	Supports Inspector	Supports Inspector

> **Note** Outlook 2002 fixes the problematic Inspector behavior found in Outlook 2000. Word is the default e-mail editor in Outlook 2002. The NewInspector event will always fire in Outlook 2002 and is not dependent upon the default e-mail editor or the mail format.

There are other circumstances where you cannot instantiate an Inspector object when a user or program code creates or modifies an item in a folder. An Outlook 2002 Office Document item does not support an Inspector object. A DocumentItem object is any document—other than an Outlook item—that exists as an item in an Outlook folder. In common usage, an IPM.Document item will be an Office Document, but it may also be any type of document, an executable file, or an HTML document. Remember that Exchange folders can contain almost any type of Document item. Moreover, Office Document items can be posted or sent directly to a folder either by a user action or by program code. In this instance, the DocumentItem objects do not support an Inspector object. The following table indicates when a DocumentItem object supports an Inspector object.

Document Item	Message Class	Supports Inspector for Outlook Document Item	Supports Inspector for Native Document Item
Web Page	IPM.Document.htmlfile	Not applicable	No
Word Document	IPM.Document.Word.Document.8	Yes, if created by Outlook 2000 or earlier	No
Excel Worksheet	IPM.Document.Excel.Sheet.8	Yes, if created by Outlook 2000 or earlier	No
PowerPoint Presentation	IPM.Document.PowerPoint.Show.8	Yes, if created by Outlook 2000 or earlier	No
Visio Drawing	IPM.Document.*.VSD	No	No

> **Caution** Earlier versions of Outlook allowed you to create custom forms based on the Outlook Office Document item. These forms wrapped a native Office document (such as a Word document, an Excel worksheet, or a PowerPoint presentation) in an Outlook Inspector. This functionality is not available in Outlook 2002. When you select the Office Document command from the New submenu of the File menu in Outlook 2002, you will see the New Office Document dialog box. When you select an Office Document type in this dialog box, you launch the hosting application and can save the document to the file system, Web storage, or an Exchange folder. You cannot create and design custom Outlook Office Document items in Outlook 2002. Outlook Office Document items still open and function correctly in Outlook 2002, but you must use an earlier version of Outlook if you want to create and design these forms.

If you post an Office document such as an Excel workbook or a PowerPoint presentation directly to a folder, an Inspector object will not be created. The NewInspector event will not fire when you add a native Office document to an Exchange folder. If you post or send an Office Document item created in a version of Outlook earlier than Outlook 2002, the NewInspector event will fire. Posting any other document, whether it is an HTML document, a .zip file, a .pdf file, or any other type of document that can be posted to a public folder, will not cause the NewInspector event to fire.

Part IV Beyond The Basics

If an application external to Outlook creates an Outlook Inspector object, the NewInspector event will not fire if an Inspectors collection object has been instantiated by Outlook VBA or an Outlook COM Add-in. An external application is an application that uses Simple MAPI to create an Outlook mail message. This limitation does not apply to applications that use Outlook as an ActiveX Automation Server to create Outlook items. For example, you can send a file as an attachment to an Outlook message by selecting the Mail Recipient MAPI command on the Send To menu of the file's shortcut menu. Right-click the file in Windows Explorer to display the file's shortcut menu. When you select this command, an Inspector window opens and the file is added as an attachment to an Outlook message. However, a NewInspector event will not fire for this message. Similarly, if you use the Send Page By E-Mail or Link By E-Mail commands in Internet Explorer, a NewInspector event will not fire. The following table illustrates when a NewInspector event fires, depending on the calling application. You should realize that the exceptions regarding mail editor settings and message format discussed earlier will also determine whether the NewInspector event fires.

Calling Application	Command	NewInspector Event for Inspectors Collection object
Windows Explorer	Send To extensions such as Mail Recipient MAPI command	No
Internet Explorer	File Send Page By E-Mail or Link By E-Mail	No
Outlook	File New Mail Message	Yes, depending on default e-mail editor and message type
Outlook	Create New Item (either through user action or program code)	Yes
Word, Excel, Visual Basic, Visual C++, or any COM-compliant ActiveX automation controller application	Outlook automation through program code	Yes

NewInspector

The NewInspector event occurs when a new Inspector object is created either through a user action or program code. The NewInspector event fires before the Inspector window is displayed. If you create an item through code and do not display the item, then the NewInspector event does not occur.

As discussed earlier, the NewInspector event is the gateway to item-level events. The following code example shows how to create item-level objects depending on the class of the item returned by the CurrentItem property of the Inspector object. Once you have instantiated these form-level objects in your VBA code, you can raise events on the form-level objects in VBA as long as you have declared the form-level objects using the WithEvents keyword. All of the traditional form-level events, such as Item_Open, Item_Read, Item_Write, and Item_Send, are available for the Item object declared using WithEvents.

The importance of this approach is that these events are now available to you in VBA or in your COM Add-in, rather than in VBScript code written for a custom form.

```
'Place these declarations in the general section ThisOutlookSession
Public WithEvents objInsp As Outlook.Inspector
Public WithEvents colInsp As Outlook.Inspectors
Public WithEvents objMailItem As Outlook.MailItem
Public WithEvents objPostItem As Outlook.PostItem
Public WithEvents objContactItem As Outlook.ContactItem
Public WithEvents objDistListItem As Outlook.DistListItem
Public WithEvents objApptItem As Outlook.AppointmentItem
Public WithEvents objTaskItem As Outlook.TaskItem
Public WithEvents objTaskRequestItem As Outlook.TaskRequestItem
Public WithEvents objTaskRequestAcceptItem As Outlook.TaskRequestAcceptItem
Public WithEvents objTaskRequestDeclineItem As Outlook.TaskRequestAcceptItem
Public WithEvents objTaskRequestUpdateItem As Outlook.TaskRequestUpdateItem
Public WithEvents objJournalItem As Outlook.JournalItem
Public WithEvents objDocumentItem As Outlook.DocumentItem
Public WithEvents objReportItem As Outlook.ReportItem
Public WithEvents objRemoteItem As Outlook.RemoteItem

Private Sub colInsp_NewInspector(ByVal Inspector As Inspector)
    Dim objItem As Object
    Set objInsp = Inspector
    On Error Resume Next
    Set objItem = objInsp.CurrentItem
    Select Case objItem.Class
        Case olMail
            Set objMailItem = objItem
        Case olPost
            Set objPostItem = objItem
```

(continued)

Part IV   Beyond The Basics

```
            Case olAppointment
                Set objApptItem = objItem
            Case olContact
                Set objContactItem = objItem
            Case olDistributionList
                Set objDistListItem = objItem
            Case olTask
                Set objTaskItem = objItem
            Case olTaskRequest
                Set objTaskRequestItem = objItem
            Case olTaskRequestAccept
                Set objTaskRequestAcceptItem = objItem
            Case olTaskRequestDecline
                Set objTaskRequestDeclineItem = objItem
            Case olTaskRequestUpdate
                Set objTaskRequestUpdateItem = objItem
            Case olJournal
                Set objJournalItem = objItem
            Case olReport
                Set objReportItem = objItem
            Case olRemote
                Set objRemoteItem = objItem
            Case olDocument
                Set objDocumentItem = objItem
        End Select
End Sub
```

The item's class is a better guide to the type of item than the item's message class. For example, all Contact items have a class value of *olContact*. If you look up the *olContact* value in the *OlObjectClass* Enum, *olContact* has a decimal value of *40*. Any contact items, whether they are default contact items with a message class of IPM.Contact or custom contact items with a message class of IPM.Contact.MyCustomContactForm, have an item class value equal to *olContact*.

Inspector Events

The Activate and Deactivate events for the Inspector object are not commonly used. However, the Close event is critical for proper operation of COM Add-ins, especially in regard to when Outlook is removed from memory.

Activate

The Activate event for the Inspector object occurs when the Inspector window becomes the active window in Outlook. The following example makes the built-in Clipboard Command bar visible in the Inspector window if the message class of the CurrentItem is IPM.Note. When the Activate event occurs, you can return the CurrentItem property of the Inspector object to examine the properties of the item.

```
Private Sub objInsp_Activate()
    If objInsp.CurrentItem.MessageClass = "IPM.Note" Then
        objInsp.CommandBars("Clipboard").Visible = True
    Else
        objInsp.CommandBars("Clipboard").Visible = False
    End If
End Sub
```

Close

The Close event occurs when the Inspector object is closed, either through a user action or programmatically. The Close event will always occur after the Deactivate event. The following example uses the Close event to hide the Assistant. As with the Deactivate event, you cannot access the CurrentItem property of the Inspector object during the Close event.

```
Private Sub objInsp_Close()
    With Assistant
        .Visible = False
    End With
End Sub
```

Deactivate

The Deactivate event occurs when the Inspector window ceases to be the active window because of a user action or program code. The same cautions mentioned earlier regarding the Deactivate event of the Explorer window apply to the Inspector window. Do not display user interface elements in the Deactivate event procedure. The following procedure hides the built-in Clipboard Command bar. In the Deactivate event, you cannot use the CurrentItem property to return properties of the item. If you attempt to use the CurrentItem property, Outlook will generate an Object Not Found error.

```
Private Sub objInsp_Deactivate()
    objInsp.CommandBars("Clipboard").Visible = False
End Sub
```

New Inspector Events in Outlook 2002

Outlook 2002 introduces a series of window events for the Inspector object. These events determine when an Inspector window has been minimized, maximized, moved, or sized. Because the Inspector window events are identical to the Explorer window events, see the section "New Explorer Events in Outlook 2002" beginning on page 343 for a description of these events.

Folders Collection Events

The Folders collection object contains all the MAPIFolder objects belonging to a parent MAPIFolder object. The NameSpace object also contains a Folders object containing all the root folders for the currently logged-on user. The Folders collection object events occur when folders are added, changed, or deleted because of user action or program code. The Folders collection events give you a powerful means to control folder names, hierarchical structure, and folder contents, in addition to traditional Exchange roles and folder permissions.

> **Note** With the proper synchronization of FolderAdd and FolderRemove events, you can actually restore deleted items and folders. Previously, this functionality was very difficult to achieve, requiring Exchange Server 5.5 scripting agents.

FolderAdd

The FolderAdd event occurs when a folder is added to a Folders collection object, through either user action or program code. The following example prevents users from deleting the Large Messages folder in their Inbox. If a user deletes this folder, a message box appears and notifies the user that the folder cannot be deleted. The folder is then moved from the user's Deleted Items folder back to the Inbox.

This example requires that you declare two collection object variables using WithEvents: *colDeletedItemsFolders* and *colInboxFolders*. When a folder is deleted from *colInboxFolders,* the FolderRemove event fires. The global variable *blnDeleteRestore* is set to *True* in the FolderRemove event procedure for *colInboxFolders*. When a folder is deleted from *colInboxFolders*, it is moved to the Deleted Items folder. The FolderAdd event procedure for the *colDeletedItemsFolders* object evaluates the *blnDeleteRestore* variable. If *blnDeleteRestore* is *True,* the procedure moves the folder that has just been added to the Deleted Items folder back to the Inbox.

Raise Events and Move to the Head of the Class   Chapter 9

```
'Place these declarations in the general section of ThisOutlookSession
Public WithEvents colDeletedItemsFolders As Outlook.Folders
Public WithEvents colInboxFolders As Outlook.Folders
Public blnDeleteRestore As Boolean

Private Sub Application_Startup()
    Set objNS = Application.GetNameSpace("MAPI")
    Set colInboxFolders = objNS.GetDefaultFolder(olFolderInbox).Folders
    Set colDeletedItemsFolders = _
        objNS.GetDefaultFolder(olFolderDeletedItems).Folders
End Sub

Private Sub colInboxFolders_FolderRemove()
    blnDeleteRestore = True
End Sub

Private Sub colDeletedItemsFolders_FolderAdd(ByVal Folder As MAPIFolder)
    If blnDeleteRestore Then
        MsgBox "You cannot delete " & Folder.Name _
        & vbCr & "This folder will be restored to your Inbox.", _
            vbInformation
        Folder.MoveTo objNS.GetDefaultFolder(olFolderInbox)
    End If
    blnDeleteRestore = False
End Sub
```

FolderChange

The FolderChange event occurs when a folder in a Folders collection object is changed, either through user action or program code. The FolderChange event fires if a user or program code renames a folder, or if an item in the folder is added, changed, or removed. The following code example prevents a user from renaming the Large Messages subfolder of their Inbox. Outlook uses the Large Messages subfolder to store messages above a certain size limit that a user does not want to download to their offline folders file. The *blnLargeMsgActive* global variable ensures that the code runs only if the Large Messages folder is the current folder in the Explorer. All the necessary event procedures have been included in this example so that you can see how events have to be chained together to achieve the intended result.

```
'Place these declarations in the general section of ThisOutlookSession
Public WithEvents objExpl As Outlook.Explorer
Public WithEvents colInboxFolders As Outlook.Folders
Public blnLargeMsgActive As Boolean
```

(continued)

Part IV Beyond The Basics

```vb
'Create objExpl in the Application Startup event
Private Sub Application_Startup()
    Set objExpl = Application.ActiveExplorer
End Sub

'Create colInboxFolders in BeforeFolderSwitch and set blnLargeMsgActive
Private Sub objExpl_BeforeFolderSwitch(ByVal NewFolder As Object, _
  Cancel As Boolean)
    If NewFolder.Name = "Large Messages" And _
      NewFolder.Parent.Name = "Inbox" Then
        blnLargeMsgActive = True
    Else
        blnLargeMsgActive = False
    End If
    If NewFolder.Parent.Name = "Inbox" Then
        Set colInboxFolders = NewFolder.Parent.Folders
    End If
End Sub

Private Sub colInboxFolders_FolderChange(ByVal Folder As MAPIFolder)
    If blnLargeMsgActive Then
        If Folder.Name <> "Large Messages" Then
            MsgBox "Can't rename Large Messages folder!", vbInformation
            objExpl.CurrentFolder.Name = "Large Messages"
        End If
    End If
End Sub
```

FolderRemove

The FolderRemove event occurs when a folder is deleted from its Folders collection object, either through user action or program code. Unlike the FolderAdd and FolderChange events, FolderRemove does not pass a MAPIFolder object for the folder that has been removed. This example is similar to the code examples for the FolderAdd and FolderRemove events. It requires that you chain a FolderRemove event for the Inbox to a FolderAdd event for the Deleted Items folder. In this instance, if a folder is deleted from the Inbox and the deleted folder contains items, the deleted folder is displayed in an Explorer window.

```vb
'Place these declarations in the general section of ThisOutlookSession
Public WithEvents colDeletedItemsFolders As Outlook.Folders
Public WithEvents colInboxFolders As Outlook.Folders
Public blnDelete As Boolean
```

```
Private Sub Application_Startup()
    Set objNS = Application.GetNameSpace("MAPI")
    Set colInboxFolders = objNS.GetDefaultFolder(olFolderInbox).Folders
    Set colDeletedItemsFolders = _
        objNS.GetDefaultFolder(olFolderDeletedItems).Folders
End Sub
Private Sub colInboxFolders_FolderRemove()
    blnDelete = True
End Sub

Private Sub colDeletedItemsFolders_FolderAdd(ByVal Folder As MAPIFolder)
    If blnDelete And Folder.Items.Count Then
        Folder.Display
    End If
    blnDelete = False
End Sub
```

> **Note** These examples are aimed at folders in a user's private information store where a Deleted Items folder exists. If you want to recover deleted items or folders from public folders programmatically, you will have to write Exchange 5.5 scripting agents or Exchange 2000 event sinks and have your Microsoft Exchange Server administrator enable deleted item recovery for the public information store using the Exchange Administrator program. You should be aware that a user can circumvent the Deleted Items folder by pressing Shift+Delete to delete an item or a folder. Additional details regarding deleted item restoration are provided in the following articles from the Microsoft Knowledge Base on the Microsoft Support Online Web site:
>
> ❑ Q178630, "XADM: How To Recover Items That Do Not Touch The Deleted Items Folders" at *http://support.microsoft.com/support/kb/articles/q178/6/30.asp*
>
> ❑ Q180117, "XADM: Recovering Deleted Items from a Public Folder" at *http://support.microsoft.com/support/kb/articles/q180/1/17.asp*

Views Collection Events

Outlook 2002 offers a Views collection object for the MAPIFolder object. If you obtain a reference to a MAPIFolder, you can instantiate a Views collection object and enumerate all the Views in the folder. In previous versions of Outlook,

Views enumeration required the use of Collaboration Data Objects (CDO) to obtain the hidden view messages in a folder. Outlook 2002 simplifies this process and lets you create and modify Views programmatically with the View object, the child object of the Views collection. Two events are associated with the Views collection object, ViewAdd and ViewRemove.

ViewAdd

This event occurs when a View object is added to the Views collection, either programmatically or by a user. The following example prints the eXtensible Markup Language (XML) for a View object in the Immediate window after the View object has been created. In order for the ViewAdd code to work correctly, you must declare a Views object named *colViews* that uses the *WithEvents* keyword. You instantiate the *colViews* object in the BeforeFolderSwitch event of an Explorer object. This technique ensures that the *colViews* object contains the Views for the current folder.

```
Private Sub objExpl_BeforeFolderSwitch(ByVal NewFolder As Object, _
   Cancel As Boolean)
     Debug.Print "BeforeFolderSwitch"
     Set colViews = NewFolder.Views
End Sub

Private Sub colViews_ViewAdd(ByVal View As View)
     Debug.Print View.XML
End Sub
```

ViewRemove

The ViewRemove event fires when a View object is removed from the Views collection. Unfortunately, there is no cancelable BeforeViewRemove event to prevent deletion of a View object from a folder.

Items Collection Events

Like the Folders collection object, the Items collection object gives you a great deal of control over what happens in folders and with the items contained within folders. You can use the Items collection events to respond to message created, changed, and deleted events. The Items collection does not have a timer event like the Exchange Event Service does, although you can readily construct a timer-based COM Add-in with a Visual Basic Timer control or Windows API calls. Unlike the Exchange 5.5 Event Service or Exchange 2000 event sinks, Items collection events do not provide server-based scalability and process isolation. Exchange

Raise Events and Move to the Head of the Class Chapter 9

2000 offers the additional benefit of supporting both synchronous and asynchronous events for event sinks.

The following table compares the Exchange 5.5 Event Service, the Exchange 2000 event sinks, and a Visual Basic COM Add-in that uses Items collection object events.

Feature	Exchange 5.5 Event Service	Exchange 2000 Event Sink	COM Add-In
Development language	VBScript	Visual Basic or Visual C++	Visual Basic, Visual C++, or any other development tool for an ActiveX DLL
Object binding	Late-bound	Early-bound	Early-bound with proper declaration of variables
Variable types	Variant only	All supported types	All supported types
Scalability	Yes	Yes	Limited
Process location	Server	Server	Client
Error Logging	Windows NT Event Service	Windows NT Event Service	Error log on client must be created by developer

ItemAdd

The ItemAdd event occurs when an item is added to an Items collection object, either through user action or program code. The following example creates an Items collection object for an Exchange public folder named Customers that contains Contact items. When a new customer is added to the Customers folder, a message is sent to a distribution list for the correct regional sales team. This example requires another event procedure in order to instantiate the collection object for the Customers folder. So that you can better understand the code, each of these event procedures is listed below. See Chapter 11 for a complete listing of the *OpenMAPIFolder* function.

```
'Place these declarations in the general section of Class module
Public WithEvents colCustomersItems As Outlook.Items

'Instantiate collection object in objOutlook Startup event

Private Sub objOutlook_Startup()
    Dim strFolderPath As String
    StrFolderPath = "Public Folders\All Public Folders\" _
        & "Contact Management\Customers"
    Set colCustomersItems = OpenMAPIFolder(strFolderPath).Items
End Sub
```

(continued)

Part IV Beyond The Basics

```
'This event procedure sends a message to a DL
Private Sub colCustomersItems_ItemAdd(ByVal Item As Object)
Dim objContactItem As Outlook.ContactItem
Dim objMsgItem As Outlook.MailItem
Set objContactItem = Item
If objContactItem.MessageClass = "IPM.Contact.Customer" Then
    Select Case objContactItem.BusinessAddressState
        Case "CA", "NV", "WA", "OR", "AZ", "NM", "ID"
        strDL = "Sales Team West"
        Case "IL", "OH", "NE", "MN", "IA", "IN", "WI"
        strDL = "Sales Team Midwest"
        Case "ME", "NH", "NY", "NJ", "MD", "PA", "RI", "CT", "MA"
        strDL = "Sales Team East"
        Case Else
        strDL = "Sales Team National"
    End Select
    Set objMsgItem = objOutlook.CreateItem(olMailItem)
    objMsgItem.Subject = "New Customer - " & _
    objContactItem.CompanyName
    objMsgItem.Save
    objMsgItem.Attachments.Add objContactItem, olByValue
    'Must use trusted COM Add-in to prevent OM guard prompts
    objMsgItem.To = strDL
    objMsgItem.Send
End If
```

ItemChange

The ItemChange event occurs when an item in an Items collection object is changed, either by user action or program code. Continuing the example of the Customers folder described earlier, the following code writes a record to a SQL Server 7 database when an item changes in the Customers public folder. The *StrClean* function in the following procedure removes single quotes that could cause an error when the SQL statement executes:

```
Private Sub colCustomersItems_ItemChange(ByVal Item As Object)
    Dim objCont As Outlook.ContactItem
    Dim strSQL As String
    Const strSep = "','"
    Dim conDB As New ADODB.Connection
    Set objCont = Item
    If objCont.MessageClass <> "IPM.Contact.Customer" Then
        Exit Sub
    End If
    On Error GoTo AddContact_Error
    conDB.Open "Nwind", "sa", ""
    strSQL = "Insert Customers Values ('"
```

```
        strSQL = strSQL & StrClean(objCont.Account & strSep
        strSQL = strSQL & StrClean(objCont.CompanyName) & strSep
        strSQL = strSQL & StrClean(objCont.FullName) & strSep
        strSQL = strSQL & StrClean(objCont.JobTitle) & strSep
        strSQL = strSQL & StrClean(objCont.BusinessAddress) & strSep
        strSQL = strSQL & StrClean(objCont.BusinessAddressCity) & strSep
        strSQL = strSQL & StrClean(objCont.BusinessAddressState) & strSep
        strSQL = strSQL & StrClean(objCont.BusinessAddressPostalCode) & strSep
        strSQL = strSQL & StrClean(objCont.BusinessAddressCountry) & strSep
        strSQL = strSQL & StrClean(objCont.BusinessTelephoneNumber) & strSep
        strSQL = strSQL & StrClean(objCont.BusinessFaxNumber) & "')"
        conDB.Execute strSQL
        conDB.Close

        AddContact_Exit:
        Exit Sub

        AddContact_Error:
        Utility.ErrorTrap 'Writes error to event log or file
        Resume AddContact_Exit
End Sub
```

ItemRemove

The ItemRemove event occurs when an item is removed from a specified Items collection object, either through user action or programmatically. The following example expands on the FolderRemove example described earlier to show how to undelete an item programmatically. This example undeletes a custom form with a message class of IPM.Post.ContactSettings if a user deletes the item from the Settings subfolder of the Inbox.

```
'Place these declarations in the general section of ThisOutlookSession
Public WithEvents colDeletedItems As Outlook.Items
Public WithEvents colSettingsItems As Outlook.Items
Public blnDeleteItem As Boolean

Private Sub Application_Startup()
    Set objNS = Application.GetNameSpace("MAPI")
    Set colSettingsItems = _
        objNS.GetDefaultFolder(olFolderInbox).Folders("Settings")
    Set colDeletedItems = objNS.GetDefaultFolder(olFolderDeletedItems).Items
End Sub

Private Sub colSettingsItems_ItemRemove()
    blnDeleteItem = True
End Sub
```

(continued)

```
Private Sub colDeletedItems_ItemAdd(ByVal Item As Object)
    If blnDeleteItem and Item.MessageClass = "IPM.Post.ContactSettings" Then
        Set objDestFolder = _
            objNS.GetDefaultFolder(olFolderInbox).Folders("Settings")
        Item.Move objDestFolder
    End If
    blnDeleteItem = False
End Sub
```

Item Events

We've covered many of the application-level events available in Outlook 2002. Do you believe that you're ready to move to the head of the class yet? You can go beyond what you've learned so far and raise item-level events in addition to application-level events. You should be aware that Outlook 2000 introduced several new item-level events, including AttachmentAdd, AttachmentRead, BeforeAttachmentSave, and BeforeCheckNames. Outlook 2002 offers an additional item-level event: the BeforeDelete event. Following the convention established for application-level events, event names that begin with Before are subject to cancellation in the event procedure.

The important point about Outlook item-level events is that they can be controlled from ThisOutlookSession with Outlook VBA or from a COM Add-in created in Visual Basic or Visual C++. Outlook 97 and Outlook 98 did not support the declaration of item-level object variables using WithEvents in order to write event procedure code. Item-level event procedures were previously created using VBScript in Outlook custom forms. Many development projects will still require VBScript in Outlook forms. VBScript behind forms provides a simple means of enabling form-level automation and allowing that automation to travel from recipient to recipient.

In theory, an Outlook custom form could contain almost no VBScript code. The event-related behavior of this form could be controlled by item-level object variables that use Visual Basic code to create event procedures. The problem with this theoretical approach is that each client receiving your custom form would need to have your COM Add-in installed in order for the form's event procedures to function correctly. Portability of event automation is problematic when your code does not travel with the form itself. In a controlled corporate environment operating in conjunction with Exchange Server, the theoretical proposition of item-level event code residing in COM Add-in event procedures becomes more feasible if the correct COM Add-ins are deployed consistently to every client in the organization. In fact, this is one area of event automation that lends itself perfectly to COM Add-ins. If you want to create event procedures for default Outlook items such as a MailItem or ContactItem, you can do so without hesitation. A common complaint by Outlook developers is that a custom form cannot be substituted for the default mail message whose message class is IPM.Note. In Chapter 13, you'll learn how to make a custom form the default mail message in place of IPM.Note by changing registry settings. This ability constitutes a hidden feature of Outlook 2000 and Outlook 2002. If you don't want to resort to registry changes, you can create event procedure code that instantiates a MailItem object variable declared using WithEvents in the NewInspector event of the Inspectors collection object. You can use that MailItem object to write additional item-level event procedures.

The following example requires a subject to be entered for a message before the message is sent. If the user fails to enter a subject after the initial InputBox is displayed, the Send event is canceled. This code also requires chained event procedures to accomplish the intended result. All the required event procedures and declarations in the example have been included so that you can see how object variables and events are linked.

```
'Place these declarations in the general section of ThisOutlookSession
Public WithEvents colInsp As Outlook.Inspectors
Public WithEvents objMailItem As Outlook.MailItem

Private Sub Application_Startup()
    Set colInsp = Application.Inspectors
End Sub

Private Sub colInsp_NewInspector(ByVal Inspector As Inspector)
    Dim objItem As Object
    Set objInsp = Inspector
    On Error Resume Next
    Set objItem = objInsp.CurrentItem
    Select Case objItem.Class
        Case olMail
            Set objMailItem = objItem
    End Select
End Sub

Private Sub objMailItem_Send(Cancel As Boolean)
    If objMailItem.Subject = "" Then
        objMailItem.Subject = _
        InputBox("Enter a subject for this message:", "Subject Required")
        If objMailItem.Subject = "" Then
            Cancel = True
        End If
    End If
Exit Sub
```

> **Note** This functionality could also be achieved by writing code for the ItemSend event of the Application object. However, the MailItem object has a much more granular event model. Using the previous example, you could write code for any one of the item-level events supported by the *objMailItem* object variable.

Adding Events to VBScript Behind Forms

By using the Script Editor, you can add code to an Outlook item event to modify the event's behavior. For example, for the Open event, you can add code to specify the current form page, or you can add code to load a ComboBox control with a recordset from a database. For the Click event, you can create a procedure that creates a custom item, includes an attachment to the current item, and then posts the item in a folder. Item events are available for all Outlook item types except for the NoteItem object. Certain events are cancelable; you can prevent them from completing by writing the appropriate code. The following table summarizes the item events in Outlook.

Event	Cancelable	Description
AttachmentAdd	No	Occurs when an attachment has been added to the item.
AttachmentRead	No	Occurs when an attachment has been opened for reading.
BeforeAttachmentSave	Yes	Occurs before an attachment in an item is saved.
BeforeCheckNames	Yes	Occurs before Outlook starts resolving names in the Recipients collection of the item.
BeforeDelete (new to Outlook 2002)	Yes	Occurs before an item is deleted. This event will not fire unless the item is displayed in an Inspector.
Close	Yes	Occurs before Outlook closes the Inspector displaying the item.
CustomAction	Yes	Occurs before Outlook executes a custom action of an item.
CustomPropertyChange	No	Occurs when a custom item property has changed.

Event	Cancelable	Description
Forward	Yes	Occurs before Outlook executes the Forward action of an item.
Open	Yes	Occurs before Outlook opens an Inspector to display the item.
PropertyChange	No	Occurs when an item property has changed.
Read	No	Occurs when a user opens an item for editing.
Reply	Yes	Occurs before Outlook executes the Reply action of an item.
ReplyAll	Yes	Occurs before Outlook executes the Reply To All action of an item.
Send	Yes	Occurs before Outlook sends the item.
Write	Yes	Occurs before Outlook saves the item in a folder.

To add or modify an event

1. With the form in Design mode, click View Code on the Form Design toolbar.

2. On the Script Editor Script menu, click Event Handler.

3. In the Insert Event Handler list box, double-click the event you want.
   With an event procedure, the word *item* refers to the current Outlook item associated with the form. For example, the following *Item_PropertyChange* procedure sets the value of the Subject field in the item when the value in the Sensitivity drop-down list box in the Message Options dialog box is changed:

```
Sub Item_PropertyChange(ByVal PropertyName)
    Select Case PropertyName
    Case "Sensitivity"
        Item.Subject = "The sensitivity value has changed."
    End Select
End Sub
```

Part IV Beyond The Basics

> **Note** Item events are not raised exclusively at the item level in Outlook 2000 and Outlook 2002. A COM Add-in application event handler can also use the WithEvents declaration to raise item-level events and write item event procedure code in VBA or Visual Basic. However, if you want an event's code to travel with the form, you should use item-level event procedures written in VBScript.

The Firing Sequence of Events

When an Outlook form is opened to compose or read an item, events are fired in the sequences described in the following table.

Event	When Fired
Open	A form is opened to compose an item.
Send, Write, Close	An item is sent.
Write, Close	An item is posted.
Write	An item is saved.
Close	An item is closed.
Read, Open	An item is opened in a folder.
Reply	A user replies to an item's sender.
ReplyAll	A user replies to an item's sender and all recipients.
Forward	The newly created item is passed to the procedure after the user selects the item's Forward action.
PropertyChange	One of the item's standard properties is changed.
CustomPropertyChange	One of the item's custom properties is changed.
CustomAction	A user-defined action is initiated.
AttachmentAdd	An attachment is added to a message. This event occurs before the BeforeAttachmentSave event (described below).

Event	When Fired
AttachmentRead	An attachment is read.
BeforeDelete	This event occurs before an item is deleted. The item must be open in an Inspector for this event to fire.
BeforeAttachmentSave	An attachment is saved in a message. This event occurs after the Send event and before the Write event.
BeforeCheckNames	Recipient names are resolved. This event occurs before the Send event.

> **Note** An item's events fire whether the item is created through program code (in VBScript or VBA) or through the Outlook user interface.

> **Caution** The order in which Outlook calls event handlers might change depending on other events that can occur. The order might also change in future versions of Outlook.

Creating a New Item

When you create a new item, the Item_Open event is fired. In Outlook, you generally create a new item by opening a form. However, for certain folders, such as the Tasks folder, you can create a new item by clicking the New Item row in the folder. In either case, the Item_Open event is fired.

Sending an Item

When you send an item, the Item_Send event is fired, followed by the Item_Write event and then the Item_Close event.

Posting or Saving an Item

In Outlook, posting an item achieves the same result as saving an item. When you post or save an item, the Item_Write event is fired. An Item_Write event can occur in several situations. It can occur when a Post item is created and the Post button is clicked on the form, when a Contact item is created and the Save And Close button is clicked on the form, or when a Task item is created by clicking the New Item row and the item is then saved by the user clicking outside the New Item row. After the Item_Write event fires, the Item_Close event fires.

Opening an Existing Item

In Outlook, an item can be opened in two ways. If the item exists in a view that allows in-cell editing, simply clicking the item in the view will open it. An existing item can also be opened by double-clicking it and viewing it in a form. In either case, the Item_Read event is fired. If the item is viewed in a form, the Item_Read event is followed by the Item_Open event.

> **Note** Sometimes you will not want the Item_Open event to fire when an item is opened by simply being clicked in a view with in-cell editing or by another process. Outlook does not provide an Item_New event. The following *Item_Open* procedure provides an escape hatch for exiting the procedure if the item is not new:
>
> ```
> Sub Item_Open
>     '1/1/4501 represents a date field with no value
>     'If the item is not new, exit sub
>     If Item.CreationTime <> #1/1/4501# Then
>         Exit Sub
>     End If
>     'Continue Item_Open code here
> End Sub
> ```

Closing an Item

When you close an item, the Item_Close event is fired. If changes have been made to the item, when you attempt to close the item, Outlook will ask if you want to save the changes. If you click Yes, the Item_Write event is fired, followed by the Item_Close event.

Preventing Events from Firing

In some cases, you might want to prevent events from occurring. For example, you might want to add code for a Reply event that opens a custom form rather than the default Message form. To achieve this functionality, you must first prevent the default behavior from occurring. To do so, assign *False* to the function value. The actual Event procedure must be declared as a Function procedure instead of a Sub procedure so that you can cancel an Item event with an *Item_EventName = False* statement.

VBScript and VBA use different syntax to cancel events. In VBScript code, you write the event procedure as a function and set the function value to *False* in order to cancel the event. In VBA or Visual Basic code, the event procedure contains a *Cancel* argument. Set the *Cancel* argument to *True* to cancel the event. The following VBScript example prevents the standard Reply event from occurring in a Mail Message form. Instead, it opens a custom Orders form when the Reply button is clicked.

```
Function Item_Reply(ByVal Response)
    Item_Reply = False
    Set MyFolder = Application.GetNameSpace("MAPI").GetDefaultFolder(6)
    Set MyItem = MyFolder.Items.Add("IPM.Note.Orders")
    MyItem.To = Item.To
    MyItem.Subject = "RE: " & MyItem.Subject
    MyItem.Display
End Function
```

The following example shows the same code located in an application-level event procedure in VBA. Unlike Outlook 97 and Outlook 98, Outlook 2002 allows you to raise events at the form level using the correct WithEvents declarations.

```
Public WithEvents objMailItem As Outlook.MailItem
'Additional code to instantiate objMailItem object as Inspector.CurrentItem
Private Sub objMailItem_ReplyAll(ByVal Response As Object, Cancel As Boolean)
    Cancel = True
    Set objFolder = _
        objApp.GetNameSpace("MAPI").GetDefaultFolder(olFolderInbox)
    Set objItem = objFolder.Items.Add("IPM.Note.Orders")
    objItem.To = objMailItem.To
    objItem.Subject = "RE: " & objItem.Subject
    objItem.Display
End Sub
```

Form-level events that can be canceled include the following:

- Item_BeforeAttachmentSave
- Item_BeforeCheckNames
- Item_BeforeDelete
- Item_Close
- Item_CustomAction

Part IV Beyond The Basics

- Item_Forward
- Item_Open
- Item_Reply
- Item_ReplyAll
- Item_Send
- Item_Write

> **Note** Many other cancelable events are available at the application level. If you want to respond to application-level events, you must write VBA code in ThisOutlookSession or create a COM Add-in.

The AttachmentAdd Event

The AttachmentAdd event occurs when an attachment is added to an item either through a user action or by a procedure that uses code to add an Attachment object. The following VBScript example checks the size of the item after an embedded attachment has been added and displays a warning if the size exceeds 250,000 bytes:

```
Sub Item_AttachmentAdd(ByVal NewAttachment)
    Const olByValue = 1
    If NewAttachment.Type = olByValue Then
        If Item.Size > 250000 Then
            MsgBox "Warning: Item size is now " _
                & Item.Size & " bytes.", vbCritical
        End If
    End If
End Sub
```

The AttachmentRead Event

The AttachmentRead event occurs when an attachment in an item has been opened for reading. If the Attachment object is blocked by the Outlook E-Mail Security Update, the AttachmentRead event occurs after the Security Warning dialog box appears. The following example saves a copy of the attachment into the My Documents folder when the user opens that attachment:

```
Sub Item_AttachmentRead(ByVal ReadAttachment)
    Const olByValue = 1
    If ReadAttachment.Type = olByValue Then
    IntResponse = MsgBox("Save to c:\my documents?", vbQuestion + vbYesNo)
        If IntResponse = vbYes Then
            ReadAttachment.SaveAsFile "c:\my documents\" _
            & ReadAttachment.DisplayName
        End If
    End If
End Sub
```

The BeforeAttachmentSave Event

The BeforeAttachmentSave event occurs just after the Item_Send event and just before the Item_Write event. BeforeAttachmentSave always occurs after the AttachmentAdd event. This event is cancelable. If you're sending an item that contains an attachment and you cancel BeforeAttachmentSave, you will also cancel the Item_Write event. The following example prevents the user from saving an .exe file as an attachment:

```
Function Item_BeforeAttachmentSave(ByVal SaveAttachment)
    Const olByValue = 1
    If SaveAttachment.Type = olByValue Then
        If Instr(SaveAttachment.FileName, ".exe") Then
            MsgBox "Cannot save this attachment!", vbCritical
            Item_BeforeAttachmentSave = False
        End If
    End If
End Function
```

The BeforeCheckNames Event

The BeforeCheckNames event occurs just before Outlook starts to resolve names in an item's Recipient collection. This event will always fire before the Item_Send event fires. If you cancel the BeforeCheckNames event, the Item_Send event will also be canceled.

The BeforeDelete Event

The BeforeDelete event is new to Outlook 2002. It fulfills the need of developers searching for a means to handle item-level deletes. Be aware that an Inspector for the item must be open in order for the event to fire. If the user clicks the item in a view without opening it and then presses the Delete button, the BeforeDelete event will not fire. For a more reliable means to detect a Delete event in a folder, consider Exchange 5.5 scripting agents or Exchange 2000 event sinks.

Part IV Beyond The Basics

The Click Event

The Click event occurs when a user clicks a control such as a command button on a form. You can create as many Click event procedures as there are controls on the form.

> **Important** The Click event is the only VBScript control event supported in Outlook.

To create a Click event procedure

- In the Script Editor, type the name of the control that you're creating the Click event for, followed by an underscore character (_) and the word *Click*.

  The following example creates an item and displays the standard Message form when *CommandButton1* is clicked on the form:

```
Sub CommandButton1_Click
  Set MyItem = Application.CreateItem(0)
  MyItem.Subject = "This is a test."
  MyItem.To = "Davide Atenoux"
  MyItem.Display
End Sub
```

> **More Info** For more information about the Click event, see "Responding to the Click Event" on page 524 in Chapter 11.

The Close Event

The Close event occurs when the form associated with the item is being closed. When the Close event fires, the form is still open on the desktop. You can prevent the form from closing by setting the function value to *False*.

The CustomAction Event

The CustomAction event occurs when a custom action defined in the form occurs through code or a user action. You define custom actions on the Actions page of a form simply by creating a new action. When a CustomAction event is fired, both the name of the custom action being executed and the newly created response item are passed to the CustomAction event. You can prevent the custom action from occurring by setting the function value to *False*.

> **Tip** You can also use the CustomAction event as a custom method. For example, you can set the CustomAction event to *False* so that the response form is not loaded. You can then add code to the *CustomAction* event procedure to accomplish the desired task. For example, you can add code to the CustomAction event to automatically create an announcement message and send it to a distribution list.

The CustomPropertyChange Event

The CustomPropertyChange event occurs when the value in one of the item's user-defined fields changes. Because the field name is passed to the procedure, you can create a *Select Case* statement to determine which field value has changed.

The Forward Event

The Forward event occurs when the user initiates the Forward action on a form—usually by clicking the Forward button. You can prevent the form from being forwarded by setting the function value to *False*. In the following example, the Forward event is prevented from firing if the message is confidential:

```
Function Item_Forward(ByVal MyForwardItem)
    If Item.Sensitivity = 3 Then
        MsgBox "This message is confidential and cannot be forwarded.", _
            vbCritical
        Item_Forward = False
    End If
End Function
```

The Open Event

The Open event occurs when an Outlook form is opened to compose or read an item. When the Open event occurs, the form is initialized but not yet displayed. You can prevent the form from opening by setting the function value to *False*.

The example on the following page checks the ReceivedTime property of a message to determine whether the form is in Compose or Read mode. If the

ReceivedTime property is not set, the Message page is shown. If the ReceivedTime property is set, the (P.2) page is shown so that the person processing the order can view it. Before you run this example, perform the following steps:

1. Add a Message field to the (P.2) page.
2. Add this example code in the Script Editor, and then click Publish Form As on the Form Design toolbar.
3. In the Display Name text box, type *TestEvent*, and then publish the form to the Personal Forms Library.
4. On the Outlook File menu, select New and then click Choose Form.
5. Select the TestEvent form in the Personal Forms Library. Notice that the Message page is shown.
6. Address the form to yourself, and click Send.
7. Double-click the sent item in your Inbox. Notice that the (P.2) page is shown.

```
Function Item_Open()
    If Item.ReceivedTime <> "1/1/4501" Then
        Item.GetInspector.SetCurrentFormPage("P.2")
        Item.GetInspector.HideFormPage("Message")
    Else
        Item.GetInspector.SetCurrentFormPage("Message")
        Item.GetInspector.HideFormPage("P.2")
    End If
End Function
```

> **Important** Note in the example that the *If* statement checks to see whether the ReceivedTime field is set to 1/1/4501. In Outlook, Date fields that display None will return a value of 1/1/4501.

The PropertyChange Event

The PropertyChange event occurs when one of the item's standard fields (such as Subject, To, Importance, or Sensitivity) changes. Because the field name is passed to the procedure, you can use the *Select Case* statement to determine which field value has changed.

In the following example, a message box shows the values of the Importance and Sensitivity fields that have changed. To see how it works, add the following code to the Script Editor. Then exit Design mode and change the values in the Importance and Sensitivity drop-down list boxes in the Message Options dialog box.

```
Sub Item_PropertyChange(ByVal FieldName)
    Select Case FieldName
    Case "Importance"
        MsgBox "The value of the Importance field is " _
            & Item.Importance & "."
    Case "Sensitivity"
        MsgBox "The value of the Sensitivity field is " _
            & Item.Sensitivity & "."
    End Select
End Sub
```

The Read Event

The Read event occurs when a user opens an existing Outlook item for editing. The Read event differs from the Open event in that it occurs whenever a user selects the item in a view that supports in-cell editing. The Read event also occurs when the item is being opened in an Inspector. This event is fired before the Open event. In the following example, the value of the Date Opened user-defined field is set when the submitted item is first opened.

Before you run this example, perform the following steps:

1. Click New in the Field Chooser, and then type *Date Opened* in the Name text box.

2. In the Type drop-down list box, click Date/Time and then click OK.

3. Drag the Date Opened field to the Message page, and then click Edit Read Page on the Form Design toolbar.

4. Resize the Message control to make room for the Date Opened control, and then drag the Date Opened field from the Field Chooser to the Read page.

5. Click Publish Form As, and publish the form in your Personal Forms Library.

6. On the Outlook File menu, select New, click Choose Form, and then select the form. Address the form to yourself, and click Send.

7. Double-click the sent item in your Inbox. Notice that the current date is now in the Date Opened field.

```
Function Item_Read()
    If UserProperties("Date Opened") = "1/1/4501" Then
        UserProperties("Date Opened") = Now
    End If
End Function
```

The Reply Event

The Reply event occurs when a user clicks the Reply button on the form. When this event occurs, the newly created Reply item is passed to the procedure. You can prevent the item from being sent by setting the function value to *False*. The following example prevents the standard Reply event from occurring and creates an item with a custom Task form. The code then copies the values from the item's Subject and To fields to the Task Response item.

```
Function Item_Reply(ByVal Response)
    Item_Reply = False
    Set MyFolder = Application.GetNameSpace("MAPI").GetDefaultFolder(13)
    Set MyItem = MyFolder.Items.Add("IPM.Task.Test")
    MyItem.To = Item.To
    MyItem.Subject = "RE: " & MyItem.Subject
    MyItem.Display
End Function
```

The ReplyAll Event

The ReplyAll event occurs when a user clicks the Reply To All button on a form. When a user clicks Reply To All, the response is sent to the sender as well as to all recipients in the To and Cc boxes on the form. You can prevent the item from being sent by setting the function value to *False*. The following example reminds the user that he or she is replying to all the original recipients of an item and allows the user to cancel the action:

```
Function Item_ReplyAll (ByVal MyResponse)
    MyResult = MsgBox("Do you really want to send this reply to all " _
        & "the recipients in the To and Cc boxes? ", _
        vbQuestion + vbYesNo + vbDefaultButton2, "Flame Protector")
    If MyResult = vbYes Then
        Item_ReplyAll = True
    Else
        Item_ReplyAll = False
    End If
End Function
```

The Send Event

The Send event occurs when a user sends an item. You can prevent the item from being sent by setting the function value to *False*. If you prevent this event from occurring, the form remains open. The following example automatically sets the expiration date on the item when it is sent:

```
Function Item_Send()
    Item.ExpiryTime = Date + 7
End Function
```

The Write Event

The Write event occurs when the user sends, posts, or saves an item. You can prevent an item from being saved by setting the function value to *False*. The following code prevents a form from changing its message class after either the *HideFormPage* or *ShowFormPage* method is called:

```
Function Item_Write
    Set objForm = Item.FormDescription
    Item.MessageClass = objForm.MessageClass
End Function
```

Firing Order of Events

For item-level events, you can clearly predict the sequence in which events will fire. However, events at the application level are less predictable. You cannot guarantee that event firing will follow a specific sequence either because different events cause a unique firing sequence or because, in future versions of Outlook, the event sequence might change. Some insights into a typical firing sequence are offered here. If you want to investigate further, it is suggested that you write Debug.Print *Object EventName* statements for each event procedure supported by a given object variable declared using the WithEvents keyword. The following list shows just such a debug sequence when a user opens a mail message, enters recipients for the message, types a subject and message body, and then sends the message. Again, don't take this sequence as invariable; it simply gives you a reasonable expectation of the event sequence when you send a mail message.

1. Inspectors NewInspector
2. MailItem Open
3. Explorer Deactivate
4. Inspector Activate

381

5. MailItem Read
6. MailItem PropertyChange To
7. MailItem PropertyChange CC
8. MailItem PropertyChange BCC
9. MailItem BeforeCheckNames
10. MailItem PropertyChange To
11. MailItem PropertyChange CC
12. MailItem PropertyChange BCC
13. MailItem PropertyChange ConversationIndex
14. MailItem PropertyChange ReceivedTime
15. MailItem PropertyChange Subject
16. Application ItemSend
17. MailItem Write
18. MailItem Close
19. Inspector Deactivate
20. Explorer Activate

> **Note** You can see from the above that PropertyChange events fire for To, CC recipient, and BCC recipient before and after the BeforeCheckNames events. In fact, the message that generated the sequence above had only a single To recipient. You'll also notice that item-level events in VBA behave similarly to item-level events in VBScript. Unfortunately, a PropertyChange event does not fire when a user enters text in the message body.

Where To Go from Here

Microsoft Knowledge Base Articles   Microsoft Knowledge Base articles are available on the Web at *http://support.microsoft.com/support*. Also see the section, "Events (Chapter 9) KB Articles," in the Microsoft Web Sites folder in the Help And Web Sites folder on the companion CD.

10

The Outlook Development Environment

This chapter introduces you to the Microsoft Outlook development environment and shows you some of the tools that you can use to create collaborative applications. Before considering the Outlook objects, properties, and methods presented in Chapter 11, "Using Visual Basic, VBA, or VBScript with Outlook," you must reconnoiter the Outlook development landscape from the perspective of Visual Basic, VBA, and VBScript. Each variant of the Visual Basic language has some distinct advantages and disadvantages for Outlook programmers, especially when considered in the shadow of the Outlook E-Mail Security Update that is built into Outlook 2002.

The Outlook E-Mail Security Update

If you're not familiar with the Outlook E-mail Security Update, you should know that this core component of Outlook 2002 blocks access to significant portions of the Outlook Object Model. It limits the programmability of Outlook, especially for users who are not connected to an Exchange server. If your users have Exchange server mailboxes, an Administrator can use the Administrative form to change the limitations imposed on certain properties and methods in the Outlook 2002 Object Model. If a user is not connected to an Exchange server, modification of the attachment and object model security built into Outlook 2002 is not supported.

Trusted COM Add-Ins

Administrators can designate selected COM Add-ins as trusted. Trusted Add-ins are available only in Outlook 2002, and as of this writing, Microsoft has shown no inclination to extend the trust mechanism to COM Add-ins running under Outlook 2000. These trusted COM Add-ins can access the complete Outlook 2002 Object Model without limitations of the object model guard.

The development environment for programming Outlook 2002 custom forms remains VBScript. Outlook custom forms cannot contain VBA code. However, VBScript behind forms can call ActiveX dynamic-link library (DLL) components built with Visual Basic or public methods and properties exposed in an Outlook COM Add-in. COM Add-ins are a special type of ActiveX DLL and therefore can be written to expose public properties and methods that can be called by VBScript code in Outlook forms. VBScript behind forms still provides a simple yet powerful way to enable form-level automation and have that automation travel between recipients.

One limitation of VBScript solutions is that they don't have a trust mechanism for VBScript code behind forms. Any blocked Outlook Object Model calls will be blocked in VBScript code behind forms unless you turn off components of the object model guard with the Administrative form for the Outlook E-mail Security Update. Given the Outlook Object Model limitations built into Outlook 2002, a more secure architecture would be to use a trusted COM Add-in and call its public methods and properties from VBScript code behind forms. In this manner, you can wrap protected Outlook Object Model calls (such as an unattended programmatic send to a Help Desk mailbox) in public methods and properties of a COM Add-in that has been trusted by the Administrative form. For comprehensive information concerning the use of the Administrative form in public folders, see Chapter 13, "Distributing and Securing Applications."

Outlook and VBA

VBA is the preferred tool for developing personal Outlook solutions or prototyping COM Add-ins. VBA provides an integrated, high-end design environment for creating solutions at the application level. VBA solutions can include all Outlook events, as well as existing Outlook 97, Outlook 98, and Outlook 2000 events at the form level. A single VBA project also can be digitally signed and distributed to users within a corporation. Be aware, however, that VBA is supported only within the context of a single running Outlook application. The biggest limitation of Outlook VBA is that you cannot run multiple VBA projects or applications within an Outlook session.

The greatest significance of Microsoft's inclusion of VBA in Outlook is that programmers can begin COM Add-in development using VBA and then convert their VBA code to a compiled Visual Basic COM Add-in. COM Add-ins greatly extend the power and functionality of Outlook by taking advantage of application-level events in the Outlook Object Model. Supported events include NewMail, Startup, Quit, SendMail, NewInspector, FolderSwitch, ViewSwitch, and SelectionChange.

Microsoft intends for COM Add-ins to replace Exchange Client Extensions, which require C++ as the development language and are difficult to write and install. From a security perspective, Exchange Client Extensions cannot be trusted with the Administrative form mentioned earlier. Developed using any COM-compliant tool, COM Add-ins can be digitally signed with certificates for security authentication and can be deployed to the enterprise with the Microsoft Office XP Custom Installation Wizard. Most important from a security standpoint is that COM Add-ins can be trusted for privileged access to the entire Outlook Object Model. Trusted COM Add-ins are not subject to the object model limitations of the Outlook E-mail Security Update. Possible COM Add-in scenarios include custom rules that fire when new mail arrives, custom and third-party applications that control the Outlook user interface to provide unique functionality, and the integration of Outlook with corporate databases.

- You should be aware that this chapter does not address client programming against the Web Storage System. If you want to program Web Storage System applications from Outlook 2002, you can use the Microsoft Internet Publishing Provider (in conjunction with OLE DB and ADO) or the SharePoint Portal Server Object Library (also known as Microsoft PKMCDO for Microsoft Web Storage System). These technologies are covered in Part V of this book, "Advanced Topics."

VBScript Versions

The table on the following page lists the versions of VBScript and their relationship to the various versions of Outlook and Internet Explorer. Outlook 98, Outlook 2000, and Outlook 2002 require a minimal install of Internet Explorer 4 or later, even if another default browser is installed on the computer. Many users of Office 2000 and Office XP will be browsing with Internet Explorer 5 or later. Users of earlier versions of Outlook can upgrade to a later version of VBScript without upgrading their Outlook version. Most of the examples in this book assume that you are using VBScript 3 or later. If you are using Outlook 97 and your installed VBScript version is still 1, you should definitely upgrade to VBScript 3 or later. Any version-specific VBScript code will be noted in the examples in this chapter.

Part IV Beyond the Basics

Host Application	VBScript Version				
	1.x	2.x	3.x	4.x	5.x
Microsoft Internet Explorer 3	X				
Microsoft Outlook 97	X				
Microsoft Internet Information Server 3		X			
Microsoft Internet Explorer 4			X		
Microsoft Windows Scripting Host 1			X		
Microsoft Outlook 98			X		
Microsoft Visual Studio 6				X	
Microsoft Internet Explorer 5 and later					X

Determining the VBScript Version in Code

Use the following function to determine the current VBScript version in code. You can also open the ScriptEngine Object form containing the *GetScriptEngineInfo* function in the VBScript Samples folder. If you require a specific version of VBScript, you can use the GetScriptEngineInfo procedure to warn the user or to initiate a download that upgrades the VBScript version. Because of a memory leak in VBScript 1 and the greatly expanded functionality in VBScript 3 and later, it is strongly recommended that you install VBScript 3 or later for any Outlook forms application.

```
Function GetScriptEngineInfo
    Dim s
    On Error Resume Next
    ' Build string with necessary info
    s = ScriptEngine & " Version "
    If Err Then ' VBScript 1.0
        GetScriptEngineInfo = "VBScript Version 1.0"
    Exit Function
    End If
    s = s & ScriptEngineMajorVersion & "."
    s = s & ScriptEngineMinorVersion & "."
    s = s & ScriptEngineBuildVersion
    GetScriptEngineInfo = s
End Function
```

The Outlook Script Editor

With the Script Editor, which is available for each form, you can add procedures to forms to control an Outlook application or another application such as Microsoft Word or Microsoft Excel. Remember, however, that if your primary purpose is to control the Outlook application rather than an Outlook form, you should be using VBA or Visual Basic instead of VBScript behind forms. In addition, you can create procedures to control Outlook folders, forms, items, controls, and properties in items. For example, you can create a procedure to automatically set a folder as the active folder, and then create and post an item to the folder. Or you can create a procedure that creates a collection of items in a folder based on a specified filter, and then change a field value for each item in the collection.

To view the Outlook Script Editor

1. In the Inbox, click New Mail Message on the Actions menu.
2. On the Tools menu of the form, click Forms, and then click Design This Form.
3. On the Form menu of the form, click View Code.

> **Tip** Customize the Inspector standard toolbar to display toolbar buttons for the Design This Form and View Code commands. If you do a significant amount of forms development work, you'll appreciate having toolbar buttons right in front of you when you want to switch to Design mode or to inspect code behind the form. Follow these steps to customize the Standard Inspector Toolbar:
>
> 1. Open a new Mail Message by pressing Ctrl+N.
> 2. Select Customize from the Tools menu.
> 3. Click Tools in the Categories list box on the Commands page of the Customize dialog box.
> 4. Drag the Design This Form command from the Commands list box to the Standard toolbar.
> 5. Click Form Design in the Categories list box.
> 6. Drag the View Code command from the Commands list box to the Standard toolbar.
> 7. Click Close to dismiss the Customize dialog box.

An Introduction to Using the Script Editor

As an introduction to using the Script Editor, this section describes how to add code to the PropertyChange event to show a message any time you change a standard field value on a Mail Message form. The PropertyChange event is triggered whenever a standard field value changes on a form. For example, if you change the standard Importance or Sensitivity options on a Message form, the PropertyChange event is triggered because a field value has been changed.

To create and test a PropertyChange event

1. On the Script Editor Script menu, click Event Handler.
2. In the Insert Event Handler dialog box, double-click PropertyChange.
3. Add the code shown in Figure 10-1.
4. Click Close on the Script Editor File menu.
5. On the Form menu of the form, click Run This Form.
6. On the Standard toolbar of the form in Run mode, click Importance: High.
7. Click OK to close the message.
8. On the File menu of the form in Run mode, click Close.

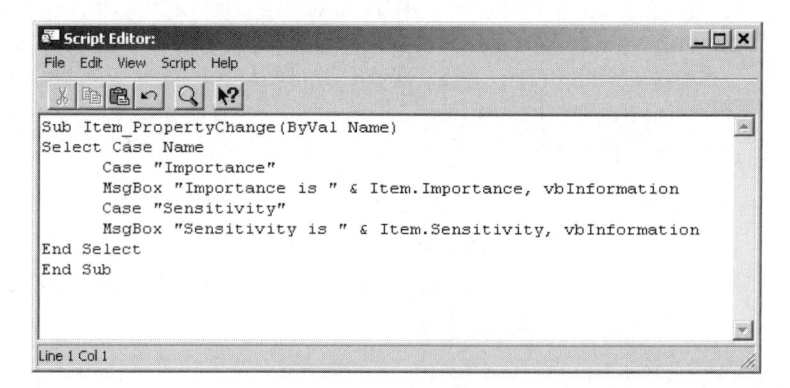

```
Sub Item_PropertyChange(ByVal Name)
Select Case Name
      Case "Importance"
      MsgBox "Importance is " & Item.Importance, vbInformation
      Case "Sensitivity"
      MsgBox "Sensitivity is " & Item.Sensitivity, vbInformation
End Select
End Sub
```

Figure 10-1 The PropertyChange event in the Outlook Script Editor.

If there is an error in the syntax of the code when you run the form, Outlook will display a message and immediately stop executing the code.

> **Note** Changes you make to a script do not affect forms that are currently running. If you want to compare the effect of a code change, run one form, change the procedure you want to test, and then run a second instance of the form (from the form that is in Design mode). You can then compare the two forms in Run mode to see how the code change affects the second instance.

Jumping to a Line of Code

As you test procedures, you will see error messages referring to specific lines of code if there are errors in your code. If you use On Error Resume Next to suppress error messages, you will not see an error message unless you explicitly trap the error. The Script Editor provides a way to jump to a particular line of code.

To jump to a line of code

1. On the Script Editor Edit menu, click Go To.
2. In the Line Number text box, type the line number, and then click OK.

Troubleshooting Code Using the Microsoft Script Editor

The Microsoft Script Editor is a tool included with Office 2000 and Office XP that helps you control the execution of a script so you can observe where run-time errors occur. You can view and change the value of a variable while the script is running, which lets you observe how different values affect the execution of the script. You can see the names of all the procedures that are currently executing. The Microsoft Script Editor lets you examine the properties of all variables in the current procedure in the Watch window, including the properties and dependent property objects of the Item object itself. The Microsoft Script Editor replaces previous versions of the Internet Explorer Script Debugger used to debug VBScript behind forms for Outlook 97 and Outlook 98.

> **Note** The Microsoft Script Editor is included in the Office XP Web Scripting Office Tools component, which you can install after installing Outlook 2002. The Script Editor is not installed by default for a typical installation.

Part IV Beyond the Basics

| To install the Microsoft Script Editor |

1. Insert the Office XP CD-ROM into your CD-ROM drive.
2. Click Start, click Settings, and then click Control Panel.
3. Double-click Add/Remove Programs.
4. On the Install/Uninstall page, click Microsoft Office XP—the exact title will vary depending on the version of Office XP installed on your computer—and then click Add/Remove on computers running Windows 2000. On computers running Windows 98, Windows ME, and Windows NT 4, click Change.
5. In the Microsoft Office XP Maintenance Mode dialog box, click Add Or Remove Features.
6. Double-click the Office Tools item to expand the item in the Microsoft Office XP: Update Features dialog box.
7. Double-click the HTML Source Editing item under Office Tools to expand the item.
8. Double-click the Web Scripting item to expand the item.
9. Click the Web Debugging drop-down item and select Run From My Computer.
10. Click Update to complete the installation of Script Editor.

| To launch the Microsoft Script Editor |

1. With a form in Design mode, on the Form menu, click View Code.
2. Enter a Stop statement at the point in your code where you want to halt code execution and begin debugging with the Microsoft Script Editor. Be certain to remove the Stop statement when you have completed the debugging process.
3. Select Run This Form from the Form menu.
4. When you see an alert box stating An Exception Of Type 'Runtime Error' Was Not Handled. Would You Like To Debug The Application?, click Yes to open the Script Editor, shown in Figure 10-2. Answer No to Would You Like To Open A Project For Debugging? If you're running Microsoft Visual InterDev 6 on the same computer with Microsoft Script Editor, you see a dialog box that offers a choice of debuggers before you enter debug mode. The wording of the initial dialog box will differ from the wording above in this case.

The Outlook Development Environment Chapter 10

5. You can now debug your code by stepping through the code, examining variables in the immediate window, and watching expressions and variables in the Watch window. Press F11 to step through the code in the Text Editor window.

6. Close the Microsoft Script Editor when you are finished with the debugging process.

Step through code with breakpoints or by inserting a Stop statement.

The current statement is highlighted.

The Watch window lets you examine the properties and property objects of the Item object.

The Immediate window lets you examine or set variable values.

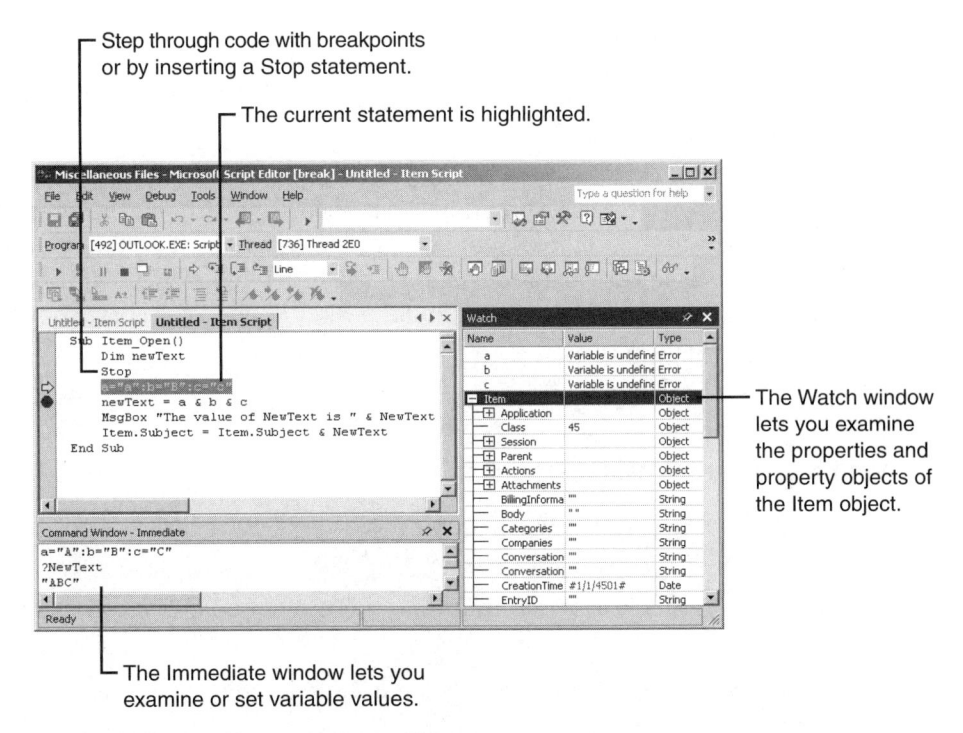

Figure 10-2 The Microsoft Script Editor.

Caution When the Script Editor is active, Outlook will not respond normally to Explorer or Inspector window commands. You will not be able to restore Outlook windows from the Windows Taskbar while code execution is paused in the Script Editor. You should close the Microsoft Script Editor window to return control to Outlook. If you attempt to inspect Item properties in the Watch window, certain Item properties will be blocked by the Outlook E-Mail Security Update component of Outlook 2002. Answer Yes to the Address Book Warning dialog box and allow access to the Outlook Address Book in order to continue debugging your code.

> **Tip** You can also obtain context-sensitive help when you are debugging your code. Follow these steps to receive context-sensitive help in the Microsoft Script Editor:
>
> 1. Place the insertion point under the keyword or operator for which you need help.
> 2. Press F1.

> **Note** The Microsoft Script Editor allows you to view the script and copy text from it, but you cannot use the debugger to interactively edit the script in Outlook. You can, however, change the value of procedure and script variables in the Immediate window and insert breakpoints into the running script.

Controlling How a Script Executes

The Debug toolbar lets you control the execution of your script at run time. Using this toolbar, you can do any of the following:

- Set and clear breakpoints that halt execution of the script at the breakpoint.
- Step through the script, executing each line one line at a time.
- Resume normal execution after stopping for a breakpoint.

> **More Info** For more information about controlling script execution, see Microsoft Script Editor Help.

Entering a Breakpoint

Once your script has halted execution at a Stop statement, you can enter breakpoints in the code window. If you are debugging an Outlook form script, you can only set breakpoints once code execution has halted due to a Stop statement. You can set or remove a breakpoint only at run time. When you set a breakpoint, a red dot is displayed in the selection margin of the Text Editor window next to the line containing the breakpoint. After setting breakpoints, you can run the application in the development environment. When execution reaches the first breakpoint, the code pauses and starts the debugger. The next line to be executed is indicated in the Text Editor window by a yellow arrow in the selection margin.

To set or remove a breakpoint

1. In the Text Editor window, move the insertion point to the line of code where you want to set or remove a breakpoint and click in the selection margin.

2. Move the insertion point to the line of code you want to insert a breakpoint into. From the Debug menu, choose Insert Breakpoint or press F9. To remove the breakpoint, choose Remove Breakpoint from the Debug menu or press F9.

- Or, as an alternative, choose the Breakpoints command from the Debug menu to display the Breakpoints dialog box. In the Breakpoints dialog box, you can click the Properties command button and set a conditional expression for a breakpoint or specify the number of times a breakpoint should be hit before stopping code execution.

Entering Commands at Run Time

Using the Immediate window of the Script Editor, you can execute script commands any time the script is halted at a breakpoint or has stepped to another statement. The command reflects or affects the state of the script at the point where execution has halted.

To enter script commands

1. On the Debug toolbar, click the Immediate window button to activate the Immediate window or choose Immediate from the Debug Windows submenu of the View menu.

2. In the Immediate window, type the command you want executed and press Enter. For example, to display the current value of the variable *Name*, type the following in the Immediate window:

```
? Name
```

To change the value of the variable, use an assignment statement, as in this example:

```
Name = "New Name"
```

Part IV   Beyond the Basics

> **Tip**   In addition to using ? to display the value of a variable in the Immediate window, you can also use the mouse pointer to display the value of a variable in the Text Editor. If you hover the mouse pointer over the variable whose value you want to inspect, a pop-up window will appear displaying the current value of the highlighted variable.

Viewing the Call Stack

The Call Stack window lets you see the names of all the procedures that are currently executing. This is especially useful if your script contains nested procedures; that is, procedures that are called within other procedures.

To view the call stack

- On the Debug toolbar, click Call Stack, or choose Call Stack from the Debug Windows submenu, available from the View menu.

Viewing the Locals Window

The Locals window displays local variables and their values in the current procedure. As the execution switches from procedure to procedure, the contents of the Locals window change to reflect the local variables applicable to the current procedure. If you have declared script-level variables in the code behind your form, these variables will not be visible in the Locals window. You can track the value of script-level variables in either the Immediate window or the Watch window.

The Locals window is updated only when execution is stopped. Values that have changed since the last break are highlighted. This list indicates some of the features of the Locals window:

- Drag a selected variable to the Immediate window or the Watch window.
- Double-click a variable to edit its value. When you change the value of a variable in the Locals window, its color will change to red.
- Click + or - to view or hide the member variables of an object variable or array.

To view the Locals window

- On the Debug toolbar, click Locals or choose Locals from the Debug Windows submenu, available from the View menu.

> **Note** The Locals window displays a variable's name, value, and type. Variables are strongly typed as strings, integers, and so forth, in the Locals and Watch windows. Don't be misled by this variable typing. From the perspective of VBScript, all variables are still typed as variants.

Viewing the Watch Window

The Watch window displays the values of selected variables or watch expressions and is only updated when execution is stopped at a breakpoint or an exception. Values that have changed since the last break are highlighted. You can use the Watch window to display script-level variables, including the Item object variable that represents the custom Outlook form you are debugging. Figure 10-3 illustrates the Item object and its properties displayed in the Watch window.

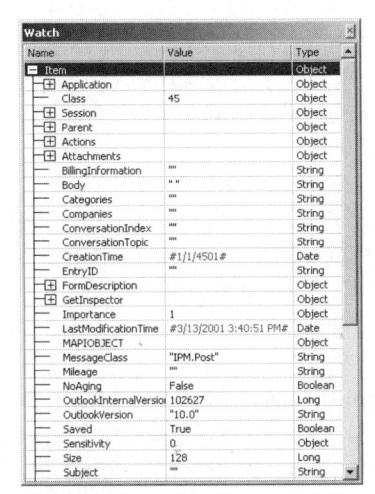

Figure 10-3 Viewing properties of the Item object in the Watch window.

To view the Watch window

- On the Debug toolbar, click Watch or choose Watch from the Debug window's submenu, available from the View menu.

To display the properties and property objects of the Item object

1. Type *Item* in an empty cell of the Name column of the Watch window and press Enter.

2. Click + or - to view or hide the member variables of the Item object.

How To Open an Item Containing VBScript

When you are designing and editing forms, you can prevent VBScript code from executing when you open a form by holding down the Shift key when you select the form. For example, to open a form in your Personal Forms Library, click Forms on the Outlook Tools menu, select Choose Form, select Personal Forms Library, and then hold down the Shift key and double-click the form you want to open. The form will then open, but the VBScript code will not execute. This method ensures that values are not inadvertently written to the fields in the form when the Open event fires as the form opens. It also helps to ensure that user-defined fields do not contain unwanted data when you publish the form.

Information Resources for Programming Outlook 2002

Web Resources

In the subfolder 1. Help and Web Sites in the Building Microsoft Outlook 2002 Applications folder, you can find folders containing items that list Microsoft Product Support Services Knowledge Base articles. These Knowledge Base articles can assist you in your Outlook programming tasks. The articles are available in many languages, so you can get help in your native language. You can get to these sites by opening the folder 1. Help and Web Sites in the Building Microsoft Outlook 2002 Applications folder, opening the Microsoft Web Sites folder, and then double-clicking the appropriate item. Each Post item is specific to a chapter in this book or an area of interest in Exchange and Outlook programming.

> **Note** There are several excellent third-party sites that also focus on Exchange and Outlook development. Open the Third Party Sites folder under the folder 1. Help and Web Sites in the Building Microsoft Outlook 2002 Applications folder to see a listing of these sites.

Sample Code

The VBScript Samples folder in the folder 4. Beyond the Basics provides sample items that let you view and run VBScript code snippets.

> **To open the VBScript Samples folder**

1. In the Folder List, open the Building Microsoft Outlook 2002 Applications folder, and then open the folder 4. Beyond the Basics.
2. Open the VBScript folder, and then open the VBScript Samples folder.

Microsoft Outlook Visual Basic Reference Help

You can use the Microsoft Outlook Visual Basic Reference Help file to view the properties, methods, and events for each object in the Outlook Object Model, as shown in Figure 10-4.

Click to view the properties available for the Application object.

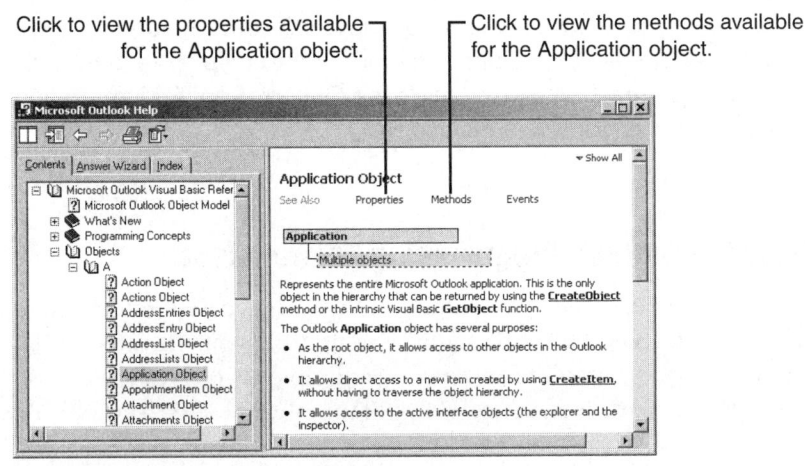

Click to view the methods available for the Application object.

Figure 10-4 Help for the Application object.

> **To use Microsoft Outlook Visual Basic Reference Help**

1. On the Script Editor Help menu, click Microsoft Outlook Object Library Help.
2. Click the Contents page, and then double-click Microsoft Outlook Visual Basic Reference if the book is not open. (Click the Show button if the Contents, Answer Wizard, and Index tabs are not visible.)
3. Double-click Objects, and then double-click the letter for the object you want help on. You can also click the Index tab and do a keyword search, or you can click the Answer Wizard tab and perform a search using the Answer Wizard.

> **Note** If you have installed Outlook Visual Basic Reference Help, you can also access Help by selecting the Advanced Customization book in the main Outlook Help window.

> **Caution** You can't use context-sensitive help in the Outlook Script Editor. If you place the cursor under a keyword or operator and press F1, Outlook will not respond. However, if you select a keyword or operator and press F1 when you're debugging code in the Microsoft Script Editor, context-sensitive help will be displayed. You can also use the Object Browser in the Script Editor environment to display help for an object, property, event, or method. Unlike the Outlook Script Editor, Outlook VBA fully supports context-sensitive help.

A Caution About the Outlook Programming Environment

The code examples in Microsoft Outlook Visual Basic Reference Help were written for both Visual Basic for Applications and VBScript. In most cases, the target programming environment for the code examples is clearly identified in Microsoft Outlook Visual Basic Reference Help. Many of the code examples in Chapter 11 are written for VBScript behind Outlook forms and must be modified accordingly if you want to use them in Visual Basic or Visual Basic for Applications. There are several distinct programming environments for Outlook forms and application development. They are illustrated in the following table.

Environment	Language	Intrinsic Objects
Code behind Outlook forms	VBScript	Item
ThisOutlookSession in VBAProject.OTM	Visual Basic for Applications	Application
COM Add-in project	Visual Basic	None
Outlook Automation from another Office XP application	Visual Basic for Applications	None
Outlook Automation from any COM-compliant development tool	Varies	None

Clearly identify the Outlook programming environment you are using and be aware of the following issues:

- There are no implicit objects in Visual Basic code. All objects must be explicitly referenced. For example, you cannot use the implicit Item object available in VBScript in Visual Basic code. All objects must be declared and instantiated on their own.

- If you do not declare constants with the CONST statement in your VBScript code, you must replace constant names in copied VBA or Visual Basic code with their numeric values in VBScript code.

The Implied Item Object

In VBScript, when you reference the active item in Outlook, the Item object is implied. Therefore, you do not need to set the Item object when referencing the active item. For example, to set the value of an active item's Subject field, you can use the following statement:

```
Item.Subject = "This is a test"
```

You can also leave out the reference to the item, as shown in this example:

```
Subject = "This is a test"
```

To test this example

1. On the Outlook Actions menu, click New Mail Message.
2. On the form's Tools menu, click Forms, and then click Design This Form.
3. On the Form Design toolbar, click Control Toolbox.
4. Resize the Message control on the form to make room for a CommandButton control.
5. Drag a CommandButton control to the form. By default, the CommandButton control is given the name CommandButton1.
6. On the Form Design toolbar, click View Code.
7. In the Script Editor window, replace the current *CommandButton1_Click* procedure with the following:

```
Sub CommandButton1_Click
  Subject = "The item is implied."
End Sub
```

8. On the form's Form menu in Design mode, click Run This Form.
9. Click CommandButton1.
10. In the Subject box of the form, you will see that the item is implied.

Object Libraries

An object library is a file with an .olb file extension that provides information to programs such as VBScript and Visual Basic for Applications about available objects. For example, the Microsoft Outlook 2002 Object Model (Msoutl.olb) contains the methods, events, properties, and constants that can be used to program the available objects. Sometimes object libraries are contained within dynamic link library (.dll) files, such as Fm20.dll, which contains the Microsoft Forms 2.0 Object Library.

When you use VBScript, Visual Basic, or VBA with Outlook, there are three primary object libraries, one advanced object library, and several helper object libraries.

- **The Microsoft Outlook 2002 Object Model** This library contains the objects, properties, methods, and events for almost all the objects that you work with in Outlook, with the exception of the Forms 2.0 Object Library objects and the Microsoft Office XP Object Library objects. When you set a reference to this object library in the References dialog box, select Microsoft Outlook 10.0 Object Model.

- **The Microsoft Forms 2.0 Object Library** This library contains the objects, methods, properties, and constants that you use to work with a Page object, a Controls collection object, and a Control object. When you set a reference to this object library in the References dialog box, select Microsoft Forms 2.0 Object Library.

- **The Microsoft Office XP Object Model** This library contains the objects, methods, properties, and constants you use to work with the CommandBars, Assistant, COMAddIns, LanguageSettings, and AnswerWizard objects. When you set a reference to this object library in the References dialog box, select Microsoft Office 10.0 Object Library.

- **Collaboration Data Objects** This library contains the objects, methods, properties, and constants you use to work with messages and folders in the Collaboration Data Objects (CDO) library. Work with CDO is typically done by more advanced programmers. CDO is called for when the Outlook Object Model does not provide access to certain Exchange properties or to hidden folders and messages. Although

CDO 3.*x* is installed with Outlook 2002, it cannot be used as a replacement for CDO 1.21. The version of CDO 1.21 that ships with Office XP is actually version 1.21s, a secure version of CDO that contains many of the same object model guards that have been built into Outlook 2002 with the Outlook E-mail Security Update. When you set a reference to this object library in the References dialog box, select Microsoft CDO 1.21 Library.

To view the objects available in the Microsoft Outlook 2002 Object Model and the Microsoft Forms 2.0 Object Library, you can use the Help file described earlier in this chapter, or you can use an object browser. To view the objects available in the Microsoft Office XP Object Model, click Microsoft Outlook Object Model Help on the Help menu of the Outlook Script Editor, and then open the book named "Microsoft Office Visual Basic Reference."

Helper Object Libraries

By using the Project References dialog box in VBA or Visual Basic, you can set references to any registered type or object library. The following table lists object libraries that might help you build your Outlook COM Add-in or Exchange application.

Object library	Name in References dialog box	Purpose	Version supplied with Office XP
Microsoft ActiveX Data Objects Library	Microsoft ActiveX Data Objects 2.5 Library	Data access and manipulation	2.5
Microsoft Direct Speech Recognition Object Model	Microsoft Direct Speech Recognition and Microsoft Direct Text-to-Speech	Perform speech and text recognition tasks	4
Microsoft Office XP Smart Tags	Microsoft Smart Tags 1.0 Type Library	Promote inter-application data transfer through Smart Tags	1
Microsoft SharePoint Portal Server Object Library	Microsoft PKMCDO for Microsoft Web Storage System	Create Web Storage System applications on SharePoint Portal Server	10.*x*
Microsoft XML Document Object Model	Microsoft XML 3.0	Manipulate and parse XML documents	3

Part IV   Beyond the Basics

Using an Object Browser

An object browser shows the objects, properties, and methods available from object libraries. Visual Basic for Applications in Outlook 2002 provides a superb object browser that you can use to view the Outlook Object Model or any other object model that you want to use. A more limited object browser is also available when you use the Object Browser command on the Script menu of an Outlook form's Script Editor. If you want to view the Forms Object Model from within Outlook's Object Browser, you must follow a few extra steps.

To use the Outlook 2002 Object Browser to view the Forms Object Model

1. On the Tools menu, point to Macro, and then click Visual Basic Editor.
2. On the Insert menu, click UserForm.
3. On the View menu, click Object Browser.
4. Select MSForms from the Project/Library drop-down list box in the Object Browser window.

> **Note**   Remove the UserForm if you do not intend to use it within the ThisOutlookSession project.

Moving Around in the Outlook Object Browser

There are now two Object Browsers available in Outlook: one browser is available in the VBScript environment for use with the Script Editor, and the other browser is available for use with Visual Basic for Applications. If you are using Visual Basic as your development environment, simply press F2 in a Code Window to display the Object Browser. With the Outlook VBScript Object Browser, you can browse through all the available objects in the Microsoft Outlook 2002 Object Library and see their properties, methods, and events, as shown in Figure 10-5. In addition, you can get help for any component in the library.

To move around in the VBScript Object Browser

1. In the Classes list box, click an object to view the properties, methods, and events for the object.
2. In the Members Of Object Name list box, click a property, method, or event to view further details, as shown in Figure 10-5.

The Outlook Development Environment Chapter 10

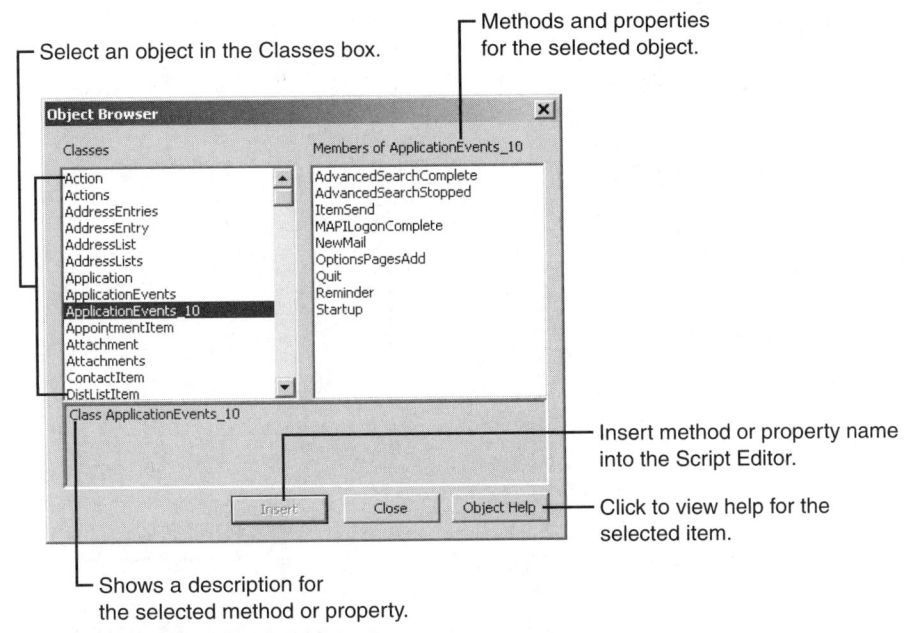

Figure 10-5 The Microsoft Outlook VBScript Object Browser.

To view the Outlook Visual Basic Reference Help topic for the selected item, click Help. To place the item or procedure in your code, click Insert.

For those of you who prefer premium fare over the standard variety, the Object Browser in Outlook Visual Basic for Applications is recommended. The Outlook Visual Basic for Applications Object Browser lets you view the object libraries for Outlook, VBA, Office, or any other object library for which you can set a reference using the Tools menu and the References command. This object browser is shown in Figure 10-6.

To display the Outlook VBA Object Browser

1. Press Alt+F11 in an Inspector or Explorer window to display the Visual Basic for Applications Editor window.
2. Press F2 to display the Object Browser.

Object Models

An object model provides a visual representation of the hierarchical structure and relationship of objects in an object library, as shown in Figure 10-7. As such, it provides a way for you to quickly see how an object library is designed.

403

Part IV   Beyond the Basics

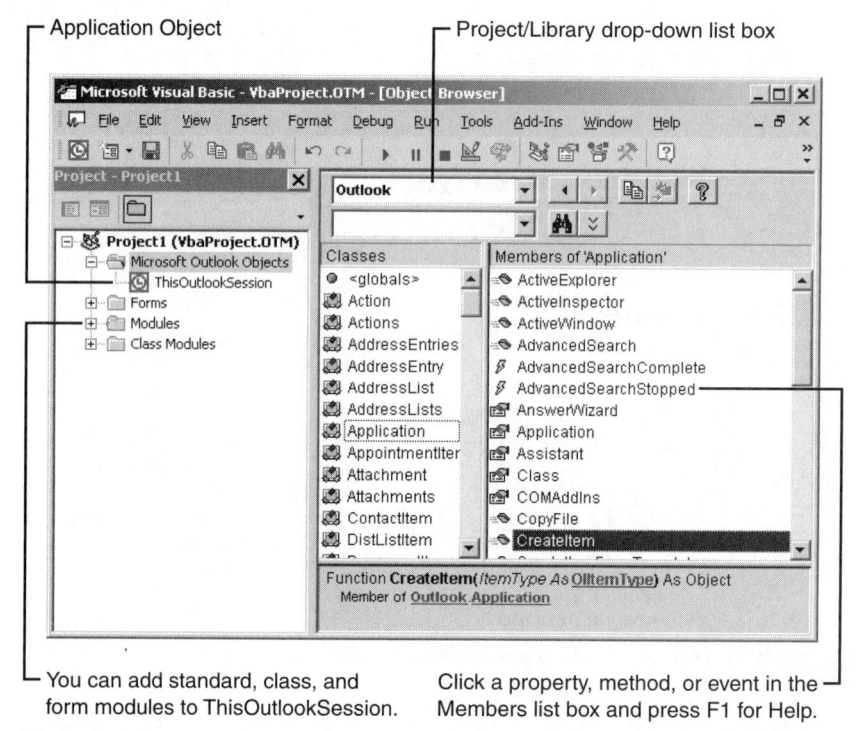

Figure 10-6 The Microsoft Outlook Visual Basic for Applications Object Browser.

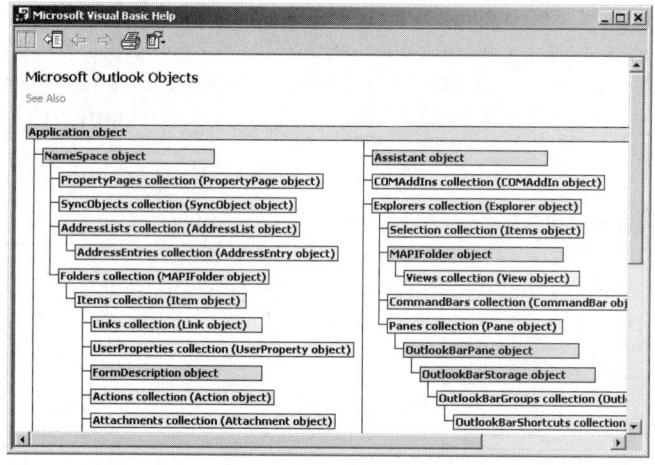

Figure 10-7 The Microsoft Outlook Object Model.

To view the Microsoft Outlook Object Model

1. On the Script Editor Help menu, click Microsoft Outlook Object Library Help.
2. Click the Contents page in the Microsoft Visual Basic Reference Help window.
3. Open the Microsoft Outlook Visual Basic Reference Help book, and then click the Microsoft Outlook Objects page. If the book is not open, double-click the book to open it.

To view the Microsoft Forms 2.0 Object Model

1. Start VBA in Outlook by pressing Alt + F11 in an Explorer window.
2. Press F2 to launch the VBA Object Browser.
3. On the Help menu of the Object Browser, click Microsoft Visual Basic Help.
4. Click the Contents tab in the Visual Basic Reference Help window.
5. Open the book named Microsoft Forms Reference.
6. Click the page named Microsoft Forms Object Model Overview.

Using the Object Hierarchy

In an object library, each object has a unique set of methods, properties, and events. Properties are attributes of the object that define it, and methods are actions that can be performed on an object. Events occur when specific actions are performed on an object—when it is opened or clicked, for example.

To use the object model, you must often move down through the object hierarchy to reference the particular object you want. For example, assume you want to display the Outlook window, which is represented by the Explorer object. Because the Application object sits at the top of the hierarchy, you must first reference the Application object before you can reference the Explorer object. In the following procedure, the *ActiveExplorer* method of the Application object is used to return the currently active Outlook window (the Explorer object). The *Display* method of the Explorer object is then used to make the Outlook window the active window on the desktop.

```
Sub CommandButton1_Click
    Set objExplorer = Application.ActiveExplorer
    objExplorer.Display
End Sub
```

Part IV Beyond the Basics

To test the code samples in the VBScript Samples folder

1. In the Folder List, open the Building Microsoft Outlook 2002 Applications folder, and then open the folder 4. Beyond the Basics.

2. Open the VBScript folder, and then open the VBScript Samples folder.

3. Double-click the item you want to open, and then click a command button to execute the sample procedure.

4. To view the sample code, click Forms on the Tools menu, click Design This Form, and then click View Code on the Form Design toolbar.

5. You can also click the Script button on the form shown in Figure 10-8. This button copies the code behind the example form and pastes it into the body of a Mail Message.

6. If you want to debug the sample code, use step 4 above to open the Script Editor window and insert a Stop statement in the procedure you wish to debug. Click Run This Form on the Form menu, and then click the command button for the procedure you are debugging.

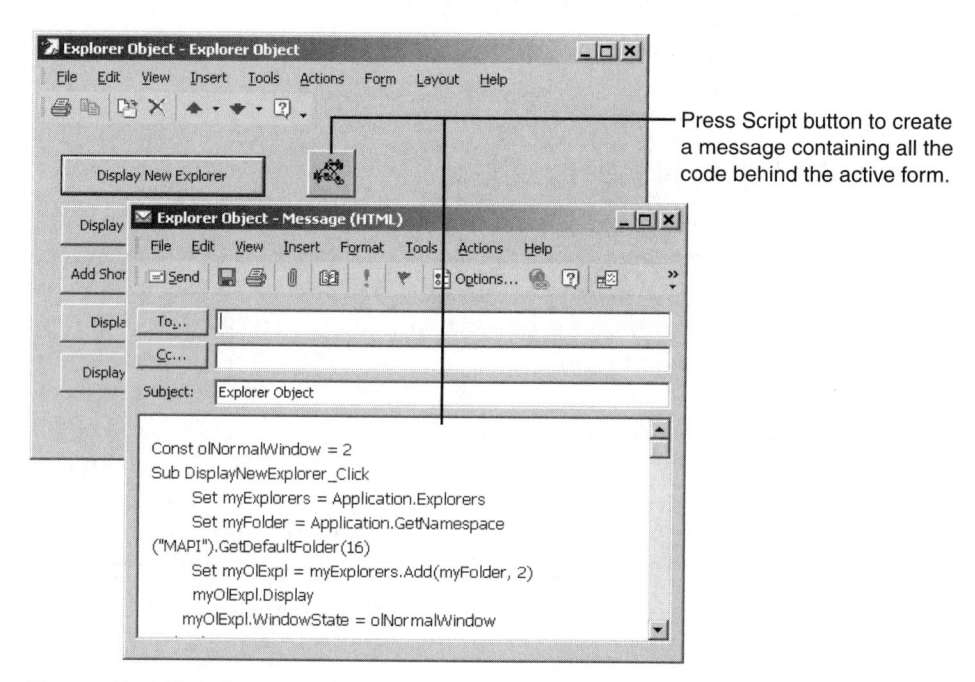

Figure 10-8 The Script button lets you quickly inspect the code behind the example form.

The following example moves further down the object hierarchy and returns a Folder object. It then uses the Name property of the Folder object to display the name of the folder in a message.

```
Sub CommandButton1_Click
    Set objFolder = Application.ActiveExplorer.CurrentFolder
    MsgBox objFolder.Name, vbInformation
End Sub
```

Getting and Setting Properties

This section covers how you either get or set the properties of an object. To get or set a property, you must reference both the object name and the property name.

Getting an Object Property

In certain cases, you want to get the properties of an object. The following procedure retrieves the text in the message box of an item and shows it in a message. Before you click CommandButton1, type some text in the message box of the form.

```
Sub CommandButton1_Click
    BodyText = Item.Body
    MsgBox BodyText
End Sub
```

> **Tip** Notice in the preceding example that the active item is referenced without moving through the object hierarchy. In this case, the item is implied, as discussed in the section "The Implied Item Object," earlier in this chapter.

Setting an Object Property

In this example, the body text of the item is set.

```
Sub CommandButton1_Click
    Item.Body = "This text appears in the message box."
End Sub
```

Using the *With* Statement

If you've installed Internet Explorer 5 or later with Outlook 2002, you will be using version 5 or later of VBScript. VBScript 5 or later supports the *With...End With* statement, which allows you to perform a series of statements on a specified object without requalifying the name of the object. For example, the following code is now supported only in VBScript 5 or later. If you use this code in a VBScript version prior to 5, the code will fail. The With...End With syntax is available in all current versions of VBA or Visual Basic.

```
Sub CreateContact
    Const olContactItem = 2
    Set myContact = Application.CreateItem(olContactItem)
    With myContact
        .FirstName = "Dolores"
        .LastName = "DelRio"
        .FullName = "DelRio, Dolores"
        .CompanyName = "XYZ Corporation"
        .JobTitle = "Senior Accountant"
        .EmailAddress = "ddelrio@xyz.com"
        .EmailAddressType = "SMTP"
        .Save
    End With
End Sub
```

> **Important** Do not jump into or out of With blocks. If statements in a With block are executed, but either the *With* or *End With* statement is not executed, you may get unpredictable behavior.

Using Variables

Variable names follow the standard naming convention rules for naming objects, properties, methods, and so on, in Microsoft VBScript. A variable name

- Must begin with an alphabetic character.
- Cannot contain an embedded period.
- Must not exceed 255 characters.
- Must be unique in the scope in which it's declared.

Generally, when you declare a variable within a procedure, only code within that procedure can reference or change the value of the variable; it has local scope and is known as a procedure-level variable. When you declare a variable outside a procedure, you make it recognizable to all the procedures in your script; it has script-level scope and is known as a script-level variable. When you're using variables in VBScript, the following limitations apply:

- There can be no more than 127 procedure-level variables (arrays count as a single variable).
- Each script is limited to no more than 127 script-level variables.

The length of time a variable exists is called its lifetime. A script-level variable's lifetime extends from the time it's declared until the time the script has finished running. A local variable's lifetime begins when its declaration statement is encountered as the procedure begins, and it ends when the procedure concludes. Local variables are ideal as temporary storage space while a procedure is running. You can have local variables with the same name in different procedures because each variable is recognized only by the procedure in which it's declared.

A variable's scope is determined by where the variable is declared. At the script level, the lifetime of a variable is always the same; it exists while the script is running. At the procedure level, a variable exists only while the procedure is running; when the procedure exits, the variable is destroyed. A global or script-level variable is available to any procedure in a form while the script is running. To set global variables, assign values to the variables before any procedures.

> **Note** The constraints listed earlier apply only to variables and procedures within VBScript code. Select the Microsoft Visual Basic Help command on the Help menu in the Outlook VBA Editor for additional information regarding variables, constants, and scope in VBA.

Using the Variant Data Type

VBScript in Outlook uses only the variant data type, which is a special kind of data type that can contain different types of information, depending on how the value is used. The Variant data type can contain several types of information—string, date and time, Boolean (True or False), currency, and numeric—with varying degrees of precision. The variant data type behaves as a number when it's used in a numeric context and as a string when it's used in a string context. If you're working with data resembling numeric data, VBScript treats it as such and processes it accordingly. If you're working with data that resembles string data, VBScript treats the data as a string. Numbers enclosed in quotation marks are also treated as strings.

The variant data type can make distinctions about the specific nature of numeric information, such as information that represents a date or time. When used with other date or time data, the result is always expressed as a date or a time. The variant data type can contain numeric information ranging in size from Boolean values to huge floating-point numbers. These various categories of information that can be contained in a variant data type are called subtypes. For a complete listing of VBScript subtypes, see "VBScript Data Types" in the VBScript documentation. Usually, you can put the type of data you want in a variant, and it will most likely behave in a way that's suited to the data it contains. You should be aware, however, of type conversion when you assign values to variables in VBScript. A classic example of a type conversion error is as follows:

```
Sub CommandButton1_Click()
    Dim A,B,C 'Variant Data Type
    A = "1" 'Assigned to string
    B = "1"
    C = A + B 'Variant result will be a string subtype
    MsgBox "The value of " & A & " plus " & B & " equals " & C & vbCr _
        & "where the subtype of C is " & TypeName(C)
    A = 1 'Assigned to integer
    B = 1
    C = A + B 'Variant result will be an integer subtype
    MsgBox "The value of " & A & " plus " & B & " equals " & C & vbCr _
        & "where the subtype of C is " & TypeName(C)
End Sub
```

> **Tip** Use the *VarType* and *TypeName* functions in VBScript to determine the subtype of *VBScript* variables. These functions can be especially useful in the Immediate window of the Script Debugger when you are attempting to debug a type conversion problem.

VBScript Naming Conventions

You will have fewer headaches in the future if you adopt a naming convention for variables in your VBScript code. Although a naming convention, in itself, will not prevent type conversion errors, the naming convention does indicate what the original programmer intended for the subtype of a given variable. While a naming convention seems superfluous in a weakly-typed language like VBScript, it will save time and reduce errors in the long run. If you are developing Outlook forms in a corporate environment, you should consult with other Visual Basic and VBScript developers. Adopt a corporate VBScript naming convention and then stick with it. The convention is summarized in the following table.

Subtype	Prefix	Example
Boolean	bln	blnSent
Byte	byt	bytRasterData
Collection object	col	colHiddenMessages
Date (Time)	dtm	dtmStartDate
Double	dbl	dblTolerance
Error	err	errOrderNum
Integer	int	intQuantity
Long	lng	lngDistance
Object	obj	objMessage
Single	sng	sngAverage
String	str	strFirstName

Declaring Constants

The first version of VBScript that shipped with Outlook 97 did not support the CONST statement. The CONST statement allows you to declare constant values and improve the readability of your code. Fortunately, the CONST statement is valid in VBScript 2 and later and thus is operational in VBScript code that you write for Outlook 2002. The extra work of declaring constants with the CONST statement may be preferable to calling a method or setting a property with a specific value. For example, which of the following statements is more readable (and more easily debugged)?

```
Set objItem = Application.CreateItem(0)
Set objItem = Application.CreateItem(olMailItem)
```

Unlike VBA code in Outlook, constants for object models external to VBScript must be explicitly declared. You can ignore the advice about constant declarations if you are only writing VBA code for Outlook. From the perspective of VBScript, Outlook's Object Model is external to VBScript. Rather than declaring constants at the procedure level, declare constants at the script level to avoid duplication. Here is a short example.

```
Const olPostItem = 6 'Script-level constant
Sub CommandButton1_Click
    Set objItem = Application.CreateItem(olPostItem)
    objItem.Display
End Sub
```

Part IV Beyond the Basics

> **Note** Versions of VBScript 2 and later support intrinsic constants for certain VBScript objects and functions. For example, use vbInformation or vbCritical to display icons when you use the *MsgBox* function instead of the specific values. See VBScript Constants in VBScript Help for a complete listing. Intrinsic constants also make your code easier to maintain and read.

To add Outlook CONST declarations to your VBScript code

1. Open the Outlook Constants item in the VBScript Samples folder.
2. Copy the necessary CONST declarations from the Outlook Constants item.
3. Paste the CONST declarations into your VBScript code. The CONST declarations typically should be placed at the top of your code before any other procedures. These CONST declarations have script-level scope in your code.

Assigning Objects to Variables

Object variables are assigned in a slightly different way from other variables. For example, if a variable is shared between procedures, you declare the variable as a script-level variable. In this procedure, the *ItemChanged* variable is declared as a script-level variable. *ItemChanged* is set to *True* whenever a standard property is changed in an item.

```
Dim ItemChanged    ' Script-level variable.
Sub Item_PropertyChange(ByVal Name)
    ItemChanged = True
End Sub
```

An object variable is a variable that is used to refer to an object. As shown in the following example, you don't need to declare the variable. Instead, you use the Set statement to assign an object to a variable. The first line of code in the following example assigns the object variable to the newly created item. Once you've set an object, you can then use the object's methods and properties to control the object. This example creates a new mail item, and then displays the item.

```
Sub CommandButton1_Click
    Set objItem = Application.CreateItem(0)
    objItem.Display
End Sub
```

Referencing Collections and Single Objects

Some objects in Outlook are collection objects, while others are single objects. For example, all the items in a folder can be contained in an Items collection object. However, a single item in an Items collection object may be represented by a MailItem object or a PostItem object. The following code uses the Items property to reference the collection of items in your Inbox. It then shows the number of items in the Items collection object.

```
Sub CommandButton1_Click
    Set objFolder = Application.GetNameSpace("MAPI").GetDefaultFolder(6)
    Set colItems = objFolder.Items
    MsgBox colItems.Count
End Sub
```

In the next example, the items in the Items collection object are referenced by index number. In this case, the code iterates through the Items collection and shows the text in the Message field for the first three items in your Inbox. (Note that items in the Inbox do not necessarily appear in the order received.)

```
Sub CommandButton1_click
    Set MyFolder = Application.GetNameSpace("MAPI").GetDefaultFolder(6)
    Set MyItems = MyFolder.Items
    For i = 1 to 3
        MsgBox MyItems(i).Subject
    Next
End Sub
```

After you set a collection object, you can reference objects in the collection by index, as shown in the preceding example, or by name. For example, to reference an item in an Items collection by name, you specify the value of the Subject field. Before you run this example, do the following:

1. Press Ctrl+Shift+I to make the Inbox your active folder.
2. Press Ctrl+Shift+S to create a new Post in the Inbox.
3. Type *VBScript Test* in the Subject box.
4. Click Post.
5. Press Ctrl+Shift+S to create a new Post item.
6. Select Design This Form from the Forms submenu of the Tools menu.
7. Click the Control Toolbox button on the Form Design toolbar.
8. Drag a command button control from the Control Toolbox to (P.2) of the form.
9. Type the code shown in the following example into the Script Editor window.

10. Select Run This Form from the Form menu.

11. Click OK in the Select Folder dialog.

12. Click CommandButton1 on (P.2) of the form.

```
Sub CommandButton1_Click
    Const olFolderInbox = 6
    Set objFolder = _
        Application.GetNameSpace("MAPI").GetDefaultFolder(olFolderInbox)
    Set colItems = objFolder.Items
    Set objItem = colItems("VBScript Test")
    objItem.Display
End Sub
```

Generally, you don't reference an item in an Items collection by name. However, you almost always reference a field property in a UserProperties collection by name. The following example sets the name of the user-defined field called Customer Name to James Allard. Before you run this example, do the following:

1. Make sure the form is in Design mode, and then click Field Chooser on the Form Design toolbar.

2. In the Field Chooser, click New, type *Customer Name* in the Name text box, and then click OK.

3. Drag the Customer Name field from the Field Chooser to the form. Add the code shown in the example to the Script Editor.

4. Click Run This Form on the Form menu to switch to Run mode, and then click CommandButton1.

```
Sub CommandButton1_Click
    UserProperties("Customer Name") = "James Allard"
End Sub
```

Where To Go from Here

Microsoft Knowledge Base Articles   Microsoft Knowledge Base articles are available on the Web at *http://support.microsoft.com/support*. Also see the section "The Outlook Development Environment (Chapter 10) KB Articles" in the Microsoft Web Sites folder in the Help And Web Sites folder on the companion CD.

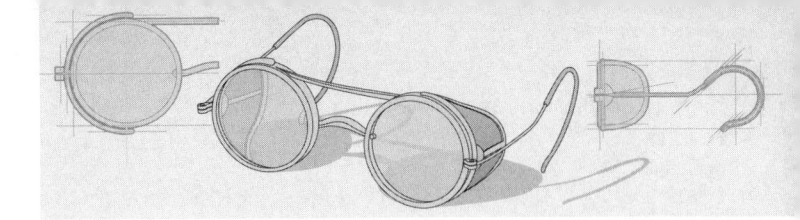

11

Using Visual Basic, VBA, or VBScript with Outlook

This chapter primarily addresses the use of Microsoft Visual Basic Scripting Edition (VBScript) in Microsoft Outlook forms. It looks at the objects of the Outlook Object Model and provides programming examples in VBScript or Visual Basic. Most of the code examples in VBScript can be extended directly in Outlook Visual Basic for Applications (VBA) or Visual Basic. Exceptions are noted accordingly. You should carefully consider the impact of the Outlook E-Mail Security Update on forms and application-level code. For additional information on the programmatic implications of the object model guard in Outlook 2002, see Chapter 13, "Distributing and Securing Applications."

This chapter is designed to give you the fundamental skills and knowledge you need to create collaborative applications using Visual Basic and VBScript. You'll find items demonstrating almost all the code examples in this chapter in the VBScript Samples folder. This chapter covers how to

- Modify command bars.
- Create a programmatic search.
- Modify views.
- Set folders programmatically for offline use.
- Snooze and dismiss reminders.
- Reference a folder collection or a folder in the Folder List.
- Create, open, send, and post standard and custom items.
- Open and close standard and custom forms.

Part IV Beyond the Basics

- Set and change field values in items.
- Hide or show a form page.
- Change the properties of a control on a page.
- Specify the recipients of an item.

To open the VBScript Samples folder

In the Folder List, expand the Building Microsoft Outlook 2002 Applications folder, expand folder 4. Beyond the Basics, expand the VBScript folder, and then click the VBScript Samples folder.

The Application Object

The Application object sits at the top of the object model and represents the entire Outlook application. The Outlook Application object has several purposes:

- As the root object, it enables you to reference other objects in the Outlook object hierarchy.
- It provides methods such as *CreateItem* and *CreateObject* so that you can create new items and reference them without moving through the object hierarchy.
- It provides methods for directly referencing the active Outlook window or form.

> **More Info**   For a complete list and description of the methods, properties, and events for the Application object, see Microsoft Outlook Visual Basic Reference Help. Also see the Visio document entitled "Outlook 2002 Object Model Extended View" in the Outlook 2002 Object Model folder under the Visual Basic for Applications folder under the 4. Beyond the Basics folder. This object model diagram shows the properties, methods, and events for every object in the Outlook object model.

> **Important**   Open the Application object item in the VBScript Samples folder to work directly with this code in Outlook.

Application Object Methods

This section covers the *ActiveExplorer*, *ActiveWindow*, *AdvancedSearch*, *CopyItem*, *CreateItem*, *CreateObject*, and *GetNameSpace* methods.

Returning the Active Window

You can use the *ActiveWindow* method of the Application object to return the topmost active Outlook window. The *ActiveWindow* method returns either an Explorer or an Inspector object, depending on the actual active window.

```
'Get the Active Outlook Window
'The ActiveWindow object is the topmost window in the running
'Outlook instance
Sub GetOutlookActiveWindow_Click
    If TypeName(Application.ActiveWindow) = "Inspector" Then
        MsgBox "The active window is an inspector", vbInformation
    Else
        MsgBox "The active window is an explorer", vbInformation
    End If
End Sub
```

The following example sets the MyExplorer object to the currently active Outlook Explorer window, displays a message that indicates the active window type, and then redisplays the item window when the ShowOutlookActiveExplorer control is clicked:

```
Sub ShowOutlookActiveExplorer_Click
    Set MyExplorer = Application.ActiveExplorer
    MyExplorer.Display
    GetOutlookActiveWindow_Click()
    Item.Display
End Sub
```

Creating a Standard Item

You can use the *CreateItem* method of the Application object to create and return Outlook standard items such as a Message item, a Post item, or an Appointment item. The following example creates a Message item using the default editor and displays it when CreateAMailMessage is clicked:

```
Sub CreateAMailMessage_Click
    Set MyItem = Application.CreateItem(0)
    MyItem.Display
End Sub
```

The next simple example creates an HTML message.

```
Sub CreateHTMLMessage_Click
    Const olMailItem = 0
    Set myItem = Application.CreateItem(olMailItem)
    myItem.HTMLBody = ""
    myItem.Display
End Sub
```

It's useful to know that you can also create a Word Envelope message in code. The following example uses the *CreateObject* method to launch Word and display a Word Envelope message. From the standpoint of the message body, Word Envelope messages are equivalent to HTML messages.

```
'Creates a Word Message item and displays it
Sub CreateAWordMessage_Click
    Const wdNewEmailMessage = 2
    Dim objApp,objMsg
    Set objApp = CreateObject("Word.Application")
    Set objMsg = objApp.Documents.Add(,,wdNewEmailMessage)
    objApp.Visible = True
    objApp.ActiveWindow.EnvelopeVisible = True
End Sub
```

The following table lists the numeric values you use as arguments for the *CreateItem* method. You can also copy the CONST declarations in the Enum OlItemType section of the Outlook Constants item in the VBScript Samples folder and paste them into your code.

Type of Item	Value
Appointment	1
Contact	2
Distribution List	7
Journal	4
Mail Message	0
Note	5
Post	6
Task	3

> **More Info** For more information about creating custom items, see "Items Collection Methods" later in this chapter.

Creating an Automation Object

You can use the *CreateObject* method of the Application object to create Automation objects, such as Microsoft Excel, Microsoft Access, or Microsoft Word objects. You can also use the *CreateObject* method to create instances of custom ActiveX DLLs that extend the functionality of Outlook. The following example uses the *CreateObject* method to create an instance of Excel, adds a workbook, and then renames the first sheet in the workbook to Outlook CreateObject Example:

```
'Launch Excel with CreateObject
Sub LaunchExcel_Click
    Dim xLApp 'As Excel.Application
    Dim xLSheet 'As Excel.Worksheet
    Set xLApp = CreateObject("Excel.Application")
    If xLApp Is Nothing Then
        MsgBox "Could not create Excel Application", vbCritical
        Exit Sub
    End If
    xLApp.Workbooks.Add
    Set xLSheet = xLApp.Sheets(1)
    xLSheet.Name = "Outlook CreateObject Example"
    'Make the Excel Application window visible
    xLApp.Visible = True
End Sub
```

> **Tip** When you are writing Automation code for VBScript in Outlook forms, you can expedite the development process by using the VBA Editor in Outlook to write the code and then pasting the code into VBScript. As noted in the example above, you must place comment marks before the As keyword in the object type declarations, or VBScript will raise an error. The beauty of this approach is that you have all the IntelliSense features of the VBA Editor at your disposal, including auto list members, syntax checking, parameter information, quick information, and code formatting. Before you begin, set references to the appropriate object libraries by using the Tool menu's References command in the VBA Editor window.

Copying an Item from the File System

The *CopyItem* method is new to Outlook 2002. It lets you copy an item from the File System to an Outlook folder. The following code example creates a Word document in the temporary folder, adds some text to the document, and then uses the *CopyItem* method to copy the document to the user's Inbox folder. Note that the *CopyItem* method accepts a string for the path to the destination folder instead of a MAPIFolder object.

```
Sub CopyItemToInbox_Click
    Dim objWord 'As Word.Application
    Dim objDoc 'As Word.Document
    Dim objSelect 'As Word.Selection
    Dim objDocItem 'As DocumentItem
    Set objWord = CreateObject("Word.Application")
    Set objDoc = objWord.Documents.Add
    Set objSelect = objWord.Selection
    objSelect.TypeText "Word document created with Automation"
    strPath = GetTempDir & "\test.doc"
    objDoc.SaveAs strPath
    Set objDocItem = Application.CopyFile(strPath, "Inbox")
    objDocItem.Display
    Set objWord = Nothing
End Sub
```

Returning a MAPI NameSpace Object

You can use the *GetNameSpace("MAPI")* method of the Application object to return the MAPI message store.

In the following example, the *GetNameSpace* method returns the NameSpace object. The Offline property of the NameSpace object is then used to display a message box indicating whether the user is on line or off line.

```
Sub CommandButton1_Click()
    Dim MyNameSpace As NameSpace
    Set MyNameSpace = Application.GetNamespace("MAPI")
    If MyNameSpace.Offline Then
        MsgBox "You are offline!", vbInformation
    Else
        MsgBox "You are online!", vbInformation
    End If
End Sub
```

> **Important** The only data source currently supported is MAPI, which allows access to all Outlook data stored in MAPI. For this reason, the *GetNameSpace* method must always appear in Outlook as *GetNameSpace("MAPI")*.

Creating Office Objects

The Application object has several child objects that are actually members of the Microsoft Office Object Model. For example, the Application object contains member objects for the Office AnswerWizard, Assistant, COMAddIns, and LanguageSettings objects. The following code example uses an animated Assistant to display the LanguageID settings for the Outlook Application object.

```
'Display the LanguageSettings
Sub DisplayLanguageSettings_Click
    Const msoLanguageIDInstall = 1, msoLanguageIDUI = 2
    Const msoLanguageIDHelp = 3
    Const msoAnimationListensToComputer = 26
    Const msoModeModal = 0, msoButtonSetOK = 1, msoIconTip = 3
    On Error Resume Next
    Dim oa 'As Office.Assistant
    Dim bln 'As Office.Balloon
    strMsg = "The following locale IDs are registered " _
        & "for this application:" & vbCr & "Install Language - " & _
        Application.LanguageSettings.LanguageID(msoLanguageIDInstall) _
        & vbCr & "User Interface Language - " & _
        Application.LanguageSettings.LanguageID(msoLanguageIDUI) _
        & vbCr & "Help Language - " & _
        Application.LanguageSettings.LanguageID(msoLanguageIDHelp)
    Set oa = Application.Assistant
    oa.On = True 'Assistant not available
    If Err Then
        MsgBox strMsg, vbInformation
    Else
        oa.Visible = True
        Set bln = oa.NewBalloon
        bln.Heading = "Language Settings"
        bln.Mode = msoModeModal
        bln.Button = msoButtonSetOK
        bln.Icon = msoIconTip
        bln.Text = strMsg
        bln.Show
        oa.Animation = msoAnimationListensToComputer
    End If
End Sub
```

Creating a Programmatic Search

The ability to create a programmatic search using the *AdvancedSearch* method of the Application object is new to Outlook 2002. *AdvancedSearch* returns a Search object, which in turn contains a Results object that you can use to iterate over the items contained in that Results object. A Results object is identical to an Items collection object. You use the *AdvancedSearch* method in conjunction with the AdvancedSearchComplete event for the Application object. When the AdvancedSearchComplete event fires, you'll know that the Search object for your query is available for further processing. Assign a *Tag* value in your call to *AdvancedSearch* so that you can identify the correct Search object in the

AdvancedSearchComplete event. See Chapter 9, "Raise Events and Move to the Head of the Class," for additional details on the AdvancedSearchComplete event and Chapter 14, "Creating COM Add-Ins with Visual Basic," for a discussion of the sample Search add-in.

AdvancedSearch takes four arguments, two of which are enigmatically explained in Outlook Visual Basic Help. Here is the syntax for a call to *AdvancedSearch*:

```
Set objSearch = objApp.AdvancedSearch(Scope, Filter, SearchSubfolders, Tag)
```

Both the *Scope* and *Filter* arguments can be understood in the context of Microsoft Exchange 2000 Web Storage queries. Although you don't have to run against an Exchange 2000 server to use *AdvancedSearch*, you should consult the Exchange SDK to gain a complete understanding of Web Storage System SQL. The Exchange SDK is available on the Web at *http://msdn.microsoft.com/exchange* and is also included on this book's companion CD. See the section entitled "Web Storage System SQL."

Fortunately, there are quicker and less painful ways to get up to speed with *Filter* and *Scope* syntax. You can use an undocumented Registry key to display a Query Builder page on the Filter dialog box associated with the View Summary dialog box. (See Figure 11-1.) After you use the Query Builder to construct your query, you can then copy the *Filter* syntax displayed on the SQL page and paste it into your code. Do not attempt to add the Query Builder page Registry setting unless you are familiar with the Microsoft Windows Registry Editor.

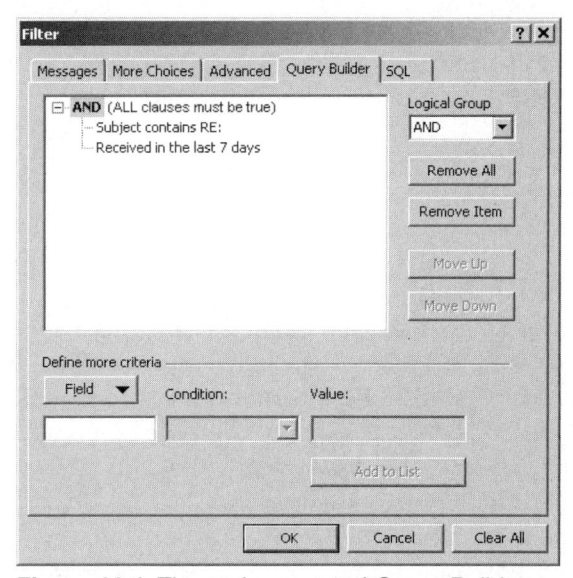

Figure 11-1 The undocumented Query Builder page on the Filter dialog box.

Using Visual Basic, VBA, or VBScript with Outlook   Chapter 11

To display the Query Builder page on the Filter dialog box

1. Click Start, point to Run, type *Regedit* in the Run dialog box, and then click OK to launch the Windows Registry editor.
2. In the Registry tree, navigate to HKEY_CURRENT_USER\Software\Microsoft\Office\10.0\Outlook.
3. Select New from the Edit menu, and then select Key from the New submenu.
4. Type *QueryBuilder* in the Key edit box. Regedit will suggest New Key #1, but you should replace that key name with *QueryBuilder*.

To build a filter using the Query Builder page on the Filter dialog box

1. In Outlook, select Current View from the View menu and then select Customize Current View from the Current View submenu.
2. Click the Filter button on the View Summary dialog box.
3. Click the Query Builder page on the Filter dialog box.
4. Use the Query Builder interface to build your query. When you construct a filter, you actually build a WHERE clause without the WHERE keyword. Notice that you can use the logical AND or logical OR operator to develop the query and move clauses up or down.
5. Click the SQL page shown in Figure 11-2 on the Filter dialog box, and clear the Edit These Criteria Directly check box. Once you clear the check box, you can copy the query by selecting it and pressing Ctrl+C to copy to the Clipboard.
6. Because you don't want to modify the view, click Cancel to dismiss the Filter dialog box. Then click Cancel again to dismiss the View Summary dialog box.

Once you have constructed your Filter string, the rest of the process is relatively straightforward. The *Scope* argument can use either an unqualified folder name such as Inbox, Drafts, Tasks, or a folder path in a Web Storage System SQL Scope clause. *SearchSubFolders* is Boolean and will work only in a Mailbox or PST store. If you're searching a public folder, you can search only one folder at a time. This is a built-in limitation of the MAPI Public Folder store. As stated previously, you should use the AdvancedSearchComplete event to process the Search object returned by *AdvancedSearch*. This next code example shows you how to construct a programmatic search and displays the user form shown in Figure 11-3 when the search is complete.

Part IV Beyond the Basics

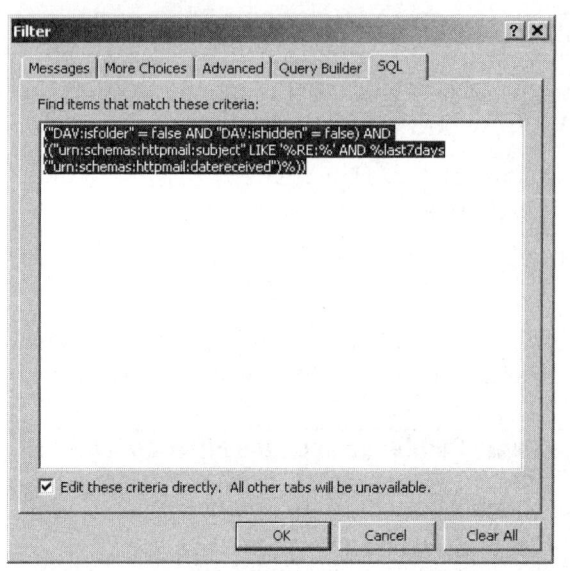

Figure 11-2 Copy a Filter string from the SQL page of the Filter dialog box to provide the *Filter* argument for the *AdvancedSearch* method.

```
Sub ShowSearch()
    Dim olApp As Outlook.Application
    Dim objFolder As MAPIFolder
    Dim objSearch As Search
    Dim strFolderPath As String, strScope As String, strFilter As String
    Set olApp = New Outlook.Application
    'Create a MAPIFolder object for Inbox
    Set objFolder = olApp.GetNamespace("MAPI") _
        .GetDefaultFolder(olFolderInbox)
    'Get the folder path
    strFolderPath = objFolder.FolderPath
    'Build a scope string
    strScope = "SCOPE ('shallow traversal of " _
        & AddQuotes(strFolderPath) & "')"
    'Build a filter string (WHERE clause without the WHERE)
    strFilter = AddQuotes("urn:schemas:mailheader:subject") _
        & " LIKE 'RE:%'"
    'Create the Search object by calling AdvancedSearch
    Set objSearch = _
        olApp.AdvancedSearch(strScope, strFilter, False, "RESearch")
End Sub
```

Using Visual Basic, VBA, or VBScript with Outlook Chapter 11

```vb
Private Sub Application_AdvancedSearchComplete _
    (ByVal SearchObject As Search)
    On Error Resume Next
    Dim objResults As Results
    Dim objItem As Object
    Dim objListItem As Object
    Dim frmAdvancedSearch As New frmSearch
    If SearchObject.Tag = "RESearch" Then
        frmAdvancedSearch.ListView1.ListItems.Clear
        'Create the Results object
        Set objResults = SearchObject.Results
        'Create a reference to first item in Results object
        Set objItem = objResults.GetFirst
        If Not objItem Is Nothing Then
            Do
                'Add item to the ListView control
                Set objListItem = _
                    frmAdvancedSearch.ListView1.ListItems.Add
                With objListItem
                    .Text = objItem.Subject
                    .SubItems(1) = objItem.SenderName
                    .SubItems(2) = objItem.ReceivedTime
                    .SubItems(3) = objItem.Size
                    'Parent is Item container
                    .SubItems(4) = objItem.Parent
                    .SubItems(5) = objItem.EntryID
                End With
                'Reference next item in the Results object
                Set objItem = objResults.GetNext
            Loop Until objItem Is Nothing
        End If
        frmAdvancedSearch.Show
    End If
End Sub
```

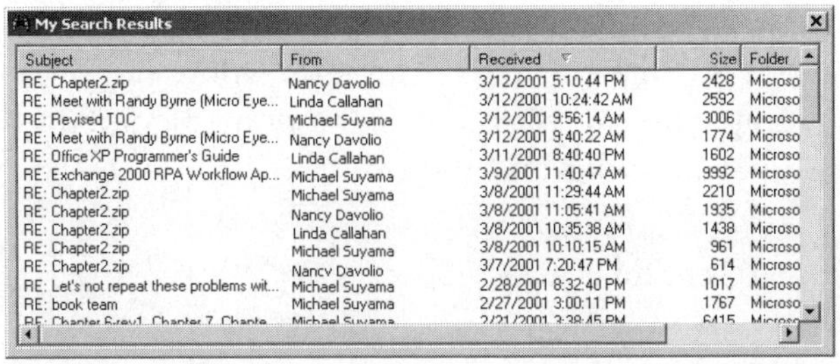

Figure 11-3 Display a custom dialog box that shows the results of a programmatic search in a ListView control.

Part IV   Beyond the Basics

The NameSpace Object

In Outlook, the NameSpace object represents the MAPI message store. The NameSpace object provides methods for logging on or off Outlook, referencing a default folder, and returning objects directly by ID. In addition, the NameSpace object provides access to a variety of methods and properties that are not normally available with the Application object.

> **More Info**   For a complete list and description of the methods, properties, and events for the NameSpace object, see Microsoft Outlook Visual Basic Reference Help.

> **Important**   Open the NameSpace object item in the VBScript Samples folder to work directly with this code in Outlook.

NameSpace Object Methods

This section covers the *GetDefaultFolder* method and the *dial* method of the NameSpace object.

Returning a Default Folder

You can use the *GetDefaultFolder* method of the NameSpace object to access folders in the root folder, also known as the Mailbox. To reference a folder in the Mailbox, you can either specify a numeric value as the argument in the *GetDefaultFolder* method or copy the olDefaultFolders constants from the Outlook Constants item in the VBScript Samples folder and paste them into your code. The table on the following page lists these numeric values.

The following example uses the *GetDefaultFolder* method of the NameSpace object to return the Contacts folder and then display it:

```
Sub CommandButton1_Click
    Set MyFolder = Application.GetNameSpace("MAPI").GetDefaultFolder(10)
    MyFolder.Display
End Sub
```

Folder	Value
Deleted Items	3
Outbox	4
Sent Items	5
Inbox	6
Calendar	9
Contacts	10
Journal	11
Notes	12
Tasks	13
Drafts	16

Dialing a Phone Number

The *Dial* method is new to Outlook 2002. If you supply a ContactItem as the argument to the *Dial* method, you will display the Outlook automatic phone dialer for that contact. The following code example uses the *Dial* method for the first ContactItem in your Contacts folder:

```
Sub DialPhone_Click()
    On Error Resume Next
    Dim objContactsFolder, objContactItem
    Const olFolderContacts = 10
    Set objContactsFolder = _
        Application.GetNamespace("MAPI") _
        .GetDefaultFolder(olFolderContacts)
    Set objContactItem = objContactsFolder.Items(1)
    If objContactItem Is Nothing Then
        MsgBox "Could not find a contact to dial." _
            , vbInformation
    Else
        Application.GetNamespace("MAPI").Dial (objContactItem)
    End If
End Sub
```

Properties of the NameSpace Object

The NameSpace object provides two properties that you use quite often. These are the CurrentUser and Folders properties.

Returning the Name of the Current User

You can use the CurrentUser property of the NameSpace object to return the name of the currently logged-on user. This example shows the current user's name in the message box when the CommandButton1 control is clicked:

```
Sub CommandButton1_Click
    Set MyNameSpace = Application.GetNameSpace("MAPI")
    MsgBox MyNameSpace.CurrentUser
End Sub
```

Referencing a Folder Collection

You can use the Folders property of the NameSpace object to reference the collection of folders in the MAPI NameSpace. The following example displays the number of subfolders in the Building Microsoft Outlook 2002 Applications .pst file:

```
Sub ReferenceAFolderCollection_Click
    Set MyNameSpace = Application.GetNameSpace("MAPI")
    set objFolder = _
        MyNameSpace("Building Microsoft Outlook 2002 Applications")
    Set colFolders = objFolder.Folders
    MsgBox "There are " & colFolders.Count & " subfolders" _
        & vbCr & "in " & objFolder.Name, vbInformation
End Sub
```

Selecting a Folder

You can use the *PickFolder* method of the NameSpace object to return a MAPIFolder object. The *PickFolder* method displays a dialog box for the user to select a folder from all available folders in the current profile. The following example displays the Select Folders dialog box and also displays an alert dialog box if the user clicks Cancel. If the user selects a folder, then the folder is displayed in an Explorer window.

```
Sub PickAFolder_Click()
On Error Resume Next
Set MyNameSpace = Application.GetNameSpace("MAPI")
Set objFolder = MyNameSpace.PickFolder
    If objFolder Is Nothing then
        MsgBox "User Pressed Cancel!", vbInformation
    Else
        objFolder.Display
    End If
End Sub
```

The Outlook E-Mail Security Update Object Model Guard

If you're using Outlook 2002 or a version of Outlook 2000 or Outlook 98 with the Outlook E-Mail Security Update installed, the code shown in *CommandButton1_Click* will display a Warning dialog box, as shown in Figure 11-4. Accessing the CurrentUser property causes the Warning dialog box to appear. The object model guard component of the Outlook E-Mail Security Update figures prominently in this chapter. Wherever possible, I will suggest workarounds for blocked object model properties and methods. Remember that developers targeting Exchanger Server users can use the Administrative form in Public Folders to designate selected COM Add-ins as trusted. These trusted COM Add-ins are not subject to the limitations of the object model guard. For details regarding the Outlook E-Mail Security Update and the use of trusted COM Add-ins to customize security restrictions, see Chapter 13.

In order to avoid the Warning dialog box, use the following code to obtain the name of the CurrentUser property:

```
Function GetCurrentUser()
    Dim objTopFolder As MAPIFolder
    Dim strTopFolder As String
    Dim olApp As Outlook.Application
    Set olApp = CreateObject("Outlook.Application")
    Set objTopFolder = olApp.GetNamespace("MAPI") _
        .GetDefaultFolder(olFolderInbox).Parent
    strTopFolder = objTopFolder.Name
    If InStr(1, strTopFolder, "-") Then
        GetCurrentUser = _
            Trim(Right(strTopFolder, _
            Len(strTopFolder) - InStr(1, strTopFolder, "-")))
    Else
        GetCurrentUser = strTopFolder
    End If
End Function
```

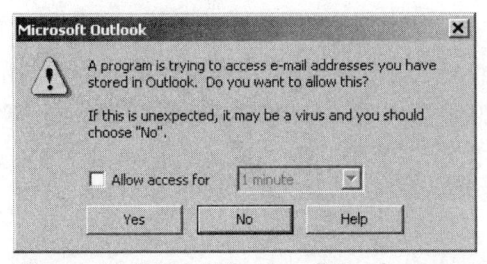

Figure 11-4 This Warning dialog box appears when you attempt to access the CurrentUser property of the NameSpace object.

Part IV Beyond the Basics

The Outlook Window (Explorer Objects)

The Explorer object represents the window in which the contents of a folder are displayed. The Explorers object is the parent collection object for Explorer objects. The following sections cover some of the methods and properties for the Explorer and Explorers objects.

Figure 11-5 illustrates elements of the Outlook user interface viewed from an object model perspective. This illustration is not meant to be all-inclusive; it shows just a few of the objects in the Outlook Object Model that you can manipulate programmatically.

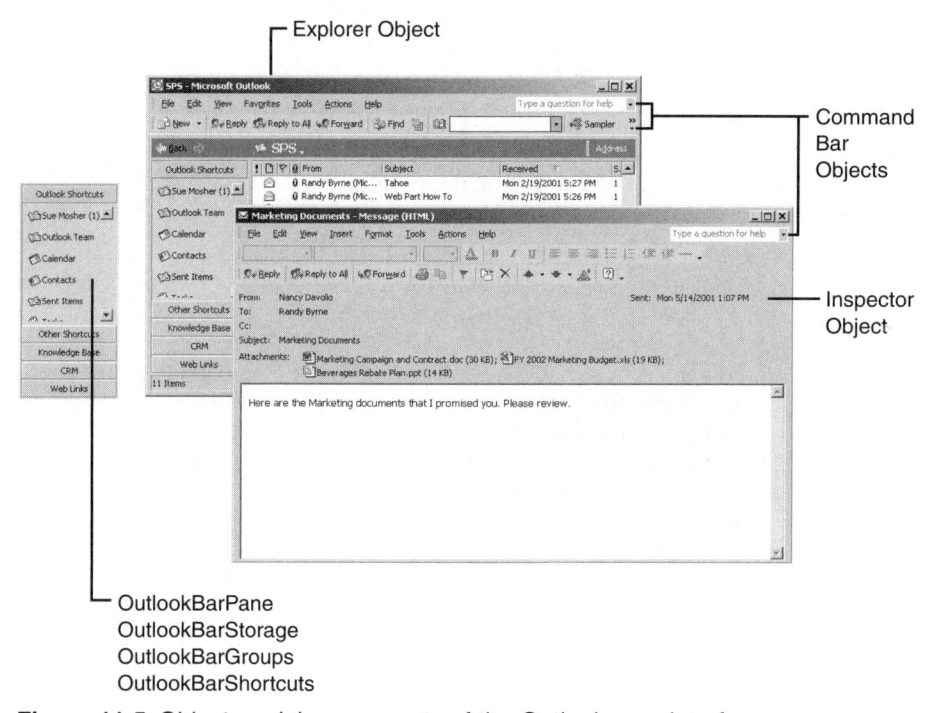

Figure 11-5 Object model components of the Outlook user interface.

> **More Info** For a complete list and description of the properties, methods, and events for the Explorer and Explorers objects, see Microsoft Outlook Visual Basic Reference Help.

Using Visual Basic, VBA, or VBScript with Outlook   Chapter 11

> **Important**   Open the Explorer object item in the VBScript Samples folder to work directly with this code in Outlook.

Explorer Methods

Creating a New Explorer Window

Outlook supports an Explorers collection object. You can use the Explorers object to add a new Explorer window for a specific folder. Use the *Display* method to present the new Explorer window. The following example creates a new Explorer window for the Drafts folder by using the *Add* method and then shows the new window on the desktop in a normal window state.

```
Const olNormalWindow = 2
Sub DisplayNewExplorer_Click
    Set myExplorers = Application.Explorers
    Set myFolder = Application.GetNameSpace("MAPI").GetDefaultFolder(16)
    Set myOlExpl = myExplorers.Add(myFolder, 2)
    myOlExpl.Display
    myOlExpl.WindowState = olNormalWindow
End Sub
```

Explorer Properties

Returning the Active Folder

You can use the CurrentFolder property of the Explorer object to return the active folder in the Outlook window. The following example shows the name of the active folder in the message box when the DisplayTheCurrentFolder control is clicked:

```
Sub DisplayTheCurrentFolder_Click
    Set myExplorer = Application.ActiveExplorer
    MsgBox "The current folder in the Explorer is: " _
        & myExplorer.CurrentFolder.Name, vbInformation
End Sub
```

Obtaining the Current View for the Active Explorer

You can use the CurrentView property of the Explorer object to return or set the current view for the Active Explorer window. The example on the following page displays the name of the current view for the Active Explorer window.

```
Sub DisplayTheExplorerView_Click
    Set myExplorer = Application.ActiveExplorer
    MsgBox "The current Explorer view is: " & vbCr _
        & myExplorer.CurrentView, vbInformation
End Sub
```

Determining Which Items are Selected in the Explorer

The Selection collection object lets you know which items are selected in the Explorer window. The Selection object, in turn, contains an Items collection that lets you iterate over selected items. If you are writing VBA code, you can respond to the SelectionChange event of the Explorer object. The following example displays the number of selected items in the Active Explorer and then asks whether the user wants to display the items:

```
Sub DisplaySelectedItems_Click
    DisplayNewExplorer_Click
    Set mySelection = Application.ActiveExplorer.Selection
    MsgBox "The number of selected items in the Explorer is " _
        & mySelection.Count, vbInformation
    If MsgBox ("Display selected items?", vbYesNo+vbQuestion) = vbNo Then
        Exit Sub
    End If
    For i = 1 to mySelection.Count
        Set myItem = mySelection.Item(i)
        myItem.Display
    Next
End Sub
```

The Panes Collection Object

The Panes collection object is a property object of the Explorer object. The Panes collection object contains the three panes of the Outlook Explorer window, as shown in Figure 11-6. These are the Outlook Bar pane, the Folder List pane, and the Preview pane.

You can create an instance of an OutlookBarPane object from the Panes collection only. The Preview and Folder List panes are not accessible from the Outlook Object Model. When you navigate an Outlook Bar's groups and shortcuts in code, you start with the Panes collection object, as demonstrated in the following code example:

```
Dim OlBarPane As Outlook.OutlookBarPane
Dim OlExplorer As Outlook.Explorer
Set OlExplorer = Application.ActiveExplorer
Set OlBarPane = OlExplorer.Panes("OutlookBar")
'Make the Outlook Bar visible if it's hidden
```

Using Visual Basic, VBA, or VBScript with Outlook   Chapter 11

```
If OlBarPane.Visible = False Then
    OlBarPane.Visible = True
End If
MsgBox "The Current Outlook Bar Group is " _
  & OlBarPane.CurrentGroup, vbInformation
```

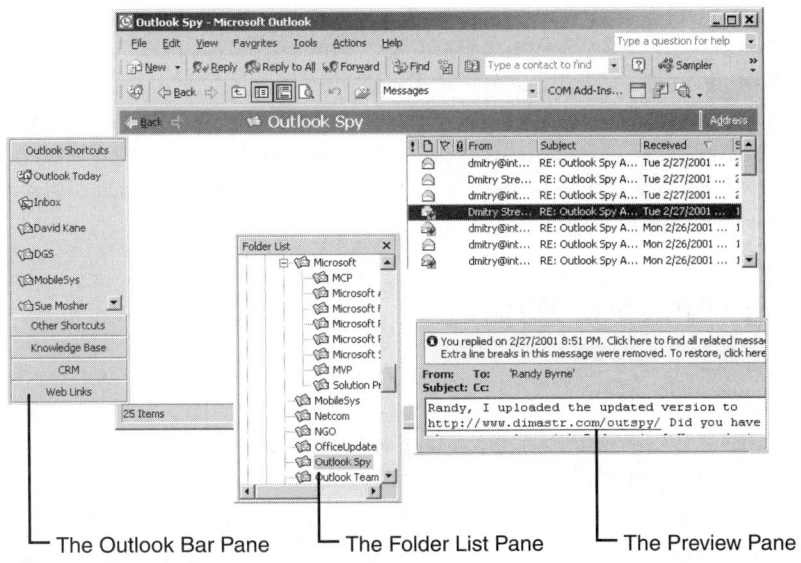

Figure 11-6 Three Explorer panes comprise the Panes collection object.

Determining Whether a Pane is Visible

You can determine whether an individual pane is visible by using the *IsPaneVisible* method of the Explorer object. To make a pane visible, you use the *ShowPane* method. The following VBScript code makes the Folder List pane visible:

```
Sub ShowFolderList
    Const olFolderList = 2
    Set objExpl = Application.ActiveExplorer
    If Not(objExpl.IsPaneVisible(olFolderList)) Then
        objExpl.ShowPane olFolderList, True
    End If
End Sub
```

> **Note**   You cannot size panes programmatically in the Explorer window in Outlook.

The OutlookBarPane Object

The OutlookBarPane object is the only object you can instantiate from the Panes collection object. It represents the Outlook Bar as well as its groups and shortcuts. Generally, you'll create a reference to the OutlookBarPane object as a means to access its dependent child objects that represent Outlook Bar groups and shortcuts. You can use the CurrentGroup property of the OutlookBarPane object to set or get the current group on the Outlook Bar. The OutlookBarPane object supports two important events: BeforeNavigate and BeforeGroupSwitch. These events inform you when a user is navigating to a shortcut or a group, respectively. For additional information on writing event procedures as well as the events supported by the OutlookBarPane, OutlookBarGroups, and OutlookBarShortcuts objects, see Chapter 9.

The OutlookBarStorage Object

The OutlookBarStorage object is an accessor object in the Outlook object hierarchy and has no methods or events of its own. OutlookBarStorage is used to access the OutlookBarGroups collection object through its Groups property. You can access the OutlookBarStorage object by using the Contents property of the OutlookBarPane object. The following VBA code demonstrates the use of the Contents and Groups property objects:

```
Dim OlBarPane As Outlook.OutlookBarPane
Dim OlBarStorage As Outlook.OutlookBarStorage
Dim OlBarGroups As Outlook.OutlookBarGroups
Dim OlExplorer As Outlook.Explorer
Set OlExplorer = Application.ActiveExplorer
Set OlBarPane = OlExplorer.Panes("OutlookBar")
Set OlBarStorage = OlBarPane.Contents
Set OlBarGroups = OlBarStorage.Groups
'This code is more efficient
'Set OlBarGroups = OlBarPane.Contents.Groups
MsgBox "There are " & OlBarGroups.Count _
    & " groups on your Outlook Bar.", vbInformation
```

The OutlookBarGroups Collection Object

The OutlookBarGroups collection object is one of two critical collection objects used to program the Outlook Bar. Using the Groups object, you can add, modify, or delete groups on the Outlook Bar. The OutlookBarGroups object also supports three events that provide an additional level of programmatic control over

Outlook Bar groups: GroupAdd, BeforeGroupAdd, and BeforeGroupRemove. The following example creates an Outlook Bar group named Web Links and positions it as the last group on the Outlook Bar:

```
Dim OlBarGroups As Outlook.OutlookBarGroups
Dim OlBarGroup As Outlook.OutlookBarGroup
Set OlBarGroups = _
    Application.ActiveExplorer.Panes("OutlookBar").Contents.Groups
Set OlBarGroup = OlBarGroups.Add(Name:="Web Links", _
    Index:=OlBarGroups.Count + 1)
```

> **Note** The *Add* method just shown uses named arguments to pass the name and index arguments to the *Add* method of the OutlookBarGroups object. You can list named arguments in any order. A named argument consists of the name of the argument, followed by a colon and an equal sign (:=), followed by the value assigned to the argument. You can also use expressions, and the value of the expression will be assigned to the argument.

The OutlookBarGroup Object

The OutlookBarGroup object represents a group on the Outlook Bar. You can manipulate the properties of the OutlookBarGroup object using its Name and ViewType properties. The ViewType property controls whether the shortcuts in the group display with a large or small icon. Use the Item property to access an existing member of an OutlookBarGroups collection object. The following example renames the Outlook Bar group named Web Links that we created in the previous example and changes the shortcuts to small icons. This enables the user to see more icons in the group before having to use the scroll bar to view other shortcuts.

```
Dim OlBarGroups As Outlook.OutlookBarGroups
Dim OlBarGroup As Outlook.OutlookBarGroup
Set OlBarGroups = _
    Application.ActiveExplorer.Panes("OutlookBar").Contents.Groups
Set OlBarGroup = OlBarGroups.Items("Web Links")
With OlBarGroup
    .Name = "Outlook Web Links"
    .ViewType = olSmallIcon
End With
```

The OutlookBarShortcuts Collection Object

OutlookBarShortcuts is a property collection object for the OutlookBarGroups object. You use this collection object to add, modify, or remove shortcuts from an Outlook Bar group. Like the OutlookBarGroups collection object, OutlookBarShortcuts supports three events you can use when you write event procedures to be executed when an Outlook shortcut has been added or removed. These events are ShortcutAdd, BeforeShortcutAdd, and BeforeShortcutRemove.

The OutlookBarShortcut Object

The OutlookBarShortcut object represents a shortcut on the Outlook Bar. A shortcut in Outlook 2000 or Outlook 2002 can launch an executable file on a local or network drive, navigate to a URL, or navigate to an Outlook folder in the folder hierarchy. The following table lists some of the common shortcuts used in Outlook 2000 and Outlook 2002.

Shortcut Function	Target Property	Example
Navigate to Outlook folder	MAPIFolder object	Set oFolder = _ objNS.GetDefaultFolder(olFolderDrafts) OlBarShortcuts.Add oFolder, "Drafts"
Open a file system file	String file URL specification	strTarget = "file:\\c:\my documents\foo.xls" OlBarShortcuts.Add strTarget, "My File"
Open a file system folder	String folder path specification	strTarget = "c:\my documents" OlBarShortcuts.Add strTarget, "My Documents"
Open a Web page	String URL	strTarget = "http://www.slipstick.com" OlBarShortcuts.Add strTarget, "Slipstick"

The Target property of OutlookBarShortcut determines what action occurs when a user clicks a shortcut on the Outlook Bar. Oddly enough, the Target property is read-only; when you set the Target property by adding a shortcut, you must remove the shortcut and add it again if you want to change the property.

> **Note** If you use an *http* URL as the target of a shortcut, Outlook will open the Web page as a Web View in the Outlook Explorer window. If you want to open the Web page in a separate window, right-click the shortcut in Outlook and select Open In New Window from the shortcut menu. In Outlook 2000, this action will open the URL in a new browser window. In Outlook 2002, this action will open the URL in a new Outlook Explorer window.

OutlookBarShortcut supports the new *SetIcon* method for Outlook 2002. Use SetIcon to set the icon for an OutlookBarShortcut object.

The CommandBars Collection Object

The ability to program the Outlook Bar gives you a significant level of control over the Outlook user interface. Using the OutlookBarGroups and OutlookBarShortcuts events, you can prevent a user from removing an Outlook Bar group or shortcut that is essential to your application. You can also dynamically add Outlook Bar groups and shortcuts. You don't have the same flexibility, however, with Outlook Bar objects as you do with all the objects belonging to Office command bars. CommandBar and Assistant objects are actually members of the Office Object Model. CommandBar objects give you the opportunity to customize Outlook in a way that was impossible in Outlook 97 and Outlook 98. That said, the following discussion gives an overview of using command bars in Outlook. How you call CommandBar objects in Outlook differs somewhat from how you call them in other Office applications.

> **Note** If you are writing a COM Add-in, you must explicitly add a reference to the Microsoft Office 9.0 Object Library or Microsoft Office 10.0 Object Library using the appropriate command in your development tool. If you are using Outlook VBA to write code in the VBAProject.otm file, Outlook automatically creates a reference to the Microsoft Office 10.0 Object Library.

Overview of Command Bars

In the Outlook Object Model, both the Explorer and Inspector objects contain a CommandBars property object. The CommandBars object for Inspector and Explorer controls all Outlook toolbars, menu bars, and shortcut menus. The CommandBar object and its children contain the following items:

- Menu bars, toolbars, and shortcut menus
- Menus on menu bars and toolbars
- Submenus on menus, submenus, and shortcut menus

You can modify any built-in menu bar or toolbar, and you can create and modify custom toolbars, menu bars, and shortcut menus to deliver with your Outlook VBA project or COM Add-in application. Use command bar customization to present the features of your application as individual buttons on toolbars or as groups of command names on menus. Because both toolbars and menus are command bars, you can use the same kind of controls on them.

Custom command bars differ somewhat from built-in command bars because they can be deleted from the Outlook environment. Built-in command bars can be modified by the user or by program code. However, built-in command bars can be restored to their original state and default behavior by using the Reset command button on the Toolbars page of the Customize dialog box.

The following table shows the built-in command bars in Outlook.

Object	Built-In Command Bar
Explorer	Menu Bar Standard Advanced Remote (Outlook 2000 only) Web Clipboard (Outlook 2000 only)
Inspector	Menu Bar Standard Formatting Form Design Clipboard (Outlook 2000 only)

Be aware that command bars are defined as either docked or, in the case of a floating command bar or menu bar, undocked. Outlook features four command bar docks—one at the left, right, top, and bottom of the Outlook window.

Outlook CommandBarButton objects represent buttons and menu items. The pop-up controls that display menus and submenus are known as CommandBarPopup objects. Both the menu and the submenu are unique CommandBar objects with their own sets of controls.

In addition to CommandBarButton and CommandBarPopup objects, the CommandBarControls object can contain CommandBarComboBox objects. CommandBarComboBox objects assume a variety of different types: edit box, drop-down list box, or drop-down combo box. Like the List Box control on Outlook forms, the CommandBarComboBox object supports both an *AddItem* method to add items to the control and a ListIndex property to retrieve the selection index.

Exploring the CommandBars Collection

One way to learn more about the CommandBars object is to write code that maps the existing built-in and custom Outlook command bars. Because Outlook supports command bars for both the Explorer and Inspector windows, the following function requires a class argument that indicates whether the Inspector or Explorer command bars and controls should be output to the Debug window.

PrintAllCBarInfo can be found in the basCommandBars module in VBA Samples.zip in the VBA Samples folder.

To use the code in the VBA Samples folder

1. Using Windows Explorer, expand the Building Microsoft Outlook 2002 Applications folder. Then expand the 4. Beyond the Basics folder, and then expand the Visual Basic For Applications folder, followed by the VBA Samples folder.

2. The code, class, and user form modules for VBAProject.otm are in VBA Samples.zip in the VBA Samples folder. You can extract these items from VBA Samples.zip by using a Zip utility program such as WinZip, which is availble at *http://www.winzip.com*.

3. You can also replace your current VBAProject.otm file with the VBAProject.otm installed by the setup program on the companion CD.

To run the *PrintAllCBarInfo* procedure

1. Open the Visual Basic Editor by pressing Alt+F11.

2. Extract basCommandBars from VBA Samples.zip in the VBA Samples folder to a file system folder.

3. Select Import File on the File menu to import basCommandBars into your Outlook VBAProject.otm.

4. Press Ctrl+G to open the Debug window.

5. Type *?PrintAllCBarInfo(olExplorer)*, and press Enter. Information on all command bars and controls in the CommandBars collection will display in the Debug window.

```
Function PrintAllCBarInfo(intClass As Integer)
    'This procedure prints (to the Debug window)
    'information about each command bar in the
    'active Explorer or Inspector window.
    'Use OlExplorer or OlInspector for intClass argument
    Dim cbrBar As Office.CommandBar
    Dim colCB As Office.CommandBars
    On Error Resume Next
    If intClass = OlExplorer Then
        Set colCB = Application.ActiveExplorer.CommandBars
```

(continued)

Part IV Beyond the Basics

```
            If Err Then
                Debug.Print "No Active Explorer found!"
                Exit Function
            End If
        Else
            Set colCB = Application.ActiveInspector.CommandBars
            If Err Then
                Debug.Print "No Active Inspector found!"
                Exit Function
            End If
        End If
        For Each cbrBar In colCB
            CBPrintCBarInfo cbrBar.Name, intClass
        Next cbrBar
    End Function
```

The following function is a helper function for the CBPrintAllCBarInfo function just shown. This function calls two other functions that enumerate the types of command bars and command bar controls. See the code in the basCommandBars module for a complete listing.

```
Function CBPrintCBarInfo(strCBarName As String, intClass As Integer) _
  As Variant
    'This procedure prints (to the Debug window) information
    'about the command bar specified in the strCBarName argument
    'and information about each control on that command bar.
    'Use olExplorer or olInspector for intClass argument
    Dim cbrBar                 As CommandBar
    Dim ctlCBarControl         As CommandBarControl
    Const ERR_INVALID_CMDBARNAME   As Long = 5
    On Error GoTo CBPrintCBarInfo_Err

    If intClass = OlExplorer Then
        Set cbrBar = Application.ActiveExplorer.CommandBars(strCBarName)
    Else
        Set cbrBar = Application.ActiveInspector.CommandBars(strCBarName)
    End If

    Debug.Print "CommandBar: " & cbrBar.Name & vbTab & "(" _
        & CBGetCBType(cbrBar) & ")" & vbTab & "(" _
        & IIf(cbrBar.BuiltIn, "Built-in", "Custom") & ")"
    For Each ctlCBarControl In cbrBar.Controls
        Debug.Print vbTab & ctlCBarControl.Caption & vbTab & "(" _
            & CBGetCBCtlType(ctlCBarControl) & ")"
    Next ctlCBarControl

CBPrintCBarInfo_End:
    Exit Function
CBPrintCBarInfo_Err:
```

```
    Select Case Err.Number
        Case ERR_INVALID_CMDBARNAME
            CBPrintCBarInfo = "'" & strCBarName & _
                "' is not a valid command bar name!"
        Case Else
            CBPrintCBarInfo = "Error: " & Err.Number _
                & " - " & Err.Description
    End Select
    Resume CBPrintCBarInfo_End
End Function
```

Listed next you'll find the output of CBPrintCBarInfo as it appears in the Debug window. This excerpt shows all the controls on the Outlook Advanced toolbar.

```
CommandBar: Advanced        (Toolbar)    (Built-in)
    Outloo&k Today    (Button)
    &Back     (Button)
    &Forward      (Button)
    &Up One Level     (Button)
    Fold&er List      (Button)
    Preview Pa&ne     (Button)
    Print Pre&view    (Button)
    &Undo     (Button)
    Ru&les Wizard...      (Button)
    Current &View     (Combobox)
    Group &By Box     (Button)
    Field &Chooser    (Button)
    Auto&Preview      (Button)
```

Using Images on Command Bar Buttons

Once you have explored the Outlook command bars and their controls, take a look at the images used on these buttons. If you plan to write code to create your own custom command bars, you need to find a source for icons that will appear on the buttons. You can use the *FindControl*, *CopyFace*, and *PasteFace* methods to copy and paste images from a built-in button to custom buttons you've created. You can also supply a *FaceID* value for your custom command bar button that corresponds to the *FaceID* for a built-in icon. The following procedure creates a temporary custom toolbar that displays built-in Office icons, as shown in Figure 11-7 (on page 443). If you hold your mouse pointer over the button, a tooltip will display the FaceID property.

To run the *CBShowButtonFaceIDs* procedure

1. Open the Visual Basic Editor by pressing Alt+F11.
2. Drag basCommandBars from the VBA Samples folder to a file system folder such as C:\My Documents.

Part IV Beyond the Basics

3. Select Import File on the File menu to import basCommandBars into your Outlook VBAProject.otm.
4. Press Ctrl+G to open the Debug window.
5. Type *?CBShowButtonFaceIDs(0, 299, olExplorer)*, and press Enter.
6. Press Alt+F11 to return to the Outlook application window. You should see the ShowFaceIDs toolbar displayed over the Explorer window.

```
Function CBShowButtonFaceIDs(lngIDStart As Long, _
        lngIDStop As Long, intClass As Integer)

    'This procedure creates a toolbar with buttons that display the
    'images associated with the values starting at lngIDStart and
    'ending at lngIDStop
    'Use olExplorer or olInspector for intClass argument
    Dim cbrNewToolbar   As CommandBar
    Dim cmdNewButton    As CommandBarButton
    Dim intCntr         As Integer

    'If the ShowFaceIds toolbar exists, delete it
    On Error Resume Next
    If intClass = OlExplorer Then
        'Delete the ShowFaceIds toolbar
        Application.ActiveExplorer.CommandBars("ShowFaceIds").Delete
        'Create a new toolbar
        Set cbrNewToolbar = Application.ActiveExplorer.CommandBars.Add _
            (Name:="ShowFaceIds", Temporary:=True)
    Else
        'Delete the ShowFaceIds toolbar
        Application.ActiveInspector.CommandBars("ShowFaceIds").Delete
        'Create a new toolbar
        Set cbrNewToolbar = Application.ActiveInspector.CommandBars.Add _
            (Name:="ShowFaceIds", Temporary:=True)
    End If

    'Create a new button with an image matching the FaceID property value
    'indicated by intCntr
    For intCntr = lngIDStart To lngIDStop
        Set cmdNewButton = _
          cbrNewToolbar.Controls.Add(Type:=msoControlButton)
        With cmdNewButton
            'Setting the FaceID property value specifies the appearance
            'but not the functionality of the button
            .FaceId = intCntr
            .Style = msoButtonIcon
            .Visible = True
            .TooltipText = "FaceId = " & intCntr
```

```
        End With
    Next intCntr

    'Show the images on the toolbar
    With cbrNewToolbar
        .Width = 600
        .Left = 100
        .Top = 100
        .Visible = True
    End With

End Function
```

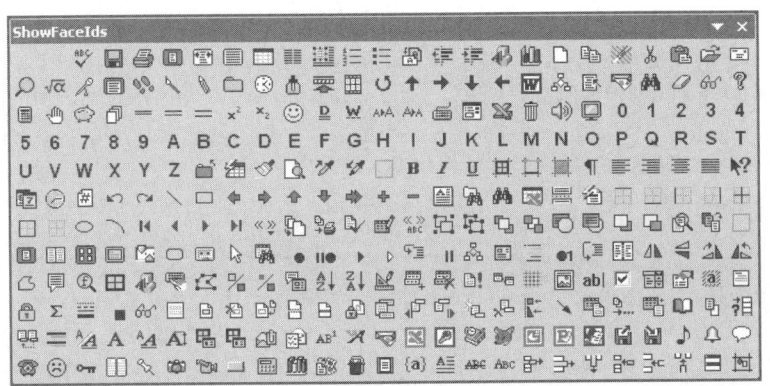

Figure 11-7 The ShowFaceIds toolbar provides a palette of images to use for custom buttons.

Use the ShowFaceIDs toolbar to provide icon images for your custom toolbar buttons. Place the cursor over the desired command button to learn its FaceID property. You can copy the code for the cmdNewButton object shown a moment ago and paste it into the code that your own button creates. Just substitute the actual value for the FaceID icon that you need for the *intCntr* variable.

Adding a Command Bar to the Collection

Use the *Add* method to add a command bar to either the Inspector or the Explorer CommandBars collection. If you are using Visual Basic rather than VBScript, you can use named arguments when you call the *Add* method of the CommandBars collection object to add a command bar. The following example adds the Items command bar to the Explorer CommandBars collection:

```
Dim cbrNewToolbar As CommandBar
Set cbrNewToolbar = Application.ActiveExplorer.CommandBars.Add _
        (Name:="Items", Position:=msoBarTop, Temporary:=False)
```

In VBScript, all variables are declared as Variants and named arguments are illegal. Here is a statement that adds an Inspector command bar:

```
Set objCommandBar= Item.GetInspector.CommandBars.Add _
        ("Command Bar Example", 1, False, True)
```

The Position property determines whether the toolbar will be docked in the Explorer or the Inspector window or displayed as a floating toolbar. If you supply the *msoBarPopUp* value for the *Position* argument, you will create a shortcut menu rather than a menu bar or toolbar. The following table shows the possible values for the Position property.

Constant	Description
msoBarLeft=0, msoBarTop=1, msoBarRight=2, msoBarBottom=3	Indicates the left, top, right, and bottom coordinates of the new command bar
msoBarFloating=4	Indicates that the new command bar won't be docked
msoBarPopup=5	Indicates that the new command bar will be a shortcut menu

The Temporary property indicates whether the command bar will be deleted when the Outlook application or the Inspector window closes. Notice that the VBScript Command Bar Example toolbar is temporary; it appears only for a specific custom form. Generally, you don't want to create persistent Inspector toolbars.

> **Note** Once you have added the command bar to the CommandBars collection, you can set additional properties that determine the command bar's appearance and behavior. For example, the Type property determines whether the CommandBar object behaves as a menu bar, toolbar, or shortcut menu.

Retrieving an Existing Command Bar

To retrieve an existing built-in or custom command bar, use the Items property with either an index value or the name of the command bar. Because the Items property is the default property of the CommandBars collection object, you don't actually have to use the Items property to retrieve a command bar from a collection. The following two statements are equivalent:

```
Set cbrItems = Application.ActiveExplorer.CommandBars.Items("Items")
Set cbrItems = Application.ActiveExplorer.CommandBars("Items")
```

Deleting a Command Bar

Use the *Delete* method to delete a custom command bar from the CommandBars collection. You cannot delete a built-in command bar with the *Delete* method. The *Delete* method is actually a CommandBar method, not a CommandBars method. The following function deletes a command bar and returns *True* if the command bar was successfully deleted:

```
Function CBDeleteCommandBar(strCBarName As String) As Boolean
    On Error Resume Next
    Application.ActiveExplorer.CommandBars(strCBarName).Delete
    If Err = 0 Then
        CBDeleteCommandBar = True
    End If
End Function
```

Using the OnUpdate Event

The CommandBars collection supports an OnUpdate event that fires whenever a command bar is changed. For additional information regarding Visual Basic events, the *WithEvents* keyword, and event procedures, see Chapter 9. The event is triggered by any change to a command, or by the state of a bar or command bar control. These changes can result from pressing a button, by changing text, or by selecting a cell. Because a large number of OnUpdate events can occur during normal usage, you should be very cautious when working with this event. I strongly recommend that you use this event primarily for checking that a custom command bar has been added or removed by an Outlook COM Add-in. To see how many times this event can fire, add the following code to VBAProject.otm. A statement appears in the Debug window every time the OnUpdate event fires.

```
'Place in Declarations of ThisOutlookSession
Dim WithEvents colCB As CommandBars

Private Sub Application_Startup()
    Set colCB = Application.ActiveExplorer.CommandBars
End Sub

Private Sub colCB_OnUpdate()
    Debug.Print "CommandBars OnUpdate"
End Sub
```

The CommandBar Object

The CommandBar object represents a command bar—either built-in or custom—for either the Outlook Explorer or Inspector window. You can modify a built-in command bar through the Customize dialog box or through program code. If you are building a custom Outlook application or creating a COM Add-in, you should consider providing a custom command bar or modifying the menus on the Outlook menu bar for your COM Add-in. Once you have created a command bar object programmatically, you should add controls to the command bar and program them to respond to events such as Click or Change.

Properties of the CommandBar Object

The following table lists some important properties of the CommandBar object. For additional information on CommandBar object properties, see Microsoft Outlook Visual Basic Reference Help.

Property	Description
AdaptiveMenus	Determines whether an individual command bar displays adaptive menus. This property can be True or False.
Enabled	Determines whether the command bar can be modified with the Customize dialog box. If the Enabled property is False, you cannot set the Visible property to True.
Position	Returns or sets the position of the command bar.
Type	Determines the type of command bar—menu bar, toolbar, or shortcut menu.
Visible	Determines whether the command bar is visible in the Explorer or Inspector window. This property can be True or False.

Methods of the CommandBar Object

The methods listed in the following table operate on the CommandBar object. For additional information on methods for the CommandBar object, see Microsoft Office Visual Basic Reference Help.

Method	Description
Delete	Deletes a custom command bar.
FindControl	Finds a control on a command bar that meets specified criteria. You can search by control type, ID, or tag property based on whether a control is visible or on a submenu.
Reset	Resets a built-in command bar to its default configuration. If you have customized a built-in command bar, those customizations are removed when you call this method.
ShowPopup	Shows the command bar as a pop-up menu at specified coordinates or at the current cursor location.

Using Visual Basic, VBA, or VBScript with Outlook Chapter 11

The *ShowPopup* method will work only for a command bar that has been added as a shortcut menu to the CommandBars collection. You cannot cause a built-in or custom toolbar to appear suddenly as a pop-up menu. The Outlook Inspector has a limited capacity to display shortcut menus because a MouseUp event is not supported using the current control container for Outlook custom forms. If you are utilizing UserForms in your VBA or COM Add-in project, use the MouseUp event of intrinsic and third-party ActiveX controls to build event procedures that display Outlook shortcut menus. The following procedure displays a pop-up menu at the current cursor location in the Explorer window:

```
Sub ExplorerPopUp()
    Dim CBCopyandPasteMenu As Office.CommandBar
    Set CBCopyandPasteMenu = Application.ActiveExplorer.CommandBars.Add _
        (Name:="Custom", Position:=msoBarPopup, Temporary:=True)
    Set Copy = CBCopyandPasteMenu.Controls.Add
    With Copy
        .FaceId = Application.ActiveExplorer.CommandBars _
            ("Menu Bar").Controls("Edit").Controls("Copy").ID
        .Caption = "Copy the selection"
    End With
    Set Paste = CBCopyandPasteMenu.Controls.Add
    With Paste
        .FaceId = Application.ActiveExplorer.CommandBars _
            ("Menu Bar").Controls("Edit").Controls("Paste").ID
        .Caption = "Paste from the Clipboard"
    End With
    CBCopyandPasteMenu.ShowPopup
End Sub
```

The next procedure uses the MouseUp event to display the Data Helper shortcut menu when the right mouse click occurs over the *lstSync* control on a UserForm:

```
Private Sub lstSync_MouseUp _
    (ByVal Button As Integer, ByVal Shift As Integer, _
    ByVal X As Single, ByVal Y As Single)
On Error Resume Next
Dim cbrShortcut As CommandBar
Select Case Button
    Case vbKeyLButton 'Left
    Case vbKeyRButton 'Right
        Set cbrShortcut = _
            Application.ActiveExplorer.CommandBars("Data Helper")
        cbrShortcut.Visible = True
        cbrShortcut.ShowPopup X, Y
End Select
End Sub
```

Protecting a Command Bar from User Modification

How do you protect a custom command bar you've developed from user modification? A user can modify your command bar either through the user interface or through program code. To prevent changes to your custom command bar, you can set the Enabled property to False to make the command bar invisible in the list of Outlook command bars for either the Explorer or Inspector window. Once the Enabled property is set to False, users cannot modify your custom command bar because they will not be able to see the command bar name in the Toolbars list. You must reset the Enabled property to True before you can use the Visible property to display the command bar. However, the Enabled property is not the most secure means of protecting your custom command bar. The following procedure can prevent a user from using the Customize dialog box to alter your custom command bar. The code disables the Customize command on the Tools menu and the Toolbars list on the View menu.

```
Sub AllowExplorerCBCustomization(blnAllowEnabled As Boolean)
    'This procedure allows or prevents access to the
    'command bar's Customize dialog box according to the
    'value of the blnAllowEnabled argument.
    Dim colCB As CommandBars
    Set colCB = Application.ActiveExplorer.CommandBars
    colCB("Tools").Controls("Customize...").Enabled = blnAllowEnabled
    colCB("Toolbar List").Enabled = blnAllowEnabled
End Sub
```

The CommandBarControls Collection Object

CommandBarControls is a collection object that represents all the controls on a command bar. You use the Controls property of a CommandBar object to refer to a control on a command bar. The Controls property is a CommandBarControls collection. If the control is of the type msoControlPopup, it also will have a Controls collection representing each control on the pop-up menu. Pop-up menu controls represent menus and submenus and can be nested several layers deep, as shown in the second example in this section.

In the following example, the code returns a reference to the New button on the Standard toolbar and displays the type of the control in a message box:

```
Dim ctlCBarControl As CommandBarControl
Set ctlCBarControl = Application.ActiveExplorer.CommandBars _
    ("Standard").Controls("New")
MsgBox "The type of " & ctlCBarControl.Caption _
    & " is " & CBGetCBCtlType(ctlCBarControl), vbInformation
```

Here, the code returns a reference to the Macros control on the Macro pop-up menu located on the Tools menu on the menu bar for the Explorer window:

```
Dim ctlCBarControl As CommandBarControl
Set ctlCBarControl = Application.ActiveExplorer.CommandBars("Menu Bar") _
    .Controls("Tools").Controls("Macro").Controls("Macros...")
```

Because each pop-up menu control is actually a CommandBar object, you can also refer to it directly as a member of the CommandBars collection. For example, the following line of code returns a reference to the same control as the previous example did:

```
Set ctlCBarControl = Application.ActiveExplorer.CommandBars("Macro") _
    .Controls("Macros...")
```

Once you have a reference to a control on a command bar, you can access all available properties and methods of that control.

> **Note** When you refer to a command bar control by using the control's Caption property, you must specify the caption exactly as it appears on the menu. For example, in the previous code sample, the reference to the control caption *"Macros..."* requires the ellipsis (...) in order to match the way the caption appears on the menu. However, you do not have to include the ampersand (&) that is returned in the control's Caption property when you refer to the control. *Controls("Macros...")* is equivalent to *Controls("&Macros...")* in the previous example.

Use the Count property of the CommandBarControls collection to return the number of controls in the collection object. To add controls to the collection, use the *Add* method. The Item property is the default property of the CommandBarControls collection object. For this reason, you do not have to use the Item property to access individual controls in the collection if you are writing Visual Basic or VBA code. *Controls("Macros...")* is the equivalent of *Controls.Item("Macros...")*. However, if you are writing VBScript code, you must use the Item property to access individual controls in the collection.

The CommandBarControl Object

The CommandBarControl object is the child object of the CommandBarControls object, and it represents a control on a built-in or custom command bar. If you want to refer to a control on a built-in command bar, you should dimension the

449

control variable as a CommandBarControl object. If you want to instantiate an object on a custom command bar, use the CommandBarButton, CommandBarComboBox, or CommandBarPopup object for your item declaration in Visual Basic. If you are using VBScript in an Outlook form, the type of the object is immaterial because all objects are Variants by default.

> **Note** If you do declare a control object as a CommandBarControl, you can still use the properties and methods of the CommandBarButton, CommandBarComboBox, and CommandBarPopup objects with it. However, dimensioning the control as the correct variable type is the preferred approach. You cannot use the read-only Type property to change the type of an existing custom control. If you want to change the control type, you must delete the control and then add it with the correct type argument in the *Add* method of the CommandBarControls object.

Adding Custom Command Bar Controls

The CommandBarControl object allows you to modify built-in controls or to add new controls on a custom command bar. Additionally, you can set the properties of the control to determine how the control will appear or what procedure will run when the user clicks the command button or selects a menu item. The difference between CommandBarControl objects is clearly demonstrated in the following code sample for a command bar named Testing. The Testing command bar, shown in Figure 11-8, uses every type of control available for a custom command bar.

Figure 11-8 The Testing command bar.

The code required to create Testing is relatively straightforward. It's presented in sections so that you can clearly understand each step of the coding process. The first order of business is to instantiate a CommandBar object so that controls can be added to the command bar's CommandBarControls collection. The next line attempts to instantiate a Testing CommandBar object from the Explorer's CommandBars collection. If Testing already exists and no error occurs, the existing toolbar is deleted before the command bar is added.

```
Sub CBTestingDemo()
    Dim cbTesting As CommandBar
    Dim ctlCBarButton As CommandBarButton
```

Using Visual Basic, VBA, or VBScript with Outlook Chapter 11

```
Dim ctlCBarCombo As CommandBarComboBox
Dim ctlCBarPopup As CommandBarPopup
On Error Resume Next
Set cbTesting = Application.ActiveExplorer.CommandBars("Testing")
If Err = 0 Then
    cbTesting.Delete
End If
Set cbTesting = Application.ActiveExplorer.CommandBars _
    .Add(Name:="Testing", Position:=msoBarTop)
```

Notice that we've added a position argument to the *Add* method in order to place the command bar in the top dock. Now we're ready to add controls to the command bar. These additional controls don't actually do anything when clicked. Four different types of controls will be added to Testing. The first is a standard button that's typical of the controls on toolbars. We've assigned the caption Color to this button and an icon that corresponds to the built-in FaceID 2167, the icon for the color palette. In order for both the icon and the caption to appear, you must set the button's style to msoButtonIconAndCaption. If you are using a built-in FaceID to provide an icon for a custom button, you must set the button's Visible property to True or the icon will not appear, even though the new button appears on the toolbar.

```
Set ctlCBarButton = cbTesting.Controls.Add(Type:=msoControlButton)
With ctlCBarButton
    .Caption = "Color"
    .FaceId = 2167
    .Style = msoButtonIconAndCaption
    .Visible = True
    .TooltipText = "Test color button"
End With
```

The next control to add to Testing is an Edit box control. Edit box controls are equivalent to edit boxes on an Outlook form. A separate object type does not exist for edit controls. Edit box controls are actually CommandBarComboBox objects. Their Type property is msoEditBox. Edit box and List box controls can show a label before the control if their Style property is set to msoComboLabel. The following code adds an Edit box control to Testing and sets its Text property to Red:

```
Set ctlCBarCombo = cbTesting.Controls.Add(Type:=msoControlEdit)
With ctlCBarCombo
    .Caption = "Color: "
    .Text = "Red"
    .Style = msoComboLabel
    .TooltipText = "Test Edit box"
End With
```

The ComboBox control uses many of the same properties and methods as the MSForms combo box that you're familiar with from Outlook forms. You can use the *AddItem* method to add items to the list and the ListIndex property to set or return the selected item in the list. Like the Edit box control, this combo box uses a caption to identify the value being selected by the user.

```
Set ctlCBarCombo = cbTesting.Controls.Add(Type:=msoControlComboBox)
With ctlCBarCombo
    .AddItem "Red"
    .AddItem "Green"
    .AddItem "Blue"
    .ListIndex = 1
    .Caption = "Test Combo box"
End With
```

Finally we'll add a Popup control to Testing and make the toolbar visible. Remember that every Popup control contains a Command Bar object and a corresponding controls collection. If you want to add items to the Popup control, use the *Add* method for the Controls property object of the CommandBarPopup object. The following code adds three button controls to the Popup control. If we added these controls as Popup controls rather than button controls, we would have submenus that could contain additional submenus or button controls.

```
Set ctlCBarPopup = cbTesting.Controls.Add(Type:=msoControlPopup)
Set ctlCBarControl = ctlCBarPopup.Controls.Add(Type:=msoControlButton)
ctlCBarControl.Caption = "Red"
Set ctlCBarControl = ctlCBarPopup.Controls.Add(Type:=msoControlButton)
ctlCBarControl.Caption = "Green"
Set ctlCBarControl = ctlCBarPopup.Controls.Add(Type:=msoControlButton)
ctlCBarControl.Caption = "Blue"
With ctlCBarPopup
    .Caption = "Test Popup"
End With
cbTesting.Visible = True
End Sub
```

> **Note** The last statement in the previous code listing makes the new custom command bar visible. Unless you set the Visible property of your custom command bar, you will not be able to see the new command bar in the Outlook Explorer or Inspector window.

Running a Procedure for a Control

Adding controls to your custom toolbar is not very useful unless they help the user perform an action. To run a procedure when a user clicks a control button or a combo box changes, you can set the OnAction property to refer to a Sub procedure or Function procedure in your project. If you are creating a custom command bar in an Outlook form using VBScript, using the OnAction property is the only way you can run a procedure for a control. If you are creating a COM Add-in, you also have the option to declare the object variable for the control using the *WithEvents* keyword and run an event procedure when the control's Click event (CommandBarButton) or Change event (CommandBarComboBox) fires.

The following code from the Items toolbar example will cause the *LaunchWordMail* procedure to run when a user clicks the HTML Word Mail icon on the Items toolbar:

```
Set cmdNewButton = cbrNewToolbar.Controls.Add _
    (Type:=msoControlButton) 'Custom button for Word Mail
With cmdNewButton
    .FaceId = 42
    .BeginGroup = True
    .Visible = True
    .Style = msoButtonIcon
    .Caption = "HTML Word Mail"
    .OnAction = "LaunchWordMail"
End With
```

> **Note** If you have more than one procedure with the name *Launch-WordMail* in different code modules, none of the procedures will run when the button is clicked. Outlook must be able to resolve the procedure name specified in the OnAction property for the procedure to run correctly. You cannot use traditional *basOutlook.LaunchWordMail* syntax to call a procedure in a specified module.

An equivalent OnAction property exists for the CommandBarComboBox controls. Combo box controls run the OnAction procedure when a change event fires. Button controls run the OnAction procedure when a Click event fires. If the Change event causes the OnAction procedure to run, you can examine the ListIndex property of the control to determine the combo box item selected by the user.

If you have multiple controls that point to the same procedure in their OnAction property, use the Parameters property of the control to determine which control has been clicked. You set the Parameters property of the control when you add the control to its command bar. The ActionProperty of the CommandBar object returns an object representing the control that has been clicked or changed. This example shows how you can use the Parameter and ActionControl properties to branch code execution depending on the Parameter property:

```
Dim ctlCBarControl  As CommandBarControl
Set ctlCBarControl = _
    Application.ActiveExplorer.CommandBars.ActionControl
If ctlCBarControl Is Nothing Then Exit Function
'Examine the Parameter property of the ActionControl to determine
'which control has been clicked
Select Case ctlCBarControl.Parameter
    Case "Next"
    'Next code here
        olItems.GetNext
    Case "Previous"
    'Previous code here
        olItems.GetPrevious
End Select
```

Showing and Enabling Controls

Use the Visible property of a control to show or hide the control on a command bar. Use the Enabled property to enable or disable the control on the toolbar. When a control is disabled, it is still visible but the user cannot perform an action on it. The following function toggles the state of a command bar control. To test this function, type *?CBCtlToggleVisible("Tools", "&Options...")* in the Debug window and press Enter to toggle the Enabled property of the Options command on the Explorer Tools menu.

```
Function CBCtlToggleVisible(strCBarName As String, _
        strCtlCaption As String) As Boolean
    Dim ctlCBarControl As CommandBarControl
    On Error Resume Next

    Set ctlCBarControl = Application.ActiveExplorer _
        .CommandBars(strCBarName).Controls(strCtlCaption)
    ctlCBarControl.Visible = Not ctlCBarControl.Visible
    If Err = 0 Then
        CBCtlToggleVisible = True
    Else
        CBCtlToggleVisible = False
    End If
End Function
```

The Visible property is not the only factor that determines whether a specific menu item is visible on a given menu. If personalized menus are turned on with the AdaptiveMenus property, you can use the IsPriorityDropped property to determine whether a menu item is visible on the command bar. If the control's Visible property is set to True, the control will not be immediately visible on a personalized menu if IsPriorityDropped is True.

> **Note** To determine when to set IsPriorityDropped to True for a specific menu item, Outlook counts the number of times the menu item was used and records the different application sessions in which the user employs another menu item in the same menu as this menu item, without using the specific menu item itself. When this value reaches a threshold, the count is decreased. When the count reaches zero, IsPriorityDropped is set to True. You cannot set the session value, the threshold value, or the IsPriorityDropped property. You can, however, use the AdaptiveMenus property to disable adaptive menus for specific menus in an application.

Determining the State of a Control

The State property of a control tells you whether a button control is in the down or up position. The State property is read-only for built-in controls. A good example of a built-in control that displays state is the Folder List control on the Advanced toolbar. When the control's state equals msoButtonDown, the button is depressed on the toolbar. If the control's state equals msoButtonUp, the button is not depressed on the toolbar. This code examines the state of the Folder List button on the Advanced toolbar:

```
Function DisplayFolderListState()
    Dim ctlCBarButton As CommandBarButton
    Set ctlCBarButton = Application.ActiveExplorer _
        .CommandBars("Advanced").Controls("Folder List")
    Select Case ctlCBarButton.State
        Case msoButtonUp
            MsgBox "Folder List Hidden", vbInformation
        Case msoButtonDown
            MsgBox "Folder List visible", vbInformation
    End Select
End Function
```

Adding Separators Between Controls

If you want to add a separator between buttons on a command bar, set the BeginGroup property for the control to True. Group separators on a toolbar provide important visual clues for the user about the relationship of controls. The following example adds a group separator before the Choose Form control on the Items toolbar:

```
Set cmdNewButton = cbrNewToolbar.Controls.Add _
    (Type:=msoControlButton, ID:=1910) 'Choose Form...
cmdNewButton.BeginGroup = True          'Group Separator
```

Finding a Control

To find a control on a built-in or custom command bar, use the *FindControl* method. The *FindControl* method takes several arguments that facilitate your search. The following example performs a nonrecursive search of the Standard toolbar for the Find A Contact combo box. If a control with a type of msoControlComboBox is found on the Standard toolbar and that control's caption is Find A Contact, the Text property of the combo box is set to the name of a contact. Setting the combo box Text property causes Outlook to search for the contact name as though a user had actually typed a name into the combo box. If the search completes successfully, Outlook displays the Inspector for the contact item.

```
Sub ContactFindMethod()
    Dim ctlCBarCombo As CommandBarComboBox
    Dim cbrMenuBar As CommandBar
    On Error Resume Next
    Set cbrMenuBar = Application.ActiveExplorer.CommandBars("Standard")
    Set ctlCBarCombo = _
        cbrMenuBar.FindControl (Type:=msoControlComboBox, Recursive:=False)
    If ctlCBarCombo = "Find a Contact" Then 'Caption is default property
        ctlCBarCombo.Text = "Susan Chainey"
    End If
End Sub
```

Using Control Events

Command bar controls raise two separate events: Click and Change. You can use these events in place of the OnAction property to run an event procedure when a user action or program code causes an event to fire. The table on the following page displays the control and command bar events.

Using Visual Basic, VBA, or VBScript with Outlook   Chapter 11

Event	Source Object	Occurs
OnUpdate	CommandBars	When any change occurs to a built-in or custom command bar, or to the state of a control on a command bar.
Click	CommandBarButton	When a button or menu item is clicked.
Change	CommandBarComboBox	When a user makes a selection in a drop-down list box or a combo box. The Change event also occurs when text is changed in an edit box.

> **More Info**   Be aware that you cannot use control events when writing VBScript code in an Outlook custom form. In this case, you must use the OnAction property to specify the Sub procedure in your code that runs when a toolbar button is clicked.

To write an event procedure for a command bar control

1. Declare an object variable by using the *WithEvents* keyword in the declarations section of ThisOutlookSession or in the class module for your COM Add-in project.
2. Select the object in the Object box of the class module's code window.
3. Select the event name in the Procedure box of the class module's code window.
4. Write event procedure code to respond to the Click or Change event.

The CommandBarButton Object

The CommandBarButton object represents a button control on a command bar. We have already discussed in detail many of the properties and methods of the CommandBarButton object. For additional information, search for CommandBarButton in Outlook Visual Basic Reference Help. The Outlook 2000 and Outlook 2002 Explorer and Inspector command bars offer major improvements over command bars in previous versions of Outlook. You can create custom command bars for an Inspector in a previous version of Outlook if you use the Office 97 CommandBars object. However, custom command bars in Outlook 97 and Outlook 98 do not persist between Outlook sessions and cannot be created for

457

Part IV Beyond the Basics

the Explorer window. You can use the *Execute* method to cause built-in commands to run, but the functionality and customization potential of toolbars is limited in previous versions of Outlook.

> **Note** For additional information regarding command bars in previous versions of Outlook, see the following articles in the Microsoft Knowledge Base:
> - Q173604-OL97: How to Use Command Bars in Outlook Solutions
> - Q182394-OL98: How to Use Command Bars in Outlook Solutions

The CommandBarComboBox Object

The CommandBarComboBox object represents a Combo box or an Edit box control on a command bar. When you add the combo box to a command bar, you specify the type of combo box in the *Add* method. The following table lists some of the unique properties, methods, and events of a CommandBarComboBox object.

Type	Name	Description
Property	DropDownLines	Returns or sets the number of items displayed in the drop-down list box. If the number of items in the list is greater than DropDownLines, a scroll bar appears in the drop-down list box.
	DropDownWidth	Returns or sets the width in pixels of the combo box drop-down.
	ListCount	Returns the number of items in the list.
	ListIndex	Returns or sets the index of the selected item in the list.
	Text	Returns or sets the text in the edit portion of the control.
Method	*AddItem*	Adds an item to the list.
	Clear	Clears the items in the list.
	RemoveItem	Removes an item from the list.
Event	Change	Occurs when a user changes the selection in a combo box or the text in an edit box.

The CommandBarPopup Object

The CommandBarPopup object represents a pop-up control on a command bar. Pop-up controls are unique in that every control contains a CommandBar property object. You can use the CommandBar object to access the child controls of a CommandBarPopup object. The following example uses the CommandBar property object to add additional buttons to the pop-up control:

```
Set ctlCBarPopup = cbTesting.Controls.Add(Type:=msoControlPopup)
Set cbTestPopup = ctlCBarPopup.CommandBar
Set ctlCBarControl = cbTestPopup.Controls.Add(Type:=msoControlButton)
ctlCBarControl.Caption = "Red"
Set ctlCBarControl = cbTestPopup.Controls.Add(Type:=msoControlButton)
ctlCBarControl.Caption = "Green"
Set ctlCBarControl = cbTestPopup.Controls.Add(Type:=msoControlButton)
ctlCBarControl.Caption = "Blue"
With ctlCBarPopup
    .Caption = "Test Popup"
End With
```

The AddressLists Collection Object

Outlook users often have several address books from which they can select recipients for a message. The AddressLists collection object contains all the address books available to a user. Using the AddressLists object, you can reference one or more AddressList objects, each of which represents a single address book.

> **Important** Open the AddressLists collection object, AddressEntries collection object, and the AddressEntry object items in the VBScript Samples folder to work directly with this code in Outlook.

The AddressLists collection object is always referenced from the NameSpace object.

AddressLists Collection Methods

This section covers the *Item* method of the AddressLists collection object.

Iterating Through a Collection of Address Lists

You can use the *Item* method of the AddressLists collection object to iterate through a collection of address books. The following example uses the Count property of the AddressLists collection object to determine the number of AddressList objects referenced by the collection. It then uses the *Item* method of the AddressLists collection object to return and display the name of each address book.

```
Sub ShowAddressLists_Click
    Set MyNameSpace = Application.GetNameSpace("MAPI")
    Set MyAddressLists = MyNameSpace.AddressLists
    MsgBox "There are " & MyAddressLists.Count & " address lists.", _
      vbInformation
    For i = 1 to MyAddressLists.Count
        Set MyAddressList = MyAddressLists.Item(i)
        MsgBox MyAddressList.Name & " is " & i & " of " _
          & MyAddressLists.Count, vbInformation
    Next
End Sub
```

The AddressList Object

The AddressList object represents a single Outlook address book that contains a set of AddressEntry objects. The AddressEntry objects, in turn, can be accessed through the AddressEntries property of the AddressList object.

> **Outlook Security** If your code attempts to access an AddressEntries collection object or an AddressEntry object, the Warning dialog box shown in Figure 11-4 (on page 429) will be displayed. See Chapter 13 for methods to eliminate the Warning dialog box.

The AddressEntries Collection Object

The AddressEntries collection object is provided by the AddressEntries property of the AddressList object. It provides access to each of the AddressEntry objects contained within a given address book.

AddressEntries Collection Methods

This section covers the *Add* and *Item* methods of the AddressEntries collection object.

Adding an Address Entry

You can use the *Add* method of the AddressEntries collection object to create a new item in an address book. The following example uses the *Add* method to create a new entry in the Personal Address Book. The *Update* method of the AddressEntry object is required to commit the new item to the address book.

```
Sub AddAddressEntry_Click
    On Error Resume Next
    Set MyNameSpace = Application.GetNameSpace("MAPI")
    Set MyAddressList = MyNameSpace.AddressLists("Personal Address Book")
    If MyAddressList Is Nothing Then
        MsgBox "Personal Address Book Unavailable!", vbExclamation
        Exit Sub
    End If
    Set MyEntries = MyAddressList.AddressEntries
    Set myEntry = MyEntries.Add _
        ("SMTP","James Allard","jamesallard@microsoft.com")
    myEntry.Update
End Sub
```

Iterating Through a Collection of Address Entries

You can use the *Item* method of the AddressEntries collection object to iterate through the items in an address book. The following example uses the Count property of the AddressEntries collection object to return the number of items in the user's Personal Address Book. It also uses the *Item* method of the AddressEntries collection object to return each item in the address book and then display its name.

```
Sub ShowAddressEntries_Click
    On Error Resume Next
    Set MyPage = Item.GetInspector.ModifiedFormPages _
        ("AddressEntries Collection")
    Set ListBox1 = MyPage.Controls("ListBox1")
    Set MyNameSpace = Application.GetNameSpace("MAPI")
    Set MyAddressList = MyNameSpace.AddressLists("Personal Address Book")
    If MyAddressList Is Nothing Then
        MsgBox "Personal Address Book Unavailable!", vbExclamation
        Exit Sub
    End If
    Set MyAddressEntries = MyAddressList.AddressEntries
    For i = 1 to MyAddressEntries.Count
        Set MyEntry = MyAddressEntries.Item(i)
        ListBox1.AddItem MyEntry.Name
    Next
End Sub
```

Part IV   Beyond the Basics

The AddressEntry Object

The AddressEntry object represents an individual item in an address book. The AddressEntry object contains information about one or more individuals or processes to which the messaging system can send messages. If the AddressEntry object represents a distribution list—that is, if its DisplayType property is set to olDistList or olPrivateDistList—it can contain additional AddressEntry objects that can be accessed through its Members property.

AddressEntry Object Methods

This section covers the *Details*, *Update*, *Delete*, and *GetFreeBusy* methods of the AddressEntry object.

Displaying Details of an Address Entry

The *Details* method of the AddressEntry object displays a modal dialog box that lets a user see (and, if permissions allow, change) the information stored in the Address Book item represented by the object.

The following example steps through the items in a user's Personal Address Book, using the *Details* method to display the information contained in each item. If the user clicks OK in the dialog box, the next entry is displayed. If the user clicks the Cancel button in the dialog box, an error is produced. For this reason, an On Error statement is included to prevent the routine from exiting immediately, and the *Err global* variable is tested to determine if it is not zero (which would indicate that the user clicked Cancel or that an error had occurred).

```
Sub DisplayEntryDetails_Click
    On Error Resume Next
    Set MyNameSpace = Application.GetNameSpace("MAPI")
    Set MyAddressList = MyNameSpace.AddressLists("Personal Address Book")
    If MyAddressList Is Nothing Then
        MsgBox "Personal Address Book Unavailable!", vbExclamation
        Exit Sub
    End If
    Set MyAddressEntries = MyAddressList.AddressEntries
    On Error Resume Next
    For i = 1 to MyAddressEntries.Count
        Set MyEntry = MyAddressEntries.Item(i)
        MyEntry.Details
        If err <> 0 Then Exit Sub
    Next
End Sub
```

Changing an Address Entry

If you have the appropriate permissions, you can change the Address, Name, and Type properties of an AddressEntry object. To commit the change to the address book, you use the object's *Update* method. The following example converts the Name property of an AddressEntry object to all uppercase characters:

```
Sub ChangeAddressEntry_Click
    On Error Resume Next
    Set MyNameSpace = Application.GetNameSpace("MAPI")
    Set MyAddressList = MyNameSpace.AddressLists("Personal Address Book")
    If MyAddressList Is Nothing Then
        MsgBox "Personal Address Book Unavailable!", vbExclamation
        Exit Sub
    End If
    Set MyEntries = MyAddressList.AddressEntries
    Set MyEntry = MyEntries.Item(1)
    MyEntry.Name = Ucase(MyEntry.Name)
    MyEntry.Update
End Sub
```

Deleting an Address Entry

The *Delete* method of the AddressEntry object removes an item from the address book. The following example steps through the items in the Personal Address Book and deletes the first item where the type is set to Sample:

```
Sub DeleteAddressEntry_Click
    On Error Resume Next
    Set MyNameSpace = Application.GetNameSpace("MAPI")
    Set MyAddressList = MyNameSpace.AddressLists("Personal Address Book")
    If MyAddressList Is Nothing Then
        MsgBox "Personal Address Book Unavailable!", vbExclamation
        Exit Sub
    End If
    Set MyEntries = MyAddressList.AddressEntries
    MsgBox "Adding a sample entry...", vbInformation
    Set MyEntry = MyEntries.Add ("SAMPLE","Sample Entry","sampleentry")
    MyEntry.Update
    MyEntry.Details
    Set MyEntry = MyEntries.GetFirst
    Do While TypeName(MyEntry) <> "Nothing"
        If MyEntry.Type = "SAMPLE" Then
            MsgBox "Deleting "& MyEntry, vbCritical
            MyEntry.Delete
        Exit Sub
        End If
        Set MyEntry = MyEntries.GetNext
    Loop
    MsgBox "No sample entries found.", vbInformation
End Sub
```

Getting Free/Busy Information for a User

You can determine whether someone is available at a given time using the *GetFreeBusy* method of the AddressEntry object. This method returns a string representing 30 days of free/busy information starting at midnight on a specified date. Each character in the string is a digit that indicates whether the person is available during a specified time period. You can specify that the string should indicate only whether the person is available, or you can specify that you want the string to indicate whether a busy time is marked as tentative or out of office.

For example, the following code example returns a string 1440 characters long (48 half-hour periods over 30 days) containing 0 for each half-hour period the person is free, 1 for each period the person has a busy time marked tentative, 3 for each period the person has a busy time marked out of office, and 2 for other busy periods:

```
MyStatus = MyAddressEntry.GetFreeBusy("7/1/98",30,True)
```

The following code example returns a string 720 characters long (24 one-hour periods over 30 days) containing 0 for each hour the person is free and 1 for each hour the person is busy, regardless of how the busy periods are designated:

```
MyStatus = MyAddressEntry.GetFreeBusy("7/1/98",60,False)
```

The following example displays the next time a person is busy. In addition to Outlook objects and methods, it uses the following VBScript functions:

- **InputBox** To prompt the user for the name of the person whose first busy time is to be checked.

- **Date** To retrieve the current date.

- **FormatDateTime** To convert the retrieved date to the format required by GetFreeBusy.

- **InStr** To determine the location (offset) of the first 1 character in the string returned by GetFreeBusy.

```
Sub GetFreeBusyInformation_Click
    On Error Resume Next
    Set MyNameSpace = Application.GetNameSpace("MAPI")
    Set MyAddressList = MyNameSpace.AddressLists("Global Address List")
    If MyAddressList Is Nothing Then
        MsgBox "Global Address List Unavailable!", vbExclamation
        Exit Sub
    End If
```

```
    Set MyEntries = MyAddressList.AddressEntries
    MyName = InputBox("Find first busy time for:")
    If MyName <> "" then
        Set MyEntry = MyEntries(MyName)
        If Err Then
            MsgBox "Could not find " & MyName, vbCritical
        Exit Sub
        End If
        StartDate = FormatDateTime(Date,2)
        MyBusyTime = MyEntry.GetFreeBusy(StartDate,60)
        MsgBox MyEntry.Name & " is busy " & InStr(MyBusyTime,"1")-1 _
            & " hours after 12:00 am " & StartDate
    End If
End Sub
```

AddressEntry Properties

You can use such properties as Name, Address, Members, Type, and Manager to retrieve useful information contained in the item.

> **More Info** For a complete list and description of the methods and properties for the AddressEntry object, see Microsoft Outlook Visual Basic Reference Help.

The following example uses the Members, Name, and Address properties of the AddressEntry object to display the name and address of each member of a private distribution list named Department:

```
Sub DisplayListMembers_Click
    On Error Resume Next
    Set MyNameSpace = Application.GetNameSpace("MAPI")
    Set MyAddressList = MyNameSpace.AddressLists("Personal Address Book")
    If MyAddressList Is Nothing Then
        MsgBox "Personal Address Book Unavailable!", vbExclamation
        Exit Sub
    End If
    MyName = InputBox("Display entries in this Personal Distribution List:")
    If MyName <> "" Then
        Set MyDistList = MyAddressList.AddressEntries(MyName)
        If Err Then
            MsgBox "Could not find " & MyName, vbCritical
            Exit Sub
        End If
```

(continued)

```
        Set MyAddressEntries = MyDistList.Members
        For i = 1 to MyAddressEntries.Count
            Set MyEntry = MyAddressEntries.Item(i)
            MsgBox MyEntry.Name & " " & MyEntry.Address
        Next
    End If
End Sub
```

Using CDO to Obtain Recipients

Collaboration Data Objects (CDO) is an object model that assists in building messaging and collaboration applications. CDO serves as a complementary object model to manipulate MAPI folders and items from Visual Basic or VBScript code. You can use CDO to access messaging objects which are not available in the Outlook Object Model. For example, the Address procedure shown next lets you present an AddressBook dialog box to the user. When the user makes recipient selections from the AddressBook dialog box, the resolved recipient names are stored in the user-defined field CDORecipients on the AddressEntry object example form in the VBScript Samples folder.

> **Outlook Security** Access to Recipients, AddressEntries, and AddressEntry objects is also blocked in the CDO Object Model by the Outlook E-Mail Security Update component of Outlook 2002. Unlike blocked Outlook objects, properties, and methods, you cannot create trusted CDO code that eliminates the Warning dialog boxes using the Administrative form in public folders. However, there are third-party alternatives for accessing CDO properties, methods, and objects in a trusted context.

```
Sub GetRecipients_Click()
    Address "CDORecipients", "Recipients"
End Sub

Sub Address(strUDFieldName, strShortName)
    Dim i
    Dim strRecip
    On Error Resume Next
    strDialogCaption = "Select " & strUDFieldName
    Set objCDO = Application.CreateObject("MAPI.Session")
    'Piggyback on existing Outlook session
    objCDO.Logon "", "", False, False, 0
    If Err Then
```

Using Visual Basic, VBA, or VBScript with Outlook   Chapter 11

```
        MsgBox "Could not establish CDO session!", vbCritical
    End If
    Set Recips = objCDO.AddressBook(Nothing, _
        strDialogCaption, False, True, 1, strShortName, "", "", 0)
    'These recipients have been resolved by forceResolution argument above
    If Not Err Then
        For i = 1 To Recips.Count
            strRecip = strRecip & Recips(i).Name & "; "
        Next
        If strRecip <> "" Then
            strRecip = Left(strRecip, Len(strRecip)-2)
            Userproperties(strUDFieldName) = strRecip
        End If
    End If
    objCDO.Logoff
End Sub
```

Installing Collaboration Data Objects

Unfortunately, CDO is not installed by default with Outlook 2002. This practice reverses Microsoft's default CDO installation for Outlook 98. CDO provides functionality for many of the examples in this book and must be installed for the examples to operate correctly. The setup program for the companion CD automatically installs CDO, or CDO can be installed manually.

To install Collaboration Data Objects

1. Insert the Office XP CD-ROM into your CD-ROM drive.
2. Click Start, click Settings, and then click Control Panel.
3. Double-click Add/Remove Programs.
4. On the Install/Uninstall page, click Microsoft Office XP and then click Add/Remove.
5. In the Microsoft Office XP Maintenance Mode dialog box, click Add Or Remove Features.
6. Double-click the Microsoft Outlook For Windows item to expand the item in the Microsoft Office XP: Update Features dialog box.
7. Click the Collaboration Data Objects item under Microsoft Outlook For Windows to expand the item.
8. Select Run From My Computer.
9. Click Update Now to complete the installation of Collaboration Data Objects.

467

Part IV Beyond the Basics

The Folders Collection Object

The Outlook Object Model provides two folder objects: a Folders collection object and a MAPIFolder object. The Folders collection object represents multiple folders. The MAPIFolder object, covered later in this chapter, represents a single folder.

The Folders collection object can contain single or multiple folders. The Folders collection object is always referenced from the NameSpace object.

> **More Info** For a complete list and description of the properties, methods, and events for the Folders collection object, see Microsoft Outlook Visual Basic Reference Help.

Folders Collection Methods

This section covers the *Add* and *Item* methods of the Folders collection object.

Adding a Folder to the Folder List

You can use the *Add* method of the Folders collection object to add a folder to the Folder List. The following example uses the *Add* method of the Folders collection object to add a folder called My New Folder to the Building Microsoft Outlook 2002 Applications personal folder (.pst) file:

```
Sub CommandButton1_Click
    Set MyNameSpace = Application.GetNameSpace("MAPI")
    Set MyFolder = MyNameSpace.Folders _
        ("Building Microsoft Outlook 2002 Applications")
    Set MyNewFolder = MyFolder.Folders.Add("My New Folder")
End Sub
```

Iterating Through a Collection of Folders

You can use the *Item* method of the Folders collection object to iterate through a collection of folders. The following example uses the Count property of the Folders collection object to return the number of folder items in the Folders collection. It also uses the *Item* method of the Folders collection object to return each folder in the collection and then display its name. You can also use the For Each…Next syntax to iterate over the objects in a collection object.

```
Sub IterateThroughAFolderCollection_Click
    Set myNameSpace = Application.GetNameSpace("MAPI")
```

```
    Set myFolders = myNameSpace.Folders _
        ("Building Microsoft Outlook 2002 Applications")
    Set MyCollection = myFolders.Folders
    For i = 1 to MyCollection.Count
        set MyFolder = myCollection.Item(i)
        MsgBox MyFolder.Name, vbInformation
    Next
    'For Each...Next provides alternative syntax
    'For Each MyFolder in MyCollection
        'MsgBox MyFolder.Name, vbInformation
    'Next
End Sub
```

> **Note** When iterating through a collection of folders or items, the folders or items are not always ordered in the collection based on the date they are received in the folder. If your code depends on a particular order in the collection, use the *Sort* method of the collection object to control the order of the collection.

The MAPIFolder Object

The MAPIFolder object represents a single Outlook folder. A MAPIFolder object can contain other MAPIFolder objects, as well as Outlook items. This section explains how to move through the Folder List by using the MAPIFolder object and its Folders property.

> **More Info** For a complete list and description of the properties, methods, and events for the MAPIFolder object, see Microsoft Outlook Visual Basic Reference Help.

> **Important** Open the MAPIFolder object item in the VBScript Samples folder to work directly with this code in Outlook.

MAPIFolder Object Methods

This section covers the *CopyTo* and *Display* methods of the MAPIFolder object.

Copying a Folder

You can use the *CopyTo* method of the MAPIFolder object to create a copy of a folder in another folder. The following example copies the Notes folder to the Inbox:

```
Sub CommandButton1_Click
    Set MyNameSpace = Application.GetNameSpace("MAPI")
    Set MyInboxFolder = MyNameSpace.GetDefaultFolder(6)
    Set MyCurrentFolder = MyNameSpace.GetDefaultFolder(12)
    Set MyNewFolder = MyCurrentFolder.CopyTo(MyInboxFolder)
End Sub
```

Displaying a Folder

You can use the *Display* method of the MAPIFolder object to display the folder represented by the MAPIFolder object, as shown here:

```
Sub DisplayAFolder_Click
    On Error Resume Next
    Set MyNameSpace = Application.GetNameSpace("MAPI")
    Set MyFolder = MyNameSpace.Folders("Public Folders")
    If MyFolder Is Nothing Then
        MsgBox "Public Folders folder not found", vbCritical
            Exit Sub
    End If
    MyFolder.Display
End Sub
```

MAPIFolder Object Properties

This section covers the DefaultMessageClass, FolderPath, Folders, InAppFolderSyncObject, Items, Parent, Child, EntryID, StoreID, UnReadItemCount, and WebViewURL properties. The Folders property is useful for accessing a folder in the folder list. The Items property is useful for retrieving a collection of items in the folder.

Referencing a Folder in the Folder List

You can use the Folders property with the MAPIFolder object to return another MAPIFolder object. The *OpenMAPIFolder* function shown on page 473 is a more efficient way to return a folder in the folder list, compared with the folder-by-folder method illustrated here. In the following procedure, the Folders property is used to move through the various branches of a personal folders list:

```
Sub ReferenceAFolder_Click
    Set MyNameSpace = Application.GetNameSpace("MAPI")
    Set MyFolder = MyNameSpace.Folders _
        ("Building Microsoft Outlook 2002 Applications")
    Set BeyondFolder = MyFolder.Folders("4. Beyond the Basics")
    Set VBScriptFolder = BeyondFolder.Folders("VBScript")
    MsgBox VBScriptFolder.Name, vbInformation
End Sub
```

Iterating Through a Collection of Items in a Folder

You can use the Items property of the MAPIFolder object to return a collection of items in the folder. The following example uses the Items property of the MAPIFolder object to return the collection of items in the Inbox folder. It then shows the Subject value of the first five items in the Items collection.

```
Sub IterateThroughACollectionofItems_Click()
  On Error Resume Next
  Set MyNameSpace = Application.GetNameSpace("MAPI")
  Set MyInboxFolder = MyNameSpace.GetDefaultFolder(6)
  Set MyItems = MyInboxFolder.Items
  For i = 1 to 5
      Set MyItem = MyItems(i)
      Msgbox MyItem.Subject, vbInformation
  Next
End Sub
```

The EntryID and StoreID Properties

The EntryID and StoreID properties of the MAPIFolder object can be used to identify a folder in Outlook. The EntryID property corresponds to the MAPI property PR_ENTRYID. When an object is created, MAPI systems assign a permanent, unique ID string which does not change from one MAPI session to another. The EntryID and StoreID properties, which are analogous to primary keys in a database table, let you identify both Folder and Item objects in the MAPI subsystem. Once you have these values, you can use the *GetFolderFromID* method to return a MAPIFolder object.

The following example displays the value of the MAPI EntryID and StoreID for the current folder in a message box, displays another message box showing the folder's UnReadItemCount, DefaultMessageClass, and WebViewURL, and then uses the *GetFolderFromID* method to re-instantiate the Folder object and display the folder:

```
Sub ShowFolderInfo_Click
    Set MyNameSpace = Application.GetNameSpace("MAPI")
    Set MyFolder = MyNameSpace.PickFolder
    If MyFolder Is Nothing Then
```

(continued)

```
            MsgBox "User pressed cancel.", vbInformation
            Exit Sub
        End If
        MsgBox "The Entry ID for the selected folder is:" & vbCr _
            & MyFolder.EntryID & vbCr & vbCr _
            & "The Store ID for the selected folder is:" & vbCr _
            & MyFolder.StoreID, vbInformation
        MsgBox MyFolder.UnReadItemCount & " of " & MyFolder.Items.Count _
            & " items are unread." & vbCr _
            & "The default message class is: _
            & MyFolder.DefaultMessageClass & vbCr _
            & "The folder URL is: " & MyFolder.WebViewURL, vbInformation
        Set MyFolder = MyNameSpace.GetFolderFromID _
            (MyFolder.EntryID, MyFolder.StoreID)
        MyFolder.Display
    End Sub
```

Making a Folder Available for Offline Use

You can programmatically make a folder available for offline use by using the InAppFolderSyncObject property. Somewhat mysteriously named, the InAppFolderSyncObject property determines whether the folder will be added to the Application Folders Send/Receive group. For additional information on Send/Receive groups and offline use, see Chapter 8, "Folders." The following code example adds the Top Accounts folder to the Application Folders group and starts a synchronization programmatically:

```
Sub SyncTopAccounts()
    Dim objFolder As Outlook.MAPIFolder
    Dim objAppSync As SyncObject
    Dim objOutlook As Outlook.Application
    Set objOutlook = CreateObject("Outlook.Application")
    Set objFolder = objOutlook.GetNamespace("MAPI") _
        .GetDefaultFolder(olFolderInbox)
    Set objFolder = objFolder.Folders("Top Accounts")
    objFolder.InAppFolderSyncObject = True
    Set objAppSync = ThisOutlookSession.GetNamespace("MAPI") _
        .SyncObjects.AppFolders
    objAppSync.Start
End Sub
```

Returning a Folder from a Folder Path

The OpenMAPIFolder procedure allows you to return a MAPIFolder object if you supply a folder path as an argument. A folder path is expressed as follows:

```
Set objFolder = OpenMAPIFolder _
    ("\Public Folders\All Public Folders\Sales\Q401")
```

```
Function OpenMAPIFolder(ByVal strPath) 'As MAPIFolder
    Dim objFldr 'As MAPIFolder
    Dim strDir 'As String
    Dim strName 'As String
    Dim i 'As Integer
    On Error Resume Next
    If Left(strPath, Len("\")) = "\" Then
        strPath = Mid(strPath, Len("\") + 1)
    Else
        Set objFldr = Application.ActiveExplorer.CurrentFolder
    End If
    While strPath <> ""
        i = InStr(strPath, "\")
        If i Then
            strDir = Left(strPath, i - 1)
            strPath = Mid(strPath, i + Len("\"))
        Else
            strDir = strPath
            strPath = ""
        End If
        If objFldr Is Nothing then
            Set objFldr = Application.GetNameSpace("MAPI").Folders(strDir)
            On Error Goto 0
        Else
            Set objFldr = objFldr.Folders(strDir)
        End If
    Wend
    Set OpenMAPIFolder = objFldr
End Function
```

> **Note** The type declarations have been commented out in the *OpenMAPIFolder* and *GetFolderPath* functions. If you want to use these functions in VBA or Visual Basic code, remove the comment marks.

Returning a Folder Path from a Folder

If you are using a version of Outlook prior to Outlook 2002, the GetFolderPath function allows you to return a string representing a folder path if you supply a MAPIFolder object as an argument. If you are using Outlook 2002, you simply use the FolderPath property of the MAPIFolder object to return a string that contains the folder path.

Part IV Beyond the Basics

```
Function GetFolderPath(ByVal objFolder) 'As String
    On Error Resume Next
    Dim strFolderPath 'As String
    Dim objChild 'As MAPIFolder
    Dim objParent 'As MAPIFolder
    strFolderPath = "\" & objFolder.Name
    Set objChild = objFolder
    Do Until Err <> 0
        Set objParent = objChild.Parent
        If Err <> 0 Then
            Exit Do
        End If
        strFolderPath = "\" & objParent.Name & strFolderPath
        Set objChild = objParent
    Loop
    GetFolderPath = strFolderPath
End Function
```

Displaying a Folder Web View

One of the exciting features of Outlook is the ability to display Web views in the Explorer View pane. The following example sets the WebViewURL for your Drafts folder to the MSDN Online Exchange Developer Center and then displays the Web view of the folder. The WebViewOn property is then set to *False* to restore the default view on the folder.

```
Sub DisplayFolderWebView_Click
    On Error Resume Next
    Set MyNS = Application.GetNameSpace("MAPI")
    Set MyFolder = MyNS.GetDefaultFolder(16) 'Drafts folder
    MyFolder.WebViewURL = "http://msdn.microsoft.com/exchange"
    MyFolder.WebViewOn = True
    MyFolder.Display
    MsgBox "Click OK to Reset Web View", vbInformation
    MyFolder.WebViewOn = False 'Reset
    'Re-instantiate the MAPIFolder object
    Set MyFolder = MyNS.GetDefaultFolder(16) 'Drafts folder
    MyFolder.Display
End Sub
```

New Outlook 2002 Folder Properties

In addition to the InAppFolderSyncObject property discussed previously, Outlook 2002 adds some MAPIFolder properties that are worth noting. The ShowAsOutlookAddressBook property determines whether a Contacts folder will be displayed as an Outlook Address Book. If the folder is not a Contacts folder, setting the property has no effect. The AddToPFFavorites property adds a public folder to the Favorites folder so that it's available for offline use. The following example adds a folder named Classified Ads to the Favorites folder:

```
Sub AddClassifiedToPFFavorites()
    Dim oFolder As Outlook.MAPIFolder
    Dim oApp As Outlook.Application
    Set oOutlook = CreateObject("Outlook.Application")
    Set oFolder = _
       oApp.GetNamespace("MAPI") _
          .GetDefaultFolder(olPublicFoldersAllPublicFolders)
    Set oFolder = objFolder.Folders("Classified Ads")
    oFolder.AddToPFFavorites
End Sub
```

The Views Collection Object

The Views collection object, which is new in Outlook 2002, is a property object of the MAPIFolder object. You can use the Views collection object to enumerate the Views in a folder or to obtain a child View object and change the View programmatically. You can also use the *Add* method to add a View to a folder. The following example creates a View named Larger View in the CurrentFolder object of the ActiveExplorer object. For a more thorough explanation of modifying Views programmatically with the XML DOM (eXtensible Markup Language Document Object Model), see the Outlook View Wizard example in Chapter 14.

```
Sub CreateLargerView()
    Dim objView As Outlook.View
    Dim colViews As Outlook.Views
    Dim objXMLDOM As New MSXML2.DOMDocument30
    Dim objNode As MSXML2.IXMLDOMNode
    Dim objOutlook As Outlook.Application
    Dim objActExpl As Outlook.Explorer
    Set objOutlook = CreateObject("Outlook.Application")
    'Get the Active Explorer
    Set objActExpl = objOutlook.ActiveExplorer
    'Obtain the Views collection for the current folder
    Set colViews = objActExpl.CurrentFolder.Views
    'Create a new view named Larger View
    Set objView = colViews.Add _
       ("Larger View", _
        olTableView, _
        olViewSaveOptionThisFolderEveryone)
    'Load the XML for the new view into XML DOM object
    objXMLDOM.loadXML (objView.XML)
    'This is the element that we will modify
    strElement = "view/rowstyle"
```

(continued)

Part IV Beyond the Basics

```
        'Get the node object for view/rowstyle
        Set objNode = objXMLDOM.selectSingleNode(strElement)
        'Change the font size to 14pt
        objNode.nodeTypedValue = "font-size:14pt"
        'Assign the XML for View to objXML.XML
        objView.XML = objXMLDOM.XML
        'Save the View
        objView.Save
        'Apply the View in the folder
        objView.Apply
End Sub
```

The Items Collection Object

Items are the discrete packages of information represented by a Mail Message, a Post item, a Contact item, a Distribution List item, a Document item, a Journal item, a Meeting Request, a Note, or a Task item. You use the Items property to return the Items collection of a MAPIFolder object. The single item object is represented by the following objects:

- **AppointmentItem object**   An Appointment item.
- **ContactItem object**   A Contact item.
- **DistListItem object**   A Distribution List item.
- **DocumentItem object**   A Document item.
- **JournalItem object**   A Journal item.
- **MailItem object**   A Mail Message item.
- **MeetingItem object**   A Meeting item.
- **NoteItem object**   A Note item.
- **PostItem object**   A Post item.
- **ReportItem object**   A Mail delivery report item.
- **TaskItem object**   A Task item.
- **TaskRequestAcceptItem**   An item sent to accept a Task request.
- **TaskRequestDeclineItem**   An item sent to decline a Task request.
- **TaskRequestItem**   An item sent to assign a Task.
- **TaskRequestUpdateItem**   An item sent to update a Task request.

This section covers some of the methods and properties of the Items collection object. Sections that follow this section—beginning with "The PostItem Object" on page 481—cover the methods and properties of specific Item objects.

> **More Info** For a complete list and description of the properties, methods, and events for the Items collection object, see Microsoft Outlook Visual Basic Reference Help.

> **Important** Open the Items collection object item in the VBScript Samples folder to work directly with this code in Outlook.

Items Collection Object Methods

This section covers the *Add*, *Find*, and *Restrict* methods of the Items collection object.

Creating a Custom Item

With Outlook, there are two basic methods of creating items. Standard items such as Message items (IPM.Note), Post items (IPM.Post), and Contact items (IPM.Contact) are created using the *CreateItem* method of the Application object, as discussed earlier in this chapter.

To create custom items, however, such as an IPM.Post.Product Idea item, you use the *Add* method of the Items collection object. For example, to create a Product Idea item (IPM.Post.Product Idea) for the Product Ideas folder, you must first return the Items collection object, and then use the *Add* method of the Items collection object to add the new item to the collection. The custom item has the methods and properties of the item upon which is it based. For example, an item with the message class IPM.Post.Product Idea contains the methods and properties of the PostItem object, in addition to the custom UserProperties defined for IPM.Post.Product Idea. If you create an item with the message class IPM.Note.Orders, you use the MailItem object.

> **Important** Before you can create a custom item, the form associated with the item must exist in the forms library of the folder in which the item is created. For example, to create a Product Idea item, the Product Idea form must exist in the Product Ideas Folder forms library or in the Personal or Organizational Forms Libraries.

The following example references the Product Ideas folder and then creates a Product Idea item and displays it. Note that the Product Idea form exists in the Product Ideas folder forms library.

```
Sub CreateACustomItem_Click()
    Set MyNameSpace = Application.GetNameSpace("MAPI")
    Set BldFolder = MyNameSpace.Folders _
    ("Building Microsoft Outlook 2002 Applications")
    Set QuickFolder = BldFolder.Folders("2. Quick Guide")
    Set ProductIdeasFolder = QuickFolder.Folders("Product Ideas")
    Set MyItems = ProductIdeasFolder.Items
    Set MyItem = MyItems.Add("IPM.Post.Product Idea")
    MyItem.Subject = "VBScript Test"
    MyItem.Body = "This is a test"
    MyItem.Display
End Sub
```

> **Important** Note that in the preceding procedure, the Body property of the single Item object corresponds with the Message field on the form. For more details about the properties of standard items, see "MailItem and PostItem Objects Properties" later in this chapter.

Finding an Item in a Folder

You can use the *Find* method of the Items collection object to find an item in a folder based on the conditions you specify.

> **Important** If you are using user-defined fields as part of a restriction argument of a *Find* or *Restrict* method, the user-defined fields must exist in the folder; otherwise, the code will raise an error and the *Find* or *Restrict* method will fail. You can add a field to a folder by displaying the Field Chooser and clicking New.

The following example uses the *Find* method of the Items collection object to return the first item in the Product Ideas folder with the value Boating in the Product Category field:

```
Sub FindAnIteminAFolder_Click ()
    Set MyNameSpace = Application.GetNameSpace("MAPI")
    Set BldFolder = MyNameSpace.Folders _
        ("Building Microsoft Outlook 2002 Applications")
```

```
    Set QuickFolder = BldFolder.Folders("2. Quick Guide")
    Set ProductIdeasFolder = QuickFolder.Folders("Product Ideas")
    Set MyItem = ProductIdeasFolder.Items.Find _
        ("[Product Category] = 'Boating'")
    MyItem.Display
End Sub
```

Creating a Filtered Collection of Items from a Folder

You can use the *Restrict* method of the Items collection object to create filters that return only those items in a folder matching the conditions you specify.

> **More Info** For more information about constructing filter expressions, see *Find* Method and *Restrict* Method in Microsoft Outlook Visual Basic Reference Help.

The following example returns the collection of items from the Product Ideas folder and then creates a filtered collection of items with only the value Boating in the Product Category field:

```
Sub CreateAFilteredCollection_Click
    Set MyNameSpace = Application.GetNameSpace("MAPI")
    Set BldFolder = MyNameSpace.Folders _
        ("Building Microsoft Outlook 2002 Applications")
    Set QuickFolder = BldFolder.Folders("2. Quick Guide")
    Set ProductIdeasFolder = QuickFolder.Folders("Product Ideas")
    Set MyItems = ProductIdeasFolder.Items
    Set MyFilter = MyItems.Restrict("[Product Category] = 'Boating'")
    MsgBox "There are " & MyFilter.Count & " Boating items.", vbInformation
End Sub
```

> **Note** The *Restrict* method does not offer optimal performance for a large collection of items in a folder. If you need to iterate over hundreds or thousands of items in a folder, use the *SetColumns* method to cache specified properties and increase performance. Only certain Item properties can be cached with the *Restrict* and *SetColumns* methods. User-defined properties cannot be cached with *SetColumns*. See *Restrict* Method and *SetColumns* Method in Microsoft Outlook Visual Basic Reference Help for additional information.

Sorting the Items in a Filtered Collection

If you want to sort the items in the Items collection, use the *Sort* method. Currently, the *Sort* method only supports sorting on built-in properties for the Item. The example below creates a restricted collection of Contacts in your mailbox that have an Email1Address value. After the restriction has been created, the *Sort* method is used on the filtered Items collection object. Finally the first item is the Sorted Items collection is displayed.

```
Sub SortAFilteredCollection_Click
    On Error Resume Next
    olFolderContacts = 10
    Set MyNameSpace = Application.GetNameSpace("MAPI")
    Set myFolder = MyNameSpace.GetDefaultFolder(olFolderContacts)
    Set MyItems = myFolder.Items
    'Create the Filter first and then sort
    Set MyFilter = MyItems.Restrict("[Email1Address] <> ''")
    'Sort by LastName in descending order
    MyFilter.Sort "[LastName]", True
    'Display the first item in the filter
    MyFilter.Item(1).Display
End Sub
```

> **Important** The *Sort* method will return an error if you attempt to sort for built-in multi-valued properties such as Companies and Categories. You also cannot sort by a user-defined field unless the user-defined field is defined in the folder. The *Sort* method is effective, from a performance standpoint, only for small collections of items.

Deleting the Items in a Collection

If you want to delete items from an Items collection object, you can't use the *For i = 1 to MyItems.Count...MyItems.Item(i).Delete...Next* routine or the *For Each myItem in MyItems...myItem.Delete...Next* routine you would normally use to iterate over the items in the collection. The following example is a generic function that will delete all the items in the Items collection passed as an argument to the function:

```
Function DeleteAllItems(myItems) 'MyItems is an Items collection object
    On Error Resume Next
    Do Until MyItems.Count = 0
        MyItems.Remove 1
    Loop
End Function
```

Items Collection Object Properties

This section explains how to use the Count property.

Returning the Count of Items in the Items Collection

You can use the Count property of the Items collection object to return the number of items in the Items collection. This provides an easy way to loop through collections to process a large number of items, as shown in the previous example. The following example returns the number of items in the Inbox and shows the number in a message box:

```
Sub CommandButton1_Click()
    On Error Resume Next
    Set MyFolder = _
        Item.Application.GetNameSpace("MAPI").GetDefaultFolder(6)
    Set MyItems = MyFolder.Items
    MsgBox "You have " & MyItems.Count _
        & " items in your Inbox.", vbInformation
End Sub
```

The PostItem Object

The PostItem object represents a message posted in a public folder. Unlike a MailItem object, a PostItem object is not sent to a recipient. This section covers some of the methods of the PostItem object. Properties of the PostItem object are similar to the properties of the MailItem object, so they are discussed together in "MailItem and PostItem Objects Properties" later in this chapter.

PostItem Object Methods

The PostItem object provides a variety of methods that you can use to control the actions of an item. This section covers the *Copy, Move, Delete, Display,* and *Post* methods.

Copying and Moving an Item

You can use the *Copy* method of the PostItem object to create a copy of an item. You can then use the *Move* method to move the copied item to a new location.

The example on the following page returns the first item in the Product Ideas folder with the value Boating in the Product Category field. It then uses the *Copy* method to create a copy of the item returned from the Product Ideas folder. If the user selects Yes in the message box, the *Move* method copies the item from the Product Ideas folder to the Drafts folder. If you want to move rather than copy the item, use the *Delete* method and place a MyItem.Delete statement after the MyItem.Copy statement.

Part IV Beyond the Basics

```
Sub CopyAndMove_Click
    Set MyNameSpace = Application.GetNameSpace("MAPI")
    Set BldFolder = MyNameSpace.Folders _
        ("Building Microsoft Outlook 2002 Applications")
    Set QuickFolder = BldFolder.Folders("2. Quick Guide")
    Set ProductIdeasFolder = QuickFolder.Folders("Product Ideas")
    Set MyItem = ProductIdeasFolder.Items.Find _
        ("[Product Category] = 'Boating'")
    If MyItem Is Nothing Then
        MsgBox "Could not find an item.", vbInformation
    Else
        strQuestion = "Copy " & MyItem.Subject & " to Drafts?"
        If MsgBox(strQuestion, vbQuestion+vbYesNo) = vbYes Then
            Set MyCopiedItem = MyItem.Copy
            'MyItem.Delete if a move instead of copy
            Set DestinationFolder = MyNameSpace.GetDefaultFolder(16)
            myCopiedItem.Move DestinationFolder
            MsgBox MyItem.Subject & " copied to Drafts.", vbInformation
        End If
    End If
End Sub
```

Creating and Displaying a Custom Post Item

You can use the *Display* method of the PostItem object to display an item on the desktop. As discussed earlier, you use the *Add* method of the Items collection object to create a new custom Post item. The following example returns the Product Ideas folder and then creates a new custom PostItem object by using the *Add* method of the Items collection object. It then displays the item in the Product Idea form. If you click the Post button on the form, the item is posted in the Product Ideas folder.

```
Sub CreateAndDisplay_Click()
    Set MyNameSpace = Application.GetNameSpace("MAPI")
    Set BldFolder = MyNameSpace.Folders _
        ("Building Microsoft Outlook 2002 Applications")
    Set QuickFolder = BldFolder.Folders("2. Quick Guide")
    Set ProductIdeasFolder = QuickFolder.Folders("Product Ideas")
    Set MyItem = ProductIdeasFolder.Items.Add("IPM.Post.Product Idea")
    myItem.Subject = "Handlebar polish"
    myItem.UserProperties("Product Category") = "Cycling"
    myItem.Body = "For cyclists who want their bikes to gleam in the wind."
    MyItem.Display
End Sub
```

Posting an Item

You can use the *Post* method of the PostItem object to post an item in a folder. The following example sets the folder to the Product Ideas folder. It then creates a new item with the message class IPM.Post.Product Idea, which is added to the Product Ideas Items collection. In this procedure, the object returned to MyItem by the *Add* method has a base message class of IPM.Post so you can use the *Post* method. The Subject and Body properties of the MyItem object are set, and then the item is posted to the Product Ideas folder.

```
Sub PostanItem_Click
    Set MyNameSpace = Application.GetNameSpace("MAPI")
    Set BldFolder = MyNameSpace.Folders _
        ("Building Microsoft Outlook 2002 Applications")
    Set QuickFolder = BldFolder.Folders("2. Quick Guide")
    Set ProductIdeasFolder = QuickFolder.Folders("Product Ideas")
    Set myItem = ProductIdeasFolder.Items.Add("IPM.Post.Product Idea")
    myItem.Subject = "VBScript is versatile"
    myItem.Body = "Let's develop new products using this technology."
    myItem.Post
    MsgBox myItem.Subject & _
        " has been posted in the Product Ideas folder.", vbInformation
End Sub
```

The MailItem Object

The MailItem object represents a message in a mail folder. This section also covers some of the methods and properties of the PostItem object. Properties of the PostItem object are similar to the properties of the MailItem object, so they are discussed together.

> **Important** Open the MailItem object and PostItem object items in the VBScript Samples folder to work directly with this code in Outlook.

MailItem Object Methods

This section covers the *Send*, *Reply*, and *Close* methods of the MailItem object.

If your code attempts to send a message programmatically, the Warning dialog box shown in Figure 11-9 will be displayed. See Chapter 13 for methods to eliminate the Warning dialog box.

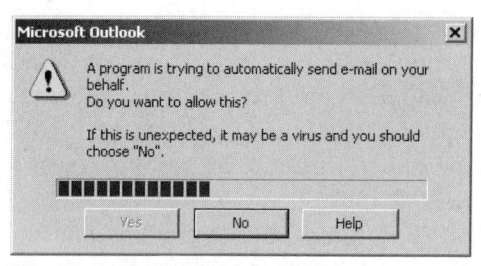

Figure 11-9 This Warning dialog box appears when you attempt to send a message programatically.

Sending a Message

You can use the *Send* method of the MailItem object to send a message to a recipient. The following example creates a Mail Message item, sets the Subject and message Body fields, and then sets the To field to your name. You can retrieve the ScriptText property of the FormDescription object for the item to set the Body property of the message. It then uses the *Send* method to send the item to the specified recipient.

> **Note** The Body property of the item only lets you set plain text as the message text. If you want to format the Body programmatically, use the HTMLBody property discussed on page 487.

```
Sub SendAMessage_Click
    Set MyItem = Application.CreateItem(olMailItem)
    MyItem.Subject = "VBScript Code for MailItem object"
    Set MyForm = Item.FormDescription
    MyItem.Body = MyForm.ScriptText
    MyItem.To = Application.GetNameSpace("MAPI").CurrentUser
    MyItem.Send
End Sub
```

Replying to a Message

You can use the *Reply* method of a MailItem object to return a Reply item. The following example creates a Reply item based on the current item, and then returns the Reply item represented by the MyReply object. The Reply item is then displayed. To run this example, you must first put a CommandButton1 control on the Read page of a Mail Message form. Exit Design mode and send the item to your Inbox, and then open the item in the Inbox and click CommandButton1. The Reply item is displayed.

Using Visual Basic, VBA, or VBScript with Outlook Chapter 11

```
Sub CommandButton1_Click
    Set MyFolder = Application.GetNameSpace("MAPI").GetDefaultFolder(6)
    Set MyItem = MyFolder.Items.Item(1)
    Set MyReply = MyItem.Reply
    MyReply.Display
End Sub
```

Closing an Item

You can use the *Close* method of the MailItem object to close an item. When you close the item, you also close the item's associated form. The following example closes the current item when the CloseAnItem button is clicked. Note that if the *blnIsDirty* script-level variable is *True*, then the user is prompted to save changes. If *blnIsDirty* is *False*, then the item is closed and changes are not saved. You could modify this procedure to automatically save changes to a dirty form. This example also illustrates how you can write event procedures in the code for your custom form to control how and when the form is saved.

```
Dim blnIsDirty

Sub Item_PropertyChange(ByVal Name)
    blnIsDirty = True
End Sub

Sub Item_CustomPropertyChange(ByVal Name)
    blnIsDirty = True
End Sub

Function Item_Write()
    blnIsDirty = False
End Function

Sub CloseAnItem_Click
    Const olSave = 0
    Const olDiscard = 1
    Const olPromptForSave = 2
    If blnIsDirty = True Then
        Item.Close olPromptForSave
    Else
        Item.Close olDiscard
    End If
End Sub
```

You can use one of the arguments in the table on the following page with the *Close* method or use CONST declarations as shown in the preceding example.

Part IV Beyond the Basics

Save Option	Value
Save all changes without prompting	0
Discard all changes without prompting	1
Prompt to save or discard all changes	2

> **Note** Unlike previous versions of Outlook, Outlook 2000 and 2002 allow you to write VBA or Visual Basic code to respond to all the events that are raised in a Message item. For additional information, see Chapter 9 and Chapter 14.

MailItem and PostItem Objects Properties

This section covers the GetInspector, Body, HTMLBody, To, and SenderName properties of the MailItem and PostItem objects.

Using GetInspector To Reference the Form

You can use the GetInspector property of the MailItem object or the PostItem object to reference the form associated with an item. You can then reference the page on the form, and then the controls on the page. The following example uses the GetInspector property of the MailItem object to return the form associated with the item. It references the Message page on the form and then sets the Visible property of the TextBox1 control to *False*.

Before you run this example, do the following:

1. If you don't have a TextBox1 control on the form, click Design This Form from Forms on the Tools menu to switch to Design mode.

2. Drag a TextBox control from the Control Toolbox to the form.

3. Click Run This Form on the Form menu to switch to Run mode, and then click CommandButton1 to hide the TextBox1 control.

```
Sub CommandButton1_Click
    Set MyPage = GetInspector.ModifiedFormPages("Message")
    MyPage.TextBox1.Visible = False
End Sub
```

Setting the Message Text of an Item

You can use the Body property of a MailItem object or a PostItem object to specify the text that appears in the Message control of a Mail Message. The following

Using Visual Basic, VBA, or VBScript with Outlook   Chapter 11

example creates a Reply item, enters text in the Message control of the Reply item, and then sends the form:

```
Sub CommandButton1_Click()
    Dim MyFolder, MyItem, MyReply
    Set MyFolder = Application.GetNamespace("MAPI").GetDefaultFolder(6)
    Set MyItem = MyFolder.Items(1)
    Set MyReply = MyItem.Reply
    MyReply.Body = "Let's go to the Napa Valley next weekend."
    MyReply.Display
End Sub
```

> **Note**   The Body property does not support Rich Text Format (RTF) or HyperText Markup Language (HTML).

You can also use the HTMLBody property of a MailItem or PostItem object to specify formatted text in the Message control. When you set this property, Outlook automatically sets the EditorType property of the associated Inspector object to olEditorHTML(2).

> **New to Outlook 2002**   The BodyFormat property provides an easier way to specify the format of a message than the HTMLBody and Body properties. Be aware that if you change the BodyFormat property from RTF to HTML or vice versa, the formatting of the message will be lost. The BodyFormat property is available only for MailItem and PostItem objects.

The following example displays the current editor type, sets the HTMLBody property of the item, and then displays the new editor type. Open the HTMLBody Object form in the VBScript Samples folder to see a more sophisticated example of using the HTMLBody property. You can create HTML dynamically in the VBScript code behind a form and then present that HTML in the body of an Item.

```
Sub CommandButton1_Click
    On Error Resume Next
        strHTML= "<body bgcolor='cyan'>" _
            & "<H1>This is HTML text.</H1>" _
            & "<body>"
    Item.HTMLBody = strHTML
End Sub
```

487

> **Note** For additional information on the Body property, see Knowledge Base article Q291153-OL2002: Working With the Message or Body of an Outlook Item.

Setting the To Field of an Item

You can use the To property of the MailItem object to set the value of a To field. The following example creates a new item and then sets the To field and Subject field values of the item:

```
Sub CommandButton1_Click
    Set MyItem = Application.CreateItem(0)
    MyItem.To = "someone@somecompany.com"
    MyItem.Subject = "How to set the To field"
    MyItem.Display
End Sub
```

> **Outlook Security** As long as you display the MailItem object and allow the user to click the Send button rather than sending programmatically, the Warning dialog box shown earlier in Figure 11-9 will not appear.

Getting the Sender Name of an Item

You can use the SenderName property of the MailItem object to return the name of the person who sent the message. The following example gets the first item in the Inbox and sets the *Recip* variable to the value of the SenderName property. It then creates a new Message item and sets its To field to the value of the *Recip* variable. When the item is displayed, the value of the SenderName property shows in the To box of the form.

```
Sub GetTheSenderName_Click
    Set MyFolder = Application.GetNameSpace("MAPI").GetDefaultFolder(6)
    Set MyItem = MyFolder.Items(1)
    Recip = MyItem.SenderName
    Set MyNewItem = Application.CreateItem(0)
    MyNewItem.To = Recip
    MyNewItem.Display
End Sub
```

> **Note** In the preceding example, the name in the To field is not resolved. To resolve a name, the name must be added to the Recipients collection object. For more information, see "The Recipients Collection Object" later in this chapter.

Getting the Sender Address of an Item

The Outlook Object Model does not provide a means to obtain the e-mail address of the item's sender. To obtain the e-mail address of the sender, you can use CDO to create a Sender object for the MAPI Message object. The Sender object exposes several useful properties, one of which is the Address property. The following VBA code displays a message box containing the e-mail address for the sender of the first item in the Inbox:

```
Sub GetSender()
    Dim objCDO As MAPI.Session
    Dim objMsg As MAPI.Message
    Dim objSender As MAPI.AddressEntry
    Dim oMsg As Outlook.MailItem
    Dim strMsg As String
    On Error Resume Next
    Set oMsg = Application.ActiveExplorer.Selection.Item(1)
    Set objCDO = CreateObject("MAPI.Session")
    objCDO.Logon "", "", False, False
    Set objMsg = objCDO.GetMessage(oMsg.EntryID)
    Set objSender = objMsg.Sender
    strMsg = "Subject: " & objMsg.Subject & vbCrLf _
        & "Sender Name: " & objSender.Name & vbCrLf _
        & "Sender e-mail: " & objSender.Address & vbCrLf _
        & "Sender type: " & objSender.Type
    MsgBox strMsg, vbInformation
End Sub
```

> **Outlook Security** When you set the *objSender* variable, you access a CDO AddressEntry object. This will cause the Warning dialog box shown in Figure 11-4 (on page 429) to appear.

Adding Attachments to an Item

You can add attachments to an item programmatically by using the *Add* method of the Attachments collection object. VBScript's FileSystemObject lets you write and read from a file programmatically. Therefore, you can write to a file and then attach the file to a message in code. Open the FileSystemObject item in the VBScript Samples folder to see this code in action.

```
Sub WriteandAttachFile_Click()
    Const ForReading = 1, ForWriting = 2, ForAppending = 8
    Const olByValue = 1, olByReference = 4, olEmbeddeditem = 5, olOLE = 6
    Dim fso
    Set fso = CreateObject("Scripting.FileSystemObject")
    strPath = GetTempDir & "\FSObject.txt"
    Set objFile = fso.OpenTextFile(strPath, ForAppending, True)
    strLine = Now & " - " & "This file demonstrates use " _
        & "of the FileSystemObject to write to a text file."
    objFile.Write(strLine)
    objFile.Close
    Set objMsg = Application.CreateItem(0)
    Set colAttachments = objMsg.Attachments
    colAttachments.Add strPath, olByValue, 1, "FileSystemObject Attachment"
    objMsg.Subject = "FileSystemObject Object"
    objMsg.Display
End Sub

Function GetTempDir
    Const TemporaryFolder = 2, SystemFolder = 1, WindowsFolder = 0
    On Error Resume Next
    Dim fso, tfolder
    Set fso = CreateObject("Scripting.FileSystemObject")
    Set tfolder = fso.GetSpecialFolder(TemporaryFolder)
    If Err then
        GetTempDir = "Could not obtain temporary folder path."
        Exit Function
    End If
    GetTempDir = lcase(tFolder.Path)
End Function
```

The DocumentItem Object

The DocumentItem object represents an assortment of different items that can be stored in Outlook folders. To clarify what a DocumentItem object represents, the terms extrinsic and intrinsic DocumentItems need to be defined. A DocumentItem object can be a file that is dragged to an Outlook folder from

Windows Explorer. It can also result from a file posted to an Exchange public folder from a source application such as Microsoft Word, Excel, or PowerPoint. These items are extrinsic DocumentItem objects, meaning that they were created by an application extrinsic to Outlook. An extrinsic DocumentItem has the following characteristics:

- The DocumentItem was created by its native application or an object model supported by its native application.

- The item does not support Outlook DocumentItem properties, methods, and events.

- You cannot create a custom Outlook form from an extrinsic DocumentItem.

Because extrinsic DocumentItem objects do not support Outlook Inspector properties and events, you cannot automate these items easily within the container of an Outlook folder. For example, you cannot write an *Item_Open* event procedure for an extrinsic DocumentItem object. Some applications—most notably Microsoft Excel—still support a native Open event that fires when a user opens the document. This event fires whether the Excel document exists in an Outlook folder or in the file system. A DocumentItem object can also be an Outlook 2000 DocumentItem that wraps an Inspector object around an Office document. You cannot create an Outlook 2000 DocumentItem in Outlook 2002. Outlook 2000 DocumentItems are supported in Outlook 2002, but you cannot design a new DocumentItem in Outlook 2002. For additional details, see "Inspectors Collection Events" in Chapter 9. A user creates an Outlook Office Document Item in Outlook 2000 only by selecting the Office Document command from the New submenu of the File menu in Outlook Explorer. There are only four types of Outlook 2000 DocumentItems that you can create from within Outlook: Word Documents, Excel Charts, Excel Worksheets, and PowerPoint Presentations. These Outlook 2000 DocumentItems are known as intrinsic DocumentItems. An intrinsic DocumentItem object has the following characteristics. Be aware that this list applies only to DocumentItems created in Outlook 2000.

- They support Outlook DocumentItem properties, methods, and events.

- They can be either a Post-type or Send-type DocumentItem. When you design an Outlook DocumentItem, you will see a dialog box asking you if you want to send the document to someone or post the document in this folder. Whatever your choice, Outlook does not distinguish between a Post or Send DocumentItem in the message class of the custom form.

Part IV Beyond the Basics

- You can create a custom Outlook form from an intrinsic DocumentItem. This custom form will have a base message class equivalent to the message class of the extrinsic DocumentItem. If you create a custom DocumentItem named Sales Analysis from a Word DocumentItem, the message class of the custom form will be IPM.Document.Word.Document.8.Sales Analysis.
- You can write VBScript code behind the DocumentItem custom form.

These Outlook DocumentItems have the same base message class as extrinsic DocumentItems. In all cases, DocumentItems are actually attachments to a message container with a message class of IPM.Document. The following table lists some important types of DocumentItems that can be placed in an Outlook folder.

Document Item	Message Class	Outlook DocumentItem with Inspector	Custom Form Built on Item	Document Open Event
Web Page	IPM.Document.htmlfile	No	No	Use DHTML to create window onload event.
Word Document	IPM.Document.Word.Document.8	Yes	Yes	No. See workaround below.
Excel Worksheet	IPM.Document.Excel.Sheet.8	Yes	Yes	Yes.
PowerPoint Presentation	IPM.Document.PowerPoint.Show.8	Yes	Yes	No.
Adobe Acrobat Document	IPM.Document.AcroExch.Document	No	No	No.
Visio Drawing	IPM.Document.Visio.Drawing.5	No	No	No.
Other Document Types	IPM.Document.<Document Class>	No	No	Depends on the object model and VBA support in the source application.

Creating a Word DocumentItem

You can create a Word DocumentItem programmatically in a folder as long as you have Word installed. Creating a DocumentItem programmatically is a two-step process. First create a DocumentItem with the correct message class in the target folder. To complete the process, use the Attachments collection of the DocumentItem to add an appropriate attachment to the DocumentItem. The following VBA example uses Word Automation to create a Word document in the temporary folder. The Word document is then attached to a Word DocumentItem created in the user's Inbox. Finally the Word document in the temporary folder is deleted. The same basic sequence would be followed if you wanted to create an Excel workbook instead of a Word document.

```
Sub AddDocumenttoInbox()
    Dim objWordDoc As DocumentItem
    Dim wdApp As Word.Application
    Dim wdDoc As Word.Document
    Dim objFolder As MAPIFolder
    On Error Resume Next
    Set objFolder = _
        Application.GetNameSpace("MAPI").GetDefaultFolder(olFolderInbox)
    Set objWordDoc = objFolder.Items.Add("IPM.Document.Word.Document.8")
    Set wdApp = CreateObject("Word.Application")
    Set wdDoc = wdApp.Documents.Add
    With wdApp.Selection
        .TypeText "Microsoft Outlook 2002"
        .TypeParagraph
        .TypeText "A great tool for communication and collaboration!"
    End With
    'GetTempDir returns trailing \
    strPath = GetTempDir() & "O2KTest2.doc"
    wdDoc.SaveAs strPath
    wdDoc.Close
    'Save the DocumentItem with wdDoc attachment
    With objWordDoc
        .Subject = "Microsoft Outlook 2002"
        .Attachments.Add (strPath)
        .Save
    End With
    'Delete wdDoc in temp folder
    Kill strPath
End Sub
```

Firing the Word Document Open Event

One problem with intrinsic DocumentItems based on Microsoft Word is that the *Document_Open* event does not fire when the DocumentItem is opened from an Outlook folder. If you build an application based on a Word DocumentItem, you'll want to be able to use the *Document_Open* event so that code can assign values to bookmarks, insert and format text, and fill tables from an external database, if necessary. In short, the *Document_Open* event is the gateway to automating your custom DocumentItem form from Word VBA code embedded in the DocumentItem, rather than from VBScript code in the *Item_Open* event.

You'll find a workaround for this problem in the Document_Open Workaround item located in the VBScript Samples folder. The workaround uses the VBScript GetObject function to return a reference to the Word Application object. Because the document embedded in the DocumentItem object represents the ActiveDocument in the Word Application object, you can instantiate a Word Document object and use the *AutoRunMacro* method on that object to fire the *Document_Open* event. In order for the following example to work correctly, you might have to lower the Macro Security settings in Word. In this example, the *Document_Open* event displays a message box indicating the word count for the document:

```
Sub Item_Open()
    On Error Resume Next
    'Get CurrentUser
    strUser = Application.GetNameSpace("MAPI").CurrentUser
    Set objWord = GetObject(, "Word.Application")
    'Use Word TypeText to insert some sample text
    strText = "The CurrentUser is: " & strUser
    objWord.Selection.TypeText strText
    objWord.Selection.TypeParagraph
    'Run the Document_Open procedure with RunAutoMacro method
    Set objDoc = objWord.ActiveDocument
    Const wdAutoOpen = 2
    objDoc.RunAutoMacro wdAutoOpen
    Item.Subject = "DocumentItem Word Document_Open Workaround"
    'Use Built-in properties to set subject and author
    Const wdPropertySubject = 2
    Const wdPropertyAuthor = 3
    objDoc.BuiltinDocumentProperties(wdPropertySubject) = _
        "Document_Open Workaround"
    objDoc.BuiltinDocumentProperties(wdPropertyAuthor) = strUser
    'Optional: Use CustomDocumentProperties to set additional fields
End Sub

Private Sub Document_Open()
    Dim strMsg As String
    strMsg = "This document contains " _
        & ThisDocument.BuiltInDocumentProperties(wdPropertyWords) _
        & " words."
    MsgBox strMsg, vbInformation, "Document Open Event"
End Sub
```

Using DocumentProperties with DocumentItem Objects

One of the great, but little known, features of Outlook is the ability to place documents in folders and expose both the BuiltInDocumentProperties and CustomDocumentProperties objects of the document in folder views. The DocumentProperties object is exposed for all applications in the Office suite, except Outlook. Each DocumentProperty object represents a built-in or custom property of a container document. DocumentProperties are, in turn, divided into BuiltInDocumentProperties and CustomDocumentProperties. Each Office application exposes a subset of the BuiltInDocumentProperties collection object. If you are building an application around a folder containing DocumentItems, you can add BuiltInDocumentProperties to folder views.

To add built-in document properties to a Folder View

1. Navigate to the folder where you want to establish the view.
2. On the Advanced toolbar, click the Field Chooser icon.
3. Select All Document Fields in the drop-down list box at the top of the Field Chooser window.
4. Drag appropriate fields to the folder View.

> **More Info** For additional information about the DocumentProperties collection object, see DocumentProperties in the Microsoft Office Visual Basic Reference Help.

To use Custom Document Properties in a folder view, you must add the CustomDocumentProperties fields to the folder as user-defined fields in the folder. The following example assumes that you have installed the Expense Statement template for Excel 2002. (If you have not installed the Expense Statement template, it will demand to be installed the first time you attempt to create a workbook based on that template.)

To create an Expense Statement Document

1. Launch Excel 2002.
2. Select New from the File menu.
3. Double-click Expense Statement on the Spreadsheet Solutions page of the New dialog box.
4. Complete the Expense Statement template by clicking the Select Employee button and adding expense report information.

Part IV   Beyond the Basics

5. Select Send To from the File menu, and then select Exchange Folder from the Send To submenu. If you are not using an Exchange Server, you can save the file to a file system folder and then drag the Expense Statement workbook from the file system to an Outlook folder.

To add custom document properties to a Folder View

1. In the folder where you placed the Expense Statement report, click the Field Chooser icon on the Advanced toolbar.
2. Select User-Defined Fields In Folder in the drop-down list box at the top of the Field Chooser window.
3. Click the New button to create a new user-defined field in the folder.
4. Enter Employee Name as the name of the user-defined field, and click OK.
5. Drag the Employee Name field into the folder view.
6. In the Field Chooser, click New again.
7. Enter Total Reimbursement/Payment as the name of the user-defined field.
8. Select Number in the Type drop-down list box.
9. Click OK.
10. Drag the Total Reimbursement/Payment field into the folder view.
11. You should now see the values of the Custom Document Property fields displayed in the view in the folder.

The AppointmentItem Object

An AppointmentItem object represents an appointment in the Calendar folder. An AppointmentItem object can represent a one-time appointment, a meeting, or recurring appointments and meetings. A meeting usually involves more than one person and is created when an AppointmentItem is sent to other users, who then receive it in the form of a MeetingItem object in their respective Inbox folders.

An appointment or meeting can be recurring—that is, set to occur more than once on a regular or repetitive basis. When this occurs, a RecurrencePattern object is created for the AppointmentItem object. An instance of a recurring appointment can be changed or deleted. This creates an exception to the recurrence pattern, and this exception is represented by an Exception object. All Exception objects associated with a given AppointmentItem object are contained in an Exceptions collection object associated with the AppointmentItem.

> **Important** Open the AppointmentItem object in the VBScript Samples folder to work directly with this code in Outlook. The object contains advanced CDO code (not shown in this chapter) that lets you programmatically set the color label property. Color appointments are new to Outlook 2002.

Working with Recurring Appointments

This section covers recurring appointments, including how to create a recurring appointment and how to deal with exceptions to the recurrence pattern.

Creating a Recurring Appointment

A recurring appointment is represented by an AppointmentItem object with the IsRecurring property set to *True*. However, you cannot set this property directly. Instead, you create a recurring appointment by calling the *GetRecurrencePattern* method of the AppointmentItem object and then saving the item. The following example illustrates how to create an appointment named Test Appointment and then call the *GetRecurrencePattern* method to make it a recurring appointment:

```
Sub CreateRecurringAppointment_Click
    Set MyItem = Application.CreateItem(1)
    MyItem.Subject = "Test Appointment"
    Set MyPattern = MyItem.GetRecurrencePattern
    MyItem.Save
End Sub
```

The *GetRecurrencePattern* method returns a RecurrencePattern object. You can change the recurrence pattern of the appointment by setting properties of the appointment's RecurrencePattern object.

Setting the Recurrence Pattern of an Appointment

When a new recurring appointment is created, it inherits a default recurrence pattern based on the time the appointment was created. To change the recurrence pattern of an appointment, set the appropriate properties of the appointment's RecurrencePattern object.

> **More Info** For more information about the properties of the RecurrencePattern object affecting the recurrence pattern, see Microsoft Outlook Visual Basic Reference Help.

The following example shows how to create a one-hour recurring appointment that occurs at noon on the second Tuesday of each month for two months, starting July 2001:

```
Sub SetRecurrencePattern_Click
    Set MyItem = Application.CreateItem(1)
    MyItem.Subject = "Monthly Appointment"
    Set MyPattern = MyItem.GetRecurrencePattern
    MyPattern.RecurrenceType = 3 'Monthly, on a specific weekday
    MyPattern.Interval = 1 'Every month (2 would be every other month)
    MyPattern.DayOfWeekMask = 4 'Which day of week (Tuesday)
    MyPattern.Instance = 2 'Which instance (second Tuesday)
    MyPattern.StartTime = "12:00 pm" 'Time each appointment begins
    MyPattern.EndTime = "1:00 pm" 'Time each appointment ends
    MyPattern.PatternStartDate = #7/1/2001# 'Earliest date appt can occur
    MyPattern.PatternEndDate = #9/1/2001# 'Latest date appt can occur
    MyItem.Save
End Sub
```

Working with a Single Appointment in a Series

To determine whether an instance of a recurring appointment occurs at a particular time, use the *GetOccurrence* method of the RecurrencePattern object. This method returns an AppointmentItem object representing the instance of the recurring appointment.

> **Important** The *GetOccurrence* method will produce an error if an instance of the recurring appointment does not start at the date and time you provide. If it is possible that your script can supply a date and time that does not match an instance of a recurring appointment (because of user input, for example), the script should be able to handle the error appropriately. Otherwise, the script procedure will fail and Outlook will display an error message.

The following example illustrates how to use the *GetOccurrence* method to determine whether a recurring appointment (created by the code in the previous section) starts on a date and time provided by the user. The On Error Resume Next statement ensures that the procedure will continue if the user enters anything that does not match the start date and time of an instance of the recurring appointment. After calling the *GetOccurrence* method, the script tests the *MyAppointment* variable to determine whether it is set to Nothing, indicating that the method failed and did not return an AppointmentItem object.

Using Visual Basic, VBA, or VBScript with Outlook Chapter 11

```
Sub CheckOccurrence_Click
    Set MyNameSpace = Application.GetNameSpace("MAPI")
    Set MyCalendarFolder = MyNameSpace.GetDefaultFolder(9)
    Set MyItem = MyCalendarFolder.Items("Monthly Appointment")
    Set MyPattern = MyItem.GetRecurrencePattern
    On Error Resume Next
    MyDate = InputBox ("Enter a date and time (m/d/yy hh:mm): ")
    Do While MyDate <> ""
        Set MyAppointment = Nothing
        Set MyAppointment = MyPattern.GetOccurrence(MyDate)
        If TypeName(MyAppointment) <> "Nothing" Then
            MsgBox "This instance of " & MyAppointment.Subject _
                & " occurs on " & MyAppointment.Start
        Else
            MsgBox MyItem.Subject & " does not occur on " & MyDate
        End If
        MyDate = InputBox _
            ("Enter another date and time (m/d/yy hh:mm):")
    Loop
End Sub
```

Once you retrieve the AppointmentItem object representing an instance of a recurring appointment, you can delete or change the appointment instance. When this happens, Outlook creates an Exception object. The properties of this object describe the changes that were made to the instance. All of the Exception objects for a recurring appointment are contained in an Exceptions collection object associated with the appointment's RecurrencePattern object.

The AppointmentItem property of the Exception object returns the AppointmentItem object that constitutes the exception to the original recurrence pattern of the recurring appointment. You can use the methods and properties of the AppointmentItem object to work with the appointment exception. The following example changes the subject of an instance of the recurring appointment created by the script in the previous section. It then uses the AppointmentItem property of the resulting Exception object to change the start time of the appointment exception.

```
Sub CreateException_Click
    Set MyNameSpace = Application.GetNameSpace("MAPI")
    Set MyCalendarFolder = MyNameSpace.GetDefaultFolder(9)
    Set MyItem = MyCalendarFolder.Items("Monthly Appointment")
    Set MyPattern = MyItem.GetRecurrencePattern
    Set MyInstance = MyPattern.GetOccurrence(#8/14/2001 12:00 pm#)
    MyInstance.Subject = "Monthly Pattern (exception)"
    MsgBox MyInstance.Subject & " starts on " & MyInstance.Start
    MyInstance.Save
    Set MyNewPattern = MyItem.GetRecurrencePattern
    Set MyException = MyNewPattern.Exceptions.Item(1)
```

(continued)

```
    Set MyNewInstance = MyException.AppointmentItem
    MyNewInstance.Start = (#8/14/2001 1:00 pm#)
    MsgBox MyNewInstance.Subject & " now starts on " & MyNewInstance.Start
    MyNewInstance.Save
End Sub
```

The following two sections describe how to use the Exception object to work with changed or deleted instances of a recurring appointment.

Determining the Original Date of an Exception

The OriginalDate property of the Exception object returns the start date and time of the changed appointment before it was changed. The following example uses the OriginalDate property to retrieve the original start date of the appointment exception created in the previous section. In addition, it uses the Start property of the AppointmentItem associated with the Exception object to provide the new start date of the appointment.

```
Sub ShowOriginalDate_Click
    On Error Resume Next
    Set MyNameSpace = Application.GetNameSpace("MAPI")
    Set MyCalendarFolder = MyNameSpace.GetDefaultFolder(9)
    Set MyItem = MyCalendarFolder.Items("Monthly Appointment")
    Set MyPattern = MyItem.GetRecurrencePattern
    Set MyException = MyPattern.Exceptions.Item(1)
    MsgBox "The changed appointment originally occurred on " _
        & MyException.OriginalDate & Chr(13) & "It now occurs on "_
        & MyException.AppointmentItem.Start, vbInformation
End Sub
```

Determining Whether an Appointment Instance Was Deleted

When an appointment in a recurring series is deleted, an Exception object representing the deleted appointment is created, and the Deleted property of the Exception object is set to *True*. The following example uses the *Delete* method of the AppointmentItem object to delete the appointment instance changed in the previous section. It then tests the value of the Deleted property of the Exception object representing the deleted appointment to determine whether the appointment was actually deleted.

```
Sub CheckIfDeleted_Click
    Set MyNameSpace = Application.GetNameSpace("MAPI")
    Set MyCalendarFolder = MyNameSpace.GetDefaultFolder(9)
    Set MyItem = MyCalendarFolder.Items("Monthly Appointment")
    Set MyPattern = MyItem.GetRecurrencePattern
    Set MyAppointment = MyPattern.GetOccurrence(#8/14/2001 1:00 pm#)
    MyAppointment.Delete
    Set MyException = MyPattern.Exceptions.Item(1)
    If MyException.Deleted Then MsgBox "The appointment was deleted."
End Sub
```

The MeetingItem Object

> **Important** Open the MeetingItem object in the VBScript Samples folder to work directly with this code in Outlook.

A MeetingItem object represents a request for a meeting received in a user's Inbox mail folder. You cannot create a MeetingItem object directly. Instead, Outlook creates a MeetingItem object in each recipient's Inbox folder when a user sends an AppointmentItem object with its MeetingStatus property set to olMeeting(1). The following example shows how to create an appointment and then send the appointment as a meeting request to a required attendee and an optional attendee:

```
Sub SendMeetingRequest_Click
    Set myItem = Application.CreateItem(1) 'Create an appointment
    myItem.MeetingStatus = 1 'Appointment is a meeting
    myItem.Subject = "Marketing Strategy Meeting"
    myItem.Location = "Conference Room B"
    myItem.Start = #9/24/2001 1:30:00 PM#
    myItem.Duration = 90
    myAttendee = InputBox ("Enter name of Required Attendee")
    If myAttendee <> "" then
        Set myRequiredAttendee = myItem.Recipients.Add(MyAttendee)
        myRequiredAttendee.Type = 1 'Required
    End If
    myAttendee = InputBox ("Enter name of Optional Attendee")
    If myAttendee <> "" then
        Set myOptionalAttendee = myItem.Recipients.Add(MyAttendee)
        myOptionalAttendee.Type = 2 'Optional
    End If
    myItem.Send
End Sub
```

The MeetingItem object replaces the MeetingRequestItem object provided by Outlook 97.

Working with Meeting Requests

Most often, you will not work directly with a MeetingItem object. For example, you do not use the MeetingItem object to accept or decline the meeting. Instead, you use the appointment associated with the meeting request.

The *GetAssociatedAppointment* method of the MeetingItem object returns an AppointmentItem object that you can use to accept or refuse the meeting request or to directly add the meeting (as an appointment) to the Calendar folder.

You can also directly access an AppointmentItem that has its MeetingStatus property set to olMeeting(1) to determine which recipients have accepted or declined the meeting request. The following sections illustrate how to work with a meeting request through the appointment associated with the meeting.

Retrieving the Associated Appointment of a Meeting

The MeetingItem object is a message containing a request to add an appointment to the recipient's calendar; it is not the appointment itself. To access the appointment associated with the meeting request, you use the *GetAssociatedAppointment* method of the MeetingItem object. This method requires a Boolean argument that specifies whether the appointment is added to the user's Calendar.

The following example calls the *GetAssociatedAppointment* method of each MeetingItem in the user's Inbox and then uses the returned AppointmentItem object's *Display* method to open the appointment. Note that the argument of GetAssociatedAppointment is set to *False* so that the appointment is not added to the user's Calendar.

```
Sub DisplayMeetingRequests_Click
    Set myNameSpace = Application.GetNameSpace("MAPI")
    Set myFolder = myNameSpace.GetDefaultFolder(6)
    Set myItems = myFolder.Items
    Set myMeetingRequest = _
        myItems.Find("[MessageClass] = 'IPM.Schedule.Meeting.Request'")
    Do While TypeName (myMeetingRequest)<> "Nothing"
        myMeetingRequest.GetAssociatedAppointment(False).Display
        Set myMeetingRequest = myItems.FindNext
    Loop
End Sub
```

Responding to a Meeting Request

To respond to a meeting request, you use the *GetAssociatedAppointment* method of the MeetingItem object to obtain the AppointmentItem object associated with the meeting request. You then use the *Respond* method of the AppointmentItem object to notify the meeting organizer whether the meeting has been accepted, declined, or tentatively added to the receiving user's Calendar.

The *Respond* method allows you to send the notification without user intervention, or it can allow the user to edit the response before sending it. The *Respond* method accepts three parameters: the first specifies the actual response (accept, decline, or tentative), while the second two are Boolean values that determine whether the user will be given the opportunity to edit the response.

Using Visual Basic, VBA, or VBScript with Outlook Chapter 11

> **Outlook Security**   Code that utilizes the *Respond* method without requiring action by the user is blocked by the Outlook E-Mail Security Update in Outlook 2002. If you run the *AutoAcceptMeetingRequest* procedure shown next, you will see the Warning dialog boxes we looked at earlier. If you want most of the code in this section to run without prompts, you will have to wrap the code into a COM Add-in and then add the COM Add-in to the list of trusted COM Add-ins.

To send the notification without requiring action by the user, you call the *Respond* method with the second parameter set to *True* and then send the AppointmentItem as shown in the following example:

```
Sub AutoAcceptMeetingRequest_Click
    Set myNameSpace = Application.GetNameSpace("MAPI")
    Set myFolder = myNameSpace.GetDefaultFolder(6)
    Set myMtgReq = _
        myFolder.Items.Find("[MessageClass] = _
        'IPM.Schedule.Meeting.Request'")
    If TypeName(myMtgReq) <> "Nothing" Then
        Set myAppt = myMtgReq.GetAssociatedAppointment(True)
        myAppt.Respond 3, True
        myAppt.Send
        MsgBox "The " & myAppt.Subject & " meeting on " & myAppt.Start _
            & " has been accepted.", vbInformation
    Else
        MsgBox "You have no meeting requests in your Inbox.", vbInformation
    End If
End Sub
```

If you want to allow the user to choose how to respond (that is, whether to send a response and whether to edit the body of the response before sending), call the *Respond* method with the second parameter set to *False* and the third parameter set to *True*, as shown below:

```
Sub PromptUserToAccept_Click
    Set myNameSpace = Application.GetNameSpace("MAPI")
    Set myFolder = myNameSpace.GetDefaultFolder(6)
    Set myMtgReq = _
        myFolder.Items.Find("[MessageClass] _
            ='IPM.Schedule.Meeting.Request'")
    If TypeName(myMtgReq) <> "Nothing" Then
        Set myAppt = myMtgReq.GetAssociatedAppointment(True)
        myAppt.Respond 3, False, True
```

(continued)

```
        Else
            MsgBox "You have no meeting requests in your Inbox."
        End If
End Sub
```

You can use the *Respond* method to display a dialog box that gives the user three choices:

- Edit The Response Before Sending
- Send The Response Now
- Don't Send A Response

Outlook immediately sends the AppointmentItem to the meeting organizer if the user chooses Send The Response Now. If the user chooses Edit The Response Before Sending, Outlook opens the item to allow the user to change recipients, the subject, or the body text before sending the response.

Instead of giving the user the choice of how to respond, you can call the *Respond* method with the second and third parameters both set to *False*. The result is the same as when the user chooses Edit the response before sending.

Determining the Status of a Recipient of a Meeting Request

An AppointmentItem object created from a MeetingItem object has an associated Recipients collection object. You can use the MeetingResponseStatus property of the Recipient objects in this collection to determine whether a given recipient has accepted or declined the requested meeting.

The script in the following example retrieves each meeting that the user has requested and then checks the MeetingResponseStatus property for each recipient of the meeting. A description of the status for each recipient is added to a text string that is displayed in a message box once the status of all the recipients has been checked.

```
Sub CheckRecipientStatus_Click
    Set myNameSpace = Application.GetNameSpace("MAPI")
    Set myFolder = myNameSpace.GetDefaultFolder(9)
    Set myItems = myFolder.Items
    Set myMeeting = myItems.Find("[MeetingStatus] = 1")
    Do While TypeName(myMeeting) <> "Nothing"
        TextStr = "The following is the status of recipients for " _
            & MyMeeting.Subject & " on " & MyMeeting.Start & ":" & chr(13)
        Set myRecipients = myMeeting.Recipients
        For x = 1 To myRecipients.Count
            TextStr = TextStr & chr(13)& myRecipients(x).Name
```

```
            Select Case myRecipients(x).MeetingResponseStatus
                Case 0
                    TextStr2 = " did not respond."
                Case 1
                    TextStr2 = " organized the meeting."
                Case 2
                    TextStr2 = " tentatively accepted."
                Case 3
                    TextStr2 = " accepted."
                Case 4
                    TextStr2 = " declined."
            End Select
            TextStr = TextStr & TextStr2
        Next
        If MsgBox(TextStr,1) = 2 then Exit Sub ' Use OK/Cancel; exit if Cancel
        Set myMeeting = myItems.FindNext
    Loop
End Sub
```

> **More Info** For more information about the MeetingResponseStatus property and the values it returns, see Microsoft Outlook Visual Basic Reference Help.

The TaskItem Object

The TaskItem object represents a single item in the user's Tasks folder. A task is similar to an appointment in that it can be sent to others (much like a meeting request) and can be a recurring task. Unlike an appointment, however, an uncompleted recurring task has only a single instance. When an instance of a recurring task is marked as complete, Outlook creates a second instance of the task for the next time period in the task's recurrence pattern.

This section shows you how to work with a TaskItem object.

> **Important** Open the TaskItem object and TaskRequestItem object items in the VBScript Samples folder to work directly with this code in Outlook.

TaskItem Object Methods

This section covers the *GetRecurrencePattern* and *Assign* methods of the TaskItem object.

Creating a Recurring Task

You can use the *GetRecurrencePattern* method of the TaskItem object to create a recurring task, in much the same manner as creating a recurring appointment. (For more information, see "Creating a Recurring Appointment" earlier in this chapter.) The following example shows how to create a task and then call the *GetRecurrencePattern* method to make the task a recurring task:

```
Sub CreateRecurringTask_Click
    Set MyItem = Application.CreateItem(3)
    MyItem.Subject = "Test Task"
    Set MyPattern = MyItem.GetRecurrencePattern
    MyItem.Save
End Sub
```

As with a recurring meeting, you use the RecurrencePattern object associated with the task to specify how often and when the task will recur. Unlike a recurring appointment, however, a recurring task does not have multiple occurrences. Instead, when a recurring task is marked as completed, Outlook creates a copy of the task for the next date in the recurrence pattern. Consequently, the RecurrencePattern object of a task does not support the *GetOccurrence* method or the Exceptions property.

Delegating a Task

In much the same way as you can invite others to a meeting by sending them an AppointmentItem object, you can delegate a task to others by sending them a TaskItem object. Before sending the object, however, you must first use the *Assign* method to create an assigned task. The following example shows how to create and delegate a task using the *Assign* and *Send* methods. Remember that the programmatic *Send* will cause the Warning dialog box to appear.

```
Sub AssignTask_Click
    Set myItem = Application.CreateItem(3)
    myItem.Assign
    Set myDelegate = myItem.Recipients.Add("James Allard")
    myItem.Subject = "Develop order confirmation form"
    myItem.DueDate = #6/12/99#
    myItem.Send
End Sub
```

When a task is assigned and sent to another user, the user receives a TaskRequestItem object. You can use this object to access the task associated with the request and to respond to the task request.

The TaskRequestItem Object

A TaskRequestItem object represents a request to assign a task in the Inbox of the user to whom the task is being assigned. The following example displays a message box containing the subject of each task request in the user's Inbox folder:

```
Sub ShowTaskRequests_Click
    Set myNameSpace = Application.GetNameSpace("MAPI")
    Set myFolder = myNameSpace.GetDefaultFolder(6)
    Set myItems = myFolder.Items
    Set myTaskRequest = _
        myItems.Find("[MessageClass] = 'IPM.TaskRequest'")
    Do While TypeName (myTaskRequest)<> "Nothing"
        myMessage = myMessage & chr(13) & myTaskRequest.Subject
        Set myTaskRequest = myItems.FindNext
    Loop
    If myMessage = "" then
        MsgBox "You have no pending task requests"
    Else
        MsgBox "Your pending task requests are:" & chr(13) & myMessage
    End If
End Sub
```

Working with Task Requests

As with a MeetingItem object, usually you will not work directly with a TaskRequestItem object. For example, you do not use the TaskRequestItem object to accept or decline the task. Instead, you use the task associated with the task request.

The *GetAssociatedTask* method of the TaskRequestItem object returns a TaskItem object that you can use to accept or refuse the task.

Retrieving the Associated Task of a Task Request

Using the *GetAssociatedTask* method, you can access the task associated with a TaskRequestItem. Properties of the TaskItem returned by this method contain additional information about the assigned task, such as its due date.

> **Important** Before you call the *GetAssociatedTask* method for a TaskRequestItem object, you must first process the TaskRequestItem object. By default, this is done automatically (unless the user has cleared the Process Requests And Responses On Arrival check box on the Advanced E-Mail Options dialog box available through the Options dialog box). You can also process a TaskRequestItem object by calling its *Display* method. Note that when a TaskRequestItem object is processed, its associated task is added to the user's Tasks folder.

The following code example displays a message box containing the subject and due date of every task request in the user's Inbox. This example is identical to the one in the previous section, but it uses the *GetAssociatedTask* method to access the DueDate property of the task associated with the task request. Note that this example assumes that the TaskRequestItem objects have already been processed.

```
Sub ShowAssociatedTasks_Click
    Set myNameSpace = Application.GetNameSpace("MAPI")
    Set myFolder = myNameSpace.GetDefaultFolder(6)
    Set myItems = myFolder.Items
    Set myTaskRequest = _
    myItems.Find("[MessageClass] = 'IPM.TaskRequest'")
    Do While TypeName (myTaskRequest)<> "Nothing"
        myMessage = myMessage & chr(13) _
            & myTaskRequest.Subject & " due on " _
            & myTaskRequest.GetAssociatedTask(False).DueDate
        Set myTaskRequest = myItems.FindNext
    Loop
    If myMessage = "" then
        MsgBox "You have no pending task requests"
    Else
        MsgBox "Your pending task requests are:" & chr(13) & myMessage
    End If
End Sub
```

Responding to a Task Request

To accept, decline, or modify a task request, use the *Respond* method of the TaskItem object returned by the *GetAssociatedTask* method of a TaskRequestItem object. The following example retrieves the first TaskRequestItem in the user's Inbox and accepts it. Like the *GetAssociatedAppointment* method discussed earlier, the *Respond* method will display the Outlook Object Model Guard dialog boxes.

```
Sub AcceptTaskRequest_Click
    Set myNameSpace = Application.GetNameSpace("MAPI")
    Set myFolder = myNameSpace.GetDefaultFolder(6)
    Set myItems = myFolder.Items
    Set myTaskRequest = _
        myItems.Find("[MessageClass] = 'IPM.TaskRequest'")
    If TypeName(myTaskRequest) <> "Nothing" then
        Set myTask = MyTaskRequest.GetAssociatedTask(False)
        myTask.Respond 2, True,False
        myTask.Send
        MsgBox "Accepted: " & MyTask.Subject, vbInformation
    Else
        MsgBox "You have no pending task requests", vbInformation
    End If
End Sub
```

Note that if you set the second parameter of the *Respond* method to *True*, you must call the *Send* method of the TaskItem.

When the *Respond* method is used to respond to a task request, the initiating user receives a TaskRequestAcceptItem, TaskRequestDeclineItem, or TaskRequestUpdateItem object, depending on the type of response. You work with these objects in much the same way as a TaskRequestItem object in that you use the object's *GetAssociatedTask* method to retrieve the TaskItem object associated with the request and then call the methods and access the properties of the TaskItem object.

The ContactItem and DistListItem Objects

The ContactItem contains two important collection objects in Outlook 2000 and Outlook 2002. The Links object lets you link child ContactItem objects to parent Item objects. Only ContactItem objects can perform as child objects of a parent MailItem, PostItem, AppointmentItem, DocumentItem, JournalItem, TaskItem, DistListItem, or ContactItem object. Another great feature of the Links object is that Link object members do not have to live in the same folder as the parent item object.

The second collection object that pertains to the ContactItem is the DistListItem. A DistListItem acts as a container for ContactItem objects and, as the name implies, is a means of creating distribution lists in both your mailbox Contacts folder and in public folders. Because the Outlook ContactItem is such a rich form with over 100 properties that support Personal Information Management (PIM), the DistListItem is also a rich container and can be manipulated programmatically by your application.

> **More Info** For a complete list and description of the properties, methods, and events for the ContactItem and DistListItem objects, see Microsoft Outlook Visual Basic Reference Help.

> **Important** Open the ContactItem object item in the VBScript Samples folder to work directly with this code in Outlook.

ContactItem Object Methods

This section shows you how to forward a Contact Item as a vCard, the Internet standard for creating and sharing virtual business cards.

Sending the Contact as a vCard

This example uses the *ForwardasvCard* method to forward a vCard attachment for a Contact in a Mail Message. The *ForwardasvCard* method returns a MailItem with the vCard file attached.

```
Sub SendAsvCard_Click
    Const olContactItem = 2
    On Error Resume Next
    Set myContact = Application.CreateItem(olContactItem)
    myContact.FirstName = "Nancy"
    myContact.LastName = "Davolio"
    myContact.FullName = "Davolio, Nancy"
    myContact.CompanyName = "AnyCompany Corporation"
    myContact.JobTitle = "Senior Analyst"
    myContact.Department = "ITSD"
    myContact.EmailAddress = "nancyd@anycompany.com"
    myContact.EmailAddressType = "SMTP"
    myContact.Display
    Set myMsg = myContact.ForwardasvCard
    myMsg.Display(True) 'Forces modal display
End Sub
```

Adding Items to the Links Collection

Use the Links collection to add Contacts to an existing item. You can add Link items to any Item type. The following example shows you how to use the *Add* method of the Links collection object to add the last three LastNames in your

Contacts folder to a Contact item that was created programmatically. Only items with a base message class of IPM.Contact can be added as a member of the Links collection for an item. You cannot add a DistListItem to the Links collection.

```
Sub AddItemstoLinks_Click
    Const olContactItem = 2, olFolderContacts = 10
    Set objContact = Application.CreateItem(olContactItem)
    objContact.FirstName = "Jane"
    objContact.LastName = "Smith"
    objContact.FullName = "Smith, Jane"
    objContact.CompanyName = "XYZ Corporation"
    objContact.JobTitle = "Senior Analyst"
    objContact.Department = "ITSD"
    objContact.EmailAddress = "jsmith@xyz.com"
    objContact.EmailAddressType = "SMTP"
    Set colLinks = objContact.Links
    'Add the last three names in your contacts folder to links
    Set objNS = Application.GetNameSpace("MAPI")
    Set objFolder = objNS.GetDefaultFolder(olFolderContacts)
    Set colContacts = objFolder.Items
    colContacts.Sort "[LastName]", True 'Descending
    For Each myContact in colContacts
        'Can only add Contacts to Links collection
        If Instr(myContact.MessageClass,"IPM.Contact") Then
            If myContact.EmailAddress <> "" Then
                colLinks.Add(myContact)
                intAdded = intAdded + 1
            End If
        End If
        If intAdded = 3 Then Exit For
    Next
    'Contact must be saved for links to work
    objContact.Save
    objContact.Display
End Sub
```

Adding Contacts to a DistListItem

The following example shows you how to programmatically add members to a DistListItem object. The trick is to create a temporary mail item and instantiate a Recipients collection item for that Mail item. Once you have added recipients to the Recipients collection, use the *AddMembers* method of the DistListItem to add the recipients to the Distribution List. For additional information on the Recipients object, see "The Recipients Collection Object" later in this chapter.

Part IV Beyond the Basics

> **Outlook Security** If your code attempts to access a Recipients collection object, attempts to access a property that relates to a ContactItem e-mail address, or uses the *GetMember* method of the DistListItem, the Warning dialog box shown earlier in Figure 11-4 (on page 429) will appear. See Chapter 13 for methods to eliminate the Warning dialog box and a detailed discussion of which properties and methods trigger Warning dialog boxes.

```
Sub AddContactstoDistListItem_Click
    On Error Resume Next
    Const olMailItem = 0, olDistributionListItem = 7, olFolderContacts = 10
    Set objDL = Application.CreateItem(olDistributionListItem)
    'Create a temporary mail item
    Set objMsg = Application.CreateItem(olMailItem)
    Set colRecips = objMsg.Recipients
    'Add the first three names in your contacts folder to links
    Set objNS = Application.GetNameSpace("MAPI")
    Set objFolder = objNS.GetDefaultFolder(olFolderContacts)
    Set colContacts = objFolder.Items
    colContacts.Sort "[LastName]"
    For Each myContact in colContacts
        'Can only add contacts with e-mail address
        If myContact.EmailAddress <> "" Then
            colRecips.Add MyContact.EmailAddress
            intAdded = intAdded + 1
        End If
        If intAdded = 3 Then Exit For
    Next
    objDL.AddMembers colRecips
    objDL.Subject = "Test DL"
    objDL.Display
End Sub
```

The JournalItem Object

The JournalItem object provides a convenient way to record activity in relationship to any Outlook item. A journal entry can be as simple as the record of a phone call or as complex as recording the number of times a specific Word document has been edited.

JournalItem Object Methods

Because the JournalItem object records activities in time, the two most important methods of the JournalItem object are the *StartTimer* and *StopTimer* methods. The following example creates a Journal Item from a contact, creates a link to the contact for the Journal Item, and then starts the Journal Item timer with the *StartTimer* method:

```
Sub LinkJournalItemtoContact_Click
    Const olContactItem = 2, olJournalItem = 4
    On Error Resume Next
    Set myContact = Application.CreateItem(olContactItem)
    myContact.FirstName = "Friedman"
    myContact.LastName = "Fern"
    myContact.FullName = "Friedman, Fern"
    myContact.CompanyName = "XYZ Corporation"
    myContact.JobTitle = "Senior Analyst"
    myContact.Department = "ITSD"
    myContact.Email1Address = "ffriedman@xyz.com"
    myContact.Email1AddressType = "SMTP"
    'Save the contact before you create a link
    myContact.Save
    Set myJournal = Application.CreateItem(olJournalItem)
    myJournal.Companies = myContact.CompanyName
    myJournal.Subject = myContact.Subject
    Set colLinks = myJournal.Links
    colLinks.Add myContact
    myJournal.Display
    myJournal.StartTimer
End Sub
```

> **More Info** For a complete list and description of the properties, methods, and events for the JournalItem object, see Microsoft Outlook Visual Basic Reference Help.

> **Important** Open the JournalItem object in the VBScript Samples folder to work directly with this code in Outlook.

Part IV Beyond the Basics

The Item Window (Inspector Objects)

The Inspector object represents the window in which an Outlook item is displayed. The Inspectors object is the parent collection object for Inspector objects. The following sections cover some of the methods and properties for the Inspector and Inspectors objects.

> **More Info** For a complete list and description of the properties, methods, and events for the Inspector and Inspectors objects, see Microsoft Outlook Visual Basic Reference Help.

> **Important** Open the Inspector object in the VBScript Samples folder to work directly with this code in Outlook.

Inspector Object Methods

This section covers the *SetCurrentFormPage*, *HideFormPage*, and *ShowFormPage* methods of the Inspector object.

Setting the Current Form Page

You can use the *SetCurrentFormPage* method of the Inspector object to set the current form page of a form. The following example shows the Details page as the current form page of a Contact form when you click CommandButton1. (To use this example, you must add a command button to a Contact form in Design mode. Add the code in the Script Editor, and then run the form.)

```
Sub SetTheCurrentFormPage_Click
    Set MyNameSpace = Application.GetNameSpace("MAPI")
    Set MyFolder = MyNameSpace.Folders _
        ("Building Microsoft Outlook 2002 Applications")
    Set BeyondFolder = MyFolder.Folders("4. Beyond the Basics")
    Set VBScript = BeyondFolder.Folders("VBScript")
    Set VBScriptSamples = VBScript.Folders("VBScript Samples")
    Set MyItem = VBScriptSamples.Items.Add("IPM.Post.Test")
    set MyInspector = MyItem.GetInspector
    MyInspector.SetCurrentFormPage("Test")
    MyItem.Display
End Sub
```

Hiding and Showing a Form Page

You can use the *HideFormPage* and *ShowFormPage* methods of the Inspector object to hide and show a form page. In the following example, the Test page of the Test form is hidden:

```
Sub HideTheTestPage_Click
    Set MyNameSpace = Application.GetNameSpace("MAPI")
    Set MyFolder = MyNameSpace.Folders _
        ("Building Microsoft Outlook 2002 Applications")
    Set BeyondFolder = MyFolder.Folders("4. Beyond the Basics")
    Set VBScript = BeyondFolder.Folders("VBScript")
    Set VBScriptSamples = VBScript.Folders("VBScript Samples")
    Set MyItem = VBScriptSamples.Items.Add("IPM.Post.Test")
    Set MyInspector = MyItem.GetInspector
    MyInspector.HideFormPage("Test")
    MyItem.Display
End Sub
```

Inspector Object Properties

This section covers the ModifiedFormPages property of the Inspector object. The ModifiedFormPages property returns the entire collection of pages for a form. The Pages collection object is covered in more detail in the next section.

Referencing a Form Page and Its Controls

You can use the ModifiedFormPages property of the Inspector object to return the Pages collection representing the pages on a form that have been modified. Note that standard pages on a form, such as a Message page, are also included in the collection if the standard pages can be customized. You must use the Pages collection object to switch to the page, which then allows you to gain access to controls on the page. The following example uses the ModifiedFormPages property of the Inspector object to return the Inspector object page in the Pages collection object. It then uses the Controls property of the Page object to reference the HideandShow toggle button control. When the HideandShow control is down (its value equals *True*), the HideAndShowLabel control is visible. When the toggle button is up, the HideAndShowLabel control is not visible.

```
Sub HideAndShow_Click
    Set myInspector = Item.GetInspector
    Set myPage = myInspector.ModifiedFormPages("Inspector Object")
    Set myControl = myPage.Controls("HideAndShow")
    If myControl.value = True Then
        myPage.Controls("HideAndShowLabel").Visible = True
    Else
        myPage.Controls("HideAndShowLabel").Visible = False
    End If
End Sub
```

The Pages Collection Object

To reference a page or controls on a page, you use the ModifiedFormPages property of the Inspector object to reference the Pages collection object, and then you reference the individual page by name or number. The following procedure uses the ModifiedFormPages property of the Inspector object to return the number of modified form pages in the Pages collection. Note that the pages are not added to the collection until the page is clicked at design time.

```
Sub ShowModifiedFormPagesCount_Click
    Set PagesCollection = Item.GetInspector.ModifiedFormPages
    MsgBox "The number of modified form pages in the Pages collection is " _
        & PagesCollection.Count & "."
End Sub
```

> **Important** Open the Page object item in the VBScript Samples folder to work directly with this code in Outlook.

The Page Object

You can use the ModifiedFormPages property to return the Pages collection from an Inspector object. Use ModifiedFormPages*(index)*, where *index* is the name or index number, to return a single page from a Pages collection. The following example references the Message page and then references the CommandButton1 control on the page. When clicked, the CommandButton1 control moves to the right.

> **Important** The Page object is contained in the Microsoft Forms 2.0 Object Library. To view the methods and properties for the Page object, consult "Microsoft Forms Visual Basic Reference" in Microsoft Outlook Visual Basic Reference Help.

```
Sub CommandButton1_Click
    Set MyPage = GetInspector.ModifiedFormPages("Message")
    Set MyControl = MyPage.CommandButton1
    MyControl.Left = MyControl.Left + 20
End Sub
```

The Controls Collection Object

To access controls on Outlook forms, you use the Controls collection object. The Controls collection object contains the collection of controls on a form page. To access an individual control in the Controls collection, you use the index value of the control or the name of the control. The Controls collection object is contained in the Microsoft Forms 2.0 Object Library. This section discusses how to reference control collections and controls on a form.

> **Important** Open the Control object item in the VBScript Samples folder to work directly with this code in Outlook.

Methods of the Controls Collection Object

The Controls collection object offers a variety of methods that let you manipulate the controls on a form. For example, you can use the *Move* method to move all the controls on a page, or you can use the *SendToBack* method to send the controls in the Controls collection to the back layer of the page.

You can use the Controls property to return the Controls collection from a Page object. Use Controls*(index)*, where *index* is the name or index number, to return a control from a Controls collection.

Adding a Control to the Form Page

You can use the *Add* method of the Controls collection object to add a control to the form. The following example uses the *Add* method to add a new CommandButton control to the ControlObject page:

```
Sub AddAControlToAPage _Click
    Set MyPage = GetInspector.ModifiedFormPages("Control Object")
    If MyPage.Controls.Count < 3 then
        Set MyControl = MyPage.Controls.Add("Forms.CommandButton.1")
        MyControl.Left = 18
        MyControl.Top = 150
        MyControl.Width = 175
        MyControl.Height = 20
        MyControl.Caption = "This is " & MyControl.Name
    Else
        MsgBox "You can only add one command button.", vbInformation
    End If
End Sub
```

Part IV Beyond the Basics

> **More Info** For more information about using the *Add* method of the Controls collection object, see "Control Reference" in Microsoft Outlook Visual Basic Reference Help.

Controls Collection Object Properties

The Controls collection object provides only the Count property. With the Count property, you can use the For...Next statement to loop through the controls in a collection. The following example returns the collection of controls on the Controls collection object page. It then displays the name of each control contained on the page.

```
Sub ShowtheControlsCollectionCount_Click
    Set Page = Item.GetInspector.ModifiedFormPages("Control Object")
    Set MyControls = Page.Controls
    For i = 0 to MyControls.Count - 1
        MsgBox MyControls(i).Name, vbInformation
    Next
End Sub
```

> **Important** Notice that the For...Next statement starts at 0. You must use 0 to reference the first item in the collection. However, Outlook returns a Count of 3. Therefore, you must specify Count -1 as the upper limit in the argument of the For...Next statement.

The Control Object

In the Visual Basic Forms Object Model, the control objects are generically represented by a Control object. Further, they are individually represented by the objects that represent the names of the individual control components, such as TextBox, CheckBox, and so on. As discussed in the preceding section, to reference a control, use the Controls property to return the Controls collection from a Page object, and then use Controls*(index)*, where *index* is the name or index number, to return a control from a Controls collection.

> **Important** The Control object and the individual control objects, such as CheckBox and TextBox, are contained in the Microsoft Forms 2.0 Object Library. To view the methods and properties for this library, use the VBA Object Browser and select MSForms in the library drop-down list box.

Unlike controls on VBA or Visual Basic forms, the control object in VBScript must be explicitly instantiated before you can access the properties and methods of the control. You must explicitly reference the control object regardless of whether the control is an intrinsic Outlook Forms control or an extrinsic custom or third-party ActiveX control. The following line of code shows you how to set a reference to a control object:

```
Set TextBox1 = Item.GetInspector.ModifiedFormPages("P.2").Controls("TextBox1")
```

A shorter alternative syntax is as follows:

```
Set TextBox1 = GetInspector.ModifiedFormPages("P.2").TextBox1
```

Setting Control References at the Script Level

If you inspect the code behind the Control object example form, you'll see that some control objects have been dimensioned as script-level variables. The *Item_Open* procedure then sets a reference to each control dimensioned as a script-level variable, and the control object has a script-level lifetime. If you follow this convention, you do not have to instantiate a control object reference in every procedure where you want to get or set control properties and call control methods. Dimension the controls as script-level variables using the same name as the control, and then instantiate those control variables in the form's *Item_Open* procedure. Don't use an alias for the control object. Name the control object on the left side of the Set statement with the same name as the actual control. This practice makes your code more readable because the name of the control in VBScript code is the same as the control name in Design mode.

Properties of Control Objects

The properties available for a control will differ for each type of control. This section covers the Value property for the CheckBox control and the Enabled property for the TextBox and Label controls.

Setting the Enabled Property of a Control

The following example uses a CheckBox control called EnableTextBox and a TextBox control called TextBox1. When the EnableTextBox control is clicked, the procedure evaluates the state of EnableTextBox. If the value of EnableTextBox is *True*, then TextBox1 and Label1 are enabled; otherwise, they are not enabled.

```
Sub EnableTextBox_Click
    Set MyPage = Item.GetInspector.ModifiedFormPages("Control Object")
    Set MyControls = MyPage.Controls
    If MyControls("EnableTextBox").Value = True then
        MyControls("Label1").Enabled = True
        MyControls("TextBox1").Enabled = True
    Else
        MyControls("TextBox1").Enabled = False
        MyControls("Label1").Enabled = False
    End If
End Sub
```

Setting the PossibleValues Property of a ComboBox or ListBox Control

Rather than use the *AddItem* method to add items to a ListBox or ComboBox control, you can use the PossibleValues property. Note that the PossibleValues property is an undocumented property. In this example, the PossibleValues property is used to add the values Red, Green, and Blue to the ComboBox1 control when CommandButton1 is clicked.

```
Sub CommandButton1_Click
    Set MyPage = Item.GetInspector.ModifiedFormPages("Message")
    MyPage.ComboBox1.PossibleValues = "Red;Green;Blue"
End Sub
```

Using the List Property to Populate a ListBox or ComboBox Control

The most powerful method to add values to a ListBox or ComboBox control is the List property. The List property populates a ListBox control or ComboBox control with a single statement. By assigning the control object's List property to a variant array, you can create a single-column or a multi-column list in the control. If you are populating controls with the results of an ADO recordset, the List property and the recordset *GetRows* method (which returns a variant array) are perfect partners. The following example from the *Item_Open* event in the Control object form creates a variant array and then assigns the array to the List property of the ListBox1 and ComboBox1 controls:

```
Sub Item_Open
    'Instance script-level control objects
    Set ListBox1 = GetInspector.ModifiedFormPages _
        ("Control Click Events").ListBox1
    Set ComboBox1 = GetInspector.ModifiedFormPages_
        ("Control Click Events").ComboBox1
    'Create a variant array to hold values
    Redim varArray(2)
    varArray(0) = "Red"
    varArray(1) = "Blue"
    varArray(2) = "Green"
    'Populate ListBox1 and ComboBox1
    ListBox1.List = varArray
    ComboBox1.List = varArray
End Sub
```

Hiding Columns in a ComboBox Control

You can hide a column in a ComboBox control by using the ColumnWidths property. The following example presents a typical problem for the designer of a mutli-column combo box. You want to present recognizable names, such as the full name of a state, but you only want to store the state's abbreviation. The PopulateStates procedure in the Control object form populates the cmbStates combo box with the abbreviation and full name for several vacation states. The ColumnWidths property is set so that the state abbreviation does not appear in the drop-down portion of the list. However, the TextColumn property is set so that the abbreviation appears in the ComboBox control when the user selects an item from the list. If you are binding the control to a user-defined field, you should also set the BoundColumn property so that the bound field uses the specified column as its value source. The *cmbStates_Click* procedure utilizes the Text, ListIndex, and Column properties of the combo box to create a message box that informs the user about their selection.

```
Sub PopulateStates
    Dim varStates()
    Set cmbStates = _
        GetInspector.ModifiedFormPages("Control Object").cmbStates
    ReDim varStates(6,1)
    varStates (0,0) = "AZ"
    varStates (0,1) = "Arizona"
    varStates (1,0) = "CA"
    varStates (1,1) = "California"
    varStates (2,0) = "HI"
```

(continued)

Part IV Beyond the Basics

```
        varStates (2,1) = "Hawaii"
        varStates (3,0) = "ID"
        varStates (3,1) = "Idaho"
        varStates (4,0) = "NV"
        varStates (4,1) = "Nevada"
        varStates (5,0) = "OR"
        varStates (5,1) = "Oregon"
        varStates (6,0) = "WA"
        varStates (6,1) = "Washington"
        cmbStates.List = varStates
        cmbStates.ColumnCount = 2
        cmbStates.ColumnWidths = "0 in ; 1 in" 'Hide col 0
        cmbStates.TextColumn = 1
        cmbStates.BoundColumn = 1
End Sub
Sub cmbStates_Click
        MsgBox "You selected the state of " & cmbStates.Text _
            & vbCr & "Enjoy your vacation in " _
            & cmbStates.Column(1, cmbStates.ListIndex), vbInformation
End Sub
```

> **Tip** When you set TextColumn or BoundColumn in a ListBox or ComboBox control, remember that the Column property is zero-based so that Column 1 is referenced as Column(0).

Resizing a Control Vertically and Horizontally

Quite often, you want controls on a form to adjust horizontally and vertically when the form is resized. To do this, you must set an invisible property called LayoutFlags. This example sets the LayoutFlags property for the TextBox1 control when you click CommandButton1.

To run the example, do the following:

1. In Design mode, add a TextBox1 control to the (P.2) page of a form.
2. Resize the control so that its bottom border is near the bottom border of the form and its right border is near the right border of the form. Don't obscure the CommandButton1 control.
3. Add the following code for the CommandButton1 control.
4. Switch to Run mode, resize the form, and notice what happens.
5. Then click CommandButton1 and resize the form. After the LayoutFlags property is set, the controls adjust to the size of the form.

```
Sub CommandButton1_Click
    Item.GetInspector.ModifiedFormPages("P.2").TextBox1.LayoutFlags = 68
End Sub
```

After you set the LayoutFlags property, you can delete the procedure from the Script Editor.

Resizing a Control Vertically

In some situations, you want controls on the form to vertically resize when the form is vertically resized. To do this, set the LayoutFlags property to 65.

To run this example, do the following:

1. Delete the TextBox1 control from the (P.2) page, and then add a new TextBox1 control.

2. Resize the control so that its bottom border is near the bottom border of the form. Don't obscure the CommandButton1 control.

3. Add the following code for the CommandButton1 control.

4. Switch to Run mode, and resize the form vertically. Then click CommandButton1, and vertically resize the form again.

```
Sub CommandButton1_Click
    Item.GetInspector.ModifiedFormPages _
        ("P.2").TextBox1.LayoutFlags = 65
End Sub
```

After you set the LayoutFlags property, you can delete the procedure from the Script Editor.

Binding a Control to a Field at Run Time

You can use the hidden ItemProperty property to bind a control to a field at run time. To run this example, do the following:

1. Add a new TextBox1 control (or use the existing one if it's already on the form) to the (P.2) page of the form.

2. Add the following code for the CommandButton1 control.

3. Switch to Run mode, click the Message tab, and type *Test* in the Subject box.

4. Then click CommandButton1. Notice that the value in the Subject box appears in the TextBox1 control because the control is now bound to the Subject field.

```
Sub CommandButton1_Click()
    Item.GetInspector.ModifiedFormPages _
        ("P.2").TextBox1.ItemProperty = "Subject"
End Sub
```

> **Note** If you create a control by dragging a plain text field to a form, you cannot bind the control to a field of a different type. For example, you cannot drag a TextBox control to a form and then bind it programmatically to a field containing an E-mail recipient type (such as the To field).

Binding a Control to a Data Source

You can bind controls on an Outlook form to a data source with ADO. However, you should be cautious when incorporating non-Exchange sources of data into your solution. If your application requires online and offline use, dynamic connections to data with ADO are not practical in the offline state. You can use ADO persisted recordsets to store data in a folder and then extract that persisted recordset to the file system when you need to access the data. This practice is limited to small sets of data that do not change frequently. Figure 11-10 illustrates a form that populates unbound controls with data from a persisted recordset stored in an Outlook folder. For additional examples of bound data controls and other methods of retrieving data in Outlook, see the Data Access Strategies For Outlook folder under "5. Advanced Topics" in the "Building Microsoft Outlook 2002 Applications" personal folders (.pst) file.

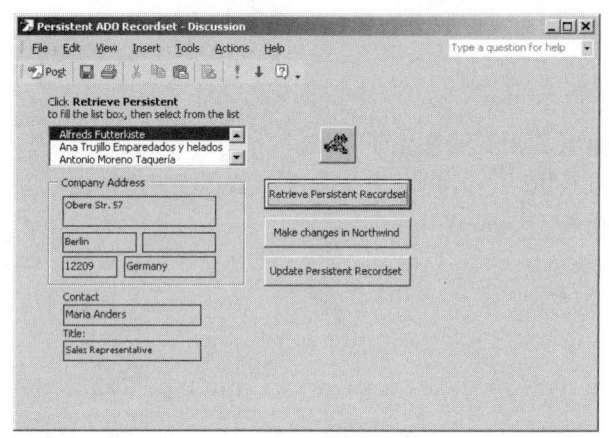

Figure 11-10 Bind controls to data with a persisted recordset stored in an Outlook folder.

Responding to the Click Event

The Click event is the only event raised by controls on Outlook forms. You must define the Click event procedure for a control in the Script Editor as follows:

```
Sub ControlName_Click
    'Event code goes here
End Sub
```

The Click event fires without exception for the Label, Image, CommandButton, ToggleButton, and Frame controls. Open the Control object item in the VBScript Samples folder and click the Control Click Events page for a practical demonstration of control Click events. However, there are many exceptions to the Click event:

- Right-clicking a control does not fire a Click event.
- Not every third-party or custom ActiveX control will fire a Click event in the Outlook forms container.
- The following controls do not respond to Click events in Outlook: TabStrip, SpinButton, ScrollBar, TextBox, and MultiPage.
- The following controls only respond to Click events when they are populated with items and an item in the list is selected: ComboBox and ListBox.
- The following controls respond to a Click event based on a change in their Value property: OptionButton and CheckBox.

An alternative to using a Click event is to write a *CustomPropertyChange* or *PropertyChange* event procedure for the bound field of the control. For example, the following procedure mimics the Buddy control available in Visual Basic by binding a SpinButton control to a user-defined field. When the user clicks the spin button, the value of TextBox2 changes. You can see this example in action on the page named "Using Control Values" in the Control Object item in the VBScript Samples folder.

```
Sub Item_CustomPropertyChange(ByVal Name)
Select Case Name
    Case "SpinButton2"
    TextBox2.Value = SpinButton2.Value
End Select
End Sub
```

The UserProperties Collection Object

The UserProperties collection object represents the custom fields contained in an item. To return a collection of user-defined fields for an item, you can use the UserProperties property of the MailItem object, the PostItem object, and so on. The UserProperty object represents a single field in the item.

> **More Info** For a complete list and description of the properties and methods for the UserProperties collection object, see Microsoft Outlook Visual Basic Reference Help.

> **Note** Standard properties in Outlook, such as Subject, To, and Body, are properties of the individual Item object. For more information, see "MailItem and PostItem Objects Properties" earlier in this chapter.

UserProperties Collection Object Methods

This section covers the *Find* method of the UserProperties collection object.

Getting and Setting the Value of a User Property

You can use the *Find* method of the UserProperties collection object to get or set the value of a user-defined field in an item as follows:

```
MsgBox "The value of the Customer Name field is " _
    & Item.UserProperties.Find("Customer Name").Value & "."
```

The syntax, however, can be shortened by three dots to increase performance and readability. Because the *Find* method is the default method of the UserProperties object and the Value property is the default property of the UserProperty object, the following statement is equivalent to the one above:

```
MsgBox "The value of the Customer Name field is " _
    & UserProperties("Customer Name") & "."
```

To set the value of a UserProperty object, simply reverse the statement as follows:

```
UserProperties("Customer Name") = "Microsoft Corporation"
```

The ItemProperties Collection Object

The ItemProperties collection object is new to Outlook 2002. This object is related to the UserProperties collection object, which contains only custom properties defined for an Item. The ItemProperties object lets you enumerate all the properties available for an Item. Be aware that certain Item properties related to an AddressEntry object will display the Security Warning dialog box. The ItemProperties collection object contains child ItemProperty objects that provide additional information about the Item property. If you use the *Add* or *Remove* methods of the ItemProperties object, you can add or remove custom properties only. The following example enumerates all the default and user-defined properties for the Company form used in Chapter 12, "The Northwind Contact Management Application."

```
Sub EnumerateContactItemProps()
    Dim oContactItem As ContactItem
    Dim colItemProps As ItemProperties
    Dim i As Integer
    Dim strPath As String
    Dim oFolder As MAPIFolder
    On Error Resume Next
    strPath = "\\Public Folders\All Public Folders\" _
        & "Northwind Contact Management Application\Companies"
    Set oFolder = OpenMAPIFolder(strPath)
    Set oContactItem = oFolder.Items.Add("IPM.Contact.Company")
    Set colItemProps = oContactItem.ItemProperties
    For i = 0 To colItemProps.Count - 1
        Debug.Print colItemProps.Item(i).Name, _
            colItemProps.Item(i).Value, _
            colItemProps.Item(i).IsUserProperty
    Next
End Sub
```

The Recipients Collection Object

The Recipients collection object represents the names that appear in the To field of the MailItem, MeetingRequestItem, and TaskRequestItem objects.

Recipients Collection Object Methods

This section covers the *Add* and *ResolveAll* methods of the Recipients collection object.

> **More Info** For a complete list and description of the properties and methods for the Recipients collection object and the Recipient object, see Microsoft Outlook Visual Basic Reference Help.

Adding Recipients to the Collection

You can use the *Add* method of the Recipients collection object to add recipient names to the Recipients collection. The following example creates a new Message item and then uses the Recipients property of the MailItem object to return the Recipients collection object that, in this case, is empty. It then adds two names to the Recipients collection object, uses the *ResolveAll* method to resolve the recipient names, and then displays the Message form. For this example, you can replace the names Nancy Davolio and Michael Suyama with names of people in your organization.

```
Sub AddRecipientsToCollection_Click()
    Dim objItem As Outlook.MailItem
    Dim colRecips As Outlook.Recipients
    On Error Resume Next
    Set objItem = Application.CreateItem(olMailItem)
    If objItem Is Nothing Then
        MsgBox "Could not create MailItem.", vbCritical
        Exit Sub
    End If
    objItem.Subject = "Outlook Object Model"
    Set colRecips = objItem.Recipients
    If Err Then
        MsgBox "The User did not allow Address Book access.", _
            vbCritical
        Exit Sub
    End If
    colRecips.Add ("Nancy Davolio")
    colRecips.Add ("Michael Suyama")
    colRecips.ResolveAll
    objItem.Display
End Sub
```

> **Outlook Security** The *AddRecipientsToCollection* procedure will cause the Warning dialog box shown earlier in Figure 11-4 (on page 429) to display. Any access to the Recipients collection object displays the Warning dialog box. If you haven't used the Administrative form to access the Recipients object, you might need to know whether the user has pressed Yes or No to allow Address Book access. The previous code example traps an error on the *Set colRecips = objItem.Recipients* statement when the user clicks No in the Warning dialog box.

Automatically Addressing an Item to All Contacts in a Contacts Folder

The following example uses the *Add* method and the *ResolveAll* method to show how you can use the Recipients collection object to create a procedure that allows you to automatically address a message to all the users in the Contacts folder in your Mailbox. In this procedure, the Contact's e-mail addresses are added to the Recipients collection object.

```
Sub AddresstoAllContacts_Click
    On Error Resume Next
    Set MyNameSpace = Application.GetNameSpace("MAPI")
    Set MyFolder = MyNameSpace.GetDefaultFolder(10)
    Set MyItems = MyFolder.Items
    Set MySendItem = Application.CreateItem(0)
    Set MyRecipients = MySendItem.Recipients
    For i = 1 To MyItems.Count
        If MyItems(i).EMailAddress <> "" Then
            MyRecipients.Add MyItems(i).EMailAddress
        End If
    Next
    MyRecipients.ResolveAll
    MySendItem.Display
End Sub
```

Automation

In addition to using VBScript or Visual Basic to program Outlook forms and COM Add-ins, you can use Visual Basic to program Outlook objects remotely. In order to enhance security, programs that automate Outlook externally will always be subject to the object model guards of the Outlook E-Mail Security Update. You use Automation when you want to control an entire session. For example, you may want to automatically send a message from within a Visual Basic or Microsoft Excel application.

To automate Outlook from another application, such as Visual Basic or Microsoft Excel, you must first reference the Microsoft Outlook 2002 Object Model. You can then use the GetObject function to automate a session that's already running, or the CreateObject function to open a new Outlook session. After the Outlook Application object is returned, you can then write code that uses the objects, properties, methods, and constants in the Outlook 2002 Object Model. The following example creates a Mail item from a Microsoft Excel 2002 worksheet when the MailSalesReport button is clicked:

```
Sub MailSalesReport_Click
    Set MyOlApp = CreateObject("Outlook.Application")
```

(continued)

Part IV Beyond the Basics

```
    Set MyItem = MyOlApp.CreateItem(olMailItem)
    MyItem.Subject = "Sales Results - " & Now()
    MyItem.Body = " Click the icon to open the Sales Results." & Chr(13)
    Set MyAttachments = MyItem.Attachments
    MyAttachments.Add "C:\My Documents\Q401.xls", OlByReference, 1, _
        "Q4 2001 Results Chart"
    MyItem.To = "Sales"
    MyItem.Display
End Sub
```

> **Note** As shown in the preceding example, the constants in the Outlook 2002 Object Model are valid when used in Visual Basic or Visual Basic for Applications.

Where To Go from Here

Microsoft Knowledge Base Articles Knowledge Base articles are available on the Web at *http://support.microsoft.com/support*. Also see "Using Visual Basic, VBA, or VBScript with Outlook (Chapter 11) KB Articles" in the Microsoft Web Sites folder under the Help And Web Sites folder on the companion CD.

12

The Northwind Contact Management Application

The Northwind Contact Management application uses the Microsoft Access 2002 Northwind sample database to populate a set of folders that showcase the contact management features of Microsoft Outlook 2002. Of course, every user has the ability to manage his own contacts using the Contacts folder in his personal mailbox. However, organizations need to manage and share contact information beyond the confines of their users' personal contact lists. Outlook 2002 improves upon the ability of previous versions of Outlook to track and manage contact activity in public folders. Public folders that contain contact items allow users to share contacts across a corporation, department, or workgroup—regardless of whether the user is on line or off line. Unlike database applications that require time-consuming table schema and stored procedure coding, Outlook contact applications can be developed rapidly using either default or custom contact items. Remember that a default Outlook contact item has more than 100 default properties that contain information associated with a contact.

With Outlook 2002, you can now use the Activity page of an Outlook contact item to create views of shared folders and to open items in those folders directly from the Activity page of the Contact form. The Links collection object lets you link one contact item to another quickly and efficiently. Think of the Links collection object as a means of implementing one-to-many relationships between items in Outlook folders. Outlook establishes your personal Contacts folder as an Outlook Address Book. Public folders that use the Outlook contact item as the default item type can also serve as Outlook Address Books, enabling you to categorize and communicate with your existing customers or sales leads.

The Northwind Contact Management application offers a practical example of what you can achieve with an Outlook application that operates seamlessly on line and off line, and it takes advantage of the synchronization features built into Outlook 2002. This application recapitulates what you have learned so far and provides us with a core application that we can extend in later chapters when we discuss Digital Dashboards in Chapter 15, "Integrating Outlook with Web Applications," and SharePoint Portal Server in Chapter 16, "Using Outlook with SharePoint Portal Server."

Overview

The Northwind Contact Management application can serve as a starting point for a customer relationship management (CRM) application. When deployed to an Exchange public folder, the application records your corporate activities for external companies and related company contacts. One company, for example, might contain more than 50 company contacts that have different job titles. When you open a company record, you can see all the related company contacts on the General page of the Company form, as shown in Figure 12-1. In addition, the company contact might be a vendor or a customer, or it might have another type of relationship with your company. The main Company form for the application lets you classify customers according to Company Type, Company Category, Territory, and Priority.

> **Note** The Northwind Contact Management application requires Outlook 2002. You can modify the application to run under Outlook 2000, but it might not run seamlessly both on line and off line. New properties and methods in the Outlook 2002 Object Model help you adjust to the on-line and offline state. Also, the Outlook View Control, an essential component of the application, must be installed separately in Outlook 2000. In Outlook 2002, however, the Outlook View Control is installed as an integral part of the program.

The possible values for these custom fields are stored in the CRM Administration form (shown in Figure 12-2) in the Setup subfolder of the Companies folder. The Setup folder is read-only to users of the application. Users can read

The Northwind Contact Management Application   Chapter 12

the lookup values from the form in this folder, but they cannot change the default values for Company Type, Company Category, Territory, and Priority. These values can be modified only by the owner of the application. Because the values are stored in a folder item rather than in the Windows registry or a database, they are available when the user disconnects from the corporate network. The best feature of the Northwind Contact Management application is that it is available either on line or off line. Changes made off line while a user is in the field are synchronized when he or she returns to the home office, and items in the public folder hierarchy are available to all users of the application.

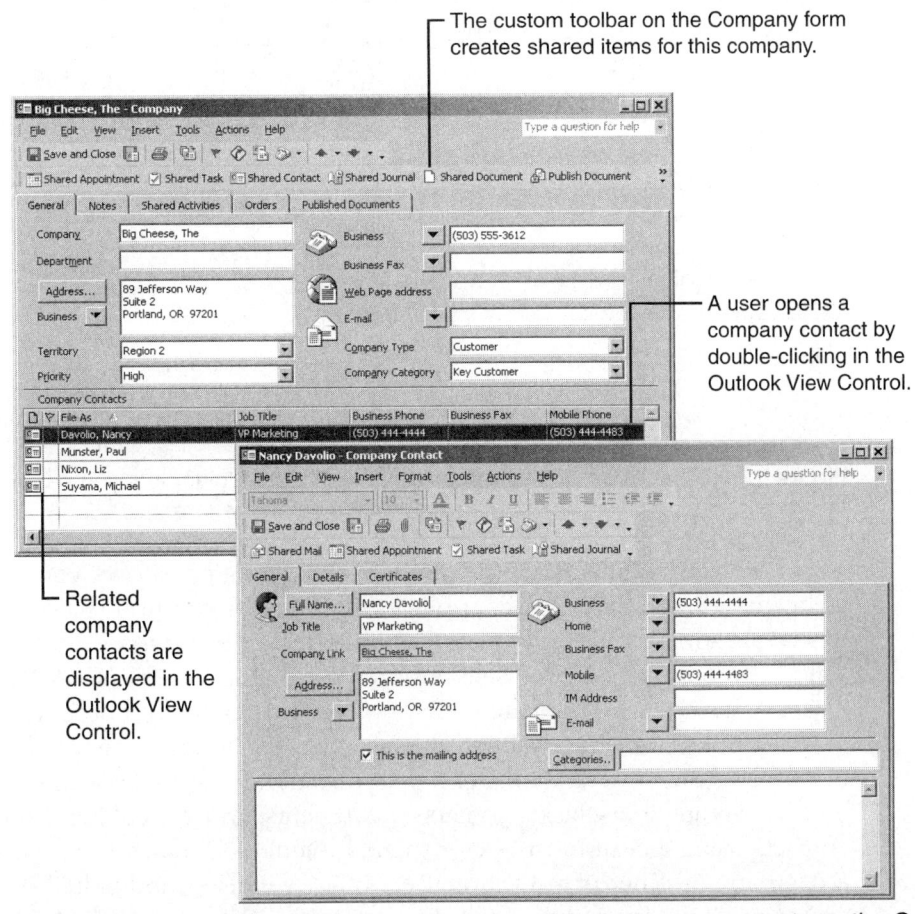

Figure 12-1 The Outlook View Control displays linked company contacts on the General page of the Company form.

Part IV Beyond the Basics

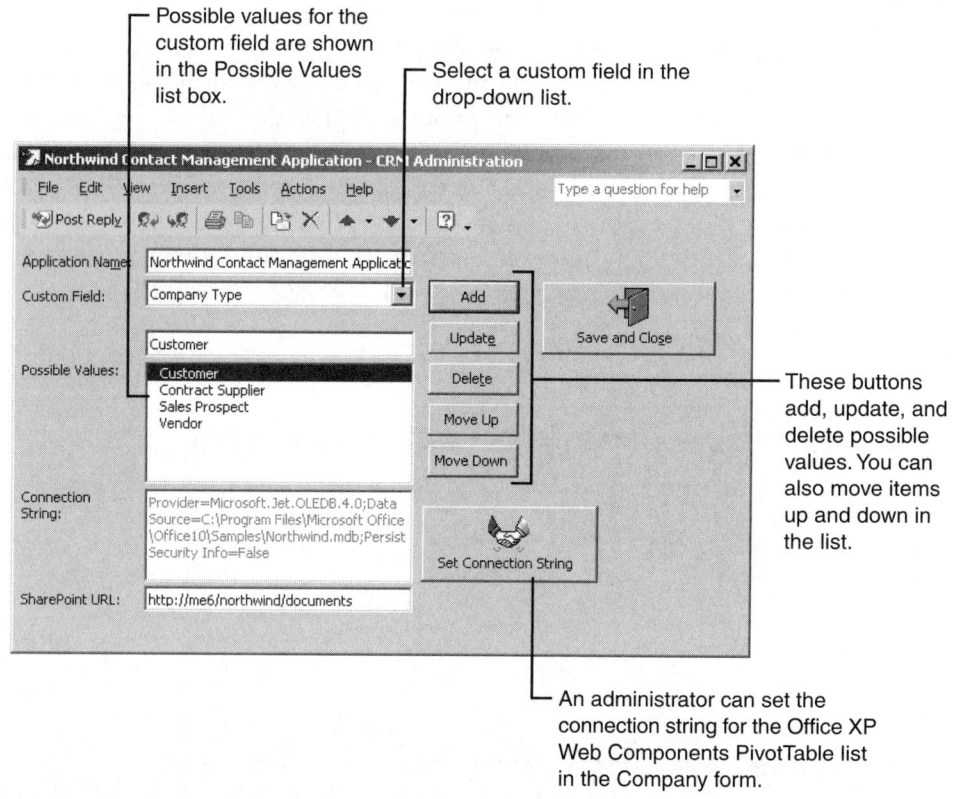

Figure 12-2 The CRM Administration form in the Setup folder lets you establish values for controls on the Company form without redesigning the form.

The Northwind Contact Management application shows you how to create a shared activities contact application in Exchange public folders. Although this application uses the familiar Northwind sample database in Access, you'll learn how to use Microsoft Visual Basic and ActiveX Data Objects (ADO) to import existing, prospective, or inactive company and contact records in an existing database into Exchange public folders. Once you've imported company information into the Contact Management application folders, you can create shared e-mail, appointments, tasks, contacts, documents, and journal items for customer contacts using a custom Inspector toolbar. Outlook contact items can represent a company or other organizational entity as well as an individual contact. You can create linked contact records for a company and view them in the Outlook View Control on the parent company form. Activities related to a given company or its linked contacts are recorded in an appropriate public folder. Consequently, shared appointments are created in the Shared Appointments folder, tasks in the Shared Tasks folder, journal items in the Shared Journal folder, and so forth.

Outlook 2002 and Automatic Activity Journaling

Outlook does not support automatic journaling of appointments, tasks, e-mail, and other activities in public folders. Automatic journaling of such activities is supported only within the context of a user's private mailbox. However, Outlook 2000 and Outlook 2002 do allow application designers to associate a Contacts public folder with other public folders in order to track shared activities on the Activities page of contact items in the Contacts public folder. The default Activities page of the Contact form features a drop-down control that lets a user display a linked folder for shared activities. Unfortunately, the built-in Activities page on the Contact form cannot be customized, so a new custom Shared Activities page uses the Outlook View Control to enhance the user experience. The Shared Activities page shown in Figure 12-3 lets a user pick the Shared Activity folder and then select any view defined for that folder. For example, if the user picks the Shared Tasks folder, she will see only the tasks created for the parent company. The Outlook View Control allows you to programmatically restrict the items displayed in the view. Users click a drop-down control to select the linked folder, and they can then select any view available in that folder.

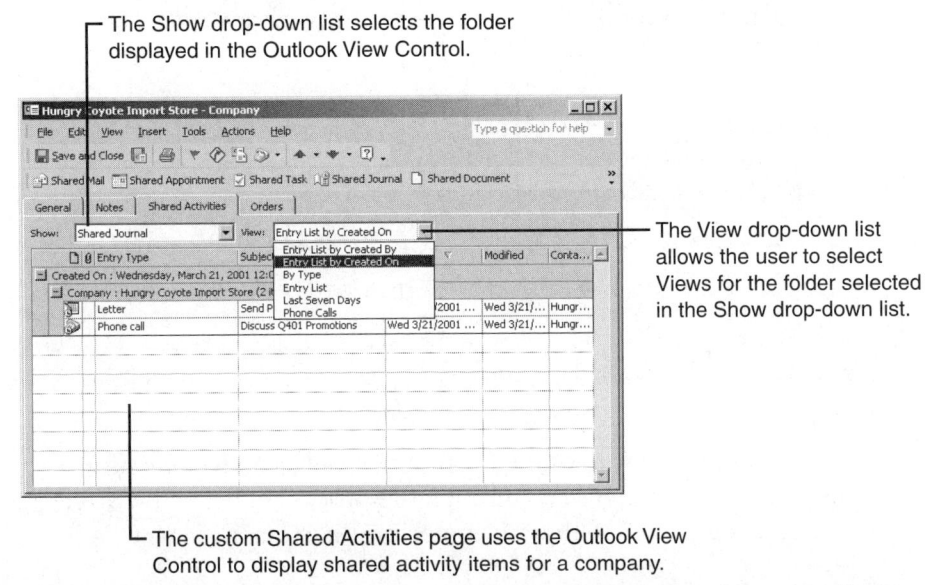

Figure 12-3 The Shared Activities page uses the Outlook View Control to display information in shared folders.

The Northwind Contact Management application also makes use of the PivotTable List ActiveX control in Microsoft Office XP. An Office XP Web Component, the PivotTable List lets a user query the Northwind database and view order information for a given customer by product category, salesperson, or order

ID directly on an Outlook form. The PivotTable List control is also used on an Access 2002 Data Access page that serves as a folder home page in a placeholder folder in the application, as shown in Figure 12-4. Placeholder folders are containers for active application subfolders that contain Outlook items such as contacts, appointments, and tasks. Think of a placeholder folder as an empty node in the public folder hierarchy. Because placeholder folders never contain items that can be modified by a user, they are excellent candidates for becoming folder home pages that provide supplementary information or functionality in your application. The Data Access folder home page in the parent folder of the Northwind Contact Management application provides a Web-based PivotTable list of Northwind orders organized by customer name.

The PivotTable list on the Northwind folder home page lets a user show sales for all salespersons or drill down to a specific individual.

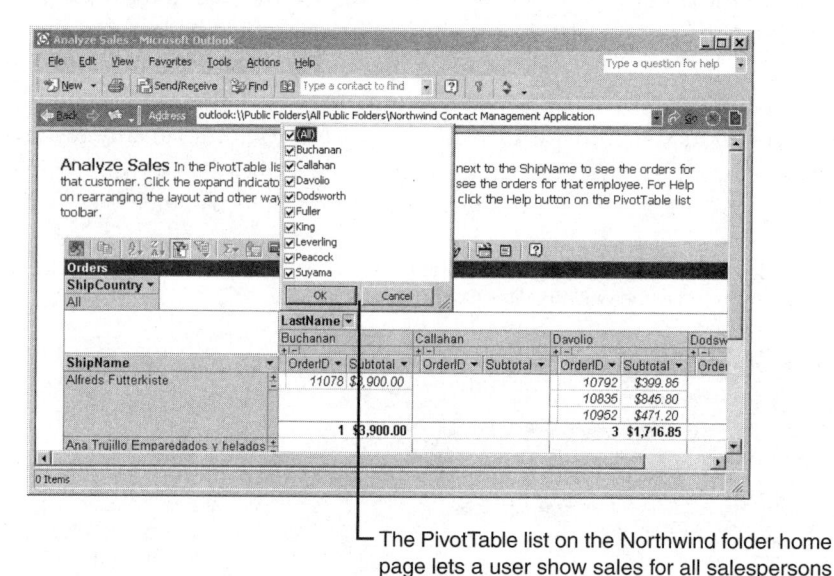

Figure 12-4 The Northwind Data Access page is the folder home page in the root folder of the Northwind Contact Management application.

To demonstrate how the Northwind Contact Management application works, the rest of this section steps through the process of using this application to track activities associated with a customer or a customer contact.

A User Navigates to the Root Folder

While reading this chapter, you should assume that the Northwind Contact Management application is published in public folders rather than in a personal folders file (.pst). The Northwind Contact Management application demonstrates how to track interactions with customers and customer contacts in public folders. The Companies and Shared Contacts folders have been populated with records imported from the Customers table in the Access Northwind sample database. In a real CRM application that tracks customer and contact activity, the Company items in the public folder would originate from company records in a corporate database. Using a third-party product, Exchange 5.5 scripting agents, or Exchange 2000 event sinks, you can choose to create bilateral synchronization between the Company items in Exchange public folders and the Company records in your corporate database. You can also elect to make the synchronization unilateral so that the corporate database records act as the sole data source for the Company items in Exchange. Note that users might be prohibited from creating new Company items in the Companies folder in a real-world contact management application. These Company items could be created in a public folder only after a company record was created in the master Companies table. In this chapter, we'll concentrate on how a user—from an inside sales associate, to a customer service specialist, to a field sales representative—records activity with a company.

> **Note** If you want to prevent users from creating Company items in the Companies folder, hide the Company form in the Companies folder. You must have owner permission on a folder to hide its forms. When a form is hidden, it cannot be created through the Outlook user interface. However, you can still create the form through code. For example, if a new customer record is created in your customer database, you could write a trigger that executes code that in turn creates the Company item in the Companies folder.

The user navigates to the Northwind Contact Management application by clicking the Companies shortcut in the Northwind Contacts group of the Outlook Bar. By default, the Companies folder shows Company items in a Phone List view grouped by country. This view makes it easy for customer representatives to quickly reference company phone numbers.

A User Searches for a Company

If a user wants to find a company in a folder that contains hundreds or thousands of company records, he would click the Find button on the Standard toolbar. The Find button displays the new Outlook 2002 Find pane above the current view, as illustrated in Figure 12-5. Let's assume that the user wants to find a company name that begins with the word *Hungry*. To find all companies that begin with *Hungry*, the user enters *Hungry* in the Look For edit box and then clicks the Find Now button. Any company name that contains *Hungry* will be displayed in the view.

Part IV   Beyond the Basics

The Create Shared Items toolbar appears only when the Companies folder is the active Explorer folder.

The new Outlook 2002 Find panel provides a quick search for company names.

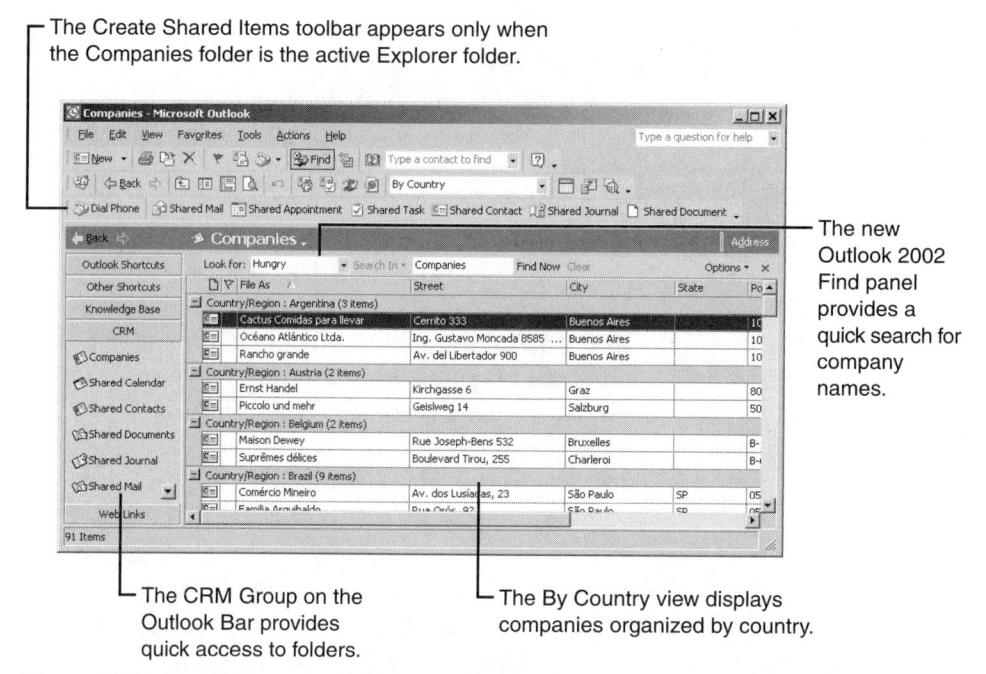

The CRM Group on the Outlook Bar provides quick access to folders.

The By Country view displays companies organized by country.

Figure 12-5 The Companies folder organized using the By Country view. The Create Shared Items custom toolbar and the Find pane are both visible.

If you examine Figures 12-1 and 12-5, you'll observe that both the Company form Inspector window and the Companies folder Explorer window share a similar toolbar. The Create Shared Items toolbar allows the user to create shared items in subfolders of the Companies folder. Users can create shared appointment, task, contact, e-mail, document, and journal items. One interesting feature of the Northwind Contact Management application is that it re-creates the standard Outlook phone dialer behavior. However, it allows the user to create a shared journal item for a phone call, rather than a private journal item. Figure 12-6 shows the New Call dialog box that contains a check box for recording the phone call activity in the Shared Journal public folder.

Viewing Shared Activities

Let's assume that you're a sales manager and you'd like to review the recent activities for The Hungry Coyote Import Store. If you click the Shared Activities page of the Company form, you will see the activities tracking power of Outlook in action. Like Outlook 2000, Outlook 2002 supports contact activity tracking in public folders. Journal entries, appointments, contacts, documents, tasks, and e-mail items can be stored in shared public folders and viewed from the Shared

Activities page of a custom Company item. In Figure 12-3 (on page 535), the Shared Activities page shows a view of shared journal items for The Hungry Coyote Import Store.

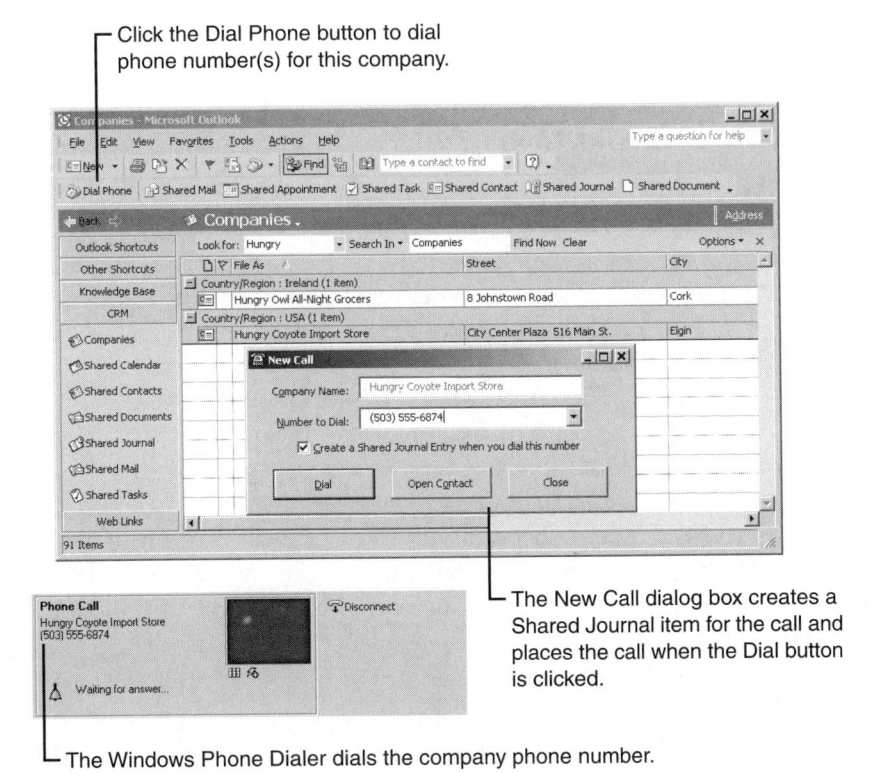

Figure 12-6 The New Call dialog box allows you to record phone call activity in the Shared Journal public folder.

Custom Views on the Shared Activities Page

You can define custom views on the Shared Activities page for each shared folder that you select in the drop-down list. Unlike the standard Activity page in an Outlook contact item, the Company custom form contains both a folder and view selector to allow a user to choose different views for a specific shared activities folder. The Shared Activities page is built with the versatile Outlook View Control. First introduced as an ActiveX control for Outlook 2000 that was available by download from the Web, the Outlook View Control is an integral component of Outlook 2002.

> **Note** For additional information about the properties, methods, and new events available for the Outlook View Control in Outlook 2002, see Chapter 15.

Viewing Sales Data in the Customer Form

The Northwind Contact Management application also demonstrates how Outlook can be integrated with other data sources, including Microsoft Access, Microsoft SQL Server, and other OLE DB or ODBC-compliant databases. The Orders page of the Company form contains a PivotTable List control. The Orders page is hidden if the user is off line or the company does not have a record in the Customers table of the Northwind database. The PivotTable List is an ActiveX control that ships with Office XP. The Office XP Web Components are the Chart, Spreadsheet, and Data Source controls. From a functional point of view, a PivotTable List is an interactive table that lets a user analyze data. Typically, the PivotTable List is placed on a Web or data access page. However, the PivotTable List control can also take up residence on an Outlook form page, as shown in Figure 12-7. You can use the list to view and organize data from the Northwind database, filter the result of a query and show selected fields, and export the data in the list to Microsoft Excel.

> **Note** The Office XP PivotTable List requires that you install Microsoft Internet Explorer 4.01 or later for it to function correctly. You must install Internet Explorer 4.01 or 5.0 or later for a successful Outlook 2002 installation anyway. However, you do not have to make Internet Explorer your default browser if you elect to use another browser. Office XP Web Components do not run in Netscape Navigator or Internet Explorer 3. To design a component-based page with Access or browse a page created with Access, you must use Internet Explorer 5.0 or later.

Recording Shared Activities by Using Links

Companies stored in a Contact form are just the starting point for the Northwind Contact Management application. What makes this application unique is its ability to track your activities with Company items in several subfolders. The most obvious feature for anyone who has used Outlook to associate contacts with trading partners is the Shared Contacts folder, a subfolder of the Companies folder. The Shared Contacts folder contains the contact names in the Customers table in the Northwind database. In a real-world contact management scenario, contact records would most likely be stored in a separate table or in multiple tables. For the purposes of our demonstration, I've simply created a separate Company Contact item in the Shared Contacts folder and created a link between the Company Contact item and its parent Company item.

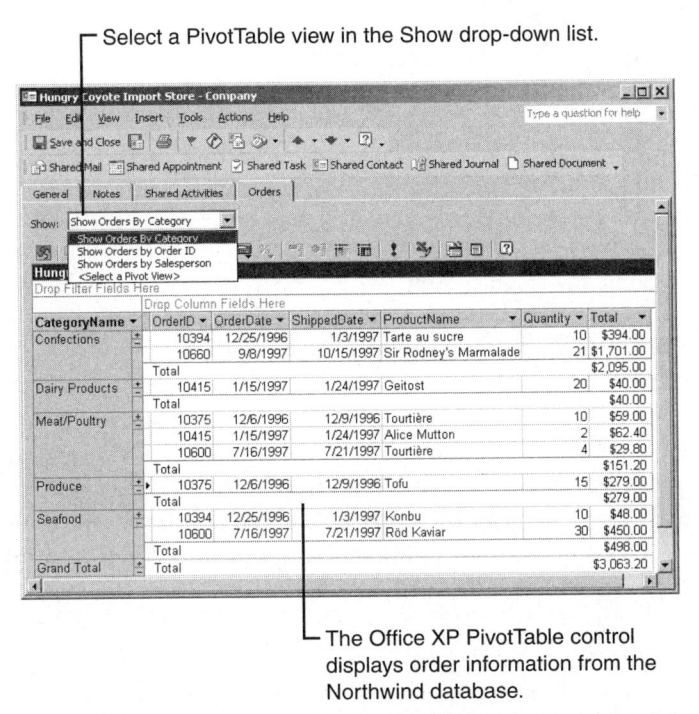

Figure 12-7 A PivotTable List control on the Orders tab of the Customers form.

Links are a means of connecting one Outlook item with another. Every item type in the Outlook Object Model supports a Links collection object. However, only contact items can be members of the Links collection. Mail, appointment, contact, journal, and task items all contain a Links collection. Remember, however, that only contact items can be members of the Links collection. The Company Contact form shown in Figure 12-8 illustrates a linked company contact. Company contacts are typically individuals that work for the company as employees. There's also no reason why company contacts can't represent organizational entities as well.

Part IV Beyond the Basics

Shared items can be created from a Company Contact item.

Double-click the Company Link to open the parent Company item.

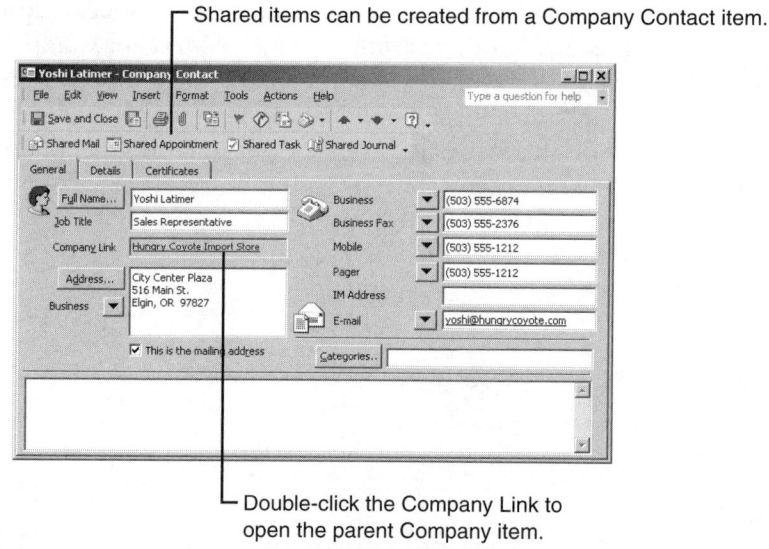

Figure 12-8 The Company Contact form.

To create additional shared contacts for a customer, click the Shared Contacts button on the Create Shared Items toolbar at the top of the Company form. Once you create those shared contacts, they are linked to the parent Company form by way of the Links collection and with a unique field generated during the Item_Write event. If you do add a shared contact, the company contact immediately appears in the Outlook View Control on the General page of the Company form. You can open any linked company contact by double-clicking the item in the Outlook View Control.

Shared Documents

The Northwind Contact Management application can associate documents with a specific company. When you click the Shared Documents button on the Create Shared Items toolbar, you have the option of creating a Microsoft Excel, PowerPoint, or Word document, as shown in Figure 12-9. Depending upon the application, you can select a document from the new Office XP Task pane or from a File New dialog box. In either case, you create the new document from a template and then save the document into the Shared Documents public folder. The Outlook Shared Activities COM Add-in provides document management functionality and is an integral part of the Northwind Contact Management application. This COM Add-in creates the Create Shared Items toolbar shown in Figure 12-5 (on page 538) and enables phone dialing, document creation, and linking.

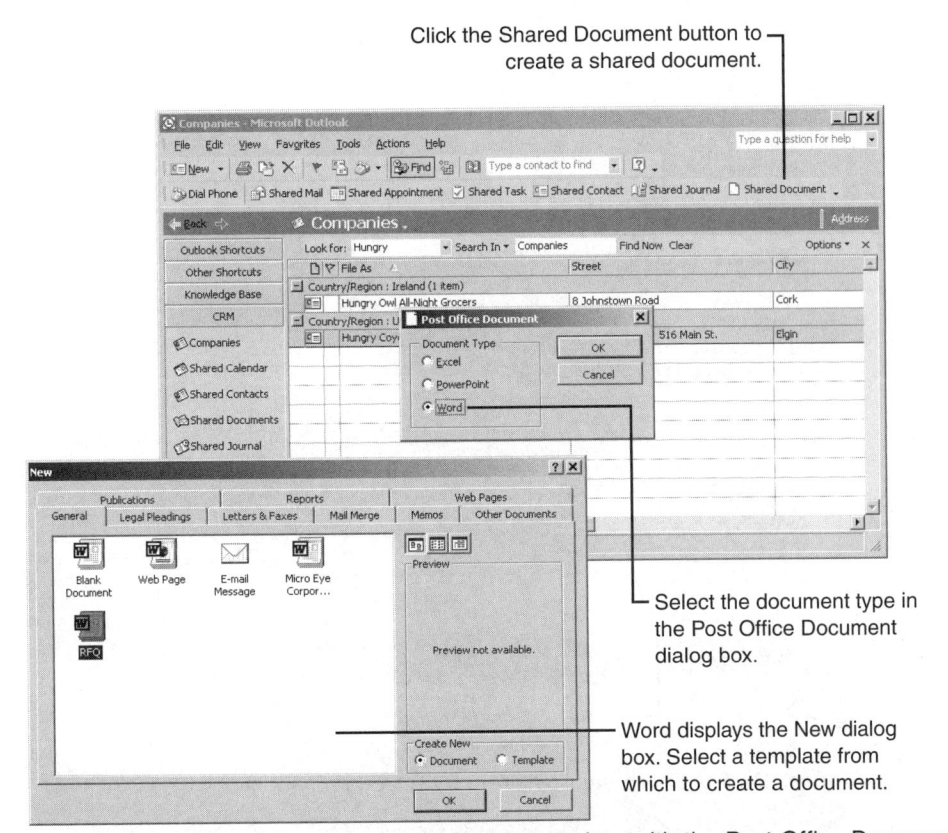

Figure 12-9 Create Office documents from a template with the Post Office Document dialog box.

Shared Appointments and Tasks

Most of the other shared items in the Northwind Contact Management application are self-explanatory. The user clicks the appropriate shared item button on the Create Shared Items toolbar to create a shared appointment, e-mail, journal item, document, or task. If a user creates a shared appointment or task, she is asked whether she wants to create a copy of the item in her personal Calendar or Tasks folder. If the user selects Yes, a copy of the appointment item is created automatically in her Calendar folder. Unlike appointment items created in a public folder, appointment items created in a user's Calendar folder can have reminders set on them. Appointments and tasks placed in your personal folders are easily synchronized with a mobile device. Figure 12-10 shows a shared appointment created for a presentation with a Company item.

Part IV Beyond the Basics

Click the Shared Appointment button to create a shared appointment.

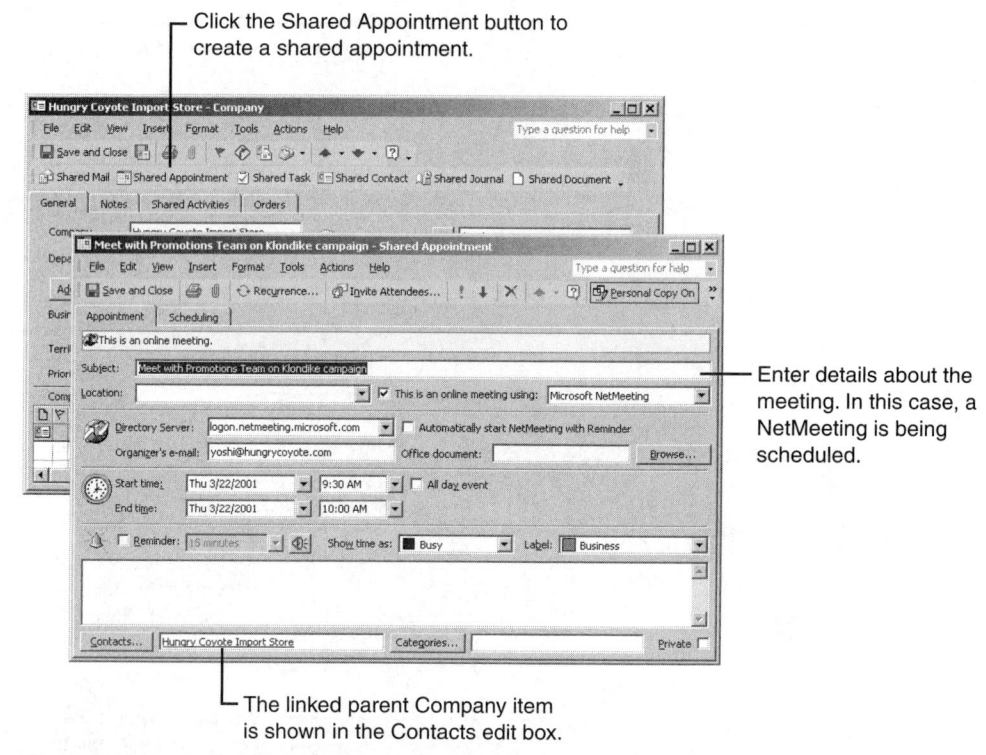

Enter details about the meeting. In this case, a NetMeeting is being scheduled.

The linked parent Company item is shown in the Contacts edit box.

Figure 12-10 A shared appointment for a Company item.

A User Sends Shared E-Mail

Unlike the other shared items, a shared e-mail message will be saved by default in the personal Sent Items folder of the user who issues the e-mail. The workaround for this is to send a blind carbon copy (bcc) of the message to the Shared Mail public folder when a user sends a shared message. The message is linked to the company or contact you send it to. You can track shared messages to a company or company contact on the Shared Activities page of the item. In order for shared e-mail to work correctly, you must expose the address of the Shared Mail folder in the Exchange Global Address List (GAL).

Setting Up the Application

Before you can run the Northwind Contact Management application, you need to copy the Northwind Contact Management application folder to your Exchange public folders. If you are not connected to an Exchange server, you can run most features of the Northwind Contact Management application from the Building Microsoft Outlook 2002 Applications personal folder (.pst) file with the exception of Shared Mail, which requires an addressable public folder. If you use the application in this manner, you won't be able to use the workgroup features that allow multiple users to share contacts, appointments, tasks, journals, and e-mail. Exchange Server is required to track and share activities for multiple users. This section explains how to install the Northwind Contact Management application in your Exchange public folders.

Reminders in Public Folders

Exchange and Outlook do not support reminders for appointment and task items in public folders. If you attempt to set a reminder on an appointment or task item in a public folder, you will see an alert box informing you that reminders cannot be set on public folder items. However, you can circumvent this limitation. After you set a reminder on the public folder item, you can do one of the following:

- ❑ Answer Yes to the Create Personal Copy Of Item? prompt. A copy of the item with the reminder set will be created in your personal Calendar or Task folder.

- ❑ Invite yourself to the appointment. You cannot assign a task to yourself. You can also create a distribution list item that contains members of your team (including yourself) and invite members of the team, if appropriate. You will see an alert box that informs you that meeting responses will not be tallied for appointments stored in a public folder.

- ❑ Create an Exchange 5.5 scripting agent or an Exchange 2000 event sink that synchronizes public folder appointments with a user's personal calendar. This solution is complex and beyond the scope of this chapter. If you'd like additional information on this technique, see the discussion "Maintaining a Group Calendar in Outlook" at *http://www.slipstick.com/calendar/scheduleall.htm*.

If you do not initially set a reminder on the item in the public folder, none of these strategies will work to set the reminder. Instead, you will have to manually set the reminder when the meeting or task item is copied to your personal folder.

Copying the Application Folders to Public Folders

These instructions assume that you have added the Building Microsoft Outlook 2002 Applications personal folder (.pst) file to your user profile. If you haven't, see the section "Add the Personal Folder (.pst) File to Outlook" in the introduction of this book.

To make it possible for a variety of people to easily record activities with company contacts, you must make the Companies folder and its subfolders publicly available. Copy the application root folder from the Building Microsoft Outlook 2002 Applications personal folder (.pst) to Public Folders.

> **Note** If you don't have permission to copy the folder to Public Folders, contact your Exchange administrator. The user that copies the files in the .pst file to Public Folders must have the ability to create Public Folders under All Public Folders or a subfolder of All Public Folders. The Exchange user that copies the folders in the .pst file to Public Folders will become the owner of the Northwind Contact Management Application Public Folders. Some organizations require that you log on to Exchange to create Public Folders with an account that has an unlimited lifetime. A typical mailbox name for a permanent recipient might be ExchAdmin. This mailbox should never be deleted. If you use the account of an individual employee who winds up leaving the company and thus has his Exchange mailbox deleted, the ownership of the public folder can be compromised and you will have to reset folder permissions.

Let's assume that you will create the Northwind Contact Management Application folder as a subfolder of All Public Folders. Your Exchange administrator might require that you create the root application folder in a subfolder of All Public Folders—for example, Test Applications. If you cannot create a subfolder of All Public Folders, adjust the target folder accordingly.

To copy the Northwind Contact Management Application folder

1. Log on to Outlook with the user profile that will assume ownership of the application folders.
2. In the Folder List, open the Building Microsoft Outlook 2002 Applications folder.
3. Open the 6. Sample Applications folder.
4. Right-click the Northwind Contact Management Application folder, and then click Copy Northwind Contact Management Application on the shortcut menu.

5. In the Copy Folder dialog box, open the Public Folders folder, select the target folder, and click OK. All the subfolders of the root application folder will also be copied to the folder you have selected.

Restricting Access to the Application Folders

To prevent users from opening the folder while you test or modify it, you need to restrict access to it. You can restrict access to the Northwind Contact Management Application folder and its subfolders in one of two ways. You can restrict access on a folder-by-folder basis with Outlook, or the Exchange administrator can apply permissions to the root application folder and propagate the permissions to all its subfolders. If you have to apply permissions to an extensive hierarchy of subfolders, it's more efficient if your Exchange administrator propagates permissions to subfolders. To propagate permissions with the Exchange Administrator program, see the section "Set Permissions for Subfolders" in Chapter 8, "Folders."

To restrict access to the application folder and its subfolders by using Outlook

1. In the Folder List, right-click the Northwind Contact Management Application folder you just added to Public Folders, and then click Properties on the shortcut menu.
2. Click the Administration page depicted in Figure 12-11.
3. Click Owners Only, and then click OK.
4. Repeat this process for each subfolder of the Northwind Contact Management Application folder.

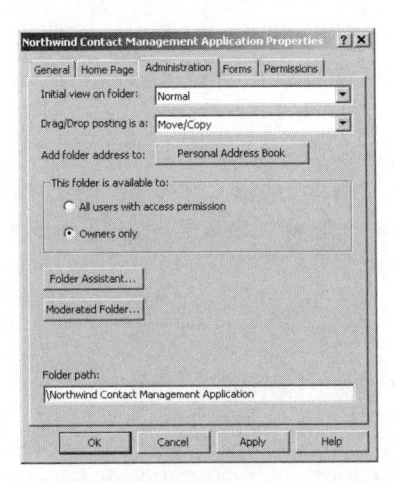

Figure 12-11 The Administration page.

Part IV   Beyond the Basics

Adding the Shared Mail Folder to the Global Address List

Your Exchange administrator will also need to expose the Shared Mail public folder to the Exchange Global Address List. Public folders can serve as recipients for mail as well as individual recipient accounts. The Shared Mail folder is added as a bcc recipient when a user clicks the Shared Mail button on the Create Shared Items toolbar.

To add the Shared Mail folder to the Global Address List

1. Launch the Exchange Administrator (Exchange 5.5) application or the System Manager (Exchange 2000) application.

2. In the Folder List, select the Shared Mail folder under the Northwind Contact Management Application folder under Public Folders.

3. Click the Properties button on the toolbar.

4. If you are using Exchange 5.5, clear the Hide From Address Book box on the Advanced page. If you are using Exchange 2000, clear the Hide From Exchange Address Lists box on the Exchange Advanced page.

5. Click OK.

Setting the Folder Home Page for the Root Folder

To establish a folder home page for the application folder

1. Right-click the Northwind Contact Management Application folder, and select the Properties command.

2. Click the Home Folder tab on the Folder Properties dialog box.

3. Check the Show Home Page By Default For This Folder check box, as shown in Figure 12-12.

4. Enter the URL for the Analyze Sales folder home page in the Address edit box. For the purposes of this example, you enter the URL for your server in the format *http://servername/virtualwebname/ Analyze%20Sales.htm*.

5. Click OK.

Creating Items in Public Folders from the Shared Database

Company items in the .pst Companies folder are linked to company contact items in the Shared Contacts folder. If you copy the Companies folder and its subfolders to All Public Folders, the links between Company items and Company Contact items will still point to the items in the .pst folders. Follow the next procedure to re-create the Company and Company Contact items in your public folders.

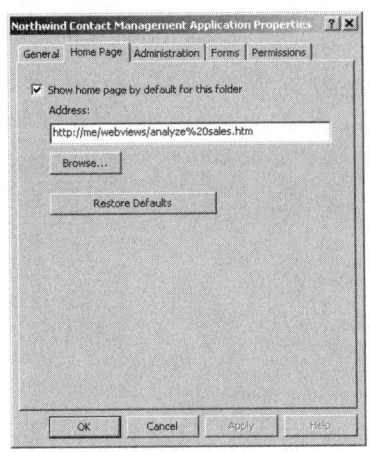

Figure 12-12 Setting the folder home page for the Northwind Contact Management Application public folder.

To re-create the items in the Companies and Shared Contacts folders

1. Navigate to the Readme and Support folder under the Northwind Contact Management Application folder.

2. Double-click LoadSample.zip. If you do not have a Zip utility, obtain WinZip at *http://www.winzip.com*.

3. Double-click LoadSample.exe in the Zip file LoadSample.zip. If you prefer, you can extract LoadSample.zip, save it into an empty folder, and then open the LoadSample Visual Basic project.

4. Click the Load Sample Companies And Contacts From Northwind DB button on the form that appears.

5. Select Northwind.mdb in the Open Northwind Database dialog box. You can select the version of Northwind installed on your local drive or on a network share point.

6. Select the Companies folder to which you want to save the re-created items. If you have installed the Northwind Contact Management application into public folders, select the Companies folder under the Northwind Contact Management Application folder.

Exposing the Shared Contacts Folder as an Outlook Address Book

Because you will be storing shared contacts in the Shared Contacts subfolder of the Companies folder, you can expose the Shared Contacts folder as an Outlook Address Book. (See Figure 12-13.) This means that users will be able to share e-mail addresses for Company Contact items stored in the Shared Contacts folder. This approach avoids the redundancy of each user storing company contact e-mail addresses in their personal Contacts folder. However, a folder owner cannot make this setting for all users simultaneously. Each user that wants to expose the Shared Contacts folder as an Outlook Address Book must do so individually.

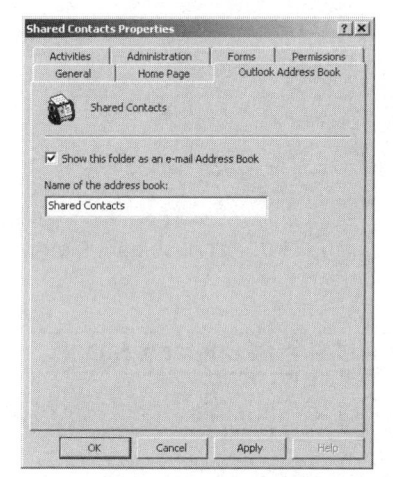

Figure 12-13 Exposing shared contacts as an Outlook Address Book.

> **Note** Rather than using individual settings to establish the Shared Contacts folder as an Outlook Address Book, you can modify the Outlook Shared Activities COM Add-in so that it establishes the Shared Contacts folder as an Outlook Address Book programmatically. Outlook 2002 introduces a new ShowAsOutlookAB property for the MAPIFolder object. In the InitHandler event of the COM Add-in, write code to set the ShowAsOutlookAB property for the Shared Contacts folder. COM Add-ins are an essential component for making your project work in the context of the entire Outlook application. While Visual Basic Scripting Edition (VBScript) behind forms enables you to program custom forms, COM Add-ins provide event-driven features that are not available from VBScript behind forms.

The Northwind Contact Management Application   Chapter 12

| **To expose the Shared Contacts folder as an Outlook Address Book** |

1. Select the Shared Contacts folder under the Companies folder in the Folder List.
2. Right-click the Shared Contacts folder, and select the Properties command from the shortcut menu.
3. Click the Outlook Address Book page on the Folder Properties dialog box.
4. Check the Show This Folder As An E-Mail Address Book check box.
5. Click OK.

Setting the Initial View on the Customers and Shared Contacts Folders

Views are an essential component of Exchange application design. As the application designer, you'll want every user that navigates to the Companies and Shared Contacts folders to initially see a specific default view. The following procedure will ensure that every user sees the correct initial view when they navigate to either of these folders. Figure 12-14 shows the procedure.

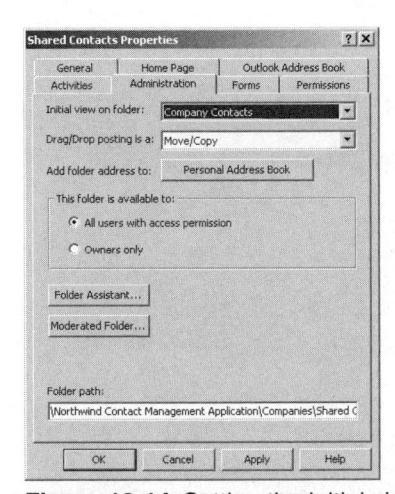

Figure 12-14 Setting the initial view on a folder.

| **To set the initial view on a folder** |

1. Select the Shared Contacts folder under the Companies folder in the Folder List.
2. Right-click the Shared Contacts folder, and select the Properties command from the shortcut menu.

551

3. Click the Administration page on the Folder Properties dialog box.

4. Select Company Contacts in the Initial View On Folder drop-down menu. Repeat the previous steps for the Companies folder, but in this case, select By Country as the initial view on the Companies folder.

5. Click OK.

Setting the Default Item for a Folder

Be certain that the Shared Appointment form is set as the default form for the Shared Calendar folder. You set the default post form for a folder on the General page of the Folder Properties dialog box. Figure 12-15 shows the General page of the Shared Calendar folder. If your default form is an Appointment form rather than a Shared Appointment form, you will lose the ability to copy appointments to the user's personal calendar. The Northwind Contact Management application uses special forms in the Shared Journal, Shared Calendar, and Shared Tasks folders to provide additional functionality. If you copy the application from the .pst folders, these default forms should be set correctly.

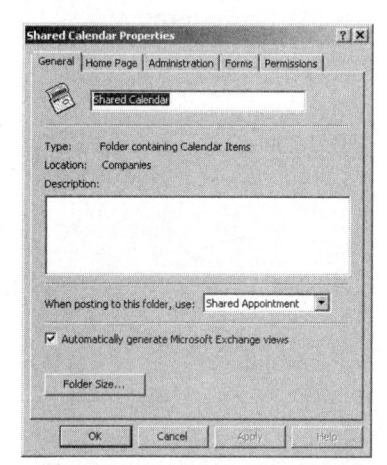

Figure 12-15 Setting the default form for a folder.

To set the default form for the Shared Calendar folder

1. Select the Shared Calendar folder under the Customers folder in the Folder List.

2. Right-click the Shared Contacts folder, and select the Properties command from the shortcut menu.

3. Click the General page on the Folder Properties dialog box.

4. Select Shared Appointment in the When Posting To This Folder, Use: drop-down list.

5. Click OK.

> **Note** You should also set the Shared Task form as the default form for the Shared Task folder and the Shared Journal form as the default form for the Shared Journal folder using the steps just outlined.

Installing the Outlook Shared Activities Add-In

Before you can run the application, you must install the Outlook Shared Activities COM Add-in. This COM Add-in is an integral part of the Northwind Contact Management application. It supplies an Explorer toolbar and additional functionality that cannot be achieved with VBScript behind Outlook forms.

To install the Outlook Shared Activities Add-in

1. Navigate to the Readme and Support folder under the Northwind Contact Management application folder.

2. Double-click OutlookSharedActivitiesCOMAddin.zip. If you do not have a Zip utility, obtain WinZip at *http://www.winzip.com*.

3. Extract OutlookSharedActivitiesCOMAddin.zip, and save it to an empty folder. All the code for the COM Add-in is contained in the Zip file as well as the compiled ShareAct.dll.

4. Select Options on the Tools menu.

5. Click the Other page, and then click the Advanced Options button.

6. Click the COM Add-Ins button.

7. Click Add on the COM Add-Ins dialog box, and then use the Add Add-In dialog box to select ShareAct.dll in the folder used in step 3.

Setting the Database Connection String

The final task to set up the Northwind Contact Management application is to create an ADO connection string for the PivotTable list that points to the shared Northwind database. The Setup form contains a user-defined field that stores a connection string. The connection string itself results from a call to the Outlook Shared

Part IV Beyond the Basics

Activities COM Add-in that provides a *GetConnectionString* method. This method uses the Microsoft OLE DB Service Component 1.0 Type Library to create a connection string for any OLE DB provider. Figure 12-16 shows the sequence of dialog boxes displayed by the Setup form.

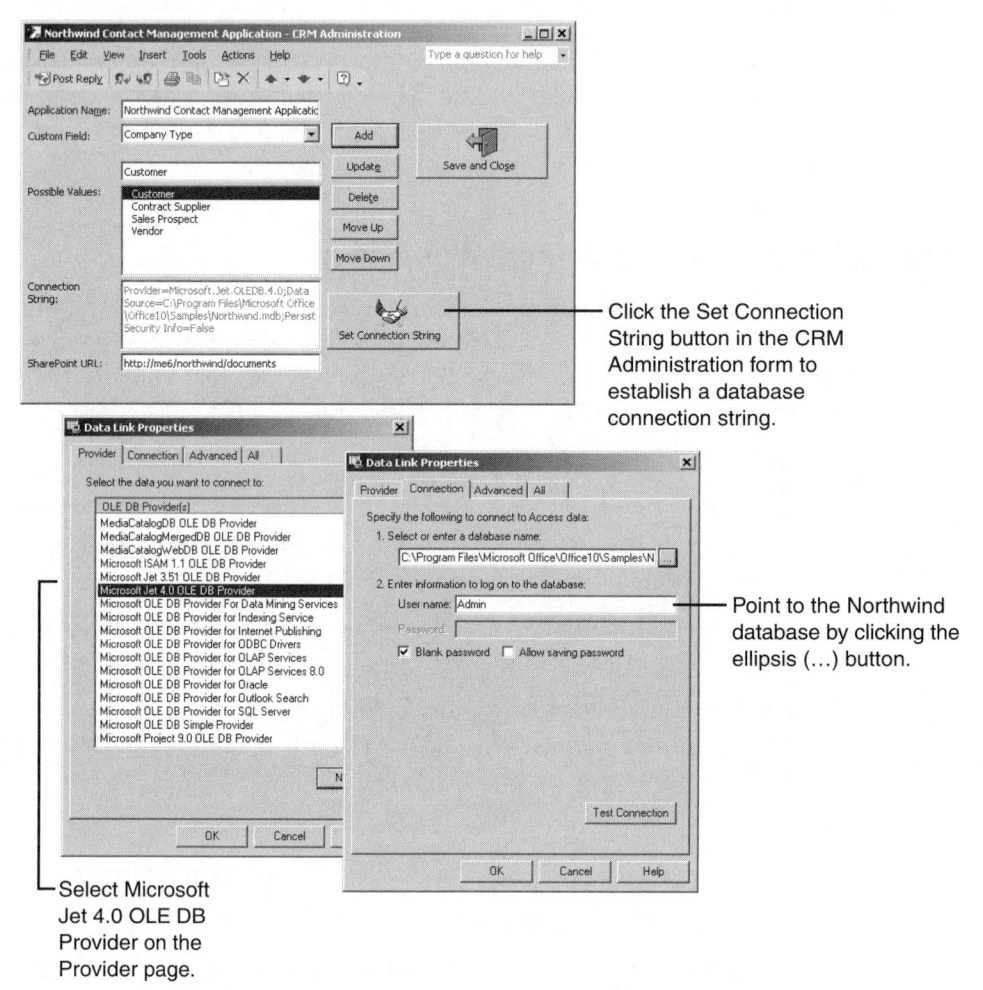

Figure 12-16 Setting the connection string for the PivotTable List control.

If you elect to extend this application beyond the sample code, you could establish a database connection for SQL Server or any OLE DB provider. You have to set up the connection string only once for the entire application.

> **Note** The following steps assume that you have copied the Northwind database from a local drive to a network share. If you want to try this application with SQL Server, you can establish a connection with the Northwind sample database in SQL Server. You will have to modify the SQL string stored in *gstrSQL* so that it uses Transact-SQL syntax.

To establish a database connection string

1. Select the Setup folder under the Companies folder under the Northwind Contact Management Application folder in All Public Folders.
2. Open the CRM Administration form in the Setup folder.
3. Click the Set Connection String button.
4. Select Microsoft Jet 4.0 OLE DB Provider in the OLE DB Provider(s) list box on the Provider page.
5. Click the Next button.
6. Click the ellipsis (…) button next to the Database Name edit box.
7. Select the location of the Northwind database. If you have copied the Northwind database to a network share, you should enter the UNC (Universal Naming Convention) path in the Database Name edit box as follows:

    *ServerName**ShareName**Path*\northwind.mdb
8. Click the Test Connection button to ensure that you have a working database connection.
9. Click OK.
10. Click Save, and the click Close.

Loading the Company and Company Contact Forms

The Companies and Shared Contacts folders of the Northwind Contact Management application already contain data loaded from the Northwind database. It's helpful to understand how the records in the Customers table in the Northwind database were converted into Outlook forms. As I stated at the beginning of the chapter, in a real-world contact management scenario you'll most likely import companies and company contacts from separate tables in one or many corporate databases. In the case of the Northwind database, the contact for the company is stored in the customer record in the Customers table. The code to load the Company and Company Contact forms is located in the LoadSample.zip file in the Readme And Support folder under the Northwind Contact Management Application folder.

> **Note** If you want to test the application in public folders, you should re-create the Company and Company Contact items in public folders so that links between the items point to public folders instead of the folders in the Building Applications with Microsoft Outlook 2002 personal folders file.

The basic task in loading the Company and Company Contact forms is to convert Access data into Outlook data. Simply put, you'll create Outlook items from Access database records. In some cases, you could use the Outlook 2002 Import and Export Wizard to create Outlook items from various data sources. However, in this case, we need to link the Company Contact items to the parent Company items. If you elect to import some of your corporate or departmental data into this application, you'll have to modify this code or create your own procedures to import data. It is necessary to write code to make the conversion work correctly.

The code required to accomplish the conversion is straightforward. You use ADO to open a connection to the Access database. You then supply a SQL SELECT statement to select all the records in the Customers table and convert those records into Company and Company Contact items in the correct folders. If you decide to modify the Northwind Contact Management application to create a custom contact management application, you'll want to modify the conversion code to suit your source database.

To observe the conversion process in action, delete all the items in the Companies and Shared Contacts folders and re-create those items. To see how to re-create those items, see "Creating Items in Public Folders from the Shared Database," beginning on page 548.

The following discussion assumes that you have Visual Basic installed on your machine. You can open the LoadSample project in the folder that you created earlier, in "Creating Items in Public Folders from the Shared Database." LoadSample displays a frmNorthwind form that has a command button. When the command button is clicked, the code behind it prompts the user for the location of the Northwind database and for the Companies folder. The code then passes the database path and a MAPIFolder object to *CreateCompaniesandContacts*. The *CreateCompaniesandContacts* procedure in the modNorthwind module creates Company and Company Contact forms in the correct folders. The *Add* method of the Items collection object lets you add a custom form to a folder, and the *Remove* method deletes existing items.

```
Public Sub CreateCompaniesandContacts _
    (strDBPath As String, objFolder As MAPIFolder)
    Dim cnnDB As ADODB.Connection
    Dim rstCust As ADODB.Recordset
    Dim oCompaniesFolder As Outlook.MAPIFolder
    Dim oContactsFolder As Outlook.MAPIFolder
    Dim oCompany As Outlook.ContactItem
    Dim oContact As Outlook.ContactItem
    Dim oLinks As Outlook.Links
    Dim oContactLinks As Outlook.Links
    On Error Resume Next
    frmNorthwind.lblStatus = "Removing existing items, please wait..."
    DoEvents
    Set cnnDB = New ADODB.Connection
    With cnnDB
        .Provider = "Microsoft.Jet.OLEDB.4.0"
        .Open strDBPath
    End With
    Set oCompaniesFolder = objFolder
    'Delete existing items
    Do Until oCompaniesFolder.Items.Count = 0
        oCompaniesFolder.Items.Remove (1)
    Loop
    Set oContactsFolder = oCompaniesFolder.Folders("Shared Contacts")
    'Delete existing items
    Do Until oContactsFolder.Items.Count = 0
        oContactsFolder.Items.Remove (1)
    Loop
    On Error GoTo CreateCompaniesandContacts_Error
    Set rstCust = cnnDB.Execute("Select * from Customers")
    Do Until rstCust.EOF
        Set oCompany = _
            oCompaniesFolder.Items.Add("IPM.Contact.Company")
        oCompany.UserProperties("Company ID") = rstCust!CustomerID
        oCompany.UserProperties("Company Type") = "Customer"
        oCompany.UserProperties("Company Priority") = "Medium"
        'CheckNull replaces database Nulls with empty string
        oCompany.CompanyName = CheckNull(rstCust!CompanyName)
        oCompany.FileAs = CheckNull(rstCust!CompanyName)
        oCompany.BusinessAddressStreet = CheckNull(rstCust!Address)
        oCompany.BusinessAddressCity = CheckNull(rstCust!City)
```

(continued)

Part IV Beyond the Basics

```
                oCompany.BusinessAddressState = CheckNull(rstCust!Region)
                oCompany.BusinessAddressPostalCode = CheckNull(rstCust!PostalCode)
                oCompany.BusinessAddressCountry = CheckNull(rstCust!Country)
                oCompany.BusinessTelephoneNumber = CheckNull(rstCust!Phone)
                oCompany.BusinessFaxNumber = CheckNull(rstCust!Fax)
                'Save before adding links
                oCompany.Save
                'Add Contact in Shared Contacts
                Set oContact = _
                    oContactsFolder.Items.Add("IPM.Contact.Company Contact")
                oContact.Account = oCompany.Account
                oContact.CompanyName = CheckNull(rstCust!CompanyName)
                oContact.BusinessAddressStreet = CheckNull(rstCust!Address)
                oContact.BusinessAddressCity = CheckNull(rstCust!City)
                oContact.BusinessAddressState = CheckNull(rstCust!Region)
                oContact.BusinessAddressPostalCode = CheckNull(rstCust!PostalCode)
                oContact.BusinessAddressCountry = CheckNull(rstCust!Country)
                oContact.BusinessTelephoneNumber = CheckNull(rstCust!Phone)
                oContact.BusinessFaxNumber = CheckNull(rstCust!Fax)
                oContact.FullName = CheckNull(rstCust!ContactName)
                oContact.JobTitle = CheckNull(rstCust!ContactTitle)
                oContact.UserProperties("Company Type") = "Customer"
                oContact.UserProperties("Company Priority") = "Medium"
                'Save before adding links
                oContact.Save
                Set oContactLinks = oContact.Links
                'Add customer parent as link
                oContactLinks.Add oCompany
                Set oLinks = oCompany.Links
                'Add contact as link to customer
                oLinks.Add oContact
                oCompany.Close (olSave)
                oContact.Close (olSave)
                rstCust.MoveNext
                frmNorthwind.lblStatus = "Loading " _
                    & CheckNull(rstCust!CompanyName)
                DoEvents
            Loop

CreateCompaniesandContacts_Exit:
        On Error Resume Next
        rstCust.Close
        cnnDB.Close
        Exit Sub

CreateCompaniesandContacts_Error:
    MsgBox "Error#: " & Err.Number & vbCr & Err.Description, vbInformation
    Resume CreateCompaniesandContacts_Exit
    End Sub
```

The CheckNull function converts database Nulls to an empty string. You must use CheckNull to prevent errors when your code populates an Outlook form from a database table. Outlook cannot accept Null values.

```
Function CheckNull(s As Variant) As Variant
    On Error Resume Next
    If IsNull(s) Then
        CheckNull = ""
    Else
        CheckNull = s
    End If
End Function
```

The Company Form

The Company form is based on the standard Contact form. It serves as the navigation hub to other Northwind Contact Management Application forms that store information about shared activities or data for this company. Shared activities constitute shared tasks, appointments, journal items, and e-mail. Shared data includes company contacts and documents created in Excel, Word, or PowerPoint. An Outlook Contact form is well suited to storing information about companies and individuals. Because you'll most likely load the Company form with data from an existing database, the form's General page has been modified to make it more appropriate for company contact information rather than that of individuals. Additionally, four user-defined fields on the Company form let you assign values for Company Type, Company Category, Priority, and Territory fields. If you elect to customize the Northwind Contact Management application, you can add to the number of user-defined fields on the Company form.

This section discusses some of the design techniques and implementations of the Company form, such as:

- Using script-level variables and constants
- Declaring form controls with script-level object variables
- Setting a restriction on the Outlook View Control to display only related company contacts
- Retrieving the possible values for the custom fields on the Company form
- Updating company contacts when values change in the parent Company form
- Creating a Create Shared Items toolbar for the Customer form

Part IV Beyond the Basics

- Tracking shared activities
- Using a drop-down list to let the user select different views in the PivotTable List control
- Determining whether the user is on line or off line and adjusting folder paths

Script-Level Constants and Variables

A relatively unknown feature of VBScript (version 2.0 or later) is its ability to declare script-level constants and variables. Script-level constants and variables are always declared at the top of the VBScript code window before any procedures. Script-level constants and variables are available to all procedures in the VBScript code behind the Company form. If you use the *Const* statement to declare Outlook and other object model constants, your form-level code will be easier to create and maintain. Provided that you declare all variables as Variants (or simply place a comment mark before the *As* keyword), you can write and debug form-level code in Outlook Visual Basic for Applications (VBA) and then paste the code into your form. The Company form also requires explicit variable declaration for all script-level and procedure-level variables because the *Option Explicit* statement is placed before any other statements or declarations. Although *Option Explicit* requires more work in the short run, in the long run it prevents many errors that can be difficult to track. Due to the noninteractive nature of VBScript, you'll save time by using *Option Explicit*.

Declaring Form Controls with Script-Level Object Variables

You should make the form-level code in the Company form behave like form-level code in Visual Basic by declaring all controls as global control variables. For example, if you place a TextBox1 control on a Visual Basic form, you can always refer to the control in form-level code as TextBox1. You can do the same in VBScript by declaring a script-level object variable for the control object in the script-level declarations. Use the same name for the control variable as for the control itself to prevent confusion. You instantiate the control-level variable in the Item_Open event of your form so that the control-level variable is a valid object variable representing the control on your form.

```
Option Explicit              'Require explicit variable declaration

'Global variables
Dim gobjPageGeneral          'General page object
Dim gobjPageOrders           'Orders page
Dim gobjPageActivity         'Activities page
```

The Northwind Contact Management Application   Chapter 12

```
Dim gobjPagePublish            'Published Documents page
Dim gstrSQL                    'Provides query for PivotTable list
Dim gstrConnect                'Connection string for PivotTable list
Dim gstrSharePointURL          'SharePoint Portal Server documents URL
Dim gstrComp                   'Path to Companies folder
Dim IsLoading                  'Boolean for load state
Dim blnOffline                 'Boolean for offline state
Dim blnChangeLinks             'Boolean to update linked contacts
Dim blnChangeCompany           'Boolean to update company name
Dim myAdmin                    'Administration form
Dim folSetup                   'Setup folder
                               'Global control variables
Dim ctlOrders                  'Office XP PivotTable list
Dim ctlViewControl             'Outlook View Control
Dim ctlViewActivity            'View control for activities
Dim cmbActivity                'Activity selector
Dim cmbView                    'View selector
Dim cmbSelector                'Selector for PivotTable view
Dim cmbCompanyType             'Drop-down list for company type
Dim cmbCompanyCategory         'Drop-down for company category
Dim cmbTerritory               'Drop-down for company territory
Dim cmbPriority                'Drop-down for company priority
Dim WebBrowser1                'Browser control
```

Initializing Form Controls

Figure 12-17 (on page 565) illustrates the duplicate control and variable naming convention and applies it to the ctlViewContacts control on the General page of the Companies form. Once the control has been dimensioned at the script level, you instantiate the control object in the Item_Open event of the form. The housekeeping chores for the form's controls have been wrapped into an *InitControls* procedure that's called in the Item_Open event. The following code shows how this works:

```
Function Item_Open()
    Dim folThis, folSetup, myRestrictItems
    On Error Resume Next
    IsLoading = True
    If CInt(Left(Application.Version, 2)) <= 9 Then
        MsgBox "CRM requires Outlook 2002 or above.", vbCritical
        Item_Open = False
        Exit Function
    End If
    'Outlook 2002 or later
    If Application.GetNamespace("MAPI").Offline Then
        blnOffline = True
    End If
```

(continued)

Part IV Beyond the Basics

```
'Determine correct folder path
If blnOffline Or Item.Size = 0 Then
    Set folThis = Application.ActiveExplorer.CurrentFolder
Else
    Set folThis = Item.Parent
End If
'Make an adjustment because this form can be opened from the
'Companies or Shared Contacts folders
If folThis.Name <> "Companies" Then
    Set folThis = folThis.Parent
End If
gstrComp = folThis.FolderPath
'Remove first \ from folder path
gstrComp = Right(gstrComp, Len(gstrComp) - 1)
'Try to retrieve the Setup folder and Admin form
Set folSetup = folThis.Folders("Setup")
If folSetup Is Nothing Then
    'Move up one folder
    Set folSetup = folThis.Parent.Folders("Setup")
    If folSetup Is Nothing Then
        MsgBox "Could not find Setup folder.", _
               vbInformation, gstrAppName
    End If
End If
Set myRestrictItems = folSetup.Items.Restrict _
    ("[MessageClass]='IPM.Post.CRM Administration'")
Set myAdmin = myRestrictItems.GetFirst
If myAdmin Is Nothing Then
    MsgBox "Could not find Administration form.", _
           vbInformation, gstrAppName
Else
    'Assign AppName to value stored in Admin form
    gstrAppName = myAdmin.UserProperties("AppName").Value
        'Assign SharePoint URL
        gstrSharePointURL = _
        myAdmin.UserProperties("SharePoint URL").Value

    'Assign ConnectionString
    gstrConnect = _
       myAdmin.UserProperties("ConnectionString").Value
End If
'Create the Inspector CommandBar
CommandBarCreate
InitControls
'Set first shared activity to Shared Tasks
cmbActivity.Value = "Shared Journal"
cmbView.Value = "Entry List by Created On"
IsLoading = False
End Function
```

```
Sub InitControls
    Dim strFolderPath, strRestrict
    Dim strRoot, i, objFolder, colItems
    On Error Resume Next
    'Get tab page objects and set global control variables
    'Setting global control object variables
    'allows you to write code for those objects
    'in other procedures without instantiating a control instance
    Set gobjPageGeneral = _
        Item.GetInspector.ModifiedFormPages("General")
    Set gobjPageOrders = _
        Item.GetInspector.ModifiedFormPages("Orders")
    'Hide the Orders page if off line or if not in Database
    If blnOffline Or Item.UserProperties("Company ID") = "" Then
        Item.GetInspector.HideFormPage("Orders")
    Else
        Item.GetInspector.ShowFormPage("Orders")
    End If
    'Set object variable for PivotTable list
    Set ctlOrders = gobjPageOrders.Controls("ctlOrders")
    ctlOrders.TitleBar.Caption = Item.CompanyName
    Set gobjPagePublish = _
        Item.GetInspector.ModifiedFormPages("Published Documents")
    'Hide the Published Documents page if off line or URL is blank
    If blnOffline Or gstrSharePointURL = "" Then
        Item.GetInspector.HideFormPage("Published Documents")
    Else
        Item.GetInspector.ShowFormPage("Published Documents")
    End If
    Set WebBrowser1 = gobjPagePublish.Controls("WebBrowser1")

    'Populate DBLookup type controls
    Set cmbCompanyType = gobjPageGeneral.Controls("cmbCompanyType")
    PopulateValues "Company Type", cmbCompanyType
    Set cmbCompanyCategory = _
        gobjPageGeneral.Controls("cmbCompanyCategory")
    PopulateValues "Company Category", cmbCompanyCategory
    Set cmbTerritory = gobjPageGeneral.Controls("cmbTerritory")
    PopulateValues "Company Territory", cmbTerritory
    Set cmbPriority = gobjPageGeneral.Controls("cmbPriority")
    PopulateValues "Company Priority", cmbPriority
    'Set up the Company Contacts View control
    Set ctlViewContacts = gobjPageGeneral.Controls("ctlViewContacts")
    gstrComp = gstrRoot & "\Companies"
    strFolderPath = gstrComp & "\Shared Contacts"
    ctlViewContacts.Folder = strFolderPath
    ctlViewContacts.View = "Company Contacts"
    ctlViewContacts.LayoutFlags = 68
```

(continued)

Part IV Beyond the Basics

```
            strRestrict = "[Account] = '" & Item.Account & "'"
            ctlViewContacts.Restriction = strRestrict
            Set gobjPageActivity = _
                Item.GetInspector.ModifiedFormPages("Shared Activities")
            Set cmbActivity = gobjPageActivity.Controls("cmbActivity")
            Set cmbView = gobjPageActivity.Controls("cmbView")
            cmbActivity.AddItem "Shared Mail"
            cmbActivity.AddItem "Shared Calendar"
            cmbActivity.AddItem "Shared Documents"
            cmbActivity.AddItem "Shared Journal"
            cmbActivity.AddItem "Shared Tasks"
            SetViews(olFolderSharedJournal)
            cmbView.Visible = True
            'Set up the Activities View control
            Set ctlViewActivity = _
                gobjPageActivity.Controls("ctlViewActivity")
            strFolderPath = gstrComp & "\Shared Journal"
            ctlViewActivity.Visible = True
            ctlViewActivity.Folder = strFolderPath
            ctlViewActivity.LayoutFlags = 68
            cmbView.Value = "Entry List by Created On"
            ctlViewActivity.View = "Entry List by Created On"
            strRestrict = "[BillingInformation] = '" & Item.Account & "'"
            ctlViewActivity.Restriction = strRestrict
            'Load the PivotTable list selector with AddItem method
            Set cmbSelector = gobjPageOrders.Controls("cmbSelector")
            cmbSelector.AddItem "Show Orders By Category"
            cmbSelector.AddItem "Show Orders by Order ID"
            cmbSelector.AddItem "Show Orders by Salesperson"
            cmbSelector.AddItem "<Select a Pivot View>"
            cmbSelector.Value = "<Select a Pivot View>"
            'Hide ctlOrders until user makes selection
            ctlOrders.Visible = False
        End Sub
```

Using the Outlook View Control to Display Company Contacts

An important feature of the General page on the Company form is the Outlook View Control that displays all of a company's linked contacts. The purpose of the Outlook View Control on the General page is to allow the user to see more information about a linked contact than is available in the Contacts edit box. The Contacts edit box shows underlined link names only and has been removed from the General page during the design process.

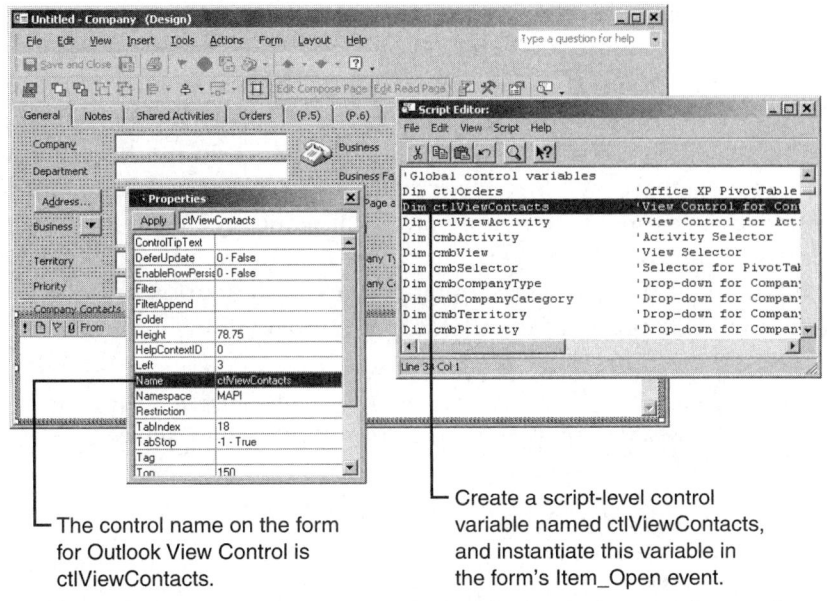

Figure 12-17 Script-level control variables duplicate the actual control names.

The control name on the form for Outlook View Control is ctlViewContacts.

Create a script-level control variable named ctlViewContacts, and instantiate this variable in the form's Item_Open event.

The Outlook 2000 View Control, which was made available on the Web after the initial release of Outlook 2000, is an ActiveX dynamic-link library (DLL) component of the Outlook Team Folders Kit. In Outlook 2002, the new Outlook View Control is an integral component of Outlook and is installed by default. Although the Outlook View Control is designed primarily for use on Web pages, it can also display Outlook information on Outlook or Visual Basic forms. The three most important properties of the Outlook View Control are the Folder, View, and Restriction properties. The Folder property is a string containing a folder path that establishes the folder represented by the control. The View property sets the view used to display the information in the folder. The Restriction property provides you with the ability to show only a subset of items in a given folder. For additional information on the properties, methods, and events for the Outlook View Control in Outlook 2002, see Chapter 15.

When a company item is created, a unique identifier is created and stored in the Account field. The Account field is a default property of a contact item. The Account field for a company item will be a combination of a substring of the company name and a randomly generated number. For example, the Account field for a company named The Big Cheese might be BigChe797909. The benefit of using this unique account number is that several types of items can be linked to a parent Company item without using the Links collection object. Because the unique ID for a company is created on the fly, this approach does not mandate that a company must first exist in a relational database such as Northwind. This Account field also facilitates the creation of Company items for companies that are prospective customers. Prospective customers do not have unique IDs in a corporate database. When a user creates a new Company item, either on line or off line, an account value is generated automatically by the following code. The PropertyChange event can generate a new account value or change the company name in related company contact items based upon modification of the CompanyName property in an existing company.

```
Sub Item_PropertyChange(ByVal Name)
Dim lowerbound, upperbound, RandomID, strRandomId, intLength
'Change INT_MAX to increase size of numeric portion of Item.Account
Const INT_MAX = 6
Select Case Name
    Case "CompanyName"
        'Only change Account field if blank
        If Item.Account = "" Then
            lowerbound = 1
            'Use Clng to force Long As 999999
            upperbound = CLng(String(INT_MAX,57))
            Randomize()
            RandomID = _
            Int((upperbound - lowerbound + 1) * Rnd + lowerbound)
                strRandomId = Trim(CStr(RandomID))
            intLength = Len(strRandomID)
            If intLength < INT_MAX then
                'Prepend 0 if not INT_MAX characters
                strRandomID = _
                String((INT_MAX-intLength),48) & strRandomID
            End If
            'Assign unique account number
            Item.Account = CleanString(Item.CompanyName) _
                & strRandomID
            Item.Subject = Item.CompanyName
        Else
            'Company name has changed, used in Item_Write
            blnChangeCompany = True
        End If
End Select
End Sub

Function CleanString(InString)
    Dim OutString, ch, i, Keysize
```

```
    'Change Keysize value to change length of alpha characters
    Keysize = 6
    For i = 1 to Len(InString)
        ch = Right(Left(InString,i),1)
        If Len(OutString) > Keysize Then
            Exit For
        End If
        If InStr("' """",ch) = 0 Then
            OutString = OutString & ch
        End if
    Next
    CleanString = OutString
End Function
```

When a programmatic search for related items occurs, the Account field in the parent company item is compared to the Account field in Company Contact items or the Billing Information field in the shared appointment, task, journal, document, or e-mail items. Like the programmatic *Restrict* method, the Outlook View Control enables you to display a subset of items in a single folder by setting its Restriction property. Only items that provide a match appear in the Outlook View Control. Be aware that the Restriction property works on Table and Card views only. If you attempt to set the Restriction property on a Calendar view, the restriction will fail and all items in the folder will be displayed.

> **Note** The Company form also stores the Northwind database CustomerID in a user-defined field named Company ID. This technique allows the Company form to display the PivotTable List control and query the database based on the CustomerID primary key. You can store primary database keys in user-defined fields in your custom form.

The code to display related company contact or shared activity items in the Outlook View Control is very straightforward. Just set the Restriction property of the Outlook View Control to filter the items displayed in the control. The code for this is shown in the *InitControls* procedure listed in the earlier discussion, "Initializing Form Controls." There are actually two Outlook View Controls on the Company form: *ctlViewContacts* and *ctlViewActivity*. The first displays company contacts on the General page, and the second displays many different item types on the Shared Activities page. Both Outlook View Controls use the Restriction property to show the subset of items related to the parent Company item.

Part IV Beyond the Basics

> **More Info** When you use the Outlook View Control to show a subset of items in a folder, be sure to consider performance. Depending upon the performance of your Exchange server and the client machine, online performance can degrade to an unacceptable level if the number of items in the folder exceeds 10,000. If you are working off line, performance can suffer with fewer items in the folder because you're depending exclusively on the client configuration. Be sure to test in both online and offline states before you release your application.

Retrieving the Possible Values for Custom Fields

An important feature of the Company form is that it enables you to set and retrieve the possible values for custom fields such as Company Type, Company Category, Priority, and Territory. You can extend the Company form with custom fields that are required by your application. Possible values are stored in a semicolon-delimited string in the appropriate custom fields in the CRM Administration form stored in the Setup folder. The *PopulateFields* procedure uses the VBScript Split function to turn the semicolon-delimited string stored in the user-defined field into an array and then sets the List property of the control to that array. Be aware that MyAdmin has script-level scope and consequently is instantiated in the *Item_Open* event procedure.

> **Note** The values of the Company Type field (and similar custom fields on the Company form) are not stored in the Possible Values edit box on the form. The Possible Values edit box is available when you right-click the drop-down control, click the Properties command, and then click the Value page. If you use the Possible Values field associated with the drop-down control, you must republish the form every time a possible value is added to the list. Because the possible values are obtained from the CRM Administration form in the Setup folder, using the Possible Values field uncouples the possible values from the Company form. You can modify the possible values for the Company Type field in the CRM Administration form. When you open a Company form after modifying Company Type, the possible values for Company Type are immediately available to the Company form; you do not have to republish the form.

The Northwind Contact Management Application   Chapter 12

```
Function PopulateValues(strField, objControl)
    On Error Resume Next
    'Use Split to create array from delimited  text field
    objControl.List = _
        Split(MyAdmin.UserProperties(strField).Value, ";")
End Function
```

Updating Company Contacts When Values Change in a Company

The custom fields on the Company form are useful for organizing companies with views. The usefulness of these fields increases when they are propagated to the related company contacts. For example, you might want to use the Mail Merge command on the Tools menu to send a Word document to all company contacts located in a certain company territory. When a new company contact is created, the values in the four custom fields (Company Type, Territory, Priority, and Company Category) are copied to the new company contact in the Shared Contacts folder. This functionality is easy to accomplish.

Other scenarios involving company contacts, however, can be more complicated. For instance, what happens when a company moves from Region1 to Region2? And what do you do when the parent company name changes? The solution to these problems can be found in the *Item_Write* event procedure for the Company form. When the CompanyName property changes, a script-level variable named *blnChangeCompany* is set to True in the PropertyChange event. When a custom field changes, the CustomPropertyChange event sets another script-level variable named *blnChangeLinks* to True. If either *blnChangeCompany* or *blnChangeLinks* is True, the following *Item_Write* code saves the changes to all child Company Contact items:

```
Function Item_Write()
    On Error Resume Next
    Dim LinkItem, colItems, colRestrictItems
    Dim objFolder, i, strRestrict
    If Item.Account = "" Then
        MsgBox "Invalid Account ID and Company Name.", _
            vbCritical
        Item_Write = False
    End If
    If blnChangeCompany Then
        Set objFolder = _
            OpenMAPIFolder(gstrComp & "\Shared Contacts")
        Set colItems = objFolder.Items
        colItems.SetColumns "Account"
        strRestrict = "[Account] = '" & Item.Account & "'"
```

(continued)

```
            Set colRestrictItems = _
                objFolder.Items.Restrict (strRestrict)
            For i = 1 to colRestrictItems.Count
                Set LinkItem = colRestrictItems.Item(i)
                LinkItem.Links.Remove(1)
                LinkItem.Links.Add(Item)
                LinkItem.CompanyName = Item.CompanyName
                LinkItem.Save
            Next
            blnChangeCompany = False
        End If
        If blnChangeLinks Then
            Set objFolder = _
                OpenMAPIFolder(gstrComp & "\Shared Contacts")
            Set colItems = objFolder.Items
            colItems.SetColumns "Account"
            strRestrict = "[Account] = '" & Item.Account & "'"
            Set colRestrictItems = _
                objFolder.Items.Restrict (strRestrict)
            For i = 1 to colRestrictItems.Count
                Set LinkItem = colRestrictItems.Item(i)
                LinkItem.UserProperties("Company Type").Value = _
                    Item.UserProperties("Company Type").Value
                LinkItem.UserProperties("Company Category").Value = _
                    Item.UserProperties("Company Category").Value
                LinkItem.UserProperties("Company Priority").Value = _
                    Item.UserProperties("Company Priority").Value
                LinkItem.UserProperties("Company Territory").Value = _
                    Item.UserProperties("Company Territory").Value
                LinkItem.Save
            Next
            blnChangeLinks = False
        End If
End Function
```

Creating a Create Shared Items Toolbar

The code that creates the Create Shared Items toolbar for the Inspector of the Customer and Customer Contact forms is essentially the same as the Visual Basic code in the Outlook Shared Activities COM Add-in that creates the Create Shared Items toolbar in the Explorer. You can examine the *CommandBarCreate* procedure in the code behind the Company form to see the complete listing. Be aware that it's possible to create toolbars for Outlook Inspector objects and cause the toolbar buttons on the command bar to run procedures in your form-level code.

Tracking Shared Activities

The Shared Activities page on the Company form replaces the built-in Activities page. The Shared Activities page shows only activities related to a given company in the subfolders of the Companies folder. When a user selects a different folder in the Show drop-down control, the View drop-down control is populated with a list of views for the folder. The Outlook View Control makes all this possible with just a few lines of code. Note that if a user selects Shared Calendar, only table type views will be available in the View drop-down control. The Restriction property for the Outlook View Control doesn't work on calendar views such as Day/Week/Month. If calendar views were included in the View drop-down control, shared calendar items for all companies would display in the view. Here is the code that changes the folder displayed on the Shared Activities page when a user clicks the Show drop-down control:

```
Sub cmbActivity_Click
    On Error Resume Next
    Dim strFolderPath, strRoot, strRestrict, strView
    If IsLoading Then
        Exit Sub
    End If
    ctlViewActivity.DeferUpdate = True
    Select Case cmbActivity.Value
        Case "Shared Mail"
            strFolderPath = gstrComp & "\Shared Mail"
            strView = "All Mail Messages"
            strRestrict = _
                "[BillingInformation]= '" & Item.Account & "'"
            SetViews olFolderSharedMail
        Case "Shared Journal"
            strFolderPath = gstrComp & "\Shared Journal"
            strView = "Entry List By Created On"
            strRestrict = _
                "[BillingInformation] = '" & Item.Account & "'"
            SetViews olFolderSharedJournal
        Case "Shared Documents"
            strFolderPath = gstrComp & "\Shared Documents"
            strView = "All Documents"
            strRestrict = _
                "[BillingInformation] = '" & Item.Account & "'"
            SetViews olFolderSharedDocuments
        Case "Shared Calendar"
            strFolderPath = gstrComp & "\Shared Calendar"
            'Note: Restrict only works on a TableView
            strView = "Active Appointments"
```

(continued)

```
                    strRestrict = _
                        "[BillingInformation] = '" & Item.Account & "'"
                    SetViews olFolderSharedCalendar
                Case "Shared Tasks"
                    strFolderPath = gstrComp & "\Shared Tasks"
                    strView = "Active Tasks"
                    strRestrict = _
                        "[BillingInformation] = '" & Item.Account & "'"
                    SetViews olFolderSharedTasks
            End Select
            ctlViewActivity.Folder = strFolderPath
            If strView <> "" Then
                ctlViewActivity.View = strView
                cmbView.Value = strView
            End If
            ctlViewActivity.DeferUpdate = False
            ctlViewActivity.Restriction = strRestrict
            ctlViewActivity.Visible = True
            cmbView.Visible = True
End Sub
```

Selecting Views in the PivotTable List

The PivotTable List control on the Orders page of the Company form enables the application user to drill down into customer order information in the Northwind database. From a programmer's perspective, the PivotTable List is a great control because it organizes and presents data for the user with minimal effort on your part. When the Company form opens, the Show drop-down control for the PivotTable List control is loaded with different PivotTable views in the *InitControls* procedure (shown earlier in "Initializing Form Controls"). The control name of the Show drop-down control is *cmbSelector*. The default text for *cmbSelector* is *Select a Pivot View*. The *cmbSelector* Click event fires when the user explicitly selects a view on the Orders page. The *cmbSelector_Click* procedure uses a *Select Case* statement to create the correct view in the PivotTable list depending upon the user's view selection.

```
Sub cmbSelector_Click
Dim objPivotControl, ActView, fldSets, Tot
Dim strSQL, strCompanyID
'Const plFunctionSum = 1
'Note: A PivotTable List supports a Constants collection object
'that contains all PivotTable list object model constants.
'Either set an object variable to refer to
'the constants collection or use an explicit reference
'as in ctlOrders.Constants.plFunctionSum
```

```
On Error Resume Next
'Company ID used to construct WHERE clause
strCompanyID = Item.UserProperties("Company ID")
ctlOrders.CommandText = gstrSQL & " WHERE CustomerID = '" _
    & strCompanyID & "'"
'Set connection string
ctlOrders.ConnectionString = gstrConnect
'Set objects for PivotTable
Set ActView = ctlOrders.ActiveView
ActView.TitleBar.Caption = Item.CompanyName
Set fldSets = ActView.FieldSets
'Set up PivotTable depending upon cmbSelector.Value
Select Case cmbSelector.Value
    Case "<Select a Pivot View>"
        'Do nothing
        ctlOrders.Visible = False
    Case "Show Orders By Category"
        'Group by
        ActView.RowAxis.InsertFieldSet(fldSets.Item("CategoryName"))
        'Row data
        ActView.DataAxis.InsertFieldSet(fldSets("OrderID"))
        ActView.DataAxis.InsertFieldSet(fldSets("OrderDate"))
        ActView.DataAxis.InsertFieldSet(fldSets("ShippedDate"))
        ActView.DataAxis.InsertFieldSet(fldSets("ProductName"))
        ActView.DataAxis.InsertFieldSet(fldSets("Quantity"))
        ActView.DataAxis.InsertFieldSet(fldSets.Item("Total"))
        fldSets("Total").Fields(0).NumberFormat = "Currency"
        'Add a total
        Set Tot = ActView.AddTotal("Total ", _
            fldSets("Total").Fields.Item(0), _
            ctlOrders.Constants.plFunctionSum)
        ActView.DataAxis.InsertTotal(Tot)
        ctlOrders.Visible = True
    Case "Show Orders by Order ID"
        'Group by
        ActView.RowAxis.InsertFieldSet(fldSets.Item("OrderId"))
        'Row data
        ActView.DataAxis.InsertFieldSet(fldSets("OrderDate"))
        ActView.DataAxis.InsertFieldSet(fldSets("ProductName"))
        ActView.DataAxis.InsertFieldSet(fldSets("UnitPrice"))
        ActView.DataAxis.InsertFieldSet(fldSets("Quantity"))
        ActView.DataAxis.InsertFieldSet(fldSets("Discount"))
        ActView.DataAxis.InsertFieldSet(fldSets("Total"))
        fldSets("Total").Fields(0).NumberFormat = "Currency"
        'Add a total
        Set Tot = ActView.AddTotal("Total ", _
            fldSets("Total").Fields.Item(0), _
```

(continued)

Part IV Beyond the Basics

```
                ctlOrders.Constants.plFunctionSum)
        ActView.DataAxis.InsertTotal(Tot)
        ctlOrders.Visible = True
    Case "Show Orders by Salesperson"
        'Group by
        ActView.RowAxis.InsertFieldSet(fldSets.Item("LastName"))
        'Row data
        ActView.DataAxis.InsertFieldSet(fldSets("OrderID"))
        ActView.DataAxis.InsertFieldSet(fldSets("OrderDate"))
        ActView.DataAxis.InsertFieldSet(fldSets("ProductName"))
        ActView.DataAxis.InsertFieldSet(fldSets("Quantity"))
        ActView.DataAxis.InsertFieldSet(fldSets.Item("Total"))
        fldSets("Total").Fields(0).NumberFormat = "Currency"
        'Add a total
        Set Tot = ActView.AddTotal("Total ", _
            fldSets("Total").Fields.Item(0), _
            ctlOrders.Constants.plFunctionSum)
        ActView.DataAxis.InsertTotal(Tot)
        ctlOrders.Visible = True
End Select
End Sub
```

> **Note** For additional information on the Office Web Components Object Model, see "Microsoft Office Web Components Visual Basic Reference," contained in the owcvba10.chm help file.

Determining Whether a User Is On Line

The Company form needs to determine whether a user is off line or on line. If the user is off line, the Orders page will be hidden because the Northwind database is on line only. Similarly, the Published Documents page requires a connection to SharePoint Portal Server, so this page is hidden if the user if off line. Previous versions of Outlook required Collaboration Data Objects (CDO) code to determine the online/offline state. The Offline property of the NameSpace object provides you with a means to test this condition. The following code fragment from the *Item_Open* procedure in the Company form sets a script-level variable that indicates whether a user is off line:

```
If Application.GetNamespace("MAPI").Offline Then
    blnOffline = True
End If
```

Obtaining a Folder Path When Off Line

Successful operation of the Northwind Contact Management application depends upon determining a folder path for a Folder object named *folThis* when the *Item_Open* event in the Company form is processed. (See the *Item_Open* event procedure code earlier in "Initializing Form Controls.") This folder path is used to locate the Setup folder and load values from the CRM Administration form. Typically, you would use Item.Parent to obtain the Folder object containing the item. When the user is on line, Item.Parent always returns the correct folder path for a company item that already has been saved. However, there are problems with this approach. Item.Parent returns a Folder object representing the path to the user's Inbox when a new company item is being created. In an offline state, Item.Parent returns the Folder object as a direct subfolder of the Favorites folder. When a new company item is created or when a user is off line, you must use Application.ActiveExplorer.CurrentFolder to obtain the correct folder path. If this approach fails, you might have to hard-code the folder path into your form-level code. The following table shows you what Item.Parent.FolderPath returns under different conditions:

New Item	State	Item.Parent.FolderPath
No	Online	Returns correct folder path *Public Folders\All Public Folders\CRM\Companies*
Yes	Online	Returns path to Inbox *Mailbox* – UserName*Inbox*
No	Offline	Returns folder path as immediate subfolder of Favorites *Public Folders\Favorites\Companies*
Yes	Offline	Returns path to Inbox *Mailbox* – UserName*Inbox*

Other Application Forms

Several additional custom forms are used to create items in the subfolders of the Companies folder. This section describes those custom forms.

The Company Contact Form

The Company Contact form is essentially a standard contact form with additional VBScript code for the Create Shared Items toolbar. (See "Creating a Create Shared

Part IV Beyond the Basics

Items Toolbar" in the previous section for more on this toolbar.) The only unique code for the Company Contact form is in the *Item_Write* event procedure. This code determines whether the Company Contact form has a linked parent. If a linked parent Company form is found, the *Item_Write* procedure of the Company Contact child form creates a link to itself in the Company form parent. The GetParentCompany helper function returns an object reference to the parent company item if the parent is found; otherwise, GetParentCompany returns Nothing.

```
Function Item_Write()
    Dim i, objParent, blnNewContact, blnFound, objForm
    On Error Resume Next
    If Item.Account = "" Then
        MsgBox gstrErrorNew, vbInformation, gstrAppName
        Item_Write = False
        Exit Function
    End If
    'New item
    If Item.EntryId = "" then
        blnNewContact = True
    Else
        blnNewContact = False
    End If
    'Get the parent
    If blnNewContact Then
        Set objParent = GetParentCompany()
    Else
        Exit Function
    End If
    Item.Save
    'Add the link, duplicates cannot exist
    If blnNewContact or objParent.Links.Count = 0 Then
        objParent.Links.Add(Item)
        objParent.Save
    End If
End Function

Function GetParentCompany ()
Dim i
For i = 1 to Item.Links.Count
    If IsObject(Item.Links.Item(i).Item) Then
        If Item.Links.Item(i).Item.Account = Item.Account Then
            Set GetParentCompany = Item.Links.Item(i).Item
            Exit Function
        End If
        Exit For
    End If
Next
```

```
'No parent found, so set to Nothing
Set GetParentCompany = Nothing
End Function
```

The Administration Form

The CRM Administration form shown in Figure 12-2 (on page 534) is located in the Setup folder. This form stores application-level values such as the Connection String for the PivotTable, the Application Name, the URL to a SharePoint Portal Server Documents folder, and the Possible Values for custom fields on the Company form. This form is essential for correct operation of the application. It provides a container for storing application-level variables whether the user is off line or on line. The Exchange Public Folder store can provide a repository for application-level values for your project. There are numerous approaches to storing application-level data in hidden or read-only folders, but this approach uses a single item in the folder to retrieve the application-level data. When the *Item_Open* event fires in the Company form, the CRM Administration form is located in the Setup folder and application-level values are read from the form. The following code uses the *GetConnectionString* method to set a connection string for the PivotTable that is stored in the ConnectionString custom field. (We'll revisit this momentarily in "The Outlook Shared Activities Add-In.")

```
Sub cmdConnect_Click
    On Error Resume Next
    Set oSA = CreateObject("OutlookSharedActivities.OutAddIn")
    strConnect = oSA.GetConnectionString()
    If strConnect <> "" Then
        UserProperties("ConnectionString").Value = strConnect
    End If
End Sub
```

Shared Item Forms

Besides the Customer Contact form, three custom forms provide additional functionality for items in the subfolders of the Companies folder: the Shared Appointment form, the Shared Task form, and the Shared Journal form.

The Shared Appointment and Shared Task forms contain a very small amount of VBScript code. This code allows the user to create a copy of a shared item in his personal Calendar or Tasks folder. You can view the code for the Shared Appointment form's *Item_Write* event procedure in the section "Creating a Personal Copy of Shared Items," beginning on page 581. The Shared Journal form does not contain any VBScript code. It uses two user-defined fields in the item, Created By and Created On, which define a custom view of the journal entries in the Shared Activities folder. These user-defined fields in the Shared Journal form let you create views that group activities by the name of the user who created the activity and the day on which the activity occurred.

The Outlook Shared Activities Add-In

The Northwind Contact Management application uses the Outlook Shared Activities COM Add-in. See the discussion on page 553, "Installing the Outlook Shared Activities Add-In," for instructions on installing this COM Add-in and its source code. The following discussion highlights some of the features of this add-in. The functionality of the add-in that relates to SharePoint Portal Server is discussed in Chapter 16. For additional details on creating COM Add-ins, see Chapter 14, "Creating COM Add-Ins with Visual Basic."

Displaying an Explorer Toolbar

When a user navigates to the Companies folder, the Create Shared Items toolbar (shown in Figure 12-5 on page 538) is displayed in the Outlook Explorer window so that the user can create a shared item without opening the form in the folder. Explorer toolbars provide a professional touch to your application and guide the user in ways that were not possible in Outlook 97 and Outlook 98. In the Northwind Contact Management application, a COM Add-in creates the Explorer toolbar.

Using the BeforeFolderSwitch Event

To provide an Explorer toolbar that appears only when a certain folder is the current folder, you write code in the BeforeFolderSwitch event of an Explorer object variable. When the correct folder is active, you make your custom toolbar visible. Otherwise you hide the Create Shared Items toolbar because it isn't appropriate to see this toolbar when some other folder is current. The following code shows or hides the Create Shared Items Explorer toolbar depending upon the current folder. If the current folder has a subfolder named Setup that contains the CRM Administration form, the Create Shared Items toolbar is displayed. Otherwise, it is hidden.

```
Private Sub objExpl_BeforeFolderSwitch(ByVal NewFolder As Object, _
    Cancel As Boolean)
    On Error Resume Next
    'Used when NewFolder is file system folder
    If NewFolder Is Nothing Then
        objCommandBar.Visible = False
        Exit Sub
    End If
    Call CBSharedItemsShowOrHide(NewFolder)
End Sub
```

The Northwind Contact Management Application Chapter 12

```
Sub CBSharedItemsShowOrHide(objFolder As MAPIFolder)
    On Error Resume Next
    Dim objFolderSetup As MAPIFolder
    Dim myAdmin As PostItem
    Dim myRestrictItems As Outlook.Items
    Dim objCommandBar As CommandBar
    Set objCommandBar = _
        golApp.ActiveExplorer.CommandBars("Create Shared Items")
    Set objFolderSetup = objFolder.Folders("Setup")
    If objFolderSetup Is Nothing Then
        objCommandBar.Visible = False
    Else
        Set myRestrictItems = objFolderSetup.Items.Restrict _
            ("[MessageClass]='IPM.Post.CRM Administration'")
        Set myAdmin = myRestrictItems.GetFirst
        If myAdmin Is Nothing Then
            objCommandBar.Visible = False
        Else
            objCommandBar.Visible = True
        End If
    End If
End Sub
```

> **Note** For additional information on command bars and the Office Object Model, see Chapter 11, "Using Visual Basic, VBA, or VBScript with Outlook." To learn more about event procedures, see Chapter 9, "Raise Events and Move to the Head of the Class."

Running a Procedure When a User Clicks a Toolbar Button

Each command bar button on the Create Shared Items toolbar is declared using the *WithEvents* keyword in the OutAddIn class. The click event for the button fires when the user clicks a command bar button and a procedure is called in basNorthwind, creating a shared item in the appropriate folder. Here is an example of the procedure that is called when the Shared Appointment button is clicked:

```
Private Sub CBBAppt_Click(ByVal Ctrl As Office.CommandBarButton, _
    CancelDefault As Boolean)
    Call basNorthwind.cmdAppointment_Click
End Sub

Sub cmdAppointment_Click()
    Call ButtonClick(olAppointmentItem)
End Sub
```

Part IV Beyond the Basics

The *ButtonClick* procedure does all the work of creating and displaying the new shared item in the correct folder. The *pintItemType* argument lets the *ButtonClick* procedure know what type of shared item is being created. GetFolder is another helper function that delivers the proper folder location where new items are created. Let's take a look at the code now:

```
Sub ButtonClick(pintItemType)
    Dim objTargetFolder As MAPIFolder
    Dim objNewItem
    Dim oItem As ContactItem

    On Error Resume Next
    If golApp.ActiveExplorer.Selection.Count = 0 Then
        MsgBox "You must select a company " _
        & "before you can create a shared item.", vbInformation
        Exit Sub
    End If
    Set oItem = golApp.ActiveExplorer.Selection.Item(1)
    If GetFolder(pintItemType, objTargetFolder, oItem) Then
        ' Create item
        Set objNewItem = objTargetFolder.Items.Add
        Select Case pintItemType
            Case olMailItem
                Call SetMailProps(objNewItem, objTargetFolder, oItem)
            Case olContactItem
                Call SetContactProps(objNewItem, oItem)
            Case olJournalItem
                Call SetJournalProps(objNewItem, oItem)
            Case olAppointmentItem
                Call SetAppointmentProps(objNewItem, oItem)
            Case olTaskItem
                Call SetTaskProps(objNewItem, oItem)
        End Select
        Call objNewItem.Links.Add(oItem)
        objNewItem.Display
    End If
End Sub

Function GetFolder(pintFolderType, objFolder As MAPIFolder, oItem)
    Dim objMyFolders As Outlook.Folders
    Dim i As Integer
    GetFolder = False
    Set objMyFolders = oItem.Parent.Folders
    i = 1
    Do While i <= objMyFolders.Count
        If objMyFolders.Item(i).DefaultItemType = pintFolderType Then
            Set objFolder = objMyFolders.Item(i)
            GetFolder = True
```

```
            Exit Do
        End If
        i = i + 1
    Loop
    If Not GetFolder Then
        MsgBox gconstErrorFolder, vbCritical, gconstAppName
    End If
End Function
```

SetAppointmentProps copies information from a Company or Company Contact item to the appointment. A similar procedure is called for each shared item created by the Create Shared Items toolbar. Because a custom form with a message class of IPM.Appointment.Shared Appointment is the default form in the Shared Calendar folder, objNewItem is created as a Shared Appointment form rather than as a standard Appointment form. A custom Appointment form in the Shared Calendar folder offers additional functionality that is not available in the default form.

```
Sub SetAppointmentProps(pobjNewItem, oItem As ContactItem)
    pobjNewItem.Companies = oItem.CompanyName
    pobjNewItem.BillingInformation = oItem.Account
End Sub
```

> **Outlook Security** The *SetMailProps* call shown in the *ButtonClick* procedure you just saw will display the Outlook E-Mail Security Update Address Book Warning dialog box when a user clicks the Shared Mail command bar button. If you want to suppress this Warning dialog box, you should add the Outlook Shared Activities Add-in to the list of trusted COM Add-ins in the Administrative form. For additional details, see Chapter 13, "Distributing and Securing Applications."

Creating a Personal Copy of Shared Items

The following code in the Shared Appointment form creates a copy of the appointment in a user's personal calendar if she toggles the Inspector command bar button to Personal Copy On. By default, the Personal Copy and Shared Folder user-defined fields are set to True. When the Shared Appointment form *Item_Write* event detects that Personal Copy and Shared Folder are True, a copy of the shared appointment item is placed in the user's personal Calendar folder.

```
Sub Item_Write
    Dim objCopyItem
    Dim objNS
    Dim objPersonalFolder
```

(continued)

Part IV Beyond the Basics

```
        Const olFolderCalendar = 9
        On Error Resume Next
        If UserProperties("Shared Appt") And UserProperties("Personal Copy") Then
            Set objCopyItem = Item
            Set objPersonalFolder = _
               Application.GetNamespace("MAPI").GetDefaultFolder(olFolderCalendar)
            objCopyItem.Move objPersonalFolder
            objCopyItem.UserProperties("Shared Appt") = False
            objCopyItem.Save
        End If
End Sub
```

Enabling and Disabling Inspector Menu Bar Commands

Certain commands on the Company and Company Contact menu bars must be disabled to make the application function correctly. For example, because our sample application is for shared appointments, tasks, and so forth, you don't want the user to select New Task For Contact on the Actions menu. If the user selects this command, the new task will be placed in her personal Tasks folder rather than the Shared Tasks folder. Consequently, we need to enable and disable commands on the Actions menu.

An effective way to control Inspector command bars is by using the Open event of the contact item. You'll run into a problem if you attempt to disable the menu bar commands through VBScript code in the Item open event of your custom form. The Inspector menu bar applies to all contact item inspectors. If a user opens a standard contact item, the Actions menu commands will be disabled incorrectly. As a workaround, you can use Outlook events to enable and disable commands on the Actions menu. You can create an object variable for items where the base message class is IPM.Contact and raise item-level events on that object variable. You should instantiate the item-level object variable in the NewInspector event of the Inspectors collection object. Whenever a new Inspector is created by a user action or program code, a new *objContactItem* object variable is created. By declaring *objContactItem* using the *WithEvents* keyword in the OutAddIn class module, you will be able to write code behind the *objContactItem_Open* event procedure to modify the command bars for the item. The following code enables or disables commands on the Actions menu of a contact item depending upon the message class of the item. For the two custom contact items in this application, commands on the Actions menu are disabled.

```
Private Sub objContactItem_Open(Cancel As Boolean)
    On Error Resume Next
    Dim objCBMenu
    Set objCBMenu = _
        objContactItem.GetInspector.CommandBars("Menu Bar").Controls("Actions")
    If objContactItem.MessageClass = "IPM.Contact.Company" _
```

```
            Or objContactItem.MessageClass = "IPM.Contact.Company Contact" Then
            objCBMenu.Controls("New Contact").Enabled = False
            objCBMenu.Controls("New Contact from Same Company").Enabled = False
            objCBMenu.Controls("New Meeting Request to Contact").Enabled = False
            objCBMenu.Controls("New Appointment with Contact").Enabled = False
            objCBMenu.Controls("New Journal Entry for Contact").Enabled = False
            objCBMenu.Controls("New Task for Contact").Enabled = False
            objCBMenu.Controls("Link").Enabled = False
            objCBMenu.Controls("Post Reply to Folder").Enabled = False
            objCBMenu.Controls("Copy to Personal Contacts").Enabled = False
        Else
            objCBMenu.Controls("New Contact").Enabled = True
            objCBMenu.Controls("New Contact from Same Company").Enabled = True
            objCBMenu.Controls("New Meeting Request to Contact").Enabled = True
            objCBMenu.Controls("New Appointment with Contact").Enabled = True
            objCBMenu.Controls("New Journal Entry for Contact").Enabled = True
            objCBMenu.Controls("New Task for Contact").Enabled = True
            objCBMenu.Controls("Link").Enabled = True
            objCBMenu.Controls("Post Reply to Folder").Enabled = True
            objCBMenu.Controls("Copy to Personal Contacts").Enabled = True
        End If
End Sub
```

Extending Your Application with Public Methods

The basic functionality of the Outlook Shared Activities COM Add-in centers around the addition of an Explorer toolbar. In this respect, this add-in is typical. However, it has some special features that allow you to extend your application beyond the addition of Explorer toolbars. For example, VBScript code behind forms cannot make Windows API calls. The Outlook Shared Activities COM Add-in wraps Telephony Application Programming Interface (TAPI) Calls in a public method *Dial Phone*. A similar approach of wrapping complex code in a method call is used for both the *ShowDocumentDialog* and *GetConnectionString* methods. Unlike a COM Add-in created with Office XP Developer, a COM Add-in created in Visual Basic can expose public properties and methods that are available to other applications or to the VBScript code behind the forms that compose your application. For example, the Post Office Document dialog box shown in Figure 12-9 (on page 543) allows the user to select from a range of templates in order to create a document that is posted to the Shared Documents folder. The following code from the Company form calls the *ShowDocumentDialog* method to display the Post Office Document dialog box:

```
Sub cmdDocument_Click()
    On Error Resume Next
    Dim objFolder, objDM
```

(continued)

Part IV Beyond the Basics

```
        'Item has to be saved, otherwise linking does not work.
        If Item.EntryId = "" then
            If MsgBox(gstrErrorButton, vbYesNo + vbQuestion, _
                gstrAppName) = vbYes Then
                Item.Save
            Else
                Exit Sub
            End if
        End If
        Set objFolder = OpenMAPIFolder(gstrComp & "\Shared Documents")
        Set objDM = CreateObject("OutlookSharedActivities.OutAddIn")
        objDM.ShowDocumentDialog _
            objFolder, Item.CompanyName, Item.Account
End Sub
```

When the user clicks the OK button in the Post Office Document dialog box, a variety of strategies are employed to create the Office document from a template. Each Office application dictates the code used to create a new Office document from a template. In Excel 2002, for example, it is possible to use the NewWorkbook and WorkBookOpen events of the Excel Application object to determine which document the user has selected from the Excel 2002 Task Pane. The following example shows how the *cmdOK_Click* procedure in frmDocument creates an Office document, sets the Billing Information field to the value in the Item Account field, and then displays the item. This functionality would be impossible to achieve in VBScript.

```
Private Sub cmdOK_Click()
    Dim strSubject As String
    Dim strFilePath As String
    Dim oMsg As DocumentItem
    On Error Resume Next
    Me.Hide
    DoEvents
    'Excel document
    If optExcel = True Then
        Set xlApp = New Excel.Application
        xlApp.DisplayAlerts = False
        If Val(xlApp.Version) <= 9 Then
            If xlApp.Dialogs(xlDialogNew).Show Then
                'User selected item
                xlApp.Dialogs(xlDialogProperties).Show
                strSubject = _
                    xlApp.ActiveWorkbook.BuiltinDocumentProperties("Subject")
                If Trim(strSubject) = vbNullString Then
                    strSubject = "Excel Document"
                End If
                strFilePath = GetTempDir & CleanFileName(strSubject) & ".xls"
```

```vb
            xlApp.Visible = True
            With xlApp.ActiveWorkbook
                .CustomDocumentProperties.Add _
                    Name:="Company Name", LinkToContent:=False, _
                    Value:=m_CompanyName, _
                    Type:=msoPropertyTypeString
                .SaveAs strFilePath
                .Close
            End With
            DoEvents
            Set oMsg = m_Folder.Items.Add("IPM.Document.Excel.Sheet.8")
            oMsg.Attachments.Add strFilePath
            oMsg.Subject = strSubject
            oMsg.MessageClass = "IPM.Document.Excel.Sheet.8"
            oMsg.BillingInformation = m_Account
            oMsg.Save
            oMsg.Display
        End If
    Else
        'Excel 2002
        xlApp.Visible = True
        xlApp.Dialogs(xlDialogNew).Show
        Exit Sub
    End If
'PowerPoint document
ElseIf optPPT Then
    Set ppApp = New PowerPoint.Application
    ppApp.DisplayAlerts = ppAlertsNone
    strSubject = InputBox("Presentation Subject:", "PowerPoint Document")
    If Trim(strSubject) = vbNullString Then
        strSubject = "PowerPoint Document"
    End If
    ppApp.Visible = msoTrue
    strFilePath = GetTempDir & CleanFileName(strSubject) & ".ppt"
    ppApp.Presentations.Add
    With ppApp.ActivePresentation
        .BuiltinDocumentProperties("Subject") = strSubject
        .CustomDocumentProperties.Add _
            Name:="Company Name", LinkToContent:=False, _
            Value:=m_CompanyName, _
            Type:=msoPropertyTypeString
        .SaveAs strFilePath
        .Close
    End With
    DoEvents
    Set oMsg = m_Folder.Items.Add("IPM.Document.PowerPoint.Show.8")
    oMsg.Attachments.Add strFilePath
    oMsg.Subject = strSubject
```

(continued)

Part IV Beyond the Basics

```
                oMsg.MessageClass = "IPM.Document.PowerPoint.Show.8"
                oMsg.BillingInformation = m_Account
                oMsg.Save
                oMsg.Display
            'Word Document
            ElseIf optWord Then
                Set wdApp = New Word.Application
                wdApp.DisplayAlerts = wdAlertsNone
                If wdApp.Dialogs(wdDialogFileNew).Show Then
                    wdApp.Dialogs(wdDialogFileSummaryInfo).Show
                    strSubject = _
                        wdApp.ActiveDocument. _
                        BuiltinDocumentProperties(wdPropertySubject)
                    If Trim(strSubject) = vbNullString Then
                        strSubject = "Word Document"
                    End If
                    strFilePath = GetTempDir & CleanFileName(strSubject) & ".doc"
                    wdApp.Visible = True
                    With wdApp.ActiveDocument
                        .CustomDocumentProperties.Add _
                            Name:="Company Name", LinkToContent:=False, _
                            Value:=m_CompanyName, _
                            Type:=msoPropertyTypeString
                        .SaveAs strFilePath
                        .Close
                    End With
                    DoEvents
                    Set oMsg = m_Folder.Items.Add("IPM.Document.Word.Document.8")
                    oMsg.Attachments.Add strFilePath
                    oMsg.Subject = strSubject
                    oMsg.BillingInformation = m_Account
                    'Set MessageClass explicitly for Word documents
                    oMsg.MessageClass = "IPM.Document.Word.Document.8"
                    oMsg.Save
                    oMsg.Display
                End If
            End If
            Unload Me
            Kill strFilePath
    End Sub
```

Application Folder Views

The Companies Folder

The Companies folder contains several custom views. Many of these views use custom fields, such as Company Type, Company Category, Territory, and Priority, to group companies. The By Territory view enables sales personnel to quickly view the companies in their territory. As shown in Figure 12-5 (on page 538), the By Country view groups Company items by their geographic location.

The Company Contacts Folder

The Company Contacts folder uses a standard view for a Contacts folder, the By Company view. This view lets you see company contacts grouped by the Company field in the Company Contacts item.

The Shared Journal Folder

The Shared Journal folder consists of three custom views that organize the shared journal items: the Entry List By Company, Entry List By Created By, and Entry List By Created On views. These views depend upon user-defined fields specified in the Shared Journal custom form. This folder provides managers with a picture of which sales personnel have accomplished an activity for a Company item on a given day. The Created By and Created On user-defined fields are set when a shared journal item is created.

Releasing the Northwind Contact Management Application

Before you release the Northwind Contact Management application for public use, you must set permissions for the Companies folder and its subfolders. You will also need to set Administration and Forms properties and check that the shared folders for the Companies folder are set correctly.

Setting Permissions

You use the Properties dialog box to set permissions for the Companies, Shared Mail, Shared Appointments, Shared Contacts, Shared Journal, Shared Documents, and Shared Tasks folders.

To set permissions for the Companies folder and its subfolders

1. In the Folder List, right-click the Companies folder under the Northwind Contact Management Application folder in All Public Folders.
2. Click Properties on the shortcut menu.
3. Click the Permissions page.
4. Set the permissions shown in the table on the following page for the folder.

Part IV   Beyond the Basics

Repeat the same steps for the subfolders of the Companies folder application, except for the Shared Journal folder and the Setup folder. In the Shared Journal folder, assign only Author permissions to the participants. This prevents users from editing each other's journal items. In the Setup folder, assign Reviewer permissions to the participants. Participants only need permission to read from the CRM Administration form in the Setup folder.

Name	Role	Assign To
Default	None	
All participants in the company activity tracking process	Editor	People responsible for tracking activities for the Companies folder and its subfolders. Use an Exchange Distribution List to simplify management.
Application designers or system administrators	Owner	People responsible for maintaining and designing applications.

> **Note**   For more information about setting permissions, see "Set Permissions" in Chapter 8.

Setting Administration Properties

Next you can set the Administration properties on the folder and its subfolders so that they are available to all users with access permissions.

To set administration properties

1. On the Administration page of the Properties dialog box, click All Users With Access Permission and then click OK.
2. Set the Initial View On Folder drop-down menu to the name of the view that will display when users first visit the folder.

Setting Forms Properties

You should also set the Forms properties for the Companies folder and its subfolders. Use the Forms page on the Folder properties dialog box to set the forms allowed in the folder.

> **To set forms allowed in the folder for the Companies folder and subfolders**

1. In the Folder List, right-click the Companies folder under the Northwind Contact Management Application folder in All Public Folders.
2. Click Properties on the shortcut menu.
3. Click the Forms page.
4. Select the Only Forms Listed Above option in the Allow These Forms In This Folder frame. Repeat these steps for the Shared Contacts, Shared Appointments, Shared Journal, and Shared Tasks folders.

Customizing the Application

The Northwind Contact Management application is a starting point for all that you can accomplish in Outlook 2002. If you want to customize the application, you can use the CRM folder under the 6. Sample Applications folder. The CRM folder contains all the forms and folders for the application, but it does not contain items that have been converted from the Northwind database. You can modify any and all of the forms in the Northwind Contact Management application to suit your company's requirements. You can also modify the Outlook Shared Activities COM Add-in that provides additional functionality for the application. As I mentioned at the beginning of this chapter, we'll extend the Northwind Contact Management application to develop custom Web Parts for a Northwind Digital Dashboard and use SharePoint Portal Server document management in Chapters 15 and 16, respectively.

Where To Go from Here

Microsoft Knowledge Base Articles   Microsoft Knowledge Base articles are available on the Web at *http://support.microsoft.com/support*. Also see "Northwind Contact Management Application (Chapter 12) KB Articles" in the Microsoft Web Sites folder under the Help And Web Sites folder on the companion CD.

13

Distributing and Securing Applications

The process of distributing and maintaining Microsoft Outlook applications varies with each organization. In some organizations, the application designer develops the application and then submits it to an administrator, who is then responsible for its distribution, maintenance, and security. In other organizations, the application designer both develops the application and serves as its administrator. In both cases, the application designer must ensure that the code used to create the application will not display the warning prompts generated by the Outlook 2002 E-Mail Security Update. Do not educate users to click through the warning prompts presented by Outlook 2002 security. If you do so, you send the message that users should not take e-mail viruses seriously. The next time a user ignores the warning alert might be the first time a serious virus spreads throughout your organization and to your external trading partners. No one wants to shoulder the blame or the expense of such a virus attack.

If you plan to run existing collaborative applications, you should test them and make sure that they run correctly with the Outlook 2002 security settings. If the applications don't run correctly, you might have to modify them. This chapter will provide you with guidelines for coding your current and future applications so that they operate without triggering the Outlook security warnings. You'll learn how to use the Administrative form in Public Folders to establish default security settings for your organization and to set custom security settings for user groups. Fortunately, the Administrative form in Outlook 2002 permits the use of distribution lists provided that you are using Exchange 2000 Server; this limitation was a major obstacle for the Administrative form that shipped with the Outlook 2000 E-Mail Security Update.

Distribute Forms

This section provides information, strategies, and instructions for distributing forms in your organization. It covers how to:

- Make forms available in the Organizational Forms Library, the Personal Forms Library, or a Folder Forms Library.
- Change the standard IPM.Note message.
- Send a form to an administrator or to another user.
- Distribute forms in a personal folder (.pst) file.
- Make forms available for offline use.

Make Forms Available in the Organizational Forms Library

Most often, the types of forms contained in the Organizational Forms Library are general purpose Message forms that you want to make available to the entire organization. The Organizational Forms Library is located on Microsoft Exchange Server, so access to the forms in this library is determined by the structure and configuration of your Microsoft Exchange Server system.

Usually, there are two types of Message forms published in the Organizational Forms Library:

- General purpose Message forms, such as the While You Were Out form and Vacation Request form, which are used to send messages from one user to another
- Message forms that make it possible for users to submit information to a public folder

> **Note** Non-message forms such as Post, Contact, and Task forms are contained in the Forms Library within the folder. If the folder is a public folder, the forms contained in the folder's Forms Library are made available to all users who have access to the folder.

Submit the Form to an Administrator

In most organizations, only administrators have permission to publish forms in the Organizational Forms Library. As such, application designers who want forms published in the Organizational Forms Library must submit the forms to the administrator.

Distributing and Securing Applications   Chapter 13

When a form is published in a forms library such as the Organizational Forms Library, the form definition (and the ability to view the form) is accessible to everyone with access to the library. Thus, when the form is published, you should send the form definition with the item. (The Send Form Definition With Item check box on the form's Properties page should be cleared.)

> **Outlook Security**   Unless you have modified the One-Off Form setting in the Default Security Settings form, Outlook 2002 prohibits you from running code behind one-off forms.

To submit a form to an Administrator

1. With the form in Design mode, click Save As on the File menu.
2. In the Save In drop-down list box, click the Outlook default template folder, such as C:\Documents and Settings\<*UserName*>\Application Data\Microsoft\Templates.
3. In the File Name text box, type the form name.
4. In the Save As type drop-down list box, select Outlook Template (.oft).
5. Click Save.
6. On the form's Actions menu, click New Mail Message.
7. On the Insert menu, click File.
8. In the Look In drop-down list box, click the folder where you saved the .oft file.
9. Select the form name you entered in step 3, and click the Insert button.
10. In the To text box, type the administrator's name, or click the To button and then select the administrator's name from the list.
11. Click Send.

Check the Form for Viruses and Harmful Code

The administrator is responsible for making sure the form is free of viral infection and harmful code. The administrator should make sure that the code behind the form does not trigger the object model warnings in the Outlook E-Mail Security Update.

Publish the Form

If the administrator finds the form to be free of viruses and harmful code, she clears the Send Form Definition With Item check box on the Properties page of the form and publishes the form in the Organizational Forms Library. You must have Owner permissions to publish in the Organizational Forms Library. Contact your Exchange Administrator to obtain the correct permissions.

To clear the Send Form Definition With Item check box

1. With the form in Design mode, click the Properties tab.
2. Clear the Send Form Definition With Item check box.

> **More Info** For more information about the Send Form Definition With Item option, see "About the Send Form Definition With Item Check Box" later in this chapter.

> **Tip** If your custom form contains ActiveX controls other than the Forms 2.0 controls provided with Outlook, or if it uses ActiveX components that do not ship with Microsoft Office XP, you will need to run a setup program for these components before the custom form will run correctly on the target machine. The following alternatives apply if you are using ActiveX controls directly on your custom forms or ActiveX components that are called by the *CreateObject* function of Microsoft Visual Basic Scripting Edition (VBScript). You can install your ActiveX controls using any of the following methods. (This list is not meant to be inclusive.)
>
> ❑ Use the Visual Studio Package and Deployment Wizard or a Windows Installer tool to create a setup package and make that installation available to users on your corporate intranet.
>
> ❑ Create a folder home page that uses CODEBASE tags to install the required ActiveX components automatically when a user navigates to the Folder Home Page.
>
> ❑ Use an enterprise management tool, such as Microsoft Systems Management Server, to install the components.

To publish the form in the Organizational Forms Library

1. With the form in Design mode, select Forms from the Tools menu and then click Publish Form As.
2. In the Look In drop-down list box, click Organizational Forms Library.
3. Type the form name into both the Display Name and the Form Name text boxes.
4. Click Publish.

Make Forms Available in the Personal Forms Library

There are three good reasons to publish a form in the Personal Forms Library:

- You want to limit the number of people who have access to a form.
- You want to publish a form in your Personal Forms Library so that you are the only person who can use the form. For example, you may want to create a customized announcement form for communicating with a specific group of customers.
- You want to test a form that will be published later in the Organizational Forms Library. In this case, you can test the form in the Personal Forms Library before you submit it to an administrator for publishing in the Organizational Forms Library.

About the Send Form Definition With Item Check Box

If you are distributing forms to users who will install the form in their Personal Forms Libraries, or if you are publishing a form to your own Personal Forms Library, you should clear the Send Form Definition With Item check box.

To clear the Send Form Definition With Item check box

1. With the form in Design mode, click the Properties tab.
2. Clear the Send Form Definition With Item check box.

By default, the Send Form Definition With Item check box is cleared. When the form is published, however, the user is prompted to either select the check box or leave it cleared. When users have access to the forms library, you do not need to send the form definition along with the item. In this case, select No to keep the Send Form Definition With Item check box clear and to minimize the size of the item.

Distribute a Form for Publishing in a Personal Forms Library

Quite often, you want to distribute a form to a specific group of users and give them instructions about how to publish the form in their Personal Forms Libraries. The following sections describe how to do this.

Save the form as an .oft file First save the form as an .oft file so you can distribute it to other users.

To save a form as an .oft file

1. With the form in Design mode, select Save As on the File menu.
2. In the Save In drop-down list box, select the default Outlook template folder, such as C:\Documents and Settings\<*UserName*>\Application Data\Microsoft\Templates.
3. In the File Name text box, type the form name.
4. In the Save As type drop-down list box, select Outlook Template (.oft).
5. Click Save.

Insert a form (.oft) file as an attachment in a message To make a form accessible to a specific workgroup, the form must be published in the Personal Forms Library of each person who needs to use the form. The easiest way to do this is to save the form as an .oft file and then insert the .oft file into the message box of a message.

To insert a form (.oft) file as an attachment in a message

1. On the form's Actions menu, click New Mail Message.
2. On the Insert menu, click File.
3. In the Look In drop-down list box, click the folder you saved the .oft file in.
4. Select the file name of the .oft file, and click the Insert button.
5. In the To text box, type the names of the people that you want to receive the attached .oft file, or click the To button and then select the names from the list. Click OK.
6. In the message box, include the instructions listed in the next procedural section to publish the attached form in the users' Personal Forms Libraries.
7. Click Send.

Include instructions about how to publish the form Along with the form's .oft file, include the following instructions explaining to users how to publish the attached form in their Personal Forms Libraries.

To publish the attached form in a Personal Forms Library

1. Double-click the attachment.
2. If the Macro Warning dialog box appears, click Disable Macros.
3. On the Tools menu, select Forms and then click Publish Form As.
4. In the Look In drop-down list box, click Personal Forms Library and then click OK.
5. Type the form name into both the Display Name and the Form Name text boxes.
6. Click Publish.
7. Click No to keep the Send Form Definition With Item check box clear. When items are published and then run from the folder where they are published, they do not need embedded form definitions. This will only slow down form loading time.

Publish a Form in Your Personal Forms Library

In some cases, you may want to create a form and then publish it in your Personal Forms Library.

To publish a form in your Personal Forms Library

1. On the form's Tools menu, select Forms and then click Publish Form As.
2. In the Look In drop-down list box, click Personal Forms Library and then click OK.
3. Type the form name into both the Display Name and the Form Name text boxes.
4. Click Publish.
5. Click No to keep the Send Form Definition With Item box clear. When items are published and then run from the folder where they are published, they do not need embedded form definitions. This will only slow down form loading time.

Make Forms Available in a Folder Forms Library

Folder forms libraries are containers for forms. Each folder contains a unique forms library. As such, a forms library can exist on the server or on the user's hard disk, depending on the location of the folder. There are several good reasons for publishing forms to the folder's forms library:

- Most often, the forms stored in the library of a folder are used to post or save information in a folder. Such forms may include a standard or custom Post, Contact, or Task form. In some cases, however, Message forms are installed in the forms library of the folder so that users can send items from the folder.

- Another reason to publish forms in the folder's forms library is to transport the forms in a personal folder (.pst) file. You can use the personal folder (.pst) file for storing and distributing forms. Making forms available in a personal folder (.pst) file is described in "Distribute Forms in a Personal Folder (.pst) File" later in this chapter.

- Forms in a folder's Forms Library are available for storage in an offline folder (.ost) file and can be used when the user is off line from Microsoft Exchange Server.

To publish a form in a folder forms library

1. On the form Tools menu, select Forms and then click Publish Form As.
2. In the Look In drop-down list box, select Outlook Folders and then click the Browse button to locate the folder forms library to which you want to publish the form. Outlook also maintains a list of recently used folder names in the Look In drop-down list box.
3. Type the form name in both the Display Name and the Form Name text boxes.
4. Click Publish.
5. Select No to keep the Send Form Definition With Item check box cleared on the Properties page of the form.

Changing the Standard IPM.Note Message

Outlook 2000 and Outlook 2002 make it possible to change IPM.Note, the standard read and compose message form for reading, composing, and sending a message. These forms can contain VBScript code in addition to Forms 2.0 controls.

Changes in the standard message form are accomplished through changes in the Windows registry. Outlook looks up a set of registry keys whenever an item is opened. It uses the message class identified in the registry to open, compose, or send a form.

Be aware that once you make these changes, the default IPM.Note will not be available for the customized mode of reading, composing, and sending. If you want to roll out customized forms that replace the default IPM.Note, you should publish the forms to the Organizational Forms Library and be certain that you have a means of pushing the required registry settings down to each desktop in your organization.

The locations in the registry where the standard forms can be changed are listed in the following table. Take the appropriate precautions, including a full backup of the entire system before you make any changes to the Windows registry. These changes should only be made after careful and extensive testing of the substitute forms.

Standard Message Mode	Registry Location
Compose and Send	HKEY_CURRENT_USER\Software\Microsoft\Office\10.0\Outlook\Custom Forms\Compose\<MESSAGE CLASS>
Read	HKEY_CURRENT_USER\Software\Microsoft\Office\10.0\Outlook\Custom Forms\Read\<MESSAGE CLASS>

Figure 13-1 illustrates the registry entries that are necessary to change the standard Read message form. For the registry settings shown, IPM.Note.Foobar Read replaces IPM.Note as the standard Read message.

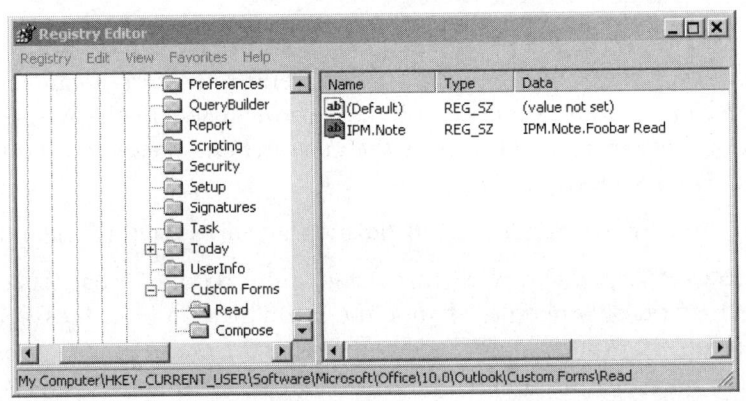

Figure 13-1 The Read key in the Windows registry causes IPM.Note.Foobar Read to become the default Read message.

Part IV   Beyond the Basics

To makes these changes for all the Outlook clients in your organization, you can create an .INF file, create a .REG file, or use VBA or Visual Basic code to make the registry changes programmatically. You can also push the changes to the desktop using the Office XP Custom Installation Wizard or Microsoft Systems Management Server. If you want to make these registry changes manually, the following procedure outlines the required steps.

To change the default Read message

1. Click the Windows Start menu, and select the Run command.
2. Type *regedit* in the Open edit box, and click OK.
3. In the Windows registry editor, select the Outlook key under HKEY_CURRENT_USER\Software\Microsoft\Office\10.0.
4. Select New from the Edit menu, and then select Key from the New submenu.
5. Type *Custom Forms* in place of New Key#1, and press Enter.
6. Select New from the Edit menu, and then select Key from the New submenu. Type *Read* in place of New Key#1, and press Enter.
7. Select New from the Edit menu, and then select String Value from the New submenu.
8. Type *IPM.Note*, and press Enter.
9. Select the Modify command from the Edit menu.
10. Type the message class of your custom form (for example, *IPM.Note.My Custom Name*), and click OK.

The Compose key has a special syntax so that you can set a replacement default message for both the Compose and Send modes of a standard message form. You can set both Compose and Send forms respectively by separating the custom Compose message class from the custom Send message class with a Null character. The exact syntax is

```
IPM.Note.Compose Form<vbNull>IPM.Note.Send Form<vbNull><vbNull>
```

If necessary, you can write this string value with a Visual Basic program. Otherwise, if you only need to change the standard Compose message, you can set a replacement Compose message class for IPM.Note in the Compose key just as you did above for the Read key. The changes you make in the registry are reflected in Outlook instantly.

Use the Send Form Definition With Item Check Box to Send a Form to Another User

In some cases, you need to use a Message form to send items to users who do not have access to the form associated with the item. For example, you may want to send a Product Announcement form to a customer. To ensure that the item appears in the form it was created with, you select the Send Form Definition With Item check box on the Properties page of the form when the form is in Design mode. You then publish the form in a forms library, as described earlier in this chapter. When you publish, select Yes when you are prompted to Send Form Definition With Item. This results in a larger file size, but the form is self-contained and can be viewed, even if the user does not have access to the forms library.

> **Outlook Security** If the recipient of the custom form has installed the Outlook E-Mail Security Update in Outlook 2000 or is running Outlook 2002, he or she will not be able to run the code behind this one-off form.

Distribute Forms in a Personal Folder (.pst) File

If you want to distribute one or more forms using a floppy disk, a CD-ROM, or a network drive, publish the form to the Forms Library of a folder that is located in a personal folder (.pst) file. You can then make a copy of the .pst file and use it for distribution. For more information about distributing a .pst file, see "Distribute a Folder in a Personal Folder (.pst) File" later in this chapter.

Make Forms Available for Offline Use

Users can set up Outlook so that they can work off line with forms and folders. For complete instructions on setting up Outlook 2002 for offline use, see "Make the Folder Available for Offline Use" in Chapter 8, "Folders." If your application has custom forms that you want to be available for offline use, you must check the Synchronize Forms box (shown in Figure 13-2) in the appropriate Send/Receive Settings dialog box. Remember that the Synchronize Forms setting is specific to an individual Send/Receive group.

Part IV Beyond the Basics

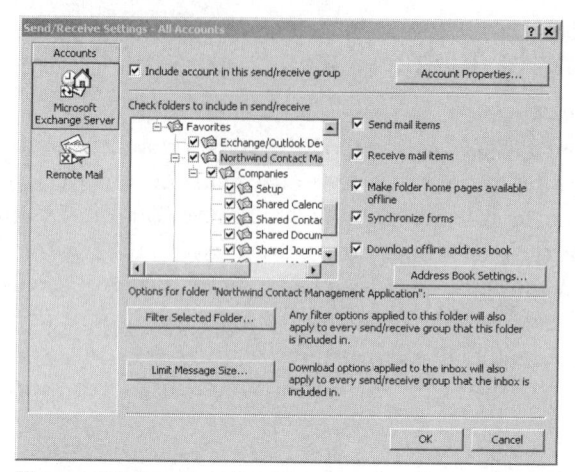

Figure 13-2 Select the Synchronize Forms check box to make custom forms available for offline use.

Manage Forms

This section describes how to copy and delete forms and change form properties using the Forms Manager. It also provides some strategies and tricks for making changes to forms.

The Forms Manager

With the Forms Manager, shown in Figure 13-3, you can copy and delete forms and change form properties.

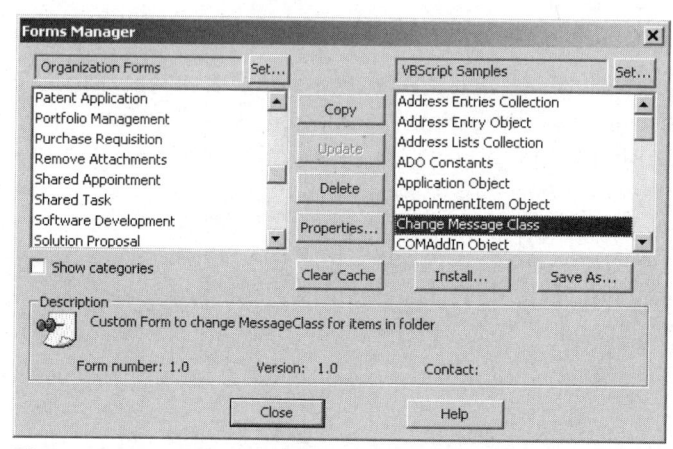

Figure 13-3 The Forms Manager dialog box.

To open the Forms Manager

1. Select Options on the Tools menu, and then click the Other page.
2. Click Advanced Options, and then click Custom Forms.
3. Click Manage Forms.

The Forms Manager dialog box allows you to manage forms in the Personal and Organizational Forms libraries simultaneously with the forms libraries of folders.

To copy a form

1. Click the left Set button to choose the forms library from which you want to copy forms.
2. In the left list box, select the forms you want to copy.
3. Click the right Set button to choose the forms library to which you want to copy forms.
4. Click Copy.

To set form properties

1. In the right list box, select the form whose properties you want to set.
2. Click Properties.
3. Select the options you want.

To delete a form

1. In the right list box, click the forms you want to delete.
2. Click Delete.

To synchronize one form with an updated version of the form, select the one you wish to update. For the update process to work, the form must be visible in both forms libraries (in both the right and left list boxes).

To update forms published in different forms libraries

- In the right list box, click the form and then click Update. Although you won't see an action, the forms will now be updated.

> **Note** The Install and Save As buttons are used to install and save forms developed for Microsoft Exchange Client.

Modify Forms

Quite often, changing a form can affect other forms or folders. When modifying a form, here are some things to consider:

- If a view or rule is based on a particular field and you remove or modify that field name, the view or rule must be updated to reflect the change.

- If fields are renamed on an existing form, their associated field values in items created using a previous version of the form do not appear on the new form.

- If the form contains VBScript code, any changes you make to the form components, such as the controls or fields, must also be changed in the Script Editor if the components are referenced in script.

- If you add new fields to an existing form, publish the modified form in a forms library, and then open old items with the new form, the new fields on the form will be blank or show the initial value for the field, if there is one.

- Forms with the same name but with different contents may cause unpredictable results. It is recommended that you use unique names or update the form in all the forms libraries in which it is published. For more information, see "The Forms Manager" in the preceding section.

Making Changes to a Form's Message Class

There are circumstances under which you will need to reset the message class of forms that have already been created in a folder. In this case, you can use the Change Message Class form that is included in the VBScript Samples folder under the folder 4. Beyond the Basics in the personal folders (.pst) file that accompanies this book. Changing the message class of a form will alter both the behavior and appearance of the form. Be aware that you should test the change thoroughly before you make changes to production items stored on your Microsoft Exchange Server. Figure 13-4 illustrates the Change Message Class form.

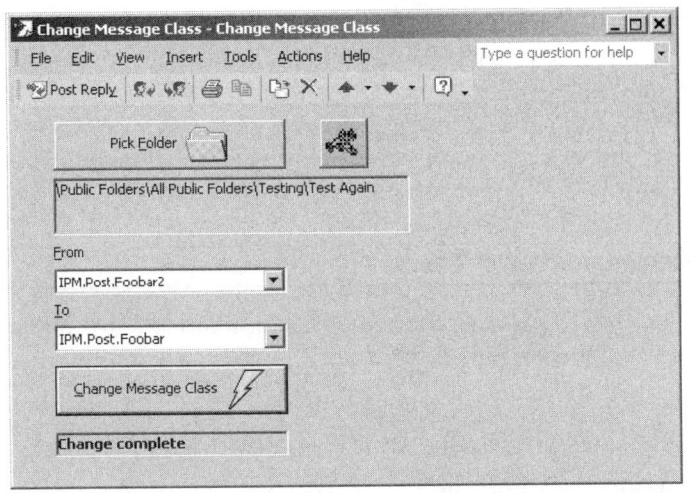

Figure 13-4 The Change Message Class form changes the message class of existing items in a folder.

To change the message class of existing forms in a folder

1. Use the Folder List to navigate to the VBScript Samples folder in the personal folders (.pst) file accompanying this book.
2. Double-click the Change Message Class item in the VBScript Samples folder to open the form.
3. Click Pick Folder to select a folder where you want to change the message class.
4. Select the From message class in the drop-down combo box. You can also type a built-in message class such as IPM.Post in the From combo box.
5. Select the To message class in the drop-down combo box. You can also type a built-in message class such as IPM.Post in the To combo box.
6. Click Change Message Class to change the message class for all forms with the From message class in the selected folder.

> **Note** The Change Message Class form uses Collaboration Data Objects (CDO) to populate the From and To combo boxes with the list of available message classes and custom forms in a folder. You can click the View Script button on the Change Message Class form to see the code that makes the form work.

Manage Changes to Forms

Let's assume you make changes to a form in an application that has been in use for several months. Rather than remove the old form, you can keep the old form in the forms library and set its Hidden property. This way, users can't create new items with the form, but they can view existing items with the form the items were created with.

To set the Hidden property of a form

1. In the Folder List, right-click the folder that contains the form you want to change. For the Organizational and Personal Forms libraries, you can right-click Inbox.
2. On the shortcut menu, click Properties.
3. Click the Forms tab, and then click Manage.
4. The Forms Manager shows the forms in the active folder's Forms Library in the right list box, as shown earlier in Figure 13-3.
5. Click the right Set button to choose the forms library containing the forms for which you want to set the Hidden property.
6. In the right list box, click the form you want to set the Hidden property for, and then click Properties.
7. Select the Hidden check box, and then click OK.

> **Note** Another way to set the Hidden property for a form is to select the Use Form Only For Responses check box on the Properties page of a form.

Install Forms Programmatically

It is not possible to perform a completely unattended form installation using the Outlook 2002 Object Model if the form has not been published in a Personal Folder or an Organizational Forms Library. If you attempt to create an item using the *CreateItemFromTemplate* method of the Application object, the Macro Warning dialog box will always appear for the .oft file if the form template contains VBScript code. It is possible, however, to automate a complex form installation over an extensive subfolder hierarchy using the *PublishForm* method of the FormDescription object. The *PublishForm* method can publish custom forms into one or more of the following form registries: Personal Forms, Organizational Forms, or active Folder Forms. Every Outlook custom form contains a

Distributing and Securing Applications   Chapter 13

FormDescription object that contains the form's general properties. You can use the Hidden property of the FormDescription object to hide the form, if necessary.

> **More Info**   For more information about the FormDescription object and its properties and methods, see Microsoft Outlook Visual Basic Reference Help.

The following procedure uses the *AddStore* method of the NameSpace object to add a personal folder (.pst) file to the current profile. The Foobar form has already been published to the Foobar Container folder in the foobar.pst file. Because the Foobar form is already a trusted form in the Foobar Container folder, you can obtain the form description for a new Foobar form and use the *PublishForm* method to publish the form to another forms library in the current profile. The following example installs the Foobar form to a public folder named Testing Permission. For this example to work correctly, you need to copy the *OpenMAPIFolder* procedure from basOutlook in the VBA Samples folder into a code module in your form installation project. After the form has been installed successfully, the *RemovePST* method of the NameSpace object removes foobar.pst from the current profile.

```
Sub TestPublishForm()
    Dim oNS As Outlook.NameSpace
    Dim oFormDesc As Outlook.FormDescription
    Dim oMsg As Outlook.PostItem
    Dim oSource As Outlook.MAPIFolder
    Dim oSourceRoot As Outlook.MAPIFolder
    Dim oTarget As Outlook.MAPIFolder

    On Error Resume Next
    Set oNS = Application.GetNameSpace("MAPI")
    'Add store with published form
    oNS.AddStore "c:\exchange\foobar.pst"
    Set oSource = OpenMAPIFolder("\Foobar\Foobar Container")
    Set oSourceRoot = oSource.Parent
    Set oMsg = oSource.Items.Add("IPM.Post.Foobar")
    Set oFormDesc = oMsg.FormDescription
    Set oTarget = OpenMAPIFolder("\Public Folders\ _
        & All Public Folders\Test Permission")
    oFormDesc.PublishForm olFolderRegistry, oTarget
    If Err Then
        MsgBox Err.Description, vbCritical
    End If
    oNS.RemoveStore oSourceRoot 'Remove store
End Sub
```

The Forms Cache

The forms cache is a local file system folder that serves as a forms storage location. The forms cache improves the load time of a form because commonly used forms are loaded from the hard disk rather than downloaded from Microsoft Exchange Server. When a form is activated for the first time, the form definition file is copied from its forms library to the user's Forms folder. The forms cache keeps a temporary copy of the form definition in a subfolder whose name roughly matches the name of the form. The Forms folder can be found in the locations listed in the following table, depending on the operating system you're using.

Operating System	Location for Forms Cache
Microsoft Windows 98 and ME	*drive*:\Windows\Local Settings\Application Data\Microsoft\Forms
Microsoft Windows NT 4	*drive*:\Winnt\Profiles\<*user*>\Local Settings\Application Data\Microsoft\Forms
Microsoft Windows 2000	*drive*:\Documents and Settings\<*user*>\Local Settings\Application Data\Microsoft\Forms

> **Note** The form table, Frmcache.dat, is also located in the Forms folder and is used to locate a form and to prevent multiple instances of the same form from being loaded in the cache.

When a form is activated, Outlook checks to see whether a form with the same message class is already in the cache. If not, it copies the form definition to the cache. In addition, if a change has been made to a form, Outlook copies the new form definition to the cache.

The user can determine the size of the forms cache. The default size of the forms cache is 2048 KB. If a user changes the size of the forms cache to 0, no custom forms can be opened on the user's system.

To specify the amount of disk space allocated for forms

1. Click Options on the Tools menu.
2. Click the Other tab, and then click Advanced Options.
3. In the Advanced Options dialog box, click the Custom Forms button.
4. Specify the disk space under Temporary Storage For Forms.

Clearing the Forms Cache

There are circumstances where the Outlook forms cache can become corrupted. If the forms cache is corrupted, users could experience one or more of the following conditions when they attempt to open a custom form:

- A user receives a "Cannot Create The Item" error message when the user opens an item.
- Forms suddenly do not behave properly.
- A user receives a message about a problem with the Frmcache.dat file.
- A user receives a "The Object Could Not Be Found" error message when the user opens an item or clicks on a mailto: link.

Clearing the forms cache does not always resolve a corrupted form problem. Sometimes, the form definition is actually corrupted on Exchange Server. In this case, you will need to delete the form using the Manage Forms dialog box described earlier in this chapter. Then you will need to republish the form from an .oft file in order to rebuild the damaged message containing the custom form description. Although the possibility of a damaged form description message in the Exchange store is small, it could occur. Consequently, you have one more reason to back up custom forms to an .oft file stored on a network or local drive which is backed up regularly.

To clear the forms cache in Outlook 2002

1. Select Options on the Tools menu, and then click the Other page.
2. Click Advanced Options.
3. In the Advanced Options dialog box, click Custom Forms.
4. Click Manage Forms.
5. Click Clear Cache in the Manage Forms dialog box.
6. Quit and then restart Outlook.

> **More Info** Because Outlook caches forms, you should avoid having more than one form with the same name in—or publishing the same form to—more than one forms library. If you do publish forms with the same name to more than one forms library (for example, a public folder and a folder in a personal folders file), you might experience forms cache corruption. Symptoms of forms cache corruption include Outlook displaying an alert message telling you that your custom form could not be opened. To reset the Outlook forms cache, you must follow the procedures outlined earlier to clear the forms cache.
>
> Forms used in a folder-based solution should be published only in the application folder. If you're developing a solution based on mail message forms, you can temporarily publish the forms in your Personal Forms Library. Once the form is finalized, you should publish the form to the Organizational Forms Library on the Microsoft Exchange Server and then delete the form from your Personal Forms Library after making a backup of the form. If, for some reason, you need to publish a form in more than one location, you should be sure to keep all forms libraries up-to-date with the current version of the form.

Form Activation

A form is activated when the user selects a form to compose an item or when the user performs an operation on a existing item. For example, the user double-clicks an existing item in a folder to open it. Outlook uses the following form-caching sequence to activate forms:

1. **Standard Forms Library** Checks for standard forms, such as Note, Post, Contact, Distribution List, Task, Journal, and Appointment.
2. **Cached Forms** Checks for a form in the forms cache.
3. **Active Folder Library** Checks for a form in the forms library of the active folder.
4. **Personal Forms Library** Checks for the form definition in the Personal Forms Library. If it is found, Outlook opens the form.
5. **Organizational Forms Library** Checks the form definition in the Organizational Forms Library. If it is found, Outlook opens the form.

Distribute and Manage Folders

After a folder is designed, you can copy it to a Mailbox folder, Personal Folders, or Public Folders. This section discusses the different methods for making a folder available for use. It also briefly discusses folder replication and archiving. For additional information on making a folder available for offline use, see "Make the Folder Available for Offline Use" in Chapter 8.

> **Important** Do not attempt to distribute folders using the Outlook Import and Export Wizard. The Import and Export Wizard is designed for importing and exporting data, not for distributing folders.

Make a Folder Available to All Users in Your Organization

You can make a folder available to all users in your organization by creating the folder in, or copying the folder to, Public Folders. Then it is up to the administrator to determine whether the folder is replicated throughout the organization. You or the administrator can set permissions for who has access to the folder and to what extent those users can work in the folder.

> **Note** To copy a folder to Public Folders, you must have permission to create subfolders for that portion of the Microsoft Exchange Server folder hierarchy.

Based on the policies of your organization, you may not have permission to copy a folder to Public Folders. You may be required to hand off the folder to your administrator, who then copies the folder and completes the design tasks according to your specifications. Alternatively, you may be given permission to copy your folder to a specific public folder and then complete the task yourself. See your administrator for specific instructions.

To create a folder in Public Folders

1. In Public Folders, right-click the folder in which you want to create the subfolder, and then click New Folder on the shortcut menu.
2. In the Name text box, type a name for the folder.

Part IV Beyond the Basics

3. Select the options you want.

4. If prompted, select a choice about creating a shortcut on the Outlook Bar and then click OK.

To copy a folder to Public Folders

1. In the Folder List, right-click the folder you want to copy, and then click Copy *folder name* on the shortcut menu, where *folder name* is the folder name you used in step 2 of the previous procedure.

2. Click the public folder you want to copy the folder to, and then click OK.

Set Permissions for the Folder

When you set permissions on the folder, you determine who has access to the folder and what functions they can perform in the folder.

To set permissions for the folder

1. In the Folder List, right-click the folder you copied to Public Folders, and then click Properties on the shortcut menu.

2. Click the Permissions page.

3. Set permissions for the folder.

> **More Info** For more information about setting permissions, see "Set Permissions" in Chapter 8.

If the folder is replicated to other servers, make sure you set the permissions so that all users who need access to the folder have the appropriate permissions.

Make a Folder Available for Personal Use

Private folders are stored in the user's Mailbox folder or in a personal folder (.pst) file. There are several reasons for storing a folder in a personal folder file:

- Users have exclusive rights to the folder. For example, many users keep a list of personal contacts in their Contacts folder.

Distributing and Securing Applications Chapter 13

- Users can access information in the folder even when they are not logged on to Microsoft Exchange Server. This can be especially useful for people who travel because they can access information in a personal folder on a laptop without a live connection to the server.

- Users can easily distribute the folder in personal folder (.pst) files. For example, many of the applications in this book were tested in public folders on a test Exchange Server. After testing, they were copied to the Building Microsoft Outlook 2002 Applications folder so they could be distributed in a .pst file.

> **More Info** If you have not yet created a Personal Folder file, see "Create a Personal Folder File" later in this chapter.

To create a folder in your Mailbox or in a personal folder (.pst) file

1. In the Folder List, right-click the Mailbox folder or personal folder you want to create the subfolder in, and then click New Folder on the shortcut menu.
2. In the Name text box, type a name for the folder.
3. Select the options you want.

To copy a folder to your Mailbox or personal folder (.pst) file

1. In the Folder List, right-click the folder you want to copy, and then click Copy *folder name* on the shortcut menu, where *folder name* is the folder name you used in step 2 above.
2. Click the Mailbox folder or personal folder you want to copy the folder to, and then click OK.

Distribute a Folder in a Personal Folder (.pst) File

A personal folder (.pst) file provides a convenient way to distribute applications using a floppy disk, a CD, or a network drive. For example, you can create folders on your Microsoft Exchange Server system in either public or personal folders. When you are ready to distribute the folders, you can create a personal folder file and then copy the folders to the file.

Part IV Beyond the Basics

Create a Personal Folder File

To create a personal folder (.pst) file

1. On the File menu, click New and then click Personal Folders File (.pst).
2. On the Save In drop-down list box, specify the location for your personal folder (.pst) file.
3. In the File Name text box, enter a name for the personal folder (.pst) file.
4. Click Create.
5. In the Create Microsoft Personal Folders dialog box, select the options you want and then click OK.

Copy Folders to a Personal Folder File

To copy a folder to a personal folder (.pst) file

1. In the Folder List, right-click the folder you want to copy, and then click Copy *folder name* on the shortcut menu, where *folder name* is the folder name you used in step 3 above.
2. Click the personal folder you want to copy the folder to, and then click OK.

Distribute the Personal Folder File

To distribute the personal folder (.pst) file, open Windows Explorer and copy the .pst file to a floppy disk, a network drive, or a CD drive.

Install a Personal Folder File Programmatically

You can install a personal folder (.pst) file programmatically if you use the *AddStore* method of the NameSpace object. If the .pst file does not exist, a new .pst file will be created using the file specification provided. The following procedure adds a .pst file named appwzd.pst located in the D:\Exchange folder.

```
Sub AddPST()
    Set oNS = Application.GetNameSpace("MAPI")
    oNS.AddStore "d:\exchange\appwzd.pst"
End Sub
```

Make an Existing Personal Folder File Available on Your Microsoft Exchange System

> **To make an existing personal folder file available on your Microsoft Exchange System**

1. On the File menu, select Open and then click Personal Folders File (.pst).
2. Specify the location you want, and then double-click the personal folder (.pst) file you want.
3. The file appears in your Folder List.

Making Changes to a Folder

If you're responsible for maintaining an application, you're often asked to make changes to the forms or folders that make up the application. For example, users may ask for enhancements to a form, additional folder views, or permissions.

If the changes to the folder are substantial, you should copy the design of the folder to another folder, make the necessary changes to the folder, and then copy the design back to the original folder. If the changes are minor, such as adding a permission or a view, you can modify the folder directly. To make changes to a folder, you must have Owner permission for the folder.

> **More Info** For more information about how to modify a folder, see Chapter 8.

Folder Replication Issues

Replication is the process by which Microsoft Exchange Server keeps folders that are in different locations synchronized. Generally, folder replication is handled by Microsoft Exchange Server administrators and involves careful planning and coordination between site administrators.

If you are an application designer, here are a few issues you should be aware of regarding folder replication:

- If a folder contains critical data that must be refreshed immediately in all locations when new data is received, the folder should not be replicated.
- Replicate applications from a central location. It often makes sense to store all applications on one server and perform all replication and updates to the application from this central location.
- Make sure each site that needs to replicate the application has appropriate permissions to support replication.

Age and Archive Folders

You can have Outlook automatically remove items of a specified age and transfer them to an archive file. Only folders in your mailbox or in a .pst file can be autoarchived. Outlook 2002 provides an enhanced user interface for folder archiving, as shown in Figure 13-5. This dialog box controls the default AutoArchive settings. If you want to use a different setting for the folder, you must use the AutoArchive page on the Folder Properties dialog box.

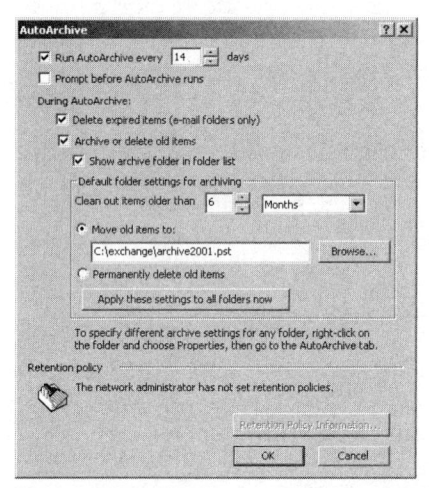

Figure 13-5 The improved Outlook 2002 AutoArchive dialog box controls the AutoArchive settings for a folder.

To turn on AutoArchiving for Outlook

1. On the Tools menu, select the Options command.
2. Click the AutoArchive button on the Other page of the Tools Options dialog box.

3. Check the Run AutoArchive Every <*number*> Days check box. Specify the number or accept the default.

4. Establish the default AutoArchive location or accept the default.

5. Click OK.

To turn AutoArchiving on for a specific folder

1. Select the folder you want to AutoArchive in the Folder List.

2. On the File menu, select Folder and then select Properties for <*folder name*>.

3. Click the AutoArchive page of the <*folder name*> Properties dialog box.

4. If you want to use the default AutoArchive settings, select the Archive Items In This Folder Using The Default Settings option.

5. If you want to establish a custom setting for this folder, select the Archive This Folder Using These Settings option.

6. Make your choices and then click OK.

Outlook 2002 Security

Perhaps the most significant new feature of Outlook 2002 is the Outlook E-Mail Security Update. Introduced in response to the damage wrought by e-mail viruses such as Melissa and ILoveYou, the Outlook E-Mail Security Update was offered originally as a patch for Outlook 2000 SR-1a and Outlook 98. This update is not available for Outlook 97. In Outlook 2000 SP2 and Outlook 2002, the Outlook E-Mail Security Update is built into Outlook. It cannot be removed, and administrative control is available only for users who are connected to an Exchange server. Administrative control is provided by an Administrative form that is located in a folder in the Public Folder hierarchy and by a registry key setting that causes Outlook to read values from the form when Outlook launches.

The Outlook E-Mail Security Update can be broken down into two functional areas: attachment security and object model guard security. The Attachment Security component prevents users from directly opening files that are potentially dangerous. These potentially dangerous files can run scripts that range in severity from a nuisance message to the destruction of data and operating system files. In addition to destroying files, e-mail viruses can compromise personal or corporate security. Object model guard security restricts access to certain objects, methods, and properties in both the Outlook Object Model and CDO. When a program attempts to access these items, a warning dialog box that allows the user to cancel the object model call is displayed. (See Figure 13-6.) An administrator can use the Administrative form to cause the blocked object model calls to fail silently without displaying the security warning dialog box. Object model calls allow hackers to propagate their viruses, typically by accessing a user's Contacts folder or the Global Address List (GAL) and then sending the virus payload to the addresses discovered through the object model.

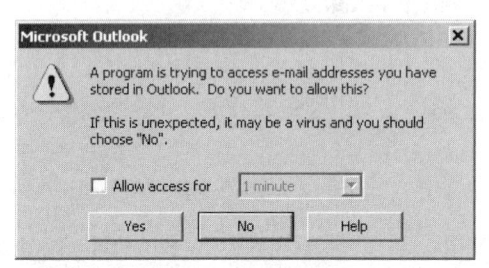

Figure 13-6 The security warning dialog box alerts the user to code that attempts to access the Outlook Address Book.

Attachment Security

The Attachment Security component of the Outlook E-Mail Security Update attempts to block access to attachment files of certain types (recognized by their file extensions) that are deemed to be potentially harmful. The blocked file types are known as Level 1 attachments. When a user sends a message with a Level 1 file attached, the warning message shown in Figure 13-7 appears. The user has the option of sending the message or canceling it. When the recipient of the message opens the message, she will see the warning shown in Figure 13-8 on the message InfoBar. This message states that Outlook has blocked access to the attachment. Access to the Level 1 attachment will be blocked only if the recipient is using a version of Outlook that has the Outlook E-Mail Security Update. Be aware that this Level 1 attachment will still be attached to the message in the Exchange store, but it cannot be opened by a user through Outlook.

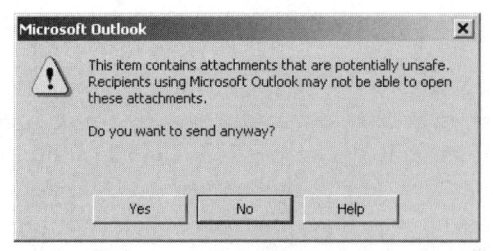

Figure 13-7 The attachment warning appears when the user sends a message containing a Level 1 attachment.

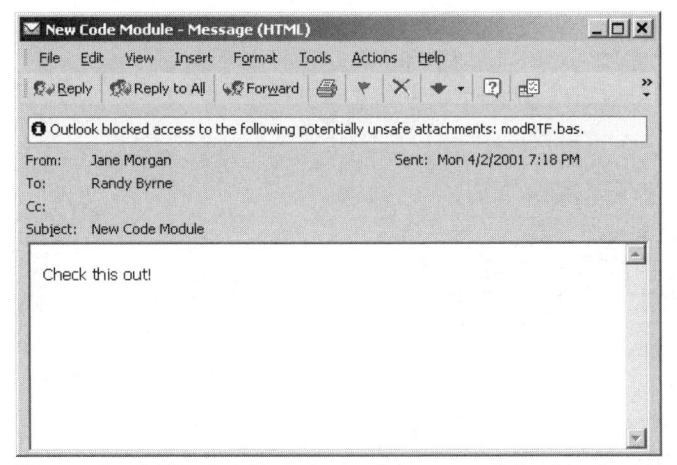

Figure 13-8 The InfoBar shows the name of the blocked Level 1 attachment.

> **Note** The InfoBar will not appear on an Outlook custom form. If your custom form uses Level 1 attachments, the user will not see an InfoBar warning that access to the attachments has been blocked.

Level 1 attachments cannot be accessed programmatically through the Outlook Object Model. For example, if you use Attachments.Count to return the number of attachments for the message shown in Figure 13-8, the count returned is zero. Any nonblocked attachments will still be available in the Attachments collection object of the message.

Outlook also recognizes Level 2 attachments, which are attachments that must be saved to disk before they can be opened. You cannot open a Level 2 attachment directly by double-clicking on it in the message or the preview pane. Figure 13-9 shows the Level 2 Attachment Security Warning dialog box. In this case, the Administrative form has been used to remove .exe files from Level 1 and to add .exe files to Level 2. By default, no Level 2 file extensions exist. You must use the Administrative form to change Level 1 file types to Level 2. Unlike Level 1 attachments, Level 2 attachments are accessible through the Attachments collection object.

In addition to Level 1 and Level 2 attachments, the Attachment Security component blocks in-place activation of OLE-embedded objects in e-mail messages, such as a Microsoft Excel worksheet or a Microsoft Word document. OLE-embedded objects can be inserted only into Rich Text Format messages. If a user attempts to activate an OLE-embedded object, the in-place activation fails silently. In Outlook 2002, OLE-embedded objects are read-only and cannot be activated in place.

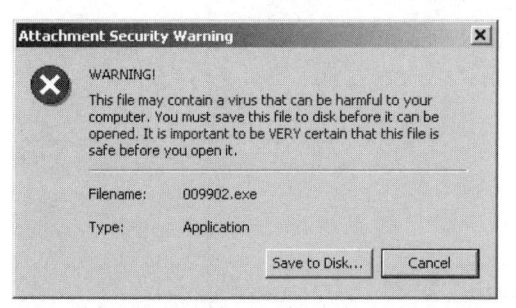

Figure 13-9 Level 2 attachments must be saved to disk before they can be opened.

The following table shows the list of Level 1 file types blocked by default. The Level 1 files blocked differ between the Outlook 2000 E-Mail Security Update and the security update for Outlook 2002. See the section "Creating Custom Security Settings" toward the end of the chapter for instructions on how to modify the list of Level 1 file types.

File Extension	File Type	Blocked by Outlook 98 and 2000 (Default)	Blocked by Outlook 2002 (Default)
.ade	Microsoft Access project extension	X	X
.adp	Microsoft Access project	X	X
.asx	Windows Media Audio/Video shortcut		X
.bas	Microsoft Visual Basic code module	X	X
.bat	Batch file	X	X
.chm	Compiled HTML Help file	X	X
.cmd	Microsoft Windows NT command script	X	X
.com	Microsoft MS-DOS program	X	X
.cpl	Control Panel extension	X	X
.crt	Security certificate	X	X
.exe	Executable program	X	X

Distributing and Securing Applications Chapter 13

File Extension	File Type	Blocked by Outlook 98 and 2000 (Default)	Blocked by Outlook 2002 (Default)
.hlp	Help file	X	X
.hta	HTML program	X	X
.inf	Setup information	X	X
.ins	Internet naming service	X	X
.isp	Internet communication settings	X	X
.js	JScript file	X	X
.jse	JScript-encoded script file	X	X
.lnk	Shortcut	X	X
.mda	Microsoft Access add-in program		X
.mdb	Microsoft Access program	X	X
.mde	Microsoft Access MDE database	X	X
.mdz	Microsoft Access wizard program		X
.msc	Microsoft Common Console document	X	X
.msi	Windows Installer package	X	X
.msp	Windows Installer patch	X	X
.mst	Visual Test source files	X	X
.pcd	Photo CD image or Microsoft Visual Test compiled script	X	X
.pif	Shortcut to MS-DOS program	X	X
.prf	Microsoft Outlook Profile Settings		X
.reg	Registration entries	X	X
.scf	Windows Explorer command		X
.scr	Screen saver	X	X
.sct	Windows script component	X	X
.shb	Shortcut into a document	X	X
.shs	Shell scrap object	X	X
.url	Internet shortcut	X	X
.vb	VBScript file	X	X
.vbe	VBScript-encoded script file	X	X
.vbs	VBScript file	X	X
.wsc	Windows script component	X	X
.wsf	Windows script file	X	X
.wsh	Windows Scripting Host settings file	X	X

Object Model Security

The Object Model Security component of the Outlook E-Mail Security Update poses the greatest challenge to your development efforts. (In this discussion, I'll refer to the Object Model Security component as the Object Model Guard.) Code written for existing applications can break, and you must carefully consider the impact of the Object Model Guard on any applications you plan to develop in the future. I strongly recommend that you rewrite existing applications to eliminate the warning dialog boxes presented by the Object Model Guard. You do not want your users to ignore the Object Model Guard warning prompts. Your help desk also will not want to be deluged with support calls from concerned users. If you cannot modify an existing application that displays warning prompts, you can use the Administrative form to allow blocked object model calls for application users. For more on this topic, see the "Creating Custom Security Settings" section later in the chapter. You can also modularize your code and place blocked object model calls in a trusted COM Add-in. For additional details, see the "Trusted Code Page" section later in the chapter.

When the Object Model Guard Operates

The Outlook Object Model Guard operates whenever code attempts to call a restricted property or method of the Outlook Object Model, CDO, or Simple MAPI. Simple MAPI, or the Simple Messaging Application Programming Interface, provides some basic messaging calls, such as MAPISendMail and MAPIReadMail. The following environments will display the Object Model Guard warnings provided that the Administrative form has not been used to change the object model restrictions:

- VBScript code behind custom forms that are published to any folder forms library, including the Organizational Forms Library.

- Outlook Visual Basic for Applications (VBA) code.

- Visual Basic code in standalone applications.

- Visual Basic code in untrusted COM Add-ins. A digital signature for the COM Add-in does not determine whether it will be trusted by the Object Model Guard. To bypass the Object Model Guard warnings, you must use the Administrative form to add the COM Add-in to the list of trusted COM Add-ins.

- Any other automation code in Visual C++, JavaScript, or another development environment that uses blocked methods and properties of the Outlook Object Model, CDO, or Simple MAPI. Extended MAPI calls are not blocked by the Object Model Guard.

Restricted Properties and Methods

The following table lists the properties and methods that cause the Object Model Guard warning dialog box to display in Outlook 2002.

Object	Restricted Properties	Restricted Methods
Action		*Execute*
AddressEntries	Any property	Any method
AddressEntry	Any property	Any method
AppointmentItem	Organizer RequiredAttendees OptionalAttendees Resources NetMeetingOrganizerAlias	*Respond* *SaveAs* *Send*
ContactItem	Email1.Address Email1.AddressType Email1.DisplayName Email1.EntryID Email2.Address Email2.AddressType Email2.DisplayName Email2.EntryID Email3.Address Email3.AddressType Email3.DisplayName Email3.EntryID NetMeetingAlias ReferredBy	*SaveAs*
DistListItem		*GetMember* *SaveAs*
ItemProperties	Any restricted property for an item	
JournalItem	ContactNames	*SaveAs*
MailItem	SentOnBehalfOfName SenderName ReceivedByName ReceivedOnBehalfOfName ReplyRecipientNames To Cc Bcc	*SaveAs* *Send*
MeetingItem	SenderName	*SaveAs*

(continued)

Part IV Beyond the Basics

Object	Restricted Properties	Restricted Methods
NameSpace	CurrentUser GetRecipientFromID	
PostItem	SenderName	*SaveAs*
Recipient	Any property	Any method
Recipients	Any property	Any method
TaskItem	ContactNames Contacts Delegator Owner StatusUpdateRecipients StatusOnCompletionRecipients	*SaveAs* *Send*
UserProperties		*Find*
UserProperty	Formula	

> **Note** The ItemProperties collection is new in Outlook 2002. This collection object allows you to enumerate the default and custom properties on an item. If you attempt to access a restricted property through the ItemProperties collection object, you will trigger the Object Model Guard warning. For example, the following statement will display the warning prompt when a user tries to access the Address Book:
>
> ```
> strSenderName = objMailItem.ItemProperties("SenderName")
> ```

Some code examples can help you understand the object model calls that trigger the warning prompts. The following example is taken from the Test Trust COM Add-in included on the companion CD:

```
Public Sub SendMailToMe(strSubject, strBody)
    On Error Resume Next
    Dim oMailItem As MailItem
    Dim oRecip As Outlook.Recipient
    'Triggers Address Book UI
    Set oRecip = golApp.GetNamespace("MAPI").CurrentUser
    Set oMailItem = golApp.CreateItem(olMailItem)
    With oMailItem
        .Subject = strSubject
        .Body = strBody
        'Triggers Address Book UI
```

```
        .Recipients.Add oRecip
        'Triggers programmatic send UI
        .Send
    End With
End Sub
```

This simple example is designed to send a message to the currently logged on user. It will display both the Address Book warning shown in Figure 13-7 and the programmatic send warning shown in Figure 13-10. In the "Trusted Code Page" section later in the chapter, you'll learn how to include this COM Add-in on the list of trusted COM Add-ins. Trusted COM Add-ins do not display the warning prompts and have unrestricted access to the Outlook Object Model. In addition, trusted COM Add-ins can expose public properties and methods to VBScript behind forms and provide unrestricted access through VBScript calls to those trusted COM objects.

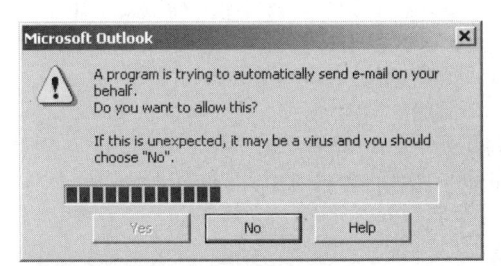

Figure 13-10 The *Send* method of the MailItem object displays the programmatic send warning.

One-Off Forms Code Disabled by Default

One-off forms are custom forms that have VBScript code stored within them instead of in a forms library. Typically these forms are used to send custom forms to recipients outside a user's organization. In versions of Outlook without the E-Mail Security Update, opening a one-off form displays a Macro Warning dialog box that lets the user enable or disable the code behind the form. Under the Outlook E-Mail Security Update, the code behind all one-off forms is disabled by default. One-off forms sent to recipients outside a user's organization can be published to the recipient's Folder, Organizational, or Personal Forms Library.

Other Object Model Security Restrictions

Outlook 2002 has some additional object model restrictions that you should be aware of. The restrictions listed here are designed to prevent hackers from sneaking in through the back door to obtain e-mail addresses to spread viruses:

- When you call the *Execute* method of a CommandBarButton object that represents the Send button on an Inspector toolbar, the programmatic send warning will be displayed.

- The *SendKeys* statement in Visual Basic or VBA will display Object Model Guard warnings when certain Outlook dialog boxes are active. This restriction prevents hackers from manipulating Outlook dialog boxes programmatically.

- By default, the Outlook E-Mail Security Update sets Outlook Macro Security to High. This setting prevents Outlook VBA macro code from running. Other Office applications—such as Microsoft Word, PowerPoint, and Excel—also have their Macro Security set to High.

- For HTML mail, the Outlook E-Mail Security Update uses the Restricted Sites zone as its default. This setting prevents the program from running scripts that are embedded in HTML messages.

Workarounds and Error Trapping

You can't suppress the Object Model Guard warnings once you make a call to a restricted property or method. However, you can work around some of the Object Model Guard restrictions in your code. For example, the following code from the NameSpace Object form in the VBScript Samples folder on the companion CD uses the IsOutlookSecure function to determine whether to call the GetCurrentUser function to replace the CurrentUser property of the NameSpace object:

```
Sub ReturnTheCurrentUserName_Click
    If IsOutlookSecure Then
        MsgBox GetCurrentUser, vbInformation
    Else
        MsgBox Application.GetNamespace("MAPI").CurrentUser
    End If
End Sub

Function IsOutlookSecure
On Error Resume Next
    strVersion = Application.Version
    If Err Then
        'Fails in Outlook 97
        Exit Function
    Else
        intVersion = CInt(Left(strVersion, 2))
        If intVersion > 9 Then 'Outlook 2002
            IsOutlookSecure = True
        ElseIf intVersion = 9 'Outlook 2000
            If CInt(Right(strVersion, 4)) >= 4201 Then
                IsOutlookSecure = True
            End If
        ElseIf intVersion = 8 'Outlook 98
            If CInt(Mid(strVersion, 5, 4)) >= 7806 Then
                IsOutlookSecure = True
            End If
        End If
```

```
        End If
End Function

Function GetCurrentUser
    Dim objTopFolder, strTopFolder
    Const olFolderInbox = 6
    On Error Resume Next
    Set objTopFolder = _
        Application.GetNamespace("MAPI") _
        .GetDefaultFolder(olFolderInbox).Parent
    strTopFolder = objTopFolder.Name
    If InStr(1, strTopFolder, "-") Then
        GetCurrentUser = Trim(Right(strTopFolder, _
            Len(strTopFolder) - InStr(1, strTopFolder, "-")))
    Else
        GetCurrentUser = strTopFolder
    End If
End Function
```

If you make a call to a restricted object model property or method, Outlook will display the appropriate object model warning dialog box. If the user cancels the restricted object model call by selecting No in the dialog box, your code will raise a trappable error. The Visual Basic error number is 287, and the error description is "Application-defined or object-defined error." The following procedure displays a message box to the user depending upon the choice he makes when the Address Book warning is displayed. The offending statement in this procedure tries to obtain the SenderName property of the first message in the Inbox.

```
Sub TrapOMGuardError()
    Dim folInbox As MAPIFolder
    Dim objItem As MailItem
    Dim colProps As ItemProperties
    Dim strSender As String
    On Error Resume Next
    Set folInbox = _
        Application.GetNamespace("MAPI") _
        .GetDefaultFolder(olFolderInbox)
    Set objItem = folInbox.Items(1)
    strSender = objItem.ItemProperties("SenderName")
    If Err = 287 Then
        'User answered No to Address Book warning UI
        MsgBox "You canceled the Address Book access. Good Job!" _
            , vbInformation
    Else
        MsgBox "The SenderName is: " & strSender, vbExclamation
    End If
End Sub
```

Part IV Beyond the Basics

CDO Security

A secure version of CDO ships with the Outlook E-Mail Security Update. Although the version returned by the Version property of the CDO Session object is still 1.21, the properties of cdo.dll show the version as 1.21s when the secure client version of CDO is installed. The Outlook E-Mail Security Update won't change the cdo.dll file installed on an Exchange Server 5.5 machine, and you should never attempt to replace the cdo.dll file on your server with a version of it intended for use on a client system.

Unfortunately, there is no method for bypassing the CDO restricted properties and methods using the trusted COM Add-ins page of the Administrative form. A trusted COM Add-in that makes calls to restricted CDO properties and methods will still display the object model warning prompts in the default configuration of Outlook 2002. You can, however, use the Administrative form to select options for restricted calls to the CDO object model. You can display a prompt for a user decision, and you can automatically approve or deny calls to the CDO object model.

The following table lists the blocked properties and methods in the CDO object model.

Object	Restricted Properties	Restricted Methods
AddressEntries	Item	*Add*
		GetFirst
		GetLast
		GetNext
		GetPrevious
AppointmentItem	Fields properties listed under Fields object Organizer	
Fields	PR_SENT_REPRESENTING_ENTRYID PR_SENT_REPRESENTING_SEARCH_KEY PR_SENT_REPRESENTING_NAME PR_SENT_REPRESENTING_ADDRTYPE PR_SENT_REPRESENTING_EMAIL_ADDRESS PR_SENDER_ENTRYID PR_SENDER_SEARCH_KEY PR_SENDER_NAME PR_SENDER_ADDRTYPE PR_SENDER_EMAIL_ADDRESS PR_DISPLAY_TO PR_DISPLAY_CC	

Object	Restricted Properties	Restricted Methods
Fields (continued)	PR_DISPLAY_BCC PR_ORIGINAL_DISPLAY_TO PR_ORIGINAL_DISPLAY_CC PR_ORIGINAL_DISPLAY_BCC	
Folder	Messages (Contacts folder only)	
Message	Fields properties listed under Fields object Sender	*Send* (when ShowDialog argument is False)
Recipients	Item	*Add* *AddMultiple* *GetFirstUnresolved* *GetNextUnresolved* *Resolve*
Session	CurrentUser	*GetAddressEntry* *GetRecipientFromID*

Like the Outlook Object Model Guard, CDO cannot access an attachment in the Attachments collection if the attachment file is a blocked file type. Also similar to Outlook, CDO will return an error when a user selects No in a warning dialog box. CDO will return the error "Collaboration Data Objects-[E_ACCESSDENIED(80070005)]," which corresponds to a long error number of −2147024891.

Administrative Options

Fortunately, there are administrative options that can override the default security settings of Outlook 2002—as long as you are connected to an Exchange server. If you use a .pst file for your mailbox or run Outlook in Personal Information Manager (PIM) mode, you cannot benefit from the Administrative form in Public Folders and must run Outlook with its default security settings. Be aware that if you don't want to modify the default security settings of Outlook 2002, you don't have to install admpack.exe, a self-extracting executable that contains the Administrative form and other components. Administrative options apply to organizations that want to modify the default security settings of Outlook 2002 or to create exception security groups for developers, power users, and so forth. You'll learn about Outlook E-Mail Security Update administrative options in the following sections. You'll also learn how to provide granularity to your security settings by creating your own default and exception security settings with the Outlook Security form.

> **Note** There is one exception to the rule concerning users that are not connected to Exchange Server. It is possible for a user that is not connected to an Exchange Server to modify the list of Level 1 attachments without using the Administrative form. Outlook MVP Ken Slovak has written an Outlook COM Add-in that lets non-Exchange users modify the list of Level 1 attachments. This COM Add-in is available for download at *http://www.slipstick.com/outlook/esecup/getexe.htm#ol2002*.

Installing Admpack.exe

To establish administrative options for your organization, you must first obtain admpack.exe. This file is available in the Office XP Resource Kit or on the CD that comes with certain editions of Office XP. You should install admpack.exe only on the computer of the Exchange administrator responsible for creating and maintaining administrative security settings. You don't need to install any additional components on the client systems that will connect to Exchange Server. However, you will have to make registry changes on client computers if you want them to use either your own default security settings or the security settings for an exception group.

> **Note** The administrator's computer on which admpack.exe is installed must be running the Windows 2000 operating system. If you want multiple Exchange administrators to manage security settings, admpack.exe must be installed on each administrator's computer.

To install admpack.exe

1. Double-click admpack.exe to begin the installation process. Answer Yes to accept the license agreement.

2. Click the Browse button to locate the folder where you will install the components of admpack.exe. Click OK to accept the folder you selected in the Browse For Folder dialog box.

3. Click OK to extract components to the folder you selected in step 2.

4. From the Start menu choose Run, and then type the following command line in the box to register hashctl.dll. The hashctl.dll file is a component of the Trusted Code control, a tool used by the template to specify trusted COM Add-ins. The *folderpath* in this command line is the folder you established in step 2.

   regsvr32 drive:\<*folderpath*>\hashctl.dll

5. Choose Run from the Start menu, and then type the following command line in the box to register comdlg32.ocx:

   regsvr32 drive:\<*folderpath*>\comdlg32.ocx

Creating the Outlook Security Settings Public Folder

The next step in the installation process is to create the Outlook Security Settings public folder. This folder should be created by the Exchange administrator who will administer Outlook security settings for your organization. If you want multiple administrators to manage security settings, you must give them Owner permission on the Outlook Security Settings public folder.

To create the Outlook Security Settings public folder

1. Create a folder named Outlook Security Settings under Public Folders\All Public Folders. This folder must exist at the root of the public folder hierarchy directly under All Public Folders. Do not change the name of the folder, or the administrative security settings will not work.

2. Right-click the folder in the folder tree, and select the Properties command.

3. Click the Permissions page shown in Figure 13-11, and assign Reviewer permission as the default permission for the folder.

Part IV Beyond the Basics

> **Note** To establish separate security settings for a mixed installation of Outlook 2000 and Outlook 2002 clients, create a folder named Outlook Security Settings for Outlook 2000 users and one named Outlook 10 Security Settings for Outlook 2002 users. The folder from which Outlook reads security settings at boot time is determined by a registry key on the client computer.

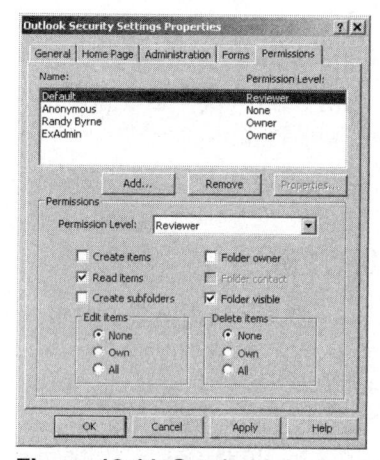

Figure 13-11 Set the default permission for the Outlook Security Settings folder to Reviewer permission.

The Outlook Security Form

The Outlook Security form shown in Figure 13-12 is a custom form that ships with admpack.exe. You can use this form to establish the default settings for your organization or to create exception security groups for certain users. The form contains three pages that control the following components of the Outlook 2002 E-Mail Security Update:

- **Outlook Security Settings** Provides a name for the Security group represented by the Outlook Security form and allows you to modify Level 1 and Level 2 file types.

- **Programmatic Settings** Lets you determine whether warning prompts will display when a user attempts to access blocked properties in the Outlook Object Model, CDO, and Simple MAPI.

- **Trusted Code** Lets you select COM Add-ins that will have unrestricted access to the Outlook Object Model.

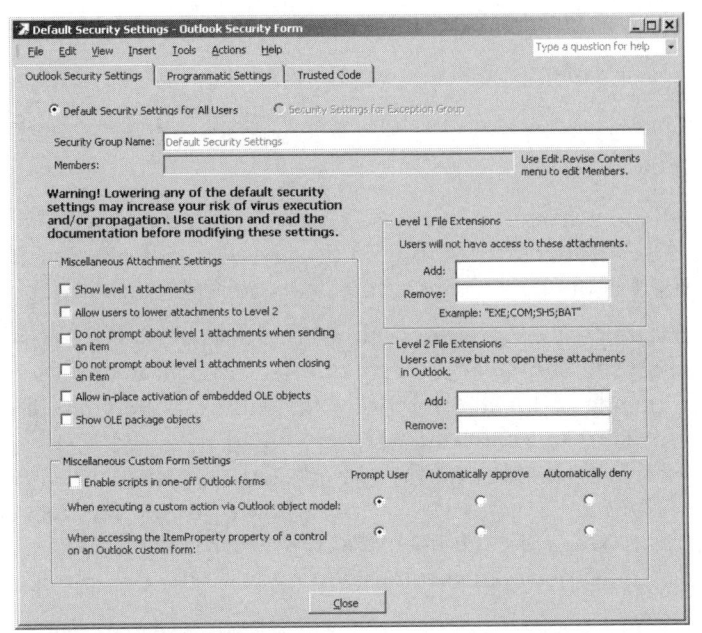

Figure 13-12 The Outlook Security form lets you customize settings for default and exception security groups.

Before you can establish custom security settings, you must install the Outlook Security form. This form is located in the folder that you created in step 2 of the admpack.exe installation on page 631.

To install the Outlook Security form

1. On the administrator's computer, double-click OutlookSecurity.oft in the folder where you extracted admpack.exe.

2. Select the Outlook Security Settings or Outlook 10 Security Settings public folder that you created on Exchange Server in the Select Folder dialog box.

3. On the Tools menu of the template, point to Forms and then click Publish Form.

4. In the Display Name edit box, type *Outlook Security Form*. The form name should change to Outlook Security Form, and the message class of the form will be IPM.Post.Outlook Security Form.

5. In the Publish Form As dialog box, click the Publish button to publish the security template in the Outlook Security Settings folder. You can now close the Outlook Security Settings template. Do not save when prompted to save while closing the template.

Part IV Beyond the Basics

6. Select the Outlook Security Settings folder in the Outlook Folder List.
7. On the Actions menu, select New Outlook Security Form.
8. Create either a default security setting or custom settings for a specific set of users:

    - To create a default security setting to be used by all users, click the Default Security Settings For All Users option. Specify the desired default security settings for your organization.

    - To create custom security settings for a specific set of users, click the Security Settings For Exception Group option and then type a unique name in the Security Group Name box that describes the group. The Outlook Security form shown in Figure 13-13 creates an exception security group named Outlook Dev Team and gives the group less restrictive security options. In the Members box, type the name of each user who must have custom security settings. Then specify the settings you need for the exception group.

> **Note** If you are running Exchange 2000 Server or later on your server, you can use distribution lists (only for server-created security groups) in the Members box. Otherwise, you cannot use distribution lists. Adding users from the Contacts Address Book is not supported.

9. Click the Close button at the bottom of the form, and answer Yes to the Save Changes option.

> **Note** To add user names to the Members box for an exception security group, create a new e-mail message, click the To button, and then select names from the Global Address List. Copy the resolved names from the To box on the e-mail message to the Members box on the Outlook Security Settings form. If a user's name is entered as a member of more than one exception security group, the settings of the most recently created exception security group will apply. This is because Outlook searches for the first item that has the user's name in the Members field.

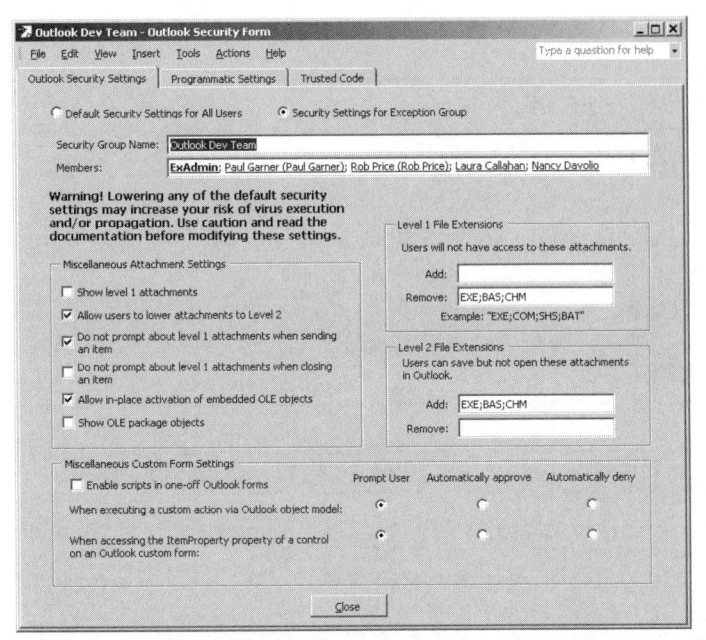

Figure 13-13 The Outlook Security form for the Outlook Dev Team group provides less restrictive security settings for its members.

Deploying Outlook Security Settings to Client Computers

Although you have created the Outlook Security Settings public folder and the custom forms for the default and exception security groups, you still have to write registry keys on client computers before these security settings can take effect. Be aware that Outlook 2002 security is in effect whether or not you make these changes. The client settings force Outlook to search for either custom or default security settings.

After you configure default and exception security groups in the Outlook Security Settings public folder, you must enable the customized settings for your users. To enable the changed settings, you might need to deploy a new registry key to the client computers, depending upon whether Office XP was initially deployed with system policies. If Office XP was deployed with system policies, the Outlk10.adm file will automatically pass your customized security settings to client computers each time users log on to the system. If Office XP was deployed without system policies, you must create a new registry key on the client computers. Outlook will respect this new registry key, even if you are not using policies. This registry key has the following path:

HKCU\Software\Policies\Microsoft\Security\CheckAdminSettings

Part IV Beyond the Basics

This table describes the possible DWORD values of CheckAdminSettings.

Key State	Description
No key	Uses Outlook 2002 default security settings
Set to 0	Uses Outlook 2002 default security settings
Set to 1	Uses default or exception security settings in custom forms in the Outlook Security Settings folder
Set to 2	Uses default or exception security settings in custom forms in the Outlook 10 Security Settings folder
Set to >2	Uses Outlook 2002 default security settings

To create a new registry key for distribution to client computers

1. Click Start, point to Run, and then type *regedit* in the Open box.

2. Click OK to start the Windows registry editor, and then expand the following subkey:

   HKEY_CURRENT_USER\Software\Policies\Microsoft\Security

3. From the Edit menu, choose New. Then click the DWORD value to add a new registry key, as shown in Figure 13-14.

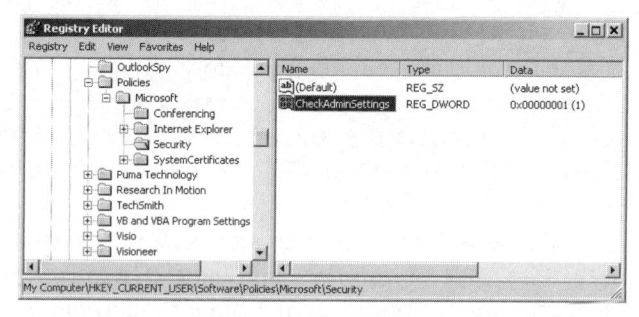

Figure 13-14 The CheckAdminSettings key causes Outlook to look for custom default and exception security settings.

4. The value name for the key must be CheckAdminSettings.

5. Select the new key name. Then choose Export Registry File from the Registry menu.

6. In the Export Registry File dialog box, type a name for the registry file and select the Selected Branch option under the Export Range group. Then click Save to create the registry file.

After the key has been created, use a push technology such as Microsoft Systems Management Server to deploy the registry key to client computers. Do not send the .reg key in an e-mail message to users because Outlook attachment security blocks .reg files as a Level 1 file type!

> **Note** The first time a user starts Outlook after setting the administrative options, he will still be using the built-in Outlook 2002 security settings. The user must quit and then restart Outlook in order for the custom default or exception security settings to apply.

Enabling Offline Use

You don't need to add the Outlook Security Settings or Outlook 10 Security Settings folder to the Favorites folder for offline use. This addition occurs behind the scenes, ensuring that your organizational default and custom security settings travel with offline users. Remember that if you don't establish the CheckAdminSettings registry key on a user's laptop, he or she will default to the built-in Outlook 2002 security settings.

User Registry Settings

It is possible for an end user to establish a Level1Remove registry key to remove file types from the Level 1 list. This is the only customization available to users who aren't connected to an Exchange server and who use a .pst file as their mail delivery location. If your Exchange administrator has not explicitly disallowed customization with the Level1Remove key, it also will be available to users who are connected to an Exchange server.

To create a Level1Remove key

1. Click Start, point to Run, and then type *regedit* in the Open box.
2. Click OK to start the Windows registry editor, and then expand the following subkey:

   HKEY_CURRENT_USER\Software\Microsoft\Office\10.0\Outlook\Security

3. From the Edit menu, choose New. Then click the DWORD value to add a new registry key.
4. The value name for the key must be Level1Remove.

Part IV   Beyond the Basics

5. Add a semicolon-delimited list of file type extensions that you want to remove from Level 1 attachment security (such as exe; chm; bas; mdb). Do not add periods before the extensions.

Administrator vs. User Settings

In general, security settings defined by the user work as though they were added to the settings defined by the Exchange administrator. When there is a conflict between the two, the settings with a higher security level will override those with a lower level of security. The following list describes some specific interactions between administrator and user security settings:

- **Show Level 1 Attachments**   When this option is set on the Outlook Security Settings tab, all file types are set to Level 2 security. The user will then need to customize the list to block access to specific types of attachments.

- **Level 1 File Extensions – Add**   When set by the administrator, this list overrides the user's settings. For example, if the user wants to remove EXE, REG, and COM but the administrator explicitly puts EXE in the Level 1 Add category, the user would have access to only REG and COM files.

- **Level 1 File Extensions – Remove**   The user's list is combined with the list set by the administrator to determine which Level 1 items are set to Level 2.

- **Level 2 File Extensions – Add**   If a user turns Level 1 files into Level 2 files and those file types are listed in the Add box, the files are treated as Level 2 attachments.

- **Level 2 File Extensions – Remove**   There is no interaction for this setting.

- **Allow Users To Lower Attachments To Level 2**   This setting allows users to demote a Level 1 attachment to Level 2. If this option is unselected, the user's list is ignored and the administrative settings control the security.

Preventing End User Customization

The option to prevent end user customization of the security settings is controlled by a registry key. The value of the key is as follows:

HKCU\Software\Policies\Microsoft\Office\10.0\Outlook

Value: DisallowAttachmentCustomization

If the registry key is present, end user customization is disallowed. If the key is not installed on the computer, end user customization is allowed. The value of the key has no effect.

Creating Custom Security Settings

You can create custom security settings either as the default for your organization or for exception security groups. This section discusses the various security settings that you can establish with the Outlook Security form.

Outlook Security Settings Page

Miscellaneous Attachment Settings

The following table describes the security options for e-mail attachments.

Option	Description
Show Level 1 attachments	Enables users to gain access to attachments with Level 1 file types.
Allow users to lower attachments to Level 2	Enables users to demote a Level 1 attachment to Level 2.
Do not prompt about Level 1 attachments when closing an item	Prevents users from receiving a warning when they send an item containing a Level 1 attachment. This option affects only the warning. Once the item is sent, the user won't be able to see or access the attachment. To allow users to post items to a public folder without receiving this prompt, you must select both this check box and the Do Not Prompt About Level 1 Attachments When Closing An Item check box.
Do not prompt about Level 1 attachments when closing an item	Prevents users from receiving a warning when they close a mail message, appointment, or other item containing a Level 1 attachment. This option affects only the warning. Once the item is closed, the user won't be able to see or access the attachment. To enable users to post items to a public folder without receiving this prompt, you must select both this check box and the Do Not Prompt About Level 1 Attachments When Sending An Item check box.

(continued)

Part IV Beyond the Basics

Option	Description
Allow in-place activation of embedded OLE objects	Allows users to double-click an embedded object, such as a Excel spreadsheet, and open it in place. If you are using Word as your e-mail editor, clearing this check box will still allow OLE objects to be opened when the embedded object is double-clicked.
Show OLE package objects	Displays OLE objects that have been packaged. (A package is shown by using an icon that represents an embedded or linked OLE object.) When you double-click the package, the program used to create the object either plays the object or opens and displays it. Use caution when displaying OLE package objects because the icon can easily be changed and used to disguise malicious files.

Level 1 File Extensions

Level 1 files are hidden from the user in all items. The user cannot open, save, or print a Level 1 attachment. The InfoBar at the top of the item will display a list of the blocked files. The InfoBar does not appear on a custom form. For information on the default list of Level 1 file types, see the table listing Level 1 file types (on pages 620–21).

The following table describes how to add or remove Level 1 file extensions from the default list.

Item	Description
Add	Specifies the file extension (usually three letters) of the file types you want to add to the Level 1 file list. Do not enter a period before the file extension. If you enter multiple extensions, separate them with semicolons.
Remove	Specifies the file extension (usually three letters) of file types you want to remove from the Level 1 file list. Do not enter a period before the file extension. If you enter multiple extensions, separate them with semicolons.

Level 2 File Extensions

The user is required to save a Level 2 file to disk before opening it. A Level 2 file cannot be opened directly from an item. The following table describes how to add or remove Level 2 file extensions from the default list.

Item	Description
Add	Specifies the file extension (usually three letters) of the file types you want to add to the Level 2 file list. Do not enter a period before the file extension. If you enter multiple extensions, separate them with semicolons.
Remove	Specifies the file extension (usually three letters) of file types you want to remove from the Level 2 file list. Do not enter a period before the file extension. If you enter multiple extensions, separate them with semicolons.

Miscellaneous Custom Form Settings

The following table describes the security settings for scripts, custom controls, and custom actions.

Setting	Description
Enable scripts in one-off Outlook forms	Select this check box to run scripts in forms where the script and the layout are contained in the message itself.
When executing a custom action via the Outlook Object Model	Specifies what happens when a program attempts to run a custom action using the Outlook Object Model. A custom action can be created to reply to a message and circumvent the programmatic send protections described earlier in the chapter. Select one of the following: ❑ **Prompt User** Enables the user to receive a message and decide whether to allow programmatic send access. ❑ **Automatically Approve** Always allows programmatic send access without displaying a message. ❑ **Automatically Deny** Always denies programmatic send access without displaying a message.

(continued)

Part IV   Beyond the Basics

Setting	Description
When accessing the ItemProperty property of a control on an Outlook custom form	Specifies what happens when a user adds a control to a custom Outlook form and then binds that control directly to any of the Address Information fields. By doing this, code can be used to indirectly retrieve the value of the Address Information field by getting the Value property of the control. Select one of the following: ❏ **Prompt User** Enables the user to receive a message and decide whether to allow access to Address Information fields. ❏ **Automatically Approve** Always allows access to Address Information fields without displaying a message. ❏ **Automatically Deny** Always denies access to Address Information fields without displaying a message.

Programmatic Settings Page

The Programmatic Settings page shown in Figure 13-15 enables you to configure settings related to your use of the Outlook Object Model, CDO, and Simple MAPI.

The table on the following page lists descriptions for each option on the Programmatic Settings page. See tables for the restricted Outlook and CDO properties and methods on pages 623 and 628 for a complete listing of restricted properties and methods for the Outlook and CDO object models. For each item, you can choose one of the following settings:

- **Prompt User**   Users receive a message allowing them to choose whether to allow or deny the operation. For some prompts, users can choose to allow or deny the operation without prompts for up to 10 minutes.

- **Automatically Approve**   The operation will be allowed, and the user will not receive a prompt.

- **Automatically Deny**   The operation will not be allowed, and the user will not receive a prompt.

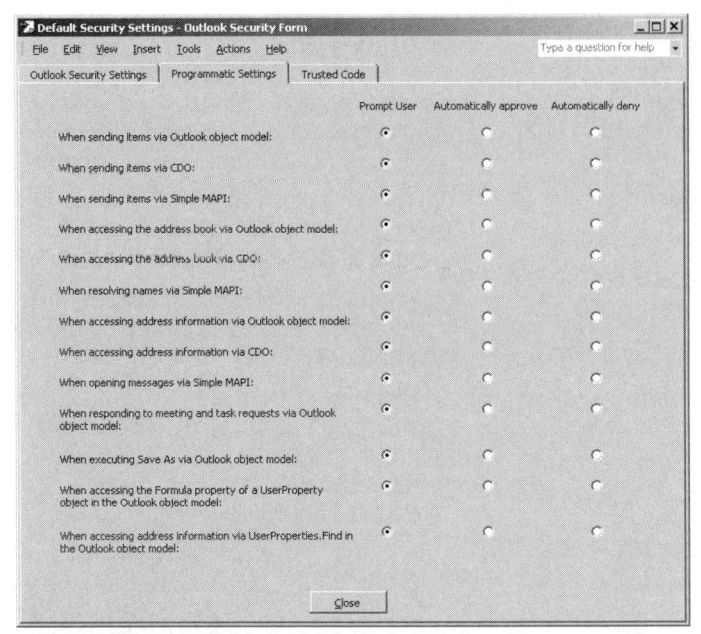

Distributing and Securing Applications   Chapter 13

Figure 13-15 The Programmatic Settings page provides granular control over programmatic security settings.

Item	Description
When sending items via Outlook object model	Specifies what happens when a program attempts to send mail programmatically using the Outlook Object Model.
When sending items via CDO	Specifies what happens when a program attempts to send mail programmatically using CDO.
When sending items via Simple MAPI	Specifies what happens when a program attempts to send mail programmatically using Simple MAPI.
When accessing the address book via Outlook object model	Specifies what happens when a program attempts to gain access to an Address Book using the Outlook Object Model.
When accessing the address book via CDO	Specifies what happens when a program attempts to gain access to an Address Book using CDO.
When resolving names via Simple MAPI	Specifies what happens when a program attempts to gain access to an Address Book using Simple MAPI.

(continued)

643

Part IV Beyond the Basics

Item	Description
When accessing address information via Outlook object model	Specifies what happens when a program attempts to gain access to a recipient field, such as To, using the Outlook Object Model.
When accessing address information via CDO	Specifies what happens when a program attempts to gain access to a recipient field, such as To, using CDO.
When opening messages via Simple MAPI	Specifies what happens when a program attempts to gain access to a recipient field, such as To, using Simple MAPI.
When responding to meeting and task requests via Outlook object model	Specifies what happens when a program attempts to send mail programmatically using the *Respond* method on task and meeting requests. This method is similar to the *Send* method on mail messages.
When executing Save As via Outlook object model	Specifies what happens when a program attempts to programmatically use the Save As command on the File menu to save an item. Once an item has been saved, a malicious program could search the file for e-mail addresses.
When accessing the Formula property of a UserProperty object in the Outlook object model	Specifies what happens when a user adds a Combination or Formula custom field to a custom form and binds it to an Address Information field. By doing this, code can be used to indirectly retrieve the value of the Address Information field by retrieving the field's Value property.
When accessing address information via UserProperties.Find in the Outlook object model	Specifies what happens when a program attempts to search mail folders for address information using the Outlook Object Model.

Trusted Code Page

The Trusted Code page shown in Figure 13-16 is used to specify which COM Add-ins are trusted and can be run without encountering the Outlook Object Model blocks. Trusted COM Add-ins have unrestricted access to the entire Outlook Object Model. Figure 13-16 shows that the Test Trust sample COM Add-in (whose compiled file name is TestTrust.dll) has been added to the list of trusted COM Add-ins. The Test Trust COM Add-in is located in the Test Trust COM Add-In folder under the Creating COM Add-Ins With Visual Basic folder in the 5. Advanced Topics folder in the .pst file on the companion CD.

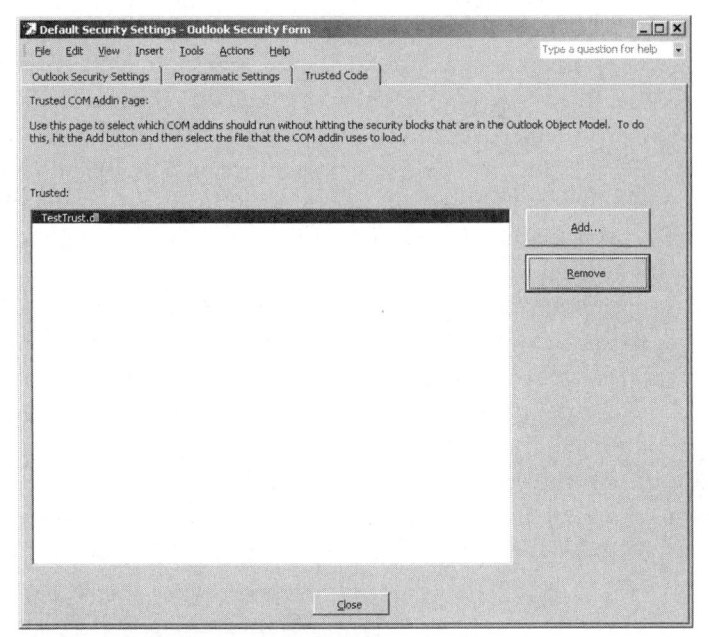

Figure 13-16 Trusted Code page.

Test Trust COM Add-In

You can use the Test Trust COM Add-in in both untrusted and trusted mode to see how the trusted code settings work with the custom Outlook security settings. The Test Trust COM Add-in will place a command bar button with a key icon on the standard Explorer toolbar. Click this button to display a dialog box that contains several commands that let you test trusted COM Add-ins. Click the Send Mail To Me button to send a message to yourself programatically. If you have not added TestTrust.dll to the list of trusted add-ins, you will see two warning prompts displayed when you send a message to yourself. If your program trusts TestTrust.dll, the warning prompts will not be displayed and the message will arrive in your Inbox.

> **Note** The Trusted Code feature of the Administrative form is available only for clients running Outlook 2002. Clients running Outlook 2000 with the Outlook E-Mail Security Update installed are unable to trust a COM Add-in.

Specifying Trusted COM Add-Ins

The process of specifying a trusted COM Add-in is relatively simple. You must register hashctl.dll on the administrator's machine before you attempt to trust COM Add-ins. The hashctl.dll file creates a unique hash value for the COM Add-in that is stored in the Outlook Security Settings custom form. This value is compared to the hash value calculated on the COM Add-in .dll installed on the client computer. If the hash values match, the COM Add-in on the client machine is granted unrestricted access to the Outlook Object Model.

Unfortunately, it is impossible to determine the version number of the COM Add-in you have trusted on the Trusted Code page of the Administrative form. I recommend that you keep a record of the version number when you add the COM Add-in to the list of trusted add-ins. Any recompilation of the COM Add-in (with or without a version number change) will require you to remove the add-in from the list of trusted add-ins and then add the new version to the list. Though it's commendable that COM Add-ins can be trusted in Outlook 2002, the Trusted Code page has several shortcomings in its ease of use and user interface design.

> **Note** COM Add-ins do not have to be digitally signed to be added to the list of trusted add-ins. Digital signatures have no bearing on whether a COM Add-in is trusted.

To specify a trusted COM Add-in

1. Copy the .dll (or other file) that's used to load the COM Add-in to a location where the administrator creating the security setting can access it. This file must be the same file used on the client computers that will run the COM Add-in.

2. On the Trusted Code page of the Outlook Security form, click the Add button and select the .dll you want to add from the location you specified in step 1. The COM Add-in will now run without giving warning prompts to Outlook 2002 users who use this security setting.

3. To remove a file from the trusted list on the Trusted Code page, select the file name and click the Remove button.

4. Click the Close button at the bottom of the form, and answer Yes to the Save Changes option.

> **Note** If you recompile the trusted COM Add-in or receive a new version of it from a vendor, you must remove the old version and then add the new version with each custom security group or default security group for which the add-in is trusted.

Building Trusted COM Add-Ins

Trusted COM Add-ins provide one way to extend Outlook without having the restrictions of the Outlook Object Model Guard. There are several important points to keep in mind when you build a trusted COM Add-in for Outlook 2002. First, only the Outlook Object Model can have restrictions removed with the Trusted Code page on the Outlook Security Settings form. You must have a mailbox on Exchange Server to take advantage of the administration options. Second, if you are developing a COM Add-in that runs in all modes of Outlook 2002 (including the Internet Only mode, in which your primary delivery container is a .pst file), your COM Add-in has no trust mechanism and must avoid blocked object model calls. For alternative solutions for all modes of COM Add-ins, see the next section, "Outlook Redemption: A Third-Party Alternative."

Third, there is no trust mechanism for a CDO 1.21 Session object at the level of a specific COM Add-in. If you want to use restricted CDO code in your add-in, you will have to modify the CDO options on the Programmatic Settings page of the security form. This CDO setting then applies to every user in the custom or default security group and leaves users vulnerable to a virus that uses CDO. Fourth, the Application object that is passed as an argument in the OnConnection event of the COM Add-in is a trusted object. Its child objects and their properties and methods are not restricted by the Outlook Object Model Guard. And finally, if you use CreateObject or GetObject to instantiate an Outlook Application object in your COM Add-in code (regardless of whether the COM Add-in .dll is trusted or untrusted on the Trusted Code page), that Application object, its dependent child objects, and their properties and methods will be restricted by the Outlook Object Model Guard.

> **See Also** For additional information on the architecture of COM Add-ins, see Chapter 14, "Creating COM Add-Ins with Visual Basic."

Part IV Beyond the Basics

Outlook Redemption: A Third-Party Alternative

If you need to make blocked CDO calls in clients running against Exchange Server or if you are writing a COM Add-in for all modes of Outlook, you have an alternative to Microsoft's Administrative Options package: the development tool known as Redemption. This tool was created by Extended MAPI wizard and Outlook MVP Dmitry Streblechenko. Redemption wraps Outlook Object Model and CDO calls in wrapper functions available through the Redemption Object Library. Redemption's object library is a standard COM component and can be called by Visual Basic, VBA, VBScript, or, for that matter, Visual C++. Extended MAPI calls are not subject to the restrictions of the Outlook E-Mail Security Update. Redemption also has its own built-in security mechanism that prevents viruses from using its object model to gain illegal access to Outlook information. An evaluation copy of Redemption can be found at *http://www.dimastr.com*.

Outlook Redemption enables you to perform the following tasks:

- Run your Visual Basic, VBA, and VBScript code without it being affected by the Outlook E-Mail Security Update
- Access properties not exposed by the Outlook Object Model (such as Internet message headers, sender e-mail addresses, and hundreds of other properties)
- Directly access the RTF body of any Outlook item
- Import .msg files
- Directly access message attachments as strings or arrays without saving them as files first
- Display the Address Book
- Force immediate Send/Receive
- Track new e-mail events with a new e-mail item passed to your handler—Outlook doesn't allow you to do this

The Redemption Object Library

Redemption exposes an object library that allows you to access blocked properties and methods of the Outlook Object Model without major revisions to your code. After you install Redemption, you can set a reference to Safe Outlook Library in the Project References dialog box. You can also inspect the objects, properties, and methods of Redemption in the Object Browser, as shown in Figure 13-17.

All Redemption objects have an Item property that must be set to an Outlook item. Once set, you can access any properties and methods available on an original Outlook item, both blocked and unblocked. For the blocked properties and functions, Redemption objects completely bypass the Outlook Object Model and behave exactly like Outlook objects but without the constraints of built-in

Outlook security. For the properties not blocked by the Outlook E-Mail Security Update, all calls to the properties and methods are forwarded to the Outlook object that you assign to the Item property.

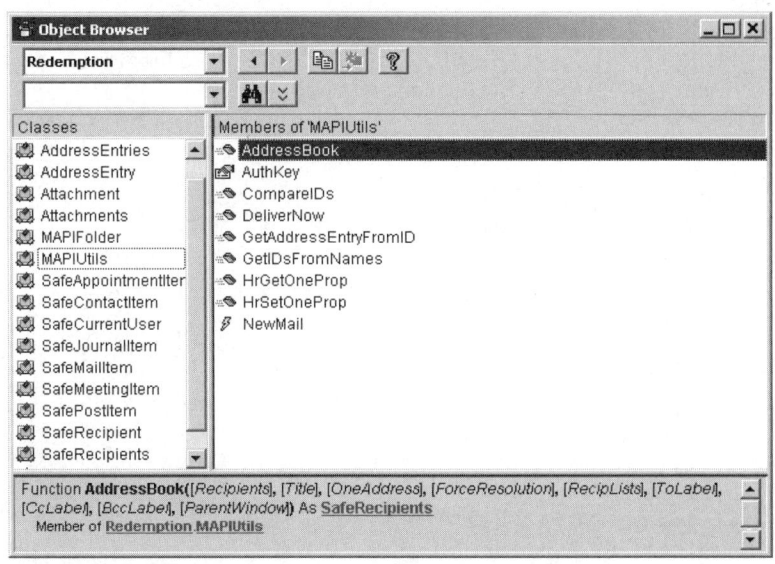

Figure 13-17 The Redemption Object Library exposes safe items that do not display warning prompts.

Using this approach means that changes to your code will be minimal. You change only the way you declare the objects; you don't change the code that actually accesses blocked and unblocked properties and methods. An additional benefit of Redemption is its ability to access all the Fields collection properties available through CDO without requiring you to actually install CDO. For additional details, see the Redemption documentation.

The most important concept in the Redemption object library is the Safe*Item. For example, a SafeMailItem object contains all the properties and methods of an Outlook MailItem object after you set the SafeMailItem.Item property to the MailItem object in your code. The following example uses Redemption to display an Address Book and then add the recipients returned by the *AddressBook* method to an Outlook MailItem represented by objSafeItem:

```
Sub DisplayRedemptionAB()
    Dim objOutlook As Outlook.Application
    Dim objItem As Outlook.MailItem
    Dim i As Integer
    Dim strTo, strCC, strBCC As String
    On Error Resume Next
    'Declare Redemption objects as Variants
    Dim colRecips, objSafeItem, objUtils
```

(continued)

```
        Set objOutlook = CreateObject("Outlook.Application")
        Set objItem = objOutlook.CreateItem(olMailItem)
        Set objSafeItem = CreateObject("Redemption.SafeMailItem")
        Set objSafeItem.Item = objItem
        objSafeItem.Subject = "Test Redemption"
        Set objUtils = CreateObject("Redemption.MapiUtils")
        Set colRecips = objUtils.AddressBook(Title:="Redemption Address Book")
        If colRecips Is Nothing Then
            'User canceled
            Exit Sub
        End If
        For i = 1 To colRecips.Count
            Select Case colRecips.Item(i).Type
                Case 1 'To
                    strTo = strTo & colRecips.Item(i).Name & ";"
                Case 2 'Cc
                    strCC = strCC & colRecips.Item(i).Name & ";"
                Case 3 'Bcc
                    strBCC = strBCC & colRecips.Item(i).Name & ";"
            End Select
        Next
        objSafeItem.To = strTo
        objSafeItem.CC = strCC
        objSafeItem.BCC = strBCC
        objSafeItem.Display
    End Sub
```

> **Note** For additional code examples that demonstrate the use of Redemption, see the Redemption Objects item in the VBScript Samples folder. You must install Redemption before you run the code in the Redemption Objects item.

If you were to use only CDO and Outlook objects in this example, the Address Book warning prompt would display twice—once for CDO recipient access and once for Outlook recipient access. Redemption allows you to eliminate the Outlook E-Mail Security Update warning prompts while running your code in a secure environment.

Where To Go from Here

Microsoft Knowledge Base Articles   Microsoft Knowledge Base articles are available on the Web at *http://support.microsoft.com/support*. Also see "Distributing and Securing Applications (Chapter 13) KB Articles" in the Microsoft Web Sites folder in the Help And Web Sites folder on the companion CD.

Part V

Advanced Topics

14 Creating COM Add-Ins with Visual Basic   653

15 Integrating Outlook with Web Applications   711

16 Using Outlook with SharePoint Portal Server   785

The Advanced Topics chapters are primarily for developers who want to use Microsoft Visual Basic to extend Microsoft Outlook in a corporate environment where Microsoft Exchange Server is installed. Chapter 14, "Creating COM Add-Ins with Visual Basic," provides you with practical templates for Visual Basic COM Add-in component creation and discusses the security issues associated with COM Add-ins. You'll also learn how to use Visual Basic to create an ActiveX control that serves as a property page in the Outlook Tools Options dialog box. Chapter 15, "Integrating Outlook with Web Applications," shows you how to use the Outlook View Control in Web pages. To polish the application, you will create Digital Dashboard Web Parts for the Northwind Contact Management application. In Chapter 16, "Using Outlook with SharePoint Portal Server," you'll discover how to use the PKMCDO object model for document checkin, checkout, and versioning. You will be able to integrate the Northwind Contact Management application with SharePoint Portal Server document management and search.

14

Creating COM Add-Ins with Visual Basic

Microsoft Outlook COM Add-ins provide an abundance of exciting new opportunities for Outlook developers. In Outlook 97 and Outlook 98, Outlook development took place primarily in the forms arena. Modification of the Outlook application environment—toolbars, dialog boxes, and property pages—required costly development of Exchange Client Extensions authored in C++. The costs associated with the C++ and MAPI development cycle discouraged the building of components that extended Outlook or fostered vertical market applications using Outlook and Exchange.

> **Note** Outlook 2002 COM Add-ins can also be trusted using the Outlook Security form in the Outlook Security Settings public folder. If you are developing a COM Add-in for Outlook 2000 and Outlook 2002 that must access blocked object model calls in Outlook and Collaborative Data Objects (CDO), you should consider a third-party alternative such as the Redemption object library. For additional details on Redemption, see Chapter 13, "Distributing and Securing Applications."

COM Add-ins are the preferred technology for extending Outlook in the 2000 and 2002 versions of the application. A COM Add-in is an ActiveX component packaged in a dynamic-link library (DLL) that is specially registered so that it can be loaded by Outlook. You can create Outlook COM Add-ins with either Microsoft Visual Basic 5 or 6. Visual Basic 5 requires some gymnastics on your part to get a COM Add-in to register correctly, so this chapter will focus instead on the use of Visual Basic 6 to create COM Add-ins. In fact, you can use any COM-compliant development tool, including Microsoft Visual C++, Microsoft Office XP Developer, or a tool from a vendor other than Microsoft, as long as that tool can create ActiveX DLLs. In this chapter, we'll discuss a variety of COM Add-ins that are available in the Creating COM Add-Ins With Visual Basic folder under the 5. Advanced Topics folder on the companion CD. Along the way, we'll cover the techniques you must be aware of when you create COM Add-in solutions.

> **Note** COM Add-ins can also be created using an ActiveX .exe file, but this approach is not recommended for Outlook COM Add-ins. Because ActiveX .exe components operate out of process, you'll incur a performance penalty if you create an ActiveX .exe COM Add-in.

Tools Needed to Create COM Add-Ins

To create an Outlook COM Add-in, you should obtain Visual Studio 98 Professional Edition or Visual Basic 5 Professional Edition. Visual Studio 98 is the preferred development tool because you can use Visual InterDev 6 to customize folder home pages, as well as Visual Basic 6 to create COM Add-ins. You can also create COM Add-ins for Outlook with Microsoft Office XP Developer. If you don't have Office XP Developer, you can develop a project using ThisOutlookSession and Outlook Visual Basic for Applications (VBA), but a solution based on ThisOutlookSession will have several limitations, including Outlook's inability to run more than one ThisOutlookSession project in a given Outlook session. If you install a custom VBAProject.otm (the project that contains ThisOutlookSession), you will overwrite the existing VBAProject.otm for the current user. On the other hand, multiple COM Add-in solutions can run in a given Outlook session. The table on the following page outlines the solutions you can create with the development tools mentioned and also lists the pros and cons of each tool.

Creating COM Add-Ins with Visual Basic Chapter 14

Tool	Solution Created	Intellectual Property Protection	Deployment	Multiple Solutions in an Outlook Session
Microsoft Office XP Developer	COM Add-in ActiveX DLL built with VBA 6.3	Compiled ActiveX DLL	Package and Deployment Wizard	Yes
Microsoft Visual Basic 5 Professional or Enterprise Edition	COM Add-in ActiveX DLL built with Visual Basic 5. Extra steps required because Visual Basic 5 does not support Add-in Designers	Compiled ActiveX DLL	Setup Wizard with extra steps required	Yes
Microsoft Visual Basic 6 Professional or Enterprise Edition	COM Add-in ActiveX DLL built with Visual Basic 6	Compiled ActiveX DLL	Package and Deployment Wizard or Visual Studio Installer	Yes

> **Note** You can use Microsoft Visual C++ to create COM Add-ins for Office XP applications. You can also use any development tool capable of creating an ActiveX DLL, as long as you meet the special requirements of Office XP COM Add-Ins. At the time of this writing, it is not clear if Microsoft Visual Studio.NET tools will participate in COM Add-in development.

The COMAddIns Collection Object

Before we cover the steps required to create a COM Add-in, you should realize that COM Add-ins are exposed in the Office XP Object Model through the COMAddIns collection object and its member COMAddIn objects. You can determine which COM Add-ins are available in a given Outlook application session by iterating over the items in the COMAddIns collection object. The COMAddIns collection object is available as a property object of the Outlook Application object. Although the COMAddIns collection object is available as a property object for each Application object in the Office suite, the COMAddIns collection object is application-specific, meaning that you can obtain the COMAddIns collection only for the Outlook Application object. The COMAddIns collection object supports only two methods, the *Update* method and the *Items* method. The *Items* method lets you access a COMAddIn object from the collection by index or by the COMAddIn's COM ProgID. The *Update* method refreshes the COMAddIns collection from the COM Add-ins that are registered in the Windows registry. Figure 14-1 illustrates a UserForm that displays the friendly names of Outlook COM Add-Ins, whether the COM Add-in is loaded in the current Outlook session, and the ProgID of the add-in.

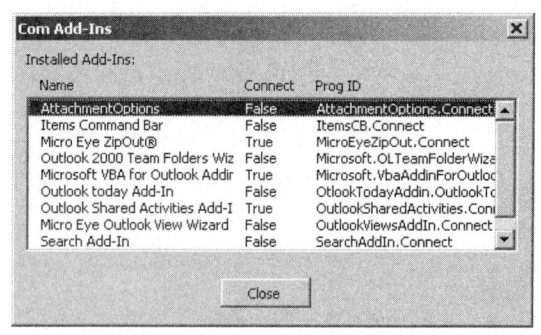

Figure 14-1 The COM Add-Ins dialog box displays the members of the COMAddIns collection that are registered.

COMAddIn Object

The COMAddIn object lets you determine the friendly name of a COM Add-in, whether the COM Add-in is loaded, and the ProgID of the COM Add-in. You can cause a COM Add-in to programmatically load or unload by setting its Connect property. If you are worried about a performance penalty in loading your COM Add-in during Outlook startup, you should consider loading and unloading your Add-in through program code instead. A more typical approach is to let the user install COM Add-ins through a setup program and then use the Outlook COM Add-Ins dialog box to determine which COM Add-ins are loaded. The following code populates the list box shown in Figure 14-1. To create a multi-column list box, create a Variant array and then fill the array with the Add-in's friendly name, connect state, and ProgID. When the array is populated, assign the array to the List property of the list box.

```
Private Sub UserForm_Initialize()
Dim avarArray
Dim intCount As Integer
Dim intAddIns As Integer
Dim objAddIn As Office.COMAddIn
Dim colAddIns As Office.COMAddIns
Set colAddIns = Application.COMAddIns
intAddIns = colAddIns.Count
If intAddIns Then
    ReDim avarArray(intAddIns - 1, 2)
    For intCount = 1 To intAddIns
        Set objAddIn = colAddIns.Item(intCount)
        avarArray(intCount - 1, 0) = objAddIn.Description
        If objAddIn.Connect = True Then
            avarArray(intCount - 1, 1) = "True"
        Else
            avarArray(intCount - 1, 1) = "False"
        End If
        avarArray(intCount - 1, 2) = objAddIn.ProgId
    Next
    lstAddIns.List = avarArray
End If
End Sub
```

Displaying the List of COM Add-Ins

Outlook's COM Add-Ins dialog box (shown in Figure 14-2) is buried deep in the Tools Options dialog box. If you are developing COM Add-ins, you'll want to customize your Standard or Advanced Explorer toolbar and place a command bar button on the toolbar to provide a shortcut to the COM Add-Ins dialog box.

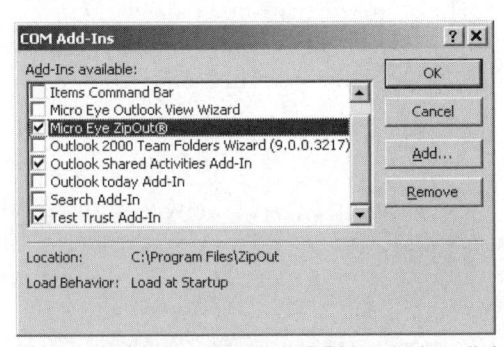

Figure 14-2 The Outlook COM Add-Ins dialog box lets you control the connection state of registered COM Add-ins.

Part V Advanced Topics

To display the Outlook COM Add-Ins dialog box

1. Select the Options command on the Tools menu.
2. Click the Other page on the Tools Options dialog box.
3. Click the Advanced Options command button.
4. Click the COM Add-Ins command button on the Advanced Options dialog box.

To add a toolbar button for the COM Add-Ins dialog box

1. Select the Customize command on the Tools menu.
2. Click the Commands page.
3. In the Categories list, click Tools.
4. In the Commands list, click COM Add-Ins. You may have to scroll through the list to find it.
5. Drag the COM Add-Ins command to the Standard or the Advanced Explorer toolbar.
6. Close the Customize dialog box.

To Load or Unload a COM Add-In

You can load a COM Add-in by checking the box next to the friendly name of the Add-in in the COM Add-Ins dialog box. Depending on the load behavior of the COM Add-In, the COM Add-in will either load immediately or it will load the next time you launch Outlook. There are circumstances in which you will want to unload a COM Add-in to debug the COM Add-in directly in Visual Basic in run mode. See "The Debugging Process" later in this chapter.

To Add a COM Add-In

If you install a COM Add-in by using its setup program, it will automatically register and appear in the list box of the COM Add-In dialog box shown in Figure 14-2. However, you can also add an unregistered COM Add-in by clicking Add in the COM Add-Ins dialog box and selecting the correct ActiveX DLL in the Add Add-In dialog box. If the ActiveX DLL you select is a valid Outlook COM Add-in, it will be registered and loaded by Outlook the next time Outlook starts.

> **Note** If you select an ActiveX DLL that is not an Office COM Add-in, Outlook will alert you and decline to load the Add-in. You cannot load other application-specific Add-ins (such as an Excel Add-in) with the Outlook COM Add-Ins dialog box.

To Remove a COM Add-In

To remove a COM Add-in, select it in the COM Add-Ins dialog box and click Remove. Removing an Add-in deletes the registry key containing the Add-in's name and load behavior. The registry contains information about COM Add-ins under HKEY_CLASSES_ROOT and HKEY_CURRENT_USER. Like any other DLL, the Add-in's ActiveX DLL is registered as a unique object in the system under HKEY_CLASSES_ROOT. In addition, information about the Add-in is placed under HKEY_CURRENT_USER\Software\Microsoft\Office\Outlook\Addins to notify Outlook that the Add-in exists. If you remove a COM Add-in from the list of installed Add-ins, the subkey identifying the COM Add-in is removed from the registry but the ActiveX DLL itself remains registered. If you add the Add-in to the list again, the Add-in's informational subkey is re-created in the registry.

Creating an Outlook COM Add-In Project in Visual Basic

The companion CD includes a template project—Outlook COM AddIn.vbp—for creating an Outlook COM Add-in using Visual Basic 6. This template project is available in the Outlook COM Add-In Template folder. It provides an easy-to-use template that lets you create Outlook COM Add-ins with a minimum of confusion. We'll assume that you have already installed Visual Basic 6 and that you want to add the Outlook COM Add-in to your development environment. The first sequence of steps will show you how to move the files for the Outlook COM Add-In template from the personal folders (.pst) file that accompanies this book to the projects folder for your Visual Basic 6 installation. Any project placed in the Visual Basic 6.0 Projects folder is available as a new project when you select New Project on the File menu in Visual Basic.

Part V Advanced Topics

To install the Outlook COM Add-in project in your Visual Basic 6.0 Projects folder

1. Expand the subfolder 5. Advanced Topics in the Building Microsoft Outlook 2002 Applications personal folders (.pst) file.

2. Expand the Creating COM Add-Ins Using Visual Basic folder, and click the Outlook COM Add-In Template folder.

3. Double-click OutlookCOMAddInTemplate.zip in the Outlook COM Add-In Template folder. You must have a Zip utility to extract this zip file. If you do not have a Zip utility, visit *http://www.winzip.com* to obtain WinZip.

4. Extract the files in the zip file to the Projects folder for Visual Basic 6. If you've selected the default installation, the Projects folder is located in C:\Program Files\Microsoft Visual Studio\VB98\Template\Projects.

To open a new Outlook COM Add-in project in Visual Basic 6

1. Launch Visual Basic 6.
2. Select New Project from the File Menu.
3. Select Outlook COM Addin in the New Project dialog box, as shown in Figure 14-3.

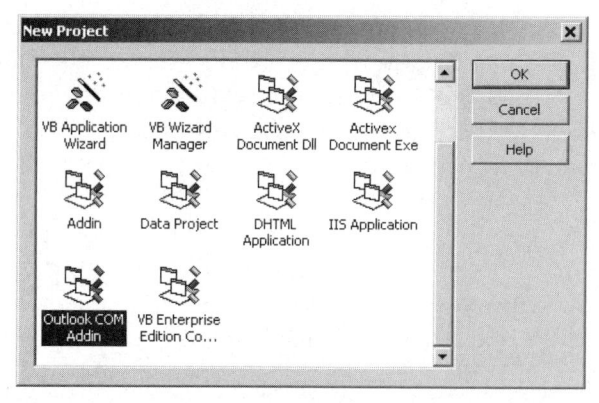

Figure 14-3 Use the Visual Basic New Project dialog box to create a new Outlook COM Add-in project after you have installed the Outlook COM Add-in project template.

4. Click OK.

Creating COM Add-Ins with Visual Basic   Chapter 14

> **Note**   Once you've opened a new Outlook COM Add-in project, you should rename the project and the base class to names you choose. These names will determine how your COM Add-in appears in the Outlook COM Add-Ins dialog box, and they will form the basis of its programmatic identifier in the Windows registry.

To add your identity to the Outlook COM Add-in project

1. Press CTRL+R to open the Visual Basic Project Explorer.
2. Click MyOutlookAddIn in the Project Explorer window.
3. Press F4 to open the Visual Basic Properties window.
4. Use the Properties window to rename the project from MyOutlookAddIn to a name that describes your project. The project name cannot contain spaces. The project name that you supply will serve as the first part of the programmatic identifier for your project.
5. Rename the Class module OutAddIn, if necessary. The class module name serves as the second part of the programmatic identifier of the class object in the Windows registry. If you compiled the MyOutlookAddIn project without changing any names, the compiled ActiveX DLL would have a ProgID of *MyOutlookAddIn.OutAddIn* in the Windows registry.
6. Rename the Connect Add-In Designer, if necessary. The Add-In Designer name also serves as the second part of the programmatic identifier for the Add-In Designer object in the Windows registry. If you compiled the MyOutlookAddIn project without changing any names, the compiled COM Add-in would have a ProgID of *MyOutlookAddIn.Connect* in the Windows registry.
7. Select Save Project As from the File Menu. Save your new project in a folder other than the VB98 folder. You should click the New Folder icon on the Save As dialog box, supply a new folder name for your project, and save all the files in the project into that folder.
8. You're now ready to begin the work of adding code to both the Add-In Designer and the class module for the COM Add-in. (See Figure 14-4.)

Part V Advanced Topics

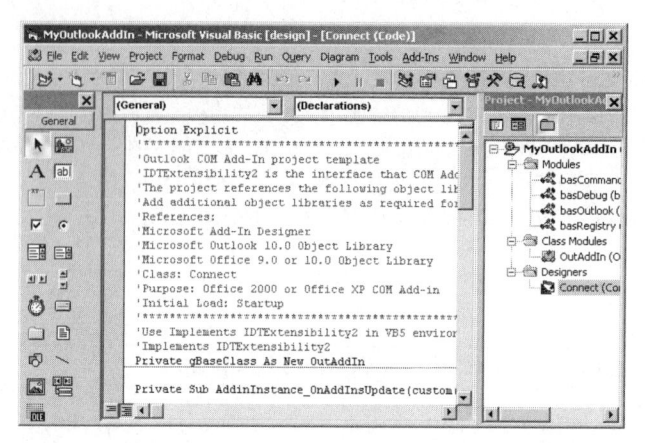

Figure 14-4 The Outlook COM Add-In project in the Visual Basic 6 development environment.

The Outlook COM Add-In Project Template

The Outlook COM AddIn.vbp template serves as the foundation for your own COM Add-ins and provides you with the following:

- **An Add-In Designer**   An Add-In Designer is a component that helps you create and register a COM Add-in. This Add-In Designer is created specifically for Outlook COM Add-ins.

- **A reference to the Microsoft Add-In Designer Object Library**   The Visual Basic 6 Outlook COM Add-In template project sets a reference to the Microsoft Add-In Designer Object Library contained in the file msaddndr.dll. When you set a reference to the Microsoft Add-In Designer, you can implement the IDTExtensibility2 Type Library, which supplies the events you can use to run code when your Add-in is connected to or disconnected from its hosting Outlook application.

- **A reference to both the Microsoft Outlook 10.0 and the Microsoft Office 10.0 Object Libraries**   You need to reference the Office 10.0 Object Library to create custom toolbars for Outlook Explorer and Inspector objects. If you are creating a COM Add-in for use in Outlook 2000 and Outlook 2002, you should change the reference to the Outlook 9.0 Object Library and the Office 9.0 Object Library. Be aware that you cannot use new Outlook 2002 objects, properties, methods, and events with this approach.

- Object variables declared WithEvents so that you can write event procedures in the OutAddIn class module in the MyOutlookAddIn project.

- Standard modules that allow you to debug your project and that contain common Outlook functions.

- A standard module that allows you to get and set Windows registry settings.

- A standard module that lets you create and manipulate Office command bar controls from a COM Add-in.

Moving ThisOutlookSession Code to a COM Add-In

The Outlook COM Add-In project does not actually contain working code. We'll examine a working COM Add-in project later in this chapter. If you've worked with Outlook VBA and developed code that you'd like to port to a COM Add-in, you might be wondering how you accomplish this conversion. You can obtain a license for Office XP Developer Edition and use the code that you've developed with Outlook VBA to create a COM Add-in solution with Office XP Developer. The conversion process is manual and involves the following steps:

1. Install Office XP Developer.
2. Press Alt+F11 to launch the Outlook VBA editor.
3. Click New Project on the File menu, and then double-click Add-In Project in the New Project dialog box.
4. Click the AddInDesigner1 project in the Project Explorer, and then select Class Module on the Insert menu.
5. Double-click ThisOutlookSession in the Project Explorer, and then point to Select All on the Edit Menu.
6. Point to Copy on the Edit menu.
7. Double-click Class1 under AddInDesigner1 in the Project Explorer.
8. Point to Paste on the Edit menu.
9. You are now ready to add the *InitHandler* and *UnInitHandler* procedures shown on pages 675 and 676, respectively, to the *OnConnection* and *OnDisconnection* event procedures in the AddInDesigner1 module. If you have additional forms, class modules, or standard modules in your Outlook VBA project, you will have to export them from VBAProject.otm and import them into your AddInProject1 project.
10. Give the Add-in project and the Add-In Designer appropriate names. Be aware that the ProgID of your COM Add-in derives from ProjectName.AddInDesignerName.

> **Note** While COM Add-ins developed with Office XP Developer can use all the features of Outlook 2002 and can be added to the list of trusted COM Add-ins so that they bypass the Outlook Object Model Guard, they cannot expose public methods and properties to other applications or to Visual Basic Scripting Edition (VBScript) code behind forms. The only instancing property for an Office XP Developer class is PublicNotCreateable. Visual Basic COM Add-ins can expose public properties and methods in a class where the Instancing property is set to MultiUse.

What Is a COM Add-In?

As stated at the beginning of this chapter, a COM Add-in is a special type of ActiveX DLL that communicates with Outlook. The Outlook COM Add-In project template provided with this book gives you a cookie-cutter tool for creating Outlook COM Add-ins. The one essential requirement for a COM Add-in is that it must contain code to implement the IDTExtensibility2 Type Library that provides the programming interface for integrating COM Add-ins with their host applications. The examples included with this book use two classes, rather than one, to build a COM Add-in. The reason for this approach is so that you can separate the code into two separate class modules when you build your COM Add-in. The first class derives from the Add-In Designer that must be added to a COM Add-in project in order to create a COM Add-in. The second class actually does the work of implementing the functionality of your COM Add-in. We'll call this class the base class of your COM Add-in. Figure 14-5 illustrates the COM interfaces of the Outlook COM Add-In project template. You should realize that you could construct your COM Add-in from only one class if you so desire. The two-class approach makes it easier to plug another base class into a standard Connect class module that handles the unique events of the IDTExtensibility2 Type Library.

From the more practical rather than theoretical perspective of this chapter, the important point to remember is that the Outlook COM Add-In project supplied with this book supports at least two public classes. The Connect class is the umbilical cord between your COM Add-in and Outlook 2002. Without the Connect class, your COM Add-in is just a garden variety ActiveX DLL looking for a client object to instantiate it. If you wanted to load this garden variety ActiveX DLL whenever Outlook started, you'd have some difficult obstacles to overcome before you could create a reliable solution. The Connect class that Implements

IDTExtensibility2 solves this problem for you. It provides a means for Outlook to instantiate your COM Add-in automatically when Outlook launches, either through a user action or program code. The Connect class for the MyOutlookAddIn project has no public methods or properties.

COM Add-In

- Connect
- OutAddIn
- IDTExtensibility2

Connect (Add-In Designer) | OutAddIn (Base Class)

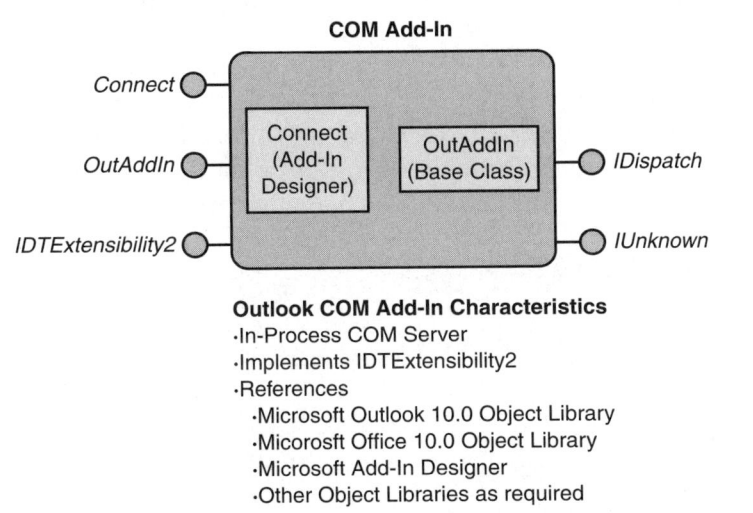

- IDispatch
- IUnknown

Outlook COM Add-In Characteristics
- In-Process COM Server
- Implements IDTExtensibility2
- References
  - Microsoft Outlook 10.0 Object Library
  - Micorosft Office 10.0 Object Library
  - Microsoft Add-In Designer
  - Other Object Libraries as required

Figure 14-5 The COM interfaces of the Outlook COM Add-In project.

> **Note** If your COM Add-in is set to launch on startup, the COM Add-in will run if a user opens Outlook from the Start menu, or if program code in an Automation controller application launches Outlook to send a mail message. If you've set your COM Add-in's initial load behavior to Load On Startup, your COM Add-in will run whenever Outlook runs.

The base class of your COM Add-in actually does the work of the COM Add-in. The base class has been isolated from the Add-In Designer Connect class so that you can plug different base classes into your Connect class. Although the OutAddIn class in the Outlook COM Add-In project template does not expose any properties or methods, you could expose public properties and methods in the base class of your COM Add-in. Those public properties and methods would then be available to any other Automation controller that can instantiate your COM Add-in base class object. Later you will see how you can use this approach to make a public method in a COM Add-in available to VBScript code in an Outlook form.

Part V Advanced Topics

Building a COM Add-In

Now that we have a template project available in Visual Basic 6, we can walk through the steps of building a COM Add-in. After you have created and saved a new project using the Outlook COM Add-In template, you need to save some settings that control the load behavior of your COM Add-in. The Add-In Designer for the Outlook COM Add-In project is a class module with a user interface that lets you set properties for the Add-in. Figure 14-6 shows the AddInDesigner dialog box for Connect.dsr in the Outlook COM Add-In template. Remember that this dialog box appears only when you are in Design mode in Visual Basic; this dialog box is not exposed to the user who actually uses your COM Add-in.

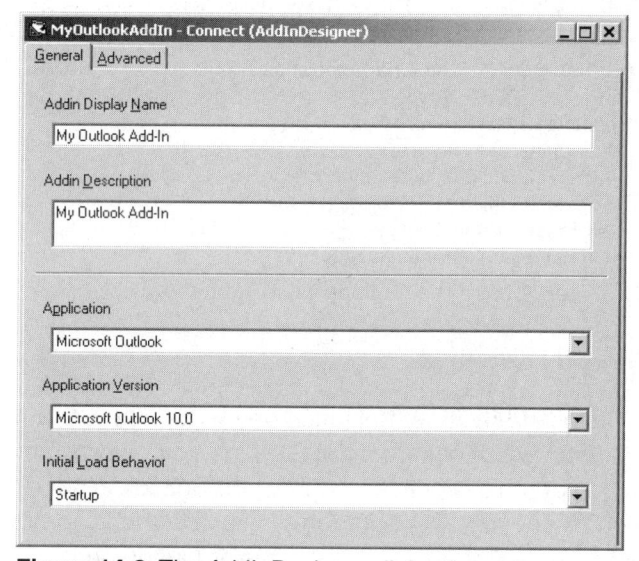

Figure 14-6 The AddInDesigner dialog box.

COM Add-In Settings

Before you can build a COM Add-in, you must make several settings in the design environment to determine how and when your COM Add-in loads. You must also select a unique project name to create the ProgID for the Add-in. Finally, you need to use the event procedures for the AddInDesigner library to connect your COM Add-in to class, form, and standard code modules.

Using the AddInDesigner Dialog Box

The properties you set in the AddInDesigner dialog box control the initial load behavior of your COM Add-in and the friendly name a user sees in the COM

Add-Ins dialog box. The following table lists the available settings in the AddInDesigner dialog box's General page.

Option	Description
Addin Display Name	The name that will appear in the COM Add-Ins dialog box in Outlook. The name you supply should be descriptive to the user. The Addin Display Name is equivalent to the Description property of the COMAddIn object. In the Windows registry, the Addin Display Name is stored in the FriendlyName key. If the name is to come from a resource file specified in the Satellite DLL Name box on the Advanced page, the name must begin with a number sign (#), followed by an integer specifying a resource ID within the file.
Addin Description	In the Windows registry, the Addin Description is stored in the Description key. This name is not available as a property of a COMAddIn object. If the description is to come from a resource file specified in the Satellite DLL Name box on the Advanced page, the description must begin with a number sign (#), followed by an integer specifying a resource ID within the file.
Application	The application in which the Add-in will run. This list displays applications that support COM Add-ins.
Application Version	The version of the application in which the Add-in will run.
Initial Load Behavior	The way the Add-in will load in Outlook. The list of possible settings comes from the registry.

The Advanced page of the AddInDesigner dialog box allows you to specify a file containing localized resource information for the Add-in and to specify additional registry data in the Windows registry. The following table describes the options available on the Advanced page.

Option	Description
Satellite DLL Name	The name of a file containing localized (translated) resources for an Add-in. The file must be located in the same directory as the Add-in's registered DLL.
Registry Key For Additional Addin Data	The registry subkey to which additional data is to be written.
Addin Specific Data	The names and values to be stored in the registry subkey. Only String and DWORD type values are permitted.

Determining the ProgID for Your COM Add-In

If you change the Add-In Designer name in the Properties window of the Visual Basic Project Explorer, you will change the class name from Connect to the name you enter in the Properties window. The class name of the Add-In Designer is used to create the programmatic identifier—or ProgID—for your COM Add-in. The ProgID derives from the combination of the Visual Basic project name and the Add-In Designer name. If your Visual Basic project name is MyProjectName and the name of your Add-In Designer is MyConnect, then the ProgID for your COM Add-in would be *MyProjectName.MyConnect*.

Where Outlook COM Add-Ins Are Registered

Outlook COM Add-ins are registered in the Windows registry under the following key:

HKEY_CURRENT_USER\Software\Microsoft\Office\Outlook\Addins

Each COM Add-in has a subkey under the Addins key based on its ProgID. If you are using Visual Basic 6 to create your Add-in, the ProgID subkey and some essential key values are automatically created for you when you compile your Add-in project or when a user installs a COM Add-in. Figure 14-7 shows the Addins key in the Windows Registry Editor.

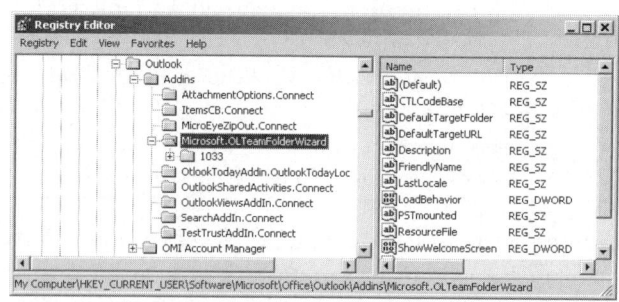

Figure 14-7 COM Add-in settings in the Windows Registry Editor.

Controlling Initial Load Behavior

You control the initial load behavior of your COM Add-in by setting the Initial Load Behavior drop-down list box on the General page of the AddInDesigner dialog box. If you are not using a Visual Basic 6 Add-In Designer to create your COM Add-in, you can set the initial load behavior directly by assigning the correct DWORD value to the LoadBehavior key in the Windows registry. Notice in the table on the following page that a value of *0x01* is added to the LoadBehavior value if the Add-in is connected.

Creating COM Add-Ins with Visual Basic   Chapter 14

> **Note** If your install program registers your Add-in under HKEY_LOCAL_MACHINE instead of HKEY_CURRENT_USER, the Add-in will be available for every user who logs on to the machine. If you examine HKEY_LOCAL_MACHINE\Software\Microsoft\ Office\Outlook\ Addins, you'll see that Microsoft has added an Add-in key for Outlook VBA. Outlook VBA is registered under HKEY_LOCAL_MACHINE as a demand-loaded Outlook COM Add-in. If you register the Add-in under HKEY_LOCAL_MACHINE, it won't be available in the COM Add-ins dialog box shown in Figure 14-2 (on page 657). HKEY_LOCAL_MACHINE registration prevents a user from disconnecting the Add-in.

Initial Load Behavior Setting	LoadBehavior DWORD	Behavior Description
None	*0x00* 0x01 (Connected)	The COM Add-in is not loaded when Outlook boots. It can be loaded in the COM Add-Ins dialog box or by setting the Connect property of the corresponding COMAddIn object.
Startup	*0x02* 0x03 (Connected)	The Add-in is loaded when Outlook boots. Once the Add-in is loaded, it remains loaded until it is explicitly unloaded.
Load On Demand	*0x08* 0x09 (Connected)	The Add-in is not loaded until the user clicks the button or menu item that loads the Add-in, or until a procedure sets its Connect property to *True*. In most cases, you won't set the initial load behavior to Load On Demand directly; you'll set it to Load At Next Startup Only, and it will automatically be set to Load On Demand on subsequent boots of Outlook.
Load At Next Startup Only	*0x10* (Reverts to 0x09 on next boot)	After the COM Add-in has been registered, it loads as soon as the user runs Outlook for the first time, and it creates a button or menu item for itself. The next time the user boots Outlook, the Add-in is loaded on demand—that is, it doesn't load until the user clicks the button or menu item associated with the Add-in.

> **Important** Be careful to test your Add-in under different hardware and software configurations before you release your COM Add-in. If you have set the Initial Load Behavior setting so that your Add-in is loaded on startup and your Add-in does extensive processing or makes a database connection, you will incur an unacceptable performance penalty when Outlook launches. Users of your COM Add-in will soon be knocking at your door. Outlook's Object Model is single-threaded and does not return control to a calling application until its thread of execution has completed.

IDTExtensibility2 Event Procedures

The next step in creating your Outlook COM Add-in is to write code for the event procedures exposed by the IDTExtensibility2 Type Library. The COM Add-in template exposes IDTExtensibility2 Type Library event procedures automatically. You do not have to use an *Implements IDTExtensibility2* statement in the Declarations section of the Connect module unless you are using Visual Basic 5 where the *Implements* statement is required. If you use the Outlook COM Add-In template supplied on the companion CD, the *IDTExtensibility2* event procedures have already been created for you. These event procedures are created in the Connect class AddInDesigner, and the IDTExtensibility2 object library is represented by an AddinInstance object. You can find each event procedure by selecting AddinInstance in the Object drop-down list box in the Code window and then clicking each procedure name for AddinInstance in the Procedure drop-down list box. Even if you are not writing code for the event procedure, it's a good idea to add a Visual Basic comment marker (a single apostrophe) inside each event procedure.

> **More Info** For additional information on the Implements statement and classes in general, see the Visual Basic 6 online documentation.

```
Option Explicit
'*******************************************************************
'Outlook COM Add-In project template
'IDTExtensibility2 is the interface that COM Add-Ins must implement.
'The project references the following object libraries:
'Add additional object libraries as required for your COM Add-in.
```

```vb
'References:
'Microsoft Add-in Designer
'Microsoft Outlook 10.0 Object Library
'Microsoft Office 10.0 Object Library
'Class: Connect
'Purpose: Office XP COM Add-in
'Initial Load: Startup
'**********************************************************************
'Use Implements IDTExtensibility2 in VB5 environment
'Implements IDTExtensibility2
Private gBaseClass As New OutAddIn

Private Sub AddinInstance_OnAddInsUpdate(custom() As Variant)
    '
    'DebugWrite "AddinInstance_OnAddInsUpdate"
End Sub

Private Sub AddinInstance_OnBeginShutdown(custom() As Variant)
    '
    'DebugWrite "AddinInstance_OnBeginShutdown"
End Sub

Private Sub AddinInstance_OnConnection(ByVal Application As Object, _
    ByVal ConnectMode As AddInDesignerObjects.ext_ConnectMode, _
    ByVal AddInInst As Object, custom() As Variant)
    On Error Resume Next
    'Evaluate ConnectMode
    Select Case ConnectMode
        Case ext_cm_Startup
        Case ext_cm_AfterStartup
        Case ext_cm_CommandLine
        Case ext_cm_Startup
    End Select
    'Don't call InitHandler if Explorers.Count = 0 and Inspectors.Count = 0
    If Application.Explorers.Count = 0 _
        And Application.Inspectors.Count = 0 Then
        Exit Sub
    End If
    'AddInInst represents COMAddIn object
    'Create and initialize a base class
    gBaseClass.InitHandler Application, AddInInst.ProgId
    'DebugWrite "IDT2 OnConnection"
End Sub

Private Sub AddinInstance_OnDisconnection(ByVal RemoveMode _
    As AddInDesignerObjects.ext_DisconnectMode, custom() As Variant)
    'Tear down the class
```

(continued)

```
    'IMPORTANT: This event will not fire when
    'RemoveMode = ext_dm_HostShutdown
    'It will fire when RemoveMode = ext_dm_UserClosed
    gBaseClass.UnInitHandler
    If RemoveMode = ext_dm_UserClosed Then
        'User shutdown removed COM Add-in
        'Clean up custom toolbars by deleting them
    Else
        'Host shutdown
    End If
    Set gBaseClass = Nothing
    'DebugWrite "AddinInstance_OnDisconnection"
End Sub

Private Sub AddinInstance_OnStartupComplete(custom() As Variant)
    '
    'DebugWrite "AddinInstance OnStartupComplete"
End Sub
```

OnAddInsUpdate Event

The OnAddInsUpdate event occurs when the collection of loaded COM Add-ins changes. When an Add-in is loaded or unloaded, the OnAddInsUpdate event occurs in any other loaded Add-ins. For example, if Add-ins A and B are both currently loaded and Add-in C is subsequently loaded, the OnAddInsUpdate event fires in Add-ins A, B, and C. If Add-in C is unloaded, the OnAddInsUpdate event occurs again in Add-ins A and B.

If you have an Add-in that depends on another Add-in, you can use the *OnAddInsUpdate* event procedure in the dependent Add-in to determine whether the other Add-in has been loaded or unloaded. Examine the Connect property of the other Add-ins to determine whether or not they are loaded. If the Connect property is *True*, then the Add-in is loaded. The following example prints the friendly name and the connect state of the COMAddIns Collection to the immediate window when the OnAddInsUpdate event occurs. This code uses a global Outlook Application object, golApp, that is instantiated during the *InitHandler* procedure called by code in the *OnConnection* event procedure.

```
Private Sub AddinInstance_OnAddInsUpdate(custom() As Variant)
    Dim oAddIn As Office.COMAddIn
    For Each oAddIn In golApp.COMAddIns
        Debug.Print oAddIn.Description, oAddIn.Connect
    Next
End Sub
```

> **Note** The OnStartupComplete, OnBeginShutdown, and OnAddInsUpdate event procedures each provide only a single argument, the *custom()* argument, which is an empty array of Variant type values. You can ignore this argument for COM Add-ins for Office applications.

OnBeginShutdown

The OnBeginShutdown event occurs when Outlook begins its shutdown, but only in the case where Outlook closes while the COM Add-in is still loaded. If the Add-in is not currently loaded when Outlook closes, the OnBeginShutdown event does not fire. When this event does occur, it occurs before the OnDisconnection event.

OnConnection

The OnConnection event occurs when the COM Add-in is loaded through the user interface or when program code sets the Add-in's Connect property to *True*. An Add-in can be loaded in one of the following ways:

Action	ConnectMode
The user starts Outlook and the Add-in's load behavior is specified to load when Outlook starts.	ext_cm_Startup
The user loads the Add-in in the COM Add-Ins dialog box.	ext_cm_AfterStartup
The Connect property of the corresponding COMAddIn object is set to *True*.	ext_cm_AfterStartup

If you revisit the OnConnection event code listing for the Outlook COM Add-In template, you'll see that an *InitHandler* procedure is called in the OnConnection event. The *InitHandler* procedure instantiates event-ready object variables in the OutAddIn class module so that you can write event procedure code using the events in the Outlook 2002 Object Model. It's worth taking a moment to discuss what happens in the *InitHandler* procedure. First, look at the parameters passed to the *InitHandler* procedure. An Outlook application variable is passed, which is a copy of the *Application* object passed to the *IDTExtensibility2_OnConnection* procedure. The *olApp* variable that is passed to the *InitHandler* procedure creates two Outlook application variables, *objOutlook* and *golApp*. The first application variable, *objOutlook*, is declared WithEvents in the OutAddIn class module so that you can raise application-level Outlook events in OutAddIn. A string variable is passed that contains the ProgID of the COM Add-in, which is useful for setting the OnAction property of custom CommandBarButtons.

The *InitHandler* procedure also instantiates *NameSpace, Explorers, Inspectors,* and other object variables declared WithEvents in the OutAddIn class module. The Friend keyword is used to make the *InitHandler* procedure available to other form and class modules in the project. However, the Friend keyword prevents the *InitHandler* procedure from being exposed as a public method of the OutAddIn class. Friend makes the procedure visible throughout the project, but not to a controller of an instance of the object. Another important aspect of the *InitHandler* procedure is that we instantiate a global Application variable, *golApp*. To be public to all code modules in the project, *golApp* must be declared in a standard module (basOutlook) rather than in a class module. Unlike Outlook VBA where a global Application object is always available, you must explicitly declare a global Outlook Application object in a COM Add-in. The *InitHandler* procedure in the OutAddIn class module is listed below.

```
'Object variables for Event procedures declared in OutAddIn class module
Private WithEvents objOutlook As Outlook.Application
Private WithEvents objNS As Outlook.NameSpace
Private WithEvents objExpl As Outlook.Explorer
Private WithEvents colExpl As Outlook.Explorers
Private WithEvents colViews As Outlook.Views
Private WithEvents objResults As Outlook.Results
Private WithEvents colReminders As Outlook.Reminders
Private WithEvents objInsp As Outlook.Inspector
Private WithEvents colInsp As Outlook.Inspectors
Private WithEvents objMailItem As Outlook.MailItem
Private WithEvents objPostItem As Outlook.PostItem
Private WithEvents objContactItem As Outlook.ContactItem
Private WithEvents objDistListItem As Outlook.DistListItem
Private WithEvents objApptItem As Outlook.AppointmentItem
Private WithEvents objTaskItem As Outlook.TaskItem

Private WithEvents objJournalItem As Outlook.JournalItem
Private WithEvents objDocumentItem As Outlook.DocumentItem

'Use gstrProgID to set the OnAction property of CB buttons
Private gstrProgID As String
'Declare CommandBar, CommandBarButton, and CommandBarComboBox
'object variables here
'Private WithEvents CBBMyButton As Office.CommandBarButton
```

```
Friend Sub InitHandler(olApp As Outlook.Application, strProgID As String)
    'Declared WithEvents
    Set objOutlook = olApp
    'Instantiate a public module-level Outlook application variable
    Set golApp = olApp
    'Declared WithEvents
    gstrProgID = strProgID
    Set objNS = objOutlook.GetNameSpace("MAPI")
    Set colExpl = objOutlook.Explorers
    Set colReminders = objOutlook.Reminders
    Set colInsp = objOutlook.Inspectors
    Set objExpl = objOutlook.ActiveExplorer
End Sub
```

> **Outlook Security** If you trust your COM Add-in using the Administrative form in the Outlook Security Settings public folder, all trusted objects, properties, and methods must inherit from the Application object passed in the *OnConnection* event procedure. If you use *CreateObject* or *GetObject* in your COM Add-in to instantiate other Outlook Application objects, these objects will activate warning prompts when you call blocked properties or methods. In the Outlook COM Add-In template, the public Outlook Application variable named *golApp* is derived from the Application object passed to the *OnConnection* procedure. Consequently, *golApp* is a trusted Application object from the standpoint of a trusted COM Add-in.

OnDisconnection

The OnDisconnection event occurs when the COM Add-in is unloaded. You can use the *OnDisconnection* event procedure to run code that restores any changes made to Outlook by the Add-in and to perform general cleanup operations.

An Add-in can be unloaded in one of the following ways:

Action	ConnectMode
Outlook closes. If the Add-in is currently loaded when Outlook closes, it is unloaded. If the Add-in's initial load behavior is set to Startup, it is reloaded when Outlook starts again.	ext_dm_HostShutdown
The user clears the check box next to the Add-in in the COM Add-Ins dialog box.	ext_dm_UserShutdown
The Connect property of the corresponding COMAddIn object is set to *False*.	ext_dm_UserShutdown

The *RemoveMode* argument of the OnDisconnection event lets you determine how the Add-in was unloaded, either by a user action (user shutdown) or by Outlook closing (host shutdown). The following code example writes a string to the Visual Basic Immediate window indicating the mode with which the COM Add-in was removed:

```
Private Sub AddinInstance_OnDisconnection(ByVal RemoveMode _
   As AddInDesignerObjects.ext_DisconnectMode, custom() As Variant)
    'Tear down the class
    gBaseClass.UnInitHandler
    Set gBaseClass = Nothing
    Dim strMode As String
    If RemoveMode = ext_dm_HostShutdown Then
        strMode = "Host Shutdown"
    Else
        strMode = "User Shutdown"
    End If
    Debug.Print "IDT2 OnDisconnection " & strMode
End Sub
```

The important task in the OnDisconnection event is to tear down the base class and other object variables before the COM Add-in is removed from memory. If you do not clean up your object variables, you might find that Outlook continues to remain in memory, even though the user has selected the Exit command from the Outlook File menu. The OnDisconnection event in the Outlook COM Add-In project calls the *UnInitHandler* procedure in the OutAddIn class module. The *UnInitHandler* procedure sets object variables to Nothing. Remember that if you declare a public Outlook Application variable in a standard module, you should use the *UnInitHandler* procedure to clean up that object reference. Otherwise, Outlook will remain in memory and your COM Add-in will not behave as expected.

```
Friend Sub UnInitHandler()
    'You must dereference all objects in this procedure or
    'Outlook will remain in memory
    'If you have created an objMailItem variable,
    'be sure to Set objMailItem = Nothing in this procedure
    Set objInsp = Nothing
    Set objExpl = Nothing
    Set colInsp = Nothing
    Set colReminders = Nothing
    Set colViews = Nothing
    Set colExpl = Nothing
    Set objNS = Nothing
    Set golApp = Nothing
    Set objOutlook = Nothing
End Sub
```

Special Disconnection Considerations for Outlook

Outlook 2002 is much better than previous versions of Outlook at completely removing itself from memory when a user quits the program. However, the considerations discussed in this section apply to both Outlook 2000 and Outlook 2002. You need to dereference all object variables when your COM Add-in disconnects. If you don't destroy your object variables by setting them to Nothing, your COM Add-in might yield some anomalous results. For example, you might declare *objOutlook* as an Outlook Application object in the declarations of your base class module. You then instantiate that object, an Explorer object, and a global Outlook Application object for use in the code listed below. If you do not dereference these object variables, you will find that Outlook remains in memory due to your COM Add-in.

```
Private WithEvents objOutlook As Outlook.Application
Private WithEvents objExpl as Outlook.Explorer

Friend Sub InitHandler(olApp As Outlook.Application, strProgID As String)
    'Declared WithEvents
    Set objOutlook = olApp
    'Instantiate a public module-level Outlook application variable
    Set golApp = olApp
    'Set additional object references as required
    Set objExpl = objOutlook.ActiveExplorer
End Sub
```

A symptom of an incomplete shutdown is when Outlook remains in memory after a user selects the Exit command from the File menu. You should carefully test your COM Add-in to determine whether Outlook remains in memory after you quit Outlook. Don't trust the behavior of your Add-in in debug mode because events are proxied by the debugger and the Disconnection event will fire, whereas it might not fire when your compiled COM Add-in is running. To determine if Outlook has remained in memory, start the Windows Task Manager by pressing Ctrl+Alt+Delete, or run a process viewer tool such as the Process Viewer Application that ships with Visual Basic 6.

The following code sets all object variables in the COM Add-in to Nothing by calling the *UnInitHandler* procedure in the Explorer object Close event. See the *UnInitHandler* listing earlier in this chapter to see how this procedure removes references to object variables.

```
Private Sub objExpl_Close()
    On Error Resume Next
    If golApp.Explorers.Count <= 1 And golApp.Inspectors.Count = 0 Then
        UnInitHandler
    End If
End Sub
```

> **Disconnection Event Workaround**
>
> There is a workaround for the problem of Outlook remaining in memory, and it is strongly suggested that you implement it in your COM Add-in. Both the Inspector and the Explorer objects support a Close event that you should use to remove references to all objects in your application. Use the Close event to remove the reference to all Outlook object variables when you are certain that Outlook is shutting down. For example, you can check the Explorers collection object's Count property. If the Count property is less than or equal to 1 during the Close event, and if Inspectors.Count = 0, you can be certain that Outlook's Explorer is shutting down.

OnStartupComplete Event

The OnStartupComplete event occurs when Outlook completes its startup, but only in the case where the COM Add-in has an Initial Load Behavior setting that forces load at startup. If the Add-in is not loaded when Outlook starts up, the OnStartupComplete event does not fire, even when the user loads the Add-in in the COM Add-Ins dialog box. When this event does occur, it occurs after the OnConnection event.

You can use the *OnStartupComplete* event procedure to run code that interacts with the application and shouldn't be run until the application has finished loading. For example, if you want to display a dialog box that gives users a choice of items to create when they start Outlook, you can put that code in the *OnStartupComplete* event procedure. When you create a COM Add-in for Outlook 2002, you can also use the MAPILogonComplete event for the Outlook Application object. In the case of the Outlook COM Add-in template, you call the *InitHandler* procedure in the OnConnectionEvent and then write the following code:

```
Private Sub objOutlook_MAPILogonComplete()
    Debug.Print "Outlook has completed the boot process"
End Sub
```

Adding Property Pages

The following sections describe how you can add property pages to the Outlook Tools Options dialog box or the Folder Properties dialog box. Property pages are discussed in the context of COM Add-in development because property pages provide a means of persisting settings for your COM Add-in to the Windows registry.

Installing the Sample Page Project

Custom property pages allow you to add your own page to either the Outlook Tools Options dialog box or the Folder Properties dialog box. Figure 14-8 shows the Sample Page property page in the Tools Options dialog box. The Sample Page example is useful because it shows you how to use common Visual Basic controls on an Outlook property page. A group of option buttons has been placed in a frame as well as a text box, a command button, a drop-down combo box, and a check box on the User Form. You'll learn how the Sample Page works and how you can add custom property pages to your COM Add-in. If you need to maintain persistent user settings for your COM Add-in, you should consider adding a custom property page .ocx to your COM Add-in project. You implement Outlook property pages as an ActiveX control created in Visual Basic or another ActiveX control creation tool. First you will learn how to create a property page ActiveX control, and then you will learn how to load that control in your COM Add-in. Before we discuss the creation of Outlook property pages, you must first install the Sample Page project from the companion CD.

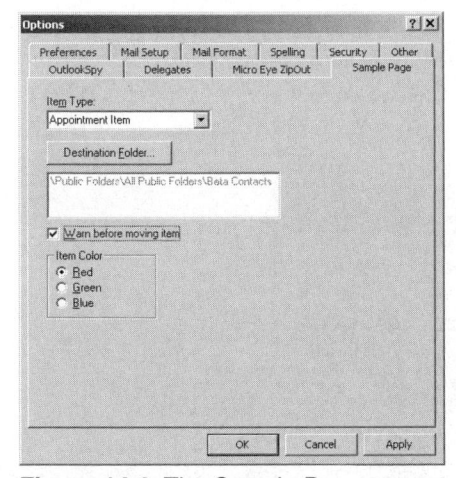

Figure 14-8 The Sample Page property page in the Tools Options dialog box.

To install and open the Sample Page project

1. Expand the subfolder 5. Advanced Topics in the Building Microsoft Outlook 2002 Applications personal folders (.pst) file.

2. Expand the Creating COM Add-Ins with Visual Basic folder, and click the Sample Page Property Page Example folder.

Part V Advanced Topics

3. Double-click SampleOptionsPage.zip in the Sample Property Page Example folder. You must have a Zip utility to extract this zip file. If you do not have a zip utility, visit *http://www.winzip.com* to obtain WinZip.

4. Extract the files in the zip file into a folder named Sample Page Property Page under the VB98 folder for Visual Basic 6. If you've selected the default installation, the VB98 folder is located in C:\Program Files\Microsoft Visual Studio\VB98.

5. Launch Visual Basic, and open the SampleOptionsPage project in the folder you created in step 4.

Creating a custom property page in Visual Basic is actually quite straightforward, once you get the hang of it. Figure 14-9 shows the SampleOptionsPage project loaded in the Visual Basic 6 development environment. The most basic rule of property page creation is that the code module for the UserControl must contain *Implements Outlook.PropertyPage* in its declarations section. An Outlook property page is an abstract object in the Outlook Object Model. You can't actually instantiate a property page object in the way that you can create a MailItem object, for example. However, the Implements keyword lets you access the properties and methods of the PropertyPage class in the same way that *Implements IDTExtensibility2* lets you access the events of the IDTExtensibility2 class. The code on the following page shows the declarations section of the SamplePage UserControl.

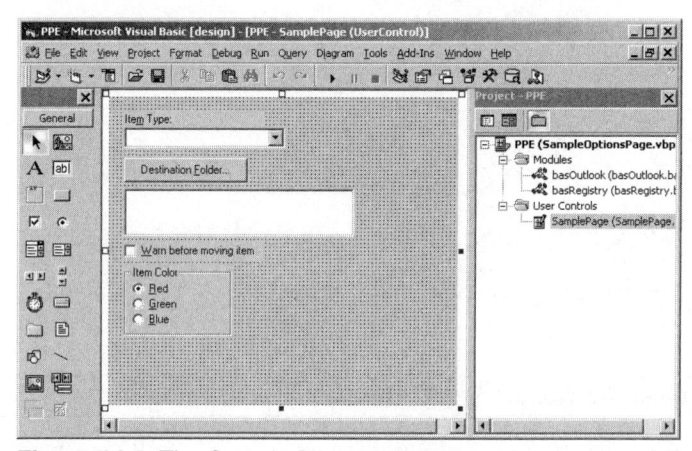

Figure 14-9 The Sample Page property page in the Visual Basic 6 development environment.

```
'************************************************************
'Outlook Property Page Example
'PropertyPage is the interface that property pages must implement.
'The project references the following object libraries:
'Add additional object libraries as required for your control.
'References:
'Microsoft Outlook 10.0 Object Library
'************************************************************
Implements Outlook.PropertyPage
Dim objSite As Outlook.PropertyPageSite
Dim gblnDirty As Boolean
Dim IsLoading As Boolean
```

Loading the Page and Persisting Settings in the Registry

Two module-level variables, *gblnDirty* and *IsLoading*, help to ensure that the property page is not marked as dirty when the control is loading. Typically, you would have the values for the constituent controls persist on your property page in the Windows registry. When the user clicks OK or Apply on the property page, you save the values represented by the controls on that page to the registry. When the user invokes the property page by selecting the Outlook Tools Options command, you have to retrieve the values you stored in the registry and set the controls on your property page accordingly. Consequently, the *InitProperties* procedure listed below sets the initial values of the controls on the property page. An extensive discussion about programming the Windows registry is beyond the scope of this chapter. Suffice it to say that *GetKeyValueEx* and *SetKeyValue* are functions included in basRegistry that let you get and set registry values.

Notice in the listing below that if the values retrieved from the registry are not blank, the registry value in each of the constituent controls of the property page is set. If the registry value is an empty string, then the default values of the controls are used on the page. By setting *IsLoading* = *True* at the beginning of the procedure, the *SetDirty* procedure is prevented from setting gblnIsDirty to *True*. Once the values of controls have been set in the *InitProperties* procedure, *IsLoading* is set to *False*. This means that any changes to the controls on the page will set gblnIsDirty to *True*, and the user will be able to click the Apply button on the property page to save her changes.

```
Private Sub UserControl_InitProperties()
    On Error Resume Next
    Dim strType, strFolderPath, strWarn, strOption As String
    Dim strKey As String
    'Determine Outlook version
```

(continued)

Part V   Advanced Topics

```
        If Left$(golApp.Version, 1) = 9 Then
            strKey = "Software\Microsoft\Office\9.0\Outlook\Options\SamplePage"
        Else
            strKey = "Software\Microsoft\Office\10.0\Outlook\Options\SamplePage"
        End If
        Set objSite = Parent
        'Set IsLoading to False so that setting controls will not dirty form
        IsLoading = True
        cmbType.Clear
        cmbType.AddItem "Appointment Item"
        cmbType.AddItem "Contact Item"
        cmbType.AddItem "Journal Item"
        cmbType.AddItem "Mail Item"
        cmbType.AddItem "Task Item"
        'Set controls based upon registry values
        strType = GetKeyValueEx(HKEY_CURRENT_USER, _
          strKey, "ItemType")
        If strType <> "" Then
            cmbType.Text = strType
        End If
        strFolderPath = GetKeyValueEx(HKEY_CURRENT_USER, _
          strKey, "FolderPath")
        If strFolderPath <> "" Then
            txtFolder = strFolderPath
        End If
        If GetKeyValueEx(HKEY_CURRENT_USER, _
          strKey, "Warn") = "1" Then
            chkWarn.Value = vbChecked
        Else
            chkWarn.Value = vbUnchecked
        End If
        strOption = GetKeyValueEx(HKEY_CURRENT_USER, _
          strKey, "ColorOption")
        Select Case strOption
            Case "1"
            optRed = True
            Case "2"
            optGreen = True
            Case "3"
            optBlue = True
        End Select
        IsLoading = False
        gblnDirty = False
End Sub
```

Marking the Page as Dirty

The *SetDirty* procedure does the work of marking the page as dirty when a user changes the value of one of the controls on the page. The *gblnDirty* variable is set to *True* so that the *Apply* procedure can reset *gblnDirty* to *False* when it completes its work. The *SetDirty* procedure notifies Outlook that a property page has changed by calling the *OnStatusChange* method of the PropertyPageSite object. The PropertyPageSite object represents the container of a custom property page. You must call the *SetDirty* procedure in the Change event for the controls on the page. For some controls, such as the combo box named cmbType, you should also use the DropDown event (or a CloseUp event if supported by the control) to call *SetDirty*.

```
Private Sub SetDirty()
    If Not objSite Is Nothing Then
        If Not (IsLoading) Then
            gblnDirty = True
            objSite.OnStatusChange
        End If
    End If
End Sub
```

Applying Changes

Once the *OnStatusChange* method has notified Outlook that the page is dirty, the Apply button on the property page changes from disabled to enabled, as shown in Figure 14-10. The user can click the Apply button to apply changes or the OK button to apply the changes and dismiss the dialog box where the property page appears. Notice in the *Apply* procedure on the following page that the *SetKeyValue* function is called in basRegistry to maintain the persistent settings for each of the controls to the Windows registry.

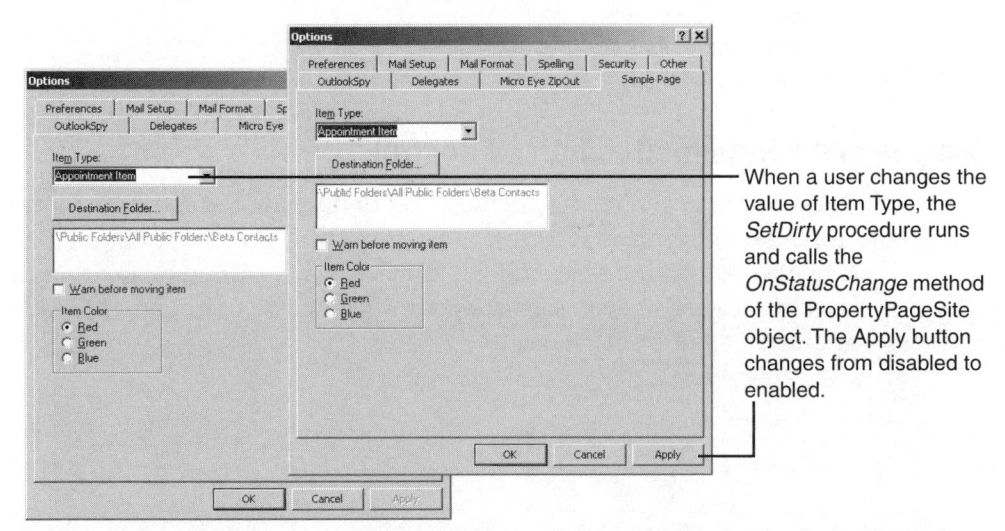

Figure 14-10 When a user changes a value on the property page, the Apply button is available.

```
Private Sub PropertyPage_Apply()
    Dim strKey As String
    If gintVersion = 9 Then
        strKey = "Software\Microsoft\Office\9.0\Outlook\Options\SamplePage"
    ElseIf gintVersion = 10 Then
        strKey = "Software\Microsoft\Office\10.0\Outlook\Options\SamplePage"
    End If

    'User clicked Apply or OK, so save changes to registry
    SetKeyValue HKEY_CURRENT_USER, _
      strKey, "ItemType", cmbType.Text, REG_SZ
    SetKeyValue HKEY_CURRENT_USER, _
      strKey, "FolderPath", txtFolder, REG_SZ
    If chkWarn.Value = vbChecked Then
        SetKeyValue HKEY_CURRENT_USER, _
          strKey, "Warn", "1", REG_SZ
    Else
        SetKeyValue HKEY_CURRENT_USER, _
          strKey, "Warn", "0", REG_SZ
    End If
    If optRed Then
        SetKeyValue HKEY_CURRENT_USER, _
          strKey, "ColorOption", "1", REG_SZ
    ElseIf optGreen Then
        SetKeyValue HKEY_CURRENT_USER, _
          strKey, "ColorOption", "2", REG_SZ
    ElseIf optBlue Then
        SetKeyValue HKEY_CURRENT_USER, _
          strKey, "ColorOption", "3", REG_SZ
    End If
    'Set dirty to False
    gblnDirty = False
End Sub
```

Compile and Distribute the ActiveX Control

Once you've completed designing and debugging the ActiveX control for your property page, you should compile the control. Your control will compile to an ActiveX .ocx control. Remember that when you distribute your COM Add-in, you must include the ActiveX .ocx control for your custom property page in your COM Add-in distribution package.

> **More Info** For additional information on the creation, compilation, and distribution of ActiveX controls, see "Component Tools Guide" in the Visual Basic 6 online documentation.

Displaying the Property Page

To display your custom property page, you only have to insert a single line of code in the OptionsPagesAdd event of either the Application object (for Tools Options property pages) or the NameSpace object (for Folder Properties property pages). Chapter 9, "Raise Events and Move to the Head of the Class," discusses how the OptionsPagesAdd event lets you display property pages. However, that discussion occurs in the context of Outlook VBA. If you want to display a property page in a COM Add-in, you need to dimension an object variable WithEvents for an Outlook Application object or an Outlook NameSpace object. For example, in the sample Outlook COM Add-In project, *objOutlook* is declared WithEvents in the OutAddIn class module. If you add the following code to the *objOutlook_OptionsPagesAdd* event procedure, the Sample Page property page will be visible in the Outlook Tools Options dialog box when your compiled COM Add-in is loaded. When you create your own COM Add-in, change the ProgID of *PPE.SamplePage* in the example below to a ProgID that matches the ProgID of the ActiveX control supplying the property page for your COM Add-in.

```
Private Sub objOutlook_OptionsPagesAdd(ByVal Pages As _
    Outlook.PropertyPages)
    Pages.Add "PPE.SamplePage", "Sample Page"
End Sub
```

Modifying Command Bars

Developing a property page is one way to add a user interface to your Outlook COM Add-in. The other (and perhaps more common) way to provide a user interface is to modify the command bars for the Outlook Explorer and Inspector windows. If you want to modify command bars, you must be certain to set a reference to the Microsoft Office 10.0 Object Library with the Visual Basic Project References command. The Outlook COM Add-In template project has set this reference for you. If you've reviewed the material in Chapter 11, "Using Visual Basic, VBA, or VBScript with Outlook," you'll know that the OnAction property is used to set the procedure that runs when a user clicks a CommandBarButton object. If you want a CommandBarButton to respond to a Click event on the Explorer toolbar, for example, you must code a call to the event procedure for a COM Add-in differently than you would in Outlook VBA.

Basic Techniques

Two procedures you should follow when you create command bar buttons for Explorer or Inspector command bars are

- To dimension object variables using the WithEvents keyword for the CommandBarControls on your toolbar and then write code in the Click event for each CommandBarButton object. Instantiate object variables for the event-ready CommandBarButton objects in the *InitHandler* procedure of your COM Add-in.

- To set the OnAction property for a CommandBarButton or CommandBarComboBox with a string that contains the ProgID for your COM Add-in. This string is prefixed by <! and ends with >. You can obtain the ProgID for your COM Add-in by setting the ProgID property of the AddInInst object passed in the OnConnection event to a public variable. Following the example of the Outlook COM Add-In sample project, you can also pass the ProgID to the *InitHandler* procedure in the base class of the Add-in. The exact syntax is as follows:

```
objCommandBarButton.OnAction = "<!" & gstrProgID & ">"
```

Step-By-Step Summary for COM Add-In Command Bars

To create an Explorer command bar button in an Outlook COM Add-in

1. In the Add-In Designer's module or the class module for the base class, use the WithEvents keyword to declare a module-level variable of type CommandBarButton. This creates an event-ready CommandBarButton object.

2. In the same module, create the *Click* event procedure stub for the CommandBarButton object by clicking the name of the object variable in the Object box and then clicking Click in the Procedure box.

3. Write code within the event procedure stub.

4. In the *OnConnection* event procedure or in the *InitHandler* procedure for your base class, check to see whether the command bar control already exists and return a reference to it if it does. If it doesn't exist, create the new command bar control and return a reference to it. You need to check whether the command bar control exists so that you don't create a new control each time your code runs.

5. When you create the new command bar control, set the Tag property for the CommandBarButton object to a unique string. The Tag property lets you easily find the control using the *FindControl* method.

6. When you create the new command bar control, set the OnAction property for the command bar control if the COM Add-in is to be demand-loaded. If you fail to set the OnAction property, the command bar button will load the Add-in the first time Outlook starts, but it will not load the Add-in when Outlook is closed and re-opened.

7. Within the *OnConnection* event procedure or in the *InitHandler* procedure for your base class, assign the reference to the command bar control to the event-ready CommandBarButton object variable.

8. Add code to the OnDisconnection event or to the *UnInitHandler* procedure in the base class to remove the command bar control when the Add-in is unloaded.

Command Bar Caveats

There are a couple of issues you should be aware of when creating COM Add-ins that display custom command bars or command bar buttons.

Custom Icons

If you want your command bar button to display custom icons, you must explicitly set a reference to the Microsoft Office 10.0 Object Library. The Office XP CommandBarButton object supports a Picture and a Mask property that let you use custom images for your command bar buttons. If you need your COM Add-in to run in both Outlook 2000 and Outlook 2002, you must set the FaceID property for the custom CommandBarButton object to a built-in CommandBarButton ID. The Picture property of a CommandBarButton object is not supported in the Microsoft Office 9.0 Object Library.

The following code will load a custom resource for a CommandBarButton object and display the button on the Standard Explorer toolbar:

```
Sub CreateButtonWithImage()
    Dim picPicture As IPictureDisp
    Dim strPicPath As String
    Dim objCB As CommandBar
    Dim objCBB As CommandBarButton
    Dim objOutlook As Outlook.Application
    Set objOutlook = CreateObject("Outlook.Application")
    'Set a reference to the Picture property and use LoadPicture
    strPicPath = "C:\Program Files\Microsoft Visual Studio" _
        & "\Common\Graphics\Bitmaps\Outline\NoMask\audio.bmp"
    Set picPicture = stdole.StdFunctions.LoadPicture(strPicPath)
    Set objCB = Application.ActiveExplorer.CommandBars("Standard")
    Set objCBB = objCB.Controls.Add(Type:=msoControlButton)
    With objCBB
        'Change the button image
        .Picture = picPicture
        .Caption = "Audio"
        .Tag = "Audio"
        .Style = msoButtonIconAndCaption
        .Visible = True
    End With
End Sub
```

Preventing Orphans

It's a good programming practice to clean up your custom toolbars and toolbar buttons when Outlook quits. If a user uninstalls your COM Add-in, custom toolbars and toolbar buttons won't be removed by the uninstall program and will appear as orphans the next time the user launches Outlook. You can delete custom command bars and command bar buttons during the *UnInitHandler* procedure, or you can set the *Temporary* argument of the *Add* method to True when you create the objects.

Adding Dialog Boxes

Dialog boxes in COM Add-ins follow the same guidelines as dialog boxes in any other Visual Basic project, with one precaution: do not attempt to show a modal dialog box directly from your COM Add-in. Outlook (and for that matter, any other Office application) cannot display a modal dialog box when that dialog box is displayed directly from a COM Add-in or an ActiveX DLL component. Figure 14-11 illustrates a Visual Basic About dialog box displayed from a COM Add-in. By displaying Visual Basic modeless dialog boxes, you can add a wealth of func-

Creating COM Add-Ins with Visual Basic   Chapter 14

tionality to your COM Add-in application. If you are connected to your network, you can display information from corporate databases, provide data entry forms, or enable users to create settings that might otherwise not be available on a custom Tools Options property page. An enormous number of third-party ActiveX custom controls are available for your dialog boxes, in addition to the intrinsic and extrinsic ActiveX controls that ship with Visual Basic.

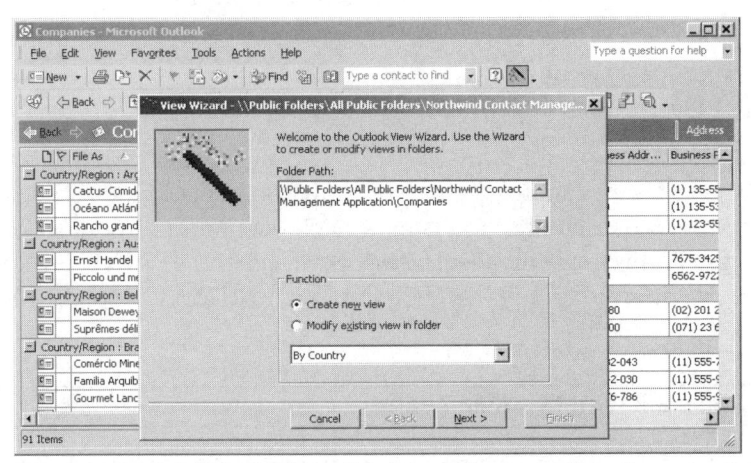

Figure 14-11 A Visual Basic dialog box displays when the user clicks the Display View Wizard command bar button.

> **Caution**   Do not display modal dialog boxes directly from your COM Add-in. You can, however, display a modal Visual Basic dialog box from a modeless dialog box that is displayed from COM Add-in code. For example, assume you have Form1 and Form2 in your COM Add-in. You can place a Form1.Show statement in the Click event for a toolbar button, but you cannot write Form1.Show vbModal in the Click event without hanging either your COM Add-in or Outlook. However, you can place a command button on Form1 that executes Form2.Show vbModal without a problem.

Visual Basic Forms

Adding dialog boxes to your COM Add-in is simple once you've designed and debugged the dialog box. It is advisable to design and test the dialog box in a standard .exe project before you move the dialog box to your COM Add-in.

Part V Advanced Topics

To add a Visual Basic form to a COM Add-in

1. Select the Add Form command from the Visual Basic Project menu.

2. Add controls and code to your form.

3. Display the form from your COM Add-in by adding *FormName.Show* to an event procedure for a CommandBarButton on an Explorer or Inspector command bar.

Forms 2.0 Forms

You can also add Microsoft Forms 2.0 forms to your COM Add-in project. Microsoft Forms 2.0 provides the familiar form design environment of Outlook custom forms. You are not, however, limited to a single Click event and a reduced property set when you use Forms 2.0 in the Visual Basic environment. If you've developed forms in Outlook VBA, you can also directly import those forms without modification into your COM Add-in.

To add a Forms 2.0 form to a COM Add-in

1. Select the Components command from the Visual Basic Project menu.

2. Click the Designers page on the Components dialog.

3. Check the Microsoft Forms 2.0 Form box in the Designers list box.

4. Select Add Microsoft Forms 2.0 Form on the Project menu.

5. Add controls and code to your form with the Forms 2.0 control toolbox. You cannot add Visual Basic intrinsic controls to your Forms 2.0 form. You must display the Forms 2.0 Control Toolbox before you can drag controls onto your form. Right-click the Forms 2.0 form, and check the Toolbox command on the context menu.

6. If you want to add Visual Basic extrinsic or third-party ActiveX controls to your Forms 2.0 form, you must do so by adding the controls to the Forms 2.0 Control Toolbox rather than the Visual Basic toolbox. Right-click the Forms 2.0 Control Toolbox, and select the Additional Controls command to add controls to the Forms 2.0 Control Toolbox.

7. Display the form from your COM Add-in by adding *FormName.Show* to an event procedure for a CommandBarButton on an Explorer or Inspector command bar.

Displaying a Dialog Box with a Public Method

You have more options for your COM Add-in than simply displaying a dialog box when a command bar button is clicked. Because a COM Add-in is a special form of ActiveX DLL component, you can also add public methods and properties to your component. The beauty of this approach is that you can then instantiate your COM Add-in component from VBScript and call the *ShowMyForm* method of your component. If you look at the OutlookSharedActivities project discussed in Chapter 12, "The Northwind Contact Management Application," you'll observe a public procedure in the OutAddIn class. Because this procedure is public, it is exposed as a method of the OutAddIn class. Figure 14-12 shows the *DialPhone* method of the OutAddIn class in the object browser in Outlook.

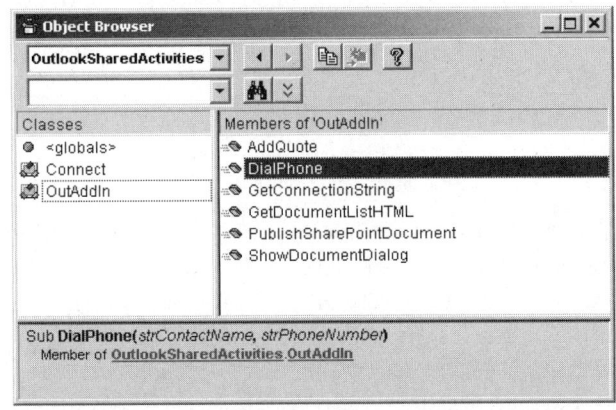

Figure 14-12 The *DialPhone* method in the Outlook Object Browser.

The following code example shows how you call the *DialPhone* method from VBScript to display the Dial Phone dialog box. The *DialPhone* procedure is also shown.

```
'DialPhone is public in order to expose it as a method
'for OutlookSharedActivities.OutAddIn
'Can be called from VBScript as follows:
Sub cmdDialPhone_Click
    On Error Resume Next
    Dim oSA
    Set oSA = CreateObject("OutlookSharedActivities.OutAddIn")
    If oSA Is Nothing Then
        MsgBox "Shared Activities Add-in not installed!", vbCritical
        Exit Sub
    End If
    oSA.DialPhone "800 Information", "1-800-555-1212"
End Sub
```

(continued)

Part V Advanced Topics

```
Public Sub DialPhone(strContactName, strPhoneNumber)
    On Error Resume Next
    With frmDial
        .txtContactName.Enabled = True
        .txtContactName = strContactName
        .cmbNumber = strPhoneNumber
        .chkJournal.Visible = False
        .cmdOpen.Visible = False
        .Show
    End With
End Sub
```

> **Important** Open the Com Add-in Example item in the VBScript Samples folder to work directly with this code in Outlook.

The Debugging Process

You can debug a COM Add-in by opening your COM Add-in project in Visual Basic and placing the project into Run mode. When you set breakpoints or watches in your code, you can interactively debug your COM Add-in. Figure 14-13 shows the OutlookSharedActivities project in debug mode. A watch has been added for the *RemoveMode* variable in the *OnDisconnection* event procedure in the Connect code module.

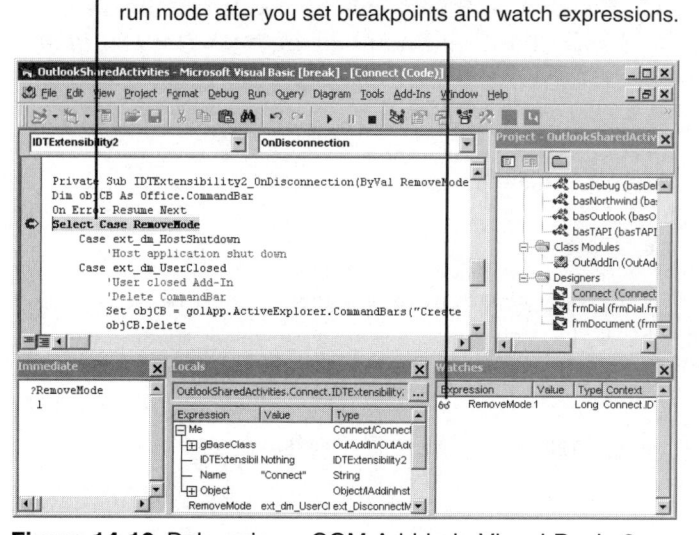

Figure 14-13 Debugging a COM Add-in in Visual Basic 6.

To debug a COM Add-in in Visual Basic 6

1. Open the Add-in project in Visual Basic 6.
2. Place any desired breakpoints, Stop statements, or watches in the code.
3. On the Run menu, click Start With Full Compile or press Ctrl+F5. This action compiles your project, alerts you to any compilation errors, and then puts the project into run mode.
4. Launch Outlook. If you've set the Add-in's load behavior to Startup or Load At Next Startup Only, the Add-in loads as soon as you start Outlook. If the Add-in's Initial Load Behavior is set to None or Load On Demand, open the COM Add-Ins dialog box and select the check box next to your Add-in to load it.

> **Note** When your COM Add-in stops at a breakpoint, you might not be able to activate the running Outlook application until you complete code execution.

Compiling Your COM Add-In

Once you've completed the debugging process, you can compile your COM Add-in and create an ActiveX DLL. This ActiveX DLL, along with any required ActiveX controls for custom property pages or for UserForms and dialog boxes, will be distributed to users of your COM Add-in.

To compile a COM Add-in in Visual Basic 6

1. Open the Add-in project in Visual Basic 6.
2. Select the *<ProjectName>* Properties command on the Project menu. Make sure that you've entered the correct company, version, and copyright information on the Make page of the Project Properties dialog box. Click OK to accept the changes you've made to project properties.
3. On the File menu, select the Make *<ComponentName>*.dll command.

Part V Advanced Topics

> ### Troubleshooting Debug Mode
>
> You might find that you have problems forcing your COM Add-in to enter Debug mode even after you've set breakpoints or watch expressions in your code. Here are a few suggestions that will help you debug your Add-in:
>
> - Make sure that you've set the Version Compatibility option for your project in the Visual Basic Project Options dialog Component page to Project Compatibility or Binary Compatibility. If Version Compatibility is set to No Compatibilty, you might discover that Outlook cannot locate your COM Add-in component and you can't enter Debug mode.
>
> - If you've already loaded your compiled COM Add-in in Outlook, you will have to unload the Add-in using the COM Add-Ins dialog box. Use the COM Add-Ins dialog box again, and reload the COM Add-in until your Add-in enters debug mode in Visual Basic. Set a breakpoint in the *OnConnection* event procedure to ensure that you're in Debug mode.
>
> - Make sure that your Add-in is actually in Run mode. I've had occasion to wonder why my Add-in was not entering Debug mode, only to discover that I had not placed my Visual Basic COM Add-In project in Run mode. The project was still in Design mode. You can't debug your component in Design mode.

Sample COM Add-Ins

Look for the sample COM Add-ins in the subfolders of the Creating COM Add-Ins With Visual Basic folder under the 5. Advanced Topics folder. All source code for the COM Add-ins is provided, in addition to a compiled ActiveX DLL for users who do not have Visual Basic 6.

Outlook View Wizard

The Outlook View Wizard illustrates how you can use the Visual Basic 6 Wizard Manager Add-in to create a Wizard dialog box that steps a user through a process. The Outlook View Wizard COM Add-in moves the user through the process of creating a View. The following *SetStep* procedure creates a View programmatically and moves the user to the next or the previous step in the process:

Creating COM Add-Ins with Visual Basic   Chapter 14

```vb
Private Sub SetStep(nStep As Integer, nDirection As Integer)
    Dim strViewName As String
    Dim colViews As Views
    Dim i As Integer
    On Error Resume Next
    Set colViews = m_Folder.Views
    Select Case nStep
        Case STEP_INTRO 'Welcome step
            'Select new view or existing view
        Case STEP_1 'Create view step
            mbFinishOK = False
        Case STEP_2 'Customize view with Outlook 10 View Control
            If optNew Then
                'Save the new view
                'First determine whether a view with the same name exists
                strViewName = txtViewName
                For i = 1 To colViews.Count
                    If colViews.Item(i) = strViewName Then
                        'The view already exists
                        Set m_View = colViews.Item(i)
                        GoTo ViewExists
                    End If
                Next
                'Set SaveOption
                If optSaveThisFolderEveryone Then
                    intViewSaveOption = _
                        olViewSaveOptionThisFolderEveryone
                ElseIf optSaveThisFolderOnlyMe Then
                    intViewSaveOption = _
                        olViewSaveOptionThisFolderOnlyMe
                ElseIf optSaveAllFoldersOfType Then
                    intViewSaveOption = _
                        olViewSaveOptionAllFoldersOfType
                End If
                'Set ViewType
                If optTableView Then
                    intViewType = olTableView
                ElseIf optCardView Then
                    intViewType = olCardView
                ElseIf optCalendarView Then
                    intViewType = olCalendarView
                ElseIf optIconView Then
                    intViewType = olIconView
                ElseIf optTimeLineView Then
                    intViewType = olTimelineView
                End If
                Set m_View = _
```

(continued)

Part V Advanced Topics

```
                colViews.Add(txtViewName, intViewType, intViewSaveOption)
                blnCreateView = True
            Else
                strViewName = cmbViews
                Set m_View = m_Folder.Views(strViewName)
            End If
ViewExists:
            m_Folder.CurrentView = strViewName
            ViewCtl1.Folder = m_Folder.FolderPath
            ViewCtl1.View = strViewName
            ViewCtl1.ZOrder
            DoEvents
            mbFinishOK = False
        Case STEP_FINISH 'Finished
            txtXML = ViewCtl1.ViewXML
            If optNew Then
                lblViewName = txtViewName
            Else
                lblViewName = cmbViews
            End If
            mbFinishOK = True
    End Select

MoveNext:
    'Move to new step
    fraStep(mnCurStep).Enabled = False
    fraStep(nStep).Left = 0
    If nStep <> mnCurStep Then
        fraStep(mnCurStep).Left = -10000
    End If
    fraStep(nStep).Enabled = True
    DoEvents

    SetCaption nStep
    SetNavBtns nStep

End Sub
```

    You can modify this Add-in for your own purposes or use it to learn about the Views and View objects. In Outlook 2002, each MAPIFolder object exposes a Views collection object that contains all the views defined for that folder. A View object can be added programmatically to the Views collection for a folder, and the View object can be manipulated through the Microsoft XML Parser (MSXML). An XML schema defines each View object. The XML property of the View object is a read/write property that lets you modify the view by changing its XML with MSXML. The View Wizard also uses the Outlook View Control to allow the user to modify the view directly in the View Wizard dialog box. The wizard then displays the XML for the modifications. You can also copy the XML for any view to the Windows Clipboard. Figure 14-14 shows the XML for the By Company Type view in the Companies folder of the Northwind Contact Management application.

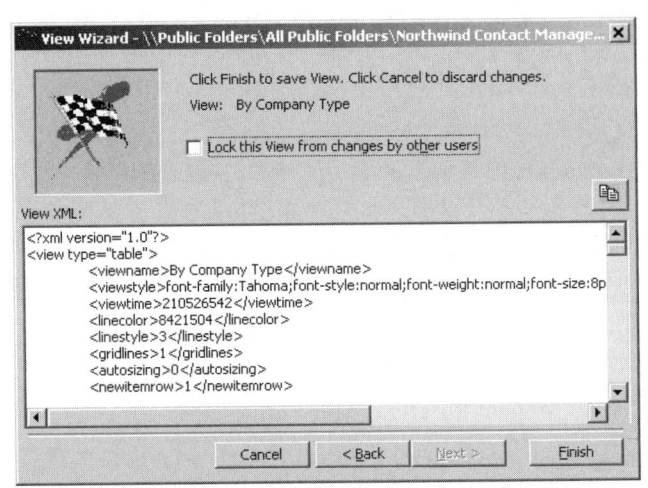

Figure 14-14 The Outlook View Wizard dialog box shows the XML for the By Company Type view in the Companies folder.

> **Note** For additional information regarding the Microsoft XML Parser, visit the Microsoft XML Developer Center at *http://msdn.microsoft.com/xml*. For additional information on XML view schema, see "XML View Definitions" in "Outlook 2002 Technical Articles" in the Help folder under 1. Help and Web Sites.

Outlook Shared Activities

The Outlook Shared Activities COM Add-in demonstrates how you can use a COM Add-in to provide an Explorer command bar to extend a forms-based application. This COM Add-in is discussed in detail in Chapter 12 and in Chapter 16, "Using Outlook with SharePoint Portal Server." This COM Add-in also exposes public properties and methods that can be called by other Add-ins or by VBScript behind forms. The forms in the Northwind Contact Management application call this COM Add-in to add documents to the Shared Documents folder and to publish documents to SharePoint Portal Server.

Part V Advanced Topics

Search

The Search COM Add-in demonstrates how to use the *AdvancedSearch* method of the Application object to display a custom dialog box with search results. You can use this COM Add-in as a learning tool or customize it to your own application requirements. Like some of the other COM Add-ins discussed in this section, the Search Add-in exposes a public method that lets other applications create a programmatic search. The code for the *ShowSearch* procedure follows. Once the search completes, the AdvancedSearchComplete event for the Application object displays the Search dialog box.

```
Public Sub ShowSearch(strDialogCaption, objFolder, _
    strFilter, blnSearchSubfolders)
    Dim strFolderPath As String
    Dim strScope As String
    Dim strTag As String
    Dim objSearch As Search
    Dim strPFStoreID As String
    If strDialogCaption <> "" Then
        strTag = strDialogCaption
    End If
    'Get the folder path
    strFolderPath = objFolder.FolderPath
    'Turn off SearchSubfolders in public folder store
    strPFStoreID = golApp.GetNamespace("MAPI") _
        .GetDefaultFolder(olPublicFoldersAllPublicFolders).StoreID
    If objFolder.StoreID = strPFStoreID Then
        blnSearchSubfolders = False
    End If
    'Build a scope string
    strScope = "SCOPE ('shallow traversal of " _
        & AddQuotes(strFolderPath) & "')"
    'Create the Search object by calling AdvancedSearch
    Set objSearch = _
        golApp.AdvancedSearch _
            (strScope, strFilter, blnSearchSubfolders, strTag)
End Sub
```

Test Trust

The Test Trust COM Add-in is a simple example of how to handle the issues that you must confront when your Add-in calls blocked methods and properties in the Outlook 2002 Object Model. Test Trust creates a toolbar button that displays a dialog box that you use to send a message to yourself. If you include this Add-in on the list of trusted COM Add-ins in the Administrative form located in the Outlook Security Settings public folder, you can observe how the trust mechanism suppresses the Object Model Guard warning prompts. Test Trust also uses the Redemption Object Library discussed in the "Outlook Redemption: A Third-Party Alternative" section in Chapter 13.

Add-In Registration

When you compile your COM Add-in in Visual Basic 6, you have actually registered the COM Add-in in the correct location in the Windows registry. When you deploy your COM Add-in, the Package and Deployment wizard handles registration automatically on the target installation system. If you are using Visual Basic 5 to create your COM Add-in, you must create registry entries for the COM Add-in programmatically. If you are using Visual Basic 5, a registry key with the ProgID of your COM Add-in and three required subkeys for the COM Add-in must be created in the following location:

HKEY_CURRENT_USER\Software\Microsoft\Office\Outlook\Addins

The following subkeys under the ProgID of the Add-in are required for correct operation of your COM Add-in.

Name	Type	Value
Description	String	A descriptive string that is not exposed by the COMAddIn object. If you need to, you can retrieve this string from the Windows registry.
FriendlyName	String	Name in COM Add-Ins dialog box. Equivalent to COMAddIn object Description property.
LoadBehavior	DWORD	Integer indicating load behavior: 0 (None), 3 (Startup), 9 (Load On Demand), or 16 (Load At Next Startup Only). These are decimal values.

Providing Security

In this section, we'll look at security from the perspectives of both the developer and the user of the COM Add-in. From the developer's perspective, COM Add-ins provide protection from anyone who wants to steal or tamper with the source code. Because COM Add-ins are compiled, source code is unavailable to anyone but the developer of the Add-in. In this regard, COM Add-ins offer a comfortable level of security for your intellectual property. Outlook VBA solutions do not provide the same level of intellectual property protection because a password for the project can be hacked, lost, or stolen.

Securing Your Intellectual Property

Let's consider what your options are as a developer if you want to offer a solution to other users. First, you can develop your solution in Outlook VBA. You might want to test an Outlook VBA solution before you move your code to a COM Add-in. So, you should be aware of how you provide security for an Outlook VBA solution. Outlook VBA solutions gain security for the developer from password protection of the Outlook VBA project.

Outlook Macro Security

If you've decided to move beyond Outlook VBA to a COM Add-in solution, your concern will shift from providing security for yourself to providing security for the user of your solution. Before discussing how you can assure users that they can trust your solution, it's important to discuss how Add-in security is implemented in Outlook 2002. In this section, we'll discuss macro security, or security that controls the running of code within the Outlook process space. Remember that Outlook macro security differs from the Object Model Guard and Attachment Security components provided by the Outlook E-Mail Security Update. Outlook VBA macro security is set on a user-by-user basis by using the Security command under Macro on the Tools menu. Figure 14-15 illustrates the Security dialog box, which allows a user to set the security level. As a side note, you should not confuse macro security with Outlook message-level security provided by either S/MIME or Exchange. They are completely separate and distinct.

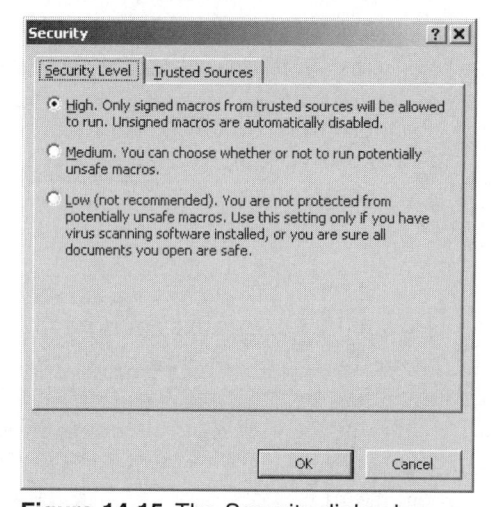

Figure 14-15 The Security dialog box.

Creating COM Add-Ins with Visual Basic Chapter 14

> **Note** If you are responsible for rolling out Outlook 2002 with an automated installation process, you can set registry settings with the Custom Installation Wizard, which will move control of security from the user to the administrator. Users will not be able to display the Security dialog box and change their security settings.

The following table summarizes the three security levels in Outlook 2002.

Type of Solution and Verification Result	High (Default)	Medium	Low
No VBAProject or COM Add-ins.	N/A	N/A	N/A
Unsigned VBAProject.	Outlook VBA macros are automatically disabled without notification, and Outlook application starts.	User is prompted to enable or disable Outlook VBA macros. Outlook VBA code is then demand-loaded.	No prompt. Outlook VBA code is demand-loaded.
Signed Outlook VBAProject from a trusted source. Verification succeeds.	Macros are automatically enabled, and Outlook application starts.	Macros are automatically enabled, and Outlook application starts.	No prompt or or verification. Macros are enabled.
Signed Outlook VBAProject from an unknown author. Verification succeeds.	A dialog box is displayed with information about the certificate. Macros can be enabled only if the user chooses to trust the author and certifying authority by selecting the Always Trust Macros From This Author check box in the Security Warning dialog box.	A dialog box is displayed with information about the certificate. The user is prompted to enable or disable macros. Optionally, the user can choose to trust the author and certifying authority by selecting the Always Trust Macros From This Author check box in the Security Warning dialog box.	No prompt or verification. Macros are enabled.

(continued)

Type of Solution and Verification Result	High (Default)	Medium	Low
Signed macros from any author. Verification fails, possibly due to a virus.	User is warned of a possible virus. Macros are automatically disabled.	User is warned of a possible virus, and macros are automatically disabled.	No prompt or verification. Macros are enabled.
Signed macros from any author. Verification not not possible because public key is missing or incompatible encryption methods were used.	User is warned that verification is not possible. Macros are automatically disabled.	User is warned that verification is not possible. User is prompted to enable or disable macros.	No prompt or verification. Macros are enabled.
Signed macros from any author. The signature was made after the certificate had expired or been revoked.	User is warned that the signature has expired or been revoked. Macros are automatically disabled.	User is warned that the signature has expired or been revoked. User is prompted to enable or disable macros.	No prompt or verification. Macros are enabled.

Obtaining a Digital Certificate

A digital certificate is a digital ID card that guarantees users that your COM Add-in emanates from a trusted source. You can sign an Outlook VBA Project or a COM Add-in with a digital certificate. There are several sources for digital certificates that provide security for your COM Add-in:

- Selfcert.exe, included on the Office XP CD, creates a personal certificate. A personal certificate lets you certify your own Outlook VBAProject.otm macro code to yourself when the Outlook security setting is High.

- You can obtain a certificate from your organization's internal certification authority. Some organizations may elect to produce in-house digital certificates by using tools such as Microsoft Certificate Services. In effect, this option lets you act as your own organizational certification authority.

- You can obtain a commercial Class 2 or Class 3 certificate from a commercial certificate authority. Use this option if you plan to distribute your COM Add-in commercially or to the public at large.

Signing an Outlook VBA Project

Outlook 2002 macro security is set to High by default. If you want to run your own Outlook VBA code, you need to install the personal certificate that ships with Office XP. This process installs selfcert.exe in the same folder where you've installed Office XP.

To install the Create Digital Certificate utility

1. In the Control Panel, double-click Add/Remove Programs.

2. In the list of currently installed programs, click Microsoft Office XP—the exact text will vary depending upon the version of Office XP you have installed—and then click Add/Remove (for Microsoft Windows 98, Windows Me, and Microsoft Windows NT 4) or Change (for Windows 2000).

3. In the Microsoft Office XP Setup dialog box, select the Add Or Remove Features option and click Next.

4. Expand Office Shared Features, and set Digital Signature For VBA Projects to Run From My Computer.

5. Click Update Now.

6. Once you've installed selfcert.exe, you need to actually add a digital signature to your Outlook VBA project. First create your personal certificate by double-clicking selfcert.exe. The selfcert.exe file is installed in the same folder where Office XP is installed, typically c:\program files\microsoft office\office10. You'll be asked to enter your name to identify your personal certificate. That's all there is to it. Next you actually sign your Outlook VBA project.

To digitally sign a VBA project

1. If user profiles are in use, log on to Windows as the user whose Outlook VBA project you want to sign. Start Outlook.

2. Open the Visual Basic Editor by pressing Alt+F11.

3. On the Tools menu, click Digital Signatures.

4. Do one of the following in the Digital Signature dialog box:
    - If you haven't previously selected a digital certificate or want to use another one, click Choose, select the certificate and click OK twice.
    - Click OK to use the current certificate.

Signing a COM Add-In

To ensure users of your Add-in that the ActiveX DLL file has not been modified by someone other than the software publisher, you need to obtain a digital certificate that will authenticate your COM Add-in. Once your COM Add-in has been signed, its ActiveX DLL file will contain a digital signature. If you examine the COM Add-in DLL in Windows Explorer, the Properties page for the file will display a Digital Signatures page containing information about the certificate. Figure 14-16 shows the Properties dialog box for a digitally signed version of Micro Eye ZipOut, a COM Add-in that performs attachment management and compression.

> **Note** Be aware that the digital signature indicates only that the file is signed by the software publisher shown in the certificate. In Outlook 2002, a digital signature does not control whether the COM Add-in will be loaded. All COM Add-ins are loaded by default, whether or not they have a digital signature.

Outlook 2002 Default COM Add-In Security Settings

Outlook 2002 macro security differs from other Office XP applications in one important respect: If you examine the Trusted Sources page of the Security dialog box in Microsoft Word 2002, you'll see a check box for Trust All Installed Add-Ins And Templates. If you clear that check box in Word, COM Add-ins will not be trusted by default unless they are digitally signed by a trusted source. Outlook 2002 has no such check box on the Trusted Sources page. All COM Add-ins are trusted to run by default. However, all Outlook 2002 COM Add-ins are subject to the security imposed by the Outlook E-Mail Security Update. From this perspective, all COM Add-ins are untrusted by default. Remember that you can modify the security imposed by the Outlook E-Mail Security Update by using the Administrative form discussed in Chapter 13. You can also trust a specific COM Add-in by using the Trusted Code page of the Outlook Security form. Trusted COM Add-ins have unblocked access to the entire Outlook Object Model.

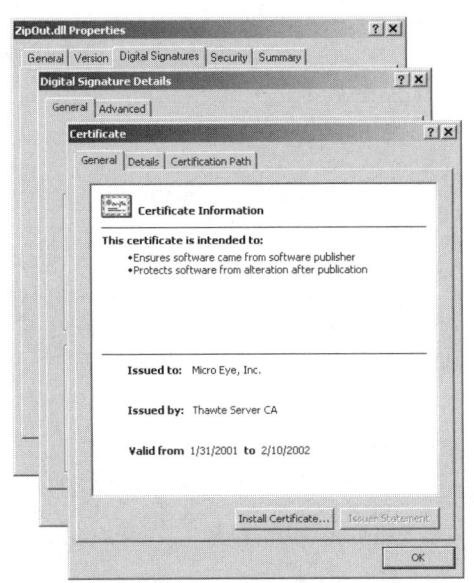

Figure 14-16 The Digital Signatures page appears on the Properties dialog box for a signed COM Add-in.

> **More Info** For additional information about obtaining a digital certificate, signing code with signcode.exe, and using command-line switches for signcode.exe, see *http://www.microsoft.com/security*.

Object Model Guard and Attachment Security

The Object Model Guard and Attachment Security components for COM Add-ins have some important implications. First, unless your COM Add-in is trusted with the Outlook Security form, many useful methods, properties, and objects in the Outlook Object Model will cause the warning prompts to display. Because you don't want to teach users to ignore security warnings, you should make every effort to write your COM Add-in so that it never causes these prompts to display. It should be a requirement of a well-written COM Add-in not to show the warning dialog boxes. The table on the following page summarizes the different security environments in which your COM Add-in might operate.

Environment	Outlook Object Model	CDO	Attachment Security
Outlook 2000 RTM and Outlook 2000 SR-1A without Outlook E-Mail Security Update	Completely trusted	Completely trusted	None
Outlook 2000 SR-1A or later with Outlook E-Mail Security Update Internet Mail Only mode	Blocked objects, methods, and properties	Blocked objects, methods, and properties	Level1 Blocked; Level2 Save to Disk
Outlook 2000 SR-1A or later with Outlook E-Mail Security Update Corporate/Workgroup mode	Blocked objects, methods, and properties unless modified with Programmatic Settings page	Blocked objects, methods, and properties unless modified with Programmatic Settings page	Level1 Blocked; Level2 Save to Disk; Custom Level1 Settings with Administrative Form in Public Folders
Outlook 2002 with PST delivery location	Blocked objects, methods, and properties	Blocked objects, methods, and properties	Level1 Blocked; Level2 Save to Disk; Level1Remove in Windows Registry
Outlook 2002 connected to Exchange Server	Blocked objects, methods, and properties unless access is unblocked on Programmatic Settings page	Blocked objects, methods, and properties unless access is unblocked on Programmatic Settings page	Level1 Blocked; Level2 Save to Disk; Custom Level1 Settings with Administrative Form in Public Folders
Outlook 2002 connected to Exchange Server and COM Add-in added to trusted COM Add-in	Completely trusted both on line and off line	Blocked objects, methods, and properties unless access is unblocked on Programmatic Settings page	Level1 Blocked; Level2 Save to Disk; Custom Level1 Settings with Administrative Form in Public Folders

Trusted COM Add-Ins

The trust mechanism for COM Add-ins in Outlook 2002 resides in the Administrative form in either the Outlook Security Settings or Outlook 10 Security Settings public folder. A digital signature on a COM Add-in has no influence on whether the Add-in will be trusted in Outlook 2002. As you learned earlier, all

COM Add-ins are trusted to load by default. Except for personal macro code in VBAProject.otm, it does not matter whether you add the Certificate Signer of a COM Add-in to the list of trusted sources. To add a COM Add-in to the list of trusted add-ins with the Administrative form, follow the steps outlined in "Specifying Trusted COM Add-Ins" in Chapter 13.

From a development perspective, here are the points you should remember when creating a COM Add-in that will run as a trusted Add-in based upon settings in the Administrative form:

- If your Add-in is included on the list of trusted COM Add-ins, it has unblocked access to the Outlook 2002 Object Model. The Application object passed in the OnConnection event of the Add-in is trusted in addition to all its dependent child objects, properties, and methods. If you use a *CreateObject* or *GetObject* method to create other Outlook Application objects, the child objects derived from these objects won't be trusted and will display warning prompts.

- If your Add-in is included on the list of trusted COM Add-ins, it will still display warning prompts when you make calls to the CDO 1.21 object model. You must lower the CDO settings on the Programmatic Settings page to avoid CDO warning prompts, or you must use a third-party alternative such as the Redemption object library.

- If you recompile your COM Add-in, it must be trusted again with the Administrative form. The trust mechanism is based on a hash value calculated from the Add-in DLL, and each time you recompile your Add-in the hash value changes. Delete the original COM Add-in from the list of trusted COM Add-ins, and then add the recompiled COM Add-in.

Deploying Your COM Add-In

This section describes some of the alternatives that you can use for deploying your COM Add-in.

> **Note** Outlook COM Add-ins do not require the distribution of Visual Basic 6 or VBA run-time files. These files are installed when you install Outlook 2002.

The Package and Deployment Wizard

Once you have developed, debugged, and secured your COM Add-in, you can create an installation setup program with either the Setup Wizard, if you are using Visual Basic 5, or the Package and Deployment Wizard, if you are using Visual Basic 6. If you use the Visual Basic 5 Setup Wizard, you must add code to the setup program to ensure that the correct registry settings will be created for your Add-in. See "Add-In Registration" earlier in this chapter for the correct registry key names and values for a COM Add-in. If you use Visual Basic 6 and the Package and Deployment Wizard, all the registration chores are handled for you automatically. The discussion that follows assumes that you will use the Visual Basic 6 Package and Deployment Wizard to package your Add-in.

Setup Checklist

Before you begin the package and deployment process, be certain that you have completed the following steps:

- Debug and test your COM Add-in under different operating systems and in different Outlook modes.

- If required, ensure that your Add-in has been digitally signed with a digital certificate.

- Make sure that you have added any required property page ActiveX controls and also third-party or extrinsic ActiveX controls required by your Add-in.

- If your Add-in requires object libraries that are not part of Office XP, make sure that you have the right to distribute those object libraries and that you've identified all the dependencies for your COM Add-in.

- Test the setup program under a variety of circumstances. Don't assume that because the COM Add-in installs on your development machine that it will install on a machine that only has Office XP installed.

The Visual Studio 98 Package and Deployment Wizard

The Package and Deployment Wizard lets you create either a standard setup package or a Web-based setup package using Active setup with Internet Explorer. There are a number of ways to start the Package and Deployment Wizard:

- You can launch the Package and Deployment Wizard as a stand-alone application. In this case, you must select the Visual Basic project that you want to package and deploy.

- If you have loaded the Package and Deployment Wizard as an Add-in, it is available from within the Visual Basic Development environment. In this case, the default project to package will be the current project.

Standard Setup Package

A standard setup package uses setup.exe to bootstrap the setup process. Setup.exe in turn calls setup1.exe, which contains the main setup program for your COM Add-in. Unlike the Setup Wizard that shipped with previous versions of Visual Basic, the Visual Basic 6 Package and Deployment Wizard places the ActiveX DLL and all dependent files into a single cabinet (.cab) file. When installation occurs, the application component and its dependent files are extracted from the cabinet file and moved to the correct folder on the local drive. A standard setup package can create a floppy, CD, or network-share type of setup. If you want the end user of your COM Add-in to be able to uninstall your COM Add-in, you should select the standard setup package option in the Package and Deployment Wizard.

Web-Based Setup

In a Web-based setup, the Package and Deployment Wizard creates a cabinet file and a Web page so that your COM Add-in component can be downloaded from the Internet or a corporate intranet. When a user accesses the Web page that hosts your COM Add-in package, the system downloads the ActiveX DLL component and dependent files to the user's computer. Internet Component Download, a feature of Internet Explorer 3 and later, causes the package to be verified for safety, unpacked, registered, installed, and then activated. The downloading occurs in the background and is controlled by the browser. User intervention is kept to a minimum or is nonexistent, depending on the security settings in the user's browser.

The most compelling feature of a Web-based setup is that it lends itself to use with folder home pages. You could design a folder home page for the top-level folder in an Exchange public folder application. When users navigate to that folder, they could read instructions for using the application, and a Web-based setup would automatically install all the COM Add-in or other ActiveX components required for the application.

> **More Info** For additional information on the Visual Basic 6 Package and Deployment Wizard, see the book *Distributing Your Applications* in the Visual Basic online documentation.

Visual Studio Installer

Visual Studio Installer uses the Windows Installer to package and deploy your COM Add-in. If you plan to distribute a COM Add-in commercially, a Windows Installer setup is the preferred installation technology. Office XP uses Windows Installer 1.1, and Visual Studio Installer has been upgraded from its initial 1.0 release to support all the features of Windows Installer 1.1. Obtain Visual Studio Installer 1.1 by visiting *http://msdn.microsoft.com/vstudio/downloads/vsi11/default.asp*. Here is just a short list of the features Visual Studio Installer 1.1 offers:

- **Application self-repair** A Repair mode is available to restore missing or damaged files necessary to the operation of your COM Add-in.

- **Rollback capability** This is an undo capability for COM Add-in installation.

- **Support for Windows Installer merge modules** Merge modules make it easier to distribute files necessary to the operation of your COM Add-in.

- **Ability to run installation on administratively locked machines** You can install a COM Add-in on a machine running Windows 2000 that has been locked administratively.

Where To Go from Here

Microsoft Knowledge Base Articles Microsoft Knowledge Base articles are available on the Web at *http://support.microsoft.com/support*. Also see "Creating COM Add-Ins with Visual Basic (Chapter 14) KB Articles" in the Microsoft Web Sites folder under the Help and Web Sites folder on the companion CD.

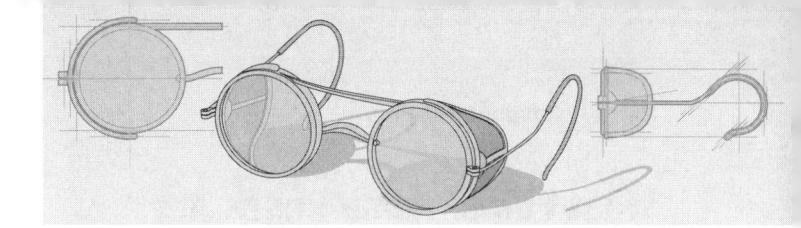

Chapter 15

Integrating Outlook with Web Applications

This chapter will introduce you to some of the methods used to integrate Microsoft Outlook with the Web. Integration includes presenting Web content in Outlook with folder home pages and presenting Outlook content in Web pages with the Outlook View Control. Those of you who missed the Outlook View Control in Outlook 2000 because it shipped as a Web download instead of with the product will be relieved to know that the Outlook View Control is an integral component of Outlook 2002. The discussion in this chapter covers client-side integration only. It doesn't include Outlook Web Access (OWA) for Microsoft Exchange 5.5, Exchange 2000, or Active Server Pages (ASP) code for rendering folder items in a Web interface.

This chapter will also introduce you to Microsoft Digital Dashboards and Web Parts. Specifically, you will learn how to use the Outlook View Control to build Web Parts for your Inbox, Calendar, Contacts, Journal, and Tasks folders. You'll also see an example of a Web Part that opens a shared Calendar folder. Finally, you will discover how to create custom Web Parts for the application presented in Chapter 12, "The Northwind Contact Management Application."

As a developer, you might be wondering what use, if any, you can make of the folder home page feature in Outlook 2002. Some Outlook developers—especially those who concentrate their efforts on form development—might be puzzled by the importance and significance of folder home pages. What are they for, and why would anyone use them? This chapter will try to provide you with answers to these questions. Folder home pages are a complementary technology to COM Add-ins; they let you customize the Outlook environment and shape a user's experience of a public folder application.

Part V Advanced Topics

What Folder Home Pages Are

Folder home pages help promote features of your application directly to the user. You can replace nested menu commands, which many users will ignore, with command buttons that appear front and center on a folder home page. The concept of bringing all the commands and features of your application to a single folder home page is known as enhancing discoverability. Those of us who make a living through our development work enjoy exploring the nooks and crannies of applications. However, many end users are interested only in the point-and-click approach to application discovery. Typically, they are too busy with their everyday work to learn about hidden features in an application. This might be termed the reality of application design: "If you don't put it right in front of them, they will ignore it." Folder home pages let you present all the important commands and data for your application in the view pane of the Outlook Explorer. We'll examine the Digital Dashboard 3.0 project used to create this folder home page later in the chapter. As you can see from the Northwind Dashboard folder home page shown in Figure 15-1, a great deal of functionality is placed on a single folder home page. You might say that everything but the kitchen sink is in there, yet, at the same time, the user experience has been streamlined and simplified. The sales personnel who will use this application will enjoy its simplicity and its straightforward approach in design.

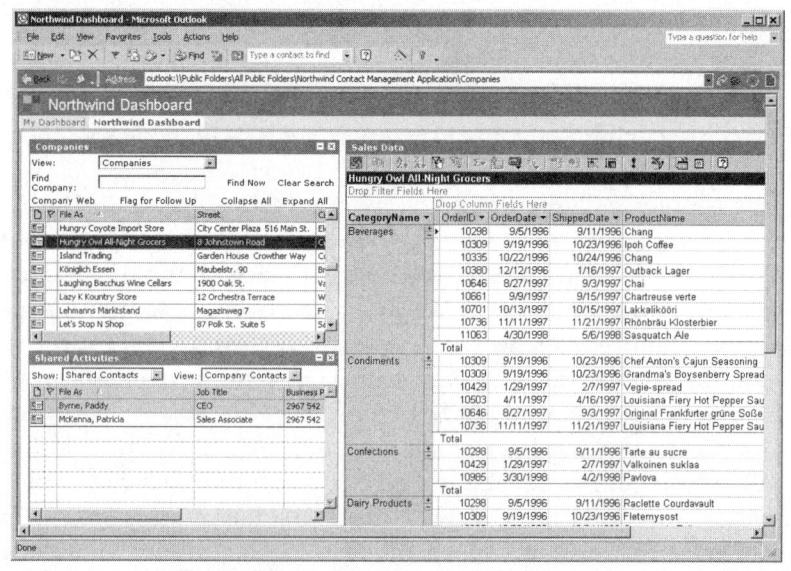

Figure 15-1 A Digital Dashboard folder home page for the Northwind Contact Management Application Companies folder.

What Folder Home Pages Are Not

It's also important to understand what folder home pages are not. Folder home pages should not be confused with Outlook Web Access, or OWA. Folder home pages represent a client-based integration of Outlook with the Web. By definition, folder home pages require Outlook. Outlook Web Access, on the other hand, does not require an Outlook client for the Windows or Macintosh environments.

Outlook Web Access

Outlook Web Access is a cross-platform technology that lets mobile users read their e-mail from a system that is independent of the Outlook client. OWA on the Exchange 2000 platform shows great improvement in both performance and scalability over Exchange 5.5. As users who read their e-mail at airport kiosks can testify, you don't need to have an Outlook client installed to read your mail from Outlook Web Access. The simplicity of Outlook Web Access also comes with some limitations. For example, Outlook Web Access cannot render Task or Journal items at this time. Furthermore, reminders are not available when you use Outlook Web Access. But you can expect Microsoft to make a significant effort to improve OWA and the Exchange 2000 Server platform in the future.

Outlook and the Web

The emergence of Web Storage System (also known as the Exchange store) applications has made it clear that browser-based applications built on the Exchange 2000 Server platform have a long life expectancy. Unlike Outlook forms, which are client based and subject to forms corruption, setup problems, security concerns, and dynamic-link library (DLL) incompatibilities, Web Storage System applications use efficient browser access to private and public stores on Exchange 2000 Server. Code executes on a secure server with ample processing power. Every item on Exchange 2000 Server is URL addressable, and items can reside in non-MAPI folder hierarchies that offer special deep-traversal search capabilities (unlike MAPI-based public folder hierarchies). Clearly Outlook's future promises more Web integration, not less. Inevitably, a future .NET version of Outlook will extend Outlook's Web capabilities, yet the implications of such a .NET version for application development remain to be seen.

Folder Home Pages Compared to Outlook Web Access

The table on the following page illustrates some of the differences between folder home pages and Outlook Web Access.

Technology	Outlook Web Access	Folder Home Pages
Client	Any browser that has the ability to render frames.	Outlook 2000 and 2002 only with Microsoft Internet Explorer 4.x or later
Client-side scripting	Yes	Yes
Server-side scripting with ASP or ASP+	Yes	Not typical when using Outlook View Control (However, folder home pages can also execute as ASP pages on a server.)
Supports event	Only if combined with Exchange 5.5 scripting agents or Exchange 2000 event sinks	Yes, using events in Outlook Object Model procedures
Supports Outlook View Control	No	Yes

Placeholder Folders and Active Folder Home Pages

Chapter 8, "Folders," briefly discusses folder home pages and presents you with some scenarios for their use in placeholder folders. The Northwind Contact Management Application uses an Access 2002 Data Access Page as a folder home page for the root folder of the application. Although the root folder does not contain Outlook items (and thus it is a placeholder to the active subfolders that do contain custom forms), it does host a folder home page that lets a user examine sales data in a Pivot Table List for current Northwind customers. Typically, a placeholder folder home page does not let the user open items directly in the placeholder folder. A placeholder home page certainly qualifies as a folder home page, but it just scratches the surface of what is possible with this technology. In this chapter, you'll see examples of what I'll describe as an active folder home page. An active folder home page such as the Northwind Dashboard shown in Figure 15-1 lets the user directly manipulate the items contained in the folder hosting the home page. To start our tour of folder home page development opportunities, we'll first take a look at the tools you can use to create active folder home pages.

Folder Home Page Security

In Outlook 2002, you can associate a Web page with any mailbox or public folder. Folder home pages either use zone security and allow script access to Outlook Object Model, or they use zone security only.

Using Zone Security and Allowing Script Access to the Outlook Object Model

This mode is the default for Outlook 2002, and it gives scripts on a Web page access to the Outlook Object Model. It also ensures that the Outlook Today ActiveX control (discussed in a moment) runs continuously. Therefore, if the Internet Explorer zone security settings specify that ActiveX controls are not allowed to run, the only ActiveX control that runs for a folder home page is the Outlook Today ActiveX control. For all other aspects of the Web page, the appropriate Internet Explorer zone security settings are used.

Access to the object model allows scripts to manipulate the Outlook Object Model, subject to the restrictions of the Outlook E-mail Security Update. If the Administrative form has been used to modify programmatic settings, these settings will control object model access on the page.

Using Zone Security Only

Zone security mode is activated directly through the Windows registry or indirectly through a system policy. In this mode, scripts on the Web page do not have access to the Outlook Object Model, and the Outlook Today ActiveX control is subject to the same Internet Explorer zone security settings as all other ActiveX controls. Thus, if the Internet Explorer zone security settings specify that ActiveX controls are not allowed to run, the Outlook Today ActiveX control will not run on the computer.

You can control security settings relating to Outlook Today and folder home pages with the System Policy Editor available with the Microsoft Office XP Resource Kit. The settings that relate to folder home pages and Outlook Today are listed under Default User. For additional information regarding the System Policy Editor, see the documentation that accompanies the Office XP Resource Kit. The following table lists some of the security settings that relate to folder home pages and Outlook Today for Outlook 2002.

Setting	Options	Value
Outlook Today availability	Outlook Today is available.	Boolean
URL for custom Outlook Today	URL for custom Outlook Today.	String
Disable Folder Home Pages	Disables folder home pages for all folders.	Boolean
Folder Home Page Security	Disables script access to Outlook Object Model.	Boolean

Part V Advanced Topics

The Outlook Today Page

Like its predecessor Outlook 2000, Outlook 2002 provides an Outlook Today page that is customizable. You might think of the Outlook Today page in Outlook 2002 as a customized folder home page at the root of your private information store. Unlike the Outlook Today page that is implemented by a custom DLL named outlwvw.dll and databinding code to an object known as a RENSTATICTABLE, folder home pages are created as straightforward HTML pages and are comparatively easy to customize using Microsoft Visual InterDev or the editor of your choice. In both Outlook 2000 and Outlook 2002, Outlook Today enforces browser security within the Outlook Today view. In Outlook 98, browser security was always disabled in the Outlook Today view, no matter what URL was being viewed. Outlook 2002 offers an enhanced security model that turns on browser security as soon as the user navigates away from the default URL.

End users can customize their Outlook Today page by clicking the Customize Outlook Today link in the page header. Developers can customize the built-in Outlook Today to brand the page with a corporate identity or to modify the page for use within different departments in an organization. You can also change the layout of the page and add links to pages on your corporate intranet. Developer customization of the default Outlook Today view in Outlook 2002 is beyond the scope of this chapter. A technical article that discusses advanced customization techniques for Outlook Today is available on the Web at *http://www.microsoft.com/office/ork/2000/download/OutToday.exe*. Although this article focuses on Outlook 2000, customization of the default Outlook Today page is almost identical for Outlook 2002.

Instead of customizing the default Outlook Today page, you can create a custom Outlook Today folder home page similar to the one illustrated in Figure 15-2. This custom Outlook Today page was created from Web Parts supplied on the companion CD and downloaded from the Microsoft Web Part Gallery. It uses the Outlook View Control to show the contents of the Inbox, Contacts, and Calendar folders. If you want to use a more extensible development platform, you should consider using the Digital Dashboard Resource Kit 3.0 to build a Digital Dashboard that can serve as a custom Outlook Today page. Digital Dashboard Resource Kit 3.0 enables you to host Digital Dashboards on a machine running Microsoft SQL Server 2000 or Microsoft SharePoint Portal Server. No matter which platform you use, you will need to set the folder home page for a custom Outlook Today page.

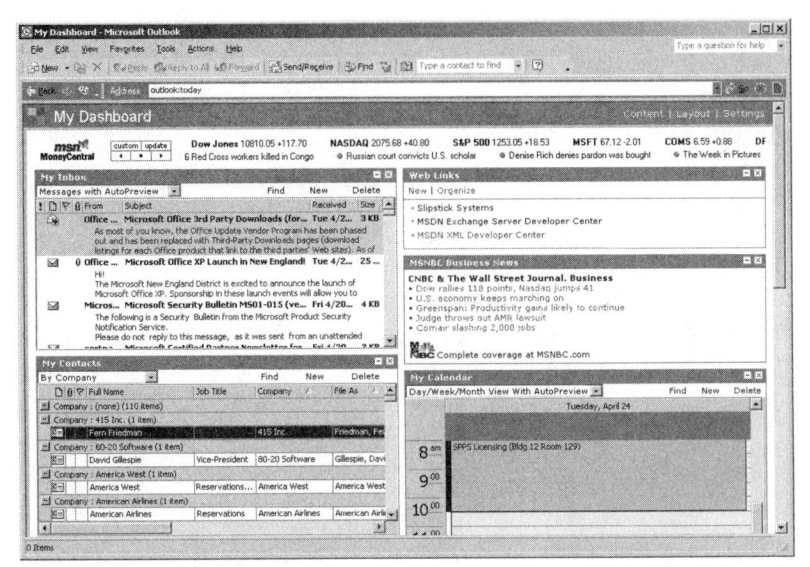

Figure 15-2 A custom Outlook Today page using a Digital Dashboard application hosted on SQL Server 2000.

> **To set a custom Outlook Today page**

1. Right-click the Outlook Today shortcut on the Outlook Bar, or select Outlook Today from the folder list and right-click it.
2. Select the Properties command on the shortcut menu.
3. Click the Home Page tab on the Outlook Today Properties sheet.
4. Enter the URL to your custom folder home page, or click the Browse button to locate your custom folder home page in the file system.
5. Check the Show Home Page By Default For This Folder box.
6. Click OK.

Tools to Create Folder Home Pages

To create folder home pages, you can use any of the tools listed next. If you become a serious folder home page developer, you will use a combination of these tools or maybe a third-party authoring tool not listed in the following table. If you want to customize your folder home pages, you should consider Microsoft

Visual Studio 98 Professional, Visual Studio 98 Enterprise edition, or a later version as the tool of choice. Because Visual Studio ships with both Visual Basic and Visual InterDev in the box, you have the two essential tools for folder home page customization in your toolkit.

Tool	Solution Created	Skill Set	Code and Debug Environment
Microsoft FrontPage 2002	HTML-based page	Intermediate	Front Page Editor
Office XP Developer	Digital Dashboards and Web Parts using Office XP Developer Support for Digital Dashboard Resource Kit 3.0	Advanced	Microsoft Development Environment 7.0
Microsoft Visual InterDev 6.0	HTML-based page with client-side script or ASP for server-side deployment in Internet Information Services (IIS) 4.0 or later; Digital Dashboards and Web Parts using Web Part Builder (DDRK 2.2 only)	Advanced	Microsoft Development Environment 6.0

The Outlook View Control

The Outlook View Control gives an Outlook folder home page the ability to display the contents of an Outlook folder, to control folder views, and to create, open, print, and delete items in the source folder. It is implemented as an ActiveX control (in a DLL file rather than as an OCX file) that can be added to a Web page, an Outlook form, a Visual Basic for Applications (VBA) UserForm, or a Visual Basic form. The View control allows folder home pages to operate with the speed and versatility that they exhibit. Unlike Outlook Web Access pages, which must convert folder items to HTML, the View control encapsulates the view pane that you see in the Outlook Explorer window and makes it portable. The Outlook View Control is an integral component of Outlook 2002, and no additional installation or setup is required.

Adding the View Control to a Form

Figure 15-3 illustrates the Outlook View Control placed on a UserForm. This UserForm is included in the VBAProject.otm accompanying this book. Before discussing the use of the View Control on HTML pages, it would be helpful to examine how the View control is used on the frmViews UserForm.

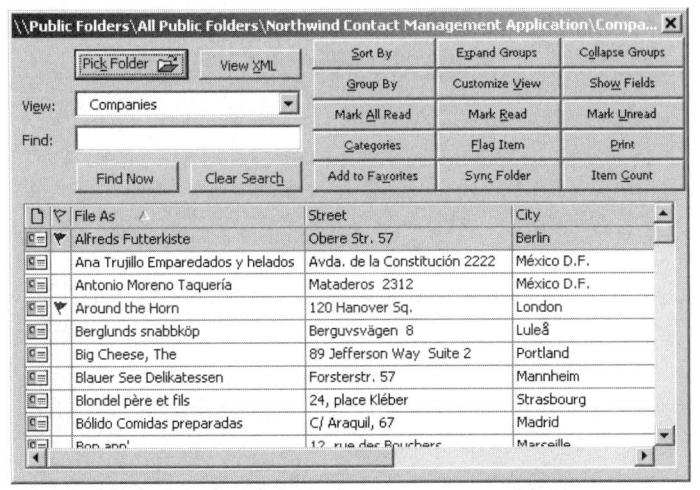

Figure 15-3 The Outlook View Control on a VBA UserForm.

To open the Outlook View Control UserForm

1. Press Alt+F8 to open the Macro dialog box.
2. Select ShowViewControlForm in the Macro Name list box.
3. Click Run.

This form demonstrates many of the features of the Outlook View Control. On first inspection, you'll notice that this control exposes a full-featured Outlook view in the UserForm on which it has been placed. If you right-click on the View control, all the normal shortcut menus of a standard Outlook view are available, including the ability to customize the view from the shortcut menu. You can drag and drop fields on the view. You can select a view from the View drop-down list box and the view in the View control will change. You can also use the command buttons on the form to demonstrate some of the methods of the control. If you double-click an item in the view, the item opens. The beauty of this control is that it's fast and relatively lightweight.

Part V Advanced Topics

Let's take a look at how the Outlook View Control UserForm is implemented. Before you can add a View control to a UserForm or an Outlook form, you must add it to the list of available controls in your Control Toolbox. The steps below assume that you're adding the control to the Control Toolbox in VBA. The steps are essentially the same if you're adding the control to a Control Toolbox in Visual Basic or Visual InterDev.

To add the Outlook View Control to your Control Toolbox

1. Press Alt+F11 to open the Visual Basic editor.
2. Select UserForm from the Insert menu.
3. If the Control Toolbox is not visible, select Toolbox from the View menu.
4. Right-click the Control Toolbox, and select the Additional Controls menu.
5. Check Microsoft Outlook View Control in the list of available controls in the Additional Controls dialog box, as shown in Figure 15-4.

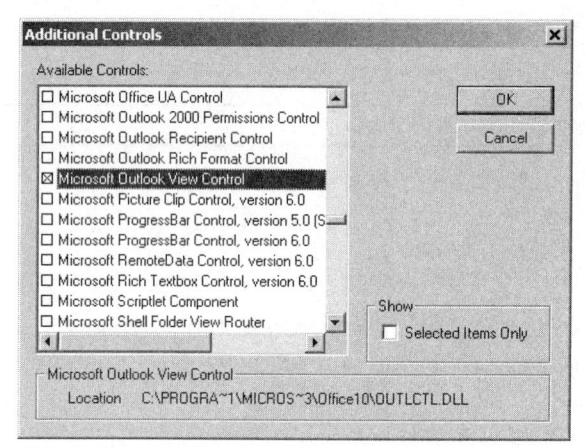

Figure 15-4 Add the Outlook View Control to your Control Toolbox.

To add the Outlook View Control to your form

1. Drag the View control from the Control Toolbox to your form. The default name of the Outlook View Control is *ViewCtl1*.
2. The View control will default to showing the contents of your Inbox.

Programmatic control of the Outlook View Control is straightforward. The control exposes many methods that are equivalent to Outlook menu commands.

The two most important properties exposed by the View control are the Folder and View properties. These properties let you manage the current folder and view that is displayed in the control. Both the View and Folder properties are strings. While you might expect the Folder property to be a MAPIFolder object, it is a string value that indicates the full path to the target folder. You can see the Folder property in the caption of the UserForm, as shown previously in Figure 15-3. To set the Folder property for the View control when you have only a MAPIFolder object (such as the MAPIFolder object returned by the *PickFolder* method of the NameSpace object), use the GetFolderPath function listed in Chapter 11, "Using Visual Basic, VBA, or VBScript with Outlook," in the section, "Returning a Folder Path from a Folder." Or you can use the FolderPath property of the MAPIFolder object to obtain a full folder path.

> **Note** The GetFolderPath function returns a folder path with one leading backslash instead of two leading backslashes. The Outlook 2002 FolderPath property returns a folder path with two leading backslashes (\\). The View Control will accept either one or two leading backslashes when you set the Folder property for the control.

Outlook View Control Properties

The following table lists the properties of the Outlook View Control.

Property	Type	Description
ActiveFolder	Object	Returns an ActiveFolder object for use when the control is hosted in a Web page.
DeferUpdate	Boolean	Causes updates to the control to be deferred until the *ForceUpdate* method is called.
Filter	String	Applies a DAV Searching and Locating (DASL) query to the view currently displayed in the control. Use this property with caution.
FilterAppend	String	Applies a logical AND of the *FilterAppend* string to the Filter property. Use this property with caution.
Folder	String	Returns or sets the path of the folder displayed by the control.
ItemCount	Long	Returns the number of items in the folder displayed in the control.

(continued)

Part V Advanced Topics

Property	Type	Description
NameSpace	String	Returns or sets the NameSpace property of the control. This property always returns MAPI.
OutlookApplication	Object	Returns an Outlook Application object for use when the control is hosted in a folder home page.
Restriction	String	Applies a filter to the items displayed in the control, displaying only those items that contain the string in the filter. Note that the behavior of the control's Restriction property differs from the *Restrict* method in the Outlook Object Model. See Restrict in the Microsoft Outlook Help Reference for additional details on logical and comparison operators.
Selection	Object	Returns a Selection collection object for the items that are currently selected in the control.
View	String	Returns or sets the name of the view in the control. Setting this property to a value that does not match a view name listed above does not cause the view to change, although this property will subsequently return the invalid view name.
ViewXML	String	Returns or sets the XML for the view displayed in the control.

Outlook View Control Methods

The following table lists the methods of the Outlook View Control.

Method	Description
AddressBook	Displays the Outlook Address Book dialog box.
AddToPFFavorites	Adds the folder displayed in the control to the user's Favorites folder. Does not display the Add To Favorites dialog box.
AdvancedFind	Displays the Outlook Advanced Find dialog box.
Categories	Displays the Outlook Categories dialog box for the item or items currently selected in the control, allowing the user to select categories for the current item or to modify the master category list.
CollapseAllGroups	Collapses all displayed groups in the control. If the view displayed in the control does not group items, this method has no effect.

Integrating Outlook with Web Applications Chapter 15

Method	Description
CollapseGroup	Collapses the currently selected group in the control. If the view displayed in the control does not group items or if an item in the view is selected, this method has no effect.
CustomizeView	Displays the Outlook View Summary dialog box, allowing the user to customize the current view in the control.
Delete	Deletes the currently selected groups or items in the control. If one or more groups are selected, the groups and all items in the groups will be deleted.
ExpandAllGroups	Expands all displayed groups in the control. If the view displayed in the control does not group items, this method has no effect.
ExpandGroup	Expands the currently selected group in the control. If the view displayed in the control does not group items or if an item in the view is selected, this method has no effect.
FlagItem	Displays the Outlook Flag For Follow Up dialog box for the selected item.
ForceUpdate	Refreshes the view in the control.
Forward	Executes the Forward action for the selected item or items in the control.
GoToDate (newDate as String)	Sets the displayed date in the control to the date specified by *newDate*. This method affects only views of the Calendar folder.
GoToToday	Sets the displayed day in the control to the current day. This method affects only views of Calendar folder and Timeline views in the Inbox and Task folders.
GroupBy	Displays the Outlook Group By dialog box, allowing the user to group items in the current view. This method has no effect if the current view does not display grouped items.
MarkAllAsRead	Marks all items as read in the folder displayed in the control. The user is prompted for confirmation before any change is made.
MarkAsRead	Marks all selected items as read in the control. The user is prompted for confirmation before any change is made.

(continued)

723

Part V Advanced Topics

Method	Description
MarkAsUnread	Marks all selected items as unread in the control. The user is prompted for confirmation before any change is made.
MoveItem	Displays the Outlook Move Items dialog box for the items selected in the control.
NewAppointment	Creates and displays a new appointment.
NewContact	Creates and displays a new contact. If the control is displaying a Contacts folder, when the new contact is saved, it is saved in the folder displayed in the control. Otherwise, the contact is saved in the user's default Contacts folder.
NewDefaultItem	Creates and displays a new Outlook item. The item type is the default item type for the folder displayed in the control.
NewForm	Displays the Outlook Choose Form dialog box, allowing a user to create a new Outlook item by selecting a form from a forms library.
NewJournalEntry	Creates and displays a new Journal entry. If the control is displaying a Journal folder, when the new journal entry is saved, it is saved in the folder displayed in the control. Otherwise, the journal entry is saved in the user's default Journal folder.
NewMeetingRequest	Creates and displays a new meeting request. If the control is displaying a Calendar folder, when the meeting request is sent, the corresponding appointment is saved in the folder displayed in the control. Otherwise, the appointment is saved in the user's default Calendar folder. Responses to the meeting request are tallied only if the appointment is saved in the user's default Calendar folder.
NewMessage	Creates and displays a new e-mail message.
NewOfficeDocument	Displays the Outlook New Office Document dialog box. This method prompts the user to select the type of Office document to create and then launches the appropriate Office application.
NewPost	Creates and displays a new post item. When the user posts the message, it is posted to the folder displayed in the control. This method has no effect if the folder displayed in the control does not support messages.

Integrating Outlook with Web Applications Chapter 15

Method	Description
NewTask	Creates and displays a new task. If the control is displaying a Tasks folder, when the new task is saved, it is saved in the folder displayed in the control. Otherwise, the task is saved in the user's default Tasks folder.
NewTaskRequest	Creates and displays a new task request.
Open	Opens the item or items currently selected in the control.
OpenSharedDefaultFolder	Displays a specified user's default folder in the control. This method takes two arguments. These arguments are the same as the arguments for the *GetSharedDefaultFolder* method of the Namespace object in the Outlook object model. An error occurs if the user running the control does not have permission to access the specified folder.
PrintItem	Prints the currently selected items in the control. If a group is selected, the items in the group are selected and printed. The Print dialog box is displayed to allow the user to specify how the items are to be printed.
Reply	Executes the Reply action for the selected item or items in the control.
ReplyAll	Executes the ReplyAll action for the selected item or items in the control.
ReplyInFolder	Creates a Post item for each currently selected message in the control. The Post item contains the text of the message it is replying to and has the same conversation topic.
SaveAs	Saves the selected items in the control as a file. The Save As dialog box is displayed to allow the user to select the location and format of the resulting file. If more than one item is selected, the items are concatenated and saved as a text file; otherwise, the user is allowed to choose from several file formats.
SendAndReceive	Sends messages in the Outbox folder and checks for new messages.
ShowFields	Displays the Outlook Show Fields dialog box, allowing the user to select the fields to be displayed in the current view in the control.

(continued)

Method	Description
Sort	Displays the Outlook Sort dialog box, allowing the user to sort the contents of the control using multiple criteria.
SynchFolder	Synchronizes the displayed folder in the control for off-line use.

Outlook View Control Events

Event support is a new feature of the Outlook 2002 View Control. The Outlook 2002 View Control events make it possible to perform some helpful tasks that you couldn't do with the Outlook 2000 View Control. For example, you can now easily trap the SelectionChange event, which fires for the folder displayed in the control and is independent of the CurrentFolder property in the Outlook Active-Explorer object. If no ActiveExplorer object exists in Outlook, the SelectionChange event still fires. With the Outlook 2000 View Control, the only way to trap a SelectionChange event was to ensure that the CurrentFolder property for the ActiveExplorer object was the same as the folder for the View Control. The Outlook 2002 View Control has done away with this requirement; instead, it fires the SelectionChange event whenever the selection changes in the view. The following table lists the events for the Outlook 2002 View Control.

Event	Cancelable	Description
Activate	No	Occurs when the View Control becomes the active element on the page, either as the result of user action or through program code.
BeforeViewSwitch (*newView* as String, Cancel as Boolean)	Yes	Occurs before the View Control changes to a new view, either as the result of user action or through program code.
SelectionChange	No	Occurs when the selection of the current view changes. Use the Selection property of the View Control to obtain a Selection collection object that contains selected items.
ViewSwitch	No	Occurs when the view in the View Control changes, either as the result of user action or through program code.

Obtaining Views for the Active Folder

One important piece of code behind the Outlook View Control UserForm is the *GetFolderViews* procedure. *GetFolderViews* returns a variant array that contains the views available in the folder displayed in the control. When a user clicks the Pick Folder button, she or he can select a different folder in the folders available to the current logged-on Outlook user. The *cmdPickFolder_Click* procedure lets the user select a different folder for display in the Outlook View Control. This procedure calls the *GetFolderViews* procedure that iterates the views in the folder by using the new Views collection object. Here's the code:

```
Private Sub cmdPickFolder_Click()
    On Error Resume Next
    Dim objNS As Outlook.NameSpace
    Dim objFolder As Outlook.MAPIFolder
    Set objNS = Application.GetNamespace("MAPI")
    Set objFolder = objNS.PickFolder
    If objFolder Is Nothing Then
        Exit Sub 'If user pressed cancel
    End If
    'Prevents cmbView_Change event from firing
    blnViewChange = True
    cmbView.Clear
    OVCtl1.Folder = objFolder.FolderPath
    Me.Caption = objFolder.FolderPath
    'Get views in the new folder
    cmbView.List = GetFolderViews(objFolder)
    If cmbView.List(0) = "" Then 'Handles error condition
        cmbView.Value = ""
    Else
        cmbView.Value = OVCtl1.View
        If Err = 380 Then 'Invalid property assignment
            'View Control active view name is incorrect
            cmbView.Value = cmbView.List(0)
            OVCtl1.View = cmbView.List(0)
        End If
    End If
    'Done - allow cmbView_Change to fire
    blnViewChange = False
End Sub

Function GetFolderViews(objFolder As MAPIFolder) As Variant
    On Error Resume Next
    Dim avarArray
    Dim i As Integer
    ReDim avarArray(objFolder.Views.Count - 1)
```

(continued)

Part V Advanced Topics

```
        For i = 1 To objFolder.Views.Count
            avarArray(i - 1) = objFolder.Views(i).Name
        Next
        GetFolderViews = avarArray
    End Function
```

Using the View Control in an HTML Page

One special feature of the Outlook View Control is that you can use it on an HTML page as well as on the page of an Outlook form. The control can be used in any of the environments listed in the table below. When the control is running purely within Internet Explorer, its scriptability is limited for security reasons. When you host the control within an HTML page with Internet Explorer as the container application, you will not be able to access the full Outlook Object Model programmatically. Access to the Outlook 2002 Object Model is also limited by the restrictions of the Outlook 2002 E-Mail Security Update.

Environment	Outlook 2002 Object Model Exposed
HTML Page in Internet Explorer 4.x or later running outside Outlook Web View	No
HTML Page in Outlook folder home page	Yes
Outlook Custom Form	Yes
Office UserForm	Yes
Visual Basic Form	Yes

Accessing the Outlook Application Object

Remember that you can access the Outlook Application object only when your Web page is hosted in Outlook. You can use either the OutlookApplication property of the Outlook View Control or Window.External.OutlookApplication to obtain an instance of an Outlook Application object. Once you have access to the Outlook Application object, you can instantiate all the child objects of the Outlook Object Model in DHTML code, subject to the limitations of the Outlook E-Mail Security Update. If the Web page is displayed as a folder home page within Outlook, the following code in the *window_onload* procedure creates an Outlook Application object named *g_App*.

> **Note** This discussion assumes that you have a basic understanding of Hypertext Markup Language (HTML), Dynamic HTML (DHTML), and Cascading Style Sheets (CSS). For additional information on HTML, DHTML, and CSS, visit *http://msdn.microsoft.com/workshop/author*.

```vbscript
<script language="VBScript">
'Script-level variables
dim g_App, g_TheExplorer, g_CommandBars, g_NameSpace
Sub Window_onload()
On Error Resume Next
Set g_App = ViewCtl1.OutlookApplication
Set g_TheExplorer = g_App.ActiveExplorer
Set g_CommandBars = g_TheExplorer.CommandBars
Set g_NameSpace = ViewCtl1.OutlookApplication.GetNamespace("MAPI")
'Alternative code
'Set g_App = window.external.OutlookApplication
End Sub
</script>
```

Using FrontPage 2002 with the Outlook View Control

When you design a Web page with the Outlook 2002 View Control, you can use any of the design tools listed on page 718 to insert the View Control into your Web page. For example, in FrontPage 2002, you can use the following steps to insert the View Control into your Web page.

To insert the Outlook View Control into a Web page using FrontPage 2002

1. On the File menu, point to New and then click Page Or Web.
2. In the New Page Or Web task pane, under New, click Blank Page.
3. On the Insert menu, select Insert Web Component.
4. In the Component Type list box, scroll to the bottom of the list and select Advanced Controls.
5. In the Choose A Control list box, select ActiveX Control.
6. Click Next.

7. Click the Customize button.

8. In the Customize ActiveX Control List dialog box, scroll down in the Control list box and check Microsoft Outlook View Control. Then click OK.

9. Select Microsoft Outlook View Control in the Choose A Control list box, and click Finish.

> **Note** Don't worry if you can't see the contents of the Outlook View Control in the Normal or Preview panes. The control might be grayed out, as shown in Figure 15-5. You can see the operational View Control when you click the Preview In Browser button on the FrontPage toolbar to display your Web page in a browser.

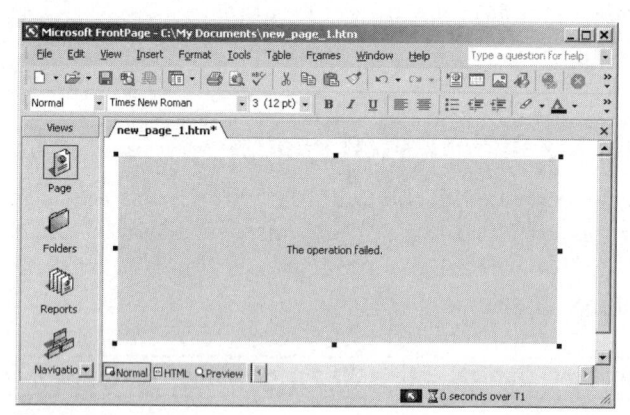

Figure 15-5 The Outlook View Control on a Web page in FrontPage 2002.

The Outlook View Control has now been inserted in your Web page, as shown in Figure 15-5. To continue using the FrontPage interface, right-click the View Control in the Normal pane. Then set properties for the control, such as the Height, Width, View, and Folder properties in the ActiveX Control Properties dialog box (shown in Figure 15-6).

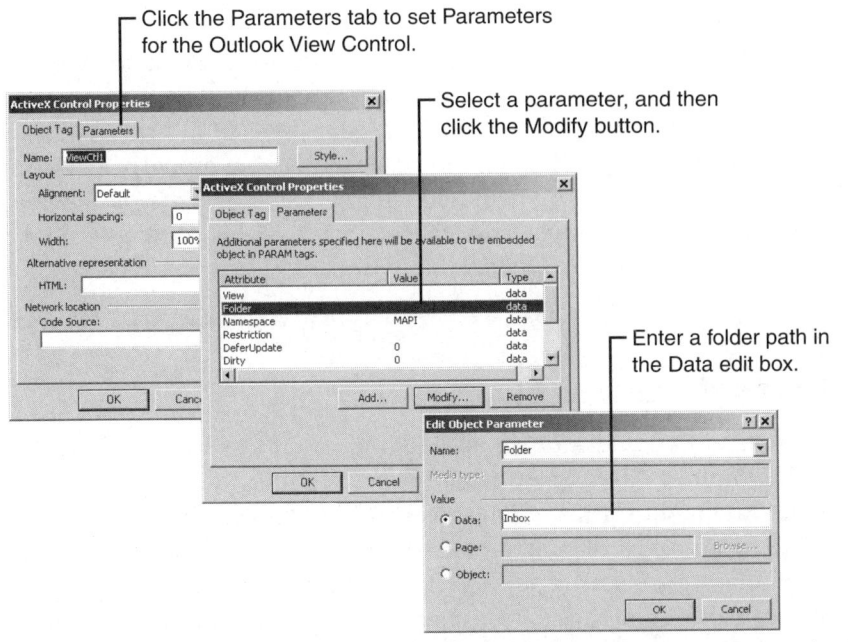

Integrating Outlook with Web Applications   Chapter 15

Figure 15-6 Use the ActiveX Control Properties dialog box to set properties for the Outlook View Control.

To set properties for the Outlook View Control

1. Right-click the Outlook View Control in the Normal pane.
2. Select ActiveX Control Properties from the shortcut menu.
3. Set properties such as Height, Width, and Border on the Object Tag page.
4. Click the Parameters tab to modify unique Outlook View Control properties.
5. Select the property to modify in the Additional Parameters list box.
6. Click the Modify button, and enter a value such as Inbox For Folder or Messages For View in the Data edit box. Use a full folder path for folders that are not default Mailbox folders, such as \\Public Folders\All Public Folders\Northwind Contact Management Applications\Companies. If you enter an invalid value for the Folder or View property, the Outlook View Control will not display data when you preview the page in a browser.
7. Click OK.

> **Note** One problem with setting properties for the Outlook View Control with FrontPage 2002 is that FrontPage sometimes sets extraneous parameters. For example, the *ViewXML* parameter of the control can sometimes contain the XML for the view in the Value property in the control's HTML markup. You should delete any Value property in the *ViewXML* parameter unless you explicitly want to use this parameter to create a custom view in the Outlook View Control.

HTML Markup for the Outlook View Control

Experienced Web designers will find it more productive to insert HTML markup for the Outlook 2002 View Control directly into the HTML for the Web page. Unlike the markup for the Outlook 2000 View Control, you do not have to add a Codebase tag to download the control in case it isn't installed on a user's machine. Because the Outlook View Control is an integral component of Outlook 2002, a Web download is not required. Here is the basic HTML markup for the Outlook View Control:

```
<object classid="clsid:0006F063-0000-0000-C000-000000000046" id="ViewCtl1">
    <param name="View" value=>
    <param name="Folder" value=>
    <param name="Namespace" value="MAPI">
    <param name="Restriction" value>
    <param name="DeferUpdate" value="0">
    <param name="Dirty" value="0">
    <param name="Filter" value>
    <param name="FilterAppend" value>
    <param name="EnableRowPersistance" value="0">
    <param name="ViewXML" value=>
</object>
```

You should supply the values for the Folder property and optionally for the View property. If you do not set the Folder property, the Outlook View Control will not operate correctly. If you do not supply a value for the View property, the Outlook View Control will display the current view in the folder specified in the Folder property. Remember that the current view is determined on a per-user basis. If the current view on your Inbox is Message Timeline, you should not expect this view to be the current view for another user's Inbox.

Outlook View Control Security

As stated previously, the Outlook View Control provides access to the Outlook Object Model only when it is hosted inside an Outlook folder home page. If the View Control is displayed inside Internet Explorer, the control disables access to the Outlook Object Model. Figure 15-7 shows a simple Web page named OutlookViewControl.htm displayed in a browser window. With the exception of the Flag For Follow Up button, any button that you click on the page displays a message box indicating that this scripting code is not available in Internet Explorer. The message box does not display automatically—you must write code to cause it to display. Which objects, properties, and methods are still available in the Outlook Object Model when you display the View Control in a Web page? Essentially, none. However, all the properties, methods, and events of the Outlook View Control are still available for your code when your page operates in a browser window.

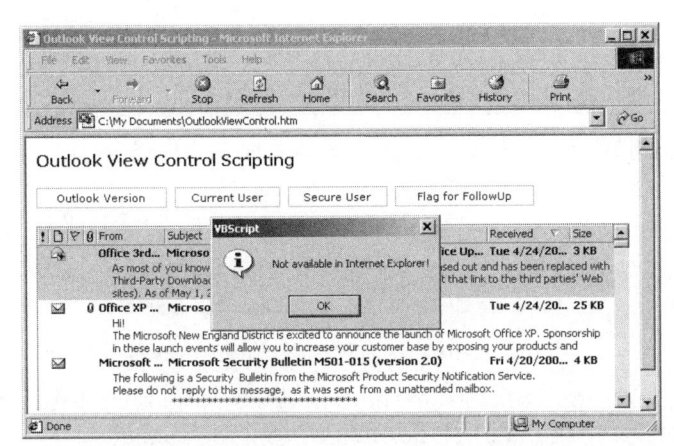

Figure 15-7 The Outlook View Control Scripting page demonstrates the security restrictions imposed by the control when it operates in a browser window.

When you use the same page as a folder home page hosted in Outlook, all the scripting code behind the buttons on the Web page operate correctly, as shown in Figure 15-8. The next set of instructions explains how to install OutlookViewControl.htm as a folder home page for your Inbox folder. Be sure to disable the page by deselecting the Show Folder Home Page By Default For This Folder box on the Home Page tab of the Inbox Properties sheet after you have completed the demonstration.

733

Part V Advanced Topics

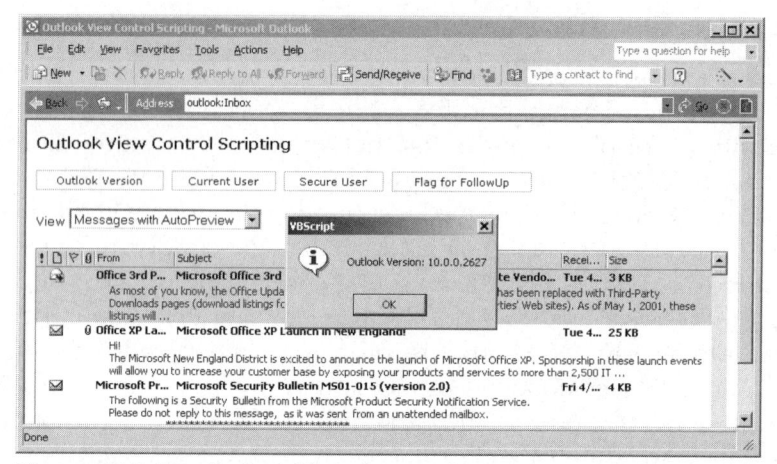

Figure 15-8 The Outlook View Control Scripting page hosted in an Outlook folder home page has access to the Outlook Object Model, subject to Object Model Guard limitations.

To use OutlookViewControl.htm as a folder home page

1. Navigate to the Outlook View Control folder under the Integrating Outlook With Web Applications folder under 5. Advanced Topics in the Building Applications with Microsoft Outlook 2002 PST file.

2. Double-click OutlookViewControl.htm. When Outlook asks you whether to open the file or save to disk, select the save to disk option.

3. Save OutlookViewControl.htm to your My Documents folder.

4. Right-click your Inbox folder in the Folder List, and click Properties. Click the Home Page tab on the Inbox Properties sheet.

5. Click the Browse button to select OutlookViewControl.htm in your My Documents folder, and check Show Home Page By Default For This Folder, as shown in Figure 15-9. Then click OK.

6. Navigate to your Inbox in the Folder List. You should see a folder home page similar to the one shown in Figure 15-8.

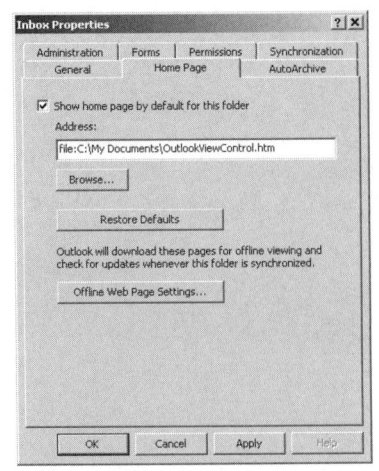

Figure 15-9 Use the Inbox Properties sheet to establish a folder home page for your Inbox.

Writing Code in a Folder Home Page

If you have written code behind Outlook forms, writing code for Web pages should not be a problem. For additional information about scripting Web pages, see *http://msdn.microsoft.com/workshop*. Any code in your Web page must be contained between <script> </script> tags. The key concept for writing the code in OutlookViewControl.htm is to determine when the page is operating in a browser as opposed to in a folder home page. Like Outlook forms, you declare script-level variables at the top of your script block. In this case, a variable named *g_App* is declared for the Outlook Application object. You can retrieve an Outlook Application object from the Outlook View Control's OutlookApplication property or from Window.External.OutlookApplication. If this object variable is Nothing, you can be certain that the Outlook Object Model is not available for scripting.

In this case, a script-level variable named *IsIEHost* is set to True. If the *g_App* variable can be instantiated, the Outlook Object Model is available for scripting, subject to the limitations of the Outlook 2002 Object Model Guard. Click the Current User button to see the Object Model Guard in action. Otherwise, your code has complete access to the Outlook Object Model as long as it's hosted in Outlook in a folder home page. The OutlookViewControl.htm will display a View

Part V Advanced Topics

control selector if it's hosted in Outlook but will hide the View drop-down control and its label if hosted in Internet Explorer. Here is the code for OutlookViewControl.htm:

```vbscript
<script language="VBScript">
'Script-level variables
dim g_App, g_TheExplorer, g_CommandBars, g_NameSpace, IsIEHost

Sub Window_onload()
    On Error Resume Next
    Set g_App = ViewCtl1.OutlookApplication
    If g_App Is Nothing Then
        IsIEHost = True
        cmbView.style.display = "none"
        lblView.style.display = "none"
        Exit Sub
    End If
    Set g_TheExplorer =  g_App.ActiveExplorer
    Set g_CommandBars = g_TheExplorer.CommandBars
    Set g_NameSpace = ViewCtl1.OutlookApplication.GetNamespace("MAPI")
    'Load the views for the Inbox
    Const olFolderInbox = 6
    Set objFolder = g_Namespace.GetDefaultFolder(olFolderInbox)
    cmbView.options.length = 0
    For i = 1 to objFolder.Views.Count
        strView = objFolder.Views.Item(i).Name
        Set oOption = document.createElement("OPTION")
        oOption.text = strView
        oOption.value = strView
        cmbView.add(oOption)
    Next
End Sub

Sub Window_onunload()
    'Maintaining state in a folder home page
    'Set the InboxView
    'Window.external.SetPref("InboxView") = ViewCtl1.View
    'SetCookie "InboxView", ViewCtl1.View
End Sub

Sub Window_onfocus()
    'Set the value for cmbView
    'Can't set the value during onload event
    cmbView.Value = ViewCtl1.View
End Sub
```

Integrating Outlook with Web Applications   Chapter 15

```
Sub btnVersion_onclick()
    If IsIEHost Then
        MsgBox "Not available in Internet Explorer!", vbinformation
    else
        MsgBox "Outlook Version: " & g_App.Version, vbinformation
    end if
End Sub

Sub btnCurrentUser_onclick()
    If IsIEHost Then
        MsgBox "Not available in Internet Explorer!", vbinformation
    else
        MsgBox "Current User: " & g_NameSpace.CurrentUser, vbinformation
    end if
End Sub

Sub btnSecure_onclick()
    If IsIEHost Then
        MsgBox "Not available in Internet Explorer!", vbinformation
    else
        MsgBox "Current User: " & GetCurrentUser, vbinformation
    end if
End Sub

Sub btnFlag_onclick()
    ViewCtl1.FlagItem
End Sub

Sub cmbView_onchange()
    ViewCtl1.View = cmbView.Value
End Sub

Function GetCurrentUser
    Dim objTopFolder, strTopFolder
    Const olFolderInbox = 6
    On Error Resume Next
    Set objTopFolder = _
        g_App.GetNamespace("MAPI") _
        .GetDefaultFolder(olFolderInbox).Parent
    strTopFolder = objTopFolder.Name
    If InStr(1, strTopFolder, "-") Then
        GetCurrentUser = Trim(Right(strTopFolder, _
            Len(strTopFolder) - InStr(1, strTopFolder, "-")))
    Else
        GetCurrentUser = strTopFolder
    End If
End Function
</script>
```

Part V Advanced Topics

> **Note** The code shown for the OutlookViewControl.htm Web page uses Visual Basic Scripting Edition (VBScript) as its scripting language. Most Outlook forms developers are familiar with VBScript, so this language offers the most productive avenue for scripting Web pages that use the Outlook View Control or the Outlook Object Model. However, most client-side scripting for Web pages is done with JScript. The Northwind Dashboard, discussed later in the section entitled "The Northwind Dashboard," uses JScript for its Web Parts. Because the Outlook View Control requires Internet Explorer to operate, you can do your scripting in VBScript instead of JScript.

Maintaining State in a Folder Home Page

You might be wondering how to maintain state in a folder home page. For example, you might want to store a value such as the current view stored in the Outlook View Control. Here are two suggestions for maintaining state in a folder home page:

- Use *Window.External.SetPref("ValueName")* and *Window.External.GetPref("ValueName")* to store values in the Today key of the Windows registry.

- Use client-side cookies to write and read the values.

Using *GetPref* and *SetPref*

Use the *GetPref* and *SetPref* methods to set REG_SZ (string) values in the HKEY_CURRENT_USER\Software\Microsoft\Office\10.0\Outlook\Today key of the Windows registry. *GetPref* and *SetPref* were originally designed to set and retrieve values for custom Outlook Today pages built using the Digital Dashboard 1.0 Starter Kit. However, there is no reason you can't continue to use these methods, as long as you use a unique value name that won't match another folder home page using these methods to set values. The following code fragments set and retrieve a value for the *InboxView* value during the Window onunload and onload events:

```
Sub Window_onunload()
    Window.external.SetPref("InboxView")=ViewCtl1.View
End Sub

Sub Window_onload()
    ViewCtl1.View = Window.external.GetPref("InboxView")
End Sub
```

Using Client-Side Cookies

The document.cookie property provides you with another means of maintaining state. A cookie is a small piece of data stored by your browser. If you want the cookie to be available outside the current browser session, you need to set the expires property for the cookie name-value pair. The expires property must be set with the Universal Coordinated Time (UTC) format shown in the SetCookie example that follows. A UTC date/time is equivalent to the GMT time zone, or Greenwich Mean Time. Be aware that some users might have browser security settings that prohibit the use of cookies. For additional information about cookies, see the DHTML documentation available at *http://msdn.microsoft.com/workshop*.

```
Sub Window_onunload()
    SetCookie "InboxView", ViewCtl1.View
End Sub

Sub Window_onload()
    ViewCtl1.View = GetCookie("InboxView")
End Sub

Function SetCookie(strName, strValue)
    document.cookie = strName & "=" & strValue _
        & ";expires=" & "Wed, 31 Dec 2003 23:59:59 UTC;"
End Function

Function GetCookie(strName)
    avarCookie = Split(document.cookie,";")
    For i=0 to Ubound(avarCookie)
        avarCrumb = Split(avarCookie(i),"=")
        If Trim(avarCrumb(0)) = strName Then
            GetCookie = Trim(avarCrumb(1))
            Exit Function
        End If
    Next
End Function
```

Using Event Handlers with the View Control

The Outlook 2002 View Control supports a limited number of events, such as Activate, BeforeViewSwitch, SelectionChange, and ViewSwitch. How do you raise those events in a Web page, and why would you want to do so? Let's answer the second question first. In the OutlookViewControl.htm Web page, a View selector on the page allows the user to change the view in the Outlook View Control. This works fine as long as the View selector on the Web page is the only place where the user can select a view. If the user changes the folder view with the View selector on the Advanced toolbar in the Outlook window, the View selector on the Web page must be adjusted accordingly.

As for how you raise events in a Web page, you write event handler code in the page. The two script blocks shown next get the job done. The first block identifies the event as BeforeViewSwitch. Notice that the event name must be supplied without the arguments that are passed in the event procedure. However, the code in the event procedure calls ViewCtl1_BeforeViewSwitch with both the *newView* and *Cancel* arguments. The second code block is written with any arguments that are passed to the event. The statement *cmbView.Value = newView* is all it takes to set the Value property of cmbView to the *NewView* string. *NewView* is the name of the view that will appear in the Outlook View Control as a result of a view change.

```
<SCRIPT LANGUAGE=VBScript FOR=ViewCtl1 EVENT=BeforeViewSwitch()>
    Call ViewCtl1_BeforeViewSwitch(newView, Cancel)
</SCRIPT>

<SCRIPT ID=clientEventHandlersVB LANGUAGE=VBScript>
Sub ViewCtl1_BeforeViewSwitch(newView, Cancel)
    On Error Resume Next
    cmbView.value = newView
End Sub
</SCRIPT>
```

Digital Dashboards

While FrontPage 2002 makes a good prototyping tool for creating folder home pages, more advanced folder home page development requires Visual InterDev or Office XP Developer and Digital Dashboard technology. Some pundits have questioned whether Digital Dashboards represent a marketing campaign, knowledge management initiative, product, or strategic technology for Microsoft. The truth is most likely a combination of all these options. Certainly the shipment of SharePoint Portal Server has made a real product from the Digital Dashboard concept. In any event, you can read about Microsoft's Digital Dashboard vision at *http://www.microsoft.com/business/DigitalDashboard*. This site defines a Digital Dashboard as follows:

> A digital dashboard is a customized solution that consolidates personal, team, corporate, and external information with single-click access to analytical and collaborative tools.

From a developer's perspective, Digital Dashboards provide a robust means of creating folder home pages and extending Outlook into new realms. Outlook can be considered the home base where most knowledge workers live, so folder home pages are the perfect place to host Digital Dashboards. You can create a corporate Outlook Today folder home page using Digital Dashboard technology, or you can create Web Parts for inclusion in Digital Dashboards distributed for use in a custom Outlook application.

Glossary of Digital Dashboard Terms

Before attempting to develop your own Digital Dashboards and Web Parts, carefully study the documentation that accompanies the DDRK. The following table provides a glossary of Digital Dashboard terms and concepts that are used in this chapter.

Term	Description
Digital Dashboard	The rendering of a set of Web Parts in an HTML page. Digital Dashboards can be nested so that one Digital Dashboard has a child relationship to its parent.
Digital Dashboard application	A Digital Dashboard plus all its support files, customization pages, and Web Parts.
Digital Dashboard factory	A set of ASP, XML, and XSL files that assemble Web Parts into a view layout suitable for rendering in a Digital Dashboard.
Web Part	The building blocks for a Digital Dashboard. Web Parts have properties that you can set to control their content, appearance, and functionality.
Web Part catalog	A library of Web Parts located on the Internet or a local intranet. Users can add Web Parts to their Digital Dashboards by importing them from Web Part catalogs.

Choosing the Digital Dashboard Platform

The Digital Dashboard Resource Kit (DDRK) 3.0, which replaces DDRK 2.2, was made available for downloading from the Web in May 2001. If you have DDRK 2.2 and want to use a File System Dashboard instead of the SQL Server 2000 Dashboard in DDRK 3.0, be aware that DDRK 2.2 Dashboards are not forward-compatible. Some changes made to Web Part schemas in DDRK 3.0 require you to modify Web Parts developed for DDRK 2.2 before using them in a DDRK 3.0 Dashboard. The Web Parts included in the Web Parts folder in the .pst file that accompanies this book will operate on DDRK 3.0 Dashboards only. If you want to use the sample Web Parts outlined in this chapter with DDRK 2.2, you will have to modify the Web Part namespace, as described later in "DHTML Events for a Web Part."

The following platforms are supported in Digital Dashboard Resource Kit 3.0:

- **SQL Server 2000 or later**   Digital Dashboards built on the SQL Server 2000 platform both offer improved scalability and use the relational table structures of SQL Server to provide additional features for user personalization.

- **SharePoint Portal Server 2001 or later**   Digital Dashboards built on the SharePoint Portal Server platform use the Document store (also known as the Web Storage System) to store Digital Dashboard parts and schema. SharePoint Portal Server uses Digital Dashboards and Web Parts as the foundation of its user interface. With its search, subscription, and document management features, the SharePoint Portal Server platform offers a wealth of features for your corporate intranet.

Downloading the Digital Dashboard Resource Kit 3.0

The Digital Dashboard Resource Kit 3.0 is the preferred development environment for current and future Digital Dashboard projects. To download DDRK 3.0 or later, visit *http://microsoft.com/digitaldashboard*. The Digital Dashboard Resource Kit (both versions 2.2 and 3.*x*) is an unsupported Microsoft product. If you require a supported Digital Dashboard platform, you should consider adopting SharePoint Portal Server in your organization. The CD version of DDRK 3.0 ships with a 120-day evaluation copy of SharePoint Portal Server. If you are using the Web download version of DDRK 3.0, you can download an evaluation version of SharePoint Portal Server from *http://www.microsoft.com/sharepoint*. If you do not have SQL Server 2000 installed on your organization's network, you can obtain an evaluation edition of SQL Server at *http://www.microsoft.com/sql*.

> Note   If you use SQL Server 2000 as your Digital Dashboard platform, installation of the SQL Server Dashboard on a Windows 2000 domain controller running SQL Server 2000 is not supported at the time of this writing. See the documentation that accompanies the DDRK 3.0 for additional information regarding system requirements.

Installing the SQL Server Dashboard

The Web Parts that accompany this chapter are designed for use with the SQL Server 2000 sample Dashboard. The following instructions assume that you have downloaded the Web version of DDRK 3.0 or later.

To install the SQL Server sample Dashboard for the DDRK

1. Be certain that you have installed all the prerequisites for the SQL Server sample Dashboard, including a version of SQL Server 2000 on Windows 2000 Professional, Server, or Advanced Server.

2. If you have downloaded DDRK 3.0 from the Web, you will download a file named sqldash.exe, which is a self-extracting executable file.

3. Double-click sqldash.exe, and click the Unzip button to extract the files to the default location, c:\sqldash.

4. The SQL Server Digital Dashboard 3.0 home page should open in your browser after the file extraction completes. Be sure to read the installation documentation before you begin setup.

5. Click the Install link on the home page, and then scroll down the page to the Installation Components section.

6. Click the Install The Microsoft SQL Server Digital Dashboard 3.0 link, and if prompted, click the Open This File From Its Current Location option.

7. Installation will begin. Follow the prompts of the installation program. You will have to supply an administrator account name and password during the setup. After setup is complete, the Welcome Dashboard for the SQL Server Digital Dashboard should open in your browser. Add the Welcome Dashboard to your Internet Explorer Favorites.

8. The URL for your Welcome Dashboard is *http://<servername>/dashboard*. This URL should redirect to the full URL for the Welcome Dashboard. Be sure to replace <servername> with the actual name of the computer on which you have installed the SQL Server Dashboard.

Installing Office XP Developer Support for SQL Server Digital Dashboard 3.0

After you've installed the SQL Server Digital Dashboard on your server, install the technology preview for the Microsoft Office XP Developer Support for SQL Server Digital Dashboard 3.0. This discussion assumes that you have Office XP Developer installed on your development computer. If you do not, you can still import the Web Parts supplied in the .pst file on the companion CD. Stay tuned to *http://msdn.microsoft.com/vstudio* to learn if a Web Part development tool becomes available for Visual Studio developers.

To install Office XP Developer Support for SQL Server Digital Dashboard 3.0

1. Install Office XP and Office XP Developer.
2. Use the Windows Explorer to open the Office Developer SQL Update folder under the Sqldash folder, and run Microsoft Office XP Developer Support for DDRK 3.0.msi.
3. Click Next after you read the Welcome information.
4. Click Next if you accept the terms of the license agreement.
5. Click Install to begin installation.
6. Click Finish to complete setup.

Now that you have installed the SQL Server Dashboard and Office XP Developer Support for SQL Server, you can create a new Dashboard Project in Office XP Developer.

To create a new Dashboard Project with Office XP Developer

1. Point to Microsoft Development Environment in the Microsoft Office XP Developer program group, select the New command on the File menu, and select the Project command.
2. In the New Project dialog box shown in Figure 15-10, select Dashboard Project in the Templates list box. Next enter the URL for your SQL Server Dashboard.Davfactory (*http://<servername>/davfactory*, where <servername> is the name of the server on which you installed the SQL Server Digital Dashboard 3.0) in the Location edit box. Then enter a project name in the Name edit box.
3. Click OK.

> **Note** If you have Office XP Developer, you can create My Dashboard and Northwind Dashboard (both discussed later in the chapter) directly through Office XP Developer. When you create the Dashboard Project using the steps just outlined, name the project My Dashboard. After you move the Web Parts from the Web Parts folder in the .pst file on the companion CD to the file system on your computer, you can import these Web Parts using Office XP Developer.

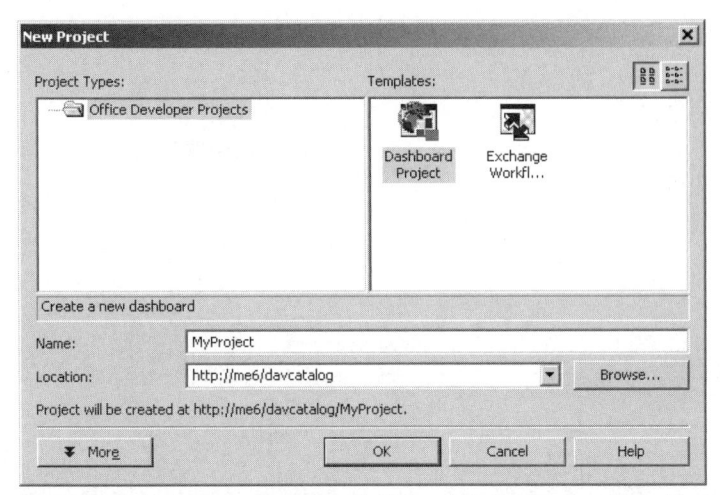

Figure 15-10 Use the Microsoft Office XP Developer New Project dialog box to create a new Digital Dashboard project.

The following discussion assumes that you will import the Web Parts in the Web Parts folder with the Administration Dashboard for My Dashboard and Northwind Dashboard. If you have Office XP Developer, you can import the Web Parts directly into a Dashboard project.

To import Web Parts into an Office XP Developer Dashboard Project

1. Open Windows Explorer, and create a local file system folder named Web Parts.

2. Open the Web Parts folder under the Integrating Outlook With Web Applications folder under the 5. Advanced Topics folder.

3. Press Ctrl+A to select all the items in the folder.

4. Drag the Web Parts from the Web Parts folder, and drop them onto the Windows Explorer folder that you created in step 1.

5. Launch Office XP Developer, and create a Dashboard project with it if you have not done so already. For example, you can create a Dashboard project named My Dashboard.

6. Select the project in the Solution Explorer, and then click Add Existing Item on the Project menu.

7. Add Web Parts from the Web Parts folder that you created in step 1. You can select multiple Web Parts in the Add Existing Item dialog box by pressing Ctrl and then clicking multiple items. The developer environment is shown in Figure 15-11.

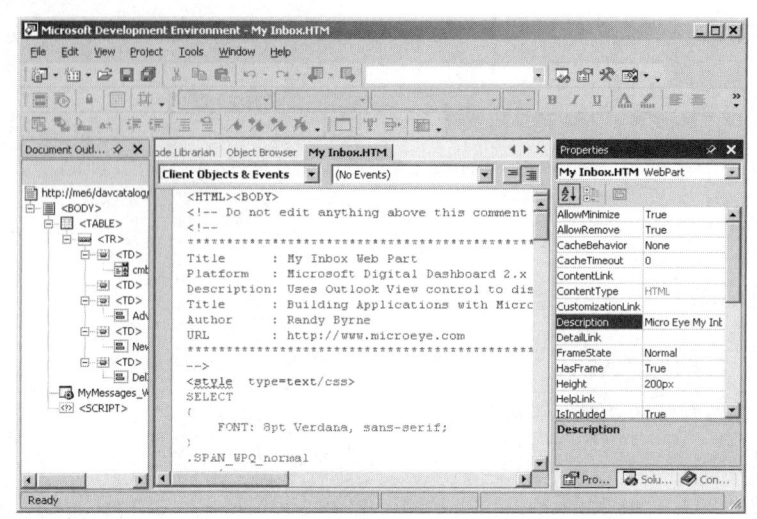

Figure 15-11 The Office XP Developer development environment with My Inbox Web Part added to a Digital Dashboard Project.

Importing a Web Part

Once you've installed the SQL Server Dashboard, you're ready to create a Digital Dashboard and add Web Parts to it. Sample Web Parts are supplied in the Web Parts folder in the .pst file on the companion CD. The portable file format for Web Parts is a Web Part Definition, or .dwp file. These .dwp files contain XML Web Part schema and can be imported into Dashboards via the Import A Web Part File link on the Dashboard's Contents page. You can also use the Import command on the Web Part List on the Administration Dashboard. You must have administrative privileges on the Dashboard to import Web Parts. You also must be using Internet Explorer 5.5 or later on the computer where you will perform the import.

> **To install the sample Web Parts to the file system**

1. Open Windows Explorer, and create a local file system folder named Web Parts.

2. Open the Web Parts folder under the Integrating Outlook With Web Applications folder under the 5. Advanced Topics folder.

3. Press Ctrl+A to select all the items in the folder.

4. Drag the Web Parts from the Web Parts folder, and drop them onto the Windows Explorer folder that you created in step 1.

Before you add the supplied Web Parts into your Dashboard project, you must first create a new Digital Dashboard named My Dashboard and a nested Dashboard named Northwind Dashboard. After you create these Dashboards, you can add Web Parts from the Web Part catalog.

Creating My Dashboard

Rather than create your first Digital Dashboard through a development tool such as Office XP Developer, you will create it through the Dashboard interface.

To create My Dashboard

1. Launch Internet Explorer, and enter *http://<servername>/dashboard*, where <servername> represents the server to which you installed the sample SQL Server Dashboard.

2. Click the Administration link to open the Dashboard Administration page.

3. Click New in the Dashboard View Web Part. Note that the Administration page is itself a Dashboard composed of special Web Parts.

4. Enter *My Dashboard* as the name and title of the Dashboard, as shown in Figure 15-12.

5. Click the Save button in the Dashboard Properties Web Part.

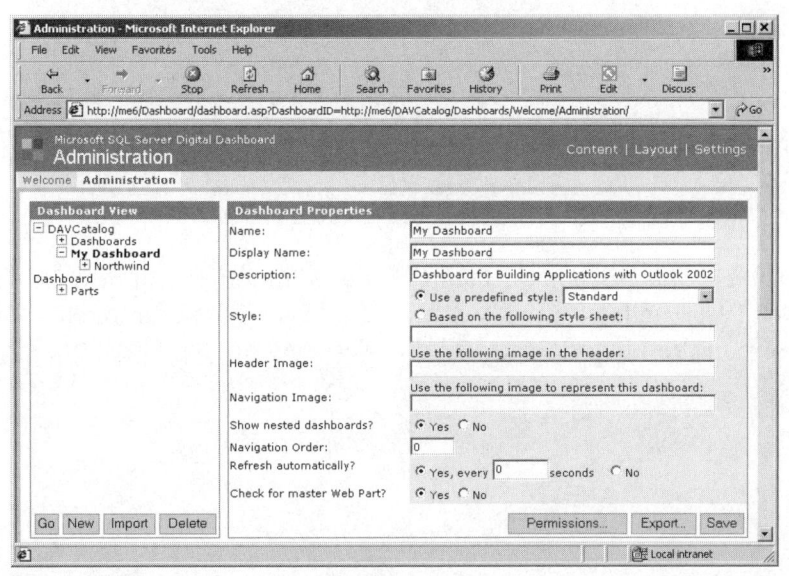

Figure 15-12 Use the Administration Dashboard to create My Dashboard.

Part V Advanced Topics

Creating a Nested Dashboard

One great feature of Digital Dashboards is that they can be nested. In this case, you will create a child Dashboard named Northwind Dashboard under My Dashboard.

To create the Northwind Dashboard

1. In the Administration page, click My Dashboard in the Dashboard View Web Part.
2. Enter *Northwind Dashboard* as the name and title of the Dashboard, as shown in Figure 15-13.
3. Click the Save button in the Dashboard Properties Web Part.

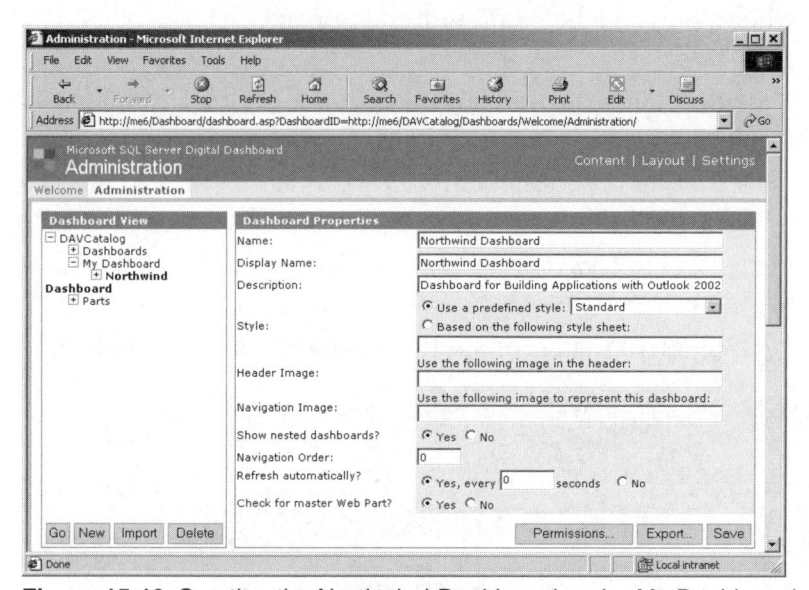

Figure 15-13 Creating the Northwind Dashboard under My Dashboard.

Each of the custom Web Parts that you imported will now be available in the Web Parts catalog for the Windows 2000 File System sample Dashboard. The next step in the process is to add the Web Parts to your Dashboards.

Adding Web Parts from the Web Part Catalog

A Web Part catalog is a list of Web Parts that are available for use in your dashboard. You can download Web Parts from the Web or import them as .dwp files. You can also create Web Parts directly with Office XP Developer. In this case, you will add Web Parts from the Web Part catalog.

To add Web Parts to My Dashboard

1. Launch Internet Explorer, and type the following URL in the Address Bar:

    http://<servername>/Dashboard/dashboard.asp?DashboardID=http://<servername>/DAVCatalog/My%20Dashboard/

2. Click the Content link, and then click the Import A Web Part File link at the bottom of the Content page.

3. Select My Inbox, My Calendar, My Shared Calendar, My Journal, My Tasks, and My Contacts using the Open dialog box. These Web Parts should be in the Web Parts file system folder that you created on page 746. You must repeat this step for each Web Part that you import. You cannot use Ctrl+Click to select multiple Web Parts.

4. Check My Inbox, My Contacts, and My Calendar on the Content page, as shown in Figure 15-14.

5. Click the Save button at the bottom of the page when you have completed importing Web Parts to My Dashboard Content. You will return to the My Dashboard page.

6. Click the Layout link, and then rearrange the Web Parts by dragging and dropping them into a layout that resembles the one shown in the Layout page in Figure 15-15.

7. Click Save.

Part V Advanced Topics

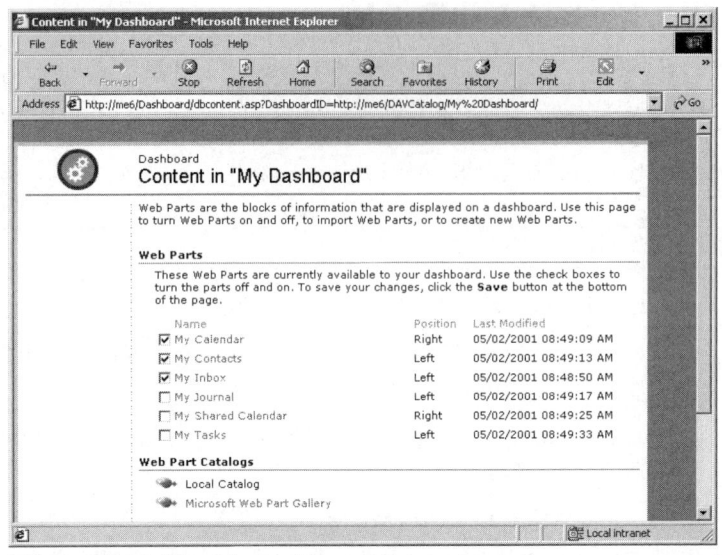

Figure 15-14 The My Dashboard Content page.

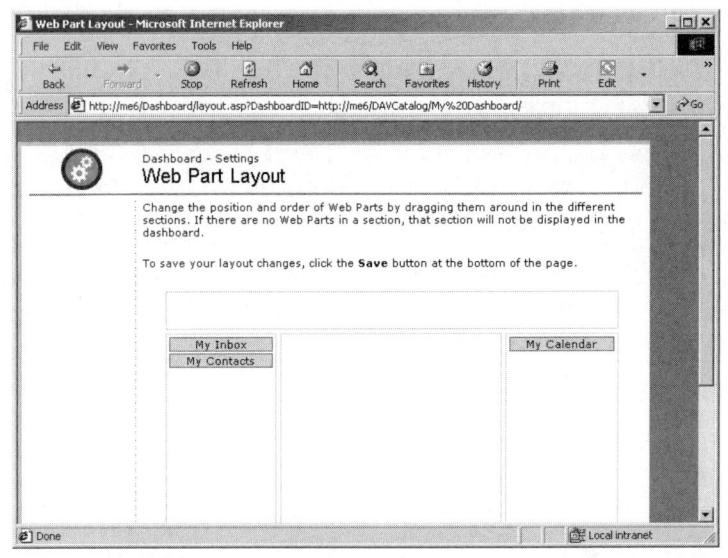

Figure 15-15 The Layout page for My Dashboard allows you to customize the arrangement of your Web Parts.

To add Web Parts to Northwind Dashboard

1. Launch Internet Explorer, and type the following URL in the Address Bar:

   http://<servername>/Dashboard/dashboard.asp?DashboardID=http://<servername>/DAVCatalog/My%20Dashboard/

2. Click the Northwind Dashboard link, click the Content link on the Northwind Dashboard, and then click the Import A Web Part File link at the bottom of the Content page.

3. Import the Companies, Sales Data, and Shared Activities Web Parts from the Web Parts file system folder you created on page 746. Check each Web Part so that it is displayed in the Northwind Dashboard.

4. Click Save to save your changes to the Northwind Dashboard catalog.

5. Click the Layout link, and then rearrange the Web Parts by dragging and dropping them into a layout that resembles the one shown in the Layout page in Figure 15-16.

6. Click Save.

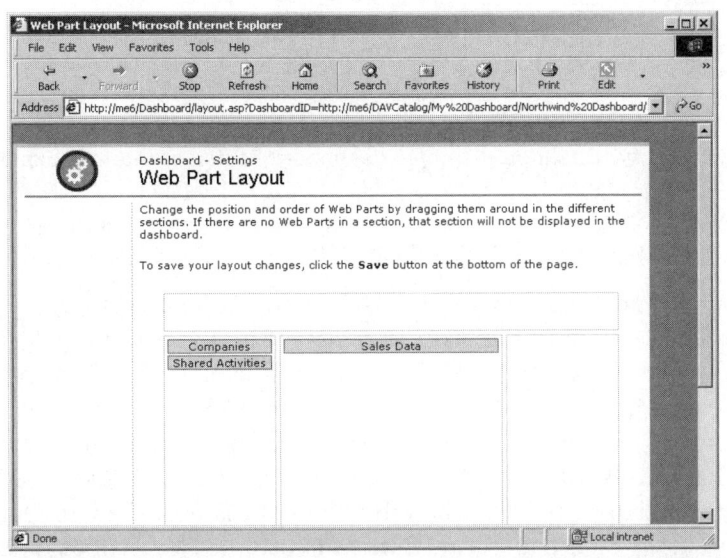

Figure 15-16 The Layout page for Northwind Dashboard allows you to customize the arrangement of your Web Parts.

Part V Advanced Topics

Features of My Dashboard

You should now have a functioning My Dashboard application similar to the one shown in Figure 15-16. If you host My Dashboard in Outlook as a folder home page, you will see the My Dashboard page shown in Figure 15-17. Notice that the Northwind Dashboard is also available when you click the Northwind Dashboard link in My Dashboard.

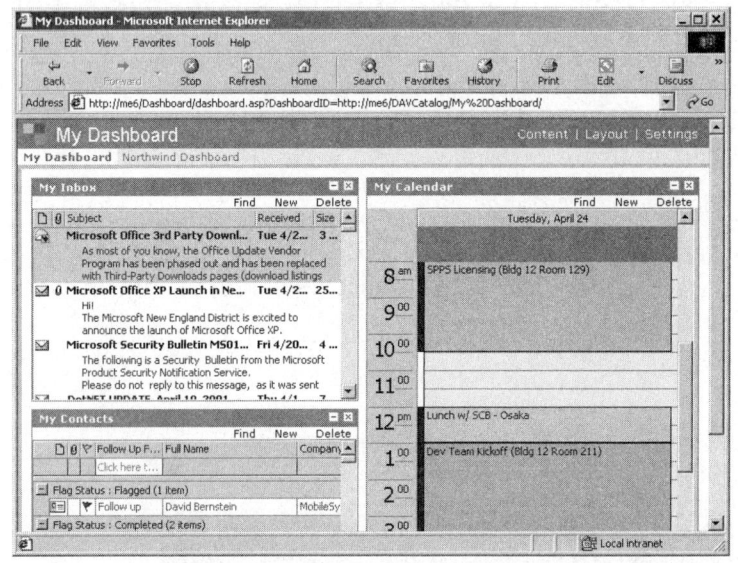

Figure 15-17 The My Dashboard sample dashboard hosted in Internet Explorer.

The Web Parts in My Dashboard have some enhancements over the standard Web Parts that ship with the DDRK. The modifications are as follows:

- The My Folder series (My Calendar, My Inbox, and so forth) of Web Parts detect whether the Web Parts are hosted in an Outlook folder home page. If they are, a View selector is displayed so that the user can select views in the Web Part. (See Figure 15-18.) The View selector contains all default and custom views for the folder. Although these Web Parts can be displayed in Outlook 2000 or Outlook 2002, the View selector will appear only when the Web Part is hosted in an Outlook 2002 folder home page. The Web Parts use the new Views object in Outlook 2002 to enumerate the views in the folder and populate the Select control. If the Web Part is hosted in a browser Dashboard rather than a folder home page Dashboard, the Outlook Object Model is not available for scripting and the View selector is hidden.

Integrating Outlook with Web Applications   Chapter 15

- The My Folder series of Web Parts contains script-level variables that let you localize the Web Parts in your own language. The Web Parts are currently localized for the U.S. English version of Office XP. You can change the view names that appear in the Web Parts to match the view names in your own language.

- The My Shared Calendar Web Part lets you open a shared Calendar folder by clicking the Share command on the Web Part. You must host this Web Part in a folder home page in order to select a Shared Calendar. This Web Part is useful for someone who has to maintain one or more shared calendars.

- The My Public Folder Web Part lets you open an Exchange Public Folder by clicking the Open command on the Web Part. You must host this Web Part in a folder home page in order to select a Public Folder. When this Web Part is hosted in a folder home page, you will be able to select folder views from the View selector.

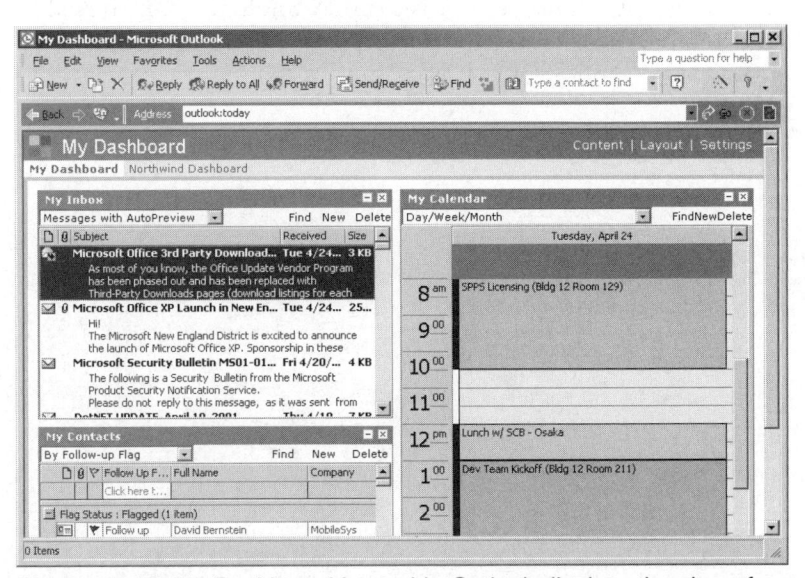

Figure 15-18 My Dashboard hosted in Outlook displays the views for each Web Part folder.

Designing Web Parts with Office XP Developer

Office XP Developer is the Web Part designer of choice, especially if you plan to use the SQL Server 2000 Digital Dashboard 3.0. If you want to deploy Web Parts for SharePoint Portal Server, you can design your Web Parts with Office XP

Developer, export them to a .dwp file, and then import them into SharePoint Portal Server. While it's beyond the scope of this chapter to cover all the nuances of Web Part design, it is helpful to take a look at the Web Parts supplied with this book and discuss the code used in them. If you need additional information about Web Parts schema, Dashboard schema, and the methods available for objects exposed by the Digital Dashboard Services Component (discussed later in the section), consult the documentation that accompanies the DDRK.

Opening and Designing a Web Part

To open a Web Part in Office XP Developer, first create or open a Digital Dashboard solution with the Open Solution command on the Office XP Developer File menu. (For a refresher on creating a dashboard, see "To create a new Dashboard Project with Office XP Developer" on page 744.) In the Solutions Explorer, navigate to the Web Part that you want to open and double-click it. You should see the Web Part in the Office XP Developer editor, and it should look similar to the illustration in Figure 15-19. Note that IntelliSense is available in the Office XP Developer editor and exposes the properties and methods of the Outlook View Control represented by MyMessages_WPQ_.

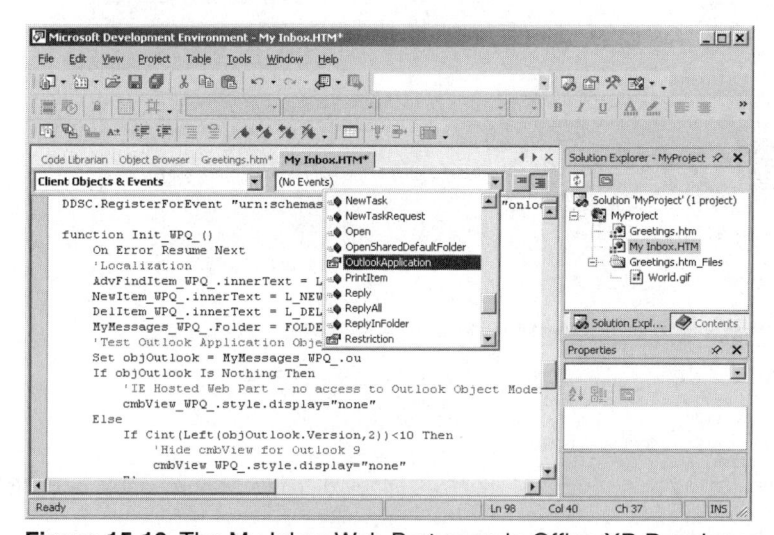

Figure 15-19 The My Inbox Web Part open in Office XP Developer.

To create and debug a new Web Part instead of importing an existing one, use the Office XP Developer development environment.

To create a Web Part in Office XP Developer

1. On the Project menu, click Add New Item.
2. Select the type of Web Part you want to create from the Template list box in the Add New Item dialog box, shown in Figure 15-20.
3. Click Open.

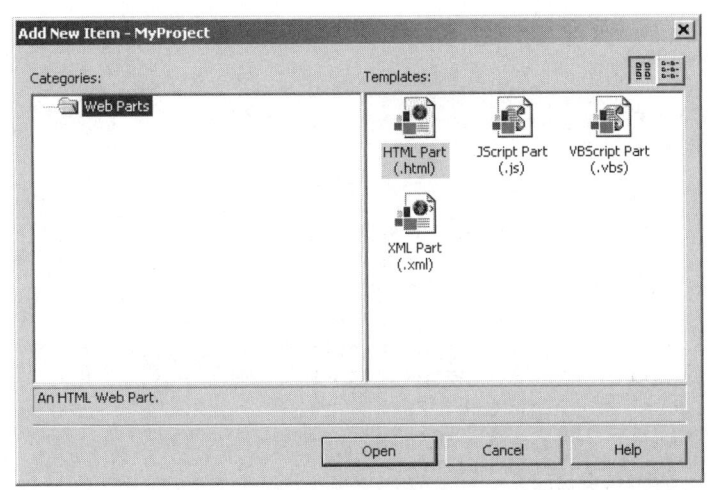

Figure 15-20 Create Web Parts with Office XP Developer.

If you are developing an HTML Web Part, the following markup will appear in the Development Environment editor. Do not remove the tags above and below the comment lines.

```
<HTML><BODY>
<!-- Do not edit anything above this comment -->

<!-- Do not edit anything below this comment -->
</BODY></HTML>
```

My Inbox HTML

The HTML for the My Inbox Web Part is fairly straightforward. It uses a table to hold the elements that appear on the command bar of the Web Part. Each element in the table is identified by a unique ID that uses the _WPQ_ token (discussed momentarily) required for Web Parts. The syntax follows.

Part V   Advanced Topics

```html
<style  type=text/css>
SELECT
{
    FONT: 8pt Verdana, sans-serif;
}
.SPAN_WPQ_normal
    {
    cursor:hand;
    color:black;
    }
.SPAN_WPQ_hover
    {
    cursor:hand;
    color:red;
    }
</style>
<table border="0" cellpadding="0" cellspacing="0" style="width:100%;">
    <tr>
        <td width="30%" align="left"><SELECT id="cmbView_WPQ_" class="select"
        style="display:none"
        onchange="cmbView_WPQ__onchange()">
        <OPTION selected></OPTION></SELECT></td>
        <td colspan="2" width="20%"></td>
        <td width="10%" align="left" valign="center">
            <span id="AdvFindItem_WPQ_"
            class="SPAN_WPQ_normal"
            onmouseover="this.className='SPAN_WPQ_hover'"
            onmouseout="this.className='SPAN_WPQ_normal'"
            onClick="advfind_Message_WPQ_()">
              Find
            </span>
        </td>
        <td width="10%" align="left" valign="center">
            <span id="NewItem_WPQ_"
            class="SPAN_WPQ_normal"
            onmouseover="this.className='SPAN_WPQ_hover'"
            onmouseout="this.className='SPAN_WPQ_normal'"
            onClick="new_Message_WPQ_()">
              New
            </span>
        </td>
        <td width="10%" align="left" valign="center">
            <span id="DelItem_WPQ_"
            class="SPAN_WPQ_normal"
            onmouseover="this.className='SPAN_WPQ_hover'"
            onmouseout="this.className='SPAN_WPQ_normal'"
            onClick="del_Message_WPQ_()">
              Delete
```

Integrating Outlook with Web Applications   Chapter 15

```
            </span>
        </td>
    </tr>
</table>
<object ID="MyMessages_WPQ_"
        CLSID="CLSID:0006F063-0000-0000-C000-000000000046"
        style="width:100%;height:100%"
        codebase="http://activex.microsoft.com/activex/controls/
    office/outlctlx.CAB#ver=9,0,2814">
        <param NAME="View" VALUE="">
        <param NAME="Folder" VALUE="">
        <param NAME="Namespace" VALUE="MAPI">
        <param NAME="Restriction" VALUE="">
        <param NAME="DeferUpdate" VALUE="0">
</object>
```

> **Note** The markup for the Outlook View Control in the My Inbox Web Part uses a Codebase tag so that the Outlook 2000 View Control can be downloaded from the Web if it isn't already installed. Because the Outlook View Control is built into Outlook 2002, the Codebase tag is ignored when the Web Part operates with Outlook 2002. Although this Web Part is designed to work with Outlook 2002, it will degrade gracefully if used with Outlook 2000.

The _WPQ_ Token

Probably the most difficult concept to grasp when writing a Web Part is that nonisolated Web Parts are assembled into a Web page by the Digital Dashboard factory. To avoid naming collisions when different Web Parts are assembled to create HTML that is passed to the client browser, Web Parts use Web Part tokens. Although several Web Part tokens exist, the one that concerns us in this discussion is the _WPQ_ token. You need to use this Web Part token when you create the IDs for your elements, script variables, and procedures in a nonisolated Web Part. The _WPQ_ token is used by the Digital Dashboard factory to ensure that your Web Part's names do not collide with the names of other Web Parts in the rendered page. Remember that a Digital Dashboard page is created from a collection of Web Parts rather than from a single HTML page or from ASP code that creates a single page. To prevent unexpected results in your Dashboard, the Web Part token is replaced with a unique ID when the Web Parts pass through the Digital Dashboard factory. For example, the Outlook View Control in the My Inbox Web Part uses the following ID: MyMessages_WPQ_.

Part V   Advanced Topics

The other My Folder Web Parts, such as My Contacts, use exactly the same ID for the Outlook View Control. What prevents these names from colliding when the Web Parts are rendered into a single page delivered to your browser? When the Web Part is rendered in the Digital Dashboard factory, the _WPQ_ is replaced by a unique identifier, such as MyMessagesWPQ3. The following components of your nonisolated Web Parts should use the _WPQ_ token to guarantee them a unique ID:

- Functions that have the same name in multiple Web Parts
- Objects that have the same name in multiple Web Parts
- Variables that have the same name in multiple Web Parts

Scripting a Web Part

Your Web Part can use JScript, VBScript, or a combination of both for HTML scripting. Because Web Parts that use the Outlook View Control require Internet Explorer 5.0 or later, you can use VBScript for your client-side scripting. My Inbox and its related My Folder Web Parts use VBScript only. The Companies, Sales Data, and Shared Activities Web Parts discussed later, in "Communicating Between Web Parts," use JScript. You can also use a combination of VBScript and JScript for Web Part client scripting depending upon your requirements. When you write code for your Web Part, Office XP Developer provides you with a powerful editor. You won't miss the Outlook forms editor when you're working in the Microsoft development environment.

Here is a partial listing of Office XP Developer editing windows that can help you create great Web Parts:

- **Source View**   You can edit your HTML and script code directly in the Source View window as well as use IntelliSense to help write your code, as shown earlier in Figure 15-19.

- **Web Part Properties**   You can use this window to set Digital Dashboard and Web Part properties.

- **Solution Explorer**   This window provides access to all the Web Parts and Digital Dashboards in your Dashboard project.

- **Document Outline**   This window shows you all the HTML or script objects available in your Web Part.

> **See Also**   For additional information about the Office XP Developer editor, see the help files that accompany Office XP Developer.

Notice that the _WPQ_ token is used to prevent collisions between script-level variables or procedures in different Web Parts. Here is the script for the My Inbox Web Part:

```vbscript
<script language = "vbscript">
'Script-level variables
'Replace these variables for localization in your language
L_FIND_TEXT_WPQ_ = "Find"
L_NEW_TEXT_WPQ_ = "New"
L_DELETE_TEXT_WPQ_ = "Delete"
'Folder constants
FOLDER_CONSTANT_WPQ_ = 6
FOLDER_NAME_WPQ_ = "Inbox"
'This code always runs
On Error Resume Next
'Register for DHTML onload
DDSC.RegisterForEvent _
    "urn:schemas-microsoft-com:dhtml", "onload", GetRef("Init_WPQ_")

function Init_WPQ_()
    On Error Resume Next
    'Localization
    AdvFindItem_WPQ_.innerText = L_FIND_TEXT_WPQ_
    NewItem_WPQ_.innerText = L_NEW_TEXT_WPQ_
    DelItem_WPQ_.innerText = L_DELETE_TEXT_WPQ_
    MyMessages_WPQ_.Folder = FOLDER_NAME_WPQ_
    'Test Outlook Application object
    Set objOutlook = MyMessages_WPQ_.OutlookApplication
    If objOutlook Is Nothing Then
        'Internet Explorer Hosted Web Part - no access
        'to Outlook Object Model
        cmbView_WPQ_.style.display="none"
    Else
        If Cint(Left(objOutlook.Version,2))<10 Then
            'Hide cmbView for earlier versions of Outlook
            cmbView_WPQ_.style.display="none"
        Else
            cmbView_WPQ_.style.display=""
            cmbView_WPQ_.options.length = 0
            Set objNamespace=objOutlook.GetNamespace("MAPI")
            'Get folder views
            Set objFolder = _
            objNamespace.GetDefaultFolder(FOLDER_CONSTANT_WPQ_)
            For i = 1 to objFolder.Views.Count
                strView = objFolder.Views.Item(i).Name
                Set oOption = document.createElement("OPTION")
                oOption.text = strView
                oOption.value = strView
```

(continued)

Part V   Advanced Topics

```
                    cmbView_WPQ_.add(oOption)
                    If strView = objFolder.CurrentView Then
                        intIndex = i - 1
                    End If
                Next
                cmbView_WPQ_.selectedIndex = intIndex
            End If
        End If
    end function

    sub cmbView_WPQ__onchange()
        On Error Resume Next
        MyMessages_WPQ_.View = cmbView_WPQ_.value
    end sub

    sub advfind_Message_WPQ_()
        On Error Resume Next
        MyMessages_WPQ_.AdvancedFind
    end sub

    sub new_Message_WPQ_()
        On Error Resume Next
        MyMessages_WPQ_.NewDefaultItem
    end sub

    sub del_Message_WPQ_()
        On Error Resume Next
        MyMessages_WPQ_.Delete
    end sub
</script>
```

The code for the other Web Parts (My Contacts, My Calendar, My Journal, My Tasks, My Public Folder, and My Shared Calendar) is essentially the same as the code for the My Inbox Web Part. The _WPQ_ token prevents collisions between Web Parts on the same page. These Web Parts use embedded HTML content, so they are not isolated on the page, and they require the _WPQ_ token to operate correctly. If you want to change the folder for the Web Part, you should change the following script-level variables after you paste the embedded content for My Inbox into another Web Part:

```
'Folder constants
FOLDER_CONSTANT_WPQ_ = 6
FOLDER_NAME_WPQ_ = "Inbox"
```

Just perform a find on folder constants in the Source View when the Web Part is open in Visual InterDev. For example, if you want to create a Web Part for the Drafts folder, use the following for folder constants:

```
'Folder constants
FOLDER_CONSTANT_WPQ_ = 16
FOLDER_NAME_WPQ_ = "Drafts"
```

Web Part Localization

Another important concept for the My Inbox Web Part is the localization of Web Part commands such as Find, New, and Delete. The My Inbox Web Part uses script-level variables such as L_FIND_TEXT_WPQ_ to store the innerText property for the element with the ID of AdvFindItem_WPQ_. If you use a version of Outlook in another language, you can replace the value of L_FIND_TEXT_WPQ_ with the equivalent of the word *Find* in your language. Change the other localization strings in My Inbox script to suit your local language. These localization strings are declared as script-level variables and are prefixed with L_.

DHTML Events for a Web Part

Just as events are critical for scripting Outlook forms, DHTML events are essential for scripting Web pages. However, the puzzling aspect of Web Part scripting is knowing how to distinguish a Web Part DHTML event from the DHTML event that occurs in the composite Web page rendered on the client. Here's how DHTML events work for Web Parts. The following line appears in the VBScript for the My Inbox Web Part:

```
DDSC.RegisterForEvent _
    "urn:schemas-microsoft-com:dhtml", "onload", GetRef("Init_WPQ_")
```

This statement calls the *RegisterForEvent* method of the Digital Dashboard Services Component (DDSC) object. DDSC is a hidden object that provides runtime services for scripting in your Web Parts. The DDSC component can raise DHTML events in a Web Part and can communicate with other Web Parts.

> **See Also** For additional information regarding the DDSC object and its properties and methods, see the section entitled "DDSC Object Model" in DDRK 3.0 Help.

The *RegisterForEvent* method takes three arguments:

- **Namespace**   A string that contains the namespace of the event provider
- **Event**   The name of the event in *Namespace* that your Web Part is registering for
- **Function**   The name of the function in your script that will run when *Event* fires

When you use "urn:schemas-microsoft-com:dhtml" as the *Namespace* argument and onload as the *Event* argument for the *RegisterForEvent* method, the Init_WPQ_ function runs when the DHTML onload event occurs on the Digital Dashboard page when the page loads on the client. Notice that you must use the VBScript GetRef function for the *Function* argument of the *RegisterForEvent* method. If you do not use GetRef, the *RegisterForEvent* method will raise an error in VBScript. Although onload is the only DHTML event registered for the My Inbox Web Part, you can register other DHTML events, such as onunload, onresize, and onerror.

> **Note** The Web Part *Namespace* argument for *RegisterForEvent* and *UnRegisterForEvent* has changed from "urn:schemas.microsoft.com:dhtml" for DDRK 2.2 Dashboards to "urn:schemas-microsoft-com:dhtml" for DDRK 3.0 Dashboards. If you want to use the Web Parts presented in this chapter with DDRK 2.2, be sure to use the correct namespace.

Writing Outlook Code in a Web Part

Examine the *Init_WPQ_* procedure carefully because that's where the real scripting occurs in the My Inbox Web Part. The idea behind this code is to change the Web Part depending on whether it's running in a secure Outlook scripting environment or in Internet Explorer.

The first chore is to set the folder for the Outlook View Control represented by MyMessages_WPQ_. Once you've set the folder for the control, an object variable named *objOutlook* is set to the MyMessages_WPQ_.OutlookApplication object. If this object is Nothing, the environment is not secure and the cmb_View_WPQ_ control is hidden by setting the style.display property to none. If the Outlook Application object is not Nothing, the code has access to the Outlook

Object Model, subject to the limitations of the Outlook Object Model Guard. The final sequence in the *Init_WPQ_* procedure is to obtain all the views for the folder represented in the view by iterating over that folder's Views collection. The code tests for the version number of Outlook to prevent an empty View drop-down list in Outlook 2000 because its object model does not support a Views collection object. A For Next loop determines the view name and sets the Option element for cmbView_WPQ_. Notice that when the current view for the folder is obtained with the CurrentView property of the MAPIFolder object, the code sets an *intIndex* variable equal to the counter in the For Next loop. This enables the code to set the correct selectedindex property for cmbView_WPQ_.

> **Note** One peculiarity of the safe scripting environment in Outlook concerns navigating away from the folder home page. Once you navigate away from the folder home page, the Outlook scripting environment is no longer considered safe. You can see a practical instance of this behavior when you click the Content or Layout links on My Dashboard. When you return to My Dashboard, the View drop-down selectors for the Web Parts are no longer visible. This means that the code has determined that the OutlookApplication object for MyMessages_WPQ_ cannot be instantiated. You must navigate away from the folder that contains your folder home page and then return in order for the View drop-down selectors to appear on the Web Parts.

> **Note** If you look at the Init_WPQ_ code carefully, you'll notice that some object variables, such as *objOutlook* and *objNamespace*, do not use the _WPQ_ convention for token replacement. This is because these variables are local in scope to the *Init_WPQ_* procedure. When *Init_WPQ_* is processed by the Digital Dashboard factory, it will be changed *to InitWPQ3* and will be a unique procedure within the scripting code for the page. Any variables used within this procedure are scoped to the procedure, not to the page. However, script-level variables are a different story. You should always use _WPQ_ for token replacement on those variables.

Part V Advanced Topics

Maintaining State in a Web Part

You can maintain state in a Web Part with techniques similar to those outlined earlier in "Maintaining State in a Folder Home Page." However, the recommended technique for maintaining state in Web Parts is to use the Digital Dashboard State Management Service. The State Management Service exposes a Property object that you can use to store values between instances of your Digital Dashboard. The following code from the My Shared Activities Web Part allows the Web Part to remember the mailbox name for the last Calendar folder opened by the *OpenSharedDefaultFolder* method of the Outlook View Control:

```
sub sharedcalendar_WPQ_()
    On Error Resume Next
    Const olxFolderCalendar = 9
    strMailboxName = _
    varPart_WPQ_. _
    Properties. _
    Item("urn:schemas-microeye-com:mysharedcalendar#mailboxname").value
    strName = _
    InputBox(L_SHARE_MBX_TEXT_WPQ_, L_SHARE_TITLE_TEXT_WPQ_, strMailboxName)
    If strName <> "" Then
        MyMessages_WPQ_.OpenSharedDefaultFolder strName, olxFolderCalendar
        varPart_WPQ_. _
         Properties. _
         Add("urn:schemas-microeye-com:mysharedcalendar#mailboxname").Value _
            = strName
        varPart_WPQ_.Save
    End If
end sub
```

Providing a Web Part Namespace

You can provide your Web Parts with a unique namespace, such as "urn:schemas-microeye-com:mysharedcalendar". A Web Part namespace is a Uniform Resource Identifier (URI) that uniquely identifies the Web Part. The full property name of the mailboxname property shown in the previous code example is "urn:schemas-microeye-com:mysharedcalendar#mailboxname." The URI portion of the property name ensures that it is globally unique and unambiguous. Once you have set the property for your Web Part, call the *Save* method of the varPart_WPQ_ object to persist the property value to Web Part storage. The varPart_WPQ_ object provides a means for the Web Part to refer to itself in scripting code. This object is analogous to the Me object in Visual Basic.

> **See Also** For additional information regarding the State Management Service and the Property object, see the documentation that accompanies the DDRK.

Exporting Web Parts

You can use Office XP Developer to export Web Parts after you have completed your design and debugging of them. As mentioned earlier, Web Parts are exported as .dwp files. Each such file contains the XML schema for the Web Part in addition to its embedded content.

To export a Web Part

1. Select a Web Part in the Solution Explorer. In this example, let's assume that you are exporting My Inbox.htm.
2. On the File menu, click Save Copy Of My Inbox.htm As. This opens the Save Copy Of Web Part As dialog box.
3. In the Save As Type combo box, select DWP file (*.dwp).
4. Accept the Web Part name, or enter another name in the File Name edit box.
5. Click Save to export your Web Part.

The Northwind Digital Dashboard

The Northwind Dashboard shows how you can use a folder home page to provide a simple but powerful user interface for an Outlook Public Folder application. The Northwind Dashboard, shown in Figure 15-21, acts as the folder home page for the Companies folder discussed in Chapter 12. The Northwind Dashboard presents a single page that integrates company, company contact, and sales data in your browser or in a folder home page. This integration is dynamic. When a user changes the selected company in the Companies Web Part, the Shared Activities and Sales Data Web Parts change accordingly.

Part V Advanced Topics

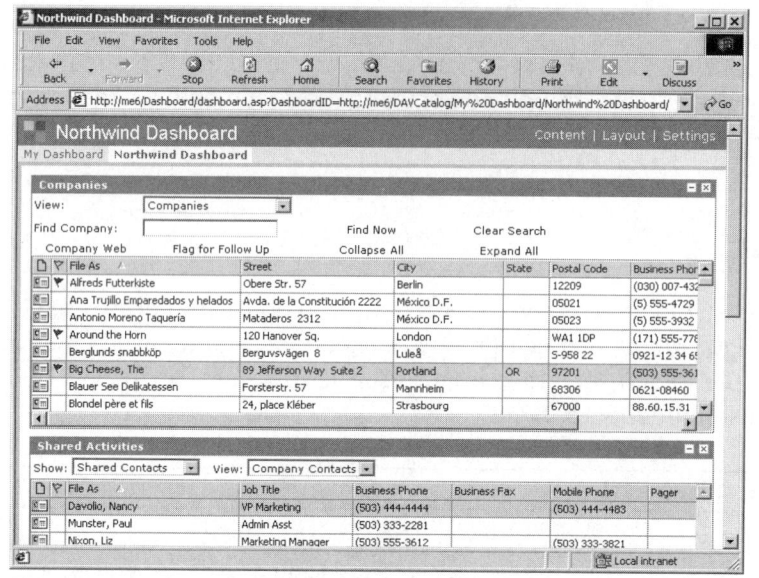

Figure 15-21 Northwind Dashboard hosted in Internet Explorer contains Companies, Shared Activities, and Sales Data Web Parts.

Northwind Dashboard Setup

In the "Creating My Dashboard" section, you learned how to create My Dashboard as well as its sub dashboard, the Northwind Dashboard. Before you attempt to run the sample Company, Sales Data, and Shared Activities Web Parts, there are some issues that you should be aware of:

- **Public Folder Path** The Northwind Dashboard Web Parts expect that the path to the Northwind Contact Management Application will be Public Folders\All Public Folders\Northwind Contact Management Application\Companies. You must install the Northwind Contact Management Application described in Chapter 12 before you can use the Northwind Dashboard. If the public folder path differs from the default, you must change the hard-coded folder paths in the script for the Companies and Shared Activities Web Parts. The scripts for the Northwind Dashboard Web Parts are written in JScript, so be sure to include an escape backslash character when you create your public folder path. This means that the path just described will become \\Public Folders\\All Public Folders\\Northwind Contact Management Application\\Companies.

- **Database Connection String**   The database connection string for the PivotTable List in the Sales Data Web Part is hard-coded into the Web Part. This Web Part expects you to have installed the Northwind database in c:\program files\microsoft office\office10\samples. If you want to extend these Web Parts for use in your own organization, you should edit the database connection string for the PivotTable List.

Web Part Flexibility

You can arrange Web Parts in the Northwind Dashboard to display information effectively. For example, Figure 15-22 shows the Sales Data Web Part directly below the Companies Web Part, which is where it's best displayed. The Sales Data Web Part expands its width to display the Office XP PivotTable List. When a user changes the selected company in the Companies Web Part, the Sales Data Web Part shows selected company sales information from the Northwind database in an Office XP PivotTable List.

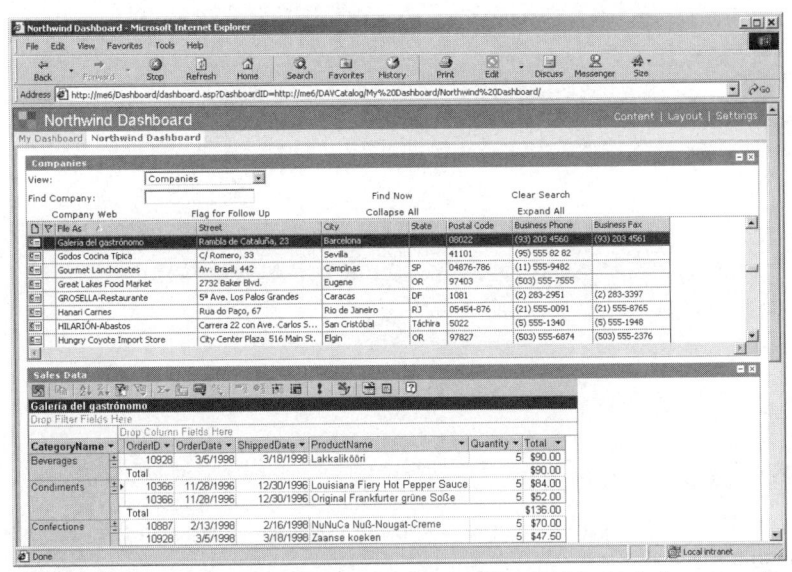

Figure 15-22   The sales information in the PivotTable List changes whenever you select another company in the Companies Web Part.

Browser Interface for a Public Folder Application

This type of interface is especially attractive for users who require enhanced discoverability. For example, the Companies Web Part contains buttons for commands that might be unfamiliar to some users. Putting such commands as Flag For Follow-Up in a visible position on the Web Part helps users learn your application without requiring complicated menu navigation.

Part V Advanced Topics

Quick Search

Another feature demonstrated by the Companies Web Part is Quick Search. If a user types any part of a company name in the Find edit box and clicks Find Now, the matching companies are shown in the Outlook View Control in the Companies Web Part. Figure 15-23 shows the results of a search for company names containing the word *the*. Notice that the result of the Quick Search is not case sensitive. This functionality results from programmatic use of the Outlook View Control's Restriction property. When the user has completed her search, she clicks the Clear Search button to return to a view of all the companies in the Companies folder.

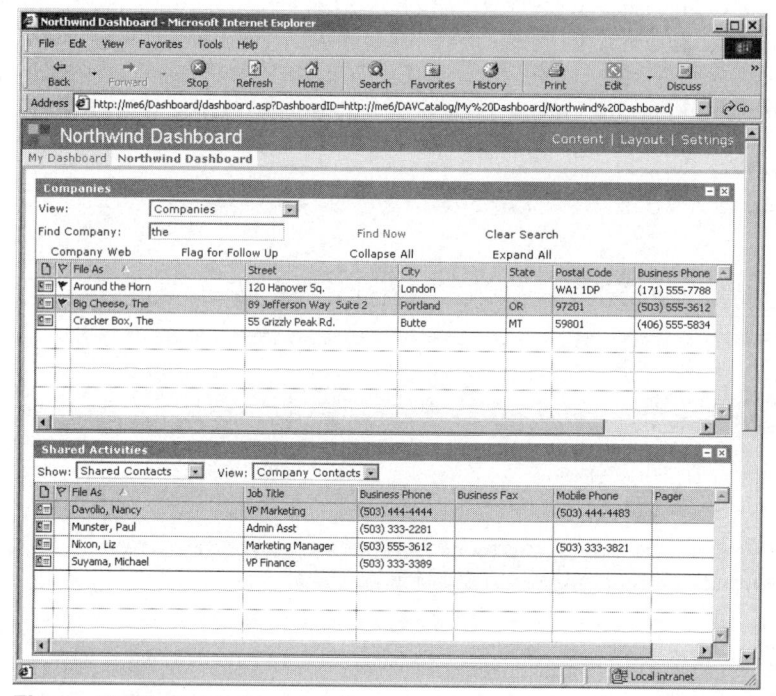

Figure 15-23 Quick Search returns company names that contain the text entered in the Find Company edit box.

The Quick Search function of the Northwind Dashboard has an interesting feature that results from an undocumented behavior of the Outlook 2002 View Control. If you enter a second value in the Find Company edit box after the initial search, the second value is treated as a logical AND to the original restriction. Returning to the previous example, if you initially enter the word *the* in the Find Company edit box, you will see three company items displayed in the Outlook View Control:

- Around The Horn
- The Big Cheese
- The Cracker Box

If you then enter the word *cheese* in the Find Company edit box and click Find Now, you will see only one company item for The Big Cheese displayed in the Outlook View Control. Click Clear Search to clear the Restriction property on the View Control and display all the items in the folder.

Track Shared Activities

Figure 15-24 shows the Northwind Dashboard with a layout that concentrates on shared activities. Analysts can view activities by company and compare the level of activity to the level of profitability. The Shared Activities Web Part derives directly from the Shared Activities page on the Company form in the Northwind Contact Management Application. A user can change the Shared Activities folder (Tasks, Calendar, Contacts, Documents, and Journal) and also change the view in the folder. Unlike the dynamic My Inbox Web Part discussed earlier in the chapter, the Shared Activities Web Part has folder and view names hard-coded into it.

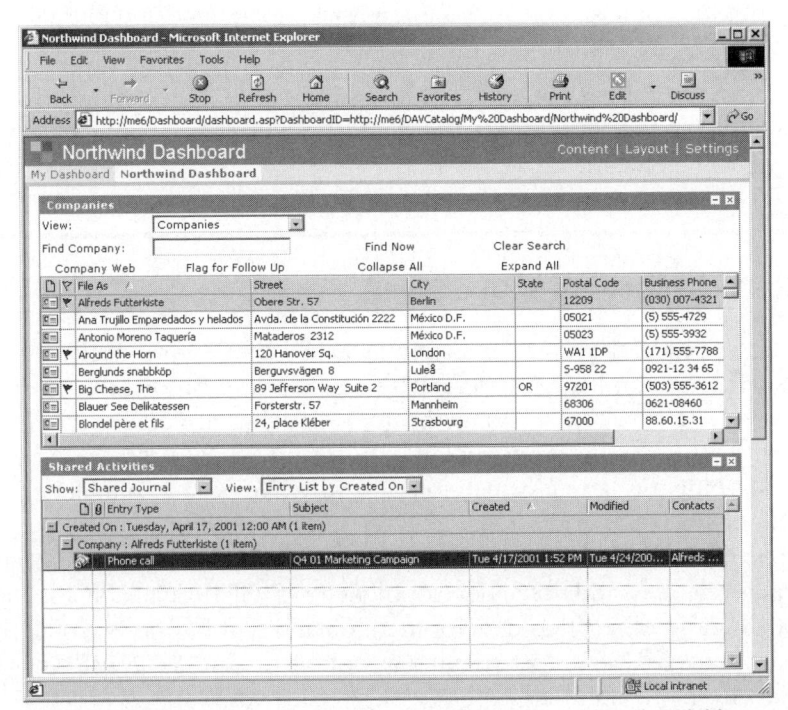

Figure 15-24 Shared Journal can track company-related activities such as phone calls and presentations.

Part V Advanced Topics

Communicating Between Web Parts

Web Part communication is what makes the Northwind Dashboard operate. Because the Outlook 2002 View Control supports events in general and the Selection Change event in particular, you can write a Web Part event handler. The Notification Service of the Digital Dashboard Services Component provides the mechanism for Web Part communication and hides the complexity of the underlying event mechanisms of DHTML events in the Web browser.

The DDSC Notification Service

By using the Notification Service of the DDSC, Web Parts indicate interest in an event and provide a handle to a function that will be called when the event runs. In the following JScript code for the Companies Web Part, the *ovcCompanies_WPQ_SelectionChange* event procedure calls the *RaiseEvent* method on the DDSC object. Three variables are made available to other Web Parts when the *PutSessionState* method is called on the DDSC:

- **Account** Contains the unique account number for the company. This account number is used to link related company contacts and other shared items, including shared appointment, task, document, and journal items.

- **CompanyID** Contains the unique company ID for the company in the Northwind database. The *CompanyID* variable is used in the WHERE clause of a SQL query that retrieves data for the PivotTable List in the Sales Data Web Part.

Welcome to the World of JScript

The code for the Companies, Sales Data, and Shared Activities Web Parts is written completely in JScript. It's a safe bet to predict that there are curly braces in your future. As an Outlook developer, you are already familiar with VBScript and most likely with Visual Basic. If you don't know JScript, learning this language would be worthwhile because it will help you write client-side code for Exchange 2000 and SharePoint Portal Server applications that run in a client browser. Once Microsoft's .NET development platform is released, additional development tools will be available for Digital Dashboards and other Web development. When that happens, you'll need to expand beyond VBScript and take a look at C# and VB.Net to increase your development options.

- **CompanyName** Contains the company name. This variable is equivalent to the CompanyName property in the custom Company form. The CompanyName property is used to supply the caption for the PivotTable List in the Sales Data Web Part.

```
<SCRIPT ID=clientEventHandlersJS LANGUAGE=JScript>

function ovcCompanies_WPQ__SelectionChange()
{
    if (ovcCompanies_WPQ_.Selection.Count == 1) {

    DDSC.PutSessionState(sNamespace_WPQ_, "Account",
        ovcCompanies_WPQ_.Selection(1).Account);
    DDSC.PutSessionState(sNamespace_WPQ_, "CompanyID",
        ovcCompanies_WPQ_.Selection(1).UserProperties("Company ID"));
    DDSC.PutSessionState(sNamespace_WPQ_, "CompanyName",
        ovcCompanies_WPQ_.Selection(1).CompanyName);
    }
    else
    {
    DDSC.PutSessionState(sNamespace_WPQ_, "Account", "");
    DDSC.PutSessionState(sNamespace_WPQ_, "CompanyID", "");
    DDSC.PutSessionState(sNamespace_WPQ_, "CompanyName", "");
    }
    DDSC.RaiseEvent (sNamespace_WPQ_, "CompanyChange");
}

function document_onkeydown(){
    //The enter key was pressed
    if (window.event.keyCode == 13)
    {
        btnFind_WPQ__onclick();
    }
}

</script>
```

The DDSC *RaiseEvent* method allows other Web Parts to become aware of the CompanyChange event. For example, you'll find that the Shared Activities Web Part calls the DDSC *RegisterForEvent* method to register itself for event messages transmitted by the CompanyChange event from the Companies Web Part. Both Web Parts share a common Web Part namespace of "urn:schemas-microeye-com:crm:companies". The following *RegisterForEvent* method code also runs the ChangeFilter_WPQ_ function when the CompanyChange event fires.

Part V   Advanced Topics

```
var sNamespace_WPQ_ = "urn:schemas-microeye-com:crm:companies";
//Error handler
try {
   DDSC.RegisterForEvent(sNamespace_WPQ_, "CompanyChange",
      ChangeFilter_WPQ_);
   DDSC.RegisterForEvent
      ("urn:schemas.microsoft.com:dhtml","onload",Init_WPQ_());
   }
catch(e){
   //Do nothing
}

function ChangeFilter_WPQ_()
{
   var sAccount = DDSC.GetSessionState(sNamespace_WPQ_, "Account");
   if (cmbShow_WPQ_.value == "Shared Contacts")
   {
   ovcSharedActivities_WPQ_.Restriction = "[Account] = \'"+sAccount+"\'";
   }
   else
   {
   ovcSharedActivities_WPQ_.Restriction = "[BillingInformation] = \'"+sAccount+"\'";
   }

}
```

This code uses the *Account* variable retrieved by the *GetSessionState* method to set the Restriction property for the Outlook View Control. Depending on the folder shown in the *ovcSharedActivities_WPQ_* View Control, the code uses the Account or Billing Information field to create the string used for the Restriction property. By using the Restriction string in this way you show only a subset of related company contacts in the Outlook View Control named *ovcSharedActivities_WPQ_*. Also note that, similar to the Companies and Sales Data Web Parts, the Shared Activities Web Part uses a *Try…Catch* construct to handle any errors that might occur when the page is loaded.

> **See Also**   For additional information on the DDSC *RegisterForEvent*, *RaiseEvent*, *PutSessionState*, and *GetSessionState* methods, see the book entitled "DDSC Object Model" in the documentation that accompanies DDRK 3.0.

The Companies Web Part

The critical function of the Companies Web Part is to raise an event to the other Web Parts in its namespace when the selected item changes in the Outlook View Control. Additional commands are placed above the View Control to enhance discoverability. For example, sales or service personnel might want to use the Flag For Follow-Up command to set reminders for company-related tasks. Like the My Inbox Web Part, the Companies Web Part displays a drop-down list for selection of available views for the Companies folder. However, the views for the Companies folder are hard-coded into this Web Part. The Init_WPQ_ function is responsible for loading the views into the Select control named *cmb_View_WPQ_*. Init_WPQ_ builds an array containing view names for the Companies folder and then passes *cmbView_WPQ_* and the array to the BuildSelect function. Here's the code:

```
<script language=javascript>
//Script-level variable
   var sNamespace_WPQ_ = "urn:schemas-microeye-com:crm:companies";
//Error handler
try {
    DDSC.RegisterForEvent("urn:schemas-microsoft-com:dhtml",
        "onload",Init_WPQ_());
    }
catch(e){
    //Do nothing
    }

function Init_WPQ_()
{   var el;
    var viewlist;
    //Load the View combo
    el = cmbView_WPQ_;
    viewlist = new Array();
    viewlist[0] = "By Company Category";
    viewlist[1] = "By Company Type";
    viewlist[2] = "By Country";
    viewlist[3] = "By Priority";
    viewlist[4] = "By Territory";
    viewlist[5] = "Companies";
    BuildSelect_WPQ_(el,viewlist);
    el.selectedIndex = 5;
    ChangeView_WPQ_();
}

function BuildSelect_WPQ_(el,newlist)
{
```

(continued)

Part V Advanced Topics

```
        var oOption;
        el.options.length = 0;
        for (i=0; i<newlist.length; i++)
        {
            oOption = document.createElement("OPTION");
            oOption.text = newlist[i];
            oOption.value = newlist[i];
            el.add(oOption);
        }
}

function cmbView_WPQ__onchange()
{
    ChangeView_WPQ_();
}

function ChangeView_WPQ_()
{
    //Change the view
    ovcCompanies_WPQ_.View = cmbView_WPQ_.value;
    //Clear the restriction
    ovcCompanies_WPQ_.Restriction = "";
    txtFind_WPQ_.innerText = "";
}
```

   The Companies Web Part also supports Quick Search. The user types a complete or partial company name into the Find Company edit box and then clicks Find Now or presses the Enter key. A Restriction string for the Outlook View Control is formed using the *txtFind_WPQ_* value, and the Restriction is applied to the View Control. When the user has completed the search, she clicks Clear Search to display all the companies in the Web Part. Here is the code that enables the Quick Search functionality in the Web Part:

```
function btnFind_WPQ__onclick()
{
    var sFind = txtFind_WPQ_.value;

    if (sFind.length > 0){
        ovcCompanies_WPQ_.Restriction = "[CompanyName] = \'"+sFind+"\'";
    }
}

function btnClear_WPQ__onclick()
{
    ovcCompanies_WPQ_.Restriction = "";
    txtFind_WPQ_.innerText = "";
    DDSC.RaiseEvent (sNamespace_WPQ_, "CompanyChange");
}
```

The Shared Activities Web Part

The Shared Activities Web Part is dependent upon the existence of the Companies Web Part. Without the Companies Web Part, the Shared Activities Web Part does not know which related company contacts or other shared items to display in its Outlook View Control. Like the Companies Web Part, the Shared Activities Web Part uses hard-coded values for select controls. The Shared Activities Web Part uses one drop-down list for folder selection and another for the views available in the selected folder.

The Shared Activities Web Part must register for two events in its script-level code. It registers for the DHTML onload event to load initial values into the Show and View Select controls. It also registers for the CompanyChange event so that it can change the shared items displayed in the Outlook View Control named *ovcSharedActivities_WPQ_* when a user selects a different company in the Companies Web Part. The key to this functionality is to use the Digital Dashboard's *RegisterForEvent* and *RaiseEvent* methods (explained earlier). The *PutSessionState* and *GetSessionState* methods provide a means of setting and getting properties.

The other important function of the Shared Activities Web Part is to allow the user to select a variety of folders and views similar to the Shared Activities page on the Company form in the Northwind Contact Management application. Most of the JScript code in the Shared Activities Web Part is in fact adapted from the VBScript code in the Company form. The following code shows you how the Shared Activities Web Part initializes its Select controls and then dynamically changes the values available in the *cmbView_WPQ_*, depending upon the value of *cmbShow_WPQ_*:

```
<SCRIPT LANGUAGE=javascript>
var sNamespace_WPQ_ = "urn:schemas-microeye-com:crm:companies";
//Error handler
try {
    DDSC.RegisterForEvent(sNamespace_WPQ_, "CompanyChange",
        ChangeFilter_WPQ_);
    DDSC.RegisterForEvent
        ("urn:schemas-microsoft-com:dhtml","onload",Init_WPQ_());
    window.status = "";
    }
catch(e){
    //Do nothing
    }
function Init_WPQ_()
{
    var el;
    var folderlist;
    //Load the Show combo
    el = cmbShow_WPQ_;
```

(continued)

Part V Advanced Topics

```
    folderlist = new Array();
    folderlist[0] = "Shared Mail";
    folderlist[1] = "Shared Calendar";
    folderlist[2] = "Shared Contacts";
    folderlist[3] = "Shared Documents";
    folderlist[4] = "Shared Journal";
    folderlist[5] = "Shared Tasks";
    BuildSelect_WPQ_(el,folderlist);
    el.selectedIndex = 2;
    ChangeFolder_WPQ_();
}

function AddOption_WPQ_(el,sText)
{
    var oOption = document.createElement("OPTION");
    oOption.text=sText;
    oOption.value=sText;
    el.add(oOption);
}

function BuildSelect_WPQ_(el,newlist)
{
    var oOption;
    el.options.length = 0;
    for (i=0; i<newlist.length; i++)
    {
        oOption = document.createElement("OPTION");
        oOption.text = newlist[i];
        oOption.value = newlist[i];
        el.add(oOption);
    }
}

function cmbShow_WPQ__onchange()
{
    ChangeFolder_WPQ_();
}

function ChangeFolder_WPQ_()
{
    var folder = cmbShow_WPQ_.value;
    var el = cmbView_WPQ_;
    var sRootFolder = \\Public Folders\\All Public Folders\\" +
        "Northwind Contact Management Application\\Companies\\";
    var viewlist = new Array();
    //Reset the View combo
    el.options.length = 0;
```

```
                switch (folder){
                    case "Shared Journal":
                        viewlist[0] = "Entry List by Created By";
                        viewlist[1] = "Entry List by Created On";
                        viewlist[2] = "By Type","Entry List";
                        viewlist[3] = "Last Seven Days";
                        viewlist[4] = "Phone Calls";
                        BuildSelect_WPQ_(el,viewlist);
                        el.selectedIndex = 0;
                        break;
                    case "Shared Mail":
                        viewlist[0] = "Messages";
                        viewlist[1] = "Messages with AutoPreview";
                        viewlist[2] = "By Sender";
                        viewlist[3] = "Last Seven Days";
                        viewlist[4] = "Sent To";
                        viewlist[5] = "Message Timeline";
                        BuildSelect_WPQ_(el,viewlist);
                        el.selectedIndex = 0;
                        break;
                    case "Shared Tasks":
                        viewlist[0] = "Active Tasks";
                        viewlist[1] = "Next Seven Days";
                        viewlist[2] = "Overdue Tasks";
                        viewlist[3] = "Completed Tasks";
                        viewlist[4] = "Task Timeline";
                        BuildSelect_WPQ_(el,viewlist);
                        el.selectedIndex = 0;
                        break;
                    case "Shared Calendar":
                        viewlist[0] = "Active Appointments";
                        viewlist[1] = "Recurring Appointments";
                        el.selectedIndex = 0;
                        BuildSelect_WPQ_(el,viewlist);
                        break;
                    case "Shared Contacts":
                        viewlist[0] = "Company Contacts";
                        viewlist[1] = "By Company";
                        BuildSelect_WPQ_(el,viewlist);
                        el.selectedIndex = 0;
                        break;
                    case "Shared Documents":
                        viewlist[0] = "All Documents";
                        viewlist[1] = "By Company";
                        viewlist[2] = "Last Seven Days";
                        BuildSelect_WPQ_(el,viewlist);
                        el.selectedIndex = 0;
                }
```

(continued)

Part V Advanced Topics

```
            ovcSharedActivities_WPQ_.Folder = sRootFolder+folder;
            ChangeFilter_WPQ_();
            ChangeView_WPQ_();
}
function cmbView_WPQ__onchange()
{
    ChangeView_WPQ_();
}

function ChangeView_WPQ_()
{
    //Change the view
    try {
        ovcSharedActivities_WPQ_.View = cmbView_WPQ_.value;
        window.status = "";
        }
    catch(e){
        //Do nothing
        }
}
```

The Sales Data Web Part

The Sales Data Web Part contains the results of a PivotTable query to the Northwind database. Be aware that the Northwind database path and the PivotTable connection string are hard-coded into the Web Part. If you install the Northwind database to a network share or use the Northwind SQL Server database, you will have to change the *sDBPath_WPQ_* and *sConnect_WPQ_* script-level variables in the Sales Data Web Part. Also, the Office XP Web Components must be installed on your computer before you can run the Sales Data Web Part. Because the Office Web Components are part of a default installation, this requirement should not pose a problem.

The HTML for the Pivot Table list is compact. Here is the required HTML for the Sales Data Web Part:

```
<OBJECT id=PivotTable_WPQ_
style="LEFT: 0px; TOP: 0px;"
classid=clsid:0002E552-0000-0000-C000-000000000046
VIEWASTEXT><PARAM NAME="XMLData"
VALUE='<xml xmlns:x="urn:schemas-microsoft-com:office:excel">
&#13;&#10;
<x:PivotTable>&#13;&#10;
<x:OWCVersion>10.0.0.2621
</x:OWCVersion>&#13;&#10;
<x:DisplayScreenTips/>&#13;&#10;
```

```
<x:CubeProvider>msolap.2
</x:CubeProvider>&#13;&#10;
<x:CacheDetails/>&#13;&#10;
<x:PivotView>&#13;&#10;
<x:IsNotFiltered/>&#13;&#10;
</x:PivotView>&#13;&#10;
</x:PivotTable>&#13;&#10;
</xml>'></OBJECT>
```

When the PivotTable is first displayed in the Northwind Dashboard, it does not display data. This is a recommended strategy, because loading data from a database during the DHTML onload event will impact the performance of the Web Part. However, when a user selects a company item in the Companies Web Part, the Sales Data Web Part uses the CompanyID property to create a query. This query is then assigned to the CommandText property of the PivotTable named *PivotList_WPQ_*, and it causes the PivotTable to display sales information grouped by category for the currently selected company in the Companies Web Part. To achieve this result, the Sales Data Web Part registers for the CompanyChange event in its script-level code by calling the *RegisterForEvent* method on the DDSC object. When the CompanyChange event occurs, the ChangePivot_WPQ_ function runs and retrieves the company ID using the *GetSessionState* method of the DDSC object. A dynamic SQL string is created and assigned to the CommandText property of *PivotList_WPQ_*. The following code shows you how to achieve this result:

```
<SCRIPT LANGUAGE=javascript>
//Script-level variable
var sNamespace_WPQ_ = "urn:schemas-microeye-com:crm:companies";
//Error handler
try {
    DDSC.RegisterForEvent(sNamespace_WPQ_, "CompanyChange",
        ChangePivot_WPQ_);
    window.status = "";
    }
catch(e){
    //Do nothing
    }
//Script-level variables
//Change the connection string for your installation//
Notice that \ must be escaped as \\
var sDBPath_WPQ_ =
    "C:\\Program Files\\Microsoft Office\\Office10\\Samples\\Northwind.mdb";
var sConnect_WPQ_ = "Provider=Microsoft.Jet.OLEDB.4.0;Data Source="+
    sDBPath_WPQ_+";Persist Security Info=False";
PivotTable_WPQ_.ConnectionString = sConnect_WPQ_;
```

(continued)

Part V Advanced Topics

```javascript
function ChangePivot_WPQ_(){
    var plFunctionSum = 1;
    var sCompanyID = DDSC.GetSessionState(sNamespace_WPQ_, "CompanyID");
    var sCompanyName = DDSC.GetSessionState(sNamespace_WPQ_, "CompanyName");

    //Create dynamic SQL string for PivotTable
    var sSQL = "Select * From (SELECT Orders.CustomerID, Orders.OrderID," +
        " Employees.LastName,";
    sSQL += "Orders.EmployeeID, Orders.OrderDate, Orders.ShippedDate, " +
        "Categories.CategoryName,";
    sSQL += "Products.ProductName, [Order Details].UnitPrice, " +
        "[Order Details].Quantity,[Order Details].Discount,";
    sSQL += "CCur([Order Details].[UnitPrice]*[Quantity]*" +
        "(1-[Discount])/100)*100 AS Total FROM ";
    sSQL += "Employees INNER JOIN ((Categories INNER JOIN Products " +
        "ON Categories.CategoryID = Products.CategoryID) ";
    sSQL += "INNER JOIN (Orders INNER JOIN [Order Details] " +
        "ON Orders.OrderID = [Order Details].OrderID) ";
    sSQL += "ON Products.ProductID = [Order Details].ProductID) " +
        "ON Employees.EmployeeID = Orders.EmployeeID)";
    sSQL += " WHERE CustomerID = \'" + sCompanyID + "\'";

    PivotTable_WPQ_.CommandText = sSQL;

    var ActView = PivotTable_WPQ_.ActiveView;
    var fldSets = ActView.FieldSets;

    //Group by
    ActView.RowAxis.InsertFieldSet(fldSets.Item("CategoryName"));
    //Row data
    ActView.DataAxis.InsertFieldSet(fldSets("OrderID"));
    ActView.DataAxis.InsertFieldSet(fldSets("OrderDate"));
    ActView.DataAxis.InsertFieldSet(fldSets("ShippedDate"));
    ActView.DataAxis.InsertFieldSet(fldSets("ProductName"));
    ActView.DataAxis.InsertFieldSet(fldSets("Quantity"));
    ActView.DataAxis.InsertFieldSet(fldSets.Item("Total"));
    fldSets("Total").Fields(0).NumberFormat = "Currency";
    //Add a total
    var Tot = ActView.AddTotal("Total ",fldSets("Total").Fields.Item(0),
        PivotTable_WPQ_.Constants.plFunctionSum);
    ActView.DataAxis.InsertTotal(Tot);
    //Set caption to company name
    ActView.TitleBar.Caption = sCompanyName;
}
</script>
```

Putting It All Together

Now that you've seen how Web Parts are built, you can display the Northwind Dashboard as the folder home page for the Companies Public Folder, as shown in Figure 15-1 on page 712. Here is a checklist that you should follow before using the Northwind Dashboard as a folder home page for the Companies folder:

- Install the Northwind Contact Management application into Public Folders as described in Chapter 12.
- Install the Office XP Web Components. The Office XP Web Components are installed by default, so this requirement should not pose an issue.
- Create the Northwind Dashboard as described earlier in the chapter in "Creating My Dashboard."
- If necessary, adjust the folder paths in the Companies and Shared Activities Web Parts.
- If necessary, adjust the database path and the ConnectionString in the Sales Data Web Part.

Setting the Folder Home Page for the Companies Folder

Assuming that you've followed the instructions to install the correct components on your computer, you can set the folder home page for the Companies folder. The next set of instructions assume that you will set the folder home page for the Companies folder in Public Folder\All Public Folders\Northwind Contact Management Application\Companies.

To set a folder home page for the Companies folder

1. In the Folder List, right-click the Companies folder in the Northwind Contact Management Application folder under All Public Folders and then click Properties on the shortcut menu.
2. Click the Home Page tab, as illustrated in Figure 15-25.
3. Check the Show Home Page By Default For This Folder box.
4. Enter the URL for the Northwind Dashboard in the Address edit box. If you installed the Northwind Dashboard according to the earlier instructions, the URL for your Northwind Dashboard should resemble the following:

*http://<servername>/Dashboard/dashboard.asp?DashboardID=http://
<servername>/DAVCatalog/My%20Dashboard/Northwind%20
Dashboard/*

5. Be sure to replace *<servername>* with the name of the computer on which you have installed the sample DDRK 3.0 SQL Server 2000 Dashboard. If you install My Dashboard and Northwind Dashboard on a SharePoint Portal Server Digital Dashboard, be sure to adjust the URL accordingly.

6. Click OK.

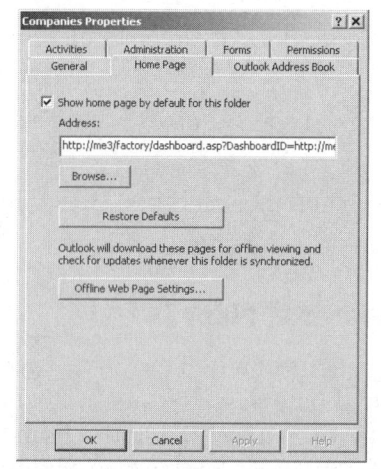

Figure 15-25 Set the Northwind Dashboard as the folder home page for the Companies folder.

Navigating to the Companies Folder

You should now be able to navigate to the Companies folder and see the Northwind Dashboard displayed in Outlook. Here are some features of the Northwind Dashboard that you'll want to test.

Using the Outlook View Control

- Double-clicking an item in the Outlook View Control will open the item.
- Right-clicking the Outlook View Control will display shortcut menus.
- Selecting a view in the View drop-down list will change the view displayed in the Companies or Shared Activities Web Parts.

- Selecting a folder in the Show drop-down list will change the folder displayed in the Shared Activities Web Part. When you select a different folder, the views listed in the View drop-down list change accordingly.

Using the Command Buttons

- Clicking the command buttons in the Companies Web Part enhances discoverability for the Northwind Contact Management application. For example, clicking the Expand All and Collapse All buttons changes the view in a Group By View, such as By Country.

- Clicking the Flag For Follow-Up command button displays the Flag For Follow-Up dialog box for the selected company in the Companies Web Part.

- Clicking the Company Web command button opens the company Web page in a separate browser window. If the company does not have a URL stored in the company item, an alert box indicating that there's no Web address for the company will appear.

Finding a Company

- Enter a find string in the Find Company edit box, and click the Find Now button to display a subset of customers in the Outlook View Control. The string you type in the Find Company edit box creates a Restriction on the View Control when you click the Find Now button and displays a subset of Company items. For example, if you enter the word *The* in the edit box and then click Find, all company names containing *The* will appear in the View Control.

- Click the Clear Search button to display all the items in the current view in the Companies folder.

Changing the Layout

- You can change the layout of the Northwind Dashboard to suit your monitor capabilities and personal preferences.

- Click the Layout link on the Northwind Dashboard page to change the layout of Web Parts.

- Drag and drop the Web Parts on the Layout page, and then click OK to accept your changes.

Part V Advanced Topics

Where To Go from Here

Microsoft Knowledge Base Articles   Microsoft Knowledge Base articles are available on the Web at *http://support.microsoft.com/support*. Also see "Integrating Outlook with Web Applications (Chapter 15) KB Articles" in the Microsoft Web Sites folder under the Help And Web Sites folder on the companion CD.

Digital Dashboard Articles and Resources

- You'll find the Digital Dashboard Resource Kit 3.0 and later available at *http://www.microsoft.com/business/DigitalDashboard*.

- The Digital Dashboard Business Process Assessment Guide is available at *http://www.microsoft.com/business/digitaldashboard/ddbpag.asp*.

- The white paper, "Integrating Microsoft Project Central into a Digital Dashboard," is available at *http://www.microsoft.com/business/digital-dashboard/ProjCen.asp*.

16

Using Outlook with SharePoint Portal Server

Microsoft SharePoint Portal Server 2001 provides an out-of-the-box portal application for companies that want to provide document management, integrated search capabilities, and content subscription to their users in an integrated Digital Dashboard application. Figure 16-1 shows an example of such an application. Like Microsoft Exchange 2000, SharePoint Portal Server uses the Web Storage System (WSS) as its core engine. Unlike traditional data repositories, the Web Storage System excels at storing multiple types of unstructured data in one data storage container. In SharePoint Portal Server, the Web Storage System is synonymous with the Document store. Using the Document store, SharePoint Portal Server offers a rich set of collaboration services, such as document-based, folder-based, and category-based threaded discussions, announcements, and query-based subscriptions and notifications.

Be careful to distinguish SharePoint Portal Server from the SharePoint Team Services product that ships with Microsoft Office XP. SharePoint Portal Server is a separate entity that requires its own server and client access licenses. While SharePoint Team Services does allow Web-based collaboration and discussions, it does not offer the advanced document management and search services of SharePoint Portal Server.

As a Microsoft Outlook developer, you're bound to be more interested in the functionality of the SharePoint Portal Server product than that of SharePoint Team Services. You can integrate Outlook-based Web Parts into the SharePoint Dashboard, and you can use the powerful search capabilities of the SharePoint engine to search the Exchange public folder hierarchy. Unlike an Outlook-based search, which searches only a single public folder at a time, a SharePoint search can scan a public folder hierarchy that includes subfolders of the root folder. A SharePoint search catalog is known as a content source. Content sources can include Web sites, file shares, public folder hierarchies on Exchange 5.5 or Exchange 2000 servers, other SharePoint Portal Servers, and Lotus Notes Servers.

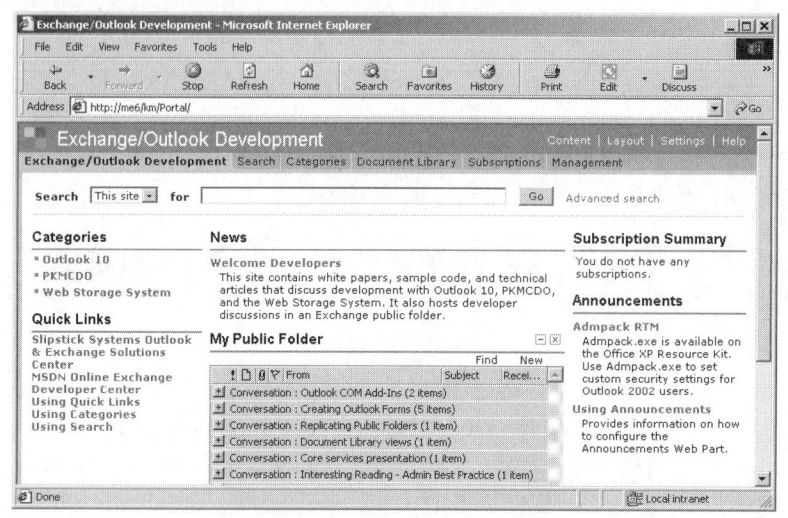

Figure 16-1 The SharePoint Portal Server Dashboard is composed of several dashboards, each containing specialized Web Parts.

From a developer's perspective, SharePoint Portal Server offers URL addressability for every item in its store, a very granular permissions structure, and data access through multiple object models. These object models include:

- ActiveX Data Objects (ADO).

- MSDAIPP, using the World Wide Web Distributed Authoring and Versioning protocol (WebDAV). MSDAIPP is the Microsoft OLE DB Provider for Internet Publishing.

- Collaboration Data Objects for Exchange (CDOEX).

- XMLHTTP COM component. The XMLHTTP COM component is part of the Microsoft XML Parser (MSXML).

Additionally, by default Office XP installs an object library known as PKMCDO, or Publishing and Knowledge Management Collaboration Data Objects. PKMCDO is consequently available as a client-side object library. PKMCDO lets you programmatically check in, check out, and publish documents to SharePoint Portal Server folders. SharePoint Portal Server development in relation to Web Parts, the SharePoint document store, and PKMCDO could justify an entire book. However, this chapter specifically covers how you can use SharePoint services to enhance Outlook folder home pages or integrate Outlook information. We'll examine a code example of a COM Add-in that lets you select attachments in a message and automatically publish them to a SharePoint Portal Server workspace. Before we discuss the sample code in this chapter, let's review the important components of the SharePoint Portal Server platform.

> **See Also** If you are new to SharePoint Portal Server development, familiarizing yourself with the Exchange SDK and the SharePoint Portal Server SDK should be your top priority. The most recent versions of the Exchange SDK and the SharePoint Portal Server SDK are available on the book's companion CD. Updates to the Exchange SDK and SharePoint Portal Server SDK are issued periodically. To download the latest version of the Exchange SDK, visit *http://msdn.microsoft.com/exchange*. To download the latest version of the SharePoint Portal Server SDK, visit *http://www.microsoft.com/sharepoint*.

SharePoint Portal Server Evaluation Edition

To follow the code samples presented in this chapter, you need a copy of the SharePoint Portal Server evaluation edition. You can obtain this edition either from the CD version of the Digital Dashboard Resource Kit 3.0 or as a Web download from *http://www.microsoft.com/sharepoint/downloads*. Follow the setup documentation carefully to avoid problems running the code examples in this chapter. To run the code examples, your Microsoft Windows NT account should be assigned the Workspace Coordinator role. Although you can install SharePoint Portal Server on a variety of platforms, you will get the best results if you install the evaluation edition on a Windows 2000 member server in a domain.

SharePoint Portal Server Platform

The SharePoint Portal Server platform is composed of many elements, including workspaces, folders, enhanced folders, documents, categories, and content sources. Each one of these components has an object model equivalent in the PKMCDO object library. Unlike Exchange 2000, in the SharePoint Portal Server platform you can enumerate these objects from client-side PKMCDO code. Let's take a look at the major elements of the SharePoint Portal Server environment.

Part V   Advanced Topics

The Workspace

The SharePoint Portal Server platform contains one or more workspaces. Each workspace contains a collection of folders, management tools, categories, and indexed information in which users in an organization can store and manage documents. You can also think of the workspace as the root-level container for all folders that comprise the workspace. In the world of Outlook and Exchange, it's convenient to think of the Exchange store as a collection of folders and items. The same concept can be applied to SharePoint Portal Server, except that the items are documents rather than Outlook items.

To establish a workspace, you use the SharePoint Portal Server Administration application and the New Workspace Wizard. When you install SharePoint Portal Server, the New Workspace Wizard prompts you to create a workspace. Let's assume that you want to create a new workspace to search for content in the Northwind Contact Management application. If you've installed the application discussed in Chapter 12, "The Northwind Contact Management Application," follow these steps to create a workspace named Northwind.

To create the Northwind workspace

1. On the computer where SharePoint Portal Server is installed, log in as an Administrator and click Start.

2. On the Programs menu, click Administrative Tools and then click SharePoint Portal Server Administration.

3. In the SharePoint Portal Server Administration console, right-click the server name in the Tree view and select Workspace on the New pop-up menu.

4. The New Workspace Wizard will start. Click Next. In the Workplace Definition screen provide a name for your workspace, as shown in Figure 16-2.

5. Click Next, and then provide a contact name and contact e-mail address for your workspace.

6. Click Finish to create the workspace.

Using Outlook with SharePoint Portal Server   Chapter 16

Use the SharePoint Portal Server Administrator Program to create a new workspace.

Enter workspace name and description in the New Workspace Wizard dialog box.

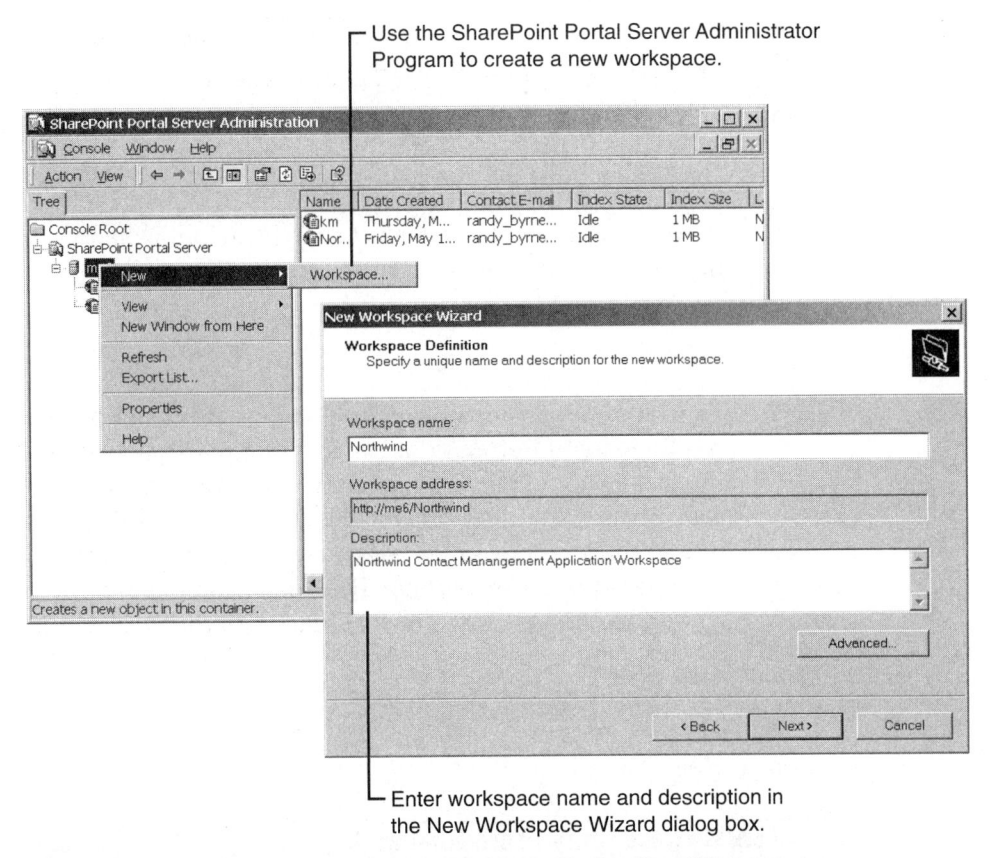

Figure 16-2 Create the Northwind workspace with the New Workspace Wizard.

SharePoint Portal Server Roles

SharePoint Portal Server uses a role-based security model to determine the level of access granted to a visitor to the Dashboard site. The following roles are supported on SharePoint Portal Server:

- **Coordinator on the workspace** Lets you configure general workspace settings, user permissions, document profiles, content sources, categories, and workspace index settings.

- **Coordinator on a specific folder** Lets you configure subfolders, user permissions, approval processes, and publishing settings for a specific folder.

789

Part V Advanced Topics

- **Author** Lets you store, manage, and search for workspace documents and indexed content from content sources.

- **Reviewer** With this role, you can review, approve, or reject documents that are submitted for publication. You can also provide feedback to the submitter of the document.

- **Reader** Lets you browse and search for published documents and indexed content from content sources. This role provides read-only access to the workspace.

> **See Also** For additional information on SharePoint Portal Server roles, see "Roles and Permissions" in SharePoint Portal Server User's Help and "Configuring Security" in SharePoint Portal Server Administrator's Help. SharePoint Portal Server User's Help is available at the root level of a SharePoint Portal Server workspace. Open a Web folder for the workspace to access this help. The Administrator's Help is located in the Docs folder on the SharePoint Portal Server Installation CD.

You need to create roles for the Northwind workspace that you just developed. Roles can be at either the folder or workspace level.

To create roles for the Northwind workspace

1. On the computer where SharePoint Portal Server is installed, log in as an administrator and click Start.

2. On the Programs menu, click Administrative Tools and then click SharePoint Portal Server Administration.

3. In the SharePoint Portal Server Administration console, right-click the Northwind workspace in the Tree view and select Properties on the Shortcut menu.

4. Click the Security tab on the Northwind Properties dialog box, as shown in Figure 16-3.

5. Change the default role for all users from Reader to Author by selecting Everyone in the User Or Group list box and then selecting Author in the Role drop-down list.

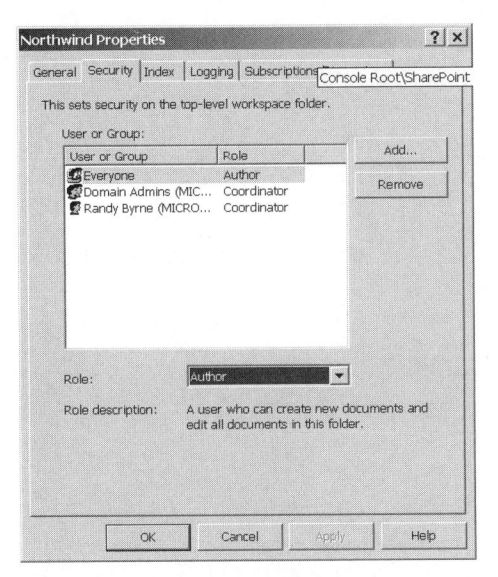

Figure 16-3 Set roles for the Northwind workspace in the Security tab on the Workspace Properties dialog box.

6. Add security groups as necessary by clicking the Add button and then selecting the group or Windows NT user account from the Select Users Or Groups dialog box. For example, you might add the Domain Admins group for your domain and assign the Coordinator role to this group. You could also create a separate security group named SharePoint Admins and assign it to the Coordinator role.

7. Click OK.

You are now ready to open the Northwind Dashboard in your browser and customize the Northwind Dashboard site. The Dashboard site is a Digital Dashboard that is generated automatically when you create a workspace. You navigate to your workspace Dashboard site by entering the following URL in Microsoft Internet Explorer:

http://<*servername*>/<*workspacename*>

When you navigate to the Northwind Dashboard site by entering *http:// <servername>/Northwind* in Internet Explorer, you will see a workspace home page similar to the one illustrated in Figure 16-4. Later in this chapter, in the section "Outlook Integration with SharePoint Portal Server," you'll customize the content of the Northwind Dashboard site.

Part V Advanced Topics

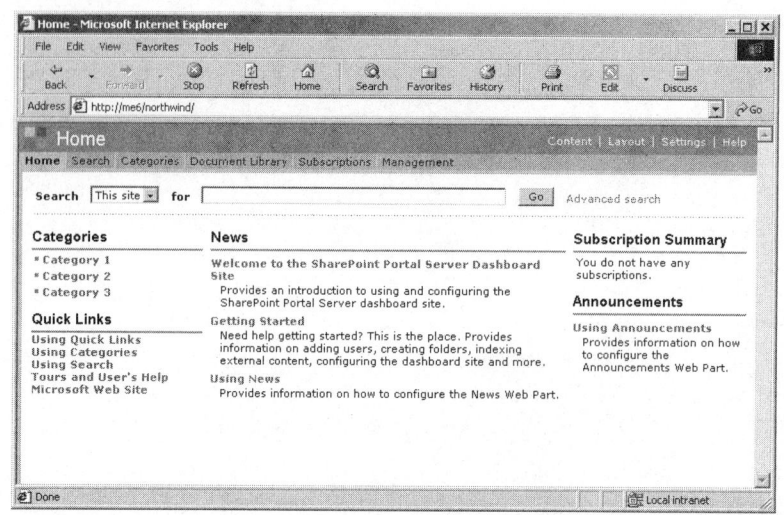

Figure 16-4 The Northwind Dashboard site before it has been customized.

Document Management

Perhaps the most important feature of SharePoint Portal Server is its ability to perform document management using a special set of workspace folders known as enhanced folders. Enhanced folders support all document management features, including check in, check out, public and private views for workspace documents, document profiling, document version history, and an approval process for making documents public. Although you can view any document through your Web browser, document check in and check out requires Office 2000 or Office XP. (We'll discuss document check in and check out states in a moment.)

The required components for SharePoint Portal Server document management are installed with Office XP by default. If you use Office 2000 for document management functions, you need to perform a separate client installation. The client installation does not install a client program per se that can be run from the Start menu. But it does install the necessary components to enable Web folders and SharePoint Portal Server document management in Microsoft Word, Excel, and PowerPoint.

> **See Also** For additional information about server and client setup procedures for SharePoint Portal Server, see the Planning And Installation help file in the Docs folder on the SharePoint Portal Server Installation CD.

When you create a workspace, a default set of enhanced folders for document management is created for you. The default document management folder is named Documents. The Documents folder is available through the Dashboard site when you click the Document Library tab on the Dashboard Site Web page. To open the Documents folder in your browser, click the Documents folder link on the Document Library page, as shown in Figure 16-5.

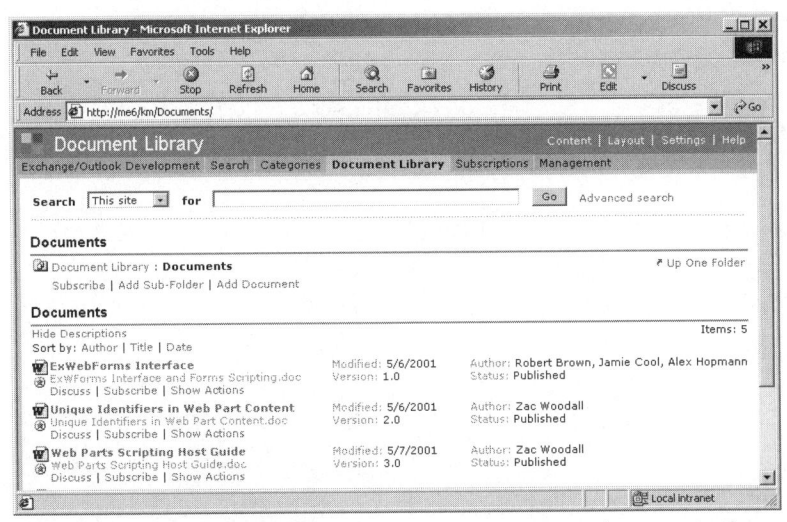

Figure 16-5 The Documents folder lets you manage documents through a browser.

Using Web Folders

Web folders provide an additional interface for the management and content of a SharePoint Portal Server. For example, you can access Document folders through Web folders in Windows Explorer, as shown in Figure 16-6.

> **Note** The Web folder interface depicted in Figure 16-6 contains hidden folders. To see these hidden folders, select Folder Options on the Windows Explorer Tools menu, click the View tab, and select the Show Hidden Files And Folders option in the Advanced Settings list box.

To establish a Web folder in Windows Explorer, you first should ensure that you have the correct permissions on the workspace to which you want to connect. Once your permissions have been established correctly, follow the steps in the next procedural section to add a Web folder.

Part V Advanced Topics

Figure shows two Windows Explorer windows with callouts:
- the KM workspace in a Web Folder view
- The Documents Folder is a SharePoint Portal Server Enhanced Folder.
- The shortcut menu contains commands for Document Management.

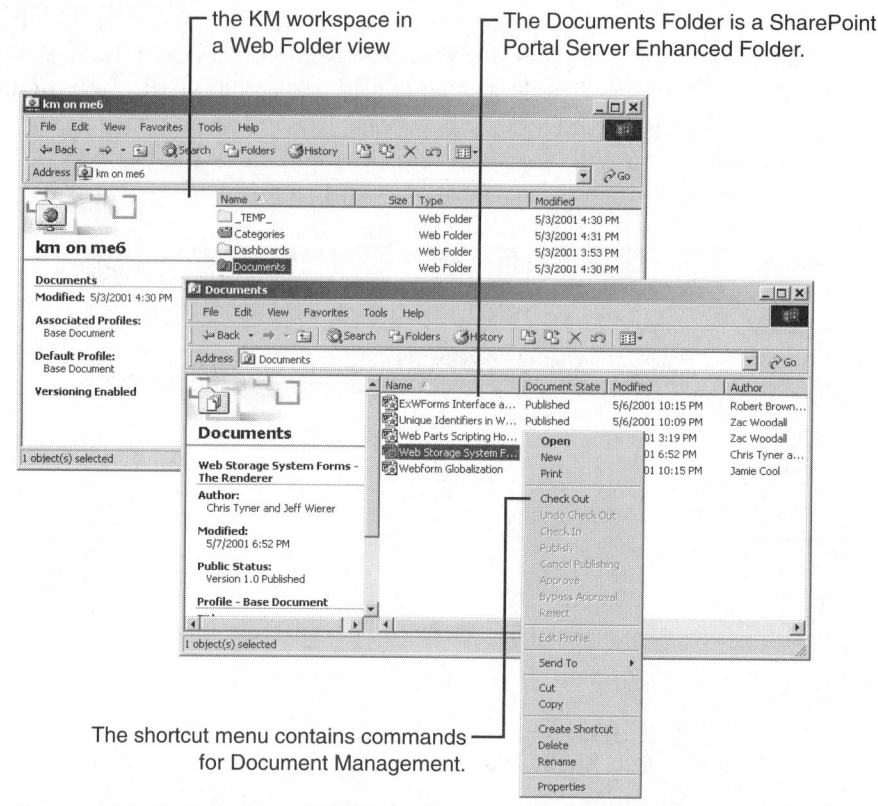

Figure 16-6 Web folders in Windows Explorer provide an additional interface for accessing SharePoint Portal Server content and administration.

To create a Web folder on Windows 98 or Windows NT

1. On the Windows desktop, double-click My Computer.
2. In My Computer, double-click Web Folders.
3. Double-click Add Web Folder.
4. Enter the URL for a SharePoint Portal Server workspace or folder, and then click Next. Assuming that you have created a Northwind workspace, enter *http://<servername>/Northwind*, where <servername> is the name of your SharePoint Portal Server computer.
5. Enter the display name of your Web folder, and click Finish.

To create a Web folder on Windows Me or Windows 2000

1. On the Windows desktop, double-click My Network Places.
2. In My Network Places, double-click Add Network Place.

3. Enter the URL for a SharePoint Portal Server workspace or folder, and then click Next. Assuming that you have created a Northwind workspace, enter *http://<servername>/Northwind*, where <servername> is the name of your SharePoint Portal Server computer.

4. Enter the display name of your network place, and click Finish.

> **Note** If you cannot successfully connect to your SharePoint Portal Server workspace, check your Internet Explorer connection settings. Select Options on the Internet Explorer Tools menu, click the Connections tab, and then click the LAN Settings button. If you are using a proxy server, be sure to check the Bypass Proxy Server For Local Addresses check box in the Local Area Network (LAN) Settings dialog box.

Check In and Check Out

Documents in SharePoint Portal Server have several states that reflect their status in the publication process. Document check in and check out as well as the document management process apply only to enhanced folders. All subfolders of the main Documents folder in a default workspace are enhanced folders. Standard folders are analogous to file system folders. They can contain HTML documents or other items, but you cannot use the document management process for SharePoint standard folders.

SharePoint document states are summarized in the following table.

Document State	Description
Checked In	A checked-in document can be viewed and read by other users. The check in process makes the latest version of the document available to other users. When a document is checked in, a new version number is assigned to the document and the previous version is archived.
Checked Out	A checked-out document cannot be viewed by other users. It can be viewed by the document author or a workspace coordinator, however. A checked-out document is one that's being edited or has been added to the Documents folder without being checked in. An author must check in a document after editing is complete in order for other users to see the changes.

(continued)

Part V Advanced Topics

Document State	Description
Pending Approval	A document in this state requires approval by a user with the Approver role before it can be published.
Published	A published document is available to all users with permissions to view or check out the document for editing. When a document is published, and there is approval routing defined for that document, the routing is initiated. A document must be checked in before it can be published.

Document Profiling

When a user checks in a document, he is prompted for properties such as title, author, keywords, and description, as shown in Figure 16-7. The SharePoint document properties dialog box is directly related to the Properties dialog box in Word, Excel, or PowerPoint that appears when you select the Properties command on the File menu. The properties in a document profile constitute metadata on the document. You can use that metadata to search or organize views of documents in a Documents folder.

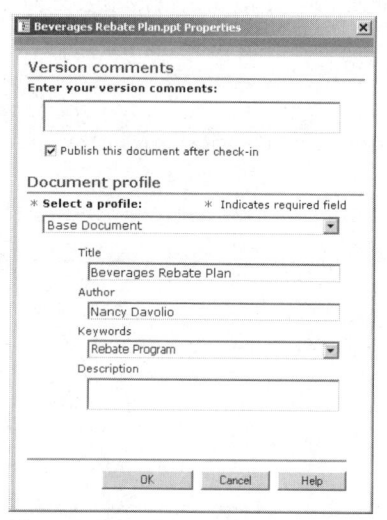

Figure 16-7 Document properties provide metadata for searching and organizing documents.

By default, SharePoint Portal Server uses a Base Document profile for document profiling. A workspace or folder coordinator can create additional document profiles that prompt a user for properties such as Categories, Company, and Subject, or for custom properties such as CompanyType and CompanyPriority. You can also modify the existing Base Document profile. For example, a coordinator for the Northwind SharePoint Dashboard can define a new document profile named Northwind Document. Follow the next set of steps to create a document profile named Northwind Document and make it available to the Documents folder in the Northwind workspace. You must be a workspace coordinator to accomplish this task.

To add a new document profile named Northwind Document

1. Open the Web folder for the Northwind workspace.
2. Navigate to the Document Profiles folder under the Management folder.
3. Double-click the Add Document Profile item.
4. The Document Profile Wizard will launch. Click Next.
5. Enter *Northwind Document* in the Name edit box, and click Next.
6. Click the New button to add custom properties. Add custom properties for CompanyName, CompanyType, CompanyCategory, CompanyPriority, and CompanyTerritory. These are all Text properties, and they correspond to UserProperties on the Company form in the Northwind Contact Management application. Do not check the Require Users To Enter A Value For This Property box in the Add New Property dialog box. Make sure that all the custom properties that you have defined are checked in the list of properties shown in Figure 16-8. Then click Next.
7. You can rearrange the order of properties by clicking the up or down arrows. Then click Next.
8. Click Finish.

Once you have created the Northwind Document Profile, you must enable it in the Documents folder. After you enable the Northwind Document Profile, the properties are available for searching documents using Advanced Search on the Search Dashboard.

Part V Advanced Topics

Click the New button to create a new property in the Add Document Profile Wizard dialog box.

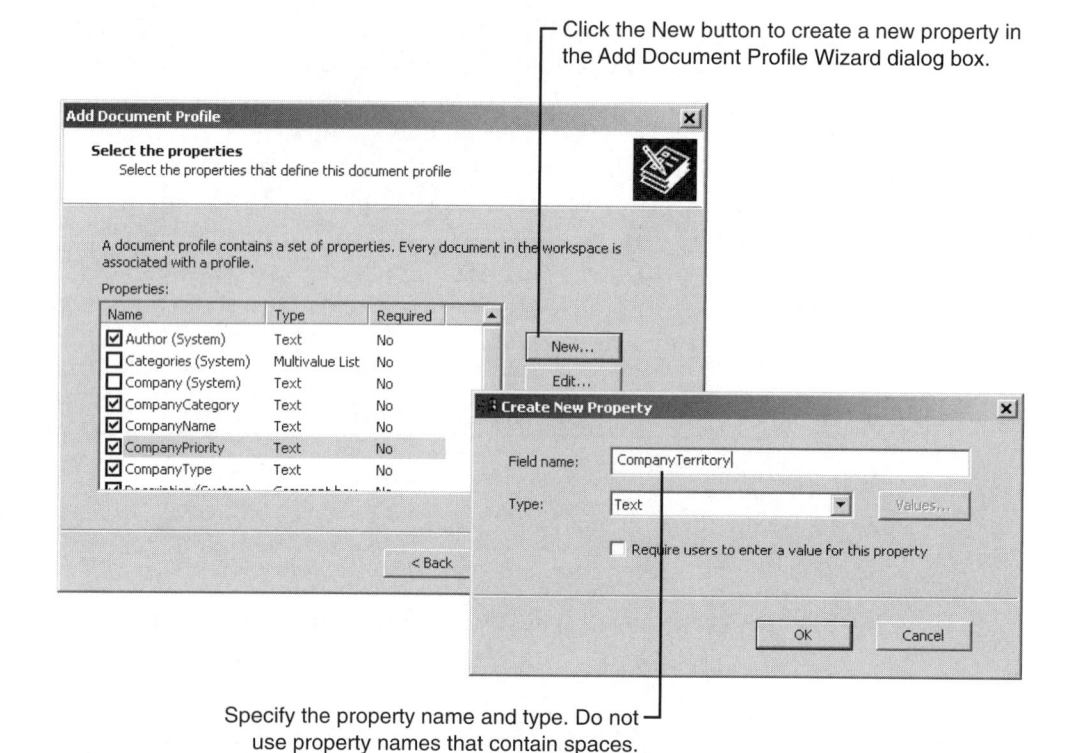

Figure 16-8 Use the Add Document Profile Wizard to define custom properties for the Northwind Document profile.

Specify the property name and type. Do not use property names that contain spaces.

To set the Northwind Document Profile as the default document profile

1. Open the Web folder for the Northwind workspace.
2. Right-click the Documents folder, and select the Properties command.
3. Click the Profiles page on the Document Properties sheet, as shown in Figure 16-9.
4. Uncheck the Base Document Profile so that it isn't available for use in the Northwind Documents folder.
5. Check the Northwind Document Profile, and select Northwind Document in the Use The Following Profile By Default For Documents In This Folder drop-down list.
6. Click OK.

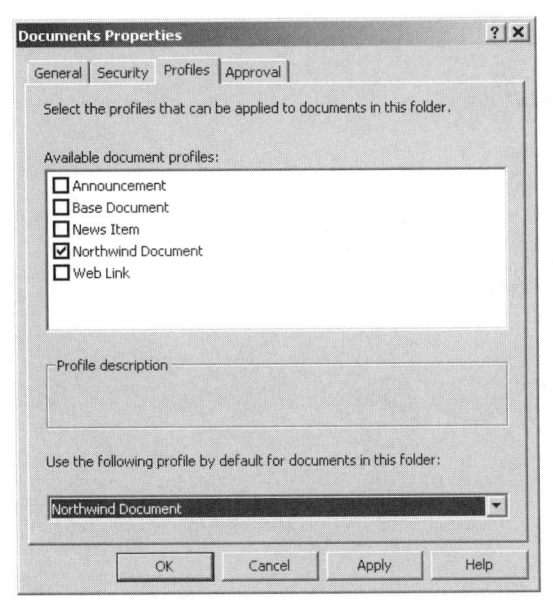

Figure 16-9 Make the Northwind Document Profile the default document profile.

> **Note** When you establish a profile for a document, you change its Dav:contentclass property. For example, a document that uses the Northwind Document Profile automatically has a Dav:contentclass property equivalent to urn:content-classes:Northwind Document. The contentclass property is analogous to the Message class of an Outlook item. For additional information on content classes in general, see the Exchange SDK. For specific information on the PKMCDO Knowledge-ContentClass object, see the SharePoint Portal Server SDK.

Approval Routing

Approval routing is another important feature of SharePoint document management. Approval routing lets you route a checked-in document to a serial or parallel list of approvers. These approvers must accept the document before it can be published to a Documents folder. By default, approval routing is turned off in the Documents folder and its subfolders. SharePoint Portal Server has two basic types of approval routing: serial routing and parallel routing. Figure 16-10 illustrates both these types.

Part V   Advanced Topics

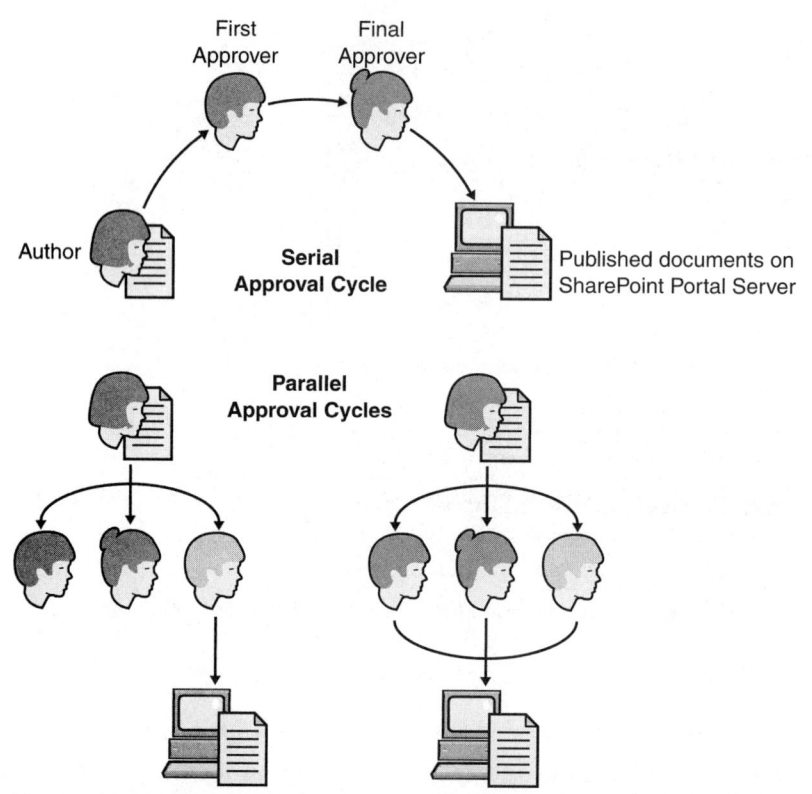

Figure 16-10 SharePoint Portal Server supports both serial and parallel routing.

When a document is waiting for approval by reviewers, it cannot be checked out or edited. If a workspace or folder coordinator wants to bypass the approval process for a specific document, she can select the Bypass Approval command on the shortcut menu for the item in the Web folder view.

If a reviewer has an e-mail address, the approval request notification arrives via e-mail. Reviewers can approve the document using the e-mail notification sent to their Inbox or the shortcut menu in a Web folder view. The following list highlights some of the most important aspects of serial and parallel routing approval:

- **Serial approval**   The first member of the approvers list receives a request-for-approval notification when a document is published to a Documents folder. After the first person on the list approves the document, the next person on the list receives a request for approval, and so on. The document is published only after all the approvers accept the document. If any person on the list rejects the document, the approval process is canceled and the document is returned to a checked-in state.

- **Parallel approval** This approval model is based on voting. The coordinator of the specific enhanced folder can choose one of two voting strategies: single or all. In the single voting strategy, one vote of approval publishes the document; in the all strategy, acceptance by all approvers publishes the document.

> **Note** Routing is automatic because of Web Storage System event sinks that are built into the SharePoint workspace. Do not attempt to modify the event sinks in the SharePoint Portal Server workspace with the Exchange Workflow Designer or the Web Storage System Explorer.

Remember that approval routing is turned off in an enhanced folder by default. Moreover, approval routing does not propagate to subfolders of a folder that has approval routing enabled. If you want to turn on approval routing, use the following steps.

To enable approval routing for an enhanced folder

1. Open the Web folder for the Northwind workspace.
2. Navigate to the enhanced folder for which you want to enable approval routing.
3. Right-click the folder, and select Properties from the Shortcut menu.
4. Click the Approval page on the Document Properties sheet.
5. Check the Documents Must Be Approved Before Publishing box.
6. Click the Add button to select users from the Select Users dialog box.
7. Select an approver in the Approvers list box, and click the Set E-Mail button to add a complete SMTP e-mail address for an approver (such as approver@mycompany.com).
8. Select the type of approval routing, as illustrated in Figure 16-11. For serial approval, select the One After Another option. For parallel approval, select the All At Once option. If you select parallel approval, you can select either All Approve or Only One Approval Required from the drop-down list immediately below the All At Once option.
9. Click OK.

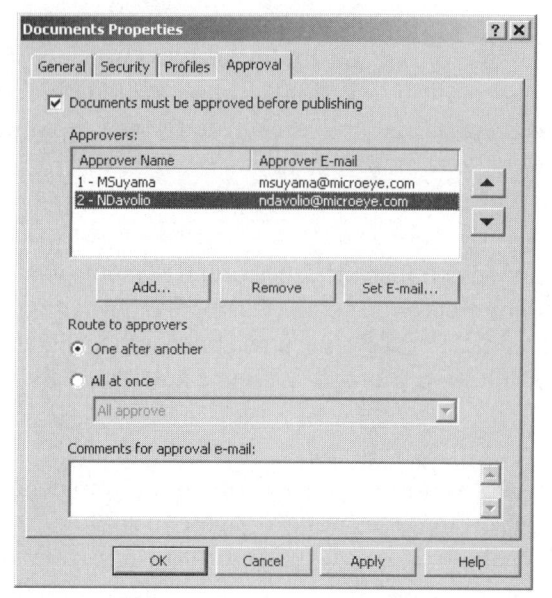

Figure 16-11 Use the Approval page to set approvers and the type of approval routing.

Using Categories

Categories provide another means of classifying and searching for documents in a SharePoint Portal Server workspace. The Northwind workspace is used to store and search for documents that are related to a company item in the Northwind Contact Management application. The Company form has a Company Category user-defined field that allows users to characterize a company according to a list of categories defined in the CRM Administration form in the Setup subfolder of the Companies folder. A user can pick only one category per company item using the drop-down control on the Company form. The Company Category field on the Company form is actually a Text type user-defined field, and it cannot store multiple values. A Keywords field for the company category on the Company form could provide this functionality but can be implemented only in a ListBox control. The drop-down ComboBox control on an Outlook form does not support MultiSelect for Keywords type values.

A SharePoint Portal Server category is analogous to a Keywords field on an Outlook form. You can establish categories by using the Web folders interface and giving the default Category 1, Category 2, and Category 3 names that suit your application. For example, you might want to establish the categories Marketing, Research, and Executive Briefing. Each of these categories can in turn have subcategories. You can then add the Categories field to the Northwind Document Profile so that users can categorize documents when they publish them to the document library. To make categorization mandatory, you can specify that a user must select a value for categories when the Northwind Document Profile is completed.

To add categories to a document profile

1. Open the Web folder for the workspace.
2. In the Management folder, open the Document Profiles subfolder.
3. Right-click the document profile with which you want to work, and then click Properties on the Shortcut menu.
4. Click the Properties page on the Document Profile Properties sheet, and then click the Select Properties button.
5. In the Properties list box, check the Categories box. You can enforce categorization by clicking the Edit button and checking the Require Users To Enter A Value For This Property box.
6. Click OK twice.

When you categorize a document, it appears in the category folders to which it belongs. While the document is not actually stored in its category folder or folders, it is displayed in those folders to simplify document searches. In the Dashboard portal, click the Categories tab to view the documents within their respective categories. With the Web folders interface, just navigate to the correct category to see all the documents in that category.

Content Indexing and Searches

One of the most powerful features of SharePoint Portal Server is its ability to search the workspace document library and additional content sources. A content source provides a starting point for crawling a file system, database, or Web site in order to include content in an index. In addition to the content of the workspace itself, the following content sources are available:

- External and internal Web sites
- Local and network file system folders
- Exchange 5.5 and Exchange 2000 Server public folders
- Other SharePoint Portal Server computers
- Lotus Notes databases

Part V Advanced Topics

Establishing the Default Content Access Account

Before you establish a content source to search, you should use the SharePoint Portal Server Administration console to establish a Default Content Access account.

To set the Default Content Access account

1. On the computer where SharePoint Portal Server is installed, log in as an administrator and click Start.
2. On the Programs menu, click Administrative Tools and then click SharePoint Portal Server Administration.
3. In the SharePoint Portal Server Administration console, right-click the SharePoint Portal Server computer in the Tree view and select Properties on the Shortcut menu.
4. Click the Accounts page on the *<ComputerName>* Properties sheet.
5. Select Default Content Access Account as shown in Figure 16-12, and then click Configure to supply the account and password for the Default Content Access account. This account should have at least read permission on content sources. Click OK after you have supplied the account and password.
6. Click OK to save your settings.

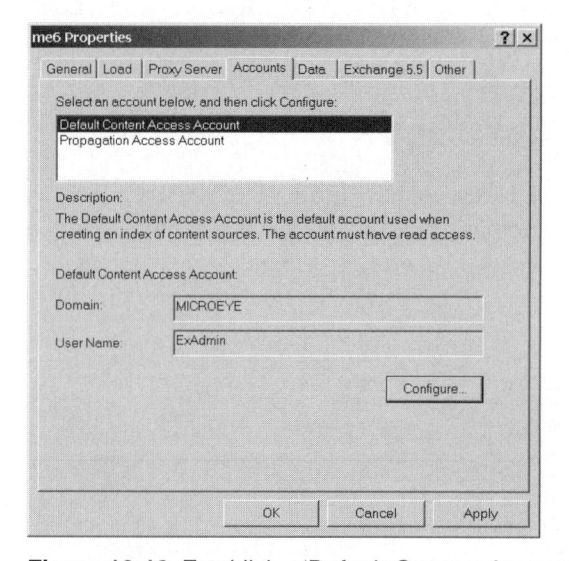

Figure 16-12 Establish a Default Content Access account for indexing content sources.

Indexing Exchange Public Folders

In the Northwind workspace, you must set up a content source for the Northwind Contact Management application in the Exchange public folder hierarchy. Depending upon whether you installed the Northwind Contact Management application in Public Folders on an Exchange 2000 server or an Exchange 5.5 server, add a content source using the Web folders interface. The following instructions detail how to set up a content source for the Northwind public folders. These instructions assume that you have installed the Northwind Contact Management application described in Chapter 12 in the public folder hierarchy on an Exchange 2000 server. Before following these steps, create a Web folder that points to the Northwind workspace, as outlined on page 794. You must have the Coordinator role assigned to you before you can administer the workspace.

To set up a content source on an Exchange server public folder hierarchy

1. Open the Web folder for the Northwind workspace.
2. Double-click the Management folder.
3. Double-click the Content Sources folder.
4. Double-click Add Content Source to launch the Add Content Source Wizard.
5. Click Next to view the Content Source Type page of the wizard shown in Figure 16-13. Select Exchange 2000 Server, and click Next.

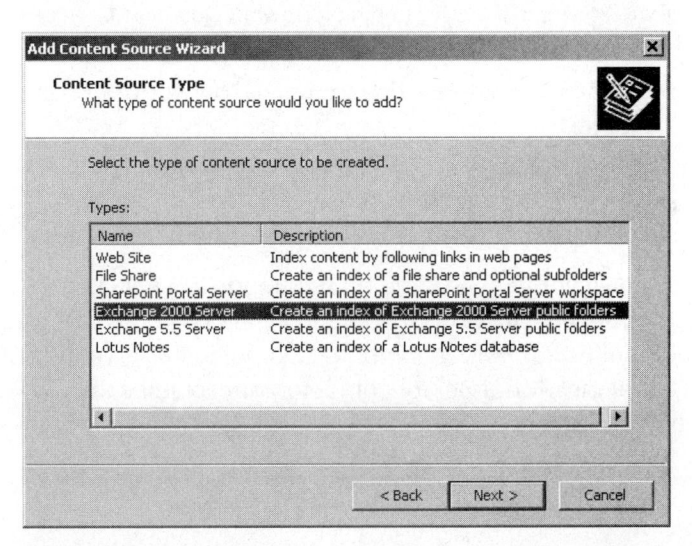

Figure 16-13 Select Exchange 2000 Server as a content source in the Add Content Source Wizard.

6. Enter the URL to the Northwind Contact Management application public folder on your Exchange 2000 server, as shown in Figure 16-14. Then click Next. Be sure to select the This Folder And All Subfolders option to search all application subfolders. The Public Folder virtual root on Exchange 2000 Server is http://<*servername*>/public. If you installed the Northwind Contact Management application as described in Chapter 12, the correct URL to enter is *http://<servername>/public/ Northwind Contact Management Application*.

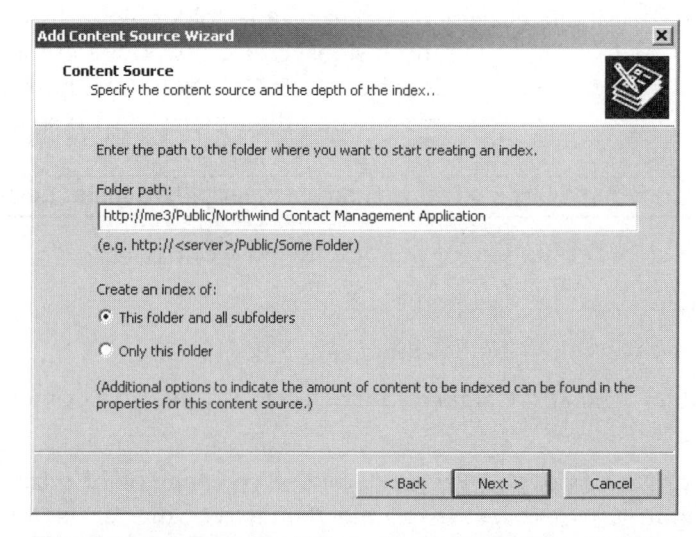

Figure 16-14 Enter the URL to the Northwind Contact Management application public folder.

7. Enter a name for your content source, or accept the proposed name, and click Next.
8. Click Finish to complete the Content Source Wizard.

> **More Info** If you are indexing an Exchange 5.5 server public folder hierarchy, you must install Collaboration Data Objects (CDO) 1.21 on the SharePoint Portal Server computer. Do not install a version of CDO on the SharePoint Portal Server computer that contains the Outlook E-Mail Security Update.

Scheduling Updates

That's all there is to creating a content source. Now you will be able to use the powerful search engine in SharePoint Portal Server to search a public folder hierarchy. Unlike searching an Outlook public folder (which does not let you search subfolders), you can search the subfolders of your content source. To ensure that your content source index is refreshed periodically, you can establish a schedule for an incremental update or a full update. Full updates include all content in the content source, while incremental updates include only content that has changed.

To schedule content source indexing

1. Double-click the content source you just created for the Northwind Contact Management application in the Content Sources Web folder.

2. Click the Scheduled Updates tab, and check the Incremental Updates box. Checking the Incremental Updates box should open the Schedule page on the Incremental Updates Properties sheet. Otherwise click the Schedule button to open the Schedule page on the Incremental Properties sheet.

3. On the Schedule page of the Incremental Update Properties sheet shown in Figure 16-15, set the frequency and other properties for the incremental update.

4. When you click OK to accept the properties for the incremental update, you will be prompted for an account and a password. The account should have at least read permission in order to crawl the public folder hierarchy.

When the indexing of the content source has completed, you can inspect the results in the Content Sources Web folder, as shown in Figure 16-16. If the update fails, you can click the Detailed Log link at the bottom of the Content Sources pane in the Windows Explorer Web folder to obtain additional information. You can also use the event viewer to examine the application log on the SharePoint Portal Server computer for additional details about indexing activities.

Searching the Northwind Workspace

After the indexing of the Exchange 2000 Public Folder has completed successfully, you can search the Northwind workspace for items in the public folder hierarchy. Remember that the power of using SharePoint Portal Server to search

Part V Advanced Topics

lies in its ability to scan an entire public folder hierarchy rather than a single public folder. For example, assume that you want to search for the name Antonio Moreno. On the Search page of the Northwind site, type *Antonio Moreno* in the Search box and then click Go. All instances of the name Antonio Moreno appear in the Matching Documents Web Part. Figure 16-17 illustrates the results of this search.

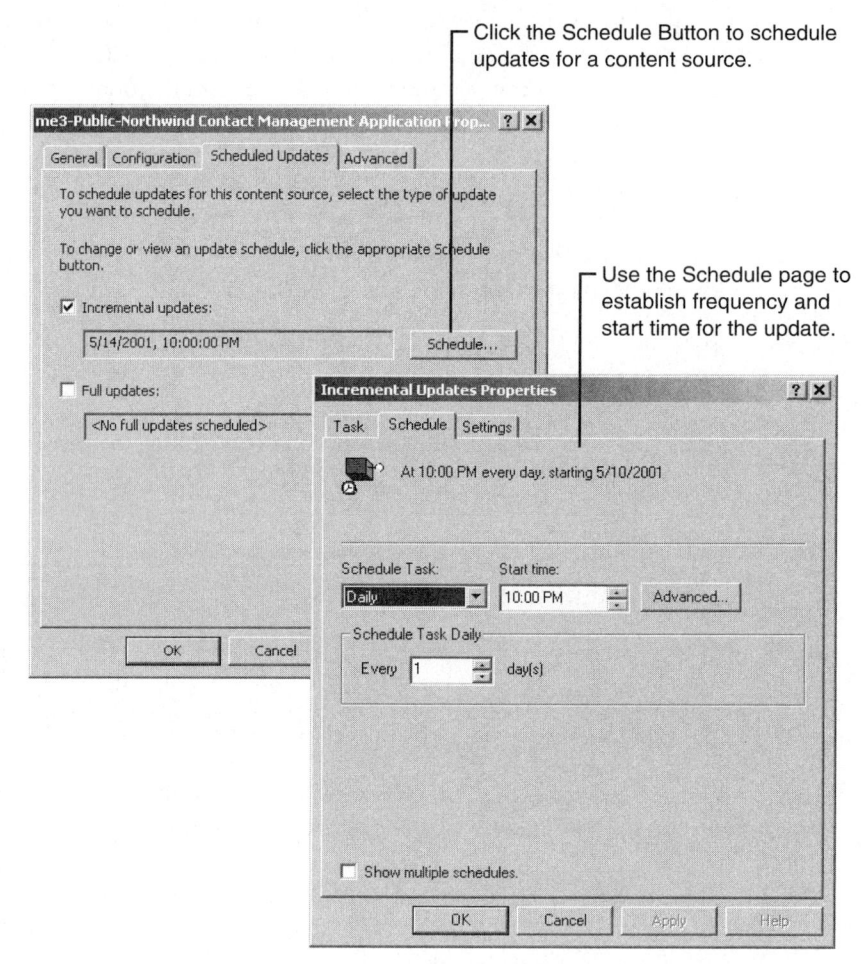

Figure 16-15 Schedule full or incremental updates to ensure that your content source index is current.

Using Outlook with SharePoint Portal Server Chapter 16

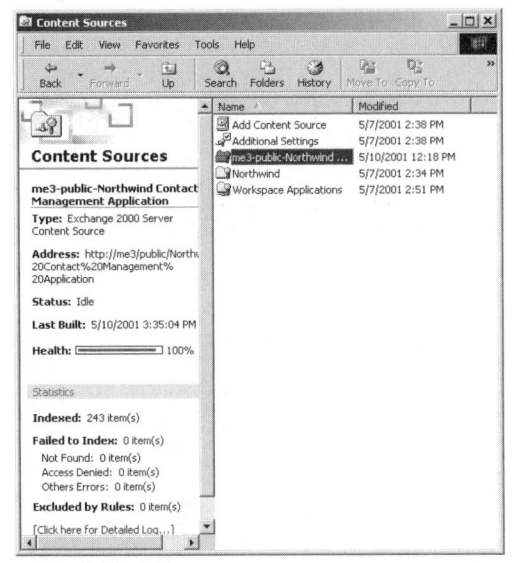

Figure 16-16 Index health and results are displayed when you click the content source item in the Content Sources folder.

> **Note** When you open a company item, you open it in Outlook Web Access. To customize the form used to view a company item in Outlook Web Access, you must create a custom Web Storage System form and register it for the Companies folder. Creating a custom Web Storage System form is beyond the scope of this book. For additional information, see the Exchange SDK on the companion CD.

Using Advanced Search

If you click the Advanced Search link in the Search Web Part, you can select a document profile for your search and conduct the search using values for custom properties. Unlike an advanced search, a simple search performs a standard, full-text search on all content sources defined for the workspace. An advanced search query, however, is typically more granular than that of a simple search. For example, suppose you want to find documents created with the Northwind Document Profile that have Alfreds Futterkiste as the CompanyName property and Michael Suyama as the author name. Figure 16-18 shows the results of this advanced search. The results of an advanced search query are typically more focused because you have greater control over the search criteria.

809

Part V Advanced Topics

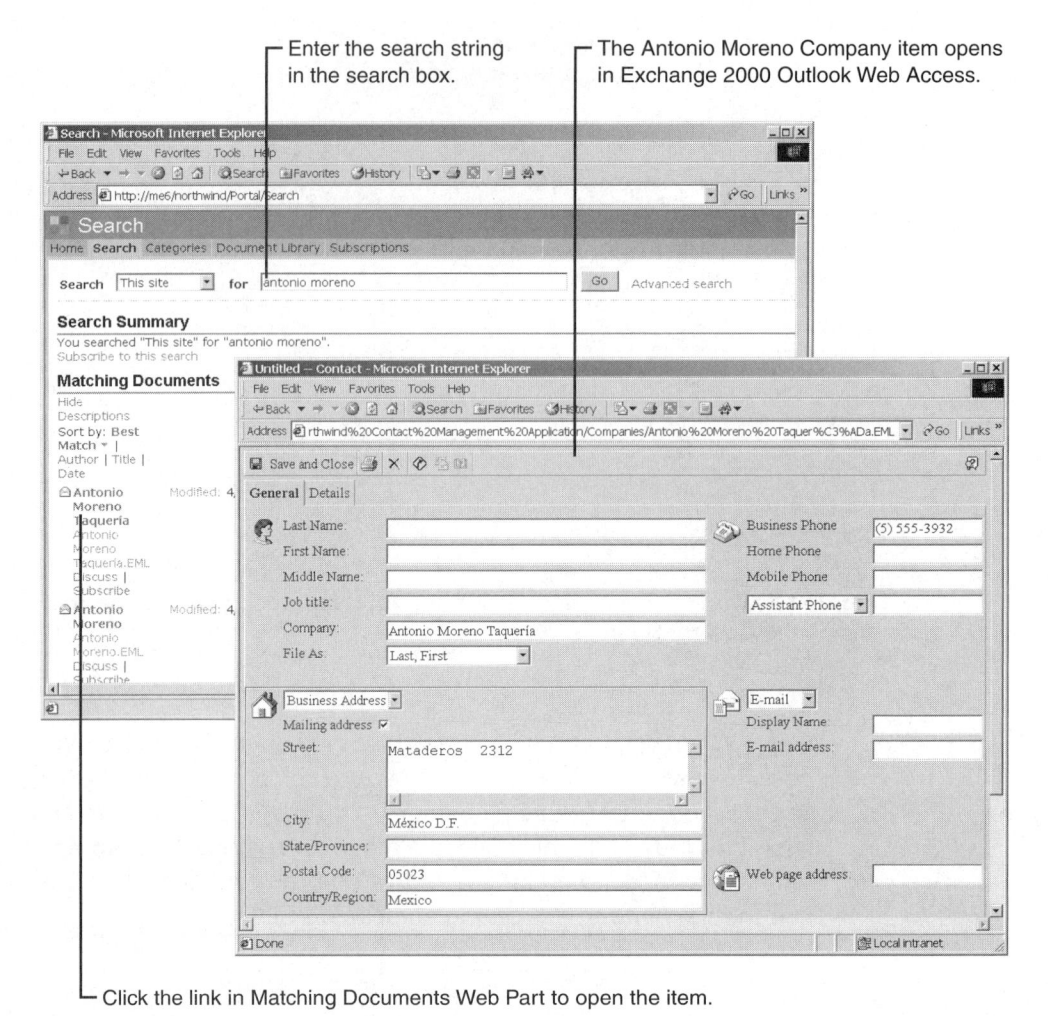

Figure shows screenshots with annotations:
- Enter the search string in the search box.
- The Antonio Moreno Company item opens in Exchange 2000 Outlook Web Access.
- Click the link in Matching Documents Web Part to open the item.

Figure 16-17 Searching for items in the Northwind Contact Management Application folder and its subfolders.

To search using Advanced Search

1. Click the Advanced Search link on the Home page or the Search page of the Northwind Dashboard site.

2. Select Northwind Document in the Search By Profile list.

3. Select Author in the Search By Properties list. Type the name of the author in the value edit box. If you select the default condition of equals (=), only values that are an exact match for the author's name will be returned.

4. Select CompanyName in the second Search By Properties list. Type the name of the company in the value edit box.

5. Click Go to perform the search.

> **Note** For additional information on searching with SharePoint Portal Server, click the Help link on the Search Dashboard in the Dashboard site.

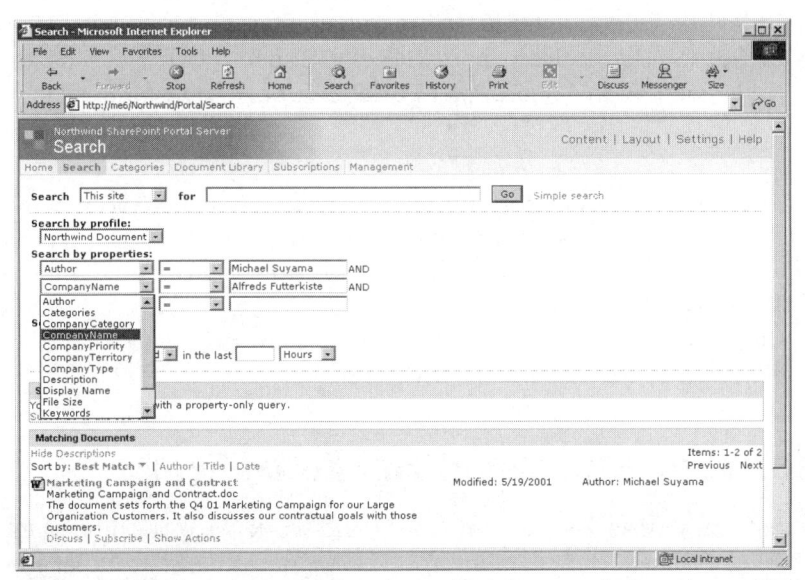

Figure 16-18 An advanced search can find documents by using custom properties defined for a document profile.

The Power of Subscription

If you carefully examine Figure 16-17 in the previous section, you will notice that you can subscribe to items or documents in the SharePoint Portal Server workspace by clicking the Subscribe link next to a document or item. Subscriptions are useful when you want to be informed about a change in a document. You can also subscribe to changes in public folder items. Subscription notifications can appear in the Subscription Summary Web Part when you visit the Dashboard site or in an e-mail notification that arrives in your Outlook Inbox. When you combine e-mail notification with the Outlook Rules Wizard or Outlook Mobile Manager for Microsoft Mobile Information 2001 Server, you have the ability to receive almost immediate notification when an item or document of interest changes. If you create a subscription, you can choose from the following notification intervals:

- Once a day
- Once a week
- When a change occurs

> **See Also** For additional information about subscriptions on SharePoint Portal Server, see "Introduction to Subscriptions" in the SharePoint Portal Server User's Help and "Specify Subscription Settings for the Workspace" in the SharePoint Portal Server Administrator's Help.

Subscriptions operate at the document level or the folder level, meaning that you can subscribe for notification about a particular document or folder. If you decide that you no longer want to subscribe to a document or folder item, click the Subscriptions tab on the Workspace portal, where you can delete existing subscriptions. To modify the frequency of an existing subscription, you must delete and then re-create the subscription.

Outlook Integration with SharePoint Portal Server

Now that you've established your Northwind workspace, it's time to integrate the Northwind Contact Management application with the SharePoint Portal Server document management and search capabilities. First you should customize the content of the Northwind Home Dashboard with the Companies, Sales Data, and Shared Activities Web Parts introduced in Chapter 15, "Integrating Outlook with Web Applications." This discussion assumes that you learned how to import the Web Parts for the Northwind Dashboard, as discussed in Chapter 15. Follow the instructions on page 751 of Chapter 15 for importing Web Parts, but instead of importing the Web Parts into the Northwind Dashboard hosted on SQL Server 2000, you should import them into the Dashboard site for the Northwind workspace.

Modifying Default Web Parts

To make room for the Northwind custom Web Parts on the home page of the Northwind SharePoint Dashboard (shown in Figure 16-19), you must modify the properties of the default Web Parts for the Home Dashboard. Many of the Web Parts for the SharePoint Portal Server Dashboard site are configured so that they

Using Outlook with SharePoint Portal Server Chapter 16

cannot be removed or minimized by a user. You must be a workspace coordinator to change the Dashboard site content, layout, and settings. Follow these steps to allow the removal of the Announcements, Categories, and News Web Parts.

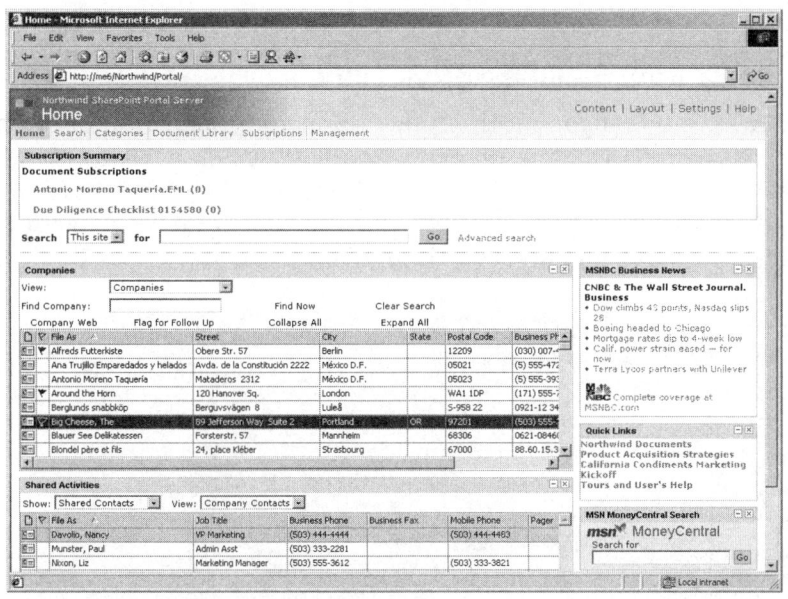

Figure 16-19 The Northwind SharePoint Dashboard integrates custom Web Parts and document management features.

To allow Web Parts to be removed from a SharePoint Dashboard site

1. Click the Content link.
2. Click the Announcements Web Part link in the Contents page.
3. Click the Show Advanced Settings link.
4. Check Allow Users To Remove This Web Part From Their Dashboard and Allow Users To Minimize This Web Part On Their Dashboard.
5. Click the Save button at the bottom of the page.
6. Repeat steps 1 through 5 for the Categories and News Web Parts.
7. After you allow removal of the Announcements, Categories, and News Web Parts, uncheck those Web Parts in the Contents page.
8. Click Save to save the contents of the Northwind SharePoint Dashboard.

Part V Advanced Topics

After you remove Web Parts from the home page of the Northwind SharePoint Dashboard, you can import other Web Parts, use a custom style, and change the layout so that your Northwind SharePoint Dashboard resembles the one shown in Figure 16-19.

Adding a URL to the CRM Administration Form

In order for the Company form in the Companies public folder to operate correctly with SharePoint Portal Server, you must add the URL for the Documents folder in the Northwind workspace to the CRM Administration form, as shown in Figure 16-20. This URL is used by the code in the Companies form to enable a user to add a document to the Northwind Documents folder.

Enter the URL for the SharePoint Portal Server Documents folder.

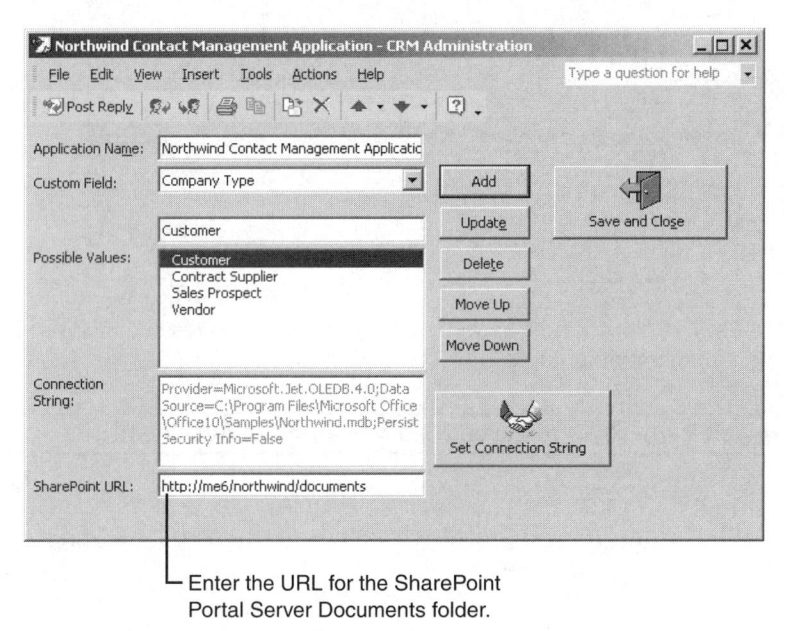

Figure 16-20 The CRM Administration form in the Setup folder contains a custom field that allows you to specify the URL for the Northwind Documents folder.

The following discussion requires that you have performed these steps:

- Installed the Northwind Contact Management application into the public folder hierarchy.

- Installed the Outlook Shared Activities COM Add-in. If the Outlook Shared Activities COM Add-in is not correctly installed, none of the SharePoint Portal Server features will work correctly.

If you have not installed these two components, see "Copying the Application Folders to Public Folders" and "Installing the Outlook Shared Activities Add-in" in Chapter 12 (on page 546 and page 553, respectively) for instructions on how to perform this installation.

To add the SharePoint URL to the CRM Administration form

1. Navigate to the Setup folder under Companies under Northwind Contact Management Application in the public folder hierarchy.
2. Double-click the CRM Administration form.
3. Enter the URL to the Documents folder in the Northwind workspace. The URL is *http://<servername>/Northwind/Documents*, where <servername> is the name of the computer on which SharePoint Portal Server is installed.
4. Click the Save And Close button.

Publishing a Document with the Company Form

If a SharePoint URL has been entered in the CRM Administration form, the code behind the Company form adds a Publish Document button to the toolbar for the Company form and displays a page on the form named Published Documents. Figure 16-21 depicts this page.

> **Note** Do not confuse the Shared Document button with the Publish Document button on the toolbar for the Company form. The Shared Document button adds a Word, Excel, or PowerPoint document to the Shared Documents public folder. It does not support document management features in that Exchange public folder, such as check in or check out. If you want to use the enhanced document management features of SharePoint Portal Server, click the Publish Document button.

When you click the Publish Document button, the following actions occur:

1. The Publish Document To SharePoint Portal Server dialog box appears, and the user selects a document to publish from the local file system or a network share.
2. The Document Properties dialog box appears, letting the user modify properties in the Northwind Document Profile, such as Author, Title, Keywords, and Description.

Part V Advanced Topics

3. When the document is published to the Documents folder, an alert message appears, informing the user whether the publication succeeded or failed.

4. The Published Documents page displays the new document on the Published Documents page of the company item.

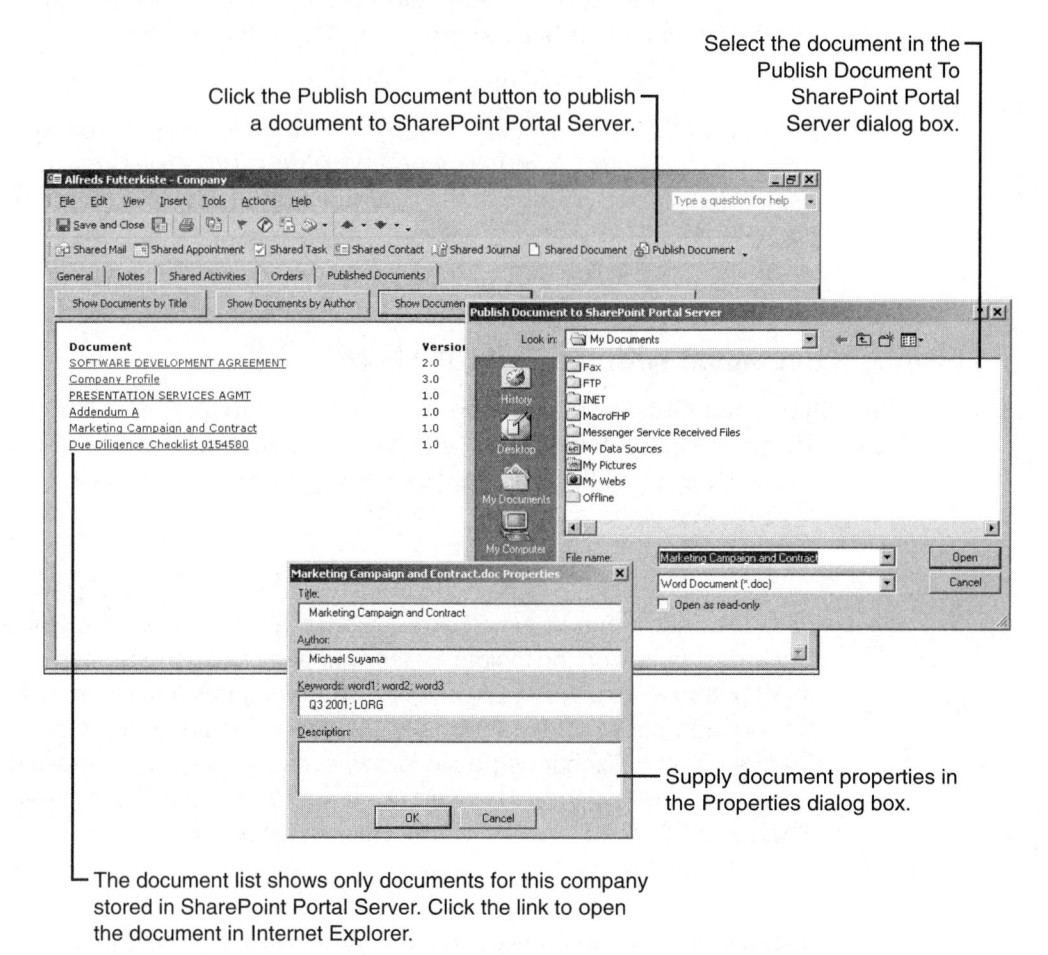

Figure 16-21 The Company form allows you to publish documents related to the company in the Documents folder of the Northwind workspace on SharePoint Portal Server.

A user can click the buttons on the Published Documents page to sort the published documents for this company by author, title, or date. Be aware that only published documents for this specific company will appear on the Published

Documents page of the form. Each document is assigned the unique Company identifier stored in the Account field on the Company form. This identifier can then be used to query the Documents folder and return a subset of documents with a matching Account string. As an added benefit, additional properties (such as Company Name, Company Type, Company Category, Company Priority, and Company Territory) are added to the document. These properties are available in the Northwind Document Profile dialog box shown in Figure 16-22.

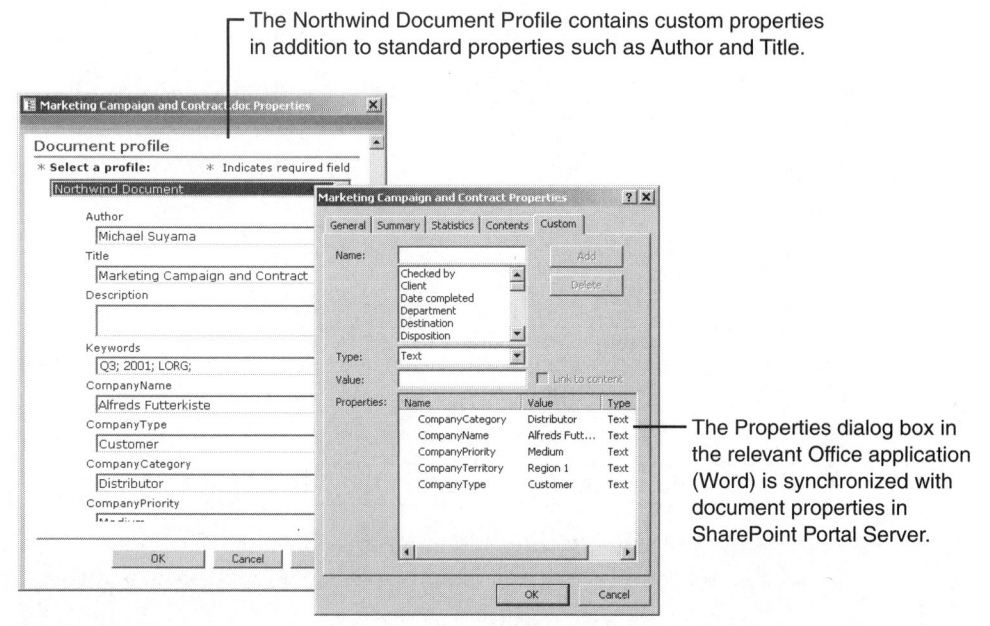

Figure 16-22 Custom company item properties are copied to the Northwind Document Profile and visible in the Document Properties dialog box.

Documents added with the Publish Document command on the Company form are checked in and published simultaneously. If you have set approval routing for the Documents folder in the Northwind workspace, the document will be published when the approval sequence is complete. Users can check out these documents and use all the powerful search and subscription features of SharePoint Portal Server.

Improving Productivity with the Office XP Places Bar

If you work with SharePoint documents consistently, consider using one of the significant new features of the Office XP common dialog boxes. The Office XP

Part V Advanced Topics

common dialog boxes enable you to customize the Places Bar for quick access to commonly used folders where you open or save documents. Figure 16-23 shows the Open dialog box in Word 2002 with the Northwind Documents place at the bottom of the Places Bar. Because Word and other Office XP applications allow you to open items directly from a Web folder, this feature is a tremendous time saver.

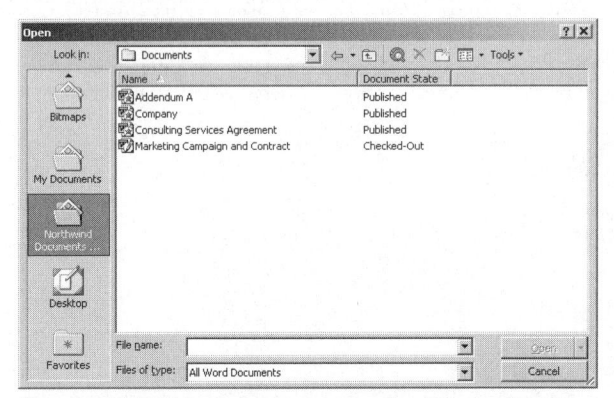

Figure 16-23 You can customize the Places Bar in an Office XP common dialog box to add a place for a SharePoint Documents folder.

To add a SharePoint Document folder to the Office XP Places Bar

1. Follow the steps outlined in "Using Web Folders" on page 793 to create a Web folder for the Document folder that you want to add to the Places Bar.

2. Click and drag the item you created in step 1 to the Windows desktop. Dropping the item on the Windows desktop creates a folder shortcut to the Documents folder on SharePoint Portal Server.

3. Launch Word, and select Open on the File menu.

4. Click the Desktop place in the Places Bar in the Open dialog box.

5. Select the folder shortcut that you added in step 2.

6. Click the Tools drop-down list at the top-right corner of the dialog box, and select the Add To My Places command.

7. You can now use the Documents place to open documents in a SharePoint Portal Server Documents folder.

The Outlook Shared Activities Add-In

You might be wondering how SharePoint Portal Server document management occurs via an Outlook form. The answer is that the form contains code that calls public methods in the Outlook Shared Activities COM Add-in. The Outlook Shared Activities COM Add-in uses the PKMCDO object model to check in and publish the file system document on SharePoint Portal Server.

Calling Methods from the Company Form

Let's take a look at the code in the Company form that enables document publication. The Publish Document command button is named *cmdPublish* and uses the click event to instantiate a Shared Activities object named *objDM*. The Shared Activities Add-in features several public properties and methods that relate to document management. In this example, you need to call the *PublishSharePointDocument* method and supply the necessary arguments for it. Then the *cmdShowDocumentsByDate_Click* procedure is called to refresh the view of documents on the Published Documents page.

```
Sub cmdPublish_Click()
    On Error Resume Next
    Dim objDM
    'Item has to be saved; otherwise, linking does not work
    If Item.EntryId = "" then
        If MsgBox(gstrErrorButton, vbYesNo + vbQuestion, _
            gstrAppName) = vbYes Then
              Item.Save
        Else
            Exit Sub
        End If
    End If
    Set objDM = CreateObject("OutlookSharedActivities.OutAddIn")
    If objDM Is Nothing Then
        MsgBox "Shared Activities Add-in not installed.", _
              vbCritical
        Exit Sub
    End If
    objDM.PublishSharePointDocument _
        gstrSharePointURL, Item.CompanyName, Item.Account, _
        Item.UserProperties("Company Type").Value, _
        Item.UserProperties("Company Category").Value, _
        Item.UserProperties("Company Priority").Value, _
        Item.UserProperties("Company Territory").Value
    'Now display the new document in the list
    Call cmdShowDocumentsByDate_Click()
End Sub
```

Part V Advanced Topics

The *PublishSharePointDocument* Method

The *PublishSharePointDocument* method in the Outlook Shared Activities COM Add-in does the real work of publishing a document. The most important point made in this book is that you can wrap complex functionality in public methods of a dual-class COM Add-in. This concept is discussed in detail in Chapter 14, "Creating COM Add-Ins with Visual Basic." In our example, the COM Add-in uses the common dialog box control and the PKMCDO object library to open the document, save it to an ADODB Stream object, set custom properties, check in and publish the document, and then display a message box that informs the user whether publication succeeded. Figure 16-24 shows the *PublishSharePointDocument* method of the OutlookSharedActivities.OutAddIn class in the Microsoft Visual Basic Object Browser.

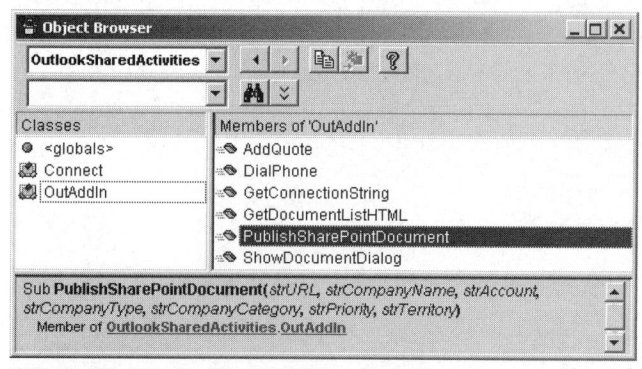

Figure 16-24 The *PublishSharePointDocument* method displayed in the Visual Basic Object Browser.

Two important objects in *PublishSharePointDocument* are the PKMCDO KnowledgeDocument object and the ADODB Stream object. The KnowledgeDocument object lets you programmatically check in, check out, and publish documents to a SharePoint enhanced folder. You use the *OpenStream* method of the KnowledgeDocument object to instantiate an ADODB Stream object. The Stream object uses the *LoadFromFile* method to read the file into an ADODB Stream object. Once you have a KnowledgeDocument object, you can add custom properties by using the object's Fields collection. You must call the *Update* method on the Fields collection before you call the *SaveTo* method on the DataSource property of the KnowledgeDocument object. The code for *PublishSharePointDocument* follows:

```
Public Sub PublishSharePointDocument(strURL, strCompanyName, strAccount, _
    strCompanyType, strCompanyCategory, strPriority, strTerritory)
    Dim oFolder As New PKMCDO.KnowledgeFolder
    Dim oDoc As New PKMCDO.KnowledgeDocument
```

820

Using Outlook with SharePoint Portal Server   Chapter 16

```
Dim oVersion As New PKMCDO.KnowledgeVersion
Dim oStream As ADODB.Stream
Dim strPath, strDocumentURL, strDisplayName, strFilter As String
Dim strMsg, strError As String
Dim i As Integer
Dim blnError As Boolean

On Error Resume Next
strFilter = "Word Document (*.doc)|*.doc|Excel Workbook (*.xls)" & _
    "|*.xls|PowerPoint Presentation (*.ppt)|*.ppt|All Files(*.*)|*.*"
With frmPublish.CommonDialog1
    .Filter = strFilter
    .FilterIndex = 1
    .DialogTitle = "Publish Document to SharePoint Portal Server"
    .ShowOpen
End With
If frmPublish.CommonDialog1.FileName = "" Then
    Unload frmPublish
    Exit Sub
End If
oFolder.DataSource.Open strURL
If Err Then
    MsgBox "Could not open the URL:" & vbCrLf & strURL, vbCritical
    Exit Sub
Else
    frmWait.Show
    DoEvents
End If
With frmPublish.CommonDialog1
    strDisplayName = .FileTitle
    strPath = .FileName
End With
'Open binary stream
Set oStream = oDoc.OpenStream
oStream.Type = adTypeBinary
oStream.SetEOS
'Load the file
oStream.LoadFromFile strPath
oStream.Flush
Set oStream = Nothing
strDocumentURL = strURL & "/" & strDisplayName
'Add custom fields to the document
oDoc.Fields("Account").Value = strAccount
oDoc.Fields("urn:schemas-microsoft-com:office:office#CompanyName") _
    .Value = strCompanyName
oDoc.Fields("urn:schemas-microsoft-com:office:office#CompanyType") _
    .Value = strCompanyType
```

(continued)

Part V   Advanced Topics

```
            oDoc.Fields("urn:schemas-microsoft-com:office:office#CompanyCategory") _
                .Value = strCompanyCategory
            oDoc.Fields("urn:schemas-microsoft-com:office:office#CompanyPriority") _
                .Value = strPriority
            oDoc.Fields("urn:schemas-microsoft-com:office:office#CompanyTerritory") _
                .Value = strTerritory
            'Update the fields collection - adds fields to WSS item
            oDoc.Fields.Update
            'Save to URL
            oDoc.DataSource.SaveTo (strDocumentURL)
            'Check for errors
            If Err = 0 Then
                With frmProperties
                    .Caption = strDisplayName & " Properties"
                    .txtAuthor = Trim(oDoc.Author)
                    .txtTitle = Trim(oDoc.Title)
                    .txtKeywords = GetKeywords(oDoc.Keywords)
                    .txtDescription = Trim(oDoc.Description)
                    .Show 1
                    DoEvents
                End With
                If frmProperties.blnProperties Then
                    oDoc.Author = frmProperties.txtAuthor
                    oDoc.Title = frmProperties.txtTitle
                    If frmProperties.txtKeywords <> "" Then
                        'Changes txtKeywords into array
                        oDoc.Keywords = _
                            SetKeywords(frmProperties.txtKeywords)
                    End If
                    oDoc.Description = frmProperties.txtDescription
                    oDoc.DataSource.Save
                End If
                Unload frmProperties
                strMsg = "Published " & oDoc.Title & vbCrLf _
                    & Replace(oDoc.DataSource.SourceURL, " ", "%20")
            Else
                'Error occurred
                blnError = True
                strError = "Error Publishing " & strDisplayName & vbCrLf _
                    & Replace(strDocumentURL, " ", "%20") & vbCrLf _
                    & "Error Number: " & Err.Number & vbCrLf _
                    & "Error Description: " & Err.Description
            End If
            'Check in and publish
            oVersion.CheckIn strDocumentURL
            oVersion.Publish strDocumentURL
            Set oVersion = Nothing
            Set oDoc = Nothing
```

```
    Unload frmWait
    If blnError Then
        MsgBox strError, vbCritical
    Else
        MsgBox strMsg, vbInformation
    End If
End Sub
```

Web Storage System Properties

Like MAPI properties used in legacy Exchange and Outlook environments, Web Storage System properties can be set on items and folders. However, Web Storage System properties are set on an individual instance of a content class and offer greater extensibility than MAPI properties. You can create new properties on any item in the SharePoint document store, even without defining it as part of the schema.

Web Storage System properties should be named according to the following guidelines:

- Properties should be created using a namespace plus an identifier. For example, urn:schemas:mycompany.com:myproperty or urn:schemas-mycompany-com-mycontentclass#myproperty.

- Property names with spaces are not recommended because XML (specifically HTTP-DAV) does not support spaces in element names.

- If your application requires that you access user-defined fields in Outlook forms, you should limit the property name to 32 characters or less. This limitation might mean you will not use a fully qualified namespace. If you do not use a fully qualified namespace, access your custom schema properties as fields in the Outlook Field Chooser or use the UserProperties collection in the Outlook Object Model.

The properties for the Northwind Document Profile are added to the namespace urn:schemas-microsoft-com:office:office. When you add a property to this namespace in SharePoint Portal Server, you are creating the equivalent of a CustomDocumentProperties property in the object model of the Office application that hosts the SharePoint Portal Server document. As you saw in Figure 16-22, the custom properties defined on a Northwind Document Profile appear on the Custom tab of the Word Document Properties dialog box. If you are perplexed by namespace and property naming issues, open a workspace document in the Web Storage System Explorer. The Web Storage System Explorer is a development tool that lets you examine and modify item properties; consider it the Web Storage System equivalent of Outlook Spy or MDBVU32. You can obtain the

Part V Advanced Topics

Web Storage System Explorer in the latest release of the Web Storage System Tools at *http://msdn.microsoft.com/wss*. Figure 16-25 shows the Web Storage System Explorer displaying properties for a document named Marketing Campaign and Contract.doc that has been published to the Documents folder in the Northwind workspace.

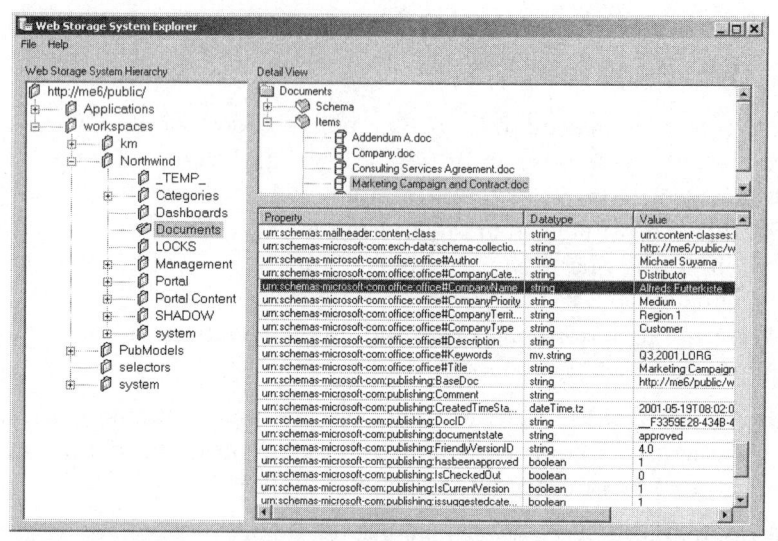

Figure 16-25 The Web Storage System Explorer lets you examine the properties of items and folders in the Web Storage System.

> **Note** When you enter a SharePoint Portal Server URL in the Web Storage System Explorer, do not use the *http://<servername>/workspace* URL that you use to open a workspace in Internet Explorer. As a connection URL, use *http://<servername>/public*, where <servername> is the name of your SharePoint Portal Server. As Figure 16-25 shows, you can then navigate to the SharePoint Portal Server workspace and its folders in the Web Storage System Hierarchy Tree View control. Expand the Items node in the Detail View Tree View control to see the documents in the folder.

> **More Info** Use the Web Storage System Explorer with care. If you modify a property or content class definition incorrectly, you can corrupt your SharePoint Portal Server workspace.

Handling Keywords

One of the important features of the *PublishSharePointDocument* method shown earlier is that it enables you to set document properties with a UserForm named frmProperties. This ensures that the document is published with the correct author, title, keyword, and description information. The Keywords property allows a user to enter keywords that help to categorize and search a document. Keywords are distinct from categories, which are established at the system level by a workspace coordinator. A user can also enter keywords delimited by semicolons in the Keywords edit box on frmProperties. You must convert those keywords to an array with the SetKeywords function shown next. Conversely, to retrieve keywords from a document item, you use the GetKeywords function to return a string that contains semicolon-delimited keywords. Both SetKeywords and GetKeywords are useful functions when you're adding documents programmatically to an enhanced folder.

```
'***************************************************************
'Custom procedure: GetKeywords(avarKeywords) As String
'Purpose: Return keywords from array
'***************************************************************
Public Function GetKeywords(avarKeywords) As String
    Dim i As Integer
    Dim strKeywords As String
    On Error Resume Next
    For i = 0 To UBound(avarKeywords)
        strKeywords = strKeywords & avarKeywords(i) & ";"
    Next
    If strKeywords <> "" Then
        If Right$(strKeywords, 1) = ";" Then
            strKeywords = Left$(strKeywords, Len(strKeywords) - 1)
        End If
    End If
    GetKeywords = strKeywords
End Function


'***************************************************************
'Custom procedure: SetKeywords(avarKeywords) As String
'Purpose: Return array from semicolon-delimited keywords
'***************************************************************
Public Function SetKeywords(strKeywords As String) As Variant
    Dim i As Integer
    Dim strValues As String
    Dim avarArray, avarSplit
    On Error Resume Next
    avarSplit = Split(strKeywords, ";")
    ReDim avarArray(UBound(avarSplit))
```

(continued)

```
        For i = 0 To UBound(avarSplit)
            avarArray(i) = avarSplit(i)
        Next
        SetKeywords = avarArray
End Function
```

Referencing the PKMCDO and CDO 3.0 Object Libraries

This function uses several object libraries that are referenced in the Shared Activities project. Extensive coverage of the PKMCDO object library is beyond the scope of this book. However, it's important to remember that PKMCDO is a client object library installed by default with Office XP or with the SharePoint Server client installation in an Office 2000 environment. Use the References command on the Visual Basic Tools menu to add a reference to the PKMCDO object library, as shown in Figure 16-26. The exact name of the PKMCDO object library is Microsoft PKMCDO for Microsoft Web Storage System.

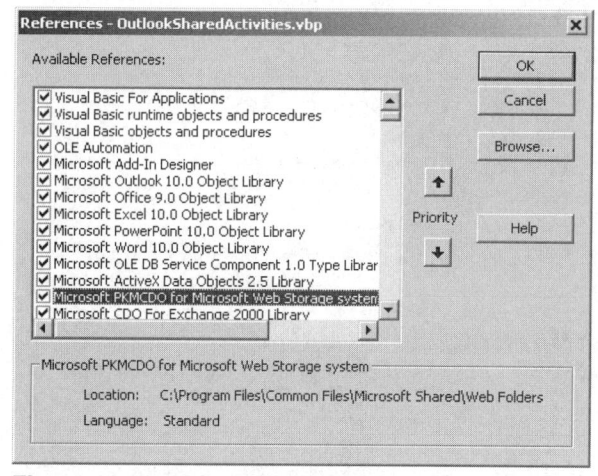

Figure 16-26 Set a reference to the PKMCDO and CDO 3.0 object libraries for the Shared Activities Add-in.

If you inspect Figure 16-26 carefully, you will notice that Collaboration Data Objects (CDO) 3.0 is also referenced for the Shared Activities project. Unlike CDO 1.21, which operates only on MAPI-based folders in Outlook, CDO 3.0 is designed to access folders and items on the Web Storage System. Somewhat of an unexpected guest in Office XP, CDO 3.0 is installed by default in addition to PKMCDO and Web folders. You reference Collaboration Data Objects as Microsoft CDO for Exchange 2000. Do not confuse this object library with Microsoft CDO 1.21 Library. Although the code in the Shared Activities Add-in only uses a tiny piece of the CDO 3.0 object model, it does provide an essential object, the Appointment object. This object lets the Add-in translate between Universal Coordinated Time (UTC) on the SharePoint Portal Server and the local time zone on the client computer. (UTC date/time is equivalent to the GMT time zone, or Greenwich Mean Time.) The subject of time zones and date storage in the Web Storage System is detailed later in the section, under "Working with Web Storage System Date/Time Values."

> **See Also** For detailed coverage of the objects, properties, and methods in CDO 3.0, see the Exchange SDK. Also see the "Where to Go from Here" section at the end of this chapter.

Displaying the List of Documents

The Published Documents page contains a WebBrowser Active X control that lets you display Web content in the control. In our example, the *GetDocumentListHTML* method of the Shared Activities Add-in creates an HTML document in the user's temporary folder and then displays that document in the Web Browser control. The Published Documents page of the Company form has several command buttons that let the user show published documents by author, title, and date. You only need to see the code for one of these buttons to get an idea of what happens. The following code is for the cmdShowDocumentsByDate button:

```
Sub cmdShowDocumentsByDate_Click
    On Error Resume Next
    Dim objDM
    'Call procedure that supplies URL for WebBrowser1 control
    Set objDM = CreateObject("OutlookSharedActivities.OutAddIn")
    If objDM Is Nothing Then
        MsgBox "Shared Activities Add-in not installed.", _
            vbCritical
        Exit Sub
    End If
    gstrFilePath = objDM.GetDocumentListHTML _
        (gstrSharePointURL, Item.Account, "Date")
    WebBrowser1.Navigate gstrFilePath
End Sub
```

Like the *cmdPublish_Click* procedure discussed earlier, the *cmdShowDocumentsByDate_Click* procedure calls a public method of the Shared Activities COM Add-in. In this case, the *GetDocumentListHTML* method returns a file path specification for an HTML file that is created in the user's temporary folder. The *Navigate* method is then called on the WebBrowser1 control to display the HTML file in the Web Browser control. The file path is stored in the script-level variable *gstrFilePath*. When the form closes, the HTML file is deleted from the temporary folder by using the *DeleteFile* method of the FileSystemObject.

```
Function Item_Close()
    Dim objFS
    On Error Resume Next
    If gstrFilePath <> "" Then
        Set objFS = CreateObject("Scripting.FileSystemObject")
        objFS.DeleteFile gstrFilePath
    End If
End Function
```

> **See Also** For additional information on the FileSystemObject in Visual Basic Scripting Edition (VBScript), see the FileSystemObject User's Guide at *http://msdn.microsoft.com/scripting/vbscript/doc/jsFSOTutor.htm*.

The *ShowDocumentListHTML* Method

This method creates an HTML document in the user's temporary folder and then passes back a file path string to the VBScript code in the Company form. This file specification is used as the argument for the *Navigate* method of the Web Browser control. To search a SharePoint folder, you establish a connection to the SharePoint Portal Server using MSDAIPP, also known as the Microsoft OLE DB Provider for Internet Publishing. Although CDO 3.0 is installed on a client computer as part of a default Office XP installation, you cannot use EXOLEDB as the provider for your ADODB Connection object. The Connection object requires a valid URL to the Northwind workspace Documents folder for its *Open* method.

Once you have created a Connection object, you create an ADO Command object and set the ActiveConnection property to the Connection object. The next step is to build a Web Storage System SQL string to return a Recordset that contains the fields that will be displayed on the Published Documents page of the Company form. The WHERE clause for this SQL string uses the unique Account property of the Company form to return only documents for the company. The *Sort* argument to the *ShowDocumentListHTML* method determines the ORDER BY clause that is appended to the SQL string. Once the Recordset is returned, you build an HTML string that contains a table for each row in the Recordset. Finally, the code uses Visual Basic to write the file to the local temporary folder. The code follows:

```vb
Public Function GetDocumentListHTML(strURL, strAccount, strSort) As String
Dim cmd As New ADODB.Command
Dim cnx As New ADODB.Connection
Dim oRS As ADODB.Recordset
Dim intFile As Integer
Dim strSQL, strHTML, strFilePath As String

On Error Resume Next
'Open an ADODB connection using MSDAIPP
With cnx
    .Provider = "MSDAIPP.DSO"
    .Properties("Prompt") = adPromptNever
    .Properties("Url Encoding") = 1
    .Properties.Item("Flush WinInet Password Cache").Value = True
    .Open strURL
End With
'Set the ActiveConnection for the Command object
Set cmd.ActiveConnection = cnx
'Build a DASL Query string to query Documents folder
strSQL = "Select " & AddQuote("DAV:href") & "," _
    & AddQuote("DAV:displayname") & "," _
    & AddQuote("DAV:getlastmodified") & "," _
    & AddQuote("urn:schemas-microsoft-com:publishing:FriendlyVersionID") & "," _
    & AddQuote("urn:schemas-microsoft-com:office:office#Author") & "," _
    & AddQuote("urn:schemas-microsoft-com:office:office#Title") _
    & " FROM Scope('SHALLOW TRAVERSAL OF " & AddQuote(strURL) & "')" _
    & " WHERE " & AddQuote("Account") _
    & " ='" & strAccount & "'"
'Order by depends upon Sort argument
Select Case strSort
    Case "Title"
        strSQL = strSQL & " ORDER BY " _
            & AddQuote("urn:schemas-microsoft-com:office:office#Title") _
            & " ASC"
    Case "Author"
        strSQL = strSQL & " ORDER BY " _
            & AddQuote("urn:schemas-microsoft-com:office:office#Author") _
            & " ASC"
    Case "Date"
        strSQL = strSQL & " ORDER BY " _
            & AddQuote("DAV:getlastmodified") & " DESC"
End Select
cmd.CommandText = strSQL
'Call the Execute method
Set oRS = cmd.Execute
'Build an HTML string
strHTML = "<html><head><title>Published Documents</title></head><body>" _
    & "<table width =100% style='FONT:8pt Verdana, san-serif'>" _
```

(continued)

Part V Advanced Topics

```
            & "<tr><td width =50%><b>Document</b></td>" _
            & "<td width = 10%><b>Version</b></td>" _
            & "<td width =20%><b>Last Modified</b></td>" _
            & "<td width =20%><b>Author</b></td></tr>"
    'Iterate over the Recordset from the query and build table rows
    Do Until oRS.EOF
        strHTML = strHTML & "<tr><td><a href=" _
        & AddQuote(oRS.Fields("DAV:href")) _
        & " target = '_blank'>" _
        & oRS.Fields("urn:schemas-microsoft-com:office:office#Title")
        strHTML = strHTML & "</a></td><td>" _
        & oRS.Fields("urn:schemas-microsoft-com:publishing:FriendlyVersionID") _
        & "</td><td>" _
        & ConvertDateTime(oRS.Fields("DAV:getlastmodified")) _
        & "</td><td>" _
        & oRS.Fields("urn:schemas-microsoft-com:office:office#Author") _
        & "</td></tr>"
        oRS.MoveNext
    Loop
    strHTML = strHTML & "</table></body></html>"
    'Open a file for output in temp folder
    On Error GoTo GetDocumentListHTML_Error
    intFile = FreeFile
    'Use the unique account as filename
    strFilePath = GetTempDir & strAccount & ".htm"
    Open strFilePath For Output As #intFile
    Print #intFile, strHTML
    Close #intFile
    'Return the file path
    GetDocumentListHTML = strFilePath
GetDocumentListHTML_Exit:
    Exit Function

GetDocumentListHTML_Error:
    Resume GetDocumentListHTML_Exit
End Function

'Helper function
Function AddQuote(strValue) As String
    AddQuote = Chr(34) & strValue & Chr(34)
End Function
```

> **See Also** For additional information on SQL syntax for SharePoint Portal Server, see the book entitled "SharePoint Portal Server Search SQL Syntax" in the SharePoint Portal Server SDK.

Using Outlook with SharePoint Portal Server Chapter 16

Working with Web Storage System Date/Time Values

The *GetDocumentListHTML* method retrieves the last modified date/time value for documents in the Northwind Documents folder. When a date/time value is stored in the Web Storage System, it is stored using the UTC format. As mentioned earlier, UTC date/time is equivalent to the GMT time zone, or Greenwich Mean Time. Unless you live in the GMT time zone, all date/time values must be converted to the date/time value for your local time zone. The ConvertDateTime function creates a CDO Appointment item with the date/time value set to the value passed in the function. By switching the time zone of the CDO Configuration object, you can convert the UTC time to local time, as shown in the following code:

```
'****************************************************************
'Custom procedure: ConvertDateTime(datUTC) As Date
'Purpose: Return local date/time from Web Storage System UTC
'****************************************************************
Public Function ConvertDateTime(datUTC As Date) As Date
On Error Resume Next
Dim intZone As Integer
Dim datDate As Date
Dim cdoAppt As New CDO.Appointment

With cdoAppt
    'Save original local time zone
    intZone = .Configuration.Fields(cdoTimeZoneIDURN)
    'Switch to UTC
    .Configuration.Fields(cdoTimeZoneIDURN) = cdoUTC
    'You must update
    .Configuration.Fields.Update
    'Set start time equal to our UTC value
    .StartTime = datUTC
    'Switch back to local time zone
    .Configuration.Fields(cdoTimeZoneIDURN) = intZone
    'Update again to force the change
    .Configuration.Fields.Update
    'Read out the UTC date changed to local time
    datDate = .StartTime
End With
Set cdoAppt = Nothing
ConvertDateTime = datDate
End Function
```

Part V Advanced Topics

The PKMCDO Object Model

An extensive discussion of the PKMCDO Object Model is beyond the scope of this book. Instead, I'll cover some of the most important objects in the PKMCDO Object Model to give you a basic understanding of what PKMCDO can do. The PKMCDO Object Model allows you to accomplish programmatically many of the tasks that you would perform in the Web folders user interface. At the top of the PKMCDO Object Model is the KnowledgeServer object. To help you understand the dependencies in the PKMCDO Object Model, the *EnumerateWorkspaces* procedure displays workspaces, folders, and documents in the Debug window. Here is the code for the procedure:

```
Sub EnumerateWorkspaces()
Dim oServer As New PKMCDO.KnowledgeServer
Dim oWS As New PKMCDO.KnowledgeWorkspace
Dim oFolder As New PKMCDO.KnowledgeFolder
Dim oCategory As New PKMCDO.KnowledgeCategoryFolder
Dim oDocument As New PKMCDO.KnowledgeDocument
Dim oVersion As New PKMCDO.KnowledgeVersion
Dim oContentClass As New PKMCDO.KnowledgeContentClass
Dim rsWorkspaces, rsFolders, rsCategories As ADODB.Recordset
Dim rsDocuments, rsVersions As ADODB.Recordset
Dim strServerURL, strWorkspaceURL As String
Dim strFolderURL, strDocumentURL As String

On Error Resume Next
strServerURL = InputBox _
    ("Enter the URL for SharePoint Portal Server (http://<servername>):", _
    "Enumerate Workspaces")
If strServerURL = "" Then
    Exit Sub
End If
If Right(strServerURL, 1) = "/" Then
    strServerURL = Left(strServerURL, Len(strServerURL) - 1)
End If
oServer.DataSource.Open strServerURL & "/Public/Workspaces"
Debug.Print "Server Creation Date: " & oServer.CreationDate & " GMT"
Debug.Print "SMTP Server: " & oServer.SMTPServerName
Debug.Print "Workspaces on : " & strServerURL
Set rsWorkspaces = oServer.Workspaces
While Not rsWorkspaces.EOF
    strWorkspaceURL = rsWorkspaces.Fields(PKMCDO.cdostrURI_HREF)
    strWorkspaceURL = strServerURL & "/" _
        & Right(strWorkspaceURL, _
        Len(strWorkspaceURL) - InStrRev(strWorkspaceURL, "/"))
    Debug.Print rsWorkspaces.Fields(PKMCDO.cdostrURI_DisplayName)
    Debug.Print Chr(9) & "(" & _
        rsWorkspaces.Fields(PKMCDO.cdostrURI_Description) & ")"
```

```
Debug.Print Chr(9) & strWorkspaceURL
'Open the workspace
oWS.DataSource.Open strWorkspaceURL
Set rsFolders = oWS.Subfolders
Debug.Print Chr(9) & Chr(9) & "Folders:"
While Not rsFolders.EOF
    strFolderURL = rsFolders.Fields("DAV:href")
    Debug.Print Chr(9) & Chr(9) _
        & rsFolders.Fields(PKMCDO.cdostrURI_DisplayName)
    Debug.Print Chr(9) & Chr(9) & strFolderURL
    If rsFolders.Fields("DAV:contentclass") = _
       "urn:content-classes:rootcategoryfolder" Then
        oCategory.DataSource.Open strFolderURL
        Debug.Print Chr(9) & Chr(9); "Category: " & oCategory.DisplayName
        Set rsCategories = oCategory.Subfolders
        While Not rsCategories.EOF
            Debug.Print Chr(9) & Chr(9) & Chr(9) _
                & rsCategories.Fields(PKMCDO.cdostrURI_DisplayName)
            Debug.Print Chr(9) & Chr(9) & Chr(9) _
                & rsCategories.Fields("DAV:href")
            rsCategories.MoveNext
        Wend
    End If
    oFolder.DataSource.Open strFolderURL
    Debug.Print Chr(9) & Chr(9) & Chr(9) & "Items:"
    Set rsDocuments = oFolder.Items
    While Not rsDocuments.EOF
        strDocumentURL = rsDocuments.Fields("DAV:href")
        Debug.Print Chr(9) & Chr(9) & Chr(9) _
            & rsDocuments.Fields(PKMCDO.cdostrURI_DisplayName)
        Debug.Print Chr(9) & Chr(9) & Chr(9) _
            & strDocumentURL
        oDocument.DataSource.Open strDocumentURL
        Debug.Print Chr(9) & Chr(9) & Chr(9) & oDocument.Author
        Debug.Print Chr(9) & Chr(9) & Chr(9) & oDocument.Title
        Debug.Print Chr(9) & Chr(9) & Chr(9) & oDocument.ContentClass
        Set oContentClass = oDocument.ContentClassObject
        'Corresponds to Document Profile Name
        Debug.Print Chr(9) & Chr(9) & Chr(9) & oContentClass.Title
        Set rsVersions = oVersion.VersionHistory(strDocumentURL)
        While Not rsVersions.EOF
            Debug.Print Chr(9) & Chr(9) & Chr(9) & Chr(9) & _
                "Checked Out: " & rsVersions.Fields _
                ("urn:schemas-microsoft-com:publishing:IsCheckedOut")
            Debug.Print Chr(9) & Chr(9) & Chr(9) & Chr(9) & _
                "Version: " & rsVersions.Fields _
                ("urn:schemas-microsoft-com:publishing:FriendlyVersionID")
```

(continued)

```
                rsVersions.MoveNext
            Wend
            rsDocuments.MoveNext
        Wend
        rsFolders.MoveNext
    Wend
    rsWorkspaces.MoveNext
Wend
End Sub
```

> **Note** The code for EnumerateWorkspaces and additional SharePoint Portal Server code examples using MSDAIPP and PKMCDO can be found in the basPKMCDO standard module in the VBAProject.otm that accompanies this book.

The KnowledgeServer Object

The KnowledgeServer object represents a SharePoint Portal Server. KnowledgeServer objects are the primary mechanism for creating and organizing workspaces. The KnowledgeServer object provides methods for creating, deleting, and enumerating KnowledgeWorkspaces. A KnowledgeServer object contains a Workspaces property that returns an ADODB Recordset object containing all the KnowledgeWorkspaces in the KnowledgeServer. You obtain a KnowledgeServer object by opening it with a SharePoint Portal Server URL. Here's an example:

```
oServer.DataSource.Open strServerURL & "/Public/Workspaces"
Set rsWorkspaces = oServer.Workspaces
```

The KnowledgeWorkspace Object

The KnowledgeWorkspace object represents a knowledge workspace, which contains content-class definitions and property definitions, as well as the root Categories folder and the root Documents folder. A KnowledgeWorkspace object contains a Subfolders property that returns an ADODB Recordset object that contains all the KnowledgeFolders in the KnowledgeWorkspace. You obtain a KnowledgeWorkspace object by opening it with a workspace URL. Here's an example:

```
oWS.DataSource.Open strWorkspaceURL
Set rsFolders = oWS.Subfolders
```

The KnowledgeCategoryFolder Object

The KnowledgeCategoryFolder object represents a category folder in the SharePoint Portal Server folder hierarchy. A KnowledgeCategoryFolder object is a special type of KnowledgeFolder object. KnowledgeFolder objects provide a physical container for KnowledgeDocument objects. KnowledgeCategoryFolder objects provide a logical grouping of KnowledgeDocument objects. They do not actually contain the KnowledgeDocument objects, because one KnowledgeDocument object can belong to one or more KnowledgeCategoryFolder objects. A KnowledgeCategoryFolder object contains a Subfolders property that returns an ADODB Recordset object that contains all the subcategories in the KnowledgeCategoryFolder. It also contains an Items property that returns an ADODB Recordset object containing all the items that have been assigned to the category represented by the KnowledgeCategoryFolder object. Here's an example:

```
oCategory.DataSource.Open strFolderURL
Set rsCategories = oCategory.Subfolde rs
```

The KnowledgeFolder Object

The KnowledgeFolder object represents a knowledge folder. All documents are stored in a set of hierarchical folders that operate similarly to file-system directories. Some folders can contain items in addition to documents, such as property definitions and dictionaries. A KnowledgeFolder object contains an Items property that returns an ADODB Recordset object containing all the items in the KnowledgeFolder. Here's an example:

```
oFolder.DataSource.Open strFolderURL
Set rsDocuments = oFolder.Items
```

> **Note** All Recordsets returned by PKMCDO have a RecordCount property equal to –1. Instead of relying on the RecordCount property, you should use a While or Do Until loop to check for the EOF of the Recordset and use the *MoveNext* method within the loop.

The KnowledgeDocument Object

The KnowledgeDocument object represents a document that is contained in the store on a SharePoint Portal Server. You can access many of the default document properties such as Author, Title, Description, Keywords, and Categories directly through the KnowledgeDocument object.

```
oDocument.DataSource.Open rsDocuments.Fields("DAV:href")
Debug.Print Chr(9) & Chr(9) & Chr(9) & oDocument.Author
Debug.Print Chr(9) & Chr(9) & Chr(9) & oDocument.Title
Debug.Print Chr(9) & Chr(9) & Chr(9) & oDocument.ContentClass
```

The KnowledgeContentClass Object

The KnowledgeContentClass object represents a SharePoint Portal Server Document Profile. Each document in SharePoint Portal Server is associated with the KnowledgeContentClass object that defines the object through its ContentClassObject property.

```
Set oContentClass = oDocument.ContentClassObject
'Corresponds to document profile name
Debug.Print Chr(9) & Chr(9) & Chr(9) & oContentClass.Title
```

The KnowledgeVersion Object

The KnowledgeVersion object provides methods such as *Approve*, *CheckIn*, *CheckOut*, *Publish*, and *VersionHistory* for managing document versions. A KnowledgeVersion object is not a dependent object of a KnowledgeDocument object. You can obtain the versions for a KnowledgeDocument object by calling the *VersionHistory* method of the KnowledgeVersion object and supplying a URL to the KnowledgeDocument object. The *VersionHistory* method returns a Recordset object that contains all the versions of the KnowledgeDocument object specified in the URL.

```
Set rsVersions = oVersion.VersionHistory(strDocumentURL)
While Not rsVersions.EOF
  Debug.Print Chr(9) & Chr(9) & Chr(9) & Chr(9) & _
    "Checked Out: " & rsVersions.Fields _
    ("urn:schemas-microsoft-com:publishing:IsCheckedOut")
    Debug.Print Chr(9) & Chr(9) & Chr(9) & Chr(9) & _
    "Version: " & rsVersions.Fields _
    ("urn:schemas-microsoft-com:publishing:FriendlyVersionID")
    rsVersions.MoveNext
Wend
```

Using Outlook with SharePoint Portal Server   Chapter 16

> **Note**   The object libraries for Word 2002, Excel 2002, and PowerPoint 2002 support SharePoint Portal Server document management with properties and methods that are native to their respective object models. Depending upon the context, you might not have to use PKMCDO to get the job done. However, the Outlook 2002 Object Model does not offer any methods or properties that pertain to document management on SharePoint Portal Server.

An Outlook COM Add-In for SharePoint Portal Server

If you don't go through the entire process of creating a Northwind workspace, installing the Northwind Web Parts, and setting up the Northwind Document Profile, there's a COM Add-in you can use to publish Outlook message attachments to SharePoint Portal Server. This COM Add-in can help you learn about the PKMCDO Object Model or quickly check in and publish message attachments to a SharePoint Portal Server Documents folder. Interestingly enough, many Outlook users still rely on attachments as their primary means of document collaboration and versioning. The sending and resending of these document attachments consumes network bandwidth and storage resources on Exchange Server. Use of these resources for attachment-based document collaboration translates to a considerable expense over time. To wean these users off sending attachment versions of a document, teach them how to use this Add-in to publish their documents to a SharePoint Portal Server Documents folder. Using SharePoint subscription notification about a version change is more efficient and less error prone than sending versions back and forth in message attachments.

Installing the SharePoint Portal Server Add-In

If you install the SharePoint Portal Server Add-in, you can examine the source code, modify it to suit your requirements, and use the Add-in to publish message attachments to SharePoint Portal Server.

To install the SharePoint Portal Server COM Add-in

1. Navigate to the SharePoint Portal Server COM Add-In folder under the Using Outlook With SharePoint Portal Server folder under the 5. Advanced Topics folder.
2. Double-click SharePointPortalServerAddin.zip. If you do not have a Zip utility, obtain WinZip at *http://www.winzip.com*.

Part V   Advanced Topics

3. Extract SharePointPortalServerAddin.zip to an empty folder. All the code for the COM Add-in as well as the compiled spps.dll is contained in the Zip file.

4. Select Options on the Tools menu.

5. Click the Other page, and then click the Advanced Options button.

6. Click the COM Add-Ins button.

7. Click Add on the COM Add-Ins dialog box, and then use the Add Add-In dialog box to select spps.dll in the folder used in step 3.

Using the SharePoint Portal Server Add-In

The SharePoint Portal Server Add-in adds the Publish Attachments command to the File menu for an Outlook Inspector. You can select one or more attachments to publish to a SharePoint Portal Server enhanced folder URL, as shown in Figure 16-27. You can optionally create a reply message that contains publication results, as illustrated in Figure 16-28.

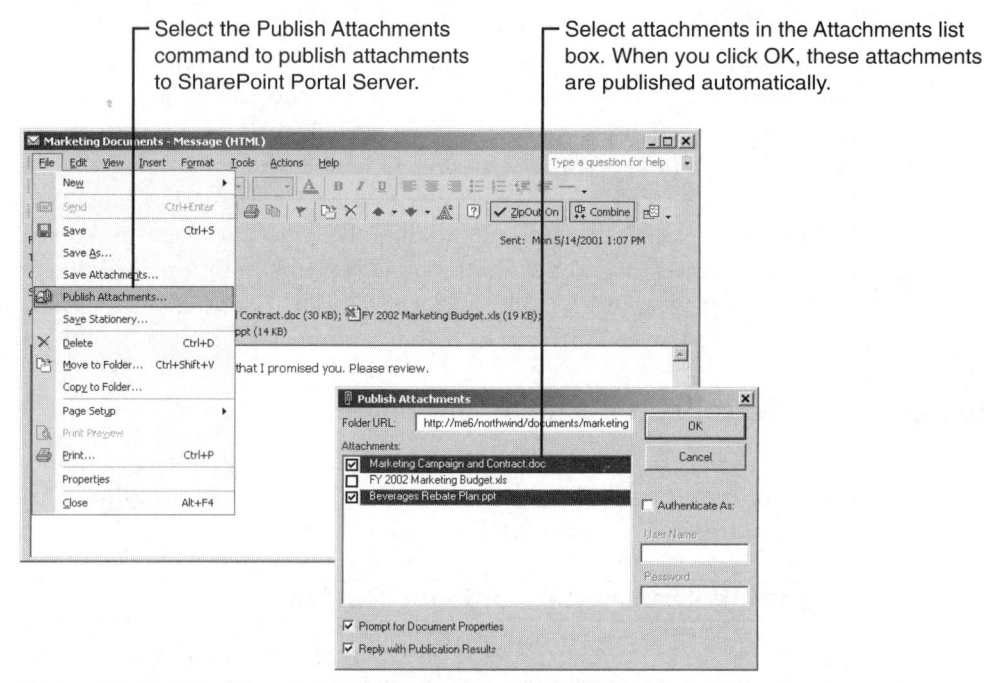

Figure 16-27 The SharePoint Portal Server COM Add-in publishes attachments to a SharePoint Portal Server Documents folder.

Using Outlook with SharePoint Portal Server   Chapter 16

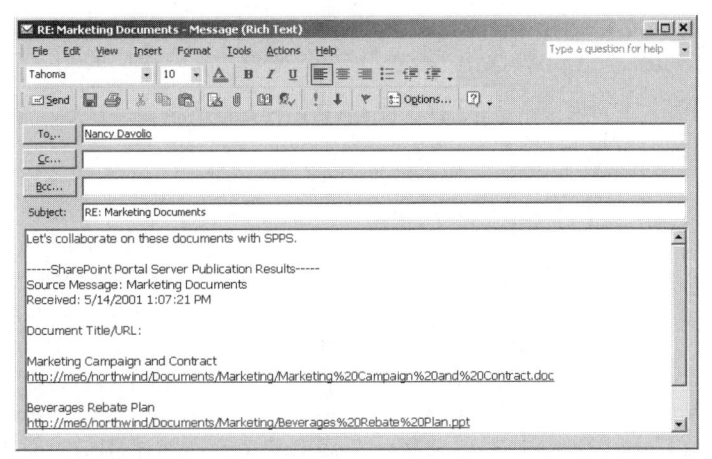

Figure 16-28 Send a reply message to the sender to share the publication results.

> **Note**   In order for the SharePoint Portal Server COM Add-in to function correctly, your SharePoint Portal Server workspace coordinator should assign you the author role or higher.

To add attachments to a Document folder

1. Open the message containing the attachments you want to publish.
2. Select Publish Attachments on the File menu.
3. Enter the URL of a SharePoint Portal Server Documents folder in the Folder URL edit box. The next time you publish attachments, the COM Add-in will remember the URL for the folder.
4. Select one or more attachments in the Attachments list box. Use Ctrl+Click to select multiple attachments if necessary.
5. Check the Prompt For Document Properties box if you want to be prompted for document properties such as Title, Author, Keywords, and Description.
6. Check the Reply With Publication Results if you want to send a reply message to the sender informing him or her of publication results.
7. Click OK.

Part V Advanced Topics

8. If you elected to complete the Document Properties dialog box, enter *Document Properties* and click OK.

9. If you elected to reply with publication results, type a message if required and click Send.

SharePoint Portal Server COM Add-In Code

The code for the SharePoint Portal Server COM Add-in is straightforward. When the NewInspector event fires, a MailItem object is instantiated. Because this MailItem object (named *objMailItem*) is declared using the *WithEvents* keyword in the declarations of the OutAddIn class, you can trap item-level events on *objMailItem*. In this case, the important item-level event is the Open event. In the Open event, the Publish Attachments menu item is added to the File menu as follows:

```
Private Sub objMailItem_Open(Cancel As Boolean)
Dim cbFile As Office.CommandBar
Set cbFile = objMailItem.GetInspector.CommandBars.Item("File")
On Error Resume Next
Set cbbSPPS = cbFile.FindControl(Tag:="SPPS Publish Attachments")
If cbbSPPS Is Nothing Then
    Set cbbSPPS = _
        cbFile.Controls.Add(Type:=msoControlButton, _
        Parameter:="SPPS Publish Attachments", Before:=7, Temporary:=True)
    With cbbSPPS
        .Parameter = "SPPS Publish Attachments"
        .FaceId = 258
        .Style = msoButtonIconAndCaption
        .Caption = "Publish Attachments..."
        .Tag = "SPPS Publish Attachments"
        .BeginGroup = False
    End With
End If
If objMailItem.Attachments.Count = 0 Then
    cbbSPPS.Visible = False
Else
    cbbSPPS.Visible = True
End If
End Sub
```

When the Close event for *objMailItem* fires, the Publish Attachments command bar control is removed from the File menu. Here's the code:

```
Private Sub objMailItem_Close(Cancel As Boolean)
On Error Resume Next
```

```
Dim cbFile As Office.CommandBar
    Set cbFile = objMailItem.GetInspector.CommandBars.Item("File")
    Set cbbSPPS = cbFile.FindControl(Tag:="SPPS Publish Attachments")
    cbbSPPS.Delete
End Sub
```

That's all there is to the code in the OutAddIn class of the COM Add-in. The other important code is contained in the frmPublish form. When this form loads, the Initialize event fires. The Initialize event for a UserForm is equivalent to the Load event for a Visual Basic form. The *Initialize* procedure checks for registry values that supply a folder URL and determine whether the Prompt For Document Properties and Reply With Publication Results boxes are checked. The procedure then uses the Attachments collection to populate the Attachments list box.

```
Private Sub UserForm_Initialize()
Dim i, intCount As Integer
Dim strURL As String
Dim blnPrompt, blnResults As Boolean
On Error Resume Next
strURL = _
    GetKeyValueEx(HKEY_CURRENT_USER, gstrRegKey, "URL")
If strURL <> "" Then
    txtURL = strURL
    blnPrompt = _
        GetKeyValueEx(HKEY_CURRENT_USER, gstrRegKey, "Prompt")
    If blnPrompt Then
        chkPrompt.Value = True
    Else
        chkPrompt.Value = False
    End If
    blnResults = _
        GetKeyValueEx(HKEY_CURRENT_USER, gstrRegKey, "Results")
    If blnResults Then
        chkResults.Value = True
    Else
        chkResults.Value = False
    End If
End If
lstAttachments.Clear
'objItem is declared as a form-level variable
Set objItem = golApp.ActiveInspector.CurrentItem
intCount = objItem.Attachments.Count
For i = 1 To intCount
    If objItem.Attachments.Item(i).Type = olByValue Then
        lstAttachments.AddItem _
            objItem.Attachments.Item(i).DisplayName
    End If
Next
End Sub
```

Part V Advanced Topics

After the form has been loaded, the code behind the cmdOK button does the actual work of publishing documents to SharePoint Portal Server. This code derives from the *PublishSharePointDocument* method in the Outlook Shared Activities Add-in discussed earlier. The lstAttachments ActiveX control supports a selected property that lets you determine whether the attachment has been selected for publication. Once the publication is complete, a reply message is prepared for the sender of the original message. This message informs the sender of the URLs for the published documents on SharePoint Portal Server. Notice that you must use the Replace function to convert the SharePoint URL to a canonical URL in order for the URL to work correctly in the body of the reply message. Canonical URLs do not contain spaces. The code for cmdOK is shown here:

```
Private Sub cmdOK_Click()
Dim oFolder As New PKMCDO.KnowledgeFolder
Dim oDoc As PKMCDO.KnowledgeDocument
Dim oStream As ADODB.Stream
Dim objMsg As MailItem
Dim strPath, strURL, strDisplayName, strMsg, strError As String
Dim i As Integer
On Error Resume Next
If txtURL = "" Then
    MsgBox "You must supply a URL to SPPS folder.", vbInformation
    Exit Sub
End If
On Error Resume Next
oFolder.DataSource.Open txtURL
If Err Then
    MsgBox "Could not open the URL:" & vbCrLf & txtURL, vbCritical
    txtURL.SelStart = 0
    txtURL.SelLength = Len(txtURL)
    txtURL.SetFocus
    Exit Sub
Else
    'Hide this form
    Me.Hide
    frmWait.Show
    DoEvents
    'Persist settings to registry
    SetKeyValue HKEY_CURRENT_USER, _
        gstrRegKey, "URL", txtURL, REG_SZ
    SetKeyValue HKEY_CURRENT_USER, _
        gstrRegKey, "Prompt", Abs(chkPrompt.Value), REG_DWORD
    SetKeyValue HKEY_CURRENT_USER, _
        gstrRegKey, "Results", Abs(chkResults.Value), REG_DWORD
    'Create message for Post Item
    strMsg = vbCrLf & vbCrLf & _
```

```vb
                    "-----SharePoint Portal Server Publication Results-----" & _
                    vbCrLf & "Source Message: " & objItem.Subject & vbCrLf & _
                    "Received: " & objItem.ReceivedTime & vbCrLf & vbCrLf & _
                    "Document Title/URL:" & vbCrLf & vbCrLf
End If
'Iterate over attachments
For i = 1 To lstAttachments.ListCount
    'Only publish selected items
    If lstAttachments.Selected(i - 1) = True Then
        strDisplayName = objItem.Attachments.Item(i).DisplayName
        strPath = GetTempDir & objItem.Attachments.Item(i).FileName
        objItem.Attachments.Item(i).SaveAsFile strPath
        Set oDoc = New PKMCDO.KnowledgeDocument
        'Open binary stream
        Set oStream = oDoc.OpenStream
        oStream.Type = adTypeBinary
        oStream.SetEOS
        'Load the attachment from the temp folder
        oStream.LoadFromFile strPath
        oStream.Flush
        Set oStream = Nothing
        'Delete the attachment from temp folder
        Kill strPath
        strURL = txtURL & "/" & strDisplayName
        'Save to URL
        If chkAuthenticateAs = True Then
            oDoc.DataSource.SaveTo _
                SourceURL:=strURL, _
                Username:=txtUserName, _
                Password:=txtPassword
        Else
            oDoc.DataSource.SaveTo (strURL)
        End If
        'Check for errors
        If Err = 0 Then
            If chkPrompt.Value = True Then
                With frmProperties
                    .Caption = strDisplayName & " Properties"
                    .txtAuthor = oDoc.Author
                    .txtTitle = oDoc.Title
                    .txtKeywords = GetKeywords(oDoc.Keywords)
                    .txtDescription = oDoc.Description
                    .Show 1
                    DoEvents
                End With
                'If True, set oDoc properties
```

Part V Advanced Topics

```
                        If blnProperties Then
                            oDoc.Author = frmProperties.txtAuthor
                            oDoc.Title = frmProperties.txtTitle
                            If frmProperties.txtKeywords <> "" Then
                                'Changes txtKeywords into array
                                oDoc.Keywords = _
                                    SetKeywords(frmProperties.txtKeywords)
                            End If
                            oDoc.Description = frmProperties.txtDescription
                            oDoc.DataSource.Save
                        End If
                        Unload frmProperties
                        DoEvents
                    End If
                    strMsg = strMsg & oDoc.Title & vbCrLf _
                        & Replace(oDoc.DataSource.SourceURL, " ", "%20") _
                        & vbCrLf & vbCrLf
                Else
                    'Error occurred
                    strError = strError & strDisplayName & vbCrLf _
                        & Replace(strURL, " ", "%20") & vbCrLf _
                        & "Error Number: " & Err.Number & vbCrLf _
                        & "Error Description: " & Err.Description _
                        & vbCrLf & vbCrLf
                End If
                'Checkin and publish
                Dim oVersion As New PKMCDO.KnowledgeVersion
                oVersion.Checkin strURL
                oVersion.Publish strURL
                Set oVersion = Nothing
                Set oDoc = Nothing
            End If
        Next
        If chkResults = True Then
            If strError <> "" Then
                strMsg = strMsg & strError
            End If
            'Create a reply message
            Set objMsg = objItem.Reply
            objMsg.BodyFormat = olFormatRichText
            objMsg.Body = strMsg
            objMsg.Display
        End If
        Unload frmWait
        Unload Me
    End Sub
```

SharePoint Development Opportunities

SharePoint Portal Server offers a wealth of development opportunities on its own or in conjunction with Office XP applications such as Outlook 2002. The Web Storage System provides a solid platform for building collaborative applications. It's up to developers like you to create outstanding solutions for the SharePoint Portal Server platform. Unlike development on the Exchange 2000 Server platform—which uses server-based technologies such as Web Storage System forms (SP1 or later), event sinks, and the Exchange 2000 workflow engine—SharePoint Portal Server development occurs on both the client and the server. PKMCDO operates as an object library on both client and server computers. Use the version of the SharePoint Portal Server SDK supplied on the companion CD to broaden your knowledge of the PKMCDO Object Model and the best practices for SharePoint Portal Server development. Based upon what you now know about Outlook 2002 and SharePoint Portal Server, you can begin to evaluate integrated Outlook and SharePoint Portal Server solutions for your own organization.

Where To Go from Here

Many resources can help you deepen your understanding of the material in this chapter. I'll list some of the most helpful ones here.

Microsoft Knowledge Base Articles   Microsoft Knowledge Base articles are available on the Web at *http://support.microsoft.com/support*. Also see "Using Outlook with SharePoint Portal Server (Chapter 16) KB Articles" in the Microsoft Web Sites folder under the Help And Web Sites folder on the companion CD.

SharePoint Portal Server Articles and Resources

- See the item entitled "SharePoint Portal Server Technical Articles" in the Help folder under the Help And Web Sites folder on the companion CD.

- The SharePoint Portal Server SDK is available at *http://www.microsoft.com/sharepoint/downloads/tools/SDK.asp*.

- See the white paper, "SharePoint Portal Server as a Collaborative Solution Platform," at *http://msdn.microsoft.com/library/default.asp?URL=/library/techart/Tahoe.htm*.

- See the "Web Storage System Schema Usage and Best Practice Guide" at *http://msdn.microsoft.com/library/default.asp?URL=/library/techart/Wssschemause.htm*.

Part V   Advanced Topics

Books on Web Storage System Development

Gomez, Alex; Jamison, Scott; Wesolowski, George. *Developing Applications with Exchange 2000: A Programmer's Guide.* Boston, MA: Addison Wesley, 2001.

Martin, Mindy. *Programming Collaborative Web Applications with Microsoft Exchange 2000 Server.* Redmond, WA: Microsoft Press, 2000.

Rizzo, Thomas. *Programming Microsoft Outlook and Microsoft Exchange, Second Edition.* Redmond, WA: Microsoft Press, 2000.

Index

Symbol
~ (tilde), 185, 187

A
Access. *See* Microsoft Access
access, restricting. *See* Administration properties; permissions
Action buttons, 143
actions, 94–100
   Address Form Like property, 218
   buttons, 143
   creating new, 96–97, 99, 144
   CustomAction event, 376–77
   function of, 116–17
   making unavailable, 95
   naming, 96
   OnAction property, 453–54
   Post To Folder, 95
   Reply (*see* Reply actions)
   Reply To Folder (*see* Reply To Folder actions)
   returning items to sender, 305
   rules, specifying based on, 304–5
   voting buttons, 218
Actions menu
   automatic inclusion of forms, 90
   disabling commands, 582–83
   hidden forms, 234
Activate event, 356–57
ActiveWindow method, 417
ActiveX, 3
   adding custom property pages, 679–81
   binding controls, 207
   Click event, 201, 207
   COM Add-ins (*see* COM Add-ins)
   compiling, 684–85
   controls, 207–8
   data objects (*see* ADO (ActiveX Data Objects))
   events, 207
   installation, 207
   licensing, 207
   Microsoft ActiveX Data Objects 2.5 Library, 401
   Microsoft Office XP Developer, 33–34
   modal dialog boxes, 688–89
   NewInspector event, 354

ActiveX, *continued*
   Outlook Extensions Library, 37
   Outlook Today ActiveX control, 715
   property page controls, 328–29, 337
   registration of controls, 132
   security settings affecting, 715
   setup programs for custom forms, 594
   third-party control events, 132
   UserForms, 31
ActiveX Data Objects. *See* ADO (ActiveX Data Objects)
Activity page, 531
AdaptiveMenus property, 455
Add Folder Address To Personal Address Book option, 294–95
adding
   columns, 25–26
   controls, 59–65, 78, 132–34, 517
   dialog boxes, 31
   fields, 20, 48–49, 135–38
   images, 204
   Web Parts, 770–72
add-ins
   COM Add-ins (*see* COM Add-ins)
   debugging tools, 35–36
   design tools, 32–34
   development tools, 36–37
   Microsoft Office XP Developer, 33–34
AddIn.vbp, 662
Add method
   Attachment collection object, 490
   Controls collection object, 517
   Items collection object, 477–78, 557
   PropertyPages collection object, 328–29
address books
   adding entries, 461
   AddressEntries collection object, 460–62
   AddressEntry object, 462–67
   AddressEntry properties, 465–66
   AddressLists collection object, 459–60
   availability of users, 464
   changing entries, 463
   deleting entries, 463

847

Index

address books, *continued*
   displaying entry details, 462
   folder addresses, adding to, 178–79
   GetFreeBusy method, 464
   programmatic security settings, 643
   purpose of, 531
   Shared Contacts folder, exposing as, 550–51
AddressEntries collection object, 460–62
AddressEntry object, 462–67
AddressEntry properties, 465–66
Address Form Like A option, 227–28, 241–42
Address Form Like property, 218
Address Information field, programmatic security settings, 644
addressing
   Add Folder Address To Personal Address Book option, 294–95
   Address Form Like A option, 227–28, 241–42
   Global Address Book, 295
   hidden, 131
   profile options, setting, 179
   To field, preaddressing, 177–79, 215
AddressLists collection object, 459–60
Administration properties, 70
   discussion applications, 106
   releasing folders, 307–8
   setting for folders, 293–96, 588
Administrative form
   Admpack.exe installation, 630–31
   CDO security settings, 628
   options to override security, 629–32
   Outlook Security form, 632–34
   Outlook Security Settings public folder, 631–32
administrators, submitting forms for publication to, 592–93, 596
Admpack.exe installation, 630–31
ADO (ActiveX Data Objects)
   binding controls to data sources, 524
   connection strings, 553–55
   SharePoint Portal Server, 786
   Web Storage System Explorer, 36
ADODB Stream object, 820
advanced properties, setting, 133, 141
AdvancedSearchComplete event, 331–32
AdvancedSearch method, 332, 421–25, 698
AdvancedSearchStopped event, 332
Advanced toolbar
   adding VBA command bar button, 313–14
   Current View list, 260
   Field Chooser, 262
   Group By icon, 270
aligning controls, 138
All Fields page, 114

Allow These Forms In This Folder options, 256
Always Use Microsoft Word As The E-mail Editor property, 144–45
Anonymous role, 69
Application Folders Send/Receive group, 286, 344
Application Folders SynchObject, 344
Application-level events
   AdvancedSearchComplete event, 331–32
   AdvancedSearchStopped, 332
   firing order, 381–82
   ItemSend, 327
   MapiLogonComplete, 332
   NewMail, 327–28
   OptionsPagesAdd, 328–29, 685
   Quit event, 329–30
   Reminder, 330
   Startup, 330–31
   VBScript with, 326
Application object
   ActiveWindow method, 417
   AdvancedSearch method, 421–25, 698
   COMAddIns collection object, 655–57
   CopyItem method, 419–20
   CreateItem method, 417–18
   CreateObject method, 419
   events raised, 323
   folder home pages, 735
   GetNameSpace("MAPI") method, 420
   list of methods, properties, and events, 416
   Microsoft Office Object Model objects, 420–21
   Outlook Object Model, 314–15
   purposes of, 416
   Reminders collection object, 332–35
   WithEvents keyword, 322
Application Quit event, 329–30
applications
   calendar (*see* calendar applications)
   contact management (*see* Northwind Contact Management application)
   creating from built-in modules (*see* customizing built-in modules)
   discussion (*see* discussion applications)
   distributing (*see* distributing applications)
   distribution list (*see* distribution lists)
   feedback collection (*see* Art Approval form)
   Internet (*see* Digital Dashboards; folder home pages)
   Product Ideas (*see* Product Ideas application)
   training management (*see* Training Management application)
   types of, 5–16
   Vacation Request (*see* Vacation Request application)
Appointment forms, 111

848

Index

AppointmentItem object, 496–501
appointments
   AppointmentItem object, 496–501
   color, 497
   creating exceptions, 498–500
   creating recurring, 497
   deleted recurring, 500
   exceptions, 498–500
   GetAssociatedAppointment method, 501–2
   meetings (*see* meetings)
   original dates of exceptions, 500
   recurrence patterns, setting, 497–98
   status of requested meetings, 504–5
approval routing, 799–801
Art Approval form, 212–20
   Address Form Like property, 218
   create form, 214–15
   folder creation, 212–13
   initial values, setting, 215
   options, setting, 215–16
   preaddressing, 215
   publishing, 217–18
   reply address specification, 216
   reviewing replies, 219–20
   Run mode, 214
   sending, 219
   specifying voting buttons, 216
   tracking item storage specification, 216–17
   using voting buttons, 219
ASP (Active Server Pages), 3
   folder home pages, 5–6, 714
AttachmentAdd event, 374
Attachment collection object, *Add* method, 490
AttachmentRead event, 374–75
attachments
   alternatives to, 837
   Attachment collection object, 490
   compressing, 37
   DocumentItem object, 490–500
   E-mail Security Update, 283
   Level 1, 618–21, 630, 637–40
   Level 2, 619, 638–39, 641
   Message field, 181, 183–86
   .oft files, 596
   Outlook E-mail Security Update, 618–21
   security settings, 639–41
   stripping from messages, 327
   types blocked by security, table of, 620–21
Attachment Security component, 705–6
Author role, 69, 299
AutoArchiving folders, 616–17
AutoLayout, 20, 136
Auto List, 29–30

automatic formatting, 281–82
automatic journaling, 534–37
automatic phone dialer, displaying, 427
automation, external, 529–30
Automation objects, creating, 419
AutoSize cells, 204

B

background colors, controls, 155
backing up forms, 88–89, 147–48
bars. *See* Outlook Bar; toolbars
BeforeAttachmentSave event, 375
BeforeCheckNames event, 375
BeforeDelete event, 375
BeforeGroupAdd event, 349
BeforeGroupRemove event, 349
BeforeGroupSwitch event, 348
BeforeNavigate event, 348
BeforeReminderShow event, 333
BeforeShortcutAdd event, 350–51
BeforeShortcutRemove event, 351
Best Fit command, 27, 50, 52–53
Beta Contacts folder, 12, 43–47
Beta Contacts form, 44–45
Beta Participants view, 43, 45, 50–54
binding
   ActiveX controls, 207
   CheckBox controls, 195
   ComboBox controls, 196
   controls to data sources, 524
   controls to fields, 134–36, 157–60, 193–99
   controls to fields at runtime, 523–24
   ListBox controls, 198–99
   OptionButton controls, 193–94
Body property, 486–87
BorderStyle property, 157
Bring To Back option, 155–57
Bring To Front option, 155–57
browsers
   Internet Explorer, 728
   Internet Explorer Script Debugger, 389
   Outlook Web Access for display to, 6
   viewing forms in (*see* Outlook View Control)
   Web Views, 19
built-in forms. *See* customizing built-in modules
built-in modules. *See* customizing built-in modules
buttons
   adding to toolbars, 341
   CommandBarButton object, 457–58
   icons, custom, 687–88
   images, using on, 441–43
   voting (*see* voting buttons)

849

Index

C

C++ coding for events, 321. *See also* Microsoft Visual C++
calculated values. *See* Formula fields
calendar applications, 12
   AppointmentItem object, 496–501
   control, ActiveX, 37
   customizing built-in modules, 41–42
   drop-down controls, 33
   Exception object, 496
   forms, creating, 126
   MeetingItem object, 501–5
   My Shared Calendar Web Part, 753
   RecurrencePattern object, 496, 498
Calendar forms, creating, 126
canceling events, 373–74
categories, 802–3, 835
Category property, 144
CCur function, 174–75
CD, companion
   add-ins, 35
   Help And Web Sites folder, 18
   third-party tools, 17
CDO (Collaboration Data Objects)
   3.0, referencing in SharePoint, 826–27
   CDOEX, 786
   COM Add-ins, 707
   installing, 467
   messaging object access, 466–67
   objects with security restrictions, table of, 628–29
   Outlook E-mail Security Update, 628–29
   programmatic settings, 642–44
   purpose of, 400–401
   Redemption, 648–50
   Sender object, 489
   SharePoint Portal Server, 786
   time conversions, UTC to local, 831
   trusted code, 647
   versions, 400–401
cells, allowing user editing, 280–81
Center In Form command, 78
Change event, 456–57
Change Large Icon property, 146
Change Message Class form, 605
Change Small Icon property, 144
Characteristics Of The New Form, Reply To Folder action, 241
CheckBox controls, 63–64
   adding with Field Chooser, 137
   binding, 195
   description of, 194
   initial values, setting, 195
   Yes/No fields, 162

child objects
   with events, 322–26
   instantiation, 325–26
Classified Ads folder sample, 248
clearing initial values, 91
Click event
   ActiveX controls, 201, 207
   CommandBarButton object, 457
   CommandButton control, 200–202
   Control object with, 524–25
   Image controls with, 205
   procedures, creating, 376
   support for, 201
clients, deploying security settings to, 635–37
Close event, 357, 376, 678
closing forms, 125
cmd parameter, 187
code
   editing (*see* Microsoft Script Editor; Script Editor)
   enabling document publication, 819–23
   one-off forms, 120–22, 625
   preventing execution, 95
   trusted (*see* trust)
Code Librarian, 17
collaborating on information, 4. *See also* discussion applications
Collaboration Data Objects (CDO). *See* CDO (Collaboration Data Objects)
collecting information, 4
collection objects, referencing, 413–14
colors
   controls, 155
   labels, 497
columns
   adding, 25–26
   Best Fit, 50, 52–53
   Column Heading row, 262
   combination, 264–67
   creating, 262
   defined, 259
   deleting, 25–26, 262
   first non-empty field, showing value, 266–67
   formatting, 26–27, 262–64
   formula, 267–68
   heading labels, changing, 263–64
   headings, adding, 49–50, 52
   order of, changing, 49
   order of headings, 103
   sizing, 27
   widths, 50, 52–53
COM Add-ins, 3
   ActiveX .exe files, 654
   Add-In Designer, 661–62
   AddInDesigner dialog box, 666–70

850

Index

COM Add-ins, *continued*
   adding, 658
   AddIn.vbp, 662
   application-level events (*see* Application-level events)
   Apply button, 683–84
   architecture of, 664–65
   Attachment Security component, 705–6
   base class (OutAddin), 664–66
   C++ coding for events, 321
   CDO, 647, 707
   changes, enabling, 683–84
   checking for, 672–73
   checklist, development, 708
   classes used, 664
   COMAddIns collection object, 655–57
   COM Add-ins dialog box, 657–58
   command bars, 437, 445–46, 685–88
   compiling, 684–85, 693–94, 707
   Connect class, 664
   Connect property, 672
   creating projects in Visual Basic, 659–63
   debugging, 692–94
   default security, 704
   defined, 654, 664–65
   deployment, 385, 708–10
   Description option, 667
   detecting loading on startup, 330
   development tools, 654–55
   dialog boxes, adding, 688–92
   digital certificates, 702–3, 705
   dimensioning object variables, 686
   dirty, marking as, 681–83
   disconnection, 675–78
   displaying Property page, 685
   event procedures, coding, 670–72
   Explorer command bar button creation, 686–87
   forms, adding, 689–90
   Friend keyword, 674
   friendly names, 656
   icons, custom command bars, 687–88
   IDTExtensibility2 event procedures, 670–72
   IDTExtensibility2 Type Library, 664
   InitHandler procedure, 673–74
   initial load behavior, 667–70
   instantiation of variables, 674
   interfaces of template project, *665*
   item-level event control, 366–67
   Items collection object events, 363
   listing, 657
   loading, 658, 667–68, 672–73, 704
   loading event, 673–75
   macro security, 700–702

COM Add-ins, *continued*
   memory leaks, 676–78
   Microsoft Add-In Designer Object Library, 662–63
   Microsoft Forms 2.0 forms, 690
   Microsoft Office 10.0 Object Library, 662, 685–88
   Microsoft Outlook 10.0 Object Library, 662
   modal dialog boxes, 688–89
   naming, 661, 667
   Object Model Guard, 705–6
   OnAction property, 686
   OnAddInsUpdate event, 672–73
   OnBeginShutdown event, 673
   OnConnection event, 673–75
   OnDisconnection event, 675–78
   OnStartupComplete event, 678
   opening new projects in Visual Basic, 660
   OptionsPagesAdd event, 685
   Outlook Object Model access, 707
   Outlook Shared Activities, 553–54 (*see also* Outlook Shared Activities COM Add-in)
   Package and Deployment Wizard, 708–9
   porting preexistent code, 663–64
   ProgIDs, 328–29, 656, 661, 668, 685–86, 699
   programming environment variances, 398–99
   property pages, adding, 678–85
   public methods, calling, 691–700
   Redemption, 648–50
   registration, 668–69, 699
   registry, saving settings to, 681–82
   Registry Key, additional data, 667
   removing, 659
   Sample Page property page installation, 679–81
   samples, 694–98
   Satellite DLL Name, 667
   Search, 698
   security, 385, 699–700 (*see also* COM Add-in security)
   selfcert.exe, 702–3
   settings, design environment, 666–70
   setup packages, 708–10
   SharePoint Portal Server, 837–44
   shutdown event, 673
   signing projects, 703–5
   template project, 659–60, 662–63
   testing, 670
   Test Trust, 645–47, 698–99
   ThisOutlookSession class module, 654
   trapping events, 322
   troubleshooting, 694
   trusted, 384–85, 632, 644–47, 675, 698–99, 705–7
   unloading, 658, 675–78
   user interface modification, 6
   user-interfaces, adding, 685

851

Index

COM Add-ins, *continued*
  variables, setting to Nothing, 677
  VBA for development, 385
  Version Compatibility option, 695
  Visual Basic for, 654
  Visual Basic forms, adding, 689–90
  Visual Studio Installer, 710
  Web-based setup packages, 709
  Windows Installer setups, 710
  WithEvents keyword, 322, 662–63
  ZipOut 2000, 37
COM Add-in security
  digital certificates, 704
  intellectual property, 699–700
  Object Model Guard, 705–6
  settings, default, 704
  source code, 699
  trust, 384–85, 632, 644–47, 675, 698–99, 705–7
combination columns, 264–67
Combination fields, 23, 162, 164–67
  automatic update option, 164
  creating, 164
  expressions, building, 165
  formatting, 166
  showing only first non-empty field, 166
  text fragments, including, 165
ComboBox controls, 59–61
  adding to forms, 78
  binding, 196
  CommandBarComboBox object, 458
  hiding columns, 521–22
  initial values, 197
  inserting values, 196–97
  List property, 520–21
  ListStyle property, 196
  list type selection, 196
  MatchEntry property, 197–98
  OnAction property, 453
  PossibleValues property, 520
  properties, setting, 78–80
  purpose of, 195
CommandBarButton object, 457–58, 686
CommandBarComboBox, 686
command bar control events, 456–57
CommandBarControls collection object, 448–59
  AdaptiveMenus property, 455
  adding custom controls, 450–52
  Add method, 449, 451
  BeginGroup property, 456
  Caption property, 449
  Change events, 456–57
  Click events, 456–57

CommandBarControls collection object, *continued*
  CommandBarButton object, 450, 457–58
  CommandBarComboBox object, 450, 453, 458
  CommandBarControl object, 449–57
  CommandBarPopup object, 450, 452, 459
  Count property, 449
  dimensioning controls, 449–50
  Enabled property, 454
  events, 456–57
  FindControl method, 456
  IsPriorityDropped property, 455
  OnAction property, 453–54
  OnUpdate event, 457
  Parameters property, 454
  purpose, 448
  State property, 455
  Visible property, 452, 454
CommandBar object, 437–48
command bars, 32, 437–48
  adding custom controls, 450–52
  adding to collection, 443–44
  built-in, 438
  button images, 441–43
  collection object (*see* CommandBars collection object)
  COM Add-In (*see* COM Add-Ins, command bars)
  controls (*see* CommandBarControls collection object)
  deleting, 445–46
  disabling, 454
  docks, 438
  events, 445
  icons, custom, 687–88
  instantiating objects, 450
  preventing user modification, 448
  printing bar information, 439–41
  resetting, 446
  retrieving existing, 444
  running procedures from controls, 453–54, 457
  separators between buttons, 456
  State property, 455
  visibility of, 452, 454
CommandBars collection object, 437–48
  Add method, 443–44
  button images, 441–43
  CommandBar object, 445–48
  deleting command bars, 445–46
  Enabled property, 448
  OnUpdate event, 445
  Position property, 444
  printing bar information, 439–41
  Reset method, 446

Index

CommandBars collection object, *continued*
    retrieving existing command bars, 444
    ShowPopup method, 446–47
    Temporary property, 444
    Type property, 444
CommandButton controls, 200–202
command buttons
    adding to toolbar with VBA, 331
    creating procedures for, 202
commands, disabling, 582–83
Companies folder, 14–15
    enabling SharePoint, 814
    Northwind Dashboard as folder home page for, 765
Companies Web Part, 768–69, 773–74
Company form, Northwind, 559–75
    code enabling document publication, 819–23
    Contacts form, based on, 559
    control declarations, 560–61
    initializing controls, 561–64
    Outlook View Control, 564–68
    PivotTable Lists, 572–74
    Possible Values edit box, 568
    Published Documents page, 827–28
    publishing documents with, 815–17
    Restriction property, 571
    retrieving possible field values, 568–69
    script-level variables, 560
    Shared Activities page, 571–72
    Shared Items toolbar creation, 570
    updating contacts, 569–70
    users, determining status of, 574
compiling
    ActiveX controls, 684–85
    COM Add-ins, 693–94, 707
Compose page, 76–84
    adding ComboBox controls, 78
    aligning controls, 80–81
    centering controls, 78
    controls, removing, 77
    defined, 127
    Frame controls, 83
    graphic, adding, 82–83
    Image controls, 83–84
    initial values, setting, 80
    labels, adding, 80–81
    Message control, 77–78
    moving controls, 81–82
    purpose of, 112–13
    sizing controls, 77
    tab order, 84, 140–41
    viewing, 129
conditions for rules, 301–4

Connection object, 828
constants
    declaring, 411–12
    intrinsic, 412
    Outlook 2002 Object Model, 530
    script-level, 560
contact applications. *See* contact management features; Northwind Contact Management application
Contact forms, 111
    Company form based on, 559–60
    creating, 126
ContactItem objects, 509–12
contact management features, 531–33
    automatic journaling, 534–37
    customizing built-in modules, 42
    database integration, 539–40
    links, 540–42
    Outlook View Control, 539–40
    PivotTable Lists, 535–36, 540
    synchronization, 537
Contact property, 144
Contacts form, customizing, 57–65
Contacts module, 42
content sources, 786, 803–7
Contributor role, 299
Control object
    aliases, 519
    Click event, 524–25
    dimensioned as script-level variables, 519
    Enabled property, 520
    hiding columns, 521–22
    instantiation, 519
    Layout Flags property, 522–23
    List property, 520–21
    PossibleValues property, 520
    purpose of, 518
    setting references to, 519
control properties
    advanced, 133, 157
    BorderStyle, 157
    colors, 155
    Control Toolbox, changing with, 187
    display, 154–55
    layers, 155–57
    setting, 21–23, 133–34
    transparent background, 157
    viewing, 154
    WordWrap, 157
controls
    ActiveX, 132, 207–8
    adding, 59–65, 78, 132–34, 517
    adding custom, 450–52

853

Index

controls, *continued*
   adding custom property pages, 679–81
   advanced properties, setting, 133, 157
   aligning, 80–81, 139
   background colors, 155
   binding to data sources, 524
   binding to fields, 79, 134–37, 157–60
   binding to fields at runtime, 523–24
   BorderStyle, 157
   Bring To Back option, 155–57
   Bring To Front option, 155–57
   changing field types, 163
   Click event, 376
   colors, 155
   ComboBox (*see* ComboBox controls)
   command bars (*see* CommandBarControls collection object)
   CommandButton (*see* CommandButton controls)
   ControlTipText, 141
   Control Toolbox, 78, 114–15
   creating with Field Chooser, 20
   date selection, 207–8
   declaring as global control variables, 560–61
   deleting, 77
   dominant, 209
   DTPicker, 207–8
   editing, 138
   enabling, 520
   Field Chooser, creating with, 20
   fields with (*see* fields)
   foreground colors, 155
   formulas, validation, 173–76
   Frame, 83
   From, 76
   help, creating for, 141
   Image, 83
   Label (*see* Label controls)
   layers, setting, 155–57
   MultiPage (*see* MultiPage controls)
   multiple, selecting, 209
   naming conventions, 140
   Post To, 76
   procedures, running from, 453–54, 457
   properties (*see* control properties)
   properties, setting, 21–23, 134
   read-only, 91–92
   removing, 77
   required input, 172–73
   resizing, 522–23
   saving information, 115
   ScrollBar, 206
   sizing, 77
   spacing, 139

controls, *continued*
   SpinButton (*see* SpinButton controls)
   State property, 455
   tab order, 139–40
   TabStrip, 206
   templates, creating, 188
   TextBox, 61–63
   time selection, 207–8
   ToggleButton, 206
   toolbox (*see* Control Toolbox)
   undoing deletions, 137
   UserForms, 31
   validating data, 172–76
   Value page, 135
   VBScript, types requiring, 206
   Visual Basic Expression Service, 23–24
   WordWrap property, 157
Controls collection object, 517–18
ControlTipText, 141
Control Toolbox, 78, 114–15
   adding controls, 132–33
   additional controls, 133, 187
   binding, 188
   customizing, 186–87
   exporting pages, 188
   Frame controls, 83
   Image controls, 83–84
   importing pages, 188
   labels, adding from, 80–81
   opening, 132
   Outlook View Control, adding to, 720
   properties of controls, changing with, 187
   saving images to, 84
   Selector tool, 82
   templates, creating, 188
Conversation field, 179
Conversation Index field, 102–3
Conversation property, 272–73
Conversation Topic property, 102
cookies, 739
copying
   controls, 86–87
   designs of existing folders, 253–54
   field values, 242–43
   folders, 253–54, 292, 470
   forms, 258, 603
   items from file system, 419–20
CopyItem method, 419–20
Count property, Controls collection object, 518
CreateItem method, 417–18
CreateObject function
   automation using, 529
   security, 647

Index

CreateObject method, 419
Creates Form Of Type property, 218
creating. *See also* adding
   actions, 96–97
   columns, 262
   Digital Dashboard projects, 744
   fields, 134–35, 160–61
   filters, 53–54
   Folder Home Pages, 286–87
   folders, 46–47, 251–52
   forms, 125–27
   items, 54–56
   Message forms, 125
   new folder views, 260–61
   personal folders, 124
   Post forms, 125
   views, 47–54
CRM Administration form, 532–34, 814–15
CRM (customer relationship management)
   applications, 532
Ctrl+Click selection method, 209
Currency fields, 162, 174–75
Current View command, 260
CustomAction event, 376–77
custom forms. *See* customizing built-in modules; forms
Custom Installation Wizard, 701
Customize Current View command, 269
customizing built-in modules, 41–70
   adding controls, 59–65
   Beta Contacts folder, 43–47
   Beta Contacts form, 44–45
   Beta Participants view, 43, 45, 50–54
   CheckBox controls, 63–64
   column headings, adding, 49–50
   column order, 49
   ComboBox controls, 59–61
   Contacts form, 57–65
   field categories for binding, 159
   filters, creating, 53–54
   form properties, setting, 64–65
   forms, built-in, modifying, 112
   item creation, 54–56
   opening forms, 58
   Potential Beta Participants view, 43–44, 47–50, 54
   publishing forms, 65–67
   renaming forms, 58–59
   testing forms, 65, 67–68
   TextBox controls, 61–63
   views, creating, 47–54
CustomPropertyChange event, 377
Custom role, 299

D

databases
   ADO (*see* ADO (ActiveX Data Objects))
   connection strings, 553–55, 766
   importing outside, 555–59
   integration with, 540
   Northwind Dashboard connection string, 766
   Null values, converting, 559
data types
   Type property, fields, 162–63
   variant, 409–11
Date And Time Picker Control, 207–8
Date fields, 162
   default value, 173
   None value, 378
Date function, 464
dates
   calculations, 170
   variant data type, 409–11
   Web Storage System, 831
date selection controls, 207–8
DblClick events, 207
DDRK. *See* Digital Dashboard Resource Kit
DDSC Notification Service, 770–72
DDSC (Digital Dashboard Services Component)
   object, 761
Deactivate event, 357
debugging
   COM Add-ins, 692–94
   Internet Explorer Script Debugger, 389
   with Microsoft Script Editor (*see* Microsoft Script Editor)
   tools, 35–36, 390
declarations
   constants, 411–12
   WithEvents keyword, 325
defaults
   contact management with, 531
   e-mail editor, 183
   mail format, 144
   new items, form for, 290–91
   security settings, 632–34
   template folder location, 89
Default user, 297
deleting
   columns, 25–26, 262
   command bars, 445–46
   controls, 77
   fields, 101, 137–38, 163
   forms, 603
   images, 204

Index

deleting, *continued*
  item-level events, 375
  items, 68, 480
  pages, 203
deployment of COM Add-ins, 708–10
Description property, 144
Design Environment folder, 45–46
Design mode, 7, 20–28
  actions, setting, 94–100
  Advanced Properties dialog box, 21–23
  advantages of, 21
  AutoLayout, 20
  Control Toolbox, opening, 132
  Field Chooser, 20
  Form Design toolbar, 20
  Properties dialog box, 21–23
  Run mode, entering, 20
  Script Editor, 24–25
  Separate Read Layout option, 127–30
  switching to, 125
  viewing forms, 20–21
  Visual Basic Expression Service, 23–24
design tools, 17–37
  add-ins, 32–34
  Design mode (*see* Design mode)
  Microsoft Office XP Developer, 17, 33–34
  Microsoft Visual Studio 98, 17, 34–35
development tools
  COM add-ins, 36–37
  Microsoft Outlook Visual Basic Reference Help, 397–98
  object libraries, 400–403
  programming environment variances, 398–99
  Script Editor, 387–95
  VBA preferred, 384–85
  VBScript, 384–86
  VBScript Samples folder, 396–97
  Web resources, 396
DHTML events, 761–62
Dial method, 427
dialog boxes
  COM Add-ins, adding to, 688–92
  creating, 31
  displaying programmatically, 691–92
  modal, 688–89
  Search COM Add-in, 698
digital certificates, 702–3, 705
Digital Dashboard Resource Kit
  building custom Outlook Today pages, 716
  downloading, 742
  versions, 741

Digital Dashboards
  Account variable, 770, 772
  adding Web Parts, 749–51
  Administration page, 747
  applications, 741
  CompanyID variable, 770
  CompanyName variable, 771
  creating new projects, 744
  DDSC Notification Service, 770–72
  DDSC object, 761
  defined, 740–41
  event handling, 770–72
  factories, 741, 757
  importing Web Parts, 74–747
  installing Office XP Developer Support, 743–45
  installing SQL Server sample Dashboard, 742–45
  My Dashboard, adding Web parts, 749–50
  My Dashboard, creating, 747
  My Dashboard features, 752–53
  namespaces, 762
  nesting, 748
  Northwind (*see* Northwind Dashboard)
  Northwind SharePoint Dashboard, 812–14
  platforms, 741–42
  SharePoint Portal Server platform, 742
  SQL Server 2000 platform, 742–45
  State Management Service, 764
  terminology, 741–42
  version compatibility, 741
  Web Part catalogs, 741
  Web Parts (*see* Web Parts)
  Web Parts samples, installing, 746
dimensioning objects for events, 324–25
disabling commands, 582–83
discoverability, 712
discussion applications, 71–72
  actions, setting, 94–100
  Administration properties, setting, 106
  backing up forms, 88–89, 93
  clearing initial values, 91
  collaboration illustrated, 72
  Compose page (*see* Compose page)
  Conversation Index field, 102–3, 274
  Conversation property, 272–73
  Conversation Topic property, 102
  copying to public folders, 105
  creating forms, 75–90
  default form for folders, setting, 103
  definition of form, including, 90
  folder creation, 75
  forms, 73–90
  grouping folder items, 102
  hiding forms, 104

Index

discussion applications, *continued*
    initial view, setting, 106
    overview of example, 72–74
    permissions, 106
    Post forms (*see* Compose page; Read page)
    Product Idea Response form, 73–74, 90–100
    properties of forms, 87–88
    publishing forms, 89–90, 93–94
    read-only controls, 91–92
    Read page, 85–87, 92
    releasing, 106
    response button, 96–97
    response form creation, 90–94
    sorting items, 102–3
    testing forms, 88, 104–5
    types of, 71–72
    views, 72–73, 100–103
discussion folders, 13, 247
displaying
    folders, 470
    items (*see* views)
Display This Page option, 130–31
DistListItem object, 509, 511–12
distributing applications, 591
    CD-ROM, using, 601
    definition, sending with forms, 601
    floppy disk, using, 601
    Folder forms libraries, 598
    folder replication, 615–16
    folders, making available to all users, 611–12
    installing forms programmatically, 606–7
    instructing on how to publish, 597
    IPM.Note, 598–600
    network drive, using, 601
    offline use of forms, 601–2
    Organizational Forms Library, 592–95
    permissions for folders, 612
    personal folder files, 601, 614–15
    personal folders, 612–15
    Personal Forms Library, 595–97
    Public Folders, 611–12
    publishing in Organizational Forms Library, 594–95
    publishing in Personal Forms Library, 597
    Read message, changing default, 600
    Send Form Definition With Item option, 594–95
    standard message form, 598–600
    submitting to administrators, 592–93, 596
    viruses, checking for, 593
distributing information, 4
distribution lists
    customizing built-in modules, 42
    Distribution List forms, creating, 126
    Distribution Lists, 297–98
    Outlook 2002 Administration form, 591

DLLs, 693–94. *See also* COM Add-ins
docks, 438
DocumentItem object, 490–500
    document properties with, 495–96
    extrinsic objects, 491
    Inspector object support, 352–53
    intrinsic objects, 491–92
    Microsoft Word, 493–94
    types of items, 492
document management, 792–803
DocumentProperties object, 495–96
Documents folder, 793, 839–40
dollars. *See* Currency fields
dominant controls, 209
Drafts folder, 125
drag operations, 294
DropDownList type, 196–97
drop operations, 294
DTPicker control, 33, 207–8
Duration fields, 162

E

editing
    controls, 138
    labels, 138
    pages of forms, 127–32
    Read page, 141–42
Editor role, 299
e-mail. *See also* items; messages
    default editor, 183
    editors, NewInspector event availability, 352
    E-mail Security Update (*see* Outlook E-mail Security Update)
    new, event tracking, 648
    sharing, 544
e-mail addresses warning dialog box, 429
E-mail Security Update. *See* Outlook E-mail Security Update
embedded commands, Folder Home Pages, 284
enhanced folders, 792–93
errors, validation, 175
Event Handler
    command, 24
    events, creating code for, 388
event handling
    Digital Dashboards, 770–72
    Outlook View Control, 739–40
events
    Activate, 356–57
    ActiveX, 207
    AdvancedSearchComplete event, 331–32
    AdvancedSearchStopped, 332

Index

events, *continued*
  application-level (*see* Application-level events)
  BeforeGroupAdd, 349
  BeforeGroupRemove, 349
  BeforeGroupSwitch, 348
  BeforeNavigate, 348
  BeforeReminderShow, 333
  BeforeShortcutAdd, 350–51
  BeforeShortcutRemove, 351
  C++ to respond to, 321
  canceling, 373–74
  carrying code with forms, 366, 370
  child objects raising, 322–26
  Click, 200–202, 524–25
  Close, Inspector object, 357, 678
  command bar controls, 456–57
  DblClick, 207
  Deactivate, 357
  defined, 311
  DHTML, in Web Parts, 761–62
  dimensioning objects for, 324–25
  Explorer (*see* Explorer events)
  firing sequence, 370–71, 381–82
  Folders collection object, 358–61
  GroupAdd, 348–49
  history of Outlook, 311
  Inspector, 356–58
  Inspectors collection object, 351–56
  item (*see* item-level events)
  ItemAdd, 327
  item-level, 351–56
  Items collection object, 362–66
  ItemSend, 327
  MapiLogonComplete, 332
  NewExplorer, 337
  NewInspector, 351–56
  NewMail, 327–28
  objects that raise, table of, 323–24
  OnAddInsUpdate, 672–73
  OnBeginShutdown, 673
  OnConnection, 673–75
  OnDisconnection, 675–78
  OnError, 346
  OnStartupComplete, 678
  OnUpdate, CommandBars, 445
  OptionsPagesAdd (Application object), 328–29, 685
  OptionsPagesAdd (NameSpace object), 336, 685
  OutlookBarGroup, 348–49
  OutlookBarPane, 347–48
  OutlookBarShortcut, 350–51
  Outlook View Control, 726
  preventing from firing, 372–74
  Progress, 346

events, *continued*
  PropertyChange, 388
  Quit event, 329–30
  Reminder, 330
  Reminders collection object, 332–35
  SelectionChange, 432
  ShortcutAdd, 350
  Snooze event, 335
  Startup, 330–31
  SyncEnd, 347
  SyncObject events, 344–47
  SyncStart, 347
  timer, 363
  tracing in VBA, 326
  trapping with COM Add-ins, 322
  VBScript to carry code with forms, 366, 370
  Views collection object, 361–62
  WithEvents declarations, 579–81
  WithEvents object variables, 321–26
event templates, 24–25
Exception object, 496, 499–500
exception security groups, 634
Exchange agents, 7
Exchange Client
  ActiveX to replace extensions, 3
  automatically generate views, 291
  COM Add-ins to replace extensions, 385
  difficulty with extensions, 653
  Extensions, 3, 385, 653
Exchange newsgroups, 292–93
Exchange Server. *See* Microsoft Exchange Server 2000
Exchange Workflow Designer, 33–34
Explorer, Outlook
  built-in command bars, 438
  COM Add-In command bars (*see* COM Add-Ins, command bars)
  displaying, 327–28
  events (*see* Explorer events)
  items selected, determining, 342
  objects (*see* Explorer object)
  panes, 432–33
  toolbar (*see* Explorer toolbar)
  window creation event, 337
Explorer events, 338–44
  Activate, 338
  BeforeFolderSwitch, 339
  BeforeItemCopy, 343
  BeforeItemCut, 343
  BeforeItemPaste, 343
  BeforeMaximize, 343
  BeforeMinimize, 344
  BeforeMove, 344
  BeforeSize, 344

Index

Explorer events, *continued*
   BeforeViewSwitch, 339–40
   Close, 340
   Deactivate, 340
   FolderSwitch event, 341
   NewExplorer, 323, 325, 337
   SelectionChange, 341
   ViewSwitch, 341
Explorer object
   Add method, 431
   BeforeFolderSwitch event, 578–79
   CurrentFolder property, 431
   CurrentView property, 431–32
   Display method, 431
   events raised by, 323
   IsPaneVisible method, 433
   Outlook window display, 405
   Panes collection object, 432–33
   purpose of, 430
   SelectionChange event, 432
   ShowPane method, 433
Explorers object, 323, 325, 337, 430
Explorer toolbar
   macros, adding to, 320
   Outlook Shared Activities COM Add-in, 578–83

F

FaceID property, 441–43, 687–88
features, new in Outlook 2002, 3
feedback, collecting. *See* approval routing; Art Approval form; responses
Field Chooser, 20, 24–25, 262
   adding fields with, 136–38
   changing field types, 163
   deleting fields, 163
   first non-empty field, showing value, 267
   formula columns, creating, 267–68
fields
   adding from Field Chooser, 136–38
   adding from forms, 135–36
   adding to forms, 20
   adding to views, 48–49
   binding controls to, 79, 115–16, 134–37, 157–60
   changing type, 163
   combination, 23
   comparing values, 174–75
   copying values, 242–43
   creating, 134–35, 160–61
   creating columns from, 262
   custom, collection object, 525–26
   CustomPropertyChange event, 377
   default values, 173
   deleting, 48, 51, 137–38
   Field Chooser (*see* Field Chooser)

fields, *continued*
   filtering using values, 277–79
   finding value of, 526
   format, selecting, 161, 163
   formulas, validation, 173–76
   formulas in, 23 (*see also* Formula fields)
   function of, 115
   initial values, setting, 80, 170–72
   location of user-defined, 265
   location on creation, 161–62
   name changes, effects of, 604
   Office Document forms, 159–60
   properties, setting, 21–23
   Properties dialog box for creating, 160–70
   PropertyChange event, 378–79
   removing from views, 101
   required, 172–73
   selecting from other forms, 135–36
   shared, 122–23
   sorting items by entries in, 271–72
   type, 161–63
   undoing deletions, 137
   user-defined, 134–36, 160–70, 265
   validating data, 23, 172–76
   viewing available, 136–37
   Visual Basic Expression Service, 23–24
files
   extensions, Level 1 (*see* Level 1 attachments)
   personal folder files, 601, 614–15
filters, 53–54, 274–79
   Advanced Filter dialog box, 277–78
   automatic formatting, 282
   conditions, 276
   field values, filtering by, 277–79
   items, using *Restrict* method, 479–80
   message classes, filtering by, 276–77
   offline folders, 306
   specifying, 276–77
finding items, 478–79
Find method
   Items collection object, 478–79
   UserProperties collection object, 526
firing order of events, 370–71, 381–82
FolderAdd event, 358–59
Folder Assistant, 295
   actions, specifying, 304–5
   advanced conditions, specifying, 302–3
   fields, selecting for conditions based on, 304
   opening, 301
   simple conditions, 301
   unmet conditions, actions on, 303
   user-defined fields, conditions using, 303–4
FolderChange event, 359–60

859

Index

Folder forms libraries, 598
folder home pages, 5–6, 283–90
   Application Folders Send/Receive group, 286
   Application object, 735
   ASP, 714
   coding in, 735–38
   cookies, 739
   creating, 286–87
   defined, 712
   design considerations, 286
   Digital Dashboards (*see* Digital Dashboards)
   dynamic database data, 287
   embedded commands, 284
   hiding, 287
   Inbox Properties sheet to establish, 734–35
   My Dashboard features, 752–53
   navigating from, effect on scripting, 763
   Northwind Dashboard, 712, 765
   offline viewing, 286–90
   Outlook Today page, custom, 716–17
   Outlook View Control (*see* Outlook View Control)
   overriding by users, 286
   vs. OWA, 713–14
   placeholder folders, 714
   purpose of, 248, 283–84
   resetting to default, 287
   searching items using, 285
   security, 714–15
   setting for Companies folder, 781–82
   setting for Outlook Today, 717
   SharePoint Portal Server, 285
   state, maintaining, 738–39
   System Policy Editor, 715
   tools for creation, 717–18
   URL for, 286
   Web interfaces from, 14
   Web page settings, offline, 289–90
   zone security, 715
Folder List pane, Panes collection object, 432–33
Folder Properties dialog box
   adding custom property pages, 679–81
   OptionsPagesAdd event, NameSpace object, 336
FolderRemove event, 360–61
folders, 247–308
   accessing with *GetDefaultFolder*, 426–27
   active, returning, 431
   Add Folder Address To Personal Address Book option, 294–95
   Address Book, adding to, 178–79
   Administration properties, 293–96
   aging, removing (*see* AutoArchiving folders)
   applications created with, 5
   arrival events, 327–28

folders, *continued*
   AutoArchiving, 616–17
   BeforeFolderSwitch event, 339
   Beta Contacts folder, 46–47
   built-in modules, based on, 11–12
   Classified Ads, 248
   copying, 253–54, 292, 470
   creating, 46–47, 251–52
   default forms, setting, 67, 103
   default template, location, 89
   Default user, 297
   deleted, recovering, 361
   descriptions, copying, 254
   Design Environment, 45–46
   designing, methods of, 249
   discussion, 247
   Discussion folders, 13
   displaying, 470 (*see also* Explorer object)
   Drafts, 125
   drag/drop operations, 294
   enhanced, 792–93
   events triggered by operations, 358–61
   Exchange agents for customizing, 7
   Folder Assistant, 295
   Folders collection object events, 358–61
   formatting columns, 26–27
   forms, creating in, 123
   forms cache, 608–10
   Forms Manager, 255–56
   Forms page, Properties dialog box, 255–56
   Global Address Book of, 178
   grouping items, 26
   home pages (*see* folder home pages)
   in-cell editing option, 27
   initial view, setting, 294
   Internet newsgroups, 292–93
   item creation, 54–56
   locations for, choosing, 250–51
   Mail Items option, 251
   MAPIFolder object (*see* MAPIFolder object)
   moderated, 296
   modifying directly, 252–53
   new, creating, 251–52
   offline use of, 305–7, 472
   opening Permissions page, 297
   Owners Only option, 293, 295
   paths, 472–74
   permissions, 69–70, 253, 295–300, 612
   personal, 45–46, 612–15
   personal, designing new folders in, 250
   personal folder files, 614–15
   placeholder, 247, 536
   planning, 248–49

Index

folders, *continued*
    preaddressing forms to, 177–79
    Properties dialog box, 27–28
    protecting from other users, 295 (*see also* folders, permissions)
    public (*see* public folders)
    purposes of, 11
    reference, 247
    reference applications, 14–16
    releasing, 307–8
    replicating, 308
    restricting access, 547
    rules, copying, 254
    shortcuts to, in Message field, 184
    shortcuts to, in Outlook Bar, 252
    showing custom views only, 27
    subfolder permissions, 299–300
    template, default, 89
    testing, 307–8
    This Folder Is Available To option, 295
    Tracking folders, 14, 248
    types of items allowed, specifying, 256
    types of items held, 251–52
    URLs for accessing, 187
    URL shortcuts, 19
    views (*see* views)
    Web, 793–95
    Web sites about, 16
    Web views of, 14, 474 (*see also* folder home pages)
Folders collection object
    Add method, 468
    events, 358–61
    Folders object, events raised by, 324
    Item method, 468–69
folder views. *See* views
font selection, 279, 281–82
foreground colors of controls, 155
Format Columns command, 264, 266
FormatDateTime function, 464
formatting
    AutoLayout, 20, 136
    automatic, 281–82
    columns, 26–27, 262–64
    default mail, selecting, 144
    folder views, 259, 279–82
    fonts, 279
    grid lines, 279
FormDescription object, *PublishForm* method, 606–7
Form Design toolbar, 20
form graphics, 82–84
form-level automation, VBScript for, 384
Form menu, View Code command, 24

forms, 109–52
    actions (*see* actions)
    activation, 610
    adding controls, 59–65, 132–34
    advantages of, 21
    All Fields page, 114
    applications created with, 5
    Appointment, 111
    Art Approval form creation, 212–20
    backing up, 88–89, 147–48
    based on templates, 126
    built-in modules, 10, 112
    cache, 608–10
    Calendar (*see* Calendar forms, creating)
    canceling events, 373–74
    CheckBox controls (*see* CheckBox controls)
    clearing initial values, 91
    closing, 125
    code, preventing execution, 95
    ComboBox controls (*see* ComboBox controls)
    Compose page (*see* Compose page)
    Contact, 111 (*see also* Contact forms)
    Contacts, 57–65
    controls (*see* controls)
    Controls collection object, 517–18
    Control Toolbox (*see* Control Toolbox)
    copying with Forms Manager, 258, 603
    creating, 125–27
    creating in personal folders, 123
    customizability of, 21
    customizing (*see* customizing built-in modules)
    default, setting, 67, 103
    definition, sending with, 601
    definitions, opening, 122
    definitions saved with items, 120–22
    deleting, 603
    Design mode (*see* Design mode)
    Design window, 109–10
    discussion (*see* discussion applications)
    displaying, 59
    distribution, 592–601
    Distribution List, 126
    editing pages, 127–32
    Exchange agents for customizing, 7
    Field Chooser, 110, 137–38
    fields in (*see* fields)
    General page, 114
    graphics, 82–84
    help, creating for, 141
    hiding, 258, 606
    hiding pages, 131
    installing programmatically, 606–7

Index

forms, *continued*
  items of (*see* items)
  Journal, 111–12
  layout, 138–41
  libraries, publishing to, 66–67, 146–50, 255
  Message (*see* Message forms)
  message classes, 122, 148–49, 604–5
  Message page (*see* Message page)
  modifications, managing, 604–7
  naming, 147–48, 610
  naming pages, 131–32
  Notes, 126
  Office Document, 111
  offline use of, 306
  one-off, 120–22, 593, 625
  opening for customization, 58
  opening process, 122
  pages, 112–14
  parts of, 112–14
  password protection for, 145
  Post (*see* Post forms)
  preaddressing (*see* To field)
  Product Idea, 73–90
  properties, 64–65, 87–88, 116, 144–47
  Properties dialog box, 110
  publishing, 65–67, 89–90, 147–51, 254–55, 594–95
  Read pages, 112–13
  renaming, 58–59
  Run mode, viewing in, 140
  saving as .oft files, 596
  scripts (*see* Script Editor)
  search order on activation, 610
  Send Form Definition With Item option, 90, 146
  Separate Read Layout option, 127–30
  setting Hidden property, 104
  shortcuts, 95
  showing pages, 131
  standard message (IPM.Note), 598–600
  tab order, 84, 87, 139–41
  Task, 111–12
  testing, 65, 67–68, 88, 104–5, 151–52
  TextBox controls, 61–63
  toolbox (*see* Control Toolbox)
  types of, 111–12
  types of applications using, 7–10
  updating with Forms Manager, 258
  viewing properties of, 258
  Web sites about, 16
forms cache, 608–10
Forms folder location, 608
Forms Manager, 255–56, *602*
  copying forms with, 258, 603
  deleting forms with, 258, 603

Forms Manager, *continued*
  library, changing, 257
  Microsoft Exchange Client forms, 604
  opening, 255, 257, 603
  properties of forms, setting, 603
  updating forms with, 258, 603
Forms Object Model, 402
Forms properties, setting for folders, 588–89
formula columns, 267–68
Formula fields, 162
  automatic updating, 168
  creating, 167–68
  date calculations, 170
  IIf function, 169–70
  text strings, building, 168–69
  uses for, 167
  validation, 173–76
formulas, 23. *See also* Combination fields
Forward. *See* responses
Forward event, 377
forward messages based on rules, 304–5
Forward option, 227
Frame controls, 83, 192
Friend keyword, 674
From controls, 76
From field, programmatic security settings, 644

G

General page, 114
GetDefaultFolder method, 426–27
GetFreeBusy method, 464
GetInspector property, 486
GetNameSpace("MAPI") method, 420
GetObject function
  automation using, 529
  security, 647
GetPref( ), 738
Global Address Book, 295
global object variables, setting to Nothing on Quit event, 329–30
grid lines, 279
GroupAdd event, 348–49
grouping folder items, 26, 102, 269–73
groups
  defined, 259
  Outlook Bar events, 348–49
groupware, 41. *See also* discussion applications

H

headings, column, 49–50, 52
  changing labels, 263–64
  order of, 103

Index

help
  creating for forms, 141
  Help And Web Sites folder, 18
  Microsoft Outlook Visual Basic Reference Help, 18, 188–89
  Microsoft Script Editor, 392
  TipText, 141
  VBA, 30
  Visual Basic Reference Help, 397–98
Help And Web Sites folder, 18
Hidden property, Response forms, 104, 233–34, 246
HideFormPage method, 515
hiding
  forms, 537, 606
  pages, 131
home pages, establishing, 548
HTML message format, 144
  coding, 418
  Restricted Sites zone default, 626
HTML pages. *See also* Web pages
  inserting Outlook View Control, 729–30
  Outlook Application Object, accessing, 728–29
  Outlook View Control, 728
hyperlinks, 184–86. *See also* URLs (Uniform Resource Locators)

I

icons. *See also* buttons
  custom, 687–88
  selecting sizes, 144–45
IDTExtensibility2 Type Library, 664
IIf function, 169–70
Image controls, 82–84
  adding pictures to, 204
  adding to forms, 83–84
  Click event, 205
  deleting pictures, 204
  form graphics, components of, 82
  sizing images, 204
images
  adding to forms, 83–84
  custom, adding to command bars, 687–88
Immediate window, 326
Implements statement, 670
Import and Export Wizard folders, 611
importing databases, 555–59
Inbox
  arrival event, 327–28
  items collection, referencing, 413
in-cell editing, 27, 379–80
indexes
  aging, control of, 283
  Conversation Index field, 102–3
  Exchange Server public folders, 805–6
  sorting by Conversation Index, 274

InfoBar, Outlook E-mail Security Update warnings, 619
initial values, setting, 170–72
  CheckBox controls, 195
  ComboBox controls, 197
  Label controls, 190
  ListBox controls, 200
  OptionButton controls, 194
  Subject field, 180
  TextBox controls, 191
  To field, 177–79
Initial View On Folder property, 70
in-place activation, 619–20
InputBox function, 464
inserting pages, 203
Inspector events, 324, 356–58
Inspector object, 514–15
  created by external applications, 354
  events, 324, 356–58
  HideFormPage method, 515
  methods, 514–15
  NewInspector event, 351–56
  properties, 515–16
  SetCurrentFormPage method, 515
  ShowFormPage method, 515
  wrapping Office documents in, 353
Inspectors collection object events, 351–56
Inspectors object, 324
Inspector toolbar
  macros, adding to, 320
  View Code command button, displaying, 387
Inspector Tools menu, Macro command, 29
Inspector window
  built-in command bars, 438
  COM Add-In command bars (*see* COM Add-Ins, command bars)
  toolbar (*see* Inspector toolbar)
installing
  Admpack.exe, 630–31
  CDO, 467
  COM Add-ins, 708–10
  Custom Installation Wizard, 701
  forms programmatically, 606–7
  Microsoft Script Editor, 390
  Outlook Security form, 633–34
InStr function, 464
Integer fields, 162
intellectual property, securing, 699–700
InterDev. *See* Microsoft Visual InterDev
Internet. *See also* Web pages
  newsgroup folders, 292–93
  Reply forms over, 234
Internet Explorer Script Debugger, 389
Internet News page, 292–93

863

Index

intrinsic constants, 412
IPM.Note, 598–600
IsPriorityDropped property, 455
ItemAdd event, 327
item-level events, 351–56, 366–81
   adding, 369
   AttachmentAdd, 374
   AttachmentRead event, 374–75
   BeforeAttachmentSave event, 375
   BeforeCheckNames event, 375
   BeforeDelete event, 375
   cancelability, 368–69
   Click event, 376
   Close event, 376
   COM Add-ins, 366–67
   CustomAction event, 376–77
   CustomPropertyChange event, 377
   deletes, 375
   firing order, 370–71, 381–82
   Forward event, 377
   Item_Open event firing, 371
   Item_Read event, 372
   Item_Send event firing, 371
   Item_Write event, 372
   list of, with descriptions, 368–69
   MailItem object, 367–68
   message subject, requiring, 366–67
   modifying, 369
   NewInspector event, 351–56
   new to Outlook 2000, 366
   Open event, 377–78
   portability, 366
   preventing events from firing, 372–74
   PropertyChange event, 378–79
   Read event, 379–80
   ReplyAll event, 380
   Reply event, 380
   Send event, 381
   VBScript, behavior modification with, 368–70
   WithEvents keyword, 370
   Write event, 381
Item method, AddressLists collection object, 460
Item object, 399–400
Item object variable, 395–96
Item.Parent, 575
ItemProperties collection object, 526–27, 624
ItemProperty property, 642
items
   as attachments, 181, 183–84
   automatic formatting, 281–82
   closing, Item_Close event firing, 372
   copying from file system, 419–20
   counting, 481

items, *continued*
   CreateItem method, 417–18
   creating, 54–56, 477–78 (*see also* Compose page)
   creation, Item_Open event firing, 371
   currently selected in Explorer, determining, 341
   custom, creating, 477–78
   default, setting for folders, 552–53
   defined, 119
   definitions, linking to, 122
   definitions, sending with, 120–22
   deleted, recovering, 361
   deleting, 68, 480
   events (*see* item-level events)
   filtering (*see* filters)
   finding, 478–79
   GetInspector property, 486
   grouping (*see* grouping folder items)
   ItemAdd event, 327, 363–64
   ItemChange event, 364–65
   Item object, 399–400
   ItemProperties collection object, 526–27
   ItemRemove, 365–66
   Items collection object (*see* Items collection object)
   Items collection object events, 362–66
   ItemSend event, 327
   iterating through, 460–61
   journal (*see* journals, items)
   linking contacts to parent items, 509–12
   message (*see* messages)
   message classes, 122
   one-off forms, 120–22
   opening (*see* Read page)
   opening, Item_Read event firing, 372
   personal information stores, 119
   posted, methods for, 481–83
   posting, Item_Write event firing, 372
   posting in folders, 483
   referencing forms associated with, 486
   reminder events, 330
   selected, determining, 432
   SenderName property, 488
   Send Form Definition With Item option, 120–22
   sending, Item_Send event firing, 371
   sorting, 102–3, 271–72, 480
   storage of, 119
   tasks (*see* tasks)
   To property, 488
   types held in folder, choosing, 252, 256
Items collection object, 362–66, 476–81
   Add method, 477–78, 557
   Count property, 481
   deleting items, 480
   Find method, 478–79

Index

Items collection object, *continued*
   objects of, 476
   referencing, 413
   Remove method, 557
   Restrict method, 479
   Sort method, 480
ItemSend event, 327
Items object, events raised by, 324
Item windows. *See* Inspector object
iteration, *Item* method, 460–61
IT Factory Development Center, 37

J

journals
   applications, customizing built-in modules, 42
   items, 512–13
   Journal forms, 111–12, 126
   JournalItem object, 512–13

K

Keywords fields, 162, 199
Knowledge Base articles, 396
knowledge folders, 834–35
KnowledgeServer object, 832–36

L

Label controls, 134, 189–90
labels
   adding to forms, 80–81
   binding to fields, 190
   color, 497
   column, 26–27
   ComboBox controls, 59–60
   editing, 138
   Field Chooser, creating with, 20
   font selection, 82
   form graphics using, 82–83
   initial values, setting, 190
   TextBox controls, 63
layers, 155–57
layout, forms, 138–41
Layout menu
   Align submenu, 138
   AutoLayout command, 136
   Center In Form command, 78
   spacing options, 139
Level 1 attachments, 618–21, 630, 637–40
libraries. *See also* object libraries
   changing in Forms Manager, 257
   form definition repositories, 122

libraries, *continued*
   Organizational Forms (*see* Organizational Forms Library)
   publishing forms to, 66–67, 146–50, 255
   table of, 148–49
lifetimes of variables, 409
lines, creating, 192
linked objects in Message fields, 181
linking, 540–42
Links collection object, 541
Links object, 509–11
ListBox controls
   binding, 198–99
   check boxes, 198
   initial values, setting, 200
   Keywords fields, 162, 199
   List property, 520–21
   list styles, 198
   multiple values, allowing for, 198
   OptionButtons, 198
   populating with COM Add-in, 656–57
   PossibleValues property, 520
   purpose of, 198
   values, adding to, 199
localization, Digital Dashboards, 761

M

Macro command, 29, 313
macros
   adding to toolbars, 320
   creating, 319–20
   limitations, 319
   Macros dialog box, 320–21
   Microsoft Word, opening, 319
   recording, 318
   running, 320–21
   security (*see* macro security)
   Send Form Definition With Item option, 120–22
   Sub procedures, 318–20
macro security
   changing, 321
   digital certificates, 702–4
   levels, 701–2
   Outlook Macro Security, 626
   purpose of, 700
   setting, 318, 700
Mailbox Folders
   accessing with *GetDefaultFolder*, 426–27
   attributes available, 250–51
   permissions for modifying, 253
MailItem object, 367–68, 483–86

865

Index

MailItem object properties, 486–90
Mail Items option, 251
managing applications, 591
   activating forms, 610
   AutoArchiving folders, 616–17
   changing folders, 615
   distributing folders, 613–16
   forms cache, 608–10
   forms management, 602–6
   hiding forms, 606
   installing forms programmatically, 606–7
   making folders available to users, 611–13
   modifying forms, 604–7
   personal folder files, 614–15
   replication, 615–16
   synchronizing forms, 603–4
MAPI (Messaging Application Program Interface), 35–37
   extended, wrapper for, 36–37
   GetNameSpace("MAPI") method, 420
   message store, 420
   NameSpace object, referencing with, 428
   programmatic settings, 642–44
   Redemption, 648–50
MAPIFolder object
   CopyTo method, 470
   Display method, 470
   EntryID property, 471–72
   Folders property, 470
   Items collection object, 476–81
   Items property, 471
   making folders available offline, 472
   paths, returning, 472–74
   properties, 474–75
   StoreID property, 471–72
   Views collection object, 361–62
   Web views of folders, 474
MapiLogonComplete event, 332
MatchEntry property, 197–98
MDBVU32, 35
MeetingItem object, 501–5
meetings, 496
   GetAssociatedAppointment method, 501–2
   MeetingItem object, 501–5
   programmatic security settings, 644
   requests for, 501–2
   responding to requests, 502–4
   status of requested meetings, 504–5
memory leaks, 676–78
menu bars, CommandBar object, 437–48
menus
   AdaptiveMenus property, 455
   automatic inclusion of forms, 90

menus, *continued*
   CommandBar object, 437–48
   menu bar commands, enabling, 582–83
   pop-up, 448–49
message classes, 122, 148–49, 604–5
Message control. *See also* Message field
   attachments to, 183–86
   rules for, 182–83
   specifying text in, 486–87
   tab order with, 139
Message field, 176, 181–86
   attachments, 181, 183
   folder shortcuts in, 184
   hyperlinks in, 184–86
   items as attachments, 181, 183–84
   linked objects, 181
   objects in, 186
   security, 182
   shortcuts, 181
   URL shortcuts in, 181–82, 184
Message forms, 8
   creating, 125
   enabling sending, 120
   field categories for binding, 159
   opening, 215
   purpose of, 111
   Reply actions (*see* Reply actions)
   To field, default value, 171
   user-defined fields, 160
   voting (*see* voting buttons)
Message page, *114*
   addressing, 131
   hiding, 131
   Message controls, limits on, 183
   Message field, 176, 181–86
   Subject field, 176, 179–80
   To field, 176–79
messages. *See also* e-mail; items
   attachments, 490
   closing, 485–86
   Read, changing default, 600
   recipients, adding, 528–29
   replying, 484–85
   save options, 486
   sender address, obtaining, 489
   sender name, retrieving, 488
   sending, 484
   standard, changing default, 600
   text, specifying, 486–87
   To field, retrieving, 488
methods. *See also specific objects*
   affected by Outlook E-mail Security Update, 623–24
   calling from COM Add-ins, 691–700

Index

methods, *continued*
   Outlook View Control, table of, 723–26
   public, Outlook Shared Activities COM Add-in, 583–86
Micro Eye ZipOut 2000, 37
Microsoft Access
   document creation from templates, 584–86
   importing data from, 555–59
Microsoft ActiveX Data Objects 2.5 Library, 401
Microsoft Add-In Designer Object Library, 662
Microsoft CDO 1.21 Library, 400–401
Microsoft Certificate Server, 702
Microsoft Date And Time Picker Control, Version 6.0, 207–8
Microsoft Direct Speech Recognition Object Model, 401
Microsoft Excel
   fields for forms, 160
   NewInspector event, 352–54
   Office Document items, 352–53
Microsoft Exchange Server 5.*x*
   Event Service vs. Items collection object events, 363
   scripting agents, 250
   subfolder permissions, 299–300
Microsoft Exchange Server 2000
   AdvancedSearch method, 421–25
   browsing folders, 12–13
   caching of folder views, 283
   content source for public folder hierarchies, 805–6
   E-mail Security Update, 283
   event sinks, 250
   Event Sink vs. Items collection object events, 363
   indexing, 805–6
   Organizational Forms Library, 592–95
   replicating folders, 308
   storage for items, 119
   subfolder permissions, 299–300
   Web Storage System Explorer, 35–36
   workflow design, 34
Microsoft Forms 2.0 Object Model
   COM Add-ins, adding forms to, 690
   Library, 400
   viewing, 405
Microsoft FrontPage
   folder home page development, 718
   Outlook View Control, inserting with, 729–32
Microsoft Knowledge Base articles, 209
Microsoft Office 10.0 Object Library, 400
   COM Add-ins, 662
   referencing Application object, 315
   referencing for COM Add-in command bars, 685–88
Microsoft Office Object Model. *See* Microsoft Office XP Object Model

Microsoft Office XP
   Application object, 420–21
   command bars, 437–48
   document creation from templates, 584
   Places Bar, 817–18
Microsoft Office XP Developer, 17
   ActiveX controls, 207
   add-in tools, 33–34
   COM Add-ins, 654
   COM Add-ins, porting preexistent code, 663–64
   Digital Dashboards, 743–44
   editing windows, 758
   Exchange Workflow Designer, 33–34
   folder home page development, 718
   Solution Explorer, 754, 758
   Web Part design (*see* Web Parts, designing with Office XP Developer)
Microsoft Office XP Object Model, 400, 420–21, 437–48
Microsoft Outlook 10.0 Object Library, 315, 662
Microsoft Outlook 10.0 Object Model. *See* Microsoft Outlook Object Model
Microsoft Outlook 2000
   NewInspector event, 352
   security settings, 632
Microsoft Outlook 2002 Object Model. *See* Microsoft Outlook Object Model
Microsoft Outlook Object Model, 312
   Application object (*see* Application object)
   calls using trusted COM Add-ins, 384, 707
   child objects, 322–26
   Outlook View Control, access from, 733, 735
   programmatic settings, 642–44
   Redemption, 648–50
   referencing, 400
   ThisOutlookSession class module, 314
   user interface components, 430
   VBA with, 312
   viewing, 405
Microsoft Outlook Visual Basic Reference Help, 18, 188–89, 397–98
Microsoft PKMCDO for Microsoft Web Storage System, 401
Microsoft PowerPoint
   fields for forms, 160
   Office Document items, 352–53
Microsoft Script Editor
   breakpoints, entering, 392–93
   call stack, viewing, 394
   Debug toolbar, 392
   editing with, 392
   effects when active, 391
   execution control, 392

Index

Microsoft Script Editor, *continued*
  help, 392
  installing, 390
  Intermediate window, 393
  Item object variable, 395–96
  Locals window, 394–95
  local variables, 394
  location of, 389
  opening, 390–91
  purpose of, 389
  script commands, entering, 393–94
  script-level variables, 394–95
  stepping through code, 391
  troubleshooting with, 389–95
  variables, displaying value of, 393–95
  Watch window, 395
Microsoft SharePoint Portal Server Object Library, 401
Microsoft Smart Tags 1.0 Type Library, 401
Microsoft SQL Server 2000 for Digital Dashboards, 742–45
Microsoft Visual Basic
  ActiveX controls, 207
  for Applications (*see* VBA (Visual Basic for Applications))
  creating COM Add-in projects, 654, 659–63
  custom property pages, 679–81
  debugging COM Add-ins, 692–93
  dialog boxes in COM Add-ins, 688–89
  Editor window (*see* VBA Editor)
  forms, adding to COM Add-ins, 689–90
  Implements statement, 670
  object referencing, 399
  Package and Deployment Wizard, 708–9
  Reference Help, 188–89
  run-time files, 707
  Script Editor, 24–25
  Scripting Edition (*see* VBScript (Visual Basic Scripting Edition))
  UserForms, 31
  Version Compatibility option, 695
  Wizard Manager Add-in, 694–97
Microsoft Visual C++
  COM Add-ins with, 655
  difficulty with, 653
  item-level event control, 366
Microsoft Visual InterDev, 37
Microsoft Visual InterDev 6.0
  choosing debuggers, 390
  folder home page development, 718
Microsoft Visual Studio 98, 17, 34–35, 654, 710
Microsoft Web Sites folder, 18

Microsoft Word
  always using as e-mail editor, 144
  DocumentItem object, 493–94
  fields for forms, 160
  macro for launching, 319
  NewInspector event, 352–54
  Office Document items, 352–53
Microsoft XML Document Object Model, 401
Microsoft XML Parser (MSXML), 696–97, 786
modal dialog boxes, 688–89
moderated folders, 296
modifying forms, management of, 604–7
money. *See* Currency fields
MSDAIPP, 786
MSXML (Microsoft XML Parser), 696–97, 786
MultiPage controls, 202–3
multiple controls, selecting, 209
My Dashboard
  adding Web Parts, 749–50
  creating, 747
  features, 752–53
My Inbox Web Part, 755–57, 759
My Shared Calendar Web Part, 753

N

NameSpace object
  AddStore method, 607
  CurrentUser property, 428–29
  Dial method, 427
  events, 335–37
  Folders property, 428
  GetDefaultFolder method, 426–27
  instantiation, 335
  list of methods, properties, and events, 426
  Offline property, 574
  OptionsPagesAdd event, 323
  PickFolder method, 428
  purpose of, 426
  SyncObject events, 344–47
namespaces
  object (*see* NameSpace object)
  Web Parts, 762, 764
naming
  actions, 96
  conventions, 140
  pages, 131–32
nesting Digital Dashboards, 748
.NET platform, 17
NewExplorer event, 337
NewInspector event, 351–56
NewMail event, 327–28

Index

New menu
    Outlook Data File command, 46
    Post In This Folder command, 290–91
New Post To Folder actions, 239
Nonediting Author role, 299
None role, 299
None value, 173, 378
Northwind Contact Management application, 531–34
    Administration form, 577
    Administration properties, 588
    ADO connection string, setting, 553–55
    automatic journaling, 534–37
    Click events, toolbar, 579–81
    Companies folder views, 586–87
    Company Contact form, 575–77, 582–83, 587
    Company form (*see* Company form, Northwind)
    content source for public folders, creating, 805–6
    Create Shared Items toolbar, 542–44, 575–76, 578–83
    CRM Administration form, 814–15
    CustomerID, 565–67
    customizing, 589
    custom views, 539–40
    database integration, 539–40
    digital dashboard (*see* Northwind Dashboard)
    disabling commands, 582–83
    Explorer toolbar display, 578–83
    Forms properties, 588–89
    home page for folders, 548
    importing contacts databases, 555–59
    initializing controls, 561–64
    item creation from shared database, 548–49
    items for folders, setting default, 552–53
    links, 540–42, 564–68
    menu bar commands, enabling, 582–83
    offline, working, 533
    Outlook 2000 with, 532
    Outlook Shared Activities COM Add-in, 553–54, 578–86
    Outlook View Control, 564–68
    parent companies, 576
    paths, folder, obtaining offline, 575
    permissions, 587–88
    personal copies of shared items, 581–82
    PivotTable Lists, 535–36, 540, 572–74, 577
    preventing Company item creation, 537
    public folder limitations, 545
    public methods with, 583–86
    Published Documents page, 815–17
    releasing, 587–89
    reminders, 545

Northwind Contact Management application, *continued*
    restricting access, 547
    retrieving possible field values, 568–69
    root folder, 536
    searching for companies, 537–38
    setting up, 544–55
    Shared Activities page, 535, 538–40, 571–72
    Shared Appointment form, 581–82
    Shared Contacts folder, exposing, 550–51
    shared documents, 542–43
    shared e-mail, 544
    shared items, 542–44
    shared items forms, 577–78
    Shared Items toolbar creation, 570
    Shared Journal folder, 587
    Shared Mail folder, adding to Global Address List, 548
    updating contacts, 569–70
    users, determining status of, 574
    view, setting initial, 551–52
    views, application folders, 586–87
Northwind Dashboard, 765–83
    adding Web Parts, 751
    arrangement of Web Parts, 767
    browser interface, 767
    command buttons, 783
    communication between Web Parts, 770–72
    companies, finding, 783
    Companies Web Part (*see* Companies Web Part)
    CompanyChange event, 771
    creating, 748
    database connection string, 766
    DDSC Notification Service, 770–72
    event handling, 770–72
    folder home page, 712
    folder home page, setting for Companies folder, 781–82
    installation checklist, 781
    layout, changing, 783
    Outlook View Control, using, 782–83
    public folder path, 766
    purpose of, 765
    Quick Search, 768–69
    Sales Data Web Part, 778–80
    setup, 766–67
    Shared Activities Web Part, 769, 775–78
    SharePoint Portal Server, opening with, 791
Northwind SharePoint Dashboard, 812–14
Notes forms, 126
Null values, 559
Number fields, 162

Index

O

Object Browser, 30
object browsers, 402–3
object hierarchies, using, 405–7
object libraries, 400–403
   Microsoft Add-In Designer Object Library, 662
   Microsoft Outlook 10.0 Object Library, 315, 662
   Microsoft SharePoint Portal Server Object Library, 401
   Microsoft Smart Tags 1.0 Type Library, 401
   PKMCDO, 826
   Redemption, 648–50
   VBA, referencing from, 30
Object Model Guard, 622–27, 705–6
object models, 403–5
   Microsoft Office XP Object Model, 400, 420–21
   Outlook (see Microsoft Outlook Object Model)
   properties, getting, 407–8
   referencing properties, 407–8
   SharePoint Portal Server, 786
Object Model Security, 622–27
objects. *See also specific objects*
   affected by Outlook E-mail Security Update, 623–24
   assigning to variables, 412
   events raised by, table of, 323–24
   Message field holding, 186
   With statement, 407–8
object variables, 412
Office Document
   command, 353
   creation unsupported in Outlook 2002, 353
   field categories for binding, 159–60
   forms, 111
   NewInspector event unavailable, 352
Office XP Developer. *See* Microsoft Office XP Developer
offline, working, 4
   distributing forms for, 601–2
   making folders available, 472
   Northwind Contact Management application, 533
   security settings, 637
   storage for items, 119
   SyncObject, 344–45
Offline Folders Forms Library, 149
offline use of folders, 305–7
OLE-embedded objects, 619–20
OnAction property, 453–54
OnBeginShutdown event, 673
OnConnection event, 673–75
OnDisconnection event, 675–78
one-off forms, 120–22, 625
OnError event, 346

OnStartupComplete event, 678
OnUpdate event, 457
Open event, 377–78
opening
   Control Toolbox, 132
   Folder Assistant, 301
   forms, 58, 122
   Microsoft Script Editor, 390–91
   VBA Editor, 312–13
   Web pages, 436
OptionButton controls, 192–94
   binding, 193–94
   captioning, 193
   Frame controls holding, 192
   initial values, setting, 194
   purpose, 192
   Value property, 194
Options command, Tools menu, 328
OptionsPagesAdd event
   Application object, 328–29
   COM Add-ins, 685
   NameSpace object, 336
Organizational Forms Library, 148
   making forms available, 592–95
   testing forms in, 150
.ost files, 305–6
OutAddin class, 665–66
Outlook Application object. *See* Application object
Outlook Bar, 32
   adding web pages, 19
   CommandBars collection object, 437–48
   events, 347–51
   OutlookBarPane object, 434
   preventing navigation, 347–51
   shortcuts, 436
OutlookBarGroup events, 348–49
OutlookBarGroup object, 324, 435
OutlookBarGroups collection object, 434–35
Outlook Bar pane
   OutlookBarPane events, 323, 347–48
   OutlookBarPane object, 434
   Panes collection object, 432–33
OutlookBarShortcut object, 436–37
OutlookBarShortcut object events, 324, 350–51
OutlookBarShortcuts collection object, 436
OutlookBarStorage object, 434
Outlook Data File command, 46
Outlook E-mail Security Update, 182, 283
   administrator vs. user, 638
   attachments, 618–21
   attachment settings, 639–41
   automation, external, 529–30

Index

Outlook E-mail Security Update, *continued*
  CDO, 628–29
  CommandBarButton object, 625
  CurrentUser property, NameSpace object, 429
  custom action settings, 641
  deploying settings to clients, 635–37
  environments affected, 622
  error trapping, 626–27
  exception security groups, 634
  functional areas, 617–18
  HTML mail format, 626
  InfoBar, 619
  Level1Remove registry keys, 637
  Level 2 attachments, 638
  methods affected, 623–24
  Microsoft Script Editor blocks, 391
  object model calls, 618, 622–27
  objects affected, 623–24
  offline use, 637
  OLE-embedded objects, 619–20
  Outlook Macro Security, 626
  Outlook Security form, 632–34
  preventing end-user customization, 638–39
  Programmatic Settings page, 632, 642–44
  properties affected, 623–24
  Redemption, 648–50
  scripts, one-off, 641
  SendKeys statement, 626
  settings, 639–50
  Trusted Code page, 644–46
  workarounds, 626–27
Outlook Extensions Library, 37
Outlook Macro Security, 626
Outlook Object Library. *See* Microsoft Outlook 10.0 Object Library
Outlook Object Model. *See* Microsoft Outlook Object Model
outlook.ost, 306
Outlook Post forms. *See* Post forms
Outlook Security form, 632–34, 639–50
Outlook Security Settings public folder, 631–32
Outlook Shared Activities COM Add-in, 553–54, 578–86, 697
  Click events, toolbar, 579–81
  Explorer toolbar display, 578–83
  menu bar commands, enabling, 582–83
  personal copies of shared items, 581–82
  public methods with, 583–86
  PublicSharePointDocument method, 820–23, 825
  SharePoint document management, 819–23
  TAPI calls, 583
Outlook Spy, 35–36

Outlook Today ActiveX control
  GetPref( ), 738
  security settings affecting, 715
Outlook Today page, 716–17
Outlook user interface, 430
Outlook VBA code. *See* VBA (Visual Basic for Applications)
Outlook View Control
  accessing, 728–29
  adding to forms, 719–21
  Application object, 735
  coding in folder home pages, 735–38
  Control Toolbox, adding to, 720
  cookies, 739
  environments accepting, 728
  event handlers, 739–40
  events, table of, 726
  folder home pages, using as, 718, 733–40
  folder home pages with, 5–6
  Folder property, 721, 732
  FrontPage 2002 with, 729–32
  GetFolderViews procedure, 727–28
  HTML markup for, 732
  HTML page using, 728
  inserting in Web pages, 729–30
  methods, table of, 723–26
  Northwind Contact Management application, 564–68
  Outlook Object Model access, 733, 735
  path, obtaining, 721
  performance, 568
  programmatic control, 720–21
  properties, setting, 730–32
  properties, table of, 721–22
  Restriction property, 567, 768, 772
  security, 733–34
  Shared Activities page built with, 539–40
  state, maintaining, 738–39
  UserForm, placed on, 719–21
  uses, 31
  using in Northwind Dashboard, 782–83
  VBScript for, 738
  views, iterating, 727–28
  ViewXML parameter, 732
Outlook View Wizard COM Add-in, 694–97
Outlook Web Access (OWA), 6, 713–14
Outlook window, 405
OWA (Outlook Web Access), 6, 713–14
Owner role, 69, 299
Owners Only option, 295

Index

P

Package and Deployment Wizard, 708–9
Page object, 516
pages, 112–14
   Compose (*see* Compose page)
   Controls collection object, 517–18
   Control Toolbox, adding to, 187
   deleting, 203
   editing, 127–32
   hiding, 131
   inserting, 203
   moving, 203
   MultiPage controls, 202–3
   naming, 131–32
   Read (*see* Read page)
   renaming, 203
   Separate Read Layout option, 127–30
   showing, 131
Pages collection object, 515–16
Panes collection object, 432–34
parentheses, 131
passwords, form protection, 145
paths, obtaining folder, 472–74, 575
Percent fields, 162
performance
   folder views, 283
   Outlook View Control, 568
permissions, 69–70
   Anonymous role, 69
   Author role, 69
   copying to new folder, 254
   Default user, 297
   discussion applications, 106
   Distribution Lists, 297–98
   folders, setting, 612
   modifying folders, 253
   Name list box, 296–97
   opening Permissions page, 297
   Owner role, 69
   planning, 249
   public folders, 298
   Publishing Author role, 69–70
   setting for folders, 296–300, 587–88
   subfolders, 299–300
Personal Address Book
   Add Folder Address To Personal Address Book option, 294–95
   folder addresses, adding to, 178–79
personal folder files, 119, 613–15
personal folders
   attributes available, 250–51
   copying folders to, 612–15

personal folders, *continued*
   creating, 45–46, 123–24
   creating folders to, 612–15
   designing new folders in, 250
   permissions, 296
Personal Folders Forms Library, 149
Personal Forms Library, 148
   publishing forms in, 595–97
   testing forms in, 150
personal information stores, 119
physical storage
   fields as, 115
   items, 119
PickFolder method, 428
pictures, custom, 687–88
PictureSizeMode cells, 204
PIM (Personal Information Management), 509
PivotTable Lists
   function of, 535–36
   requirements, 540
   setting connection strings, 577
   view selection, 572–74
PKMCDO (Publishing and Knowledge Management Collaboration Data Objects), 786, 820, 826–27, 832–37
placeholder folders, 247, 536, 714
Places Bar, Office XP, 817–18
Plain Text mail format, 144
Pop-up controls, 459
pop-up menus, 448–49
portal applications. *See* SharePoint Portal Server
Post forms, 9–10, 111–12
   actions, making unavailable, 95, 99
   Compose page, 76–84 (*see also* Compose page)
   creating, 125
   discussion applications using, 75–90
   field categories for binding, 159
   Read page, 76
   Reply To Folder actions (*see* Reply To Folder actions)
   testing, 151
Post In This Folder command, 290–91
PostItem object, 481–83
PostItem object properties, 486–90
Post To control, 76
Post To Folder action, 95
Post To Folder form, 73–74
Potential Beta Participants view, 43–44, 47–50, 54
preaddressing forms. *See* To field
predefined roles, table of, 299
preventing events from firing, 372–74
Preview pane, Panes collection object, 432–33

Index

procedures
   COM Add-ins, 670–72
   running from controls, 453–54, 457
   Sub procedures for use as macros, 319–20
Product Category view, 72, 100–103
product feedback applications, 71–72
Product Idea form, 73–90
   backing up, 88–89
   Compose page, editing, 73–84
   properties, setting, 87–88
   publishing, 89–90
   purpose, 73
   Read page, editing, 85–87
Product Idea Response form, 90–100
   actions, setting, 94–96, 98–99
   backing up, 97, 99
   creating, 90–94
   publishing, 97–98, 100
   purpose of, 73–74
   setting Hidden property, 104
Product Ideas application, 71–106. *See also* discussion applications; Product Idea form; Product Idea Response form
Product Ideas folder, 13, 75, 89–90
profiles, 836
ProgIDs, 328–29, 656, 661, 668, 685–86, 699
Programmatic IDs. *See* ProgIDs
Programmatic Settings page, 642–44
programming. *See* development tools; VBA (Visual Basic for Applications); VBScript (Visual Basic Scripting Edition)
Progress event, 346
properties
   adding with ItemProperties object, 527
   AddressEntry, 465–66
   Administration, 70, 106
   advanced, 21–23, 133
   affected by Outlook E-mail Security Update, 623–24
   CheckBox controls, 63–64
   ComboBox controls, 59–60, 78–80
   CommandBar object, 445–48
   controls (*see* control properties)
   enumerating for an item, 526–27
   Explorer object, 431–32
   of fields, 21
   of folders, 27–28
   of forms, 64–65, 87–88, 116, 143–47
   Forms Manager, setting with, 603
   MailItem object, 486–90
   MAPIFolder object, 474–75
   NameSpace object, 427–28
   object models, referencing, 407–8
   OnAction, 453–54

properties, *continued*
   Outlook View Control, setting, 730–32
   Outlook View Control, table of, 721–22
   pages, creating in VBA, 328–29
   PostItem object, 486–90
   removing with ItemProperties object, 527
   setting for objects, 407–8
   SpecialEffect, 205
   TextBox controls, 61
   validation, 172–76
   Value property, 194
   With statement, 407–8
PropertyChange event, 378–79, 388
property pages, adding to COM Add-ins, 678–85
Protect Form Design property, 145
protocols supported for hyperlinks, 185–86
.pst files, 119. *See also* personal folder files
Public Folder Forms Library, 149
public folders
   addresses, 294–95
   attributes available, 250–51
   copying folder to, 68–69, 612
   groupware, creating, 41–43
   indexing, 805–6
   limitations, 545
   Northwind Dashboard, 766
   Outlook Security Settings, 631–32
   permissions for modifying, 253, 612
   permissions philosophy, 298
   Public Folders, creating folders in, 611–12
PublicSharePointDocument method, 820–23, 825
Published Documents page, 815–17, 827–28
publishing
   definition registration, 122
   documents, SharePoint, 815–23
   Folder forms libraries, 598
   forms, 65–67, 89–90, 147–51, 254–55
   forms in Organizational Forms Library, 594–95
Publishing Author role, 69–70, 299
Publishing Editor role, 299

Q

Query Builder page, displaying, 422–25
Quick Synchronization groups, 344
Quit event, 329–30

R

Read event, 379–80
Read message, changing default, 600
read-only controls, 91–92
Read page
   copying controls to, 86, 141–42
   defined, 128

Index

Read page, *continued*
  deleting controls, 85
  editing, 85–87, 141–42
  properties, setting, 142
  purpose of, 112–13
  Run mode, 142
  tab order, 87, 142
  viewing, 129
Recipients collection object, 527–29
RecurrencePattern object, 496, 498
Redemption, 36–37, 648–50
  blocked CDO calls, 648
  extended MAPI wrapper, 36–37
  object library, 648–49
reference applications, 14–16
reference folders, 247
references, VBA, 316, 319
registration of COM Add-ins, 699
registry
  property pages for persistence, 678
  saving Property page settings, 681–82
  standard forms, changing, 598–99
registry keys
  additional data, COM Add-ins, 667
  client security settings, 635–37
  Level1Remove, 637
  preventing end-user customization, 638–39
  removing COM Add-ins, 659
releasing folders, 307–8
ReminderAdd event, 333
ReminderChange event, 334
Reminder event, 330
ReminderFire event, 334
ReminderRemove event, 334–35
reminders
  public folder limitations, 545
  removing, event upon, 334
  snoozing, 335
Reminders collection object, 332–35
Reminders collection object events, 332–35
Reminders dialog box, 333
Reminders object, 330
Reminders object events, 324
Remove method, Items collection object, 557
replicating folders, 308, 615–16
Reply. *See* responses
Reply actions, 221–24
  Address Form Like A option, 227–28
  characteristics of new forms, 226
  copying of field values, 228–30
  creating new, 223–28
  field sharing, 228–29
  Form Action Properties dialog box, 225

Reply actions, *continued*
  form opened, specifying, 226
  including original message, 227
  menu command, 226
  naming, 225–26
  publishing Reply forms, 231–32
  Reply To Folder (*see* Reply To Folder actions)
  response settings, 226–27
  Show Action On option, 228
  Subject field prefixes, 228
  testing, 233
  This Action Will option, 228
  viewing properties, 224–25
  When Responding option, 227
ReplyAll event, 380
Reply buttons, 380
Reply event, 380
Reply forms
  hiding, 233–34
  Internet-enabled, 234
  not available, 234
  publishing, 231–32
  testing, 233
  This Action Will option, 228
  Vacation Request application, 230–31
reply messages based on rules, 304–5
Reply option, 227
Reply to All option, 227
Reply To Folder actions, 95
  action name, 240
  Actions page, Course Catalog entry, 238
  Address Form Like A option, 241–42
  Characteristics Of The New Form, 241
  Create Offering action, 239–42
  disabling standard Reply to Folder, 238–39
  field values, copying, 242–43
  Form Action Properties dialog box, 240
  form name, 240–41
  hiding Response forms, 246
  menu command, placement, 240
  New Post To Folder actions, 239
  options, viewing, 240
  original message, option to include, 241
  publishing, 244–45
  Reply To Folder option, 228, 241–42
  Response form creation, 241, 244
  Show Actions On option, 242
  Subject field, copying, 242
  Subject Prefix, 242
  testing, 245
  This Action Will options, 242
  Training Management Application, 235–37
  When Responding box, 241

874

Index

Reply To Folder option, 228, 241–42
required fields, 172–73
responses
  defined, 143
  handling (*see* actions)
  hiding forms, 233–34
  Reply To Folder actions, 244
  Response option, 228
  voting (*see* voting buttons)
restaurants and accommodations applications, 72
Restrict method, Items collection object, 479
Reviewer role, 299
role-based security, SharePoint Portal Server, 789–91
roles. *See also* permissions
  assigning to users, 298–99
  Author, 69, 299
  predefined, table of, 299
rules
  actions, specifying, 304–5
  advanced conditions, specifying, 302–3
  conditions, 301–4
  copying to new folder, 254
  defined, 300
  fields, selecting for conditions based on, 304
  Folder Assistant, opening, 301
  multiple arguments within conditions, 302
  multiple conditions within, 302
  returning items to sender, 305
  simple conditions, specifying, 302
  syntax of, 302
  unmet conditions, actions on, 303
  user-defined fields, conditions using, 303–4
  uses for, 301
Rules Wizard, 312
Run mode
  from Design mode, 20
  Read page, 142
  viewing in, 140

S

Safe*Items, 649
Sales Data Web Part, 778–80
sample code, VBScript, 396–97
Sample Page property page installation, 679–81
Save As command, programmatic security settings, 644
Script Editor, 24–25, 110, 117–18
  changes, comparing results, 389
  Event Handler, 388
  events, creating, 388
  help, 397–98
  item event modification, 368–70
  line number of code, going to, 389

Script Editor, *continued*
  Microsoft Script Editor (*see* Microsoft Script Editor)
  object browser, 402–3
  purpose of, 387
  Stop statement, entering, 390
  viewing, 387
  Visual Basic Reference Help, 397–98
scripting Exchange agents, 7
Script menu, Event Handler command, 24
script tags, 735
ScrollBar controls, 206
Search COM Add-in, 698
searching
  AdvancedSearchComplete event, 331–32
  AdvancedSearch method, 421–25, 698
  AdvancedSearchStopped event, 332
  items using Folder Home Pages, 285
  SharePoint Portal Server, 785–86, 807–11
security
  Administration properties, 293–96 (*see also* Administration properties)
  Administrative form, 629–32
  administrator vs. user, 638
  COM Add-ins (*see* COM Add-in security)
  CommandBarButton object, 625
  custom action settings, 641
  custom settings, 639–50
  default, 704
  deploying settings to clients, 635–37
  digital certificates, 702–3
  E-mail Security Update (*see* Outlook E-mail Security Update)
  environments, table of, 706
  exception security groups, 634
  folder home pages, 714–15
  High, 701–2
  HTML mail format, 626
  intellectual property, 699–700
  ItemProperty property, 642
  level, setting by users, 700–702
  Level 1 attachments (*see* Level 1 attachments)
  Level 2 attachments, 638
  levels, 318
  Low, 701–2
  macro, 700–702, 704
  Medium, 701–2
  Message field attachments, 182
  object model calls (*see* Outlook E-mail Security Update, object model calls)
  Outlook Macro Security, 626
  Outlook Security form, 632–34
  Outlook Security Settings public folder, 631–32
  Outlook View Control, 733–34

875

Index

security, *continued*
  planning permissions, 249
  preventing end-user customization, 638–39
  programmatic settings, 632, 642–44
  Redemption, 648–50
  rollout, controlling, 701
  scripts, one-off, 641
  selfcert.exe, 702–3
  Send Form Definition With Item option, 120–22
  SendKeys statement, 626
  settings, 639–50
  SharePoint Portal Server, 789–91
  trusted code, 644–46
  URL shortcuts, 19
  VBA, 317–18
Security command, Tools menu, 700
Select Form command, 254
selecting multiple controls, 209
SelectionChange event, 432
Selection object, 432
selfcert.exe, 702–3
Send button, ItemSend event, 327
SenderName property, 488
Sender object, 489
Send event, 381
Send Form Definition With Item option, 120–22, 146, 594–95
Send Form Definition With Item property, 145–46
Send/Receive groups
  Folder Home Pages using, 288
  SyncObject, 344–47
Send/Receive Settings command, 288, 306
Separate Read Layout option, 127–30, 183
separators for controls, 456
Services dialog box, 179
SetCurrentFormPage method, 515
SetPref( ), 738
setup, COM Add-ins, 708–10
Shared Activities COM Add-in, 826–27
Shared Activities Web Part, 769, 775–78
shared fields, 122–23
SharePoint Portal Server, 785–846
  Administration console, 804
  advanced searches, 809–11
  approval routing, 799–801
  categories, 802–3, 835
  check in/check out, 795–96
  COM Add-in, 837–44
  Connection object, creating, 828
  connection troubleshooting, 795
  content sources, 786, 803–7
  Coordinators, 789
  CRM Administration form, adding URL to, 814–15

SharePoint Portal Server, *continued*
  default content access account, 804
  default profiles, setting, 798
  development opportunities, 845
  Digital Dashboards, 742, 812–14
  document management, 792–803
  Documents folder, 793
  Documents folder attachments, 839–40
  Document store, 785
  enhanced folders, 792–93
  evaluation edition, 787
  Folder Home Pages, 285
  hidden folders, 793
  Keywords property, 825–26
  knowledge folders, 834–35
  KnowledgeServer object, 832–36
  listing documents, 827–28
  Microsoft PKMCDO for Microsoft Web Storage System, 401
  Northwind Document, creating, 797–98
  Northwind SharePoint Dashboard, 812–14
  object models used, 786
  Outlook Shared Activities COM Add-in, 819–23
  parallel routing, 800–801
  Pending Approval state, 796
  PKMCDO, 786–87, 832–37
  Places Bar, Office XP, 817–18
  profiles, 796–99, 803, 836
  properties of documents, 796–99, 825–26
  Published Documents page, 815–17, 827–28
  Published state, 796
  publishing documents, 815–17
  purpose of, 785–86
  role-based security, 789–91
  SDK, 787
  searches, 785–86, 807–11, 828–30
  serial routing, 800–801
  Shared Activities COM Add-in, 826–27
  ShowDocumentListHTML method, 828–30
  states of documents, 795–96
  subscriptions, 811–12
  time conversions, UTC to local, 831
  updating content source indexes, 807
  URL addressability, 786
  Web folders, 793–95
  Web Part removal, 812–14
  Web Storage System Explorer, 823–24
  Web Storage System properties, 823–24
  Web Storage System (WSS), 785
  workspace, 788–89, 834
SharePoint Portal Server COM Add-in, 837–44
  attachments, 839–40
  cmdOK button, 842

Index

SharePoint Portal Server COM Add-in, *continued*
   code, 840–44
   frmPublish form, 841
   installing, 837–38
   Publish Attachments menu item, adding, 840
   using, 838–40
sharing information, 4
Shift key, 95
ShortcutAdd event, 350
shortcuts
   Message field, 181, 184
   Outlook Bar, events, 350–51
   OutlookBarShortcut object, 436–37
Show Actions On option, 242
ShowDocumentListHTML method, 828–30
ShowFormPage method, 515
showing pages, 130–31
ShowPopup method, 446–47
Simple MAPI, NewInspector event, 354
sizing images, 204
Smart Tags, 401
Snooze event, 335
sorting, 259
   by Conversation Index, 274
   items, 102–3, 271–72, 480
   Items collection object, 480
   items in views, 102–3, 271–72
   Sort method, 480
spacing controls, 139
SpecialEffect property, 205
speech recognition, 401
SpinButton controls, 205–6, 208
Spy. *See* Outlook Spy
SQL Server 2000 for Digital Dashboards, 742–45
Standard Inspector Toolbar, 387
startup
   OnStartupComplete event, 678
   Startup event, 330–31
state, maintaining
   cookies, 739
   folder home pages, 738–39
   Web Parts, 764
sticky notes forms, 126
storage. *See* physical storage
streamlining office procedures, 4
structuring information, 4
Sub-category property, 144
subfolder permissions, 299–300
Subject field
   Conversation property, 272–73
   defined, 176
   functions of, 179
   initial value, setting, 180
   prefix, setting in Reply actions, 228

Subject Prefix, 242
Sub procedures for use as macros, 319–20
SyncEnd event, 347
synchronization of contacts, 537
Synchronize Forms box, offline use of custom forms, 306
SyncObject events, 323, 344–47
SyncObject objects, 344–45
SyncStart event, 347

T

tab order, 84, 87, 139–42
TabStrip controls, 203, 206
TAPI (Telephony Application Programming Interface), 583
task applications, 41–42
Task forms, 111–12, 126
TaskItem object, 505–6
TaskRequestItem object, 507–9
tasks
   Assign method, 506
   creating recurring, 506
   creating Task forms, 126
   GetAssociatedTask method, 507–8
   GetRecurrencePattern method, 506
   operation of, 505
   programmatic security settings, 644
   responding to requests, 508
   retrieving associated, 507–8
   sending, 506–7
   Task forms, 111–12, 126
   TaskItem object, 505–6
   TaskRequestItem object, 507–9
Team Folder Wizard, 5
TeamScope Outlook Extensions Library, 37
technical users group applications, 72
Template property, 144
templates
   controls, placing in Toolbox, 188
   default folder location, 89
   forms based on, creating, 126
   Script Editor, 24–25
testing
   folders, 307–8
   forms, 88, 151–52
   views, 291–92
Test Trust COM Add-in, 645–47, 698–99
TextBox controls
   adding with Control Toolbar, 61
   adding with Field Chooser, 137
   attachments in, 191
   function of, 190
   initial values, setting, 191

877

Index

TextBox controls, *continued*
  labels, adding, 63
  multiple lines, 191
  properties, setting, 61–63
  SpinButton controls with, 205–6
Text fields, 162, 172–73
text strings, building in formula fields, 168–69
Third Party Web Sites folder, 18
This Action Will options, 242
This Folder Is Available To option, 295
ThisOutlookSession class module
  COM Add-ins, development, 654
  defined, 314
  porting to COM Add-ins, 633–34
  WithEvents keyword, 321
tilde (~), 185, 187
time. *See also* dates
  selection controls, 207–8
  Time fields, 162
  variant data type, 409–11
  Web Storage System, 831
TipText help, 141
title bar, source of, 179
To field, 176–79
  contacts, preaddressing to, 177
  default value, 171
  folder, preaddressing to, 177–79
  preaddressing, 215
  programmatic security settings, 644
  To property, 488
ToggleButton controls, 206
toolbars
  adding buttons, 341
  Advanced (*see* Advanced toolbar)
  CommandBar object, 437–48
  command button, adding with VBA, 331
  macros, adding to, 320
toolboxes. *See* Control Toolbox
Tools menu
  Address Book command, 179
  Macro command, 313
  Options command, 256, 328
  Security command, 700
  Select Form command, 254
  Send/Receive Settings command, 288
Tools Options dialog box
  adding custom property pages, 679–81
  adding pages with VBA, 328–29
To property, 488
tracking folders, 14, 248
Tracking items
  reviewing, 219–20
  voting buttons specifying, 211–12, 216–17

Training Management application
  Actions page, Course Catalog entry, 238
  Course Catalog Entry form, 236–42
  Course Offering form, 236, 239
  Create Offering action, 239–43
  Evaluation form, 237
  field values, copying, 242–43
  hiding Response forms, 246
  item types used, 235
  overview, 235–37
  publishing, 244–45
  Signup form, 237
  testing, 245
Training Management folder, 13
troubleshooting
  COM Add-ins, 694
  scripts (*see* Microsoft Script Editor, troubleshooting with)
trust
  COM Add-ins, 384, 632, 644–47, 675, 705–7
  Test Trust COM Add-in, 698–99
TypeName function, 410
Type properties of fields, 161–62

U

undoing control deletions, 137
uninstalling custom toolbars, 688
updating forms with Forms Manager, 258
URLs (Uniform Resource Locators)
  cmd parameter, 187
  folders, accessing with, 187
  Message fields holding, 181–82, 184–86
  protocols supported, 185–86
  shortcuts, 19
  spaces in, 185
Use Form Only For Responses property, 146
UserForm, Outlook View Control, 719–21
user interfaces
  COM Add-ins, 6
  Explorer events, 338–44
  Object model components, *430*
UserProperties collection object, 525–26
users
  instructing on how to publish, 597
  returning currently logged-on, 428
Use Voting Buttons check box, 216

V

Vacation Request application
  Actions page, 223
  Approve Vacation button, 223
  backing up Reply form, 231

878

Index

Vacation Request application, *continued*
  buttons, 221–22
  copying of field values, 228–30
  field sharing, 228–29
  Form Action Properties dialog box, 225
  hiding response forms, 233–34
  options, setting, 225–28
  overview, 221–22
  publishing, 231–32
  Reply forms, 230–31
  testing, 233
  Vacation Approved form, 222, 224, 230
  Vacation Denied form, 222
  Vacation Report form, 222
  viewing properties, 224–25
validating data, 172–76
Value property, 194
variables
  displaying value of, 393–95
  global object, setting to Nothing on Quit event, 329–30
  Item object, 395–96
  lifetimes, 409
  naming conventions, 408, 410–11
  objects, assigning to, 412
  scope, 408–9
  script-level, 560
  typing, 395
  variant data type, 409–11
  VBA, 30
variant data type, 409–11
VarType function, 410
VBA (Visual Basic for Applications)
  adding command bar button to advanced toolbar, 313–14
  adding macros to toolbars, 320
  add-ins, 32–34
  Add methods (*see Add* method)
  AdvancedSearchComplete event, 331–32
  AdvancedSearchStopped event, 332
  application-level events (*see* Application-level events)
  Application object, 314
  Auto List, 29–30
  availability, controlling, 312
  canceling events, 373
  child object instantiation, 325–26
  child objects raising events, 322–26
  vs. COM Add-ins, 317
  COM Add-ins, developing, 654
  COM Add-ins, porting preexistent code, 663–64
  declarations with *WithEvents* keyword, 325
  digital certificates, 702–3

VBA (Visual Basic for Applications), *continued*
  dimensioning objects for events, 324–25
  Editor (*see* VBA Editor)
  Editor window, 29–30
  event tracing, 326
  event trapping, 321–26
  Explorer events (*see* Explorer events)
  Explorers object, NewExplorer event, 323, 325
  features, 28–29
  Folders collection object events, 358–61
  help, 397–98
  Immediate window, 326
  Inspector events, 356–58
  Inspectors collection object events, 351–56
  item-level events (*see* item-level events)
  Items collection object, 362–66
  ItemSend event, 327
  libraries, 30
  limitations, 384
  location of projects, by OS, 317
  macros, creating, 319
  MapiLogonComplete event, 332
  multiple instancing of objects, 325–26
  NewExplorer event, 337
  NewMail event, 327–28
  Object Browser, 30, 402–3
  objects with events raised, table of, 323–24
  OptionsPagesAdd event, 328–29
  Outlook Bar events, 347–51
  Outlook Object Model, 312
  preferred development tool, 384–85
  programming environment variances, 398–99
  Quit event, 329–30
  references, 315–16
  Reminder event, 330
  Reminders collection object, 332–35
  Rules Wizard, custom scripts for, 312
  run-time files, 707
  saving projects, 316–17
  security, 317–18
  security for intellectual property, 700
  security levels, effects on, 701
  selfcert.exe, 702–3
  signing projects, 703
  Startup event, 330–31
  Sub procedures, 318–20
  SyncObject events, 344–47
  ThisOutlookSession class module, 314
  UserForms, 31
  variables, 30
  Views collection object, 361–62
  Visual Basic Reference Help, 397–98
  WithEvents keyword, 321–26

Index

VBA Editor, 312–18
    adding command bar button to advanced toolbar, 313–14
    Automation coding with, 419
    Call Stack window, 315
    Code window, 314–15
    digital certificates, signing projects with, 703
    docking windows, 315
    events in Procedures list, 322
    Immediate window, 315
    macros, creating, 319
    modules, inserting, 319
    navigating, 314–15
    Object Browser window, 315
    Office object library, 315
    opening, 312–13
    Outlook Application object, 315
    Outlook object library, 315
    Project Explorer window, 314–15
    Properties window, 314–15
    references, 315–16
    running macros, 320
    saving projects, 316–17
    securing projects, 317–18
    Sub procedures, 318–20
    ThisOutlookSession class module, 314–15
VBAProject.otm, 316–17, 326
VBScript (Visual Basic Scripting Edition), 117–18
    adding item-level events, 369
    canceling events, 373
    carrying event code with forms, 366, 370
    COM Add-ins, 384
    CommandButton controls, 200–202
    CONST statement, 411–12
    Control object, 519
    control types requiring, 206
    declaring constants, 399
    help, 397–98
    item event modification, 368–70
    Item object, 399–400
    modifying item-level events, 369
    naming conventions, 410–11
    object browser, 402–3
    Outlook View Control, 738
    preventing execution on opening, 396
    programming environment variances, 398–99
    Samples folder, 396–97, 406–7
    Script Editor, 24–25
    script-level variables, 560
    trust, 384
    TypeName function, 410
    variables, limitations on, 408–9

VBScript (Visual Basic Scripting Edition), *continued*
    variant data type, 409–11
    VarType function, 410
    versions, 385–86
    Visual Basic Reference Help, 397–98
    Web Parts, 758–61
    With statement, 407–8
VBScript Samples folder, 16
    opening, 396–97
    testing code samples, 406–7
vendor services applications, 72
View Code command, 24, 387
View Control. *See* Outlook View Control
viewing. *See also* views
    forms in Design mode, 20–21
    forms in folders, 255
    Script Editor, 387
View menu
    Current View command, 260
    Show Folder Home Page command, 287
views, 259–83
    adding fields, 48–49, 52
    automatically generating Microsoft Exchange views, 291
    automatic formatting, 281–82
    BeforeViewSwitch event, 339–40
    Beta Participants view, 43, 45, 50–54
    caching, 283
    cells, allowing editing, 280–81
    columns (*see* columns)
    Conversation Index property, 274
    Conversation property, 272–73
    creating custom, 47–54, 100–103
    creating new, 47–48, 51, 260–61
    Current View list, 260
    custom, 25–27
    Customize Current View command, 269
    deleting fields, 48
    design considerations, 283
    discussion applications, 72–73, 100–103
    editing, allowing user, 280–81
    Field Chooser, 262
    fields, creating columns from, 262
    filters (*see* filters)
    Folder Home Pages, 283–90
    font selection, 279
    formatting, 259, 279–82
    grid lines, 279
    Group By icon, 270
    grouping folder items, 269–73
    groups defined, 259
    indexed fields, 102–3
    initial, setting, 106, 294

Index

views, *continued*
   Initial View On Folder property, 70
   Only Show Views Created For This Folder option, 261
   order of headings, 103
   Outlook View Control, 539–40
   Outlook View Wizard COM Add-in, 694–97
   performance, 283
   Potential Beta Participants view, 43–44, 47–50, 54
   Product Category, 100–103
   purpose of, 100
   removing fields, 101
   rendering time, 283
   showing custom only, 27
   sorts (*see* sorting)
   standard views, 261
   switching, 54
   testing, 291–92
   type for new, choosing, 260
   validation rules, 269
Views collection object, 361–62, 475–76
Views object, events raised by, 324
viruses
   effect on Outlook 2002 design, 3
   forms, checking for, 593
   Outlook E-mail Security Update, 182
Visual Basic. *See* Microsoft Visual Basic
Visual Basic Editor. *See* VBA Editor
Visual Basic Expression Service, 23–24, 165
Visual Basic for Applications. *See* VBA (Visual Basic for Applications)
Visual Basic Reference Help, 18, 397–98
Visual C++. *See* Microsoft Visual C++
Visual InterDev. *See* Microsoft Visual InterDev
Visual Studio. *See* Microsoft Visual Studio 98
voting buttons
   actions, 218
   Address Form Like property, 218
   Art Approval form overview, 212
   function of, 211–12
   reviewing replies, 219–20
   specifying, 216
   Tracking items, 211–12
   tracking item storage specification, 216–17
   Use Voting Buttons check box, 216
   using, 219

W

warning prompts, security. *See* Object Model Guard; Outlook E-mail Security Update
Web applications
   Digital Dashboards (*see* Digital Dashboards)
   Outlook content in Web pages (*see* Outlook View Control)

Web applications, *continued*
   Web content in Outlook (*see* folder home pages)
Web-based setup of COM Add-ins, 709
Web folders, 793–95
Web pages
   adding to Outlook Bar, 19
   coding in, 735–38
   inserting Outlook View Control, 729–30
   opening, 19, 436
   Outlook View Control using, 728
   settings, offline, 289–90
Web Parts
   adding to dashboards, 749–51
   catalogs, 741, 749–51
   communication between, 770–72
   Companies (*see* Companies Web Part)
   creating, 755
   DDSC Notification Service, 770–72
   DDSC object, 761
   defined, 741
   designing with Office XP Developer, 753–65
   DHTML events, 761–62
   editing windows, XP Developer, 758
   event handling, 770–72
   exporting, 765
   folders, changing, 760–61
   HTML markup, 755
   importing, 745–47
   localization of commands, 761
   My Dashboard, 752–53
   My Inbox, 755–57, 759
   My Public Folder, 753
   My Shared Calendar, 753
   namespaces, 762, 764
   Northwind SharePoint Dashboard, 812–14
   opening for customizing, 754
   Outlook code in, 762–63
   properties, 758
   removal, 812–14
   Sales Data, 778–80
   samples, installing, 746
   scripting, 758–61
   Shared Activities, 769, 775–78
   SharePoint Portal Server, designing for, 753–54
   state, maintaining, 764
   version compatibility, 741
   WPQ tokens, 755–58, 763
Web Storage System (WSS)
   applications, 713
   books on, 846
   date/time, UTC, 831
   Explorer, 35–36, 823–24
   Microsoft PKMCDO for Microsoft Web Storage System, 401

Index

Web Storage System (WSS), *continued*
    properties, 823–24
    SharePoint Portal Server, core of, 785
Web Views, 19
When Responding box, 241
While You Were Out form, 592
windows, returning active, 417
Windows Explorer, Web folders, 793–94
Windows Installer setups, 710
With...End With statement, 407–8
WithEvents keyword, 321–26
    button declarations with, 579–81
    COM Add-ins, 662–63
    command bar control event procedures, 457
    firing order, 381–82
    item-level events, 370
    Property pages, COM Add-ins, 685
Word Envelope messages, coding, 418
WordMail, spaces in hyperlinks, 185
WordWrap property, 157

workflows, 33–34
workspaces, 788–89, 834
Write event, 381
WSS (Web Storage System). *See* Web Storage System (WSS)

X

XML (Extensible Markup Language)
    Microsoft XML Document Object Model, 401
    Outlook View Wizard, 696–97
    Web Parts, 765

Y

Yes/No fields, 162

Z

ZipOut 2000, 37
zone security, 715

Get the end-to-end *guidance* and *ready examples* you need to create powerfully extensible databases with Microsoft Access Version 2002.

Learn how to connect to structured data sources—and extend your solutions to the Web—with code and instruction straight from the source. Highly regarded author Rick Dobson takes you inside the enhanced capabilities of Access 2002 to give you expert guidance and rich, adaptable code samples to help you write, test, and debug extensible database applications faster and more intuitively. This in-depth analysis covers ActiveX® Data Objects (ADO), Microsoft® SQL Server™, XML, and Web development, using best practices and real-world examples to build comprehension and help expedite developer productivity. The book's code samples appear on the companion CD-ROM so you can study and reuse them for your own projects.

U.S.A. $59.99
Canada $86.99
ISBN: 0-7356-1405-9

Microsoft Press® products are available worldwide wherever quality computer books are sold. For more information, contact your book or computer retailer, software reseller, or local Microsoft® Sales Office, or visit our Web site at mspress.microsoft.com. To locate your nearest source for Microsoft Press products, or to order directly, call 1-800-MSPRESS in the United States (in Canada, call 1-800-268-2222).

Prices and availability dates are subject to change.

Microsoft

mspress.microsoft.com

The *definitive guide*
to programming the
Windows CE API

Design sleek, high-performance applications for the newest generation of smart devices with this practical, authoritative reference. It fully explains how to extend your Microsoft® Windows® or embedded programming skills to the Windows CE handheld and Pocket PC environments. You'll review the basics of event-driven development and then tackle the intricacies of this modular, compact architecture. Investigate platform-specific programming considerations, and use specialized techniques for handling memory, storage, and power constraints. Dive into serial, network, and RAPI communications. Advance your skill with modules, processes, and threads, and build or modify code to meet the requirements of new devices such as the Pocket PC.

U.S.A. **$59.99**
Canada $86.99
ISBN: 0-7356-1443-1

Microsoft Press® products are available worldwide wherever quality computer books are sold. For more information, contact your book or computer retailer, software reseller, or local Microsoft Sales Office, or visit our Web site at mspress.microsoft.com. To locate your nearest source for Microsoft Press products, or to order directly, call 1-800-MSPRESS in the United States (in Canada, call 1-800-268-2222).

Prices and availability dates are subject to change.

Microsoft®

mspress.microsoft.com

Randy Byrne

A veteran developer for Microsoft Outlook, Randy Byrne is the President and CEO of Micro Eye, Inc., a Microsoft Certified Partner specializing in collaborative application development using Microsoft Exchange and Outlook. As a Microsoft Most Valued Professional (MVP) for Outlook, he has extensive experience with the concerns of the Outlook development community. He received his Bachelor's degree from Yale University and a graduate degree from the University of California at Berkeley. A resolute fan of the Outlook Object Model, he contributes regularly to *Exchange and Outlook* magazine. He is a speaker at numerous industry conferences, including Microsoft TechEd, the Microsoft Exchange Conference, and the Exchange/Outlook Developer's Summit. Micro Eye, Inc., is located in the Sacramento area of Northern California.

Goggles

In 1268 the English philosopher Roger Bacon recorded the earliest statement about the optical use of lenses. Over the centuries, glasses came to be used for protection as well as for vision correction. Made of plastic or toughened glass, goggles are specifically designed to protect the eyes from flying debris or harmful liquids. Welders, for example, wear deep-tinted goggles to protect their eyes from the actinic rays of welding flames. Machinists and other factory workers wear glasses or goggles of great strength to shield their eyes from flying particles of metal. Watertight goggles permit divers to see under water.

Tools are central to the progress of the human race. People are adept at building and using tools to accomplish important (and unimportant) tasks. Software is among the most powerful of tools moving us forward, and Microsoft is proud to create tools used by millions worldwide and to contribute to continuing innovation.

The manuscript for this book was prepared and galleyed using Microsoft Word 98. Pages were composed by Microsoft Press using Adobe PageMaker 6.52 for Windows, with text in Garamond and display type in Helvetica Condensed. Composed pages were delivered to the printer as electronic prepress files.

Cover Designer: Methodologie, Inc.
Interior Graphic Designer: James D. Kramer
Indexer: Bill Meyers
Principal Copy Editor: Holly Viola
Principal Desktop Publisher: Dan Latimer
Interior Artist: Michael Kloepfer

Get a **Free**
*e-mail newsletter, updates,
special offers, links to related books,
and more when you*
register on line!

Register your Microsoft Press® title on our Web site and you'll get a FREE subscription to our e-mail newsletter, *Microsoft Press Book Connections.* You'll find out about newly released and upcoming books and learning tools, online events, software downloads, special offers and coupons for Microsoft Press customers, and information about major Microsoft® product releases. You can also read useful additional information about all the titles we publish, such as detailed book descriptions, tables of contents and indexes, sample chapters, links to related books and book series, author biographies, and reviews by other customers.

Registration is easy. Just visit this Web page and fill in your information:

http://mspress.microsoft.com/register

Microsoft®

Proof of Purchase

Use this page as proof of purchase if participating in a promotion or rebate offer on this title. Proof of purchase must be used in conjunction with other proof(s) of payment such as your dated sales receipt—see offer details.

Building Applications with Microsoft® Outlook® Version 2002
0-7356-1273-0

CUSTOMER NAME

Microsoft Press, PO Box 97017, Redmond, WA 98073-9830

MICROSOFT LICENSE AGREEMENT
Book Companion CD

IMPORTANT—READ CAREFULLY: This Microsoft End-User License Agreement ("EULA") is a legal agreement between you (either an individual or an entity) and Microsoft Corporation for the Microsoft product identified above, which includes computer software and may include associated media, printed materials, and "on-line" or electronic documentation ("SOFTWARE PRODUCT"). Any component included within the SOFTWARE PRODUCT that is accompanied by a separate End-User License Agreement shall be governed by such agreement and not the terms set forth below. By installing, copying, or otherwise using the SOFTWARE PRODUCT, you agree to be bound by the terms of this EULA. If you do not agree to the terms of this EULA, you are not authorized to install, copy, or otherwise use the SOFTWARE PRODUCT; you may, however, return the SOFTWARE PRODUCT, along with all printed materials and other items that form a part of the Microsoft product that includes the SOFTWARE PRODUCT, to the place you obtained them for a full refund.

SOFTWARE PRODUCT LICENSE

The SOFTWARE PRODUCT is protected by United States copyright laws and international copyright treaties, as well as other intellectual property laws and treaties. The SOFTWARE PRODUCT is licensed, not sold.

1. **GRANT OF LICENSE.** This EULA grants you the following rights:
   - a. **Software Product.** You may install and use one copy of the SOFTWARE PRODUCT on a single computer. The primary user of the computer on which the SOFTWARE PRODUCT is installed may make a second copy for his or her exclusive use on a portable computer.
   - b. **Storage/Network Use.** You may also store or install a copy of the SOFTWARE PRODUCT on a storage device, such as a network server, used only to install or run the SOFTWARE PRODUCT on your other computers over an internal network; however, you must acquire and dedicate a license for each separate computer on which the SOFTWARE PRODUCT is installed or run from the storage device. A license for the SOFTWARE PRODUCT may not be shared or used concurrently on different computers.
   - c. **License Pak.** If you have acquired this EULA in a Microsoft License Pak, you may make the number of additional copies of the computer software portion of the SOFTWARE PRODUCT authorized on the printed copy of this EULA, and you may use each copy in the manner specified above. You are also entitled to make a corresponding number of secondary copies for portable computer use as specified above.
   - d. **Sample Code.** Solely with respect to portions, if any, of the SOFTWARE PRODUCT that are identified within the SOFTWARE PRODUCT as sample code (the "SAMPLE CODE"):
     - i. **Use and Modification.** Microsoft grants you the right to use and modify the source code version of the SAMPLE CODE, *provided* you comply with subsection (d)(iii) below. You may not distribute the SAMPLE CODE, or any modified version of the SAMPLE CODE, in source code form.
     - ii. **Redistributable Files.** Provided you comply with subsection (d)(iii) below, Microsoft grants you a nonexclusive, royalty-free right to reproduce and distribute the object code version of the SAMPLE CODE and of any modified SAMPLE CODE, other than SAMPLE CODE (or any modified version thereof) designated as not redistributable in the Readme file that forms a part of the SOFTWARE PRODUCT (the "Non-Redistributable Sample Code"). All SAMPLE CODE other than the Non-Redistributable Sample Code is collectively referred to as the "REDISTRIBUTABLES."
     - iii. **Redistribution Requirements.** If you redistribute the REDISTRIBUTABLES, you agree to: (i) distribute the REDISTRIBUTABLES in object code form only in conjunction with and as a part of your software application product; (ii) not use Microsoft's name, logo, or trademarks to market your software application product; (iii) include a valid copyright notice on your software application product; (iv) indemnify, hold harmless, and defend Microsoft from and against any claims or lawsuits, including attorney's fees, that arise or result from the use or distribution of your software application product; and (v) not permit further distribution of the REDISTRIBUTABLES by your end user. Contact Microsoft for the applicable royalties due and other licensing terms for all other uses and/or distribution of the REDISTRIBUTABLES.

2. **DESCRIPTION OF OTHER RIGHTS AND LIMITATIONS.**
   - **Limitations on Reverse Engineering, Decompilation, and Disassembly.** You may not reverse engineer, decompile, or disassemble the SOFTWARE PRODUCT, except and only to the extent that such activity is expressly permitted by applicable law notwithstanding this limitation.
   - **Separation of Components.** The SOFTWARE PRODUCT is licensed as a single product. Its component parts may not be separated for use on more than one computer.
   - **Rental.** You may not rent, lease, or lend the SOFTWARE PRODUCT.
   - **Support Services.** Microsoft may, but is not obligated to, provide you with support services related to the SOFTWARE PRODUCT ("Support Services"). Use of Support Services is governed by the Microsoft policies and programs described in the user manual, in "on-line" documentation, and/or in other Microsoft-provided materials. Any supplemental software code provided to you as part of the Support Services shall be considered part of the SOFTWARE PRODUCT and subject to the terms and conditions of this EULA. With respect to technical information you provide to Microsoft as part of the Support Services, Microsoft may use such information for its business purposes, including for product support and development. Microsoft will not utilize such technical information in a form that personally identifies you.

- **Software Transfer.** You may permanently transfer all of your rights under this EULA, provided you retain no copies, you transfer all of the SOFTWARE PRODUCT (including all component parts, the media and printed materials, any upgrades, this EULA, and, if applicable, the Certificate of Authenticity), **and** the recipient agrees to the terms of this EULA.
- **Termination.** Without prejudice to any other rights, Microsoft may terminate this EULA if you fail to comply with the terms and conditions of this EULA. In such event, you must destroy all copies of the SOFTWARE PRODUCT and all of its component parts.

3. **COPYRIGHT.** All title and copyrights in and to the SOFTWARE PRODUCT (including but not limited to any images, photographs, animations, video, audio, music, text, SAMPLE CODE, REDISTRIBUTABLES, and "applets" incorporated into the SOFTWARE PRODUCT) and any copies of the SOFTWARE PRODUCT are owned by Microsoft or its suppliers. The SOFTWARE PRODUCT is protected by copyright laws and international treaty provisions. Therefore, you must treat the SOFTWARE PRODUCT like any other copyrighted material **except** that you may install the SOFTWARE PRODUCT on a single computer provided you keep the original solely for backup or archival purposes. You may not copy the printed materials accompanying the SOFTWARE PRODUCT.

4. **U.S. GOVERNMENT RESTRICTED RIGHTS.** The SOFTWARE PRODUCT and documentation are provided with RESTRICTED RIGHTS. Use, duplication, or disclosure by the Government is subject to restrictions as set forth in subparagraph (c)(1)(ii) of the Rights in Technical Data and Computer Software clause at DFARS 252.227-7013 or subparagraphs (c)(1) and (2) of the Commercial Computer Software—Restricted Rights at 48 CFR 52.227-19, as applicable. Manufacturer is Microsoft Corporation/One Microsoft Way/Redmond, WA 98052-6399.

5. **EXPORT RESTRICTIONS.** You agree that you will not export or re-export the SOFTWARE PRODUCT, any part thereof, or any process or service that is the direct product of the SOFTWARE PRODUCT (the foregoing collectively referred to as the "Restricted Components"), to any country, person, entity, or end user subject to U.S. export restrictions. You specifically agree not to export or re-export any of the Restricted Components (i) to any country to which the U.S. has embargoed or restricted the export of goods or services, which currently include, but are not necessarily limited to, Cuba, Iran, Iraq, Libya, North Korea, Sudan, and Syria, or to any national of any such country, wherever located, who intends to transmit or transport the Restricted Components back to such country; (ii) to any end user who you know or have reason to know will utilize the Restricted Components in the design, development, or production of nuclear, chemical, or biological weapons; or (iii) to any end user who has been prohibited from participating in U.S. export transactions by any federal agency of the U.S. government. You warrant and represent that neither the BXA nor any other U.S. federal agency has suspended, revoked, or denied your export privileges.

6. **NOTE ON JAVA SUPPORT.** THE SOFTWARE PRODUCT MAY CONTAIN SUPPORT FOR PROGRAMS WRITTEN IN JAVA. JAVA TECHNOLOGY IS NOT FAULT TOLERANT AND IS NOT DESIGNED, MANUFACTURED, OR INTENDED FOR USE OR RESALE AS ON-LINE CONTROL EQUIPMENT IN HAZARDOUS ENVIRONMENTS REQUIRING FAIL-SAFE PERFORMANCE, SUCH AS IN THE OPERATION OF NUCLEAR FACILITIES, AIRCRAFT NAVIGATION OR COMMUNICATION SYSTEMS, AIR TRAFFIC CONTROL, DIRECT LIFE SUPPORT MACHINES, OR WEAPONS SYSTEMS, IN WHICH THE FAILURE OF JAVA TECHNOLOGY COULD LEAD DIRECTLY TO DEATH, PERSONAL INJURY, OR SEVERE PHYSICAL OR ENVIRONMENTAL DAMAGE. SUN MICROSYSTEMS, INC. HAS CONTRACTUALLY OBLIGATED MICROSOFT TO MAKE THIS DISCLAIMER.

DISCLAIMER OF WARRANTY

NO WARRANTIES OR CONDITIONS. MICROSOFT EXPRESSLY DISCLAIMS ANY WARRANTY OR CONDITION FOR THE SOFTWARE PRODUCT. THE SOFTWARE PRODUCT AND ANY RELATED DOCUMENTATION ARE PROVIDED "AS IS" WITHOUT WARRANTY OR CONDITION OF ANY KIND, EITHER EXPRESS OR IMPLIED, INCLUDING, WITHOUT LIMITATION, THE IMPLIED WARRANTIES OF MERCHANTABILITY, FITNESS FOR A PARTICULAR PURPOSE, OR NONINFRINGEMENT. THE ENTIRE RISK ARISING OUT OF USE OR PERFORMANCE OF THE SOFTWARE PRODUCT REMAINS WITH YOU.

LIMITATION OF LIABILITY. TO THE MAXIMUM EXTENT PERMITTED BY APPLICABLE LAW, IN NO EVENT SHALL MICROSOFT OR ITS SUPPLIERS BE LIABLE FOR ANY SPECIAL, INCIDENTAL, INDIRECT, OR CONSEQUENTIAL DAMAGES WHATSOEVER (INCLUDING, WITHOUT LIMITATION, DAMAGES FOR LOSS OF BUSINESS PROFITS, BUSINESS INTERRUPTION, LOSS OF BUSINESS INFORMATION, OR ANY OTHER PECUNIARY LOSS) ARISING OUT OF THE USE OF OR INABILITY TO USE THE SOFTWARE PRODUCT OR THE PROVISION OF OR FAILURE TO PROVIDE SUPPORT SERVICES, EVEN IF MICROSOFT HAS BEEN ADVISED OF THE POSSIBILITY OF SUCH DAMAGES. IN ANY CASE, MICROSOFT'S ENTIRE LIABILITY UNDER ANY PROVISION OF THIS EULA SHALL BE LIMITED TO THE GREATER OF THE AMOUNT ACTUALLY PAID BY YOU FOR THE SOFTWARE PRODUCT OR US$5.00; PROVIDED, HOWEVER, IF YOU HAVE ENTERED INTO A MICROSOFT SUPPORT SERVICES AGREEMENT, MICROSOFT'S ENTIRE LIABILITY REGARDING SUPPORT SERVICES SHALL BE GOVERNED BY THE TERMS OF THAT AGREEMENT. BECAUSE SOME STATES AND JURISDICTIONS DO NOT ALLOW THE EXCLUSION OR LIMITATION OF LIABILITY, THE ABOVE LIMITATION MAY NOT APPLY TO YOU.

MISCELLANEOUS

This EULA is governed by the laws of the State of Washington USA, except and only to the extent that applicable law mandates governing law of a different jurisdiction.

Should you have any questions concerning this EULA, or if you desire to contact Microsoft for any reason, please contact the Microsoft subsidiary serving your country, or write: Microsoft Sales Information Center/One Microsoft Way/Redmond, WA 98052-6399.

CW01163848

MODERN CHINA IN PICTURES

NEW WORLD PRESS

First Edition 2013

Text by Wang Xu, Zhang Kaiyuan and Zhang Jing
Edited by Li Shujuan and Qiao Tianbi
Revised by Paul White and Penelope Colville
Photos edited by He Yuting
Cover design by He Yuting

Copyright by New World Press, Beijing, China
All rights reserved. No part of this book may be reproduced in any form or by any means without permission in writing from the publisher.

ISBN 978-7-5104-2632-2

Published by
NEW WORLD PRESS
24 Baiwanzhuang Street, Beijing 100037, China

Distributed by
NEW WORLD PRESS
24 Baiwanzhuang Street, Beijing 100037, China
Tel: 86-10-68995968
Fax: 86-10-68998705
Website: www.newworld-press.com
E-mail: frank@nwp.com.cn

Printed in the People's Republic of China

[Preface]

Significant Changes in a Century of Vicissitudes

One hundred years went by from the 1911 Revolution to 2011. The year 2012 marks another 100 years since the end of the Qing Dynasty in 1912. This past century has been full of twists and turns. As Li Hongzhang, a Chinese general and statesman of the late Qing Empire, wrote in 1872: "This is a great change unprecedented in the 3,000 years of Chinese history." However, it was only the beginning. The 20th century saw drastic and complete changes spread across China. Even in the 21st century we can still feel the momentum of these changes, and are spurred on by their impact.

As we look back at this volatile 100 years, we can't help asking: What exactly were the changes? This book tries to answer that question through a palette of daily-life pictures.

On the evening of October 10, 1911, gunshots were fired in Wuchang City, and the centuries of dynastic rule quickly came to an end. China opened a brand-new chapter in its history. However, the road ahead was still full of hardships in spite of the founding of the Republic of China. The country was tortured by secession and unrest while waiting for a revolution and rebirth. The wave of "modernization" challenged every corner of old China. Men's pigtails were cut off and the binding of girls' feet was forbidden by law. Loose robes with wide-open sleeves and large belts swiftly dropped out of fashion. Cities with foreign-style buildings sprang up. Trains rumbled across the countryside, and steamboats chugged up and down rivers and lakes, bringing an ancient nation on to the fast track of modernization. The changes in the physical world also had an impact on the Chinese people's mentality, as their minds opened up under the influence of Western philosophy. With educational reform, old-style private schools were abandoned, while public schools were set up to spread new thinking and concepts. Progressive thought finally triumphed in the course of the New Culture Movement, heralding a brand-new era.

In 1927 the government of the Republic of China was founded in Nanjing. However, the long-awaited stability and revitalization were yet to come. During the 22 years of rule by the Kuomintang (KMT), the country and its people still had to endure political turbulence, foreign invasion and endless wars. Yet it was also a time of vigor and changes. The Chinese people made significant achievements in this period in economic growth, culture, education, art and social progress. The burgeoning cities became dazzling highlights against the background of backwardness, turbulence and poverty. In these sleepless cities, high-rises were built everywhere, and their wide streets were lined with neon lights. People from all walks of life pursued the modern life: gentlemen in suits, and ladies with wavy hair in cheongsam dresses were eye-catching. In just a decade, imported goods, such as matches, candles, soap and light bulbs, as well as trolleybuses and running water, became daily necessities. Moreover, the new environment also gave rise to a prosperous culture. Books and newspapers, films and theatrical performances abounded in that era, which produced noted scholars and writers. It was also an era of multiple choices and diversity. Hu Shi and Lu Xun called for "national spirit," while Zhang Ailing and Huanzhu Louzhu touched people's hearts with romantic novels. Film actors and actresses enjoyed popularity, while Peking Opera performers were also highly applauded by enthusiasts. The classics and modern fashions, and tradition and modernity clashed and merged with each other, and gave birth to something new. However, this new life failed to awaken China's countryside or benefit Chinese farmers. Conflicts and difficulties were still out there. China still had a long way to go.

On October 1, 1949, the People's Republic of China was founded. China's history then embraced a great turn. A socialist regime was established, the country returned to peace and stability, and the economy also recovered. There were painful experiences later, such as the Great Leap Forward and "three-year famine," and problems with the planned economy and centralized regime, but the country kept its momentum. What's more important is that the grass-roots people won and maintained their dignity and rights. The people became the owners of their own lives, and worked with full vigor. Meanwhile, the working people had more access to department stores, cinemas, hospitals, schools and parks. Enjoyment that had once been reserved for the rich was now within the reach of everyone. During those early years, China was not prosperous, and the people led spartan lives. But they were optimistic and industrious, as they were in full control of their own lives. There was no longer the extravagance and decadence of the old era, and simplicity and friendliness became the social norms. People sang revolutionary songs and danced the *yangko* (a popular folk dance) to herald the new era and new life, displaying a vigorous People's Republic of China with high aspirations.

In 1966 the Cultural Revolution broke out. This "extreme-Leftist" movement, led by the Party and central leaders, brought about disastrous turmoil and internal frictions. The Cultural Revolution also dealt a heavy blow to Chinese culture. During that time, fanaticism, over-excitement, blind faith and other absurdities were prevalent. Meanwhile, the people struggled through this "revolutionary" period. They kept their pace of life by working to pay for basic daily necessities, and their pursuit of beauty and a free life never ended. Although people dressed almost the same and lived similarly across the country, colored clothes and long plaits would occasionally sneak in. Festivals were still celebrated with fireworks and dumplings, as well as with the occasional small parties. The general public hung on to their lives, which brought humanity to those chaotic years.

In 1978 the convening of the 3rd Plenary Session of the 11th National Congress of the CPC Central Committee opened another new chapter in China's history, with the country's opening to the outside world. The Chinese government faced up to its backwardness, and led the Chinese people to boldly and resolutely set out on the grand course of reform and opening-up, with full emancipation of the mind. From then on, China strove to integrate itself into the rest of the world and catch up with the global trend. This was a significant change for the country and the nation, and touched every aspect of life. Along with rapid economic development, people had access to more wealth. As the people's income increased, delicacies, fashionable garments and luxurious houses became available. Health, culture and enjoyment were the next topics on the list. A new sense of individuality enriched people's lives. The resumption of the university entrance examination brought with it an enthusiasm for studying, and rebuilt faith in "knowledge is power." The opening of China's first stock market stimulated everyone to speculate and invest. The Chinese people are fully aware of these changes.

Entering the new century, China's development is an irrefutable fact, and the "Chinese miracle" will continue unabated. In line with the basic national policy of reform and opening-up, the national power is being enhanced, the economy is becoming more and more prosperous, and the people's lives are improving by the day. The enhanced economic strength and abundant merchandise give rise to multiple and diversified selection and taste, as well as a colorful social life. It is impossible to describe China and the Chinese people in one word. The only thing we can be sure of is that, as the Chinese people more and more have their basic needs satisfied, they are beginning to focus more on moral cultivation. They are becoming more interested in social causes and charity work to fulfill self-achievement and share their benefits with others. It can be clearly seen that a vigorous and optimistic society is coming into being. Currently, China is on the fast track of modernization, and the century-long dream of our ancestors is about to become true. Certainly, as a developing country, China still has a long way to go. In particular, after 30 years of reform and opening-up, some deep-rooted conflicts and problems have become prominent in the course of pursuing the grand objective of seeking development and wealth. Hope for the future and potential risks coexist. People are calling for equality, justice and harmony. This is our era. This is the finishing line of an old century, yet it is also the starting point of a new century. At this moment, let's take a look back to trace this colorful and complex progress of change. Together, let's relive the life of the people and experience the events in that era of change.

Wang Xu
June, 2012

CONTENTS

Chapter 1
A Difficult Start (1911-1927) /1
A Difficult Start /2
Changes in Clothing Fashions /6
Agriculture, Commerce and Daily Life /12
Changes in Family Life /13
Transportation /16
Urban Transformation /24
New Culture 30
Artistic Revival /34

Chapter 2
Years of Crisis (1928-1949) /37
Economic Development /38
Urban Landscape /46
Lifestyle /58
National Education /64
Films and Operas /70
Anti-Japanese War /77
Economic Hardships /84
Liberation of the Farmers /86

Chapter 3
A New World (1950-1965) /89
Transportation /90
Industry /94
Society /96
Urban Landscape /100
Lifestyle /106
Education /134
Culture /138

Chapter 4
Freeze-Frame of a Symbolic Era
(1966-1976) /147

A Fiery Era /148

Chapter 5
Catching Up with the World (1977-2000) /179

Tidal Wave of the Era /180
Wave of Economic Growth /191
Food Priority /202
Return of Beauty /214
Transportation /226
Marriage and Family /232
Education /242
Sports and Entertainment /260
Films, Music and Performances /266

Chapter 5
Merging with the World
(2001-2012) /281

Transportation /282
Fashion Leaders /294
Modern Industry and Agriculture /298
New Urban Landscape /313
Lifestyle /328

Chapter 1
A Difficult Start
(1911-1927)

A Difficult Start

The Imperial Palace

Also known as the Forbidden City, this was the residence of the emperors of the Ming (1368-1644) and Qing (1644-1911) dynasties. It is the largest integrated ancient building compound in the world. The edifices are of brick and wood. The design of the Imperial Palace reflects the autocratic nature of China's ancient dynastic regimes. The magnificent architecture and luxurious decorations also showcase the extravagant lifestyle of the imperial family and nobility. The Imperial Palace was out of bounds to the general public, hence the appellation Forbidden City. After the Qing regime collapsed in 1912, the Forbidden City was turned into a museum in 1914. In 1925 it became the Palace Museum.

The last emperor of the Qing Dynasty – Aisin-Gioro Puyi (1906-1967)

The 15-year-old Prince Puyi at his home in Beijing, photographed in 1921. In 1908 Puyi became the last emperor of the Qing Dynasty at the age of 3, with the reign tile of "Xuantong." Three years later, the 1911 Revolution against the dynasty was led by Dr. Sun Yat-sen. This was followed by uprisings in a number of China's southern provinces. On February 12, 1912, the Qing regime released the Imperial Edict of Abdication, declaring the end of the dynasty and the termination of the feudal monarchy which had ruled China for over 2,000 years.

Opium Den

In the 19th century British merchants smuggled large quantities of opium from India to China trying to make up for Britain's trade deficit with the latter. This led to the First Opium War in 1840. The corrupt Qing regime was defeated and was forced to allow more opium to be imported, worsening China's trade deficit and severely injuring the health of many Chinese people.

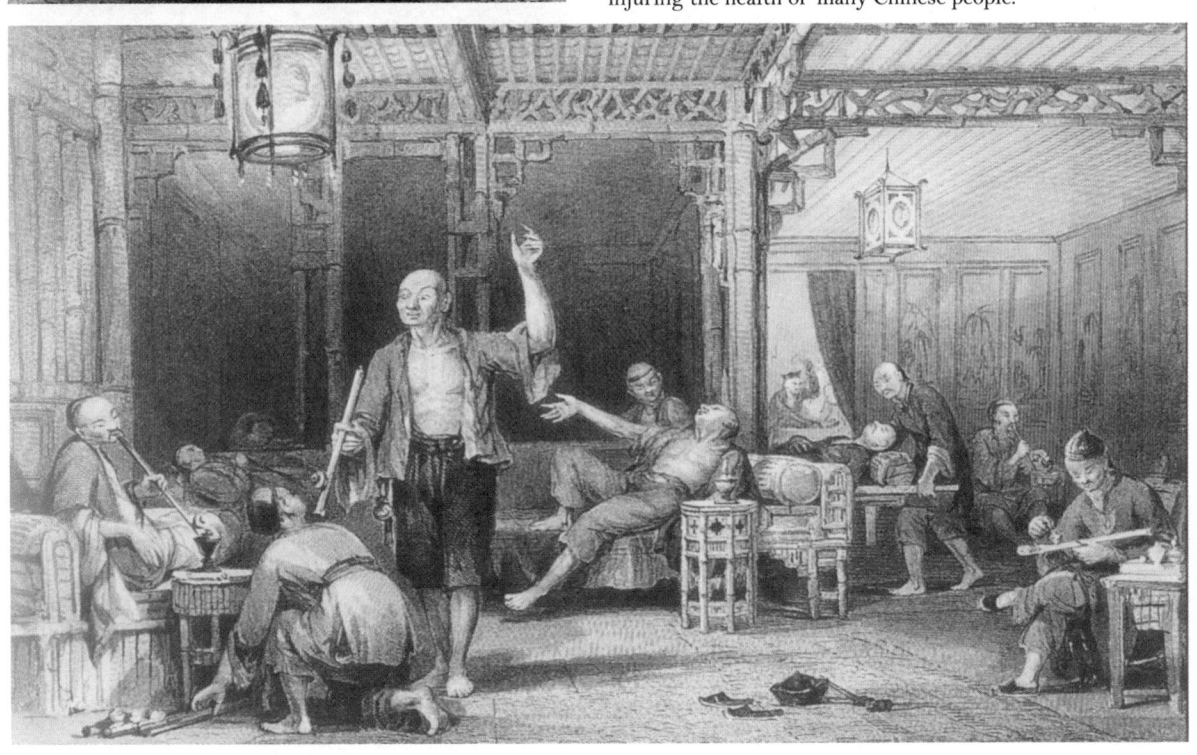

{ Chapter 1 } A Difficult Start (1911-1927)

Aristocratic women of the late Qing with bound feet – three-inch "golden lotuses"

In Chinese feudal society women of the Han ethnic group (not the ruling Manchu ethnic group), whether rich or poor, considered bound feet an asset to beauty. In the late Qing Dynasty, foot binding and opium consumption were vehemently criticized as public nuisances detrimental to health and humiliating to national dignity. The Republic of China (1912-1949) government discouraged foot binding and opium. Foot binding, however, lingered on in the rural areas. This undesirable custom, as well as that of opium smoking, disappeared after the founding of the People's Republic of China in 1949.

An illustration of the late Qing Dynasty, showing a mother binding the feet of her small daughter

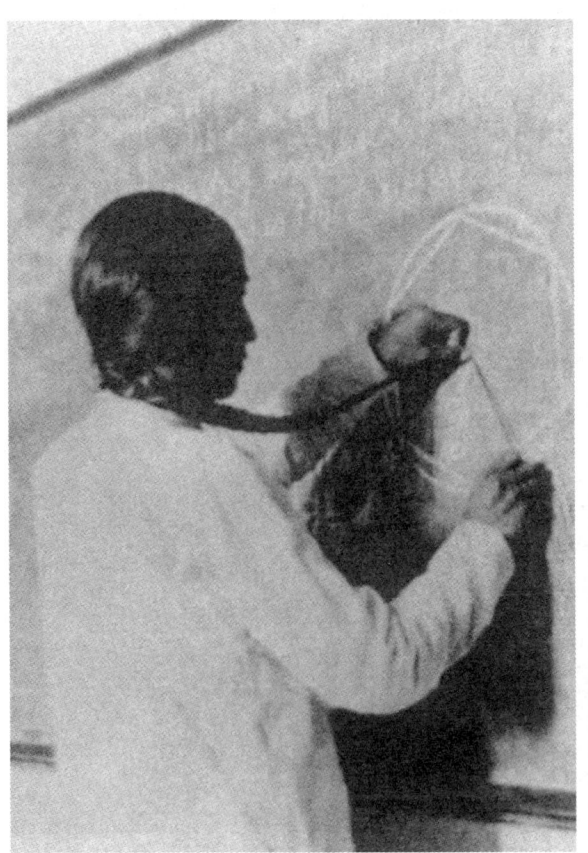

A geometry teacher using his pigtail as compasses for drawing a circle, late Qing Dynasty

In the Qing Dynasty, at the order of the Manchu ruling caste, Chinese men had to shave their foreheads and wear their hair in a pigtail at the back. In the late Qing Dynasty, some leading personages influenced by Western culture, campaigned against this fashion. The picture shows a clash between Eastern and Western culture at that time.

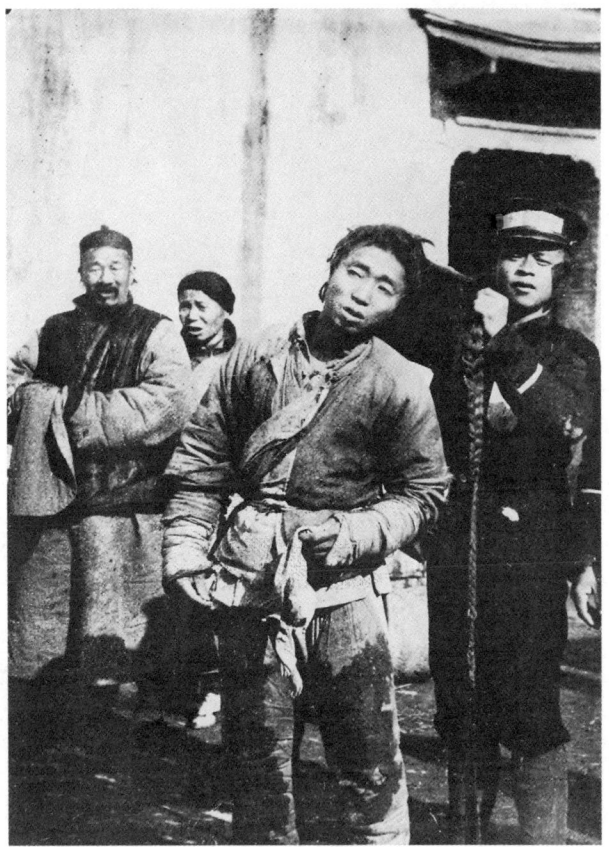

A soldier cutting off a farmer's pigtail which was once a symbol of the Qing Dynasty rule

In 1911 the Qing government began to allow people to cut off their pigtails if they so wished. During the Republic of China period (1912-1949) the government actually banned the pigtail. Even policemen and soldiers were mobilized to cut off the pigtails of passers-by. However, it was not until the 1930s that the pigtail finally disappeared.

{ Chapter 1 } A Difficult Start (1911-1927)

Changes in Clothing Fashions

Late Qing officials in casual wear
Officials of the Qing Dynasty wore long gowns and thick-soled boots. The man in the middle is also wearing a jacket.

Manchu noblewomen, late Qing Dynasty

Wealthy Han women in everyday dress, late Qing Dynasty

During the Qing Dynasty (1644-1911) male dress featured a long gown with a round collar and wide sleeves, over which a jacket was sometimes worn. Female dress for Manchu women featured a gown with a round collar and narrow sleeves, and a wide lower hem, with a jacket. They had distinctive headgear, and wore embroidered shoes with high soles. People of the Han ethnic group generally wore the fashions of the Ming Dynasty (1368-1644).

In the late Qing Dynasty traditional women's garments also changed subtly, with a preference for short, slim and comfortable wear. It was at this time that the *cheongsam* made its appearance as a typical Chinese female garment.

Yuan Shikai (1859-1916) in ceremonial dress as the president of the Republic of China

In the early years of the Republic of China, the Clothing Code stipulated a long gown or Western-style suit as ceremonial dress for officials.

Officials in formal attire in the early Republican period

Upon the founding of the Republic of China in 1912, the government stipulated changes in hair styles and dress as symbols of the end of autocratic rule and the beginning of modernization. Government officials took the lead in this regard. The picture shows the first cabinet members of the government in Beijing in March 1912.

Tang Shaoyi, State Premier, first on the right; Cai Yuanpei, Education Minister, first on the left; Song Jiaoren, Agriculture and Forestry Minister, second on the left; and Duan Qirui (in military uniform), Defense Minister, center at the back.

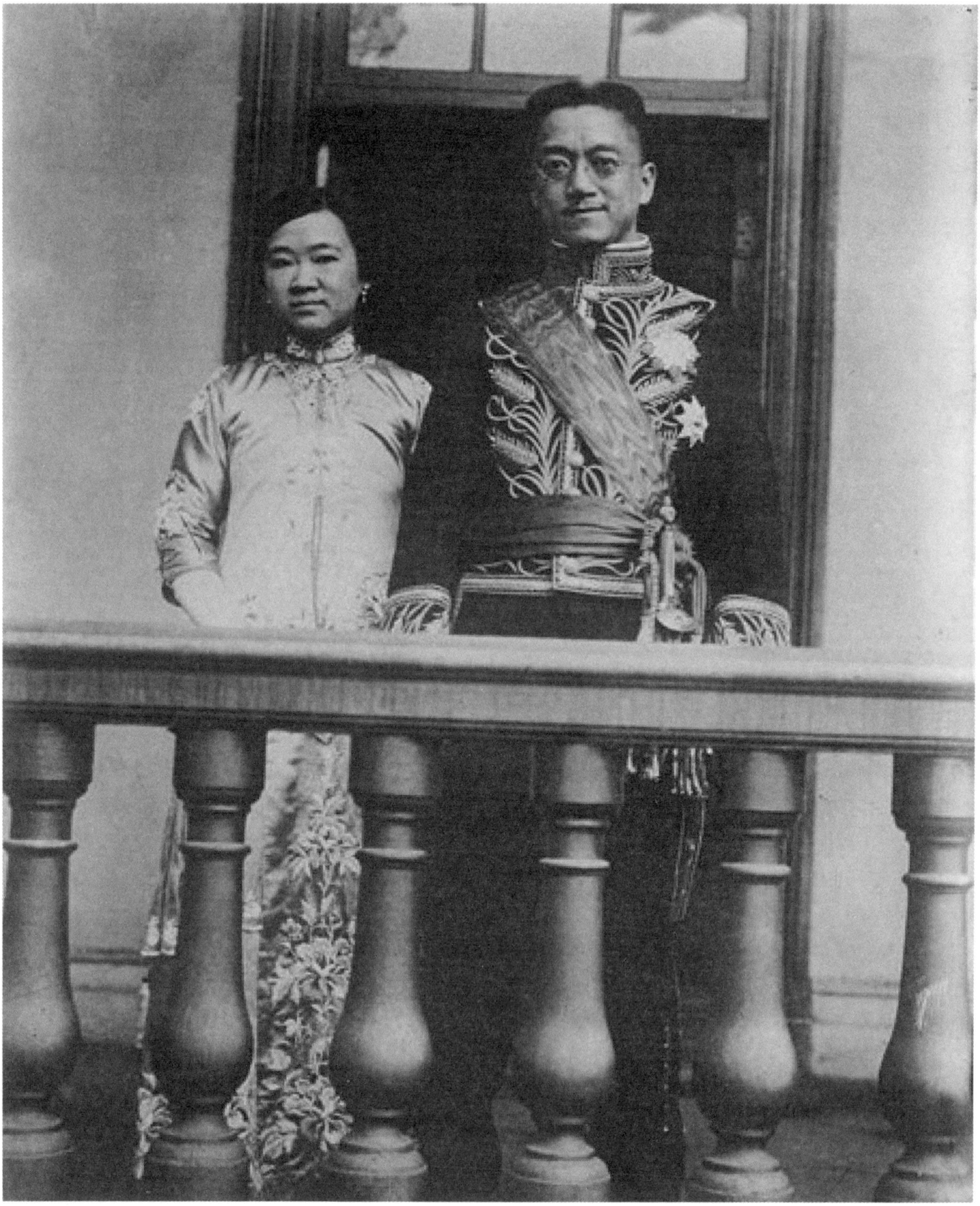

Dr. Sun Yat-sen in a Chinese tunic suit

The history of the Chinese tunic suit can be traced back to 1923, when Dr. Sun, founder of the Republic of China, believed that Western attire was much too complicated and stiff, while the Chinese long gown and jacket were conservative and uncomfortable. Thus he asked someone to design a new uniform, which was named after Dr. Sun Yat-sen (the "Zhongshan (Yat-sen) suit"). There are numerous arguments about the origin of this suit, some people seeing in it the Japanese student uniform, military uniform, or clerk uniform of Southeast Asia. Nevertheless, the Chinese tunic suit was popular among the revolutionaries and young people, thanks to its convenience, comfort, elegance, modernity and Chinese features. It was also accepted by the general public and became the national dress for men.

Zhang Zongxiang, a diplomat, and his wife in the early Republican period

After the founding of the Beijing government, a special code was drafted to regulate the dress code for officials and the general public. Western-style ceremonial dress was recommended, completely following Western practice for solemnity and elegance, featuring a top hat, tuxedo, white shirt and bow tie.

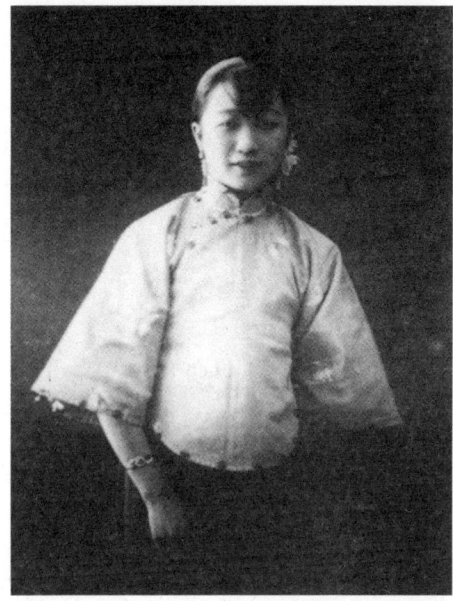

A fashionable lady in the early Republican period

Significant changes also took place in female dress in the early years of the Republic of China. The traditional *cheongsam* got a lower hem and shorter sleeves, while the waistline was cut to highlight slimness.

{ Chapter I } A Difficult Start (1911-1927)

Agriculture, Commerce and Daily Life

A food market in Yichang, Hubei Province, 1917

Buying cabbages on a Beijing street for the winter, 1925

Despite the revolution, most people still went about their ordinary, everyday lives.

Changes in Family Life

A wedding in Beijing during the early Republican period

The bridegroom wears the standard male Chinese attire of that time – a long gown with a jacket. He wears a congratulatory red blossom on his chest, and he holds the red veil which has just been removed from the bride's face. The bride wears a phoenix coronet and a ceremonial robe, decorated with pearls and pieces of jade. The newlyweds are surrounded by relatives and friends to show that their marriage has the function of connecting the family bonds. The Western hat worn by the bridegroom and the men in Western suits behind the couple forecast an upcoming change.

A marriage photo showing an East-West combination

A marriage photo dating from 1927. Their dress combines traditional and modern styles, with both Eastern and Western elements. The bridegroom sports a fashionable parted hairstyle, but is dressed in a long gown and a jacket. The bride wears a Western-style white wedding veil. This would have shocked tradition-minded people, as Chinese custom regarded white as a funeral color. The stylized flower on the bride's head is a feature of female Chinese opera characters.

Newlyweds, 1920

The simple and cozy background in the photograph implies that the young couple is creating a happy world for themselves alone. The traditional attitude of treating women as inferior to men is shifting towards equality between men and women, who are expected to support each other.

A centenarian poses with his five-generation family

For thousands of years, the Chinese people have cherished the practice of living together with as many descendants as possible. This showed that the head of the family was very successful in raising a moral and fortunate family. However, in the Republic of China period the average number of people per family was 5.2-5.3, and a big family with several generations living together was rare.

A spoiled baby boy, Beijing, 1919

A boy child is still highly prized in China. The photographer vividly captured this boy's naivety. A healthy, vivacious and curious boy was also thought to symbolize the end of turmoil and decline in the years of modern China, and the prospect of a bright future.

However, the reality was different, as poor medical conditions gave rise to a high mortality rate in modern China (156‰ in 1936). The baby in the picture is dressed like a tiger in the hope that he could grow up as strong as a tiger.

{ Chapter 1 } A Difficult Start (1911-1927)

Transportation

A blueprint for "North Harbor" described in the Industrial Development Plan by Dr. Sun Yat-sen

As it emerged in the Republican age, China was hampered by backward industrial and economic conditions. Determined to change this situation, Dr. Sun Yat-sen drew up his Industrial Development Plan as a grand blueprint for the country. It was intended to construct 100,000 miles of railways to connect China's costal, inland and border areas; one million miles of roads across the country; opening up and overhauling water channels and canals to develop inland river shipping and hydroelectric power; and constructing world-class harbors comparable to New York Harbor in the north, central and south coastal areas. However, because of political turmoil and the Japanese invasion, the North Harbor plan was never realized.

The Beijing-Zhangjiakou Railway opens on October 2, 1909.

Dr. Sun Yat-sen poses for a photograph at the Zhangjiakou Station, September 6, 1912

In modern China, the construction and management of railways were monopolized by the Western imperialist invaders. From 1876 to 1911, 9,400 kilometers of railway lines were constructed in China, of which 41% was constructed and operated by Westerners, who extended 39% of the loans to build them; only 20% was owned by China, including state and private operations.

The Beijing — Zhangjiakou Railway was 200 km long — from Fengtai in Beijing to Zhangjiakou, capital of Hebei Province. The construction was started in September 1905 and completed in August 1909 (It opened for use in October that year). It was the first railway designed and completed by the Chinese without foreign funding or expert assistance. The project was overseen by Zhan Tianyou, who accomplished remarkable engineering feats during the construction, such as the herringbone track at the Qinglongqiao Station and the 1,092-m-long tunnel at the Badaling section of the Great Wall. The completion of the railway was a milestone in China's engineering history, and it promoted confidence and national pride in the Chinese people.

Western cargo ship moored beside Chinese ships in Haihe Harbor, Tianjin (early Republican period)

In 1842 China was defeated in the First Opium War, and forced to open up Guangzhou, Xiamen, Fuzhou, Ningbo and Shanghai as treaty ports. This was followed by more cities opening up after each further defeat. The Western invaders penetrated from coastal cities to inland areas via China's major rivers. They brought a large quantity of imported goods, but also robbed China of resources and wealth. China was dragged into the capitalist orbit, and embraced Western civilization unwillingly.

Launch of a US vessel built at the Jiangnan Shipyard, 1919

The predecessor of the Jiangnan Shipyard was the Jiangnan Machinery Manufacturing Administration (established by Governor-general of Jiangxi, Anhui and Jiangsu Zeng Guofan in September 1865). The Administration was the earliest and most famous Westernized enterprise in China, and enjoyed rapid growth in the late Qing Dynasty thanks to its commercialized operations. In 1918 the total tonnage of the Shipyard reached 60,400, surpassing the monopoly of Britain's S. C. Farnham & Co. and becoming the pace-setter of shipbuilding in China. In the period 1918-1921 the shipyard built four merchant ships for the US. It was praised by the local media as "opening up a brand-new chapter in China's industrial development."

Traditional horse-drawn carriage

This common transportation means in old China had vanished forever by 1920.

Rickshaws in southern China, 1900 ←

The rickshaw, a two-wheeled vehicle pulled by a man, was introduced into China from Japan in the late 19th century. Most of the rickshaw pullers were peasants who flocked to the large cities looking for work. There were 36,500 rickshaws in Beijing in 1924, with 29,000 for business use. At the same time there were 55,000 rickshaw pullers, accounting for 7% of the total population of Beijing. The rickshaw puller was at the bottom of the social scale, and often lived in dire poverty.

Tramcars were put into use in Beijing in December 1924. They were called "jingle cars" because of the ringing of their bells.

Tramcars were introduced into Hong Kong in 1904, and spread to the concessions and inland treaty ports. Tianjin and Shanghai began tramcar operation in 1906 and 1908, respectively. The Japanese and Russian invaders also set up tramcar systems in Dalian, Harbin, Changchun, Shenyang, Fushun and other cities. Beijing was a late-comer in this regard, because of the opposition rickshaw pullers.

{ Chapter 1 } A Difficult Start (1911-1927)

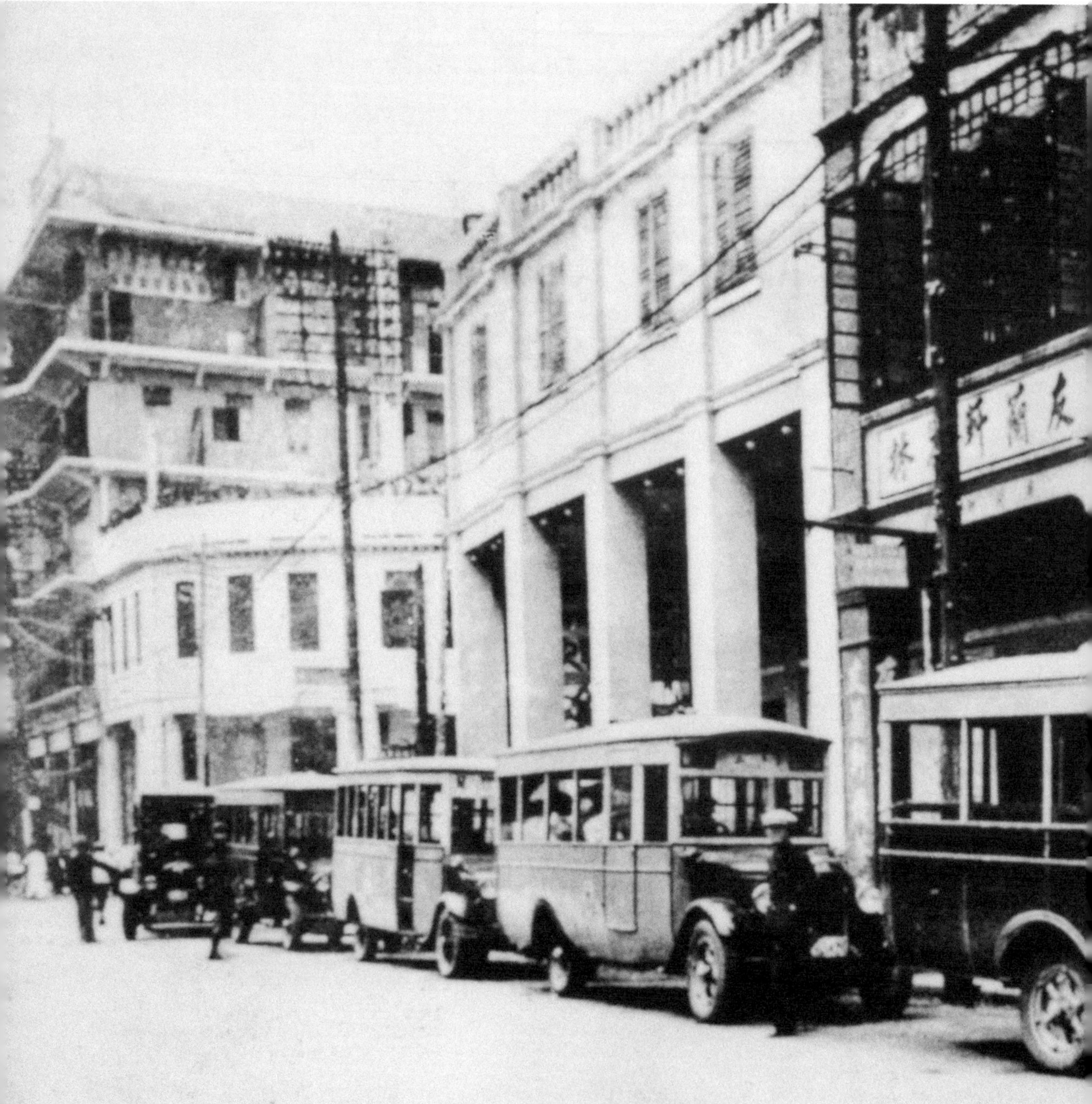

Petrol buses in Guangzhou, late 1920s

China's first petrol buses began operation in the Shanghai concessions on March 5, 1908 with a total road coverage of 6.04 km. They spread to Beijing, Tianjin, Wuhan, Guangzhou and Nanjing in the 1930s and 1940s. However, they never successfully competed with the tramcars.

{ Chapter I } A Difficult Start (1911-1927)

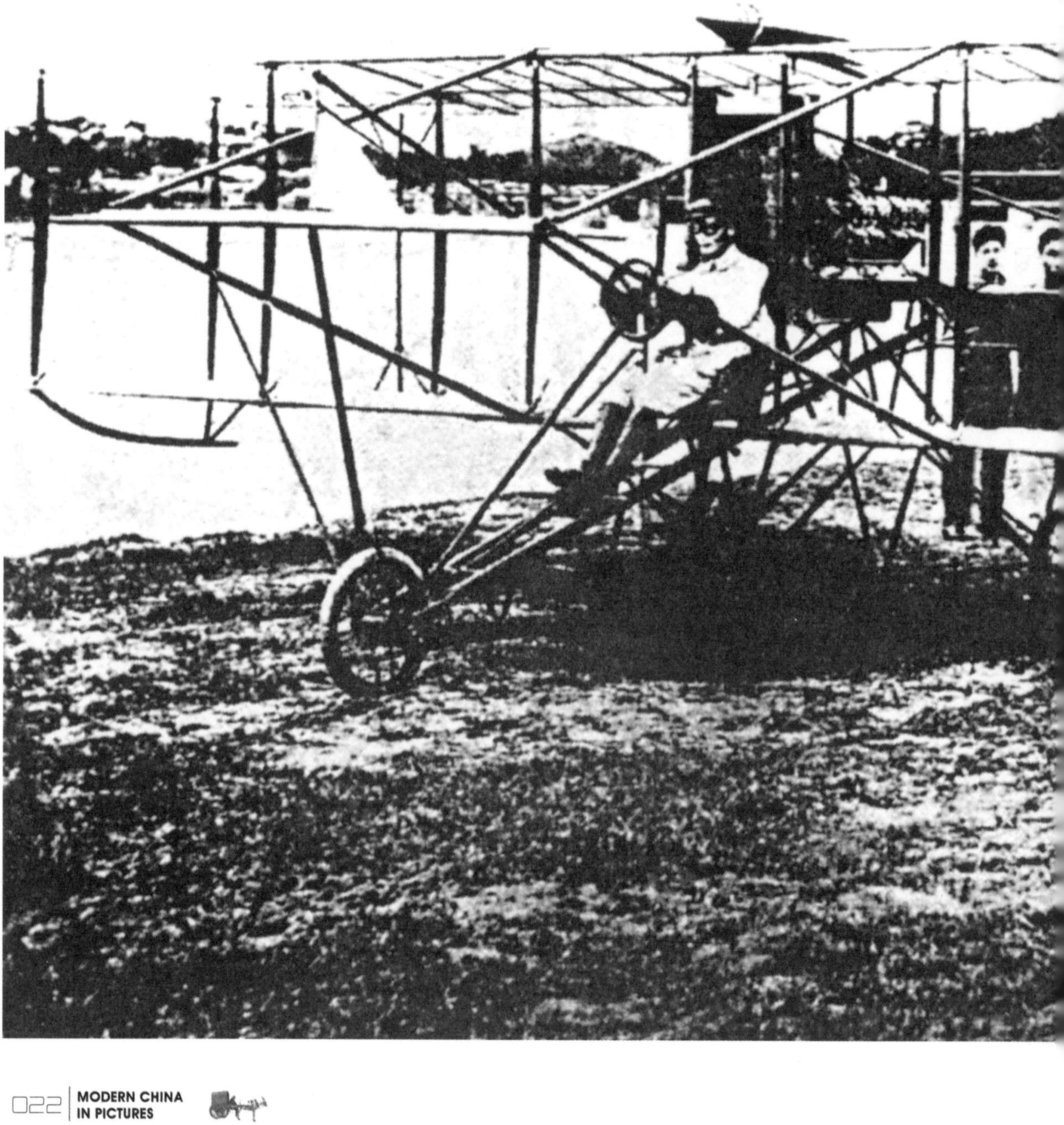

Feng Ru piloting his plane

Feng Ru (1883-1912) was China's first aviator and airplane designer. He was regarded as the father of China's aviation industry. He moved to the US with his father at the age of 12, and studied and worked in San Francisco, New York and other places. Diligent and persistent, he often worked part-time during the day and studied mechanics in the evening. He became an inventor several years later. In 1907, with funding from Chinese compatriots, Feng Ru began to develop an airplane in Oakland, San Francisco, and had a successful test flight in 1910. In 1911 he gave up a well-paid job in the US, came back to China with two airplanes, and actively engaged in the revolutionary cause. When the 1911 Revolution broke out Feng Ru was appointed by the Guangdong Revolutionary Government as the head of an air squadron. He died tragically at the age of 29 during a flying exhibition in Yantang, Guangzhou, on August 25, 1912.

Urban Transformation

Gulou Street, Beijing, Republican period

Urban construction transformed Beijing, and a new type of road was constructed, with rails for tramcars in the middle and pedestrian lanes on both sides. Electricity was also introduced. However, Beijing was still a typical Chinese city, backward when compared to Shanghai and Tianjin. Although it was the political center of the country, Beijing lacked industrial development, and its economy was highly dependent on consumption and the service sector. Located far from any port and free from foreign concessions, Beijing was slow to modernize.

Qianmen Street, Beijing, 1900

Beijing was a typical Chinese city at this time, with dirt roads, low houses and shambling carriages. Qianmen Street was crammed with all kinds of illegal settlements. It is unbelievable that this could have been the capital of a centuries-old empire. It is said that the first public toilet in Beijing was set up by the invading Eight-Power Allied Forces in 1900.

Nanjing Road, Shanghai, 1911

Shanghai's Bund, 1920s

Haizhu Bridge over the Pearl River during the Republican period (Guangzhou Province)

The Huangsha (Guangzhou) Station of the Guangzhou-Wuchang Railway, 1912

Guangzhou was the first treaty port in China, and in 1757, when the Qing Dynasty ordered all trade contacts with the outside world to be severed, only Guangzhou was excepted. Guangzhou, in fact, was once the third-largest city in the world, after Beijing and London. In modern times, Shanghai replaced Guangzhou as China's foreign trade center. But in the 19th century Guangzhou was still the political and economic center of south China, as well as one of the country's most important harbors. It was also a hotbed of revolution. The Guangzhou Uprising (1895) and the Huanghuagang Uprising (1911), which were organized by the Tung Meng Hui (Chinese Revolutionary League), took place in Guangzhou. Dr. Sun. Yat-sen set up a revolutionary government in Guangzhou three times during the Republican period. The city also gave birth to the first period of cooperation between the Kuomintang and Communist Party of China (CPC), as well as being the home of the Whampoa Military Academy. In December 1927 the CPC staged an uprising against the right wing of the Kuomintang in Guangzhou.

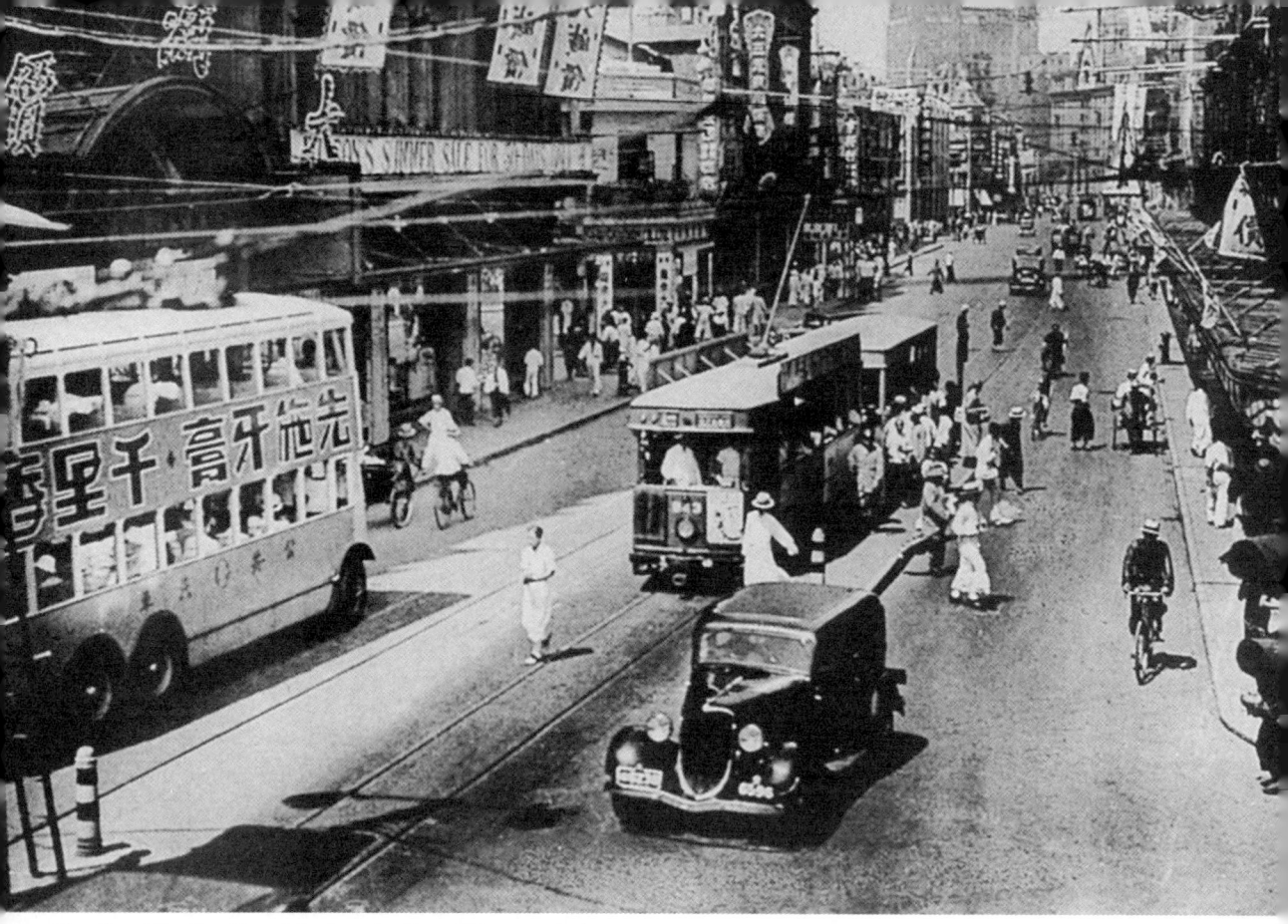

Bustling Nanjing Road during the Republican period

By the Treaty of Nanking in 1842 Shanghai became one of five treaty ports. Before long, British invaders set up the first concession in Shanghai, which was followed by US and French concessions (the British and US concessions were later combined). The concession played a key role in modern Chinese history, as it served as a stepping stone for foreign invasion on the one hand, and a conduit for introducing Western philosophy and culture into China on the other. Given its superb harbor and geographic location, Shanghai was transformed in a decade from a small coastal county into the largest and most prosperous harbor, economic and financial center and international metropolis in the Far East. It was nicknamed "flourishing foreign concession," "Paris of the East" and "No. 1 city in China." Some Western-style streets also emerged, such as the commercial center on Nanjing Road, and the financial hub of the Bund.

View of Wuchang, Hubei Province, Republican period

Wuchang, Hankou and Hanyang used to be known as "the three cities of Wuhan." Each of these three cities had its own characteristics: Wuchang served as a political and business center; Hankou was a Westernized concession and the center for bulk commodity trading and financial activities; Hanyang was a major industrial zone. During the late 19th century Governor-general of Hunan and Hubei Zhang Zhidong promoted the Westernization Drive by setting up the Hanyang Iron Plant and Hubei Firearms Plant here.

The Great Hutong of Tianjin, Republican period

The Great Hutong, also known as Guyi Street, was the first commercial street for garments in Tianjin. It was once home to eight of the city's 12 major silk and satin stores. During the Second Opium War of 1860 Tianjin was invaded by British and French forces and opened up as a treaty port. Other Western invaders then set up their own concessions in the city. There were once 9 concessions in Tianjin, set up by Britain, France, the US, Russia, Germany, Japan, Italy, Austria and Belgium. Tianjin gradually became the largest city in North China.

New Culture

The "Red-brick Building" – the original main building of Peking University

The Imperial University of Peking was established in 1898, as the first modern Western-style university. The main courses offered also favored Western knowledge. It was the highest education institution in China. In 1912 the university was renamed Peking University.

Cai Yuanpei (*third left, front row*), first president of Peking University, shown with the university's faculty, January 4, 1917

In 1917 leading educator and democratic revolutionary Cai Yuanpei assumed the post of first president of Peking University. He began to reform the university by "following the principle of free-spiritedness and inclusiveness." A number of China's best scholars, such as Chen Duxiu, Li Dazhao and Hu Shi, were employed as professors. The school management was also improved. These measures helped to create a free and open atmosphere for study, and gave birth to new thinking and new concepts. Peking University was also one of the springboards of the New Culture Movement and the May 4th Movement in 1919.

Students and professors of the Shanghai Patriotic Women's School

Christianity was introduced into China in the late Qing Dynasty and started to found schools as a means of proselytizing. The first institutions of higher education for women were set up by Christians. Progressive Chinese educators soon began to follow suit. The traditional concepts of "women being inferior to men" and "ignorance being the highest virtue" gradually vanished, and education for women became popular. In 1901 Cai Yuanpei and Zhang Binglin organized the China Education Association in Shanghai and opened the Patriotic Women's School (predecessor to the modern Shanghai Patriotism School) in the following year. The school stressed the principle that "revolutionary spirit for men and women shall be equally nurtured by providing education as its foundation stone." The school had wide influence in China.

The library of the North China Union College for Women, Beijing, 1919

In 1864 a missionary from the US Congregational Church, Eliza Jane Bridgman, set up the Bridgman Women's School in Beijing. By the late 19th century it was the best school for women in China, with Westernized primary and junior education. In 1905 university courses were included, and the school was renamed the North China Union College for Women. As the first women's university in China, it nurtured a number of leading women scholars, such as Xie Wanying (pen name Bing Xin), a prestigious author. In 1920 the university was combined with Huiwen University and Tongzhou Union University to become Yenching University.

Artistic Revival

A scene from a performance of The *Legend of White Snake*, late 1920s, with Mei Lanfang as White Snake (*center*), Cheng Yanqiu as Xu Xian (*right*) and Shang Xiaoyun as Green Snake (*left*)

In 1927 the Shuntian Newspaper hosted a poll of the best female-character performers in Peking Opera. Mei Lanfang, Shang Xiaoyun, Cheng Yanqiu and Xun Huisheng were selected by the readers as the Best Four Performers of Female Characters in Peking Opera. These four actors, all men, owed much of their skill to efforts made by intellectuals devoted to Peking Opera, such as Qi Rushan and Luo Yinggong. These people also designed scenarios and gave Peking Opera much-needed publicity. All these efforts contributed to making Peking Opera China's national opera.

A scene from a performance of *South Heaven Gate*, with Tan Xinpei as Cao Fu (*right*) and Wang Yaoqing as Cao Yulian (*left*)

From 1883 Peking Opera matured, and reached its prime in 1918, with a number of exceptional performers emerging. Tan Xinpei (1847-1917) was one of the most famous performers in the history of Peking Opera. Specializing in the roles of old gentlemen, Tan was known for his smooth, mellow and diversified voice. He was much emulated and admired by junior performers. He also created the first school of Peking Opera — the Tan School. Wang Yaoqing (1881-1954) was an early performer of female characters (usually played by male actors) in the opera. As an opera reformer, Wang designed the role of "Hua Shan" (young female characters), and abolished the walking-on-stilts performance, which mimicked the old practice of binding women's feet. Wang was also an influential opera educator. He had hundreds of disciples.

A scene from the film *Dingjun Mountain*, 1905, with Tan Xinpei as Huang Zhong

In 1905 Ren Qingtai, owner of the Fengtai Photography Studio, set up a movie camera in his courtyard and invited Tan Xinpei, an influential opera performer, to perform the opera *Dingjun Mountain* in front of the camera. The film was shot in direct daylight for three days, without script or props. It was then shown at the Da Guanlou Theater in Qianmen Street. *Dingjun Mountain* was the very first film shot by Chinese, signifying the birth of cinematography in China.

A Quyi orchestra "Green Bamboo Society"

    Quyi, a traditional Chinese performance much simpler than opera, was very popular in the late Qing Dynasty and the Republican period. The performance techniques were transferred only from masters to disciples. In this picture, the old man (*first left*) is the master, the young man (*second left*) playing the drum is his disciple and also the singer, accompanied by the other instruments of a four-stringed Chinese lute, two-stringed bowed instrument and three-stringed plucked instrument.

A scene from *Orphan Saves His Grandparents*, 1923, written by Zheng Zhengqiu and produced by the Shanghai Star Film Co.

    In the 1920s Chinese films blindly copied their Western counterparts, which led to a number of vulgar and absurd films being produced and landed the Chinese film industry in recession. An exception was the film *Orphan Saves His Grandparents*, reflecting family ethics and people's joys and sorrows, and highlighting the traditional virtues of faith, loyalty and honesty. The film was first shown on December 28, 1923, and was an immediately success. It was the first Chinese feature film to be successful both commercially and artistically. The popularity of this film led a surge in this field; 175 film companies sprang up in China in the period 1922-1926.

Chapter 2
Years of Crisis
(1928~1949)

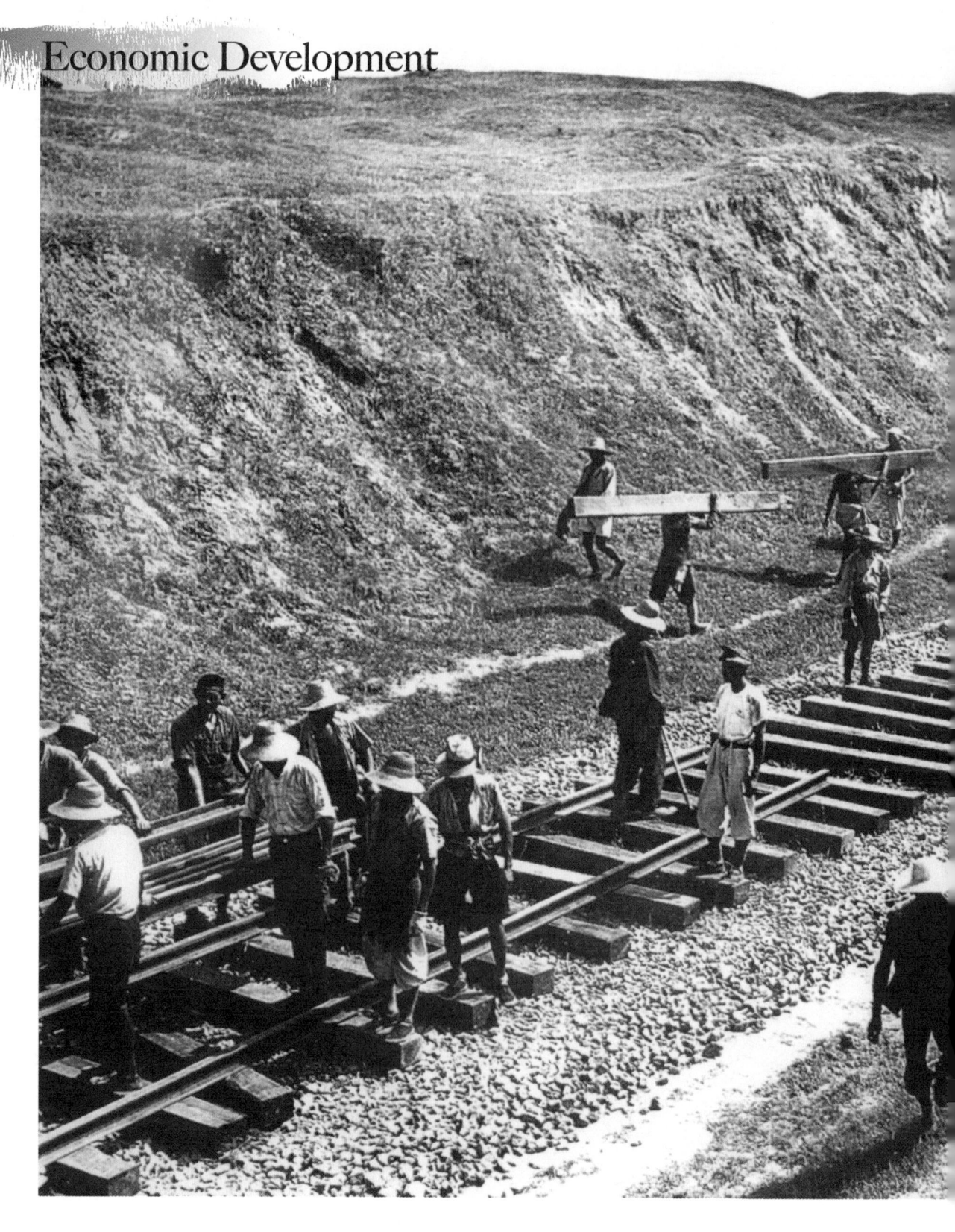

Economic Development

Railway construction, 1948

The National Government, based in Nanjing, drafted a large-scale railway development plan in 1928, but China's railways developed very slowly against the background of endless wars and social turmoil. During the decade from 1928 to 1937, a total of 4,500 km of railways were constructed. After the Anti-Japanese War broke out in 1937, the National Government limited railway construction to the southwest and northwest regions, which were far from the frontline, and 1,900 km of railways were completed during that time. However, the Japanese invaders constructed 6,600 km of railways in their occupation area in the period 1931-1945. During the whole rule of the Kuomintang (1928-1948), a total of 13,000 km of railways were built in China.

Launch of a new ship at the Jiangnan Shipyard, 1935

Cargo loading and unloading on the Huangpu River, Shanghai, 1930s

Harbor at Dalian, 1930s

China's shipping business enjoyed major development and prosperity after 1927. Although foreign shipping businesses accounted for 70% of such business in China, the quantity and capacity of local shipping companies were greatly enhanced. By 1936 there were 27 large and medium-sized shipping companies with ship capacity above 5,000 tons, including 14 with capacity of more than 10,000 tons.

The Minsheng Company was the leader of these shipping companies. In 1925 Mr. Lu Zuofu, who had been involved in education for years, started the company in Chongqing with only 50,000 yuan in capital and one steamship. The company enjoyed rapid growth due to its sound management and high quality of service. By 1935 the company had 2,836 employees, and 42 ships totaling 16,884 tons. Its equity reached 1.2 million yuan and total assets 7.3 million yuan, handling 61% of the Sichuan-Yangtze shipping business. After the Anti-Japanese War broke out, Lu was appointed director of the land-water transport management committee of the military commission of the National Government. In the fall of 1938 Wuhan fell to the Japanese. Thousands of refugees and more than 100,000 tons of supplies piled up in Yichang, which was being bombed by the Japanese. Lu mobilized all the ships and employees of the Minsheng Company to transport the stranded people and supplies around the clock despite the bombardment. In a period of 40 days, all the refugees and supplies were evacuated to Sichuan Province before Yichang fell. This emergency evacuation helped preserve a great number of human resources and materials for the Anti-Japanese War. It was known as "China's Dunkirk evacuation."

Lu Zuofu and the ocean liner of the Minsheng Co.

(Chapter 2) Years of Crisis (1928-1949)

Transportation in Peiping, 1930

While new types of modern transportation were being introduced to China, traditional wooden-wheeled (maximum load one ton) carts were still the most common heavy-duty transportation means in northern China, especially for food and coal. Such carts greatly damaged the asphalt roads that were expanding in the cities. The Peiping (Beijing) authorities forced modifications to them several times and banned them eventually.

Camel train crossing the Lugou Bridge in Beijing, 1930s

Camel transport had a long history in Beijing. Camels carried coal from Mentougou in the west to Beijing proper, and even brought goods from Inner Mongolia and Northwest China. Camels had been used in Beijing since its construction as Dadu, the capital city of the Yuan Dynasty, in the 13th century. They disappeared in the 1950s.

A textile mill in Yangshupu, Shanghai, 1930s

The textiles industry was one of the first modern industries in China. In 1935 the productivity of all cotton and textile companies totaled 4.95 million spindles. Shanghai, Tianjin, Qingdao and some other coastal cities were the major textiles producers. At the end of 1945 the National Government combined 69 textiles factories set up by the Japanese into the state-owned China Textile Co. Textiles factories used to employ mainly women workers, which helped to emancipate women from the home.

Electric street lights in Tianjin, 1930s

During the Republicn period, China's power industry enjoyed rapid growth, with the total power generation expanding from 27,000 kw in 1911 to 631,000 kw in 1936. In 1928 the National Government set up a construction commission to manage the state-owned power plants. Before the outbreak of the Anti-Japanese War in 1937 the total power generation of the state-owned power companies accounted for 60% of that of the whole country. In early 1949 national power generation totaled 1.8586 million kw, of which 1.6852 million kw was from coal-fired plants.

China's first civil airplane, "Hankou," about to take off, January 1929

In June 1928 the Ministry of Communications of the National Government began to develop civil aviation. On July 8, 1928 the first civil air route — from Shanghai to Nanjing — was opened. In August 1930 the China Aviation Co., a joint venture with the US, was established in Shanghai. In February 1931 the China-German joint venture Euro-Asia Aviation Co. was founded in Shanghai (later christened Central Aviation Co.). By the end of 1936 China Aviation and Euro-Asia had operated a dozen routes, with a total of 13,700 km. By 1937 the two companies had transported 90,793 passengers, 787 tons of cargo and 643 tons of mail. During the Anti-Japanese War China's aviation industry continued to develop. By 1947 China Aviation operated on a total of 50,000 km and Central Aviation Co. covered 30,000 km, both on domestic and international routes.

Dyke construction on the Lankao-Kaifeng section of the Yellow River, July 1935

In the 1930s and 1940s China suffered repeated natural disasters. A flood in 1931 was one of the most disastrous of the 20th century, affecting 672 counties and cities in 16 provinces. The Yangtze and Huai river basins were the worst affected. In eight provinces (Hunan, Hubei, Anhui, Jiangxi, Zhejiang, Jiangsu, Shandong and Henan) the total number of refugees was 51.27 million, and 9.73 million sq m of farmland was ruined. More than 400,000 people died in that year due to the flood, and the economic loss was RMB 2.254 billion.

To harness the two rivers using modern technology, the National Government set up the Yangtze River Committee in 1922 (reorganized in 1928 and 1935) and the Yellow River Committee in 1933.

Urban Landscape

The Shanghai Bund, 1930s

The tallest building in the picture is 77-m-high Sassoon House, built in 1929. It is currently the north section of the Peace Hotel, No. 20 Zhongshan East Road. It was built by Victor Sassoon of Britain. The building to the right is the Bank of China, relocated by the National Government from Beijing in 1928. It was originally taller than Sassoon House, but Sassoon insisted that, as this area was part of a foreign concession, the bank building should be lower than his. A lawsuit heard in London decided in favor of Sassoon, quoting the Treaty of Tianjin. The bank building was the only large building designed solely by Chinese architects at that time.

Postcard illustration featuring the Shanghai Municipal Government building

In 1929 the National Government drafted the Plan for a Great Metropolitan Shanghai, to make the city China's economic capital. The new city center was located in the northern part of Shanghai, away from the foreign concession area. Work was started on modern buildings and roads, but was halted by the Japanese invasion.

The Shanghai Municipal Government building was completed in 1933. The building reflected the Kuomintang's aspiration to "display traditional Chinese culture," with flying eaves, arches, carved beams and painted rafters.

View of Xiaguan, Nanjing, 1930s

Following the 1911 Revolution, the provisional government of the Republic of China was located in Nanjing. Dr. Sun Yat-sen was elected provisional president. In 1927 Chiang Kai-shek set up a new National Government, also in Nanjing. The city served as the capital of China for more than 20 years. At this time, the National Government drafted ambitious plans for large-scale construction in Nanjing to make it the political center of the country.

Nanmen Street, Nanjing

The Qinhuai River in downtown Nanjing

{ Chapter 2 } Years of Crisis (1928-1949) 049

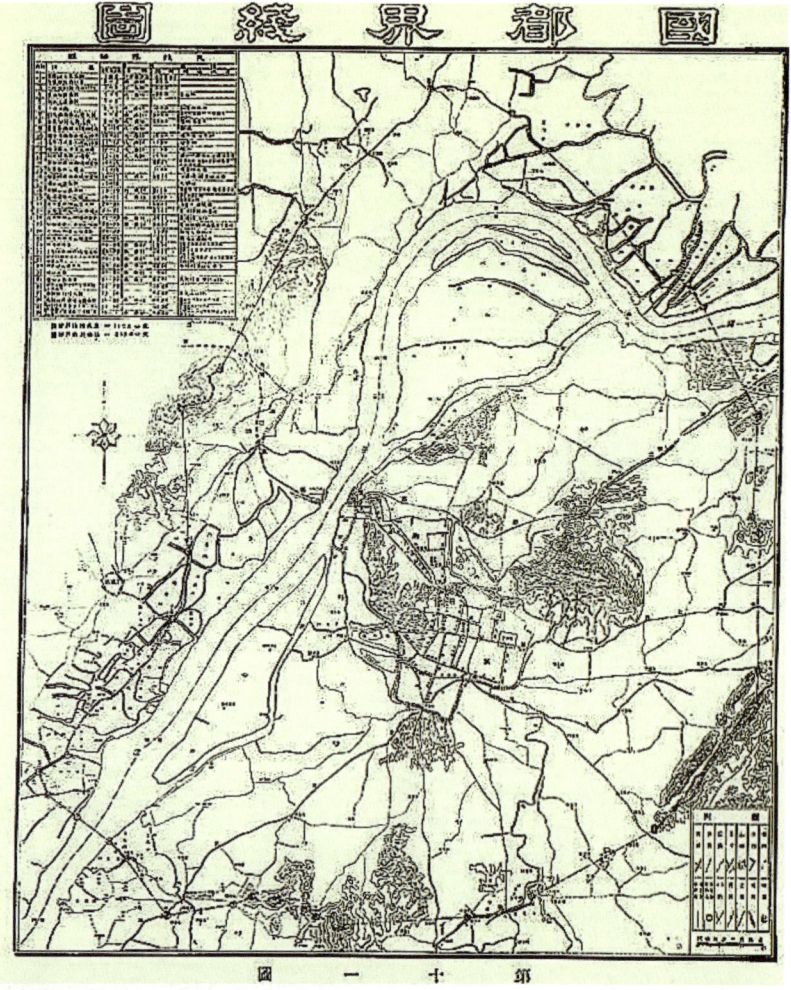

The blueprint for new Nanjing, 1929

In 1927 Sun Ke (son of Dr. Sun Yat-sen) organized the Urban Construction Committee, and invited US architect Henry Killam Murphy (designer of Tsinghua University, Jinling Women's University and Yenching University) and engineer Ernest P. Goodrich to be advisors to the committee, assisted by Lu Yanzhi (designer of the Mausoleum of Dr. Sun Yat-sen). Under the leadership of Murphy, the Capital Plan for Nanjing was drafted and released on Dec. 31, 1929. The Plan was the first urban planning document in the modern history of China.

The renovated Xinjiekou area at the center of Nanjing, 1946

Beijing's Qianmenwai Street viewed from the Qianmen Gate Tower, 1930s

The train station at East Qianmen, Beijing, 1930s

The Japanese invaders occupied Northeast China in 1931, and threatened Beijing (then called Peiping) and Tianjin. Even in this situation the attempt to modernize this ancient capital went on. The city's infrastructure construction was developed.

[Chapter 2] Years of Crisis (1928-1949)

The Archway at Xisi, Beijing, under renovation, 1935

After 1928 Beijing was no longer the capital of China, and the local government and inhabitants turned to culture and tourism to attract funds. In 1935 the local government launched a project to preserve and renovate Beijing's abundant historical and cultural relics. However, the July 7 Incident (Marco Polo Bridge Incident) of 1937 brought the Japanese invaders into the city, and the cultural protection work was halted.

Tianjin's East Train Station in 1935

During the 1930s and 1940s Tianjin was the largest city in North China, with a developed economy, and prosperous industry and commerce. Up until the early 1940s the city was divided into various foreign concessions. At the same time, Qing dynasty loyalists and ex-warlords flocked here, making Tianjin a breeding ground of political feuds and conspiracies. In 1931, after seven years in Tianjin, Puyi, the last emperor of the Qing Dynasty, was spirited out of the Japanese concession, and reemerged in Northeast China, where the Japanese made him the emperor of the puppet state of Manchukuo.

A view of Wuchang, Hubei Province, 1930s

A ferry landing in Wuhan, 1940s

In the 1930s Wuhan was the hub of finance, commerce and inland shipping on the central reaches of the Yangtze River. With a strong industrial base, Wuhan — together with its subordinate cities of Wuchang, Hankou and Hanyang — had a radiating effect towards South China. Wuchang was regarded as the political center; Hanyang was the industrial area; and Hankou was the commercial hub, with its numerous stores and warehouses.

Yanjiang Road, Haizhu Park and a residential area of Guangzhou, 1930s

In the 1930s Guangzhou, being close to Hong Kong and with contacts with Southeast Asia through its well-connected land and water transportation network, had a well-developed economy. The city was also famous for its resorts and leisure spots. It had more than 33 places of interest, ten parks, and more than 30 hotels, including the luxurious Aiqun Hotel. The city was also home to more than 100 bars, tea houses and Western-food restaurants, catering to all walks of life.

The Pearl River at Guangzhou, 1930s

Lifestyle

Public telephone in Shanghai, 1930s and 1940s

As China's largest metropolis, Shanghai was in the forefront of the country's modernization. More and more people gained access to electric lights, telephones and tap water. The city also quickly got efficient tramcar and bus connections.

Local beauties in Beihai Park, Beijing, in the 1930s, clad in the fashionable *cheongsam* dresses of the time

In the late 19th century parks were laid out in the foreign concessions of China's big cities. On October 10, 1914 the Beijing Municipal Government opened the Altar of Land and Grain (today's Zhongshan Park) area to the public as a park. This was the first of its kind in Beijing. On Aug. 1, 1925 Beihai Park was opened to the public.

Female students wearing the uniform of Southwest Associated University in Kunming, 1945

Starting in the 1930s, the cheongsam became the standard dress for all Chinese women, from housewives to the nobility, even at diplomatic events.

Photos of ordinary families, 1930s

{ Chapter 2 } Years of Crisis (1928-1949)

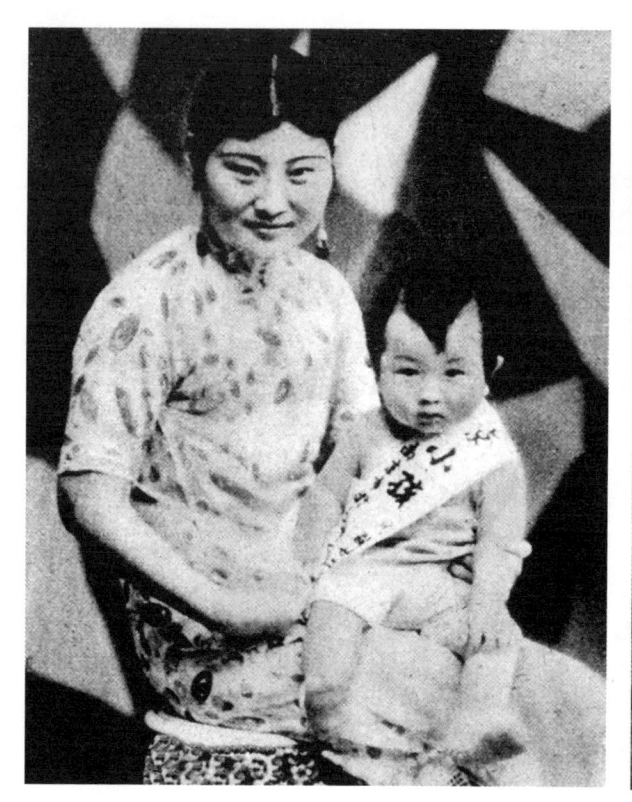

A healthy baby and mom, 1930s

China was poor and weak at that time, and was ridiculed as the "Sick Man of East Asia." Thus, there was great concern with the people's physical fitness.

A young rural woman with her one-year-old child, 1937

In spite of the changing social scene, women in China were often forced into marriage, especially in rural areas. In 1938 fewer than 1% of Chinese women remained unmarried after the age of 20. Most married women were kept at home, being completely isolated from social activities.

The winners of a child health contest in Chongqing, 1942

With the development of modern medical science, from the 1930s on, local governments and communities hosted child health contests to promote sound child rearing.

National Education

Classroom in a primary school, 1930s

Female students doing gymnastics in Beijing, late 1930s

From the late 1920s to the outbreak of the Anti-Japanese War, China was relatively stable, and education made remarkable progress. In 1935 the National Government approved the Interim Guide for Compulsory Education, and officially started four-year compulsory education. In 1937 the government released the Interim Regulations on Compulsory School Enrolment for Eligible Children. The government worked together with the educators, with the result that, in the period 1929-1936, the enrolment ratio for children at pre-school age rose from 17.1% to 43.4%. The contents of education covered ethics, general knowledge, physics, esthetics and diligence. The 1930s also saw significant development of vocational and tertiary education. In 1936 there were 108 institutions above college level, including 42 universities, 36 independent institutes and 32 vocational schools. Altogether, there were 272 schools, 1,095 departments and 41,922 students.

Tao Xingzhi, a leading Chinese educator, with boys of the Yucai School, 1939

China embraced a wave of popular education in the 1920s. Well-known educators like Cai Yuanpei, Tao Xingzhi, Liang Shuming and Yan Yangchu turned their attention to rural education, and began educational experiments in Jiangsu, Hebei, Shandong, Sichuan and Peiping (today's Beijing). Tao Xingzhi (1891-1946) promoted rural education and lifetime education, and put forward three principles, namely "life is education," "society is a school" and "integration of teaching, learning and practicing."

A private school, 1940s

Along with the rise of modern education, private schools flourished. According to a survey by the National Government, in the period 1935-1936 there were more than 10,000 private schools, with 110,000 teachers and 1.88 million students. These schools mainly imparted the traditional classics of the Confucian School, and learning by rote was stressed.

The commencement ceremony of Nanjing's Jinling Women's College, 1947

Jinling Women's College was the first college for women in China. It was established in Nanjing in 1915 by US Christians. The school management was transferred to the Chinese after 1927. In addition to basic courses in arts and science, there were also courses specially aimed at women, such as household affairs and medical science. The college was well-known at home and abroad for its high-quality education. From 1919 to 1951 the college graduated 999 women.

Prof. Hua Luogeng of Southwest Associated University and his family, 1938

As Peiping and Tianjin fell to the Japanese after 1937, teachers and students from Peking University, Tsinghua University and Nankai University set up the National Temporary University in Changsha, capital of Hunan Province. One month later they had to pack up and flee again as the Japanese invaders closed in on Central China. On April. 2, 1938 the university was set up in Kunming, capital of Yunnan Province, and renamed National Southwest Associated University. Classes started May 4 that year. The university existed for eight years, until May 4, 1946, and graduated more than 2,000 students. Among the graduates, there were 170 academicians of the China Academy of Sciences and Academy of Engineering. Nobel Prize-winners Yang Zhenning and Li Zhengdao were also graduates of this university.

Life at Southwest Associated University was very hard. Prof. Hua Luogeng was working at the Department of Mathematics of the university. He and his wife and five children lived in a restructured cattle shed. The cattle were kept in the lower story, while he and his family lived above them. Despite the hardship, he struggled on and wrote dissertations and works totaling several million words, including the influential Additive Prime Number Theory.

Films and Operas

A shot from *Red Peony*, 1931

Red Peony, which debuted on March 15, 1931 at Shanghai's Xinguang Grand Theater, was the first film with sound in China. Hu Die, a top actress of the time, played the lead role. It was an immediate success in Shanghai, and its popularity quickly spread across the country and even to Southeast Asia.

Hu Die, leading Chinese actress, 1930s

Hu Die (1907-1989) was one of China's first-generation actresses. Her career spanned the 1920s to the 1960s. She played a variety of roles in humorous, martial arts and realistic films. She was the most popular actress of the time. In the early 1930s it was rumored that she was having an affair with General Zhang Xueliang. During the Anti-Japanese War she was put under arrest, only regaining her freedom in 1945.

A scene from *Street Angel*, 1937

Written by Yuan Muzhi and starring Zhao Dan and Zhou Xuan, *Street Angel* was shot in 1937. The film used a neo-realistic approach in presenting the bustling life of Shanghai, vividly depicting the miseries of lower-class life. Its songs are still popular today.

{ Chapter 2 } Years of Crisis (1928-1949)

A scene from *Life at the Crossroads*, 1937

Life at the Crossroads was shot by the Star Co. in 1937. It is a representative work by Shen Xiling, a realistic film artist. The story was inspired by Shen's contact with jobless intellectuals and exiled students from northeast China. The film reflects the pain and struggle of intellectuals against the social background of prominent national and class conflict, and calls for these intellectuals to face up to reality, break out of the ivory tower, leave the crossroads and embrace the revolution. The film pioneered some successful film language and shooting techniques. It was the highest accomplishment of sound films in China in the 1930s.

Zhou Xuan, Film Diva

Zhou Xuan (1920-1957) was one of China's most famous film stars of the 1930s and 1940s. She was born into a poor family, but established herself in Shanghai in the 1930s, with remarkable achievements in film acting and singing, nominated by the media as one of the seven best singers in Shanghai. In the film *Angel on the Road*, Zhou played the part of Miss. Hong, an innocent and lovely lower-class girl. With her "golden voice," she sang the songs in the film.

A scene from *Eight Thousand Miles of Cloud and the Moon*, 1947

This film debuted in February 1947. It was written by Shi Dongshan, and was starred in by Tao Jin and Bai Yang. The film is an epic story that vividly captures the period of the Anti-Japanese War. It contrasted the patriotic youth fighting selflessly in the Anti-Japanese War with reactionary warlords and bureaucrats who profiteered from the war. The film provided an insight into the social reality of the area controlled by the Kuomintang during and after the war. The film was an immediate success at home and abroad, and was highly praised by progressives and general audiences.

A poster and a scene from *Spring in the City*, directed by Fei Mu, 1948

The film vividly depicts the travails of four young people immediately after the Anti-Japanese War. It was a pioneering film in the 1940s, delving into people's complex souls and uncovering delicate emotional feelings. It is a valuable piece of art in the history of Chinese cinematography.

Scenes from *Fourth Son of the Yang Family Revisiting His Mother*, Guangzhou, 1928

During the 1920 and 1930s the stable social life and emerging urban culture coincided with the heyday of Peking Opera. A number of influential performers and schools emerged. Flourishing at this time were the Four Best Female Character Performers, namely Mei Lanfang, Shang Xiaoyun, Cheng Yanqiu and Xun Huisheng, and the Four Best Male Character Performers, namely Yu Shuyan, Yan Jupeng, Gao Qingkui and Ma Lianliang. Other outstanding performers were Tan Fuying, Yang Baosen and Xi Xiaobo.

Mei Lanfang was the most popular among the many influential performers of modern Peking Opera. With support from experts, Mei successfully transformed Peking Opera with a number of new pieces. During the 1920s and 1930s Mei Lanfang made performance tours of Europe, the US and the Soviet Union, which were very successful. Meanwhile, he liked to wear modern clothes and enjoyed modern hobbies (photography, swimming and making phonograph records). He also received an honorary doctor's degree of art from Pomona College in the US. Mei was an epitome and pioneer of East-West cultural exchanges, as well as a fashion leader of his era.

Mei Lanfang with Charlie Chaplin

In 1930 Mei Lanfang headed a performance tour of six cities around the US. The photo shows Mei with Charlie Chaplin during Mei's performance in Los Angeles.

Mei Lanfang disembarks in Europe

Mei Lanfang made a performance tour of European countries April-August 1935, and his troupe received a warm welcome.

Anti-Japanese War

An orphan left behind by the Japanese bombing of Shanghai's South Station on August 28, 1937

Following their invasion of North China, the Japanese invaders seized Shanghai on August 13, 1937 after a three-month siege. The once-prosperous city was severely damaged in the war.

Kuomintang air crew waiting to go into combat in 1939

During the eight years of the Anti-Japanese War, the Chinese air force downed 1,226 Japanese fighter planes, hit (or damaged) 230 airplanes, and destroyed 8,546 enemy tanks. The Chinese air force lost 2,468 fighter planes and 6,164 men. The youngest pilot martyr, Gao Jingang, died at the age of 16.

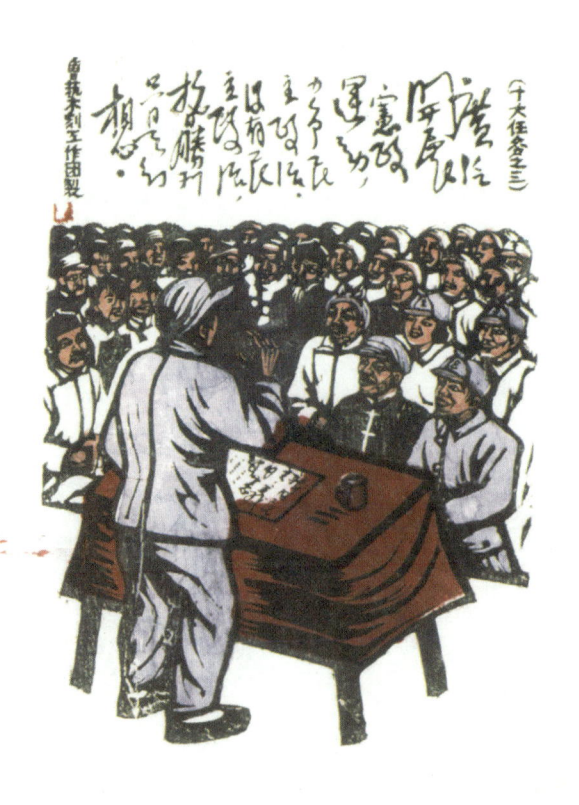

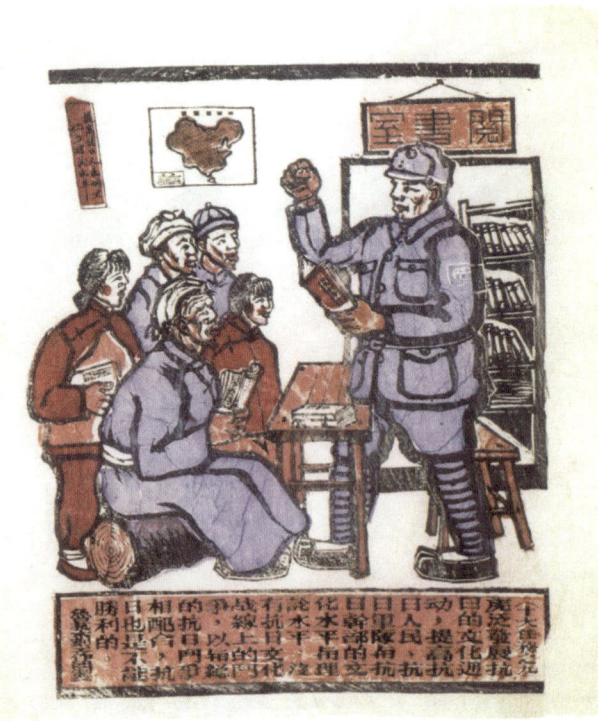

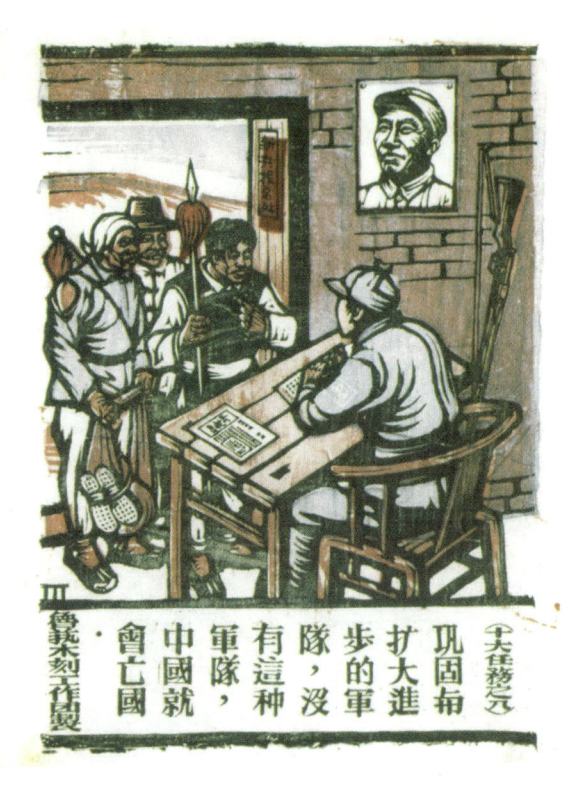

The Ten Tasks of the Anti-Japanese War, New Year woodblock-prints using a chromatography technique created jointly by Hu Yichuan, Luo Gongliu, Zou Ya, Huang Shanding and others of the Woodblock Print Group of Lu Xun Academy of Arts (The originals are now housed in the National Museum).

On February 1, 1940, the Communist Party of China's Central Committee released the Decision on the Status Quo and Main Tasks. The decision pointed out that, in the context of a strategic stalemate, the Party would focus on ten tasks in order to make use of the situation to its own advantage and avoid a reversal. The ten tasks were publicity about fighting traitors and anti-Communist intrigues, giving full play to the united front, promoting constitutional government, highlighting democratic politics, mobilizing the general public to participate in the Anti-Japanese War, implementing rent and interest reduction, enlarging the anti-Japanese base areas, expanding the progressive army forces, developing an anti-Japanese culture campaign, and consolidating the organization of the Communist Party.

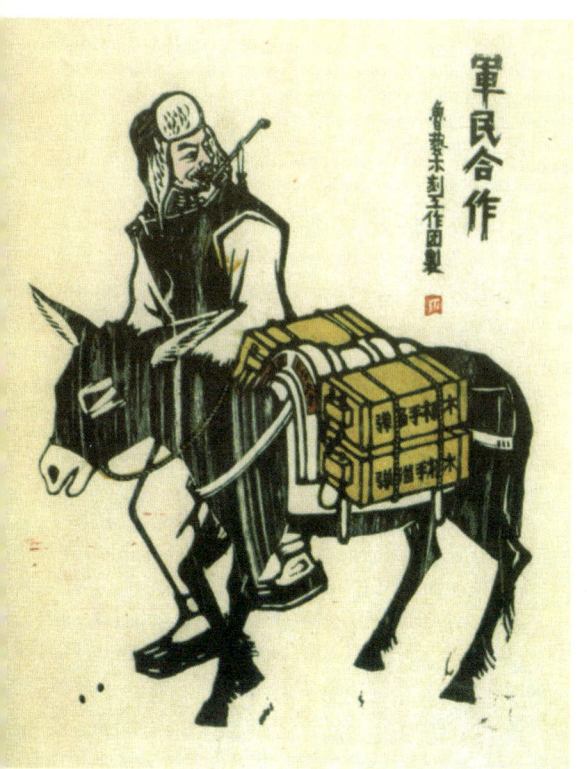

Cooperation between the Armed Forces and the People, colored New Year woodblock print by Hu Yichuan and others of the Woodblock Print Group of Lu Xun Academy of Arts

Rent Reduction Dispute, a black-and-white woodblock print, created by Gu Yuan in 1943 (The original is in the National Museum)

During the Anti-Japanese War, the Chinese Communist Party implemented the policy of rent and interest reduction. Poor farmers and tenants, who had been exploited and enslaved for thousands of years, were able to stand up and fight for their rights against their landlords.

Following the outbreak of the Anti-Japanese War, a large number of artists flocked to Yan'an to contribute their talents to the revolution. Woodblock prints were the most popular genre for anti-Japanese publicity, as wood was abundant, and the creation and reproduction costs and tool requirements were low. At the end of 1938 the Lu Xun Academy of Arts in Yan'an set up a special woodblock print group. In late 1938 several artists from the group, who were working then at the Taihang Mountains Base Area, decided to use the traditional form of New Year prints to produce works showing cooperation between the liberation army and the public, in celebration of the 1940 Spring Festival. They ushered in a new chapter in China's art history using traditional woodblock prints.

Brigade 359 of the People's Liberation Army reclaiming wasteland at Nanniwan

Chairman Mao Zedong with farmers

Cadres and soldiers spinning at the Shanxi-Gansu-Ningxia Base Area

As the Anti-Japanese War entered a phase of strategic stalemate in late 1942, the base areas set up by the Communist Party of China faced numerous attacks both from the Japanese invaders and the Kuomintang reactionaries, including economic blockades. The Party put forward the policy of "developing the local economy to ensure self-sufficiency," calling on the army and the ordinary people to earn their own livings and overcome economic difficulties through a grand production drive. After that, the base areas saw significant increases in agriculture, industry and commerce.

The reclamation of Nanniwan was a shining example of success in the grand production drive. Located 45 km southeast of Yan'an, it was a wasteland. In March 1941 Wang Zhen led Brigade 359 to reclaim 747 hectares of land there, and later to harvest 72,000 kg of grain, bring the local food self-sufficiency rate to 78.5%. By 1942 the cultivated area had been expanded to 1,787 hectares, and 183,000 kg of grain was harvested. Nanniwan became the symbol of the grand production drive.

Economic Hardships

Going to market with thousands of "gold yuan" notes, late Republican period

Bank run in the late Republican period

Homeless beggers, late Republican period

The Communist Party of China and the Kuomintang clashed in a civil war immediately after victory in the Anti-Japanese War. The Kuomintang government struggled to control inflation. A total of 660 trillion yuan — more than 400,000 times the size of China's currency in the early years of the Anti-Japanese War — was printed before the issuance of the "gold yuan" notes (August 19, 1948). The Associated Press made the following comment on July 24, 1947: In 1937, 100 yuan could buy two cows; in 1938, only one; in 1941, one pig; in 1943, one rooster; in 1945, one fish; and in 1947, 100 yuan was not enough for a box of matches. The "gold yuan" notes too succumbed to inflation. In June 1948 the issue of "gold yuan" notes was increased to 130 trillion — 240,000 times the initial issue 10 months previously. By May 1949 the price of 60 kg of grain was 400 million "gold yuan" notes.

Poverty and unemployment increased rapidly, and millions of beggars roamed the streets of the cities. Some sold their sons and daughters for money, some committed suicide, still others starved or froze to death in the streets. In Shanghai the number of bodies found in the streets was 19,091 in 1946; 25,400 in 1947; 39,359 in 1948; and 43,140 in the first four months of 1949.

Liberation of the Farmers

Measuring land before redistribution during the land reform following 1949

Poor farmers and tenant farmers receiving livestock

Farmers happy with their own land

In the 1930s the Chinese Communist Party led the farmers in the base areas to launch land reform. During the Anti-Japanese War the base areas adopted the policy of reducing rents and interest. This policy was intended to maintain the united front, with both peasants and landlords fighting against the Japanese invaders.

In 1947, the Chinese Communist Party released the Guiding Law on Land Use, stipulating that abolition of landlordism and redistributing the land to the farmers equally, depending on the rural population. By 1949 some 145 million rural dwellers had benefited from the reform. Poor and middle and lower farmers were given their own farmland and means of production. The people's initiative was mobilized, and they engaged in revolution and production wholeheartedly. This grassroots support was the wellspring of the political, economic and military strength of the Chinese Communist Party during the civil war against the Kuomintang. The rural population contributed greatly to the success of the war of liberation.

Chapter 3
A New World
(1950~1965)

Transportation

A train crosses the Tengri Desert on the railway line, opened in 1958, from Baotou in the Inner Mongolia Autonomous Region to Lanzhou, capital of Gansu Province.

Model Qian Jin (QJ) No. 101 steam locomotive manufactured in Datong, 1964

{ Chapter 3 } A Brand New World (1950-1965)

The Dalian Locomotive Co. manufactured China's first internal combustion locomotive of 4,000 hp, 1959.

The new Beijing Train Station was built, 1959.

Railways had become a popular means of passenger transportation.

The first railway opened in September 1825, when British engineer George Stevenson drove his "Rocket." Even in the early 19th century half of China had no railways, but after the founding of the People's Republic of China in 1949 railway construction became a priority for economic development.

Different types of means of transportation were seen in Beijing, and trucks were also common for carrying passengers who did not consider it dangerous standing on them.

Industry

A textile workshop, 1960s

Angang Seamless Steel Pipe Plant, 1950s

Launching of China's first 15,000-dwt-oil tanker "Daqing No. 27," 1960s

When the PRC was founded in 1949 China's industry was backward, with heavy industry located in the northeast, and textiles and other types of light industry in the east. By 1965 China had set up a complete industrial system, and was no longer limited to producing basic necessities and primary industrial products.

{ Chapter 3 } A Brand New World (1950-1965)

Society

Members of the Cuimei Production Team drying newly harvested grain, Fujian Province, 1965

With the regaining of social stability and establishment of socialist relations of production, China's agriculture made significant progress.

Shop assistants at a silk store in Shanghai celebrate the establishment of public-private ownership.

Celebrating the establishment of public-private ownership

The CPC began to reform the ownership system with joint state-private ownership in the private sector. By 1956 China had basically completed the socialist reform of agriculture, the handicrafts sector, and industry and commerce.

Steel making during the Great Leap Forward

In the period 1958-1960 the CPC launched the nationwide Great Leap Forward Campaign, in an attempt to increase social production as rapidly as possible. The results were disastrous, as quality was sacrificed to quantity. This was especially so in the sector of steel making. The target here was to surpass the productivity of the US and Great Britain. All cities and counties across China, even in Tibet, were involved in the campaign to expand steel output. Although the total output almost met the target, the products were unusable. The Great Leap Forward seriously skewed the national economy, and resulted in difficulties in the years that followed.

Urban Landscape

Trams were a common sight in Shanghai until the 1970s.

A bus with a gas-supply tank on its roof, 1963. The girl with the bag is a conductor. →

{ Chapter 3 } A Brand New World (1950-1965)

East Chang'an Avenue, the main thoroughfare in Beijing, in 1963. The building on the right is the old Beijing Hotel.

Known as the "No.1 avenue in China," Chang'an Avenue is 42 km long and bisects Beijing from east to west.

New buildings on West Chang'an Avenue, Beijing, 1962

Wangfujing, the main commercial street in Beijing, 1950s

Known as "The First Shop of New China," the Beijing Department Store opened on Wangfujing, 1955.

Guangzhou's waterfront, 1950s

Lifestyle

In the first 15 years of the PRC ordinary Chinese had a relatively high happiness index, in spite of their low incomes. They took delight in simple pleasures.

During the 1960s China experienced unprecedented natural disasters for three years running. Poor harvests and shortages of light industrial products followed. Queues for food were common sights, while in the countryside there was a severe shortage of food. Each family had a household registration book, and food and oil coupons. Meat, sweets and fruit were seldom-seen luxuries. However, the people were optimistic that such difficulties would soon be overcome.

Up until 1960 wheelbarrows were still commonly used by peddlers in Beijing. In the background of the photograph is the White Pagoda.

All businesses, no matter how small, came to be operated by state-owned companies from the early 1960s.

A peddler selling goldfish on the street in the 1960s – 0.02 RMB for a small one and 0.05 RMB for a big one

MODERN CHINA IN PICTURES

A street photographer at work in Beijing. The cloth background shows the capital's Tian'anmen Square.

Refrigerators were luxury goods in those days. Popsicles costing 0.03-0.05 RMB were kept in bamboo-cased thermos bottles. ←

{ Chapter 3 } A Brand New World (1950-1965)

Small restaurants in Beijing provided simple menus. Fried eggs and cabbage fried with meat slices usually cost 1 RMB. Boiled soybeans with white liquor was also a popular dish.

For people in North China, the staple diet was usually steamed bread, a baked cake or steamed bun. During the hard time, bread was made from sorghum. The cheapest bread would cost 0.1 RMB.

Citizens queuing up for special purchases for the Spring Festival

A vegetable market in Beijing during the Spring Festival of 1963

During the Spring Festival the government allocated large amounts of fish, meat, eggs and vegetables to enable people to eat well at least once a year. But in winter, when food was scarce, especially in the northern part of China, cabbages, carrots and potatoes comprised the main course of the Spring Festival dinner. Cabbage cores could be prepared as a salad, the leaves could be used in soup, and the lower part could be stir-fried. Even the filling of the Spring Festival dumpling was no doubt from cabbages.

Beijingers purchasing cabbages, a staple of the winter die

The winter is especially cold in north China, and there were few varieties of vegetables at that time. Cabbages were the main course for many households throughout the winter, due to their low price and ease of storage. During the era of the planned economy, cabbages were stored and transported by the government. Given the huge demand, people had to wait in queues, register, take a number tag and have their quota verified before final purchase. Most families would buy as much as 100-150 kg of cabbage, more than enough to sustain the family until the first month of the lunar year.

A state-owned company's canteen used oil drums as tables.

Street peddlers, Beijing, 1950s

{ Chapter 3 } A Brand New World (1950-1965)

A photo of a mother and her son, 1949

A small bamboo cart worth 5 RMB also served as a bed for a small child

{ Chapter 3 } A Brand New World (1950-1965)

A typical Chinese rural family at dinner

A family photo, 1958

In the 1950s and 1960s photo taking was quite expensive. A photo shop would charge 2-4 RMB, with which one could buy vegetables for a week. At that time, most families had only a few photographs, and they were put in the most eye-catching place, behind glass.

A family photo, 1960s

{ Chapter 3 } A Brand New World (1950-1965)

An ordinary family

The main room of a house, also called the central room, was where people put their most valuable objects, such as a clock, vase or bust of Chairman Mao.

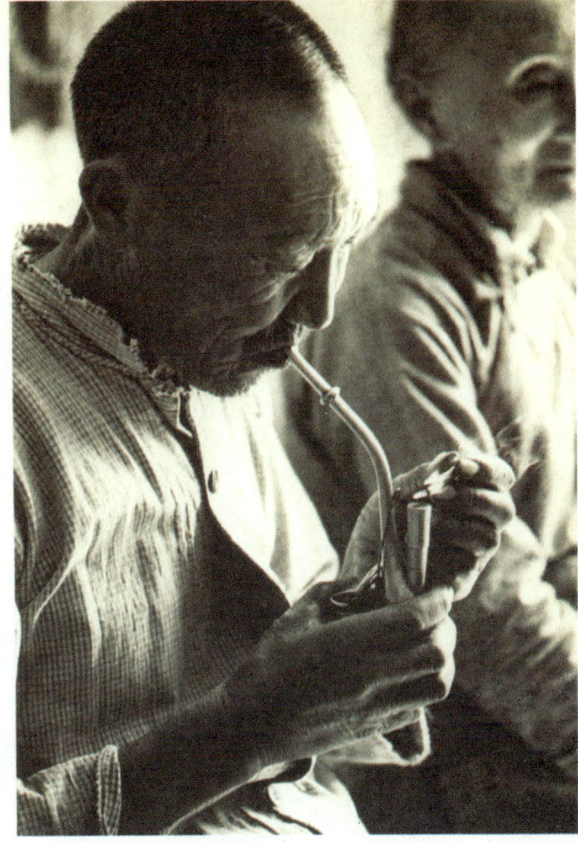

Ordinary people relax on the street.

At that time, homes were small. People spent most of their time outdoors, with women doing household chores outside, seniors sunbathing and children doing homework, since lighting cost money. There were few vehicles on Beijing's streets, and so traffic accidents were rare.

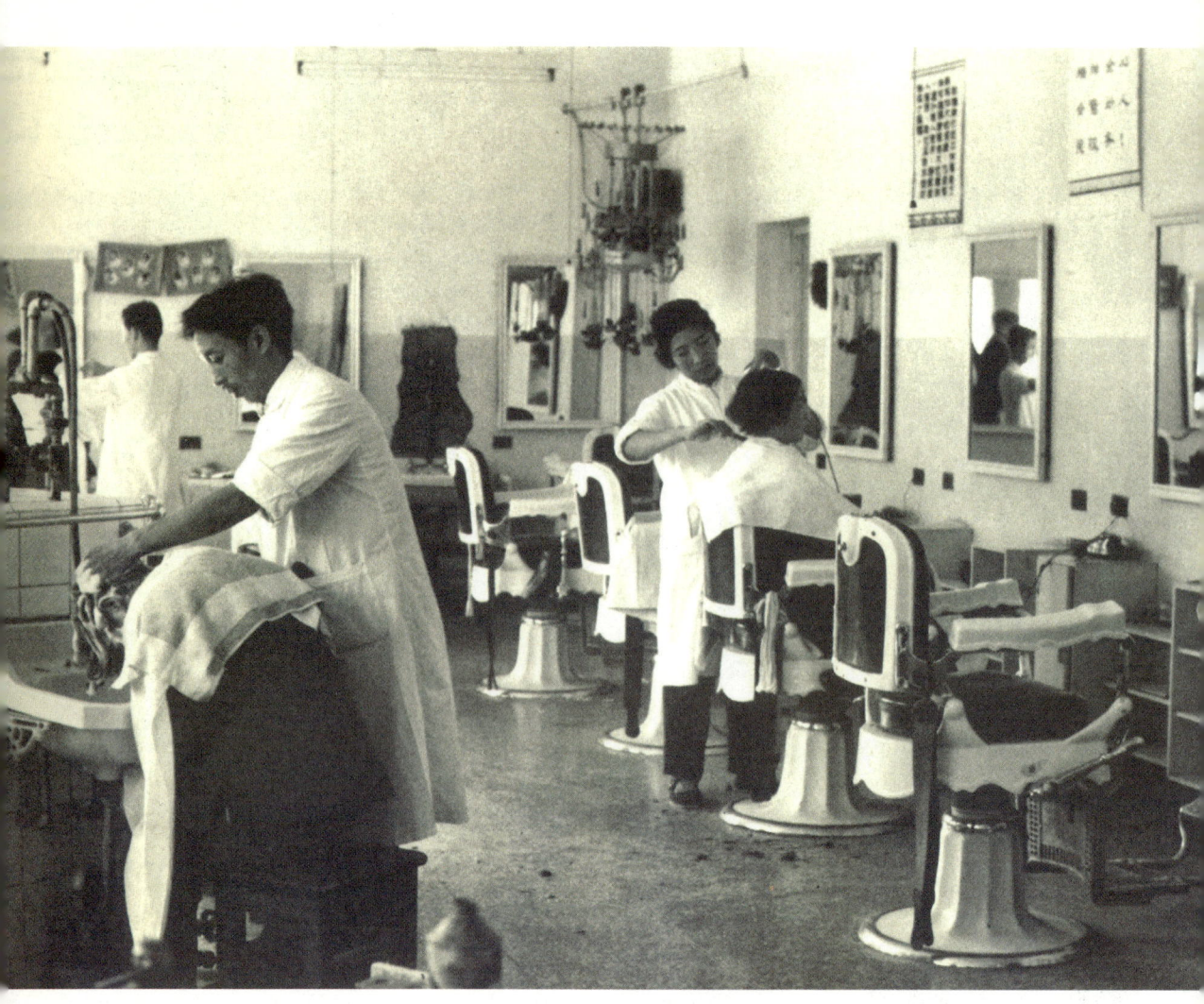

At a barber's

Some 50 years ago, commodities were scarce, and culture dull. Taking a haircut at a barber's was considered a luxury; most people would have a haircut at a barber's once a year.

Summer clothes showcased at the Xiamen Fashion Exhibition in April 1956.

The two women on the left are wearing dresses of a Soviet design of the 1950s. When Soviet leaders visited China earlier, they had suggested that Chinese women wear colorful clothes to reflect the prosperity of socialism. Such dresses mostly featured short sleeves, round collars, long skirt and cloth belt. They had a multiple floral or checked pattern and were made of cotton. In the late 1950s this Russian style went out of fashion as Sino-Russian relations worsened.

Trying on new clothes for the Spring Festival, December 1959

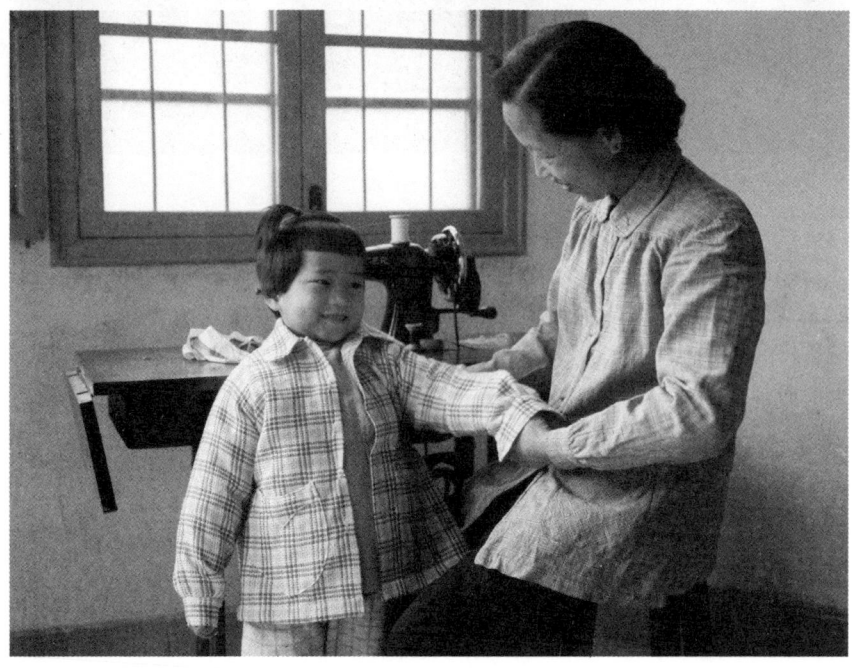

A mother helps her daughter to try on a new jacket, 1950s.

Colored clothes would always draw attention and admiration.

{ Chapter 3 } A Brand New World (1950-1965)

Small department stores were everywhere, but the goods were invariably the same, distributed by the wholesale department.

Inside the Dong'an Department Store. This store preserved the atmosphere of the traditional culture of Beijing.

{ Chapter 3 } A Brand New World (1950-1965)

Wristwatches, TV sets, sewing machines and bicycles were luxuries 40-50 years ago. TVs were available only to families of officials, and there was only one channel. A wristwatch would cost about 100 RMB, an enormous sum in those days.

In the 1950s and 1960s commerce was underdeveloped in China due to limited production. The supply of daily necessities was insufficient. In 1955 the Wangfujing Department Store opened. A retired employee recalled the scene on the day of the opening: "Thousands of people surrounded the store, and when the nine doors all opened at the same time they all rushed in like a tidal wave."

{ Chapter 3 } A Brand New World (1950-1965)

Group dance at a military camp, 1951

Children play in a courtyard during a winter vacation.

Before China carried out the family planning policy in 1978, most families had two or more children. Regarded as the "flowers of the motherland," however, they were not at all spoiled, and quite independent. They did not have lots of homework after school. Compared with children today, they were much happier, though they did not have nice food to eat nor beautiful clothes to wear.

Ice skating on Kunming Lake, Summer Palace

Education

Beihai kindergarten, 1950s

Students from Beijing Soviet Middle School meet Soviet students on the 40th anniversary of the October Revolution, at the Xijiao Friendship Hotel, November 2, 1957

Back to school, 1950s

Handicraft and radio course for schoolchildren

When the People's Republic of China was founded, in 1949, 80% of the population was illiterate, primary school enrollment was no more than 20%, and junior middle-school enrollment was only 6%. Primary school enrolment increased to 57% in 1963. Middle school enrollment also increased significantly, with junior middle schools having a total of 2.635 million students, and senior middle schools 433,000 in 1963.

Students of Peking University in their leisure time, 1950

The Library of Peking University, 1965

In 1949 there were only 120,000 students studying in higher-education institutions. By 1965 this number had increased to 1.09 million.

Students of the Jinggang Mountain Affiliate School of the Jiangxi Communist Labor University setting out to work on farmland, 1960s

Before the enrollment expansion for the university entrance examination in the 1990s the percentage of people in China who could receive higher education was low, so college graduates tended to become an elite corps.

Culture

Simple street entertainment in Beijing, 1950s

Such traditional shows utilized a series of pictures, matched with singing and storytelling.

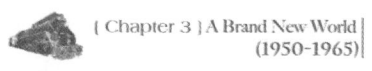

Browsing at the Xinhua Bookstore on Wangfujing Street in 1954

Reading books was a major pastime in those days. As the rate of illiteracy improved reading books and newspapers became part of daily life. The first Xinhua Bookstore was established in Yan'an in 1937, and later became the official bookstore of the country. Xinhua Bookstores could be found all over China. The name plate was inscribed in the calligraphy of Mao Zedong.

Art and painting counter at the Xinhua Bookstore on Wangfjing Street

Film stars of the 1960s

China's cinematography enjoy significant growth before the Cultural Revolution broke out, with several masterpieces produced, such as *The Whitehaired Girl*, *Young Man in the Countryside*, *Lin's Store*, *Underground Secret Service*, *Red Detachment of Women*, *Sino-Japanese War*, *Underground War*, *Landmine War*, *Eternal Radio Wave*, *Railway Guards*, *Madam Li Shuangshuang* and *Song of Youth*. The characters in these films left great impressions on people, and the theme songs were even more popular, and sung by generations. The cinema was a big attraction because TVs were not widely available at that time.

A scene from *The Battle of Shangganling*, 1956. The theme song, *My Motherland*, was an instant hit.

A scene from *Young People in Our Village*, 1959

A scene from *Struggles in an Ancient City*, 1963

{ Chapter 3 } A Brand New World (1950-1965) | 143

After the founding of the PRC in 1949 film makers began to draw inspiration from daily life, and created a number of excellent films which are still very popular today.

A scene from *Underground War*, 1965

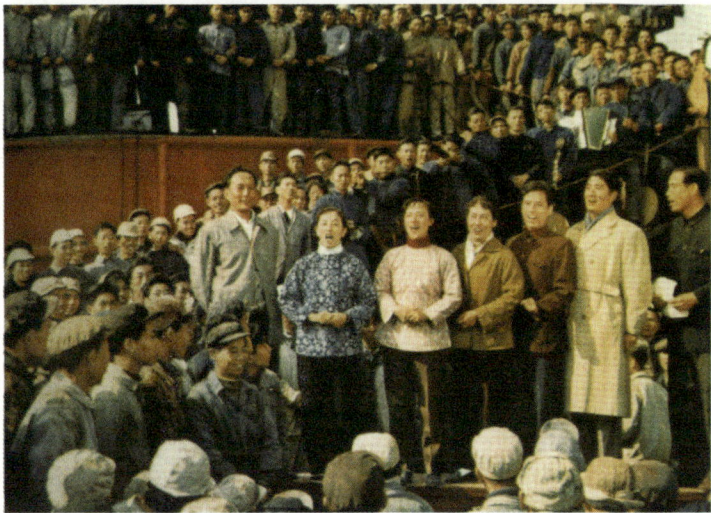

Film stars from Shanghai performing for ordinary people, 1962

Chang Xiangyu, a renowned Yuju Opera actress, performs Chaoyang Village for the members of a people's commune, 1960.

After the founding of the PRC, film, drama and opera actors became actors for the laboring people. They injected new vitality into the cultural development of New China.

Leading Peking Opera stars perform in Hong Kong (*left to right*: Zhang Junqiu, Ma Lianliang, Qiu Shengrong)

A scene from a performance by Ma Lianliang, 1963

In the rural areas, where there were no cinemas, opera performances enjoyed special popularity. An influential opera performer enjoyed the highest income at that time, for example, Ma Lianliang received 600 RMB per month, which was ten times the income of an ordinary worker, and even 200 RMB more than that of Chairman Mao.

Lei Feng with children

In the 1950s and 1960s there emerged a bunch of pacesetters and models who were adored and emulated by all the people. Lei Feng was a model of ethics and integrity, while Wang Jinxi (1923-1970) was an outstanding representative of the working class.

Lei Feng (1940-1962) was a soldier in the People's Liberation Army. He took the initiative in helping others and contributing to society selflessly. He lost his life while fulfilling his duty. People were impressed by the words he left in his diary. The "Lei Feng Spirit" inspired generation after generation.

"Iron man" Wang Jinxi at Daqing Oilfield

In the late 1950s oil was discovered in Daqing, Heilongjiang Province. Thousands of workers flocked to the frozen land in the northeast of China to work on the oilfield. Wang Jinxi was among them. Wang led his team to Daqing from the Yumen Oil Field in Gansu Province in March 1960. He became known as the "Iron Man." Wang died of stomach cancer at the age of 47 in 1970, but his "Iron Man Spirit" has continued to inspire generations to contribute to China's development.

Chapter 4

Freeze-Frame of a Symbolic Era

(1966~1976)

A Fiery Era

People enjoy themselves during the National Day celebrations in 1966, not realizing that the Cultural Revolution, which had just been launched, would bring disasters to China.

Typical girl's dress during the Cultural Revolution

Such a dress was regarded the most beautiful for most people during the Cultural Revolution.

Putting on a new dress

{ Chapter 4 } Freeze-Frame of a Symbolic Era (1966-1976)

A photo of newlyweds, 1969

This is the typical photo taking posture at that time, with both wearing a Chairman Mao badge and the bride holding the book of *Quotations from Chairman Mao*.

Everything was simple during the Cultural Revolution. Black, blue or yellow working clothes or military uniforms were worn; solemn yet simple ceremonies were held; and serious yet optimistic expressions were the norm. People belonged to the group, the country and the nation.

Typical wedding ceremony during the Cultural Revolution, early 1970s

The Three Major Items — watch, sewing machine and bicycle

A family photo, 1969

{ Chapter 4 } Freeze-Frame of a Symbolic Era (1966-1976)

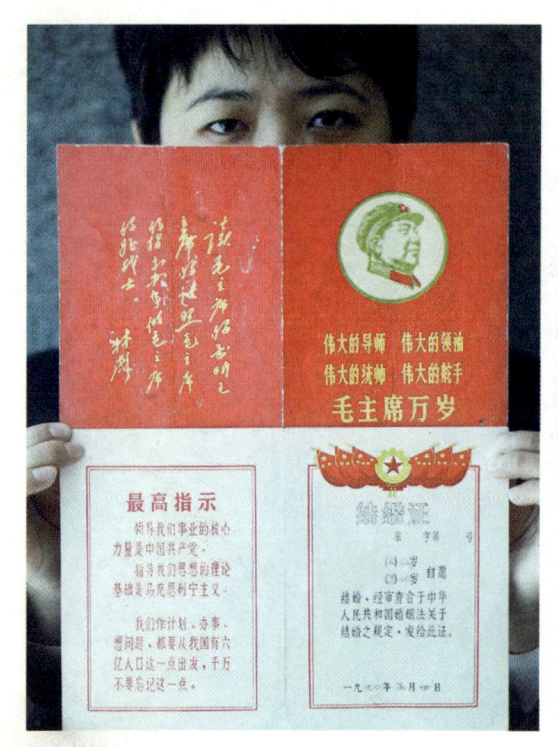

Marriage certificate during the Cultural Revolution with profile of and quotations from Chairman Mao.

At that time marriage and divorce were subject to the decisions of Party committees.

Ma Xulong (center) and Xu Tianlan, pupils at the Shanghai Huaihai Primary School, give water to a policeman on a hot day, 1969.

Exemplary deeds were widely publicized by the Party. Students and children became models of ethics and morality.

The *Dance of Loyalty* was popular at that time.

    The Dance of Loyalty was a type of group dance showing loyalty to and extolling Chairman Mao. Some well-known varieties of the dance were *Pilot Required for Taking the Helm, Beloved Chairman Mao, Up on the Golden Mountain of Beijing* and *Celebrating the 9th CPC Meeting with Aspiration*. These pieces were danced together with musical accompaniment and the chanting of quotations from Chairman Mao.

A popular dance during the Culture Revolution

A scene from *Tale of the Red Light*

A scene from *Bandit of Tiger Mountain*

Fuzhou Experimental Primary School students learning to sing *Sha Family Creek* – a revolutionary opera, 1969

Dominating the decade-long Cultural Revolution was a handful of modern revolutionary dramas, which were called "model operas." The characters were simply divided into revolutionaries and counterrevolutionaries, with the former defeating the latter.

{ Chapter 4 } Freeze-Frame of a Symbolic Era (1966-1976) | 155

Red Guards on an experience-sharing trip

With the support of the central government, students from all over the country flocked to Beijing, and Beijing students traveled around the country to share their experiences. Accommodation and other travel expenses were provided by the government.

A propaganda group gives a street performance, 1967

Reading quotations from Mao Zedong on a bus, 1967

Students of worker and rural background at Tsinghua University, Beijing, 1967

The university entrance examination was abolished when the Cultural Revolution broke out in 1966, and was not reintroduced until 1971. During that time, universities directly recruited students from factories, mines and the countryside. The students would go back to their original work upon graduation. Political behavior and individual attitude were the key criteria for recruitment, knowledge and capability being considered less important. Peking University and Tsinghua University piloted such recruitment criteria in the spring of 1972, followed by other universities.

Massive labor engagement in agriculture

Dazhai was a poor village in Xiyang County, Shanxi Province. The villagers reclaimed wild slopes by terracing, with the result that the grain output per hectare increased sevenfold. In 1964 Chairman Mao Zedong urged the whole countryside to "learn from Dazhai." This village was a model for agriculture until the late 1970s.

A military medical team going to the countryside to serve poor farmers

People in Sichuan Province celebrate the publication of the *Selected Works of Mao Zedong*.

Students of Shaoshan Middle School, Beijing, go to the countryside at the call of Chairman Mao: "The vast world can develop one's ability."

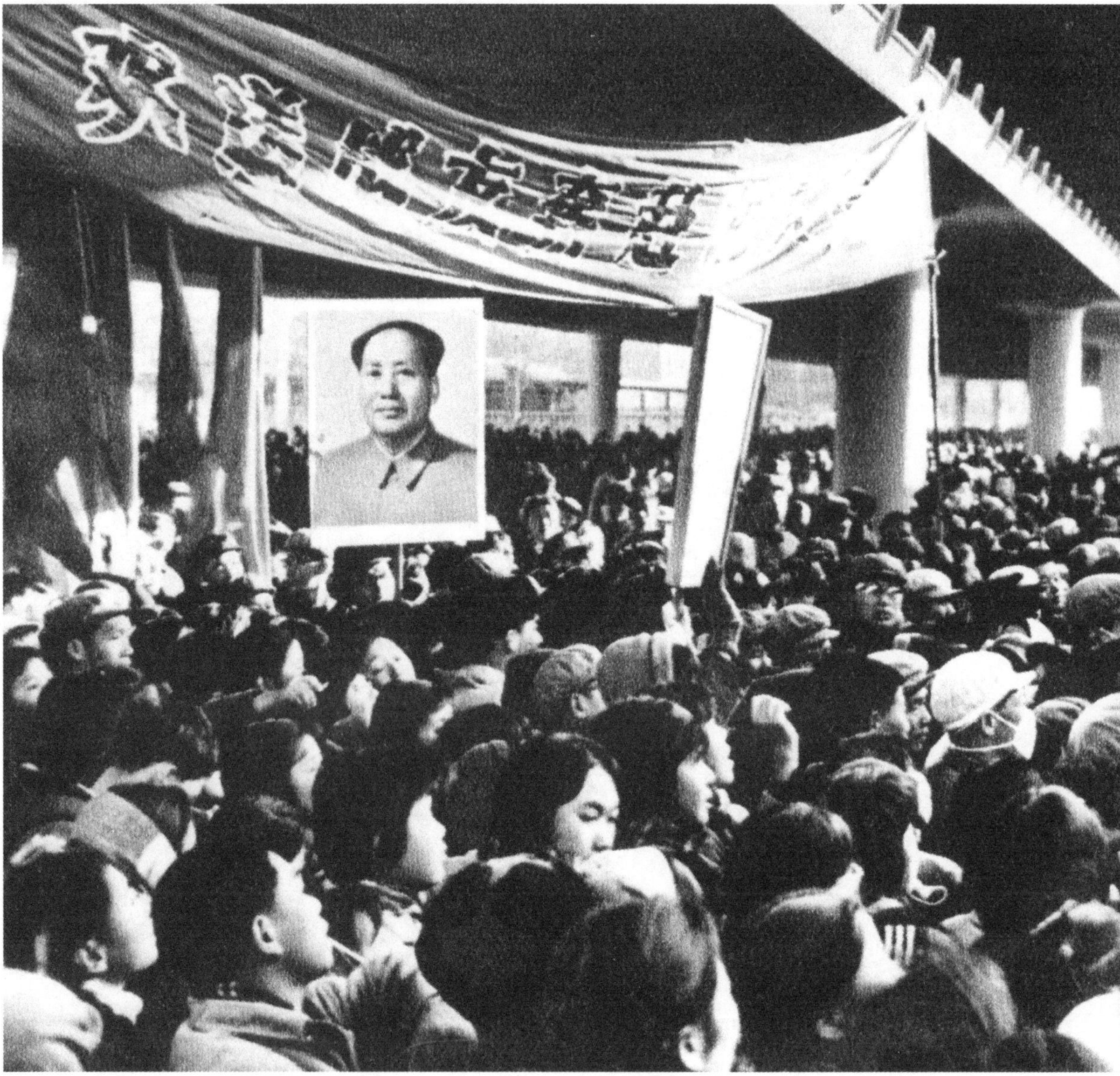

Seeing off young people going down to the countryside to learn from the peasants, at Beijing Railway Station

{ Chapter 4 } Freeze-Frame of a Symbolic Era (1966-1976)

Young graduates help with a water conservancy project at Tongxi Commune, Yueyang County, Hunan Province, in 1969.

Starting in the late 1950s, the Chinese government began to arrange for students and young graduates to assist the countryside. After the Cultural Revolution broke out the university entrance examination was halted and production was disrupted. Educated young people couldn't find jobs in urban areas. So in 1969 students and young graduates were dispatched to the countryside and settled in rural households to participate in agricultural production. Millions of young people were sent to the countryside each year until 1976.

"Barefoot doctors" treat patients in the fields, 1969

In 1969, following Chairman Mao's direction to "focus medical services on the countryside," medical staff moved to the rural areas, and clinics at people's communes began to train rural medics, known as "barefoot doctors."

Frozen pork on a Beijing street

Frozen meat was a common sight in the streets of cities in northern China during the Spring Festival. At that time there were no refrigerators in small stores. Meat was set out in the cold streets, and sold out quickly.

Vegetables displayed on shelves were just for show at that time

Plastic string bags and military satchels were universally used in the 1970s. There were no such things as brand-name handbags or sturdy shopping bags.

{ Chapter 4 } Freeze-Frame of a Symbolic Era (1966-1976)

Long braids were all the fashion for young women, the longer the more beautiful.

Secondary school students engaged in military training, 1972

Cameras were luxury goods.

At 0.8 RMB for a cartridge of film, plus 0.2 RMB for developing, this was quite an expense hobby at that time. There were no photos larger than six inches square.

{ Chapter 4 } Freeze-Frame of a Symbolic Era
(1966-1976)

The photo stand in Tian'anmen Square was constantly busy. Soldiers especially were keen to have their photos taken.

{ Chapter 4 } Freeze-Frame of a Symbolic Era (1966-1976)

Photo coloring at a photo studio

It was difficult to take a color photo at that time, and artificial photo coloring was highly professional work. Nevertheless, people were eager to get their black-and-white photos colored.

Plastic sandals

For primary and middle-school students there were only three types of shoes: cotton-padded shoes, simple cloth shoes and plastic sandals. The soles of the cheapest shoes were made from used tires. There are no such shoes today.

Children playing at soldiers in the street

A popsicle would cost 0.03 RMB.

A rural boy trying on city clothes

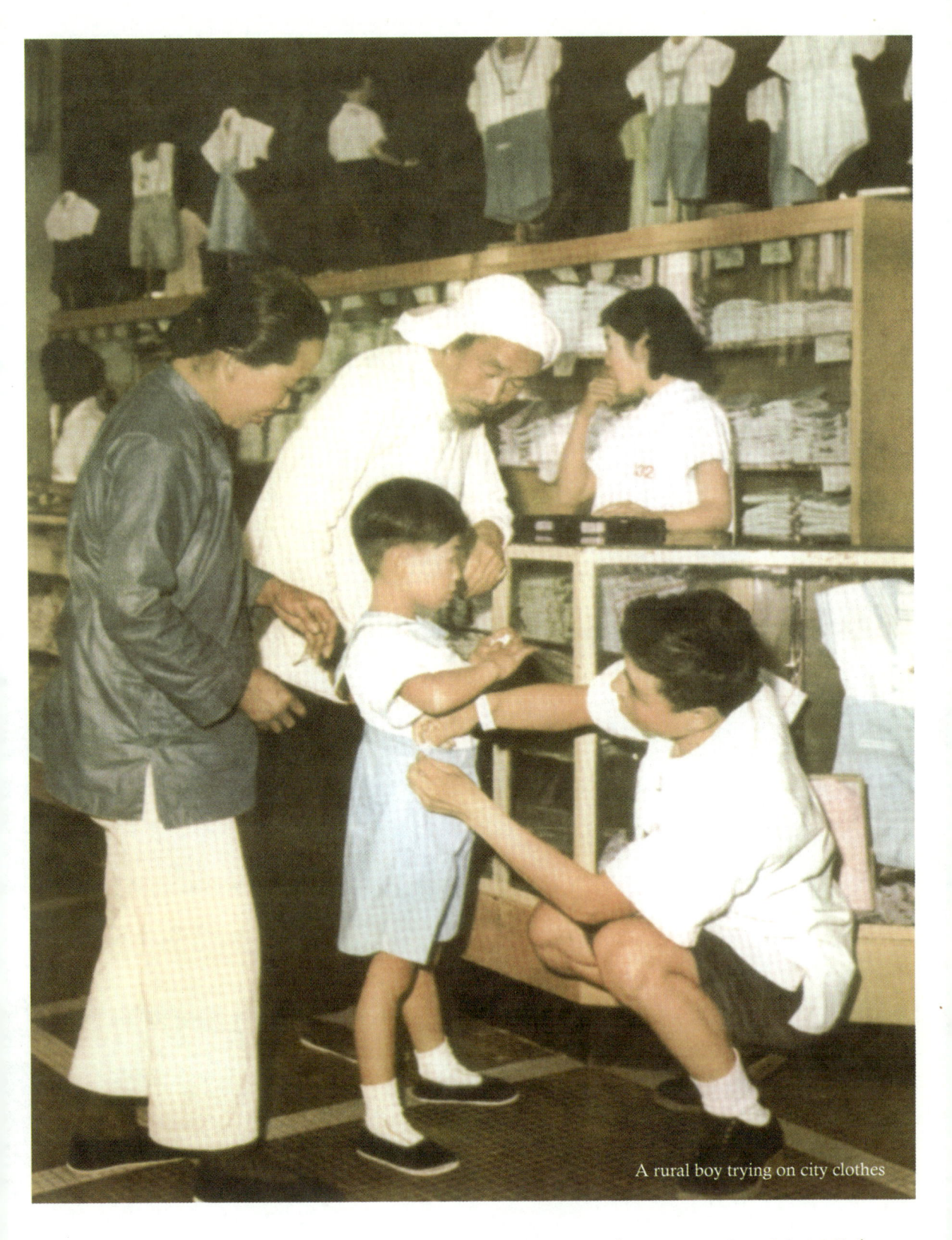

{ Chapter 4 } Freeze-Frame of a Symbolic Era (1966-1976) | 175

176 | MODERN CHINA IN PICTURES

{ Chapter 4 } Freeze-Frame of a Symbolic Era
(1966-1976)

Picture story books were very popular with children and even young adults.

Chapter 5
Catching Up with the World
(1977~2000)

Tidal Wave of the Era

People scramble to buy papers with news of the communiqué of the 3rd Plenary Session of the 11th CPC Central Committee, 1978

Farmers in Xiaogang Village, Anhui Province, pioneered the all-round contract arrangement, late 1970s.

The Cultural Revolution ended in 1976, but the people's minds and the country's development were still constrained by various factors. In December 1978, the 3rd Plenary Session of the 11th CPC Central Committee was convened in Beijing. The meeting reinstated the guiding principles of "emancipating the people's minds and seeking truth from facts." The Party began to correct all the errors made during and before the Cultural Revolution, decided to shift the focus of the country's work to economic development and adopted the policy of reform and opening-up. China entered the new era of Reform and Opening up.

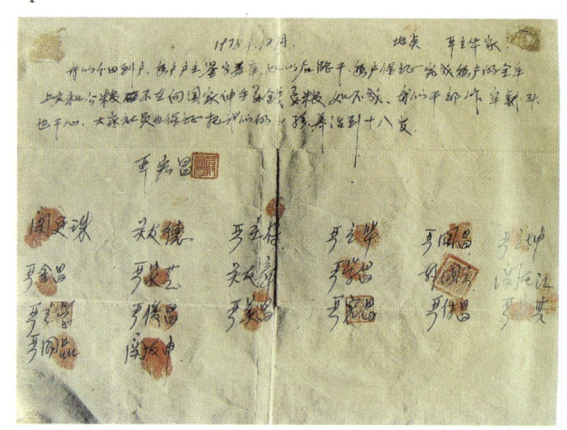

Households from Xiangang Village signed the contract arrangement, December 1978.

In the countryside the People's Commune system, featuring public land ownership, lasted for nearly 20 years. Agricultural production suffered, and poverty was a severe problem. In order to improve their livelihood, 18 households of Xiaogang Village decided to break the traditional production relations in late 1978. They adopted the "all-round contract" system and secretly distributed land to each household. At that time, such a practice was considered to be restoring capitalism. The 18 households left their fingerprints on the contract agreement. The arrangement required that the state quota would be met first, then the community quota. The remainder would be at their own disposal. If the head of the production team was sentenced to prison due to the land distribution, all his due farm work would be contracted to the other farmers, and they would support his family. This was what became later known as the "household contract responsibility system." This new type of production relations was followed by other villages in Anhui and Sichuan provinces expressly or discreetly, with the result that local productivity grew dramatically. After heated discussion the Central Government formally acknowledged the practice in 1980. By 1983, 93% of the rural production teams had adopted this system. The household contract responsibility system was the precursor of the reform and opening-up era.

Significant growth of modern agriculture

The household contract responsibility system spurred the enthusiasm of Chinese farmers, unshackled rural productivity, and promoted rural modernization. China's total agricultural output increased from 304.75 billion kg in 1978 to 407.3 billion kg in 1984. Now, after 30 years of rural reform, China supports 22% of the world's population with only 7% of the world's total farmland.

Deng Xiaoping visiting Shenzhen, the first special economic zone, for the first time, January 1984

In 1980 China chose Shenzhen, a city adjacent to Hong Kong, to be the very first economic zone, which was an important step in reform and opening up. Later, Zhuhai, which is adjacent to Macao, also became a special economic zone. The establishment of such economic zones showed that China was opening up to embrace the rest of the world. However, there were still disputes and concern over the property and orientation of economic zones. As a result, Deng Xiaoping, chief architect of the reform and opening-up policies, decided to personally visit South China to confirm the achievements of Shenzhen and Zhuhai. All disputes and concerns were then dispelled. China opened up further to the outside, and people's minds were emancipated profoundly.

Landscape of Shenzhen, early 21st century

High-rises are everywhere; the zone is still under construction. The rise of Shenzhen is a miniature of China's reform and opening-up. In the late 1970s Shenzhen was a small border city with 30,000 people and little traffic. By 1999 Shenzhen had become a metropolis of one million people and ranked among the top cities in China in GDP.

A street scene in Shenzhen, late 1970s

Cargo loading and unloading at Shanghai Harbor, 1990

A Sino-US cooperation project, MD-82 civilian airliner, 1985

Tian'anmen Square, 1970s

People's dress was drab, and bicycles clogged the streets.

← Following the advent of the reform and opening up, China's economy maintained a double-digit growth rate. China now leads the world and is a major industrial power in terms of total value and output, foreign direct investment and import of industrial products.

{ Chapter 5 } Catching Up with the World (1977-2000)

Beijing street, 1970s

    Political slogans still adorned posters. Following the turmoil and stagnation of the Cultural Revolution, and the campaign of "educated youth going to the countryside," China's urban construction lagged, with low-standard and dingy housing. But with the reform and opening up, China's urban construction was restarted.

Longfu Temple area, Beijing, 1982

In the early 1980s private restaurants opened for business, and private tricycle hauliers were seen everywhere on the streets.

Urban renovation in Shanghai, 1992

Urban construction was temporarily halted during the Cultural Revolution. People's living conditions worsened with the rise in population. But following the introduction of the reform and opening-up policies, especially in the urban renovation campaign during the 1990s, high-rises and new types of residential areas mushroomed. People's living conditions were significantly improved. In the 1990s cities began to erect commercial residential buildings. There was no more waiting to get a house allotted. People could buy a comfortable house with their own earnings.

Shenzhen street, 1993

Bustling Nanjing Road in Shanghai, 1994

From 1950 to 1978 China's urbanization rate increased from 11% to 17.92%, an annual increase rate of 0.28 percentage points. But from 1978 to 1998 urbanization increased from 17.92% to 33.35%, an annual increase rate of 0.77 percentage points. In 1957, there were only 10 cities with 1 million people each in China (excluding Hong Kong and Taiwan). There were 13 such cities in 1978, 23 in 1986 and 38 in 2000. As the number of mega cities increased, urban living conditions also improved. Meanwhile, urbanization also brought about problems involving the polarization of the rich and the poor, migrants, social security and urban sanitation.

Landscape of the eastern region of Guangdong Province, 1990s

Wave of Economic Growth

Under the planned economy system, the department stores established by the government were the places where commodities of all varieties were concentrated. In a few large cities there was more than one large department store, but only one in smaller places. In 1986 there were only 25 large department stores and 17,000 retail outlets nationwide. The bustling department stores reflected the shortage of commodities and the slack market under the planned economy system.

A department store, 1970s

A textile store, 1970s

[Chapter 5] Catching Up with the World (1977-2000)

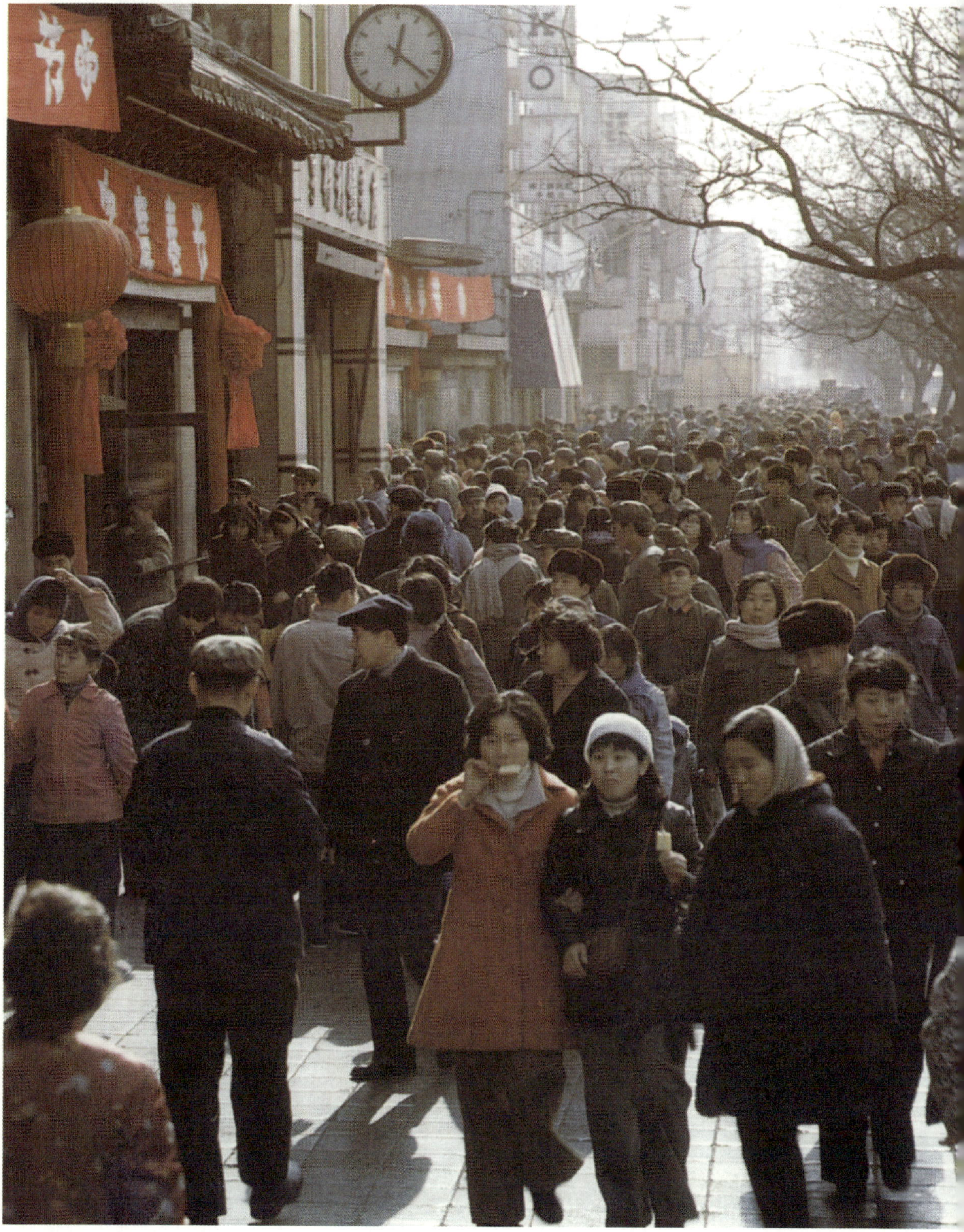

Wangfujing Street, downtown Beijing, 1980s

At a time when business was not well developed, Xidan and Wangfujing streets were the only commercial and shopping centers in Beijing. People from all over Beijing and even from neighboring cities flocked to these two places during Spring Festival and holidays.

{ Chapter 5 } Catching Up with the World (1977-2000)

Inside the commercial building in Shanghai, 1992

Women selecting clothes, 1995

Following the introduction of the reform and opening-up policies, China's retail business embraced prosperity in terms of total number and scale. Joint ventures were also opened. All this contributed to a flourishing urban commercial scene. In the period 1992-1996 the retail revenue of department stores increased by 21% on average, with the highest profit increase of 64%. In 1991 there were 94 stores with revenue over 100 million RMB. This number had increased to 624 by 1995, an increase of five times in five years. The sales volume of the top 100 stores increased from 31.8 billion-RMB-worth to 80.5 billion-RMB-worth, nearly double. This was a golden era for China's retail industry.

An advertisement for a Japanese electronic watch on a Beijing street, 1980s

With the reform and opening up, imported products became available on local Chinese markets. Western household appliances were enormously popular among urban people. On March 15, 1979, the *Wenhui* newspaper led the way in carrying a banner advertisement for a Swiss watch brand. This was the first advertisement for a foreign brand since the reform and opening up started.

In the planned economy there was no competition and no need for promotion and advertisement. There were few ad companies in 1979, yet in the period 1983-1986 the number of companies doing ad business increased by 44.9%, with sales revenue increasing by 55.3% annually. People began to understand the new market economy.

An advertisement for clothing in Taiyuan, capital of Shanxi Province, 1995

A clown attracts clients to an American-style restaurant in Tianjin

{ Chapter 5 } Catching Up with the World (1977-2000)

People scrambling to purchase stocks

By the end of 1990 China's securities market had ridden its first wave of prosperity. However, people at that time did not have any sense of risk. After 1990 people across China and from Hong Kong and Macao rushed to Shenzhen to buy stocks. Some waited outside the Shenzhen stock exchange from early in the morning to get the limited 200 entry tickets for each day. They scrambled into the exchange the moment it opened for business. People poured their money into the stock market, some even borrowed money just to buy stock. However, the best time of Chinese stock market from December 19, 1990 to May 26, 1992 didn't last long. Only six months after May 26, 1992, the Chinese stock market suffered a huge plummet of 73%. After that, Chinese investors became more realistic.

Stock fever in Dalian, 1994

There was a fever of security investment in Shanghai, 1992.

{ Chapter 5 }　Catching Up with the World (1977-2000)

Russian buyers in Yabao Street, Beijing, 1992

Yabao Street became the center for Russian dealers, 1995.

Beijing's Silk Market, 1992

Until 1978 today's Silk Market was merely a small alley near Jianguomenwai Dajie, Beijing. It is not known when people began setting up stalls there. As the alley is located in the embassy area, it was patronized by foreigners, and the number of stalls increased. In 1985 the Silk Market was formally established here. With a good geographical location, a broad variety of commodities and timely changes in the styles of commodities, particularly those of Chinese silk products, the Market attracted a large number of foreigners who called the alley "SILK STREET."

Foreign dealers and taxis were common sights around Hongqiao Market.

With the reform and opening up, some foreign dealers began to appear in Chinese markets. The first group came from Poland and Iran, followed by the Soviet Union, Yugoslavia and Turkey. They were attracted to China by abundant and cheap merchandise, such as real silk, cotton ware, pearls, cloth shoes, flashlights, ball pens, blankets and pillow cases. It was said that an ordinary pearl necklace (6-7 RMB) from the Hongqiao Market was worth around 100-300 roubles in the Soviet Union, which was enormously profitable. In the period 1980-1990 there emerged several large markets for foreign trade, such as those at Hongqiao, Xiushui and Jinsong. The Hongqiao Market was the largest market for second-hand goods and pearl necklaces in China. The Xiushui (Silk) Market, nicknamed "little Paris," was in the vicinity of foreign embassies and known for its clothes business.

Food Priority

Stacks of cabbages for winter was a major scene every year, Beijing, 1979

Right through the 1980s, cabbages were the staple food in northern China during the winter. But following the introduction of the policies of reform and opening up, productivity was enhanced, and the people's living standard improved. Vegetables also became abundant, and cabbages were sold on the market together with other vegetables and fruits.

Housewives collect their rations of cabbages, 1980s

{ Chapter 5 } Catching Up with the World (1977-2000)

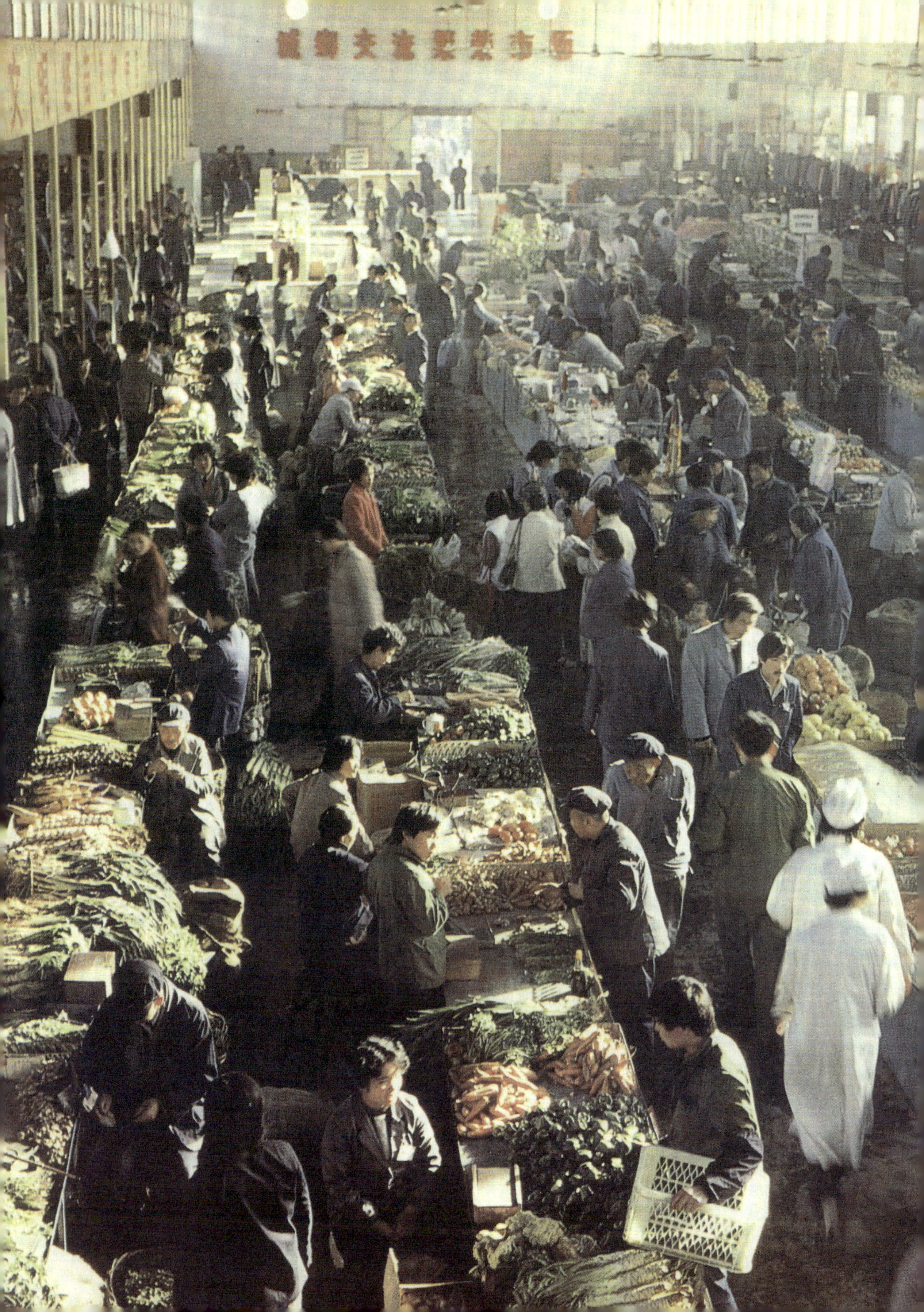

The Dongdan Vegetable Market, Beijing ←

The Dongdan Vegetable Market used to handle a record 50,000 customers a day. At holiday times, such as the Spring Festival, there were hundreds of people waiting outside the gates of the markets waiting for them to open. These vegetable markets were gradually demolished in the 1990s.

Filling bowls with rice, 1980s

Restaurants in Beijing, 1980s

There were only 1,000 restaurants (all state-owned) in Beijing in the late 1970s. A street with more than two restaurants was considered a busy street. Most people patronized restaurants only during holidays or for a celebration. Restaurants were crammed full at meal times. People sometimes had to wait for more than two hours in line to get a seat.

Mutton hotpot – a popular dish in Beijing, 1980s

There were around 10,000 restaurants in Beijing by 1985. Economic growth and increased incomes also stimulated people to spend more on food. However, the courses served in the 1980s were fairly ordinary, and mutton hotpot was quite an innovation.

Interior view of the Heping Western-style Restaurant, 1979

Before the reform and opening-up era, Beijing only had the Moscow, Heping and Dadi restaurants which served foreign (Russian-style) food. In September 1983 Pierre Cardin opened a branch of his Maxim's restaurants in Beijing. It was also the first joint-venture restaurant in China.

A celebration in a restaurant, 1980s

A family dinner of a senior official, 1980s.

The dinner consisted of four courses and one of soup, plus steamed bread. This was regarded as a lavish dinner for a family at that time.

The Big-Bowl Tea Stand in Tian'anmen Square, 1980s

In 1979, Yin Shengxi, a staff member of the community administration of Beijing's Xuanwu District, decided to try his luck with the market economy, with the initial purpose of creating jobs for unemployed youth in his community. With several unemployed young people, he opened a tea stand at Qianmen, and began to sell "Big-Bowl Tea" (0.02 RMB per bowl). It attracted lots of tourists, with thousands of bowls of tea sold each day. With the money accumulated from the tea stand business, Yin founded the Big Bowl Tea Commercial Co. in 1988. Later he opened the Lao She Teahouse, named after the author of the renowned novel *Teahouse*.

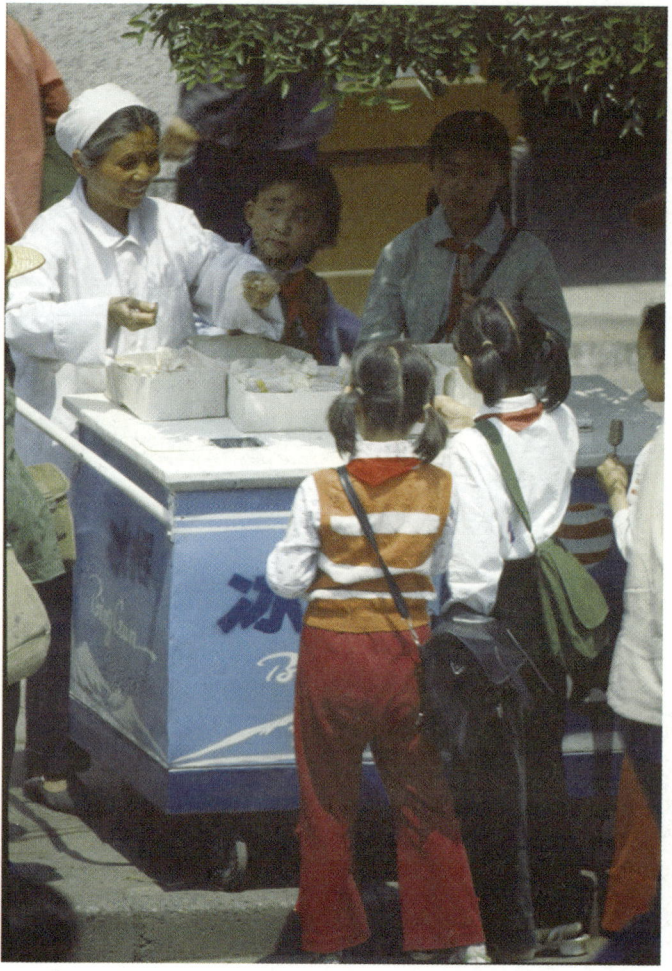

"Popsicle cart"

In the 1980s the only things sold on the streets of Beijing in the summer were popsicles with either red bean or hawthorn flavor (0.03 RMB), cream or chocolate flavor (0.05RMB). The sellers were mostly elderly, and sold popsicles from a cart. The one in the picture is a very sophisticated one; most carts were simply wooden boxes on wheels, containing a block of ice insulated with cotton wadding.

A bottle of "Beibingyang" (The Arctic Ocean) brand soda pop was once a luxury for children in Beijing

"Beibingyang" is an indelible memory for people brought up in Beijing in the 1970s and 1980s. Even in the early 1990s many stores and snack shops had to use large buckets of cold water as makeshift refrigerators, due to a shortage of proper refrigerators. As a major cold drinks and popsicles manufacturer, the Beibingyang Food Co. made over 100 million RMB in the period 1985-1988.

[Chapter 5] Catching Up with the World (1977-2000)

The first Kentucky Fried Chicken outlet in China opened on November 12, 1987 at Qianmen, Beijing.

Kentucky Fried Chicken restaurants had spread all over China by 2000. This one is located in Haikou, capital of South China's Hainan Province.

On Nov. 12, 1987, the first Kentucky Fried Chicken restaurant opened for business in China. The store was located in the Qianmen commercial area. Western food was considered a luxury at that time. An average Kentucky Fried chicken meal would cost 8 RMB, which was expensive considering that people's monthly income was only around 20-30 RMB at that time. Young people especially regarded Kentucky Fried Chicken restaurants as fashionable, and some even organized wedding ceremonies there. Encouraged by this enthusiasm, the company quickly began expansion in China. By 1992 there were only ten Kentucky Fried Chicken outlets in China, but by 1995 there were 71. Western food was no longer unaffordable.

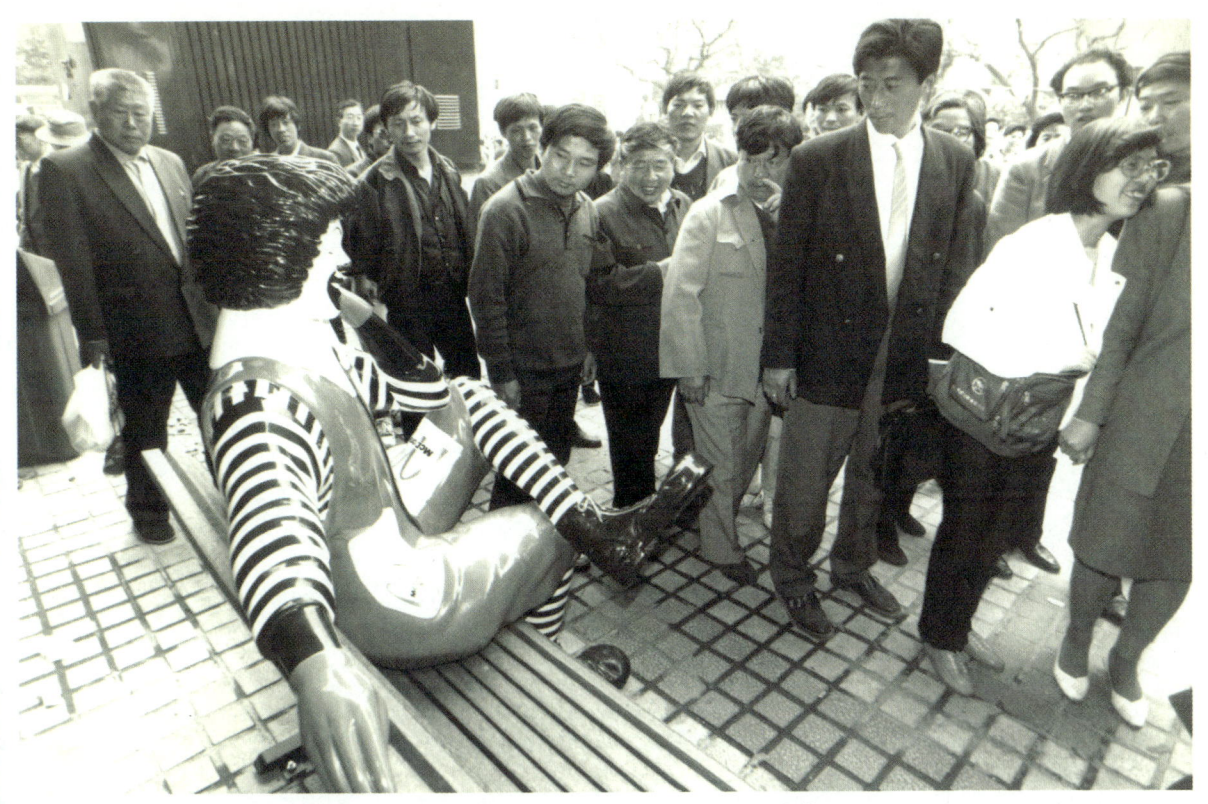

The first MacDonald's restaurant in China opened for business in Wangfujing Street, downtown Beijing, in 1992.

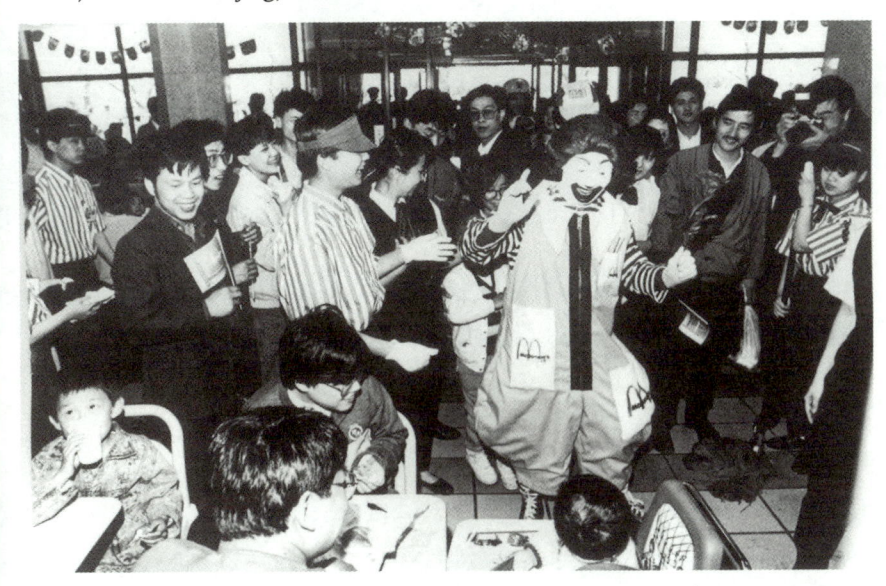

Opening ceremony of the first MacDonald's restaurant in China, 1992

Chapter 5 Catching Up with the World (1977-2000)

Return of Beauty

A couple poses for a photo in a park, 1979. The Chinese tunic suit was still the acceptable dress code of the time.

During the Cultural Revolution people dressed in a similar unisex design with color variations limited to blue, green, black and grey. The tunic and pants set dominated fashion forms. Foreign journalists in China used to joke that the Chinese had no personalities worth mentioning, but were just "busy ants in blue and grey."

Fashionable young girls in colorful accessories were very eye-catching in Beijing, 1979.

{ Chapter 5 } Catching Up with the World (1977-2000)

Revival of the suit and tie, late 1970s

During the 1970s, the Chinese tunic suit (described by foreign media as Mao Zedong's style) was the dress code for formal occasions as well. Chinese men had only the green military uniform as an alternative. By the late 1970s, the suit came back into favor as the attire for dignified and special events. At the 13th CPC Central Committee meeting held in 1987, Party Secretary Hu Yaobang and the five standing members of the Political Bureau of the CPC Central Committee attended the press conference in formal suits, a form of approval which certainly boosted the popularity of these suits. Clothing stores began to sell suits, and photo shops even began to rent them to satisfy customer needs.

Flares and bell-bottoms adopted by the female *avant garde*, 1980s

As the 1980s unfolded, the cadre suit, military uniform and Lenin-style female fashions were abandoned by Chinese women. At the extreme end of early-adopters, bell-bottoms and flared trousers featuring tight waists rose in popularity. Although their loudspeaker shape was considered somewhat outrageous, the stylish trousers were spotted in imported films and caught the attention of many young people daring enough to challenge the status quo of fashion. Wearing designs like this was quite dangerous at that time, as most people were still under the spell of ideological indoctrination. Suspicious of reform and opening up, and of anything nontraditional, they subjected the wearers of bell-bottoms to harsh criticism. Governments and schools went so far as to forbid such trousers, and violators were reprimanded and had to make a self-criticism, as was the requirement during the Cultural Revolution. Some agencies even set up checkpoints at their entrances to cut off the flared portion of such trousers on the spot.

Jeans shared the same fate. The iconic American denim pants became all the rage in 1982, and were once the emblem of "hooligan dress." Despite the resistance, people strove to break down any barriers and embrace new definitions of beauty, fueling a mass catch-up with international fashion that proved unstoppable. By the late 1980s and early 1990s, people became accustomed to changing fashion trends. The reform and opening up ushered in a tolerance for diversity and a broadening of public taste, which illustrated China's advancing modernization and social maturity.

Going from straight to curly at the hairdresser's

Choice of hair styles exploded following reform and opening up, and what nature didn't provide, modern products and technology could.

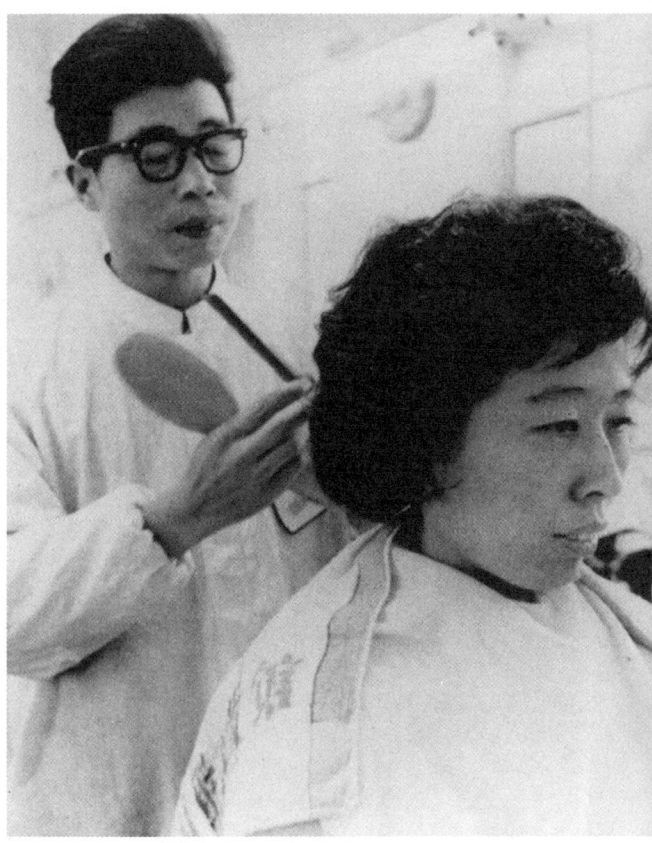

Cosmetology joined fashion trends in clothes and hair.

Women began to get rid of dull and tame styles, and experiment with chemical perms and waves. Entering the 1980s, a diversity of women's styles, long or short, or straight, curly or wavy hair, was becoming common. The distinction between mainstream and new alternatives blurred in every art and craft. People's pursuit of beauty never changed, it just had more models of expression.

A woman takes a break to freshen up before a visit to the Forbidden City

The natural look, an absence of rouge and powder, was the standard aesthetic during wartime, but it was far from meeting the demands of modern times. Makeup application was no longer just for the stage, it was a craft that had to be mastered by every woman in her daily life. For the past three decades, Chinese women have refined and matured their art as they shifted from heavy to light makeup.

A new generation strut their stuff in Tian'anmen Square, 1980s

Budding fashionists in Zizhuyuan Park, Beijing, 1980

{ Chapter 5 } Catching Up with the World (1977-2000)

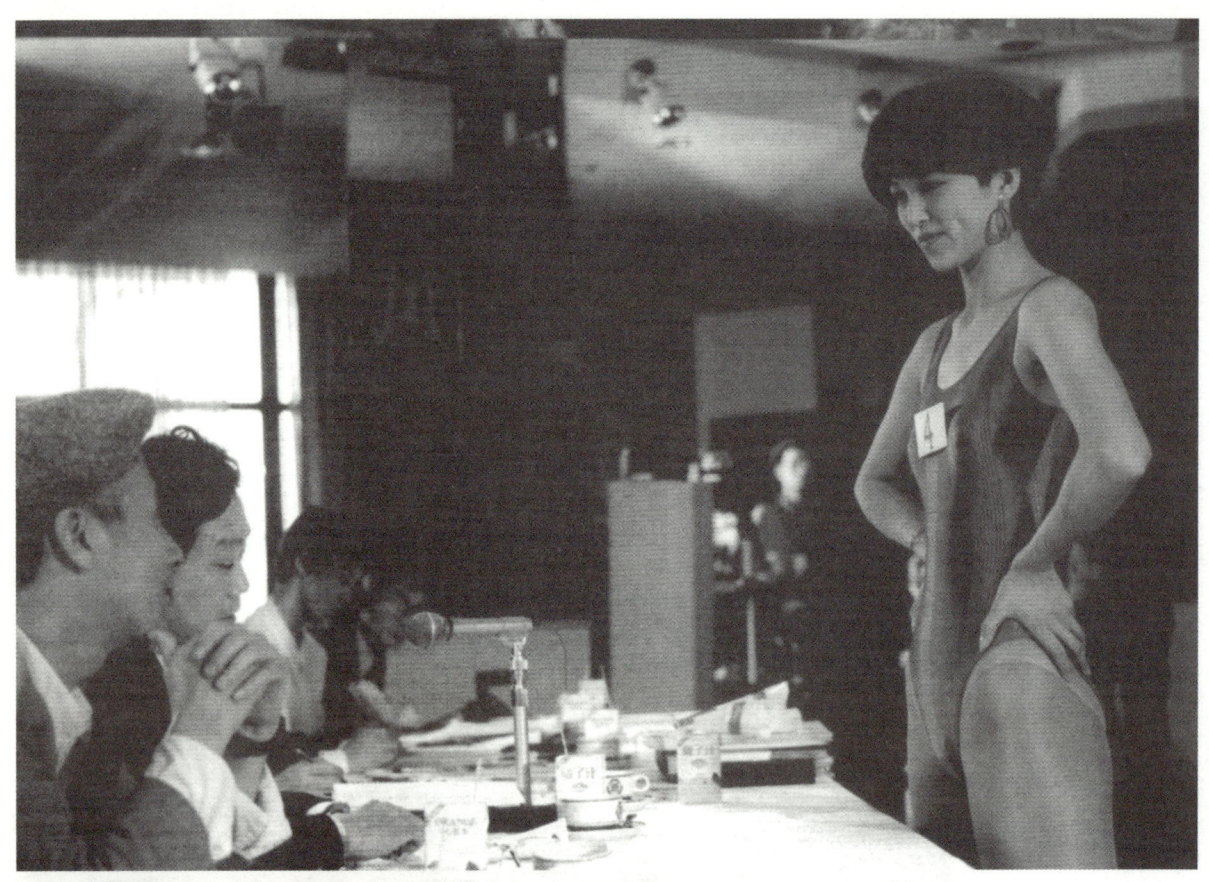

Model examination held in Guangzhou, 1987

On Sept. 17, 1989, Ma Ling, a 21-year-old actress opens Ma Ling Fashion Design Co. in Beijing.

She was the first fashion designer in China to use her own name for her design company and brand of clothes.

In 1995, at the China Mr.& Miss Bodybuilding Contest, Xu Qinhua, a female athlete from Shanghai, won the third place in the Miss Bodybuilding Contest, and was also presented with an award for "best performance."

In 1986, when the nation's first body-building convention was held in Shenzhen, candidates wore bikinis on the platform in accordance with the international standard. This was the first time the bikini had been seen in China, and it caused an uproar and vociferous criticism. There are still segments of society that regard skimpy swimsuits and tantalizing underwear designs as unfit for public showcases, but most people by that time had became accustomed to the phenomenon.

Being a fashion leader is not an easy role at any time in history, and keeping up with trends in the 1980s was an economic juggling act for many average Chinese. In 1982 a Shanghai family of four averaged a monthly income of 113 RMB, and the clothes budget might have been about 8-9 RMB (the purchasing power of 1 RMB then equaled 15-20 RMB in 2008). In 1985, a man's undershirt was 0.5 RMB or less, while a dress shirt was 3 to 5 RMB. A high-quality satin dress for a woman set her back 18 RMB. Batik and plangi clothes cost around 100-200 RMB, and a woman's leather overcoat ran as high as 300 RMB at that time. Clearly many items were unaffordable for ordinary people.

The 1990s versions of "those in the know" about fashion

Modern international fashion trends have found unique modes of expression in the Chinese market, and nurtured a flowering of taste that satisfied women's exploitation of the disarming power of glamour. Back in 1984, it started with the highly acclaimed film *Red Skirt in Fashion* which triggered a flood of all types and colors of red, yellow and other skirts into the country's clothing market and filled the streets with great swirls of color. The skirt and the pursuit of beauty became one and the same.

By the mid-1990s, the mini-skirt heralded another wardrobe benchmark that fascinated both women and men. In some cases, the skirt was so outrageously short that social conservatives condemned the item as obscene. Nevertheless, the fashion industry for females enjoyed significant growth for decades to come. Diversified lines turned out designs for the slim build that is the dominant body type of the Eastern female, and catered to the taste for elaborate styling that balanced the famously demure Oriental temperament.

Fashion model shows the public how to pull off cutting-edge designs, 1990s

In 1979, Pierre Cardin visited Beijing and hosted an informal fashion show at the Cultural Palace of Nationalities. The catwalk featured tall and elegant French models and was an instant success in the capital. The Chinese fashion sector was galvanized.

The first fashion show organizer, Shanghai Fashion Show Team, was set up in 1980. On the night of February 9, 1981, they staged the country's very first fashion show in the Friendship Cinema. Organized by Chinese from top to bottom, it lasted for 70 minutes. A model named Xu Ping was to make an appearance wearing a sleeveless ceremonial robe, but the garment was strongly disapproved of by her parents. She had to wear some concealing ribbons on her arms in the finale. The Team produced another show at the Agricultural Exhibition Center in Beijing on May 1, 1983, which if anything was an even greater success. The 1990s added a new occupation in China: fashion model.

Young girls respond to the heat of summer in style, Jinan, Shandong Province, 2005.

By this time, what to wear was a question with many right answers. It was harder by now to be obviously ahead of the fashion pack in this era of diversified tastes, rapidly evolving trends, and growing personal income levels. Styles that might once have been thought strange and weird were no longer a social taboo or indicators of rebellious behavior.

21st century femininity

China's garment industry underwent significant changes in just 30 years. A Polish journalist wrote of the capital in 1989, "look back several years and you would see a Beijing the color of grey, its citizens drably dressed in clothes of the same color and monotonous design; some called Beijing 'the world's countryside.' But today's Beijing is a fascinating jumble of a city with fashion-conscious girls dressed in Western style." He would probably be more amazed by the evolution of the Chinese fashion scene had he come back 20 years later.

Transportation

Countless bikes parked in front of Tian'anmen Gate, 1984

In the 1980s, China was known as the kingdom of bikes. By the late 1980s, there were around 500 million in China, or one for every three people. The bicycle was the very first product to be popularized in China, and became an exemplar of China's industrial progress. Right before reform and opening up, Deng Xiaoping defined "prosperity" as each family having at least one "Flying Dove" brand of bike.

However, the two wheeled self-propelled vehicle gradually lost its luster during the 1990s when the State Council released the first Policy on the Automobile Industry in 1994. The private ownership of automobiles was encouraged and became fashionable. Back in 1978, there were only 77,000 automobiles in Beijing, but by 1997, the number was one million. Bikes gradually moved out of the picture and by the late 1980s, accounted for just 63% of people's travel choices, declining to 30.3% by 2005, and finally to 17.9% by the first half of 2010. It is a fact that the bike no longer dominates Chinese streets, but when faced with a traffic jam, air pollution, or sore muscles and backache brought on by driving cars, we can't help thinking about the green and healthy travel mode provided by the simple bicycle.

Streams of bikes on Chang'an Avenue, 1986

Bicycles clog a wide boulevard in Shanghai, 1991

{ Chapter 5 } Catching Up with the World
(1977-2000)

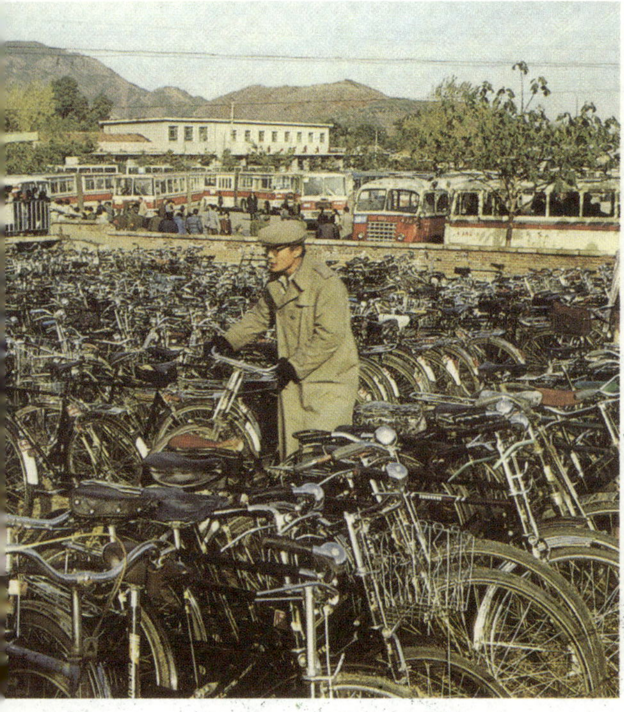

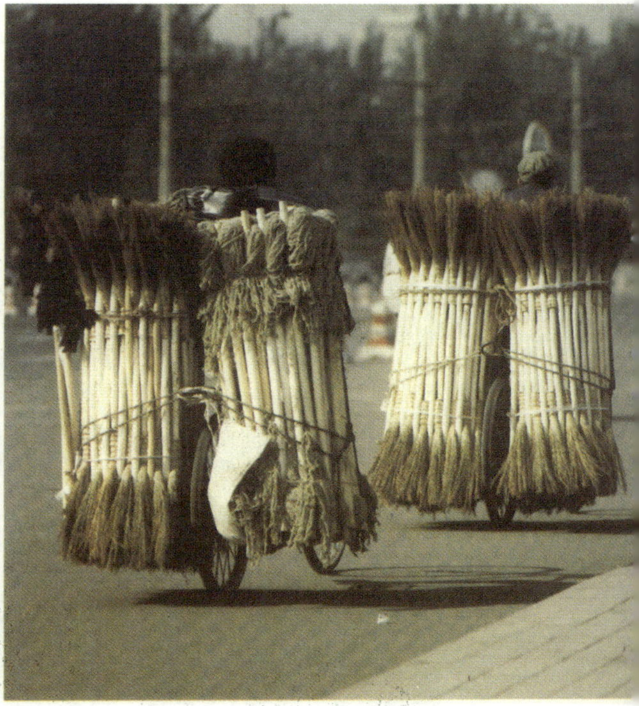

Cyclists on Chang'an Avenue in the 1980s

The bicycle left a great impression on the Chinese and even influenced their way of life. It was a kind of cultural phenomenon, through which we understood the lifestyles, attitudes, interests and wisdom of the Chinese at that time.

Under the planned economy the bicycle was a scarce and desirable good. People had to save up to buy one, and coupons were issued especially for bike purchases. Not surprisingly, it was fairly common for a bike to be used as a dowry in a marriage. Entering the 1980s, bikes became an ordinary consumer good, but for a long time people still nursed that special association and feeling for the two-wheelers.

{ Chapter 5 } **Catching Up with the World** (1977-2000)

Gridlock in Beijing, 1986

The newly-completed Sanyuanqiao Bridge on the East 3rd Ring Road of Beijing, late 1980s, as yet not dominated by a torrent of cars

Taxis in Beijing, 1990s

At the beginning of reform and opening up in 1978, a taxi represented an expensive and scarce service. People had to make reservations for them. In the 1990s, the market operations for taxi services matured and an increasing number became available, making it very convenient for people to move about in cities. In the very beginning, the most popular model was a type of yellow minibus. It was also very cheap (ten RMB for flag-fall price, and one RMB for every mile added later), but best of all, it was large enough to accommodate 10 people at a time. It could even carry a bike or large appliances, so it was much loved by the people. This type of yellow minibus could be found everywhere; they merged into traffic streams with ease and stopped anywhere and everywhere without fear of violating any regulations, which earned them the moniker of "road hopper."

In the early 1990s, such minibuses were common in many cities, but by the mid-1990s, they gradually gave way to a type of red car, the "Xiali." City streets in China were once crawling with such red taxis. There have been several rounds of taxi upgrading since then and the two-tone taxi is accepted as a common transportation mode for most urbanites.

Some major cities in China were already experiencing the precursor of the traffic jam by the mid-1980s. In 1984, Beijing experienced its very first city-wide traffic jam. Crossroads were the point where traffic jams started, and trucks and bikes were most often the culprits. Beijing constructed new roads and limited the hours trucks could access the inner city, which alleviated the problem to some extent. However, the second-largest traffic jam happened in 1995, with private cars cramming the 2nd and 3rd ring roads in full gridlock. The situation today is far from improving. In December 2001, a heavy snowfall paralyzed all roads in Beijing and turned the capital into a parking lot. Traffic jams are a big headache for most Chinese cities.

Marriage and Family

A soldier and his girlfriend go skating in a Beijing park, 1978

In the early 1980s, a famous crosstalk show (Chinese-style comedy dialogue) took on the topic of how the young demonstrated their love. In the 1950s, holding hands was the way to express love; in the 1960s, lovers went about arm-in-arm; in the 1970s, they wrapped their arms around each other's waists; by the 1980s, they had their arms slung over each other's shoulders and, in the 1990s, perhaps the girl would completely encircle the boy's neck. This is the progression of the public expression of love in China. Entering the 1980s, young people began expressing the dreams they held for their lives and especially their love lives. Young men and women no longer hid their interest and affection but pursued the object of their desire in an open and enthusiastic fashion.

Young lovers, 1980s

Love on wheels, 1980s

A marriage photo displayed in a photo studio window, late 1970s

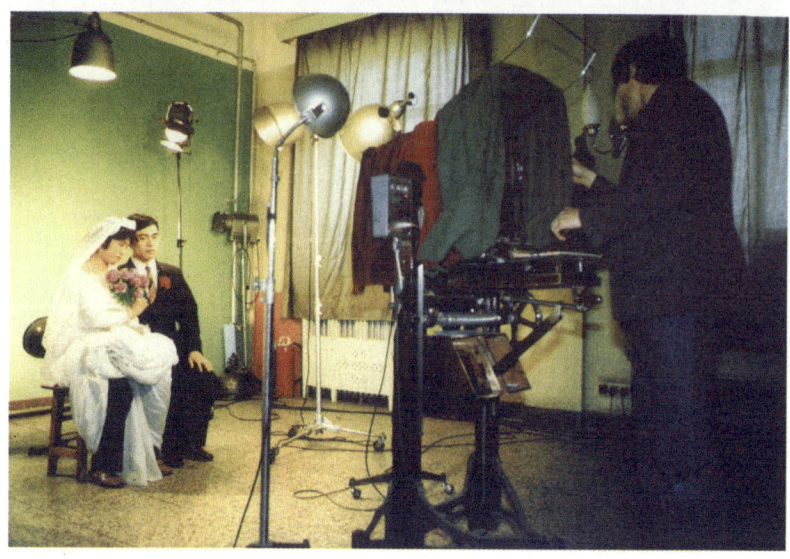

Newlyweds pose for their wedding photos, 1982

Marriage in an alley in Guangzhou, 1983

By the early 1980s, people's living conditions had improved, but were still very modest, so people were very careful with the wedding budget. The couple's home or the canteen hall of their workplace was good enough for the ceremony, a wedding photo, a couplet poem immortalizing their happiness, a few candies, a couple of wedding dinners, plus the best wishes of friends and relatives; these were all the necessities for a formal marriage. As living conditions approached middle-class abundance, the marriage ceremony also underwent appropriate changes. The wedding dinner became more lavish, and the ceremony more likes a carnival. People's standards for a mate shifted from choices that prioritized "background and political consciousness" to "education and income."

In spite of public criticism, dowries and wedding ceremonies became extravagant. In the late 1980s, a professional wedding service company opened in Beijing, ushering in the modern wedding service industry. By the 1990s, a wedding photo portfolio, motorcade, and dinner were bare necessities.

[Chapter 5] Catching Up with the World (1977-2000)

A married couple pose for a wedding photo, 1997

There has been a fashion for long-married couples, even old couples, to take wedding photos to relive their lost weddings. In their wedding photos there are often their sons and daughters.

A wedding ceremony in Anchang Town, Zhejiang Province, 2000

While nuptial culture was becoming socially formalized, people began to pay more attention to the ceremony itself. Newlyweds began to focus on the style and genre of their wedding, sometimes selecting historical themes in addition to stressing color-coding, music, flowers and decorations. The traditional ceremony was losing ground to the clever wedding theme. There were more cases of outdoor weddings, night weddings, bicycle weddings and other gimmicks that were sure to grab public attention.

[Chapter 5] Catching Up with the World (1977-2000)

Divorce rates soared as reform and opening up took hold.

According to the Ministry of Civil Affairs, divorce rates in China have been steadily rising since reform and opening up. Changes in beliefs about marriage and a simplified divorce procedure are driving the trend. Divorce is no longer regarded as a shame or kept secret like a skeleton in the family closet, and people's work units and local government no longer intervene in individual marriage breakups. Divorce is the business of the people concerned.

When the People's Republic was founded in 1949, the population of the Chinese mainland was only 540 million; this number increased to 800 million in 1969. The population increase fueled economic growth, but also exerted great pressure on public services and natural resources. The Chinese government gradually realized the necessity of controlling population growth, and in September 1980, the CPC Central Committee formally called for all Party and Youth League members to follow the policy of "one child for one couple." In September 1982, the 12th CPC Central Committee meeting adopted family planning as a basic state policy. Two months later, when it was written into the Constitution, couples had the obligation to follow this family planning policy.

Thirty years after the family planning policy was adopted, China's birthrate is finally on the decline. According to national census data, China's total population was 1.27 billion in 2000, and 1.34 billion in 2010, showing an increase of 73.9 million in a decade, with an annual growth rate of 0.57%. China is now one of the world's countries with the lowest population growth. The implementation of the one-child policy contributed positively to reducing resource consumption, promoting employment, alleviating family burdens and improving the quality of life for subsequent generations.

A poster promoting family planning in Beijing, 1992

Condom vending machine put into trial use in Guangzhou, 1999

For a long time, the Chinese avoided talking about sex. With the family planning policy in place, the Chinese now paid more attention to promoting reproductive health and sound child rearing, a consciousness which is conducive to changing people's views and behavior.

Family planning campaigns in urban centers

Entering the new century, China began to adjust its family planning policy. For example, families in some regions and cities are now allowed to have a second child, and the focus has switched to an emphasis on reproductive health and maternal and infant healthcare. These efforts are intended to strike a balance between population growth and sustainable development.

Aging population growth posing a major problem for China

On the one hand, family planning was a great success, but it also brought about social problems, such as lack of resources to care for a population characterized by a large percentage of aging people, and an imbalanced gender ratio. Currently, seniors over 60 account for one tenth of the total population and are expected to reach a quarter by 2030. By 2050, one out of three Chinese will be over 60. China is still a developing country, and elder care is expected to be a huge burden and challenge for the country, as well as for individual families, which will be compelled to support their senior members. In addition, the gender ratio of baby boys to baby girls is 120:100. This means that in only ten years, the number of males will surpass the number of females by 50-60 million. Currently this is a hidden but serious risk for Chinese society.

Education

School pupils sporting oversized hair bows in Fuzhou, 1977

A schoolboy doing his homework while ignoring street noise and bustle, a common sight in the 1970s and 1980s

A rural school teacher guides her students, 1984

Since the founding of New China, significant progress has been made with respect to universal access to basic education. However, the barriers for Chinese children in remote rural areas mean they still rarely get proper or complete schooling. Even in developed regions, access to a basic education and adequate study conditions is far from being secure.

In 1986, the Compulsory Education Law of the People's Republic of China was enacted, which stipulated that China implement a nine-year compulsory education system (six years of primary and three years of junior middle school). The law protects children's right to education, regardless of their location, ethnic group or gender. This greatly enlarged the enrolment rate of eligible children in the countryside, and put expansion of the education system onto the fast track. By 1999, there were 582,300 primary schools in China, with 13,549,600 students, and the enrollment rate for primary schools reached 99.09%. Ninety-one percent of populated regions had implemented a primary school education system, and junior school education was also coming along very well. By 1999, there were 64,400 junior middle schools, with 58,116,500 students and an enrolment rate of 88.6%.

"I wanna go to school," 1991

Su Mingjuan was born to a rural family in 1983 in Anhui Province. Her parents supported the family by fishing, breeding silkworms, raising pigs and farming. In May 1991, Xie Hailong, a photographer, visited her county to take some photos for the Hope Project. He spotted Su in her first-year class and was attracted by the child's eagerness to learn. He took her picture and titled it, "I wanna study." Su's image and her academic keenness made her a poster child for the Hope Project and a kind of natural ambassador for the initiative.

Su becomes a white collar success, 2007

The Hope Project changed Su's destiny as it did those of tens of millions of other poor children. Between 1989 and 2009, the Hope Project accumulated 5,670 million RMB, which was used to support the education of 3.46 million rural poor people, construct 15,940 Hope Schools in remote and impoverished regions, and help train 56,000 rural teachers. In 2005, Su graduated from the Polytechnical School of Anhui University and secured a job at the Anhui branch of the Industrial and Commercial Bank of China. She remained a champion of educational causes as a representative of the recipient children, as well as other issues affecting the public interest. In 2008, she worked as an Anhui Province volunteer for the Beijing Olympic Games.

Parents accompanying their children to piano lessons, 1990s

Fierce competition spurred parents to invest all they could on the education of their children, so that "they would not be behind the starting line." From exam preparation courses to nurturing natural talents, all types of supplementary courses and special training schools mushroomed overnight. Not only were junior and senior high students taking such courses, even primary school students and kindergarten kids had to do so too. Most parents believed that this would help children to acquire unique skill sets that would help them stand out in academic and employment competitions.

The first university entrance examination following the resumption of the higher-education system, 1977

During the Cultural Revolution, China's tertiary education system was virtually shut down and had to subsequently recover from severe damage. In September 1977, under the leadership of Deng Xiaoping, the Ministry of Education held a meeting on university enrollment and decided to resume the university entrance examination, which had been suspended for nearly a decade. This university entrance exam probably was, and remains, the largest of its kind in the world. The very first to be held in the wake of the Cultural Revolution was organized in Dec. 1977. Some 5.7 million flocked to take it and 273,000 passed. In the summer of 1978, the second university entrance examination was organized with 6.1 million sitting for it; 402,000 passed. The two sessions resulted in 11.6 million students being enrolled. Although the enrollment rate was rather low, the resumption of the regimen showed that China once again embraced knowledge and respected talent.

A mother preparing for the university entrance exam while caring for her infant, 1980

On October 21, 1977, the mainstream media reported on the resumption of the university entrance exam, mentioning that sittings would be organized nationwide in December. The news broke merely a month before the exam date. Middle-aged and young people rushed to begin their review of subjects immediately, and lined up in bookstores to buy textbooks and related materials. Printing presses worked around the clock to meet the demand for scholarly materials, but fell far short. As a result, many resourceful people scoured waste disposal sites in the hope of uncovering discarded old books, or painstakingly copied someone else's text by hand. Libraries were also filled to the maximum at all hours. This unprecedented situation lasted until the 1980s.

University students in class, 1978

In the spring of 1978, both the mature and the fresh wave of high school graduates were returning to academe to satisfy their ambitions and aspirations. Now with their special background and social experience, they pursued a university education with zeal. After graduation, they applied themselves devotedly to sharing what they had learnt to benefit the whole of society and change the world as they knew it. Statistics tell the story that they had already made a great contribution to the progress of the country and the world: between 1979 and 1997, 829,100 of them graduated from universities and colleges, more than two and a half times the number that had achieved this in the previous 30 years.

Student dorm, 1983

Frequent academic exchanges boosted the steady increase in the presence of foreign professors, 1980

Culture and Entertainment

Old people killing time in the afternoon, 1977

Life in China had a slow and comfortable pace, early 1980s.

The newspaper was the main source of information, 1978

There were very few newspapers published during the Cultural Revolution. The only authoritative media were the *People's Daily*, the *PLA Daily* and *Red Flag*. These papers only covered official news. During the late 1980s, other versions emerged, along the lines of evening news and youth news. Other papers were resumed or created to focus on areas of invigorated interest or rapid change, such as the urban landscape and evolving lifestyles.

The Chinese picture-story book enjoyed great popularity, 1982

The picture-story book is similar to a comic book, but based on a literary classic or on real life, with pictures accompanied by a short explanatory sentence. The picture-story book surfaced in the early 1920s in Shanghai, and was in its heyday around 1949. During the Cultural Revolution, their creation was generally banned for a decade. After 1978, the form was revived and entered another period of popularity and prosperity. More than 2,100 picture comic books were issued in 1982, with print-runs of 100,000. This was 20 times the printing capacity of the 1960s. In 1980, the Central Academy of Fine Arts opened a course in comic strip creation, which was popular for more than a decade.

However, other forms of entertainment have proliferated since the late 1980s, and the comic book genre's most experimental and leading works started to be produced abroad. Thus the traditional picture story book lost ground in its most significant market — youth.

Beauty merged with the wall calendar and a hot new item for pre-Spring Festival sales emerged in 1992 and 1993

　　In the 1980s, wall calendars were enormously popular. Markets were filled with stands selling wall calendars on New Year's Day. Government agencies and institutions commissioned or purchased calendars as gifts for employees or business partners at festival time. People collected them enthusiastically and thought nothing of getting as many calendars as possible to show off.

Art exhibition on a street in the capital, 1979

Between the late 1970s and early 1980s, individual art exhibitions were a common part of the streetscape. These sub-stream art shows had neither sponsors nor financial support, and sometimes failed to attract viewers as well. Artists were passionate about their work and aspired to independence from the world of dealers. This trend lasted until the late 1980s, spawning exhibitions that ranged into the ridiculous and weird. However, they became an indelible symbol of the era,

China's bohemians in a Beijing art village, 1993

In the 1990s, some artists took their pursuit of freedom and individuality into deserted factory facilities in the suburban fringes of Beijing, or farther afield into villages on the outskirts of the capital. Here, cheap rents, open spaces and tranquil environments provided great opportunities for avant-garde artists who had grown dissatisfied with the mainstream genre of painting. Gradually art villages began to appear. Some well-known ones include Yuanmingyuan and the 798 Art Zone which remain vibrant today. Initially, places like this were demolished since they were considered risky enclaves that attracted vagrants and vagabonds. By the late 1990s, and certainly by the 21st century, art villages were not only a widely accepted phenomenon, they had expanded to become vibrantly successful economic and tourism districts showcasing the great vitality of modern Chinese art.

Black and white sets usher in China's TV era, 1978

On May 1, 1958, Beijing TV (the predecessor of CCTV) began broadcasting. At that time, few people knew what a television was. Ordinary people considered watching TV a foreign habit. Even in the 1970s, the household TV set was still a very scarce item, because only by lottery could anyone get a coupon to purchase one. Television was a service and a privilege largely accessible only to those with an official position or enough money. Sometimes people pulled strings to get a TV set, but by the late 1970s and early 1980s, it had become largely available to ordinary people. Often it was the case that several households living in a courtyard house or sharing a neighborhood would crowd into one family dwelling where the owners were willing to share their viewing time. Later on, TV became almost ubiquitous and the sets were upgraded from black and white to color.

{ Chapter 5 } Catching Up with the World (1977-2000)

Unlike the TV, the radio and tape player/recorder was widely available in the 1970s and 1980s. These heavy and cumbersome appliances were key to bringing forms of culture to the rank and file. People got to know the diva Deng Lijun (Teresa Teng) and various bands. People learned pop songs, and the era of the fan emerged. Fashionable young people wore their hair long and donned bell-bottomed trousers, wandering the streets with their heavy and clumsy "ghetto-blasters" in hand. The tape player was made obsolete by the Walkman, VTR recorder, VCD and DVD. These gadgets brought a lot of fun into Chinese households at a time when sources of entertainment were scarce. People are still fond of talking about tape players.

The tape recorder – the bigger the better, 1980

A man fiddling with his newly purchased radio/tape player/ recorder near Chang'an Avenue, early 1980s

{ Chapter 5 } Catching Up with the World (1977-2000)

A fashionable youth with his trusty Walkman in 1982

The portable Walkman became available in China in the 1980s and replaced the large and heavy tape player. It was much loved by young people, who enjoyed having a status symbol to show off, as much as taking their pop music with them wherever they went.

"Walkie-talkie" ownership was synonymous with wealth in the 1990s

"Walkie-talkie" was the nickname given the earliest mobile phone — a Motorola 3200. On Nov. 21st, 1987, the first mobile phone model and service became available in Guangdong Province. The price of the phone was 20,000 RMB, with a service admission fee of 6,000 RMB. The call charge was 1 RMB/min. This was of course beyond the financial reach of the general public. The earliest owners were mostly businessmen, and the "Walkie-talkie" was synonymous with wealth, fame and social status.

A computer company in a small alley, Zhongguancun District, Beijing

Computer fever hits China in the early 1990s

In the 1960 and 1970s, computer was hi-tech stuff for a technology elite and little known to the general public. By the early 1980s, computers had become available to ordinary people. Some primary and middle schools began to offer computer courses. In Feb. 1984, two pupils in Shanghai demonstrated computer use to Deng Xiaoping, who declared on the spot that "computer education shall start in primary school," and it became so in eligible institutions. Computers also led to the rise of R&D and commercial business concentrations, such as the well-known Zhongguancun, once a street, and now a district, devoted to electric and electronic products. A computer is a must for every family now, and an important tool in daily life.

Sports and Entertainment

The skating rink in Beihai Park, Beijing, 1979

Northern China knows bitter winters, but the freezing weather also fosters healthy attitudes to bodybuilding and exercise in the long cold months. From Harbin in the Northeast right to Beijing and Tianjin, ice skating was very popular in winter. At that time, indoor skating rinks were not available and people made use of the icy surfaces of their local lakes and rivers. A park with a large lake area was much sought after by skating parties, and before the 1980s, for about 70-80 years, Beihai Park was such a well-known destination. At its peak, the rink area expanded to 30,000 square meters, accommodating 3,000 people. Masquerade skating events were organized where Beijingers turned up dressed as legendary figures, and onlookers considered it a major winter people-watching opportunity.

Hula hoops become all the rage, 1990s

In the 1990 Asian Games, a performer whirling a large hoop around her waist attracted people's attention, and from that moment the hula hoop took the country by storm. The simple circular plastic tube with small balls filling its hollow interior to make a whooping sound, performed the role of primary bodybuilding equipment for most families. People could be seen everywhere either in the early morning or after dinner whirling the hula hoop around their waists. The astonishing hula hoop fad in China mirrored the madness of its popularity in the West decades earlier, and inspired the pursuit of a healthy lifestyle.

Playing the guitar and catching water fleas were among the pastimes of urban children in the 1980s.

Mu Tiezhu, basketball star, 1981

At 2.28 meters, Mu became the icon of Chinese basketball in the 1970s and 1980s. His excellent skills made Mu the core of the Bayi Basketball Team. He once set a domestic scoring record of 80 points in one game. Under his leadership, the Chinese basketball team won its first gold medal in the Asian Games. Mu was declared the No. 1 center of Asian basketball in the 1980s, and remained a star and a legend of the sport in China. Once he was swarmed by fans while attempting to make his way into Donglaishun Restaurant, and only with great difficulty escaped the crowd to take refuge inside. People were not only amazed by his skills on the court, but also inspired by the indomitable young spirit he embodied, enhanced by his height, perseverance, sense of honor and charm.

Ma Junren and his trainees rise to fame, 1993

During the Stuttgart Track and Field Championship, Chinese athletes Wang Junxia, Qu Yunxia and Liu Dong took gold medals for the 10,000 meters, 3,000 meters and 1,500 meters, respectively. The world was amazed that they were all from the female track & field team managed by Ma Junren. In the World Marathon Championship held in October of the same year, Ma led his trainees to snatch the top four positions. He and his team broke record after record in global sports events, and people marveled at this new era in the mid- and long-range race he engineered. Ma proudly announced, "I can pick any of my trainees and make him or her a record breaker." His success was hailed by all Chinese. Rumor had it that the secret of Ma's success was the ingestion of turtle meat and turtle blood, and the trend of eating turtle meat caught on quickly. However, Ma's moment in the spotlight didn't last long, as cases of doping overtook his image. He was also criticized for his cruel training methods — some charge actual torture — of his trainees. Finally, the trainees decided to speak out, and Ma's team evaporated. Ma tried to train another group of athletes, but they never set any records.

Young people enjoying disco music at home, 1978

On the Chinese New Year's Eve of 1979, a ballroom dancing event was organized at a networking party in the Great Hall of the People. This kind of dancing was once dismissed as a holdover of "feudalism, capitalism and revisionism," but the party was a clear signal that this dance form was no longer taboo. Trend-conscious young people began to try various other styles of dancing. Disco was in vogue. People gathered in parks regularly in the latest fashions to walk on the wild side with some free-style moves. However, these more informal dances were banned for their "vulgarity and moral corruption." Those throwing private dance parties in their homes were even accused of "organizing an immoral activity" and their supposed corruption was penalized by the law. However the trend toward public recreation and entertainment was unstoppable. By 1985 there were several dance clubs in Beijing, some designed to accommodate thousands. In 1987 the Ministry of Culture and the Ministry of Public Security jointly released the Notice on Improving Dance Hall Management, thus giving the green light to China's entertainment sector.

Students dancing in the open air in Beijing, 1981

Rocking it up on the stage of the Hard Rock Café, Beijing, 1994

{ Chapter 5 } Catching Up with the World (1977-2000)

Films, Music and Performances

Coal carrier and a film poster for Notre Dame, 1979

The French film Notre Dame was dubbed into Chinese by the Shanghai Film Dubbing Workshop in 1972, and was well received due to its seamless translation.

A film poster for *Xiaohua*, 1979

Born into a poor family, the lead character in the movie *Xiaohua* soon lost touch with her relatives in China's social turmoil. As an adult she joined the People's Liberation Army and became a resolute and daring female soldier. During her exploits she became reunited with her family. This story was initially intended for the war film genre; however, its young directors made the decision to blaze a new trail in response to the call for "mind emancipation" from the Central Committee of the CPC. Against the backdrop of war, the film innovatively explored the "human interest dimensions" emphasizing the character's personal joys and sorrows. The film's motives were questioned and criticized on its first review screening. Even the theme song *Sister in Search of Brother* (sung by the famous diva Li Guyi) was labeled decadent music. When the film was sent for final review and approval, the Beijing Film-making Studio organized a review panel made up of party committee members, and representatives of the artistic and technical committees. After heated debate, the head of the studio gave his approval. The film attracted great attention. It put more focus on the humanity and individual sensibility of the heroine, and catered to the needs of the general public as they faced massive social changes at the beginning of reform and opening up. *Xiaohua* is considered a timeless classic in Chinese cinematic history.

A scene from *Love on Lushan Mountain*, 1980

Love on Lushan Mountain was the first romantic drama made in the wake of the Cultural Revolution, and featured an unprecedented kissing scene. The leading lady was played by Zhang Yu, who also broke a wardrobe record by changing costumes 43 times during the filming. Zhang won an award for Best Actress as well as taking the 1st Golden Rooster Awards and Hundred Flowers Awards for a role that touched the heart of everything that mattered in the 1980s China. The stunning success of the film led the Lushan tourism office to set up a small theater that screened it around the clock. At the end of 2002, it took the Guinness record for "the world's longest show time in one theater."

The cast of *Reign Behind a Curtain* was drawn from both China and Hong Kong, with mainland actress Liu Xiaoqing playing Empress Cixi, 1983

People never seem to tire of hearing how Cixi seized control of the Qing Dynasty and controlled affairs of state like a puppet master from behind a curtain. The director was already famous; Li Hanxiang from Hong Kong was joined by actor Liang Jiahui, also from Hong Kong, playing Prince Gong. This film, together with an earlier one called *Burning of the Imperial Palace*, opened up a new chapter in co-productions between the mainland and the island. Director Li successfully combined historical facts with rumors and speculation to reinterpret this pivotal event in modern Chinese history. The film won a special award from the Ministry of Culture in 1983, and later took Best Actor (Liang Jiahui), and Best Art Direction at the 3rd Academy Awards of Hong Kong.

The US blockbuster makes a comeback in Guangzhou, 1984

In 1978 dubbing Superman was a major project for the Shanghai Film Dubbing Workshop, and became another huge success. Early in 1980 Superman II also got a great reception in China. With the founding of the PRC, US film was no more. Beginning in 1978, some Western films with progressive themes were permitted in China. However, US commercial films were still not permitted due to political concerns. After some negotiation, *The Fugitive* (Warner Bros, with Harrison Ford starring) was screened in Beijing, Shanghai and four other cities on Nov. 12th, 1994. This was the first US blockbuster to reach audiences in China, and the population has enjoyed them ever since.

Leading lights of the fifth generation of film directors: Zhang Yimou (*second left*) and Chen Kaige (*first right*). Zhang eventually rose to fame in the 1990s but at the time of this photo was still a greenhorn. The fifth-generation film director is an example of the special jargon used to describe the evolution of Chinese cinema. This generation of young artists graduated from the Department of Film Direction of the Beijing Film Academy (BFA). The Departments of Cinematography and Fine Art were added later. They brought about significant changes in society and culture, and most of them were caught up in the social turmoil of China at a young and impressionable age. Some were sent to the countryside, others joined the army. They experienced first hand the joys and sorrows of the lower social ranks at that time, in the decade-long turmoil bridging the 1960s and 1970s. Armed with a strong sense of history and cultural awareness, they were keen to explore China's cultural traditions and national identity through film-making, and eagerly experimented and innovated, embraced new ideas, and ultimately defined a new approach to the art. Although only a few fell into the fifth-generation category, they gave expression to new perspectives with each film they made, indelibly influencing China's film industry.

Some of the fifth-generation members enjoy international acclaim. Chen Kaige (born in 1951, graduated from BFA in 1982) and Zhang Yimou (born in 1950, also a graduate of BFA) are the best known. Chen's works are enriched with humanity, typically focused on the individual and the triumph of the human spirit. In this sense he is a pioneer among the fifth generation. Zhang's works are emblematic for art direction; he uses strong color contrasts and dramatic sets to present the themes and motifs of a story. Audiences are impressed both with the vivid detail and the grand themes of his works. Both directors are still at the forefront of film making, and their current projects are as full of vigor as their early works.

A scene from *Yellow Earth*, 1984

Yellow Earth is regarded as the surfacing of the fifth generation of Chinese film directors. It was the first time Chen and Zhang worked together. Laced with the authentic folklore of the Northwest, using sharp visual contrasts, and exploring the director's reflections on Chinese culture, the film almost belongs to a genre of its own. Its legacy was a direct impact on the approach to storytelling and genre defining in film that influenced the directors that followed them. Together they comprised the so-called fifth generation. Chen won numerous international awards for this film, and became a leading figure in the national film industry.

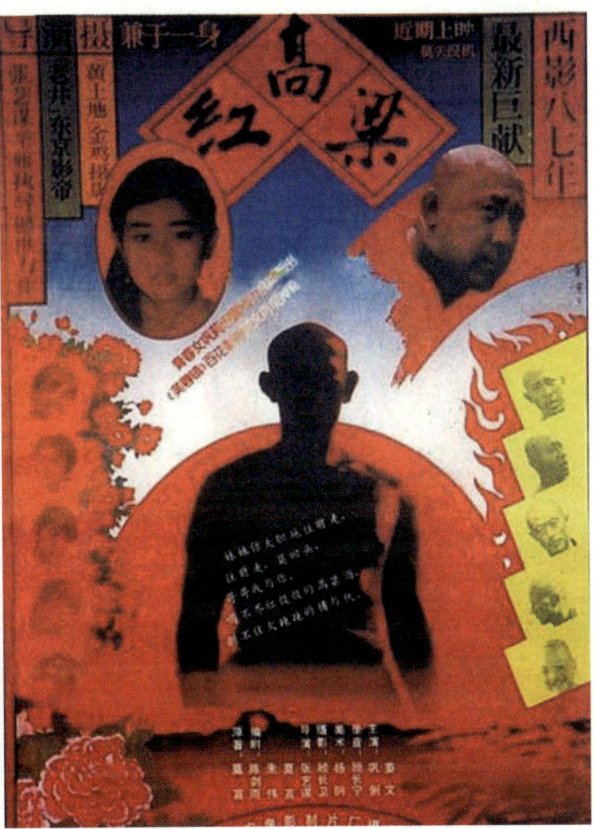

A film poster for *Red Sorghum*, 1987

Red Sorghum is a story about grandparents living in remote northwest China. It highlights the humanity and vitality of the couple, paying tribute to this kind of life in the special parlance of film. It won a Golden Bear Award for Best Story at the 1988 Berlin Film Festival. Zhang subsequently rose to fame, and the leading man (Jiang Wen) and leading lady (Gong Li) also became instant stars in China.

[Chapter 5] Catching Up with the World (1977-2000)

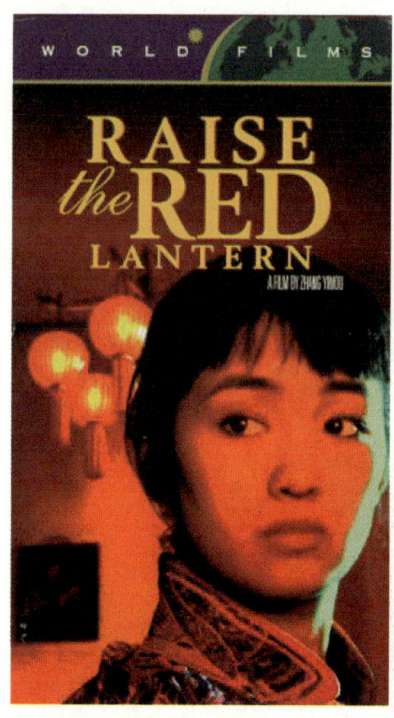

A film poster for *Raise the Red Lantern*, 1991

This film was another major work by Zhang, weaving together the historic, cultural and humanist dimensions of Chinese society through the lens of a concubine struggling in feudal China to survive the horrid and vicious family to which she is attached. But her fate is sealed and her personality becomes twisted instead; she remains a slave to the feudal regime in body, and finally, in spirit. The film electrified China as a work of art, but also launched a long dispute regarding artistic license, since use of a red lantern as depicted is false folklore.

Actors playing the roles of Mao Zedong and Chiang Kai-shek take a break together, 1992

Following the founding of the PRC, films involving Kuomintang figures invariably stereotyped them as either demon or clown. After reform and opening up, China's relationship with Chinese Taiwan and the rest of the world improved greatly, and the Chinese people began to reflect upon their history without political interference. Scripts began to deepen the characters of Kuomintang officials, including Chiang Kai-shek, and take a more objective approach to interpreting their motives and actions. The film *Bloody War at Tai'erzhuang* (1986) acknowledged the Kuomintang's effort against the Japanese invaders, and the film was even appreciated by Chiang Kai-shek's son, Chiang Ching-kuo.

The rebirth of Peking Opera

During the 1996 National Day celebrations, the Mei Lanfang Opera Troupe hosted a special performance of "The Essence of Mei Lanfang" at the newly built Chang'an Grand Theatre. Mei Lanfang's role was played by his son Mei Baojiu (in the middle), and the four other players, who hailed from the Chinese mainland, Hong Kong and Chinese Taiwan, were all disciples of Mei's school of performance.

The end of the Cultural Revolution was also marked by a revival of exemplary plays. Traditional performance arts began to make a comeback, but were faced with challenges, not the least of which was the loss of competent performers and avid young audiences. In response, the operatic performers began to break out of stereotyped performance models and plays, and created new forms of theater with innovations in singing style, accompaniment, backgrounds and props. Some even tried to incorporate Western opera and drama techniques into Peking Opera. The traditional art form continues to evolve with great vitality, despite heated disputes over direction and taste.

Teresa Teng, diva from Chinese Taiwan

New songs by Teng released on the Chinese mainland

No one had more widespread influence on the Chinese mainland than Teresa Teng (1953-1995). After the Cultural Revolution, tape recorder-players became available to Chinese families, and this paved the way for Teng's discovery and swift popularity. Her sweet, gentle voice and amiable appearance were an unprecedented and exciting experience for young people who had been constrained by revolutionary propaganda for so long. Her standards, such as *So Sweet*, *Story of a Small Town* and *The Moon Is My Heart*, echoed the pursuit of individuality that preoccupied the young. Her songs were sung by many, and even her curly hair and brightly colored dresses were copied. Her voice was once criticized as decadent and her albums banned from sale in China, but this didn't stop people from adoring her.

In the early days, some people even tried to use their tape recorders to record from another player, and these crude copies spread her songs from person to person. Many mainland divas tried to imitate her style in the early 1980s. Even today, a lot of her fans still love and play her songs, despite the fact that Teng died more than a decade ago, and she never gave a single concert on China's mainland. In 2008, *A Wish for Eternal Lovers*, one of Teng's masterpieces, was played on the Shenzhou VII spaceship. In 2009, an online survey called for nominations for outstanding cultural figures in China. Teresa Teng topped the list with 8.5 million votes, an astonishing testimony to the endurance of her art and influence.

Cui Jian, godfather of hard rock in China

In 1986, Cui Jian ignited audiences everywhere he played with his famous lyric *I Ask Time and Time Again.* The beat and rhythm, together with his characteristic vocals, set free a long-suppressed spirit in the Chinese. His song *Nothing to Lose* was a smash hit in the late 1980s. Whoever heard this song was impressed by his roaring delivery, and felt the courage to face life and destiny. Following Cui's lead, hard rock music spread like wildfire across the country and stirred up emotions and desires in the populace.

Pavarotti in Beijing, 1986

Pavarotti in concert, 1986

In 1986, the world-famous Italian tenor Pavarotti brought the 200-strong Genoa Theater Troupe (plus some fans) to China. In June-July, the troupe staged 6 performances of La Boheme at the Tianqiao Theater in Beijing. Despite the somewhat substandard equipment at the theatre, the Genoa Theater Troupe rehearsed with great gusto. Chinese audiences were correspondingly very eager to pay tribute to Pavarotti and most appreciative of his live performances. Each show concluded with a standing ovation. It is said the longest lasted for 6 minutes, generally considered long for an opera.

At another performance held at the Beijing Exhibition Theater, he returned to the stage 15 times to acknowledge the ovation, and generously gave 5 encores on top of the 12 selections he sang. The encores lasted even longer than the original performance time. The July 4 concert held in the Great Hall of the People made history; Pavarotti became the first foreigner to give a concert inside the famous venue, which turned out to be the largest indoor concert of his career. Although the Great Hall is not deemed suitable for opera, the show was still very successful, and Pavarotti himself was also greatly moved. When he retired afterwards into a Red Flag Limousine, he commented, "This is the pinnacle of my career."

People say that Pavarotti's trip to China opened up a window for the Chinese to appreciate Western opera, as well as erecting a milestone in the cultural exchange between China and Western countries. Pavarotti clearly cherished the China tour, declaring it "one of my most fabulous experiences, and one I will never forget."

Concert by Richard Clayderman, 1992

In 1992, French pianist Richard Clayderman came to China for a public performance. His cross-over style of classics with modernism, plus his sensitive performance and impressive background, won Clayderman immediate popularity. He was known as the "prince of the piano." Since then Clayderman has come to China for 13 appearances. He adapted and played a lot of Chinese music, including *Red Sun*, *Big River*, *Butterfly Love*, and *Fickle Love*, which surprised and delighted Chinese music fans. Meanwhile, Clayderman also contributed to promoting the piano in China. As an idol of pianists, his elegant style changed the stereotyped concepts held by the Chinese on how the classics should be played. Piano lessons for children enjoyed a wave of popularity across the country, and grand and upright instruments were sold out in every city.

A scene from *Turandot*, Forbidden City, 1998

 Zubin Mehta, a renowned Indian conductor, led musicians from the Florence Festival Theater in a reinterpretation of Puccinni's classic *Turandot*, infusing it with Eastern elements and setting the story in Beijing. On the night of September 5, 1998, it opened in the Forbidden City itself, directed by Zhang Yimou in the Imperial Ancestral Temple which had been turned into a grand theater. An audience of 3,500 people from around the world was invited to enjoy the show. Zhang Yimou infused Chinese culture into this Italian opera giving it new layers of mystery and exoticism. The grand staging within the temple completed what was, for the lucky audience, an amazing experience.

Foreign singers at the Beijing International Tourism Festival

China is no longer constrained by the caution and trepidation it felt 30 years ago. China and the Chinese people embrace artists and performance troupes from around the world with enthusiasm and pleasure. Political and ideological filters are no more, and people can enjoy the world's art and its entertainers to their heart's content. China is integrating with the world, and the world is beginning to learn more about China.

Chapter 6

Merging with the World

(2001~2012)

Transportation

Train designed and manufactured by Qingdao Sifang Rolling Stock Co. in use on the Baotou-Shenmu Railway, 2002

In order to accelerate the speed of the country's trains and meet the demand for short route travel among China's cities, Qingdao Sifang Rolling Stock Co. designed and manufactured a train unit for the Baotou-Shenmu Railway. With a maximum velocity of 100 kph, the unit was praised both for its high speed and roomy accommodations. However, with the progress of science and technology, its internal-combustion hydraulic power engine soon became virtually obsolete, and the unit is now used only on the Baotou-Shenmu Railway. Compared with other electrified train units, it is now the slowest.

The Beijing-Shanghai Electrified Railway, 2006

Bidding farewell to the internal-combustion locomotive, China started a new journey in transportation with the 1,464-km-long Beijing-Shanghai Railway. As an integral part of China's railway network, this route connects the Bohai and Yangtze Delta regions, parts of China that enjoy advanced social and economic development. This route also has the distinction, both at home and abroad, of carrying the highest volume of rail transportation loads. The route opened for use in 2006, with a designed speed of 200 kph. It accelerated travel speeds, reduced transport costs, improved logistics and enhanced carrying capacity.

The first train on the Qinghai-Tibet Railway crosses Hete Bridge, Lhasa.

The building of the Qinghai-Tibet Railway was a powerful phase in the strategy to develop China's West, and one of four landmark engineering feats in China. The railway starts from Xining, Qinghai Province, in the east and ends at Lhasa, capital of the Tibet Autonomous Region. The 1,956-km-long route makes this the longest stretch of rail at the highest latitude in the world. It made and broke several records that guarantee it a prominent place in the history of world railway construction. Marshalling human resources and logistics, it opened for use on July 1, 2006. A wave of Tibet tourism followed, contributing to cultural exchanges, and a revving up of industrial and tertiary industry development in the remote region. The railway brought a host of blessings to farmers on route as well, and attracted private investors and consortiums both domestic and foreign who sought access to the optimized investment structures of a new and open Tibet.

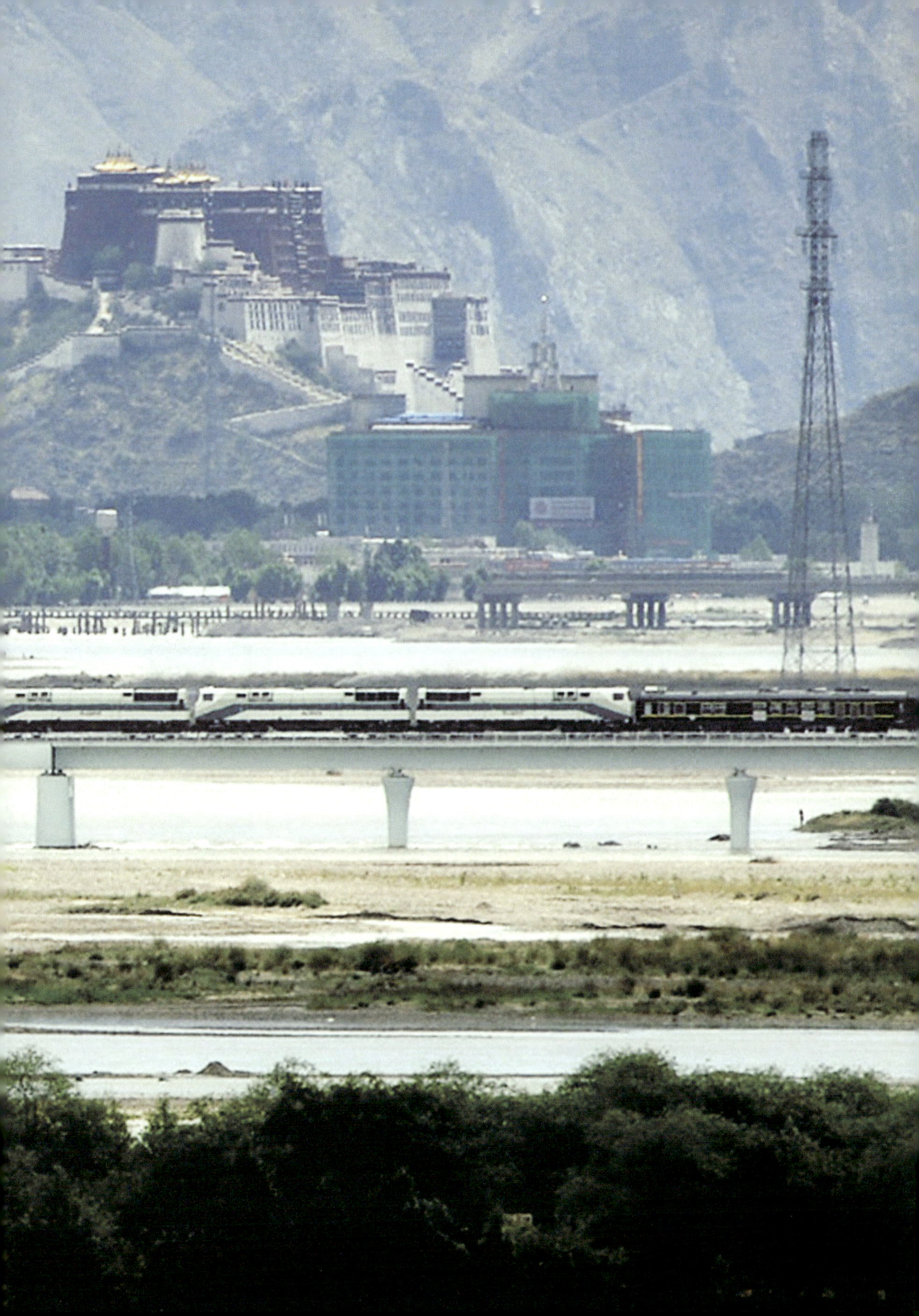

Maglev high-speed railway in Shanghai

The Shanghai Maglev High-speed Railway, the very first commercial maglev route in the world, was completed in 2002, with a maximum design speed of 430 kph, which put it second only to air travel. The route is 30 km long, starting from Subway Line 2 and ending at Pudong International Airport. It not only serves as a high-speed transport route connecting the airport with the city, but a tourism sightseeing option as well. Entering the 21st century, continuous economic development and social progress require the development of a high-speed rail transportation system in line with the country's increasing transportation loads. The high-speed maglev was among the solutions.

The first high-speed railway line in western China under construction, 2011 – Chengdu-Mianyang-Leshan Route

On the night of Dec. 29, 2008, construction began on the first intra-city high-speed railway line in western China, the Chengdu-Mianyang-Leshan route. The modern trunk line connecting these three cities contributed to the urbanization drive in western China, social and economic integration, coordinated regional development, and the opening up and development of more domestic and international markets.

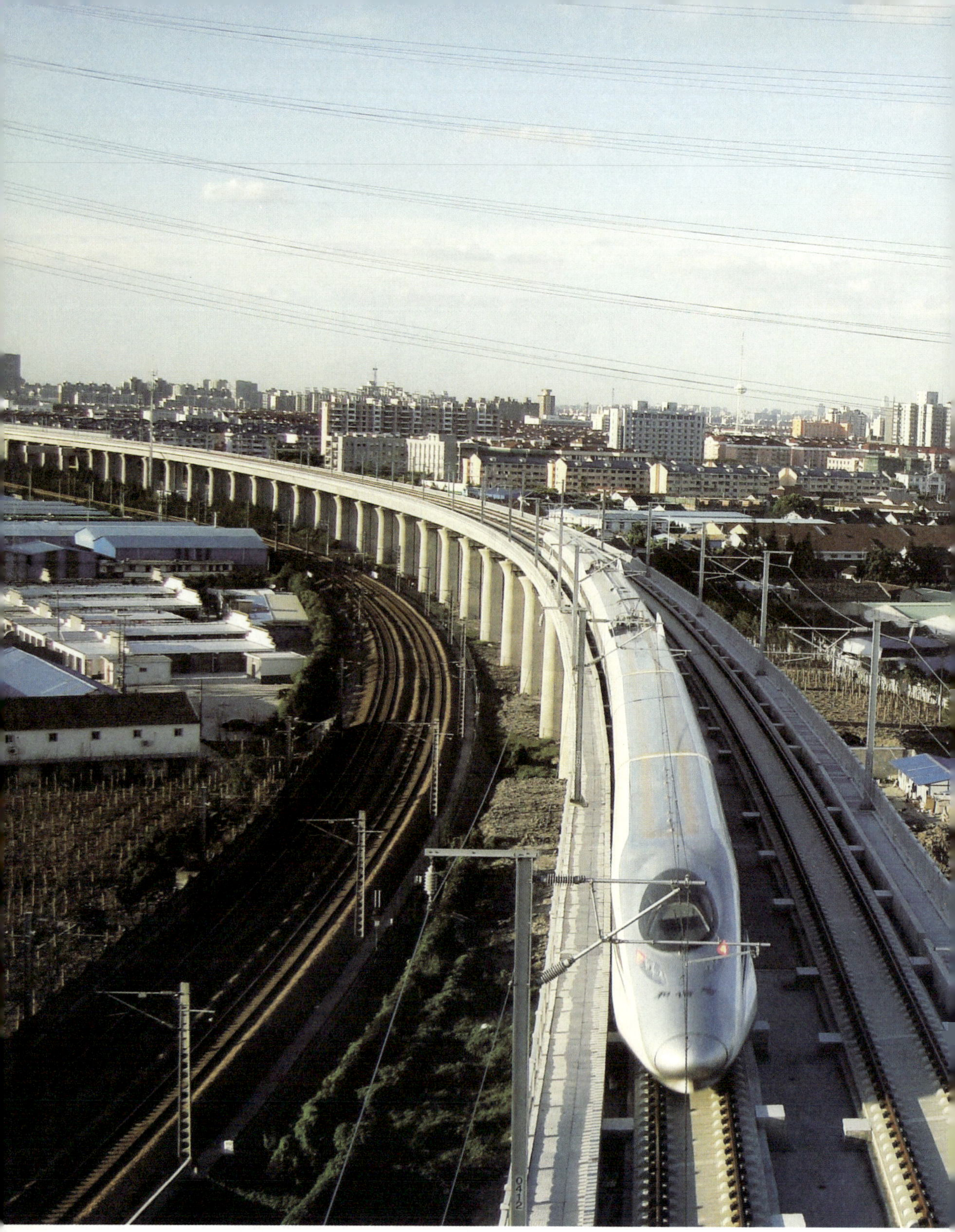

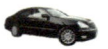

The first homegrown China Railway High-speed (CRH) train with IPR, 2008

China successfully designed its own technology for a high-speed train unit that suited the country's geographic challenges. On June 29, 2008, the first 16-car CRH was completed, boasting a design speed of 200-250 kph. These homegrown units draw upon advanced technology and enjoy intellectual property right (IPR) protection. Prior to the 2008 Beijing Olympic Games, the first CRH was put into operation on the Beijing-Tsingtao route to meet the upcoming transportation demand.

Shanghai-Hangzhou CRH opens for service, 2010

The Shanghai-Hangzhou route connects these two cities, stretching the high-speed transport network into the Yangtze Delta region that is home to a dense population and a flurry of economic exchanges. It contributes to simultaneous and coordinated activity among cities in the delta, accelerates logistics for its mobile population, capital and information, and promotes the integration of the Yangtze Delta region. The carrier for this route is the CRH380A, a new-generation powered train unit. With a designed speed of 350 kph, this technically advanced train holds the world record for running speed.

A breakthrough in arch bridge design both for Chinese and world engineering, the experience gained during its construction set the stage for China's railway technology to go global.

MODERN CHINA IN PICTURES

Ningbo Harbor ranks among the major harbors of the world

Ningbo Harbor has a 1,200-year-long history, but today it is a multi-functional and comprehensive deepwater port. Serving as river, estuary and sea port, Ningbo is a mega feeder port of ships to various parts of China and is also among a very few oceanic node ports in the world. Its 21st century makeover moved Ningbo Harbor onto the fast track of container transportation. The harbor ranked among the top 10 ports in the world in 2008, and jumped to world No. 1 in cargo throughput in 2011. The development of the harbor gave rise to an oil refinery and sectors devoted to garment manufacturing, agriculture and other businesses. The cucumber, strawberry, tomato and other products grown in this area reach the tables of Japanese and Korean consumers within 24 hours, earning it the title of "international vegetable basket."

Light rail service opens in Beijing, 2003

On January 28, 2003, a light rail service opened in Beijing. This U-shape route is 40.8 km long, and is the longest urban high-speed rail route in China. Each train is made up of three carriages, with a load capacity of 600 passengers. Its minimum interval is 4 minutes, and maximum design speed 80 kph.

Worsening traffic jams in Beijing, 2010

The new millennium also ushered in the traffic jam, a phenomenon that continues to be a big headache for China's urban giants. Economic growth is raising the average disposable income, so private car ownership is increasingly common. In Beijing for example, by July 10, 2011, autos on the capital's roads totaled 4,927,000. Meanwhile road construction in Beijing lagged behind the needs of drivers and their vehicles. The traffic jam is now a factor in formulating local travel plans.

China is one of the world's largest luxury car markets

The Chang'an Automobile debuts in Cuba

Booming automobile market in Beijing, 2008

Improved livelihoods and broader consumption capacity have changed Chinese demands for consumer goods; the bike, watch, and sewing machine were eclipsed by the computer, automobile and housing. Private auto ownership increases by 20% annually and currently stands at 30 million, more than 20 times the figure before reform and opening up. The picture illustrates the booming auto market.

Fashion Leaders

Textile mill, Jiangsu Province, 2010

Hai'an has ancient roots — 5,000 years of history in what is now Jiangsu Province - and also enjoys a national profile as a revolutionary base. Hai'an was home to a number of influential figures in Chinese history and is known as the birthplace of silk. It currently has the largest production base for high-quality silkworms, topping Jiangsu's silkworm output for 24 consecutive years. The textile and silk industry in Hai'an has given rise to a complete industrial chain of weaving, printing, dyeing and finished product assembly. Its embroidered clothing is known to the world as a "treasure of the East."

A textile workshop of the Youngor Group in Ningbo, the largest clothes export company in Zhejiang Province

Reform and opening-up breathed new life into private companies. Established in 1979, Youngor acquired Xinma Apparel Group, the core menswear business belonging to KELLWOOD, and became one of the major menswear companies in the world. After 30 years of development and diversification, Youngor now has three pillars: clothing, real estate development and equity investment. It has emerged as a large-scale multinational company with more than 50,000 employees, and its Youngor Group Co., Ltd. is a listed company.

Fashionable clothes on the street, 2010

The significant changes brought about in the 1980s have also affected how the Chinese dress. The time when everyone wore clothes of the same style and color has long passed; today, the color, style and texture of clothes changes by the minute. Long before they entered the new century, the Chinese expected to express their individuality via their wardrobe. Today, "following suit" is unthinkable, and what is in fashion has become hard to define by style or color.

The 2000 World Brand Exhibition

China goes for luxury.

First trip to Shanghai

{ Chapter 6 } Merging with the World (2001-2012) | 297

The Three-Gorges Dam is the largest hydro-power project in the world, with comprehensive flood control, power generation, navigation features and a water supply role.

The Chinese plans to treat and use the water resources from the Three Gorges of Yangtze River were in place long before 2009 when the Three-Gorges project was finally completed. It is the largest engineering project in China's history, and also the largest hydropower station in the world. The project generated great controversy and endless disputes from the first day of construction. However, three benefits are indisputable, namely, flood control, power generation and shipping facilitation, with anti-flood measures being a life-saving public good.

Dayawan Nuclear Power Plant goes into commercial operation, May 2007

Energy sourcing while limiting environmental problems poses a severe challenge to modern China. Giving full play to nuclear power is a sound way to increase the power supply and reduce GHG emissions. Currently there are 11 operating nuclear reactors in China, with 10 new reactors expected to come on stream soon, meaning that in the coming decade, the number of nuclear power plants built in China will be three times all the planned reactor construction in all other countries combined. Dayawan Nuclear Power Plant went into commercial operation in May 2007, making its mark as the largest joint project ever undertaken by China and Russia. The plant enjoys geographic, geologic and hydrologic advantages, and is capable of 60-70 billion kwh of power generation with an output value of over 25 billion RMB.

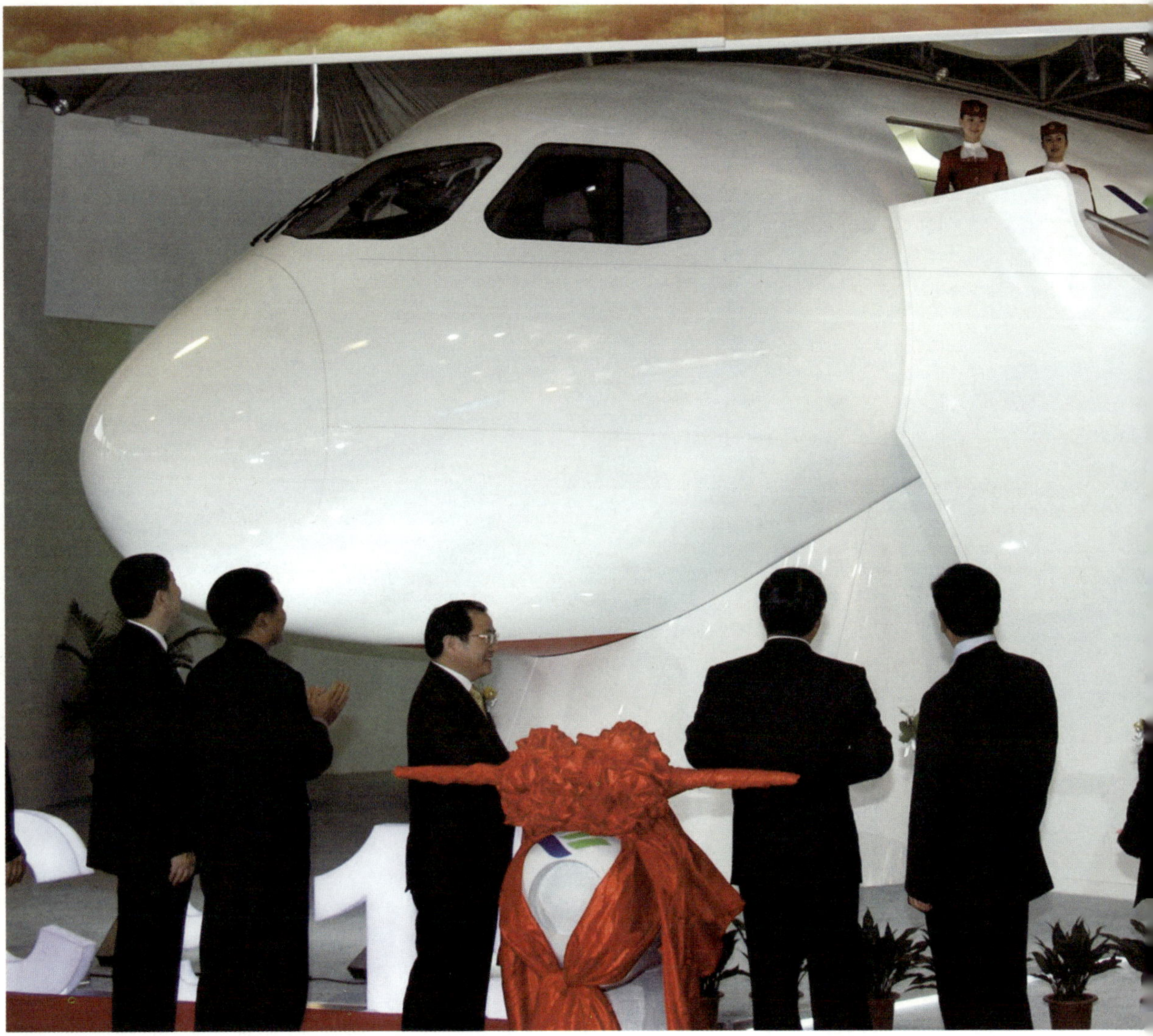

C919 airliner prototype produced by China goes on show at the International Aviation and Aerospace Exhibition, November 2010

In C919, C stands for the first letter in China, and is also the first letter in COMAC (Commercial Aircraft Corporation of China Ltd.). The code implies that China will compete with Airbus and Boeing. The first number, "9", means eternity, and the final digits "19" reflect a seating capacity of 190 people. The future evolution of the C919 may be named C929, where "29" refers to 290 passengers.

Astronaut Yang Liwei walks unaided from the cabin of his space ship, Shenzhou V, at 6:23 on October 16, 2003, after completing the first orbit of the Earth by a Chinese astronaut.

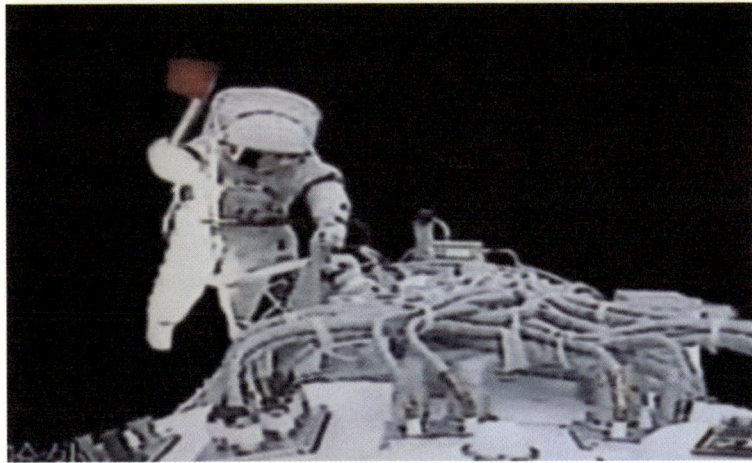

On September 25, 2008, the Shenzhou VII manned spaceship was launched, and astronaut Zhai Zhigang made China's frist space walk.

On September 25, 2008, China's third manned spaceship — Shenzhou VII — headed into space, carrying astronaut Zhai Zhigang who was the first Chinese to carry out tests on outside the spacecraft. Manned spaceship flights reflect the strength of a country's science and technology sectors, but the "walk in space" is a clear mark of a country's advancements in aviation and aerospace. This launch signaled to the world that China is now a potential partner or collaborator in aerospace programs. The Chinese left their footprint in outer space, erecting a milestone of China's exploration in this field but also laying the foundation for China to set up a space station in the future. The launch was broadcast and covered by the Chinese media in an open and transparent fashion, expressing the country's intentions with respect to the peaceful use of outer space.

At about 10 o'clock on June 29, 2012 the return capsule of the Shenzhou IX manned spacecraft landed safely in Inner Mongolia, after manual docking between the Shenzhou IX and the orbiting Tiangong-I lab module. In the picture, the three Chinese astronauts Jing Haipeng, Liu Wang and Liu Yang, salute after leaving the return capsule.

{ Chapter 6 } Merging with the World (2001-2012)

海洋石油 117
HAI YANG SHI YOU

Launching of China's first Floating Production Storage and Offloading (FPSO) of 300,000 tonnage in Shanghai, 2006

As early as the 15th century, China already had the most advanced shipbuilding capacity and the largest oceanic fleet in the world, reaching Asian and African countries seven times. But China's shipbuilding capacity lagged behind soon after its zenith. Following reform and opening up, attention once more returned to China's shipyards and the Central Government moved to restore their former glory. China's capacity is so advanced now that some of the world's leading ships are manufactured right here. On December 8, 2006, a 300,000-ton FPSO manufactured by Shanghai Waigaoqiao Shipbuilding Co., Ltd. was launched to much fanfare in Shanghai. This ship features cutting-edge technology, with a deck area that could accommodate three football fields. This FPSO can process 190,000 barrels of quality crude oil, and its oil storage capacity is two million barrels.

Modern agriculture in China, 2008

The modernization of agriculture is still an integral part of China's economic and social development. A key turning point and priority in this process is the creation of an agricultural industrial system. In 2007, the Chinese Government moved to equip the agricultural sector with a better command of its physical conditions, introduced modern science and technology, promoted a modern operational mode, led agricultural reform with modern concepts, and trained farmers, so as to promote the general modernization of this core economic field.

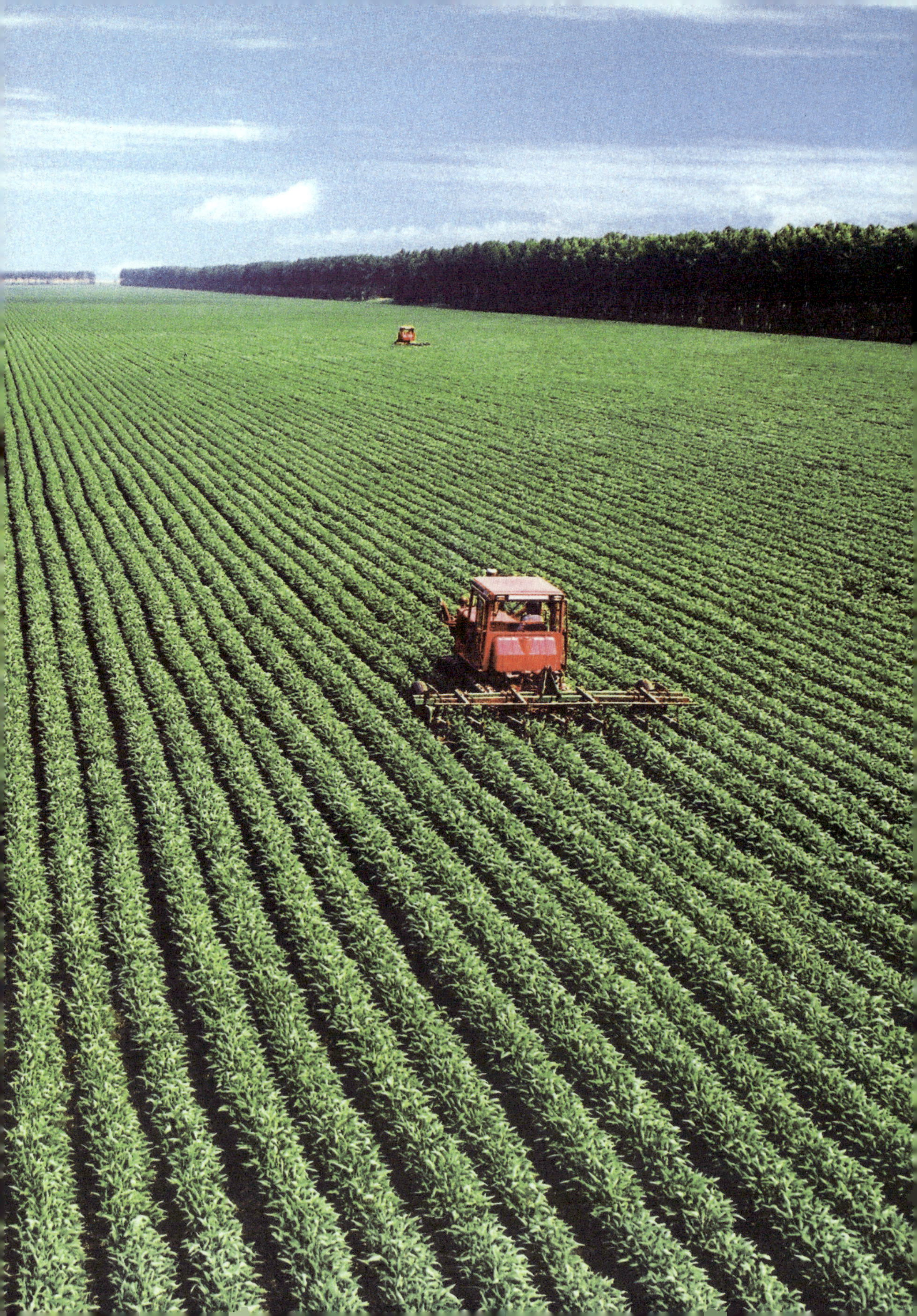

Jiang Peng, a pig breeder, is excited by a technical manual given to him by village official Wang Ya (on the right).

A college graduate from a program in livestock-raising, Wang took the job as assistant director at Hexin Village, a position that gave full play to his knowledge of pig breeding. Making contact with other pig breeders and providing a guide book free of charge was a friendly way to encourage change. The village saw improvements and was able to expand its business scale despite a downturn in the pork market. The county launched a project called "one university graduate per village" in 2006, and now there are 120 graduates working as village officials in 100 villages.

China's toy export sector enjoys strong growth, with the US being the most significant destination.

New Urban Landscape

Chang'an Avenue in 2009

The decorative lights along Chang'an Avenue are major sources of illumination during festivals. These lamps were designed and erected on the 10th anniversary of the People's Republic of China in conjunction with the expansion project of Tian'anmen Square and ten monumental architectural projects underway at that time. Experts from the Soviet Union also assisted in the design of this lamp model. Finally, it was Premier Zhou Enlai who selected the ball-type lamp from among several proposed designs. In 2009, the lighting facilities were part of large-scale renovations and subject to upgrading for celebrations marking the 60th anniversary of the People's Republic of China. Mercury lights and lights without electrodes replaced the incandescent type, so that the lighting of Chang'an Avenue has reached international advanced standards and can be manipulated for color and intensity.

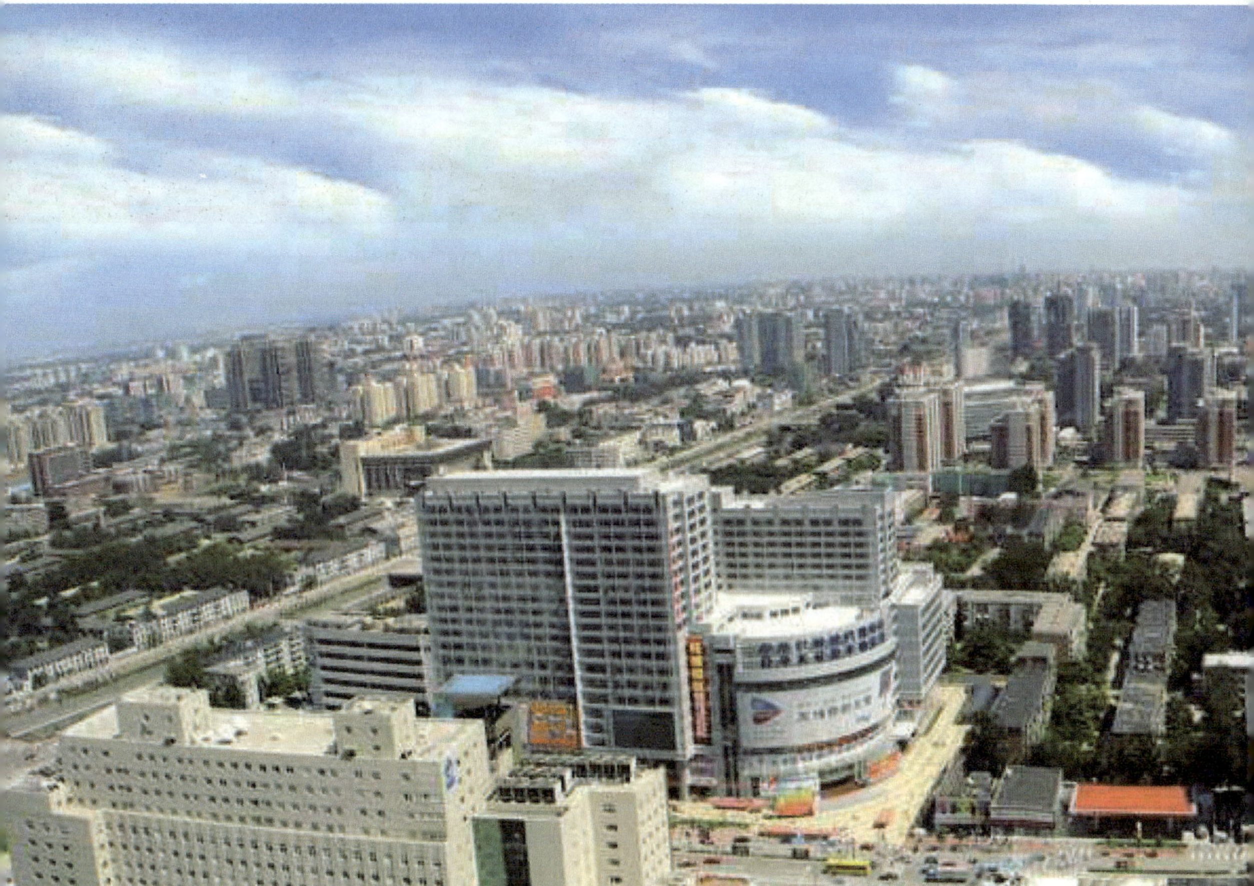

China's Silicon Valley, 2008 – Zhongguancun

China's hi-tech center, Zhongguancun is home to high-end talent in IT innovation. It is a showcase of China's strategic choices and serves as the breeding ground for this emerging industry that is of such strategic importance to the nation. Zhongguancun is a platform for resource integration and innovation, a haven for venture capital seekers and a global village for open cooperation. The miracle of Zhongguancun is the epitome of the modernization drive in Chinese cities.

Nanjing Road, Shanghai, 2010

Nanjing Road is still today among the most famous and prosperous commercial streets in China. It became known as the No. 1 commercial street in China when it became the first of its kind to open up for business in the city of Shanghai. Nanjing Road runs through a world-class commercial district, comparable to 5th Avenue in New York, the Champs Elysee in Paris, Oxford Street in London or the Ginza in Tokyo. It is home to numerous brands, and serves as a window on Shanghai and a shopping center for buyers at home and abroad.

Beginning in 1978, Nanjing Road underwent significant changes both in its outer appearance and interior decoration. All the brands of the world flock to this road to take their place in the large new commercial buildings that stand side by side with century-old department stores, brand flagships and signature outlets. The classic, the modern and the romantic intertwine to create the distinctive feel of this century-old commercial street. Elegance and fashion predominate in a place that becomes a neon wonderland after dark, one of the great nightscapes of Shanghai.

City God Temple, Shanghai, 2010

With more than 600 years of history, Shanghai's City God Temple is a piece of architecture that has also changed with the times. In the past, there used to be various peddlers around the Temple, such as tinkers, bucket binders, figure modelers, magicians, peep show touts, tooth extractors, fortune-tellers… but these people are no more, gone with snuff boxes, dental cream, thermos stoppers, thimbles and feather dusters. The place that used to be a showcase of life at the grassroots now welcomes tourists from around the world.

{ Chapter 6 } Merging with the World (2001-2012)

Unusual signature products on display

Shanghai Innovative Industrial Park is home to a number of stores featuring unusual signature products. On March 26, 2007, these stores hosted a fair to showcase ceramics modelled on Chinese clothing styles, attracting visitors from home and abroad. These handmade vases are inspired by traditional Chinese clothes, such as the traditional Chinese men's outer garment, the Cheongsam with its blue patterns, the Chinese cape and even traditional underwear. These novelties are well received by visitors for their traditional Chinese flavor.

Changing a hairstyle in a minute

The view beyond the window

Feature product fair at Shi Kumen, Shanghai

{ Chapter 6 } Merging with the World (2001-2012)

Landscape along the Pearl River in Guangzhou, 2010

In 2010, the torch for the Asian Games was lit in Guangzhou. The Pearl River coursing through Guangzhou was successfully treated for pollution and bade farewell to industrial discharge. The river is now crystal-clear like the Seine at Paris.

{ Chapter 6 } Merging with the World (2001-2012)

Landscape along the Haihe River, Tianjin, 2008

The Haihe River and its neighborhood testify to Tianjin's transformation over the past 600 years, in particular its recent urban construction drive.

Xinjiekou, Nanjing, 2009

Xinjiekou is the name of a street in Nanjing. When Nanjing became the national capital in 1927, Xinjiekou gradually became the center of its emerging commerce, finance and entertainment, and also claimed to be the No. 1 commercial center in China. This century-old street has become a business complex for shopping, catering, accommodation and recreation.

{ Chapter 6 } Merging with the World (2001-2012)

Migrant workers fixing steel bars in Hai'an City, Jiangsu Province

A farmer gazing at Jinan City

{ Chapter 6 } Merging with the World (2001-2012)

Migrant workers coming to Nanjing, 2004

In 2003, China abolished a series of unjustifiable regulations, removing barriers to rural people wishing to work in cities. And the government moved to protect the rights and interests of these mobile populations. China's central government called on local governments to eliminate the eligibility review and approval process for migrant workers joining urban enterprises, to cancel the occupational limits for migrant workers, and to abolish the administration fee for reviewing and registering such workers. The original bureaucratic restrictions were gradually replaced by a temporary residence permit. Migrant workers in urban areas are entitled to similar employment legislation and social insurance coverage as urban people.

A veteran standing on the square dressed in the uniform of the 1970s complete with two Chairman Mao badges, an eye-catching sight for passers-by

{ Chapter 6 } Merging with the World (2001-2012)

Lifestyle

The produce section of a supermarket, 2010

In 1978, the supermarket was introduced into China, and was originally referred to as a self-service grocery store. Beijing's first supermarket opened for business in 1983 in the city's Haidian District, serving mostly foreign buyers. In the early 1990s, foreign supermarkets began to enter China, and years later, domestic supermarkets followed suit. The state-owned vegetable store was history, and people today are quite accustomed to buying vegetables from the produce section of the supermarket. The diversified supply of vegetables creates a very different experience from the limited choice and enforced use of coupons that characterized the planned economy. People have increased demands on the dining experience as well, as they require not only delicious food, but a nutritionally balanced diet as well. The demand for fresh and more fruits and vegetables, and the rejection of high-fat and high cholesterol food, all signal the arrival of a more sophisticated shopper and eater. Edible wild herbs and grains, once eaten simply to satisfy hunger, have become trendy new health foods.

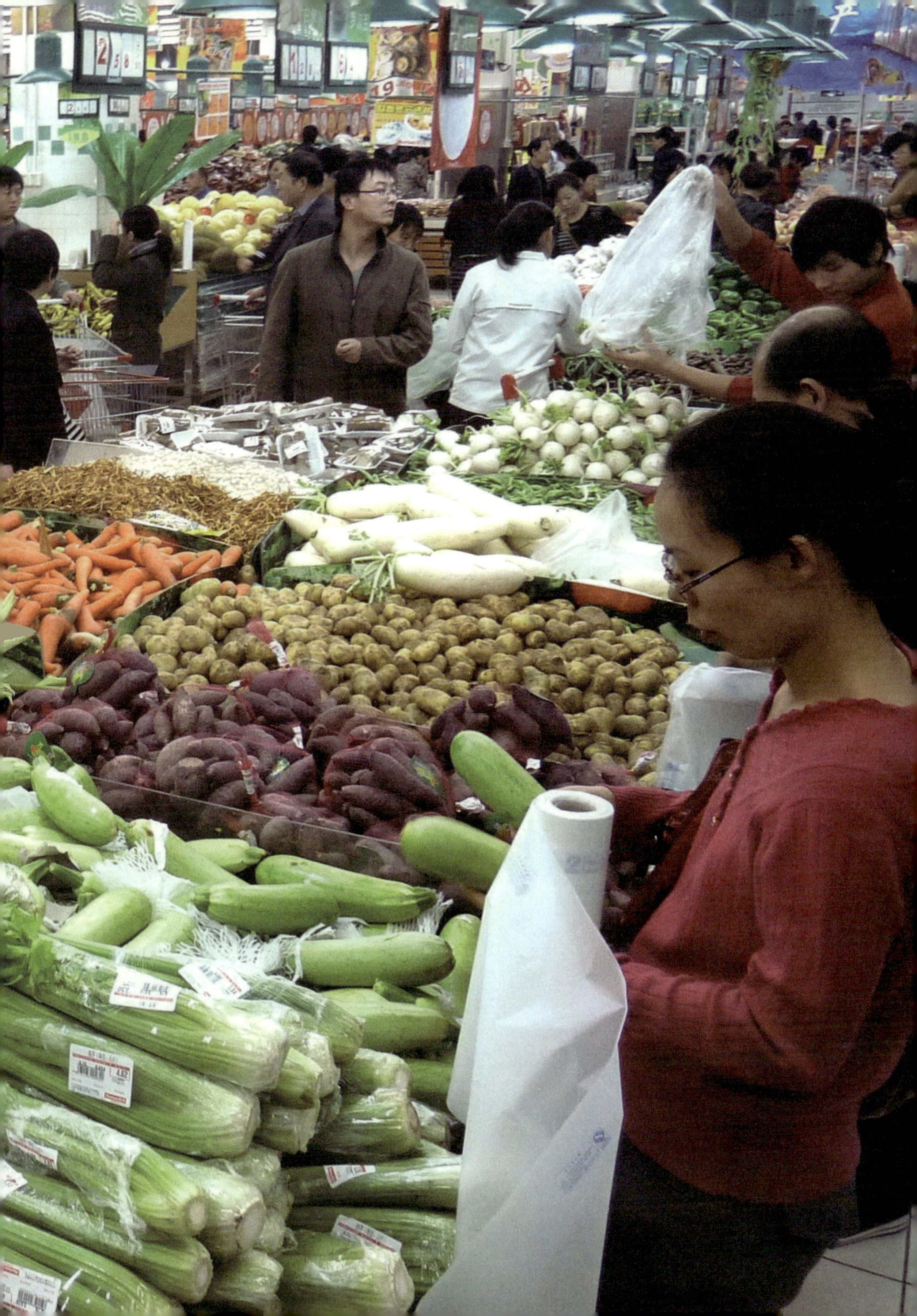

The creative wedding photo is the hallmark of young Chinese newlyweds, 2010

This is the pose a young couple chose for their wedding photo at an overpass in Beijing. Chinese youths have become increasingly fashion-conscious and globally aware. The wedding photo is no longer a memento hung on the wall to recall a moment of happiness and sweetness; it is more a showcase of individuality, romance and innovation in a partnership.

Touched by the scene in Shanghai

On September 29, 2008, a wedding service company displays a range of wedding photos with novel themes on Guanqian Street, Suzhou, and draws the sidewalk strollers.

On November 16, 2008, Yang Qinglan, a 72-year-old lady from a county in Henan Province lines up for her wedding photo at a wedding service store.

With the encouragement of their descendents, many elderly people from the countryside have began to stage the wedding photo they didn't commission at the time.

{ Chapter 6 } Merging with the World (2001-2012)

A newly-wed couple running for joy on their way home

Emotions run high in a pub in Shanghai

332 | MODERN CHINA IN PICTURES

Father and daughter touring a park, 2003

Improved living standards mean parents have more time to play with their children, and do so in more diverse ways. This girl holds a sunflower and straddles her father's shoulders to attend a festival in a park.

{ Chapter 6 } Merging with the World (2001-2012) | 333

Olympic Games fever during the summer of 2008 in Beijing

A 100-year-old woman with bound feet doing morning exercises

On May 20, 2009 Li Tao, a 100-year-old woman with bound feet, did morning exercises in Luopu Park, Luoyang City, Henan Province.

{ Chapter 6 } Merging with the World (2001-2012)

Foreign students in Henan learn Shaolin martial arts.

"Kungfu Panda" doing physical exercises on a cold winter morning

On December 17, 2011 a giant panda introduced from Sichuan Province to Taihu National Wetland Park, Suzhou City, Jiangsu Province, braved the bitter cold to do morning exercises outside its cage.

The golden years after retirement

Grandpa and grandson enjoy blowing bubbles.

{ Chapter 6 } Merging with the World (2001-2012)

The Xi'an Federation of Trade Unions took the initiative to hold a re-employment fair for laid-off workers in 2005.

On March 13, 2005, the Xi'an Federation of Trade Unions organized the 2005 re-employment job fair, convincing 340 companies to offer 7,500 job opportunities to laid-off workers. Many companies and communities also dispatched buses to carry their unemployed to the fair. More than 20,000 jobseekers attended, with 2,800 signing work contracts on site, and 3,600 eligible people establishing contact with companies who intended to find them placements.

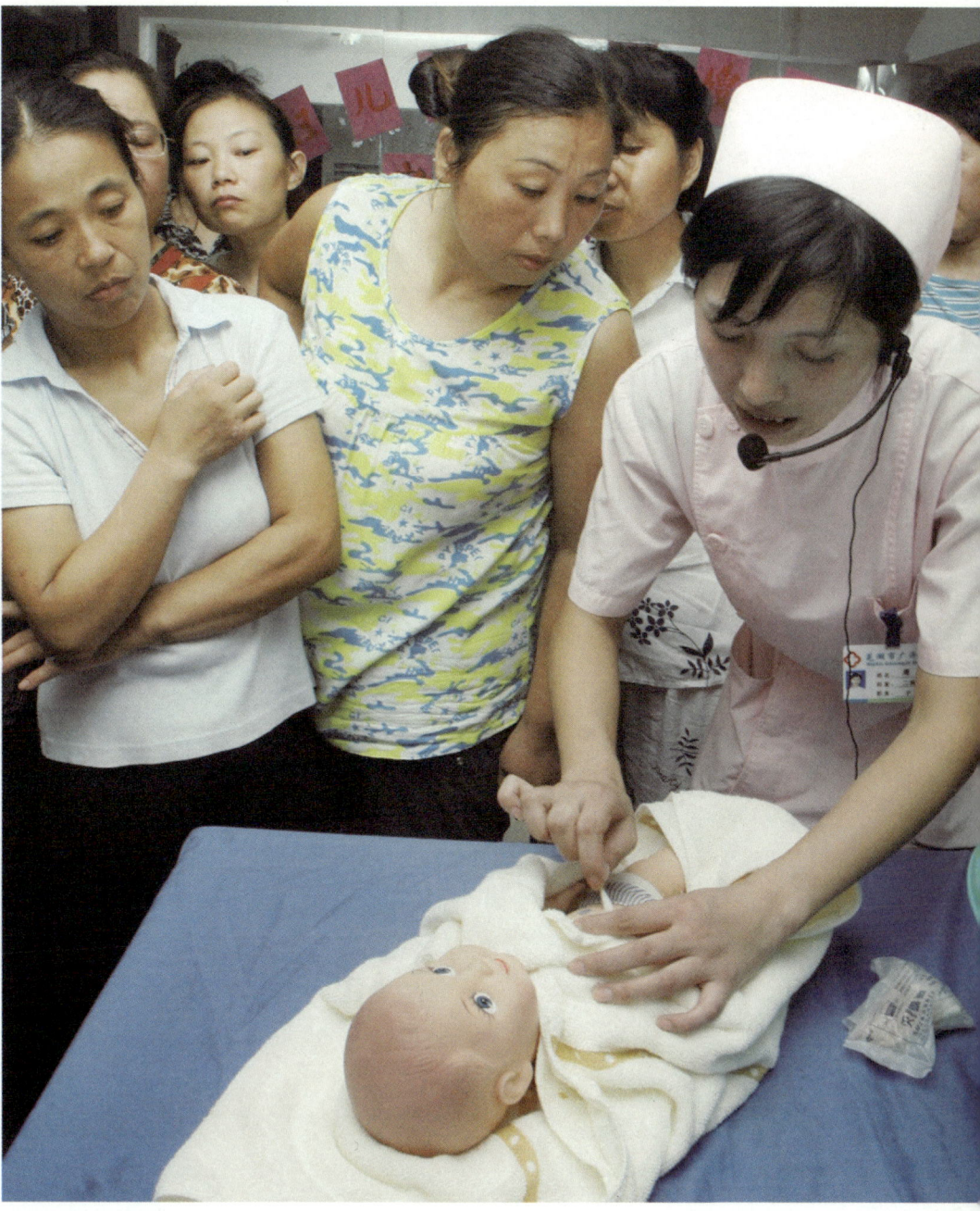

A nurse demonstrates baby care for laid-off women workers at the Mothers and Children Activities Center in Wuhu, Anhui Province.

Laid-off and unemployed workers bejing trained in culinary, in repair skills at the Sunshine Employment Training Center in Shandong Province.

Chinese netizens rank No. 2 worldwide.

Chinese netizens send and receive 30 SMS messages per week.

By the end of December 2011 the number of netizens in China had reached 513 million, with an increase of nearly 56 million in that year alone. The Internet penetration rate stood at 38.3%, an increase of four percentage points over the close of 2010.

The five years following 2006 saw the Internet penetration rate rise dramatically to 10.5%, in steady jumps of about 6% each year. In 2008 and 2009 nearly 90 million netizens came on line each year. In 2011, however, there were signs of a slowdown.

Yangzhou City publishes the first 3D newspaper, 2010.

As chairman of the Pet Breeding Association in Chengdu Province, Li is known for dog breeding and has made a fortune raising them, 1994.

Citizens of Jinan, capital of Shandong Province, scrambling for condoms on November 30, 2003, on the eve of World Aids Day →

A condom manufacturer took the opportunity to promote its product and gave out 3,000 free samples to lucky attendees.

Obesity appeared in China with the greater diversity of available cuisines.

Obese young people from Shandong and Hebei Province stay at the Xiaotangshan Hospital in Beijing during summer and winter holidays to attend weight loss camps. They try to get rid of excessive fat through exercise, proper diet, medical treatmen and Qigong.

In 2011 members of the Liqun roller-skating team of the armed forces of Zhejiang Province joined roller-skating fans from Zhejiang University by the West Lake of Hangzhou City.

Smile competition as school begins

On August 24, 2012 a "competition for smiles" was held at Yuxinnan Primary School, Handan City, Hebei Province.

图书在版编目（CIP）数据

图说百年中国：英文 / 王煦等著. -- 北京：新世界出版社，2012.4
 ISBN 978-7-5104-2632-2

 Ⅰ. ①图… Ⅱ. ①王… Ⅲ. ①中国历史：近代史－图解－英文②中国历史：现代史－图解－英文 Ⅳ. ①K250.8

中国版本图书馆CIP数据核字(2012)第039772号

Modern China in Pictures
图说百年中国（英）

文字撰写：王　煦　章开元　张　静
翻　　译：孟　岳（同文世纪）
责任编辑：李淑娟　乔天碧
图片编辑：贺玉婷
英文审定：徐明强　Paul White　Penelope Colville
图片提供：CNSPHOTO　新华社等
装帧设计：贺玉婷
版式设计：知行兆远
责任印制：李一鸣　黄厚清
出版发行：北京 新世界出版社
社　　址：北京市西城区百万庄大街24号（100037）
总编室电话：+ 86 10 6899 5424　68326679（传真）
发行部电话：+ 86 10 6899 5968　68998705（传真）
本社中文网址：http://www.nwp.cn
版权部电子信箱：frank@nwp.com.cn
版权部电话：+ 86 10 6899 6306
印　　刷：北京画中画印刷有限公司
经　　销：新华书店
开　　本：787 × 1092　1/16
字　　数：200千字　　印　张：22.25
版　　次：2013年1月第1版　2013年1月北京第1次印刷
书　　号：ISBN 978-7-5104-2632-2
定　　价：78.00元

新世界版图书　版权所有　侵权必究
新世界版图书　印装错误可随时退换